AF658042

THE NEW BJP

'The transformation of the BJP from a small player in the political scene to the premier, possibly new dominant formation in India has led to much comment but not as much quality scholarship as one might have expected. Dr Mehta brings to this subject the keen energy of a journalist and observer with the patience of an archivist. His analysis has much that will excite, surprise, and provoke critical thought even as it informs and gives a sense of perspective.

'It is especially notable how work on the growth of the Sangh and the party in the last two decades are matched by careful examination of key moments in the early years of the Bharatiya Jan Sangh. A book that will be indispensable for the study of contemporary India.'

—**Professor Mahesh Rangarajan**, Vice Chancellor, Krea University

'I've had the pleasure of reading drafts of all the chapters of Nalin Mehta's manuscript on the Bharatiya Janata Party. In my opinion, it is going to be a classic, a book that will be read widely and for a long time. Its readership will include scholars, political activists and anyone whose job or interest lies in understanding contemporary India and the processes that have shaped it.

'First, the book is founded on an impressive original database, assembled for the first time for this project. This database enables Mehta to test and analyse the changing characteristics and growth spurts of party membership in ways that have not been done before.

'Second, Mehta uses his energy and connections as a journalist to reinforce the book with extensive interviews. Again, they are new and original, not re-hashes of other journalists' work. They are detailed and often colourful. More important, they enable Mehta to test the findings of the database by asking questions of both senior and rank-and-file party members. Do people on the ground "fit" with what the data appear to be saying?

'Third, Mehta is a journalist and media analyst, but he is also a scholar with a PhD and a groundbreaking book, appreciated both by academics and general readers, on the explosion of the Indian television industry in the 1990s. His scholarship has enabled him to give a historical depth to the new book—to go back to original sources to explore how individuals, parties, organisations and ideas rise and fall.

'Fourth, Mehta can write. In the manuscript, he finds his voice as a detective, an analyst and a storyteller. It is a voice that only someone with his varied experience can achieve.

'Fifth, the book raises big questions for political and social studies. To what extent, and how, do individuals shape political parties? To what extent do communications limit or empower political organisations? How unique is India's recent political experience and how much is it part of trends and processes? What is to be learned from India about political organisation and democratic government in the twenty-first century? The book's focus on the way that the political convictions of a few can be disseminated and organised using twenty-first-century technologies has international significance.

'This is an important and readable book. It is going to be around for a while.'

—**Professor Robin Jeffrey**, Visiting Research Professor,
National University of Singapore; Emeritus Professor,
Australian National University, Canberra & La Trobe University, Melbourne

'Mehta's masterful account of the evolution and rise of the BJP deftly weaves an enormous amount of material into an expansive and authoritative account of modern India. This brilliantly revealing portrait of the inner workings of the party—its ideological bedrock, organisational structure and economic outlook—is brimming with insights about India's cultural contradictions, political alliances and searing religious tensions. Mehta's benchmark study deftly brings together the freshness and vigour of on-the-ground reporting with scholarly precision and vivid descriptions of India's political, economic and social systems. An urgent investigation of Indian democracy, its electoral system and voting patterns; written with anthropological attentiveness to local idioms, gender structure, caste conflict and class relations: a major achievement.'

—**Professor Assa Doron**, Professor of Anthropology and South Asia,
Founding Director, South Asia Centre,
Australian National University, Canberra

'This is a remarkably well-researched and thoughtfully constructed account of the rise of the BJP under Prime Minister Modi. It is a book that must be read by any political scientist interested in post-1991 India. Its use of textual and quantitative data is a brilliant example of empirical academic work. It will greatly improve the discourse on India's political economy.'

—**Professor Shubhashis Gangopadhyay**, Dean, Indian School of Public Policy; Visiting Professor, University of Gothenberg, Sweden; Visiting Professor, University of Groningen, Netherlands

'Nalin's work in this book re-establishes hope in the future of political journalism in the country. For a variety of reasons, some well-known and some less-known, political journalism in India has been losing its bite and its objectivity. Nalin combines deep data analysis, extensive research, wonderful ground reporting and balanced perspective in a crisp text with attractive charts to show how to inform and engage people with political writing even in these polarised times. This book is a must-read for anyone looking to look beyond the noise and understand modern India. It will appeal to diverse audiences: specialist as well as general.'

—**Rohit Saran**, Chief Editor, Times Internet

'Nalin Mehta's wonderful book on the BJP is a dispassionate inquiry into the genesis of the Hindutva mind space. Delineating a complete arc from its foundation to its evolution to its dominance, this study shows immense depth in going beyond traditional paradigms to investigate the party's edifice. It is a fascinating exploration of the BJP using the microscope of modern-day technology, data analysis, interviews and archival work. This book is a political equivalent of what we in the statistical world would call "Principal Component Analysis", boiling down a complex set of factors into clear, informed and robust explanations.

'For a psephologist, it provides rare insights into several other dimensions and surrogates that can be used to estimate a party's core and growing support. The conclusions shine a light on several unknown equations that blend ideology, policy and technology deployment in voter mobilisation. These are hitherto less captured within paradigms of electoral forecasting. The book also provides new scaffoldings beyond caste and community to construct the quantitative narrative of the electoral math that resulted in the stupendous victories of the Bharatiya Janata Party in recent years.

'The book provides rare glimpses into the subtle presence of the Hindu sentiment in various debates within the annals of the Congress party even when India was first coming into her own as an electoral democracy. It leaves no stone unturned to cover every aspect of the ideological and social mobilisation journey of the BJP and its predecessor, the Bharatiya Jan Sangh. As the political debate moves beyond the hard-wired constructs of state-led development vs capital-led development and Mandal vs Kamandal, this book provides rare insights on how to construct the voters' mind map.'

—**Jai Mrug**, psephologist and Director,
VotersMood Research; CEO, M76 Analytics

'This is a rare book that balances data-driven commentary with a compelling narrative derived from scores of interviews. By using software to go through lakhs of documents, and by using his considerable energies to conduct dozens of interviews, Nalin has managed to make numbers interesting and to make stories substantial. The book is a masterful, evidence-based history of how the world's largest political party came to be. I look forward to the conversations this sparks, and the research avenues it opens up.'

—**Rishabh Srivastava**, CEO, Loki.ai;
Founder, DataNarratives.com

'A gripping narrative that is built on a fascinating foundation of academic rigour, insightful political observation and comprehensive data analysis. A must-read for every student of Indian politics and history, irrespective of political allegiance or adherence. The data analysis and deep research may leave even experts stunned.'

—**T.M. Veeraraghav**, former Resident Editor, *The Hindu*;
former Visiting Professor, National Law School, Bengaluru

'Excellent book ... The year's first great political read ... Nalin Mehta's *The New BJP* ... asks and addresses a fundamental question: How did a party with an appeal largely restricted to the trading classes in urban and semi-urban India, manage to become the first choice of the rural population in India's Hindi heartland? And of women? It's a question few others have asked before ... Mehta sets out to answer the question with a combination of history, ground-level and inner-party insights, and lots of data ... I'm enjoying every bit of a book that is the perfect read ...'

—**Sukumar Ranganathan**, Editor, *The Hindustan Times*

'I don't think I have ever read a better book about a political party. The combination of political stories, statistical rigour and deep insights is absolutely impressive. Supporters of BJP and opponents will all be wiser after buying. Run and buy ... Whatever you think of BJP I strongly recommend this book. It brilliantly describes how BJP has grown to India's lead party. Many lessons for politically interested people everywhere.'

—**Erik Solheim**, former Under Secretary General, United Nations and Executive Director, UN Environment Program, and former Minister of International Development as well as Environment, Norway

'Nalin Mehta's expansive take on the ruling party is as much a thesis of political science as a commentary of a beat journalist … it is neither a hagiographical "Modi-Shah Nama" nor a Modi bashing trope. This was an ambitious project based on extensive research and analytics going beyond stereotypes and folklore … It is a seminal work written sans bias. It has to be similarly read with an open mind to have more informed debates on the "new BJP".'

—*The Hindu BusinessLine*

'Wonderful book … an exhaustive look at the at the factors behind the rise of the BJP to a position of hegemony in Indian politics. How did India become a BJP-centric polity, from first being ruled mostly by the Congress, to a period of coalitions drawn from regional players and socialists and then a bipolar system? Mehta examines all these templates. The rise of the BJP has been a process, with setbacks as well as triumphs, and Mehta does a deep dive into the process.'

—*The Hindu*

'Nalin Mehta's new book *The New BJP: Modi and the Making of the World's Largest Political Party* is considered a classic in non-fiction. It covers the evolution and rise of Bharatiya Janata Party (BJP) with the help of enormous data never unearthed before and extensive field work. It is a must-read book for anyone interested in understanding how Narendra Modi's party became the world's largest political party.'

—*Gulf News*

'Mehta's latest book *The New BJP* breaks the mould. It is a well-researched massive tome analysing the rise and expansion of the BJP objectively with hitherto "unseen data" … It is written in an easy-flowing style. Unconventional data analysis and simple graphics are Mehta's strength areas. Such is his force of arguments that you can't leave it half read. By all means, this is a landmark book.'

—*The New Indian Express*

'Fascinating account and gripping narration with startling insights … The book compels discourse and debate as it opens a new vista for all those engaged in politics, policy making as well as public communications. Equally important, the book offers a fresh perspective to those who are otherwise averse to party politics … With impeccable credentials as a dispassionate analyst, Professor Nalin Mehta offers a new perspective for news media's punditry … The book avails new digital research tools, including never before availed ones, like the three unique indices—the Mehta–Singh Social index, the Narad and PollNiti indexes … The book is not only a "revisionist history" of BJP and social engineering, but a landmark in public discourse …'

—**Professor N. Bhaskar Rao**, Founder, Centre for Media Studies

'While I was reading it, I couldn't help wonder if Nalin Mehta wrote this as a quick crash course for the opposition: why BJP keeps winning despite so and so and why they might keep on winning. Best Indian non-fiction of 2022? Absolutely. '

—**Rahul Jaimini**, Co-Founder, Swiggy

'Whether you are a BJP supporter or hater, this well-researched book gives the reader a deep understanding of why the saffron party is on an election-winning spree … Mehta goes beyond the usual saffron politics cliches. His analysis is supported by comprehensive data. Unbiased and honest, Mehta throws light on the much-touted welfare schemes of the government; their hits and misses and the idea of a New India. The book is replete with rare historical records, interviews and starting insights into the way both the party and the country function. A riveting read that the gives you a peek into the ground realities, myths and changing politics in Naya Bharat.'

—*Deccan Chronicle*

'Fascinating-myth breaking research on the BJP. It's a very thick book but very authentic and must-read to understand the BJP … Shandaar [fabulous] book. It has such information and research which will help break your preconceived notions.'

—**Ashutosh**, Founder, *Satya Hindi News*

'Magnum opus … explains Modi and the making of the world's largest political party.'

—**Vishweshwar Bhatt**, Editor-in-Chief, *Viswavani* (Kannada)

'Why does the BJP keep winning elections? No one can fill their bellies with just ideology. *The New BJP* provides answers through hard data on party composition, women's vote, etc. … Was incredulous at the findings in this book. It's so far from what one has been reading in academia and in the media … But data does not lie … Boggles the mind.'

—**Manjula Narayan**, National Books Editor, *Hindustan Times*

'Reads dangerously close to the truth … Nalin Mehta and his team have done monumental research and have come up with an impressive amount of data in chapter after chapter…. Nalin Mehta does an excellent job of mapping India's transition from the default position of reliance on Congress to that of viewing BJP as an agent of change.'

—*The Federal*

'It's an essential book for our times. A huge achievement, really well argued, well written, easy to read and accessible. '

—**Priya Sehgal**, Executive Editor, NewsX

'It's the most definitive book on the BJP.'

—**R.K. Radhakrishnan**, Senior Associate Editor, *Frontline*

'A very important book on the BJP in an age when the party is omnipresent and must be understood … *The New BJP* by Nalin Mehta is essential reading.'

—**Saba Naqvi**, senior journalist

'Rich data analysis (which is woefully missing in mainstream political reportage) + on-ground reporting insights make it a riveting read. Kudos on this blockbuster.'

—**Harsha Subramanian**, Head of News Partnerships, India, Meta, and former Executive Producer and India Media Group Head, Bloomberg

'With factual authority and academic rigour … *The New BJP* is an essential read for those who want to unravel the secrets behind the saffron surge…. Rather than indulging in the usual political commentary, based on subjective reasoning, Nalin Mehta's book uses crunching of hard data to dig facts and insights … with a factual base that cannot be contested.'

—*india.com*

'From rich data to dispassionate analysis, Nalin Mehta's *The New BJP* is a work of empirical ambition. Using innovative statistical measures, it traces the BJP's historic journey to become India's largest political party. Nalin Mehta's *The New BJP* [is] … the most ambitious attempt at using fresh data and analytical tools to dissect different facets of the current BJP's widening electoral appeal and social base, its policy measures and political messaging, especially the style and substance of its digital outreach…. the book marks a point of departure in "treatises on BJP"…. Nalin Mehta has offered a work of empirical ambition, with a blend of data-rich insight, the analytical frame of a political scientist, and journalistic reportage.'

—*Newslaundry*

‘What I like about this book is that the author’s analysis is heavily backed by data. He uses a data-based approach to understand the themes that the BJP is focusing on, and its trends and trajectories. The book does an excellent job of detailing how Hindutva actually works on the ground in India …’

—**Narayani Basu**, ‘Best books on BJP’ recommendation in *The Indian Express*

‘This book written by Nalin Mehta is a testament to history … Gorgeous book and extraordinary effort by Nalin Mehta. This one will define a lot of our contemporary political history.’

—**Vani Tripathi Tikkoo**, former Member, CBFC

‘Excellent new book.’

—**Andy Mukherjee**, Bloomberg Opinion columnist

‘Provide[s] valuable insights … Seamlessly blends a variety of methodological techniques ... the rich set of new materials Mehta has collected is truly impressive.’

—*India Today*

‘Nalin Mehta … sets aside emotions and biases to objectively examine the factor that led to the growth of the BJP over the last 15 years … it is a weighty volume that looks beyond the narrative of Hindutva politics … explains how the party has grown beyond its core base’.

—*Mint Lounge*

‘Nalin Mehta’s book is a deep-dive into the BJP’s post-2014 phase with adequate references which locate the transformations in a historical context.’

—*The Tribune*

‘Am loving it.’

—**Ashwin Sanghi**, bestselling novelist

‘Mother of all books.’

—**Ravi Subramanian**, bestselling novelist

‘Monumental tome … Mehta combines a journalist’s account of political processes on the ground with an academic’s keen eye for data detail in what could be termed as perhaps the most comprehensive, extensive, and crucial study on the astronomical proportions the BJP has acquired in recent years … [It is] a political scientist’s delight.’

—*The Book Review*

THE NEW BJP

MODI AND THE MAKING OF THE WORLD'S LARGEST POLITICAL PARTY

NALIN MEHTA

First published by Westland Non-Fiction, an imprint of Westland Publications Private Limited, in 2022

Published by Westland Non-Fiction, an imprint of Westland Books, a division of Nasadiya Technologies Private Limited, in 2022

No. 269/2B, First Floor, 'Irai Arul', Vimalraj Street, Nethaji Nagar, Allappakkam Main Road, Maduravoyal, Chennai 600095

Westland, the Westland logo, Westland Non-Fiction and the Westland Non-Fiction logo are the trademarks of Nasadiya Technologies Private Limited, or its affiliates.

ISBN: 9789395073011

10 9 8 7 6 5 4 3 2 1

Typeset in Adobe Devanagari by Jojy Philip, New Delhi – 110015
Printed at Manipal Technologies Limited, Manipal

For Rakesh Mehta, rock and inspiration;
Madhu Bala, who never gives up; and
Robin Jeffrey, for always being there.

CONTENTS

PART III
IDEOLOGY, ECONOMIC THINKING AND GOVERNANCE

PART IV
THE UMBILICAL CORD

PART V
BEYOND THE DOMINANT NARRATIVE: THE SOUTH, THE NORTHEAST AND WOMEN

CONCLUSION

INTRODUCTION

A 'Jai Sri Ram' Sticker and a Family Argument: The BJP and a Personal Retracing

My family's first domestic political fight, as far as I can remember, was over the Ram Temple. My grandfather brought a 'Jai Sri Ram' (Victory to Lord Ram) sticker from somewhere and pasted it on the front of my father's Bajaj 150 scooter. Dad blew his top.

My grandfather could not understand this reaction. 'Ram is our God. We worship him every day in this house. What's your problem with a sticker that has his name?' he asked with furious indignation.

'Yes, but this is now a political slogan. I am in the Army,' responded my father. 'It would be treason to sport a political sticker and drive this scooter while wearing my uniform,' I remember him saying.

It was September 1990. L.K. Advani, then president of the Bharatiya Janata Party (BJP), had just started his 10,000-km Rath Yatra (literally, 'chariot journey'), from the ancient reconstructed temple of Somnath on the western Gujarat coast to the disputed Babri Masjid site in Ayodhya in the heart of Uttar Pradesh (UP).

India's current prime minister, Narendra Modi, had just started making his name in Gujarat as a local BJP apparatchik. His name first appeared as a politician in the pages of *The Times of India* in 1988, as the organiser of an anti-Congress rasta-roko agitation on farmer demands in Gujarat,[1] but not many outside the state had heard of him. That wider recognition would not come until he became a key organiser of the Yatra's Gujarat leg in 1990.[2] The first fissures of the Yatra—with 'Jai Sri

Ram' as its rallying cry—and what it meant for India were being felt in our household.

My grandfather was a Punjabi refugee from what is now Pakistan's Toba Tek Singh district. Most of the family had made it alive to this side of the border in 1947, but Partition, and its Hindu–Muslim killings, left a deep psychological scar. One of his brothers joined the Rashtriya Swayamsevak Sangh (RSS) when they reached Delhi, although we seldom spoke of it at home. My grandfather, a defence ministry civil servant, never joined the Sangh. But the bloody flight from his beloved village of Kamalia near Faisalabad in Pakistani Punjab and the painful rebuilding of a new life from nothing in Delhi left in him a gaping, lifelong wound and a distrust of Muslims. It made him deeply sympathetic to Hindu nationalist causes. My father, born in Nehru's India, a year after Gandhi was assassinated, became an unapologetic Nehruvian secularist. When he joined the Indian Army, it still had a recruitment rule that denied entry to known RSS members on security-clearance grounds.[3]

The 'Jai Sri Ram' sticker ignited an argument in which neither side could understand the other. My father saw it as a political statement—one that he, as a serving Army officer, refused to make. My grandfather framed the issue as one of religious belief. When my father pulled the sticker off, insisting that he could not be seen driving a vehicle with religious messaging on it, my grandfather's religiosity was deeply offended. 'How can you remove Ram?' he shouted. Matters were getting out of hand when my grandmother stepped in and said quietly: 'Stop the political talk. No politics in the house. We have lost too many people to it already.' And that was that. Or my memory of it.

It was my first personal experience of politics, an early baptism in the wider debate on Hinduness, Indianness, secularism—the complex meanings underpinning the interface of religious identity and politics that the Rath Yatra had set off. Many Indians went through versions of this same family debate as it replayed in multiple family WhatsApp groups, in drawing rooms and in discussions with friends on 5 August 2020. On this day, Prime Minister Narendra Modi presided over the consecration of the new Ram Temple, which the Supreme Court had ruled could be built on the site of the demolished mosque. The debates were now different in detail. The BJP was in its sixth year of continuous majority power in India, but the underlying touchpoints of cultural and political contention that its rise had engendered—on what it means to be Indian in a Hindu-majority but non-sectarian State—were essentially the same.

A couple of months after the appearance of the 'Jai Sri Ram' sticker, I accompanied my father when he went to pick up my mother from her Union government ministry office in Delhi's RK Puram. Her co-workers, lower-level bureaucrats, had set up a shrine to the Hindu gods Ram, Shiva and Krishna in a corner of their shared office space. Next to it, someone had pasted a new sticker. It sported the visage of a martial Ram with a bow and arrow and a one-line message: 'Mandir Vahin Banaayenge' (We will build the temple right there). This was another rallying cry of the Ram Janmabhoomi movement—an assertion that the temple would only be built on the site of the Babri mosque, no matter what. My father, who was in his olive-green Army uniform, stiffened when he saw the slogan inside the government building. 'They have taken an oath to be apolitical in government service,' he said. 'All this should be fought outside, not here.' I was too young to understand it at the time, but my mother's office wall reflected another fissure that the Ram movement had opened up: on the role of the State and its officials when their private religious and political beliefs clashed with expected behaviour, especially when these beliefs were being vehemently, and politically, contested.

By the time L.K. Advani's rath, a souped-up Toyota truck rejigged to look like a medieval chariot, wound its way through India, I was in boarding school. We were participating in school debates with topics like 'There Is No Place for Religion in a Democracy: For or Against' or 'Our Culture Is Our Greatest Strength: For or Against'. Most students did not really care about these topics; they were just school assignments. Yet, in an India without internet or mobile phones, in the secluded, sheltered surroundings of our elite boarding school, a couple of senior boys were excited enough by the Ram movement to keep a daily pictorial scrapbook on the Rath Yatra and its day-to-day travails, with cuttings from newspapers and weekly magazines. The din of the Ram Mandir movement was all around us, challenging our young minds. One of these scrapbook-boys went on to become a successful IT entrepreneur, another a high-flying corporate banker.

I do not know what happened to that scrapbook, but Narendra Modi would have featured in it. The BJP was yet to win Gujarat, but his role in the Somnath–Gandhinagar leg of the Yatra meant that, by 1991, he was already being hailed in the press as the 'architect of the BJP's phenomenal growth in Gujarat'.[4] In 1992, less than a month after the demolition of the mosque, with Ayodhya still under curfew—and some BJP leaders in detention—he was being counted as one of the party's next-gen leaders, important enough to be mentioned among the key functionaries who met for an emergency session of the party's national executive in Delhi. The gathered BJP brass, led by senior leaders like future prime minister Atal Bihari Vajpayee, demanded immediate access to Ram Lalla idols for 'darshan' in the curfew-hit town. They called on the government to allow in devotees to Ayodhya on 26 December 1992 for the yearly 'Pragat Utsav'—a festival commemorating the appearance of the Ram idols in the Babri Masjid in 1948.[5]

Earlier that year, as chief organiser of the BJP's Kanyakumari-to-Kashmir Ekta Yatra, Modi accompanied the then BJP president Murali Manohar Joshi to unfurl the Indian tricolour in Srinagar's Lal Chowk in a symbolic ceremony. The flag-hoisting was preceded by the creation of the eponymously named 'Kesari Vahini' (literally, 'saffron vehicle'), which comprised some 6,00,000 volunteers who had been mobilised from around the country. Its slogan, as Modi told reporters, could not be clearer. 'Article 370 *hatao, atankawad mitao, desh bachao*' (Remove Article 370, wipe out terrorism, save the country).[6] The BJP leaders were airlifted from Jammu to curfewed Srinagar, where they hoisted the tricolour before being flown back. Given the rise of Dr Joshi in the BJP's leadership, what stood out then was Modi's salience as an apparatchik. He was part of the party's tapestry, no matter who headed it. Clearly, in 1990–1993, Modi was a rising star, being noticed for defining party campaigns that presaged some of his signature moves as prime minister two decades later.

Pooja, Then Quran, Followed by a Ram Temple Donation: An Older Syncretic Culture in UP and Its Questions

Reporting on another offshoot of the Ram Temple agitation in 2002, I discovered that my new mother-in-law from UP had herself been to kar-seva twice: before and immediately after the temple demolition. This was yet another example of how the political tumult of the 'outside' world plays out in complex, unexpected ways in our 'inside' family worlds. I spent most of 2002 covering the post-Godhra riots in Gujarat, which had started with the burning of fifty-nine kar-sevaks on their way back from Ayodhya. The election that followed was the making of Narendra Modi as a mass leader. Midway through that campaign, as I discussed the political rhetoric with a bureaucrat in Ahmedabad, she mused aloud about its psychological wellsprings. 'It is almost like they are taking revenge for Somnath, as if taking account for all those centuries of humiliation,' she muttered half-seriously.[7] Later that day, when I questioned my devout mother-in-law about what motivated her kar-seva, she insisted it was personal belief. She had grown up in Ayodhya's Kanak Bhawan,[8] within sight of the Babri Masjid. 'Hamaare Bhagwan hain (He is my God)' was her gentle but firm answer each time I attempted a wider discussion on her beliefs.

What about the underlying politics of the movement? What did she think it meant for Muslims? I could never draw her into a deeper dialogue on the questions I was used to discussing in my professional circles—the 'idea of India', 'secularism vs communalism', 'minority rights'. Her answer started and ended with faith. It confounded me because her gentle religiosity did not square with the aggression, machismo and anti-Muslimness I had seen in many of the movement's stormtroopers. Just when I was bracketing her in my mind as a one-dimensional Hindu nationalist, a new familial twist emerged.

My father-in-law, another devout Hindu, was equally supportive of the Ram Temple. The surprise was that his daily morning pooja at a Hindu altar was followed by another, more discreet ritual: the reading of the Quran in a closed room. The morning aarti and prasad would be followed by a religious recitation of the Islamic 'Bismillah-ir-Rehman-ir-Rahim', as he physically ran his hands in reverence over the lines of the Quranic pages. In a Kayasth family of feudal landlords in UP's Fatehpur, the origin myth of this syncretic tradition went back to the legend of a Muslim peer[9] (Sufi saint) who apparently came down to their forebears seven generations ago. The family story was that the peer advised their ancestor to keep a Quran in the house, read it daily in secret, but to remain Hindu and not convert. That tradition had survived to the present day.

In a town that once had Muslim overlords, the practice may have begun as a social defence mechanism. The fakir story may simply have been an 'invented tradition'. Yet, it was also a fascinating story of secret and multiple selves, of a remarkable cross-pollination of religious traditions born out of centuries of co-existence and an outstanding example of the legendary Ganga–Jamuna tehzeeb of UP, a fusion of Hindu and Islamic traditions born out of centuries of co-existence. The Kayasths mastered Persian, then Urdu, as scribes and close associates of various Muslim rulers or landed gentry. They were far from an orthodox, closeted elite. This was not really multiculturalism in the modern sense. The original impulse may have been a survival instinct in a time of conflict, but the tradition had survived.

My new relatives in Fatehpur, I noticed, were more religiously 'Hindu' than anyone I knew, but still greeted each other with the Urdu 'salaam', not the Hindi 'namaste'. The black-and-white photos of their ancestors on the walls depicted two kinds of cultural layering. There were colonial-era photos of impassive-looking feudal nobility dressed in starched suits and British uniforms. But the oldest family portrait, preceding the British era, depicted a gentleman in the dress of Muslim aristocracy, with a beard and headgear in the Islamicate style. They had retained their Hinduness in the internal domain, but their external cultural selves had changed with the ruling zeitgeists. Now they were changing again.

The befuddling result of this syncretism was that the same family was involved in both Ram Temple kar-seva as well as a daily reading of the Quran. They had contributed ₹40,000 to the construction of the new Ram Temple after Prime Minister Modi led the consecration ceremony in Ayodhya. Yet, they had continued, till recently, to also provide yearly donations for the upkeep of the local Mansingh Masjid, a mosque still prefixed with their Hindu surname and built over 150 years ago by an ancestor. The Masjid was built on family land that was later sold off. Its nineteenth-century spires, built opposite what was once the family mansion's main gate, are surrounded today by a row of modern houses but it still retains its Hindu nomenclature. At the centre of its prayer hall is a foundation plaque in black stone, recording its founding by a Mansingh, accompanied by a verse from the Quran.

For my father-in-law, the Quran was a treasured family 'virasat' (heritage), part of his lived daily tradition. Yet, his household also distributed motichoor ke laddoo as ritual prasad to neighbours to celebrate the Ram Temple consecration ceremony. The laddoos had been specially sent out from the Ayodhya temple, where Modi performed the rituals, to several households across UP, and had reached them via relatives in Allahabad.

Their story encapsulates for me the multiple contradictions of India, the complexities of Hinduism and Hindu nationalism beyond simple binaries, and equally, the questions it raises for the future of older, syncretic traditions. This ability to straddle two religious worlds, well-studied by anthropologists, historians and writers, would be familiar to many Indians from a small-town or rural milieu. Even now, dargahs (shrines to revered figures, often Sufi saints or dervishes) draw people of all faiths, and Indians, cutting across religions, look to pirs and other religious figures to ward off evil.

This is why an understanding of the nature of the BJP's growth, its structures of power and modes of mobilisation is critical today. The answers may be surprising.

Hindu nationalism, and the political idea of a Hindu-focused India, is not a new ideational construct. It was already a fully developed alternative political ideology by the time of independent India's first election in 1951-52. It evolved into a political force in the form of the BJP's predecessor, the Bharatiya Jan Sangh,[10] which stood in direct opposition on first principles to the Nehruvian notion of a republic that drew a sharp distinction between the State and the Hindu religious and cultural identity.

The Jan Sangh was created in 1951 for precisely this purpose: to politically oppose the Nehruvian idea of India. As the BJP's Home Minister Amit Shah describes it, 'When under Nehru ji India's development, agricultural, foreign, defence and education policies were being created, then [Jan Sangh founder] Dr Syama Prasad Mookerjee and several people like him felt that if the country goes on the path of the policies being developed by the Nehru government then it won't even find the way to turn back.' The alternative they presented had, in the BJP's view, the 'smell of the soil of this nation' as opposed to the 'pungent smell of Western thinking' that it believes Nehru represented.[11]

This ideological counterpoint proved politically unwinnable in Indian elections for years. Yet, its driving impulse was clear. In Shah's words, there was a 'big fundamental difference' between the ideology of the Congress and the Jan Sangh: Nehru's Congress wanted to build a 'new India [navnirman] whereas the Bharatiya Jan Sangh wanted to use its *ancient cultural heritage* and majestic splendour as the basis to *completely rebuild* [punarnirman] India' (emphasis added). It was to present this 'alternative thinking' that the Jan Sangh was 'born under Dr Syama Prasad Mookerjee which is now in front of the nation in the form of the Bharatiya Janata Party'.[12]

It took over seven decades for this alternative to become electorally acceptable on a national scale. This book shows how the shift in the BJP's political fortunes occurred, what changed, what it started doing differently, and the strategies that powered this change. It unpicks how a fundamentally reshaped BJP, under Narendra Modi, built on the advances of previous years but significantly reordered itself using digital technologies and revamped internal management practices to drive this growth. It uses fresh empirical evidence to demonstrate how the new BJP built novel caste alliances, reshaped class relations, tapped into gender structures and developed a new targeted politics of welfare within an India searing with religious tensions. These changes transformed the BJP into the primary pole of Indian politics as well as the world's largest political party.

To be clear, this is not a book about whether what the BJP stands for is right or wrong for India or whether Hindu nationalism, as opposed to Hindu traditionalism, in a Hindu-majority democracy is good or bad. Nor is it about the pros and cons of cultural nationalism vis-à-vis territorial nationalism. It is the story of how the BJP won India in electoral battlefields. It is about why it won (or did better than earlier) in more elections than it lost (or performed poorly in) since 2014. It answers the question of why Narendra Modi remained India's most popular electoral leader until mid-2021, at the time of writing, despite a below-par economy, and how the BJP did it.

In a deeply polarised polity divided between those who oppose the BJP, and compare its rise to something like the early rise of the 'Nazis' in Germany,[13] and those who welcome it as a vital Hindu cultural corrective to the cultural foundations of the nation, and where television news channels only shout to the converted on either side and social media is deeply split into echo chambers, this book is a non-partisan, empirical and evidence-based study. Such a method and approach to studying the BJP has never been more necessary. Unless facts are assessed and sifted, rational debate is not possible. *The New BJP* aims to shed fresh light on the modes of political power in India, the mechanics of the BJP's election triumphs, the role of technology in politics, how the party won power nationally and what this portends for Indian politics.

I have deliberately chosen to set aside personal value judgements and my own opinions on the pros and cons of 'secularism' versus 'Hindu nationalism' as a guiding philosophy for India. These ideas do appear throughout this book in the manner in which they were deployed by political parties, how they were contested by politicians, how their meanings and messaging changed over time and what they stand for today. My purpose is not to show whether one idea of India is superior to the other. That normative battle of ideas is for other books, political theorists, lawyers, constitutional experts, politicians or their proxy pamphleteers on both sides, wider civil society and the Indian citizens to continuously debate and contest.

Within these pages, I have a very specific purpose: to investigate, enquire and uncover why large sections of India agreed more than ever before with the BJP's political ideas and expressed this through their vote in successive elections from 2014 onwards. It started from a fundamental personal belief that it was vital at this point in India's national journey to understand the levers of its political growth dispassionately. One needed to step away from the sound and fury of toxic television studios, venomous social-media trolls, political slugfests and daily hand-wringing over what was happening to India (by those who opposed the BJP) or celebrations over the country's new turn (by those who supported it), and work instead with empirical evidence, facts and a fresh cross-disciplinary understanding beyond the multiple cultural divides that the party embodies.

Why did the BJP start winning on this scale? Was it only because of a cultural shift in India? Or was its edifice of expansion built on creating a much wider, deeper superstructure of new constituencies of voters who aligned with it for reasons beyond the cultural divide? How did the BJP's growth patterns differ across India's regions, in new catchment areas where it had never held sway before or in areas where it failed to make inroads? In other words, what really was happening in India, how did the BJP systematically become the country's largest political party and its fulcrum of power? These are the fundamental questions I seek to answer. There are, of course, a variety of ways to address such questions. My training as a student of politics and as a journalist covering Indian politics over twenty years impels me to favour a fact-based narrative. I draw on written sources, field visits, interviews and conversations as well as archival and documentary evidence.

The germ of this project was born out of my daily work as a political analyst and editor working with micro-level election data. Since 2017, when the data scientist Rishabh Srivastava and I started putting together micro-constituency and booth-level voting data sets across elections, using layers of subjective queries and artificial intelligence (AI) filters to study them, we started seeing confounding patterns that challenged the conventional understanding of Indian politics that I had long been used to. These counter-intuitive patterns also started showing up more and more in ground-level conversations with key actors when I travelled across several states, in both north and south India, covering elections. That experience began the hunt to dig below the surface to decipher what really was happening and why these trends were not reflecting in most opinion polls as they should have.

This book is the outcome of pursuing answers to those early questions our data algorithms threw up. About 80–90 per cent of what is in here, I did not know about when we started. It emerged from a deep dive into the BJP and its structures across states, constituencies and domains.

What's New in This Book about the BJP

The New BJP is built on insights gained from several new digital tools that have never before been used in India for political analysis of this kind and on this scale. To create the basis for a deeper, fuller understanding of the BJP, Srivastava and I created a new archival data-mining software, Narad (Normative Analysis of Reporting and Discourse). This allowed us to put together a large, original digital database of 11,588 BJP-linked documents between 2006 and 2019 (consisting of 17.9 million words) that has been assembled for the first time. The use of new AI and machine-learning techniques to examine this vast digitised BJP archive allowed us to see patterns that we would otherwise have missed.

This newly created database on BJP literature includes 8,579 BJP speeches, press releases and party articles published over thirteen years (between 2005 and 2019; 4.98 million words), 168 issues of the BJP fortnightly magazine *Kamal Sandesh* (2009–2019; 2.69 million words), 230 issues of the RSS weekly magazine *Organiser* (May 2015–December 2019; 6.12 million words), 1,305 speeches by Prime Minister Modi (2014–2019; 3.44 million words) and 216 documents of the RSS outfit Vanvasi Kalyan Ashram (literally, 'jungle-dweller benefit hermitage') which works in tribal areas (June 2018–December 2019; 43,000 words). We compared and contrasted this offline literature with social-media posts by seventy-five leaders from the BJP, the Congress and several regional parties between January 2016 and December 2019 (4,76,827 posts in all). This included all Facebook posts by the BJP, the RSS, the Congress, Narendra Modi, Amit Shah and Rahul Gandhi from their official pages in the same period (a total of 40,251; 1.2 million words). After cleaning up the data, we created a specially developed digital analysis tool, the Narad Index, which measures how communication patterns change over time. The findings surprised us, and various chapters in the book, across subjects, are suffused with the insights we gained from them.

We further supplemented the digital archive and the Narad Index by creating a centralised digital repository of 218 interactive data dashboards, which we called 'PollNiti'. This repository consists of over 100 data-analytics dashboards on constituency-level political information from national and state elections spread over four decades of politics (1980–2019); eight economic data dashboards consisting of national and state-level economic data stretching over seven years (2012–2019); and 110 social-media-analytics dashboards tracking dozens of politicians over three years (2016–2019). Many of these data sets were drawn from public sources. Some we constructed ourselves over time.

We cleaned them all up, digitised them, linked them to each other to get a holistic understanding and added our own layering of editorial filters—rural–urban seats, Muslim-significant seats, night-light data from commercial satellite imagery to see constituency-wise patterns of economic change in the Northeast, representation of women at various levels, among others. We built over a hundred such machine-led editorial filters—all interchangeable and interactive—on top of these multiple interlinked data sets to aid analysis and to find patterns that the human eye would otherwise miss. Some of the insights gained from these new digital tools are in the book. All of them are available to researchers online at *PollNiti.com*.

Realising that data alone can sometimes be misleading or offer only a partial understanding—it can tell us the what, not the how—my collaborating researchers and I met with a range of leaders at various levels of the BJP, the RSS, the Congress and regional Opposition parties across several states. We conducted over 150 on- and off-the-record interviews and conversations at different levels of politics, from the ground up to high-management levels, and with domain experts in several Indian states. I thought this would be the most difficult part, but then again, in my experience, politicians like to talk about their craft—if you are not chasing them for daily deadlines and the short-lived small scoop. I found most of the politicians I spoke to deeply thoughtful about their work, the systems they used and the implications of it all. What we learnt from these wide-ranging conversations greatly enhanced our understanding of the party and its political mobilisation processes.

Interestingly, almost all of my interviews with BJP leaders (barring those from south India) were conducted in Hindi. Almost all senior, mid- and district-level BJP leaders I spoke to in the Hindi belt, including ministers, were monolingual. Hindi is also the language of choice for most of Prime Minister Modi's speeches and for all of Home Minister Amit Shah's speeches. All translations in the book are mine.

My Hindi is pretty good—I began my career as a Hindi TV reporter and anchor, and can type in Hindi—but I still occasionally found some of the usages difficult, especially when it came to technical governance-related terms. This sometimes led to awkward situations. In Mathura, when a district-level BJP leader talked of his party's mahapaur being a Dalit, I asked, 'At what level is a mahapaur?' There was an embarrassed silence. The leader was too polite to laugh, but my journalist colleagues did, even as they informed me that 'mahapaur' means mayor. The point is that almost every BJP leader I met in UP, including two deputy chief ministers, spoke high-order Hindi and did not engage in English at all. This meant that a lot of the work for this book involved translation and the rechecking of specific word meanings and nuances with colleagues whose formal Hindi is better than mine.

Finally, the present can only be understood in the context of the past. Significant parts of this book are drawn from original primary work from three traditional historical archives. The BJP archive at Rambhau Mhalgi Prabodhini, which also serves as the party's political training centre, has kept meticulous records of BJP and RSS literature as well as party documents since the early 1980s. A lot of my understanding of the BJP is drawn from the documents I found there. As far as I know, they were made available for the first time to an outsider for a historical account such as this. Second, in 2018, the BJP launched an e-library of digitised party records from the 1950s to the present day. This resource proved invaluable in reconstructing the party's early evolution and its current thinking as seen through party documents. Finally, the Nehru Memorial Museum and Library (NMML) archive at Teen Murti House in Delhi, the newspaper records stored there and *The Times of India*'s digitised archive available on the academic database ProQuest provided a great deal of original material for this story on how key debates unfolded over time.

What Does This Book Do?

When the BJP was launched in 1980, it was derided in one memorable tongue-in-cheek press account as a 'vegetarian but tasty party'.[14] The green and saffron colours of the new party were the same as that of the Janata Party, the united Opposition front that its predecessor Jan Sangh had merged into in 1977 to fight Indira Gandhi's Emergency. When the BJP emerged out of Janata Party in 1980, it retained the colours but flipped them into vertical lines, unlike the horizontal pattern of the original. The BJP leaders added a lotus to their new flag. They told reporters that they had chosen the flower as their official symbol, and for the flag, because it was a symbol of resistance used by Indian revolutionaries against the British in the 1857 War of Independence. The lotus, of course, also has a strong mythological and cultural significance in Hinduism. It is associated with Vishnu, the protector, and Lakshmi, the goddess of wealth, and is also the national flower of India.

My account of the BJP's political journey is divided into five parts.

Part I shows how the BJP's growth was built on its transformation into the predominant rural party in its core-strength areas: the Hindi-speaking states of north India. This is a big claim to make about a party that was once derided as an urban force with a narrow upper-caste base. This part then focuses on how such a turn was achieved: through a politics of targeted social welfare aimed at 'labharthees' (beneficiaries of the government's welfare schemes), aided by digital tools, new caste alliances and a major expansion of its social base, primarily to Other Backward Classes (OBCs) and to a lesser extent to Scheduled Castes (SCs), and, finally, its approach to the Hindu–Muslim question.

The heart of its findings—how the BJP radically changed its positioning on caste after 2014 by giving a far greater space at all levels to those lower down the caste order than any other party in UP—comes from the Mehta–Singh Social Index, another original database that I created with my colleague, the journalist Sanjeev Singh. We studied the caste background of 4,415 political leaders in UP spread across three decades and four parties (BJP, Samajwadi Party [SP], Congress and Bahujan Samaj Party [BSP]). This included the caste backgrounds of all 2,560 Lok Sabha candidates fielded by these four parties in UP between 1991 and 2019; all 1,612 assembly election candidates fielded by the four parties in 2017; all 104 UP government ministers appointed between 2016 and 2019 (stretching across Akhilesh Yadav's SP and Yogi Adityanath's BJP governments); all forty-one state-level BJP office-bearers in UP and all ninety-eight district-level BJP presidents in 2020. The findings—which were rechecked multiple times—entailed a massive district-level investigation in each of UP's seventy-five districts.

Our checks included a process of blind review by separate teams working simultaneously on the same investigation to compare results, followed by a qualitative checking of lists with a cross-section of long-time Hindi journalists, academics and district-level politicians in the state, followed by random qualitative checks on specific regions with a cross-section of senior UP politicians across party lines. Despite being political junkies and having reported on the state for years, our findings on caste representation in the Mehta–Singh Index stunned us.

Part II delineates the BJP's tools of growth and political expansion. The Narad Index provides new insights into how the party calibrated its political messaging across time. A separate chapter examines how the BJP used social media and digital reach as a mass force multiplier in a country that underwent a mobile data revolution after 2015, and where digital is increasingly relevant. It takes a close look at how the party uses communication technologies and digital tools for political mobilisation, how funding patterns vary in the digital sphere, how other parties tried to replicate its online successes and why they failed, and, finally, how much digital really does matter. Simultaneously, the BJP launched the largest membership drive India has seen by a national party since the pre-Independence Congress. It restructured management oversight systems to create a deep ground organisation base at the voting-booth level with the aid of digital technologies that allowed greater precision than ever before. These methods differ from what has been deployed by other political bodies, and is at the heart of what helped turn the BJP into the world's largest political party.

Part III examines the role of ideology and governance. It examines the BJP's major ideological touchpoints—its anti-Congress-ism, its strident criticism of Nehru, its unifocal attention on the Kashmir question, the driving impulses of recent debates like the Citizenship (Amendment) Act, 2019 (CAA)—which, at their core, are also about the place of Hindus and Muslims in a democratic India from a historical perspective. It reconstructs the prehistory of these debates in the 1950s, linking them with what came before the BJP: the Jan Sangh. Many of India's current political debates are exact replicas of the debates that started back then. This section shows why these arguments did not win elections for decades, and what changed so that they became politically potent.

This section also examines the BJP's economic thinking at a time when India's high growth rates seem to have become a feature of the past, especially after the disruptions of COVID-19. It examines whether there is a Modi/BJP model of economics, and if it is different from the economic model of the last BJP government led by Atal Bihari Vajpayee.

Furthermore, it examines some of the policies of the state governments that the party leads to more closely comprehend this economic model.

The BJP cannot be understood without an understanding of the RSS. Part IV examines the RSS, how it has expanded in the last few decades, what it stood for by 2020 (as opposed to its positioning a decade ago), its role in social mobilisation, and specific measurable connections between the BJP and the RSS at the personnel level. In particular, it studies the BJP–RSS linkages in the Modi government, in the party nationally and in a state-level regime in Madhya Pradesh to provide a new understanding of this changing equation. This section also outlines the role of Sangh Parivar outfits, in particular the Vanvasi Kalyan Ashram, in mobilising tribal groups in favour of the BJP's political project.

The party may appear like a political monolith, but its geographies of influence vary a great deal across India. Under the veneer of a uniformist ideology, the BJP operates very differently in different parts of the country. The final part of this book traces the differences in the BJP's growth story in two new catchments areas: its southern-states model, where the party's mobilisation and appeal is very different from its core areas in the Hindi heartland, and its model of mergers and acquisitions in the north-eastern states of India. A party's failures tell us as much as its successes. In particular, this section examines the BJP's strategies of expansion in Karnataka—home to India's Silicon Valley, Bengaluru—and whether they can be replicated in other states like Kerala, Tamil Nadu, Andhra Pradesh or Telangana. Similarly, the Northeast, home to Assam, a state with India's largest proportion of Muslims after Kashmir, and several states with Christian majorities, offers a different model of adaptability and tactical alliances for a party that, in north India, is suffused with Hindu messaging and a religiosity that is central to its politics.

Identities of influence matter as much as geographies. The book closes with a study of how the BJP specifically focuses on rural women voters, and examines the cross-cutting national cleavage of gender. A shift in the overall women vote towards the party has driven the BJP's recent growth story. The last part of the book examines how this occurred, how the party dealt with questions of gender and what this portends for the future.

Critics and Opposition leaders have often argued that this new BJP-dominated India puts the country's democracy in danger. The Congress's

P. Chidambaram summed up this critique in early 2019 when he argued that 'fear is dominating India', that key institutions of the state had been captured by the ruling party. As he put it, 'people tell me that they think twice. Before they email, they think twice and they think even more before picking up a phone. Democracy is in danger.'[15] The BJP, of course, denies such charges. While its supporters and opponents will continue to argue on these matters, the fact is that, between 2014 and 2020, the BJP has won more elections in India than it has lost. It is important to understand why.

This is especially so in an era where, as one articulate MLA told the psephologist and journalist Prannoy Roy, 'Elections have become like exams. There are a number of papers that have to be passed. You don't have to do brilliantly in each paper; but in order to be elected, your average marks should be *at least* distinction. Voters today will not accept only pass marks … to merely pass today means that you have failed, you'll be voted out.' Election data, as Roy (not known to be close to the BJP) has shown, consistently point to the fact that since 2002, India has been in a 'wiser voter' phase, where voters have rewarded performing governments far more than in the past.[16] The BJP has been winning more exams, to take this analogy forward, than any other political party. By emerging as the dominant player in what was a fragmented party system since the early 1990s, it has led the game-changing shift in Indian politics, the biggest in three decades. It is winning elections because enough people in India, outside of its traditional vote banks, agree with its politics. This book explains how.

Why Modi Is the New Nehru for the Indian Cultural Right

Such a comparative study is important because Modi's political ascendance, and what it means for India, is as impactful and far-reaching as the political imprint left by the country's first prime minister, Jawaharlal Nehru. Modi may be the mirror opposite of most things Nehru stood for, but in terms of impact, the tectonic shifts he has heralded in Indian politics are Nehruvian in scale. So deep and wide-ranging is the societal impact of Moditva that, of all Indian prime ministers, he can be compared with only Nehru.

This may seem like a strange comparison to make. Nehru, after all, is the most reviled name in the Indian Right's political lexicon. He is often lampooned as soft, wimpish and placatory, as opposed to

Modi, who embodies, for his political supporters, strength, manliness and resoluteness.

So, what are the similarities? At a fundamental level, just as Nehru created the Nehruvian order—championing a new idea of India as a modernist, reforming and rights-based society after Independence, one that came to be accepted by both the elites and most mass voters as the dominant narrative of what it meant to be Indian[17]—Modi's two successive national electoral triumphs in 2014 and 2019 embody an alternative idea of India: soaked in a hard nationalism and an unapologetic espousal of Hindu identity wrapped within the idea of a more efficient welfare-focused state.

Ideationally, Indira Gandhi did not represent a radically new narrative of the nation from her father's. She inherited the Nehruvian template on secularism and socialism but significantly altered it by centralising power as part of a hard-nosed realpolitik approach. Indira's India, in many ways, was a negative mutation of Nehru's foundational ideas of the Indian republic. It hard-coded into the earlier ideology of developmentalism a new socialist rhetoric, an insidious leadership cult, the principle of dynastic succession in politics and a severe reduction of inner-party democracy. It may, in practice, have hollowed out and made redundant many of the key principles of Nehruvian India—but it did so in the name of those same ideals. Indira did lead India to victory in the 1971 war, which reshaped the map of South Asia. Among her other achievements, she also heralded the drive to food self-reliance with the Green Revolution. On balance, though, her record, which included the imposition of the Emergency, is chequered. Her political positioning was always framed within a narrative of continuing the legacy of Nehru's India. Other Indian prime ministers, Congress and non-Congress, had vastly differing approaches to governance, but in terms of big ideas, they too largely worked within the same broad framework of nationhood that was formulated at Independence. They did not upend it.

The Modi era, by contrast, represents a radically different attempt at a moral reordering of the nation. In another era, Nehru too single-handedly went against the dominant thinking in the post-Gandhi Congress, led by party satraps who were steeped in Hindu traditionalism, to frame the first Indian election primarily as a contest between what he called 'communal organisations' like the 'RSS and the Jan Sangh' and the forces of progress. He framed communalism as the 'foremost question'[18] before the country in that election, at a time when the Jan Sangh had been born only four days before voting started, the Hindu Mahasabha had only recently turned into a political party and the RSS was not contesting elections. The major Opposition parties of the time were not Hindu nationalist; they were socialist. The Jan Sangh only won 3 per cent of the votes in 1952, the Socialist Party 10.5 per cent and the Kisan Mazdoor Praja Party 5.7 per cent.

Within these pages, I reconstruct the politics of independent India's first election in 1951-52 to show that Nehru defined his position in this manner not necessarily because he thought that the Jan Sangh was politically strong—it was not—but because the ideals it represented enjoyed deep support within the Congress leadership itself, specifically on the question of the Hindus who still remained in Pakistan and the Nehru government's policies towards them. After Jan Sangh founder Syama Prasad Mookerjee's exit from the Nehru cabinet to form his own party, the objections he raised to Nehru's policies on Hindu cultural grounds[19] enjoyed such support within the Hindu-traditionalist wing of the Congress that it led to the most serious internal challenge that Nehru faced to his own leadership until the Sino-Indian War of 1962.[20]

This challenge was exemplified by the stunning election of Congress's UP chief Purshottamdas Tandon as Congress president on 2 September 1950, when he defeated Acharya Kriplani, whom Nehru supported. Not since Mahatma Gandhi took on Subhas Chandra Bose after his victory as Congress president at the Congress's 1939 Tripuri session had the party seen such a schism at the top. Tandon's elevation was specifically seen at the time as a signal from the Congress to Nehru for a 'reorientation of policy', especially on 'India–Pakistan relations', 'refugees' and 'propagation of Hindi'.[21] Nehru responded by asking his party for a renewed mandate on his Pakistan policies and the 'communal question' in a specially convened Nasik session of the All India Congress Committee (AICC) on 21–22 September 1950. At that session, in a masterful speech delivered at a rain-soaked ground full of slush, the prime minister threatened to resign if his policies were not endorsed. He said he would 'go out and fight independently for the idea of the Congress'.[22] This battle between the 'secular' Nehru and the 'Hindu traditionalist' Tandon, who termed it a 'fight to decide whether Congress will live or die',[23] led to a year-long internal power struggle for the control of the party structure, primarily on the 'Hindu' issues raised by Mookerjee. Nehru's victory was not certain, and for a while, there was a distinct possibility of either a split within the party or the Congress, without Nehru as the helm, taking a turn rightwards.[24] It culminated in Nehru's resignation from the Congress Working Committee on 9 August 1951[25] and a final show of strength that Nehru won, becoming party president in addition to prime minister. Tandon resigned. Chapter 9 of this book shows that the alternative ideas of the Hindu nationalists were not represented only by them—they enjoyed deep sympathies within the Congress leadership and were fought for as much within the party as outside.

Modi is both the outcome and harbinger of these ideas.

For one, like Nehru, he is uncompromising and unambiguous about his party's ideology and ideals. As he emphasised in a victory speech after his second national election win in 2019, his party's journey from 'do se dobara (from two to once again)' stood out because 'we never stepped back from our path, never let our ideals dim. We never stopped, nor got tired, nor did we bend … We will never leave our ideals, nor our sanskaar.'[26] This stout defence of ideas is not that different from Nehru's stringent insistence in the 1952 election campaign on what he called 'an all-out war on communalism', against 'sinister communal elements' that would 'bring ruin and death to the country'.[27]

Second, Modi is unambiguous on the secularism question and what his party sees as its cynical manipulation. 'For thirty continuous years especially,' he has argued emphatically, 'it was such a printout, such a tag that had become so fashionable. That whatever you do, you put it on. It was like doing a Ganga bath to get good credit [punya]. The name of this tag—and it was totally fake—was secularism.' As he later told his National Democratic Alliance (NDA) partners, minorities were made to live in fear because of vote-bank politics and this must end with 'sabka saath, sabka vikas' being extended to 'sabka vishwas'.

Third, like Nehru's conception of an Indian 'tryst with destiny' and India awakening after a 'long slumber'—as he outlined in his famous speech on the eve of Indian independence in 1947—Modi offers to his supporters the vision of a radical break with the past and of a future 'new Bharat'. This is unlike Indira, whose politics was largely about fixing the present, continuing the skeletal outline of the Nehruvian dream and retaining power. The conception of a new Bharat is a recurring theme in Modi's discourse. As he stressed in his 2019 victory speech, for example, 'You will have to leave the thought process of the twentieth century. This is the twenty-first century, this is a new Bharat.'[28] If the Nehruvian order and idea of development was represented by Nehru's characterisation of big dams as the 'temples of modern India', in Modi's India, outside the realm of identity politics, this is best symbolised by toilets as the new vehicle of upward mobility and progress.

Fourth, just as Nehru saw economics essentially as a tool for development and delivering millions out of poverty, so does Modi. His declaration that there are only two castes of Indians now, those that are poor and those engaged in alleviating poverty, is intellectually not dissimilar to the Nehruvian idea of a welfare state and what came to be known in the 1940s as the 'Bombay Plan' to harness private capitalism for nationalist goals.[29]

Fifth, if Nehru was 'chacha', or uncle, to an entire generation of Indians and appealed especially to newly empowered women voters, Modi too has assiduously courted students and a new generation of young voters with his direct outreach to exam-taking students and an aggressive new wave of women voters. My generation grew up in India of the 1980s with the legend of the republic's first prime minister who loved kids. We read children-oriented collections of his, like *Letters from a Father to His Daughter*, which were sold in all government publishing outlets, and celebrated his birthday on 14 November each year as Children's Day. (India switched from the UN-mandated date of Children's Day to Nehru's birthday after his death in 1964.) The result was that several generations of Indian children grew up with Nehru embedded in their mental maps as an icon of political life.

Similarly, since 2014, Modi has spent several episodes of his monthly All India Radio show *Mann ki Baat* focused on students, youth and especially on the stress of examinations.[30] In a country with the world's largest youth bulge and arguably one of the most competitive systems of school examinations anywhere, this specific outreach to pre-voting age students has been so far understudied by political scientists and journalists. However, it is clear that the power of India's biggest mass medium—radio, simulcast in multiple regional languages and on private radio networks—combined with the digital reach of the government's interactive MyGov.in has made it a fundamental outreach tool for reshaping the mental maps of a new generation.

A good example is Modi's book *Exam Warriors*, which was published in 2018 in multiple languages and became India's number one non-fiction bestseller for a while.[31] The book itself emerged out of an early episode of *Mann ki Baat* in February 2015 on how students in grades X and XII should deal with the stress of annual board examinations. Anyone growing up in India knows how these examinations are perceived to be make-or-break events for students' careers. When Modi first addressed these issues like a school counsellor on his radio show, many critics dismissed it as yet another publicity venture. That was a mistake. His book systematically took this gambit forward, subliminally combining the role of psychological counsellor, intimate friend and guide. *Exam Warriors*, an e-version of which is available on the Narendra Modi app, combines activities for children with a space for building their own timetables and their own 'personal diary', seamlessly interwoven with personal thoughts on how the prime minister himself handles stress in his daily work and has dealt with it during key political milestones in his political journey. So, Modi advises students in these pages on how they can use 'PlayStation' as a 'refreshing element' while they study, even as he tells them that he himself 'never accesses a mobile phone or any other gadget' during meetings.[32] Political messaging also forms a subtle backdrop to advice on yoga asanas or how to remain stress-free. As Modi wrote, 'Like you have exams, I had one of my own exams—the Gujarat elections of 2012. The day polling ended and the votes were cast, I moved ahead and began to work on the tasks at hand. I still remember going to oversee preparations for the upcoming Vibrant Gujarat Global Summit and reviewing an irrigation project. For me, the vote, like your answer sheet, was a one-way ticket. Prepare, write, move ahead.'[33]

Sixth, if Nehru was Gandhi's anointed heir, Modi has explicitly sought to appropriate the Mahatma's legacy. Take, for instance, his call for a national renewal mission coinciding with the seventy-fifth anniversary of

Gandhi's Quit India movement. When Gandhi died in 1948, Nehru turned to the radio to deliver one of his most emotional speeches, saying that the 'light has gone out of our lives'. Modi has used his radio programming in particular to drive home his appropriation of Gandhi. It is not an accident that his signature Swachh Bharat programme was symbolically launched on 2 October 2014, Gandhi's birth anniversary. The very next day, Modi launched his *Mann ki Baat* radio show, telling Indian viewers that 'when it comes to cleanliness, the most inspiring icon is Mahatma Gandhi'. This is why, he said, he had launched his clarion call to make India 'dirt-free by the 150th birthday of Mahatma Gandhi'.[34]

Similarly, it is significant that the first episode of the show also featured a clarion call to Indians to start wearing khadi, the home-spun cotton that was synonymous with Gandhi and the freedom movement, again. As Modi put it, 'Whenever we think of Mahatma Gandhi, we are reminded of khadi … I am just requesting you to use at least one khadi product, like a handkerchief, or a bath towel, a bed sheet, a pillow cover, a curtain or anything of that kind.'[35] As an aside, the Khadi and Village Industries Commission (KVIC) reported that, following this appeal, khadi sales went up by three times over a five-year period from 2015-16 to 2020. The KVIC attributed this rise in sales to the prime minister.[36] In case anyone missed the point, it also issued evocative calendars in 2017 featuring Modi in a Gandhi-like pose, spinning the charkha.[37]

Finally, for no other prime minister, since Nehru, has the narrative and image of being a global leader been so crucial to their domestic persona as it has been for Modi. Foreign policy has seldom been a vote-winner in Indian politics. Yet, for Nehru, his pivotal role in global affairs, his creation of the Non-Aligned Movement (NAM) and his outsized role as spokesperson for the postcolonial developing world were inseparable from his influence at home and his irreplaceability as a domestic leader. Of course, globalism was a key part of Indira Gandhi's politics too. She used the pageantry of NAM summits and domestic events like the 1982 Asian Games to play statesman. Rajiv Gandhi's youthful image symbolised a new India, and Manmohan Singh's erudition led to US President Barack Obama praising him as a 'man with uncommon wisdom', who even appeared 'holy' to the 'Western eye'.[38] But no one since Nehru has made the perception of foreign clout as central to their local imagery as Modi has.

In his first three speeches to the nation during the first national lockdown imposed due to the pandemic in 2020, it was telling how much of Modi's discourse focused on the term 'vaishvik mahamaari corona', or global epidemic. He stressed on what other, more developed countries, with greater resources than India, were doing and how India's response compared with theirs. In his third speech, for example, when he announced a ₹20 lakh crore package, he made it a point to emphasise that the US had devoted about 10 per cent of its GDP in its package and that India was doing the same.[39] The global is both local and fundamental to his political positioning.

Liberals sniggered at images of Modi hugging Obama during the US President's India visit and over his quip that his relationship with Obama was 'tu-tarake ka rishta' (colloquial Hindi idiom for an informal friendship where friends address each other with the informal 'tu' as opposed to the respectful 'aap'). They debated whether the semantics made any sense, but they missed the significance of the domestic political signalling. A status of equality and clout with global leaders, including with Obama's successor Donald Trump, was fundamental to Modi's domestic positioning as well. It is no coincidence that the semi-official book on the *Mann ki Baat* series, produced with the 'cooperation of the Narendra Modi app team' and written largely for an Indian audience, starts with an endorsement by the then Japanese prime minister Shinzo Abe. Or that Obama featured in the first *Mann ki Baat* radio show of 2015 alongside Modi.

Whether you believe in Narendra Modi or firmly oppose his politics, the point is that he represents a new epoch in Indian politics. No prime minister since Nehru has embodied so much political power. Modi has not only led his party to two successive victories at the national level, he also presided over its replacing of the Congress as India's predominant national party, ushering in a new era of party politics.

The Congress under Nehru and Indira dominated Indian politics for decades due to what was called the 'Congress system', to quote Rajni Kothari's elegant phrasing.[40] The BJP, committed to ushering in a 'Congress-mukt Bharat', Congress-free India, has filled the vacuum created by the decline of the Congress with its own BJP system. The how and why of that is the story this book tells.

PART I

THE HINDI HEARTLAND

LABHARTHEE SAMMELANS, CASTE RE-ENGINEERING, HINDUTVA AND THE WELFARE WHEEL

1

THE BJP AS THE PARTY OF THE VILLAGE

An Introduction

'How many people didn't get a toilet in this village? Raise your hands,' said UP Chief Minister Yogi Adityanath on the microphone. It was late night in Kandhai Madhopur village in central Uttar Pradesh's Pratapgarh district. The chief minister was sitting under a banyan tree, legs dangling off the edge of a large, specially constructed saffron stage. He was surrounded by over 3,000 villagers, some of whom had climbed trees and rooftops to get a better glimpse of him. An angry chorus rose from the crowd as several hands went up. Yogi leant into the mike again, asking, 'Who is the DPRO [District Panchayati Raj Officer] here?'

The officer, standing amidst a row of apparatchiks on the stage, stepped up gingerly, saying within earshot of the crowd, 'Five hundred toilets have been approved this year, sir. Fifty, last year.'

'Note this,' responded Yogi to him on the mike. 'And you note it too,' he said, looking meaningfully at the crowd. 'By tomorrow all labharthees should get the money into their bank account. If it doesn't reach the bank accounts, then accountability will be fixed.'

He moved on to his second public question. 'How many ration cards have been made in this village?' Again, a cacophony of responses from the gathered crowd. Yogi gestured to the row of officers nearby. 'Where is the DPRO, CDO [Chief Development Officer], DM [District Magistrate]? All three can come up here.' As they came forward, he asked on the mike,

'When was ration card issuance done here in this village?' The DM, the highest-ranked official in the district, whispered an answer to the chief minister, who then made another announcement: 'Organise a camp in the village tomorrow itself and give out ration cards here as per eligibility.' There was loud applause from the crowd. 'Within a week, make sure this is done across the entire panchayat so ration cards under Antyodaya [a Union government scheme] and Paatra Grahasthi [a state government scheme] are all given out as per eligibility.'

One by one, he read out the names of government schemes in operation in the village, got officers to list out the names of beneficiaries from government lists, personally read out some of these lists and asked villagers to tally them with their own experience. How many water handpumps had been reported broken in the village? How many had been repaired? When? How many Nirashrit Mahilas, destitute women, were getting government pensions? (Seventy-five, with thirty more names sanctioned in the new year.) How many Divyang, differently abled, pensions? (Sixty-five, and seventeen new ones sanctioned.) In each case, figures and names were read out from government lists, villagers were asked to verify them, vigorous debates ensued between those who felt they had been wrongly left out and the officials present, and the latter were asked to resolve the matter.

The audience's most vigorous reaction came when Yogi Adityanath asked about the Pradhan Mantri Awas Yojana, the Union government's scheme for housing for the poor. A man in a saffron scarf, sitting on an overlooking tree, shouted that he had been left out. The chief minister invited him onstage—'Say it from here on the mike and on stage'—to loud cheers from the crowd.

'I had filled a form,' complained the saffron-scarf man, now standing on stage and looking him in the eye, 'but didn't get anything.'

'Just filling up a form won't do it,' responded Yogi, as the public gathering threatened to get out of control. 'Labharthee names on the list are decided according to eligibility criteria set by the 2011 Socio-Economic Survey Report,' he explained. 'Selection is done only on that basis. Neither the DPRO nor the Gram Pradhan [Village Head] or Gram Development Officer can do anything about it ... Under PM Awas Yojana, the list of those 136 people who have been sanctioned houses in the village this year based on the survey report [109 in the previous year] has been hung up on a board in the Gram Sabha Sachivalaya [Village Council Secretariat]. Check your names there. For those who are left out … it is for them that this camp is being organised tomorrow so everyone eligible gets the benefit of these schemes.' Yogi then asked the district officer to read out the full list for the crowd to verify.

A bespectacled and moustachioed bureaucrat now took the mike and started intoning, somewhat surreally, from the list of those being given money for government housing. 'The people whose dreams have been fulfilled with this allotment are … 1. Pramod Bharat, Scheduled Caste 2. Laxman Bhagwati, Scheduled Caste …' and so on.

This village meeting in Pratapgarh, held in April 2018, exactly a year after Yogi Adityanath became the chief minister of UP following a landslide election win for the BJP, was the first in a new 'chaupal', or village gathering, initiative he started. It targeted political outreach on the government's social-welfare programmes ahead of the 2019 general elections. The immediate aim was to build a layer of political mobilisation and public accountability around government spending, directly linking it to the BJP's efforts. When, for example, villagers complained that they had only received ₹10,000 of the ₹12,000 that Yogi said they were entitled to under the Swachh Bharat scheme, he explained, 'Please note this and understand: you are to get Rs 10,000 in the first tranche for each personal toilet. The remaining Rs 2,000 comes after its geotagging and verification has been done.' He added, 'I request you all to get full information on government schemes. Accusations and counter-accusations won't solve anything … and if any corrupt officers ask any labharthee for money, we have arranged that not only will they be jailed and an FIR filed, their property will be confiscated, because people's exploitation can only prosper where people don't have enough knowledge of government schemes and people are not aware enough, which in turn encourages corrupt elements.'

Furthermore, this strategy seamlessly blended the BJP's focus on social-welfare spending with the politics of social engineering and a planned outreach to attract those lower down the caste order into its fold. The choice of villages where this outreach took place (4,487 in UP) was dictated by caste composition, with party leaders targeting those with a greater share of lower-caste populations first. As Yogi summed up that night, 'Honourable PM [Modi] has chosen more than 20,000 villages in the country which we are reaching out to because SCs and deprived sections constitute more than half the population of these villages. We will reach out to them in the first phase, in the second phase to other villages, and then, in the third phase, to the whole nation. So, if 136 houses were approved in this village this year and 500 personal toilets, people should have this information. Which scheme is coming and which scheme will have what benefits? What does the Jan Dhana Yojana mean for them in benefits? When the PM talks of DBT [Direct Benefit Transfers] transactions, and if that money goes directly into labharthee accounts, what is the benefit of this? If someone has a Jan Dhan account, they can benefit from every government scheme. They can get money for a toilet, money for a house, get chulha [stove] subsidy benefits, benefits from pension schemes and many other schemes.' The messaging was plain to see and specially crafted for the cameras.

Yogi Adityanath followed up the midnight meeting with dinner at a local Dalit family's house and stayed the night in the village with his cabinet ministers. The headlines on Hindi news channels the next day were dominated by what Aaj Tak, the Hindi channel, called his 'Nayak' turn, in a reference to the Anil Kapoor-starrer *Nayak*, where a local reporter-turned-chief minister held public hearings of officials. TV coverage of the event also showcased the smiling wife of Dayaram Saroj, the Dalit host, proudly talking about her dinner guest and recounting the menu for the cameras: 'bhindi ki sabzi, raita, gurh, lauki ki sabzi, aam ki chutney, kheer, roti [okra, yoghurt, jaggery, bottle gourd, mango chutney, rice pudding, bread].'[1]

'Hindutva Gives Gati, Welfare Is What Keeps the Wheel Spinning'

Chief Minister Yogi Adityanath's chaupal and the manner in which it was conducted perfectly encapsulates some of the dominant strands of the BJP's political mobilisation since 2014 in UP—India's most populous state and the one that sends the highest number of members to Parliament. First, a strong rural focus in the politics of welfare. Second, an explicit attempt to draw lower castes into the ambit of the BJP and the wider Hindutva umbrella with the messaging of inclusivity. Third, his very presence as chief minister conveyed the party's implicit message of Hinduness: a saffron-clad monk and the head of the ancient Gorakhnath Peeth, seat of the Nath monastic order, in the seat of power in Lucknow. As Yogi Adityanath said in Pratapgarh, 'The tradition I come from has for centuries been working with society's deprived Dalits, sitting among them and running a campaign of "Alakh Niranjan" [a term traditionally used by Nath yogis as a synonym for the Creator]. I have come to carry forward that same tradition. This for me is a way of seva [service], not politics.'[2]

The BJP's electoral dominance in the Hindi heartland generally, and UP specifically, has powered its political ascendance nationally since 2014. It was enabled by a complete transformation of the party at many levels. This metamorphosis transformed the BJP into the central pole of politics beyond India's cities and towns, turning it into the default political party of the village in the Hindi heartland. It has long been seen primarily as an urban-focused party—a tag that was not entirely true even earlier. However, since 2014, under Narendra Modi as prime minister, and Amit Shah as party president (2014–2019), the BJP has made deep changes to its DNA, i.e., its social and cultural composition. This transformation has had a cataclysmic impact on Indian politics.

Part I of this book takes a deep dive into the politics of India's most populous state as well as the larger Hindi heartland. It is based on game-changing new data on caste and representation that fundamentally rewires our previous understanding. We see how, after 2013, the BJP has repeatedly confounded opponents and conventional wisdom to achieve electoral blitzkriegs in rural and rurban India, significantly deepening its roots as a political party.[3] This shift, and the mechanisms that brought it about, upended the conventions of Indian politics as we know them.

Chapter 2 establishes the magnitude of the newly acquired rural depth of the BJP. Chapters 3, 4 and 5 explain how and why the party's political advancement came about. The facets of this progress have not truly been understood so far in their entirety. The broad assumption has been that the BJP somehow kept winning elections because of the Narendra Modi phenomenon, his unique brand of personality politics and an appeal to Hindu sentiments alone—and that somehow this would easily fall apart after Modi. Far from it. Modi's appeal is real and tangible, and he has undoubtedly been the primary catalyst for the turnaround. However, the party's surge in the Hindi heartland—in the rural areas and among the lower strata of caste and class—is built on deeper structural shifts undertaken on his watch.

The BJP made fundamental changes at three levels.

One, it radically changed its party structure to become the most socially representative party in UP across Hindu castes. If you leave aside Muslims—and that is an important qualifier—after 2013, the BJP has given positions of power and influence to more social groups and castes than any other party in the state. Chapter 3 shows, with new data, how this happened across several registers: the BJP's political candidates in national and state elections, its state-level office-bearers, district-level presidents, and the ministers it appointed once it had formed a government. The old BJP that was dominated by upper castes is long gone. And the electoral dominance of the new BJP is directly linked to this transformation. While the party retained its urban base, middle-class following and upper-caste support, it significantly expanded its caste representation, becoming the default party of those lower down the social and economic order. Though it had made significant inroads earlier into OBCs under the leadership of its first OBC chief minister in UP—Kalyan Singh, between 1991-92 and 1997–1999)[4]—the recent shift is much more expansive and far-reaching. K.N. Govindacharya, then general secretary of the party, argued in 1993 that the party would have to change the 'chaal, charitra aur chehra (working style, character and face)'[5] of its leadership to bring in aspirational and newly assertive castes and classes if it wanted to start winning. Nearly three decades on, this is substantially if not wholly the case in most of UP, and at the heart of the BJP's resurgence.

Two, the BJP built a grassroots party structure around most of the 1,47,164 voting booths in UP.[6] Chapter 4 shows that this new party cadre was deployed not just to get voters out to booths during election cycles but also, significantly, for targeted grassroots mobilisation around government welfare programmes—such as free housing, LPG gas connections and direct benefit cash transfers to farmers—outside of election campaigns.

While all parties spend money on welfare programmes, this kind of precision-targeted political mobilisation around government lists of welfare beneficiaries in villages is new to north India. It has been done before more in southern states, notably in Tamil Nadu, which also has cadre-based parties like the All India Dravida Munnetra Kazhagam (AIADMK) and the Dravida Munnetra Kazhagam (DMK).

Three, the BJP refocused on an unapologetic Hindutva messaging, going back to its core ideology. As UP Deputy Chief Minister Dinesh Sharma told me in his office in Lucknow's Vidhan Sabha premises, 'The core reason for the BJP's victory is that we did not change our core principles. When we lost, we still remained strong on our ideals, as we did when we won. People's belief in us grew because we didn't do the politics of gain and loss.'[7] Chapter 5 examines at length what this means for Muslims, who constitute 19.2 per cent of UP's population (14.2 per cent nationwide).[8] While this was a key driver of the BJP's growth, it is also important to acknowledge that a focus on Hindutva as a cultural force alone could never, by itself, have delivered the massive Hindi heartland vote shares and mandates that the party has won since 2013.

Hindutva sentiment is not new in Indian politics. The big question to ask is: why did the BJP never win such victories before? Even at the height of the Ram Janmabhoomi movement, in 1989, the Communist Party of India (CPI) beat the BJP at the epicentre of the movement, in Ayodhya, when its Mitrasen Yadav was elected as an MP. 'Even when the Mandir movement was at its peak, temple politics did not always win in Ayodhya itself. At that time, when sentiments around Ram were at their peak, caste consciousness beat Mandir politics in the Faizabad seat in Ayodhya with the victory of a Yadav candidate,' points out senior Lucknow-based journalist Pranshu Mishra.[9] The BJP's vote share was lower than the combined votes of the socialist and pro-Dalit parties and Congress in UP's provincial elections, even in 1991.[10]

The master key, as BJP's campaign managers recognised after 2014, is the politics of welfare and caste representation. At Lucknow's Lok Bhawan, where Chief Minister Yogi Adityanath functions from, a senior official working closely with him pointed this out to me as he explained the chaupal outreach programme: 'The BJP vote base basically is a mindset that we call Hindutva. This gives speed [gati] but the job of spinning the wheel is direct benefit transfers, social benefits, this is it. *Hindutva is like the elephant's teeth. The real teeth is welfare. Hindutva gives you speed if you are going in a particular direction, but welfare is the wheel that makes it all run* [emphasis added].'[11] Importantly, 'welfare' or 'development' here is not used in its usual sense of building 'hard infrastructure' but rather the redistribution of direct individual benefits using cash transfers through a dozen-plus schemes streamlined and funded by the Union government. How its leaders embraced this changed the party as a political outfit and created what can be called a new BJP system of politics. This new model is fundamentally different from what has been called the Congress 'system', which was based on a politics of 'consensus' and underpinned its political dominance in India from the 1950s to the 1990s.[12]

2

BECOMING THE HINDI HEARTLAND'S PREDOMINANT RURAL PARTY

The BJP has emerged as the predominant rural party in the Hindi heartland between 2014 and 2019. There is compelling evidence of this. In order to better understand the spatial geography of the party's growth, Jai Mrug, psephologist and founder of the polling agency VotersMood Research (VMR), Rishabh Srivastava and I classified 225 parliamentary constituencies in the ten Hindi-speaking states of north and central India (UP, Madhya Pradesh, Rajasthan, Bihar, Chhattisgarh, Jharkhand, Haryana, Himachal Pradesh, Uttarakhand and Delhi) into three categories: urban, rurban and rural. We did this by taking district-level census demographic data, systematically overlaying it onto Lok Sabha constituencies and geotagging them. Jai did the initial theoretical classification, defining urban seats as those with urban populations above 80 per cent, rurban as seats having an urban population between 33 and 60 per cent and rural seats as those with less than 33 per cent urban population. I did the political mapping and analysis, and Srivastava produced the data analytics. We were astonished by the patterns this exercise uncovered.

Hindi-speaking states are the central power engine of the BJP's national political dominance, accounting for almost 60 per cent of its 303-seat majority in the 2019 Lok Sabha polls. The party won over 78 per cent of the 225 Hindi heartland seats in 2019, over 84 per cent in 2014. These triumphs were essentially fashioned on the bedrock of a new rural constituency that the party created for itself in the Hindi heartland between 2014 and 2019. It grew deep roots here in new areas outside urban centres, which powered its re-election and electoral ascendance. Over half the Lok Sabha seats in the region are rural: 127 of 225. UP has roughly the same ratio of rural seats: forty-six of eighty.

No Longer a City-only Party

The most striking illustration of the BJP's rural growth comes from vote shares. In the Hindi heartland's 127 rural constituencies, the BJP managed to win over 40 per cent vote share in only 16.5 per cent seats in 2009. In 2014, it more than tripled that number to 57.4 per cent of rural seats and upped it further to a whopping 74.8 per cent in 2019. This rising rural depth of the party gave it a rural hegemony, way above its nearest competitors. In multipolar contests within India's first-past-the-post election system where dozens of candidates contest from individual seats, a 40 per cent threshold on vote share is a premier performance benchmark for political parties, indicating a decisive presence: especially so in contests with three or more major players.[1] Now, about half the states in the Hindi heartland are multiparty polities. (The exceptions are Madhya Pradesh, Rajasthan, Himachal Pradesh, Chhattisgarh and Uttarakhand, which are two-party polities, with the Congress in direct competition with the BJP.) In 2009, the Congress was ahead of the BJP in these 127 rural constituencies, winning over 40 per cent vote share in 23.6 per cent of the seats. Yet, that number collapsed to 8.6 per cent in 2014 and 11.8 per cent in 2019. In other words, the Congress shrank in rural seats, becoming over six times smaller than the BJP in the decade between 2009 and 2019 (Figures 2.1, 2.4).

This pattern becomes even more telling when we narrow-focus on UP. Of the forty-six rural Lok Sabha seats, the BJP won over 40 per cent vote share in just 6.5 per cent seats in 2009. Yet, in 2014, it won such ascendance in over half these seats, and in as many as 82.6 per cent seats in 2019. When a party wins more than 40 per cent vote share in over 80 per cent of rural seats in a state characterised by multiparty contests, it only means one thing: it has become the default party of the village there.

To put this in context, let us compare the BJP's rural depth with that of its competitors in UP: the SP, the BSP and the Congress. In the 2009–2019

Figure 2.1: The BJP Significantly Expanded in the Rural Hindi Heartland, While the Congress Shrank (2009–2019)

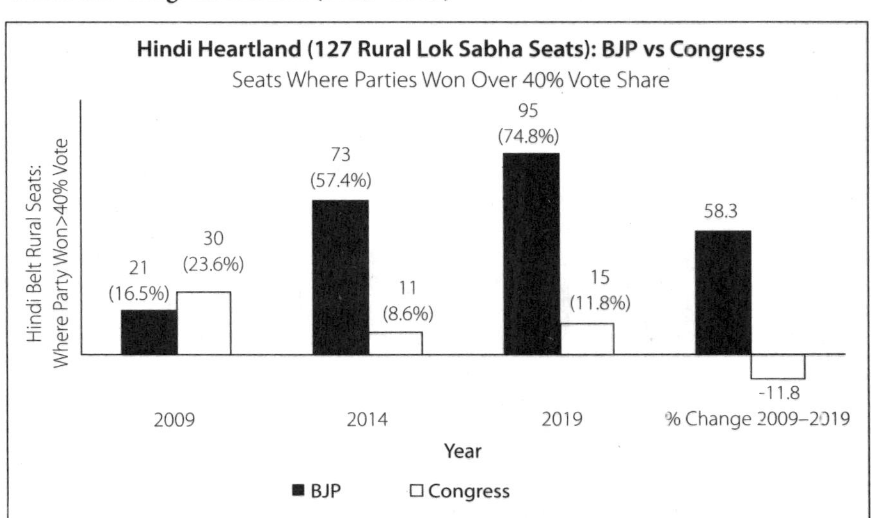

Source: Election Commission of India (ECI) data. Analysis by Nalin Mehta, Rishabh Srivastava, PollNiti.

period, while the BJP transformed into the dominant pole of politics in these rural areas, the support base of its main competitors either remained stagnant or drastically went down on the very same seats. The SP was way ahead of the BJP in 2009, winning more than 40 per cent votes in 17.3 per cent rural UP constituencies that year, but went down to 6.5 per cent in 2014. It recovered to 23.9 per cent in 2019, but the BJP still had three times that number. The BSP made major gains in rural UP in 2019, but even so had such deep-rooted vote-share support in only 26 per cent of the constituencies, while the Congress seriously declined to just a couple of such seats: Rahul Gandhi's Amethi and Sonia Gandhi's Raebareli (see Figure 2.2).

These deep-seated vote-share shifts in favour of the BJP also reflected in seats won. In the Hindi heartland, the BJP won less than one-third of the rural seats in 2009, but as much as 77.9 per cent in 2014 and 70.8 per cent in 2019. Similarly, in UP, the party went from winning just 8.6 per cent of rural seats in 2009 to 82.6 per cent in 2014 and 76 per cent in 2019. Figure 2.3 spatially maps how the BJP's advances in rural areas changed the political map of UP and the Hindi heartland in the space of a decade.

FIGURE 2.2: The BJP Significantly Expanded Its Rural Base in UP, While Key Rivals Shrank (2009–2019)

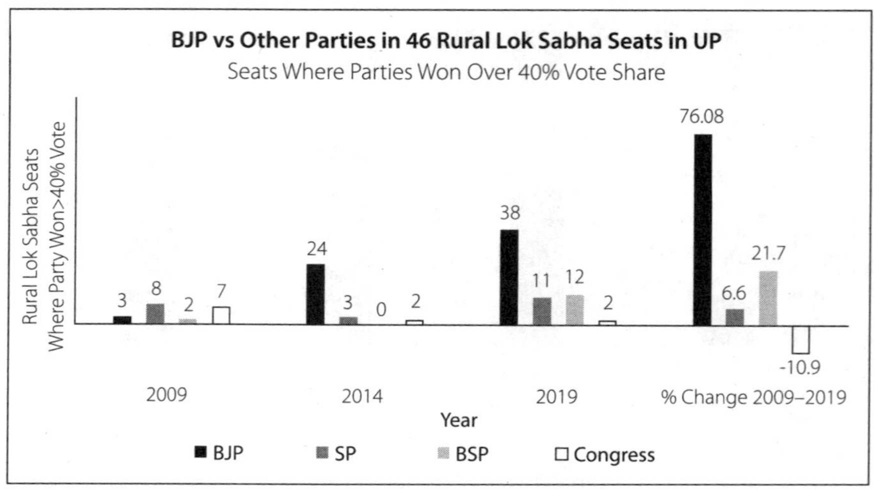

Source: ECI: Analysis by Nalin Mehta, Rishabh Srivastava, PollNiti.

Yet, the overall seat-share changes tell an incomplete story. They are often built on a lower voting base that could be overturned anytime. Mapping how deeper vote shares change is more meaningful as a way of tracking structural change. Our analysis found that, in 2019, the BJP not only retained most of its numbers in the Hindi heartland overall, and UP in particular, it actually made significant advances in rurban and rural areas.

'A Party of Both the Rural and the Town': The BJP's Rurban Rise

It is not just rural seats. The BJP showed the same pattern of growth in rurban seats as well. Of the seventy-nine rurban seats in the Hindi heartland, its MPs got elected from 24 per cent in 2009, 91.1 per cent in 2014 and 86 per cent in 2019. Again, until 2014, these poll victories could have been dismissed as only skin-deep and easily reversible. In 2019, however, the BJP gained significant voter depth in these areas, even though its seat share reduced slightly. In these very same Hindi heartland rurban seats, the party won more than 40 per cent votes in only 13.9 per cent constituencies in 2009, 82.2 per cent in 2014 and an astounding 94.9

per cent in 2019. Zoom in further on UP, and we see the same pattern of horizontal widening of the BJP's rurban base. Of twenty-eight rurban seats in UP, it went from winning just 20.7 per cent in 2009 to 96.4 per cent in 2014 and then to 75 per cent in 2019. Again, vote shares in these rurban parliamentary constituencies show a growing base for the party: more than 40 per cent of votes in zero seats in 2009, 78.5 per cent in 2014 and a whopping 92.8 per cent in 2019 (see Figures 2.4 and 2.5).

When I put these numbers to Keshav Prasad Maurya, the BJP's deputy chief minister in UP, in June 2020, his response was unambiguous. 'The BJP is a party of the poor,' he said. When we met at his residence at Lucknow's Kalidas Marg, the first COVID-19 lockdown was on. Besides the regular security metal detectors at the entrance, there were now also two gates with overhead sprinklers that blew clouds of sanitising liquid over visitors. Once inside, we observed all social-distancing norms as we conversed in his residential office. I had just travelled 1,000 km across UP researching rural areas for this book. When I asked him whether he thought that the BJP was now predominantly a rural party, he answered emphatically: 'BPL cards were always there. They were made in 2002. But when we went to the people for 2017 and 2019 elections, there were many who had reached the sky from the ground but still had BPL cards. We studied this deeply and worked to ensure that those who deserved it really get a voice, get toilets, gas connections, health services, get food in their house. This is the work we did and so BJP is the party of the poor.'[2] I examine these claims in detail in Chapter 4. For now, Maurya's assertion is a substantial one to note for a party that was once seen as a purely urban party.

Importantly, the BJP made these rural and rurban gains without losing its urban support base (see Figure 2.4). This is why, when I put the same question to the BJP's other deputy chief minister in UP, Dinesh Sharma, he answered, 'The BJP in real terms is now a party of both the village and the town. It is not only of the village, and not only of the town.'[3] The numbers clearly show two trends: the 'ruralisation of the BJP', and the 'proletarianization' of the party, as the social scientist Diego Maiorana concluded when he analysed post-poll survey data from the National Election Studies, collected by the Centre for Developing Societies in 2019. The BJP performed 'exceptionally well in rural areas', he found. Similarly,

Figure 2.3: The BJP Advances, Powered by Deep Inroads into Rural Areas (2009–2019 Lok Sabha Polls)

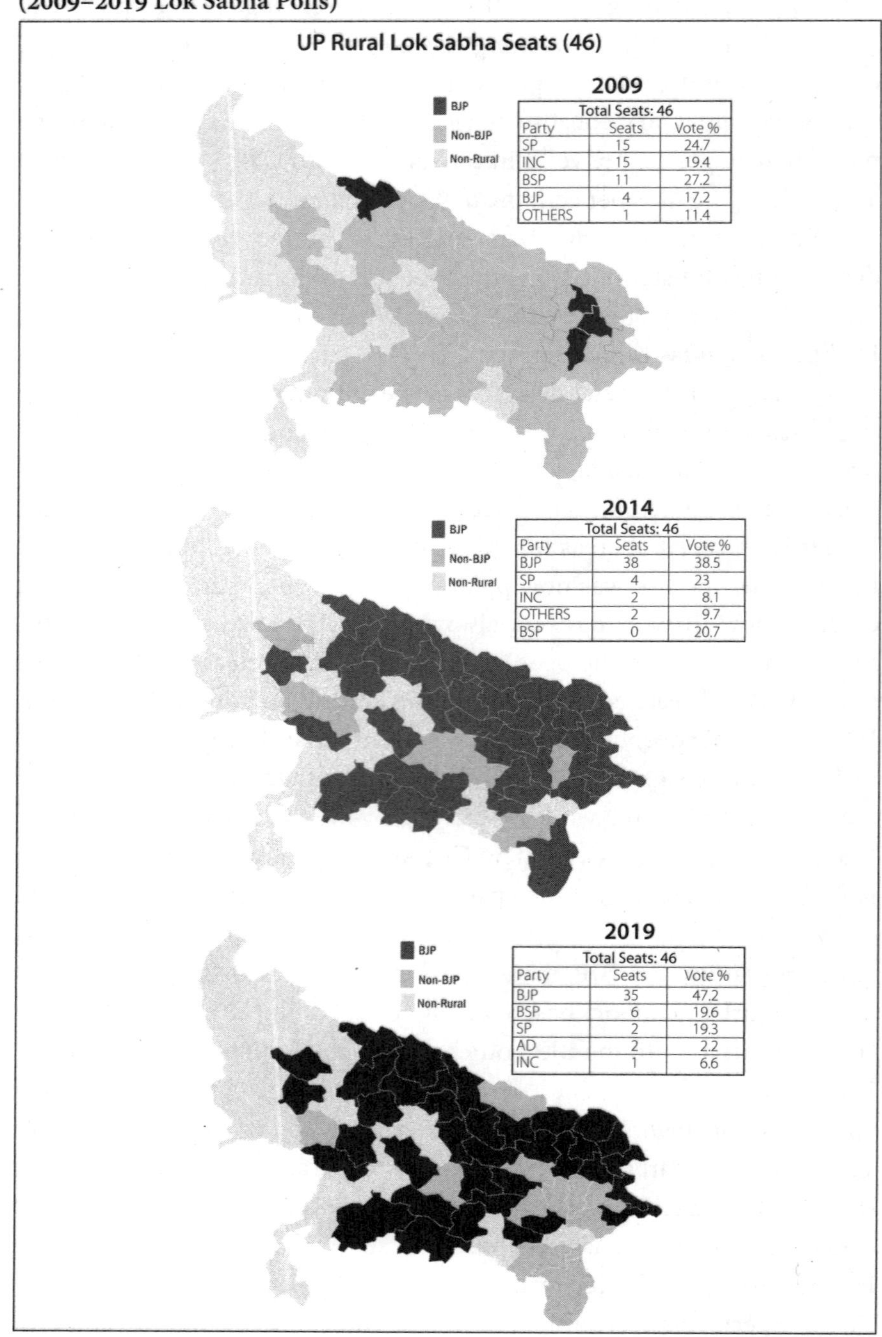

2009

Total Seats: 46		
Party	Seats	Vote %
SP	15	24.7
INC	15	19.4
BSP	11	27.2
BJP	4	17.2
OTHERS	1	11.4

2014

Total Seats: 46		
Party	Seats	Vote %
BJP	38	38.5
SP	4	23
INC	2	8.1
OTHERS	2	9.7
BSP	0	20.7

2019

Total Seats: 46		
Party	Seats	Vote %
BJP	35	47.2
BSP	6	19.6
SP	2	19.3
AD	2	2.2
INC	1	6.6

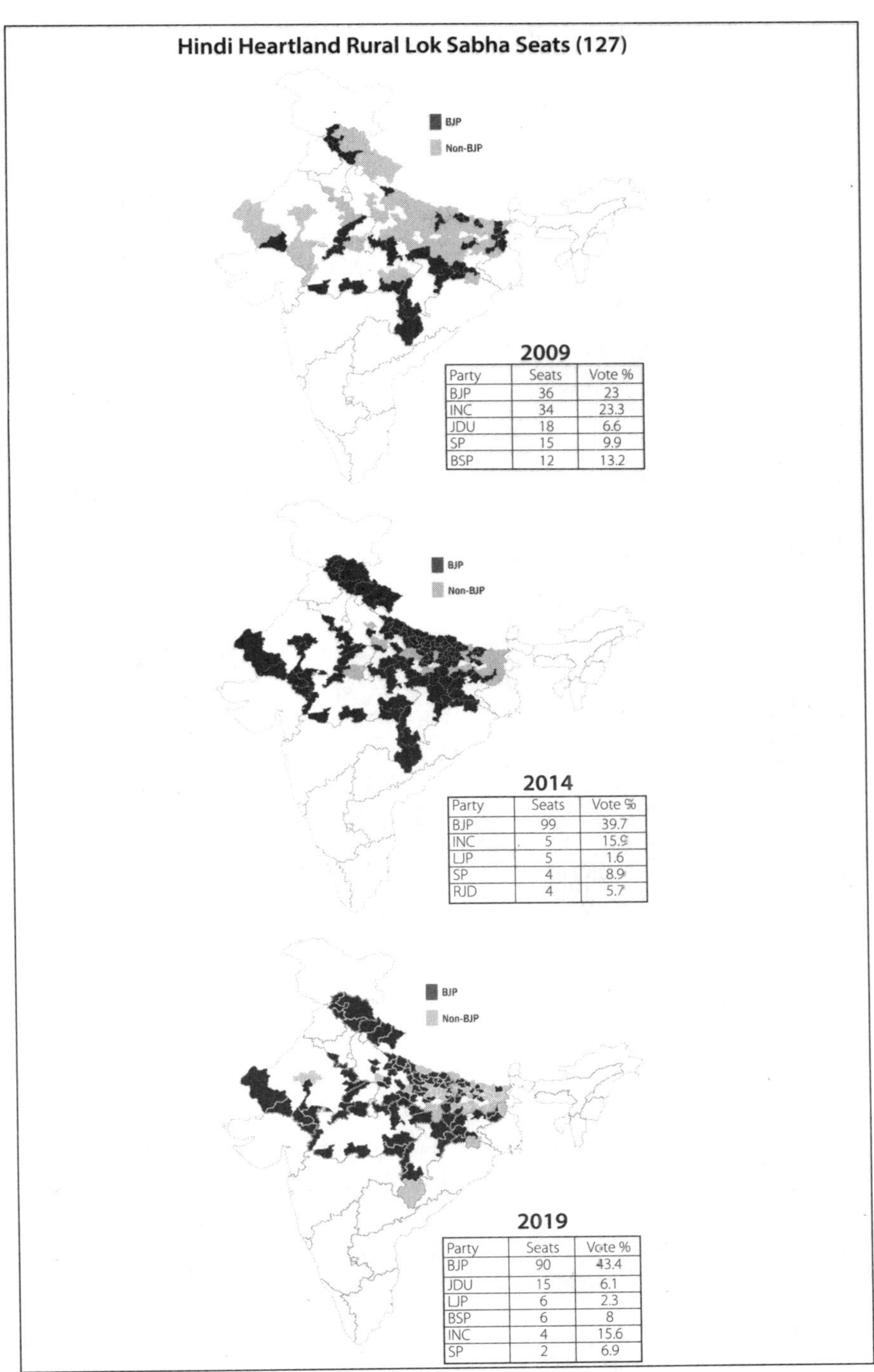

2009

Party	Seats	Vote %
BJP	36	23
INC	34	23.3
JDU	18	6.6
SP	15	9.9
BSP	12	13.2

2014

Party	Seats	Vote %
BJP	99	39.7
INC	5	15.9
LJP	5	1.6
SP	4	8.9
RJD	4	5.7

2019

Party	Seats	Vote %
BJP	90	43.4
JDU	15	6.1
LJP	6	2.3
BSP	6	8
INC	4	15.6
SP	2	6.9

Source: ECI data. Analysis by Nalin Mehta, Rishabh Srivastava, PollNiti. Graphic by Rajiv Pundir.

Figure 2.4: The BJP's Urban, Rurban and Rural Growth in the Hindi Heartland's 225 Lok Sabha Seats (2009–2019)

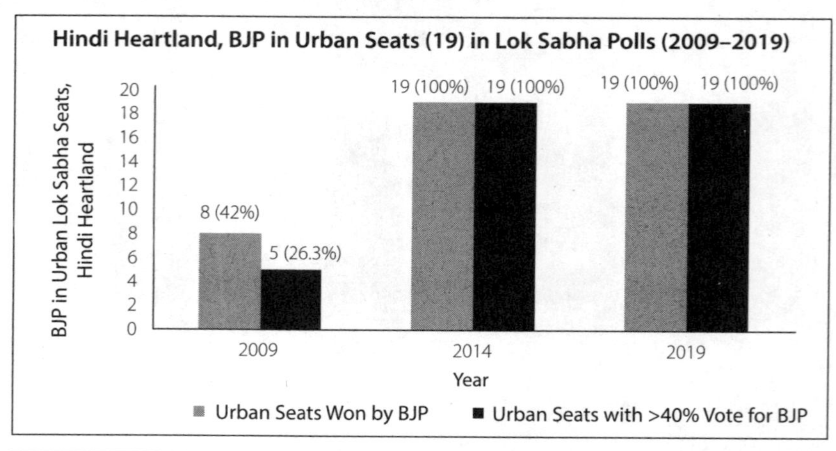

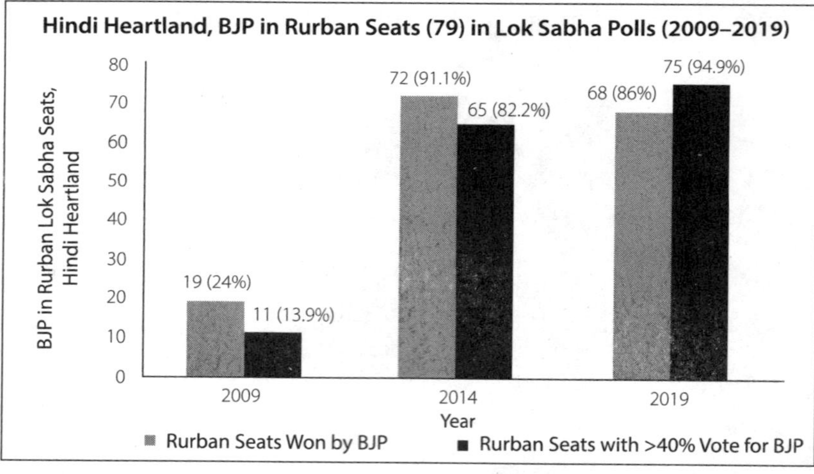

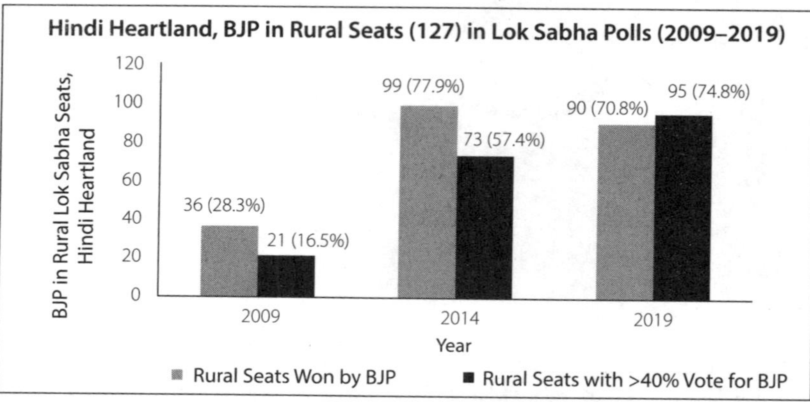

Source: ECI data. Analysis by Nalin Mehta, Rishabh Srivastava, PollNiti.

Figure 2.5: The BJP's Urban, Rurban and Rural Growth in UP's 80 Lok Sabha Seats (2009–2019)

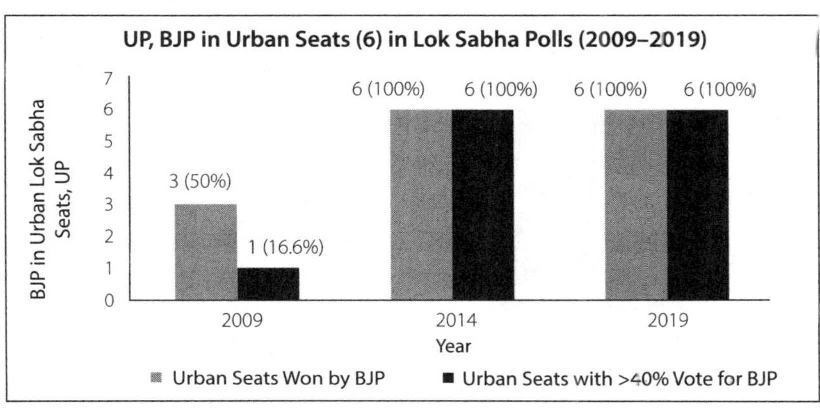

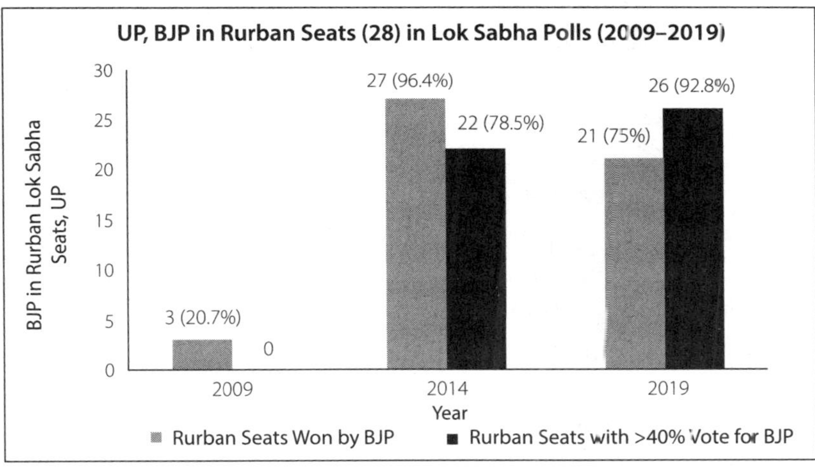

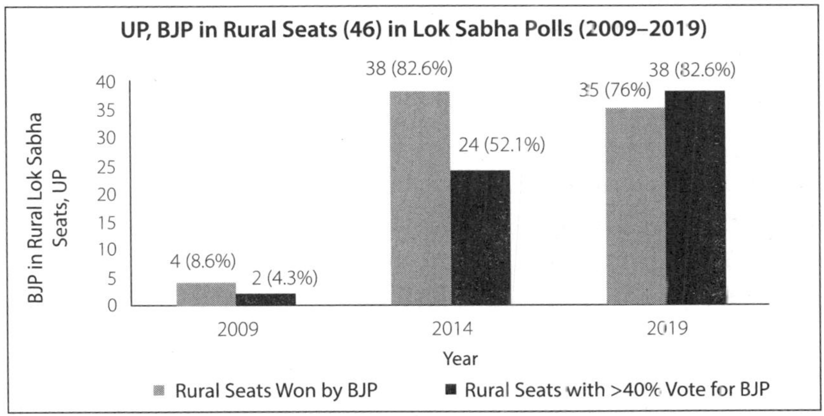

Source: ECI data. Analysis by Nalin Mehta, Rishabh Srivastava, PollNiti.

the more rural or rurban a constituency, the more likely that the BJP would do better there.[4]

The BJP's New Catchment Areas of Bengal and Karnataka Are Also Driven by Rurban, Rural Growth

Interestingly, this phenomenon is not restricted to the Hindi heartland. Even in the BJP's new catchment areas in the South (Karnataka) and in the East (West Bengal), almost all of the party's growth is primarily in rurban and rural areas. In Karnataka, it won 91.3 per cent of rurban Lok Sabha seats in 2019, all of them with greater than 40 per cent vote share. The BJP won three of these seats, with more than 60 per cent of the votes, thirteen with more than 50 per cent of the votes and five with more than 40 per cent vote share. Just as in the northern Hindi heartland, Karnataka saw a deepening of the BJP's rurban base in the decade of 2009–2019. We see the early stages of this same pattern of growth in West Bengal, where the party won 56.6 per cent rural seats and 41 per cent rurban seats in the 2019 general election. Here, too, it scored more than 40 per cent vote share in ten rural and ten rurban seats each.[5]

The BJP's rise in rurban and rural areas under Modi and Shah signifies a return to its initial growth patterns of the early 1990s, when it first became a dominant force on the back of the Ayodhya agitation. Except, it is now evident on a much wider scale in the Hindi heartland and UP, while also being replicated in the new catchment areas of Karnataka and West Bengal. 'This is a very important and interesting phenomenon. Rurban areas, in particular, are a cradle for aspirations: both economic and social,' Jai Mrug argued as we discussed these findings. 'Rurban areas are home to a putative middle class, for which the BJP has always held an appeal. The population balance in rurban areas is such that there will always be a socio-economic aspiration for upward mobility because some urban-like people are always there—people who are better off than most average voters actually. Historically, the BJP first grew in the cities, but its real expansion from the 1980s was in the rurban areas, which became its bastions. Rurban vote bases have always been more steady and solid in Indian politics, compared to urban

Figure 2.6: The BJP's Growth in New Catchment Areas Also Based on Rurban or Rural Growth

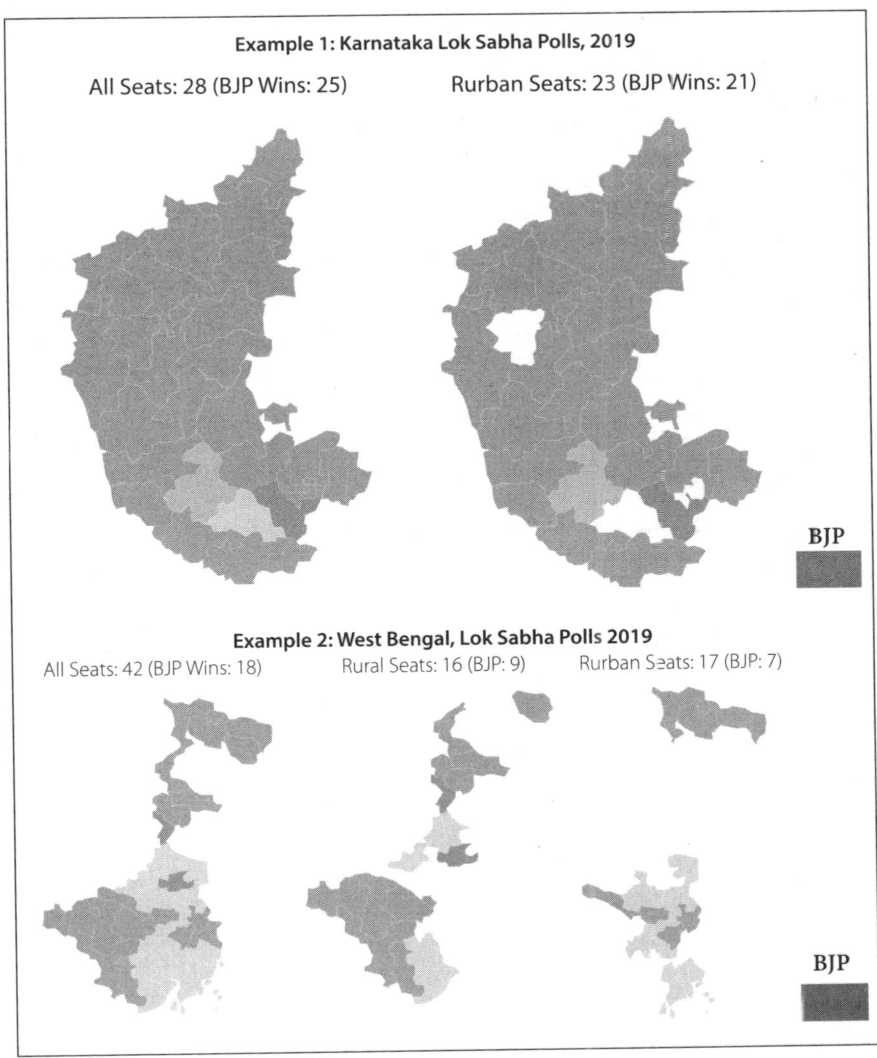

Source: ECI data. Analysis by Nalin Mehta and Rishabh Srivastava, PollNiti.

bases that shift faster, like what happened with the Congress in Delhi after Sheila Dikshit.'[6]

The BJP's rurban growth also signals the rise of a soft Hindutva vote. Almost all of the rurban areas where it initially grew in the North, and now in Karnataka and Bengal, have some history of sectarian identity politics. This is vote-growing on the back of an 'aspirational class plus Hindutva,' argued Mrug. 'At a time of great social flux, a party that has a sharper ideology and positioning compared to others who are bits of everything, like the Congress, always looks more attractive.'

The BJP's early dominant image of a city-based party was a vestige of the Jan Sangh era—an image that stuck long after its use-by date. Even in 1989, when the BJP won only eight Lok Sabha seats in UP, all of these wins were in rurban or rural areas. Most of those early BJP inroads had two things in common: a rural base with a large Muslim population and communal tensions: Bareilly (rurban and with communal tension), Aonla (large Muslim population and rurban), Saidpur (large Muslim population), Kaiserganj (large Muslim population and rural), Etah (rural western UP and home to the BJP's first OBC chief minister in UP, Kalyan Singh), Jhansi (rurban), Jaunpur (rural) and Robertsganj (rural). The party had won urban seats like Kanpur and Lucknow as early as 1967, when it won 100 UP assembly seats under the leadership of Deendayal Upadhyaya. However, by 1989, its mainstay was rurban UP, especially pockets of communal polarisation. 'Wherever there is a rural population and a history of Muslim dominance, it automatically becomes a foundational ground for the BJP,' Mrug pointed out. 'If it is a rurban space like Bareilly, that is "sone pe suhaga" [the glitter on the gold].'[7]

In that sense, UP 1991 was an early prototype for UP 2014 and 2019, which lay at the heart of the new model that Amit Shah and Modi built. In 1991, the party won over half the seats in UP in an epochal election in which the BSP's Mayawati herself lost from Muzaffarnagar to a BJP candidate, Mangal Lal Premi. That initial BJP upsurge as a major electoral force in the 1990s was built on the conjunction of three forces: caste realignment and the co-option of OBCs led by Kalyan Singh, the creation of a new Hindu political identity and a robust party cadre.

The Ram Janmabhoomi movement dated back to 1984, but it was only after the V.P. Singh government announced the Mandal Commission Action Plan for giving reservations to OBCs on 15 August 1990 that L.K. Advani's Rath Yatra took shape. Lord Ram was projected as a unifying symbol across caste divides to rally the proponents of reservation (OBCs and Dalits) as well as its opponents (upper castes) to the BJP's cause. 'The

BJP model today is essentially an enlarged version and replication of that 1991 western UP formula: aspirational, upwardly mobile MBC [Most Backward Classes] aligning with BJP,' said Mrug. 'As their economic situation became better, it was better to scale up that experiment across UP ... Amit Shah revived the old formula and the BJP went for it full on. They did social engineering with non-Jatavs and non-Yadavs. It was done deliberately, but the time for it was ripe anyway. Amit Shah was the right man at the right time for the BJP.'[8]

It is to this story, and how the new BJP transformed itself, that we now turn.

3

THE CASTE GAME

How the BJP Became the Most Socially Representative Party in UP (Barring Muslims)

The BJP has long been considered an upper-caste-dominated party by scholars who study it. This perception might have been true in its early years but new caste data that I have put together for this book shows that research and scholarship on the party have lagged behind the party's reality. In June 2020, Prime Minister Narendra Modi pointed out in a video address to his party workers that the BJP was represented by 113 OBC, 43 ST and 53 SC MPs in the Lok Sabha.[1] In other words, a full 37.2 per cent of BJP Lok Sabha MPs were OBC, 14.1 per cent ST and 17.4 per cent SC. This meant that a whopping 68.9 per cent (209) of all its 303 Lok Sabha MPs elected in 2019 were non-upper castes and from castes that were traditionally considered lower down in the caste hierarchy. This is strikingly on par with the widely accepted national share of the population of these castes: 69.2 per cent. The charge of upper caste domination is difficult to make with such electoral representation. Furthermore, if you leave out seats reserved by law for SCs or STs alone, non-upper castes still accounted for almost 60 per cent of BJP MPs elected from general constituencies. Within this, as many as 50 per cent (113) of the BJP's Lok Sabha MPs elected from general constituencies were OBCs.[2]

Yet, this Modi statement flew in the face of assertions in recent political science research on India that claimed a significant resurgence of upper-caste dominance between 2009 and 2019 within the BJP. Most recently, the Paris-based Sciences Po's Christophe Jaffrelot, declared that the 2019 poll marked 'the revenge of the upper-caste elite,' aligned with the 'BJP against the Dalits' and OBCs' assertiveness'.[3] Jaffrelot and Ashoka University's Gilles Vernier argued that the decade of 2009–2019 saw an erosion of OBC representation in the Hindi belt. As they put it, 'the last decade has seen *the return of the savarn (upper caste) ... and the erosion of OBC representation ...* along with the rise of the BJP. The trend started in 2009, but the Modi wave of 2014 has confirmed it and the last [2019] elections have resulted in a certain consolidation of this come back to the pre-Mandal scenario [emphasis added]'.[4] Specifically, they have claimed that within the Hindi belt, upper castes accounted for a whopping 44.9 per cent of the BJP MPs in the Lok Sabha, OBCs only for 19.7 per cent and SCs for 18.5 per cent.[5] In Parliament, overall, they claimed that BJP dominance was driven by 36.3 per cent upper-caste MPs within the party and only 18.8 per cent OBCs (the lowest OBC representation in a major party, compared to the Congress and the regional parties) in a recent academic caste profile of the 2019 Lok Sabha. 'Upper caste representation among BJP MPs is significantly higher' than its rival parties, they argued. They further emphasised that this 'over-representation of upper-castes largely stem from the Hindi-belt states dominated by the BJP.'[6]

It is impossible to square these two claims. Modi claimed a preponderance of lower classes in BJP's elected representatives. Jaffrelot and Vernier, using a database on the social backgrounds of elected legislators co-produced by Ashoka University's Trivedi Centre for Political Data,[7] claimed a growing upper-caste stranglehold on the BJP in the Modi–Shah years. One is right. The other is clearly wrong. I found this to be a strange conundrum. It is usually easy for neighbours, relatives and local journalists to establish the caste one belongs to. It is unusual for there to be uncertainty on such matters. Caste is an easily demonstratable fact. There can't be grey areas on facts, though there can be differing interpretations of what they mean.

The Mehta–Singh Social Index and Why Scholars Got the BJP's Caste Matrix Wrong: BJP No More an Upper Caste-Dominated Party

To uncover the facts, critically reassess the emerging picture and get to the root of this issue, I decided to take a fresh look at the caste backgrounds of political leaders in UP cutting across four parties—BJP, SP, BSP and Congress—as they evolved over time. Working closely with the journalist Sanjeev Singh, I investigated the caste backgrounds of UP politicians across five domains to create what we called the Mehta–Singh Social Index for this book. Our findings show how empirically wrong the caste researchers at Ashoka University were. We then pursued this enquiry beyond just MPs and MLAs elected by political parties. Legislators do form a critical group, but to get a fuller picture, the Mehta–Singh Social Index also looked at the changing caste patterns of BJP state-level officer-bearers, district-level presidents and ministers stretching across the BJP and its rival governments in UP. Overall, we studied the castes of:

- 2,560 Lok Sabha candidates fielded by the BJP, SP, Congress and BSP in each of UP's 80 Lok Sabha constituencies and in every single national election over three decades (1991–2019);
- 1,612 Vidhan Sabha candidates fielded by the four parties in 403 assembly constituencies in the 2017 state election;
- 42 state-level BJP office-bearers in UP in 2020;
- 101 government ministers in UP, stretching across BJP chief minister Yogi Adityanath's council of ministers (54) in 2020 and SP chief minister Akhilesh Yadav's council of ministers (47) in 2012.
- 98 district-level BJP presidents in UP in 2020.

All of these political structures needed re-examining because looking at one piece of the caste puzzle is not enough and can sometimes be misleading. The point of creating the Mehta–Singh Social Index and doing this 360-degree caste sweep of UP politics was to get a holistic picture of how representative or unrepresentative the BJP has been of castes, how this changed over time and how it compared with rival political formations.

It was vital to do this exercise from scratch. This is because caste in UP is notoriously difficult to pinpoint by only looking at names on a list, as we learnt from experience. Vermas from Noida are Gujjars (OBC), Vermas from eastern UP are SC, Vermas from near Bulandshahar are Sunars (OBC), Vermas from the Awadh region are Kurmis (OBC) and those from eastern UP are Kayasths. Similarly, Chaudharys from Ballia are Yadavs, those from western UP are Jats, while those from four UP districts are Kurmis. Kushwahas can be both upper-caste Rajput or OBC. Rawats from Uttarakhand are Rajputs/Thakurs while Rawats from UP are Pasi Dalits (SC). Likewise, Chandras can be SC or Thakur/Rajput. Tyagis are Brahmins in western UP but some Tyagis in eastern UP are SC. Some Tyagis from Meerut are also Bhumihars. Similarly, while Bhargava is often considered a Brahmin surname, we found at least one BJP Dalit candidate with this surname contesting from a reserved SC seat in 2017. No wonder, sometimes even local residents get the castes of people in nearby regions wrong. Former UP chief minister, Jagdambika Pal, for example, is a Thakur.[8] Yet, for years he has been invited to attend caste-based OBC sammelans because many thought he was one too. This is because, if you are a Pal from Basti (like the former minister), you are a Thakur (like the former chief minister), but if you are a Pal from anywhere else in UP, you are an OBC. This is why a revisionist look at caste names was essential. As a pollster who has worked for several political parties in the state told me, 'We see a candidate from afar and assume that he is from a particular caste, you reach the town and ask people and it turns out it's a totally different caste altogether.'[9]

This is why creating the Mehta–Singh Social Index was essential. We did it by bringing together a core group of senior journalists, each with over twenty years of political reporting and a deep micro-understanding of UP politics. We then added a specialised layer of UP-based Hindi journalists to the core group. Going back to the basics, once we collected the lists of political candidates, office-bearers and ministers, each name was individually verified by members of this core group from the constituency each politician belonged to. This meant calling a vast network of local political party chiefs, regional political leaders, local notables, university professors, journalists and other informants in each constituency. We kept records of each call, each message and every bit of information that was received from any source. Each name was verified by members of the wider Mehta–Singh Social Index Project network and then re-verified by our central project team after ascertaining the antecedents of the source. To be doubly sure, we double-checked some of this data through a parallel, blind peer-review process. The pollster Jai Mrug kindly agreed to run a pro bono caste-identification exercise for all political candidates from the BJP, SP, BSP and Congress who stood for Lok Sabha elections in UP. His agency, VMR, did so with their own team of survey researchers in each of UP's eighty constituencies for three national elections between 2009 and 2019. They did this independently of the Mehta–Singh Social Index Project team, mostly through meetings and phone calls with district-level presidents of the various parties. We then compared the two lists—prepared by two different teams with different skill sets. We cross-referenced these lists to see if there were any inconsistencies, mistakes or errors. To our pleasant surprise, the lists were mostly in agreement, but we closed important gaps through this process and gained valuable insights.

Finally, along with members of the core Mehta–Singh Social Index Project team, I travelled to several towns in UP—Lucknow, Raebareli, Amethi, Etah, Fatehpur, Kaushambi, Mainpuri, Pratapgarh, etc.—and checked early versions of the list with local politicians across party lines (BJP, SP, Congress and BSP, independent) as well with experienced Hindi journalists in the districts. The core team did a final round of checks with local political leaders in each district. At each stage, we found some corrections in the caste lists, which taught us valuable lessons in the complexity of caste names in UP. 'There is a bhayaanak [terrible] confusion on many OBC jaati names,' one pollster told us. By the end, though, the checks and balances we built into this exercise made us supremely confident that the Mehta–Singh Social Index is by far the most thorough independent analysis over time of caste representation among political-party candidates and representatives in UP.

BJP's Big Caste Shift: What the Mehta–Singh Social Index Topline Numbers Tell Us

The findings of the Mehta–Singh Social Index shed new light on the BJP's social engineering experiments with caste in UP. They offer a radically different picture from what most conventional scholarship has been telling us about the party's power structures. They force a major rethink of traditional assumptions about the BJP and shed new light on the reasons behind its recent electoral successes. The Mehta–Singh Social Index Project demonstrates that, in the decade between 2009 and 2019:

- The BJP systematically increased OBC representation in very significant numbers at every level of its political organisation in UP: from district-level presidents to state-unit leaders to the council of ministers to assembly and national election candidates.
- OBCs became by far the single most represented caste category in the BJP at every organisational level.
- OBC representation in the BJP is far higher than acknowledged by scholars so far. This difference is of large magnitude and not just an incremental one.
- Not only did the BJP systematically increase OBC representation, this expansion was primarily based on non-Yadav OBCs (over twenty sub-categories like Kurmis, Jats, Sainis, Mauryas, etc.). These castes did not have such representation in the previous OBC-dominated Akhilesh Yadav-led administration of the SP, which was dominated by Yadavs.
- Similarly, the BJP systematically increased SC representation, though to a lesser extent than OBCs. Again, it did so by focusing on non-Jatav SC sub-castes (over seventeen sub-categories such as Pasis, Dhobis, Valmikis, etc.) that did not have such representation in the previous SC-led administration under BSP's Mayawati where Jatavs were dominant.
- This social engineering by the BJP was done without losing the support of the upper castes.
- Yet, the entry of so many OBC and SC representatives into the party's power structures in UP meant that they became numerically much more significant in the party and upper-caste representation in the party significantly reduced in electoral politics.
- Essentially, the BJP became far more representative of all castes in UP (barring Muslims) compared to its rivals. In the process, upper-caste dominance in the party was significantly reduced.

- Crucially, while the BJP initially increased OBC representation in the early 1990s with leaders like Kalyan Singh (a Lodh OBC and the party's first chief minister in UP), OBCs were not dominant in the party's structure, as they became after 2013. Caste representation in the BJP for those lower down the caste order earlier followed the Congress model, with a leader like Kalyan Singh becoming a totem figure for the caste to mobilise around. What is happening now is significantly different. Instead of totem-pole figures, a large number of people from these castes are being given positions within the party, from the booth-level upwards, i.e., being given space in the wider tent.
- The numbers clearly demonstrate that the idea of BJP being an upper-caste-dominated party can no longer be supported, at least in UP. There is a huge chasm between the changes in the BJP since 2013, how it reshaped its organisational DNA after 2013 and the scholarly understanding of it. This means a significant overhaul is needed of our understanding of the BJP, the subterranean forces that are driving its growth and the scholarly understanding of it, which has hitherto remained behind the curve in this regard.

More specifically, to give a bird's-eye view of the numbers, OBCs and SCs accounted for as many as 57.5 per cent of the BJP's UP Lok Sabha candidates in the 2019 general election, 52.8 per cent of its candidates in the 2017 assembly poll that it swept, 50 per cent of its office-bearers in the state in 2020, 48.1 per cent of Chief Minister Yogi Adityanath's council of ministers and 35.6 per cent of the BJP's district-level presidents (see Figure 3.1). These findings show that the Ashoka University database, which is the basis of most academic and journalistic writings on the caste of Hindi heartland politicians, got its facts wrong on this score. Ashoka's researchers missed the enormity of the larger process of incorporation of key groups such as OBCs and SCs into the BJP's fold. Put simply, they read the caste-names wrong. At best, this was shoddy research caused by a lack of understanding of ground realities. The basic factual mistakes in the core database unfortunately led scholars and observers who use it to come up with an incorrect or incomplete assessment of the evidence and a skewed understanding of the BJP's growth. This led to as seasoned

Figure 3.1: BJP OBC and SC Representation in BJP Leadership in UP: Topline View

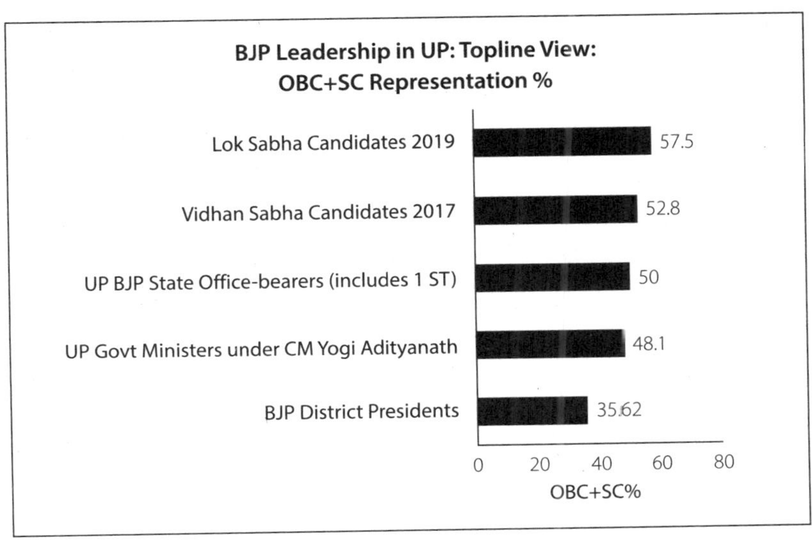

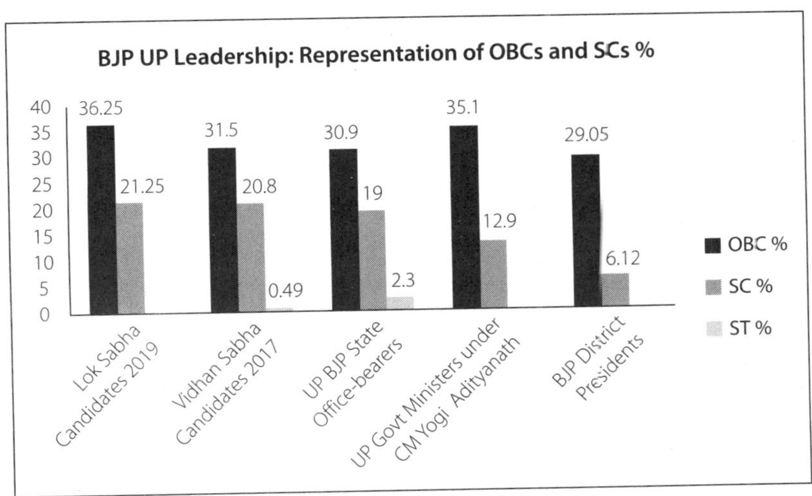

Source: Fieldwork and analysis by Mehta–Singh Social Index. Lok Sabha and Vidhan Sabha candidates analysed from ECI data. Figures for Vidhan Sabha 2017 include figures for some seats contested by BJP alliance partners. UP BJP office-bearers analysed from party list issued on 23 August 2020. UP BJP government ministers' list is accurate as of 30 October 2020. UP BJP district presidents' list is based on party listing as of 25 July 2020.

and fine a scholar as Jaffrelot to mistakenly infer continued dominance of upper castes in the BJP.

These numbers revealed by the Mehta–Singh Index showcase why it is misleading to characterise the new BJP under Modi and Shah as a party dominated by upper castes. In reality, it is quite the reverse. The BJP, between 2013 and 2019, saw a remaking of not only its social-support base but also of its internal organisational systems with OBCs being given centre stage. In a state where OBCs are 54.5 per cent and SCs 20.7 per cent of the population,[10] the BJP was ahead of all major political parties in proportionally representing candidates from these castes in the Lok Sabha and Vidhan Sabha polls and inching closer towards it in other political structures. The BJP in UP, after 2013, put up significantly more OBCs as candidates than its political rivals: SP, BSP and Congress. It also gave them more space in its internal power structures in the state, radically shifting its organisational DNA. This internal change was reflected in the upward swing in its political fortunes. To be sure, upper castes, which number about 24.2 per cent in UP, are still over-represented and remain integral to the party, but the proportion is much less than before.[11] The BJP's pattern of mobilisation is also in complete contrast with Congress-dominant UP in the pre-1989 era, well documented by scholars like Jaffrelot and Zoya Hasan.[12] It is also at variance with the pre-1990s Janata Party, or SP and BSP (from the 1990s) whose political fulcrum revolved around core OBC or SC groups while aggregating others. The great increase in representation of OBCs and SCs in the BJP's structures changed the perception of the party on the ground, in relation to its explicitly caste-based political opponents: SP (with OBCs) and BSP (with Dalits). What matters in politics is not necessarily absolute numbers but change: the perception and direction of it. Here, the direction of change in the BJP and how it started sharing power with castes that had been relatively ignored by national parties is unmistakeable.

In this regard, the most striking feature of the new BJP is the rising representation of women in the UP state-level leadership. Women accounted for 23.8 per cent of the BJP's state-level office-bearers in 2020, including one-fourth of its vice presidents and almost one-third of its secretaries. (see Figure 3.2). Chapter 17 specifically details the importance

Figure 3.2: BJP Increased Women Share in Leadership, OBC and SC Got Big Share

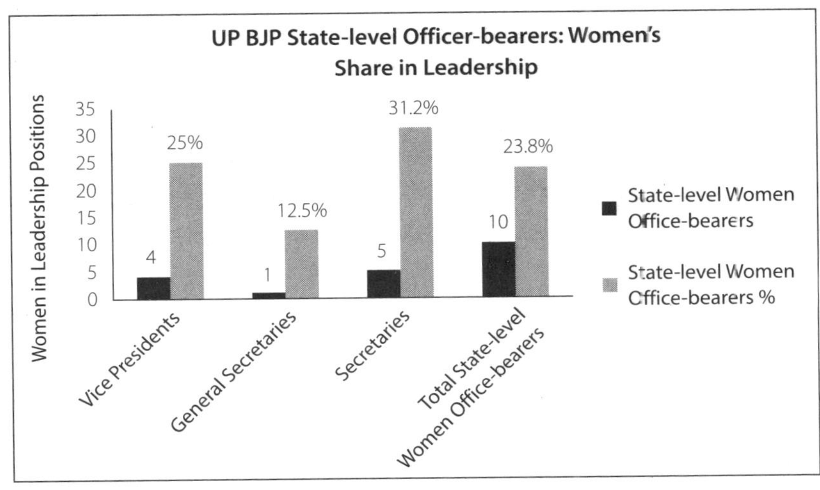

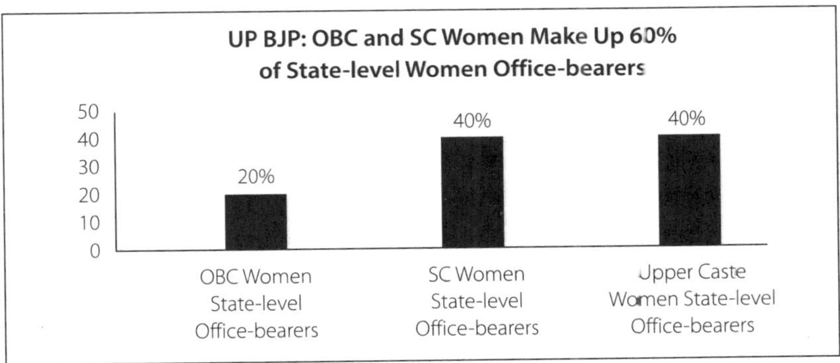

Source: Fieldwork and analysis by Mehta–Singh Social Index. UP BJP office-bearers analysed from revised party list issued on 23 August 2020.

of the BJP's strategies with women outreach overall and how they changed. Crucially, for our purposes here, OBC and SC women accounted for as much as 60 per cent of BJP's state-level women office-bearers. While upper-caste women retained a big chunk of positions (40 per cent), their numbers were significantly dwarfed by those of non-upper caste women appointees. This shows how deep-rooted and structural the BJP's shift to OBCs and SCs was. It was implemented at various levels of the party leadership.

The BJP's New 'Sanjeevani'

The rise of OBCs as the most numerically preponderant caste in the BJP's power structures in UP is a new phenomenon. 'There is a zameen asmaan ka antar [difference between the earth and the sky] between the BJP of pre-2014 and the BJP of post-2014,' says the Hindi journalist Brijesh Shukla, who has covered UP BJP's politics for three decades. 'The earlier BJP was full of swarans (upper castes) such as Brahmins, Baniyas and Thakurs. When Narendra Modi got command of the party, he completely inverted its structure. The new BJP does not focus on swarans. Swarans come to it in [the] name of nationalism. It focuses on getting backwards, smaller castes, poor: these are the people BJP has focused its attention on since 2014 and they became its new "Sanjeevani" [the life-saving divine herb that Hanuman used in the Ramayana to revive an injured Lakshman after he had been near-fatally injured in battle] before 2019.'[13]

Of course, the early BJP in the 1980s and the '90s was also built on the shoulders of OBC leaders like the party's first chief minister in UP, Kalyan Singh, in whose tenure (1991-92) the Babri Masjid was demolished; Uma Bharti, its first chief minister in Madhya Pradesh (2003-04); and former Akhil Bharatiya Vidyarthi Parishad (ABVP) leader Shivraj Singh Chouhan, a five-time MP from Vidisha who later became the BJP's longest-serving chief minister in Madhya Pradesh (2005–2018, and again from 2020). Their rise epitomised the BJP's political response to the caste-based Mandal agitation of the early 1990s, which became the crucible of a number of caste-based political parties like SP (led by Yadavs), BSP (led by Dalits), RJD (Yadavs in Bihar) and several others. OBCs were in the vanguard of the BJP's rise in that period, which was characterised by what became known as the politics of 'Kamandal' (Hindutva) versus 'Mandal'. BJP sought to draw those lower down in the caste hierarchy into a larger identity predicated on a united Hinduness. Caste-based parties, on the other hand, sought to give them political representation outside of the erstwhile mainstream parties, arguing that they would never have a fair share within the old framework. The challenge for the BJP was to combine the forces of 'Kamandal' and 'Mandal' while also incorporating the Dalit leader and Constitution-maker B.R. Ambedkar as an icon in its own pantheon. Its stagnation from the late-1990s was linked to an inability to balance these competing imperatives. The BJP's decline in UP in the 2000s, in that sense, was directly linked to losing its incipient support and leadership base among OBCs, which had been at the centre of its initial rise as a political force. The BJP's political fortunes started changing in 2014 only *after* it made a big shift in its caste strategy. It began embracing OBCs and sharing power with them in meaningful ways.

OBC Dominance in BJP's UP Lok Sabha Candidates from 2014 Onwards

This was most apparent in the big proportional shift on caste that the BJP made in candidates it fielded in the 2014 and 2019 general elections. The party had only put up fifteen OBC candidates out of eighty candidates in 2009 (see Table 3.1). In 2014, it significantly upped this to twenty-six OBCs, and then to twenty-nine in 2019. This made OBCs the single largest nominated caste category in the BJP's 2019 Lok Sabha candidates list, followed by Brahmins at eighteen (22.5 per cent) and Thakurs at thirteen (16.25 per cent). Furthermore, if we exclude the seventeen reserved SC seats in UP, OBCs (or the Mandal classes) made up a hefty 46 per cent of BJP candidates from general constituencies—almost half of its candidates. The rise in OBC numbers is significant because they are not fielded from reserved seats, unlike SC candidates, whom the party has to field anyway as seventeen (21.25 per cent) Lok Sabha seats in UP are reserved only for SC candidates. By fielding OBCs in such high numbers across two national elections (more than those fielded by any of its rival parties), the BJP was signalling a big shift in its caste orientation. Most of these candidates won. This shift in caste representation was central to the BJP's changed imagery in UP.

BJP Fielded More OBC Candidates Than Any Other Party in UP in 2017 Assembly Polls

The party made exactly the same caste shift towards OBCs in the 2017 assembly elections as well. It gave tickets to as many as 127 OBC (31.5 per cent) candidates (see Figure 3.3). Just as it did in 2014 and 2019 Lok Sabha elections, the rise of OBC candidates as the single biggest caste category

Table 3.1: BJP Significantly Increased OBC Candidates: Caste Composition of BJP Lok Sabha Candidates in UP, 2004–2019

Caste	*2004*	*2009*	*2014*	*2019*	*2019, Caste %*	*2019*	*Cumulative Caste Categories, 2019*	*% 2019*
Brahmin	18	19	18	18	22.5	General Category	33	41.25
Thakur	16	16	13	13	16.25			
Kayasth		-	-	-				
Bhumihar	1	1	1	1	1.25			
Bania	1	2	3	1	1.25			
Punjabi Khatri	1	2	-	-				
Sikh						Minorities	1	1.25
Muslim	2	1	-	-				
Parsi		-	1	1	1.25			
OBC	**21**	**15**	**26 (2 Yadavs)**	**29 (1 Yadav)**	**36.25**	**Castes that have reservation in govt jobs and education**	**46**	**57.5**
Scheduled Castes (SC)	17	15	17	17	21.25			
Did not contest		9	-	-				
Total	80 (contested 77)	80	79	80				

Source: Fieldwork and analysis by Mehta–Singh Social Index. Lok Sabha candidates analysed from ECI data. Figures for 2014 and 2019 include two seats contested by its pre-poll alliance partner Apna Dal (Soneylal).

for the BJP in the 2017 UP provincial election was the real measure of its political shift. The number of SC candidates remained constant because SC seats are reserved and all parties have to field them anyway. If you take out reserved seats, OBCs accounted for as many as 40 per cent of BJP candidates. Overall, the next highest caste category after OBCs in the BJP's assembly candidate list was SC: eighty-four (20.8 per cent); Brahmins: seventy-five (20.3 per cent), followed by Thakurs: seventy (17.3 per cent).

To put this in perspective, the BJP fielded more OBC candidates (127) in 2017 than SP, the main caste-based OBC party in UP. SP fielded only 100 OBCs, and that too mostly Yadavs, who comprise a small though socially dominant chunk of this group. The BJP also fielded almost as many *SC* candidates (eighty-four) as the main party of the Dalits, BSP (eighty-six). It did field more upper-caste candidates than these parties in percentage terms, but crucially, its combined OBC+SC representation was virtually the same as SP's and significantly higher than BSP's (see Figure 3.5). This radical shift in the social composition of its candidates reflects the critical importance of cultivating a new leadership in OBC communities for the BJP. SP was under no such compulsion due to its historical support base with these groups. The BJP, however, used its new caste-representation policy to attract many such groups to its side. These numbers reflect a radical shift in the BJP's attitude to caste: it wasn't just talking the talk. It was walking it in the form of tickets the parties distributed.

'I felt this sitting in the assembly in the last few years,' agreed one of the longest-serving independent MLAs in UP when I presented him with these findings. He was speaking off the record, but as a legislator who has continuously been a member of the state assembly since 1991, his response was telling. 'Come to the assembly in Lucknow and you will see the difference when you look at the origins of MLAs. There has been a big shift. We felt it beyond doubt and your numbers show what we have been feeling,' he said.[14]

The BJP's OBC turn in UP was predicated on a major social shift within the party's organisational structures in the state, starting from 2013. Amit Shah moved to Lucknow in early 2014 and took up residence on Rana Pratap Marg, near the *Times of India*'s (then) office in the city.[15] He was not BJP president at the time, but general secretary in charge of UP, and the party was led by Rajnath Singh, a Thakur leader and

Figure 3.3: Caste Composition of BJP, SP, BSP, INC Vidhan Sabha Candidates, UP, 2017

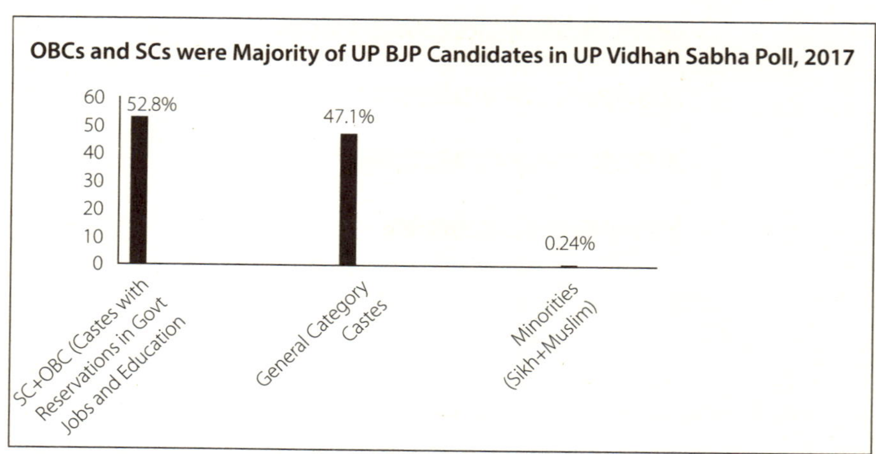

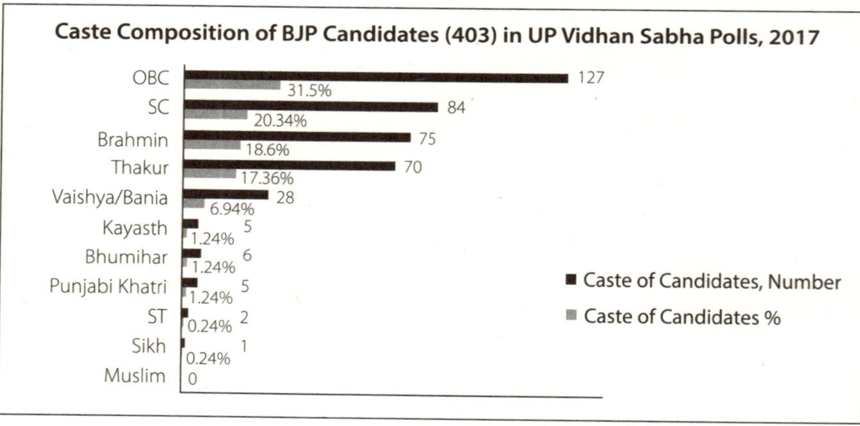

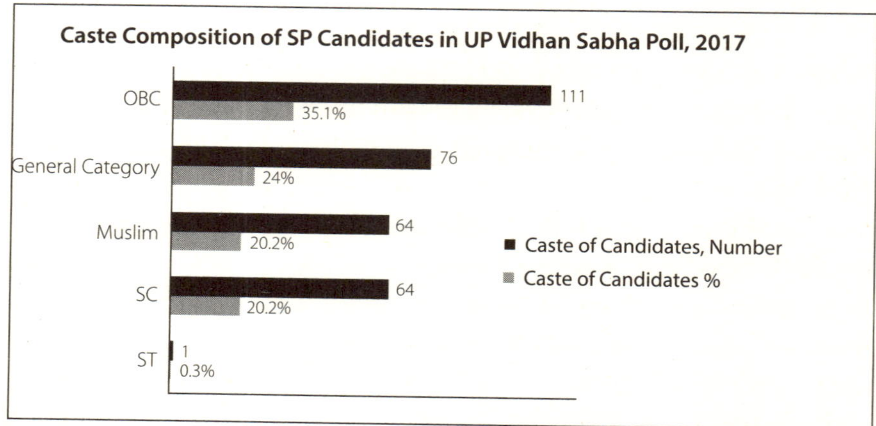

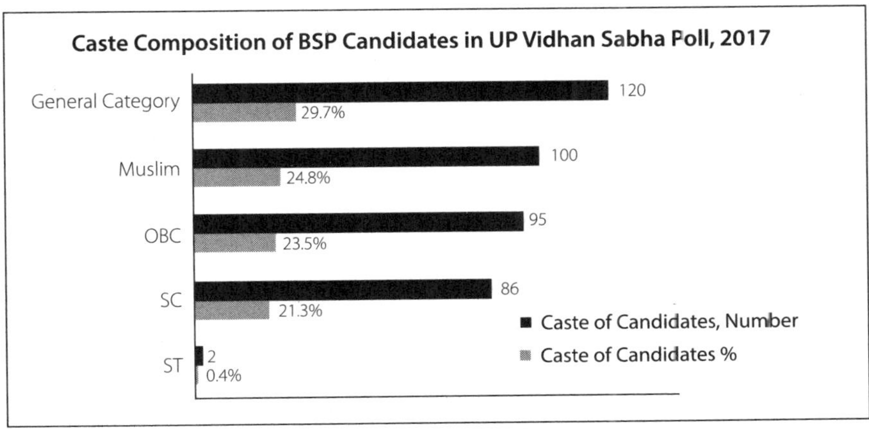

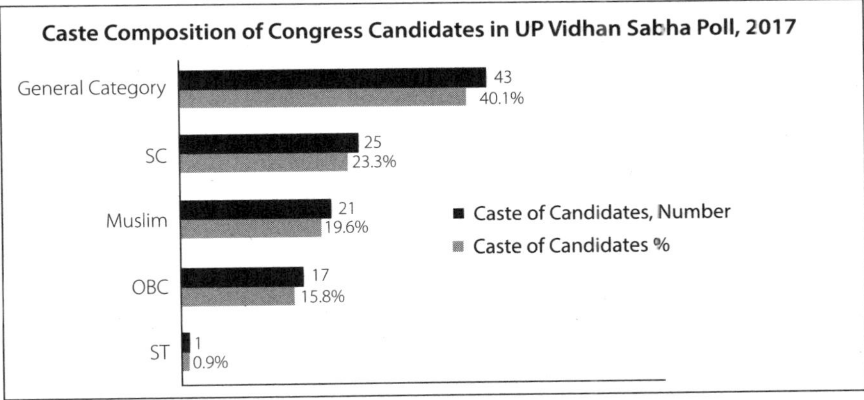

Source: Fieldwork and analysis by Mehta-Singh Social Index, using ECI data.

Note: BJP list includes 20 candidates fielded by its allies. Of these, 80% were OBC, SC or ST (8 OBC, 7 SC and 1 ST).

former UP chief minister himself. This was at a time when the BJP had not tasted significant electoral success in UP for over a decade. Shah's decision not to stay in a hotel and to take up a house signalled a new 'intent to the party's rank and file that the new leader wanted to stay here for the long haul.'[16] Shah had spent the years 2010–2012, when he was barred from entering Gujarat by the Supreme Court, living in Delhi but studying UP politics and travelling across the state. He says he learnt 'what was wrong with the BJP' during this time. The party had not fought panchayat elections in the state for twelve years, resulting in a whole 'army of politically conscious citizens', who, in his words, 'should have been with us joining other parties simply because we could not provide them with a political avenue'. Shah not only announced that the BJP would henceforth contest 'each election' in UP, he also started a new OBC outreach. He saw it as part of an effort to focus on communities that had not been supporting the BJP so far, what he called the hitherto 'dark zone' of the state of BJP.[17]

Nishads, Pasis and Suheldev's Resurrection: The BJP's Systematic Dissection of the OBC/SC Vote

Crucially, even as the BJP started shifting towards OBCs, it focused on sub-groups within this broader category that had earlier received less attention. This is significant because OBCs comprise as many as seventy-six different castes (such as Kurmis, Rajbhars, Nishads and so on) in UP.[18] The Yadavs, dominant under SP, make up only a small share (8.7 per cent) of the total population of UP[19] but had the bulk of the power during SP's regime. Similarly, UP's SC population officially consists of sixty-six castes.[20] Jatavs, who make up 54.2 per cent of UP's Dalits have always been the dominant caste in BSP. Not so much the other Dalit castes: Pasis, who make up the next 15.9 per cent of Dalits, followed by Dhobis, Koris, Valmikis, Khatiks and so on.[21] The BJP, after 2013, focused specifically on these non-Yadav OBCs and non-Jatav SCs. The key thing with some of the smaller castes is that, while they may be small in numbers, many of them are heavily concentrated in specific constituencies, which make them pivotal in electoral contests.

Three examples showcase the kind of political methods and symbols with which the BJP wooed the smaller and relatively ignored castes. Rajbhars (OBCs) account for a very small sliver of UP's population (an estimated 2.6 per cent)[22] but the party wooed them aggressively. Prime Minister Modi, as an example of this outreach, travelled to Ghazipur in December 2018 to launch a commemorative stamp on Raja Suheldev, an eleventh-century king of Shravasti, said to be both a Rajbhar and a Pasi icon, who many believe led some of the local resistance against the forces of the Afghan invader Mahmud of Ghazni centuries ago.[23] The BJP also joined hands with the Suheldev Bharatiya Samaj Party. Its leader Om Prakash Rajbhar became a cabinet minister for backward classes in Yogi

Adityanath's government, though the two allies continually had public spats until he left the alliance in May 2019.

Similarly, Nishads (OBCs) are estimated to make up 12 per cent of UP's population but are spread across the Ganga riverbank and comprise several boatmen sub-castes like Manjhis, Kewats, Binds and Mallahs. In May 2019, Amit Shah addressed several rallies in constituencies where Nishads form a sizeable chunk of voters. 'A grand memorial for Nishadraj worth Rs 34 crore will be built at Shringverpur,' promised the BJP president. In the epic Ramayana, a Nishad king had ferried Ram, Lakshman and Sita across the Sarayu river when they went into exile. Just as Yogi Adityanath had earlier promised a huge statue of Ram in Ayodhya as part of the BJP's Hindutva mobilisation, Shah's promise of an eighty-foot statue of the Nishad king was meant to draw the caste to the BJP's political project, while complementing its own ethno-religious mobilisation effort. The Yogi Adityanath government committed to building this statue at Shringverpur, near Allahabad, because that was the spot where local folklore believed Ram had crossed the river and it was said to mark the capital of the ancient Nishad kingdom.[24]

The party 'opened the horse stables'[25] for Nishads, who are influential in about twenty UP Lok Sabha constituencies, after it suffered an unexpected reverse in the Gorakhpur parliamentary by-election of March 2018.[26] It famously lost Gorakhpur—the citadel of Yogi Adityanath and a seat which he, and his adopted father before him, had not lost since 1984—to a Nishad candidate in the by-election forced by Adityanath's vacation of the seat to become chief minister of UP. That 2018 victory of Praveen Nishad, son of Nishad Party founder Sanjay Nishad, who fought on behalf of SP, sent a serious warning signal to the BJP ahead of the 2019 general election. It marked the first coming together of bitter rivals SP and BSP in a Mahagathbandhan, or Grand Alliance, previously unthinkable in UP politics. The success of the alliance in the strongest of BJP seats in the state—Gorakhpur has long been among the highest-margin seats for the BJP in the country—demonstrated that caste arithmetic could best the personality-based alchemy of politics and Hindu mobilisation. So the BJP refocused its own caste coalition at the ground level. Within a year, Praveen Nishad, the man who had felled the BJP in the chief minister's hometown, had himself switched to the BJP.[27] Ironically, he gave up the Gorakhpur seat and fought the 2019 election as a BJP candidate from the nearby seat of Sant Kabir Nagar, and won again—this time as a saffron candidate.[28]

Reclassifying Castes: Yogi Adityanath's Policy Moves on OBCs

The BJP further wooed non-Yadav OBC castes in 2019 with two promises. The first was the Yogi Adityanath-led state government's decision to accept the demands of seventeen non-Yadav OBC castes to reclassify them as SCs (traditionally considered lower down the caste hierarchy). In this, the BJP emulated the SP government that preceded it. It issued an order for reclassifying these castes as SCs on the grounds that they had missed out on the benefits of reservation because more dominant castes had cornered the lion's share of these. This reclassification, issued in June 2019, was stayed three months later by the Supreme Court. Still, the political point was made.[29] The castes that the BJP pushed for reclassifying included Nishad, Bind, Mallah, Kewat, Kashyap, Bhar, Dhivar, Batham, Machua, Prajapati, Rajbhar, Kahar, Pottar, Dhimar, Manjhi, Tuhaha and Gaur.[30]

This followed a hugely significant earlier move by Yogi Adityanath's government as soon as it came to power in 2017 when it began talking about a proposed caste-wise division, and quotas within the 27 per cent government jobs and education seats reserved for OBCs in UP. Using the same argument, that these castes had been left out in practice by dominant OBC castes, a four-member social-justice committee specially set up by Yogi Adityanath's government presented a report in December 2018. It suggested a further carving out and streamlining of OBC reservation quotas into three broad categories. Headed by Justice Raghvendra Kumar, the committee suggested that the most prosperous of the OBC castes (Yadavs, Kurmis, Chaurasias, Patels) should only get 7 per cent of the reservation seats and be reclassified as Backward Castes. It further recommended that a second category—Most Backward Classes (including Gujjars, Lodhs, Kushwahas, Shakyas, Telis, Sahus, Sainis, Malis and Nishads)—should get 11 per cent of the pie. Finally, that a third category—Most Backward Castes (including Ghosis, Qureshis among Muslims, Rajbhars, Binds and Nishads)—should get 9 per cent reservation.[31] At the time of writing, this has not yet been implemented, but the BJP's political messaging on rejigging caste benefits was clear. At its heart was a targeted political strategy to remap the OBC vote and draw in the castes that had felt subsumed by Yadav dominance.

Sharing the Spoils of Power: The BJP's New OBC Tilt

Since 2017, the BJP has not only given election tickets to castes like Nishads and Rajbhars but also visibly shared power with them. It is not a coincidence, for example, that it fielded four Rajbhar and five Nishad candidates (a very small proportion of its 403 candidates) in 2017, and yet, Yogi Adityanath made it a point to feature a Rajbhar (Anil Rajbhar) and a Nishad (Jai Prakash Nishad) minister in his council. This means there has been a radical shift in the profile of its leadership structures in UP at three levels: the state party organisation, ministerial portfolios, and among its district-level presidents. By 2020, OBCs accounted for over 30 per cent of the BJP's top office-bearers in the state and SCs over 16 per cent. The share of SCs (see Figure 3.4) is important because, unlike parliamentary or assembly elections, party organisational posts do not have state-mandated reservations. Representation here is even more reflective of a party's political positioning. Of the party's apex state leadership—consisting of its president and almost four dozen vice presidents, general secretaries and secretaries—thirteen were OBCs, the highest of any caste, followed by ten Brahmins and seven Thakurs. By 2020, OBCs and SCs together accounted for 46.5 per cent of the BJP's top brass in UP.

Figure 3.4: Caste Composition of UP BJP Office-bearers, 2020

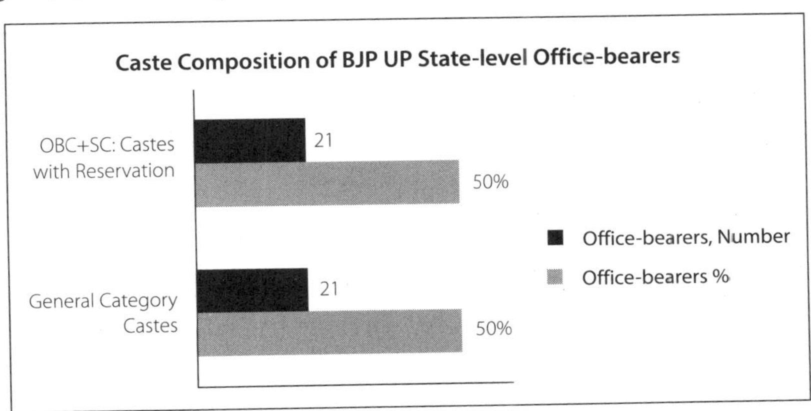

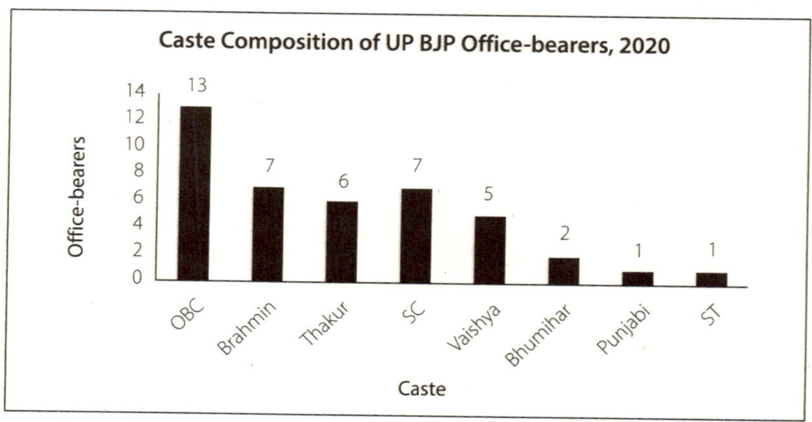

Source: Fieldwork and analysis by the Mehta–Singh Social Index. UP BJP office-bearers analysed from revised party list issued on 23 August 2020. Data includes president, vice presidents, general secretaries, secretaries and two morcha presidents (Mahila Morcha and Yuva Morcha) since these are not caste-specific categories. Other morcha leaders have been excluded from this list because these are caste-specific posts.

It is not a coincidence that we see exactly the same caste break-up in Yogi Adityanath's council of ministers. While one of the dominant media narratives around his government has been of a renewed Thakur dominance, the fact is that OBCs again constituted the single highest caste category in his council. Nineteen (35.1 per cent) of fifty-four ministers in the BJP state government in 2020 were OBCs. This was thrice the number of Thakurs (six, 11.1 per cent) and almost twice the number of Brahmins (ten, 18.5 per cent).

The nature of the BJP's shift becomes clearer when we compare it to what came before. It had almost exactly the same percentage of OBC+SC ministers (48.1 per cent compared to 48.9 per cent) as Akhilesh Yadav's preceding SP government did. This is a striking number when you consider that the BJP has always been seen as a party of upper castes, while the caste-based SP purports to be a party of social justice, and explicitly so in OBC terms. Significantly, Yogi Adityanath's government has more OBC ministers than Yadav's (see Figure 3.5). The big difference is that, while most of Akhilesh Yadav's fifteen OBC ministers were Yadavs, only one of BJP's nineteen OBC ministers happened to be a Yadav—a clear reflection of the new social coalition of non-Yadav OBCs and non-Jatav Dalits that the BJP had forged in UP (see Figure 3.5). The

Figure 3.5: Ministers in Yogi Adityanath's Government More Representative Across Castes Than Ministers Appointed by Akhilesh Yadav's Preceding Government

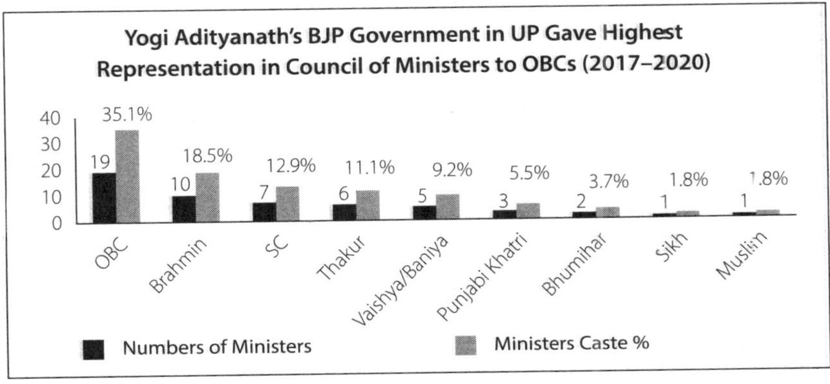

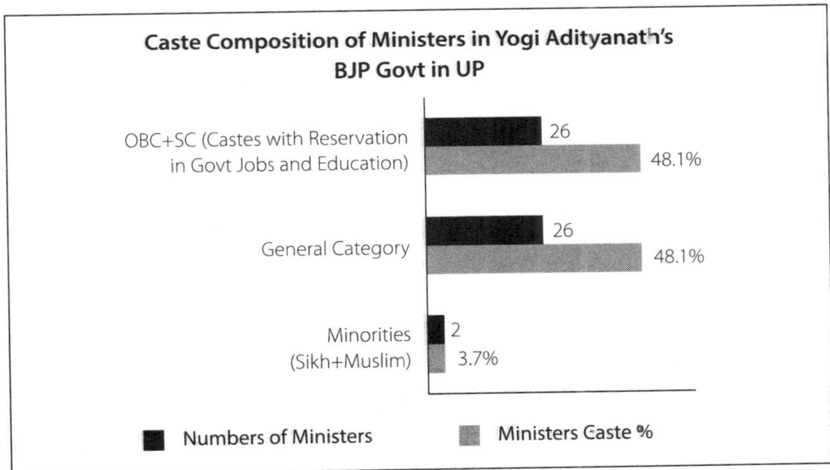

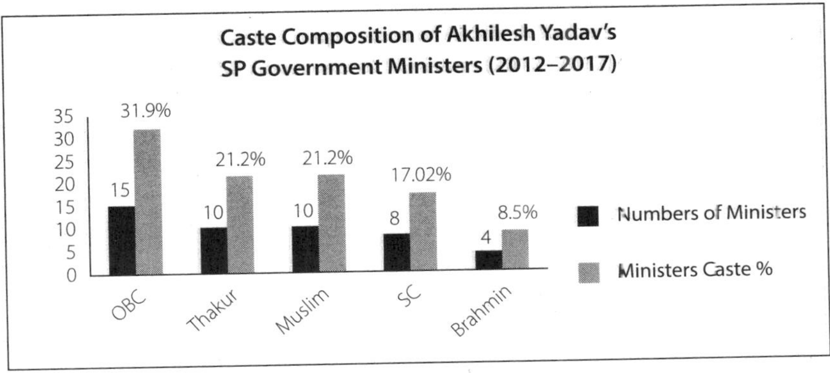

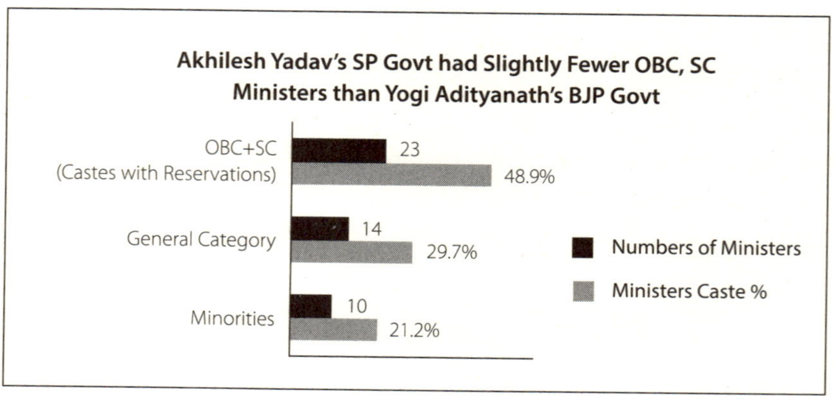

Source: Fieldwork and analysis by Mehta–Singh Social Index. Based on Yogi Adityanath's Council of Ministers list, accurate as of 30 October 2020. Akhilesh Yadav's Council of Ministers as per list issued by UP government in 2012.

other big difference was on the subject of Muslims, which is discussed separately in Chapter 5.

The changed representation of these castes in the BJP's political structures—its election candidates, ministers and office-bearers—was part of a planned political outreach. As Dinesh Sharma, UP deputy chief minister, says, 'The work we did at the ground level sent a message at the ground level that while other parties gave caste slogans, we worked on a caste-blind [jaati-viheen] basis. When Jan-Dhan accounts were opened, they were opened for all castes, when toilets were constructed, they were constructed for all castes—for Muslims as well as SCs and backwards. When there is no favouritism in government schemes, people believe it is a casteless structure. SP talks of backwards but goes with only one caste [Yadavs] among backwards. Mayawati talks of Dalits but goes forth with only one caste [Jatavs] among Dalits. Whereas BJP has worked to take along all castes.'[32]

In politics, signalling matters, and one key element of it is leadership structures. For this reason, Keshav Prasad Maurya, a non-Yadav Kushwaha OBC leader from Kaushambi, was made state BJP chief in 2016. Son of a tea vendor and farmer, he cut his teeth in politics as an activist in the Ram Janmabhoomi movement, but first won political office only in 2012 as a first-time MLA from Sirathu.[33] 'Who had heard of Maurya before that in the state,' a local political leader pointed out. Yet, his appointment, first as state party chief, and later as one of the two deputy chief ministers in Yogi Adityanath's government, reflected the BJP's OBC push. Similarly, Swatantra Dev Singh, a Kurmi OBC leader from Mirzapur, Bundelkhand, was appointed the state unit chief in July 2019, after Yogi Adityanath, a Thakur, became chief minister in 2017.

Modi, OBCs and the BJP's Caste Messaging

Crucially, Modi himself is OBC, classified in government records as a Modh Ghanchi, a caste of oil-pressers in Gujarat. Much has been made of the prime minister's humble origins as a tea-seller. In terms of caste, the fact of his OBC status has been both explicit and implicit in the BJP's political messaging, especially in the Hindi heartland. Modi's caste was not always OBC. While Muslim Ghanchis in Gujarat were classified as OBCs in 1993, Hindu Modh Ghanchis were added to the list by the state government in 1994 and by the Union government in 1999.[34] These circulars turned Modi into an OBC leader at forty-nine, halfway into his political career, but well before he first won elected office in 2001 as Gujarat chief minister. Initially, Modi and the BJP did not make much of his OBC status, except when there was a controversy in 2014. The Congress's then state leader Shaktisinh Gohil, current Rajya Sabha MP, accused Modi of being a 'fake OBC' in 2014 during the latter's campaign for prime ministership.[35] That verbal skirmish on Modi's OBC status passed below the national radar, since no major national Opposition leader repeated it. Modi himself chose not to respond to the diatribe, though his office issued a strong rebuttal. By 2019, though, the BJP's OBC inroads were deep enough for the charge to be repeated by BSP chief Mayawati at the height of the national election campaign in 2019. She accused Modi of being a 'zabardasti ka pichhda' (pushed backward by force). It was telling that Mayawati chose to make the jibe at her first rally with SP's Mulayam Singh Yadav in twenty-four years. Flanked by Yadav, she argued that Modi was not a backward caste person by birth,[36] comparing him with the SP leader, whom she called a 'real leader' of the Backwards.[37] It was an early indication of how serious a threat the BJP had become to the SP's OBC vote bank. Mayawati and Mulayam tried to reignite the image of 1993—the unity of Backwards and

Dalits—to take on the BJP's Hindutva plank. By questioning his caste and class background, Mayawati sought to reinforce the image of her party and her alliance as a defender of the 'pichhda' and the 'Dalit'. The gambit did not pay off.

Modi's response to the political thrust against his background reflected both a mix of his own positioning as a son of the soil—which is so central to his political imagery—as well as his party's tactics of splintering the OBC vote to pick it up piece by piece. Significantly, he chose to respond at an election rally in the Yadav bastion of Kannauj, with a quintessentially unique and direct play on words. As he put it:

> You must have seen in so many previous elections that after the first 1-2-3 phases, they start asking what jaat [caste] is Modi from? Somebody says Modi is from a 'neech jaati' [Backward Caste]. Somebody says he is 'neech' [lowly, a reference to Priyanka Gandhi's comment in 2014] ... I have never been in favour of politics in the name of caste. Till my opponents did not abuse me, this country did not even know what my caste is. But now I am grateful to Behenji, Akhilesh ji, Congress and all the Mahamilawatis [great adulterators] that they are openly discussing my pichhdapan [backward identity] ... Behenji and Mihamilawati people, my caste is small, so small ... I was not born in a pichhda [backward] but in an ati-pichhda [most backward] caste. You are making me say it from my mouth, so I am saying it ... I have never been an advocate of backward–forward [caste] politics. When my country is backward then what is forward? I want to make the whole country forward. But when you are talking of Forwards and Backwards and distributing proof-certificates of my caste, then let me tell you that my caste is ati-pichhdee [most backward] and it is very small.[38]

Modi's characterisation of his social origins as being from a 'most backward caste' went to the heart of the BJP's electoral positioning as the protector of those lowest down in the social hierarchy. The symbolism of having a prime minister who is an OBC leader has been central to the BJP's politics in the Hindi heartland. It is one reason why the party did not need to put in place an OBC chief minister in UP (just as it did not need a Jat chief minister in Haryana or a Maratha chief minister in Maharashtra). UP Deputy Chief Minister Dinesh Sharma explained this by saying, 'We have a Backward leadership. Modiji is, as it is, way above caste, but if people say that they have a Backward leadership, then well, BJP has given the prime minister in the form of Backward leadership. Though we don't talk about this issue, but the public watches everything and knows everything. Because of the way we work, they don't have any counter against our leadership.'[39]

By way of context, India's first and only OBC prime minister before Modi was H.D. Deve Gowda (1996-97), who headed a rickety coalition and became prime minister as a post-election consensus choice between regional parties, not through a national mandate. Modi is the OBC leader who led his party to national election victories, not once but twice. The BJP can credit itself with having the first full-term prime minister from the Mandal classes, twice.

Sharma's response sums up how Modi himself approaches the OBC question in public, though not very often. But when he does, he is very explicit. His messaging is always wrapped up in the larger binary of what he calls the politics of the 'Naamdar' (those with big names, i.e., in his view, the Congress) and 'Kaamdar' (those who work, i.e., in his view, himself). The clearest illustration of this was in Rajasthan's Alwar in November 2018, when he linked the caste debate to Rajiv Gandhi's opposition to the Mandal Commission. As he put it:[40]

> Parliament was discussing the Mandal Commission Report in the context of reservations for OBCs and this Naamdar Rajiv Gandhi, just take out the Parliamentary debate records and check—the poison Rajiv Gandhi spat out, the language he used, the criticism he made, the echoes of it can still be heard within the walls of India's Parliament. This is a reflection of their mindset. Brothers and sisters ... Among Congress leaders, someone abuses my mother, someone asks questions on my jaati, I am not surprised. Whosoever it is who says such things, the person who makes them say it is always a Naamdar. Everything happens at their signal. Congress knows everything at whose saying it happens, in a party where no one can say a word otherwise ... When the election in Gujarat was happening, even then there was a big attack regarding my caste. Then when they saw the people's anger, he [Gohil] was suspended and then after two months they hugged him again.

OBCs and Caste Policy Moves by the Modi Government

The BJP accompanied its state-level moves on caste with parallel moves at the national level, which form the focal point of the party's political messaging to OBCs. Parallel to the Yogi Adityanath government's appointment of a panel to reorganise OBC reservations in 2017, the Union government under Modi set up a similar five-member commission. Headed by former chief justice of the Delhi High Court, Justice G. Rohini, it was tasked in October 2017 with deciding how to further sub-divide the 27 per cent quota among the 2,400-plus OBC castes (which range across five broad categories) nationally.[41] The Rohini Commission was initially asked to finish its work in twelve weeks, but has received several extensions since, the latest one being a six-month extension in July 2021.[42] Additionally, the National Commission for Backward Classes (NCBC) was given constitutional status by an act of Parliament in August 2018.[43] This constitutional change happened towards the end of the first Modi government. However, earlier, after consultation with nine states, the commission had also submitted a detailed report to the government on the sub-categorisation of OBCs nationally.[44] It asked the government for permission to implement this work nationwide. Much like the state-level report submitted in UP, this recommendation was pending with the government at the time of writing. Yet, its political potential was obvious.

The change in the status of the Backward Classes Commission is a theme that has constantly featured in Modi's election speeches ever since. Speaking in Dhanbad during the Jharkhand election campaign in December 2019, for example, he declaimed that the 'demand for giving the OBCs Commission constitutional status was on for many years.'

> Congress governments used to come, make promises at time of elections, click pictures with OBC leaders and forget about it after elections got over. Congress used to keep it hanging, so in each election, this issue could be revived. This was their politics of selfishness. But BJP gave this commission constitutional status to solve the problem of backwards classes–OBCs so that backward classes get justice. You must have seen that people were spreading lies that Modi will come, BJP will come and remove reservation. Recently in Parliament we took a decision to increase SC–ST reservation for ten years. This is the result of BJP's national policies.[45]

Finally, and importantly, even as the BJP homed in on the OBC narrative, the party did not lose its focus on the general category (or upper castes) either. So, in January 2019, the Modi government, through another constitutional amendment bill, legislatively also enabled 10 per cent reservation for economically weaker sections (EWS, i.e., the poor among the non-reserved, general category castes).[45] As Modi also emphasised in Dhanbad, 'Every family has been demanding reservation for the poor in the general category. Every poor person in general category was demanding this for years, running a campaign, but Congress kept postponing legitimate demands, burying them, keeping them hanging. This was the result of the selfish policies of Congress and its associates. BJP, in the interest of the poor, gave 10 per cent reservation to the poor from the general category also. This is our national policy.'[47] In his public outreach, Modi often stresses that the Ministry of Tribal Affairs was carved out as a separate ministry under Atal Bihari Vajpayee in 1999 and that his own government increased funding for the welfare of SCs and STs from ₹66,159 crore in 2013-14 to ₹1.26 lakh crore in 2019-20.[48]

The BJP's Last-mile Sangathan Re-engineering

The BJP's leadership changes at the top levels of the party in UP were accompanied by a major structural shift at its lowermost organisational levels as well. In 2013, Amit Shah pushed for the party to elect its district presidents. UP has seventy-five districts. The BJP has ninety-eight district-level presidents, with more than one president in several larger districts. From 2013 onwards, it has held three rounds of organisational elections for district presidents: in 2013, 2016 and 2019. Each round, held in preparation for a major election, brought with it new, younger leadership at the lower ranks of the party. Many of these new district presidents were OBC leaders who became vociferous advocates for the party within their communities. The assumption was that voters above fifty years of age were more unlikely to shift old political allegiances, so the BJP focused specifically on politically ambitious youth from these castes.

After 2013, Modi and Shah ensured that the changes at various levels of the organisation reflected caste realities on the ground. Realising the continuing centrality of caste in Indian politics, they made a big bet on

OBCs in UP, inducting members of the caste group at every level of the party as never before. These castes had been a part of the BJP's initial resurgence in UP in the 1990s, with leaders like Kalyan Singh, Uma Bharti and Vinay Katiyar. Modi and Shah revived that old formula but with a twist. In the older BJP, OBC leaders were important at higher levels, but the power-sharing did not necessarily happen at the lower organisational levels. The older BJP model was closer to the Congress style of politics—getting charismatic caste leaders who became totems but did not really represent their caste interests beyond wielding that identity. The underlying power structures remained the same.

OBCs Constitute the Biggest Chunk of UP BJP's District Presidents

My analysis of the BJP's UP district presidents in June 2020 on the Mehta–Singh Social Index showed that OBCs make up the highest chunk of the BJP's district presidents in UP. Twenty-nine (29.5 per cent) of its ninety-eight district presidents were OBCs (almost all non-Yadav), the highest caste category. This was followed by Brahmins at twenty-one (21.4 per cent) and Thakurs at eighteen (18.3 per cent). The ascendance of OBCs at this micro-level of the BJP's organisational structures forms a striking contrast with a much lower number of Brahmins and Thakurs as well as the continuing marginality of Dalits at this level. This suggests (Figure 3.6) that the caste shift within the BJP is an ongoing project. Overall, upper castes taken together do dominate among district presidents and SCs remain very few (six, 6.1 per cent). The change started with the OBCs at the ground level and is very much a work in progress—especially with SCs, who are the target group for the BJP's next phase of consolidation.

The point, as one politician explained, is that, on caste, voters do not necessarily see these representation numbers in isolation but with a broader sense of where a party is going. Politics is about balancing vying factions. At the local level, if someone from a particular caste gets a ticket, then someone else gets made district president and yet another person may get a Vidhan Sabha ticket. In 2014, for example, when he was on the campaign trail in Pilibhit, the journalist Brijesh Shukla remembers being told emphatically by local politicians that the BJP would win that seat.

Figure 3.6: Caste Composition of the BJP's District Presidents in UP, 2020

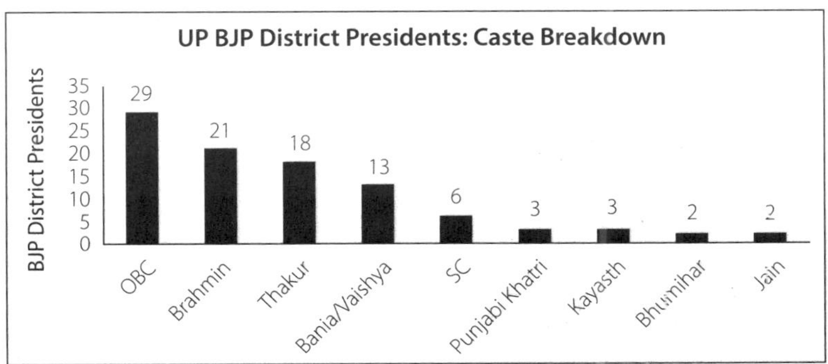

Source: Fieldwork and analysis by the Mehta–Singh Social Index. Data analysed from the UP BJP district presidents' list, accurate as of 25 July 2020.

When he asked why, they pointed out that the SP had just removed its district president, who happened to be a Maurya OBC. He was replaced by a Yadav. The BJP promptly appointed the out-of-favour Maurya district president as its own district president in Pilibhit. 'People take these things very seriously and they matter a lot,' he recalled. These micro-adjustments at the ground level are what moved OBC voters towards the BJP. 'In reality, castes want a share. Now fake hissedaari [sharing] will not work. It won't happen with Modi's tweet, or with Rahul Gandhi's tweet. It will happen with real power-sharing.'[49]

Booth Committees, Reorganised Party Structure and Caste Balancing

K.P. Maurya, the OBC leader who led the party as state unit chief in the UP campaign of 2017, says that the reorganisation of the state into regions and the creation of a booth-level structure was fundamental to the party's strategy. 'We held six booth-level sammelans, one in each region, where our national president came [in 2016-17]. This sent a very big message. We repeated this process at the district level, then at the Vidhan Sabha level and then at the Lok Sabha level. In terms of organisation, we have created such a strong structure that BJP on this basis has created such a factory that it can produce as many MPs and MLAs as you want for the nation's service.'[50]

Significantly, the party was very mindful of caste in these local structures as well. Of UP's 1,47,164 voting booths, it set up booth presidents and fifteen-member booth-level committees in 1,20,000 booths during Rajnath Singh's tenure and while Amit Shah headed UP affairs. 'They left out some booths that were in Muslim-dominated areas like in Rampur or Moradabad,' says Pravin Kumar, the biographer of Yogi Adityanath and resident editor of a big daily in Lucknow. 'Amit Shah ensured equal representation at the booth level for all caste segments. So, in these fifteen-member booth committees, three would be Brahmins, three Thakurs, three Baniya, many more OBCs were brought in.' Importantly, while the BJP had always had notional district-level elections, these were held seriously and ruthlessly in 2013, leading to a major turnover in the party's district-level leadership. This was done to finetune the organisation and they were 'particular about the other caste combinations. That is why they won so many election victories.'[51] (Chapter 8 details how these organisational structures were set up and how they operated.)

The party became so mindful of caste numbers for OBCs that, in many districts, it 'held off appointments of presidents till they found Lodh Rajput OBCs'.[52] A case in point is that of Lucknow, where Mukesh Sharma, a Brahmin, was the city BJP president. When it came to appointing the district president, there was tremendous pressure to appoint someone from among the upper-caste leaders. The party leadership postponed the announcement, dropped many names that came before them and put off a decision till they found an OBC, Shrikrishna Lodh, who was named district president.

The BJP's primary aim was to have a 'sangathan [organisation] in each booth', explains Deputy Chief Minister K.P. Maurya when I ask him about the significance of these district-level elections. Once booth-level committees and presidents were elected, he says, the 'booth president was given the status of a malik [boss]. Earlier they didn't get much status, were not given the kind of respect they should get. Earlier, ordinarily we used to look for them only when we had to give them an election bag. The organisation was only up to this level earlier. But BJP moved much far ahead of this and organised booth presidents first by region, then by district and then by Vidhan Sabha. We did many sammelans with them.'[53] Maurya became party president in April 2016 and these sammelans started in July

2016. 'The last programme was held in Ramabhai Ambedkar Park, which was addressed by PM Narendra Modi. This was a sammelan of booth presidents where we first gave the slogan "*Ab ki baar 300 paar*" [this time we'll cross 300] and we got 325 seats.' Once this structure was in place, the party used it for specific outreach to key target groups. It held a series of 'separate OBC sammelans with OBCs, women sammelans and youth sammelans,' says Maurya. 'We had many Q-and-As here where we put our views before the public and these conversations had a big impact.'[54]

Essentially, the BJP under Amit Shah replicated the booth-level political organisation lessons that the party had learnt in Gujarat. Dinesh Sharma, who had served as party secretary in Gujarat with Shah, before moving back to the UP unit, attributes the entire post-2013 shift in the state's party organisation to Shah. When I asked him whether the BJP was replicating the Gujarat organisational model in UP, he concurred. 'This is correct that in Gujarat we had a sangathan up to the booth level and the primary basis of our victories in Gujarat was the sangathan,' he said. 'Today we have the same situation in Uttar Pradesh too. We have a sangathan till the booth level and the basis of our victory is the sangathan. Whoever the sangathan puts up is the candidate. Earlier it was that if you don't put so and so person, then the party will get finished. Now whether you put Mister A or Mister B from a particular place, it doesn't matter—in the Gujarat style ... We did this in Gujarat ... We all keep contributing a little bit like squirrels, but victory is the result of our combined hard work.'[55]

Shah, he says, focused attention from 2013 onwards on bringing in a new generation of youth workers into the party. This was at the heart of the BJP's turnaround. 'The person who gave the organisation a new character as the creator was Amit Shah,' he says. 'His Chanakya-neeti created workers in every booth and not just workers, spirited workers. This created a large group of youth who had a feeling of dedication to the party.'[56]

Crucially, the BJP focused on building a middle line of leadership in the districts, with a new line-up of Backward Caste leaders. The key thing with some of the smaller Backward Castes is that, while they may be small in numbers, many of them are heavily concentrated in specific constituencies. When they embraced the BJP, it made a huge difference to winnability. For example, Mohanlalganj in Lucknow is a Pasi-dominated seat and Pasis are the most dominant SC caste after Jatavs in UP's Awadh region. So, the BJP specifically focused on building a Pasi leadership, with leaders like Kaushal Kishore, who won the parliamentary election from Mohanlalganj in 2019 and heads the BJP's state SC unit. Similarly, the party focused on projecting several non-Yadav and non-Jatav leaders from the MBCs: leaders like Ashok Katariya from Bijnor, Rama Shankar Katheria in Agra and the Kurmi leader Anupriya Patel from its alliance partner Apna Dal. In Muzaffarnagar, the party bet on Sanjeev Baliyan. While he gained a reputation as a local Hindutva rabble-rouser, Baliyan also symbolised the BJP's understanding of local caste structures and its on-the-ground social engineering.

The only other party to build such a line-up of second-line local leaders in UP was the SP in Mulayam Singh Yadav's heyday. Yadav, says the journalist Pranshu Mishra, 'allowed local leaders to grow: like Azam Khan, Ramakant Yadav. They did their own thing in their areas but always remained behind Netaji. BSP, on the other hand, didn't create a local leadership. It only relied on its cadre but never allowed locally recognisable leaders to be created. Congress only always had feudal leaders in the last couple of decades and no cadres.'

What Modi and Shah did in UP was a far more fundamental structural change—infusing members of OBC castes in significant proportions at every level that matters: parliamentary and assembly candidates, state-level apex leadership, council of ministers and district- and booth-level leadership. This major shift in the BJP's organisational DNA led to the creation of a new political system. 'BJP's organisational bouquet is such, whether it is the PM, whether the state president, whether organisational general secretaries, whether regional president, whether district presidents and after that our candidates—we have without any discrimination tried to give people what is their right. We went to the people for their support in elections with this leadership, with this confidence and right that the very grand bouquet that BJP has built, they can say that my [people's] face is also in it. In that the biggest face is that of the PM. If today the Backward Classes are with the BJP, it is because of this and they see that if they get due respect, it is so only and only in the BJP,' Maurya explains to me at his home on Lucknow's Kalidas Marg. 'Within BJP, there is a bouquet of various classes and people. When a person looks at it, he feels that he is represented, feels that my person is also there, I also have a space.'[57]

The BJP, the evidence clearly shows, is no longer a party of 'savarns'. At least in UP. 'What Modi has done with caste on the ground has broken new ground,' concludes Brijesh Shukla. 'Rahul Gandhi and others are not understanding this. They think they can win on Twitter. Actually, BJP was playing a very long-term game thinking of the long-term with caste. How will its opponents fight it if they don't understand this?'[58]

How the BSP Became a Party of the Rich: A Question of Money

In politics, a party does not have to be perfect on a particular metric. It only has to be better than its opponents. We have already seen how the BJP compared with SP on OBC mobilisation. What worked in its favour was also the fact that its other opponent, BSP, while remaining a party of Dalits, had also become a party of the rich by 2019. Originally set up by Kanshi Ram as part of the great Dalit political revolution, under Mayawati, the party began to change character.

Consider this: in UP in 2004, the BSP had only 1.3 per cent candidates who had assets greater than ₹5 crore. That percentage quadrupled by the next election to 21.5 per cent in 2009, then doubled to 45 per cent in 2014 and went up as high as 67.57 per cent by 2019 (see Table 3.2). The BSP may have retained its Dalit vote base, but it was predominantly fielding only rich candidates in the elections. This change happened after Mayawati won power with the party's first full majority mandate in UP politics in 2007. One reason for so many rich candidates may have been that, after 2007, the BSP allegedly started selling its party tickets to the highest bidder—an allegation that many have made in the past. While I could not verify this independently, the data shows that the BSP started fielding a disproportionately high number of rich candidates.

When we started enquiring about their backgrounds during the research for the Mehta–Singh Social Index, we found that many BSP candidates were the hardest to get a fix on. Often, even the district presidents of the party did not know who a particular candidate was. This meant that, in many cases, they had no political reputation at all and were not known in political circles, but had still contested as party candidates. This problem came up more often in the case of the BSP candidates than any other party. Whether they were paying for these tickets or not, one thing was clear: the preponderance of so many rich candidates meant that the BSP was certainly not as representative of Dalits as it was purported to be. In the 2017 election, for example, it fielded more upper-caste candidates (114) than SCs (eighty-two).

Table 3.2: Percentage of Lok Sabha Candidates with >₹5 Crore Assets in UP (BJP, BSP, INC, SP), 2004–2019

Party	*2004*	*2009*	*2014*	*2019*
BJP	2.67	10.29	29.49	50.65
BSP	1.3	21.05	45	67.57
INC	4.35	15.15	37.3	50.77
SP	6.06	12.33	30.76	43.24

Percentage of Lok Sabha Candidates with >₹5 Crore Assets in India (BJP, INC), 2004–2019

Party	*2004*	*2009*	*2014*	*2019*
BJP	2.72	11.08	29.67	43.19
INC	11.3	22.25	40.8	49.64

Source: Mehta–Singh Social Index. Association for Democratic Reforms data from ECI affidavits filed by candidates, analysis by Rishabh Srivastava. Some of the increase in assets in 2019 was also due to a change in law that required candidates to additionally also declare offshore assets, and those of their spouses, children and Hindu Undivided Family.

While there is no doubt that the BSP's rise in its early years contributed to what the Dalit thinker Chandra Bhan Prasad calls a Dalit 'social revolution', these numbers empirically show why the party seemed to be 'freezing' up by 2020. It had once 'scaled Everest' in political terms, as Prasad has argued. However, as the Dalit middle-class has grown in recent years, the BSP's brand of 'monument symbolism' appears to have 'outlived its shelf-life'.[59] Simultaneously, the party reduced the representational opportunities it once offered to Dalit politicians. This shift, in the absence of a clear Dalit party alternative, opened up new opportunities for the BJP as it looked to pick up non-Jatav votes.

Much is made of the BJP being the richest party in India (as Chapter 7 details). Yet, this change in the central BJP coffers happened after it came to power in 2014. Until 2014, it was the Congress that had the money advantage. At the level of candidates, the BJP's UP candidates were actually the second-poorest among major state parties in 2004 (2.67 per cent with assets above ₹5 crore) and the poorest (10.29 per cent with assets above ₹5 crore) in 2009 and 2014 (29.49 per cent). All through these years, the Congress, the SP to some extent, and the BSP to a much greater extent, fielded richer candidates than the BJP in UP during Lok Sabha polls.

Yes, the net worth of BJP candidates did increase substantially by 2019, when as many as half of its UP candidates were worth more than ₹5 crore—turning it into a party with the second most prosperous Lok Sabha candidates in the state by 2019. But this was still on par with the Congress (50.7 per cent), not too different from the SP (43.2 per cent) and much lower than the BSP (67.5 per cent). While the BJP did become a much richer party, in terms of the people it fielded, the proportion of rich candidates was still within the Indian average for political parties—unlike the BSP, which is way above that average.

This trend is also borne out at the national level. Across all Indian states, the BJP's candidates with assets over ₹5 crore went from 2.72 per cent in 2004 to 29.67 per cent in 2014 and 43.18 per cent in 2019. By 2019, the BJP also became by far the richest party in India. This does give it structural advantages. But it is important to remember that this advantage only accrued to it by 2019. In individual candidate terms, the Congress, at the national level and on average, fielded richer candidates than the BJP, even in 2019. Nationwide, the number of its rich candidates was substantially higher than the BJP's in 2014, double that of the BJP in 2009 and four times higher in 2004.

The common liberal assumption that the BJP is winning elections because it has more money simply does not hold up. In other words, the BJP, even now, is still far away from the backlash that the BSP faced because it started fielding a disproportionately high percentage of rich candidates in UP.

Conclusion

This chapter has shown how caste remains the central lever of power in Indian politics, how the BJP rearranged its caste matrix, giving much greater representation to OBCs, and the upward impact this had on its political fortunes. This is not to argue that caste groups are monoliths, or that everyone in a particular caste group votes the same way. Far from it. However, the BJP's strategies underscored how powerful caste identities remain the truest indices of social power in India. In a different context, the American journalist Isabel Wilkerson, in her book *Caste: The Origins of Our Discontent*, has used the C-word to show how the deeply embedded racial attitudes in the United States mirror the inbuilt social inequities of the caste ladder in India.[60] While India and the US are very different societies, and caste dynamics keep changing, the point is that political representation matters immensely. The BJP's leaders understood this, and the changes they made to their organisation in terms of caste representation at every organisational level played a vital role in its electoral triumphs.

This chapter has provided new evidence to show how our understanding of the BJP's caste representation has so far not kept pace with ground realities. The revelations of the Mehta–Singh Index should lead to much-needed soul-searching as well as a correction of methodologies and dominant narratives among academic experts who study caste patterns in political representation. These findings put a very serious question mark not only on their academic research—which ignored observations from a whole host of journalists on the ground in UP, all pointing strongly to a contrary trend[61]—but also on the poor oversight mechanism of the university research centres that churned out the wrong data and the peer-reviewed academic journals that published them. There is need for both introspection and more transparency. We can have differing interpretations of facts, of course, but only if the data itself is correct. When institutions that are the touchstones of academic credibility produce misleading data, it skews our basic understanding of society and erodes public trust. We hope the findings of the Mehta–Singh Index will start a much-needed debate.

In terms of the wider political terrain, these changes on caste-representation by the BJP came on the back of ten years of successive rule in UP by the state's regional caste-based parties: first the BSP (2007–2012) and then the SP (2012–2017). Unlike in the 1990s, these parties were no longer challengers or rebels with a cause but an integral part of the power structure. In tandem with the BJP's expansion, both parties saw a contraction of their voter base even while they were in power, while the Congress sank into insignificance. At the same time, the Modi period has also seen in UP a solidification and retrieval of savarns who had drifted away from the party in the early 2000s. However, upper-caste mobilisation is not the story of this phase of Indian politics, as this chapter has demonstrated. The expansion of the BJP's vote base, its new MPs, MLAs and office-bearers has been tilted in favour of OBCs in the new BJP. They made up exactly half of its MPs elected from general-category seats nationwide. Within UP, OBCs (mostly non-Yadav) constituted over one-third of the party's Lok Sabha candidates and ministers in Yogi Adityanath's government, and almost one-third of its Vidhan Sabha candidates, state-level officer-bearers and district presidents. Similarly, the BJP significantly upped SC (mostly non-Jatav) representation among its MPs, MLAs, state-level office-bearers and ministers. So much so that OBCs and SCs, taken together, came to occupy half or more than half of the leadership positions at virtually every level of the party, barring its district presidents.

This Mandalisation of the BJP—caste mobilisation without caste wars or confrontations[62]—brought the party's composition closer to the overall population composition of UP than any of its rivals had managed. The unprecedented inclusion of these castes in the party's power structures, combined with an unprecedented cadre expansion, especially with those under forty-five years of age, constituted a significant political innovation that was at the heart of the BJP's post-Modi electoral dominance. Whether this pattern will hold or not is unclear, but these caste alignments were supplemented by a new politics of welfare and DBTs that worked in lockstep with the party's new booth-level cadre mobilisation in UP. It is to this story that we now turn.

4

THE BJP'S POLITICAL MOBILISATION OF WELFARE

'Labharthees'

'I have been gram pradhan for five years and got about Rs 40 lakh in this time period to spend on the village,' Hemant Chauhan told us, sitting by the ancient Shakumbhari Devi temple near Saharanpur in western UP. 'In comparison to that, we have seen about Rs 2 crore each coming in yearly into the village separately through just two schemes. Personal toilets under Swachh Bharat and money for houses under PM Awaas Yojana-Gramin [PMAY-G].'

Chauhan holds an MBA degree and used to work for Johnson & Johnson as a marketing executive in Lucknow and Dehradun before he decided to move back to the Shahpur Bans Must village in Behat tehsil, near the ancient Shakti Peeth of Shakumbhari Devi, in 2013. Because he was well-educated, the villagers decided to elect him as the pradhan, a position that allowed Chauhan to play a vital role in the management and administration of a plethora of government schemes that touched the life of the village. We were chatting about these schemes in his village in June 2020, discussing whether things were really different under the Modi government as compared to Manmohan Singh's time, when he startled me with the stark comparison on governmental spending in his area.

So, was the size and scale of the welfare money the big political differentiator for the Modi government? Did previous governments not spend similar amounts on these schemes? Indeed, was not the toilets scheme simply a renamed, repackaged mega-version of Manmohan Singh's Nirmal Bharat Scheme, rechristened Swachh Bharat? Just like the PMAY-G was a reworked version of what was once called the Indira Awas Yojana? Sure, he answered, but 'you people don't understand the real difference'. After Modi came to power, the money for these schemes 'comes directly into the labharthee's bank account, whether for toilets or for houses'. A villager wanting to get a toilet made, if eligible under Swachh Bharat, gets ₹12,000;[1] while those under the poverty line wanting a pucca house under PMAY-G get ₹1,20,000 in their bank account.[2] 'Imagine, if they got Rs 12,000 for fixing a toilet but it cost only Rs 5,000 to do it,' Chauhan said sardonically. 'The rest of the money is theirs.' The discussion had clearly hit a raw nerve. 'What if they just got some plastering done and got their name written on the list? Whether a toilet is made or not made, the money is with the labharthee. It's the same thing with the houses. People are getting a moti rakam [fat amount], Rs 1,20,000, to build a house. So much money may not be required.'[3] His heart seemed to be in the right place, but the pradhan was clearly not thrilled by the DBTs flowing into villagers' bank accounts. Yet, his micro-perspective had nailed the radical shift that such transfers had caused in the political economy of his village.

Earlier, villagers had to go with their 'arms outstretched' ('haath phaila ke') before local officials to get their entitlements, often for a large cut.[4] Now, the money came directly into their accounts. The officials could still demand a cut in return for sanctioning the payment, or if the villager wanted to be approved as a beneficiary for other schemes. But the fact that the money reached the beneficiary first increased his bargaining power. In a country where Rajiv Gandhi, as prime minister, had famously argued that only 15 paisa of every rupee that is spent on the poor actually reached them, DBTs, for all the faults in the system, drastically shifted the power dynamic in the village. Money went into bank accounts earlier too, but wily village pradhans could make fake job cards for schemes like the Mahatma Gandhi National Rural Employment Guarantee Scheme (MGNREGS)—say fifty fake ones in a village of 200. Once Aadhaar cards were linked to bank accounts, this became much more difficult. Of course, leakages, corruption and systemic inefficiencies still remained, as a range of studies have documented. Yet, from the villagers' point of view, the scope for pilferage was reduced. 'You cannot move Rs 2 from here to there,' a long-time observer of such schemes in Lucknow told us. 'They have made their system so strong that through government the money goes directly into people's accounts—if it is Rs 200, Rs 200 reaches. The mentality has been that if it was Rs 2,000 earlier, then only Rs 200 would reach the village. So, people think that this guy has brought magic. The big difference is that you don't have to beg with your hands outstretched before anyone. That is what has changed.'[5]

Direct Benefit Transfers: Origins and Modi's Ramp-up

The village in Saharanpur exemplified the sea change in the rural welfare economy that DBT had wrought. Equally, it was an example of how an idea pushed through by Manmohan Singh at the fag end of UPA-2 was appropriated by the Modi government politically. The DBT programme was formally launched with much fanfare by Manmohan Singh's UPA-2 government on 1 January 2013. Then Rural Affairs Minister Jairam Ramesh even coined a political slogan for it: 'Aapka Paisa, Aapke Haath' (Your Money in Your Hands). It was launched after months of internal sparring among Congress ministers on the usage of Aadhaar. Once the objections were overcome, however, it was hailed at the time as the 'world's largest cash-transfer scheme'.

The political potential of it was clear even then. One observer saw it as the 'most historic one-shot transformative social policy instrument in India', 'on a par with the abolition of the *zamindari* system, the Green Revolution, banks nationalisation, the Right to Information and the National Rural Employment Guarantee Scheme'.[6] Political editors covering the BJP and the Congress both noted at the time that the launch of the scheme had brought the 'spring back into the step of Congress leaders'[7] after months of being on the defensive as they headed into an election year. The UPA initially launched DBT on a trial basis for twenty-four Union government schemes in forty-three districts.[8] The first trials took place in Rajasthan and then in Andhra Pradesh, but it took a few months to get over the teething problems. The DBT trials were, in fact, ushered in by the Congress a few months before even the banking system moved to accepting Aadhaar numbers for paperless Know Your Customer verification through UIDAI in September 2013.[9] However, initial feedback on the early experiments was not great. By the time many of the issues identified in these trials were fixed, the Congress had lost the elections and the BJP had come to power in 2014.

The Modi government inherited a structure for DBT transfers in 2014 that had already gone through the testing phase, with several schemes and the backend tech stack in place to build on with Aadhaar. Modi gave the initiative full political backing. To its credit, the new government doubled down on DBTs and expanded it fifteen-fold to 434 schemes by 2018-19.[10] Government data shows that the initial 10.8 crore beneficiaries of DBT reported in 2013-14 (many of whom were added under UPA) went up by seven times to 76.3 crore beneficiary accounts by 2018-19. Actual direct cash payments into people's bank accounts went up by over twenty-nine times from ₹7,367 crore in 2013-14 to ₹2.14 lakh crore in 2018-19. If you add transfers in kind, then total transfers went up by forty-four times in the same period (see Table 4.1).

Table 4.1: DBT Transfers Grew at a Fast Pace in NDA-1: DBT Transfers (2013-14 to 2019-20)

Year	*Schemes (No.)*	*Beneficiaries (No. in Crore)*	*DBT (in Cash), ₹ in Crore*	*DBT (in Kind), ₹ in Crore*	*DBT Total, ₹ in Crore*
2013-14	28	10.8	7,367.7	-	7,367.7
2014-15	34	22.8	38, 926.2	-	38, 926.2
2015-16	59	31.2	61, 942.4	-	61, 942.2
2016-17	142	35.7	74, 689.4	-	74, 689.4
2017-18	437	77.7	1, 70, 292.2	20, 578.7	1, 90, 870.9
2018-19	434	76.3	2,14,092	1,15, 704.3	3, 29, 796.3

Source: Collated from Minister of State for Finance Anurag Singh Thakur, Answer to Lok Sabha Unstarred Question No. 1183, 19 September 2020; Minister of State for Finance P. Radhakrishnan, Answer to Lok Sabha Unstarred Question No. 2827, 28 December 2018; Cash and kind break-up of total 2017-18 and 2018-19 transfers is from DBT Mission, Government of India, https://dbtbharat.gov.in/[11]

That these direct cash transfers for a wide range of schemes—LPG, rural housing, toilets—became the basis for a new kind of political mobilisation for Modi and the BJP has long been clear. (Chapter 10 details how they became a vital part of the government's economic policy, and a crucial part of the BJP's arsenal in combating the economic and political costs of the coronavirus lockdown in 2020.) The journalist Pravin Kumar remembers travelling through a village, Harchandpur, near Raebareli, in March 2019, just before the Lok Sabha election. While driving through, he noticed a festive atmosphere, almost like a village fair, with a lot of people out on the road. He remembers stopping and asking residents if they were celebrating a festival. They told him they had just received the first instalment of ₹2,000 in a DBT into their accounts under the PM-Kisan Scheme. Two such instalments (of a total of three annual payments) were made to 4.74 crore registered farmers in February and March 2019, just before the elections, with the ECI's consent. The scheme itself was formally launched by Modi on 24 February 2019 in Gorakhpur, the UP chief minister's constituency, by transferring the first instalment to 1.01 crore farmers, amounting to ₹2,021 crore.[12] On the campaign trail in UP that year, the prime minister often referred to these payments in his speeches. As he told a Kannauj audience, 'This money is yours, it is your right, you own it. Not even Rs 2 from this money can be taken away by any government. And this won't be paid once. It will be paid thrice a year to you.'[13]

Similarly, a few months earlier, in Telangana, over 5.7 million farmers received two payments of ₹4,000 for each acre of land they cultivated per crop season as part of the Telangana Rashtra Samithi (TRS)-led state government's Rythu Bandhu (Farmer's Friend) Scheme. The last of these instalments of ₹4,000 was made in October 2018 through DBTs, just a month before the Telangana state election in November 2018, after due permission from the ECI. This DBT, until then the largest such pre-election cash transfer in India, was said to have played a major factor in shoring up political support for the TRS and its return to power.[14] The Modi government followed a similar playbook with PM-Kisan and other schemes in 2019.

Now, all governments since Independence have spent money on development. The large numbers of Congress-era schemes that were renamed under the Modi regime is a case in point. At one stage, the Congress listed almost three dozen such schemes on its website—the implication being that the Modi government had somehow stolen its ideas and was taking unfair advantage of them by rebranding them.[15] Several scholars have written about the Modi government's mid-term pivot to welfare and redistributive policies with these schemes. Their diagnoses have ranged from the rise of a new kind of welfare populism to pointing to a strategy of personally linking the prime minister's imagery with that of these schemes as a benefactor of the poor, practising what has been called the politics of 'vishwas'.[16] Yamini Aiyar, for example, has argued that 'more than the policies themselves, what distinguished Modi's approach to welfare was the presentation and handling of them in ways that enhanced the Modi persona. Policies that the government said had priority had the initials PM (for 'Prime Minister') added as a prefix before their names, suggesting the idea of a connection between Modi himself and the beneficiaries.'[17]

This by itself is hardly new in India. Among the thirty-two schemes that the Congress accused the Modi government of renaming/repackaging, three were previously named after Rajiv Gandhi, two after Indira Gandhi and one after Nehru. The BJP chose to name three after Deendayal Upadhyaya, one after Atal Bihari Vajpayee and nine carried the generic prefix 'Pradhan Mantri'. Schemes have been named after leaders of the ruling political party for decades. In itself, this is not surprising. In UP, as chief minister between 2012 and 2017, Akhilesh Yadav provided 15 lakh free laptops to college students as part of a government scheme, each carrying photos of him and his father Mulayam Singh Yadav.[18] His government also bought 1.8 crore school bags for children with his photo and the party symbol embossed on them. Ironically, many of these school bags with the SP symbol were later distributed by the Yogi government.[19] Tamil Nadu, too—which once distributed free TV sets to the poor under Karunanidhi's DMK regime, and mixers, grinders and fans under Jayalalithaa's AIADMK government—has long had such welfare schemes branded with the personality of individual chief ministers.

The BJP's Labharthee Model in UP: Sammelans and DBT Welfare Lists

The big question to ask is whether such schemes make a difference and whether people vote for them. Also, what did the BJP do that was different from normal political practice? The first difference is the transformative power of DBTs, the change in local power equations they heralded, and the massive scale-up of these schemes. That the entire bureaucratic and technology backend had been tested and was ready to be plugged into play by the time Modi came to power was the BJP's good fortune. The party capitalised on it by doubling down on it politically and scaling it up in a big way. The cash transfers created a new class of labharthees who could be politically harnessed. They played a vital role in the expansion of support among non-traditional BJP voters in rural areas. As a senior official in the UP chief minister's office (CMO) told me in Lucknow's Lok Bhawan, 'Direct transfers played a big part. If someone gets even Rs 50 in a direct transfer in his bank, then he remembers it, as opposed to the thousands of crores you spend on the public. That no one cares about or remembers at the time of elections. This creation of personal labharthees was crucial and we worked very hard to politically mobilise this with labharthee sammelans.'[20]

A Lucknow journalist argued, 'You can make roads paved with silver and gold but nothing will happen [in terms of votes]. It is about what you get personally. That is what matters and this is why cash transfers changed the game.' A senior functionary recounted a telling conversation with a roadside cobbler, who plied his trade opposite a doctor's clinic in Lucknow, just before the 2019 elections. When asked who would win, the cobbler unequivocally replied: 'Modi'. Why, asked the questioner, who was also carrying out a survey of twenty Jatavs each in several constituencies. The cobbler himself was a 'haathi-waala' (BSP supporter; the haathi, or elephant, is the party's poll symbol). So, why did he think Modi would win?

'Yes, I will vote for haathi,' he said, 'but in my village, one person has got a house [money for one] from the government.'

Did he get a house himself?

'No,' said the cobbler. 'But I will get it. I have ummeed [hope].'

The cobbler was a diehard BSP supporter, but he had seen people in his village benefiting, and thought that he too could benefit at some stage. The possibility made him more receptive to the party.[21]

DBT and the BJP's Targeted Meetings

Yet, if spending money on welfare alone was enough to win back power, then few democratic governments anywhere would lose power. DBT as a policy tool is not some secret weapon. Liberal economists have been aggressively recommending it for years, and state governments cutting across party lines, like the TRS in Telangana and the Kamal Nath-led Congress government in Madhya Pradesh (2018–2020), have all deployed them.[22] This brings us to the second major shift that the BJP made. The party skilfully deployed its grassroots organisation, which had been reshaped in 2013, as a tool to specifically target labharthees. It combined precision-use governmental beneficiary lists with last-mile political workers to initiate a concerted campaign of political mobilisation that broke new ground in north Indian politics.

Yogi Adityanath's November 2018 village chaupal gathering in Pratapgarh (described in Chapter 1) was one such meeting. When he started that late-night assembly by asking people if they had received scheme benefits, the loudest voices in the crowd shouted 'no'. The initial response seemed to indicate that the vast majority of people in the village had not received anything. But once the chief minister read out some beneficiary lists himself, asked the DM and the DPRO to read out other lists and engaged in public dialogue with those who had grievances, it turned out that more than half the village had indeed benefited. 'On labharthees, the issue is that, when someone gets something, mostly they keep quiet,' a senior government officer who works closely with Yogi Adityanath's office explained later. 'You see any political rally, say of Modi's. When the camera shows labharthees, they don't show any obvious reaction. They keep sitting quietly. When the guys in front clap, they will all clap. If they don't clap, then no one will clap. It will look like whatever is being said does not concern them.' In that first Pratapgarh chaupal, he and some of his officers deliberately mingled with the audience and sat with them. His account of the crowd dynamic is worth repeating in full:[23]

> Whenever Yogi would ask a question about schemes, we saw that there were essentially fifteen–twenty boys who, each time, would shout 'nahin' [no]. They must have had a problem with the village pradhan and they kept saying that he ate all the toilets, that he was a thief. They insisted they hadn't got anything. The vast majority was silent because whosoever gets anything, they usually keep quiet. Many don't tell anyone it is from the government. They tell people they got it with their own money or from the family. That is why they keep quiet. We were worried because it was a large crowd and people were watching from rooftops and had climbed trees. A chief minister dealing with such a bawaal [disturbance] is rare. But Yogiji is used to street politics.
>
> He responded by first calling those who said they hadn't got anything on stage. He asked them one-by-one to list what they didn't get. Then he called the CDO there with the beneficiary lists. He questioned one of the complainants, are you under the poverty line? He said no. Yogiji said, how will you get it if you are above the poverty line? Then he asked one who was saying he hadn't got a house if he already had a house. He said yes, but it is old. Yogiji said, don't you know only those people get houses who don't have a pucca one. Many people still kept complaining, so Yogiji read out the lists—how many people have got what. As the names were being read out, and the villagers heard the names, the people's attitude changed. They realised that things had been received. As names were read, he would say whose name is this, stand up. Slowly but surely, the disturbance and perception changed. We realised that day that the person who gets something mostly remains quiet. This is how we changed the narrative.

Yogi Adityanath's chaupals were a logical extension of a booth-level initiative of direct mobilisation around welfare schemes that the BJP's UP unit started in 2016. 'Labharthee sammelan' is a term that comes up a lot when you speak to the state's BJP leaders. Deputy Chief Minister Dinesh Sharma explained that these beneficiary meetings were systematically organised around specific schemes in each booth area. 'For this, we did labharthee sammelans,' he said. 'Someone got a gas chulha, someone got a toilet. We did separate sammelans with those who got gas cylinders and separate sammelans with those who got toilets. We did these kinds of activities at the booth level.'[24] The first aim of these meetings was to hammer home the political linkage of these schemes with Modi. 'Our opponents can shout as much as they like,' says Sharma. 'Labharthees know that these toilets got made by Modiji. They know that the Kisan Samman Rashi is theirs, which Modiji gave them. This is unlike before. There was a saying that do a good deed and put it in the well. Now it is, do a good deed and put it to the people, in the people's darbar. That is what we did with these sammelans.'

Furthermore, these labharthee sammelans also served as a second layer of checks and balances on welfare schemes outside of the government machinery. The BJP launched a big campaign centred on this in each district and vidhan sabha constituency of UP. This was done with the 'sangathan and government working on this in coordination', said Deputy Chief Minister K.P. Maurya. This involved a whole host of the party's senior-most state leaders, its MPs and MLAs, being tasked with visiting specific constituencies to hold public meetings with labharthees. Not only were they asked to visit villages as part of a planned campaign, they each had to spend the night there too, to get a better sense of the mood and what was really happening. 'We used to mostly plan to spend the night in villages,' said Maurya. 'Whether it was the CM, deputy CM, state president, district president or any other office bearer, everyone used to spend a night pravas in some village or the other. The aim was that for those who benefited—whether with gas cylinders under Ujjwala, or houses under PMAY—we would go and assess at every level if there was any wrongdoing. We designed these visits to check if anyone who was supposed to get benefits didn't get them, to see who was left out. If there were weaknesses, we focused on fixing them so that those who needed benefits got them.'[25]

The BJP's booth-level presidents and booth-committee members were central to this drive. Maurya cites the example of ration cards as a case in point. 'BPL [Below Poverty Line] cards were made in 2002. When we went to the people between the 2017 and 2019 elections, it had already been seventeen years since they were made and that is a long time. There were many who had reached the sky from the ground in this time but still had BPL cards. In these visits, we did a deep analysis of this and focused on getting BPL cards for those who really deserved them so that they could get their rights, get toilets, gas connections, health services and food.' The BJP's booth-level workers specifically worked with government beneficiary lists to organise these meetings. When I asked an official in the CMO about the level of coordination between the party and the government on how these government lists of labharthees were used for political mobilisation, the answer was clear. 'When it is a party programme, the party does it; when it is a government programme, the government does it,' said the senior official. 'There is a list in each area on how many people got houses; there is a list on how many got toilets; there is a list on how many got gas connections. The administration has these lists and they talk about it. The government's work the government does on its own for follow-up and feedback with these lists. When the party does it, it is different. The sangathan's people do it on their own. They take the list from the DM.' When I queried if BJP workers took these lists from the DMs, he said, 'Yes, they take the list and they do their own work. They work separately.'[26] (Chapter 8 further details how the BJP was reorganised at the micro voting-booth level for this purpose.)

The use of beneficiary lists was fundamental to this mobilisation, and at the very heart of the BJP's political project. When I asked Maurya about how these beneficiary lists were used, his answer too was unequivocal. 'Yes, the government has these lists. We have these lists: who got benefits, who didn't get benefits. If someone's name is on the beneficiary list or not, we know.' So, this was a targeted mobilisation, I said. 'What targeted?' he responded. 'Please understand that our PM is a poor son of Maa Bharti who is leading the country, the government has made so many schemes for the welfare of labharthees and has done this work of giving such a large part of the government's treasury to the people. This country has also seen a time when Rajiv Gandhi himself as PM said that only 15 paise of every rupee that the government spends on the poor reaches them. But now we can say with pride that, since PM Modi's government was formed, when he sends Re 1 to the poor, Re 1 reaches.'[27]

Yogi Adityanath's Welfare Model: Recreating the BJP as a 'Party of the Poor'

When Yogi Adityanath took charge as chief minister in 2017, he made effective execution of all Union schemes his top priority. As his biographer told me in Lucknow, 'They have nothing much of their own.'[28] The BJP began focusing on what one leader called 'double-engine ki sarkar'[29]—the state government working in tandem with the Union government. A senior officer told me, 'Yogiji's approach is that when the Union government announces schemes, his attempt is that maximum to maximum people here get benefits from our end. Money is coming from there [Union government], it is not from us [state government]. So, we try to get maximum bhaagidari [sharing] that we can do with the Centre—Rs 30 lakh crore, Rs 40 lakh crore … We ensure that it is implemented with maximum support. Toilets were there earlier also. When Yogiji came, he took it up with full strength. He got 2.5 crore toilets made, got houses made—more than what was not done in last fifteen years in one go. When he holds meetings with bureaucrats, he says, please get this report done. We should get maximum beneficiaries and maximum results. He works hard.'[30]

The chief minister, a saffron-clad monk, was initially not taken seriously by the UP bureaucracy. At the very outset, he modelled his management style on Modi. 'When he started as CM, Modi suggested to him that you take a presentation from each department on work they have done and what they will do in next 100 days,' says a senior official in the CMO. Yogi put in place a structured three-monthly review system of government programmes. As the officer explained: [31]

> When he [Yogi Adityanath] started, he would take meetings till 1 a.m. in the morning. That gave him an idea of what is happening initially. Officers took him lightly. They thought he is a Yogi, they thought they knew him and that he would forget. But his memory is very strong, he remembers figures—for example, he will listen to a presentation and say this is Rs 600 crore, it is not Rs 630 crore.
>
> After that, he started doing reviews every three months. He would call them for a review and some officers would repeat old statistics. He would say, you showed the same figures last time, the data is old. Then they would say, 'Oh, Sir, some work was left'. He told them to come again next month. The thing is that you cannot repeat a lie again and again. You will have to deliver, come what may. IAS/IPS officers are smart anyway. They understood that they won't be able to manage without doing work and he will keep following up. He doesn't give any option.
>
> It is like, if you as an editor assign a story to someone and after some time he is still sitting on his seat, you will ask—where is the story, how

long will it take? He will say, Sir, I couldn't do it today. Then what about tomorrow, you will question. Why haven't you done it for three days? You will either make this reporter work or get a new person. If you remove him, the new person will also think that he will have to do the work anyway, come what may, even if they are corrupt. They don't have any option. And he doesn't have any other work. He sits at 8.30 a.m. in the morning on the files.

He wakes up at 3 or 4 a.m. He does pooja etc till 5 a.m. and his other stuff by 8 a.m. Then he is at his office desk by 8.30 a.m. By 9 a.m., we reach. From 10, he starts taking meetings. When he is out of town, it's like a Sunday. If a person works like this, if you do 30 per cent of that, you will see results. Even if you are the most corrupt of corrupt persons, you will still have to show results.

This focus on delivery of government schemes exemplified the social-welfare focus of the BJP. For example, within 100 days of coming to power, Yogi Adityanath's government issued the first public report card of its work on welfare schemes. Unlike detailed government reports, this was aimed at the general public, filled with colourful pages and photographs, enumerating results across a number of schemes, from those addressing sugarcane farmers to village electricity to water for fields.[32] The UP government has since continued to publish similar periodic report cards.[33] A detailed analysis of the performance of these schemes is outside the purview of this book. But the political focus on governmental schemes was clear (more details in Chapter 8).

Between 2013 and 2019, the BJP swept four elections in UP: two Lok Sabha polls (2014 and 2019), one assembly election (2017), nine by-elections and municipal elections in 2018. Senior state BJP leaders attributed this upswing in political fortunes in great measure to the political mobilisation around welfare. They attribute it to what they call 'sushasan' [good governance] and a victory of welfare politics. The election results over six years showed that the initial win of 2014 was not a 'momentary victory', says Dinesh Sharma.[34]

Many people tried to portray the 2014 win as a mere coincidence, but the way Modiji worked for the welfare of the poor, no party has touched those things in that manner. Jan Dhan accounts for the poor, toilets, gas connections, construction of houses, Samman Rashi for farmers, cheap fertilisers, right price for crops, all these were key. Between 2017 and 2020, we paid Rs 96,000 crore loans of sugarcane farmers ... These measures touched the villages and farmers ... Our successive election victories demonstrated this ... This is why our vote share grew in rural areas. Go to the villages and you will see toilets in houses, gas cylinders and electricity. Earlier, we politicians didn't give anything, only talked of caste, but now the public benefits.

Significantly, UP reported the highest number of total DBT fund transfers of all states in 2018-19. Partly this is by virtue of it being India's most populous state. Even so, it was ahead by a wide margin on DBT in a state-by-state comparison of the highest-spending states (see Figure 4.1).

Figure 4.1: UP Highest in DBT Fund Transfers Among All States

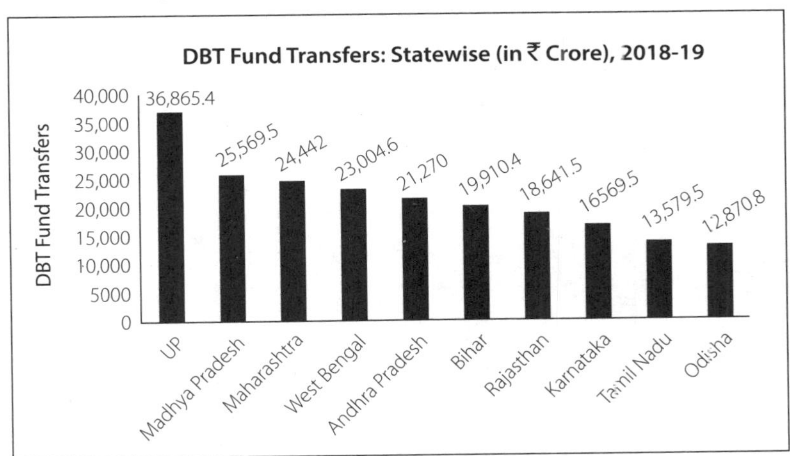

Source: Based on schemes for which state-wise data has been reported. As reported by DBT Mission, Government of India, 'State-Wise DBT Fund Transfer', https://dbtbharat.gov.in/page/frontcontentview/?id=NjU=

'Izzat Ghar': The Case of Household Toilets

The pace of construction of household toilets under Swachh Bharat and housing under PMAY-G illustrate the Yogi government's focus on implementing Union government schemes. UP constructed 17.1 million household toilets between 2014-15 and 2019-20, taking the overall tally to 23.8 million in UP and 164.18 million nationally (see Figure 4.2).[35]

Figure 4.2: Construction of Household Toilets in UP Grew at the Same Pace as Construction Nationwide: Swachh Bharat

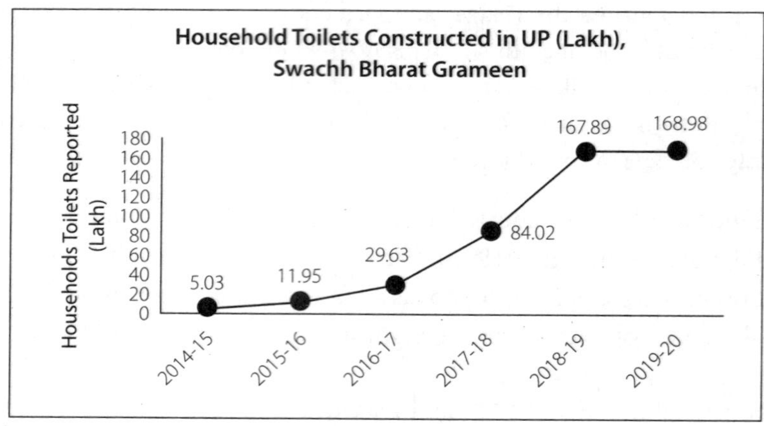

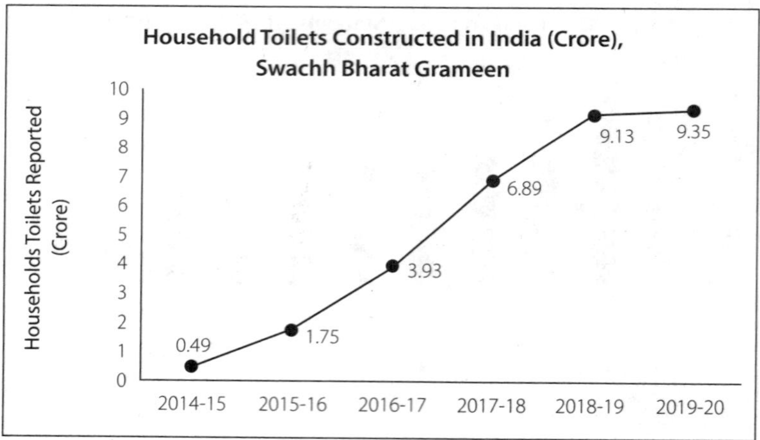

Source: Swachh Bharat Mission Gramin Dashboard, Ministry of Jal Shakti, Governmentt of India, https://sbm.gov.in/sbmdashboard/IHHL.aspx

Importantly, these toilets are not built by the government. Beneficiaries receive ₹12,000 in their bank account and have to get it constructed themselves. They receive ₹10,000 in the first tranche, and the remaining money after the construction is verified and geotagged. Revealingly, Modi began referring to these toilets as 'Izzat Ghar' or 'House of Respect' after seeing this title-plate on some toilets built in Varanasi in 2017. In a country where a lack of toilets has been one of the most obvious yet underrated of gender divides, this terminology for toilets specifically targeted women. As Modi told an election rally in UP in 2019, 'Modi's campaigning is being done by that daughter in whose house a toilet was built under the Swachh Bharat Mission. For a young daughter, this was the making of an Izzat Ghar.'[36] In October 2017, the Union government even issued a circular to all states, asking Hindi-speaking states to start formally referring to Swachh Bharat toilets as 'Izzat Ghar' and non-Hindi speaking states to come up with similar nomenclature in their own languages.[37] (Chapter 17 investigates the gender-specific politics around such schemes in detail.)

The Women Factor: Housing and DBT

Modi often says in his election speeches that 'Modi's campaign is being done by the poor brother and sister who, under Pradhan Mantri Awas Yojana got a pakka ghar [permanent house], got its keys and went there to stay.'[38] The PMAY-G was formally launched on 20 November 2016. By November 2020, a whopping 17.5 million houses had been sanctioned under this scheme for the poor. Over 12 million of these approved houses had already been constructed[39] and over 1.6 million (1.4 million completed) were in UP. Just as with household toilets, these houses are not constructed by the state but funded by it. Beneficiaries (those who lived in kaccha/dilapidated houses) received DBT of ₹1,20,000 to build their own houses (₹1,30,000 in hill states) and were also entitled to receiving ninety days of unskilled labour under MGNREGS in a scheme that was funded in a 60:40 ratio by the Union and state governments.[40] Importantly, governmental policies ensured a good balance of minority groups and disadvantaged castes among the beneficiaries. Government data shows that 23.08 per cent of houses were sanctioned for STs, 21.7 per cent for SCs and 12.03 per cent for religious minorities during this period nationwide. In UP, over one-third of houses went to SCs and 11 per cent to minorities (see Figure 4.3 and Table 4.2).

The BJP did not just focus on DBT schemes; it added an extra layer of political mobilisation using grassroots booth-level organisation structures. Crucially, most of the outreach to labharthees happened outside of election cycles. In effect, the party sangathan became the foundation for a new kind of system. This mobilisation around welfare

Figure 4.3: Housing Construction through DBT has Grown: Keeping in Mind Caste Groups

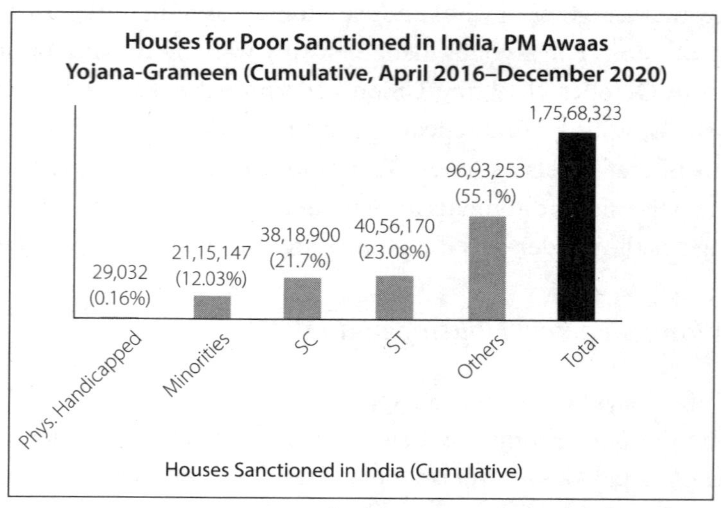

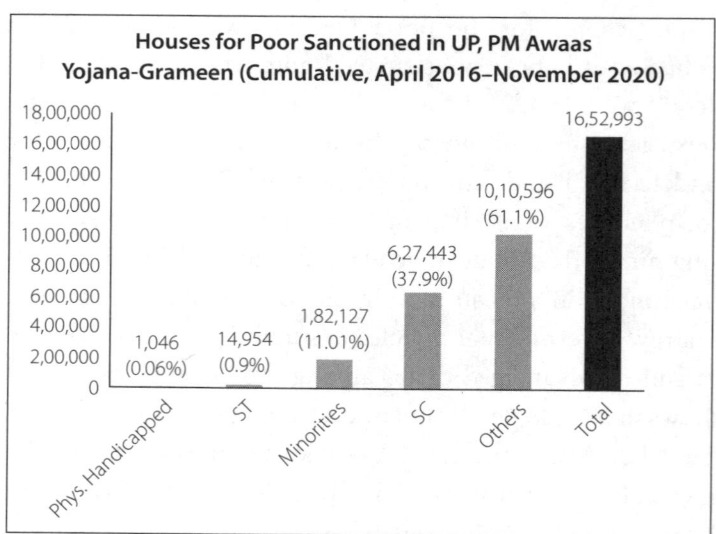

Source: Data from PM Awaas Yojana–Gramin, Awassoft Dashboard, 'C2- Category-Wise Houses Sanctioned and Completed', 27 November 2020, https://rhreporting.nic.in/netiay/SocialProgressReport/Categorywisehousescompletedreport.aspx was new. 'We always had a sangathan,' says Sharma. 'Now we added some new points to it. When you come to power, you learn something. This is the first time we came to power on our own at the Centre, since the government in Atalji's time was a coalition.'

Table 4.2: Central Government Funds Released Under PMAY-G (2016-17 to 2018-19, in ₹ in lakhs)

Year	*UP*	*India*
2016-17	2,45,959.01	15,85,280.27
2017-18	4,94,806.43	29,99,560.46
2018-19	27,758.51	29,32,675.97
Total Funds Released by Centre	10,18,351.25	75,17,516.70

Source: Minister of Rural Development Narendra Singh Tomar, Answer to Lok Sabha Unstarred Question No. 1936, 3 March 2020, http://164.100.24.220/loksabhaquestions/annex/173/AU1936.pdf[41]

BJP leaders are right to argue that they are not winning on Hindutva alone. As one official told me, 'Many others came before with Hindutva. There was Swami Chinmayanand and others earlier. What happened to them? If it was only Hindutva, Yogi Adityanath would also have got wiped out.'[42] This is why, they told us, Hindutva is the 'gati', it was welfare that was the wheel. In this view, the BJP took major steps that transformed it into what Maurya called the 'party of the poor'. As UP Deputy Chief Minister Dinesh Sharma put it, 'Congress used to have a slogan, "Garibi Hatao" [Remove Poverty]. Garibi did not go, the garib [poor] would go. Modiji gave a slogan to remove poverty and we have made visible progress, with poverty numbers going down.'

The truth is that poverty numbers have been consistently going down in India since 2004-05. India lifted 138 million people out of poverty between 2004-05 and 2011-12.[43] What the BJP has done is to systematically add a new layer of micro-level political mobilisation around welfare in a way that has not been done before. It turbo-charged older systems of social-welfare delivery and pushed newer delivery systems like DBTs on a massive scale.

In Mathura, for example, when I met a group of BJP district-level officials in July 2020, they told me that a large proportion of their daily work was the checking of beneficiary lists in their areas. 'Right now, we are doing a collection of how many BPL cards were made by us,' said Hemant Agarwal, BJP's Mathura district vice president. 'How many chulhas we distributed, how many cards we distributed in Ayushman Bharat, how many toilets we made. This listing is being done. It is being audited ... So, for example, PM Awas Yojana has houses, those lists come to us. We check them from our side. We see if it is correct or not, whether there are complaints or not, if there is a problem or not.'[44] Through the pandemic-induced lockdown, the party's city unit had conducted targeted Zoom meetings with separate local groups of beneficiaries, scheme by scheme: those with BPL cards who had recently been allocated electricity connections across UP, those who received chulhas under a government scheme and so on.

Nobody can claim that the governmental systems worked perfectly, or that there are no flaws in them. That would obviously be wrong. The point is that the BJP, using its ground machinery and targeted messaging, was able to reap the political benefits of its welfare spending, thus evolving a new model of politics in north India.

As one of the longest-serving independent MLAs in UP told me, 'BJP has done work but it also has an old speciality: to do work which may be worth very little, as much as a speck of hair, but to dress it up so that it looks like a wonder.'[45]

5

THE BJP'S MUSLIM MODEL

Hindutva, the Politics of Exclusion and Why the BJP Still Wins Muslim Seats

I was waiting in Deputy Chief Minister Dinesh Sharma's antechamber in Lucknow. Also patiently awaiting their turn were at least two delegations of over fifty Muslim religious leaders, dressed in white kurta-pyjamas and prayer caps. Another delegation was already inside, closeted in conversation. I wondered why they were there. It was early June 2020. Perhaps it was because the state government had just announced that UP's mosques, which had been closed for two months due to the first COVID-induced national lockdown, could reopen but with 'wuzu' (hand-washing) now only allowed at home and no hugs or shaking of hands. These rules were similar to those for Hindu temples—which too could reopen, but with no bell-ringing, exchange of prasad, kirtans or bhajans, touching of gods and goddesses, or any footwear in the precincts. My colleagues and I got called inside for our interview before we could ask our fellow waiters in the antechamber why they had come. But such a large presence of Muslim notables in the deputy chief minister's office was a powerful visual metaphor for the big questions that have always been at the heart of the BJP's relationship with religion, its belief in Hindutva as a primary marker of Indianness, and the implications of this identity politics for India's Muslims.

So, I put two questions to Sharma at the end of our interview. How exactly does the BJP view Muslims? And how has it been winning in UP without the support of a community that makes up 19.2 per cent of the state's population (higher than the national average of 14.2 per cent[1])? 'Look, now the times have changed,' he replied. 'When you came, you saw so many famous maulanas, national-level maulanas, sitting with me. Three more are coming in a while to meet me. They are international-level maulanas. In one section of Muslims, the thinking has changed—I won't say for the whole section—and this was a reason to worry for the Opposition. It was scared that Muslims also should not go with BJP, so they started false campaigning on the CAA, especially with Muslims, and created a conspiracy to create misunderstandings. This is because a section of Muslims, especially educated Muslims, are getting attracted to the BJP.'[2] We ran out of time as he finished, and another group of maulanas entered his office, this time accompanied by leaders from the BJP's local Minority Cell, which coordinates the party's work with minority religions.

It was evident that Sharma was very pleased by the visits of these Muslim leaders. However, his response to the Muslim question needs to be read in conjunction with his unequivocal emphasis on what he considered the primary reason for the BJP's electoral successes: its core ideology. 'The fundamental reason for BJP's victory is that we didn't change our set guiding principles,' he insisted . 'When we lost, we still remained steadfast on our guiding principles. When we won, then also we remained steadfast in our policies. We didn't do the politics of loss and profit ... BJP's agenda remained the same as it was before through our manifesto: to remove Article 370, Triple Talaq, CAA, the construction of the Ram Temple. These four–five issues were there, and with them, nationalism as a centre-point. This has a direct impact on the people.'[3] Ever since the BJP's rise to power, this emphasis on its core ideology has been the primary fault line in the ideological debate between its supporters and those who oppose it. The party's critics have argued that its ascendance has raised serious questions about the fate of Indian secularism,[4] signalled the rise of a new kind of 'toxic majoritarianism'[5] and resulted in the gutting of Indian democracy to reduce Muslims to second-class status.

The BJP's response to this critique has always been to refer back to its 2014 election slogan of 'Sab Ka Saath Sab Ka Vikas'. It insists that there has never been any religious bias in the implementation of its governmental welfare schemes and accuses the secular liberal chattering classes and the Opposition of misrepresenting its politics. Narendra Modi pointedly referred to this in his May 2019 acceptance speech. Calling the verdict a riposte to the secular critique, Modi argued in his moment of triumph that this was one of the primary lessons of the election. 'This dramebazi has been on for years, but for thirty continuous years especially,' he said in a speech at the BJP's headquarters in Delhi. 'It was such a printout, such a tag that had become so fashionable. That whatever you do, you put it on. It was like doing a Ganga bath to get good credit [punya]. The name of this tag—and it was totally fake—was secularism. There were slogans chanted, "Seculars unite, Seculars unite". You would have seen that from 2014 to 2019, that entire jamaat [community] stopped talking only. In this election, not even one political party dared to wear the mask of secularism to misdirect Hindustan. They got exposed.'[6]

The truth is that, while it has not won successive elections because of Hindutva and its core supporters alone—that would simply not be possible—there is no question that, after 2014, the BJP sharpened its focus on an assertive Hinduness as an idiom of the party. This goes beyond iconic issues or historic symbols—there is now an emphasis on Hinduness and nationalism being synonymous. The ascent of Yogi Adityanath, the saffron robe-wearing mathadheesh of the Gorakhnath peeth, as chief minister in UP is symbolic of this hard turn to first principles. Yogi, like Modi, has often argued publicly that secularism, as it has been practised in India, is a 'false' narrative—drawing from L.K. Advani's original critique of pseudo-secularism in the 1980s—that Hinduism as a religion is essentially secular, and therefore India as a country is secular essentially because it is Hindu.[7] As he put it, soon after taking charge as chief minister in 2017, 'The government should be panth-nirpeksh [community-neutral], not dharm-nirpeksh [religion-neutral]. We should understand the difference between panth and dharm. Secularism as a word means panth-nirpeksh not dharm-nirpeksh. This is why this word should be debated seriously. Secondly, what is the meaning of secularism in the country? If panth-nirpekshta is secularism, then nobody is a bigger secular than the Hindu who speaks of "*Sarve bhavantu sukhinah*" [May all be happy], "*Vasudhaiva kutumbakam*" [The world is one family], "*Ekam satya vipra bahudha vadanti*" [There is only one truth (or true being) and learned persons call it by many names]. But in this country, what have so-called secularists turned the meaning of secularism into? Those who abuse Indianness, those who oppose sanaatan tradition, those who abuse Indian greats—they will be great secularists. We don't need this kind of secularism in this country ... Secularism must mean *sarv panth samabhaav* [equal respect for all sects]. No government or state can run by taking any one upasna vidhi [worship system] alone. It must respect all. In this matter, you will see that our government respects *sarv panth samabhaav* and its spirit.'[8]

Hindu Counter-mobilisation in UP and the Hindi Heartland's Muslim-significant Seats

Electorally, much has been made of the symbolism of the BJP's decision from 2014 onwards of not fielding a single Muslim candidate in any UP national or state election. Its critics interpreted this policy as a signal to Muslim voters that they do not impact its fortunes. In a state where one in every five voters is Muslim, such a strategy would once have been political suicide. Yet, the BJP has won election after election with it. The fact is that the BJP in UP specifically, and in the Hindi heartland more generally, has been winning a large number of seats with significantly high Muslim populations, ranging from Kairana, Muzaffarnagar and Meerut in western UP to Bareilly in central UP and Bahraich in the eastern part of the state. Just as it did with rural seats, the party, between 2014 and 2019, cemented itself as the dominant pole of politics in these seats. This is not because it won greater Muslim support, but because of Hindu counter-mobilisation in these areas. What often happens in many such constituencies is that rival parties tend to field Muslim candidates, while the BJP fields a Hindu candidate who then benefits from a consolidation of the Hindu vote.

There are nineteen Lok Sabha seats in the Hindi heartland where over 30 per cent of voters happen to be Muslim. For our purposes here, let's call them Muslim-significant seats. Of these, the BJP won only five seats (19.6 per cent of the votes) in 2009, fourteen (41.6 per cent) in 2014 and seven (39.6 per cent) in 2019. This would imply that its support base in these Muslim-significant seats declined in 2019. However, when we look at vote shares, it is clear that the party grew much deeper roots in these seats during the past decade. In 2009, BJP won only one of the nineteen Muslim-significant seats with more than 40 per cent vote share, which, as we have seen before, is a performance benchmark that indicates a decisive presence.[9] That number went up to nine in 2014 and to thirteen in 2019. In other words, the BJP in 2019 won more than 40 per cent of the vote in 68.4 per cent of Muslim-dominated seats in the Hindi heartland (see Figure 5.1). In sharp contrast, the Congress, which had won the largest number of these Muslim seats in 2009 (six seats, 16.4 per cent vote share), got reduced to a rump by 2019 (one seat, 11 per cent vote share).

Figure 5.1: The BJP Expanded Its Base in Muslim-significant Seats, While the Congress Shrunk in the Hindi Heartland (Lok Sabha: 2009–2019)

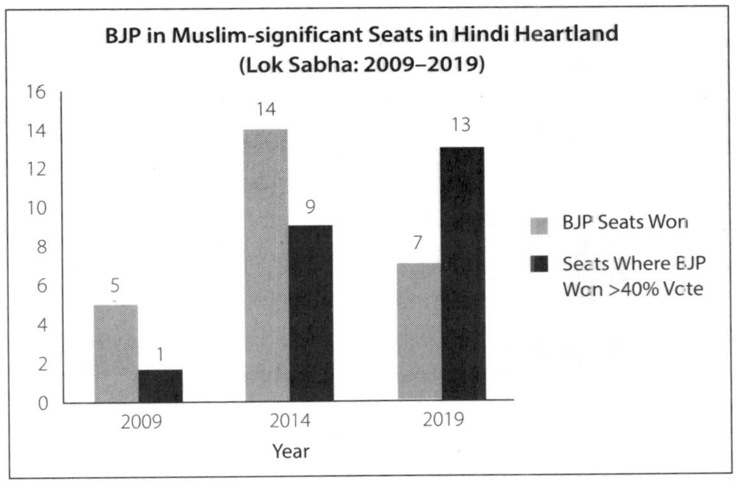

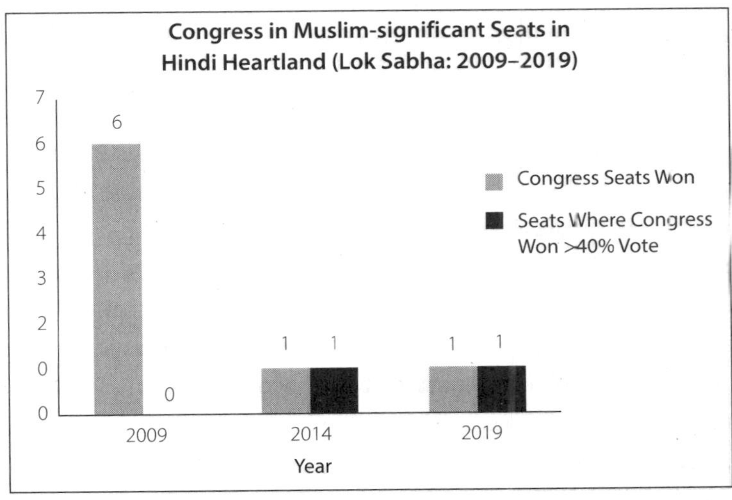

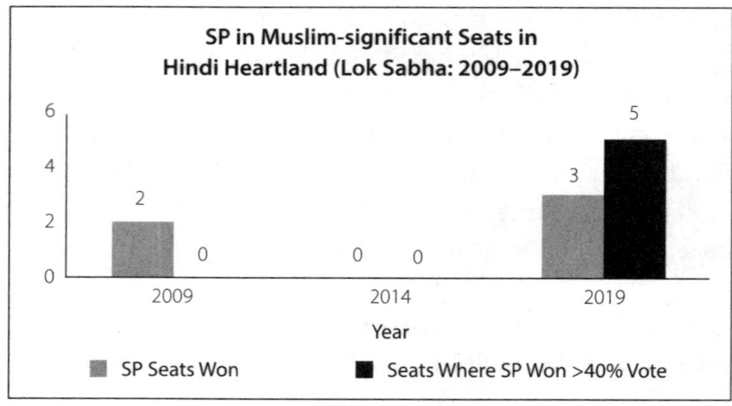

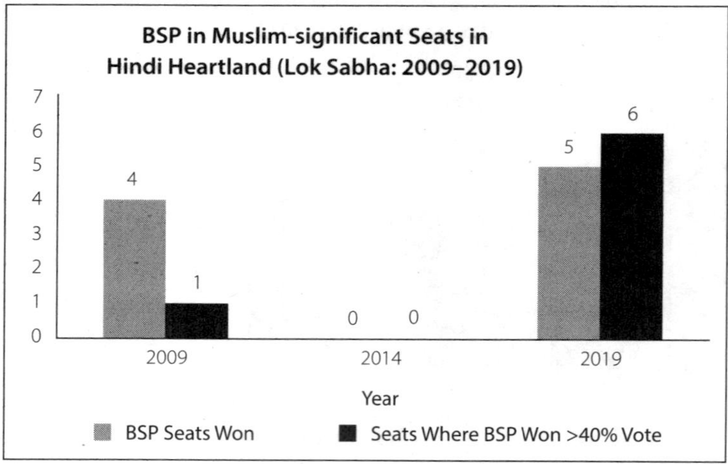

Source: ECI data. Analysis by Nalin Mehta and Rishabh Srivastava, PollNiti. We are thankful to Jai Mrug for classification of seats with 30 per cent or more Muslim voters.

Similarly, in UP, the BJP won only one of thirteen Muslim-significant seats in 2009, all thirteen in 2014, and only five in 2019. A superficial reading of this would imply that Muslims were attracted by Narendra Modi's messaging in 2014 but many turned away in 2019. Vote shares tell the deeper story. In 2009, the BJP won only 15.2 per cent of the votes in Muslim-significant seats. This dramatically increased to 44.6 per cent in 2014 and 45.6 per cent in 2019. Moreover, the BJP in UP had not managed to attract more than 40 per cent of votes in even a single Muslim seat in 2009. In 2014, it did so in eight seats, and by 2019 in as many as eleven seats. In other words, the BJP won more than 40 per cent

Figure 5.2: The BJP Expanded Its Base in Muslim-significant Seats in UP (Lok Sabha: 2009–2019)

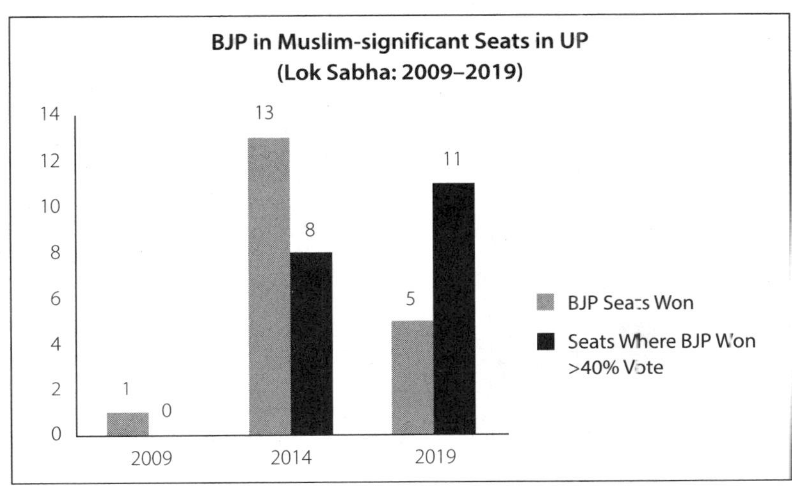

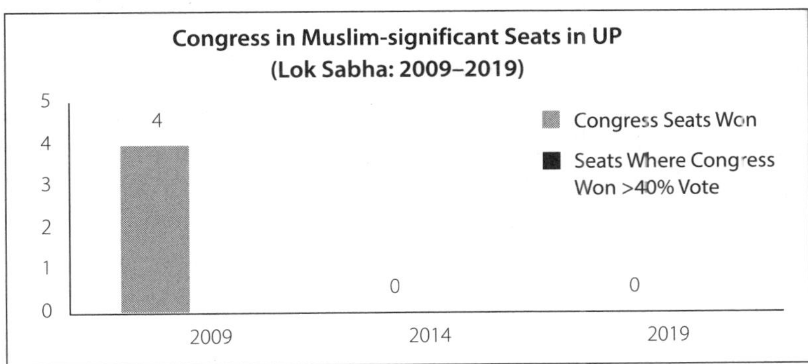

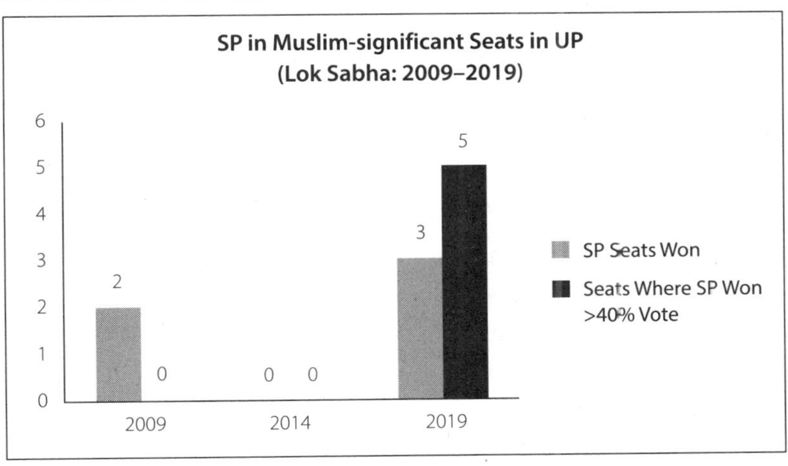

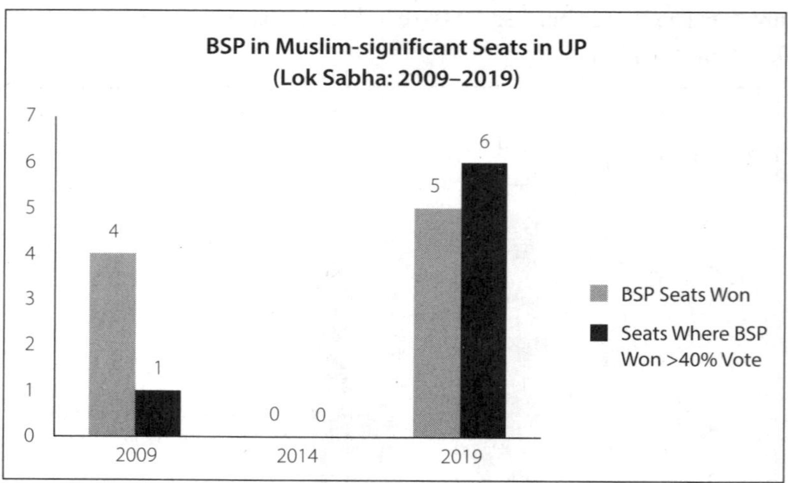

Source: ECI data. Analysis by Nalin Mehta and Rishabh Srivastava, PollNiti. We are thankful to Jai Mrug for classification of seats with 30 per cent or more Muslim voters.

of the vote in an overwhelming majority—as many as 84.6 per cent—of Muslim-significant seats in UP in 2019. Essentially, the BJP's fortunes rose in Muslim-significant areas because of the much sharper counter-mobilisation by Hindus in the party's favour.

In other words, while other parties mostly fielded Muslim candidates in these seats, hoping to attract what they saw as a monolithic chunk of Muslim voters, the community's vote often ended up being split between them. The BJP, on the other hand, always fielded a Hindu candidate in such seats. It benefited from a consolidation of Hindu voters in response to a perceived Muslim political mobilisation, which had the potential to override other issues of difference among them. With the Muslim vote divided between rival candidates, the BJP often needed a lower winning threshold in Muslim-significant seats. The party won fewer Muslim-significant seats in 2019 even though it attracted more votes than earlier because of the SP–BSP alliance against it. Yet, the alliance also resulted in a sharper polarisation among voters along Hindu–Muslim lines. Again, like in the wider Hindi heartland, the Congress went from being a strong force in UP in 2009 (four seats, 17.7 per cent votes) to zero seats in 2019. This pattern of the rise of the BJP and the decline of the Congress even in Muslim-significant seats is consistent across both UP and the Hindi heartland.

That the BJP gained from greater Hindu vote consolidation in its favour after 2014, while religious minorities stayed away from it, has long been evident in voter surveys. Shreyas Sardesai, for example, studied NES data in both 2014 and 2019 to show that, for two national elections in a row, the BJP under Narendra Modi and Amit Shah was able to overcome caste hierarchies among Hindus and systematically construct a Hindu category of voters versus others. Yet, the study did not find sufficient evidence to support claims that a large part of the Hindu support for the BJP-led alliance was on account of anti-minority sentiments.[10] Outside of UP, nationwide, the BJP won more than 50 per cent of the Lok Sabha seats in ninety 'minority-concentration' districts identified in 2008 by the previous UPA government. Of seventy-nine such constituencies, the BJP won forty-one, a gain of seven over 2014. Overall, the party also fielded a handful of Muslim candidates in 2019, though not one of them managed to win.[11]

The Yogi Factor: Why It Works in Muslim-significant Seats

This Hindu counter-mobilisation works much more strongly in Muslim-significant areas, where Muslims can be projected as the 'Other', than it does in areas where Hindus are a comfortable majority. As a senior official in Yogi Adityanath's office explained to me, 'The mathematics [ganit] is that where Hindus are in a majority, where almost everyone is a Hindu, there Yogiji's impact is not that much in relative terms.' However, 'wherever Muslims are strong, say 30 per cent, Hindus there vote together for him. The reason is that they know that the Muslims are in front and they know what problem they can face. They know what happens there and they realise it immediately.'[12]

BJP leaders point to western UP, with its large Muslim concentration of voters, as a case in point. This is a region where, historically, the BJP had not done well, dominated as it was by the BSP and the Rashtriya Lok Dal (RLD). Yet, in 2019, Yogi Adityanath launched the party's campaign from the region's famous Shakumbhari Devi shrine. BJP leaders say that his presence changed the local poll dynamics. A senior official put it thus: 'In western UP, we knew there would be a big impact if Yogiji went. People said he won't have any impact there, but we knew BJP will rise there and so as he went. You must understand Muslims in western UP are well off, rich and dominant. The Muslim there is not only economically rich but physically big too. He is not like a weak person. He gives you an equal challenge, he fights, he does division of assets, takes you on when it comes to land, on markets. He confronts you on everything. So, Hindu messaging works there.'[13]

It is not only in UP that the polarising impact is seen. This effect is exactly why, after Modi and Amit Shah, Yogi Adityanath remains the most sought-after leader in the BJP for state units fighting elections. BJP leaders understood his potential as a vote-catcher and catalyst for Hindu consolidation, especially in areas with a Muslim presence, over a decade ago. In Chhapra, Bihar, for example, the journalist Sanjeev Singh recalls that, even in 2005, people used to ask for Yogi to campaign. 'The calculation in those days was that if you got him for a meeting, it would make a difference of 5,000 Hindu votes. But yes, you would then not get a single Muslim vote. The Hindu vote, you would cement though.' It is not a coincidence that, in the Bihar assembly polls of November 2020, Yogi Adityanath was the most sought-after non-local BJP star campaigner after Modi.[14] The results showed that he ended up having a 66.6 per cent strike-rate in the constituencies he travelled to.[15] In the 2019 general election too, Yogi was the most in-demand BJP chief minister for the party's official election rallies. He addressed more rallies than any other BJP chief minister: 135. This was followed by Jai Ram Thakur with 106, Devendra Fadnavis with ninety-one, Vijay Rupani with eighty-six and Vijendra Singh Rawat with fifty-eight.[16] While all parties tend to designate their star campaigners, the number of rallies they actually address is often indicative of how much local candidates think they will add to their chances of winning. Yogi Adityanath's in-demand status as a campaigner, in that sense, reflects instrumental judgements on his impact that the party was making, not just ideological signalling.

A Post-symbolism BJP: Muslim Representation, Ideological Maximalism and Electoral Winnability

Much has been made of the symbolism of the BJP not fielding any Muslim candidates from the crucial state of UP in the national elections of 2014 and 2019 and the state assembly polls of 2017. From Sikander Bakht to Najma Heptulla and Mukhtar Abbas Naqvi to Shahnawaz Hussain, the BJP has always had symbolic Muslim leaders in the past. Yet, it has hardly ever fielded Muslim candidates in UP over the past three decades between 1991 and 2019. Consider this: the BJP fielded zero Muslim candidates in the state when it first became a rising power there at the height of the Ram Janmabhoomi movement in 1991. Even in 1996, it fielded only one Muslim candidate each in 1998 and 1999. This phase of UP politics coincided with the Vajpayee era of coalition politics when the BJP went up to a high of two Muslim candidates in 2004—the highest number (2.5 per cent) that the party has ever fielded in UP. Of course, such representation was always only a symbolic gesture. Muslim leaders were never a major part of its political mobilisation.

What the BJP did, first in the UP assembly election of 2017, and then in the 2019 Lok Sabha polls, was to do away with the symbolism (see Table 5.1). It took a political call that it did not need Muslims to win elections. In fact, in purely electoral terms, doing away with the symbolism and being unambiguous in its messaging increased the BJP's winnability, as the data shows. This was particularly true in Muslim-significant areas. While the party decided that it did not need Muslim leaders to draw voters, it did

Table 5.1: Not Just Now, the BJP Hardly Ever Fielded Muslim Candidates in UP in the Lok Sabha Elections: BJP, Congress, BSP, SP Muslim Lok Sabha Candidates in UP (1991–2019)

Year	*BJP*	*Congress*	*BSP*	*SP*
1991	0	6	n.a.	6
1996	0	2	21	12
1998	1	10	11	10
1999	1	8	13	11
2004	2	8	20	10
2009	1	9	12	11
2014	1	9	12	15
2019	0	8	6	4

Source: Fieldwork and analysis by Mehta–Singh Social Index. Lok Sabha candidates analysed from ECI data.

feel that a symbolic Muslim presence was important for governance. So, though the BJP did not field a single Muslim candidate in the 2017 assembly polls, Yogi Adityanath did appoint a Muslim minister, former first-class cricketer Mohsin Raza, as minister for Minority Welfare, Muslim Waqf and Haj.[17] Similarly, in the Lok Sabha, though the BJP did not field a single Muslim from UP in 2019, it appointed Mukhtar Abbas Naqvi as the cabinet minister in charge of Minority Affairs. Naqvi, the first elected Muslim for the BJP in the Lok Sabha in 1998,[18] had also served as a minister in the Vajpayee government, along with Shahnawaz Hussain, who served as a national party spokesperson before being appointed cabinet minister in Nitish Kumar's NDA alliance government in Bihar in February 2021.

The BJP was more restrained in its Hindutva idioms and symbolism in the earlier days—especially at the national level between 1996 and 2009—because it needed alliances. After 2014, under Modi, it unapologetically doubled down on Hindutva, which worked in terms of electoral winnability. Its political message now had a clear and distinctive branding. The psephologist Jai Mrug argues that, in a time of great social flux, voters are attracted to a party that has a 'clear positioning, as opposed to one that stands for many things and is a bit of this and a bit of that. Not being defensive about Hindutva helped BJP with younger voters.' It is indeed worth investigating if more strident Hindutva rhetoric earned the BJP a higher appeal among younger voters. In this context, the political scientists Rahul Varma and Pradeep Chhibber have shown through studies of voter surveys that nationalistic sentiments were heightened in India and a 'new form of ethno-political majoritarianism delinked from religious Hindu nationalism was key to the party's ability to attract new voters'.[19]

This return to core ideological principles is a strategy that the RSS had long recommended. In fact, each time the BJP lost elections in the past, the RSS had publicly argued that the reason was a dilution of ideology. After the party finished poorly in the UP assembly election of 2007, for example, the *Organiser* editor R. Balashankar wrote a signed piece, arguing that the 'BJP lost steam midway. Its campaign got stuck between half-hearted Hindutva and development governance. An aggressive Hindutva approach would have ensured greater success ... but the party was extremely restrained.'[20] The same happened in 2004. After Vajpayee's surprise loss, an RSS spokesperson told the media, 'The BJP has lost its way because it abandoned Hindutva'.[21]

Vajpayee's early 1980s experiment with turning the BJP into the 'asli [real] Janata Party' had ended in failure. Writing scathingly of that experiment, former Jan Sangh president Balraj Madhok wrote that the BJP 'adopted its two-coloured flag and Gandhian socialism as its ideology and claimed the Jan Sangh whose name, saffron flag and ideology it discarded'. That gambit ended in the party being reduced to two seats in the Lok Sabha in 1984. The BJP returned to its core issues of Ayodhya, Kashi and Mathura thereafter: temple issues Madhok said he had first raised in the Lok Sabha on 30 September 1961. Juxtaposing the ebbs and flows of the BJP's electoral fortunes with the embrace and distancing of its core ideological principles, Madhok argued that there could only be one conclusion:[22]

> This partial return to the Jan Sangh brought rich dividends to the BJP. Its tally in the Lok Sabha rose from two to 86 in the 1989 general election, to 121 in 1991 and to 163 in the 1996 election. However it began to distance itself from the Jan Sangh ideology after 1996 in search of new allies to enable it to form a government. Its decline had begun. In the 1998 elections, it could win only 180 seats and its growth rate came down to zero in the 1999 poll. There is now a growing realisation in the rank and file of the BJP and RSS that discarding the Jan Sangh in 1980 was a folly. While the ideological spread of the Jan Sangh has remained intact, the credibility of the BJP is going down ... It is necessary that nationalist forces should come together. This demands the return of the BJP and the reunification of the Bharatiya Jan Sangh under the saffron flag.

Essentially, he was saying that the BJP won when it was unambiguous about its first principles and declined when it diluted them to focus on wider issues. As one long-standing UP MLA asked me: 'Why does Yogi Adityanath have such support?' His answer:[23]

> Does he meet people well? Do people know him as a polite person? No. The reason is basically mukhar [in your face] and ugra [aggressive] Hindutva. This is why BJP is rising. In elections, Yogi is in demand as a campaigner in each state, the most after Narendra Modi and Amit Shah.

> Why? Because of Hindutva. We are seeing an awakening of Hindutva, it is a punarjaagaran [reawakening]. Those who espoused Hinduism earlier were put aside. Do you think Muslims are with SP because of its idea of Samajwaad [socialism] or Ram Manohar Lohia's ideology or socialism or because of a community mobilisation? Now that is different with Hindus too, to some extent.

An illustration of this is Yogi Adityanath's decision to end the tradition of iftar parties to mark Ramzan in Lucknow, just as Modi ended it in Delhi. He even declared on the floor of the UP assembly that, as a proud Hindu, he saw no reason for him to celebrate Eid. Yogi said that he was not one of those people who wear 'janeu' (sacred thread) inside the house and don skull caps outside when needed. 'I am not like them because I am a Hindu and have no reason to celebrate Eid,' he said. He added, however, that his government would 'continue to work for a peaceful Eid'.[24] This is why Yogi Adityanath's government, soon after coming to power, also doubled the grants for Hindu pilgrims undertaking holy visits to the Kailash Mansarovar from ₹50,000 to ₹1 lakh each.[25] This was somewhat akin to the Haj subsidies the Union government had paid for decades, until 2018.[26] 'There was a time when such things [iftar] were a necessity,' said a UP MLA. 'Not anymore.' Once party leaders saw that ending such symbolic moves did not harm them electorally, they saw no reason to rethink the strategy. 'The fact that BJP started winning in Muslim-dominated seats shows that parties had been wrong earlier about the supposed power of the Muslim vote. They were not that big as people thought,' the MLA said.

Contrary to received wisdom, many leaders in UP emphatically made the point to me that one reason why support for the SP and the BSP declined was because they gave so much importance to Muslim representation. The SP in 2017 fielded sixty-five Muslims (20.7 per cent of its candidates), the BSP fielded as many as ninety-eight (24.4 per cent). 'Elections are won by karyakartas [workers],' one Opposition MLA told me. 'They make the *chunaav ki haava. Chunaav ko charhate hai* [the election's momentum. They make the election rise]. If my top ten guys get angry and stay at home, then *chunaav nahi charhega* [the election momentum won't rise]. If Muslims are fielded by SP in, say, Meerut and such places, then it is an issue. *Unka chunaav charhta nahin hai* [their election momentum does not rise]. BJP has an advantage there. Politics has changed in the last seven years. Cadres have shifted. SP is not growing. The committed BSP cadre of old who used to wear a blanket and be out on the road for a month on cycles are not doing that anymore. While cadres of other parties are depressed, BJP guys are on a high.'[27] While representation matters a great deal in electoral democracy, for many political leaders, the metric of success is winnability. On that metric, the BJP's punt worked.

How do these larger debates on secularism, the place of Muslims and their gradual marginalisation play out in the village? When we asked Chouhan, the village pradhan in Saharanpur, to compare Yogi Adityanath with his predecessor, Akhilesh Yadav, the answer was clear. The 'biggest impact has been on law and order at the panchayati level,' he said. 'No community is able to be haavi [dominant] on the other, whether Muslim or Hindu. Earlier, Muslim leaders, especially in western UP, were very haavi. There were local leaders here who had clout in police stations and Hindus wouldn't speak against Muslims earlier. That psychological advantage has come to Hindus these days.' He was the Hindu pradhan of a village that was primarily Muslim, in an area of UP where the minority population is high. 'It's a question of balance. Earlier the default power was with Muslims, now it is with Hindus. Earlier Muslim leaders could do whatever they wanted to in these three–four districts. Basically, law and order is better. Earlier girls used to run away a lot. They don't anymore because of this.'[28] This was only his perception, of course, but it offered a window into why so many voters moved to the BJP.

When they are questioned about Muslims, BJP leaders always point to government schemes, saying there is no religious bias in them. On that count, they are not wrong. Chouhan's village by the Shakumbhari Devi temple is a case in point. Nine houses were approved to be built in the village in 2020, under PMAY-G: six were for Muslim households, three for Hindu ones. Twenty-three houses had been approved in 2019. Of these, twenty-one were for Muslim families, two Hindu. In the neighbouring village, ninety-eight houses were approved in 2020. Of these, twenty-eight were for Hindus or Dalits, seventy were for Muslim families.[29] This is because Muslims made up the bulk of the population in the region. Of course, it was their right to have access to these schemes, and it would have been unconstitutional for the state to discriminate against them even if it wanted to. Government data shows that 11.9 per cent of over 18 million houses sanctioned in India under PMAY-G between 2016 and 2020 was for religious minorities. In UP, the minorities accounted for 10.9 per cent of such grants.[30] Similarly, they accounted for 10 per cent of all loans under the Pradhan Mantri Mudra Yojana (PMMY), which provides credit to micro-enterprises to bring them into the formal financial system.[31]

I asked the pradhan if access to welfare schemes meant that some Muslims were voting for the BJP. He answered, 'The poor will vote. If you get rations for five kids and you earn for two, you will vote. It is a simple, straight thing if you get benefits.'

In a state where the government put up name-and-shame banners identifying those who protested against the CAA in March 2020, the BJP has clearly bet its political fortunes on an uncompromising, maximalist approach based on its ideological positions. This does not mean that it has no interest at all in wooing minorities. The slogan 'Sabka Saath, Sabka Vikas aur Sabka Vishwas' (With All, for Everybody's Development and Everybody's Trust) is a case in point. As Modi declared in a speech after winning the Lok Sabha 2019 polls: 'They [minorities] cannot be handed over to them [Opposition], who benefit because we keep quiet.'[32] Like CAA, his government's primary Muslim-linked legislation on criminalising triple talaq was aimed as much at a wider messaging to Hindus as it was to the minorities. The one outstanding issue in the BJP's core manifesto targets that it has not yet fulfilled is the promulgation of a Uniform Civil Code. The triple talaq law, by demolishing an element of Muslim personal law, therefore had wider significance for the party. Modi, of course, presented it as a progressive step for Muslim women and as a welfare measure for the community. As he said in a 2019 rally in Dhanbad:[33]

> We had said that the bad practice of triple talaq, which had turned the lives of crores of sisters to a life of hell, we will save our sisters and mothers from this badness. Today we have made a strong law against triple talaq. This law has protected the lives of lakhs and crores of our Muslim sisters and daughters. This has freed them of a big worry in life. Did I not fulfil my promise? I never worried about vote banks. My intention is to work for the benefit of people. Did I do it or not? Some people have this misunderstanding that the law the Modi government has made for triple

> talaq will only benefit Muslim sisters. It will surely help Muslim sisters but it will help Muslim brothers even more. For any brother, if his sister comes home after triple talaq, won't her brother be troubled? If a daughter comes home after triple talaq, won't her father be deeply troubled? A daughter, father, mother and whole family gets destroyed, and this is why by bringing this law against triple talaq we have also helped Muslim men.

The fact that instantaneous triple talaq has long been banned in almost two dozen Islamic countries—including Pakistan, Turkey, Indonesia, Egypt, Saudi Arabia[34]—allowed the BJP to present the changes in Muslim personal law as a progressive, developmental and gender-positive measure. Simultaneously, its base welcomed this particular change as yet another strike on what they saw as the political favouritism to minorities, or 'pseudo-secularism', that had been ushered in during the era of Congress hegemony.

The Owaisi Factor: 'F-Team to B-Team' and the Rise of a New Muslim Party

Asaduddin Owaisi's sprawling white mansion in Shastripuram, with its arched windows and white-pillared courtyards shaded with palm trees, spreads over several acres of a hillock. It has a splendid view of Hyderabad—a picturesque sweep across both Old Hyderabad, which his family lineage represents, as well as New Hyderabad, which his politics seeks to reshape. The four-time Hyderabad MP, barrister from London's Lincoln's Inn and president of the city's All India Majlis-e-Ittehadul Muslimeen (AIMIM, or the All India Council for the Unity of Muslims) has become the face of a new kind of Muslim politics and electoral response to the rise of the BJP.

When we drove up to his house to interview Owaisi on a sunny late-November day in 2018, he was in the middle of the Telangana election campaign. We had met earlier that day over a sumptuous free-wheeling biryani-and-kebabs lunch at TRS Working President K.T. Rama Rao's working office, and Owaisi had consented to meet us again for a formal interview.

The Hyderabad MP is a fascinating figure. A former fast bowler for the South Zone University cricket team,[35] he had once ridden into

Telangana Chief Minister K. Chandrashekhar Rao's house on a Bullet motorcycle for a political meeting in December 2018.[36] Owaisi represents a party that traces its historical lineage to 1926, when it started political life as MIM, an outfit in the Nizam's Hyderabad. MIM was linked to the Nizam's Razakars, who had defied India's moves to integrate Hyderabad after Independence, and were banned in 1948 after 'Operation Polo', the Indian military action that ended the armed resistance. The party was then revived in 1957 by Abdul Wahed Owaisi, Asaduddin's grandfather, who restructured MIM into AIMIM after swearing allegiance to India's Constitution. The party has been a key political pillar in the Greater Hyderabad area ever since.[37] Yet, until the ascent of Asaduddin Owaisi, it had remained a local Hyderabad player.

When we met, AIMIM had seven MLAs in Telangana's 119-member state assembly and had already started making moves in national politics as a 'Muslim' party out to represent constituencies with large Muslim populations. It had already registered a noticeable presence in some municipal polls in Muslim-significant areas in Maharashtra (Nanded-Waghela city), Karnataka and UP. By 2020, it had garnered for itself one Lok Sabha MP (Aurangabad) and two MLAs in Maharashtra, two more Members of Legislative Council (MLCs) in Telangana and, importantly, five MLAs in Bihar's 2020 assembly poll.

Not surprisingly, AIMIM's rise in each of these places had been at the expense of the Congress, which had benefitted from minority vote-bank politics in the past. Consequently, Owaisi has often been accused by Congress leaders of 'being a partner with the majoritarian right-wing radicalisation' in a mutual game of political extremes on the Muslim question.[38] Owaisi, who has always scoffed at these charges of being the BJP's 'B-team', met us in his anteroom wearing his trademark pin-striped sherwani and skullcap. As we interviewed him for our election show, surrounded by framed verses from the Koran on the walls, I asked him about the Congress's charge that his party, by splitting the anti-BJP vote, in effect ended up helping the BJP. 'This is clear frustration on their [Congress's] part,' he responded indignantly, arguing that he was being blamed for the Congress's own failures. 'They don't want to do serious introspection. For example, I didn't contest in Delhi, Haryana, J&K or Jharkhand elections. I can go on and on, but you [Congress] still don't win. In Hyderabad municipal elections, of 150 municipal corporators, how many does Congress Party have?'[39] It was a fair point. Owaisi then went on to explain why he felt Muslims needed new representation, arguing that parties they had voted for before had failed. Ergo, the need for a 'Muslim' political party. As he put it:[40]

> My political struggle and argument is that we should not only vote but contest elections so that democracy is strengthened, and the reality of our Indian democracy is that if you don't have a political voice then your issues of development and education won't be taken forward. This is the crass reality and to prove that [see] Sachar Committee, Mishra Commission, Kundu Committee, NSSO data. Wherever you have a semblance of political representation, all these parameters improve.

Since 2014, the BJP's rise and the Congress's shrinkage has certainly created the political space for a party that represents 'Muslim' interests in a way that existing 'secular' parties do not. This became evident as early as 2009, when the Peace Party in UP, founded by the surgeon Dr Mohammad Ayub, set itself up as precisely such a vehicle for Muslim and Dalit interests. It ended up winning significant vote shares (8–12 per cent) in four Lok Sabha constituencies in the state: Gonda, Domariyaganj, Basti and Sant Kabir Nagar.[41] The Peace Party, which also won four MLAs in the 2012 UP assembly polls, later faded away. It is this breach that AIMIM sought to fill as it expanded outside of Hyderabad.

Owaisi himself was aligned with the Congress till 2012. He famously voted in favour of Manmohan Singh's Indo-US nuclear deal in Parliament in 2008 after the then UP chief minister, BSP's Mayawati, declared that Indian Muslims were against the deal.[42] Owaisi had stated in Parliament then that he was voting to save the Congress-led government, specifically to pre-empt the possibility of a BJP government coming to power.[43] Yet, he ended a fourteen-year alliance with the Congress—at the national as well as state level—in 2012, citing the 'communal policies' of the then Congress government in Andhra Pradesh.[44] Did he worry about being pigeonholed by his opponents and reduced to a stereotype, I asked him. 'What really bothers me is this language of Congress party wherein they don't want, in real terms, a political leadership to develop of weaker sections, which includes Muslims,' he responded with a barely concealed smirk and twinkle in his eye. 'This is the mentality of Congress Party. If you oppose them, you become communal, you become vote-katua [cutter], you become B-team. So definitely I have progressed, thankfully. From 1998–2012, I was F-team of Congress Party. After leaving Congress Party, between 2012 and 2018, I have come up to B-team. So hopefully I will become A-team in another coming two–three years.'

Owaisi, who first became an MLA in 1994 from Hyderabad's Charminar, has a political career going back at least three decades. Yet, his national salience as a 'Muslim' politician has also risen in direct proportion to the BJP's ascendance and his assertive response to it. When he took oath for the fourth time as an MP in 2019, his walk to the podium was accompanied by some BJP MPs chanting slogans of 'Jai Sri Ram' and 'Vande Mataram'. He responded by first asking them to continue their chanting and then proceeding to read out his oath to the Indian Constitution in chaste Urdu, in the name of Khuda ('Khuda ke naam se'). He concluded with three slogans: 'Jai Bheem' (a nod to B.R. Ambedkar), 'Takbeer Allah-u-Akbar' (God is Great) and 'Jai Hind' (Hail India). It was another example of the complex interplay between the BJP's hardliners and Owaisi's own political positioning.

In Bihar, in 2020, Owaisi's party won five assembly seats in Seemanchal, which has over 30 per cent Muslim population, at the expense of the Congress and the RJD. Ironically, his impact also resulted in a Hindu counter-mobilisation: of thirty-two Muslim-significant seats, the BJP won twelve.[45] As a parliamentarian, Owaisi, who was once awarded the Sansad Ratna Award, has a record of asking questions on an eclectic range of policy issues. Of the 160 questions he raised in Parliament between July 2019 and November 2020, for example, only five pertained to minority issues.[46] Yet, in his political persona, he has emerged as the 'Muslim' counterpoint to the BJP's Hindutva narrative, focused on minority identity issues as much as the BJP is, in a sort of inverted mirror image.

The BJP's strategy of counter-polarisation in Muslim-significant areas was in evidence again in November 2020 when Yogi Adityanath, who was campaigning in the Greater Hyderabad Municipal Corporation (GHMC) elections, asked why Hyderabad—which has a 43.4 per cent Muslim population—could not be renamed Bhagyanagar. Yogi was campaigning as part of a phalanx of top BJP leaders, including Amit Shah, J.P. Nadda,

Smriti Irani, fronting the BJP's drive to create a new bridgehead in Telangana against the TRS–AIMIM alliance. As he put it, 'Some people were asking me if Hyderabad could become Bhagyanagar. I said, why not? I told them, look, in UP when the BJP government came, we renamed Faizabad as Ayodhya and Allahabad as Prayagraj—where Ganga and Yamuna meet and where the Kumbh is organised—which was its Puranic name. Then why can't Hyderabad be renamed as Bhagyanagar?'[47] The name-change gambit symbolised an extension of the counter-polarisation strategy to new catchment areas in the South.

The BJP had won four crucial Lok Sabha seats in Telangana in 2019—Secunderabad, Nizamabad, Adilabad and Karimnagar. In 2020, the scale of central-leadership firepower that it deployed in a municipal poll in the state capital reflected the party's ambitions of using that initial bridgehead. It aimed to expand in Owaisi's home citadel with a political strategy that had earlier delivered electoral returns in the Hindi heartland as well as in neighbouring Karnataka (see Chapter 15). Yet, in a city where almost every second voter is Muslim, the BJP finished as the second-largest party with forty-eight seats (up from four previously) in the Greater Hyderabad municipal polls. Furthermore, it finished within striking distance of the ruling TRS, which went down drastically to fifty-five seats. Owaisi's AIMIM, fighting in its own bastion , retained its earlier share of forty-four seats. Tellingly, at just two seats, the Congress barely moved the needle.[48] The BJP's meteoric rise in Hyderabad's 2020 municipal poll demonstrated once again the electoral value of Hindu counter-mobilisation. And the increasing irrelevance of the Congress in Muslim-significant areas amid such polarisation.

'Love Jihad' Laws, Political Positioning and the BJP

Two BJP state governments announced plans for a 'love jihad' law in November 2020: UP and Madhya Pradesh. While Madhya Pradesh's planned legislation sought to regulate interfaith marriage with the provision of a five-year jail term for forcible conversion,[49] an ordinance passed by the UP cabinet sought to put the onus of proof on defendants to prove that they had not converted for marriage. It enshrined in law a one- to five-year jail term if they could not do so.[50] 'Love jihad', as an *Organiser* cover story defined it in 2014, refers to what Hindutva groups call a 'trap of Muslim organisations to seduce Hindu girls, to use Hindu women for physical desires, to convert them, to sell them or to use them for terrorist activities'.[51] Legally, the term first appeared in a Kerala High Court judgement in 2009, when Justice K.T. Sankaran asked the government to consider enacting laws to prohibit such 'deceptive' acts.[52] The term is said to have first gained currency among Hindutva groups in Gujarat in 2007, followed by Kerala and Karnataka in 2009.[53] These laws are in addition to the anti-conversion laws that already exist in eight Indian states[54] and the provisions of the Special Marriage Act, 1954, which in any case require details of interfaith couples looking to get married to be displayed on a notice board for a month at the marriage office.[55] For critics like the scholar Christophe Jaffrelot, the new 'love jihad' laws 'illustrate the transition from a de facto to a de jure Hindu Rashtra, something already evident from the Citizenship Amendment Act (2019). This process is bound to transform India officially into an ethnic democracy, like Israel—where mixed marriages are practically impossible.'[56]

While these legislations raised significant questions about individual freedoms on marriage and religion,[57] the final word on these laws is yet to be written. The Allahabad High Court, for example, struck down two previous judgements against interfaith marriages on 24 November 2020, observing that the 'right to choose a partner, irrespective of religion, is intrinsic to the right to life and personal liberty'. The two-judge bench of Justice Pankaj Naqvi and Justice Vivek Agarwal ruled that the previous judgements were 'not laying good law'. Furthermore, they observed that 'none of these judgments dealt with the issue of life and liberty of two mature individuals in choosing a partner or their right to freedom of choice as to whom they would like to live'.[58] This important judgement set up the legal contours of a simmering political debate which is still unfolding. While that debate will go on, whichever way the court battles on these laws turn, from a political standpoint, the BJP's positioning on the issue has been unambiguous.

Even as the party sharpened its positioning on minorities and the minority question after 2014, this identity-based ideological positioning has not been the only reason for its electoral victories. Chapter 3 has shown how, from 2013, the BJP drastically changed its caste representation at all levels of the party: district-level presidents, state officer-bearers, state ministers, Lok Sabha candidates and Vidhan Sabha candidates. It pivoted towards OBCs, who became the single largest caste category that the party put up at all levels. OBCs and SCs together account for 45–55 per cent of BJP representatives at all the levels we studied under the Mehta–Singh Social Index. This new data showed a decline in upper castes and a major rise in representation of castes lower down the social order. By sharing power with these castes at all levels of the party, the BJP became more socially inclusive, leaving aside Muslims.

The new data provided in Part I of this book call for a fundamental rethink of older models of studying the BJP, which continue to frame it essentially as an upper-caste party. That BJP is long gone. The new BJP is differently oriented caste organism altogether. It also created a new model of political mobilisation around labharthees, in a way that has not been done in north India before, as Chapter 4 shows. This has similarities to the practice of Dravidian parties who have long used such modes of personal-welfare-based politics. Together, the resetting of the caste matrix, welfare politics and Hindutva created a new BJP model of politics. It turned the party into a party of the poor and transformed it into the dominant pole of politics in rural India, the default party of the village.

PART II

COMMUNICATION

WHAT THE BJP FOCUSES ON AND WHERE IT SPEAKS

6

WHAT THE BJP SAYS

The Changing Patterns of Its Discourse

Whether they support the BJP, oppose it or are politically neutral, most Indians already have a broad mental map of what they think the party stands for and what it communicates. Our perceptions are based on WhatsApp messages, Instagram posts, Facebook threads, newspaper headlines and Twitter wars. Whether we vote for the party because we think it stands for a strong Hindu cultural identity, for the idea of a New India or non-dynastic politics, or whether we believe it to be a divisive, fascist or exclusivist political force bent on reshaping India into a nativist Hindu nation, most of us have already made up our minds about the BJP.

The question is: how does the party communicate its ideas? Which ones does it privilege, and when? How does it convey these ideas to different audiences? Which ones does it prioritise or underplay, and at what times? How does it calibrate its messaging at different times in the political cycle?

For the first time, we have data spread across years to see what the BJP communicates. Most analyses of political communications so far have been based on impressionistic accounts or small survey samples. Technology now gives us the tools to see the BJP's political communications—both online and offline—in its entirety.

Introducing the Narad Index

To understand and draw up the big picture of what the BJP and the wider Sangh Parivar talk about, data scientist Rishabh Srivastava and I set up an archival data-mining software called NARAD—Normative Analysis of Reporting and Discourse, which we have been referring to as 'Narad'. Using this software, we digitally analysed over 11,558 BJP-linked documents in the 2006–2019 period, consisting of 17.9 million words.

We analysed documents in two languages: Hindi and English. The size of the Hindi public, with over 528 million Indians listing it as their first language, is far greater than the English-speaking audience (which 2,59,678 Indians listed as their first and 82.7 million as their second language).[1] The Hindi public sphere is where the game of jostling political narratives plays out most predominantly. It is also where the BJP has the greatest political impact. Hindi is the most widely spoken first and second language in India, while English is the second most widely spoken second language.[2] We ran the algorithm over the thousands of Hindi and English documents we had to see how patterns of discourse between the BJP and its linked outfits changed.

Specifically, this meant running a data-sorting algorithm over:

i. 8,579 speeches by BJP leaders, party press releases and articles that it published over the fourteen years between 2005 and 2019 (4.98 million words);
ii. 168 issues of the BJP fortnightly magazine *Kamal Sandesh*, published between 2009 and 2019 (2.69 million words);
iii. 230 issues of the RSS weekly magazine *Organiser*, published between May 2015 and December 2019 (6.12 million words);
iv. 1,305 speeches by Prime Minister Modi between 2014 and 2019 (3.44 million words);
v. 216 documents of the RSS outfit Vanvasi Kalyan Ashram, which works in tribal areas, from June 2018 to December 2019 (43,000 words).

In the offline world, the BJP's press releases, articles and the speeches delivered by its leaders gave us a sense of what the party was communicating to external audiences; the *Kamal Sandesh* (literally, Lotus Message)[3] gave us a sense of what it was saying to its cadres; the *Organiser*[4] told us what the wider Sangh Parivar was talking about; and the Vanvasi

Kalyan Ashram outreach outlined for us what one of the Sangh outfits working with tribal children focused on. These were compared with 1,060 articles published in the Congress magazine *Congress Sandesh*[5] from 2015 to 2019 (0.63 million words).

We compared this with politics in the online world. A similar approach was used to analyse Facebook posts of political groups and leaders. We also downloaded and analysed all Facebook posts made by the BJP, the RSS, the Congress, Narendra Modi, Amit Shah and Rahul Gandhi on their official Facebook pages between January 2016 and December 2019. Cumulatively, this amounted to 40,251 posts and 1.2 million words. Similarly, we studied the Twitter accounts of seventy-five political leaders from both the BJP and the Congress between January 2016 and December 2019: 4,76,827 posts. (See detailed methodology note in Appendix 4 at the end of this book.)

Once we cleaned up all this data and identified key issues, we created what we call the Narad Index. It measures the number of times a topic (or related keywords in English and Hindi) is mentioned per 100 words, thus allowing us to see patterns of political communication holistically. The more times a particular topic, say the Congress, is mentioned, the higher it ranks on the Narad Index. We took care to define both Hindi and English keywords for each topic.

Our guiding principle was simple: human cognition could have unconscious biases and memory is slippery. We wanted to see what the data told us. As political junkies who read everything about politics, we thought we knew all there was to know about the BJP. Yet, we were surprised by the data patterns we found and what this said about the party.

The fact is that, in election after election since 2014, both at the Union and state levels, the BJP has won more elections than it has lost because it managed to attract enough swing voters beyond its core ideological base. The BJP's core Hindu base is not enough for it to cross the winning line—like in Delhi, where it won 32.19 per cent of the vote in 2015 (38.51 per cent in 2020), but was still routed by the Aam Aadmi Party (AAP).[6] The BJP wins when it manages to attract enough non-core voters beyond the party faithful. How the BJP attracts these floating non-ideological voters needs to be clearly understood, along with the strategies it adopts to this end. Why do they vote for the BJP? Is it false consciousness, are they deluded or plain stupid—as the liberal imagination would have it? Or is there something we are missing in the party's messaging that voters do not miss? Politics is as much about what the parties stand for as it is about how they convey their messages. We all think we know how the BJP communicates. Now, for the first time, we have the exhaustive data that allows us to draw a comprehensive picture of what the party talks about, how and to whom. And the data paints its own story of why the BJP is rising.

The BJP Speaks More about the Congress Than about Itself

It wasn't until 2019 that the BJP began to talk more about the Congress than it did about itself. That was the first time the party, then in its fifth year in power, started talking more about the principal Opposition party than it talked about itself or its prime minister.

We put all BJP press releases, articles and speeches by party leaders between 2006 and 2019 through the Narad algorithm. When measured this way, we found that, in 2019, the BJP spoke more about the Congress than on any other topic, including Modi, terrorism, defence or Kashmir (see Figure 6.1).

This was extraordinary for several reasons. It broke a historical pattern. There had been election years before, but the BJP had never spoken so much about its rival. Interestingly, even in the 2006–2013 period, when it was out of power, on the Narad Index, the party's emphasis on the ruling Congress was less than half of what it was in 2019. It hovered between 0.291 per 100 words in 2006 and 0.281 in 2013 (see Figure 6.2). After coming to power, however, it started focusing much more on the Congress, going up from 0.391 in 2014 to 0.714 in 2019 on the Index. In other words, mentions of the Congress in the BJP's official communications increased by 82.6 per cent between 2014 and 2019. Normally, Opposition parties speak more about the government in power that they are trying to dislodge; it is unusual for ruling parties to diss their political rivals in the same measure.

Tellingly, even in 2014, the year Narendra Modi first won power as the challenger to Delhi's throne after ten years of the UPA being in power, the

Figure 6.1: How the BJP banked on the Congress and Modi to win

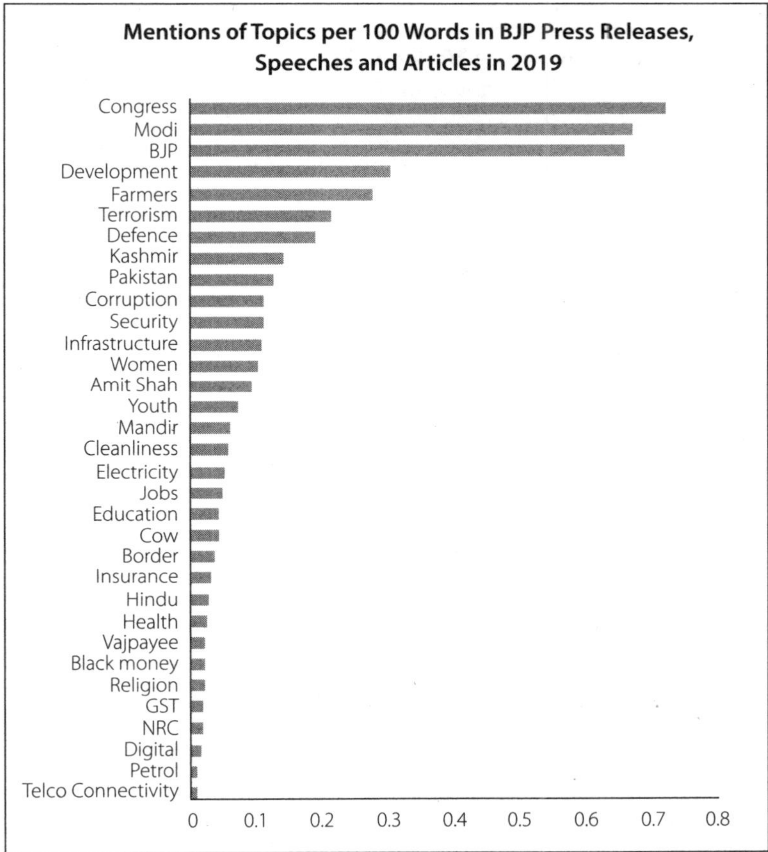

Source: Narad Index, Nalin Mehta and Rishabh Srivastava; for more details see Appendix 4/online on nalinmehta.in

BJP's focus on its rival was less than half of what it was in 2019 (see Figure 6.2)—and that election was largely about anti-incumbency.

In 2014, its focus on the Congress did jump up a notch to 0.391, but this was not out of character with the historical pattern. The number started declining soon thereafter, in 2015, as the BJP government found its feet in its first two years of power. Those early years were dominated by positive messaging by the party. The Narad Index shows that, in the first two years of the Modi government, the BJP focused much more on development, infrastructure and farmers in its messaging.

Figure 6.2: The BJP's Emphasis on the Congress is New, Increased Sharply After 2016

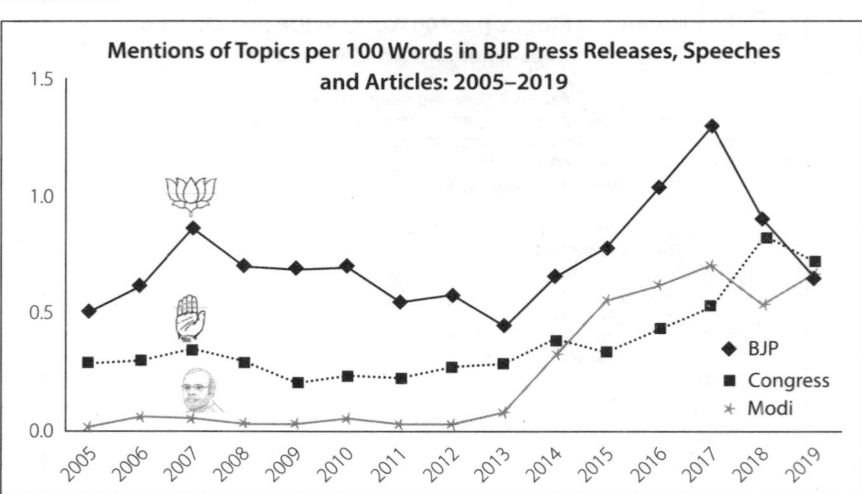

Source: Narad Index, Nalin Mehta and Rishabh Srivastava; for more details see Appendix 4/online on nalinmehta.in

This big political communication shift first began in 2016 when we started seeing a dramatic upswing in Congress-related talk by the BJP. Over the next three years, the BJP steadily ramped up the volume of its anti-Congress talk—and by the 2019 general election, this talk had overtaken its communication on all other issues.

Why did the BJP make this shift? The answer lies in a 2018 blog by then Union finance minister, the late Arun Jaitley, who asked whether the Congress was becoming 'ideologyless', and if what he called 'anti-Modism' was its only ideology. Paradoxically, that was the year when the BJP spoke more about the Congress than it did in the fourteen years (2005–2019) we tracked. Referring to Rahul Gandhi's comment a couple of days earlier on the entrepreneurial skills of shikanjiwalas, dhabawalas and mechanics, Jaitley took a dig at the Congress leader's dynastic origins: 'The great grandson of the man who authored "*The Discovery of India*" [Jawaharlal Nehru] could with his customary inaccuracies one day give to this country his monumental work on "The Rediscovery of Coca Cola" ... Dynastic political parties are family and personality dominated. Ideology takes a back seat. You can oppose the OBC when it suits you. You can shed crocodile tears for them when the opportunism so requires. You can run down jobs created by frying *pakodas*. You can quantify on the virtues of running a *dhaba*. The leader's ill-informed instincts become the ideology. This can only happen to a party which becomes ideologyless; pushes itself to the fringe; is willing to act as a tailender to regional parties. All this because its only obsession is a person called Narendra Modi.'[7]

Now, as the primary ideological opponent of the Congress, it was natural for the BJP to speak so much about its rival. Yet, the remarkable increase in its anti-Congress discourse points to a key political lesson that the party's strategic planners drew on: comparing the BJP to the Congress. In this messaging, the Congress's failures became the BJP's greatest strength. Essentially, the party positioned itself as everything its main rival was not. At the heart of the new communication was one core message: that the Congress remained a dynastic party, while the BJP, generally, was not. This was a core message at a time when most Indians had become disenchanted with claims about entitlement based on birth.[8]

A good illustration of this is what then party president Amit Shah told a gathering of intellectuals at Budha Mal castle in Palampur in May 2017: 'Out of 1,650 small and big parties in the country, only and only BJP is one in which internal democracy survives—it is one where every three years from the booth to the national president, elections are held in a timely manner as per its constitution. *You cannot tell who its next president will be, but who the Congress's next president will be, everyone knows. Everyone knows who will be the next president of regional parties, but our party's democracy is such that even a booth-level worker can become party president and a poor man's son can become prime minister* … The Congress is only worried about its next generation whereas Prime Minister Modi is worried about the country's next generation. This is the fundamental difference between the Congress and the BJP [emphasis added].'[9]

The BJP is constantly reminding voters not just of what it stands for, but what it stands against. Modi had famously told voters, you have given the Congress sixty years, give us at least five years to rule. From his third year in power, the party started talking more about what it had replaced than what it had done. The BJP draws a great deal of its voters from this anti-Congress-ism and for being what the Congress is not. As long as the Congress remains weak and dominated by dynastic politics, the BJP will continue to draw in voters at the national level on the principle that it is the alternative.

In other words, Rahul Gandhi remains Narendra Modi's greatest asset.

The BJP Speaks of the Congress Less in Internal Messaging than to Outsiders

It is interesting that the Congress is not so preponderant in the BJP's internal messaging. When we examined the pages of *Kamal Sandesh*, the party's fortnightly mouthpiece, we found that, though the Congress remained high as a pet topic (see Figure 6.3), it was not among the top five topics. More importantly, it has consistently been dropping off in intensity (see Figure 6.4).

Figure 6.3: Congress Not That High in Internal BJP Communications: *Kamal Sandesh*

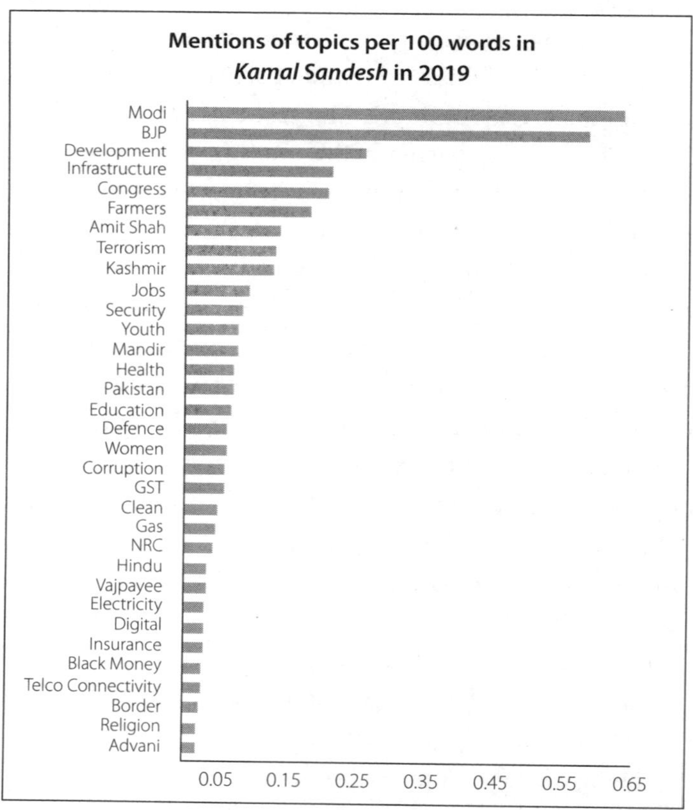

Source: Narad Index, Nalin Mehta and Rishabh Srivastava; for more details see Appendix 4/online on nalinmehta.in

Figure 6.4: Communication on the Congress Dropping Off in *Kamal Sandesh*, 2009–2019

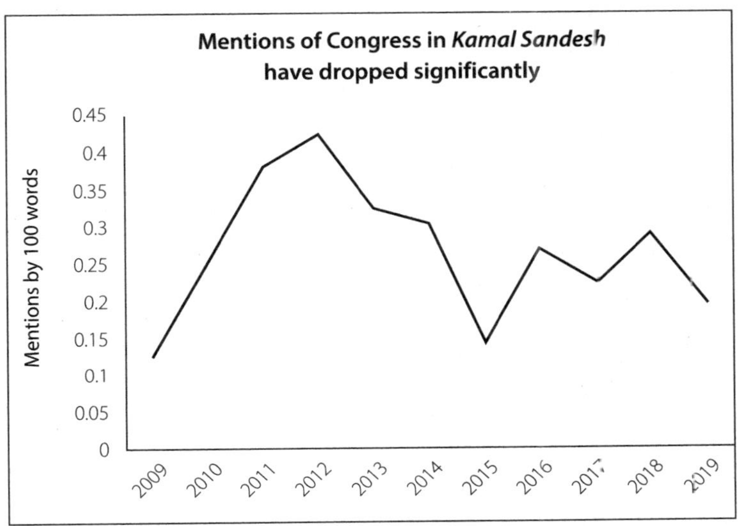

Source: Narad Index, Nalin Mehta and Rishabh Srivastava; for more details see Appendix 4/online on nalinmehta.in

Clearly, when the BJP targets external audiences, it focuses more on the Congress. It doesn't do so as much when it is talking internally to its own cadres and to the converted. *Kamal Sandesh* subscribers—the BJP's core supporters—have already made up their minds about the Congress, the party calculates. The strategic focus on the Congress and its ills in external publicity platforms is, therefore, a tactical move tied to electoral impulses and timed to the cycle of elections. It is as much a necessary voting-gathering tactic as it is a reflection of the BJP's political ideology.

Brand Modi as Force Multiplier: The Political Power of Insults

Insulting Modi Helps the BJP

In May 2018, the BJP put out a press release on its official website: '*Congressi netaon dvara Pradhan Mantri Modi ko kahe gaye apshabd*'

(Insults to Narendra Modi by Congress leaders). The document listed twenty-nine such insults. Some of these were recent: Mani Shankar Aiyar calling Modi a 'neech aadmi' (lowly man), Anand Sharma's diatribe on his 'ill mindset', Manish Tiwari and Digvijay Singh's retweet on Modi's birthday of a meme which said '*ise kehte hai choo*** ko bhakt banana or bhakto ko permanent choo**** banana*', Pramod Tiwari's equation of Modi with Hitler and Mussolini, Manish Tiwari likening him to Dawood Ibrahim and Ghulam Nabi Azad calling him 'Gangu teli'.

Others compared Modi to mythological villains, and some of these remarks were from as far back as when he was Gujarat chief minister and not yet a challenger for Delhi. Then Congress general secretary Digvijay Singh, for instance, compared Modi with Rakshas-raj (king of the demons) Ravan and cabinet minister Jairam Ramesh referred to him as 'Bhasmasur', the mythological demon.

Then there were the animal insults. Gujarat Congress leader Arjun Modvadia compared Modi to a monkey with rabies, Salman Khurshid said he attracted people as does an acrobatic monkey, Hussain Dalvai equated him to a chooha (rat) in 2012, Beni Prasad Varma to a mad dog and B.K. Hariprasad to a 'gandi naali ka keeda' (an insect from a dirty drain) in 2009. The oldest insult was Sonia Gandhi's 'maut ka saudagar' (merchant of death) comment, which is said to have turned the 2007 Gujarat election against the Congress.[10]

It is not very often that a political party publishes a list of insults to its top leader in such graphic detail. Even more interestingly, the BJP made no attempt in the press release to counter any of the insults. It did not even comment on them. It went to great lengths to collect these accusations, some over a decade old, and then simply publicised them. The insults themselves were the subliminal message.

A central belief of Modi followers since 2002 has been that he has been unfairly maligned by a lobby of privileged Modi-haters. For this group, any attack on Modi strengthens him. In this view, he is the permanent underdog who pulled himself up by his bootstraps and whose rise the erstwhile elites he ousted from positions of power are unable to stomach. This persona of the genuine 'son of the soil' who was in touch with his roots, represented the real India and was in permanent combat with an out-of-touch elite was one that Modi had perfected in the 2002 Gujarat riots. In this discourse of outsiders versus original inheritors, every abuse hurled at Modi ended up making him stronger.

There is no doubt that Narendra Modi brings a premium to the BJP. We now have the data to substantiate how and when that shift in perspective began. The party speaks about Modi more than it speaks about anyone else (see Figures 6.1 and 6.2). If 2014 was a personality contest, 2019 was a personality contest on steroids.

The numbers on the Narad Index clearly illustrate this shift. In 2014, even though Modi was its face and electrified the campaign, the BJP spoke much less about him than it would do later. The Index shows that it spoke twice more about itself (0.657) than it did about Modi (0.325) that year, when it was a party challenging the in-power UPA. By 2019, the BJP was significantly more dependent on Brand Modi. In five years, the velocity of the party's Modi-speak doubled (0.661), so much so that it was now talking more about Modi than it was about itself (0.649).

Figure 6.5: How Modi-Speak Changed on the Narad Index (2005–2019)

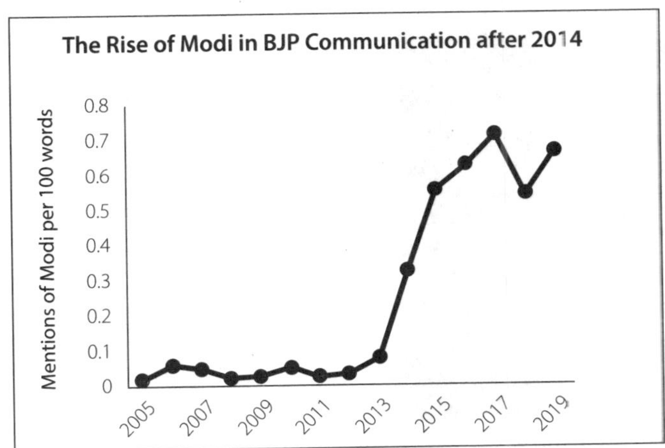

Source: Narad Index, Nalin Mehta and Rishabh Srivastava; for more details see Appendix 4/online on nalinmehta.in

Clearly, the BJP was betting that a lot more people were voting for it because of Modi and his charisma. Modi mentions grew by over 100 per cent between 2014 and 2019, while Congress mentions grew by 82.6 per cent. Anti-Congress-ism and the Modi factor became synonymous with the BJP discourse, with the prime minister held up as the personification of everything the Congress was not.

The Modi cult has been central to the rise of the BJP since 2014. It is also very unusual for the party. When L.K. Advani was leading the party in 2009, its communication was not as dominated by messaging about a great leader. Advani was the man who had single-handedly built the BJP into a political force, who had spearheaded the Ram Janmabhoomi movement and turned the party into a national force. Yet, in 2009, mentions of him were fourth highest of all topics, unlike Modi's dominance in 2019.

Furthermore, the volume of Modi mentions (0.661) in 2019 was three times that of Advani mentions (0.208) in 2009.

Figure 6.6: Modi 3x of Advani in BJP Outreach: A Comparison of its Prime-ministerial Candidates in Election Years (2009, 2019)

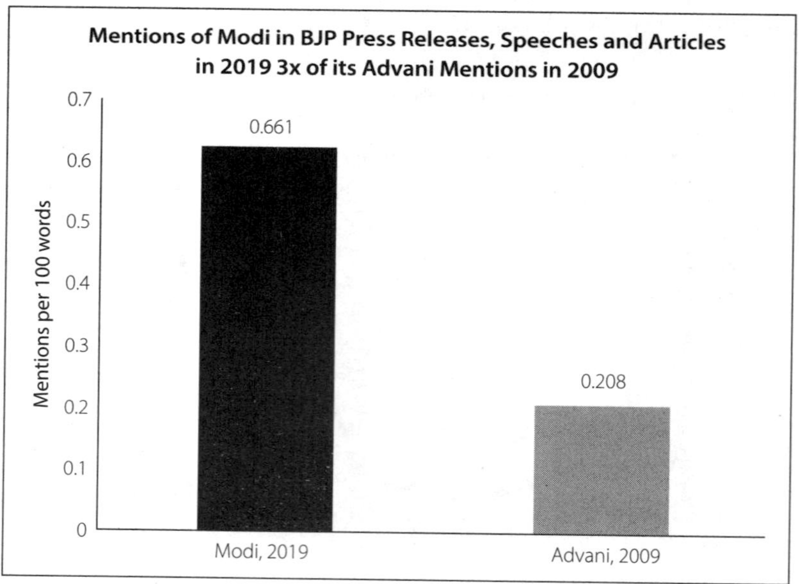

Source: Narad Index, Nalin Mehta and Rishabh Srivastava; for more details see Appendix 4/online on nalinmehta.in

Modi's personality has been even more crucial to the BJP than the last major leader around whom the party ran such personality-centric poll campaigns: Prime Minister Atal Bihari Vajpayee. Ahead of the 1998 general election, the party heralded Vajpayee with 'The Man India Awaits' advertisements. Vajpayee's persona, which morphed into 'The Man India Trusts' in BJP imagery by 1999, seemed to typify the party's identity from the mid-1990s to 2004.[11] However, we do not have comparable data for the Vajpayee years to pinpoint the Modi–Vajpayee difference for the party on the Index. Yet, the Advani–Modi statistical comparison does illustrate how Modi-centric the party has become during his years as prime minister. (Chapter 7 showcases how this reflects even more clearly in the BJP's digital media strategy.)

The BJP Focuses on Farmers and Development More than Terrorism and Mandir

One of the big puzzles for those who oppose Narendra Modi and the BJP is why the party continued to grow in agrarian and rural India even in 2019. Despite tanking job-creation numbers, agrarian distress and declining growth numbers, it continued to attract voters beyond the core base. This continued to be the case until the Modi government passed three new agriculture laws in September 2020, which sought to reform Indian farming and introduce private procurement of farm produce.[12] These legislations led to massive protests by farmers, especially from Punjab and Haryana. Suspicious that they might in the future lose governmental Minimum Support Price (MSP) guarantees on their crops at state-run Agriculture Market Produce Committee (APMC) mandis, farmers' unions began a protest in Delhi, which was ongoing a year later at the time of writing. Prime Minister Modi assured the protestors that MSP would remain—that his government had significantly increased procurements under it[13]—and that the APMC mandis would not be done away with. Eventually, however, the government withdrew the three laws.[14] A detailed analysis of this unfolding saga and its impact on farmers is beyond this book's scope. While these laws and the protest movement could significantly change the nature of the BJP's engagement with farmers, this section looks at how the party retained farmer support until 2019.

The assumption so far has been that voters are turning rightwards because of the BJP's cultural nationalism and identity politics. Insights gleaned from the Narad Index show that the truth may be a bit more complicated. At a time when combative BJP ministers and spokespersons assume an increasingly aggressive take-no-prisoners approach on Hinduness and redefining nationalism, it is easy to miss the fact that, below the top layer of aggression, there are other layers in the party's political outreach. While the headlines tend to be dominated by the controversial identity-based stuff, below the radar, the BJP has been focusing a great deal on the messaging to farmers and on the narrative of development. One of the findings that greatly surprised us was that, in its public outreach, the BJP speaks far more on these topics than about its core issues—terrorism, the Ram Mandir in Ayodhya or national security.

In its press releases, published articles and speeches by party leaders during 2014–2019, the party's communications focused most on development and on farmers—after the Congress, Modi and the party itself (see Figure 6.7). Part I of this book, on the Hindi heartland, showed how the party politically mobilised the labharthees of DBTs at the booth level. In other words, it sought to mobilise a new rural base, using new strategies and tools of communication to present all the plus points of what Vajpayee propagated as 'India Shining' (the BJP's 2004 slogan), without its negatives. We now have a clear picture of how it communicated this.

Figure 6.7: BJP Focused on Farmers and Development More than Its Core Ideological Issues

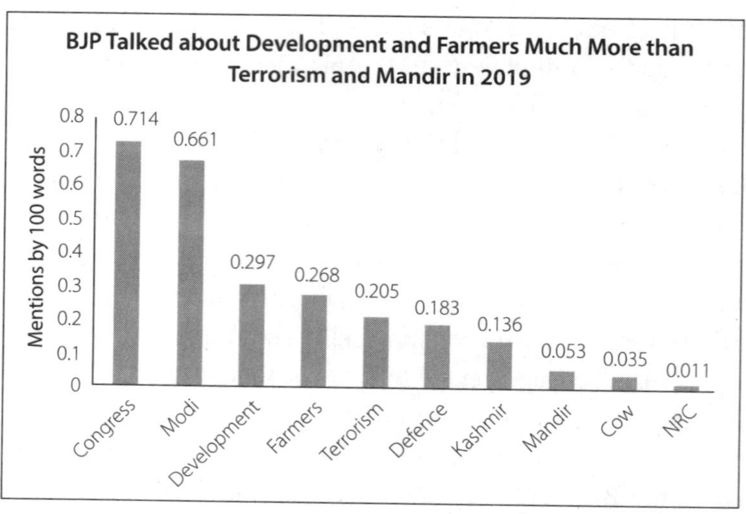

Source: Narad Index, Nalin Mehta and Rishabh Srivastava; for more details see Appendix 4/online on nalinmehta.in

The focus on farmers has been relentless since Modi came to power. The BJP doubled the intensity of its outreach to them in 2015 and has consistently increased it since, with mentions rising by 90 per cent between 2014 and 2019. For example, in January 2019, the BJP's national convention meeting at Delhi's Ramlila Maidan passed a resolution on agriculture. Titled 'Properly Farmer-Prosperous India' [sic], the resolution congratulated Prime Minister Modi for his 'pro-farmer' policies and for running a government that focused on the 'annadata' (provider of food).[15]

Modi's promises of doubling farmer income were still a long way from fruition, but the resolution listed some of the measures the government had taken.

First, it pointed to the increase in MSP for rabi and kharif crops to 1.5 times of the input cost, which was as per the Swaminathan Commission recommendations from UPA-2.[16] 'This decision of the Government,' the resolution declared in a self-satisfied tone, 'is helping farmers to get almost 50% more profit on their produce. On crops like Bajra and Udad, this profit has increased in the range of 65% to 96%.'

Second, the party extolled the fact that the Modi government had increased the budget allocation for agricultural issues from ₹1,21,082 crores between 2009 and 2014 to ₹2,11,694 crores between 2014 and 2019.

Third, it congratulated the government for its 'water to every field' programme, arguing that the 'per drop—more crop' scheme under the Prime Minister Agriculture Irrigation Scheme has given a 'new dimension' to the micro-irrigation systems in the country. The Modi government has allocated 16.21 per cent more resources and money to this scheme, which is an outlay of ₹5,460 crore.

Fourth, on crop insurance, it claimed that the 'pro-farmer Modi government has worked without any biases' and that the NDA government had increased the crop insurance scheme by six times (₹13,000 crore) as compared to the UPA government in 2013-14 (₹2,151 crore). 'Before year 2014, the number of insured loaned farmers and non-loaned farmers was 29 lakh and 6.37 crores respectively; which after the coming of the BJP-led NDA government has increased to 2.75 crores and 8.16 crore respectively. Earlier farmers were getting Rs 4,718 under the scheme which has now increased to Rs 5,400. In 2017-18, the Government paid four times more than the total premium collected from farmers under the claims of this scheme. Today 10.78 crore hectares land of the country has come under the insured area. The BJP government led by Prime Minister, Sh. Narendra Modi, has done all this.'

Fifth, it argued that 7.24 lakh metric tonne pulses and grains were procured between 2010 and 2014, whereas under the BJP-led government, 78.6 lakh metric tonne food grains and pulses were procured as of December 2018. These figures were almost eleven times more than the total procurement under the last UPA government.

Sixth, the party claimed that it solved a critical last-mile issue for farmers by forming an E-National Agriculture Market (eNAM) to connect all 585 agriculture markets in the country on one platform. This online agriculture platform, in 2019, had 1.41 crore registered buyers and sellers, and 2.25 crore tonnes of agriculture produce worth ₹58,930 crore had been marketed through it.[17]

Seventh, in the realm of policy changes, import duty on wheat was increased to 20 per cent and on tuar pulse to 10 per cent. Import duties on some other agricultural products were also implemented to make the country self-reliant and to support farmers. The document concluded by saying, 'We will keep this development of agriculture continue [sic] for a longer duration to realize the "New India" we have been thinking and working towards. We also take this "sankalp" that in 2022, the "New India", which we are conceptualizing, will have an independent, able, strong and prosperous farmer as our "annadata", who will also be a significant vehicle to take Country's economy to new heights.'[18]

Publicity documents like these form by far the third-highest component of the BJP's outreach. Beneath the more headline-grabbing controversial stuff on Hindutva and cultural identity, consistent messaging like this went a long way in retaining the farmer vote in 2019. In fact, the party's outreach to farmers was even greater during the Advani years and peaked during the 2009 election. After that, however, it dropped the ball on this key constituency until Modi won power in 2014. On his watch, the party has assiduously courted the farming community (see Figure 6.7).

The story of vikas, or development, is even more interesting. In November 2017, then BJP president Amit Shah addressed a press conference at Sindhu Bhawan in Gandhidham, Kutch. The Gujarat assembly elections were just round the corner and the BJP was under pressure. Rahul Gandhi was about to be anointed Congress party chief. Taking him on, Amit Shah told reporters:[19]

> The Congress Vice President makes fun of vikas. I challenge Rahul Gandhi to fight in the name of vikas. For Congress, vikas is a joke, for BJP it is an attitude [mizaaj] … The Congress is visible during elections but after elections no one knows where it disappears … Rahul Gandhi comes to Gujarat and makes fun of vikas but the people of Gujarat want answers to these questions from Rahul Gandhi. Why did Congress central governments keep the Narmada project on hold for so long? Why didn't they give permission to put and close doors on the Narmada dam? Why wasn't Kutch given a special desert grant? Why wasn't Gandhinagar given a grant and why did the Congress do an injustice to Gujarat for years in granting crude oil guarantees …
>
> From independence to now, the Congress has deprived the country of vikas, put obstructions in the path of progress and been anti-poor but it comes to Gujarat to ask question of Gujarat's vikas … Gujarat's people want to ask Rahul Gandhi what did you do for Gujarat's development from independence to now? From 2001-2014, under Narendra Modi, the BJP government's time in Gujarat has been Gujarat's golden age. When Rahul Gandhi comes to Gujarat, he should study the statistics on Gujarat's development and not spread lies.

It was typical of the BJP's discourse on development back then. It was aggressive, based on Modi's record in Gujarat and on questioning the Congress. The party was still very focused on its record back then and what it could do in power. It rode to power in 2014 at the Centre on the slogan of vikas. Once the BJP government took over, mentions of vikas increased substantially during the first two years, 2014–2016.

However, from 2018 onwards, that focus almost halved, as the government shifted tack to other issues. Yet, it is still 60 per cent more than it was in 2014 and way higher than most other cultural topics. The vikas discourse remains the fourth highest in the BJP's communications outreach, way above its core issues.

Terrorism, Cow and Temple Are Core Issues but Underplayed in Volume

In October 2008, the BJP issued a press release written as an open letter to 'Congressmen and your other pseudo-secular friends'. It selectively quoted Gandhi's writings on proselytisation and cow slaughter, saying that even Mahatma Gandhi, who cannot be accused of having any ill will towards Christianity, was constrained to say the following:[20]

> I disbelieve in the conversion of one person by another. My effort should never to be to undermine another's faith. This implies belief in the truth of all religions and, therefore, respect for them. It implies true humility. (Young India: April 23, 1931)
>
> It is impossible for me to reconcile myself to the idea of conversion after the style that goes on in India and elsewhere today. It is an error which is perhaps the greatest impediment to the world's progress toward peace. Why should a Christian want to convert a Hindu to Christianity? Why should he not be satisfied if the Hindu is a good or godly man? (Harijan: January 30, 1937)
>
> [...]
>
> My fear is that though Christian friends nowadays do not say or admit it that Hindu religion is untrue, they must harbour in their breast that Hinduism is an error and that Christianity, as they believe it, is the only true religion. So far as one can understand the present (Christian) effort, it is to uproot Hinduism from her very foundation and replace it by another faith. (Harijan: March 13, 1937)
>
> [...]
>
> **What Gandhiji said on Cow and Cow Protection**
> (From his Collected Works)
>
> **PLACE OF THE COW**
> [...] She is the mother to millions of Indian mankind. Protection of the cow means protection of the whole dumb creation of God [...]
>
> I worship it and I shall defend its worship against the whole world.
>
> **THE COW IN HINDUISM**
> The central fact of Hinduism is cow protection. [...] Cow protection to me is one of the most wonderful phenomena in human evolution. It takes the human being beyond this species. The cow to me means the

> entire sub-human world [...] Cow protection is the gift of Hinduism to the world. And Hinduism will live so long as there are Hindus to protect the cow
>
> **COW-SLAUGHTER**
> Cow protection to me is not mere protection of the cow [...] Cow-slaughter and man-slaughter are in my opinion the two sides of the same coin.

Gandhi's quotes on the cow were specific to the anti-imperial context they were uttered in. But the recourse to Gandhi was yet another tool to reinforce the BJP's positioning on this issue. It was illustrative of how clear the BJP has long been about where it stands on its core issues: issues of identity politics symbolised by issues like cow protection, its commitment to a Ram Temple, or the idea of a strong nationalist state with a tough posture on terrorism and national security.

The narrative of the 'tukde-tukde' gang, or the nationwide agitation around the Citizenship Amendment Bill, or the aggressive 'desh ke gaddaron ko, golee maaro saalon ko' (traitors to the nation, shoot those scoundrels) sloganeering by a Union minister in 2020—such ideological wedge issues have been the front edge of the political sledgehammer for the BJP's publicity machinery. It has dominated and shaped the political discourse as well as the party's public image.

It is surprising then to look at the BJP's official public communications in their entirety and discover that the discourse around development, farmers and infrastructure was far higher than that on its core issues (see Figures 6.1, 6.7). The party's core issues are central to its political positioning, but they form part of a wider, cohesive pattern of strategic communications.

Of course, after the Pulwama terrorist attack and the Balakot air strikes by the Indian Air Force in early 2019, the BJP's mentions of terrorism rose by 400 per cent in 2019 (see Table 6.1). Yet, interestingly, this was still far lower than how intensely the party focused on it a decade earlier, in 2006–2008 (see Figure 6.8). That it spoke much more about terrorism in 2008 is understandable, since that was the year of the Mumbai terror attacks. But, even in 2006 and 2007, the focus on terrorism was high, with the BJP accusing the UPA government of being weak on terror.

Figure 6.8: The BJP's Communications on Core Ideological Issues (Terrorism, Defence, Kashmir, Hinduism, Temple) Changed Strategically Over Time: Mentions in Press Releases, Articles Speeches (2005–2019)

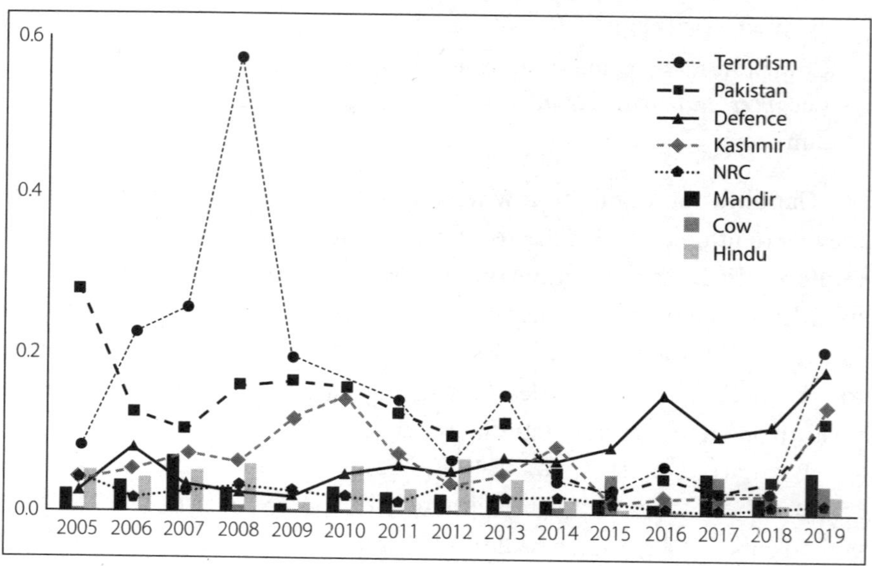

Source: Narad Index, Nalin Mehta and Rishabh Srivastava; for more details see Appendix 4/ nalinmehta.in

The pattern we have seen is that, over the past decade, the party has gradually reduced its public-outreach communications focus on core issues and increased attention on wider issues. Its leaders dialled up the temperature on the BJP's core identity issues in the public domain based on political needs, but the messaging on development and farmers was always larger during the Modi years.

Table 6.1: Terrorism, Security Rose Sharply in 2019, but Still Lower than Focus on Larger Issues in BJP Communications

Topic	*Mentions per 100 words in 2019*	*% Change: 2014–2019*
Congress	0.714	82.6
Modi	0.661	103.4
BJP	0.649	-1.2
Development	0.297	60.5
Farmers	0.268	90.1

Topic	*Mentions per 100 words in 2019*	*% Change: 2014–2019*
Terrorism	0.205	400
Defence	0.183	173.1
Kashmir	0.136	44.7
Pakistan	0.119	124.5
Corruption	0.106	16.5
Security	0.106	82.8
Infrastructure	0.101	-41.3
Women	0.096	174.3

Source: Narad Index, Nalin Mehta and Rishabh Srivastava; for more details see Appendix 4/online on nalinmehta.in

This does not mean that the BJP withdrew from, or became ambiguous about, its ideology, whether it was the CAA and National Register of Citizens (NRC) or the Ram Temple. Far from it. The party doubled down on them. For example, in the middle of the 2019 election campaign, Amit Shah told BJP booth-level workers in Dehradun: 'The Ram Temple should be constructed only on the Ram Janmabhoomi and as quickly as possible … Rahul Gandhi, Akhilesh Yadav and Sister Mayawati should first clarify their position on whether they want a Ram Temple on the Ram Janmabhoomi or not? I say clearly that the BJP is committed to the Ram Temple on the same spot.'[21] A week earlier, he was telling his party's booth workers in Lucknow and Kanpur, 'I want to make it clear to all Congress leaders that you have no right to take the name of the Ram Janmabhoomi because you have always placed hurdles in the path of the construction of a Ram temple … The central government took over 42 acres of the Ramjanmabhoomi Nyas's land in 1993. From 1993 to 2014, for 16 years Congress governments in power kept this matter hanging … The Nyas asked for its land back and we decided to give its land back and sent the matter back to the Supreme Court. Under the leadership of Narendra Modi, the government's decision to return 42 acres of land to the Ramjanmabhoomi Nyas is a historic step.'[22]

This was before the Supreme Court's decision on the Ram Temple dispute on 9 November 2019, which handed the land over to a government trust that would be set up to build the temple, with equal land being given to Muslims elsewhere in Ayodhya for a mosque.[23] Modi's dramatic fronting of the Ayodhya temple's Bhoomi-pujan ceremony on 5 August 2020, presiding over it like a Hindu suratrana (literally, protector of the gods), exemplified this core focus.[24]

Chariot of Hindutva, Riding on the Wheels of Development

The BJP operates at three levels in its political communications. It has a sophisticated and differentiated messaging strategy on what issues it targets at which interest group. When it speaks to the public at large, its messaging, the data shows, is predominantly focused on four themes—anti-Congressism, the personality pull of Narendra Modi and his image as a strong leader, and finally, a wider focus on development, farmers and infrastructure.

This implies that anti-Congressism remains its biggest talking point and its biggest external strength. Until the Congress gets its act together to effectively counter the BJP, its dynastic stasis remains an electoral asset to the BJP. Its core ideological issues of toughness on terrorism, the Ram Temple, the cow and the NRC are lower down in the pecking order. The BJP does enough to assure core voters about its hard-line positioning, but in comparison, reaches out much more to others with wider messaging to draw them into its tent. The data shows that, even in the 2005–2009 period, it had started focusing on wider issues of development and on farmers much more than the core issues. However, this shift did not work then, because the Congress still had a credible leadership.

Second, when the BJP addresses its own core constituency in party communications, it focuses less heavily on the Congress. Here, too, the greater focus is on wider issues of development.

Third, this does not mean that the BJP has withdrawn from its core agenda. In fact, talk of its core agenda has consistently been on the rise since 2017, even though it is less voluminous in percentage terms when compared to other issues in its discourse. Far from retreating on its core issues, the BJP has increased its stridency on them. It has, in effect, transformed the syntax of Indian politics—from triple talaq to the Ram Temple (with every major political party supporting the building of the Ram Temple in August 2020) and on Kashmir (no major party opposed the repeal of Article 370 in Parliament in August 2019). The shift in political cultures on Hinduness, started by L.K. Advani in the 1980s, has reached its logical culmination under Narendra Modi. By 2020, even alternative political forces, like Arvind Kejriwal's AAP in Delhi, found it difficult to oppose the CAA and NRC.

However, contrary to popular perception, the BJP is not a one-trick pony. Its core voters know what it stands for, but the party has been aggressively courting new voters through a much more varied overall discourse than is clear from the media headlines alone. This is the central insight of the Narad Index and its findings in this chapter. Even as the BJP rode the chariot of Hindutva, which signalled its ideological differentiation, it rode on the wheels of development, with Modi as its charioteer.

Finally, the BJP can afford to talk less frequently about its special issues, when compared to its discourse on development, because the party communicates to its followers in multiple voices. In fact, the RSS speaks only about these ideological issues, giving the BJP leeway to calibrate its political messaging appropriately. (I have analysed how the RSS communicates in Part IV of this book.)

7

MODI@DIGITAL

Why the BJP Wins on Social Media[1]

When Modi Hung Out with Ajay Devgn on Google+

Before Akshay Kumar, there was Ajay Devgn. Soon after Google+ launched in India, Narendra Modi, then chief minister of Gujarat, appeared on the new digital platform to participate in a live and interactive Google+ Hangout session, moderated by the actor Ajay Devgn. It was 31 August 2012. Modi was heading into his third state assembly election contest and Google was aggressively promoting the Hangouts feature. The broadcast proved to be a happy meeting ground for both politician and platform. The video chat had to be delayed, starting an hour later than 8 p.m. as scheduled, because Google+ 'systems crashed' with 'so much of traffic in lakhs' that it took 'us an hour to manage that', an apologetic Devgn told viewers who had logged in. 'I have been watching thirty–forty friends from Google here for the past hour who been have working hard to figure out how to clear the traffic,' began Modi. 'Traffic policemen on the road don't get as much trouble as the trouble my friends here were facing,' he quipped as he too apologised for the delay, before going on to thank Google and say that the platform was 'catching the pulse of the globe'.[2]

The chat itself had been advertised for four days prior to 31 August on the chief minister's personal website, www.narendramodi.in, and drew in 20,000 advance questions. Modi answered eighteen of them in the 114-minute broadcast, which was ultimately seen by over 7,88,000 viewers.[3] Presaging all the touchpoint messages of strong nationalism, developmentalism, techno-governance and a new modernity rooted in tradition that would eventually define Modi's nationwide messaging, the chat also encapsulated the core communications style that would ultimately define Brand Modi. Even the choice of topic, 'Strong and Glorious India long cherished by Vivekananda', served to subliminally connect the Gujarat chief minister to the robust Hindu-ness and cultural confidence symbolised by Swami Vivekananda, who captured the Indian imagination in 1893 with his unapologetic defence of Hinduism at the Parliament of the World's Religions. Further, with Modi becoming the first politician in India to appear on Hangouts, the chat underscored his image as a leader who embraced digital change and technology, as did his messaging on Google.

At a time when most mainstream media houses would not interview Modi without asking questions about the post-Godhra violence in 2002, the choice of moderator was crucial. Devgn had just delivered a hit with the Hindi film *Singham* a year earlier, and starred in the successful *Bol Bachchan* and *Son of Sardar* in 2012. Choosing an actor at the height of his career to anchor the session added to the novelty and spectacle of the event.

It was an early version of the celebrity model that drove the Modi interview with the Bollywood actor Akshay Kumar, which helped change the political narrative in India ahead of the 2019 general elections. As with the 'non-political' interview with Kumar, the 2012 Hangouts session with Devgn focused far more on the personal side of the man, with topics ranging from the intricacies of the Modi kurta to the rise of the Asian century.

The story goes that Google+ had first approached Rahul Gandhi for a session. As a young first-time MP who was still new to politics, he would have been the perfect fit for a young tech platform looking to engage youth through celebrities. Gandhi is said to have refused the offer, and the company then approached Modi, says journalist Brajesh Kumar Singh, who covered the event in Ahmedabad. Modi's response, he recalls, was: 'How quickly can we do this?'

Among global politicians, only then US president Barack Obama and then Australian prime minister Julia Gillard had been on Hangouts thus far. The platform was looking for celebrities to engage with in India.

Bollywood stars Shah Rukh Khan and Aamir Khan, as well as cricketer Mahendra Singh Dhoni, were among the celebrities who had featured on Google Hangouts. Modi became the first politician to join this list.[4]

At the time of the Devgn Hangout in 2012, Modi had 8 million followers on Twitter (rising to 61.5 million by September 2020), 6 million on Facebook (growing to 45.8 million by 2020).[5] He was already way ahead of all other Indian politicians (barring Shashi Tharoor at the time) on social media.[6] Rahul Gandhi, for example, did not even join Twitter until March 2015, and started tweeting under his own name only from March 2018.[7] Modi, however, was willing to go the whole hog with a social platform, using it to directly reach his voters, bypassing what he may have seen as the distorting lens of the media. To a question on the chat from a self-confessed fan on how he managed to stay calm despite media criticism, Modi said he welcomed criticism as such, but argued that what he faced in the country was not criticism but allegations by vested interests.

Modi's dominance of the digital world first became a national talking point in 2014, when he used social media and his hologram rallies to great effect. Yet, his embrace of technology as a force multiplier in politics predates this general election. Modi first deployed 3D holograms of himself not in 2014, but in the 2012 Gujarat assembly elections. Soon after that, in March 2013, while addressing the Google Big Tent summit, again via Google Hangouts, he argued: '"Technology in Politics" plays a crucial role … The internet has therefore truly empowered the citizen. It has forced the politician to perform, not just promise. In a way, it has become a challenge for the political class. The time has come for the political class to adapt to this change and reinvent itself! It needs to stop running away. It needs to embrace the internet's many powerful facets … In this age of internet democracy, citizens are netizens, who transcend the geographical borders of countries and continents. No wonder it is called the Wired Republic.'[8] All of this was indicative of how Modi viewed digital communication long before he became the BJP's prime ministerial candidate.

From pioneering the use of campaign audio and video cassettes in the 1980s during the Ram Janmabhoomi movement to adapting early to satellite television in the 1990s, and from Modi holograms in 2014 to dominating Facebook and WhatsApp in 2019, the BJP has always operated at the confluence of technology and politics.[9] In the late 1980s and up to 1992, the party powered its outreach on the Ram Temple movement with roadside ₹1 sales and mass distribution of audio cassettes containing fiery speeches on Ram by two women sanyasins—Uma Bharti (later member of Parliament and Madhya Pradesh chief minister) and Sadhvi Ritambhara from Ludhiana. The BJP's Ram Temple movement also rode the VCR boom, in the pre-internet and pre-satellite TV days, right into middle-class homes, through video cassettes containing religious songs like 'Pran Jaye Par Vachan Na Jaaye' (Let Go of Life but Not Your Word) and speeches. In many ways, these strategies reshaped direct political communications in India.[10]

By 1991, the party had begun hiring ad agencies like the Chennai-based RK Swamy BBDO Pvt Ltd, which created its 1991 election campaign using video cassettes produced at Delhi's Jain TV studios as well as devised the election taglines 'Enough is enough' and 'Let's Go With Ram Rajya, Let's Go With the BJP'.[11] In the 2000s, Modi took this party lineage of using technology for political packaging to another level—by using top Bollywood stars, first-mover advantage and deep usage of digital media, the use of top consultants—all of which ran parallel to the governance messaging campaign run by the party's foot soldiers.

In a country with more mobile phones than any other (except China), low data rates and a fast-urbanising population, the political use of digital technologies had changed the traditional modes of mobilisation. Where political messages were earlier mediated through gatekeepers like the media and opinion leaders who filtered them for the masses—in what was a two-step flow of information—the party now had the means to go directly to the people, and on a scale that was unimaginable earlier. The use of massive databases, data analytics and mass customisation allowed the BJP to send tailor-made messages in one single step directly to those it wanted to reach out to.[12]

By 2020, for example, the Narendra Modi app, named 'NaMo', was sending to all who signed up on it customised and signed birthday messages from the prime minister, addressing voters by name. Such technologies were available to all parties. But the BJP adopted digital technology to a much greater extent than other political parties. It did not win elections only because it was better placed on digital platforms, but its dominance and focus on them acted as a great force multiplier and tool for pushing its messaging to voters and for mobilisation.

Figure 7.1: Personalised NaMo App Email Birthday Greeting to One of Its Subscribers

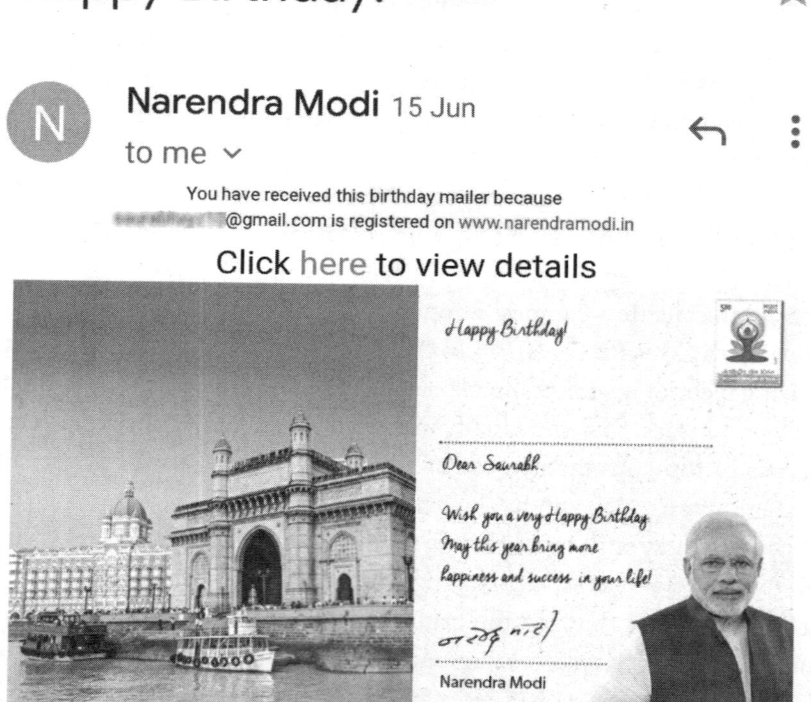

Signed and customised birthday greeting by name from Prime Minister Modi to a NaMo app subscriber on 15 June 2020, sent to the author by the subscriber. The Gateway of India image reflected the subscriber's location in Mumbai. A similar image to another subscriber, for instance, came with an image of the capital city's Qutub Minar.[13] *Picture used with permission of the recipient of this personal message.*

Politics after Jio: Making the Digital Divide Irrelevant

In 2018, as part of a special training programme for political functionaries in the party's various organisational departments, the BJP published a 'quick guidebook for handling media and social media'. Roughly half of its eighty pages were devoted to strategies for tracking and using social media. Uploaded on the party's website as part of a national training programme—the Pandit Deendayal Upadhyaya Prashikshan Mahabhiyan—the official guidebook gave a clear message to office-bearers on how to use the medium:[14]

> Political parties generally start campaigning when elections are near. However, successful political parties are always trying to reach out to people, communicating with them, disseminating correct information and addressing grievances, if any. Social media makes this easier and BJP workers must be in the forefront of this initiative. They are closest to the people/voter and what they do and say will have a large say in defining the image of the party in the minds of potential voters. However, the primary objective of your social media effort is to engage with citizens to disseminate right kind of messages so as to enhance BJP's image and to improve its voter-base. There are many other benefits to using social media. Some of them are:
>
> i. Use of Social Media is mostly free
> ii. You have a huge audience which can be reached with less effort and minimal cost.
> iii. It's another communication tool to be utilised alongside more traditional methods.
> iv. You can engage easily with your target segment.

The publishing of the handbook was a visible marker of how the party internally approached its digital outreach ahead of the 2019 general election. It was also intimately connected with, and aimed at leveraging, the digital revolution that unfolded in India between 2016 and 2019.

This is critical because the 2019 general election was India's first national election that unfolded in a truly digital India—with the second-highest smartphone penetration in the world[15] and the highest average data usage per smartphone, reaching 9.8 gigabytes (GB) per month at the end of 2018.[16] In terms of political impact, this digital transformation has been comparatively understudied. From the invention of the Gutenberg press in medieval Europe, which powered the Reformation and the European Renaissance, to mobile phones, whenever a new mass technology has emerged, it has changed the nature of society and politics.[17]

For a long time, discussions on the impact of digital technologies on Indian politics have been on the margins of scholarly studies because of the perception of a digital divide—that such an impact was limited to a small section because the vast voting multitudes simply did not have access to the internet. While this may have been true in the past, the availability of cheap data on mass mobile telephony between 2016 and 2019 has caused the digital divide in India to shrink.

Figure 7.2: BJP Training Manual on Handling Media and Social Media, 2018

Source: BJP e-library. Available at: http://library.bjp.org/jspui/handle/123456789/2572

Internet users in India increased eightfold from 65.3 million in May 2014 to nearly 600 million in May 2019.[18] Estimates vary on how many of these were active. Yet, most accounts agree that, by 2019, about half of India's voting population[19] now had access to information avenues that were simply not possible earlier. In early 2019, Google, for example, estimated 400 million active internet users in India, with an average of 40 million being added each year. Even more significantly, Google reported that more than half of its searches were now coming from 'Bharat', or non-metro cities. This was driven by the fact that India's average mobile data consumption per user was on par with developed markets.[20] In just four years, monthly data usage in the country increased by over twenty-nine times, rising from 0.26 GB per person in 2014 to 7.69 GB per person in 2018, by official estimates (see Figure 7.3).

Figure 7.3: India's Cheap Data Revolution through Mobiles Also Transformed Indian Politics

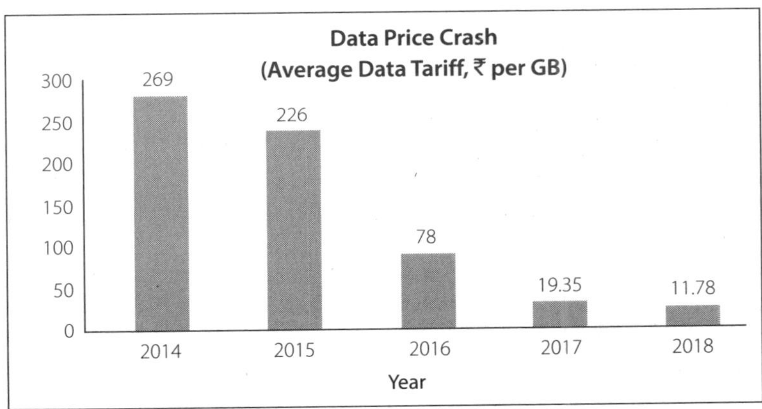

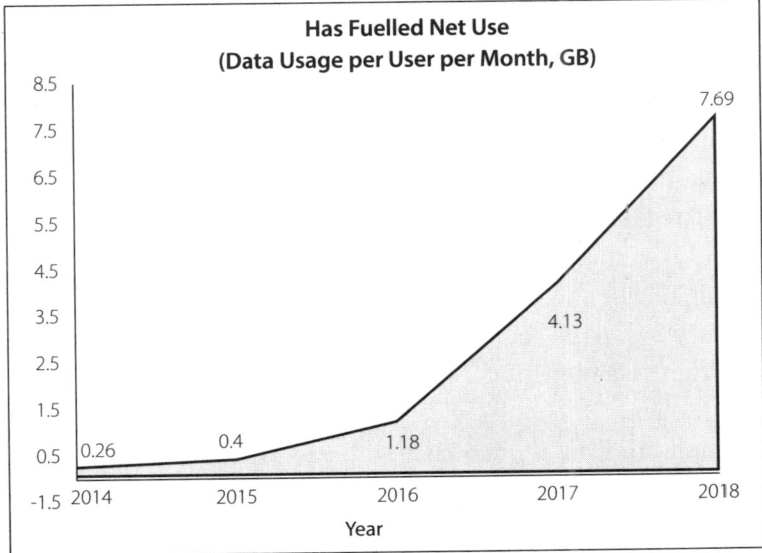

Source: Yearly data from Telecom Regulatory Authority of India, Government of India, 'Wireless Data Services in India: An Analytical Report' (New Delhi: TRAI, 2019)

By May 2019, roughly one in every three Indians was using apps or digital tools like Facebook (up from 9 per cent in 2014), WhatsApp or YouTube.[21] This cheap data revolution, triggered by the launch of the Jio phone network in September 2016, also transformed Indian politics. Digital penetration figures show that widespread adoption of technology may have been the single biggest politics-shifting event of the past decade, altering the neural structures of how local political mobilisation works.

The 2019 general election was, in that sense, India's 'first post-Jio-election', as the journalist Saba Naqvi has perceptively argued. As she put it, 'Some commentators have asked whether this was a post-caste and post-identity mandate, and thereby, a post-Mandal one … I believe that the change has been driven by technology in general, and the telecom revolution ushered in by Jio in particular.'[22] This data revolution created possibilities for political parties to reach voters one-to-one on a larger scale than had ever been possible before. It made traditional media channels obsolete and far less influential, allowing political parties to create their own media channels.

Crucially, this expansion broke down the digital divide. Chatting over coffee at Googleplex, Google's headquarters in California, on a hot, sunny day in May 2019, Caesar Sengupta, the man who then headed the company's initiative to get the Next Billion Users worldwide and Digital Payments, told me that, by 2019, 95 per cent of digital video consumption was already in regional languages, not English. By then, he said, Google had begun to receive more voice searches, as opposed to text searches, from India than any other country in the world. This was driven by the growth of regional languages online. He estimated that Hindi internet users would overtake English users by 2021. Marathi was the next biggest, but Tamil, Telugu and Kannada exhibited the 'highest internet adoption rates'. Also, by 2019, about two-thirds of Google Pay payments were coming from small towns and rural India, outside the eight big metros.[23]

Ajit Mohan, Facebook's vice president and managing director for India, emphasised in a video chat with me in July 2020 that there was 'clearly a shift from offline to online'. This was why Facebook had bought a 9.9 per cent stake in Jio in early 2020. As had Google, which took a 7.7 per cent stake. 'The fabulous thing Jio did,' he concluded, 'was to bring 400–450 million online with access to affordable mobile broadband, followed by Vodafone and Airtel.' Speaking of a new effort to bring millions of small retailers online, he explained that 'a lot of the effort we are doing now addresses the other side of it, now that we have 500 million plus people online'.[24] The fact of Indians going online on their phones was reshaping consumer businesses, making older models of media outreach obsolete. The same logic applied to politics too.

BJP Dominates Political Advertising on Facebook and Google

One way to understand how political parties approached this digital shift is to track the money they claimed to spend on online advertising. The BJP outstrips the rest in its declared spending on advertising in the digital domain. Ahead of the 2019 general elections, Google and Facebook began Ads Transparency initiatives in India. This meant that, for the first time, these two Big Tech companies began reporting the exact number of declared political advertisements they received, the entities involved and the amounts spent. Between February and May 2019, they declared cumulative political online advertising of ₹58.67 crore. The money spent on both platforms was similar, though Facebook's ad library received a far higher volume of individual advertisements. Google declared 12,276 political advertisements worth ₹29.3 crore. Facebook, in its India Ad Library, declared a total of 1,32,419 advertisements worth ₹29.28 crore.[25]

The BJP dominated digital political spending on both Google and Facebook in this period. On Google, it accounted for 41.4 per cent (₹12.19 crore) of political advertising. Tamil Nadu's DMK scored a distant second with 13.6 per cent (₹4 crore) and the Congress was third with 10 per cent (₹3 crore). On Facebook, the BJP accounted for 14.7 per cent (₹4.3 crore) of political advertising, and the Congress came in a distant second with 6.1 per cent (₹1.8 crore).

Overall, this trend in electoral spending mirrors offline trends on party earnings. It is not an outlier. In 2017-18, the BJP declared a total income of ₹1,027.34 crore, while the Congress declared an income of 199.15 crore.[26] The gaps in online spends between the two parties, in that sense, is reflective of the relative size of their political war chests offline.

Furthermore, the volume of declared political advertising on digital platforms is extremely low when compared to total declared campaign expenditure. The Congress declared ₹820 crore to the ECI as campaign expenditure in 2019. The BJP declared over ₹1,264 crore as its campaign spending in 2019 to the ECI, in comparison to ₹714 crore it declared as election expenditure in 2014.[27]

Moreover, there are serious definitional issues on what counts as political advertising. Most political spending on digital platforms is not done directly by the parties themselves but by affiliates or sympathetic groups that are technically separate. This allows for plausible deniability. Clearly, political parties are spending significantly larger amounts on digital platforms—for digital messaging, digital war rooms and troll armies—than is declared. What gets reported and pre-certified as political advertising is only a small fraction of the larger political mobilisation activities. For example, a divisive but anonymous WhatsApp or ShareChat forward depicting a particular religious community adversely may carry political weight as a signalling device to polarise the public. Such a forward is undoubtedly political in nature, but will never be classified as political advertising. It is also almost impossible to trace the origins of such messages.

Even the certified spending figures on Big Tech platforms can be deceptive, with much of the advertising money being spent by groups that support the party from outside. Consider Facebook: while the BJP was the highest declared spender among political parties in February-March 2019, seven of the top ten spenders on its advertisers' list for this period were entities sympathetic to the party. These ranged from pages like 'My First Vote for Modi', 'Bharat ke Mann ki Baat' and 'Nation with NaMo'.

By mid-2020, serious questions began to be raised about the neutrality of tech platforms and their alleged political biases. The *Wall Street Journal* (*WSJ*) broke a story accusing Facebook's then public policy head for India, South Asia and Central Asia of ensuring that posts by some BJP leaders—flagged as hate speech by Facebook's community guidelines team (which is supposed to ensure that posts on the platform follow certain minimum standards)—were not removed. This was allegedly done, according to the *WSJ*, because it was felt that such actions would anger the ruling government. Facebook's public policy officials also wrote internal messages, according to the report, supporting the BJP and its political triumphs, and disparaging its main political rival.[28] While Facebook denied any inappropriate bias, the BJP government hit back, accusing the company of bias against the ruling party. The then Union IT Minister Ravi Shankar Prasad wrote to Facebook CEO Mark Zuckerberg that the 'Facebook India team, right from the India Managing Director to other senior officials, is dominated by people who belong to a particular political belief.' He argued that the Facebook India management had deleted some pages run by people sympathetic to 'right-of-centre ideology' or reduced their reach on its platform before the 2019 general election.[29] There was an echo here of how, in the US, Facebook refused to flag as fake news a statement by US President Donald Trump, even though other tech platforms like Twitter had done so.[30] The final word on this issue is yet to be written—one man's hate speech is another man's freedom of speech, as the BJP has argued—but the political battles around such judgement calls illustrate the highly contested nature of the digital space that Indian politics now operates in.[31]

'The Internet Hindu' and Digital Politics: BJP Leads but Congress Is Not a Write-Off

'Internet Hindus are like swarms of bees,' tweeted the TV journalist Sagarika Ghose in 2010. 'They come swarming after you at any mention of Modi, Muslims or Pakistan.'[32] This was possibly the first articulation of the idea of the Cyber Hindu and the dominance of the political right-wing online. It's not simply about troll armies or the daily vitriolic battles that are fought on Twitter. The Times Group's mega 'Pulse of the Nation' e-poll in May 2018, which asked users whom they would vote for in the general elections, gave us an insight into the political disposition of mass online audiences. Users could only vote once from a mobile number, results were masked until the final day to prevent rigging and the online poll was conducted in nine different languages.

Of the 8,44,646 people who voted, 73 per cent said they would vote for Modi as prime minister if general elections were to be held at that moment. Two other surveys—in December 2017 (over half a million respondents) and February 2019 (over 2,00,000 respondents)—yielded similar results: with over 70 per cent of those taking the survey in each case saying they would vote for Modi. He did win resoundingly in 2019, of course, but not by these margins.[33] The party's online ascendancy was far higher than its offline sway. As *India Today* magazine had concluded in a cover story in November 2013 after a similar e-poll of its own: 'The Internet is saffron.'[34] Such numbers fuel the assumption that somehow digital platforms are tailormade for groups like Hindu nationalists, who find it easier to dominate online with polarising messaging. The truth is somewhat more complicated, at least on Twitter.

To understand what was really happening, data scientist Rishabh Srivastava, journalist Sanjeev Singh and I set up a 'Twitter Listening Post' in early 2016. Over two and a half years—January 2016 to May 2019—we monitored seventy-five political accounts from across political parties and the messaging on a total of 4,76,827 tweets posted by them. We found a clear pattern where, from late 2017 onwards, Rahul Gandhi started making big strides. This started unfolding a little after the UP assembly election of February-March 2017 which the BJP had swept. While Modi's Twitter following was over five times that of Gandhi's—and he remained way ahead of Gandhi in terms of followers, reach and total posts (see Figures 7.4, 7.5 and 7.6)—on a per tweet basis, Rahul Gandhi started winning on engagement metrics over these two years. This was in spite of the fact that Gandhi put out only 1,497 tweets (between June 2017 and May 2019), as compared to 8,201 by Modi. Surprisingly, in average-per-tweet terms, he was beating Modi on Twitter in the number of retweets, likes and replies to his posts (see Figure 7.4). Modi's cumulative engagement metrics, however, remained way higher.

One could argue that Gandhi got more comments because he was often abused more by the Twitterati, but the fact that he was getting more retweets and likes per tweet is still revealing. It shows that he was building an alternative online audience to Modi's. It was smaller for sure—about one-fifth the size of the prime minister's—but it was there. This was crucial progress, given that the Congress party was playing catch-up, having given the BJP a free run on social media for a long time.

We found the same patterns when we analysed Twitter data using Facebook's CrowdTangle tool: Gandhi's growth rate was faster on Twitter (349 per cent) than Modi's (57 per cent, albeit from a much larger base) from mid-2017 to 2019 and the interaction rate for his posts (0.45) was

Figure 7.4: Rahul Gandhi vs Narendra Modi on Twitter (2017–2019)

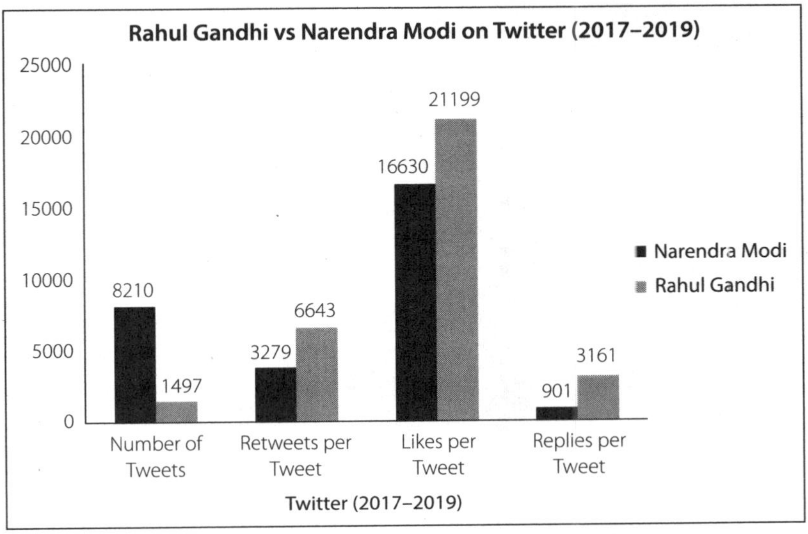

Source: 'Twitter Listening Post': Sanjeev Singh, Rishabh Srivastava, Nalin Mehta, https://pollniti.com/twitter.html

higher than Modi's (0.05%). Again, Modi remained way ahead on size (see Figures 7.5 and 7.6), but Gandhi was holding his own.

Table 7.1: Rahul Gandhi vs Narendra Modi; BJP vs Congress on Twitter: Followers (2017–2019)

Name	*Total*	*Growth (in Million)*	*Growth %*
Rahul Gandhi	9.67	+7.52	+349.22
Narendra Modi	47.73	+17.35	+57.10
BJP	11.16	+6.05	+116.3
INC	5.26	+3.32	+171.42

Source: CrowdTangle Intelligence Report Data analysed by Nalin Mehta, Rishabh Srivastava (31 May 2017–31 May 2019)

Importantly, this Twitter trend was replicated when we started examining second-level Congress and BJP leaders in the states. In particular, we looked at Congress leaders in Rajasthan, Madhya Pradesh and Chhattisgarh in the months leading up to state assembly elections in

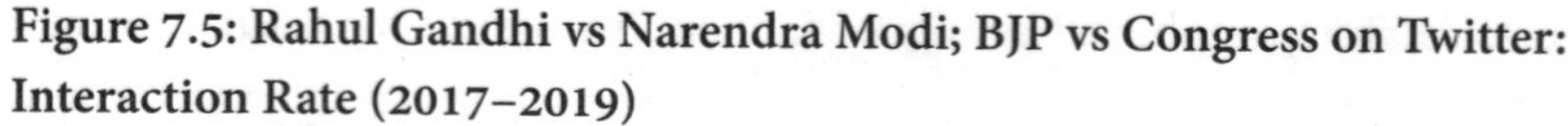

Figure 7.5: Rahul Gandhi vs Narendra Modi; BJP vs Congress on Twitter: Interaction Rate (2017–2019)

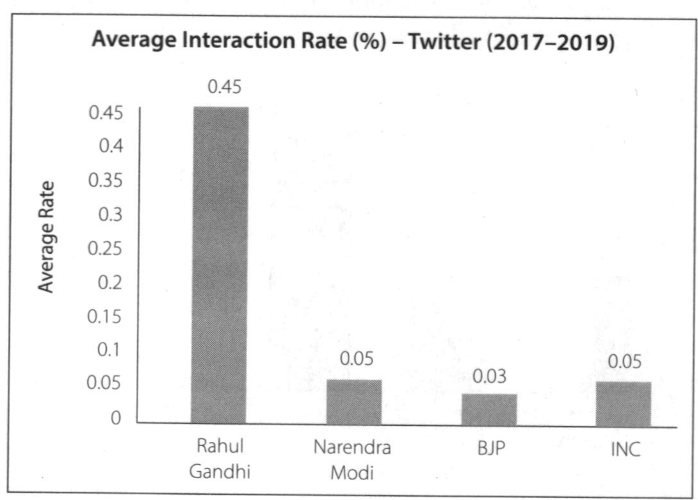

Source: CrowdTangle Intelligence Report Data analysed by Nalin Mehta, Rishabh Srivastava (31 May 2017–31 May 2019)

December 2018. In all these three states, Congress official handles and those of its key leaders (Ashok Gehlot and Sachin Pilot in Rajasthan; Kamal Nath and Jyotiraditya Scindia [before he switched to the BJP on 11 March 2020] in Madhya Pradesh; Bhupesh Bhagel and T.S. Singh Deo in Chhattisgarh) significantly outperformed official BJP handles and those of its main leaders (Vasundhara Raje Scindia in Rajasthan; Shivraj Singh Chouhan in Madhya Pradesh and Raman Singh in Chhattisgarh) on key engagement metrics. Our data recorded in the months of October-November 2018 clearly shows that the Congress was winning the Twitter battle at the regional level in these states.

In each case, the BJP had a larger following, but these Congress handles were getting much more likes, retweets and replies on the tweets they were putting out on jobs, demonetisation and GST. They were able to rebrand themselves as a viable alternative to online audiences. Retweets and likes, because they represent how users are receiving messages, are a better way to track the efficacy of digital media messages than just the messages themselves or their volume. Sanjeev Singh has published some of the findings of this analysis of Twitter data in three separate research papers. They show a clear correlation between Twitter trends and the final electoral results in these states. Causation, though, is much more tricky territory and needs more in-depth studies.[35] Between late 2018 and February 2019, hashtags sympathetic to the Congress 'started trending on Twitter much more than those related to the Bharatiya Janata Party (BJP) and causes sympathetic to it'. Joyojeet Pal, professor at the University of Michigan and senior researcher at Microsoft Research, whose team studied 1,42,000 topics that trended on Twitter in a four-month period at this time, found that the Congress was winning the sentiment game on Twitter until the BJP turned the tide from February 2019 after the Pulwama attack.[36]

What does all this mean? For one, it shows that Hindu nationalists do not have an indelible hold on social media, i.e., their dominance is not an automatic result of the nature of their messaging. Social media dominance is an outcome of the effort and attention that politicians put into it and how they engage with their audiences. The Congress, between 2017 and 2019, showed that it could fight the BJP on Twitter. The problem, however, is that Twitter remains the smallest of all the major social media platforms in India. It had only reached one-fifth of Indians by 2019. Facebook is far bigger. So, even though Rahul Gandhi was giving Modi a fight on Twitter, it tended to be a platform for debate among opinion-makers, not of mass outreach to voters. It was as if the larger shrinkage of the Congress was being replicated on social media.

The Congress seems to have missed a trick because Facebook and Instagram, which is dominated by younger people, are much bigger platforms in India, reaching about a third of voters. We saw the same higher engagement per post replicated for Rahul Gandhi on these platforms as well. However, unlike Twitter, he was so far behind Modi in overall size on these platforms that his gains proved to be irrelevant.

On Twitter, for every Rahul Gandhi follower, Modi had about five followers. In the case of Facebook, this ratio was as high as 1:14, on Instagram 1:34.[37] On Facebook, Narendra Modi's 44.02 million followers and 135.76 million interactions between May 2017 and May 2019 totally dwarfed Rahul Gandhi's 2.83 million page likes and 33.28 million interactions. Yet, in average rate of interactions per post, Gandhi was ahead of Modi (see Appendices 5–10). On Instagram, Modi (22.52

million followers and 222.44 million interactions) was over twenty times bigger than Gandhi (8,55,900 followers and 8.68 million interactions). This huge gap between the two leaders meant that any traction Gandhi got was ultimately rendered irrelevant. The BJP was so far ahead on Facebook and Instagram that the Congress was not even on the same playing field.

Modi on LinkedIn: Differentiated Communication Strategies

The big difference between the BJP and the Congress is that while the latter, until 2019, concentrated on Twitter, the BJP had 360-degree coverage on digital platforms: the prime minister has a LinkedIn account, his team maintains a Pinterest board and his YouTube channel in November 2019 had posted some 12,124 videos and had 4.26 million followers (compared to Rahul's 713 videos with 186,000 followers).[38]

Modi opened a LinkedIn account at the height of the Lok Sabha election campaign in 2014.[39] His first post, 'ICT for One Nation-One Mission', was typical of his messaging to aspirational middle-class Indian voters.[40]

> I believe in the Mantra of 'IT+IT=IT' (Information Technology + Indian Talent = India Tomorrow). ... We need to work to create an atmosphere whereby India becomes the home of the next Apple, Google, Facebook, Twitter and Amazon! ... With a policy driven and result oriented approach, I see no reason why India cannot become the next hub of cloud infrastructure ... We have heard of e-governance but now is the time to move towards m-governance (Mobile governance) ... The role of the Internet is paramount now. We need to think of a future where every home and office has internet and High Speed Data access becomes a basic utility, much like electricity, water and telephones. Handheld devices like mobile phones, tablets etc. need to be better deployed to fulfill the aspirations of the masses. We need to be a lot faster on taking the Internet to every doorstep and this calls for a time-bound programme to expand internet and broadband connectivity both in urban and rural areas.

The prime minister's LinkedIn account, which had gathered over 3 million followers by November 2019, perfectly exemplifies his approach to digital outreach: message discipline combined with maximum outreach.

While the Congress was over-focused on one platform, the BJP's approach of saturation coverage across all platforms was in line with the advice in its official media handbook for social-media managers. The handbook is surprisingly exhaustive on how to measure impact and asks party workers to use measurement tools as diverse as Keyhole, Lucidya, Mention, Audiense, Tweetreach, Followerwonk, Buffer, Sumall, Quintly, Cyfe, Klout, Viralwoot and Additomatic. It concludes by telling its users, 'This isn't an ordered list—all of these apps are great. Give a few of them a try and gain some insights that will help you reach your goals!'[41]

So, how did the Congress assess its social-media strategy after the 2019 election? When I put this question to senior Congress leader and the party's chief whip in the Rajya Sabha, Jairam Ramesh, he was candid about the gaps. Ramesh, who held several ministerial portfolios in the previous UPA government, helmed the party's poll campaign coordination in 2004, 2009 and 2014, and was part of its nine-member core group committee for the 2019 Lok Sabha elections. Chatting over tea in his book-lined government apartment in central Delhi's Lodhi Estate, he agreed that the 'gap was closed in 2019, no doubt about it'. He said, 'The disparity in the campaigns on social media was not as great as it was in 2014. We caught up fairly well on Twitter.' However, he conceded that 'we were heavily outflanked on Facebook and even more outflanked on Instagram. On Instagram, Facebook and WhatsApp, the BJP was decidedly ahead.'[42]

What about the Congress's gains on Twitter? The BJP's National Head for Information and Technology Amit Malviya responds with a dismissive wave of the hand. A former vice president at Bank of America and HSBC, Malviya is the son of an Army officer and quit a lucrative career in banking in his late thirties to take up a full-time position with the BJP in 2015. We met at his digital keycard-protected office at the BJP's headquarters in Delhi from where he plots the party's daily digital-media operations. 'First of all, my comparison is not with the Congress party,' he said. 'We don't even look at what they're doing because they're a farce. Rahul Gandhi's Twitter account is on steroids. I said this on record that his retweets are not organic. They are basically bot-driven. That is the reality. If the man was getting 10,000 retweets for every damn thing he said, then you should be more popular than the kind of popularity he enjoys today. So, let's not get into these metrics. The metrics can be gamed. We are not in the business of gaming metrics. We are in the business of winning elections and that's what we have done fairly successfully. So, I am not even going to go down that path. You say they upped the game. They didn't, because if they did, the end data would show something, right? I'm happy to have a BJP Twitter account at 1.2 crore with the kind of retweet numbers that it has. As long as I'm making the impact, I don't want an account which has 10,000 retweets and doesn't make an impact on it. Most people get social media wrong. Social media is not about the metrics that you've seen. It's really about what's the kind of impact that you're making.'[43]

He's speaking like a party spokesperson, but he does have a point about Facebook: 'Rahul Gandhi's Twitter account is on steroids, but when you look at his Facebook account, the same post gets hardly any traction. How's it possible, because Facebook is a much larger community than Twitter? So, you know, these are all good things for newspaper columns in the run-up to the elections. Their metrics are not good. If you really want to compare Rahul Gandhi's Twitter account performance, compare it to Smriti Irani, who is someone he was contesting against and she beat him.'

So, was the Congress relying more on bots than the BJP? Joyojeet Pal, whose team studied Twitter patterns of 18,000 political accounts, also found results similar to ours on Twitter: Congress and Rahul Gandhi started doing better on retweets between 2017 and 2019. 'Congress on average gets retweeted more than BJP but on aggregate BJP is way higher,' he said. 'The catch is we don't know how many of these are bots. But at a measurement level we should take the aggregate number. Rahul speaks less but when he speaks, he gets more traction.'[44]

Gandhi just tried, says Pal, to 'redo what Modi was doing in the 2014 campaign and did it well, but just that gaming in and of itself is not sufficient. It's also about which topics to pick, how certain topics can be made to trend. It is not just what one person says. In that sense Rahul got some elements right but didn't have the organization to match up.'[45]

The main difference between the BJP and the Congress was about a political mindset that combined digital with offline campaigning. 'The Congress is still in the old traditional campaigning mindset,' says Jairam Ramesh. 'They don't realise that there has been a generational shift. They don't realise that the population has become much more connected and much more urban. It is a mindset issue. If you WhatsApp or email any senior Congress leader, you are unlikely to get any response, but if you do it in the BJP, chances of getting a response are pretty bright.'

'Our mindset was still traditional, our resources were limited,' he says. 'That got reflected in our social media campaign. We had a good campaign in terms of substance. Whether we were able to get it out is a question. Our manifesto is a good example. We had a better manifesto than the BJP, but the outreach of that manifesto was pretty poor. We weren't able to get it out enough. This has always been one of the weaknesses as far as the Congress is concerned. Compared to 2014, in 2019, we were better. We have to look at it in comparison to what we were doing in the past. Compared to what our competition was doing, we fell short, but compared to what we were doing, it has been a remarkable transformation.'

Jairam showed me WhatsApp pictures of Congress workers protesting in the Northeast. 'For example, in the last five minutes,' he says, 'I am getting images of our workers who are agitating outside the RBI office in Agartala on the economic slowdown and they are putting it on Facebook. This is something that was unheard of even two-three years ago and is not something that is being done centrally. It is being done by our people in Agartala.'

Is that not part of the problem? That the Congress has often seen social media as something external to it, whereas for most public institutions and consumers, digital platforms are intrinsic to what they stand for. 'I am not defending the disparity that exists,' he says. 'We have a lot of catching up to do.'[46]

The BJP's Batman vs the Congress's Bhakt ka Chashma

When Rajiv Saxena, a Dubai-based accountant, and corporate lobbyist Deepak Talwar were brought back to India by a team of law enforcement officers in January 2019, the BJP's official handle was quick to compare Modi to the superhero Batman. 'Last time we saw such swift extradition, it was Batman extraditing Lau from Hong Kong and delivering him to Jim Gordon,' the BJP said. Then it quoted Bruce Wayne: '"Everything's impossible until somebody does it." This time it's PM Narendra Modi.' For a party more used to sanskari talk, the pop-culture reference was surprising, but the tweet quickly went viral. As one user responded, 'Wait. Did BJP just make a Batman reference?' Another one said, 'Did you actually tweet this Batman analogy? You just earned a few more votes for this?'[47]

It is an example that Amit Malviya relates proudly when you ask him about the BJP's communication strategy. In this view, for the party, social media is an alternative, direct outreach platform to the narratives of the mainstream media. 'When I came in here, one of the things that I decided to do was to focus on content. Media has its own priorities. It wants to report on things that it thinks people are interested in, not necessarily what people are wanting to read. It has a certain bent, it has a certain ideological persuasion and their news reportage also reflects that somewhere. There is very little focus on the actual work that happens in the government. So, the thing that we started consciously doing here is to start putting out positive content about what the government is doing. That strategy worked exceedingly well for us because when I took over [in July 2015], our Twitter presence was 17 lakh. By the end of 2019 general election, we have crossed five crore and this was all organic growth. Similarly, on Facebook, we were at about 70 lakh, and by the time of the 2019 election, we had got about four and a half crore followers. Most of it is organic. I realised that a lot of people were coming for content. We used graphics, memes, small videos, snippets. We used more creative content which included different voices of the people, first-party beneficiary account and a lot of youth-centric content. We used a lot of content that people would relate to. We started drawing heavily on movie characters like Batman or Spiderman or those from Bollywood. That worked extremely well for us.'

Recalling the Batman tweet, he says, 'It caught the imagination of a lot of young people and people said, wow, you know, the BJP is about Batman! My vote is for the BJP and that kind of stuff. Then we made one full series on the youth. We called it "My First Vote for Modi". A lot of what we showed there was very young people ... So, if you were speaking about women's security, we showed a young couple who are probably seeing each other in college. The guy wanted to drop a girl home and she was saying, "Don't worry, I can walk back home and I will be fine." It was that kind of approach. So, we changed the language of communication and we use modern technology to do that. The idea was to make our content very relatable, if that's the word.'

The Congress too tried various kinds of content, from comedy to satirical videos like its caustic 'Bhakt ka chashma' (devotee's spectacles) clip, which shows a young man looking to buy goggles and being taken for a ride as he tries on a magic saffron pair that tints the way the world looks to him. Where there is poverty, the saffron goggles show a vision of prosperity; where there is sickness, they show neat and clean hospitals; and where there are pakoda sellers, they show happy, degree-wielding job holders. The problem for the Congress was that it just did not have enough reach on these videos.

Why did the Congress not saturate its social platforms beyond Twitter? Jairam Ramesh, who has directed several of the party's election campaigns in the past, blames it on resources. 'I have no reliable data,' he says, 'but I have been told they [the BJP] have 500 people working 24x7 on social media. We had twenty-five people working social media 24x7 in Delhi. If you add the number of people in other states doing social alone, then, nationwide, that number would not exceed sixty. BJP had at least ten times that number. In terms of manpower resources and in terms of financial resources, we were easily outflanked and it was visible in the disparity in presence.'[48]

Question the BJP's IT Cell head on this claim, and Malviya's response is: 'Rubbish!' 'I have a twenty-two-member team here and eight people for technology and data analytics,' he told me. 'Why do I need fifty people or 500 people or whatever the number they give you? It is incorrect. If I can't do this at twenty-two people, then I can't do it with fifty or 500 or whatever number they gave you.'

When pushed on the numbers, he responded, 'The fact is that I'm one, I've created thirty-six state units and each of those state units are doing whatever they can do. With their own limited resources, they have their own things because I can't be having an opinion on what's happening in Andhra politics, right? So, I basically created a cookie-cutter model which has now been implemented in all our states. So, people in Assam are doing it, people in Bengal are doing it, people in Odisha are doing it. It's a very efficient way of doing it. Of course, it's very people-centric. If I have a good guy in any of the states, that state is much, much more robust than say a state with a less talented person.'

Another area where the BJP focused its attention was WhatsApp. In September 2018, *Hindustan Times* reported that the BJP was creating a new kind of worker: a 'cell phone pramukh'. The idea was to have around 9,00,000 of these, one for almost every polling booth or station. (India has

10,35,000 booths in all.) Prime Minister Modi, the newspaper reported, met a group of senior BJP leaders that month, and the details of this campaign were presented by a senior official in his office.[49] By December 2018, the BJP's national general secretary (organisation), Ram Lal, publicly announced that 'a chain of WhatsApp groups linking Panna Pramukhs up to national level leaders will be set up'. Panna Pramukhs are booth-level BJP workers who are responsible for keeping in touch with voters named in one page (panna) of an electoral roll in a constituency. (The BJP's structure of IT heads and panna pramukhs is detailed in Chapter 8.)[50]

While the Congress was trying to replicate Modi's 2014 digital strategy, focusing on Rahul's messaging, the BJP was already working at much more intricate and subtle levels. As one social-media manager told me, 'The BJP worked at much more local levels, infiltrating WhatsApp groups in RWA societies, office groups and alumni or friend networks. While Congress was sharing official messages of its leaders, a lot of pro-BJP messaging was done in these networks.'

Of course, what the BJP's opponents look at as 'infiltrators' on WhatsApp groups are really sympathisers who believed in their party's ideology enough to play this role for it in their own networks. There is nothing to stop Opposition parties from playing the same game, but they need a critical mass of followers who are motivated enough.

How many WhatsApp groups did the party actually set up? Malviya says, 'I don't have a number to give you. A lot of people in the media continuously keep asking how many WhatsApp groups you have or what is your reach? The answer is, I don't know. I don't make these groups. When we first started doing these training workshops, a lot of the leaders would tell me, "Amitji, my phone number is with everyone, everyone messages, what do we do? I asked them, what do you do? They said, we exit the group. I said, don't exit the group, put material on your work on these groups." So, they realised that WhatsApp, which they thought was becoming a handicap, was actually a strength for them.'

In West Bengal, by one account, the BJP reportedly set up about 55,000 WhatsApp accounts in 2019 to take on Mamata Banerjee,[51] and in Karnataka, about 20,000 groups in 2018.[52] Ask Malviya the real number and this is his response: 'Twenty thousand is a small number, it's like small change. No, it's in lakhs and even I don't know how many lakhs.'

Insults vs Multifaceted Political Messaging

From late 2017 onwards, when Rahul Gandhi's following on Twitter showed an upswing, he made two changes to his digital strategy. First, he started tweeting in Hindi. This made a huge difference because, in eight key heartland states, Hindi has far greater reach than English. In a country where 95 per cent of online video consumption was already in regional languages by 2019, and where Google expected Hindi internet users to exceed English internet users by 2021, this was vital.[53] Second, he started using what Joyojeet Pal calls 'insulting or confrontational language'. Tracking tweets by 4,931 politicians in this period, Pal found that Gandhi's rising Twitter popularity coincided with his adoption of confrontational language. The BJP's social-media warriors were the ones to originally start this game of verbal aggression, having successfully branded him as 'Pappu'. Now he was fighting back with slogans like 'chowkidar chor hai' (the guard is the thief).[54]

In fact, Gandhi's strategy was similar to what Modi had followed in his early years as chief minister, when his communications had a much more aggressive tone. As a prime-ministerial candidate in 2014, he shifted to greater use of sarcasm and wordplay, such as with his usage of the term 'shehzada' for Gandhi. He switched to a more statesmanlike tone on social platforms after becoming prime minister, leaving the hard messaging to the next rung of BJP leaders or to the trolls.[55] Even as prime-ministerial candidate in 2014, a comparative study found that Modi was much less insulting than global peers leading right-wing parties, such as US President Donald Trump in the 2016 general election, Nigel Farage in the 2016 UK Brexit referendum and Geert Wilders in the 2017 Dutch election.[56]

Modi was different from other global right-wing leaders, the study concluded. 'Narendra Modi practiced the gentle touch of innuendo with the highest level of wordplay in his tweeting, among all four,' the study said. 'In a context where the majority of social media users themselves are firmly part of the economic and social elite, Modi's Twitter output aimed to legitimize a populist movement by changing its off-street rhetoric. Unlike the other three politicians, Modi sits atop more than just an "establishment"—his political party is cadre-based and has deep roots in a community. Modi did not have to enact a populist agenda online to reach that base—it already came to him naturally through the RSS's wide network. For him, social media is a place for reserved populism. Unlike Trump or Wilders, he benefits from exhibiting restraint because his ability to wield the stick has never been in doubt.' [57]

The second big differentiator for Modi online is his focus on reaching out to celebrities. He focused on this right from his early years online when he started following a range of celebrities—from Rajinikanth in Tamil Nadu to Bill Gates in Silicon Valley to spiritual leaders like Baba Ramdev and Sri Sri Ravi Shankar. Over the years, he began broad-basing his messaging beyond the political, reaching out to cricket celebrities, as during the cricket World Cup in 2011. Bollywood and cricket personalities prefer to engage with less political content online. Modi made adroit use of this by engaging celebrities through challenges like the #SwacchBharat campaign, the Fitness Challenge or with his #SelfieWithModi campaign.[58]

Why Digital and Ground Campaigning Can't Be Differentiated Anymore

When the Congress Curiously Reduced Digital Advertising

The Congress did not lose only because it was outgunned on digital media. While the BJP remained dominant on social-media platforms, the Congress had put up a fight online. It lost also because of other reasons that had to do with the party's larger strategy, tactics and messaging. That said, in the last month of the 2019 general election campaign, the digital advertising trail shows a dipping trend for the Congress, which is curious. On Google, from sometime around 22 April 2019, a full month before the election campaign ended, Congress's spending on digital media dropped sharply (see Figure 7.6). While spending by the BJP also dipped after April—since only the last three phases of the seven-stage campaign were left—the Congress dip was much sharper. This is particularly inexplicable because these last phases included constituencies in states where the Congress was in a direct one-to-one fight with the BJP or its allies: Madhya Pradesh, Rajasthan, Haryana, Punjab and Himachal Pradesh. Also, while BJP's spending saw an uptick in the final week of the campaign, Congress's spending dropped even faster in this last phase.

Figure 7.6: Political Advertising Trend on Google by BJP and Congress in 2019 Elections[59]

Google Advertising Volumes and Money Spent by BJP and Congress (2018-19)

Party Name	*Digital Advertisements*	*Amount Spent*
BJP	12,014	18,30,36,750
INC	425	3,04,47,500

Source: Google, 'Political Advertising for India'; dataset analysed by the author for 31 May 2018–28 April 2019, https://transparencyreport.google.com/political-ads/region/IN?hl=en

Advertising Spending Patterns by BJP and Congress on Google (March–April 2019)

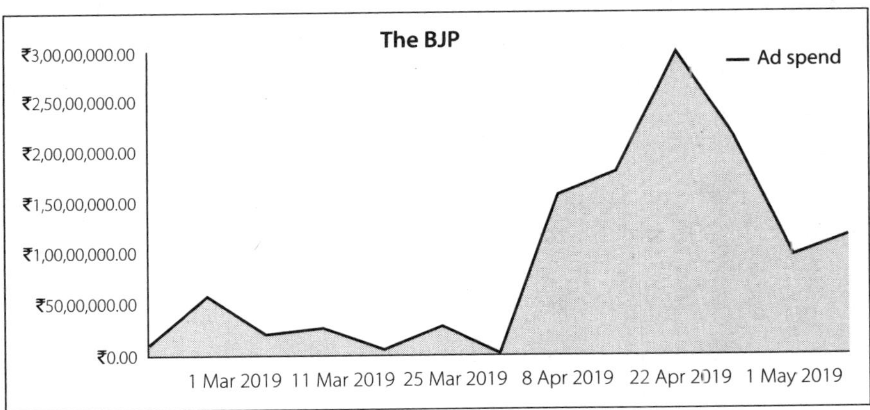

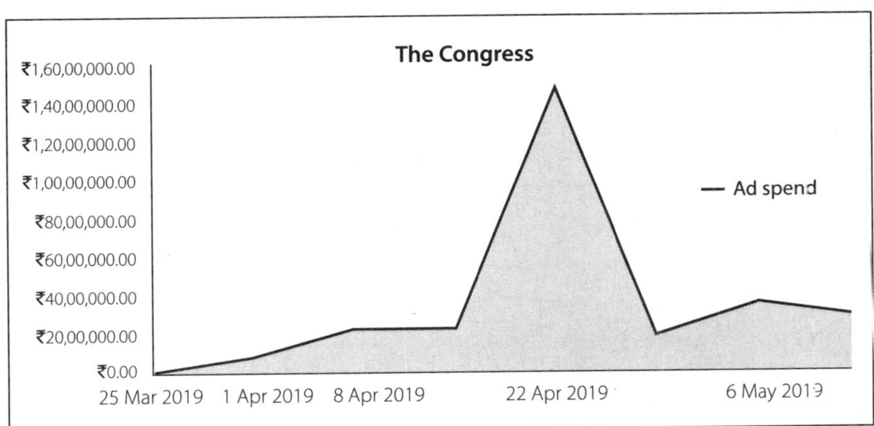

Source: Google, 'Political Advertising for India', dataset analysed by author for 31 May 2018–22 May 2019, https://transparencyreport.google.com/political-ads/region/IN?hl=en

Why this happened is unclear and needs further investigation, but the Congress, at least in this final lap of the poll, seemed to have taken its foot off the accelerator.

Where the BJP Scored: Campaign Gaps and Ground Game

It is useful to see these digital trends in tandem with the offline campaigning patterns of Narendra Modi and Rahul Gandhi. Modi addressed 142 rallies during the 2019 campaign, travelling a cumulative 1,33,349 km, as recorded by the *Times of India*'s detailed rally-by-rally campaign tracker. Rahul Gandhi, the challenger, in contrast, addressed a fewer number of rallies (115), travelling less than the incumbent (1,23,466 km).[60] It is striking that, in the first half of the campaign, Gandhi clocked up more rallies and distance mileage than Modi on the campaign tracker. In the last month, however, while Modi went all-out on rallies and travel, Rahul fell behind.

Even more revealing is where both leaders chose to focus their energies. In UP, which accounts for the most Lok Sabha seats (eighty) and which the BJP swept, Modi addressed thirty-one rallies (13,455 km) compared to Gandhi's twelve (6,564 km). We saw similar trends in most big battleground states, where the number of Modi rallies far outstripped those by Gandhi: West Bengal (Modi: seventeen, Gandhi: three), Bihar (Modi: nine, Gandhi: five), Maharashtra (Modi: nine, Gandhi: four), Odisha (Modi: eight, Gandhi: two). While rally numbers are but one indicator in a complex matrix of factors, they are indicative of a political party's ground-game emphasis.

While Modi seemed to be concentrating on difficult states where the BJP was facing challenges (like UP, with the BSP–SP alliance, or new catchment areas for the party like West Bengal and Odisha), the rally pattern shows that Gandhi travelled more than Modi to states where the Congress already seemed strong: Kerala, Karnataka, Punjab, Rajasthan (after the assembly elections in December). As Congress leader Jairam Ramesh says, 'I don't think we should make the mistake of saying that BJP was winning only because of social media. They are able to supplement social media with door-to-door campaigning by the RSS. Actually, its success is largely due to the fact that it can do good old-fashioned door-to-door campaigning which Congress has lost the art of doing. We used to do that in the 1950s, '60s and '70s. I have seen records of that. After that, we started depending on a charismatic figure and felt that there was no need to do this kind of campaigning.'

'It is easy to over-emphasise the importance of social media,' he says. 'Social media plays a supplementary role in my view, an atmosphere-creating role, but it is not a decisive role. It doesn't substitute for ground politics. I agree BJP was able to deploy good old-style door-to-door campaigning much more effectively and, of course, they also have a multiplicity of campaigners. It enables them to play the good cop, bad cop routine. PM can be above the fray and it is left to Amit Shah and the others to do all the mudslinging and run an incendiary campaign. We also have a multiplicity of voices but unfortunately, the media focuses only on the Gandhis because they think only that is important.'

The BJP's Rollover Ticket Strategy

One of the under-appreciated facets of the 2019 general election is that the BJP changed 115 of its sitting MPs who, it thought, would lose due to local anti-incumbency. The party ended up winning 86 per cent (ninety-nine) of these seats. The ruthlessness on ticket distribution helped the party overcome the hazard of incumbency. This is an old strategy for Modi and Shah, one they had used in the Gujarat assembly elections in the past, where it was common for a large number of sitting MLAs not to have their tickets renewed. Now they replicated it in Delhi. It is possible that, in a wave election, as this one was, the BJP would have won many of these seats anyway. People vote due to a complex matrix of factors, but last-mile campaign strategies do make a difference. In this, the contrast between the two parties was stark.

Message Discipline Mattered

The difference in social-media strategies between the BJP and the Congress illustrates how message discipline works. One reason why the BJP's official social-media handles send out a far greater volume of content than the Congress handles is because, even though Modi was the

Figure 7.7: BJP Won Almost All Seats Where It Replaced Its MPs

Total Seats Where BJP Replaced Sitting MP: 115

Party	*Seats Won in Constituencies Where BJP Replaced Sitting Candidates*
BJP	99
BJP Allies	8
UPA	5
Others	3

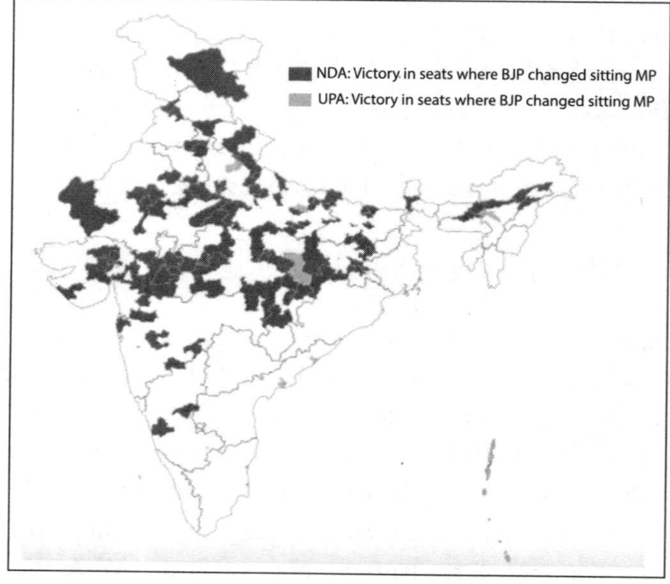

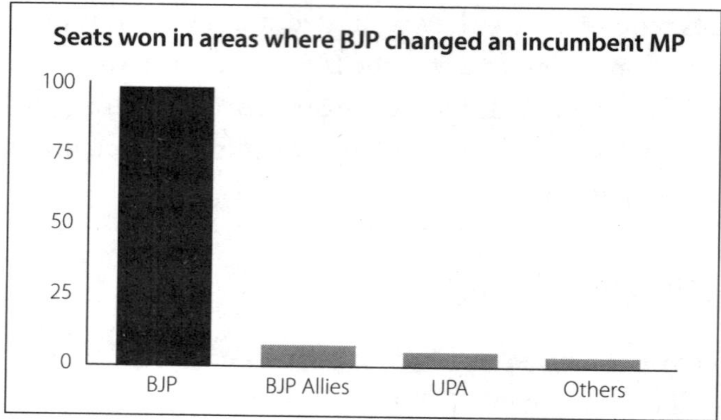

Source: Pollniti, Analysis by Nalin Mehta, Rishabh Srivastava, https://pollniti.com/live.html#, *24 May 2019*

dominant narrative, they put out content from a number of BJP leaders. As one social-media manager said, 'The Congress only largely retweets Rahul Gandhi.' Moreover, in terms of operational message discipline, while every Modi tweet would be retweeted by all the BJP ministers, most senior Congress leaders chose not to echo Rahul's 'chowkidar chor hai' line from their own social-media handles. Rahul himself did not retweet his sister Priyanka Gandhi, who was made in-charge for eastern UP, even once during the campaign. Jairam Ramesh tries to explain this by saying, 'In the public sphere, people are looking only for Rahul or Priyanka tweets. They are not looking for anyone else's tweets. In that sense, BJP is a flatter organisation than Congress. It [the Congress] is a command-and-control organisation, although in reality BJP is also command-and-control party. There is Modi and Shah and then there are others, but they are able to run it in this way.' At the end of the day, social-media strategies are reflective of the organisation they represent and can only be as strong as their backend.

NaMo App vs the Congress's Shakti Platform

The gulf between the trajectories of the NaMo app and the Congress's Shakti platform is reflective of this. By March 2019, the NaMo app had been downloaded 10 million times across Android and iOS platforms, and sold merchandise worth over ₹5 crore. The app, which came pre-configured on Jio phones, has a closed Twitter-like ecosystem, allowing users to post their own content, and also serves as an important two-way system for information-gathering and for surveys.[61]

The NaMo app gave the BJP distinct advantages. Modi conducted a large number of live interactions with party workers using the app. 'The prime minister did a great deal of his direct outreach to booth-level party workers through the app,' says Malviya. 'We used technology to connect with our grassroots workers and we did five constituencies at a time, with the PM speaking to booth-level karyakartas down to the bottom of the pyramid, which was quite impactful. This was pure digital play. It was a lot about who he is as an individual, what he does and so on. For a party, which was a cadre-based party, to have the prime minister of that party speak to the booth-level broker is a different high all together.'

The BJP conducted over two dozen such interactions on the NaMo app between September and January 2019. 'We used to do five Lok Sabha constituencies at a time,' says Malviya. 'This would happen say once or twice a week, depending on how we could organise it.' I asked him how the BJP's digital-media team works operationally, and he says, 'The prime minister's app is managed by the BJP. We have a full dedicated team that does, we do everything that is required to leverage that app. The BJP social media is a content team which is basically like a small newsroom. We cover all rallies of our prime minister and now that of the working president's. Small snippets of their speeches are put out immediately after they have finished. So that if people can't watch all 50 minutes of a speech say, they at least consume fifteen minutes of it in small capsules on social [media] and YouTube. These capsules are two-three minutes each and the narration that we give it makes it interesting.'

Further, the BJP's digital strategy is predicated on training its cadres on how to use digital tools for mobilisation. 'Essentially the bedrock of what we did,' says Malviya, 'is really to train our cadres right down to the booth on how to use technology, how to use WhatsApp and how to get information. So, if they said whatever Modiji's government is doing doesn't feature in the newspapers, we said why do you need to read the newspaper? Go to the Narendra Modi app. All this information is there in its sections. Go to the BJP on Twitter and its Facebook page. They have all the information. So, they knew where to get the information from. And then you go and create such a massive network and also sensitise them to the fact that they can use this information effectively. You do that [at] every level. I've spent the best part of my last four-five years training people in my party in terms of how to look at the Narendra Modi app, how to look at Twitter, Facebook to use it very routinely for political communication.'

'The content we put on these platforms is not very different,' he says. 'How we treat it is different. For Instagram, the content we put is more yuppie and cool. Twitter is more political. Facebook is more sedate yet impactful. We do things differently on different platforms, but essentially the message is the same.' The big difference here is that the BJP sees its digital strategy as a core strategic force multiplier for its organic offline ground game. The digital is intrinsic to the strategy and intertwined with the offline. For the Congress, its digital strategy has been an adjunct.'

In contrast to the NaMo app, the Congress's Shakti platform, which reportedly registered 60–80 lakh users, was created as an internal feedback tool for the party leadership to reach out to grassroots workers, and is said to have informed party decision on issues like Rafale and the 'chowkidar chor hai' campaign. Shakti started as a data-collection project that linked party workers' voter IDs to their mobile numbers through a simple SMS. It was meant to enable direct outreach between the top leadership and booth-level workers. However, after the Congress's electoral defeat, it was engulfed in allegations of large-scale 'bonus registrations', 'fake users' and of 'BJP infiltration'.[62] One report quoted a party general secretary as saying in an internal note that 'between 75-80% of *Shakti* registrations are bogus in each state … Crores of rupees have been sunk by the party in sending SMSes to mostly non-INC people. Consequently, the Congress has a huge database of fake workers with incorrect mobile numbers masquerading as INC workers.'[63]

An early variation of Shakti was tried in Karnataka in late 2017, before the May 2018 assembly elections in that state. Anonymous Congress insiders were later quoted in a report by *The Economic Times* (*ET*) as saying that fake data immediately became a problem. 'There was heavy pressure to collect data at the booth level, so 30%-40% of data had random names and random phone numbers,' said a Karnataka-based Congress functionary to *ET*. Karnataka has around 55,000 booths. So, if the Congress wanted eight–ten people per booth, 4–5 lakh members had to be found. As some insiders claimed, this effort was subverted by fake data.[64]

Incentivising data collection and linking preferential treatment to data volume created a special problem. 'District committee heads were catching every Tom, Dick and Harry, and were enrolling them,' a Karnataka Congress functionary told *ET*. At one stage, the party even held a competition, in which the prize for most enrolments was a meeting with Rahul Gandhi. The end result, party insiders say, was fake data of anywhere between 50 to 70 per cent across states. 'Only 30-35% were your normal karyakartas [workers].'[65]

The party's data head, who spearheaded the Shakti initiative, has denied these allegations. He emailed his colleagues on 23 May 2019, after the results: 'I have spent most of the day today wondering what we could have done differently, why we were not able to catch such a big trend with all the analysis and the surveys and so on. I have concluded there is not much we could have done. I think each of [sic] should be truly proud of your contribution and effort. We fought for a cause and while it may not have been fulfilled yet, we shall continue the fight until it is fulfilled.'[66]

Finally, the NaMo app is not just a messaging-dissemination platform for the BJP. It is also a built-in social network that works like Twitter, where any user who signs up on the platform can post any piece of content (images, videos, website links). Like Facebook and Twitter, allowing unmoderated content means the app can also be used to spread fake news. As the journalist Samarth Bansal reported in 2019, 'The user-generated content is clearly a problem, which makes the problem similar to other platforms. But the NaMo app has another unique aspect: the promoted accounts on the app's news feed, called "My Network". The feed, like on every social media platform, allows users to see all posts from people they follow in one place. But this section also promotes posts from a set of accounts … The promotion of such accounts on the NaMo app makes its millions of users vulnerable to misleading information.' A typical sample of such a post is one by Sanjay Gupta: 'Of the total 40,000 rape cases in India in the last ten years, 39,000 had a Muslim rapist. Still, Congress and Rahul Gandhi say that Hindus are rapists and terrorists. Shame on Congress and Gandhi family!' Another one says '92% of the Muslims voted in Karnataka elections, 86% Christians voted, but just 58% Hindus. 42% Hindus didn't even vote.' Neither is substantiated by data.

The BJP's Malviya is emphatic that the app cannot be responsible for what its users post. 'It is user-generated, anybody can write anything. You can also write in something and it may be wrong. If it is not kosher, how am I going to respond?'[67] As he told Bansal at the time, there is 'some scope for misinformation' on the platform and 'multiple posts have been taken down'.[68]

Cyber Yoddhas, Hate Speech, Fake News and Digital Tools: The BJP View

There is a view that the BJP has been more adept at weaponising social media.[69] How does the party respond to charges of abusive language and hate speech by the IT cell? Malviya argued that the digital domain, where everyone could proclaim their own history and story, allowed the party to bypass traditional gatekeepers of information, build and propagate its own narrative and broadcast it. His response is worth recording in full:[70]

> For a very long time, the narrative was controlled by those who were in power because the only mediums for that were tax-funded institutions and media houses who depended on the state's largesse for their survival. So, you read and heard what the establishment wanted you to do. India is no exception. Then came the internet. It was disruptive in some ways, but not as disruptive as social media is. Social media is really true, it is the spanner in the works.
>
> Now there are people who have opinions who write about it and it gets shared widely. The most read historians today are amateur historians who actually challenged the more established order or the historic narrative. This is similar to the case with politics. The most credible authors are not the ones who occupy exalted positions and media houses, but the ones who have written comprehensively with truth and facts on their side. This change has happened at different levels. Everybody's not going to the same school. They don't speak the same English. Therefore, sometimes how people in some of these smaller towns express themselves comes across as offensive or comes across as being crass.
>
> Most people who otherwise thought that it was their ordained right to pontificate, now when they get challenged on social media, they ignore the argument and focus on the language. I'm not saying for a minute that that's acceptable, but I'm trying to just tell you that, if I don't like something, there are various ways of saying it. I can say it in Oxford English or I could just use an expletive and express myself. But the point remains that you've been questioned, you're being challenged, your narrative is being challenged. You've been called out.
>
> That's what social media has done. To say that the right is more abusive is complete bunkum. The liberals are more illiberal, more intolerant. They are more abusive, but they are like a bunch of well-knit and a closely knit group of individuals. On the other hand, the right-wing is a more diffused network of very competent, well-meaning well-read individuals who actually have a life. And we have a job to go back to. The leftist are surviving on doles from the state government or languishing in campuses and out on the streets protesting, that's really the difference between the two.

> Somebody could call me a troll for having an opinion. But I was a banker who had a million-dollar salary. Somebody could call me a troll, but that doesn't make me a troll.

The BJP attributes such importance to its digital work that when Amit Shah, as BJP president, was asked why he thought Modi had won his first national election in 2014, he responded by listing three reasons: the support of rural Indians, the support of Adivasis, Dalits and OBCs, and the party's work on cyber communications. Speaking to a convention of the BJP's Social Media Workers at Kota in September 2018, he declared that the work of the 'cyber-yoddhas' (cyber-warriors) and 'young workers' was the 'most important' factor behind the victory. A 'small social media cartoon', Shah argued, could often have bigger public impact than a big leader 'shouting his throat out' in a speech. The party's cyber yoddhas, in his view, had the 'ability to change the atmosphere of the whole election campaign'.[71]

Shah illustrated his point by recalling an incident to do with fake news and WhatsApp groups during the 2017 UP assembly poll campaign. The UP BJP, he said, had created WhatsApp groups that included 32 lakh members ahead of the election. This was done so the party could push its own political narrative through the social network. He said of the WhatsApp groups, 'Every morning at 8 a.m., they sent a message, *Satya Jaaniye* [Know the Truth]. Whatever newspapers used to print wrong news about the BJP, their truth was put on WhatsApp. It used to go viral. Whichever paper had printed this, social media volunteers and public also would attack it. They would ask, why did you print such a lie? Print the truth. Your job is to print the truth. So, they [newspapers] got scared and gradually became neutral type. It [social media] has such power.'

One day, a boy on the social media team did some chalaakee (cleverness), said Shah. He posted a fake message on WhatsApp saying Akhilesh Yadav had slapped his father Mulayam Singh Yadav. 'He had not slapped him,' said Shah. 'Netaji and Akhileshji were 600 kilometres apart. But he put it. The state social media team, without understanding it, circulated it below also. It spread everywhere. By 10 a.m., I started getting lots of calls: "Bhai Sahab, you know Akhilesh has slapped Netaji"; "what kind of son is he"; "he didn't become his father's, how will he become ours". It spread. Such work should *not* be done but he spread a kind of atmosphere.'

As the audience of BJP social-media workers broke into laughter, Shah repeated his point. 'It is work that is doable [*karne jaisa*], but don't do it. Did you understand?' Again, he paused for effect, as the audience erupted in applause. 'This is work that is doable, but don't do it. We can do good work also,' he repeated for emphasis. 'The message that we want to spread—whether it is sour, sweet, true or false—that we can take to the public. But this spread could be done because we were ready with WhatsApp groups of 32 lakh people.'[72]

Conclusion: A Tale of Two Websites

In late April 2020, a month into the first COVID-19 national lockdown, I logged in to the BJP website. Its homepage had been taken over by a '#thank you corona warriors' banner. The theme dominated the party's communications. Curious to see what messaging the Congress was running, I then checked out the main Opposition party's website. Its

Figure 7.8: BJP and Congress Website Home Pages on 28 April 2020

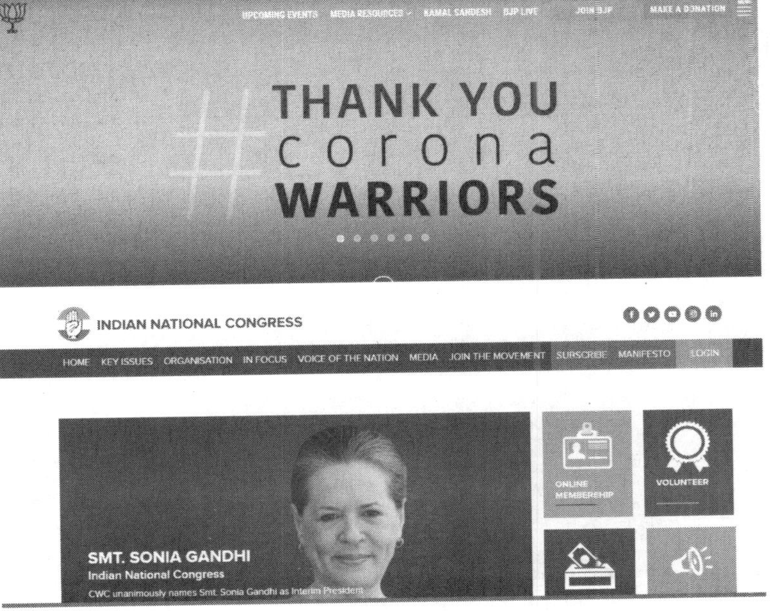

homepage was dominated by a story on Sonia Gandhi being unanimously elected interim party president by the Congress Working Committee. This story was already a few months old at the time—an announcement made in August 2019.[73] Seven months later, in April 2020, it still remained the dominant item on the party's home page. In an environment where things change on a minute-to-minute basis, the home pages of the two rivals offered a striking visual metaphor of how the parties approached

Figure 7.9: BJP and Congress Website Homepages on 20 August 2020

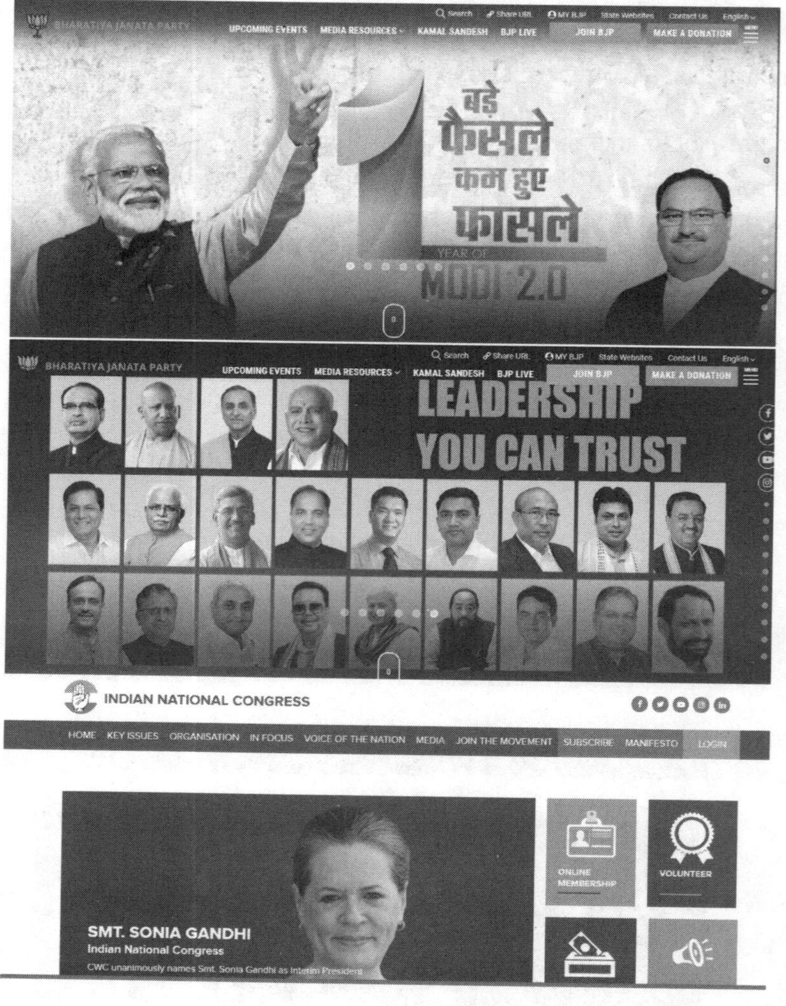

their digital political messaging. I took screenshots of both and put them away in my research files.

Four months later, in late August 2020, I went back to both websites. The BJP's homepage was now dominated by triumphalist messages on the Modi 2.0 government completing its first year in power. Modi and new party president J.P. Nadda were centre stage as part of a rotating loop of six homepage images that a visitor could browse. One of these showcased the mugshots of all the party's chief ministers and deputy chief ministers. The '#thank you corona warriors' message was still there, but it was one among these six rotating images. On the Congress website, though, nothing had changed. It was still dominated by exactly the same story of Sonia Gandhi being re-elected party president that I had seen on its home page in April 2020. Not even a comma had been changed. A full year had passed since that announcement. The CWC was to meet again, later that very week, to decide on its next interim president—but the Congress website remained static in the interim.

The two homepages encapsulated the difference in the digital communication strategies of the BJP and the Congress.

8

HOW THE BJP BECAME THE WORLD'S LARGEST POLITICAL PARTY

Organisational Restructuring and the Use of Digital Technologies

It would have gone unnoticed any other Sunday morning. Vinay Sahasrabuddhe, then BJP vice president, MP and head of the party's Good Governance and Policy Research cells, woke up, planted a party flag outside his Ashoka Road residence in central Delhi and tweeted a picture of himself with it.[1] 'As directed by the @BJP4India leadership hoisted Party flag at my residence and thereby paid tributes to all those whose painstaking efforts made us the largest political Party of the world!' read the accompanying message. 'We are proud of our Party's democratic credentials.'[2]

This was at the height of India's first COVID-19 lockdown. Prime Minister Modi had called on every Indian to light a lamp at their doorstep at 8 p.m. that evening to honour all healthcare and essential services workers. Normal work had long been suspended across the country. But Sunday, 6 April 2020, was also the BJP's Foundation Day, the fortieth anniversary of its inception. And so, in the middle of the national emergency, the party's leaders decided to continue what they call 'sangathan' (organisation) work, but with a COVID-19 twist.

Party President J.P. Nadda had issued an eight-point directive to all party workers. In view of the lockdown, they were to celebrate Foundation Day by planting a 'new party flag' at their residence, ensuring that they maintained 'social distancing while hoisting', and provide food packets to the needy, as well as two home-made masks to 'each person in our booth'. Seamlessly merging the impulses of routine political mobilisation with the imperatives of a national health emergency, Nadda's directive told party workers that 'since BJP will be celebrating its 40th Foundation Day', they should get forty others to donate to the PM Cares Fund and also contact 'forty houses in your booth' and get their signatures on five thank-you letters for police, doctors, safai karamcharis, and bank, postal and government employees.[3]

The voting booth has been at the heart of the BJP's organisational growth efforts since 2014. The party's decision not to forgo its anniversary celebrations and to adapt its voting-booth mobilisation plans for outreach work even during the lockdown reflected how important 'sangathan' work was to the leadership.

A few minutes later, Vinay Sahasrabuddhe tweeted again—this time with photos of himself in a mask, distributing food to local workers: 'In observance of @BJP4India's Sthapna Divas [Foundation Day], remained on fast and distributed home cooked food to few Sanitation and Maintenance Labourers in our residential area, while insisting that they must use masks and take care of hand washing regularly!'[4]

How the BJP Became Larger than the Chinese Communist Party and the RSS

The BJP's cadre growth and membership numbers have not elicited adequate attention outside party circles.[5] This is because the BJP and the RSS have long had a symbiotic relationship, and the RSS's cadre network—which has been the focus of relatively more scholarly and journalistic attention—often helps the BJP in elections. However, the party is distinct from the RSS. While Sangh cadres have always been sympathetic to the BJP, they were never the BJP's own cadres. (A senior RSS leader once famously asked, 'Which other party is there in the country [for us to support], Sonia Gandhi?'[6]) This means that, although the BJP has gained politically from the wider work of RSS workers, it does not control them. It is true that the party has focused on building its own cadres from the day it was born, but its network was not robust enough and widespread enough at the mohalla (street) level in large swathes of India until the early 2000s. So, for decades, it remained deeply dependent on Sangh cadres for voter mobilisation during elections—a situation that had its own pitfalls.

This is why the BJP's Rajya Sabha MP Swapan Dasgupta rightly argued in 2009 that 'One of the enduring political myths of India is the belief that, like the Communist Party of India (Marxist), the Bharatiya Janata Party is a cadre-based outfit. This misconception, spread assiduously by both the media and professional saffron watchers in academia who bank on press clippings as primary source material, is centred on the assumption that the Rashtriya Swayamsevak Sangh is the BJP's dedicated volunteer army. Consequently, the BJP is expected to replicate the disciplined drill of the RSS. When it fails to do so—and the failures are becoming more and more apparent—the party is judged far more harshly than, say, the Congress whose projected image as a big umbrella party has outlived its degeneration into a dynastic outfit.'[7]

Dasgupta's deeper point was that the BJP's party workers, while mostly on the same ideological wavelength, were not as uniformly controlled and the party's organisational structure was not as efficient as that of the RSS. Moreover, the BJP's election ground game in many parts of the country was not dissimilar in structure and efficiency (or inefficiency) to that of other political parties. As has been shown by several scholars of the Sangh as well as the Hindu nationalist movement, for years, the post of organisational secretary (later, sangathan mantri) was key to the office-level work of the party. This was as true of the BJP in 1980 as it was of its predecessor, the Bharatiya Jan Sangh, in the pre-1977 period.[8] Early Jan Sangh leaders from the RSS, like Nanaji Deshmukh, who played a key role in forging anti-Congress alliances with other Opposition parties in 1967, and Sundar Singh Bhandari, exemplified the crossover into the party for key organisational roles in the 1960s and 1970s. But after the BJP led an alliance government in New Delhi from 1998 to 2004 under its first prime minister, Atal Bihari Vajpayee, power clearly began to accrete in the government as opposed to the party, but also, at another level, with the prime minister and party vis-à-vis the RSS. This was an organic process, but it was interrupted by the BJP's defeat in the general election of May 2004.

In the Modi period, however, the BJP has not only twice secured national electoral majorities, it has followed up these triumphs by vastly expanding its presence in the body politic in a way that few in the Sangh or the BJP would have imagined possible even at the turn of the century. While explaining how, why and when this shift unfolded, this chapter also explores possible shifts in the relationship between Nagpur and Delhi.

Between 2014 and 2020, the BJP created a robust organisational structure of its own at the ground level. In its expansion, it has overtaken the Chinese Communist Party (CCP). This massive expansion of the party base, in fact, replicates many organisational techniques of the RSS. It is important to note that China is a one-party state and Communist Party membership is a prerequisite for career advancement, whereas India is a multi-party democracy. In that sense, the BJP's accomplishment within a democratic framework has come against greater odds.

BJP leaders often exult about their party being the largest political party in the world.[9] Critics, on the other hand, tended to either not believe the membership numbers or dismissed the party's organisational growth as inconsequential—as only a vote-gathering machine that somehow comes into play only during election time. Yet, this structural and organisational transformation has been a fundamental enabler of its political power. Not only did district-level expansion help the BJP upend several traditional assumptions of politics in many states, it also fundamentally changed the balance of power between the party and the Sangh.

By 2020, the BJP's cadre network had dwarfed that of the RSS. It remained tied to the Sangh for ideological reasons, but structurally, it was not quite so dependent on the RSS to mobilise votes. If anything, the RSS was now more dependent on the BJP.

Consider this: in August 2014, when Amit Shah became BJP president, the party claimed to have 35 million members.[10] The CCP, then the world's largest political party, was over double the size of the BJP at 87.79 million.[11] The maximum RSS daily shakha strength in 2014—an estimated 4.49 million active members—was about one-seventh of the BJP's members. (The RSS does not officially report its primary membership, but annually reports its daily, weekly and monthly shakhas and training camp numbers.

For our purposes here, I have made an informed estimate of active RSS members from these reports. First, I discounted the monthly and weekly shakhas—assuming that some people who go to daily shakhas may also be going to the weekly and monthly ones. Then, I used the RSS's officially reported number of daily shakhas in a year to make three projections: based on whether the average number of attendees at each shakha was fifteen, fifty or one hundred. The calculation gave us an approximate minimum and maximum range for RSS membership numbers. In our comparison of the RSS, the BJP and the CCP, we used the upper range: one hundred attendees on average per RSS shakha. This gave us an estimated maximum of 4.49 million RSS members in 2014.)[12] In other words, to the BJP's 35 million members in 2014, the RSS had a maximum of 4.49 million.

The BJP tripled in size between 2014 and 2015, the year it surpassed the CCP.[13] Its reported strength of 110 million primary members in 2015 positively dwarfed the CCP's 88.76 million that year. By then, the party was also roughly twenty times the size of the RSS. By 2019, it had expanded to 174 million signed-up members. This was about twenty-nine times the estimated size of the RSS (see Figure 8.1).

Figure 8.1: Membership Patterns of BJP, Chinese Communist Party and RSS

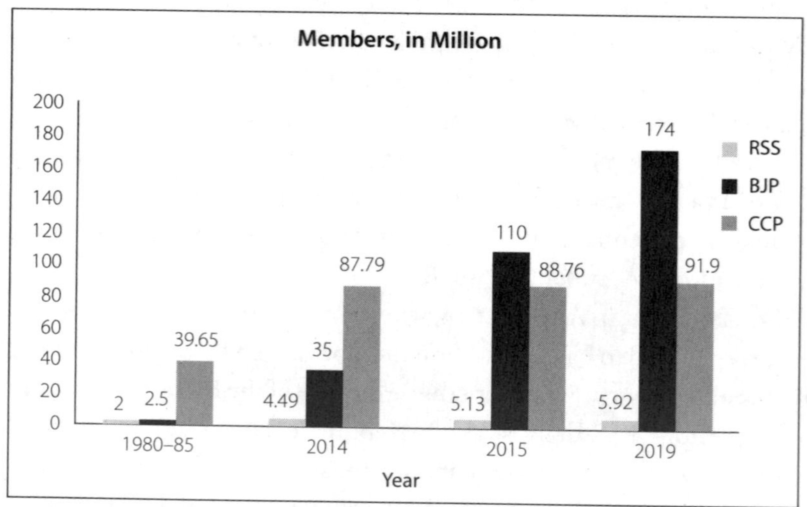

Source: RSS Annual Reports, CCP Organisation Department, BJP, Multiple Media Sources[14]

Put plainly, the BJP grew its membership almost five-fold between 2014 and 2019, during Modi's first government and under Amit Shah's presidency. India's ruling party, in 2019, was claiming membership numbers that were almost twice the size of the CCP.

This does need to be qualified. The BJP has not only been the party in office at the federal level since 2014, it had held power in as many as seventeen of India's twenty-eight states by the end of 2019. It is not uncommon for membership numbers of ruling parties to increase for instrumental reasons. Equally, the RSS has often been significant in states where the party has not been in power until recently, such as Maharashtra, where the BJP was in power only in 1995–1999 and 2014–2019, even while it remained home to the RSS headquarters in Nagpur.

Even if we assume that one-third of the members claimed by the BJP in 2019 were 'transient'—those attracted to the ruling dispensation and in danger of leaving if the party lost power—the BJP would still be much larger than the CCP (20 per cent) and nineteen times bigger than the RSS.

There is no precedence for this kind of mass-enrolment campaign by a ruling party in independent India. The last time such a party-building exercise was conducted at the national level was when the Congress was built, district by district, during the British Raj. This chapter explains how, in a similar fashion, the BJP's expansion of its membership, organisational restructuring and national office-building exercise made it the largest political party in the world.

The BJP achieved its growth by seamlessly meshing a major offline restructuring of its internal organisational structures with the adoption of new technologies and digital tools. Leveraging digital technology gave party leaders the ability to organise a large-scale campaign and verify the expansion in a way that simply was not feasible earlier.

The physical restructuring of the party occurred at the lowest rungs: at the voting booth and district levels. It was based on three fundamental pillars: decentralisation and empowerment of local-level functionaries, reservation of key posts for previously under-represented social groups (OBCs, SCs and women) and the creation of new structures of management oversight at multiple levels. For greater management efficiency and accountability, it adopted digital tools on an industrial scale, like the Zoom app for internal meetings, WhatsApp groups for conversations in real time and verifiable telephone-number listings for every single member enrolled in the party. A mindless embrace of digital tools alone would have been largely useless had it not been backed up by systemic management technique changes. But once the systems were in place, the active use of digital tools that were easily accessed across all generations of devices enabled the BJP to expand its membership with an exactitude that could only have been dreamed of even a decade earlier.

The party's highest growth came in the states of the Hindi heartland (see Figure 8.2).

Figure 8.2: BJP's Membership Growth Driven by Upsurge in Hindi States, 2015

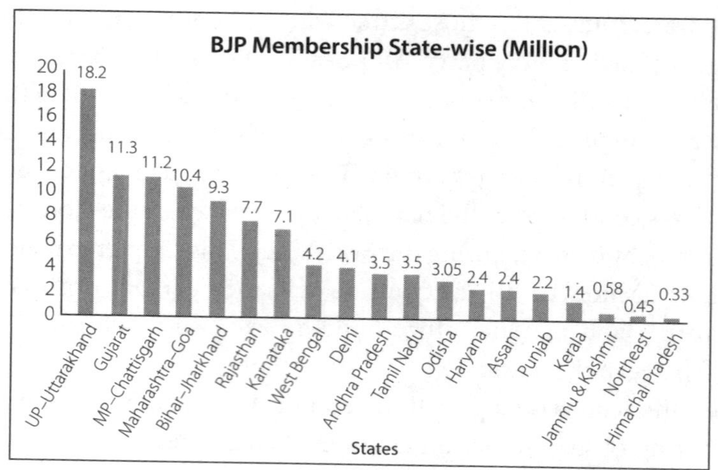

Source: BJP on Twitter, 30 April 2015, https://twitter.com/BJP4India/status/593728757547962369

This growth was bolstered by the construction of over 500 new party offices in approximately two-thirds of India's districts. Extraordinarily, these offices were not just created as functional physical spaces replicating the offices of old, but were each equipped with the best digital technology available at the time. Most also contained an archive. If the revamped structure was the fresh lifeblood of the party, the construction of so many more offices sought to build a modern physical foundation for the new BJP under Modi.

The BJP's cadre growth has significant political implications. It is clear that the party believes this massive expansion, among other factors, contributed significantly to its electoral victory in 2019. Amit Shah said as much in May 2019, about a week before the results were declared. Speaking at a joint press interaction with Narendra Modi at the BJP headquarters, he claimed that the party would win a minimum of 300 seats (a claim that proved correct): 'Look, from 2014 onwards, we have fought a battle for 50 per cent [of seats],' he said. 'The way the Narendra Modi government performed, let me give you two statistics. The central government had over 22 crore beneficiaries of its programmes and we got 17 crore votes in the last [2014] election. In the last [2014] election, we had 2.5 crore workers. This time [in 2019] we have 11 crore workers. We are fighting this election as a 50 per cent campaign, and you may not remember, but in states like Himachal Pradesh, Gujarat, Tripura, we crossed 50 per cent.'[15]

This was more than just a fourfold growth of the number of party workers. The manner of enrolment as much as the scale and pace suggested a new process of political mobilisation at work, where party, government records and welfare programmes each reinforced the other.

The spurt in party membership was the outcome of two major year-long enrolment campaigns: in 2014 (1 November) and 2019 (6 July).[16] It must be noted that both campaigns were launched not before but immediately after the party's election victories. This suggests more long-term aims in party-building and the creation of a system that is more than just a vote-catching machine. Importantly, the first of these, the Sadasyata Maha-Abhiyan (Mega Campaign for Membership), launched on 1 November 2014, did away with previous methods of filling paper forms to enrol members, switching entirely to digital form-filling and phone-based SMS and digital verification methods.[17] It was launched with the specific aim of increasing the party's strength fivefold in order to overtake the CCP cadre numbers.[18]

Party leaders say that each unit was given specific membership targets to meet, which were based on the votes the BJP had polled in each state in previous elections. For example, in West Bengal, BJP leaders say they had 1,44,478 members before the campaign started. Yet, the party had won 87,81,478 votes in the state in the 2014 general elections. 'Many other states had similar figures,' argue Anirban Ganguly and Shiwanand

Dwivedi in a biography of Amit Shah, the party president who designed the expansion plan. He 'based his core strategy on decreasing such wide gaps'.[19] Each state-level target was fixed accordingly.

Figure 8.3: The BJP Switched from Paper Enrolment Forms to Digital Membership Enrolment with OTP Verification

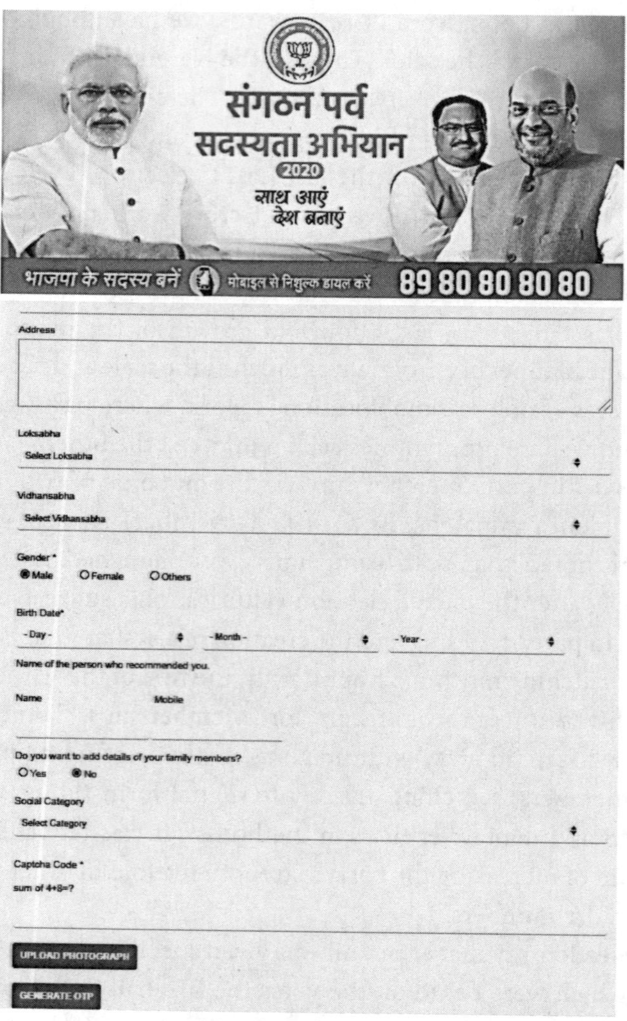

Address

Loksabha

Select Loksabha

Vidhansabha

Select Vidhansabha

Gender *

Male Female Others

Birth Date*

- Day - - Month - - Year -

Name of the person who recommended you.

Name Mobile

Do you want to add details of your family members?

Yes No

Social Category

Select Category

Captcha Code *

sum of 4+8=?

UPLOAD PHOTOGRAPH

GENERATE OTP

Source: BJP Digital Membership Form on Narendra Modi app, 2020, https://www.narendramodi.in/sadasytaparv2019/card/1562399333286

Some caveats are in order. One could argue that the BJP's membership numbers are exaggerated, that its new technique of using missed calls—wherein anyone giving a missed call on the party's recruitment helpline is enrolled as a member after due verification—could be gamed, or simply that some of these growth numbers were fudged. Certainly, critics who question the party's growth allege this.

Yet, the party's growth on independently verifiable digital platforms also dwarfs that of the RSS. The NaMo app, which the BJP used as the focal point of its recruitment drive, had been downloaded over 10 million times on Google Play Store by August 2020—that is the number of Indians who have physically downloaded the app on their phones, as opposed to only passively receiving the party's messaging. Even this number is more than the maximum estimated strength of the RSS. Similarly, the BJP had almost thrice as many Facebook followers (16 million+) as the RSS (5.5 million) in August 2020. Modi's Facebook followers (45.8 million) were eight times more than the RSS's (5.5 million). We see a similar pattern on Twitter where, by August 2020, the BJP's following (14.5 million) was over six times larger than that of the RSS (2.1 million) and Modi's (61.5 million) was about twenty-nine times bigger (see Figure 8.4).

It is important to remember, of course, that the RSS has historically been media-shy. It is also not a political organisation that fights elections. It does not need to cultivate a social-media presence as the BJP does. Yet, the magnitude of the difference between its reach and that of the BJP's on online platforms mirrors the vast gap in their offline membership estimates too. We can quibble about the exactitude of the reported numbers, but broadly speaking, all reported parameters point in the same direction: the BJP is now many times bigger than the RSS and about double the size of the CCP.

New Digital Recruitment Techniques: A Case Study from Mathura

To understand what this expansion meant for the lowest rung of the BJP, I travelled to Mathura in July 2020. COVID-19 cases were surging across UP. Wearing face masks and fortified by the feverish use of hand-sanitisers,

Figure 8.4: Narendra Modi and the BJP Far Bigger than RSS on Social Media Platforms in 2020

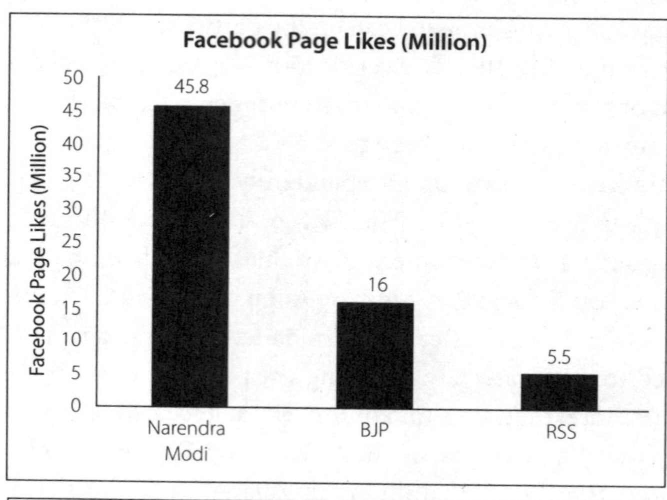

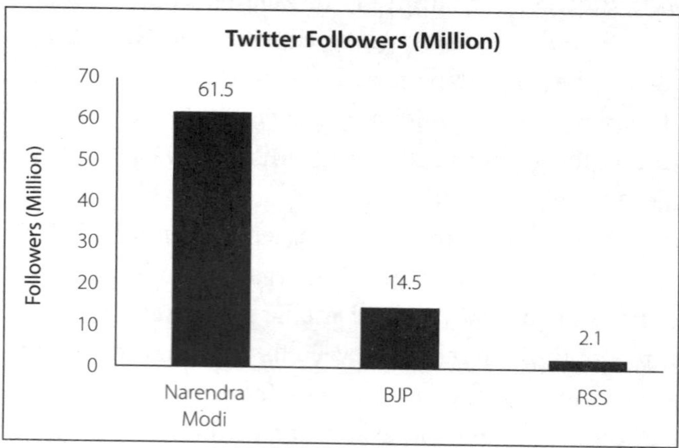

Official Mobile App of Narendra Modi

Source: Social media handles of the RSS, the BJP and Narendra Modi; Google Playstore, 30 August 2020

I visited the office of a local BJP municipality parshad (councillor) to meet with half a dozen senior local party functionaries. We chatted over sumptuous helpings of ghevar (a traditional milk dessert), milky tea and biscuits. The party's Mathura unit had claimed as many as 1 million new members in the recent membership drive—among the highest enrolment numbers in UP. For a district with a total population of 2.5 million (Census of India, 2011), it was an astoundingly large figure. I asked my hosts—all dedicated BJP karyakartas of over two decades' standing—how they enrolled members, how was it different from before, how accurate these numbers were and what it meant for their daily work as political workers. Their answers were eye-opening.

In the Vajpayee years, they explained, the party used to charge ₹3 as a membership fee for ordinary members, who had to fill in a paper form to join the party for a six-year term. This basic fee was increased in the early 2000s to ₹5. The party also had another higher category of more involved workers, the sakriya sadasya, or active members, who paid up ₹100 for a three-year term. Their active status allowed them to stand for and contest local party positions.

When Amit Shah launched the first post-Modi membership campaign in 2014, the party made a number of innovations. It abolished the paperwork required for new members and replaced it with digital enrolment. All an aspiring member had to do was call a toll-free number—18002662020—and the membership fee was waived off. This is why Opposition leaders initially reacted to the BJP's recruitment drive with mirth. 'If it were not tragic for democracy, it would be comic,' Congress spokesperson Abhishek Manu Singhvi said in March 2015. 'If by pressing a button you can get one crore membership in one week, you can imagine the commitment to ideology, the commitment to a party.'[20] What many did not factor in was that the party followed up each of these missed calls with a verification link sent directly to the caller's phone. 'After the missed call, you get a link sent to your phone. On that, you fill your name and verification and send back. Only then do you become a member,' said District Vice President Hemant Agarwal.[21]

Moreover, digital enrolments allowed the party to create a new technology-enabled layer of checks and balances for its existing rank and file. In earlier recruitment drives, party officials charged with executing them had to fill up names of new members 'on paper', said another long-time local leader.[22] But that system could be manipulated by ambitious local party officials looking to gain easy brownie points with their superiors by fudging numbers. To get around that problem, the BJP created a new rule. It told party members that only those who enrolled 100 new members would qualify to be a sakriya sadasya (active member). This was important, because active-member status is a compulsory qualification for any party post. The catch was that the any 100-new-member lists claimed by an aspiring member would now be verified in the new system by higher-ups through digital and phone records.

Technology reduced the possibility of fudging and collusion by local networks of power, even as it allowed the creation of centralised databases that could be checked and rechecked for accuracy at any level, even by a distant call centre. 'Now that system is not there that we can sit in a room, make up members, send the list up and forget about it,' explained a

Figure 8.5: BJP Cadre Work at the Height of the Pandemic-induced Lockdown, April 2020

Vinay Sahasrabuddhe, then BJP vice president and Rajya Sabha MP, planting a party flag outside his Delhi house in the middle of the national lockdown, as per BJP Foundation Day instructions to party cadres, 6 April 2020.

Source: https://twitter.com/vinay1011/status/1247033508112949249?s=20

district party official. 'Now we have to give phone numbers, Aadhaar card number. It is then tallied at that end by them [higher-ups in the party]. Then a call will come from there that so-and-so's number doesn't tally. They actually check and send it back to us. At times, they would send the full list back—saying you have made a wrong list. People's numbers are not tallying. People are saying no, we never joined, they put our name as a member without asking us. Then we have to make the list again. Earlier we could do a lot of farzi wara [fake scam]. That system is totally over now.'[23]

Finally, apart from the demand that they get 100 new party members, the BJP also doubled the membership fee of its sakriya sadasya from ₹100 to ₹200. 'Sakriya sadasya means that such a person can become a member of any party forum, can contest mandal president elections and district

Figure 8.6: BJP's Organisational Work Continued During the 2020 National Lockdown

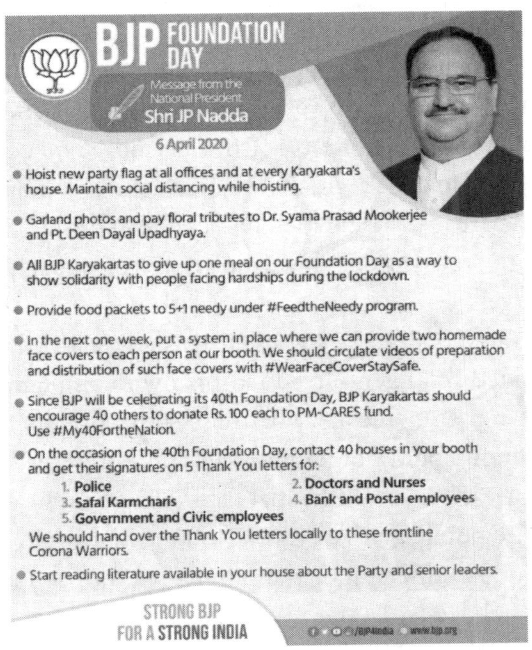

BJP President J.P. Nadda's message to party workers, 6 April 2020. They were asked to celebrate BJP's Foundation Day during the lockdown by planting a party flag outside their house while observing social distancing, to distribute food packets and to get signatures from people in their voting booth area on thank-you notes for COVID-19 workers.

Source: https://twitter.com/vinay1011/status/1246991332519772160?s=20

president elections also,' said Agarwal. 'So that gives an incentive to get 100 members if you want to rise in the party.'[24] The fee also created a more robust system of local funding. In Mathura, for example, of each ₹200 that came in from sakriya sadasya membership fees, half was kept for the district unit and half was sent to the state unit.

Along with this membership drive, Shah also initiated a new party funding scheme at the district level, called 'Aajivan Sahyog Nidhi' (Lifetime Support Scheme), which entailed annual voluntary collections by the party from 'dedicated party workers, big industries and big moneyed people' who 'give of their free will what they want to give'. This scheme runs once a year. Again, 50 per cent of the money raised in this fashion remains with the district concerned and the remaining 50 per cent goes to the state unit.[25]

'Win a Booth, Win an Election': A Worm's-eye View of the BJP

'Why should I make a WhatsApp group of karyakartas?' shouted the angry BJP booth president on the phone. A BJP call centre had contacted him. It was a follow-up call to check whether he had actually completed the work that his boss, the area's district chief, had earlier reported as concluded to his higher-ups: the making of WhatsApp groups of all party workers at the voting-booth level.

When the party's call-centre worker insisted on an answer, the booth president exploded in anger. He added his own complaints: 'After three years you have remembered us. For three years our members' work is pending. One drain could not be made in our gali [street] in three years and ten houses are in water. With what face will I go in the gali to ask votes for someone. The public gives us *gandi gandi gaali* [dirty abuses].'

'I understand, I understand,' the other man, himself a party worker, kept repeating helplessly, in the way that call centre helpline personnel often do, even as the local leader's anger washed over him.

This recording was played for me by the booth worker's district party leader. I was quizzing him on the role of WhatsApp in party management. He responded by saying, 'Let me show you something I should not be showing you. It is against me, but let me make you hear it.' With that, he played this recording on his phone. It had been WhatsApped to him, he said, by the party's IT Cell. They informed him of the problem they had identified at the booth level in his area, asked why he wasn't aware of it and asked him to solve it.

The recording reflected a new layer in the multiple management-oversight systems the BJP had put in place in UP: random checks on the work of the lowest-level members and their performance through a centralised state call centre that had the numbers of all workers across all levels. 'They connected from there [Lucknow] and sent it to me. Our work is to make lists [of party officials] and to send these to Lucknow,' explained the local party official. 'Our IT Cell is sitting there. A group of 300–400 people is sitting there. They work like a call centre. Daily they pick a place and their work is to make checks like this: like today they pick Mathura, tomorrow it will be Agra and so on.'[26]

This system of real-time monitoring was one of the new tech/data-enabled management systems introduced in UP from 2014 onwards. The membership drive was accompanied by centralised data-collection as well as a reshuffling of the party's organisation.

The Importance of the 'Small' Man: A New 'Chair' for Booth Presidents

The BJP's internal reordering was based on a simple organising idea: that the voting booth is at the heart of winning elections. This thesis became the endpoint of all organisational work. When BJP leaders speak of strengthening the foundations of the party, it is the booth level they focus on. Because the lowest grassroots unit of any Indian election process is the voting booth, the BJP has centred much of its structural shift and reorganisation since 2014 on the logistical aspect of getting voters to these booths.

Narendra Modi illustrated this point when speaking to the party's women leaders in Karnataka in May 2018: 'For me, this is the most important thing. And that is to win the polling booth. If we win the polling booth, then no power in the world can defeat us in the assembly election. So, where does victory reside? It resides in the polling booth. Everything else is the impact of that. We have to win the polling booth and the fight has to be fought there.'[27]

This last-mile focus on mobilising the voter at the booth level has driven the expansion-drive strategy in many states. In Karnataka, N. Ravi Kumar, the party general secretary for the state and MLC, summed up this approach to me in early 2020: 'Ten years back, nobody cared about booth-level workers in the party. They only cared about MLAs, MPs or zila panchayat presidents. Now a booth-level president is important in our structure.'[28]

This was in consonance with the mantra that I had heard repeatedly in the BJP's Lucknow office, as well as among the party's higher echelons. For instance, UP Deputy Chief Minister K.P. Maurya had said that the new BJP started giving 'malik ka darza' (status of owner) to newly appointed booth presidents (as quoted in Chapter 3). A few weeks later, I quizzed several booth- and district-level officials in Mathura about whether this claim rang true to them, in practice. They agreed. 'The BJP has six presidents. The party is standing on the shoulders of a presidential system of *six presidents*,' said one. In Mathura, for example, it was about the 'the booth president, the Mathura nagar president, the district president, the Braj region president (one of six administrative regions in UP in the BJP system), the state president and the national president.'

Crucially, while all these units and functions existed earlier too, the formal institutionalisation of the booth president and the importance given to this rung of the party leadership ladder was an innovation. The importance of the policy should not be underestimated, said one booth president. To put this in perspective, the whole of Mathura district—consisting of five state assembly constituencies and one Lok Sabha seat—had about 2,100 polling booths in 2020.[29] The BJP, after 2014, appointed presidents in each of these booth areas. Suddenly, the city of Mathura was full of party officials with an important-sounding presidential title.

As a BJP city corporator and former booth president in UP told me, 'Whatever you say, if you make a small man a booth president, he says "I am a president" with pride. He will remain at his work. Earlier, we used to have only zila [district] and nagar [city] presidents. There were only two presidents in a city. Whereas now, *adhyakash hee adhyaksh hain* [there are presidents and presidents].'[30]

The party also instituted another practice to encourage the new booth presidents. 'A very good thing happened in this time,' exclaimed the party's Mathura district general secretary, Pradeep Goswami. 'Whatever meetings happen in any area, whether of PM or of sangathan [organisation] president, that area's booth president will be honoured on the stage. This was to develop the booth. Whether it is a small meeting like in a nukkad, this area's booth president we have to *always give a chair.* If we give that chair, the booth president will move a little forward. He gets honoured and comes forward to work. So, his graph rose in the party.'[31]

The result was greater local reach and a more empowered local cadre. If a booth president complains about an MLA or an MP, said a local corporator, 'he is now taken seriously'. If he complains about 'us', he summed up, '*hamaare kaan khare ho jaate hain* [our ears perk up]. That is the big change.'[32]

The new BJP's party structure is built upwards from the booth. While there are variations between BJP state units, the basic principle of strengthening the voting-booth ranks is common everywhere. In Karnataka, in February 2020, the party had counted over 8,00,000 lakh active party workers. Sitting in BJP's Bengaluru office in Malleshwaram, N. Ravi Kumar, the party's state general secretary, explained the break-up of this number and how the organisational tree branches upwards. The state has '58,000 booths, so we have 58,000 booth presidents. Then we have two secretaries per booth, so that means 116,000 booth secretaries. Then we have 58,000 booth pramukhs. Each booth has a thirteen-member committee, so that amounts to 13* 58,000 people, i.e. 754,000 members. Then there are thirty-seven districts and district committee members are 160. We have 300 mandals in the state and sixty members in each mandal—like karyakari member, executive member, mandal president, vice president, general secretary and so on.'[33]

Nationally, India has 10,35,000 voting booths. The BJP claims that it had set up booth-level committees in 83 per cent of these (8,63,000) between 2014 and 2019. The party also identified 1,64,000 clusters of booths (each cluster acting as a nodal point for five–seven booths each). The BJP termed these clusters 'Shakti Kendras', or Power Centres. It had set up operations in 92 per cent of these (1,52,000) within the 2014–2019 period.[34]

The BJP's 2019 election campaign was built on the cascading layers of this organisational structure. While popular attention focused on the big leaders and the Modi–Gandhi contest, the BJP began its poll campaign first with nationwide booth sammelans (meetings). The membership-expansion drive after the 2014 election, in that sense, provided the deeper foundation for the 2019 poll campaign. The drive itself had been predicated on two major pillars.

The first was the Vistarak Yojana (Expander Scheme), which began in April 2017 from Naxalbari in West Bengal, where the Naxalite movement had begun in 1967. The yojana encompassed thousands of party workers—characterised as vistaraks—who agreed to spend between fifteen days, six months or a year in specific booths. The party claims that 2,77,922 vistaraks committed to fifteen-day booth visits.[35]

The second was the Shakti Kendra Yojana, which involved the setting up of cluster heads to supervise four–five voting booths each. The party held over 150 cluster meetings and organised 482 election-organisation committees for the national campaign, manned by 7,830 workers. Almost 3,000 party workers worked full-time and without a salary in 2,566 assembly constituencies for about two years.

A significant part of Narendra Modi's personal election campaign in 2019 was focused on booth-level workers through the NaMo app, as part of a programme called 'Mera Booth Sab Se Mazboot' (My Booth Is the Strongest). Away from the media glare, Modi held live video interactions with booth-level workers in almost every Lok Sabha constituency—in clusters of five each—through the NaMo app in the months leading up to the campaign. As part of these video meetings, the BJP claimed that Modi interacted in 2019 with over 10,000 BJP workers and over 7,000 beneficiaries of Union government schemes like the Jan Dhan Yojana or Ujjwala.[36]

The final thrust of the campaign included using the party's ground-level structures for outreach to beneficiaries of government-funded social-welfare programmes. For this, the BJP set up 161 call centres in 2019, manned by 15,862 callers, most of whom were party workers. Between them, they specifically targeted 24 crore 81 lakh beneficiaries who had gained from government programmes.[37] While the call centres targeted them through phone calls, the party's booth-level workers worked on reaching them directly. This outreach culminated on 26 February 2019 with an announcement by the BJP that it had organised a nationwide programme wherein lamps had been lit in the houses or localities of all these beneficiaries on a single evening.[38]

Even if half of this claim was true, it could only have been made possible through the grassroots reach of its booth-level workers.

Six Presidents, Six Committees and Reservations in the Party's Structure: The New UP Model

In tandem with creating new booth heads in UP, the BJP also instituted a caste- and gender-based reservation system for local-level party posts. We have already seen how, after 2014, the party brought in a new generation of OBCs at the district president level in UP (see Chapter 3). It also created a system of reservations at its lowest levels for women and castes that had traditionally not identified with the party. At the booth level, for example, each president works with a twenty-one-member karyakarini (executive council) of officer-bearers (vice presidents, general secretaries and so on). After 2014, the party began to reserve two seats each for OBCs and SCs and five seats for women among these members. 'This is fixed,' said a district-level leader. 'We have to have that in those twenty-one-member bodies at every level. Whatever level it is, we have to have SC, OBC, women, like this.'[39]

This was such a major change from the BJP's usual catchment of members that, initially, it was difficult to find enough candidates to fill these reserved cadre posts. 'The people weren't there,' a district general secretary explained to me. Many of the early reserved quotas for women, for example, were filled by relatives of local leaders. 'If you want to fill five women, then you make someone's wife, someone's sister and so on. If we had to choose five women, then four we did only to fill the quota but one woman that was genuinely new. That one woman turned into ten—but those ten new ones came from that first one. They came slowly. They did not come together.' The same thing initially happened with Dalits and backward quotas. 'Because five backwards had to be named in each list,' said the leader, 'we put anyone's name down. But we had been talking about it at different places. If we talked to fifty people, then maybe five came in, but these five became the starting point for reaching out to others.'[40]

The new quotas were a means of breaking into new communities. A Brahmin district general secretary spoke to me about the initial internal reluctance to the party's new organisational quotas and the impact of the change. He recalled that he went to have tea for the first time in a Valmiki basti. 'I am a Brahmin,' he said. 'I have a mandir in my house. If anyone comes, they cannot enter my house without having a bath. But this was sangathan work and we were told to enrol Dalits. I myself went to a Valmiki basti and had tea. Many people next to me said, how can we do this? They said no. The day I had tea in one Valmiki's house, one thing changed. After that, if I had to organise a crowd for a rally, through that one person's medium, in whose house I had tea, I could fill one bus of people for the rally from his Valmiki basti. This experience taught me that if just one cup of tea can bring you fifty people for a bus for Delhi–Lucknow, then imagine the possibility if you work with them more. I found it was more uneasy to work with Brahmins and Baniyas. With Dalits, it is easier if you work with them, because you get respect faster if you honour them.'[41]

These quotas were politically instrumental, for sure. But they also brought in a new base of voters to the party. The BJP believes that many voters in that Valmiki basti gravitated to the party for the first time in the assembly elections that followed. In Mathura city, for example, the upper-caste population is about 65 per cent. But in July 2020, the BJP's elected mayor in the city was a Dalit in a non-reserved post.[42] 'If in such a seat, our mahapaur [mayor] is SC, then you can imagine yourself,' summed up another local party official.[43]

A Digital Party: Lists, Zoom Calls and Targeted Politics during the National Lockdown

This restructuring and expansion of the BJP was accompanied by the creation of an effective oversight mechanism. When I met a group of district-level BJP workers in UP in July 2020, in the middle of the COVID-19 lockdown, they explained how their work was assessed through a detailed reporting system. Each level had to provide regular reports that were cross-checked by a designated supervisor from the level above. As one of the cluster in-charges in Mathura explained, 'Just before we met you, we were having a virtual meeting. One programme barely ends, and within two days, we get a list from the party for new programmes. At each level, we check if the president below us is working or not. From there, it will go to the national team. If they are not working, if they are not going to the field, we will appoint another one.'[44]

Even as the party decentralised, systematised digital lists of its active members right down to the booth level allowed greater oversight from the regional, state and national leadership. Where senior leaders were once dependent on local power networks that had their own dynamic, these databases allowed them greater direct outreach to the lowest-level worker. 'We get a phone [call] daily from Lucknow,' said one district-level leader. This was through a centralised call centre that put through calls between state-level leaders and booth-level workers. 'They ask which all booths you went to, what are the issues, what work is going on? They want full feedback. It is not like they don't know what is happening at the local level even if I say something ulta-seedha.'[45] Another explained that when local district officials sent lists of their office-bearers up the chain of command, 'often they sent the list back, saying the phone numbers are not matching. They would have called and checked … Or sometimes they call a few presidents. They try two-three times. If there is no response, they come back to us, saying so-and-so booth president of yours is not working. Or such-and-such phone number is wrong. The big change is that they do this monitoring of our work. It is multi-layered and real-time.'[46]

The creation of a digital pipeline of communication, based on a booth-level enumeration and a centralised database, enabled party leaders to switch seamlessly to daily digital meetings with party workers on the Zoom app when physical outreach became restricted during the 2020 lockdown. In UP, a district vice president told me in July that his workers had not had 'even one minute of rest' during the lockdown. His team, he said, had never used Zoom before, but started doing 'per day meetings' on the app. 'Sometimes we have zila meeting on Zoom app, sometimes mahanagar meeting, sometimes IT heads' meetings, sometimes Yuva Morcha meeting, sometimes a meeting of the Mahila Morcha.' He claimed emphatically that, by July 2020, the BJP had conducted 45 lakh such meetings.

There is no way to independently verify this claim, but the sheer scale of the BJP's shift to Zoom was undeniable. This shift was clearly visible on social-media platforms from April 2020 onwards. Typically, each meeting was followed by party officials taking screenshots and posting pictures of them on social media handles for further publicity (see Figures 8.6 and 8.7).

Figure 8.7: A BJP Virtual Meeting in UP's Deoband, Voting Booth Numbers 387 and 388, July 2020

Source: Pictures posted on Facebook by BJP Workers After a Virtual Rally, July 2020. From Pankaj Tyagi, general secretary, BJP, Saharanpur district, July 2020

This digital turn provided the BJP with a valuable means of two-way organisational communication with its cadres amid the economic strife and uncertainties caused by the pandemic. The party institutionalised Zoom-level meetings as a listening tool and as a platform to keep cadres continually engaged. A measure of the importance of these meetings was that, in UP, the party required its ministers and legislators to attend every sub-district-level Zoom meeting, each of which involved a few hundred workers. 'It is compulsory for them to attend,' said a district vice president in Mathura proudly. 'Even ministers and MPs are not exempt. Then only there will be motivation. Even Hemaji [Hema Malini, Bollywood actress and Mathura MP] had to attend. If only karyakartas and those at the bottom are made to sit in such meetings and those on the top are exempt, they will question what is the point.'[47] The BJP saw these virtual meetings as much as an internal HR measure as it was a tool of political mobilisation. A district-level leader in UP explained the organisational purpose of these daily digital Zoom conversations during the lockdown:[48]

> The main point is that between karyakarta and party, saamanjasya [coordination] should not break. If saamanjasya breaks, then bad feelings will take over. At this time, there are bad feelings about this Corona epidemic. Everybody is troubled. That should not take birth. If the karyakarta breaks away, then it's a problem. The karyakarta should not break. That is why this is done to keep in sampark [contact] with the karyakarta.
>
> Even if they don't listen to him, and the neta says what he wants to say, but the conversation is on. The karyakarta feels at least they are heard somewhat and some conversation is on. Many karyakartas are happy that at least they got some hearing like this. Through Zoom app many are happy that at least somebody met them, saw them. He feels obliged that he is being taken seriously. This is digital India and a digital party.

Crucially, during the lockdown, at least in UP, the BJP continued its targeted outreach to beneficiaries of government schemes, which had powered its politics in the state before the pandemic. It simply switched to having the Labharthee Sammelans on Zoom. The high penetration of mobile phones in rural UP and the availability of digitised lists with phone numbers enabled this. It was one reason why, even as the Coronavirus ravaged the economy in 2020, the BJP leaders I met in UP remained confident that they had not been damaged too much politically (this was before the second wave of the pandemic hit the state in early 2021). In July 2020, in the week I travelled to Mathura, the party's city unit had conducted Zoom meetings between Deputy Chief Minister Keshav Prasad Maurya and local groups of beneficiaries: those with BPL cards who had recently got electricity connections, those who had received chulhas under a government scheme and so on. Such meetings, local officials told me, had been conducted 'scheme by scheme'.

How did they manage this, I asked. A district-level party official explained: 'All [government] departments today have lists. We do aadaan-pradaan [exchange] of those lists. The lists also have phone numbers. Without a phone number, nobody becomes a labharthee. So, for example, PM Awaas Yojana has houses, those lists come to us. We check them from our side. We see if it is correct or not, whether there are complaints or not, if there is a problem or not ... We had full names. That is how we can now approach them and call them for Zoom calls. Then only we can connect them with the Zoom app.'[49]

Data was key to this entire outreach. 'Our work in the lockdown has not stopped,' said the district leader. 'But it has all gone online.' What did this mean for their daily work as party workers at the district, I asked. 'One mahamantri has a permanent duty on the computer for this only,' he responded with a wry smile. 'For this work with data and database.'[50]

WhatsApp Groups, Social Listening, Outreach and IT Heads

There has been a lot of attention on the use of WhatsApp in India for spreading fake news (see Chapter 7). But the BJP's use of it as a fundamental tool of party organisation has been relatively underappreciated. Alongside its leadership structure at the district levels, the party instituted a parallel governance structure for IT after 2014. These new IT teams mirrored the BJP's organisational structure at every administrative level, working in coordination with it. For instance, the party leadership has divided UP into six regions. An IT head was appointed for each of these. So, if we take Braj region (one of the six), the IT head had a second tier of IT heads for each district that came under his jurisdiction. Within districts, each mandal also had an IT head. Mathura, in the Braj region, for example, has thirty-two mandals. Each of them has a separate IT head. Their work centred on organising digital meetings and getting each booth president in the city to create official BJP WhatsApp groups in their areas.

'IT heads are different and sangathan heads are different,' explained a BJP district general secretary over hot chai in Mathura's Holi Gate area. 'If we want to do an online meeting here in Holi Gate mandal, then the district IT head will check the IDs and the Holi Gate IT head will coordinate. Others will connect with him.'[51]

A key priority of the IT heads is to organise WhatsApp groups at the booth level. Of approximately 2,100 polling booths in Mathura, local leaders estimated that they had active WhatsApp groups in 70 per cent (1,500–1,600) of them by July 2020. For the party, these WhatsApp groups performed two functions: as platforms to disseminate outward uniform messaging, but equally for socials listening from the ground up. Amit Shah outlined this approach in an address to the BJP's social media workers in September 2018 in Kota, Rajasthan.

Their work, Shah told them, had three objectives: one, data, research and analysis; two, actioning data through electronic means by samvad (communication) from 'bottom to the top and from top to the bottom'; and three, maximum spread of messaging. To achieve these aims, he asked them to organise in three ways: put together a team for data, research and analysis, a team for expansion and a creative team. 'This [political] war is such,' he said, 'only he can win who has the strength for spreading [faelaav].' He argued, 'Neither fire nor air have the power, have the power that is with those who have the power to spread [faelaav]. The one who spreads [*jo fael jaata hai*] becomes powerful, and youth have the capacity to spread.' Before the UP election in 2017, he claimed that the BJP had as many as 32 lakh people in its WhatsApp groups in the state (15 lakh and 17 lakh).[52]

The use of digital technology would not have been as impactful without the physical reordering of the party and its ground-level sangathan. The impact of this booth-based structure was such that, when the BJP faced nationwide protests against the Citizenship (Amendment) Bill, it was able to mount a swift counter-protest response.

In Karnataka, for example, in February 2020, the party's central high command targeted reaching 3,00,000 houses with the BJP's counter-messaging on the CAA. The Karnataka unit state says that, using this structure, it accessed 3,21,000 households and distributed party pamphlets on the issue to each of them within a month.[53] The party's general secretary in Karnataka, N. Ravi Kumar, told me that most of its mobilisation programmes, like the one in favour of CAA, are built around such databases. 'For any abhiyan [campaign] at the national level, there is a call centre for important office-bearers to coordinate,' said Kumar, whose job revolved around coordinating such party work.

He gave me a useful illustration of how this worked in practice. 'If the BJP president has given a call to do some action, like holding marches or reaching out to households, then our office becomes the nodal point in our state. The BJP's organisation secretary, B.L. Santhosh, will first do a video call with state general secretaries in thirty states. Then, we at the state level will do video calls with all district general secretaries and presidents. We use a lot of technology for this. WhatsApp is big for this and video calls. These calls are then followed up by meetings at the ground level, at mandal, shakthi kendra and district level. There are 224 assembly constituencies in Karnataka with about six–seven zila panchayats in each constituency. We will do meetings in each zila panchayat conducted by the mandal padadhikary [office-holder].'[54]

The party's ground-level machinery of booth workers mobilises with very specific action points during elections. In March 2018, Amit Shah held a day-long pre-poll preparatory conclave with BJP's office-bearers, MPs and booth-level presidents in Karnataka at the Royal Orchid in Yelahanka. One of the outcomes of this meeting was a list of sixteen steps the booth workers were asked to follow. They were to implement the following to-do list in order to identify and engage with sixteen categories of people in their booth area:[55]

*Appoint a page pramukh [page head, explained in the next section]
*Mobile lists: Create a list of everyone with a mobile phone in their booth and list their mobile numbers. Call them yearly for flag-hoisting on national days, on the BJP's foundation day, for Vajpayee Jayanthi and to create other occasions for interaction
*Two-wheeler lists: It was important to identify those with two-wheelers because two-wheelers can be used to transport voters to the booth on voting day
*Focus on:
Youths under 35
Farmers

Businessmen
Dharmadhikari: religious leaders like swamis and temple priests
Influential people: five to six per booth
Shopkeepers
Doctors
Old BJP karyakartas
Disgruntled Opposition leaders: Those who may in the future be persuaded to defect from other political parties and join the BJP. Go and meet them and stay in touch with them

*Set up:
Social media power:
Control room for every assembly segment
Control room at every district level
Shakti Kendra at zila panchayat level
WhatsApp group for every 100 people at booth level.

The detailing may vary across states but there is a common, broadly tech-centred organisational approach. It is not that the BJP did not have a local cadre before. In UP, for example, the party had begun booth-level cadre-building work in the 2002–2004 period when Vinay Katiyar was the state unit's chief. Booth-level heads were appointed even then and committees were organised around them, though they were not designated as presidents. What changed after 2014, when Sunil Bansal as general secretary started reorganising the UP unit, was a deepening of the older system and a much greater degree of precision through data and usage of digital technologies. As one UP district vice president told me, 'after Corona happened', the party could switch to 'virtual meetings' on such a large scale only because it had the 'full database ready'. By 2020, in UP's districts, he said in each of the 300 polling booths in his Vidhan Sabha constituency, the party had multiple lists of: five people with motorcycles, five with smartphones, five influential people, five who could provide funds. 'Such lists are ready at the booth level,' he said. 'These lists are over and above the lists of our office-bearers and their committees at these booths. This work is happening because of that policy' of depth of organisation.

Panna Pramukhs and Vistaraks: An Idea from Gujarat

The BJP's booth-level mobilisation is driven deeper during election periods by two new local entities that are largely active only during the campaign season: panna pramukh (page head/in-charge) and vistaraks (expanders).

A panna pramukh is essentially in charge of a single page (panna) of the voting list in their area's voting booth. To understand how this works in practice, let us zoom in on Karnataka. As Ravi Kumar explained, 'A very important part is played by the panna pramukh for the party. There are thirty-two pages in a booth-level voter list in Karnataka. So, thirty-two panna pramukhs will be there for a voting booth, one for each page. Their job is to go to five-six houses, whose members are listed on that page, and to connect with them at least a couple of times in a year, election or no election, so 100 per cent connect is there for the party.'[56]

Of course, appointing last-mile workers like panna pramukhs is one thing; getting them to win over voters is another. The idea is to essentially build a network of local relationships. Yet, it has obvious operational pitfalls as well. 'Basically, it has its own strength and its limitations,' says BJP's Vinay Sahasrabuddhe, who as party vice president was co-in-charge of the BJP's membership expansion campaign. He explained what the party expects from its page in-charges and how they are supposed to build local relationships:[57]

> If I am a panna pramukh and there are about thirty names on my list, the party instructs me *ke bhaiiya sab ke ghar jaao, baat kar ke aao* [Brother, go to each one's house and talk to them], which I dutifully do. Then the party also tells me that, before the day of the voting, I should also make calls to each of these people. But there is a catch—the idea is to build a relationship and kinship. It all depends on the manner in which you approach this. Imagine if you are a panna pramukh and you start feeling important that you are in charge of twenty–twenty-five people. You go to interact with families with this in mind, normally with three–four people, and if there are ladies at home in say the afternoon, they can also get scared, that so many people have come saying press your finger on the *kamal ka phool* [lotus symbol] vote button. Do you think anyone will ever say no? They all say yes-yes, we will do it. Just appointing the panna pramukh doesn't mean that you have already won the people's hearts.

> So, that is not exactly the relationship we expect. What we expect is something different. It is easy to make a phone call and just say that remember I called earlier, now please remember that the *kamal ka phool* button is the second from the bottom on the voting machine, so please press it. Nobody says to your face, if they do, it is their strength. It only works if there is a regular relationship-building. Then it means something. There is no point in becoming a panna pramukh if you are just making phone calls during election time. It has no benefit. Only if you are in regular touch and build relationships, then panna pramukh brings benefits.

The BJP has worked out very specific instructions for its booth-level workers so they can stay in touch with constituents in the manner the party wants them to.

The panna-pramukh model, which was first tried successfully in Gujarat by the BJP, was expanded to UP in the 2014 and 2019 general elections, as well as the 2017 assembly elections, and to Karnataka in the 2018 assembly elections. Typically, the BJP sorted each voter on a voting list page given to a panna pramukh into three categories: A (those who would surely vote for the BJP), B (those who may swing either way) and C (those who will vote against the BJP). The job of the panna pramukhs was to convert C category voters to B and B category voters to A.

In tandem with the panna pramukhs, in 2017 in UP, the BJP instituted a parallel system of constituency oversight through the deployment of what the party called 'vistaraks' (expanders). In each of the 403 UP Vidhan Sabha constituencies and eighty Lok Sabha seats in 2019, it posted a vistarak. These were deeply ideological party workers who volunteered to spend between six to twelve months working in constituencies away from their homes. They were deployed in constituencies '100/150/200 km away' from their own seats for long periods. Their job was to function as external listening posts for the central leadership in these areas. The vistaraks could not interfere with the local leadership but were tasked with providing daily parallel feedback and 'whole detailed ground reports' to the party on what was really happening, over and above what the local units were telling their superiors. As one local leader told me, they would provide inputs like 'the president is not working, or is not intervening or this community [biradari] is not voting for us or voting for us. This issue is there or not there.'

Vistaraks were volunteers who undertook this intelligence-gathering work free of cost. The party provided them with boarding and lodging. As the leader explained, 'If, for example, I give the party one year or so, they would send me 100/150/km way to Faizabad or Azamgarh. I will be given one vidhan sabha there. The sangathan there would keep doing its own work separately. From that sangathan I only get my stay, food and stay in touch … Apart from that, I cannot interfere in the sangathan there, but the whole day I will move around for the party's work: in different communities [samaaj], in meetings, in party meetings, in offices.'

These workers provided a parallel channel of ground information to the party's planners. The role of ideology was paramount here. 'Our biggest success was that we could take out such workers,' said the local leader. 'The party thought of this, yes, but that many people were ready to do this and came out, this was a big thing for a year.' The importance of the vistaraks was that, when a 'neta goes, people speak to him because everyone want to engage with a leader, but when a normal guy comes with a thaila [bag], he understands things differently and engages with him differently.'[58]

BJP vs Congress vs JD-S: A Ground Game Example from Karnataka

Parties do not win elections through organisational structures alone. That is not the claim being made here. The point is that building a ground game gives the party a better chance of success. In close elections, it could make all the difference.

In Karnataka, for example, the Bengaluru-based political journalist Sandeep Moudgal pointed out what this kind of party organisation means in real terms for the BJP, in relation to its political opponents—the Congress and the Janata Dal (Secular) (JD-S). 'When they hold campaign rallies, for Congress and JD-S, this means getting together a crowd of people. Congress and JD-S both rely on local leaders to get people in for a rally. In Congress, when they organise a Rahul Gandhi rally here, for example, they would pass instructions from Delhi to someone here, who would then pass instructions to the next ten leaders, then to the next ten and then next ten leaders. By the end, it will be very haphazard. In the BJP, when a senior leader visits, it is different. They will first talk directly to the ten leaders on the ground. Then they would send a recce team, followed by a dedicated team of three-four leaders which comes from outside to each place to do ground work and to ensure coordination between local people and people from outside. BJP has booth-level workers in 80 per cent of booths. BJP's organisation is much more advanced compared to Congress, and the building blocks of their structure are the difference. The focus in BJP is on booth workers and efficiency. Yeddyurappa did the ground work initially, now they have worked to build an organisational structure around that foundation.'[59]

Interestingly, the Congress tried to emulate this strategy in the 2018 assembly elections in Karnataka. Digvijay Singh, as the state-in-charge for the Congress, tried to build a cadre mentality at the booth level. But, at the end of the day, 'Congress is a brass party. It is the leader which generates a crowd in Congress, not the other way round. Congress simply couldn't match the organisation of BJP.'[60]

For BJP leaders, the fundamental difference between them and their opponents is the 'importance of organisation'. 'The difference on the ground is the importance of the karyakarta. In the Congress and the JD-S, they are only active when elections come. Even if there are no elections, we are doing our work regularly,' says Ravi Kumar.

A Party Office in Each District

Politics is often about ideas. But ideas by themselves cannot effect change. They need to be disseminated effectively, else they remain ineffectual. This is why a political party's organisational structures are as important as its ideology. As the American general Omar Bradley put it, 'Amateurs talk strategy. Professionals talk logistics.'

Building the logistical structure required to power its organisation is precisely what the BJP has focused on since winning the general election in 2014. 'Victories in elections are often achieved,' Amit Shah has argued, 'but strengthening the organisation in a sustained manner is a much more difficult task and this is the opportune period when we have won elections ... We have to lay the firm foundation so that for the next hundred years the BJP can emerge as a mighty and magnificent edifice.'[61]

The most visible marker of what the BJP's leaders mean by a 'firm foundation' lies in their decision to buy land and build party offices in almost every Indian district. In its national executive meeting in April 2015, the party made a decision to own an office in 635 of the country's 694 districts.[62] A measure of the ambition of this task is that, until 2017, it owned land for offices in only 190 districts (27 per cent of India).[63] Since then, it has focused on achieving this goal at breakneck speed.

Karnataka is a good case study for how this process unfolded. 'In two years, we will build our own offices in all thirty districts of the state,' Ravi Kumar declared confidently to me in February 2020. We were meeting in his office at the party's brand-new building in Bengaluru. I had asked him how the party was moving along on building district offices. 'We already have offices of our own in ten districts [Ballari, Mysuru, Mangalore, Udupi, Chamarajanagar, Mandya, Hubli, Davanagere and Shivamogga],' he answered. 'In eighteen other districts, we have purchased the land already.'[64]

The southern Karnataka district of Mandya reflects the speed at which the party moved. When Sandeep Moudgal visited it in May 2018 for the Karnataka assembly elections, the BJP did not own an office there. 'They had a small place and were operating out of there,' he said. In his recollection, during the 2019 Lok Sabha elections, B.L. Santosh, the BJP's national organisation secretary, visited Mandya and told the local party officers, 'whatever you guys need you will get. If you need space or if you need money, both will come.' The local unit then, as a first step, took a place on lease at ₹1,80,000 a year and set up a party office there. 'Now they have an office in Mandya,' he pointed out to me in February 2020. 'It was sanctioned within ten days by the BJP leadership.[65]

The BJP has been focused on building district party offices because it sees them as the skeletal structure holding together the party organisation. As Ravi Kumar explained, party offices are important because they act as organisational focal points for joint activity. 'Everyone will come to our office,' he said. 'State president and general secretary are active within the party. They are meant to call for programmes each month. They have to do it as part of their jobs. In each programme, there is a call centre at the mandal level and at the district level to call people. If a big event happens, for example, Delhi election results will come tomorrow, if our party gets a majority, then, in all 300 mandals, small gatherings will be held to observe Vijay Utsav. There is an email to everybody that will be sent and the district office will be key.'[66]

This is a sentiment I also heard from party workers up north in Mathura, where the BJP built a new district office in 2018. The building was closed because of the national lockdown when I visited in July 2020, but it had replaced the BJP's old office in the city, which had been rented from the nagar palika. 'It is totally hi-tech,' explained a local party official. 'You don't need to go out for anything else. It has a different office for the zila president, different for the mahanagar president, a very big badhiya hall for meetings, internet, computers, phones. It has everything. There is a guest house. If a minister or national office-bearers come, we have four-five rooms for them to stay. They are very good. You will like them.'[67] Another proud local official said, 'It has all the facilities that should be there in an office. Earlier we had nothing. We couldn't even get it cleaned earlier.'[68]

By April 2018, the BJP had completed the task of purchasing land for district offices in 522 districts of the country and construction had started on most of these. According to Anirban Ganguly and Shiwanand Dwivedi, 322 of these land purchases were made in a single twelve-month period: April 2017–April 2018.[69] The size and scale of this construction spree can be gauged by the fact that, on a single day in 2019, 6 February, Amit Shah simultaneously inaugurated as many as fifty-one district offices in UP, in a ceremony at Bulandshahr along with UP Chief Minister Yogi Adityanath.[70] Similarly, in February 2020, his successor as party president, J.P. Nadda, inaugurated sixteen BJP offices in a single day in Tamil Nadu[71] and eleven district offices in Bihar through video conferencing.[72] The BJP even inaugurated a party office in the newly constituted Union Territory of Ladakh at a height of over 11,000 feet in November 2019.[73]

In February 2018, the BJP national headquarters in Delhi itself moved to a massive new complex on Delhi's Deen Dayal Upadhyaya Marg, a road named after a key figure in the BJP's pantheon of reverence. Though Upadhyaya served only briefly as Jan Sangh president in 1967-68 before his untimely demise, he left his stamp as general secretary on the party and its successors. Spread over an area of over 1.7 lakh square feet, the new seventy-room party office, the BJP claims, is the largest such political party office in the world.[74]

Figure 8.8: BJP's Office-building Spree: The Party Purchased Land in 522 Districts

Amit Shah and UP chief minister Yogi Adityanath holding a havan to inaugurate simultaneously fifty-one district offices of the BJP in UP, 6 February 2019

Source: http://amitshah.co.in/2019-02-06-inaugurated-51-district-bjp-offices-from-bulandshahr-uttar-pradesh/

Figure 8.9: Narendra Modi Merchandise at the New BJP HQ Office, November 2019

Source: Author's collection

It is certainly a far cry from the old Lutyens Delhi Bungalow at 11 Ashoka Road that served for decades as the party's headquarters. A visitor entering the imposing pink granite edifice of the new building is greeted by a hologram of the party's lotus symbol alternating with portraits of its founding fathers at the reception. Its basement is equipped with a full-fledged memorabilia shop—selling everything from monogrammed BJP watches to NaMo T-shirts—and a well-stocked bookshop with party literature.

Unlike the old party offices in Lutyens Delhi, where visitors could walk in and out of any room, this feels more like a modern corporate office. The inner sanctums of key departments on its five floors, for example, are closed off with automated doors that only open with digital key cards operated by authorised personnel and staff members.

The office-building spree has not been without controversy. In the western state of Rajasthan, where the BJP was then in power, the state's urban development and housing (UDH) department sanctioned land for BJP offices in twenty-eight of the state's thirty-three districts in 2017. Department officials told journalists that the land was to be allotted on district lease committee (DLC) rates of the area, with no concession to the ruling party. The state minister for UDH who sanctioned it, the BJP's Srichand Kriplani, told the *Deccan Herald*, 'In 28 districts land will be allotted for BJP offices. We have almost finalised land in all the districts except two. Rajasthan will lead in the land allotment to BJP.' The minister claimed that the decision was taken in public interest and that 'any party can approach government and seek land for the construction of their office'.

The decision, however, was heavily criticised by the Congress, then in Opposition in the state. 'This is illegal and BJP is in power, which is why it is allocating land for its own offices,' Archana Sharma, a Congress spokesperson, told the newspaper.[75]

Why the BJP Is Building Libraries, State Unit Archives and New Party Histories

If the new district party offices are the physical manifestation of the BJP's organisational vigour, its drive to create libraries and research documentation centres in each of its state unit offices is envisaged as the lifeblood, meant to create an ideological bonding among its cadres. It is important to understand the vital importance of these party libraries and how the BJP's strategists view them.

The process started in December 2016 with the creation of the Nanaji Deshmukh Memorial Library at the BJP office in Raipur, Chhattisgarh. Personally inaugurated by the then party president Amit Shah, and supported by the then BJP state government,[76] this new library was created as a repository of a rare collection of around '10,000 books and documents ranging from BJP ideology' to works of the 'founding fathers of RSS, BJP & RSS'.[77] The BJP sees history as a primary tool of ideological mobilisation for its cadres and ideas. The library project, therefore, has a central role as the emotional cement the party believes is essential to bind together the cadres that animate the brick-and-mortar buildings it has built in the districts. 'The Model State Libraries will function as Knowledge Resource Centres,' declared Amit Shah on Twitter. 'Karyakartas can acquire knowledge in the party's ideology & history.'[78]

These books and manuscripts are not just contained in a physical library. They have all been digitised as part of the BJP's massive e-library project and are available free of cost to its workers and the public at large as tools for training and ideological learning.[79] Since 2016, the BJP has added to its website a massive e-library of thousands of digitised documents. In May 2020, this e-library (http://library.bjp.org/jspui/) had as many as fifty-seven categories of documents. The vastness of their range is instructive. There are digitised and fully searchable versions of archival party documents going back to the earliest days of the Jan Sangh in the 1950s as well as operational party training manuals currently being used by party leaders, such as guidebooks on handling media and social media, a training guidebook for women workers, a party manual on farmers, and my personal favourite: a 'Personal Secretary/Personal Assistant Training Guidebook'.[80] These documents, created as tools for periodic cadre-training workshops, are now available online for the general public at the click of a button. The digitisation is meant to make party mobilisation work easier.

The BJP's e-library archive stretches far beyond the training documents or official archives that one would expect from a reasonably well-organised political party. The party has also put online PDFs of a wide range of historical materials that have nothing per se to do with its political mobilisation but agree with its wider historical vision of India.

So, a reader can find the Mysore scholar Shamashastry's 1915 translation of the *Arthashastra*; the entire body of work by the colonial historian Jadunath Sarkar on Aurangzeb and Shivaji; the works of other nationalist colonial historians like Radhakumud Mookerjee and K.M. Munshi, a senior minister in the Nehru government who was pivotal in rebuilding the Somnath temple of Gujarat; entire issues of *Prabuddh Bharat*, the journal of the Ramakrishna Mission, going back to the 1900s. It even has colonial documents dating back to 1785, such as William Chambers's *A History of the Marratta State*, published in 1787, and *A History of English Education in India* (1895) by Syed Mahmood.[81] All of these documents have been digitised, catalogued and cross-referenced, using library digitisation and cataloguing techniques that mirror the professional techniques used by academic libraries globally. As the digital archive of a political party in India, it is certainly unrivalled.

Moreover, each party state unit was asked to create a history of its own unit by collecting old documents, talking to older cadres and archiving these records. The BJP's Anirban Ganguly and Shiwanand Dwivedi have documented a revealing conversation Shah had with the Madhya Pradesh party unit's library and documentation department during a review meeting, which illustrates the importance of this history project for the party. 'Did the *Ram Janmabhoomi* movement take place?' Shah asked. When the department members said yes, he asked, 'how many documents relating to the *Ram Janmabhoomi* movement are available in the state office? If somebody requires some information related to *Ram Janmabhoomi* movement right now, what documents do we have in the office at this point of time?'[82] Then Shah explained his reasons for investing in such archives. They were meant to document the lives of the party's eminent leaders for its workers. Crucially, they also aimed to provide an alternative view of history—one from the party's ideological standpoint—for global researchers. The project aims at nothing less than writing a new political history of India. As Shah told party workers in Bhopal, 'With the kind of changes that the country is undergoing at this moment, researchers from around the world would be gradually approaching us with great interest to know more about the Bharatiya Janata Party in the next fifteen to twenty years. But if we do not have records, then what will we give them? Are we only going to tell them that here is a table, this is a room, that is a chair and we have provision for food here…? We must do our documentation as if we are preparing to write the entire political history of India in 2021.'[83]

This theme of encouraging research on the party is one that Prime Minister Modi too often returns to. In May 2019, at a press conference at the BJP headquarters after the Lok Sabha polls, he told journalists, 'whenever any one of you wants to do any research, I will tell the party president that we should pass on this information to those interested journalists'. The point, Modi argued, was that 'how you run such an organisation is a very big thing' in a 'democratic set-up'. 'Mobilising such a big human resource and getting them to do such targeted activities is very hard and big work by itself,' he explained. 'Only after that you can fight an election as an organisation. This is democracy's real strength by itself.'[84]

Between 2016 and 2019, the BJP created new Nanaji Deshmukh Libraries and e-libraries in six states: Raipur (Chhattisgarh),[85] Bhopal (Madhya Pradesh),[86] Jaipur (Rajasthan),[87] Bengaluru (Karnataka),[88] Ranchi (Jharkhand)[89] and Jammu (Union Territory of Jammu & Kashmir).[90] Each of these was personally inaugurated by Amit Shah, who specially flew down for the events.

Former civil servant Dr Aseervatham Achary played a key role in creating the libraries as the BJP's coordinator for its documentation and library department. He told me that both Amit Shah and his successor as party president, J.P. Nadda, saw these libraries as 'high priority'. 'They took personal interest in monitoring progress of these projects at every level and ensured they are inaugurated well within the timeframe,' he said. 'No other party has even thought of hosting a vast repository of knowledge resources in the digital format.' The rare manuscripts and archival party documents online that his team hosts, he pointed out, were 'managed scientifically' and by 'employing tools as prescribed by library science'. I asked him who the target audience was. His answer: party karyakartas, research scholars, students, intellectuals, party spokespersons, journalists from print and electronic media. 'It aims to become a reference library for intellectuals,' he concluded.[91]

When I asked Vinay Sahasrabuddhe how different the BJP's expansion under Amit Shah's presidency was compared to that of his predecessors, he counted the work of building party offices and the focus on archives as the two primary differentiators. 'Number one is the level of activism with which he has worked on the party or organisation,' he said. 'I don't think any of his predecessors can claim that. Rajnath Singh and Nitin Gadkari had their own sets of qualities. Amit Shah focuses on party functions and structures more intensely. He practically travelled to almost all the districts and he kept party workers engaged in one campaign or another, one after the other. At the same time, he paid a significant amount of attention to institutionalisation of the political party. For example, his keenness that, for every district headquarter, we should have our own premises. Today, in more than 300 districts, it has been completed [this was in August 2019]. His insistence that every party office must have its own library. It has been completed. Then there is big party membership drive and his idea of writing the history of every BJP unit.'[92]

Of course, the archival exercise did not work uniformly in all states. When party workers were asked to start taking pictures of every event they organised and uploading them as part of an ongoing archival project, some did better than others, while many remained laggards. 'Questions will always be raised,' Sahasrabuddhe told me. 'But the attempt should be made. What he used to tell us is that if you do any activity, take a picture on your mobile phone and send it. Then send a small description of it, so we remember who said what. At least the idea was initiated. How it goes ahead one doesn't know. The party did not have this earlier.'

'Structured functioning matters a great deal,' he adds. 'It is my observation that the entire political mainstream of activism in our country is like *kafan bandh ke nikle hain* [literally, as if they have set out with coffins on their heads, to mean that they set out rashly, as if prepared to die]. We should do things in a systematic way, with a longer-term view. But when political activity happens, mostly these structural things take a backseat and people just put a coffin on their head and jump across. We are trying to change that with this systemic organisational work.'[93]

The work he describes includes creating histories. As Shah told BJP workers in Bhopal, 'In twenty years scholars from across the world will want to study the history, evolution, characteristics ideology and various dimensions of our party. It is already happening, and there should be material which we should be able to provide them with. We should have a system of collecting, recording and documenting the history of our party across the country.'[94]

Training: Notes from Rambhau Mhalgi Prabodhini

In September 2019, I spent a couple of very fruitful days researching this book at the Rambhau Mhalgi Prabodhini—a unique training and research academy, registered as a charitable trust—nestled in the Western Ghats in Thane, on the outskirts of Mumbai. Spread over 15 acres of a leafy hillside, the picturesque institute runs training modules for corporations and individuals on leadership. It also provides political training to BJP politicians.

Training is a crucial part of the party's organisational restructuring and Prabodhini fulfils a vital purpose in that deeper ecosystem. Its state-of-the-art facilities and infrastructure are, by my reckoning, on par with India's best B-schools. Apart from its educational and social sector work—it has official affiliations with the United Nations' ECOSOC, University of Mumbai and the National Skills Development Corporation—Prabodhini holds ten or twelve events a year on its own for training practising politicians (from gram panchayat leaders to parliamentarians) as well as offering certificate courses in leadership for those wishing to work in public life. 'These events are open for all political parties,' said Sahasrabuddhe, who is also vice chairman of the academy. 'So, if anyone from any other political party wants to attend, they are welcome to do so.'[95] When asked what kinds of themes make up the courses, another functionary mentioned topics like media management. 'We have developed many courses. These include training on things like "bhashan kala"—how to give speeches and ideas on Hindutva.'[96]

Separately, Prabodhini also hosts twelve or thirteen events on average each year that are organised by the BJP. In the year that I was there, for instance, it had hosted party training sessions for BJP MLAs from Arunachal Pradesh as well as for state legislators who had defected to the BJP from Maharashtra's Nationalist Congress Party (NCP) from the Pimpri Chinchwad areas and other constituencies. 'They want to know about the party,' said one executive involved in the training. 'They don't want to know who is Deen Dayal Upadhyaya. We do training from gram panchayat to pradhans to MPs.'[97] In the institute's garden is a corner where visiting BJP dignitaries plant saplings. There were saplings planted by visiting top leaders from Nagaland, by the then chief minister of Uttarakhand, Ramesh Nishankh Pokhariyal, and by the then chief minister of Karnataka, B.S. Yeddyurappa.

The rest of the year, the institute runs its own courses and corporate training programmes. The week I was there, for example, it was hosting executives from three separate companies for training retreats. Its dining halls cooked separate menus on demand for each of the corporate contingents. Prabodhini also runs a start-up incubator, the Atal Incubation Centre, a postgraduate programme in leadership politics and governance managed by its Indian Institute for Democratic Leadership as well as other educational initiatives on leadership. The students I encountered had all enrolled for the postgraduate programme. There was a medical doctor and several executives with about three–four years of experience, all of whom had taken time off from work and wanted to engage with politics.

The manner in which Prabodhini was created and how it grew is illustrative of the fact that the BJP's focus on training its cadres and on historical documentation is not new. It dates back to the early 1980s. Named after veteran BJP parliamentarian Rambhau Mhalgi, Prabodhini was the brainchild of the late BJP leader Pramod Mahajan, who was also its first chairman.[98] The 15-acre campus—more a high-end resort with a swimming pool than a paathshala—is part of a wider 215-acre complex that also contains several Sangh-related institutes: a gaushala (cow shelter), an Ayurvedic centre and an institute for agricultural research. Prabodhini was originally set up in 1982, and moved to its present campus in 1999. In 2003, construction work on the campus was completed, and it was formally inaugurated by the then prime minister Atal Bihari Vajpayee.[99]

At the heart of this complex lies a vast library named after B.R. Ambedkar, with a meticulously kept archive of well-preserved BJP documents, many of which animate this book. Used as I am to visiting political party offices, the functionaries of which often have little sense of history, I found the Prabodhini archive's professional documentation to be on par with the finest archive in India, the NMML at Teen Murti House in Delhi.

Interestingly, much of the early part of this archive, from the 1980s, focuses on the Communist Party: its writings, press clippings on its work and books on the Left movement. Sahasrabuddhe says that, when he started the library in the 1980s, many of the early titles it procured were on the Left. 'We are a centre for studying politics,' he says. 'We study all parties. We were deeply interested in Communism and we built on it in the library. Communist party leaders, when I used to interact with them in those days, used to be surprised that we kept their writings.'

Figure 8.10: The Training Centre: View of Rambai Mhalgi Prabodhini

Source: Author's collection, September 2019

This discovery allows for an interesting insight. The focus on history, on documentation and cadre mobilisation is something that the BJP has adapted not just from the RSS but also from the Communist movement. Early BJP leaders, while being ideologically opposed to the Left, were often inspired by the personal ideals of many of its senior leaders. As a senior BJP leader told me with grudging admiration, 'There are many things you learn from Communists in their approach. For example, when CPI's D. Raja retired, he stayed in VP House in Delhi. As a Member of Parliament he was allotted it, and he was allocated a bungalow also, but his party said it will decide how many rooms in a bungalow you are supposed to use for your personal use. This ethic is written in their constitution also. If you visit the CPI(M) website, you will find it there. That is remarkable.'

A senior BJP leader attributed the focus on intellectual pursuits and research to the influence in Maharashtra of the Rashtra Seva Dal (RSD). It was formed by socialist leaders S.M. Joshi, N.G. Goray and Shirubhau Limaye with the expressed objective of countering the growing influence of the RSS during the pre-Independence years. As a senior BJP leader from Maharashtra said, 'Especially in Maharashtra, there is special tussle between the RSS and RSD. In the 1940s, in Maharashtra, the situation was such that any boy of ten-plus years would go to either an RSS shakha or an RSD shakha. They also had shakhas like RSS, but they always paid attention to intellectual development, unlike the Sangh. Sangh has a tradition of saying don't debate, but focus instead on winning the heart of the person in front of you. We used to be told, we will win minds later, first win the heart. But the socialists did not think like this. They developed an intellectual climate, which we did not develop, relatively speaking. Early socialist leaders like Madhu Limaye were on par intellectually with Vajpayee and Advani. Sangh-vaalaas, the joke went in Maharashtra, were perfect below the neck, above the neck they had nothing. This changed after the Emergency, but even now there is not that much change. We frequently admit that.'

BJP's Cadre-building: The Prehistory of the Modi–Shah Era

The focus on cadre training in the BJP goes back to Advani's tenure as party president in the early 1980s. Advani was 'one of the strongest advocates of training and used to come quite often to Prabodhini'. Sahasrabuddhe recalls: 'Advaniji was fond of recalling a story on the need for training politicians by Shail Chaturvedi, a humourist-poet who was present at the BJP's 1980 plenary session. As the story narrated by Advaniji went: a newly appointed minister told his driver that he will drive the car today. The driver turned around and said that, in this case, he will get down. Try and drive, he said, your soul will get shaken. This is a car, not a government that can run *bhagwan bharose* [trusting in God alone].'[100]

While the massive spurt in the BJP's expansion started under Amit Shah in 2014, much of the early work for it had started under the first presidency of Rajnath Singh between 2005 and 2009. 'I started seeing a party which was in construction mode,' recalls Vani Tripathi Tikoo, who served as national secretary during that time. 'It was very much like when the old building gets demolished and a new one is constructed. The question was how you deconstruct the old and you start building on the new. Narendra Modi emerged at the same time as an important national leader. He was already very powerful in Gujarat and Rajnath Singh built a brand-new team at the centre after the debacle of the 2004 campaign.'[101]

At the central level, this was the period when the BJP started inducting new faces in key positions in its various cells: Smriti Irani started to gain importance as president of the party's women's wing, several young legislators from Bihar became national executive members of the youth wing, Piyush Goyal was made the party's national treasurer and Arvind Gupta was brought in to revamp the IT Cell. 'I saw several rank newcomers getting important positions in various cells of the party,' recalls Tikoo.

This rebuilding took on another dimension under Nitin Gadkari, who served as party president in the 2009–2013 period. Gadkari, a politician from Nagpur who had a strong equation with the RSS, also brought with him Mumbai-style corporate governance. 'He was an MBA by training and refused to accept the kurta-pyjama culture of the party,' recalls a party leader who worked closely with him. 'He was different from the Delhi and UP political class. He dressed in shirts and pants, spoke his mind, even using cusswords in meetings, and would be hands-on with the party cadres.' The result was that a 'a cadre, which was befuddled, upset and down on morale after the defeats of 2005 and 2009 revived with this. Under Gadkari, for the first time, the party's way of functioning was broken into smithereens and a brand-new corporate style was constructed. All of us had a hellish time for many, many months. The first thing he broke down was the metaphorical physical resemblance to an old Lutyens' zone bungalow, which changed and turned into a highly corporate-style functional office of the BJP. That was what emerged.'[102]

Amit Shah's massive expansion drive between 2014 and 2019 was preceded by an earlier version under Gadkari, which yielded the party a new line of second- and third-rung leadership. 'In most of the states,

Gadkari unleashed the most successful membership campaign for the BJP, and the lakhs of new members that we got in those three years of his presidency just indicated the fantastic relationships that he had been able to form with the state units,' says another BJP leader.[103] Gadkari also brought in a new generation of party leaders in several states, against the wishes of the old guard. He brought in Harsh Vardhan, Vijendra Gupta and Satish Upadhyaya in Delhi to replace V.K. Malhotra, who had fronted the Delhi unit for decades. Each of them successively became presidents of the Delhi unit. In Maharashtra, he promoted Devendra Fadnavis, who was later handpicked by Modi and Amit Shah to be the state's chief minster in 2019, and leaders like Vinod Tawde as general secretary. In Madhya Pradesh, he promoted Narendra Singh Tomar and in Rajasthan, Anil Madhav Dave. He also brought into his central team leaders like Dharmendra Pradhan from Odisha as general secretary, J.P. Nadda from Himachal Pradesh and Nirmala Sitharaman as party spokesperson. Each of these leaders went on to hold major ministerial and party roles in the Modi–Shah era.

The recasting of the party—in terms of format, style of functioning and a generational shift—began under Shah's predecessors. Under Singh and Gadkari, it underwent a major transformation from the organisation that Vajpayee and Advani had built through the 1980s and '90s. Modi and Shah took that structural transformation to another level after 2014.

In 2014, by the time Rajnath Singh was back for his second stint as party president (2013-14), the party used its now re-energised membership base to even design its election slogans. 'For the first time, we started asking people what the sloganeering campaign would be. We got 30,000 slogans from all across the country,' recalls Tikoo, who was part of campaign-organisation meetings.

The party's 2014 slogan 'Ab ki baar Modi sarkar' (this time, Modi government) came from one of these volunteers. 'It was not [advertising executive] Piyush Pandey, it was not [lyricist and ad executive] Prasoon Joshi, and Prasoon has, I think, openly accepted it also. It was one of the volunteers who wrote about those slogans on the digital platform. So Piyush and Prasoon thought of giving it a final shape. That is how that slogan came.'[104]

When the BJP Wanted to Disband Itself: The Blueprint that Drove the New BJP

It is difficult to imagine now, but there was a time when Atal Bihari Vajpayee, as BJP president, actually thought of disbanding the party. The party, which had imagined itself from Day One as an 'alternative to Cong (I)'[105] had suffered a crushing defeat in 1984, winning just two parliamentary seats in that year's national election. Vajpayee, its most popular national leader, had himself lost his parliamentary seat from Gwalior to Congress's Madhav Rao Scindia. Crestfallen, he commissioned a special twelve-member working group in 1985 to review the party's functioning and to answer some tough questions on why the BJP found itself 'miles away' from its objective after its first five years.[106]

One of these questions was whether the BJP's creation itself had been a mistake and whether it should dissolve itself and return to its Jan Sangh avatar. In its first two years, as now, the BJP had focused on the nuts and bolts of building an organisation. As a review by L.K. Advani had noted in 1983, the organisation's aim was 'almost entirely on enrolling members, forming committees, and thus building the party's organisational infrastructure right from the Panchayat level to the level of Parliament'.[107] In its first two years, the BJP's primary membership went from 2.2 million to 3.9 million. By 1983, it had succeeded in setting up district committees in 80 per cent of Indian districts, except the Northeast.[108] Yet, the party was virtually wiped out electorally in the Rajiv Gandhi wave of 1984 after Indira Gandhi's assassination. Vajpayee's response was to set up a working group, headed by Krishanlal Sharma and including the late Pramod Mahajan,[109] to answer two questions:

1. Whether the party's defeat was because of its decision to merge Jana Sangh with the Janata Party in 1977 and withdraw from the Janata Party in 1980? Were both the decisions wrong?
2. Should the BJP go back and revive the Jana Sangh?

Tasked with drawing up an 'Action Plan for the future on all fronts—ideological, organisational, agitational, constructive and electoral', the Working Group surveyed 4,000 party workers across the country, toured the states and met another 1,000 friends of the BJP. It answered in the negative to both questions.[110] The Working Group found that the party had taken 'a correct decision when it decided to merge with the Jana Sangh in the Janata Party, a wise decision when it decided to come out of the Janata Party to form BJP and a right decision when it chose to be BJP'.[111]

It was an important turning point for the party. It also provided the kernel for many of the underlying principles that appeared to drive Modi–Shah's massive expansion three decades later: the focus on district-level party offices, training of cadres, emphasis on full-timers, leadership tours and agitations and a return to ideology.

Among the BJP's shortcomings, the Working Group found that there was a communication gap between the leadership and the grassroot levels; 'lack of political training in a systematic manner to educate the workers on political, economic, ideological and organisational matters'; 'lack of agitations at national level on national issues'; and a 'poor response from women'.[112] At a deeper level, the Working Group argued that the BJP was facing an existential crisis because it had veered away from its core ideological identity—making alliances and diluting how it portrayed its core beliefs as a 'party with a difference'. 'We must admit that we have belied our expectations,' the report said. It was not 'popular support which is wanting but our strong will to take initiative for becoming the pivotal point of the change in the country. The Party must catch up with the time and play its historic role for providing a credible national alternative.'[113] The party's return to Hindutva under L.K. Advani followed soon thereafter. In less than five years, the BJP passed the Palampur Resolution in 1989, committing itself to the building of the Ram Temple.

To win elections, the report recommended expanding the membership of the party beyond its core cadres. The BJP had built a 'cadre party', but its leaders felt that this 'by itself will not enable us to reach our goal'. It had to expand membership and to make 'conscious efforts to enrol members from all sections of society' to get a mass following. This meant getting 'workers as leaders'. Just giving enough representation to various social sections did 'not provide any weightage or leverage to that section'.[114] Those who joined the BJP 'must be shaped into leaders of that section', the report recommended. This was essentially a call for making the party a vehicle for upward social mobility for ambitious politicians looking to make a career in politics. Both Narendra Modi and Amit Shah, who began their careers as ordinary party workers, fit the bill. The fact that so many second-line BJP leaders started with such grassroots backgrounds and rose to the top echelons of their party is an important factor in the rise of the BJP.

The 1985 report also emphasised 'training for the management of elections to be imparted to party cadres'. Specifically, it asked for cadre-training camps at the district level, state and national levels at least once a year.[115] This is exactly why institutions like Rambhau Mhalgi Prabodhini were created, and why this training culture is at the heart of the BJP's expansion efforts.

This post-mortem also emphasised the need to enrol full-timers. 'Everyone recognises the fact that politics has become very exacting and requires more and more hour to be devoted. The more and more full-time workers can be put in the field, to that extent, the grass-roots level work picks up.'[116] This focus on full-time workers is precisely what Amit Shah emphasised during his tenure as party president, during which the party saw the most expansion.

The report provided a template for leadership tours and agitations. 'Agitate or Vegitate [sic]', it declared. 'Whether it is true or not with regard to other institutions or organisations working in other fields, it is quite true for parties and much more so to a party like BJP.'[117]

It will not be an exaggeration to say that the intellectual roots of Shah and Modi's leadership styles lie in these recommendations. In 2014, the BJP reinvented its tradition of pravaas—outstation trips by its leaders—mandating that all national office-bearers must visit nine states in one year. They would do so by rotation, ensuring that all states were covered. Amit Shah, for example, started his own pravaas from Naxalbari, where an armed revolt in the 1960s gave the Naxal movement its name. Between August 2014 and 2018, as party president, he had addressed 1,027 party organisation programmes, travelling 7,90,000 km or 519 km a day on average.[118] In his first year and a half as president (August 2014 to end 2015), he stayed overnight on 102 occasions in various states.[119] This data indicates the heavy emphasis that the BJP's top brass puts on organisational work, compared to its national rival, the Congress.

In conclusion, the 1985 report extolled the value of the 'Party office' as the 'nerve centre of the Party activities' recommending that a 'well-equipped, efficient, effective functioning office is a must at national level, State level and district level'. In particular, it found that the BJP had no offices in a large number of Indian districts. Hence, it laid down: 'Party offices in a manner in which we require should be set up in all the districts throughout the country within a year.'[120] Again, the roots of Amit Shah's district office building drive can be traced back to this three-decades-old document. Although it took the BJP another three decades to follow through on the recommendations—only after it came to power under Modi, and had the resources to do so—the template used, with some modern modifications, was rooted in the party's learnings in its earliest years.

The role of party structure as a tool of political mobilisation is relatively understudied in India. But, in a rapidly urbanising and demographically young India, it should not be underestimated. Some of the BJP's electoral successes in recent years accrue as much to this grassroots work as to its larger ideological shifts. As Amit Shah put it, 'That era has gone when two leaders in Delhi would shake each other's hands in a drawing room and behind them a voter will follow like a bonded labourer. A voter decides his vote himself and uses it on the basis of what is better for his area, his country and for himself.'

Modi and Shah undoubtedly brought with them a new energy and a different leadership style to the BJP from 2014 onwards, and it completely changed how the party was run in the Vajpayee and Advani years. Naturally, this also created heartburn among the old guard. As a senior state BJP leader, not considered close to them, told me on condition of anonymity, 'They took the party to another level. There is no question about that. But they don't have a personal touch. They focus on delivery, which is good, but personal touch is missing. But you cannot deny that their style and result-oriented approach also brought victories.'

PART III

IDEOLOGY, ECONOMIC THINKING AND GOVERNANCE

9

ROOTS OF THE BJP

The Jan Sangh Story

Among the little-known delights of Delhi's parliament building is an exhibition of robotic mannequins for children, showcasing eight politicians who created modern India. At the flick of a button, the figures spring into action one by one, spouting lines about what they stood for. They are part of a light-and-sound display on the foundation story of the republic. One of these eight mannequins is of Syama Prasad Mookerjee, Hindu nationalist ideologue, India's first minister for industries and founder of the Akhil Bharatiya Jan Sangh, which preceded the BJP as India's primary Hindu nationalist party between 1951 and 1977. Mookerjee was one of several non-Congress leaders—like the Constitution-maker B.R. Ambedkar—inducted by India's first prime minister, Jawaharlal Nehru, into his founding cabinet.[1]

Mookerjee, who was acting president of the Hindu Mahasabha during 1940–1944, had joined Nehru's cabinet with 'specific approval' from the Mahasabha's driving force, Hindutva ideologue Vinayak Damodar Savarkar.[2] He served most of his ministerial term as a vice president of the Hindu Mahasabha before exiting the outfit because it refused to allow membership to non-Hindus.[3] Later, Mookerjee quit the Nehru government over the protection of Hindus left behind in East Pakistan. He is now enjoying a revival of iconicity since the Modi government came to power.

Less than a month before Home Minister Amit Shah stood up in Parliament with his 5 August 2019 proposal to revoke Article 370, which gave Kashmir special status, he was foreshadowed by a cover story on Mookerjee by the RSS magazine, *Organiser*. The publication had revisited Mookerjee's mysterious death in 1953 while he was in detention in Kashmir. He travelled there in support of the Dogra-led Praja Parishad's opposition to the state being granted special status. Mookerjee's own views on Kashmir are enshrined in his slogan, '*Ek desh mein do vidhaan, do Pradhan aur do nishaan, nahin chalenge, nahin chalenge* [In one country, two constitutions, two premiers and two symbols will not work, will not work]'.[4] *Organiser*, commemorating the leader's birth anniversary, 6 July, published his photo on its cover with the headline, 'Live Up to the Legacy'.[5]

Coincidence or not, that was exactly what Amit Shah did four weeks later in the Lok Sabha, making his announcement just a few rooms away from where Mookerjee's mannequin stood. It is impossible to understand today's BJP, its positioning and its politics without understanding the journey of its previous political avatar.

The Jan Sangh, from its inception, was designed as a fully formed ideological alternative to the Congress. A good illustration of this is an often-quoted but famously wrong analysis of Indian politics in 1967 by a correspondent of *The Times* (of London), Neville Maxwell. He wrote a two-part series titled, 'India's Disintegrating Democracy', which predicted that the coming election would 'surely' be its last. This part of his prediction is better known. What is less known is that this analysis was based on his survey of political alternatives to the Congress. *The Times* found the Jan Sangh and 'its sword hand, the Rashtriya Swayamsevak Sangh, a secretive and sinister para-military organisation … waxing in north India'. The Jan Sangh, *The Times* correspondent wrote, possibly with the recent cow agitation in Delhi in mind, 'feeds on and nourishes the chauvinist and xenophobic elements of Hindu nationalism'.[6]

Just as it coloured the opinion of the foreign press, the face-off also defined and animated the campaigning in that year's national election, the first after Nehru's death. Predictably, when some Jan Sangh supporters interrupted the then prime minister Indira Gandhi's public meetings, she lashed out. 'What were parties like the Jan Sangh doing when the country was under foreign rule?' she asked with an oratorical flourish. *Organiser* gleefully pounced back, saying, 'Even we didn't expect her to know that the Jan Sangh came into being *after* the British were gone.'[7]

The Jan Sangh, closely intertwined with the RSS, never came close to challenging the Congress's electoral dominance, even though it had become large enough to feature as one of the primary poles of ideological opposition in some poll contests. The Jan Sangh's alternative idea of India as a country deeply rooted in Hindu ideals, as opposed to Nehru's idea of a republic rooted in a distinction between the state and religious identity, did not win enough political traction. Ultimately, the Jan Sangh was forced to merge into a common Opposition front in 1977 and then reincarnate itself as the BJP in 1980. It is striking, all the same, just how much of its intellectual foundations from the 1950s are woven into the fabric of the modern BJP in the 2020s.

Why Hindu Nationalists Hated Nehru: The Jan Sangh's Founding Moment

Virtually from the moment of its birth, the Akhil Bharatiya Jan Sangh cast itself as the cultural and political opposite of the Congress. When its founding delegates met in Delhi to create a new national party on 21 October 1951, the meeting opened with the 'singing of the Vande Mataram and the chanting of Vedic mantras'.[8] On the stage sat the party's founder, Syama Prasad Mookerjee, with other party leaders. They were framed by a white backdrop, displaying pictures of the seventeenth-century Maratha king Shivaji and the sixteenth-century Rajput warrior Maharana Pratap: both Hindu chieftains who became emblems of Hindu nationalism because they had battled Muslim emperors.[9]

State-level units had already been formed in some provinces (Bengal, Punjab–PEPSU, i.e. Patiala and East Punjab States Union, Himachal Pradesh, UP). Now, 500 delegates from across India converged on Delhi to merge into a national outfit.[10] They were meeting to usher in the birth of a political alternative to the Congress, one that would be predicated on a Hindu cultural identity.

The national party was formed just four days before voting began in the new republic's first general election.[11] This political context was crucial. Three weeks earlier, Prime Minister Jawaharlal Nehru, speaking at

Ludhiana's Dresi Maidan, had launched the Congress election campaign in Punjab, calling 'communalism the greatest enemy of the country' and rallying voters for an all-out 'war against communalism'. Addressing an audience of over a lakh people who had turned out to hear him in the 'mid-day heat', Nehru described the idea of a 'Hindu Rashtra' as 'fantastic' and 'ruinous'.

Anticipating the birth of the Jan Sangh, India's first prime minister 'appealed to the people not to lend their ears' to leaders of what he called 'communal organisations such as the Hindu Mahasabha, the RSS and the Jan Sangh'. These communal forces, he thundered, 'had reduced the Hindu religion to a "kitchen religion". For them, religion meant what one should eat and what not, and where and how.' In his 100-minute address, Nehru framed communalism as the greatest political question of the day. 'This fight against communalism is the foremost question before us today,' he declared. 'We cannot afford to make any compromise in this regard.'[12]

Dr Syama Prasad Mookerjee, founding president of the Jan Sangh, stoutly denied the charge of communalism in his opening speech at the party's inaugural function. He stressed that the 'party would be open to Indians irrespective of caste and creed. The party would strive to ensure full protection and equal rights of citizenship to all minorities.'[13] Within two weeks, Mookerjee would be telling an audience in Calcutta's Deshpriya Park that his party was a 'sincere friend of Muslims'. Presaging L.K. Advani's charge of pseudo-secularism in the 1980s, he argued that the Congress could only look after Muslims through police and guns, but the Jan Sangh would see to their interests 'with love and sincerity of purpose'.[14] Nehru and Mookerjee had been cabinet colleagues for thirty-three months between August 1947 and April 1950, but clearly there had been no meeting of minds.

This theme of communalism—Nehru attacking the Sangh and Mookerjee defending his party—became a recurrent theme in the political exchanges between the two sides in that first election for India. Only three years had passed since Mahatma Gandhi had been murdered by an assassin who justified his actions in court by arguing that what he saw as the Mahatma's Muslim appeasement was, in his view, an impediment to Hindu rights.[15] Thousands of Hindu and Sikh refugees of Partition were still parked in camps across Delhi, West Bengal, Assam and Tripura. Nehru made this the central issue of independent India's first election. Communalism has, in the past, 'separated the people … and led to India's enslavement,' he declared. 'Whatever the proposed aim of those who spread communalism, their activities only weakened the foundations of freedom.'[16]

Three Internal Debates that Shaped Nehru vs Jan Sangh Battles: the Congress, the RSS and Mookerjee

Mookerjee, a brilliant lawyer from Bengal who had trained at London's Lincoln's Inn and served as vice chancellor of Calcutta University (1934–1938), had started his political career as a Congressman when he was elected to the Bengal Legislative Council in 1929. He quit the party a year later, getting re-elected from the same constituency as an independent in 1931, and subsequently joined the Hindu Mahasabha on 'encouragement from its president, Veer Savarkar' and from RSS chief Dr Keshav Baliram Hedgewar.[17] Mookerjee left the Mahasabha in May 1949, while he was still serving as Nehru's minister, because he opposed both its decision to turn itself into a political party and its reluctance to give membership to non-Hindus—something he had been pushing for since 1945.[18]

Mookerjee's decision to subsequently resign from Nehru's cabinet in 1950, protesting the newly independent nation's attitude to Hindu minorities in Pakistan, did not lead only to the creation of the Jan Sangh. It also focused attention on an issue that would become the lightning rod in key debates between Hindu nationalists and Nehru on the nature of India's obligations to non-citizen Hindus. This 1950s dispute reached its denouement seventy years later with the Modi government's enactment of the politically contentious CAA. Promulgated in August 2020, the legislation amended the Citizenship Act of 1955 to give citizenship to any Hindus, Sikhs, Buddhists, Jains, Parsis and Christians from Afghanistan, Bangladesh and Pakistan who chose to come to India.[19] The impulse driving the CAA thus lies in the founding moment of the Jan Sangh itself.

The dispute on Hindu refugees also led to a bitter internal fight within the ruling Congress—between the Nehruvians and the party's own Hindu traditionalists. It eventually came to constitute the single biggest threat

Nehru faced to his leadership from within his party after Gandhi's death, until the China war. The outcome of this political battle on what newly democratic India stood for foregrounded the political palimpsest in which the Jan Sangh was created.

Under the Delhi Pact on migrations between East Pakistan and West Bengal, jointly signed by Nehru and Pakistan Prime Minister Liaquat Ali Khan on 8 April 1950, both governments agreed to guarantee the safety of religious minorities on their side.[20] Mookerjee, along with another cabinet minister, M.C. Neogy, resigned from the government in protest the day that Khan was slated to arrive in Delhi.[21] He argued that Pakistani assurances on minority rights were untrustworthy since it was now an Islamic state. He felt that Nehru had acted weakly on the migrant question and went so far as to imply a military solution to protect Hindu minorities—whom he saw as the remnants of the Hindu nation—in East Pakistan.[22] Rather than trusting Pakistan, Mookerjee felt 'it would be better to propose an outright exchange of population', because it was feared Hindus had 'lost all sense of security in Eastern Pakistan'.[23]

Nehru's response was based on a different idea of the nature and function of the Indian state, 'even when those principles were unpopular with the masses'. He told Parliament that 'protection in Pakistan can only be given obviously in Pakistan. We cannot give protection in Pakistan.' He argued, 'There is no other way. So long as there is a Government dealing with a situation [on Hindu minorities], you have to deal through that Government.' For Nehru, as the political historian B.D. Graham summed it up, 'India could not interfere in the internal affairs of another polity, in this case Pakistan, even when the question at issue was the future of Pakistan's Hindu minorities'. For Mookerjee, 'the mere fact that that they were Hindus was sufficient justification for India's taking action'.[24] A Hindu anywhere, in this conception, was India's concern. More so if they were in Pakistan.

These disagreements and Mookerjee's exit from Nehru's government created a deep schism within the Congress. Mookerjee had, as an early historian of the Jan Sangh noted, 'acted out what many Congressmen would have liked to have done themselves'.[25] The fissure became public when Mookerjee explained the reasons for his resignation in Parliament. His speech was 'intermittently cheered by a section of the House', noted a reporter watching the proceedings. But by the time he concluded, he was 'loudly cheered by the *House as a whole* [emphasis added]'.[26] This was a remarkable indicator of wide support for his ideas in a Lok Sabha in which two-thirds of the MPs were from the Congress (364 of 489). The schism within the Congress partially explains why it took over a year for Mookerjee to form the Jan Sangh after he walked out on Nehru. This intense ideological debate and the struggle for power within the party, which very briefly opened up the tantalising possibility of a Congress without Nehru as its leader, formed the subtext to the pre-launch discussions of the Jan Sangh's founders. Mookerjee had been exploring the possibility of founding a party since 1950 through backchannel conversations with the RSS. Yet, as Graham argued, he made no public moves to do so till April 1951. This delay is especially interesting because the first general election was initially planned for mid-1951, not late 1951.[27]

Even as Mookerjee mulled over his options for creating a new Hindu-nationalist political party, Hindu-traditionalist leaders within the Congress launched an offensive against Nehru. The evidence suggests that both Mookerjee and the RSS may have had good reasons to wait for the outcome of this power struggle. Two leading early historians of the Jan Sangh and the RSS, Bruce Graham and Walter Andersen, agree that Mookerjee may have 'first wanted to see who would win the struggle for power within the Congress'.[28]

RSS pracharak Vasantrao Oke had been in touch with Mookerjee since 1949 on the idea of starting a new party. So was Sangh supremo M.S. Golwalkar. The ban on the RSS after Gandhi's murder (February 1948–12 July 1949) had just been lifted by the Government of India. Some of its younger leaders, especially in Punjab and Delhi, were pushing for the RSS to turn itself into a political party.[29] However, its constitution expressly forbade political participation. Golwalkar himself remained opposed to the idea, but he acknowledged the internal debate, saying, 'I do not know. After the ban has been lifted ... they [RSS workers] can if they like convert the Sangh into a political body. I for myself cannot say anything. I am not a dictator. Personally, I am outside politics. But why should people drag us into politics? We are happy with them as politicians and ourselves as Swayamsevaks.'[30] While the RSS made up its mind on its future political course, its leaders were also 'keenly interested in the struggle' within the

Congress.[31] Both Mookerjee and the RSS, in that sense, may have felt that they could work with a Congress that was led by a Hindu traditionalist—such as its Uttar Pradesh Congress Committee President Purshottam Das Tandon, who was also the speaker of the Legislative Assembly of India's most populous province—rather than Nehru.[32]

When Nehru Resigned, Trounced the Congress's Hindu Traditionalists on Mookerjee's Questions: The Fight for the Congress's Soul

The sequence of events is instructive. Soon after leaving the Nehru government, Mookerjee attended a large meeting of refugee groups in Delhi on 29 July 1950. He was welcomed at the Old Delhi railway station by crowds of Hindu-nationalist young men holding up banners like, 'We Do Not Want Nehru's Anti-Hindu and Cowardly Government' and 'NehruLiaquat Pact Murdabad' (Death to the Nehru–Liaquat Pact).[33] The anti-Nehru tenor of the conference, which brought together 5,000 delegates and 15,000 visitors from across the country, could not be clearer. Yet, Purshottam Das Tandon, a close confidant of Deputy Prime Minister Sardar Vallabhbhai Patel, chose to 'preside' over the refugee conference.[34] In a ninety-minute speech, he made it clear that the Nehru–Liaquat Pact had 'failed to stop the migration of Hindus' from East Pakistan. 'Reports of dacoities in Hindu homes, molestation of women' and 'requisitioning of Hindu houses' were received 'even after the Pact', he added. This was precisely why Mookerjee had walked out of Nehru's government. Now a major Congress leader was publicly challenging the prime minister's flagship initiative. The conference concluded with a resolution on the 'Indo-Pakistan Agreement', which declared that Pakistan had failed to implement the Delhi Pact in its territory.[35]

Within two months, the sixty-eight-year-old Tandon defeated J.B. Kripalani, better known as Acharya Kripalani, in a contest for Congress presidency at the party's Nagpur session on 2 September 1950. Tandon's victory, by 1,306 of 2,618 votes, showed how deeply divided the Congress was on Nehru's refugee and Pakistan policy. The victory was construed in Congress circles as the 'most significant pointer to the Government as to the direction in which popular opinion in the country would like their policies and programmes to be reoriented in the coming years, particularly in regard to Indo-Pakistan relations, rehabilitation of refugees, propagation of Hindi and development of cottage industries'.[36] Kripalani later said that Patel had personally called several Congress chief ministers and solicited their support for Tandon's election.[37] Nehru, on the other hand, reportedly wrote a letter on the eve of the election to G. Ramachandran in which he 'strongly disapproved Mr Tandon's candidature'.[38]

When Tandon won, Nehru saw the election result for what it was: a direct challenge to his writ by the Hindu-traditionalist wing of the Congress. 'Communal and reactionary forces had openly expressed their joy at the result,' he responded in a bitter public statement, demanding a mandate for his policies from his party at its upcoming Nasik session on 20-21 September 1950.[39] The importance of this showdown can be gauged by how Tandon framed it on his way to Nasik. Speaking to reporters at Jhansi railway station, Tandon declared that he and other party leaders were 'going to Nasik to decide finally the question of *whether the Congress must live or die* at this stage [emphasis added]'. The fact that this statement was uttered in the presence of another Hindu traditionalist, UP Chief Minister Govind Ballabh Pant, underscored the nature of the rift.[40] Another UP Congress leader put this in context, saying that 'contradictions within the Congress, artificially suppressed so far', between the forces of 'reaction and progress' were now coming to a head.[41] So important was this session that the US embassy in Delhi sent an observer to attend it.[42]

As both Nehru and Tandon headed to Nasik for a show of strength, newspapers openly wrote about the possibility of a 'split' in the Congress, which in turn could 'possibly result in another exodus of Muslims from India and accelerate the migration of Hindus from Pakistan'.[43] Interestingly, Tandon seems to have met both Nehru and Patel after his election to have a 'free and frank exchange of views' on Nehru's policies. Old friends from UP, now divided by ideas, Nehru and Tandon had agreed to continue working together. Yet, the divide was so deep that the possibility of Nehru resigning from the government and the Congress Working Committee was discussed in these meetings. The prime minister had been persuaded not to do so for the moment, but a newspaper reported that he had 'not made up his mind' on resigning.[44]

Amidst a heavy downpour that practically turned the Nasik meeting into a swamp, Nehru took the stage. He went straight for the jugular: a threat to resign. 'I am Prime Minister,' he told the Congress's delegates, 'because you have chosen me.' As he put it:[45]

> If you want me as Prime Minister you have to follow my lead unequivocally. If you do not want me as Prime Minister, you tell me so and I shall go. I will not hesitate. I will not argue. I will go out and fight for the ideals of the Congress as I have done all these years.

Speaking specifically on the 'Hindu-Muslim' refugee question and the internal party critique of his policies, Nehru drew a distinction between democratic principles and mob rule. The bottom-line was that he was not prepared 'to accept for a single moment the theory trotted out by certain sections of Congressmen and others that democracy means that whatever people feel regarding any matter is to be accepted.' The prime minister thundered: 'If that is called democracy then I say, hell with such a democracy.' And then he questioned, 'What has happened to the minds of Congressmen? Do they want today to bow before what a mob says and compromise their principles? ... I do not agree that Congressmen should do what the large majority of people ask to be done.' Nehru's emotional and hard-hitting speech won him a standing ovation. The same Congress leaders who earlier that month had voted Tandon in, passed Nehru's 'Resolution on Communalism' with an overwhelming majority.[46] At least one newspaper noted that Sardar Patel had sat in silence through the entire proceedings as Nehru's resolutions got passed. The Sardar's 'complete silence' was 'much commented upon', but 'perhaps there was nothing to it apart from his ill health'.[47]

Nehru's speech won him the immediate battle, but tensions between the 'secularists' and the 'Hindu nationalists' continued to simmer. He left Nasik with a 'disturbing suspicion' that, while his partymen may have been shamed into siding with him, they may not really have bought his argument. He was 'deeply troubled,' he said, by a 'feeling of different pools in the country and different pools and ideas within the Congress'.[48] The Congress's Hindu traditionalists hit back within a year by forcing Communications Minister Rafi Ahmad Kidwai's exit from Nehru's cabinet on 2 August 1951. Kidwai, a key Nehru confidant, resigned as a Union government minister after months of feeling sidelined in internal party decision-making by Tandon and his group, whom he accused of working in an 'undemocratic manner' against the principles of the Congress. In a strong statement against the Congress President, Kidwai publicly asked, 'Is there a parallel in the world where the executive head i.e. the President of an organisation is the very antithesis of everything that the organisation stands for? What is there in common between Shri Purshottamdas Tandon and the policies of the Congress—economic, communal, international and on refugees?'[49] This was when Nehru decided to take the bull by the horns.

In a sudden 'bombshell' move, the prime minister formally resigned from the Congress Working Committee and the party's Central Election Board. This was the first time he had ever done so. It was also the last. He was throwing down the gauntlet. A full year of 'controversy between him and the Congress President' led to this ultimatum on 7 August 1951.[50] The prime minister had spent a year in bruising battles with the Hindu traditionalists, but he was now in a stronger position within his party. Patel's death in December 1950 had also deprived the Hindu traditionalists of a powerful supporter.

By resigning, Nehru had forced the party's hand. He first won a vote of confidence in the Congress Parliamentary Party on 21 August. By 8 September, he was also elected Congress president, forcing Tandon to resign from the position. Independent India's first election was just a month away. With this victory within his own party, Nehru was now 'monarch of all that he surveys in this country', as summed up by a newspaper report.[51] It had been nothing short of a battle for the control of the party machinery. The Congress's Hindu traditionalists agreed with Mookerjee's critique of Nehru's Pakistan policy but when push came to shove, they chose not to split the party and failed to oust Nehru. As prime minister, Nehru had largely 'kept away' from organisational matters until his decisions were publicly challenged. It was Patel who had largely managed the party machine until his death. Now, Nehru wrested control.

The bitter war 'between two forces within Congress—the secular nationalists and the Hindu traditionalists' was closely watched by both the RSS and the Hindu Mahasabha. 'Nehru's victory was by no means certain even as late as August 1951, and until the outcome of the struggle was clear, the Hindu traditionalists hesitated to form a strong party to challenge the party,' Graham observed.[52] If Nehru had lost the leadership, it is not inconceivable that both Mookerjee and the RSS would have been comfortable with a Congress that could have turned Hindu nationalist. Nehru's triumph meant that such an option was out of reach. The Jan Sangh had become inevitable: it was launched nationally the very next month.

Nehru vs the Sangh: The Debate in India's First Election Campaign

Nehru single-handedly changed the political discourse on the Hindu refugee question and secularism in a very divided Congress. His refusal to concede to majority opinion, his deep personal commitment to the democratic ideal of a non-Hindu state, and his ability as a mass politician to impose his will through oratorical ability and sheer force of personality swung the debate on the Hindu–Muslim question. This explains the deep personal antagonism to Nehru that persists among Hindu nationalists to this day.

Nehru defined the fight against Hindu nationalism as India's primary political challenge. In December 1951, speaking at a rally in Bhopal, he bunched together the Jan Sangh, the Hindu Mahasabha[53] and the Ram Rajya Parishad as forces that would make the country weak. 'They had no economic or political programme,' Nehru argued. They were 'raising false slogans of religion and culture to confuse the people'. It was deplorable, that 'leaders of these organisations should have the cheek to exploit the religious sentiments of the people to further their political ends'.

The prime minister pointed out what might be seen as an early example of fake news: that 'fantastic lies' were being spread about the Hindu Code Bill, and that he had been told by some people in Gwalior that, under the Hindu Code, 'brothers and sisters would marry each other'.[54] The Sangh, Nehru felt, was funded by jagirdars, zamindars and capitalists, not because they were religious-minded but because they were taking shelter behind such groups to shield privileges that were now under threat.[55] Nehru was pitting the mass of Indians who were not privileged or monied against those with lineage, power and wealth. His reference to Gwalior in central

India, an old Hindu Mahasabha base and home to the royal dynasty of the Scindias, was telling, as he blended into his narrative the class, privilege and religiosity of his opponents.

Nehru had threatened to crush the Jan Sangh. In response, the new party was on the defensive from Day 1. In rally after rally, Mookerjee kept returning to the theme that this was a sign of 'dictatorship' and 'Hitlerism'.[56] On the specific charge of being a communal party, he accused the Congress, in turn, of deliberately misleading the Muslims. He declared at an election rally in Champaran in December 1951 that the safety of the minority lay 'not in backing the Congress' but in 'the goodwill of the majority'. Far from the Jan Sangh being a party of 'Seths', as Nehru had

Figure 9.1: Nehru Framed Independent India's First Election as a Contest between Communal and Secular Forces; Jan Sangh Joined Other Hindu Nationalist Parties against Congress

ALL INDIA BHARTIYA JAN SANGH

INDIAN NATIONAL CONGRESS

AKHIL BHARTIYA HINDU MAHASABHA

AKHIL BHARTIYA RAM RAJYA PARISHAD

The Jan Sangh adopted the Hindu lamp of purity as its election symbol. The Hindu Mahasabha poll symbol featured a Hindu warrior on horseback while the Ram Rajya Parishad, which promised to usher in the rule of Ram, showcased a rising sun. Nehru, in his campaigning, with the Congress poll symbol of two bullocks defined the contest as a battle against the combined forces of Hindu nationalism: referring to these parties and RSS as one category. Poll symbols from ECI.

sneered, Mookerji countered that most capitalists and landed magnates were with the Congress.[57] Repeated references to the Jan Sangh as being reactionary and communal, in fact, were an attempt to 'sidetrack grave issues of a national character and hide the failures and weaknesses of the Nehru government'.[58]

'The stronger the Jan Sangh is growing,' he declared, 'more infuriated is Mr Nehru. I do not mind his criticisms of our programme or policy but he is now indulging in fantastic allegations which have no relation to the truth. For instance, in his Allahabad speech, he is reported to have said that Jan Sangh is being supported by Princes and Jagirdars in Rajasthan. This is the reverse of truth. The Jan Sangh has evoked spontaneous support from large sections of the masses whose interest the Party has undertaken to promote.'[59]

This early exchange typified India's template of secular vs Hindu nationalist politics in the first few years after independence. If the Congress thought that the Jan Sangh was communal, the Jan Sangh accused its rival of minority appeasement. In the Jan Sangh's eyes, as Deendayal Upadhyaya, then the party's general secretary, would say in 1962, the alignment of Muslim communalists, the grant of Congress tickets to 'notorious pro-Pakistanis' and the appeasement by the Congress of Muslim separatism and collaboration posed a threat to the country.[60]

Fundamentally, for the Jan Sangh, the India–Pakistan problem was really only an extension of the Hindu–Muslim question before Partition. Future prime minister Atal Bihari Vajpayee summed this up in 1973, while introducing a compendium on Sangh policies:[61]

> At the time the Jana Sangh was born, the country was enmeshed in problems arising out of partition. Congress hopes that the creation of a separate Pakistan would put an end to an agonising chapter of communal violence and animosity had been falsified. The Hindu-Muslim conflict had only become enlarged into an Indo-Pak confrontation. Pakistan's aggression in Jammu-Kashmir State continued. In East Pakistan (now Bangladesh), Hindus were being decimated in a systematic manner. There was widespread discontent in the public mind regarding the Government's Pak-policy which in effect was only an extension of Congress' Muslim-appeasement policy.

These are the psychological wellsprings of the BJP's promulgation of the CAA, which remained as valid in 2020 as they were in 1973. This is precisely why, when faced with opposition to the Bill, the Modi government doubled down on it, rather than backing off.

Early Echoes of CAA, Article 370 and the Hindu Question: From the Jan Sangh's Day 1

CAA and the Unfinished Agenda of Partition: The 1950s Debate on Hindu Refugees

It is striking how many of the BJP's big-ticket political actions in 2019 can be traced back to Syama Prasad Mookerjee's inaugural address to the Jan Sangh on 21 October 1951. Presaging the debate over CAA, which triggered protests across India in 2019-20, Mookerjee had declared in his speech that the unfinished agenda of Partition—which he wanted annulled—must be solved. 'The Government of India was honour-bound to see that the minorities in Pakistan got a square deal,' he argued.[62] The Jan Sangh's early focus on non-Muslim refugees from Pakistan puts the modern politics of the BJP in context.

The party clearly saw Nehru's attitude to Hindus in Pakistan as a show of weakness on the part of India that needed correction. Speaking in Jodhpur in December 1951, Mookerjee declared that, 'Partition of India might have been agreed to by the Congress with the best of motives. It is, however, amazing that partition problems, mainly arising out of a policy of weakness and appeasement of Nehru government and also the blatantly communal and anti-Hindu policy of Pakistan should not be taken in hand and attempted to be solved ... One such problem relates to the protection of minorities in Pakistan, especially in East Bengal. The other was the problem of rehabilitation. These were not communal problems but political and international.'[63]

This runs quite close to what Narendra Modi or Amit Shah argued in 2020, while making a case for CAA. Replying to questions in Parliament in December 2019, Amit Shah was categorical: 'It would have been nice if Partition did not take place on the religious line, but it did. Muslim majority areas went to Pakistan and rest became India. Had India not been divided on religious lines, there was no need for Citizenship (Amendment) Bill ... Those who have suffered are the ones who can best tell their story ... We cannot say no to shelter to those who have come here seeking protection for their daughters.'[64]

In 1958, the Jan Sangh even passed a resolution demanding the rehabilitation of refugees who could not be settled in West Bengal in the nearby areas of Assam, Bihar, Orissa, Tripura, Manipur and Dandakaranya. An eight-member committee was set up in Calcutta for this.[65] An early prestige battle for the party was the fate of 9 million Hindus who remained in East Pakistan. By November 1952, the refugee influx had ended, 80,000 refugees remained in camps, and a new passport system was started. When the CPI started an 'Indo-Pak friendship week', the Jan Sangh's S.P. Mookerjee rejected it, questioning how agreements could be reached with a 'persistent wrong-doer'. He suggested that the communists could go to East Pakistan 'with their families' and try to mobilise public opinion against the passport system. Speaking at the All India Convention for Minority Rights, Mookerjee called for the passport system to be withdrawn.

His hard line on East Pakistan was predicated on three reasons. Hindus, he argued, were being converted in many parts of Pakistan. Nehru's approach of providing a 'healing touch', he dismissed scornfully as 'quack remedies'. And finally, the public mind was 'deeply agitated over the whole problem of the fate of minorities in Eastern Pakistan'.[66]

This is why, in 1956, the Sangh passed a resolution saying it was 'profoundly shocked' at the 'sudden reversal of the Government of India's policy with respect to the exodus of Hindus from East Bengal and restricting the issuance of migration certificates to Hindu migrants'. This virtual banning of Hindu migration from East Bengal 'at the behest of Pakistan', the resolution said, 'has indeed been an abject surrender to the forces of communalism let loose in the Islamic Republic, and it is calculated to result in the extermination of the Hindus in East Bengal'. It urged the government to give up the 'weak-kneed' policy immediately.[67]

The debate over the BJP's CAA in 2019-20 occurred in a very different India from that of the 1950s. Yet, the idea underpinning it lies at the very heart of the primary political fault-line on Pakistan's Hindu minorities that led to the founding of the Jan Sangh itself. The BJP may have politically overextended itself in 2019 with the twinning of CAA, meant for religious minorities in Pakistan, with a future NRC, which was meant to detect and deport illegal migrants already in India. The NRC was to follow in a 'chronology', said the home minister, after CAA. When this ignited nationwide protests and raised fears over the citizenship of minorities, the BJP seemed to put the NRC, which it had championed between April and December 2019, on the political backburner.[68]

Prime Minister Modi drew a line under this in an election rally in Delhi's Ramlila Maidan on 22 December 2019 when he insisted: 'Those Muslims who were born on Indian soil should not be concerned by CAA and the NRC. They have nothing to do with these things.'[69] He said that there had been 'no discussion on the word NRC' within his government since it came to power in 2014.[70] Home Minister Amit Shah followed suit two days later with the same clarification and the government subsequently informed Parliament in February 2020 that there had been no decision to prepare an NRC at the national level.[71]

For Mookerjee, in 1952, the treatment of minorities in Pakistan was nothing less than a policy of 'squeezing out Hindus', which he considered an 'indirect aggression on India'.[72] This line of thinking eventually led to CAA.

It is no coincidence that Amit Shah, while defending the CAA in Parliament in December 2019, responded to the Opposition's questions by referring to the Nehru–Liaquat Pact of 1950 a number of times. He emphasised that India had honoured its obligations of equality and protection of minorities, as the Pact had envisaged, but that Pakistan—as an Islamic state with restrictions on equality for minorities—had not. This, he argued, was why CAA was necessary. On the question of why Muslims were left out from the ambit of the law, he argued that 'where there is an Islamic state, Muslims cannot be termed religious minorities'. He insisted that the law had nothing to do with the existing citizenship of Indian Muslims and they had nothing to fear. 'This is not a law for taking citizenship, this is a law for giving citizenship,' he said.[73]

A detailed examination of the legal debate on CAA is outside the scope of this book. The law has been challenged in the courts on several grounds. The point is that, leaving the National Population Register (NPR) aside, the BJP's move to enact CAA in 2020 was the outcome of a long-held article of belief: to correct what Hindu nationalists always saw as a historic wrong. The fundamental belief that underpinned CAA—the defence of religious minorities in Pakistan and India's obligations to them—was literally a core political aim of the party from the day of the Jan Sangh's birth.

Interestingly, the 1950s debate on Hindu refugees also led to the First Amendment of the Constitution, which introduced more restrictions on free speech. The Supreme Court, on 26 May 1950, had lifted a ban on the leftist Bombay publication *Cross Roads* (which had been critical of Nehru's foreign policy) and also nullified a pre-censorship order on the RSS publication *Organiser* (which was critical of Nehru's refugee policy) in Delhi. The apex court ruled in a 5–1 judgement that such restrictions on free speech were unconstitutional.[74] At the time, the original Article 19(2) of the Constitution, which guaranteed free speech, had very limited restrictions. The lawyer and scholar Abhinav Chandrachud has shown that between March and June 1950, worried about open talk of war, Nehru wrote two letters to Patel complaining about 'Hindu Mahasabha propaganda' and 'the Calcutta press as well as Syama Prasad Mookerjee' as 'chief culprit[s]' that could harm the Delhi Pact with Pakistan. Because of the Supreme Court's unambiguous judgement, Patel wrote back on 3 July 1950 that there were 'no legal powers to deal with either Press or men like Syama Prasad Mookerjee'. He suggested that they would soon have to 'consider constitutional amendments'. Nehru then wrote in October 1950 to Law Minister B.R. Ambedkar with an opinion that the right to free speech needed to be amended. Ambedkar agreed, and Parliament passed the First Amendment to the Constitution on 2 June 1951.[75] Among the new restrictions to free speech were imperilling 'public order', inciting an offence or affecting 'friendly relations with foreign States'.[76]

The Early Hard-coding of Kashmir into the Party Agenda

In the earliest example of the BJP's present position on Kashmir, on the very first day of the establishment of the Jan Sangh, the party president announced that India should withdraw the Kashmir issue from the United Nations (UN) as 'the state was an integral part of India' and that the part of Kashmir under Pakistan administration should be liberated.[77] The Modi government's lightning strike on Article 370 in August 2019, through the Jammu and Kashmir Reorganisation Act, 2019, fulfilled a foundational demand that has animated the BJP and its predecessor from their very inception. This party objective is older even than the Ram Temple in Ayodhya, which the party formally embraced as a political goal only with the 1989 Palampur Resolution. The 'integration' of Kashmir, by contrast, was a fundamental party goal for the Jan Sangh right from 1951.

As early as February 1952, the Jan Sangh passed a political resolution emphasising the fact that India's constitutional provisions on Kashmir were 'of a temporary character'. The Sangh Central Working Committee's (CWC's) first resolution on internal affairs too asked for India to withdraw the issue from the UN.[78] It laid out expectations for the kind of state that Kashmir would eventually be when it 'integrates with India'. That same year, it declared that the State Constituent Assembly's decision to have a separate flag for Kashmir and its recommendations that the state be an autonomous republic within the Indian republic were a 'clear violation of India's sovereignty and the spirit of the Indian Constitution'.[79]

The BJP, in 2019, positioned the abrogation of Article 370 as the correction of a 'historical blunder'. 'In Jammu and Kashmir, Sardar Patel was right and Nehruji was wrong,' declared Union Law and Justice Minster Ravi Shankar Prasad in September 2019—again pitting 'secular' Nehru against 'Hindu traditionalist' Patel.[80] This may be an oversimplification of a complex historical story. Patel was, after all, the home minister of India at the time and Article 370 was passed with his consent. A fuller examination of Patel's role and how the Kashmir debate unfolded within the Congress at the time of accession is outside the scope of this book. But even if Patel was not the 'key architect' of Article 370, as the historian Srinath Raghavan has argued, the evidence does not indicate that he could have ensured full integration of Kashmir even if he had taken a more hands-on role.[81]

Between 1952 and 1972, the Jan Sangh passed as many as twenty-four political resolutions on Kashmir—almost one-third of all its resolutions on the wider issue of national unity. The revocation of Article 370 has also been a permanent fixture on BJP poll manifestos.

Revealingly, in 1953, when Jan Sangh leaders sat in a conference to finalise a new constitution for the party, they simultaneously passed a

Figure 9.2: Jan Sangh Saw Kashmir as Its Most Important Internal Political Concern (1951–1972)

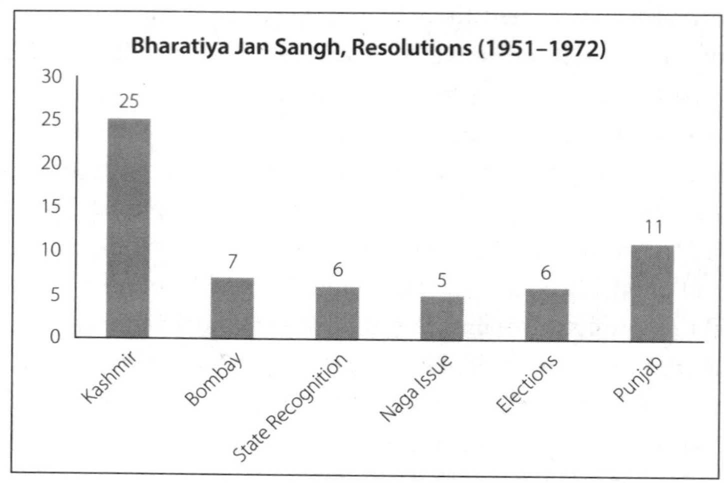

Source: Author's statistical analysis of all Jan Sangh Resolutions on Internal Affairs (1951–1972). Bharatiya Jan Sangh Party Documents, 1951–72, Vol. 4: Resolutions on Internal Affairs (New Delhi: Bharatiya Jan Sangh, 1973)

resolution demanding the 'full accession of Kashmir State to India failing which the integration of Jammu and Ladakh with Indian territory'.[82]

By the time the Jan Sangh was formed, Kashmir's special constitutional status, and Sheikh Abdullah's National Conference's insistence on retaining it, had come under strong attack from the Hindu community of Jammu, led by the Praja Parishad, and Buddhist groups from Ladakh. The Praja Parishad had been set up by RSS pracharak Balraj Madhok (later a founding member of the Jan Sangh) in November 1947, with the aim of forcing full integration of the state with India. In India's only Muslim-majority state, it received support from Dogra landowners, who were part of the ruling class under the erstwhile Maharaja's reign, but who now felt threatened by land reforms. In Jammu and Kashmir, 'deep-seated communal differences lay just below the surface of party-politics'. The Praja Parishad's agitation, organised around the slogan '*Ek Vidhan, Ek Nishaan, Ek Pradhan*' (One Constitution, One Symbol, One Premier), gained momentum when three Hindu nationalist parties—the Jan Sangh, the Hindu Mahasabha and the Ram Rajya Parishad—decided to back it. The Kashmir agitation became a key Jan Sangh priority after the 1952 general election. Syama Prasad Mookerjee's arrest in Kashmir and his mysterious death on 24 June 1953 while in police custody ended the agitation.[83] But it only served to underscore the centrality of the Kashmir question for the Jan Sangh's politics.

On 25 January 1954, the Jan Sangh demanded the full integration of Kashmir into the Indian Union. Its CWC passed another resolution on this in Bombay, titled 'Integrate Kashmir', saying that 'any continuance of the present uncertainty about Kashmir under Article 370 is undesirable'. In the Jan Sangh's view, only S.P. Mookerjee's death and the Jan Sangh's agitation saved India 'from second dismemberment' and 'rarely has history vindicated a stand in so short a period and in so unequivocal a manner'.[84] By 1955, it was demanding, as its CWC did in Jodhpur, 'This State should be completely merged with India and fully brought on the level of other States. All the remaining Fundamental Rights of Indian citizens should be extended to the citizens of Kashmir and the National Flag of India should be honoured in the State as the highest flag and not on the same level with the State flag of Kashmir.'[85]

The Jan Sangh passed resolution after resolution on the integration of Kashmir, right up to 1960. In 1958, at Delhi, it concluded that, while the writ of the Indian state should extend to all parts of Kashmir, 'abolition of permit system and all such discriminations between the citizens of the state and those of the rest of India are some of the essential steps that need to be taken in this connection ...'[86] This is exactly what Narendra Modi and Amit Shah did on 5 August 2019. Narendra Modi, after all, had accompanied the then BJP president Murali Manohar Joshi on his Ekta Yatra (Unity Journey) in December 1991–January 1992, to hoist the tricolour in Srinagar's Lal Chowk.

Exactly as the BJP argued in 2019, the Jan Sangh, in the 1950s, blamed the resistance in Kashmir on its ruling party elites. 'The ruling circles of Kashmir are interested in perpetuating the discrimination because it pays them. They try to perpetuate their hold over the Government through rigged elections and authoritarian methods. What is worse, the wrath of the people against the authorities in Kashmir (who have developed a vested interest in this position and who defend it in the name of internal Autonomy of the State) is in the ultimate, diverted against the Government and the people of India.' This is why it asked for 'immediate steps' to 'delete the transitional article 370' and to bring Kashmir in line with 'other States of India without any further delay'.[87]

Again, in 1966, the CWC reiterated its demands, arguing that Article 370 was a big hindrance to integration because it had 'created a psychological barrier' between Kashmiris and other Indians. In the Jan Sangh's view, Article 370 was 'exploited by anti-national elements and Pak agents to the detriment of vital Indian interests'.[88]

This is the historical legacy Prime Minister Modi and Amit Shah have delivered as an article of faith.

Jan Sangh and Its Target of Congress-mukt Bharat in the 1950s

In early 2014, Narendra Modi issued his now-famous call for a Congress-mukt Bharat (Congress-free India). The roots of this idea too can be traced back to Mookerjee's inaugural address to his party. Speaking to party delegates in their 1951 meeting, Mookerjee said that he saw the Jan Sangh emerging as the main Opposition party for all those who had a 'deep-rooted discontent and frustration' with the Congress. Instead of trying to solve their grievances, he argued, the Nehru government was trying to 'gag all those who sought to ventilate the people's grievances'. 'The Congress has lost the support of the people and was therefore attempting to perpetuate its rule by stifling all opposition. The drift today towards dictatorship was further felicitated by the absence of a well-organised opposition party.'[89]

The Jan Sangh was forged in a spirit of anti-Congressism from its founding moment. As Mookerjee was to say in 1951, 'We want Jana Sangh to grow up as an opposition party and prepare itself to serve as an alternative Government of this country.' This idea was also accompanied by a deep sense of victimhood. In August 1966, Balraj Madhok, president of the party, delivered a lecture at the Ahmedabad Junior Chamber that was titled 'What Bharatiya Jana Sangh Stands For'. He started by telling his audience, which consisted of the who's who of Gujarat's magnates, 'Bharatiya Jana Sangh is the one party which has been most condemned and maligned all these years without a hearing. From the day the Jan Sangh came into being, the late Pandit Jawaharlal Nehru, the ruling Congress

Party and its ideological allies as also the Communist Party started their volley against it. Perhaps, they instinctively felt that this new party might trounce them one day. Even though the first general elections were held only three months after the Jana Sangh was born yet the Jan Sangh was the main target of the Congress, Pandit Nehru, the Communist Party and everybody else. So many things have been said about us—Jana Sangh is a communal party, it is a reactionary party, it has no economic programme and so on.'[90] At the heart of this conception was the fervent belief that the Congress would soon wear itself out and wither away. From the 1960s onwards, as Madhok told his listeners, the Jan Sangh was convinced that 'in the next few years *Congress Party is going to disappear* as the ruling party in the country'.[91] It is not too difficult to see how this core belief informed the slogan of 'Congress-mukt Bharat'.

The RSS and the Jan Sangh: Cadre, Control and Power Equations

From its very inception, the Jan Sangh sought to distinguish itself from the existing Hindu nationalist parties: the Hindu Mahasabha[92] and the Ram Rajya Parishad (literally, Ram Rule Assembly, which was formed in Rajasthan with the aim of ushering in 'Ram's rule' by Swami Kalpatri in 1947).[93] Mookerjee, who had quit the Hindu Mahasabha earlier, emphasised that the new party had no connection with the Mahasabha.

Yet, it was the Jan Sangh's close relationship with the RSS, which supported it but was not a political party, that raised questions from the very beginning. Mookerjee addressed this issue directly in his inaugural speech to the party, acknowledging the RSS lineage of several members. He said emphatically, 'There are members of the RSS who in their individual capacity, have come in to the Jana Sangh and are working on it. But there are also large numbers of other people in the party who have nothing to do with the RSS.'[94]

Mookerjee and RSS chief Golwalkar had even met to discuss the contours of this relationship prior to the party's formation. Golwalkar later recalled this conversation in a 1956 article, saying 'we [he and Mookerjee] met often'. He added that in these conversations he had insisted that 'RSS could not be drawn into politics', would not 'play second fiddle to any political or other party' and would not be a 'handmaiden to political parties'.[95]

Yet, in practice, while the early Jan Sangh relied on Mookerjee's national stature as a Hindu traditionalist, to a large extent it was built on the strength of the RSS cadre. Most of its 'key organisers came from the RSS'. These included Deendayal Upadhyaya, secretary of the UP Jan Sangh; Atal Bihari Vajpayee, all-India general secretary who had joined the RSS in his student days; Professor Mahavir; and Balraj Madhok, founder of the Punjab Jan Sangh and an RSS pracharak from Jammu.[96]

This meant that when Mookerjee died in 1953, the nascent party was engulfed in a major leadership tussle: between the more liberal Hindu traditionalists who had come with him and those who came from the RSS. Between 1951 and 1967, the party had twelve presidents, with an average tenure of 1.3 years each (see Table 8.4). The organisation only gained leadership stability from 1967 onwards: first with Deendayal Upadhyaya, then with Atal Bihari Vajpayee and later with L.K. Advani. The latter two served as party president for four years each until the Jan Sangh merged into the Janata Party in 1977. All three men had been in the RSS.

Table 9.1: Jan Sangh Presidents: 1951–1975

S. No.	*Jan Sangh President*	*Year*	*Origins*
1.	Syama Prasad Mookerjee (died in Kashmir in custody, under mysterious circumstances)	1951–1953	Bengal; former Acting President, Hindu Mahasabha
2.	Mauli Chandra Sharma (resigned, later expelled from party)	1954	Delhi; ex-Congress, initially associated with Hindu Mahasabha
3.	Prem Nath Dogra	1955	J&K; instrumental in forming Jammu Praja Parishad
4.	Debaprasad Ghosh	1956–1959	West Bengal
5.	Pitambar Das	1960	UP; connected with Swadeshi movement
6.	Avasala Rama Rao	1961	Andhra Pradesh
7.	Debaprasad Ghosh	1962	West Bengal

S. No.	*Jan Sangh President*	*Year*	*Origins*
8.	Raghu Vira (died in car accident)	1963	Rawalpindi, Punjab; ex-Congress (resigned over differences on Nehru's China policy)
9.	Debaprasad Ghosh	1964	West Bengal
10.	Bachhraj Vyas	1965	Rajasthan; RSS
11.	Balraj Madhok (later expelled from party)	1966	Punjabi Khatri from Jammu; RSS, and key founder of Jammu Praja Parishad
12.	Deendayal Upadhyaya (killed on a train, under mysterious circumstances)	1967–1968	UP (Mathura); RSS
13.	Atal Bihari Vajpayee	1968–1972	Madhya Pradesh (Gwalior); RSS
14.	L.K. Advani	1973–1977	Sindhi from Karachi, RSS

The short tenures of the early Jan Sangh leaders pointed to conflict at the top of the party structure between Mookerjee loyalists and those from the RSS. As B.D. Graham has argued, 'The essential clash in 1954 was between the young RSS organisers, intent upon making the Jana Sangh more centralized and disciplined, and Sharma's relatively weak group of secondary leaders, trying ineffectually to defend what remained of Mookerjee's project for an open and democratic party.'[97] The clash was typified in a formal statement issued by Mookerjee's successor, Mauli Chandra Sharma, on 4 November 1954:[98]

> Acute differences of opinion on the question of interference by the RSS in its affairs of the Jana Sangh have been growing for over a year. Many RSS workers have entered into the party since its inception. They were welcomed, as RSS leaders had publicly declared that it was a purely cultural body having nothing to do with politics and that its members were perfectly free to join any political party. In practice, however, it did not prove to be so.
>
> The late Dr Mookerjee was often seriously perturbed by the demands of RSS leaders for a decisive role in matters like the appointment of office-bearers, nomination of candidates for elections and matters of policy. We

> however hoped that the rank and file of the RSS would be drawn into the arena of democratic public life through their association with the Jana Sangh.
>
> A vigorous and calculated drive was launched to turn the Jana Sangh into a convenient handle of the RSS. Orders were issued from their headquarters through their emissaries and the Jana Sangh was expected to carry them out. Many workers and groups all over the country resented this and the Delhi State Jana Sangh as a body refused to comply.

Madhok (who was later expelled from the party) also complained about this kind of pressure. As late as March 1973, he wrote to the then party president, L.K. Advani, complaining that 'the organizing secretaries who happen to be the real power in the Jana Sangh, having been conversant only with the working system of the RSS want to run Jana Sangh on the same lines. They have nothing but, contempt for democratic forms, norms and conventions. Dissent of any kind is anathema for them. They want to suppress all dissidents in the name of discipline. They are interested more in control than in the growth of the party. That is the real problem and dilemma of Jana Sangh which will have to be resolved one day. The sooner it is resolved, the better it would be for the RSS, the Jana Sangh and the country.'[99]

The RSS imprint on the Jan Sangh accrued from its cadre strength. In 1954, the Jan Sangh had only 1,43,000 members. This went up to 2,10,000 by 1959. In contrast, in 1951, the RSS already counted 6,31,500 active members. More significantly, by 1950, while the Jan Sangh had created 2,000 local centres nationwide, the RSS already had 5,000 centres.[100] The RSS held the levers of power.

When Deendayal Upadhyaya took over as party president in 1967, he consolidated the cultural Hindu nationalist underpinning of the party by dividing the party organisation into zones, writes the scholar Pralay Kanungo. Each zone was headed by a former RSS pracharak: Balraj Madhok (North), Nanaji Deshmukh (East), Sundar Singh Bhandari (West), Jagannath Rao Joshi (South). Their work was coordinated by Vajpayee and J.P. Mathur. All these men shared the 'RSS ideology'.[101]

The questions that Sharma and Madhok raised about the RSS would show up again in the problem of 'dual membership' of RSS members that was to plague the Jan Sangh when it merged with the Janata Party in

Figure 9.3: Deendayal Upadhayaya Comic at the BJP Headquarters, Delhi. He is One of Only Two Jan Sangh Leaders Whose Life Story is Enshrined in Comic Form and Promoted by the BJP

The comic depicts Deendayal Upadhyaya saying that Indian nationalism is predicated on 'Bharat Mata' (Mother India), not just India. 'Without the word "Mata", Bharat will remain only a piece of land,' he says in the comic. Upadhayaya is also the only political leader in whose name the Modi government has rechristened some Central government schemes. Images from 'Deendayal Upadhyaya Chitrawali' published by Prabhat Prakashan, Deen Dayal Shodh Sansthan, New Delhi.

1977 as part of a grand Opposition alliance to take on the Congress. The Janata government of Morarji Desai fell in 1979 after many of its leaders, including Deputy Prime Minister Chaudhary Charan Singh, questioned the 'dual membership' of former Jan Sangh members.[102]

The 'Rule of 75': Why Did the Jan Sangh Not Win Elections?

In 1969, a young Jan Sangh worker and lawyer in Bombay, Narandas Mehta, the youngest to contest Bombay Municipal Corporation elections in 1961, put forward a new thesis on why the party was not winning elections. Aimed at starting a major rethink among the top leadership,

Figure 9.4: Congress and Bharatiya Jan Sangh Vote Shares in Lok Sabha Elections

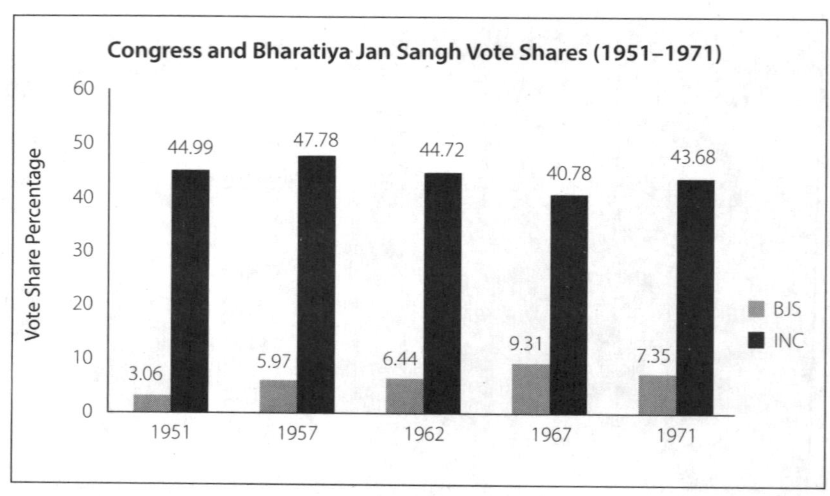

Source: ECI. Analysis by author

Figure 9.5: Bharatiya Jan Sangh Seat Share in Lok Sabha Elections (1951–1971)

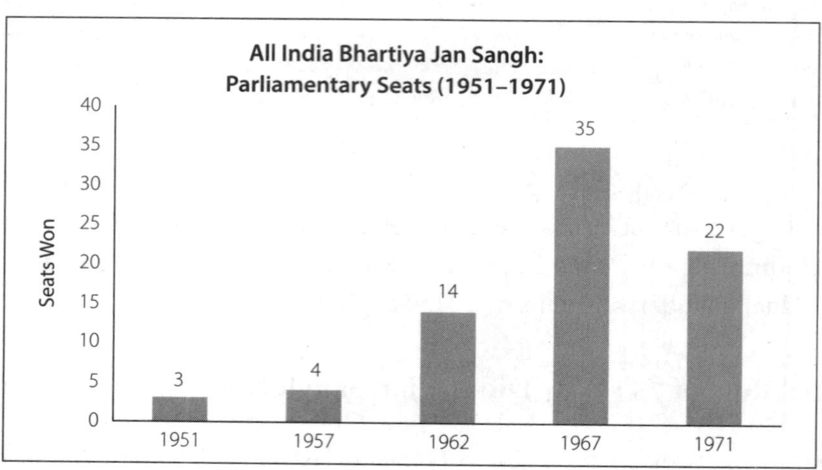

Source: ECI. Analysis by author

this provocative treatise, titled *Bharatiya Jana Sangh and the Rule of 75%*, was published by the party's Bombay branch.

What was this Rule of 75? After a study of the Lok Sabha and assembly election results until then, Mehta argued that the Jan Sangh's problem was not that it did not win seats nor that its ideology was unwinnable. It was a question of electoral tactics, retention of gains and holding on to wins. 'At least in 75% of the seats won in previous election[s],' he argued, 'Jana Sangh fails to retain the same. In other words, the Jana Sangh cannot retain more than 25% of the seats won in the previous elections and loses the 75% of the seats won in the previous elections. This is precisely *The Rule of 75%*.'[103]

Mehta's critique needs some context. In absolute terms, the Sangh went from just three seats and 3.06 per cent vote share in the 1951 Lok Sabha elections to four seats (5.97 per cent) in 1957, fourteen (6.44 per cent) in 1962, thirty-five (9.31 per cent) in 1967 and twenty-two (7.35 per cent) in the 1971 general elections (see Figures 9.4 and 9.5). So, it was winning more seats in successive elections.

A Shift to Alliances with Ideologically Different Parties: The Change of 1967

The year 1967 was a turning point, with the Jan Sangh's decision to enter into electoral alliances with parties that did not share its ideology. After Mookerjee's death, the party had chosen to follow a 'closed' strategy. Its own social base remained narrow: primarily in urban areas, and among upper castes and traders. The Jan Sangh's cultural messaging had limited political impact at a time when, at the provincial level, the Congress was itself highly Hindu traditionalist. The ruling party's provincial leaders may have lost the larger secular–communal debate to Nehru in 1950-51, but at the district level, and below the elite levels of discourse, the ideological boundaries between Hindu nationalists (from the Jan Sangh and the RSS) and Congressmen remained 'fuzzy' through the 1950s. Below elite levels of discourse, there was little distinction between Congress attitudes on issues of Hindu nationalism and those of the Jan Sangh.[104]

When the Jan Sangh did make alliances, it did so with local power groups that had a narrow upper-caste base. In 1951, for example, it made small alliances with the Uttar Pradesh Praja Party, the Zamindar Party in Punjab and the Purusharthi Parishad in Ajmer.[105] Until the 1960s, it only entered into local seat adjustments, such as with the Swatantra Party.

By the late 1960s, the Jan Sangh had changed its policy. The key progenitors of this change were Nanaji Deshmukh and Atal Bihari Vajpayee—who advocated pre-poll alliances with diverse players, including the communists. This shift led to the Jan Sangh joining the Samyukta Vidhayak Dal (SVD), a grand alliance of Opposition parties against the Congress, in the national and state elections of 1967. Their combined might took the Congress to its lowest point ever in Parliament until then, and the party lost power in several states. New SVD governments came to power in several states with the Jan Sangh as a key partner. In UP, for example, the Jan Sangh won ninety-eight of 425 state assembly seats (the highest after the Congress's 199), as part of the SVD alliance. Jan Sangh leaders joined the new UP government in an alliance that included two communist parties and several others. 'Jan Sangh's Ram Prakash Gupta, Baldev Prakash, V.K. Saklecha became deputy chief ministers in Uttar Pradesh, Punjab and Madhya Pradesh respectively. Vijay Kumar Malhotra became chief executive councilor in Delhi's Metropolitan Council, and L.K. Advani, the Chairman (Speaker); Hans Raj Gupta was elected Mayor of Delhi Municipal Corporation; Vijay Kumar Mitra, Ram Deo Mahto and Rudra Pratap Saran became ministers in Bihar.'[106]

This began a new phase of expansion in the Jan Sangh, culminating in the party's merger with the Janata Party. The BJP headquarters in Delhi still sells a comic book on Nanaji Deshmukh, depicting his key role in ending the Jan Sangh's isolation and beginning an era of alliance-building after a meeting with the socialist leader Ram Manohar Lohia.

By 1967, a contemporary press account observed: 'Few political parties have risen so spectacularly as the Bharatiya Jana Sangh.' Between 1962 and 1967, its membership more than doubled from 6,00,000 to 13,00,000, and it emerged as the 'major opposition party in north India'. The 1962 war and rehabilitation work done by RSS workers marked an important watershed. When the Indian Institute of Public Opinion predicted that the Jan Sangh could well 'become India's largest opposition party in the next two or three years', *Organiser* splashed it across the front page. For good measure, it took a dig at the party's English-language critics: 'Those who

Figure 9.6: Nanaji Deshmukh Comic Depicting Alliance-formation with Socialist Leader Ram Manohar Lohia

The socialist leader Ram Manohar Lohia is depicted in the comic in a meeting with Nanaji Deshmukh. Deshmukh is seen telling Lohia that he wants to be friends because Lohia showed courage in openly defying Nehru. Lohia asks how they can be friends, since Deshmukh is from the Jan Sangh. Deshmukh responds that he will always remain with his party, but that he had good relations with several non-Jan Sangh leaders, including those from the Congress, like Charan Singh, Lal Bahadur Shastri and Dr Sampurnanand. Images from 'Nanaji Deshmukh Chitrawali' published by Prabhat Prakashan, Deen Dayal Shodh Sansthan, New Delhi.

always used to scoff are today in a mood to praise, if not to pray.'[107] The Jan Sangh's political fortunes were clearly on the upswing. As *Weekend Review* noted, it 'is the only party (of the right) which does not owe its origin to the Congress dissidence movement'. More generally, 'the Jana Sangh appears to provide an ideal inlet for those pent-up nationalist forces in India which view with alarm the erosion of traditional values in the name of progress'.[108]

The Jan Sangh's problem, as young Narandas Mehta saw it, was that of holding on to past gains: it kept losing seats it already held. In the 1962 general election, the party substantially increased its vote share, winning fourteen new Lok Sabha seats, but lost all five seats it had held until then.[109]

That it stood second in as many as fifty-two seats showed that the party was making key advances, but it was not creating sustainable vote banks. One of the Jan Sangh's leading lights in the capital, Balraj Madhok, lost his New Delhi seat in 1962. In UP, Brajraj Singh, deputy leader of the Jan Sangh in the Lok Sabha from 1962 to 1967, lost from Aonla in 1967, a result that party leaders viewed as 'shocking and tragic'. Even Deendayal Upadhyaya, 'the great personality and the architect of the Jan Sangh', lost by over 69,000 votes a by-election in Jaunpur that had been necessitated by the death of the sitting MP.[110] The same trend was replicated in Punjab and Haryana, areas full of Partition refugees, where the party lost all the three seats it had gained.

In contrast to the Jan Sangh, Mehta observed with dismay that the Communist Party retained more than 75 per cent of the seats it had won in the previous election. Not a single Jan Sangh MP, including Vajpayee and Madhok, until that point had been elected to Parliament thrice. In contrast, the Communists had several three- or four-time MPs: men like A.K. Gopalan, Hiren Mukerji, Renu Chakravarty, Indrajit Gupta, S.M. Bannerji, Anandan Nambiar and Sarju Pande. In August 1967, Mehta and a group of Jan Sangh workers met Vajpayee in Bombay when he came to address workers in Matunga. They presented their thesis, along with facts and figures. Vajpayee gave them a 'patient hearing', accepted their findings and said, '*ab aisa nahin hoga* [this will not happen from now on]'.[111] The 1967 SVD alliances briefly changed Jan Sangh fortunes. Yet, in the 1969 mid-term elections to state assemblies in UP, Punjab and West Bengal, once again the party lost 79 per cent (117 of 149) of the seats it had won previously. All the Jan Sangh ministers were defeated in UP in 1969, as were its state president and key leaders in Punjab, all from seats they had won earlier. Furthermore, it lost its urban base in key cities—Amritsar, Jullunder, Gurgaon, Ambala, Lucknow, Bhiwani, Karnal, Pathankot and so on.

So why was the Sangh failing to hold on to its political gains, unlike the communists? This conundrum greatly animated the senior leadership of the Sangh and the pages of *Organiser* in the late 1960s. Party leaders identified several factors.

They argued that the Congress, the party in power, concentrated its firepower against the Jan Sangh, focusing on wresting back seats wherever the latter advanced. Besides, the Jan Sangh was handicapped by the fact that it did not have enough leaders with stature, *Organiser* editor K.R. Malkani argued in the magazine's February 1969 issue. This was a 'essentially a matter of length in public life'. Party leaders speculated that the wave of anti-Congressism that had driven Opposition politics had subsided. At the state level, senior leaders felt that the Jan Sangh had been hamstrung by its alliances. Many of them also argued that, in Punjab, its alliance with the Akali Dal had 'antagonised' Hindu voters. In Bengal, they felt the anti-communist vote ended up going to the Congress since it was felt that the Jan Sangh would not be able to defeat the communists, while in UP, it was felt that casteism cost the party dearly, since Jat–Ahir votes were going to Charan Singh's Bharatiya Kranti Dal (BKD).[112]

Mehta argued that none of these tactical reasons held up to deeper scrutiny. If the Congress was focusing on wresting back seats the Jan Sangh had won, it was doing that just as strongly with the communists. The Communist Party was capable of 'maintaining these seats in spite of severe Congress opposition in these constituencies while Jana Sangh succumbs in such circumstances'. If it was a question of stature, then no new entrants could ever hope to make it in politics against the Congress. Besides, the Communist Party's young guns were managing to win elections, but not the Jan Sangh's. For example, while 'Sri Ram Prakash Gupta, the young Jana Sangh leader failed to defeat Congress in UP, the young and dynamic Jyoti Basu was able to shatter the Congress and bring Communist Party Marxist into power in Bengal'.

If the wave of anti-Congressism had subsided, then, between 1967 and 1969, the Congress would not have gone from 127 seats to fifty-five in West Bengal, from 128 to 118 in Bihar and from forty-seven to thirty-eight in Punjab, Mehta argued. Such excuses, he felt, were 'a big lie': 'This is only trying to fool one's own self as well as the ordinary Jana Sangh workers.' In Punjab, for example, though the Jan Sangh's state president and finance minister, Dr Baldev Prakash, was defeated from Amritsar, the Communist Party's Satyapal Dang won the same seat, despite being in alliance with the Akali Dal. Similarly, in UP, Sangh candidates were defeated in urban areas like Lucknow and Bareilly, where there was no significant caste-based voting by Jats or Ahirs. [113]

Lessons the Sangh Learnt from the Communists on Winning Elections

Mehta concluded that the reason the Jan Sangh was not growing was because of deeper strategic failures: too much dependence on floating voters, no mass base among the working classes, lack of contact with the masses and an inability to use power to infiltrate institutions. These lessons, which he drew from the Communist Party, are all significant in contemporary politics too. Mehta forcefully argued that the Jan Sangh was too dependent on white-collar office-goers, small traders, upper middle-class intelligentsia and professionals. These voters 'were uncertain … hence are carried away by the winds blowing at the time of elections'. This is what happened in Lucknow, where the Jan Sangh's candidate, Radhey Shyam, lost his security deposit. 'In Amritsar, Ludhiana, Jullunder, Ambala, also white collared floating voters shifted again to Congress.' The Communist consolidation, on the other hand, was based on its focus on an 'illiterate, uneducated but faithful class'. The Jan Sangh 'never concentrated its strength on Harijans, backward class, oppressed people, slum dwellers or other toiling masses', Mehta said. In terms of voting numbers, these groups mattered much more. In many ways, he was setting the template for what became the BJP's greater mobilisation in the 1990s, and especially later under Modi and Shah.

The third lesson that Sangh leaders drew was that too much intellectualism lost it votes. Election reverses taught its top brass that focusing on esoteric intellectual issues did not mean anything to voters. As Mehta memorably put it: [114]

> As soon as the Jana Sangh worker is elected to assembly or parliament he goes to the hungry, roofless, and half-naked masses and says, 'We shall sever diplomatic relations with China', 'We shall recognise Dalai Lama as the head of the Government in Exile in for Tibet', 'Recognise Formosa', 'Recognise Israel', 'Forge Better Relations with South-East Asian countries', 'Tit for Tat policy with Pakistan', 'Abrogate section 370

> of the Indian Constitution giving special status to Jammu and Kashmir', 'Make Hindi national and official language', 'Crush Naga and Mizo rebels': as if by shouting the above slogans the down trodden masses will be uplifted …
>
> Such policy matters can well be presented before the organisations like the Rotary Club, Lions Club, Junior Chamber, Bombay's Progressive group or before intellectual class of lawyers, graduates, professors, college students and businessmen … the first general secretary of Bharatiya Jana Sangh Prof. Dr. Bhai Mahavir defended such speakers … and bravely declared that these are the planks and fundamentals of Jana Sangh and no Bharatiya Jana Sangh leader can afford to bypass such matters … True, we also agree. But before whom all these policy matters are to be placed? Before the hungry, roofless and half-naked masses? Definitely not …
>
> May I humbly submit to Dr. Bhai Mahavir that for the Communist Party, the recognition of East Germany, North Korea, North Vietnam is the fundamental plank of the party, but they never emphasise these matters before the masses, working class and proletariat.

Jan Sangh leaders realised that they were top-heavy and a party of intellectuals (albeit of the opposite kind vis-à-vis the prevailing Left/liberal mindset), and they did not have enough feet on the ground. They began to focus on creating a cadre using strategies employed by the RSS. 'We were told day in and day out that workers cannot be created through public meetings or newspapers. But we now find that the RSS now a days hold big public meetings and runs a chain of newspapers throughout the country.' The idea was to create empowered local groups of leaders with the autonomy to act within the party's basic ideology. Here, the Sangh looked up to leaders like D.B. Thengde of the Bharatiya Mazoor Sangh, who would tell his workers, 'You are allowed to make a mistake, but with one condition, that is you should not repeat the same kind of mistake. I shall allow you to commit another kind of mistake.'[115]

After the Jan Sangh joined governments for the first time in 1967, Mehta argued they did not leverage their election gains for power-sharing. Unlike the aggressive BJP of Maharashtra 2019, which refused to compromise with the Shiv Sena, the Jan Sangh, despite being in power in UP, Bihar, Punjab and MP in 1967, did not ask for big portfolios. It had ninety-nine of 215 government MLAs in UP, but did not get powerful portfolios like Home, Finance or Labour. 'As against this we find that with 43 MLAs the Communist Party Marxist could manage to get the important portfolios. This helped them to improve their position in the mid-term poll in Bengal raising their strength from 43 to 60.'[116]

Finally, Mehta argued that generally 'all political parties and especially the Congress and the Communists make use of the Government Offices to propagate and popularise the principles of their respective parties. The Jan Sangh performance in this respect is totally poor. Jan Sangh therefore failed to consolidate its strength in the masses and met with reverses, whereas the Communist Party Marxist with portfolios like finance, labour could penetrate deep in the labour field and consolidate the party gains.'[117]

Mehta's booklet is fundamental to understanding the BJP's politics today. In the course of participating in electoral politics, the Jan Sangh was learning lessons that the BJP would later implement. Anyone looking to understand the BJP's focus on ideological penetration, realpolitik, cadre mobilisation and its take-no-prisoners approach under the Modi–Shah duo has only to look at this churn in the Jan Sangh in the 1960s.

Those early leaders looked to emulate the Left's growth strategies and learnt the following lessons from their own failures: do not depend too much on the middle classes, focus on the rural poor, do not be overly focused on intellectuals, build a cadre and leverage power well. Ironically, the communist parties have since withered away, while the BJP has adapted its tenets to great effect.

What Did the Jan Sangh Stand for?

In August 1966, Balraj Madhok, president of the Jan Sangh, delivered a seminal lecture at the Ahmedabad Junior Chamber: 'What Bharatiya Jana Sangh Stands For'. His speech, combined with another document the party published a year earlier, 'Bharatiya Jana Sangh: Principles and Policies', provided the most succinct summary of how the party saw itself and how it hoped to reshape India. Apart from its position on Kashmir, its anti-Congressism and its links with the RSS, the Jan Sangh's primary energies remained focused on responding to the question of communalism and the ordering of Hindu–Muslim relations.

Pakistan, Indian Muslims and the Idea of India as 'One Culture, One Nation'

The Jan Sangh did not accept the Partition of India. Committed as it was to the idea of Akhand Bharat (united India), it always saw Partition as reversible. It believed India was 'one country, one nation' from 'Kashmir to Kanyakumari and from Attock to Cuttack'. Its leaders saw Partition as a 'mistake', a 'blunder, which should and could have been avoided'. As Madhok put it:[118]

> If India then had a leader of the type of Abraham Lincoln, he would have invited Civil War rather than submitted to the partition of the country, which has not solved any problems but which has created many more new problems. This partition of India is as unnatural as the partition of Germany, as the partition of Korea or Vietnam. We are convinced that this will end ... we consider it our patriotic and nationalist duty to keep the idea of Indian unity alive.

In post-Partition India, for the Jan Sangh, this translated into a belief that 'mere territorial and constitutional unity is not enough for nationalism; the foundation of one culture is essential for it'.[119] If the country had been divided on the basis of religion, in this world view, it needed to get back to being one culture. The Sangh 'has been repeatedly reminding the nation', its leaders thundered, 'that considering Muslim culture as separate entity became the basis of Two-nation theory and it was this Two-nation theory that resulted in the tragic partition of the Motherland. Hence it urges that "for the promotion of unity and nationalism, feeling of one culture should be imbibed maintaining the diversities in our national life and different modes of worship."'[120] Its leaders also had a visceral dislike of Nehru whom they saw as their primary ideological opponent.

In this idea of 'one culture' was embedded the remembrance of historical wrongs. 'What we call West Pakistan today was actually created in 1020 AD,' Madhok argued. 'We lost Sindh in 2712 AD. We lost Peshawar in 1008 AD. We lost Lahore in 1020 AD. If we had thought they were lost for all times, then we could not have gone back to Peshawar, we could not have gone back to Sindh. In the course of history, every country has ups and downs. But it does not mean that our country will remain partitioned for all time.' Notice the 'we' in this construction—the country, in his perception, was Hindu.

The place of the Muslim too is clarified. 'The Muslims of this country are not foreigners,' said Madhok. 'About ninety eight percent of them are Hindu converts. Their forefathers were the same as mine. Their culture is the same as mine. Culture has little to do with religion. The whole of Europe is Christian. But Germany has its own German culture. France has its own French culture and Italy has Italian culture. Similarly, whatever the religions of India may be, India has one culture and that is the Indian culture we stand for. That culture has its roots in the Vedas. In the course of our long history so many currents from left and right, from outside and inside, have come and joined it. But just as the streams, which join Ganga become Ganga; its water remains "Ganga-jal", we do not call its water "Ganga-Jamuna Jal" or "Ganga-Gandak Jal", similarly other currents that have come into India's cultural stream have become indistinguishable part of our culture.'[121]

Herein lay the rub. If everything was indistinguishable, then what was the place of each community in a society with clear religious differences. If it was the Hindu past that was to be reclaimed, then what was the status of the rest? What about the composite culture, the Ganga–Jamuna Tehzeeb, that was built up by secular nationalists over the late nineteenth and early twentieth centuries? To this, Madhok had a clear answer. The 'talk of composite culture is wrong, is unrealistic and is dangerous. Indian culture is one.'[122] The Sangh did not think this was a communal answer. The 'charge about communalism against Jana Sangh is just like spitting on the moon,' Madhok declared. 'Anyone who spits on the moon, simply spits on his own face.'[123]

In 2020, Modi spoke of 130 crore deshwasis (country residents) and of 'Sab Ka Saath Sab Ka Vikaas', but we can find early versions of this talk from the 1960s. As Madhok put it, 'When we talk about people of this country we mean 50 crore people and not that one percent of people who hold all the power in this country. Therefore, we judge the progress of this country by the progress that the common man has made ... the progress of the individual is the index of the progress of the country.' This is exactly how Modi frames his politics today. As he told a rally at Ram Lila Maidan in December 2019, 'Muslims are being misled ... I have always ensured that the documents will never come in the way of development schemes and their beneficiaries.'[124]

On the question of who is an Indian, the Jan Sangh's position had very clear echoes of Savarkar's idea that India is the motherland for those whose holy lands are in India. As the party president declared:[125]

> We are Bharatiya, we are not Bharatiya Lok Sangh. Lok means people. Anybody who lives in India is not a Bharatiya 'JAN'. Only he is a Bharatiya 'Jan' who loves India and looks towards India as his mother. We had discussed a lot whether our name should be Bharatiya Lok Sangh or Bharatiya Jana Sangh. We chose the word 'JAN' deliberately, because the word 'Jan' has a particular connection. Only he can be called a 'Jan' of India who looks upon Bharat as his own Janani and who owns this history, owns its past and owns its present. It is open to all of them, whatever their form of worship may be.

To be Indian, in this view, meant being Hindu—just as for the ancient Persians, for whom the sound of 'S' and 'H' were interchangeable, Sindhustan became Hindustan. 'It is strange that we take pride in calling ourselves Indians but we are ashamed in calling ourselves Hindus. The word Hindu has no religious connection. For every Indian whatever his religion may be, he is a Hindu. I will refer you to the book "SEVEN PILLARS OF WISDOM" by Lawrence of Arabia. There while describing the population of Mecca, he says that the population of Mecca is made up of Turks, Arabs and Hindus. Read that book. Indian Muslims are called Hindus. Throughout the world every Indian was known as a Hindu, whatever his religion may be. Therefore the word Hindu really means Indian. But if you take in the narrow sense, then we are not a Hindu body. We like being called Hindu in the broader sense, not in the narrower sense.'[126] Politically, the Jan Sangh had a fully formed ideology predicated on the centrality of Hinduness to Indianness: the exact opposite of the idea of citizenship advocated by Nehru.

This point of ideological difference is fundamental to understanding the early animosity between Nehru and the Jan Sangh and the visceral dislike that bhakts today have for India's first prime minister. In 1973, Vajpayee would sum the party's position thus: '... if today the Jana Sangh has become the prime target of attacks from our rulers and their communist and Communalist allies, this is essentially because these elements are increasingly becoming conscious of the fact that unlike other Opposition parties, Jana Sangh is not a splinter party formed by any group of malcontents belonging to another party, nor is it a lobby of any vested interests, but it is a party which offers a powerful alternative to the Ruling Congress and seeks to inspire and consolidate the people on the three-plank credo of Nationalism, Democracy and Justice.'[127]

On Muslims and the Antecedents of the Civil Code and Triple Talaq

Exactly like the BJP in 2020, the Sangh in the 1960s responded to charges of communalism by seeing itself as a victim of malignant targeting by opponents whom it saw as communal. When asked about his views on the Uniform Civil Code in Ahmedabad, Madhok argued that the Congress was a communal organisation. 'It lives in communalism. It has a vested interest in communalism. Actually if you go into the results of the last three elections, you will find that it is the communal votes of the Muslim votes or Christian votes, which have been the mainstay of the Congress.'[128]

Jan Sangh leaders understood that most minority groups would not vote for it. The logical culmination of this thought process was for the BJP to ignore the Muslim vote altogether in the 2017 UP election, when the party did not give a single ticket to a Muslim candidate. Why waste time in courting them, its strategists may have reasoned.

One of the triggers of this deep divide was the debate over the Uniform Civil Code. 'When the Hindu Code was being made, Government gave clear assurance in reply to a motion moved by Shri H.V. Kamath that this code will be common to all Indians. But the Muslims were exempted from it in spite of the fact that assurance to that effect was given in the Parliament. Actually, Muslim women need the protection of a common civil code more than anybody else. Anybody who knows anything about Mohmedan law will bear me out. Yet they are being exempted with dangerous results. I heard of a case in which somebody wanted to marry a second time became a Muslim and got a second wife. These things are happening again and again. So we are opposed to it. Civil code must be common to all irrespective of caste or creed and so long as Government does not do it, we will be justified in calling the Congress a communal party and not a nationalist party.'[129]

Fifty-three years after Madhok's call to end triple talaq as a gender-justice initiative, the BJP evoked the same argument in Parliament when it passed a legislation making the practice illegal. As Modi tweeted on the day the Triple Talaq Bill was passed in Parliament, 'An archaic and medieval practice has finally been confined to the dustbin of history! Parliament abolishes Triple Talaq and corrects a historical wrong done to Muslim women. This is a victory of gender justice and will further equality in society. India rejoices today!'[130]

Could Muslims Be Members of the Sangh?

The right wing was no more a monolith than the liberals were. There were two views on Muslim membership between the hard-line and the liberal wings. The Jan Sangh's answer was, yes, Muslims could be members if they accepted the primacy of Hinduness in the past and its great heroes. 'Those who consider BHARAT MATA from Kashmir to Kanyakumari, as their motherland, who own its great heritage, who own its great heroes. Who own its great past and who want to work for its better future, they make one nation whatsoever their caste, creed or race. Therefore, we do no not bring in the question of religion in the question of nationhood. That is why our doors are open to all.'[131] This is, in fact, one reason why S.P. Mookerjee decided to form the Jan Sangh 'when he failed to persuade his parent organisation Hindu Mahasabha to open its doors to all.' In Madhok's telling, he told the Mahasabha that in free India, there was 'no place for any organisation which may be open to followers of only one religion. When Hindu Mahasabha refused to accept his advice, he resigned from it, and formed Jana Sangh.'[132] The early leadership of the Jan Sangh did have minority representation. Its first president of Madras State was the late Dr V.K. John, a devout Roman Catholic. Its secretary in Jammu and Kashmir was Shaikh Abdul Rehman.

Much like L.K. Advani's articulation of it in the 1980s, the Jan Sangh's nationalism, in its view, was meant to be above tokenism: 'Jana Sangh is nationalist not because we have Muslims or Christians among us but because our outlook is nationalist, our thinking is nationalist and our policies are nationalist. We do not believe that coming of Muslims makes us nationalist. Even if there was not a single Muslim in Jana Sangh, even if there was not a single Christian in Jana Sangh, even then the Jana Sangh would be nationalist. It is wrong to think that an organisation becomes nationalist only when people of a particular religion join it. There would be nothing more wrong and irrational, than this approach.'[133]

Early Jan Sangh documents are full of references to 'bharatiya sanskriti' (Indian culture) and Sanskritic terms—Dharma, Artha, Kama and Moksha—as a guiding philosophy for its political ideals. The problem was that it was difficult to quantify what this meant, except a harking back to a golden past.[134] This is what got rolled into what the BJP would later call 'Integral Humanism' in the 1980s. The point the Jan Sangh made was that 'most of the political parties in India are inspired by Western ideologies. They are linked with one or other political movement of the West and are mere replicas of the corresponding institutions there. They cannot fulfil the aspirations of Bharat. Nor can they provide any guidance for a world standing at the cross-roads … They fail to perceive the revolutionary elements in Bharatiya *samskriti* … Integral humanism must necessarily make a balanced approach of both Bharatiya and as well as Western ideologies.'[135]

In Madhok's summing up, 'Rig Veda says: God is one. Wise men call Him by many names. You may call Him Indra or Varuna. You may call Him Ram or Rahim. You may call Him Allah or anything else. It does not matter so long as you think that the goal is one. That is the basis of Indian tolerance, that is the reason why we welcome Parsis and other oppressed people when they came to this country … So long as Indian culture, which is essentially vedic Hindu culture, survives in India there is nothing to fear for Muslims, Christians and others. They will live with us as equal citizens. But if that culture is not there, I do not know what will happen. Therefore, roots of secularism, roots of tolerance, in India are not Gandhi or Nehru or Congress or this or that party. The roots lie in Indian culture and philosophy as set out in the Vedas.'[136]

The Jan Sangh's Holy Cow

The cow first appeared on the Jan Sangh manifesto in 1962, when it declared: 'The Bharatiya Jana Sangh will amend the Constitution to prohibit the slaughter of the bovine species and enact necessary legislation.'[137] The party also promised to establish dairies, goshalas and gosadans. From the beginning, the Jan Sangh saw the cow as absolutely essential for the Indian economy. As its party president declared in 1966, 'In our ancient literature three things have been described as mother. First, is the real mother. Second is the motherland. Third is the cow. Cow and bull have been the mainstay of our economy. I may tell you that cow is the only animal which approximates in many ways to the human body. Firstly, cow gives birth after nine months. Cow's milk is the nearest approximation to that of mother's milk. Therefore, cow has rightly occupied a special place in the Indian economy and sentiment.'[138]

The Jan Sangh argued that men do not live on bread alone, but by sentiment. 'Cow is a question of sentiments for millions of our people. If we are a democracy, as we profess to be, then we must pay attention to the sentiments and emotions of the large majority of our people. If we do not do that, then we are not democratic.'[139] In fact, the Government of India appointed a committee in 1952. The committee was clear on the point that even today, 'cow can be an asset to our economy. Of course, there are many cows which are useless and they should be sterilised. So from the economic point of view also cow will be an asset and not a liability. Therefore ban on cow slaughter must be put from an economic, social and sentimental point of view.'

As Madhok told a questioner, 'In the directive principles of our Constitution, we have already laid down that cow-killing would be stopped in the whole of India. At that time, Jana Sangh was not in existence. At that time we had no member in the Constituent Assembly. It was the Congress-dominated Constituent Assembly which made the Constitution of India. So far as our approach is concerned, cow is an animal which has been absolutely essential for Indian economy from the earliest time.'[140]

In 1966, the working committee of the Jan Sangh adopted a resolution extending support to the all-party Cow Protection Movement for a total ban on cow slaughter. The resolution said that the Constitution must be amended to enact a law banning cow slaughter and said the blame should not be shifted to state governments. It charged the Centre with 'disregarding national sentiments and taking recourse to evasive and dilatory tactics to mislead the people' when the primary responsibility for cow slaughter extended to the Union government.[141]

That same year, on 7 November, thousands of sadhus and others attacked the Parliament building in Delhi, demanding a national ban on cow slaughter. Indira Gandhi defused the crisis by getting the home minister to resign and setting up a high-powered committee, under A.K. Sarkar, retired chief justice of the Supreme Court, on 29 June 1967, to examine the issue of a national ban. The committee was given six months to submit its report.

One of the members of the Justice Sarkar Committee was RSS Sarsanghchalak M.S. Golwalkar. The committee met for twelve years but produced no report. As the Congress's Jairam Ramesh says, the only accounts of the committee are in two memoirs. Ashok Mitra, the Marxist economist, and Verghese Kurien, the founder of Amul—who were both members—have written about it, and quite delightfully.[142] The committee was ultimately wound up in 1979 by Prime Minister Morarji Desai, without any report being submitted. Jairam Ramesh, who researched the cow issue, says that perhaps an account may still be preserved in the home ministry's deep archives, but there is no record of it in any public archive.

Be that as it may, the committee did end up defanging the cow slaughter issue for a few years. The Jan Sangh's 1971 manifesto, for example, did not mention it.

Interestingly, Indira Gandhi herself was very circumspect on cow slaughter. Jairam Ramesh unearthed a 1967 letter from then American ambassador Chester Bowles to Dillon Ripley, who was at the Smithsonian Institution. Ripley wanted to study the ecological consequences of India's large cattle population. Bowles replied that the prime minister did not like this idea because it was a sensitive issue and must be dealt with only by Indians.[143]

Historically, while the issue of cow slaughter has remained a central tenet of the Jan Sangh's—and later the BJP's—worldview, the importance placed on it has ebbed and flowed with the politics of the time. A case in point is the environment ministry's guidelines in May 2017 which restricted sale of cattle for slaughter. This had a huge impact on states like West Bengal, Kerala and several Northeast states, where cow slaughter is not banned.

Apart from the immediate political (and human) impact of a rise in lynchings of suspected cow smugglers, the cultural impulse for protecting cows also had an immediate economic impact. For instance, Tamil Nadu's leather industry, which is a major export-earning industry and a major employer, was badly affected. 'I am not surprised Tamil Nadu has been vociferous,' Jairam Ramesh, who was also once the Union environment minister, told me. 'There is an economic angle which also needs to be looked at.'

In UP, for instance, the economic offshoot was that panic prevailed in the ₹50,000-crore meat industry after a state-wide crackdown on illegal slaughter houses and mechanised abattoirs initiated by Chief Minister Yogi Adityanath in May 2017. Officially, the state government stated that it was only acting against illegal units, but the closure of some slaughterhouses with a valid licence in western UP set alarm bells ringing.[144]

As All India Meat and Livestock Exports Association (AIMLEA) Secretary Fauzan Alavi told a newspaper at the time, 'A licensed exporter, for example, can't even think of slaughtering a cow—not because it's legally banned, but also because we share the same sentiments for the holy animal as our Hindu brethren. But, suddenly we are being made to feel that we are not doing business, but committing crime. Taking a signal from the top, lower-rung officers are knocking at our doors with a threat to close down business. Within four days of government formation, four licensed slaughterhouses—all 100 per cent export units—have been closed in UP. Authorities checking these slaughterhouses ordered their closure on such flimsy reasons as one non-functional CCTV camera, slight variation in building plan and so on. The government's officials come to check the slaughterhouses carrying locks and seals with them.' As AIMLEA representatives waited for an audience with the chief minister, they argued that, of the 5 lakh people they employed, only '25% of the workforce was Muslim. The rest are Hindus and mostly OBCs. About 50% employees are women.'[145]

There was another problem with the restrictions on cow slaughter. 'The meat industry is the by-product of the dairy business. Have you ever seen any buffalo loitering on the roads and eating plastic bags or garbage? It is just because buffalos, when they turn unproductive, are sold to slaughterhouses, while farmers leave their unproductive cows to wander. Since a farmer earns by selling even his unproductive buffalo, buffalo-rearing is on the rise while cows are becoming economically unviable. Of the total milk production, buffalos have a 55% share. If there is a threat to the meat industry, the dairy trade would also collapse and farmers would be the biggest losers. India is at the top in the dairy business because it tops in meat production.'[146]

The Union government diluted its restrictions on cow slaughter a year later, in April 2018, doing away with the clause on 'restrictions on sale of cattle for slaughter'.[147]

The Sangh and Swatantra

The Jan Sangh had toyed with a proposal for a merger with the Swatantra Party in 1964. This was during its years of leadership turmoil in the mid-1960s. *The Times of India* reported on 23 January 1964 that a 'proposal to merge the Swantantra Party with the Jan Sangh to form a new organisation, called the National Democratic Party is reported to be under consideration by its leaders. After a preliminary study at the all-India level, the proposal has been circulated among the State units of the party for opinion ... A merger proposal was initiated on the eve of the general election, but it could not be pursued.' In fact, the Punjab units of both parties informed their central leaderships of support for the proposal.[148]

These proposals ultimately went nowhere. By then the leadership issue in the Jan Sangh had been settled, first under Deendayal Upadhyaya, then Vajpayee and Advani. The BJP emerged as a new party in 1980 out of the debris of the Janata Party. It had a new name, a new party symbol and a new start, but it retained the Jan Sangh DNA.

The old party's last two presidents had been Vajpayee and Advani. The BJP's first two were also Vajpayee (1980-1986) and Advani (1986-1991). As a rising party, its politics often adjusted to the ebbs and flows of external constraints, but now that the BJP has power by itself, it has inched closer to the ideological identity and the first principles of the Jan Sangh, adopted in the 1950s, than ever before. From Shaheen Bagh to cow slaughter, in virtually every public controversy on its core principles since 2014, the BJP's responses have been a direct extension of the lines that its forebears took in the Jan Sangh.

10

WHEN RIGHT IS LEFT

The BJP's Economic Model in New India

It is widely believed that the Narendra Modi government was given the idea of demonetisation—which caused the withdrawal of 86 per cent of the Indian currency in circulation on 8 November 2016—by a Pune-based think tank, ArthaKranti Pratishthan (Institution for Economic Revolution). As Anil Bokil, a member of the think tank later recalled, the proposal for withdrawing all high-denomination cash from the economy as a lightning strike on black money was first presented to Modi in July 2013, when he was still chief minister of Gujarat.[1] His decision to go through with it as prime minister has been termed 'one of the unlikeliest economic experiments in modern Indian history'.[2]

When Vajpayee Wanted Demonetisation

The idea of demonetisation is an old one in the BJP's economic thinking. As far back as 1971, Atal Bihari Vajpayee, then Jan Sangh president, announced that his party would demonetise currency to eliminate black money if it was voted to power. In an interview to a business daily, the BJP's first future prime minister said, 'in order to unearth the hoarded black money let us forthwith demonetise high denomination currency'.[3] Demonetisation as a crucial tool for controlling black money and tax evasion had emerged as a central theme in the Jan Sangh's economic ideation. In this early version, demonetisation was to be accompanied by a form of development bonds for rural areas, with no questions asked on sources of income. As Vajpayee put it:[4]

> If we come to power, our solution would be this: we would for a specified period of time, allow people to invest in the industrial development of the backward areas of this country and also in the essential fields of production. We would not ask them to disclose the source of their money.
>
> This along with demonetisation, would be the most practical way of solving the problem. Now for several years you and I and everybody have been hearing of the increase in the volume of black money. Various economists have made alarming estimates. Everyone knows that black money is wrecking our economy but can you solve a problem by just talking about it. Even the finance minister says now that black money is operating as a parallel economy. Well it is operating but what have they done about it? So let us be honest and try to tap this hoarded wealth for the development of the country and at the same time plug all loopholes in the tax evasion.

Modi revived the idea of demonetisation. Yet, this early Vajpayee intervention shows that the kernel for it was always there in the Jan Sangh's economic thinking. The BJP's predecessor, on two occasions, had passed economic resolutions specifically demanding that Congress governments take recourse to demonetisation: on 18 November 1972 and 16 July 1973.[5] It was not alone in doing so.

A deep dive into newspaper archives reveals that, from the mid-1960s to the mid-1970s, three future prime ministers of India—Vajpayee, I.K. Gujral and Chandra Shekhar—had demanded demonetisation during parliamentary debates on the economy.[6] For almost a decade (1967–1974), the idea enjoyed such cross-party support that it regularly featured in the parliamentary questioning of finance ministers after the presentation of the annual budget.[7] The state government of UP, led by Charan Singh and consisting of an anti-Congress coalition that included the Jan Sangh, even passed a cabinet resolution on 3 July 1967 demanding that the then prime minister, Indira Gandhi, demonetise 'all currency notes above Rs 10' to 'arrest the deterioration in the economy'.[8] These debates formed the political backdrop for the Union government's appointment of a committee, led by a distinguished bureaucrat, to study the problem of black money. The Wanchoo Committee report (1971), kept secret for a few months but later presented to Parliament, unanimously recommended demonetisation.[9]

Through the 1970s, this idea took such a hold of the country's political imagination that even several prominent Congress leaders—a group of 100 AICC members,[10] the West Bengal Congress Committee[11] and a number of ruling-party MPs[12]—demanded it. So pervasive was this talk that, at least on one occasion (in August 1973), rumours of sudden demonetisation led to panic-selling of ₹100 notes in Delhi and a sudden increase in the price of gold, forcing a clarification from the finance minister.[13] Not surprisingly, this culminated in the post-Emergency Janata government's decision to withdraw high-denomination currency notes (₹1,000, ₹5,000 and ₹10,000) in January 1978.[14] The Jan Sangh, of course, was part of that government.

Foreshadowing the debate around Modi's 2016 decision, Opposition parties responded in 1978 by accusing the Janata Party of pushing the move for political motives ahead of the impending elections to forestall opponents with secret funds.[15] Indira Gandhi alleged that selective leaks of the news to 'certain private banks' prior to the announcement had allowed them to exchange notes in advance for commercial benefits.[16] Thereafter, the idea of demonetisation as an effective economic instrument faded away from public debate.[17] The last time it was mentioned in major newspapers was in 1991, the year Manmohan Singh, as finance minister, initiated economic reforms.[18]

This pre-history shows how powerful the idea of demonetisation was for the early Jan Sangh and other Opposition parties in the 1970s, the decade in which Narendra Modi came of age as an RSS pracharak. It is not unreasonable that he would have been familiar with this history when, as a state government head four decades later, he was presented with a demonetisation proposal. It could well have played a role in influencing his decision as prime minister.

Why Demonetisation Did Not Hurt Modi

When the national lockdown of 2020 induced the sharpest contraction in quarterly GDP growth since 1996—which is when quarterly numbers began to be collected—Congress leader Rahul Gandhi tweeted a series of videos linking India's economic slowdown to demonetisation. Framing the 2020 GDP growth numbers as the 'bhayanak' (terrible) outcome of the 2016 gambit, Gandhi argued that Modi's bid for a 'cash-free' India 'broke' the economy, leading to what he called a 'labourer-farmer-small trader-free India'.[19]

Most economists agree that demonetisation was indeed a monetary 'shock' that slowed growth, though they argue about the size of its effect.[20] Yet, the question that has flummoxed all BJP critics is why Brand Modi remained relatively impervious to the problem of falling job-creation and declining economic indicators, which would have brought low any other government. Whichever side of the ideological fence you are on, there is no denying that the 2019 general election campaign was built on the simple axis of whether you were personally for or against the prime minister. Similarly, the 2017 UP assembly election was widely regarded as a mini-referendum on Modi's demonetisation decision. Both campaigns were fronted by the prime minister and both yielded sweeping victories for the BJP, powered by rural voters who were precisely the people whose economic interests had ostensibly been hurt. If anything, however, the 2017 UP poll results exemplified a considerable deepening of the BJP's

Figure 10.1: India's Economic Trajectory Under the Modi Government: GDP Growth Rate

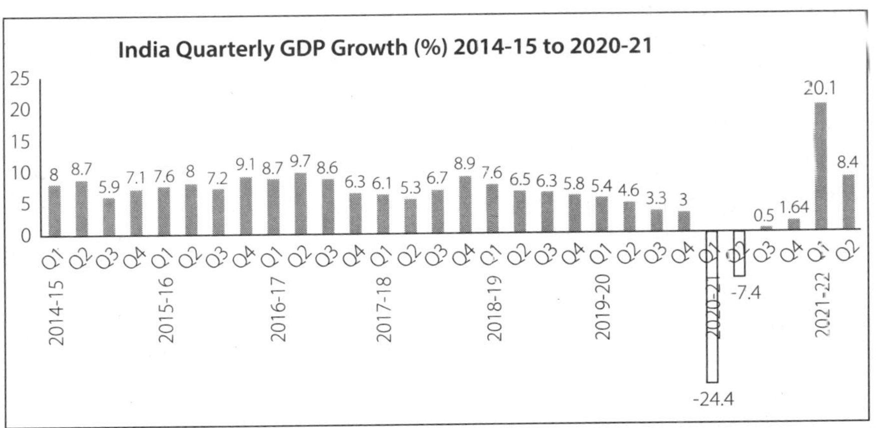

Source: 'Annual and Quarterly Estimates of GDP at Constant Prices: 2011–12 Series', Ministry of Statistics and Programme Implementation. Available at: http://mospi.nic.in/data[21]

rural voter base, which further expanded in 2019 across all Hindi-speaking states (as Chapter 2 shows).

Consider the job numbers when Modi was asking voters for a second term before the April–May 2019 general election. While the quarterly employment survey was being rejigged using a new methodology, and economists continued to argue about the quality of the government's economic numbers overall,[22] survey data from the independent Centre for Monitoring Indian Economy (CMIE) released right in the middle of the poll campaign in April 2019 showed that unemployment had increased to 7 per cent, the highest point since October 2016. It went up to as high as 8 per cent in October 2019 before settling around the 7 per cent mark by December 2019.[23]

Plot these job numbers on a national map and the densest unemployment rates of over 10 per cent were bang in the middle of the BJP's core Hindi heartland base: Rajasthan, Haryana, UP, Bihar and Jharkhand. Madhya Pradesh was not too far behind. Yet, the BJP's majority in Parliament was powered by these same states. In fact, even during the poll campaign here, it wasn't jobs or candidates but other local factors that dominated. In UP, for example, the entire election rested on the caste debate and whether the constituency-level arithmetic of the SP–BSP alliance could trump Modi's chemistry or not. We know that, ultimately, the alliance could not pull it off.

Does this mean that the economy does not matter politically in contemporary India? The idea that politics follows economics has been conventional wisdom, at least since the American political strategist James Carville put up a notice saying 'The economy, stupid' outside Bill Clinton's campaign office in 1992. Was this wisdom checkmated in India by Modi's cocktail of personality politics and a virulent Hindutva-infused, post-Balakot muscular nationalism? Conversely, were the country's economic concerns overhyped by naysayers, as the government argued? Or were people being hoodwinked by clever propaganda and identity politics, as the Congress argued? In other words, were Indian voters voting against their own economic self-interest, much like white male Republican voters in the US backing President Donald Trump?[24]

The Opposition's beliefs were best exemplified by the Congress's caustic '*Bhakt ka chashma*' campaign video in 2019 (see details in Chapter 7).[25]

Figure 10.2: Unemployment Rates in India, by State

Source: CMIE unemployment data. Graphic visualisation by Rishabh Srivastava, Nalin Mehta: PollNiti. Available online: https://pollniti.com/data/unemployment.html

The broad assumption among the elite is that people are gullible, are not as aware of their own realities as they should be, and are being carried away by a 'propaganda machinery', as Congress scion Priyanka Gandhi put it.

But the poll dynamic may be far more complicated than that. This is best shown by the Reserve Bank of India's (RBI) periodic consumer-confidence surveys, conducted in dozens of cities. One of the metrics on which responses were collected was on what people thought their own employment prospects had been in the twelve months prior to the survey. The results how that their expectation had risen sharply just after the Modi government came to power in 2014, but collapsed horribly after demonetisation.

In fact, people's confidence in their own employment prospects fell to much worse than UPA-2 levels in 2017-18 before briefly recovering in March 2019 (see Figures 10.2, 10.3 and 10.4).

Figure 10.3: The Rise and Fall of Public Expectations about Their Own Jobs (2012–2020)

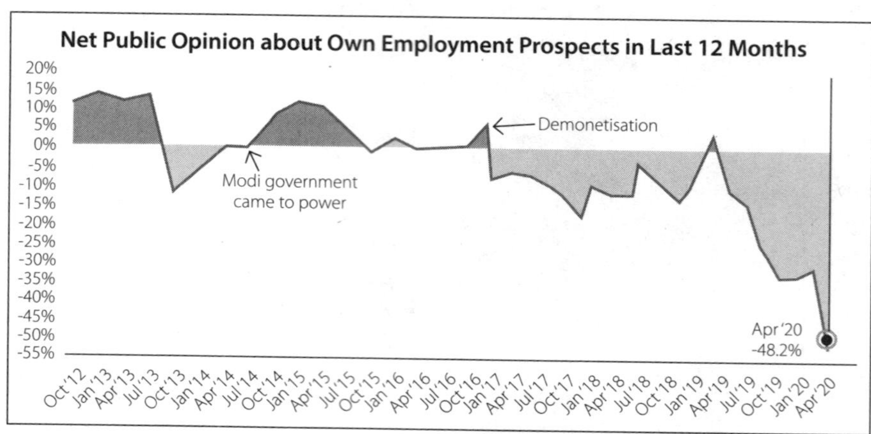

Source: RBI Consumer Confidence Surveys. Analysis and graphic visualisation by Rishabh Srivastava, Nalin Mehta: PollNiti. Available online: https://pollniti.com/data/rbi-consumer-confidence-survey.html

Yet, when the same people were asked about their future prospects, and that of the country's, as opposed to what they thought had happened in the past year, their opinions changed drastically. Unlike the complete despondency on this question at the end of UPA-2, net future expectations about the economy in India clocked in at 48.6 per cent positive in March 2019. This, astoundingly, was at a higher level just before the elections than it had been in 2014. Politics is about emotion and perception. It seems that, while people were personally unhappy in economic terms in the present, they were much more positive about their prospects in the future, as well as the overall economic direction of the country.

Now, Indians have historically been much more hopeful about the future than their counterparts in developed Western countries.[26] Even considering this, the distinction between what they believe is good for them and what they see as good for the nation is striking. This explains why Modi shifted the election discourse from jobs to wider touchpoints like nationalism, dynasty politics and other similar themes.

These survey numbers also explain why Brand Modi fared better in the 2019 election than the economic numbers might have suggested. There is no question that Modi's second government, especially after the

Figure 10.4: The Rise and Fall of Public Expectations on India's Economic Future (2012–2020)

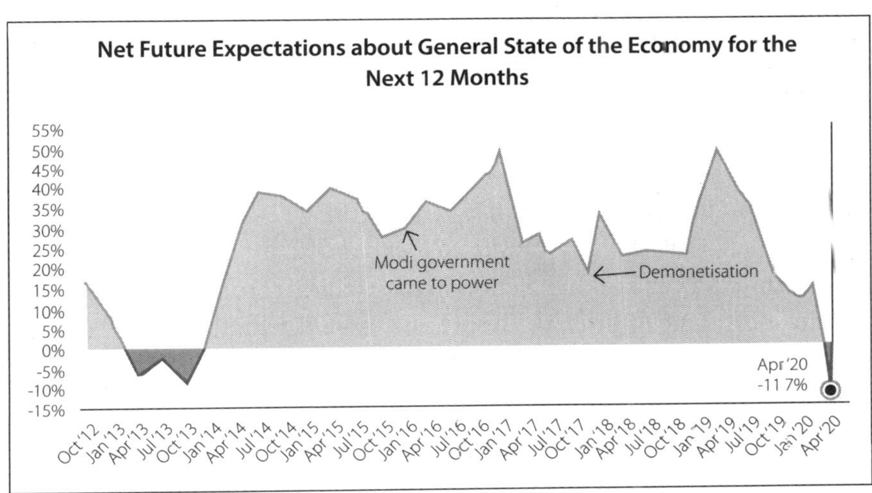

Source: RBI Consumer Confidence Surveys. Analysis and graphic visualisation by Rishabh Srivastava, Nalin Mehta: PollNiti. Available online: https://pollniti.com/data/rbi-consumer-confidence-survey.html

Figure 10.5: The Rise and Rise of Public Expectations on Their Future Jobs (2012–2020)

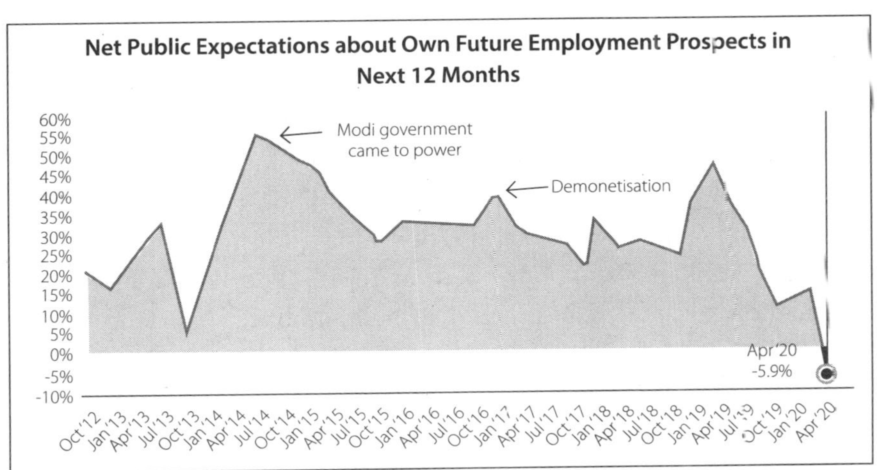

Source: RBI Consumer Confidence Surveys. Analysis and graphic visualisation by Rishabh Srivastava, Nalin Mehta: PollNiti. Available online: https://pollniti.com/data/rbi-consumer-confidence-survey.html

pandemic disruptions, faces a huge economic challenge, with several worrying indicators pointed to an upcoming reckoning. Yet, RBI surveys showed that people did not feel the economy had reached a crisis point until at least mid-2020, for this to override other factors.[27] Voters were worried, but their concerns may have been mitigated by the novelty of the targeted DBT schemes (as shown in Part I of this book), as well as their judgement on the political alternatives to Modi, the party's new caste alliances and its cultural signalling.

The fact that the BJP politically expanded in north India's rural constituencies after demonetisation suggests that its broad social signalling and the messaging of a rich vs poor class war worked at the time. The poor were 'willing to overlook their own hardship, knowing that the rich and their ill-begotten wealth were experiencing even harder hardship: "I lost a goat but they lost a cow."' In other words, this seems to have worked as a 'credibility signalling device', to quote from the economist Arvind Subramanian's analysis.[28] Retaining voter loyalty after five years in power was a major feat by Modi's BJP in 2019—just as it was for Manmohan Singh's UPA in 2009 (albeit on a much smaller scale).

The Coronavirus Crisis, Welfarism and the BJP's Political Response

The RBI voter perception numbers did show a decline in 2020-21(Figures 10.4 and 10.5). The disruption of the COVID-19 lockdown and the huge migrant crisis that followed led to speculation that Modi's political leeway may not endure. By September 2020, 10.4 million (1.04 crore) Indian migrants had moved across states. The Union government claimed that under the Pradhan Mantri Garib Kalyan Yojana (Poor Welfare Scheme), launched on 20 June 2020, it had distributed financial assistance worth ₹688 billion (68,820 crore) to 420 million (42 crore) Indians by 15 September 2020. While it did not keep a central count of migrant deaths, the government told Parliament it had distributed free rations to 800 million Indians (80 crore) during the lockdown months under a scheme that continued until 20 November 2020.[29]

To narrow-focus on a key BJP-ruled state, UP saw the return of 3.8 million migrants due to the national lockdown.[30] Some leading economists had criticised Chief Minister Yogi Adityanath's post-lockdown 'administrative' approach of issuing a 'Request for Proposal' for a 'consultant' to create a 'One Trillion Dollar Economy for Uttar Pradesh' by 2025,[31] but the state government's district-wise mapping of coronavirus migrants is revealing. UP registered 3.4 million migrants district-wise, and they were skill-mapped across ninety-four job categories. The range this survey covered is hugely diverse: from ayahs, carpenters, blacksmiths and escalator-fixers to nutritionists, gym-trainers and beauticians. By September 2020, 2.4 million of these migrants had been employed for tasks under MNREGS. Furthermore, as many as 5.3 million people in the state had received direct cash transfers of ₹1,000 in financial assistance from the state during the lockdown; 2.9 million of them got a second instalment as well.[32]

The numbers on welfare-spending through DBTs indicate how the BJP managed to partly mitigate the political impact of the economic miseries caused by the lockdown in 2020. The Modi government's critics, such as the Congress's former finance minister P. Chidambaram, have argued that more stimulus was needed—greater cash transfers, rations and financial decentralisation to the states[33]—along with a paradigmatic shift in economic management. While that may be so, by-elections held in fifty-nine constituencies across eleven Indian states in November 2020 suggest that the pandemic-induced recession had failed to dent the BJP's political momentum until that point. In these elections, across many parts of India—and the first after the lockdown—the BJP won almost two-thirds (forty-one) of the seats up for grabs. Significantly, these wins included major victories in the worst-hit Hindi heartland states (nineteen of twenty-eight in Madhya Pradesh, six of seven in UP), sustained political dominance in Gujarat (all eight), wins in South India (two of two in Karnataka; one of one in Telangana) and new advances in the Northeast (four of five in Manipur).[34]

Like the 2017 UP elections, which followed demonetisation, these nationwide by-polls in late 2020 were in part also seen as a political referendum on the Modi's government's handling of the pandemic. Far from shrinking, the BJP's political footprint had expanded significantly. Simultaneously, its NDA alliance managed to retain Bihar after three terms in power—despite facing serious incumbency, a spirited Opposition challenge and a severe migrant crisis. This is why Modi argued that the BJP's victories in these polls a few months *after* the first lockdown were even more significant than the Lok Sabha triumph of 2019. As he put it in a speech in November 2020, 'There is no one in the world who has not been effected by Corona … [However,] from the Janata [public] Curfew war until now, the way we fought this epidemic, these election results also show approval for that. In the time of Corona, from rations to employment for the poor, the level at which efforts were made in India, this is an approval of that.' The poll victories, he declared, were an endorsement of his direct-welfare policies. 'In our place, it is often said that bank accounts, gas connection, a house, self-employment opportunities, good roads, good railways, good railway stations, better airports, new modern bridges being built on rivers, internet connectivity—such issues don't matter in elections. You must have heard this. The public is again and again telling such people that these are the real issues … Those who don't understand this, this time too, in place after place, they lost their election deposits. This is the biggest reason for the love the country is showing to the BJP today in polls.'[35] He was referring to the fact that thirty-one of the BJP's forty-one seats in the November 2020 by-polls came at the expense of the Congress.[36]

The BJP Model of Economics: Low Inflation at Centre and in States (2014-19)

Depending on who you speak to, there are four broad views on Narendra Modi's economics. His detractors, BJP MP Swapan Dasgupta points out, have portrayed him as a 'man who is a master of expediency and who, at the same time, lacks any coherent political ideology beyond Nation First. This has also been a charge against the BJP.' The BJP and the Modi government, in this view, largely 'shied away' from the articulation of an economic philosophy,[37] or perhaps they never had an economic ideology after all, the economy being subservient to a cultural agenda.

The second view is that Modi took a sharp left turn in his first term. As the India Today Group's editorial director, Raj Chengappa, summarised in his post-Budget 2020 analysis, 'In his first term, saddled with back-to-back droughts that caused untold distress to farmers, and charged with being a "suit-boot Sarkar" by the Opposition, Modi took a sharp turn to the left and projected himself as a messiah of the poor, the downtrodden and farmers. He adopted a form of Swadeshi Socialism in his first term that is best remembered for the slew of development schemes that provided toilets, houses for the poor, cooking gas at subsidised prices and promised that highways and rural roads would be built at a rapid pace.'[38]

The third view is the governmental one: that the economic slowdown was cyclical, caused by external forces, and that a lot of economic activity was happening outside of formal numbers—for instance, with Mudra loans for small businesses—and that eventually India would right itself. In this view, the government did introduce reforms like Goods and Services Tax (GST) and the insolvency and bankruptcy code, and Modi's second term would move forward with greater reforms to achieve its goal of a US$ 5 trillion economy by 2024.

A fourth, more nuanced view is that the NDA is essentially a continuation of the UPA's economic model, with better branding and marketing. As former deputy chairman of Planning Commission, Montek Singh Ahluwalia, told me, 'As far as programmes are concerned, the NDA has more or less maintained most of the earlier programmes of UPA, though many of them have been renamed and modified in some ways. The question to ask is whether they are being better implemented. This calls for credible independent evaluation. GST is an important tax reform which was actually put on the agenda by the UPA, but opposed at that time by the BJP-ruled states. It is good that the Constitution was amended to enable GST, but I feel the design of the GST has got mangled with far too many rates and heavy compliance obligations on smaller firms. Demonetisation is called a reform, but in my view, it was a negative development which imposed a huge and unnecessary burden on the informal sector. The insolvency and bankruptcy code is a very important reform. I hope it proves to be a success. There are some areas where the NDA government has actually reversed the reform process. The decision to raise import duties, with the possibility of further increases ahead, is a major reversal of the policy of gradually reducing import duties, which has been in place for thirty years and was followed by several governments, including the Vajpayee government. It is not consistent with the objective of improving export performance and joining global value chains.'[39]

The big question to ask is whether there is, in fact, a BJP model of economics. Is there one common thread that binds Narendra Modi, Atal Bihari Vajpayee and other BJP-ruled states as part of a coherent economic vision? Or are they all different regimes driven by leaders with differing personalities and economic priorities? Modi came to power with the image of an economic reformer and his record on that has been mixed, but is there a thread binding his economic ideas with that of other BJP leaders in power?

The answer is yes. Despite falling growth in the Modi years and job creation that is way below what is needed, one reason why the BJP has not yet paid a political price is its relentless focus on keeping inflation down until 2019. Low inflation, mostly below 5 per cent, was probably the single biggest economic achievement of the first Modi government—and the biggest failure of UPA-2. When Rishabh Srivastava and I mapped inflation data, it became clear that inflation had consistently been higher under Congress-led UPA governments than under either the Vajpayee- or Modi-led NDA governments. Under Vajpayee, between 1999 and 2004, the inflation rate went down from 4.67 per cent to 3.77 per cent. Under Manmohan Singh, it went up from 3.77 per cent in 2004 to 10.91 per cent in 2013. During Modi's first term, it went down from 6.3 per cent in 2014 to 3.72 per cent in 2019 (see Figure 10.6). This was especially true for food prices, where hikes arguably hit the poor the hardest. It becomes particularly evident when looking at the difference between food inflation and headline inflation (see Figure 10.7). Under the BJP, this difference was far lower than it was under the Congress (an anomalous 2019 notwithstanding). Under Vajpayee, food inflation went down from 4.3 per cent in 1999 to 2.3 per cent in 2004. Under Manmohan Singh, it went up from 2.3 per cent in 2004 to as much as 13.4 per cent in 2013. Under Modi, it went down from 6.1 per cent in 2014 to -0.4 per cent in 2018, before going up anomalously to 7.5 per cent in 2019.

Economists will tell you that the reason the Modi government managed to keep inflation and food prices down is because of low crude oil prices, which helped to bring down interest rates on everything from home loans to government bonds. That is true. Yet, there is a clear political design in focusing on this metric alone—one that becomes clearer when we look at the record of BJP-run state governments. Between 2014 and

Figure 10.6: BJP Regimes Keep Inflation Lower: Inflation Rate % (1997-98 to 2019-20)

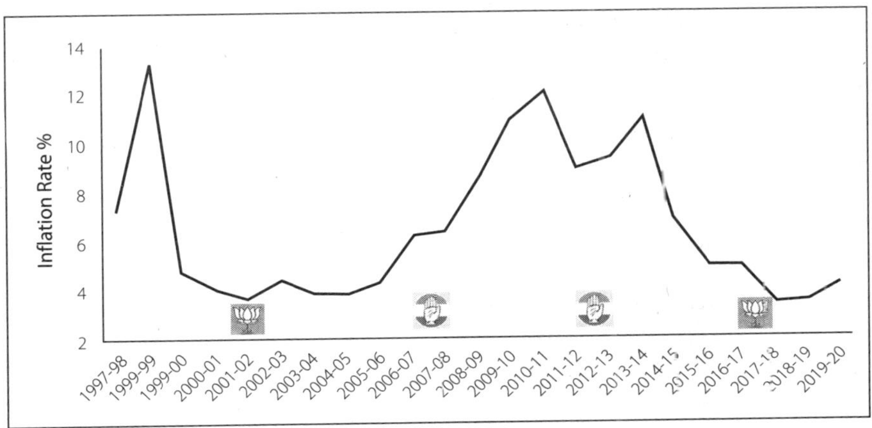

Source: World Bank. Analysis and graphic visualisation by Rishabh Srivastava, Nalin Mehta: PollNiti

Figure 10.7: BJP Regimes Keep Not Just Headline Inflation but Food Wholesale Price Inflation Down as Well

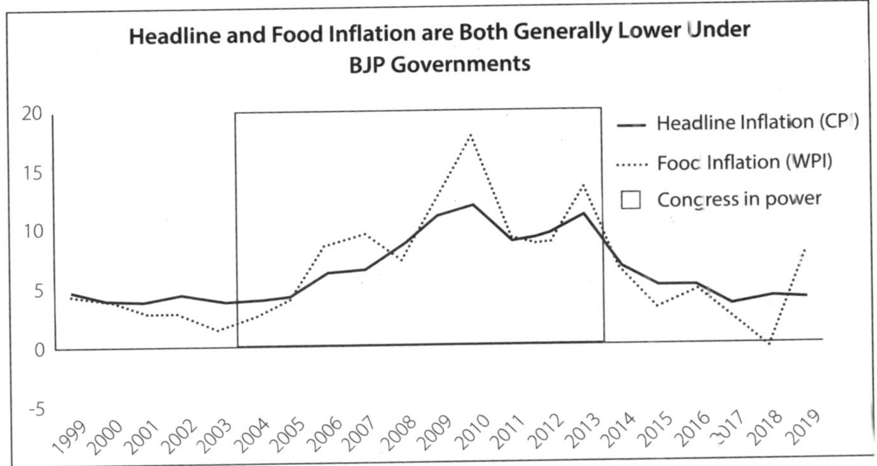

Source: World Bank. Analysis and graphic visualisation by Rishabh Srivastava, Nalin Mehta: PollNiti

2019, most BJP state governments (where they were in power on their own) kept inflation at a rate lower than the national rate (see Tables 10.1 and 10.2). On average, they kept inflation down to -0.14 per cent below national inflation levels. This included states like Bihar (0.80 per cent), Haryana (-0.38 per cent), Himachal Pradesh (-0.84 per cent), Gujarat

(-0.42 per cent), Madhya Pradesh (-0.57 per cent) and Maharashtra (-0.22 per cent). Non-BJP states, in contrast, saw average inflation rates that were 0.16 per cent higher than the national average. To be sure, states like UP, which have had a BJP government in power since 2017, had inflation rates lower than the national average even earlier. In general, though, the data shows a marked pattern of lower inflation in BJP state governments when compared with non-BJP state governments.

Table 10.1: BJP State Governments Also Keep Inflation Low (2014–2019)

Average Deviation from National Inflation Rate %

BJP-ruled states	-0.14
Non-BJP-ruled states	0.16

Source: Ministry of Statistics and Programme Implementation (MOSPI). Data analysis by Rishabh Srivastava and Nalin Mehta: PollNiti

Table 10.2: BJP State Governments Kept Lower Inflation vs Non-BJP State Governments (2014–2019)

State	*2014*	*2015*	*2016*	*2017*	*2018*	*2019*	*Average Deviation**
Andhra Pradesh	-0.77	1.89	1.71	-0.34	-1.76	-1.63	
Assam	1.07	-0.73	-1.33	-0.38	2.60	1.87	0.69
Bihar	1.38	-0.65	-0.36	-1.16	0.81	-2.50	-0.80
Chhattisgarh	0.77	1.47	0.20	-1.66	-0.53	-2.26	0.05
Delhi	0.38	-0.01	-0.16	1.98	-0.98	-0.19	
Goa	1.16	-0.66	1.09	0.02	-0.14	-1.40	0.01
Gujarat	-0.60	0.03	0.66	-0.59	-1.31	-0.70	-0.42
Haryana	-0.52	-0.59	-0.68	0.76	-0.05	-1.19	-0.38
Himachal Pradesh	0.57	-0.08	-1.00	1.62	-1.83	-2.33	-0.84
Jammu and Kashmir	-0.56	1.74	-0.43	3.65	2.08	0.10	
Jharkhand	-0.69	-0.56	1.10	0.08	0.47	-0.47	0.13
Karnataka	0.28	1.83	0.40	-0.26	-1.11	1.64	
Kerala	1.15	-0.20	-0.83	2.38	1.20	2.13	

State	*2014*	*2015*	*2016*	*2017*	*2018*	*2019*	*Average Deviation**
Madhya Pradesh	-0.36	-0.32	-0.91	-1.10	-0.15	0.77	-0.57
Maharashtra	-0.75	-0.21	-0.46	0.50	-0.18	-0.16	-0.22
Odisha	0.61	1.15	1.57	-1.80	-0.44	-0.97	
Punjab	-0.51	-0.81	-1.03	0.46	0.24	0.12	
Rajasthan	0.36	1.12	0.64	0.23	-1.50	0.48	0.17
Tamil Nadu	-0.26	0.95	-0.46	1.22	0.18	0.93	
Telangana	-1.38	0.21	1.46	0.85	-0.38	-1.34	
Uttar Pradesh	0.34	-1.09	-0.04	-1.34	0.19	0.67	-0.16
Uttarakhand	-0.93	-1.59	-1.32	0.13	0.63	1.06	0.61
West Bengal	0.38	-1.91	0.48	-0.56	2.34	-0.55	

Positive values = Higher state inflation than national.

Source: Ministry of Statistics and Programme Implementation (MOSPI). Data analysis by Rishabh Srivastava and Nalin Mehta: PollNiti

Figure 10.8: The Falling Engines of Economic Growth

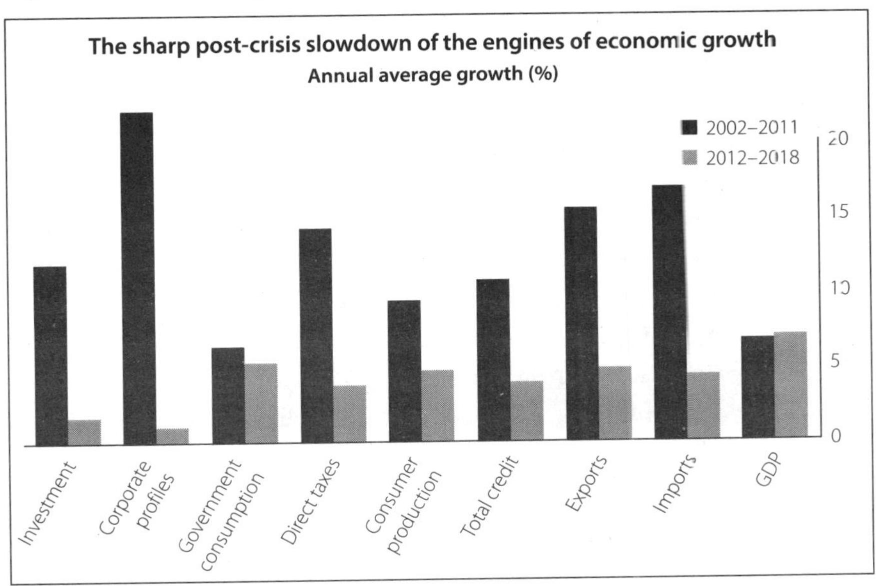

Source: Data from Arvind Subramanian and Josh Feldman, 'India's Great Slowdown: What Happened? What's the Way Out?', CID Faculty Working Paper, Harvard University, 2019[40]

While the economy may have entered a larger structural slowdown, economic growth was spluttering and job creation was low (see Figure 10.8), the BJP's focus on low inflation may help explain why the political blowback was relatively less than other governments would have felt for a performance like this. The focus on low inflation rates served as a useful political device in the face of a shrinking economic environment. It provided political cover to the BJP, at least until 2019. Since then, however, a sharp rise in inflation rates at the national level, exacerbated by the pandemic, and rising fuel prices reduced political headroom for the BJP and raised a political challenge for the party.[41]

Not So Right-wing: The Roots of the Modi Model of Economics

Why the BJP Says It Is Not a Right-wing Party

The day Narendra Modi won his second term on 23 May 2019, he made only one big economic assertion in his victory speech, which was telecast live from the BJP headquarters in Delhi. He argued there are only two castes of people now in India. 'There is one caste in India of people who are poor,' he said, 'and another caste of those who are trying to help make the country free of poverty. There are those who want to come out of poverty and then there are those who want to free the nation of poverty. These are the only two castes in the country and we must strengthen these both in the twenty-first century.'[42] Ideationally, this political articulation on removing poverty as a national goal was closer to Indira Gandhi's election-winning slogan of 'Garibi Hatao' (Eradicate Poverty) from 1971 than many would expect from a right-wing government.

When he was first elected in 2014 on a slogan of 'Acche Din' (Good Days) and 'Minimum Government, Maximum Governance', many in India's middle classes switched support because they saw him as a pro-market, epoch-defining economic reformer, like Margaret Thatcher in the United Kingdom or Ronald Reagan in the United States. The author Gurcharan Das, for example, argued in *Financial Times* that this could be India's 'Thatcher moment'. 'I have never voted for the BJP,' he wrote, but 'chose Mr Modi because he is India's best chance to restore economic growth and reward us with a "demographic dividend"'.[43] For the world's press, looking to understand the kind of leader Modi would be, Reagan and Thatcher were the most common economic comparison at the time.[44] There were those among his opponents who described him as being closer to Vladimir Putin,[45] but the most widely held assumption was that, in economic terms at least, this was a reformist leader who would be 'pro-business', 'right-wing' and a huge break from the past—one under whose watch India would embark on the next stage of economic reforms. Of course, definitions of what constitutes 'right-wing' and 'left-wing' politics have evolved over time and may elude neat classifications, but the BJP was expected by many, as a 'right-wing' party, to be more supportive of free markets, privatisation and deregulation.

In reality, however, its governance record shows that beneath the surround sound of Hinduness lies a concerted focus on creating a targeted social welfare net. That is why it is crucial to examine the BJP's foundational economic idea of 'swadeshi' (home-made) and the inherent contradiction this may have with the forces of economic liberalisation. This chapter shows how the party negotiated these pulls and pressures as it melded its governance aims with its electoral ambitions.

The idea of the BJP as an Indian Thatcherite or Reagan-type right-wing economic reform party was always a simplistic view, belied by the party's own history and evolution. As Vinay Sahasrabuddhe, the BJP's vice president, told me over a dinner meeting in Delhi, 'We are *not* right-wing in the traditional sense in economic terms. What we are pursuing can be labelled as a mixed economy. So, we are never capitalist, and of course we are not socialist. This label that we are a right-wing party is not acceptable. Neither is it a factual description of us.' Sahasrabuddhe was not only a Rajya Sabha MP, he was party vice-president at the time, chairman of the Indian Council for Cultural Relations and also headed the BJP's Department of Policy Research and its Department of Good Governance. He ran the BJP's Training Cell for over a decade, and remains a key moving force behind the Rambhau Mhalgi Prabodhini. As such, his views are an important insight into party's thinking on policies. When I asked him if, in economic terms alone, it was a misnomer to call the BJP a right-wing party, he replied, 'absolutely'. How does the BJP define its economic positioning? As 'centrist', he responded.

So, does the BJP stand for free markets in the way that American Republicans or the British Conservatives have traditionally done? 'I repeat the remark by the economist Vijay Tendulkar who said that that the prefixes of left and right have lost their meaning,' he replied. It is a comment that flies in the face of the traditional understanding of the BJP. As Sahasrabuddhe said, 'This misunderstanding is across the world. Unlike in India, there is a constituency perhaps in certain parts of the world which cherishes the idea of being a rightist. We are not like that. For example, in India, political correctness drives you to "tom-tom" leftism because leftism has a premium ... As far as BJP is concerned, economically and socially, we are not a revolutionary party. We are not a traditional party as such. There is modernity in our approach but that doesn't make us a right-wing party.'[46]

If the BJP is not right-wing economically, then what does it stand for? A political party's economic philosophy cannot, 'unlike Jack's beanstalk, grow into a giant tree overnight nor can it, like Macduff, "be ripped untimely" from its mother's womb'.[47] In that sense, it is instructive to look at how its economic ideas evolved over time, and how some of its foundational ideas continue to have an afterlife.

The Jan Sangh Phase: When Karl Marx Was as 'Out of Date' as Adam Smith

Much like demonetisation, the pedigree of some other key economic initiatives of the BJP government can be traced back to the foundations of the party. In 2018, for example, Modi appealed to Indians to buy Indian products.[48] It was an easy step from there to the all-encompassing idea of 'AatmaNirbhar Bharat' (Self-Reliant India), which became Modi's signature economic slogan in 2020 after the national lockdown. The intellectual roots of this strain of swadeshi thinking in the BJP go back to the Jan Sangh. As Vajpayee argued in 1971, as party president, 'Let us use only what is produced in this country. This will release Indian initiative for invention and enterprise. The Swadeshi cult was so successful before independence. Why should it not be successful now?... You have got to enthuse them. Today people are getting crazy over imported things and even pay fabulous prices for them. If the cult of Swadeshi is not revived, the slogan for import substitution would be hollow ... what we need today is realism. It is no use borrowing ideas from textbooks on socialism and communism. We have been hearing of socialism for decades but how much of it are we having this country today? The majority of the people in this country today live in abject poverty ... and we have to take a pragmatic approach to solve the problems.'[49]

In his second term, Prime Minister Narendra Modi told cabinet colleagues to slash their ministerial expenses by at least 20 per cent. He cut down personal staff at his own residence-cum-office by 50 per cent—from over fifty staffers to twenty-five—and the PMO's staff by 15 per cent.[50] Again, this idea of austerity at the top can be traced back to an older Jan Sangh focus on cutting down on wasteful expenditure. As Vajpayee said in 1971, 'our plan envisages a 10 per cent cut in Government expenditure which can easily be done if all useless foreign travels, cultural delegations and wasteful diplomatic and embassy expenditure is stopped'.[51]

The Modi government's budget in 2019 reduced income tax slab rates for those in the lowest income brackets (even though the removal of exemptions for those above that meant that while the government gave by one hand, it took from another), while increasing income tax brackets for those higher up in the food chain. The Jan Sangh had always been in favour of lower tax rates for those who earn less. For example, when S. Bhoothalingam recommended in the 1960s that annual incomes under ₹7,500 be exempt from income tax, the Jan Sangh wholeheartedly supported this idea. 'Do you know that the government is spending more money on the collection of income tax (upto Rs 7500/- bracket) than it actually realises from the assesses,' Vajpayee asked at the time. 'What is the use of having such a tax slab where the cost of collection of a tax is higher than the tax realisation. In the Public Accounts Committee [Mr Vajpayee was the Chairman of the Committee] we studied the problem and found that if incomes upto Rs 7500/- are exempted from taxation it would lead to no loss of revenues because the loss would be more than balanced by the saving in expenditure. What is more, the income tax staff and officers would be free to concentrate on the higher brackets of income and thus they will be able to check evasion with greater efficiency.'[52]

In the 1960s, the Jan Sangh essentially stood for a mixed economy, rejecting both capitalism and communism. As an economic resolution adopted by the party in 1965 noted, 'The capitalist system of economy which accepts the "economic man" as the central point of all its activities is inadequate. The selfish desire to acquire more and more profit is the motivating force in this system, with competition as its regulator. This does not conform to the Bharatiya [Indian] philosophy. Socialism originated in its reaction to the problems created by Capitalism. Its objectives are commendable but its end result has failed to profit mankind. The reason is the analysis of society and individual by Karl Marx, the propounder of scientific socialism, is basically materialistic and inadequate.'[53] Furthermore, the party, in one of its economic policy documents, categorically stated that it considered 'Karl Marx as out of date as Adam Smith'. As a party document supporting the idea of bank nationalisation noted, "*Das Capital*" [sic] is as irrelevant to the existing conditions as *The Wealth of Nations*. Even in USA, the industry is not that free. After approximately century of free banking, it was placed under official control after the depression of the 1930s. The Government extended to deposits the sort of protection it had conferred on bank notes in 1863.'[54]

This world view explains why even when Indira Gandhi nationalised the fourteen largest commercial banks in India in 1969,[55] the Jan Sangh did not oppose the move in principle. It only protested the manner of implementation. When I discussed this with the Congress's Jairam Ramesh, he said, 'Most people don't realise how left the Sangh was.' He picked up his phone to show me a scan of a late 1960s newspaper clipping with the blaring headline 'Jan Sangh Urges Takeover of All Big Foreign Firms', reporting on a party economic resolution that called for the nationalisation of all foreign banks operating in the country. 'Even [the late] Arun Jaitley [Modi's first finance minister] was surprised when I sent him this,' he said. 'This was a very clear strand in Sangh thinking.'[56]

In fact, apart from cultural issues, there was very little to separate the Jan Sangh and the Congress in the first two decades after Independence. A comparative study done by *The Times of India* of the Congress, the Praja Socialist Party (PSP), Communist and Jan Sangh manifestos in February 1957 found that 'in the final analysis, the electoral battle can be fought not so much on their broad programmes—which are very similar—as on their ability to implement these honestly and efficiently. Practically, *everybody is a Socialist today*.' Essentially, the four main parties of the time agreed on the need for establishing a socialist State. The 'differences between the Congress, the P.S.P. and the Communist Party' were 'mostly on degree rather than kind'.[57] The similarity between the broad ideas in the four manifestos was such that responsible 'Congressmen, Praja Socialists, Communists and Jan Sanghis separately emphasised here today: "Beware of deception". They agreed that differences among the four lay not so much in four roads to Socialism as of four buses of different makes and design on the highway to socialism or economic democracy. And each of them said: "We want the voter to know that any other bus than ours will not take him to the desired destination—the Socialist Paradise."'[58]

The main difference was that, while the Congress wanted to nationalise strategic industries, the Jan Sangh wanted to nationalise only basic and defence industries. All parties agreed that the private sector's role was to aid the development of India. All four said much the same on welfare schemes, unemployment, women and minorities. The only difference really was the Jan Sangh's emphasis on 'the entire panorama of Indian life, with the single purpose of reviving Bharatiya culture' and its focus on 'Akhand Bharat'.[59] As then Jan Sangh President Balraj Madhok argued in 1966, 'we are not guided by any "ism". We neither believe in socialism nor in capitalism nor in communism. The only "isms" we believe in are realism and nationalism. All our policies must be guided by the national interest and all our policies must be made with an eye on the Indian conditions.'[60]

By 1973, the Sangh's approach had become practical, not based on theoretical dogmas. As Vajpayee put it, 'It rejected both complete nationalisation as well as free enterprise and favoured a middle course. It advocated nationalisation of defence industries but in respect of other industries suggested an approach which under overall State regulation, "encouraged private enterprise to expand in the interests of consumers and producers" alike. The three-pronged approach—growth in production, equity in distribution and restraint in consumption—commended by the Jana Sangh in 1951, is as valid today as it was then.'[61] Note the restraint on consumption. The Jan Sangh was always very leftist on luxuries. For instance, when there is an increase in purchasing power in rural areas, the party noted that 'some of them want to have refrigerators, transistors, fans and the like'. 'Let them have these,' Vajpayee famously argued, 'but let us impose a heavy consumer tax on these luxuries.'[62]

Similarly, the Jan Sangh called for a basic minimum income for citizens as well as a cap on their private incomes and the size of their houses. It recommended that residential plots in urban areas should not be more than 100 square yards. It was against 'palatial buildings adorned with spacious gardens and swimming pools etc' which it saw as 'nothing but a vulgar display of wealth'.[63] It wanted incomes to be capped to 'a maximum of Rs 2000 p.m. and a minimum of Rs 100 p.m. with efforts to raise the minimum so that in the foreseeable future the highest and the lowest incomes may bear a ratio of 10:1'[64] The focal point of all its policies, as Vajpayee summed it up, was 'the *Daridra* (the poor) in whom it has seen the manifestation of *Narayana* (divinity). Making him happy and contented was for the Jana Sangh the highest form of worship.'[65]

The Post-1992 Phase: When the BJP Put 'Economics Before Mythology'

Before 1991, the BJP was known as a party of shopkeepers and supported decentralisation of the economy for small-scale businesses. Yet, the biggest challenge to its positioning emerged with the economic reforms of 1992, unveiled by the Congress's Narasimha Rao and Manmohan Singh. Through the 1980s, the BJP had largely carried forward the Jan Sangh's ideas of a swadeshi-focused economic vision centred on 'Gandhian Socialism', but it started growing politically after it refocused on identity politics rather than these concerns. It spelt out its first economic policy in 1986, but as the journalist R. Vijayaraghavan wrote in a perceptive analysis, the party 'had always been consumed with political and quasi-religious concerns' and took relatively 'little note of major economic policy issues'.[66]

One reason for this was that, until this point, the party had not been a serious contender for power. But things changed after 1989, when it won eighty-five of 529 seats in Parliament, and then 1991, when it won 120 seats. It now had 'visions of forming a Government at the Centre' and needed to chart a clearer economic vision to acquire greater 'legitimacy' in the electoral arena.[67]

With the reforms, the BJP was confronted with a serious ideological challenge. In 1992, the party's leaders realised that, having set the agenda for two successive elections with the revivalist Ram Janmabhoomi movement, they found themselves 'ill-equipped on economic policies' and 'found it increasingly difficult to participate in the debate on the changes initiated by Dr Manmohan Singh'. So, they engaged in a series of top-level meetings to redefine their economic policy, starting in Sarnath in March 1992, then Baroda in March and finally Gandhinagar in May that year.

A little over a year before that, Ayodhya had reverberated with the BJP slogans of '*Yeh to bas jhanki hai, Mathura Kashi baki hai*' (This is just the trailer, Mathura and Kashi [temples] are still left). The fact that the first gathering of 150 top party leaders to discuss a new BJP post-reform economic policy met at the Buddhist centre of Sarnath (and not the nearby temple town of Kashi) was symbolic in more ways than one. As journalist Nilanjan Mukhopadhyay reported at the time, after 'following a confrontationist path for close to five years', the BJP was grappling with 'new issues and realities' as it sought to position itself as a more centrist party and a serious challenger to the Congress.[68] This was the party's third major economic vision statement—the first came in the 1970s, drafted for the Jan Sangh by Subramanian Swamy, and the other in 1986.

These conclaves showed that, throughout 1991-92, the BJP's economic policy remained in ferment. On 14 March 1992, for example, L.K. Advani expressed broad support for Manmohan Singh's reforms and the government's economic policies. Yet, within twenty-four hours of that announcement, the party reversed its stance completely, with Murli Manohar Joshi calling the Union budget 'highly inflationary' and 'anti-poor'. At a time when Narasimha Rao was opening the doors of the economy with liberalisation, Joshi announced 26 March as 'Anti-Budget Day' with protest rallies around the country, to be followed by a 'protest week' at the level of the states.[69] The party rejected the Dunkel proposals on the General Agreement on Tariffs and Trade (GATT) and wanted them renegotiated. It initially supported economic reforms, but then called Rao's budget a 'great fraud' on Parliament.[70]

The BJP's Economic Policy Statement of 1992, titled 'Humanistic Approach to Economic Development—A Swadeshi Alternative', was essentially a mixture of 'non-Nehruvian socialism and market-related theories with a touch of the old paranoia towards foreign investment'.[71] It reflected the party's wariness of unbridled capitalism. The BJP remained torn between the legacy of its older socialist economic ideas and the support for reforms among some of its prominent younger leaders. This tension was reflected in the 1992 policy statement, which declared that it drew inspiration from both Gandhi's ideal of Ram Rajya and Deendayal Upadhyaya's idea of integral humanism. Though 'Communism has collapsed', it began by saying, the 'resurrection of unbridled capitalism will not provide the key to the solution of our myriad problems. It will only lead to consumerism and increasing debt burden fettering generations to come.' For the BJP, it was essential that the 'spirit of Swadeshi and self-reliance cannot be lost'.[72] The preamble to the policy noted that 'SWARAJ and SWADESHI are indivisible'. It emphasised a middle path and the creation of what it called a new 'Indian Way'. 'India cannot be, and should not be a carbon copy of any other country,' it said. It 'must liberalise, industrialise and modernise—but it must do so the Indian Way ... We have to evolve our own Model—a model that will be integral, humanist, holistic, reconciling our own needs with the experience outside.'[73] From this idea of economic nationalism flowed the party's approach to foreign capital, which carried the scepticism of its pre-1991 ideology. The BJP document argued that 'consumer goods will not be kept open for foreign investment[,] while existing multinationals in the consumer goods sector will have to dilute their control within five years, existing employees being given preference in the equity dilution'.[74]

This tension between economic nationalism and foreign capital continued to dog the Vajpayee government between 1999 and 2004. It was exemplified by the opposition to foreign capital, led by Dattopant Thengadi, one of the senior-most figures of the wider Sangh Parivar. This opposition was at the heart of the BJP's position on the Dunkel proposals, as well as on the larger debates about globalisation, liberalisation and privatisation. In this, the economic conservatives within the BJP found ready allies among the Left's trade unions. The RSS, in its economic thinking at least, was much closer to the Left than any other political formation in India.

As RSS ideologue Rakesh Sinha, a nominated Rajya Sabha MP since 2018, wrote in 2001, 'Yesterday's Right has become today's Left. The RSS has been accused as pro-United States and "Right-reactionary" by the Indian Left and Nehruvians who must now be dumbfounded by radical ideological overtures of the RSS which is appealing to the Left trade unions to join hands against the hegemonic politics of America and the capitalist economic order ... A traditional watertight compartmentalisation of politics and elites between the Right and the Left has harmed the country in evolving a realistic path of economic development.'[75] In economic terms at least, it was left-of-centre.

The BJP's initial suspicion of the reforms was not too dissimilar to the critique offered by what came to be known as the Bombay Club: a group of leading Indian industrialists who, in the early 1990s, argued that a rapid opening up of the Indian economy would hurt domestic industry since it suffered from several handicaps.[76] In his presidential address in Bangalore in 1994, Advani said, 'Government's impassioned advocacy of globalisation often smacks of diffidence and helplessness ... We cannot shut ourselves from the rest of the world but we have to be careful to see that we are not swamped by the world either.'[77]

This approach enabled the BJP to end the initial isolation it had faced with the hard cultural nationalism of the Ram Temple movement. It allowed the party to mobilise those who had been left out or felt threatened by the reforms process, including leading Indian businessmen. By 1993, it had emerged as the 'new darling of industrialists'. More businessmen began 'putting money on the party than ever before'. Some were investing in a political formation that they saw as a rising force: '*Jis taraf hawa ka rukh hai ham usee taraf jhuk jaate hai* [where the wind is blowing, we bend that way],' a businessman told a leading magazine in 1993.[78] Some business leaders saw the BJP as a useful ally in articulating their concerns on the economic reforms, even as other, more reform-minded, leaders remained opposed.

In 1994, for example, the Confederation of Indian Industries, regarded as one of the most pro-reform voices in Indian business, stunned pro-liberalisation advocates in corporate India by taking a position that would have sounded like 'chamber music' to the ears of pro-swadeshi businesses. In a seven-page document titled *MNCs: India Strategy Needs Rethink*, it virtually signalled a 'revolt against foreign investment', accusing foreign firms of betraying their Indian partners in joint ventures by selling antiquated technology and duping Indian customers.[79] This was very similar to the kind of concerns the BJP had also been raising in its policy statements on economic reforms. At a time when the party needed political alliances to consolidate its gains, espousing these concerns on reforms also opened up the possibility of alliances with other Opposition leaders who had protectionist leanings and a socialist lineage, such as George Fernandes and Ramakrishna Hegde, both of whom entered into alliances with the BJP.

In the 1990s, the party specifically positioned its economics in opposition to the Manmohan Singh–Narasimha Rao model. It argued for a simultaneous focus on the domestic swadeshi industry and for caution on the impact of foreign investments, even as it supported the opening up of the economy. Jay Dubashi, one of the architects of its New Economic Policy, summed up this approach: 'BJP's economic philosophy stands on three pillars: economic development or growth; social stability or harmony; and self-reliance or swadeshi. In fact, the best way to remember the word *swadesh*, in which *swa* stands for *swalamban* or swadeshi for self-reliance, *de* stands for development and *sh* for social harmony.' This model was in contrast to what the BJP saw as the three pillars of what it called the 'IMF–Manmohan Singh model': (i) fiscal stabilisation, (ii) restructuring and (iii) foreign investment. The BJP's big fear was that India would fall into debt traps, like Mexico, Brazil or the Soviets had.[80] The party did not have a problem with the first two tenets of the Rao–Singh outlook, but saw foreign investment as 'the most dangerous element in the new policy'. It was 'totally opposed to the Rao government's approach' to foreign investment. As the BJP saw it, Manmohan Singh's liberalisation was predicated on the idea that 'India cannot progress without foreign capital'. Dubashi, on the other hand, stressed that, while the BJP was not opposed to globalisation, it wanted to first build a strong 'indigenous economy that can withstand external pressures without caving in. After nearly half-a-century of mollycoddling, even organised Indian industry, let alone the rest of the economy, is no position to stand up to competitive pressures from outside.'[81] Put simply: local industry had to be defended. This is why the BJP opposed Coca-Cola's takeover of Parle for $50 million (₹150 crore) which it thought was 'injurious to our economy and therefore anti-national'. Coke's annual turnover in 1993 amounted to US$ 14 billion, or ₹42,000 crore, and a profit of US$ 3 billion. In the BJP's view, Coke had paid for two-thirds of the Indian soft-drink market with less than a week's profit.[82]

These tensions came to a head during the Vajpayee regime, when the party shifted to a pro-market view. The change of registers caused a lot of disquiet in the party's traditional support base. Symptomatic of this was the RSS-affiliated Swadeshi Jagran Manch's (SJM's) opposition to the Vajpayee government's ban on the sale of non-iodised salt. In September 2000, the SJM announced a Dandi-to-Parliament 'Namak Andolan' to be organised between the birth anniversary of Pandit Deendayal Upadhyaya (25 September) and Gandhi's birth anniversary (2 October). The SJM claimed that such a ban would play into the hands of MNCs who wanted to take over the ₹1,500 crore Indian salt market. Vajpayee retreated—on 12 September, a day before the prime minister left for a US visit, the government withdrew the ban.[83]

While the SJM had made 'driving out' MNCs part of what it called a 'second freedom struggle' and raised a new war cry, 'MNCs quit India', the rollback on salt followed a major pushback within the BJP itself. The 'Quit India' theme had echoed in the BJP national executive meet on 26 August 2000. It was led by Sushma Swaraj, K.R. Malkani and Pyarelal Bharadwaj. The news magazine *India Today* noted that Vajpayee and his finance minister, Yashwant Sinha, had offered a pro-reform economic resolution at the executive meet but were thwarted. The opposing swadeshi faction in the party managed to dilute it. One example they cited was the influx of Chinese toys, which had forced 50 per cent of Indian manufacturers in the ₹1,000 crore industry to shut shop.[84]

There were clearly two opposing camps in the BJP. It now faced the pressures of what happens when an ideological cadre-based party turns into a market-driven mass organisation. The reformist camp was exemplified by people like Jagdish Shettigar, convener of the party's economic cell, who argued that 'some of the SJM's resolutions are socialistic. There's no rationale behind its criticism.' In his view, the SJM was 'criticising everything from e-commerce to agriculture and disinvestment'. Another BJP minister who supported disinvestment complained that 'they cook up numbers to support completely untenable arguments'.[85] The point was, as RSS ideologue K.N. Govindacharya told *India Today*, 'activities of the RSS and the SJM in economic areas' would 'only act as pressure and will strengthen the government's resolve to protect national interests at world fora like the WTO [World Trade Organization]'.[86] The economic policy, by focusing on 'Antyodaya' (taking care of the last man—the poorest of the poor) to realise 'Swadeshi', had introduced a new complex dynamic within the party's thinking. It pitted the adherents of swadeshi against the reforming instincts of those sections of the industrial middle classes, the professionals and managerial elites, who had moved to the BJP on account of its ostensible commitment to the values of 'economic realism' and 'pragmatic efficiency'.[87]

The BJP in the 1990s, therefore, constantly sought to walk a fine line between 'its pro-liberalisation stance in response to the interests of its traditional support base and the "new-entrants" from amongst the middle classes.' The party also sought to take away the political constituency of the Left and the Janata Dal to prevent them from exclusively occupying the 'anti-multinational' space in India.[88] In articulating this balancing act, L.K. Advani, the original architect of the BJP's Ram Temple movement, made it clear that the party was opposed to the jingoism of the SJM. He declared in 1994 that 'if the BJP is to take its place in the Indian polity as a "modern party", it will have to articulate an economic policy that is taken seriously not merely in India but in the world'.[89] In response, S. Gurumurthy's 170-page draft on economic policy became the starting point of yet another major internal party debate.[90]

As internal BJP tussles on economics played out in public, Congress leader Mani Shankar Aiyar argued that the 'BJP, having run out of steam on Ayodhya, and having its forward gear put into reverse by the Joshi yatra, now finds itself so caught up in internal contradictions over economic policies that it is unable to evolve the "third model" of development it had promised its cadres.'[91] As an RSS leader told a newspaper, in some ways, it was like a 'spider caught in its own web'.[92] The party was going into parliamentary debates without its right hand knowing what its left hand was doing. The internal turmoil was so public that Aiyar even published a tongue-in-cheek economic vision document for his political rival.[93]

So intense was this internal warfare that the industrialist Rahul Bajaj, in 1998, publicly articulated how confusing the BJP's positioning appeared to some. 'I don't think the BJP is very clear what their policy would be,' he said. 'People in the party are speaking with different voices.' All wings of the party united against the WTO's ask that tariff barriers come down, and against unhindered capital flows and investments like that of Coca-

Cola, which they said they would not allow. As Shettigar declared, 'India is not there to protect the interest of foreign investors, whether FDI [foreign direct investment] or FII [foreign institutional investment]. We are supposed to protect our own interest.'[94]

RSS ideologue S. Gurumurthy's views on foreign capital at the time are instructive. In 1998, he pointed to the South-East Asian economies as a model for India to emulate, telling a news magazine that India should not allow any 'controlling equity' to foreign companies. As he put it, 'Japan and Korea do not permit controlling equity. FDI in the consumer sector, including automobiles, must go. However, the methods can be worked out without prejudice to our economic interest. During the nationalisation spree of the '70s, Unilever was permitted to hold more shares. Something on that line can be worked out. And no FDI in food sector. Because it infringes on our culture. Coca-Cola is not a drink but a sign of American machismo. The variety of Indian cuisine should not be supplanted by factory-produced junk.' What he wanted was a level-playing field. 'India can be essentially only built by Indians,' said Gurumurthy. 'But whenever someone from London comes to FIPB [Foreign Investment Promotion Board], he is given undue respect while Indians are not even treated professionally. It is our duty to protect Indian companies.' He also drew a sharp distinction between the BJP, the RSS and SJM. In his view, while the BJP looked to address current economic issues, 'we [the RSS and SJM] look at economic issues from a 25-year point of view. The BJP has to temper the current trends from the standpoint of wider national interest.'[95]

This background of contesting ideas from the 1990s has provided the subtext to Prime Minister Modi's economic outlook. So, even as he sought to position India as a competitive destination for foreign investments as part of economic diplomacy during foreign tours and liberalised the FDI regime in several sectors, his government became focused on the idea of AatmaNirbhar Bharat. On balance, 'if self-image is any indication', the BJP has 'consciously shied away from projecting itself as a party of the Right', argued BJP MP Swapan Dasgupta in 2020. This reluctance also stems from how the BJP interpreted the political impact of Vajpayee's economic policies between 1999 and 2004. 'Atal Bihari Vajpayee, never very comfortable with questions centred on the economy, always saw the Jana Sangh/BJP as a party of the Centre,' wrote Dasgupta. 'Despite this ideological baggage, the Vajpayee government did take certain decisive steps that identified it with the conventional Right globally.'[96] These steps, like disinvestment, did not go down well with a large section of the Sangh Parivar, and after the BJP lost the 2004 general election, 'the party's internal assessment blamed the Vajpayee Government's privatisation policy for leaving the BJP's middle-class supporters dispirited.'[97]

Modinomics: What the Government Says and What It Has Done

Word View: Key Words that Define Modi-era Budgets

If newspapers are any barometer of popular sentiment, a glance at *The Times of India*'s front-page headlines on post-budget days between 2014 and 2019 provides a ballpark sense of how perceptions of the Modi government's economics changed over time. If 2014 ('FM makes money for you') and 2015 were long on euphoria and hope ('Make it, India'), by 2016, the winds were clearly changing ('Glowing in the wind', 'But it's bad news for the "rich" as govt shifts focus'). By 2017, the Modi government had clearly started veering leftwards ('Wooing have-nots, hitting have-notes') and by 2018-19, it was in full election-mode ('It all adds up to 2019'; '20,19 ... Modi goes full steam'). In Modi's second term, the budget frontpage headlines remained lukewarm ('FM stumps rich, bats for investment' in 2019 and 'New tax deal for the common man' in 2020, or 'Long, wobbly flight to recovery' in *The Economic Times*).[98]

Because Narendra Modi was seen by many as a reformist economic figure when he swept to power in 2014, it is useful to check just how keen his government has been on reform and change. A verdict on this is best left to the economists, but one way to decipher it is to use discourse analysis, that is, pay closer attention to what various finance ministers have been saying over the years.

Data scientist Rishabh Srivastava and I analysed all the budget speeches by finance ministers from 1951 to 2020 to create word clouds of what they considered important and to spot patterns of change over time. A few key themes stand out about the Modi government in this analysis. We found that the Vajpayee government's finance ministers between 1999 and 2004 focused on words like 'disinvestment' and 'privatisation' about twice as much as Modi's finance ministers (see Figure 10.9) and about the same as UPA ministers. The word 'privatisation' itself first found its maiden budget speech mention in 1992-93, just after liberalisation in 1991. In the middle of Vajpayee's tenure in 2001-02, 'privatisation' had the most number of mentions (twelve). Later, between 2005-06 and 2008-09 (during the global financial crisis), and 2013–2015, there was no mention of it at all. The word was mentioned only four times in the 2019-20 budget.

Figure 10.9: FM Word Play: Vajpayee's Finance Minister Focused on Disinvestment Twice as Much as Modi's Finance Ministers (Budget Speeches: 1950-51 to 2020-21)

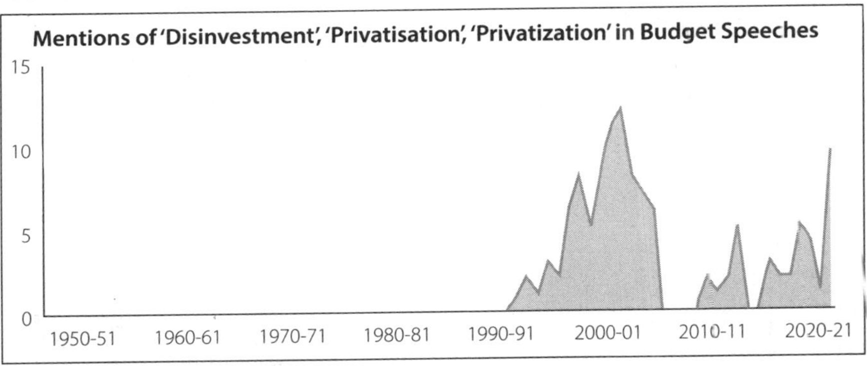

Source: Budget speeches by Union finance ministers. Analysis by Rishabh Srivastava, Nalin Mehta, PollNiti

In practice, Modi was an 'incrementalist' on privatisation in his first term. As the economics commentator Swaminathan A. Aiyar has pointed out, Modi made a 'number of small changes' but avoided a 'sweeping liberalisation of the economy'. In his second term, that approach started changing. In late 2019, the government slashed the corporate tax rate from 30 per cent to 22 per cent (plus surcharges), and to 15 per cent for greenfield investments in manufacturing made by April 2023. This was followed, in October 2021, with the announcement of the Tata Group as the winning bidder for Air India, one of the country's biggest public sector companies. This cleared the way for the 'cash-strapped Maharaja going back to the founder exactly 68 years after India has nationalised its private airlines in 1953'.[99] The closure of the Air India disinvestment process, coming after several earlier attempts failed, signalled a big shift in intent.[100] While the government's disinvestment targets have steadily risen, the fact is that until big companies like Air India and Bharat Petroleum were privatised, it would not be seen as a serious effort. As Aiyar argued, 'The star on the auction block, Bharat Petroleum, is India's sixth largest company by sales. The Container Corporation of India is a major logistics company specialising in moving railway containers. The Shipping Corporation of India is the country's biggest. The other two candidates are smaller and will probably be bought by larger public companies and don't constitute genuine privatisation. But the first three companies are highly profitable and respected.'[101] Figure 10.10 shows how both disinvestment targets as well as actual rates steadily increased through the Modi years.

Figure 10.10: Disinvestment Grew Steadily, at Incremental Pace: Targets and Actuals (2009-10 to 2018-19, Crores)

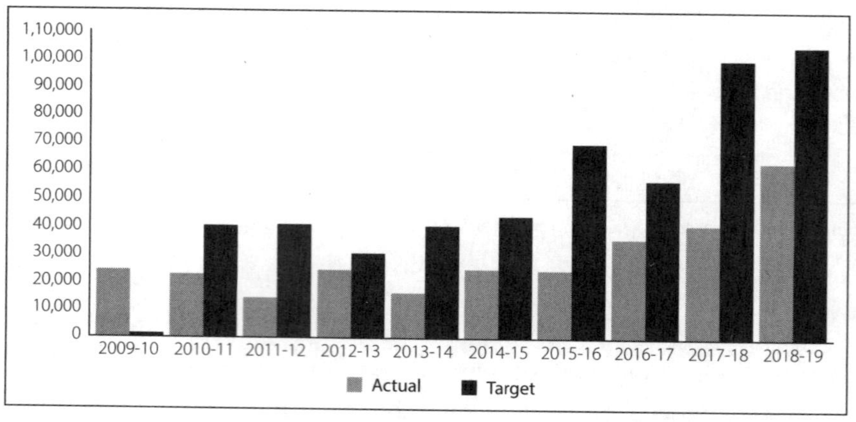

Source: Business Today, 2019. Available online at: https://www.businesstoday.in/budget/2019/infographics/disinvestment.jsp

Second, the Modi government focused on 'infrastructure' much more than the previous regimes. Apart from a few dips, mentions of 'infrastructure' in budget speeches has been on the rise in the past decade. With fifty-two mentions in the 2018 budget speech, it is clear that the sector is a top priority for the government. The word got thirty-eight mentions in the 2020-21 budget. Importantly, a heavy emphasis on infrastructure runs as a common thread across three regimes: of Vajpayee, Manmohan Singh and Modi (see Figure 10.11). The data shows that Vajpayee introduced a paradigm shift in the discourse on 'infrastructure'. Manmohan Singh greatly expanded on it. Modi inherited this legacy as prime minister and spiked it to significantly higher levels.

Figure 10.11: The Modi Government's Focus on Infrastructure Is Greater than That of Any Previous Regime (Budget Speeches: 1950-51 to 2020-21)

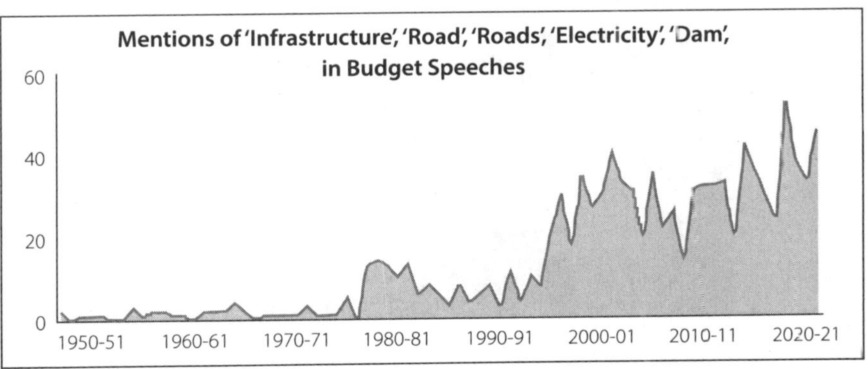

Source: Budget speeches by Union finance ministers. Analysis by Rishabh Srivastava, Nalin Mehta, PollNiti

In practice, the Modi government significantly upped total infrastructure expenditure (₹726 crore in 2018-19 to ₹972 crore in 2020-21).[102] The biggest increases were in railways, where private operators have been offered 150 routes in public–private partnerships, and in highways, where the government aimed at a build-up of 11,000 km in 2018, up from 9,328 km in 2017-18, and more than twice the rate at which UPA-2 built (see Figures 10.12 and 10.13).[103] Railways have long been a state monopoly, but the government's domination of the sector is expected to ease up with private players taking up several services.

The proposal for leasing certain railway services to private players was expected to supplement the government's 'asset recycling' plan, as Swaminathan Aiyar put it. Since 2018, the government has been 'auctioning rights to operate, maintain and share toll revenue from existing infrastructure—roads, ports, power stations and transmission lines. Cash from old infrastructure is recycled into new.' In March 2018,

Figure 10.12: Infrastructure Allocations in Modi Government Budgets (2018-19 to 2020-21)

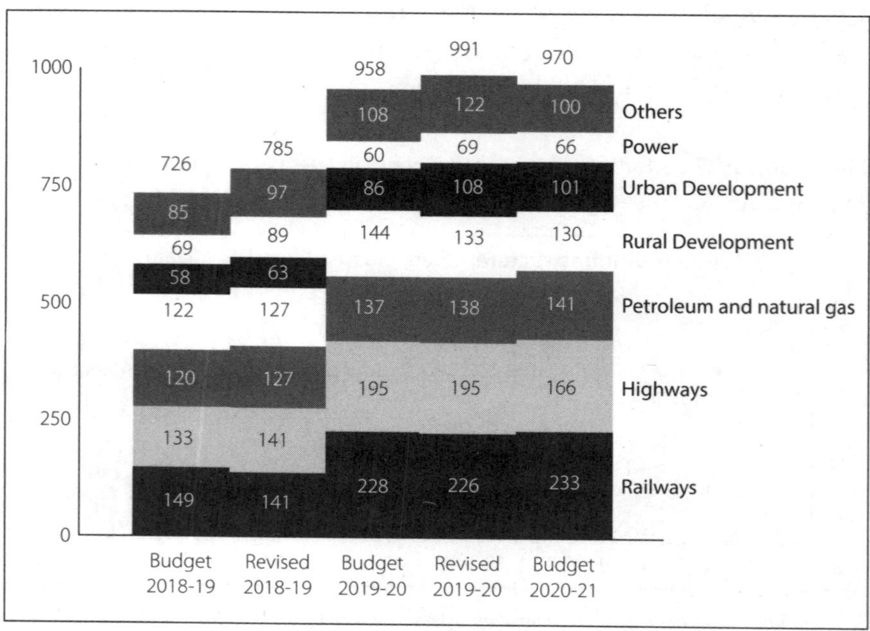

Source: Past budgets analysis on infrastructure spending by India Today, 2020[104]

Figure 10.13: Modi Government Focused Heavily on Building Highways: Highways Constructed per km 2009-18

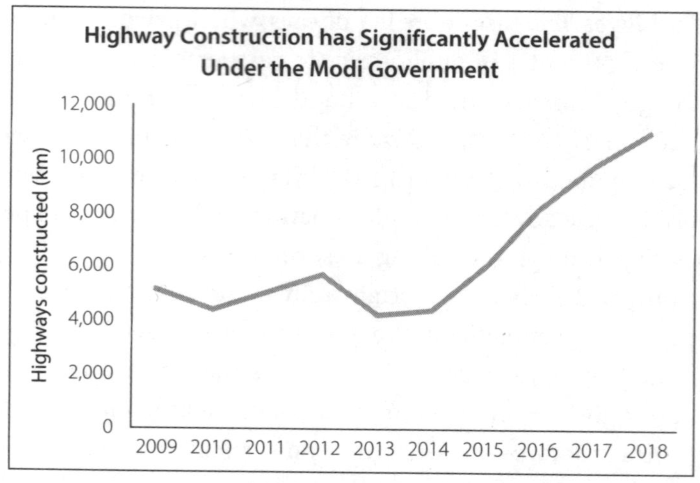

Source: Ministry of Road Transport and Highways. Analysis and graphic by Rishabh Srivastava, PollNiti

for example, a sale of 680 km of roads fetched ₹97 billion.[105] Most experts, however, believe that the big infrastructural push will depend significantly on private investment. Road Transport Minister Nitin Gadkari focused on a hybrid annuity model after 2015, wherein projects are guaranteed 40 per cent of payments annually on completing targets, and private players must raise the remaining funds themselves. Yet, raising private capital from the banks was proving to be a struggle as of early 2020.[106]

Third, the Modi government focused a great deal on digitisation (see Figure 10.14). The term 'digital' hardly ever found a mention in budget speeches over the years. That, however, changed in 2017 as a result of demonetisation and the government's push towards a less-cash economy. In Budgets 2017-18, 2018-19 and 2019-20, the term was referred to twenty-nine, ten and sixteen times respectively.

Figure 10.14 Modi Government Made a Strong Push for Digitisation, Especially After Demonetisation (Budget Speeches: 1950-51 to 2020-21)

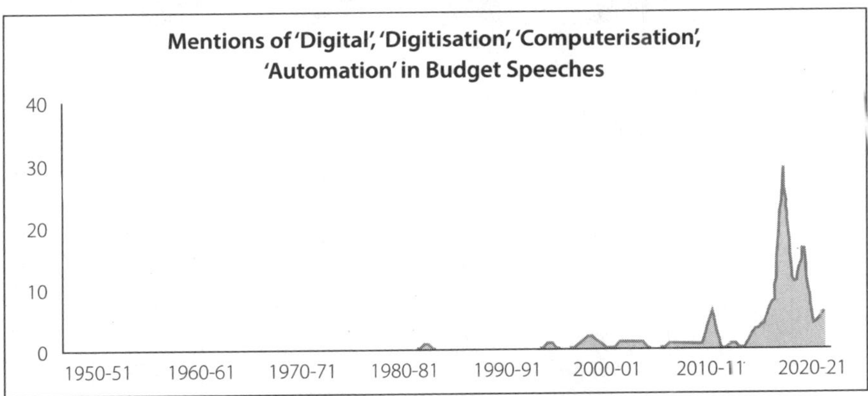

Source: Budget speeches by Union finance ministers. Analysis by Rishabh Srivastava, Nalin Mehta, PollNiti

This went hand-in-hand with a steady increase in digital payments. 'Cash is king, but digital is divine' was the motto laid down by an RBI report on digital payment growth in early 2020.[107] While the first part of the motto still holds true, Indians are definitely waking up to the second. Led mostly by the ease and proliferation of web-based transactions, the use of non-cash payments—cards, e-wallets, e-money—is on the rise. Total digital payment transactions by volume more than tripled between

2016-17 and 2019-20 (see Figure 10.15). The national lockdown of 2020 dampened economic growth and reduced the actual money value flowing through digital transactions, but the number of people adopting digital payments kept growing.

Figure 10.15: Digital Payments on Upward Path in India (2016-17 to 2019-20)

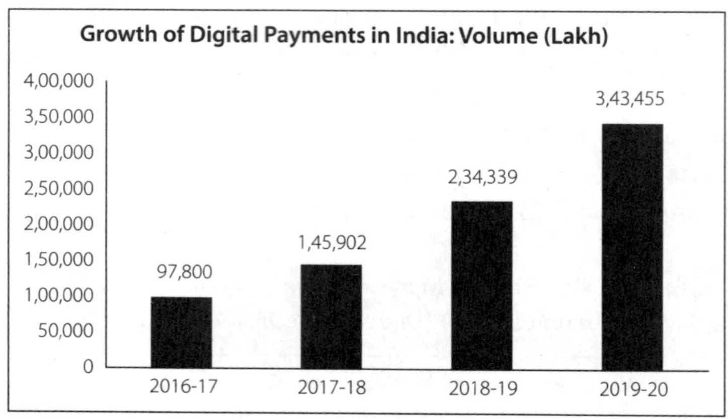

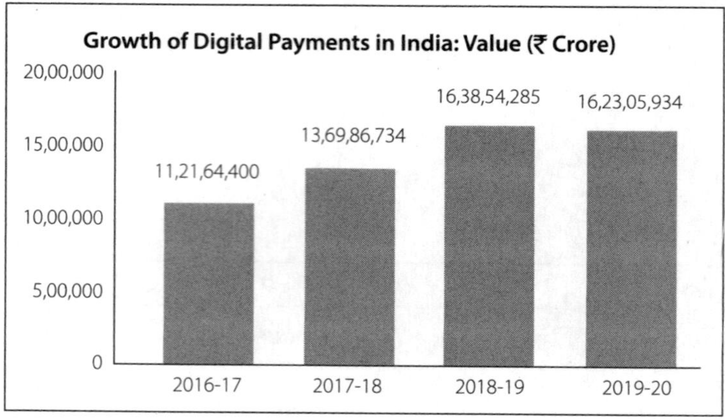

Source: RBI Annual Report, 2020; RBI Bulletin, 2019[108]

In mid-2019, just before India voted in Modi for a second term, I discussed the growth in digital money transactions with Caesar Sengupta, then head of Google's Next Billion Users Project. He stressed that India was ahead in digital payments compared to any other country in the world. 'When we started, the unified payments interface (UPI) was a very new system and had only existed for about eight or nine months,' he said. 'We have been absolutely stunned by how it has expanded. The last number we gave out in February 2019 was 45 million users and what was even more surprising was the amount of actual money passing through the system, which at that point was already above $80 billion annualised. There was a Morgan Stanley report a few months back which said 5-6% of India's GDP is now moving through UPI. That's stunning and it's happened in 18 months.'[109]

The biggest growth has been in UPI, a real-time payment system developed by the National Payments Corporation of India (NPIC), and e-money transactions, which were a very small share of total digital payments in 2016-17. Since then, UPI has become the largest mode of digital payments by volume, followed by e-money and debit card payments. Cash did make a comeback as the preferred choice of payments two years after demonetisation, but overall, digital transactions have grown by 46 per cent in value and 140 per cent in volume since demonetisation.[110] UPI, for example, clocked over a billion transactions in October 2019, and every month since then. By 31 January 2020, there were 38 crore Jan Dhan account holders in India, with 29 crore of these holding RuPay debit cards.[111]

It is important to remember here that the plumbing for the digital expansion under Modi was laid down in the Manmohan Singh era. Journalist Sanjiv Shankaran remembers going to a village in Odisha in 2009 with then RBI governor D. Subbarao to inaugurate a point-of-cash machine. While the machines themselves were available, the backend network needed to operate them was simply not up and running. The technical basis for the digital payments structure—IndiaStacks (a set of APIs that enables a unique digital infrastructure for cashless service delivery)—was developed under the UPA and further enabled under Modi. It is this network that has enabled the expansion of digital payments.[112]

Fourth, in terms of political emphasis at least, we saw a significant spike in mentions of health and education in the second half of Modi's first term in government—much more than the emphasis on these during the UPA, which focused on a rights-based social agenda (see Figures 10.16 and 10.17). One would have thought that health would have figured prominently in budget speeches over the years. In fact, it was only in 1988-89 that finance ministers started mentioning 'health' prominently in their budget speeches. The word was mentioned twenty-seven times in the 2018-19 speech by the then finance minister, Arun Jaitley, while announcing the 'world's largest healthcare programme'. However, it was mentioned just once in the 2019-20 budget before seeing a huge spike in 2020-21 during the pandemic.

Figure 10.16: Modi Government Significantly Upped Talk on Health and Education Towards End of Its First Term, Much More than UPA-2 (Budget Speeches: 1950-51 to 2020-21)

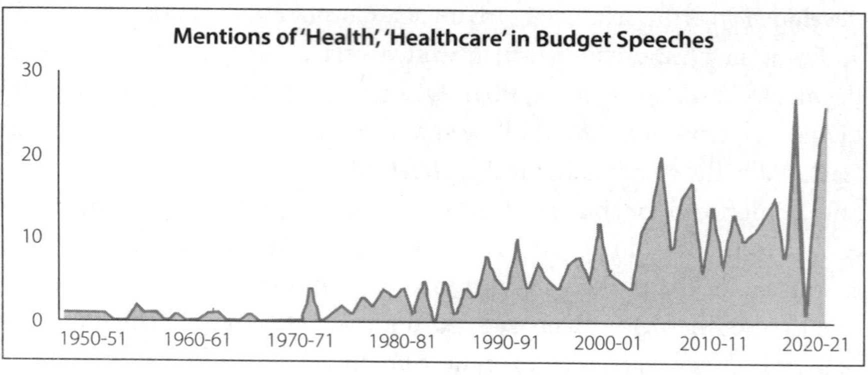

Source: Budget speeches by Union finance ministers. Analysis by Rishabh Srivastava, Nalin Mehta, PollNiti

Figure 10.17: Modi Government Significantly Upped Talk on Education Towards the End of Its First Term, Much More than UPA-2 (Budget Speeches: 1950-51 to 2020-21)

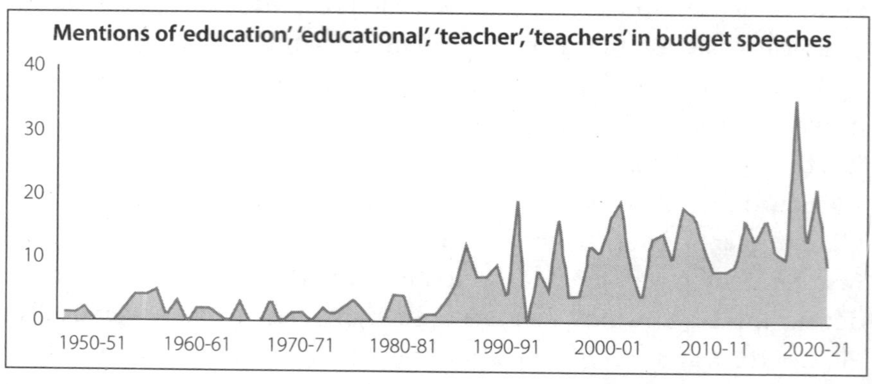

Source: Budget speeches by Union finance ministers. Analysis by Rishabh Srivastava, Nalin Mehta, PollNiti

On education, the paradox is that, though a wide range of IITs and other government colleges were built in the years after Independence, 'education' or 'teacher' were never popular words in budget speeches. The 1991-92 budget speech changed that when then finance minister Manmohan Singh mentioned it nineteen times. Budgets 2001-02 and 2007-08 also saw significant mentions. The 2018-19 budget speech had a slew of announcements on improving the quality of education and mentions jumped to thirty-five—the highest ever. The word was mentioned thirteen times in the 2019-20 budget speech.

In practice, however, there has been a gap between the government's intentions and its spending on health and education. Health spending grew by 12 per cent and education spending by 6.7 per cent between 2015-16 and 2019-20. When you factor in inflation, the per capita real growth in health expenditure translates to 6.5 per cent and per capita real growth in education expenditure stands at 2.2 per cent, according to calculations by the economist Nishant Chadha.[113] As a percentage of the GDP, India's health spending is 1.5 per cent, much less than the National Health Mission's target of 2.5 per cent by 2025 (see Figures 10.18, 10.19 and 10.20).[114]

Figure 10.18: Social Spending Increased Substantially in Government Expenditure (2012-13 to 2019-20)

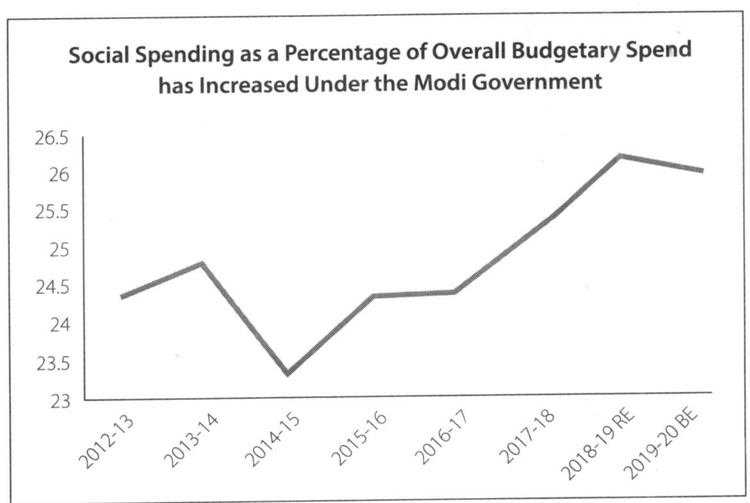

Source: Budget documents. Data analysis by Rishabh Srivastava

Figure 10.19: Growth in Health Spending in Government Expenditure

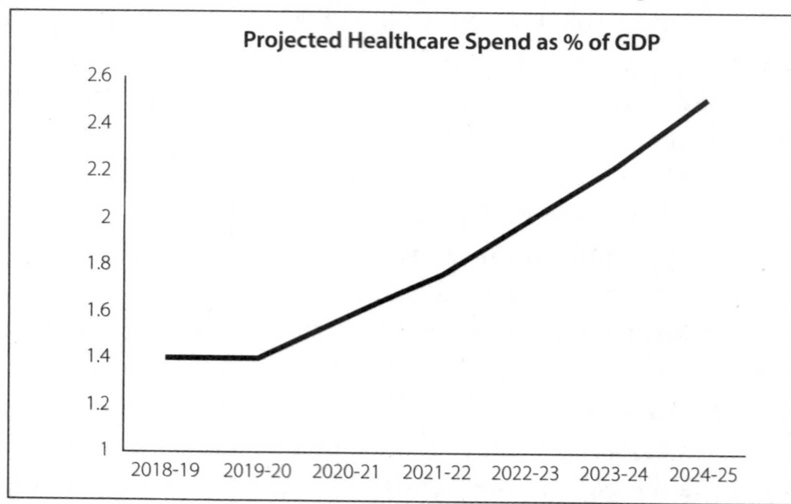

Source: Budget documents. Data analysis and visualisation by Rishabh Srivastava

Figure 10.20: Spending on Education—Actual and % of GDP (2014-15 to 2020-21)

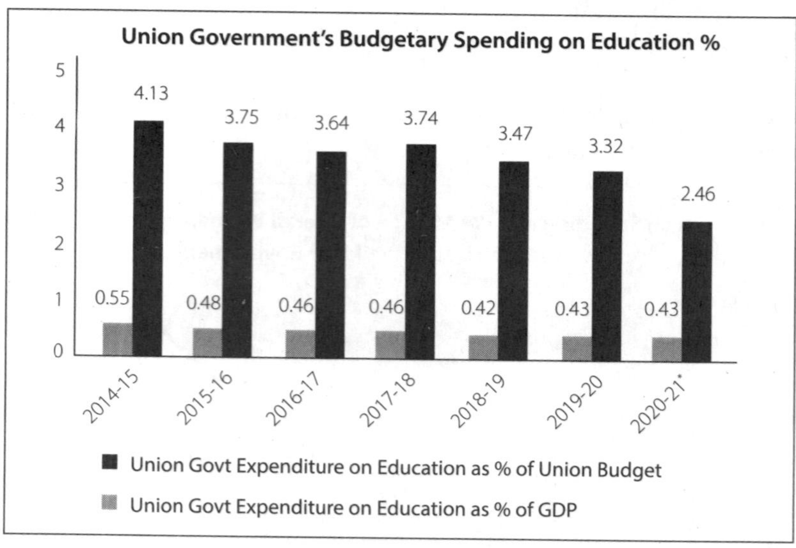

Research by Sanjiv Shankaran.

Source: HRD expenditure data from Union Budgets (Expenditure Budget). GDP at current prices data from RBI, Handbook of Statistics on the Indian Economy, 2020-21, 15 September 2021, available on https://www.rbi.org.in/scripts/AnnualPublications.aspx?head=Handbook%20of%20Statistics%20on%20Indian%20Economy.

* *Budget data for 2020-21 is the Revised Estimate; Actual spend will be available in February 2022.*

At a deeper level, this reflects a structural problem in government finances: the government simply does not have the funds to pay for its expanding expenditures. The economist Rathin Roy has pointed out that 'the government is simply not able to, year after year, collect the taxes that it says it will collect, and the shortfalls are large'. In 2020, even before the disruptions of the national lockdown, Roy estimated that the government was 0.7 per cent of GDP short of its target on tax collection. Another problem is that 'the government is simply not able to, year after year, disinvest to the extent it wants to disinvest'.[115] This means that, in 2020, the Union budget actually contracted in size, and the only sector in which spending grew substantially was agriculture (13 per cent in 2020). Other than infrastructure, 'no development expenditure allocation' increased by 'more than nominal GDP growth rate of 6.5%' in any sector.[116]

A related problem is that the state of government finances may be much worse than its appears on paper. Former revenue secretary Subhash Garg, who quit his position in mid-2019, blogged in early 2020 that the fiscal deficit reported by the government in July 2020 was understated and, in fact, stood at 4.66 per cent and 4.39 per cent in FY19 and FY18, respectively, rather than the 3.4 per cent and 3.5 per cent the official data had shown.[117] Similarly, Roy calculated off-budget spending to be about 0.7 per cent of GDP. In the same vein, the comptroller and auditor general

Figure 10.21: Black Money Is a Key Modi Government Focus Area (Budget Speeches: 1950-51 to 2020-21)

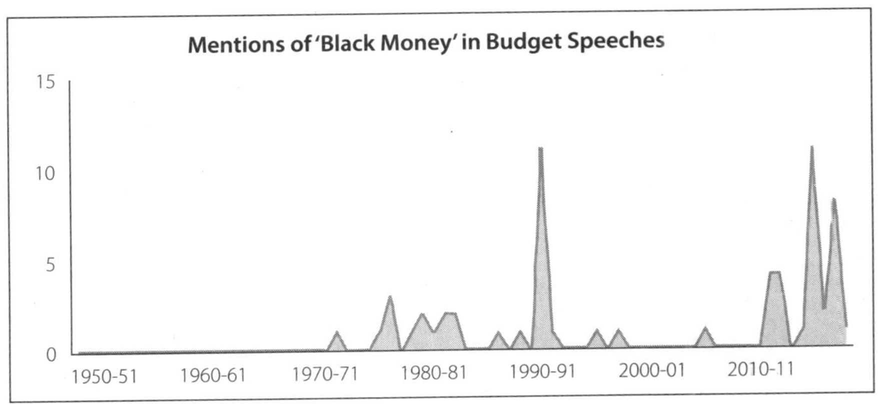

Source: Budget speeches by Union finance ministers. Analysis by Rishabh Srivastava, Nalin Mehta, PollNiti

made it clear in a presentation to the Fifteenth Finance Commission that a lack of fiscal transparency had led to government debt often being under-reported in government papers.[118]

With the Central government simply not having enough money, references to black money became much more frequent under the Modi regime. The focus on expanding the tax net in a country where only 4.18 per cent[119] of the population pays tax is understandable, but it also led in practice to a culture of what even a government supporter like former Infosys CFO and Board member Mohandas Pai called 'tax-terrorism'.[120] Not since the early 1990s has any government focused on a discourse on black money the way the Modi government has.

Is Modi a Socialist? Summing Up His Government's Economics Approach

What does all this amount to? The journalist Brajesh Kumar Singh, who has closely tracked Modi's career since his first days as chief minister in Ahmedabad, says the Modi government is the 'most left-wing government since independence'.[121] He argues that the Modi model has focused on four broad elements: building a social welfare net (with schemes like Jan Dhan, Ujjwala, and now Jan Arogya), betting on infrastructure spending, creating tent-pole social-sector projects (like toilets with Swachh Bharat in his first term and water with Jal Nidhi in his second), keeping inflation down and focusing on increasing the taxation base.

When Modi came to power, he derided the MNREGA programme as the biggest failure of the Congress. 'That people after sixty years of independence are digging holes to get paid is the best testament to your failure,' he declared in Parliament, pointing to Congress leaders.[122] Yet, after Rahul Gandhi's 'suit-boot ki sarkar' jibe,[123] his government doubled down on MNREGA, increasing its funding to higher levels than were seen under UPA-2. Modi did undertake reforms like GST and the insolvency code, but undertook less privatisation, in his first term, than Vajpayee and focused on big marquee projects like the bullet-train corridor with Japanese funding. In other words, Modi has largely been a statist. He has presided over an increase in government funding for social-welfare programmes as well as had a generic focus on making government systems more efficient.

So, is Modi a socialist? In an interview in late 2019, the BJP's Rajya Sabha member Rajeev Chandrasekhar told me that he put this very question to the prime minister. 'I've asked him, sir, are you, are we Socialist? He said—and I don't mind being quoted—he has told me very clearly: "I believe in free markets and opportunities and growth for those private sector companies that follow the law and do so through innovation, through fair competition, not through political connections. I want a robust private sector, but I want a private sector that is ethical, that is focused on the business. And why do I want it? Because only that will increase the fiscal headroom of the government through taxes and indirect taxes. So, as a government, as a political party, I believe in a strong safety net for these 300–400 million Indians that still need to be taken out of poverty. I need the fiscal headroom for that, and for that fiscal headroom, I need a strong private sector. So, on the left side of my mind, I am strongly private sector oriented. On the right side of my mind, I am a strong statist, in the sense that the state and the welfare state must intervene strongly, solidly in a clear corruption free-manner to help these 30 crore people."'[124]

Is it right, then, to compare Modi with Thatcher or Reagan? Chandrasekhar had asked the prime minister about this too: how, early on, people had made a comparison with Thatcher when he came to power. He said that Modi's response convinced him that this was a wrong comparison to make. In fact, did the policies of the government on social welfare make it, in practice, more left than the Left? 'Absolutely,' Chandrasekhar said.

'So, I asked him [Modi] this question if he wanted to be a Thatcher and he said: "Absolutely I don't want to be, I'm not getting some Nobel prize in economics. I don't want to be known as rightist, centrist or leftist. I want strong commerce, trade, industry in this country. I want that to be driven by the private sector. I want that to be done by private capital. I want the fiscal headroom that this creates and the state revenues to be spent wisely in a manner so that, in the next five to eight years, a whole new middle class is created. So that the middle class that today we say is 100 million, we can expand to 300–400 million over the next five, seven years. And imagine what kind of a consumption economy, what kind of an economic powerhouse that would be." So, think of this as being a socialist for a transition period, spending more and more of the government money, making sure you create a larger and larger middle class. When you are forward-thinking like that, suddenly it doesn't sound leftist, rightist, socialist or free-market.'

Did this mean, I asked, a statist approach with some of the guiding instincts of Singapore, but without its low tax rates? No, responded Chandrasekhar. It meant an Indian state with a focus on the local economy and exports. 'Only, if you look at a large enough Indian market, build a large middle class, can you create an export industry of the scale and size of China ... Just imagine if 500 million people enter the middle class, what will happen. There would be factories here to make things for 400-500 million Indians: making biscuits, water and so on. That kind of a scale will create an export capability that is unparalleled ... What China did in the last ten years, we will have to do in the next ten years. Feeding their burgeoning middle class has caused them [China] to create export capacity for the rest of the world. We can do the same thing. If we create a large enough domestic market alone can we export. We cannot create industries that are for export only. That is why in India today, we have textile factories that export but we have to import almost every synthetic garment from abroad. Finished products we get from Bangladesh and China, cheaper. Textiles we export because the same textile manufacturers are not making products for India.'

Whether India is competitive enough to benefit from the shift of global businesses from China or not, this ambition repeatedly comes up in conversations with senior BJP leaders. The deputy chief minister of UP, Dinesh Sharma, offered the same argument when I met him in June 2020 in Lucknow. The state government's aim, he said, was to ensure that firms leaving China come to UP and 'don't go to Vietnam or elsewhere'.[125]

Was India not losing the opportunity for exports, with businesses leaving China already going to other places that were more competitive, I asked Chandrasekhar. 'I am not saying wake up after six years,' he responded. 'I'm saying that the process that Modi has started will eventually end up in creating a huge middle class, but the middle class doesn't go from 200 to 500 million suddenly. It will progressively grow.'

BJP leaders see a clear distinction between their approach to social-welfare spending and that of the Congress. The difference, in their view, lies in targeting and higher efficiency. 'The Congress's way of public spending was statistical. They would say "I spent Rs 40,000 crore". Here,

Narendra Modiji is saying something else. He is saying, "I helped 2.5 crore Indians get subsidised cylinders. Twenty-five crore Indians have got DBT." He is not talking about numbers. He is talking about the number of Indian citizens who are getting money into their bank accounts, who are getting subsidies,' Chandrasekhar said. 'He's targeting. The biggest difference between Congress and Narendra Modi was that if he is spending Rs 30,000 crore and they were spending Rs 30,000 crore, but God knows where their Rs 30,000 crore were going. But here, in our view, Rs 30,000 crore is the sum of the beneficiaries—the 2.5 crore who got cylinders and the 25 crore who got DBT and others. He's adding up the math and getting that Rs 30,000 crore used properly. If you do that for a full five-year period like this, and you back it up with grants, jobs, Mudra loans and so on, you are potentially lifting people out of poverty faster than we did in the last sixty years.... If the niyat, the effort, the capability and the execution remain at this level and the focus is unrelentingly on getting these 35-40 crore people out of poverty permanently, then boss, this is a juggernaut country.'[126]

Would it be fair, then, to say that the BJP is economically left-wing? A few months later, I put this question to the civil servant and former deputy chairperson of the Planning Commission, Montek Singh Ahluwalia. 'This right-left binary has become a little jaded,' he responded. 'I think you are implying that the BJP was expected to be more pro-private sector but it isn't. Part of the problem is because, in the words of Arvind Subramanian, the private sector is now "stigmatised". As Amartya Sen has said, India doesn't really have a genuine right-wing party in economic terms.'[127]

This is a view that many in Delhi's economic establishment, on both sides of the political divide, agree with. Says a senior former bureaucrat who has worked in a previous prime minister's office, 'Any country that privileges philosophy over plumbing will get both wrong. I saw the first budget of Mr Jaitley, God bless him, and thought to myself they were gone. UPA's last budget was crazy. Essentially, it took all the earnings of next year and postponed all expenditures to next year. If a CFO of any private company would have done it, he would have been sacked or in jail. Modi government continued this approach of pushing the can further down the road.'[128]

Another senior economist, then on the Economic Advisory Council to the Prime Minister, compared Modi's economic approach to Indira

Gandhi's. There is a view in the government, 'like it was under UPA-2', this economist said, 'that economic growth is my birthright and would come anyway, so why bother so much'. In that sense, 'these guys are more left than the Left'. When you question them on economic policy, 'it becomes a question of loyalty—*aap kis ke saath hain?* [who are you with?]. We gave twenty-eight notes on how things can be changed. We should have been taking advantage of the China exodus after the financial crisis. But companies are going to Kenya and Vietnam. They don't see it. They say, *yeh* growth *kee baat aap chor deejiye* [put aside this talk of growth]. We have just pulled so many million people out of poverty. The tragedy is that if this government, with its large majority, can't reform India, no one else can. Then, we are doomed as a country.'

Another big issue that Modi critics identify is a relative lack of external expertise in the government. They are only relying on 'bureaucrats', said the former PMO bureaucrat. 'They have set up committees but it is only a handful of babus who call the shots … Anyone who has fixed salary can't do entrepreneurship,' he said. This changed somewhat in 2019, when the government announced a series of lateral appointments of external experts at the joint secretary-level in nine ministries[129] and added several economists to the Economic Advisory Council to the Prime Minister.[130]

The challenge of balancing change with limited resources had other ramifications, which showed up most clearly in the defence sector: a key priority area in the discourse of the Modi government. In early 2020, when China broke the decades-long mutual agreement on patrolling the disputed Line of Actual Control on the eastern border, the Indian military's long-festering challenge of funds to buy modern defence armaments came back into public focus. While the Indian Air Force's new Rafale jets from France became the showpiece of the government's publicity on defence, underneath the chest-thumping lay the deeper problem of ensuring enough funds for other modern military equipment and ammunition.

The China crisis broke at a time when the urgency of reform and positive winds of change in the newly revamped Ministry of Defence—with India's first-ever chief of defence staff (CDS) and a new Department of Military Affairs—were just about beginning to be felt.[131] Yet, this very reform cloaked the single most fundamental challenge that faced India's military. India may be the fourth largest defence spender in the world, with the defence budget getting the highest allocation of all ministries. Yet, in 2020, for the first time, the standing army was slated to be spending more on pensions (38.1 per cent) than on salaries for its serving soldiers and civilian employees (37.5 per cent) or what it would spend on modernisation (8.8 per cent). Just a few months before the China-border crisis became public, the defence ministry, a PRS analysis showed, was slated to spend almost as much on pensions (28.4 per cent) in the year as it would on salaries (30.2 per cent). This left less than half of India's allocated defence spending for other tasks. The current system was clearly unsustainable, and a radical change of the kind that the CDS started talking about was a necessity. While the Modi government increased funding for defence each year, the fact remained that, as a percentage of GDP, defence spending was at its lowest point since 1962.

Those who have studied economic reforms know that seldom has India undertaken paradigmatic shifts at the level of governmental systems unless pushed by a deep crisis that renders the current systems untenable. So it has been with Defence. At a time when the fiscal deficit is ballooning and government expenditures are stretched, there is simply no money for expansion unless it can be found through a major internal reboot of the way India has traditionally organised its soldiering.

State–Centre Funding and a New Paradigm

What does the lawyer who fought the Ram Janmabhoomi case in the Supreme Court on behalf of Ram Lalla have to do with the issue of government funding? Quite a lot. In early 2020, the same lawyer, K. Parasaran, also provided legal advice to the Finance Commission on a new structure to divide up taxation income between the Centre and the states. Under the Indian system, tax earnings are divided between the Centre and the state based on a formula set up by successive Finance Commissions. Ever since the Fourteenth Finance Commission, which increased the proportion of funding for state governments (up from 32 per cent to 42 per cent) in 2015, the Modi government has talked of how this helped its slogan of cooperative federalism. In reality, the states have been complaining that their share of the money actually came down with this new division, since the government also reduced Central government spending on schemes, while reducing funding earmarked by the erstwhile Planning Commission, which was replaced by the Niti Ayog.

That share of the states could go down further. In early 2020, the Fifteenth Finance Commission, headed by N.K. Singh, obtained a legal opinion from Parasaran on whether the division of money between the Centre and the states ought to happen only after the share of defence spending was first subtracted by the Central government. This would, in effect, reduce the total pot that would be divided and radically decrease the share of the states. The new scheme of division came after an amendment to the Terms of Reference (ToR) of the Fifteenth Finance Commission by the government in July 2019, when it was asked to 'examine whether a separate mechanism for funding of defence and internal security ought to be set up and if so how such a mechanism could be operationalized'. Further, the first report of the Fifteenth Finance Commission, tabled in Parliament on 1 February 2020, made it clear that the Finance Ministry 'has proposed setting up a non-lapsable fund, levy of cess, monetization of surplus land and other assets, tax-free defence bonds and utilizing the proceeds of disinvestment of defence public sector undertakings'.[132]

States had earlier objected to the change in the Finance Commission's mandate, fearing that, instead of a two-way distribution of net central taxes between the Centre and the states, such a fund could reduce their share if a three-way distribution were to be carried out by the Fifteenth Finance Commission. 'Constitutionally, defence is in the Union list, not in the state list. If you do a carve-out for defence, who gets to control the money? Do you then have some sort of a defence board in which there are states' representatives? It will open up a whole can of worms. It will almost certainly be challenged by states,' former principal economic adviser to the Planning Commission, Pronab Sen, told the newspaper *Mint*.[133]

Parasaran's legal advice on the proposal argued that every Indian citizen should contribute towards funding the defence and internal security needs of the country. Accordingly, the Commission's final report, tabled in Parliament on 1 February 2021, recommended the creation of a non-lapsable 'Modernization Fund for Defence and Internal Security' (MFDIS). The government accepted the recommendation 'in-principle', and Finance Minister Nirmala Sitharaman informed the house that 'sources of funding and modalities will be examined in due course.'[134] The detailing of how such a fund would operate in the future was still a work in progress at the time of writing in October 2021. This is partly because the proposed structural change in defence funding is being reviewed in tandem with the unfolding of the wider process of armed forces reform initiated by the Modi government. It is linked to the creation of the new institution of the CDS and the related move to restructure the Army, Air Force and Navy's existing operational structure of nineteen separate commands into a much smaller number of combined geographic 'theatre' commands.[135]

Interestingly, Parasaran harked back to ancient texts, and the economic thinking in the Vedas and the Puranas, to justify his legal opinion in favour of a change in the defence funding mechanism. 'Parasaran has opined that it (funding for defence and internal security) transcends any definition of classification. He has traced the evolution of the world through *Vedas*, *Puranas* and *Arthashastra*, that this is the primary obligation of every citizen of India, obligation for which he must contribute in some way or the other to ensure security and stability of India. This transcends in a way the artificial constructs [of Centre and states],' N.K. Singh said in an interview.[136]

The BJP has long believed in a more unitary state with a federal structure. If the new proposal for division of money is implemented, it would certainly be a step in that direction. Combined with the battle over GST and the sharing of resources with the states—especially over how the Union government's financial obligations to states would be fulfilled after the pandemic, which Finance Minister Nirmala Sitharaman called an 'act of God'—this indicates a new phase in Centre–state relations and questions of financial autonomy. How these events play out will have huge implications for Indian federalism.

PART IV

THE UMBILICAL CORD

11

THE BJP'S RSS LINK

The Foundational Moment

'BJP Will Never Sever RSS Link'

Exactly two weeks after the BJP was founded in 1980, its first general secretary, L.K. Advani, addressed the first convention of its Gujarat unit with a clear message. The BJP, he bluntly asserted, 'would never sever its link with the Rashtriya Swayamsevak Sangh'.[1] Nine months earlier, the Janata Party, which the Jan Sangh had merged with in 1977, along with other Opposition parties, had banned its members from having membership of 'any organisation having faith in a theocratic state'.[2] That political union—originally of five parties—broke up because many in the Janata Party questioned the 'dual' RSS membership of many ex-Jan Sangh members—a link they saw as synonymous with 'communalism'. This dispute proved to be the tipping point.[3]

After Indira Gandhi swept back to power in the 1980 election, Jagjivan Ram—the ousted Janata government's erstwhile deputy prime minister—announced on 28 February that he would 'not leave' the RSS 'dual membership issue' undecided and would 'pursue it to the end'.[4] This proved to be the final straw: the ex-Jan Sangh faction and several other leaders walked out of the Janata Party and created the Bharatiya Janata Party on 5 April 1980. They had with them fifteen of the Janata Party's twenty-eight Lok Sabha MPs, all fourteen of its Rajya Sabha MPs, five former cabinet ministers, eight former ministers of state and six former chief ministers. The newly formed BJP claimed that it was the 'real' Janata Party, not a breakaway faction.[5]

When Janata Party leader Chandra Shekhar challenged the BJP's inheritance claim, arguing that the remaining rump was actually the 'real' Janata, the ECI initially seemed to disagree. It gave the BJP 'national party status' and froze the Janata Party's election symbol for a few months (which meant that Chandra Shekhar's Janata Party could not contest elections on it) until the Commission could take a final call.[6]

As Advani told his party's newest delegates in Gujarat, the RSS question had been so central in this break-up that, until this dispute, the Janata Party had never taken a single decision by vote. The only time it would do so was to 'oust' the Jan Sangh members. 'This step by the Janata Party proved a blessing in disguise,' he said, 'not only for us but also for Indian politics itself.'[7]

The BJP's umbilical-cord attachment to the RSS and the exact nature of the relationship between the two has been a central question from the party's very foundational moment. In fact, its first few weeks in this new avatar perfectly encapsulated the old tensions around the RSS–Jan Sangh relationship as well.[8]

In its inaugural convention in New Delhi on 5–6 April 1980, the BJP tried to downplay talk of the RSS link. The visual backdrop on the stage at this session was different from the martial-Hindu-heroes imagery of Chhatrapati Shivaji and Maharana Pratap on display at the Jan Sangh's founding ceremony twenty-nine years earlier. Instead, the backdrop now displayed images of Mahatma Gandhi; Jayaprakash Narayan, the Gandhian socialist icon whose call for 'total revolution' against Indira Gandhi in the 1970s had galvanised the united anti-Congress Opposition front during the Emergency; and the Sangh's late idealogue Deendayal Upadhyaya.[9] Seeking to appropriate the legacy of the Janata Party, Atal Bihari Vajpayee, the BJP's first president,[10] declared at the convention that the new party would fight the upcoming elections on the basis of the '1977 election manifesto of the Janata Party because there was nothing wrong in the Janata Party's policies and programmes'.[11] Advani too announced that there would be 'no compromise' in accepting 'Gandhism as the ideology of the new party', insisting that its economic ideas were closer to Gandhi's than even the Congress Party's.[12]

The new party's emphasis on being inclusive of non-Jan Sangh and non-RSS members was reflected in the fact that non-Sangh luminaries from the Janata Party—like the eminent lawyer Shanti Bhushan, father of the present-day civil rights lawyer Prashant Bhushan; the legal luminary Ram Jethmalani; and the former Congressman Sikandar Bakht—were all given a prominent place on the inauguration dais. Bhushan declared he was convinced that the real 'Janata' (the party, but also a play on the word for 'people') was represented at the convention.[13] Interestingly, two of the three members in the committee that was tasked with drafting the BJP's new constitution that day were not from the Sangh: Jethmalani, a Sindhi refugee of Partition, and Bakht, a Delhi Muslim.[14] It was also Bakht who proposed Vajpayee's name for party president, seconded by the party's Rajasthan satrap, Bhairon Singh Shekhawat.

As a contemporary account noted, initially, the BJP 'appeared to play down its Jana Sangh–RSS antecedents to project itself as the standard-bearer of the idealistic and morally high-minded JP movement of the mid-seventies'.[15] The new party, in its first big policy statements, was looking to claim 'direct descendance from the JP movement and so to stand for the same principles that characterised the movement'. Simultaneously, it seemed to give the impression of 'wanting to jettison the communalist baggage with which, because of its communal Jana Sangh-RSS associations, it would otherwise be lumbered'.[16]

Essentially, caught between trying to attract a larger group of new voters and seeking to retain its traditional base of those who felt that a Hindu majority should not be apologetic about trying to build a social order on 'Hindu principles', the party's initial public position on the RSS question appeared to reflect a 'heightened sense of ambivalence'. It seemed to neither 'wholly repudiate nor unreservedly embrace' its RSS legacy.[17] The twists and turns on its RSS connection and its stance on Hindu questions suggested, to quote a newspaper editorial at the time, that the party, in these early days, was somewhat 'schizophrenic'.[18]

Clearly, this confusion over the RSS and its role needed to be resolved. Within a month of Advani's clear exposition on the BJP's unbreakable ties to the RSS, the party issued a policy statement which made it clear that it no longer seemed to 'want to or to be able to play down its Jana Sangh-RSS origins'.[19] Even as it reiterated its commitments to the beliefs of the JP movement and its new adage of 'Gandhian socialism', it declared that those who belong to 'social or cultural organisations ... working for the uplift of the masses and not engaged in political activity' (read RSS) could join the new party. Further, it reiterated that membership of one would not repudiate membership of the other.[20] In short, the BJP came out 'openly in favour of "dual membership", the rock on which relations between the undivided Janata Party foundered'.[21]

While the BJP's decision to stand by its earlier belief in the innocuousness of 'dual membership' underscored its determination to not disown its Jan Sangh–RSS lineage, it also sought to harness and inherit the larger political legacy of the Janata Party. And so, in the party's first national plenary session in Bombay on 28–30 December 1980, Vajpayee declared that the BJP had embraced the 'samata' (equality) that B.R. Ambedkar had argued for. He also invoked a new notion of 'positive secularism'.[22] This, Vajpayee indicated, was akin to what was practised by the Maratha king Shivaji towards minorities in the seventeenth century: the Chhatrapati had a Muslim personal attendant during his Agra captivity and is also known to have launched his Konkan campaign in 1661 after seeking the blessings of the Muslim saint Yakutbaba of Kelshi (Ratnagiri).[23]

Later in the 1980s, L.K. Advani would redefine the political landscape with his charge that the Congress was 'pseudo-secular', but already in 1980, the BJP was arguing that it stood for a notion of secularism that embraced tolerance but not appeasement. It was at the time a small north Indian party still, and this early idea of 'positive secularism' was meant to blunt the criticism of those who saw the party's 'refusal to disown the Jan Sangh–RSS aspect of its heritage to mean that it is advocating Hindu communalism'. Essentially, the BJP was trying to present a new face in the hope of 'gaining fresh adherents other than its traditional loyalists even while retaining the old ones'. It did not want those loyalists to have second thoughts. But not everyone was convinced. Some thought the party was seeking to 'run with the hare and hunt with the hounds', seeking to 'proclaim its secularism' without disowning what they saw as its 'reputedly communalist past'.[24]

The formal adoption of 'Gandhian socialism' as a founding ideology created new tensions with the BJP's traditionalists. When the party's thirty-three-page inaugural policy statement, which specifically mentioned this as a core principle, was circulated for discussion ahead of its first plenary,[25] BJP vice-president and Gwalior royal Vijaya Raje Scindia publicly circulated her own five-page counter-draft with an angry refutation of the idea. She argued that the slogan would create confusion in the minds of the rank and file because it was a slogan that was being raised only to 'appear progressive'. It would make the BJP look like a 'photocopy' of the Congress and make it 'lose its originality', Scindia thundered. Her specific objection was to the word 'socialism', not because she objected to the idea of equity it represented, but because of the semantics of its Western origins. The Sangh's Indian concepts of 'jan-kalyanwad' (people's welfare) and 'ekatm-manavwad' (integral humanism), she stressed, 'are wider in scope than socialism'.[26]

Scindia's public protest was in tandem with that of a section of RSS workers in the party who argued internally that the appropriation of Gandhi's name was unnecessary. Senior leaders like Vajpayee and Advani, who also had RSS origins, were clearly looking to broaden the party's appeal beyond its core constituency by appropriating Gandhian ideals, just as the Janata Party had. The dissident group argued that no such tactic was needed now that the BJP had walked out of the Janata Party. Echoing Scindia, this group argued that, while they supported the party's push for economic decentralisation, 'there was enough support for it in Indian history and the introduction of Gandhism in it was unnecessary'.[27] A vocal section of this opposing group came from Madhya Pradesh, led by then state BJP secretary Kailash Sarang. This was a state where the Jan Sangh had grown deep early roots.[28]

Eventually, a novel compromise was worked out. Scindia was prevailed upon to publicly withdraw her dissent note on the adoption of 'socialism' as party ideology. In a hurriedly organised press conference, she announced that she had done so after the party's senior leaders explained to her that the BJP's socialism actually had an 'Indian content', unlike that of Karl Marx. She said she had changed her mind after it was explained to her that the 'socialism' the party was adopting was actually the 'jan-kalyanwad' of Indian tradition and the 'integral humanism' advocated by Deendayal Upadhyaya.[29] When Madhya Pradesh leader Bhai Mahavir's attempts to bring around other dissidents failed, Vajpayee himself intervened, declaring that the party 'will not go back on Gandhian socialism'. After this, the resolution on adopting Gandhian socialism as a founding ideology was voted in with overwhelming support.[30]

Narendra Modi's appropriation of Gandhi's imagery draws from, and builds on, this earlier history. An image depicting the Mahatma's spectacles was adopted as the official logo of the Swachh Bharat Mission (launched on the Mahatma's birth anniversary in 2014 for a five-year drive until his 150th birth anniversary in 2019).[31] Earlier, in 2010-11, as Gujarat chief minister, Modi had led a move to build a large Mahatma Mandir Convention Centre in the state capital of Gandhinagar. He also led an initiative where representatives of all 18,066 villages in Gujarat would bring sand in urns and empty them into the foundation of the Mahatma Mandir. This Convention Centre included a memorial to Gandhi's Dandi March and a large charkha (spinning wheel) installation. A special road was built connecting the Mahatma Mandir with the Gujarat Legislative Assembly building.[32] The resistance by a section of the party in that first plenary session of 1980 to adopting Gandhian nomenclature seemed like something from the distant past.

Another much-commented on sign of internal discord in 1980 was the absence of former RSS pracharak and senior Jan Sangh leader Nanaji Deshmukh at that plenary. Deshmukh was, at the time, considered one of the six leading lights of the Jan Sangh. He had played a vital role in forging alliances with the socialist leader Ram Manohar Lohia, which had powered the Jan Sangh's growth in the late 1960s and '70s. His absence from the founding moment of the BJP, a successor to the Jan Sangh, was conspicuous enough for newspapers to interpret it as a sign of discord. When asked, L.K. Advani denied any such rift. He clarified that Deshmukh himself had asked Vajpayee to exclude him from active participation in 'organisational affairs' when the new party was formed.[33] He had moved instead to Gonda, Madhya Pradesh, and later to Chitrakoot, to work on rural education and farming cooperatives. His absence was important enough for Vajpayee to bring it up in his opening speech, clarifying that Nanaji Deshmukh was away because he was doing 'constructive work and not out of any differences'.[34]

Deshmukh, who was posthumously awarded the Bharat Ratna (Jewel of India)—India's highest civilian honour—by the Modi government in 2019, never returned to politics. He did, however, speak in favour of the Congress's Rajiv Gandhi on the eve of the 1984 general election after Indira

Gandhi's assassination, saying he deserved 'cooperation and sympathy' for larger causes.[35] The 1984 election resulted in just two of 514 parliamentary seats for the BJP: the lowest point in its electoral history. Rajiv Gandhi won a full majority in Parliament, the last time any party did so until Modi's triumph in 2014. At least some reports of the time said that many BJP 'active workers who were RSS people generally preferred the Congress (I)' in the 1984 poll.[36] Whether this is true or not, it was indicative of an unease within the party about the turn away from issues of cultural Hindu nationalism.

The Jan Sangh's foray into the Janata Party had been an organisational experiment that ended in failure. Yet, up until the late 1980s, the BJP continued its experiment with ideological flexibility, a legacy of its dalliance with the Janata Party. It pivoted back to cultural nationalism in 1986 with the Ram Temple agitation after the Rajiv Gandhi government enabled the opening of the locks on the disputed Babri Masjid for 'Hindu worshippers' on 1 February.[37] The BJP formally embraced the political aim of building a Ram Temple—an agitation initiated by the RSS-affiliated Vishwa Hindu Parishad (VHP, or World Council of Hindus)—through the Palampur Resolution on 9–11 June 1989. That resolution categorically framed the Ram Temple as an article of faith and committed the party to building it at the site of the Babri Masjid. It said:[38]

> The BJP holds that the nature of this controversy is such that it just cannot be sorted out by a court of law … The BJP calls upon the Rajiv Government to adopt the same positive approach in respect of Ayodhya that the Nehru Government did with respect to Somnath. The sentiments of the people must be respected, and Ram Janmasthan [Ram's birthplace] handed over to the Hindus—if possible through a negotiated settlement or else, by legislation. Litigation certainly is no answer.

The Palampur Resolution announced the BJP's return to the politics of cultural nationalism, and was followed by the Somnath–Ayodhya Rath Yatra that catalysed its next phase of growth.

The BJP, the Sangh and Leadership

While the BJP and the RSS are separate organisations, the Sangh has played a critical role in shaping the party and its wider outlook as well as its political ground game. The BJP–RSS linkage is organic, ideological, and has political ramifications. The debate on 'dual membership' that broke the Janata Party was fundamentally about contesting ideas of nationhood (though Sangh leaders were also right to point out that the issue only surfaced as a convenient tool to fight other political battles *after* the Janata Party had acquired power with the support of RSS cadres).

The BJP has never been led by a party president who did not have an RSS history. Each of its eleven presidents between 1980 and 2020 were affiliated with the Sangh or its affiliates in the early part of their careers.[39] Prime Minister Modi began his career as an RSS pracharak, as did Prime Minister Vajpayee.

As Gujarat chief minister in 2007, Modi told an interviewer: 'I have originally been a swayamsevak of the Rashtriya Swayamsevak Sangh. We are trained to think from a national perspective … it is my RSS upbringing that makes me do well whatever task I am entrusted with … I do not have a single instance of the Sangh parivar creating any problem for me. The Sangh parivar is with me. They have always backed me, helped me, guided me. The Sangh parivar is my eternal strength.'[40]

Similarly, as prime minister in 2000, Vajpayee told a VHP audience in New York, 'I may be Prime Minister today, may not be tomorrow. But one thing that nobody can rob me of is being a swayamsevak [literally self-helper, volunteer; also a term for Sangh workers].'[41]

His deputy prime minister, L.K. Advani, too, publicly proclaimed that 'if there is any admirable quality in me, I owe it to the RSS'.[42]

This is why, for anyone wishing to understand the growth of the BJP, it is vital to understand specifically what the RSS stands for and how it has evolved over time. This section of the book answers three broad sets of questions.

First, how much has the RSS grown over the years? What role does it play in political mobilisation? What are the mechanisms it uses to expand in new areas? What is the role of the wider Sangh Parivar in the BJP's expansion? What is the quantifiable role and influence of the RSS within the BJP and the governments it controls?

Second, which ideas does the RSS privilege most, and when? Which ones does it give importance to and which ones does it underplay? How does it communicate these ideas to different audiences? How does it calibrate its messaging at different times in the political cycle?

Chapters 12 and 14 answer the first set of questions. Chapter 12 provides a detailed analysis and macro picture of the RSS's national expansion over the past three decades. To delineate this further, it provides a case study of how the RSS grew in Karnataka between 2014 and 2020. It also puts together a new empirical analysis of the exact nature of the BJP–RSS linkages by quantifying, for the first time, exactly how many leaders with a verifiable RSS background occupy key positions within the BJP leadership, the Modi government and one major state government run by the BJP (Madhya Pradesh).

Chapter 14 expands the ambit of this study from political growth patterns alone to wider social trends. It studies education initiatives run by the wider Sangh Parivar through a network of educational institutions—specifically studying the Vanvasi Kalyan Ashram, which works with tribal children—to delineate how it grew, its modes of expansion and prospects. This chapter outlines the RSS's missionary model of expansion using education in new catchment areas, shedding light on the BJP's social modes of mobilisation.

Chapter 13 answers the second set of questions on what the RSS stands for in the 2020s by using the Narad Index to compare what the RSS says publicly with the communication patterns of the BJP, the Congress, Prime Minister Modi as well as a range of other leaders—both offline and on social media. Taken together, this section of the book details the RSS, its evolution, its ideological nuances and its modes of influence.

12

THE GROWTH OF THE RSS

In October 2000, I was reporting on a massive three-day camp to celebrate seventy-five years of the founding of the RSS.[1] The Rashtriya Raksha Mahashivir (Great National Security Camp), set up near the Mughal emperor Akbar's tomb on the outskirts of Agra, brought together the Sangh's top brass and over 75,000 volunteers from sixteen districts in the Braj prant (region) of western UP. They were put up in a specially constructed tent city spread over 400 acres and divided into thirty-five townships. This was a year after the Kargil War, and so, the giant main gate to the tent city, christened Mahabalipuram (Great Warrior Abode), replicated an iconic war photo of victorious Indian soldiers flying the tricolour on top of an imposing mountain peak that the Indian Army had recaptured in that war with Pakistan. Inside the tent city, the centrepoint was another massive tableau: of Lord Krishna holding aloft Mount Govardhan on his little finger (depicting a story from the Krishna legend set in nearby Vrindavan).

Over the next three days, a number of the Vajpayee government's leading lights visited the camp. Some of them, including Deputy Prime Minister L.K. Advani and UP Chief Minister Ram Prakash Gupta, standing prominently in the front row during public meetings, performed the rhythmic RSS salute (with right hand folded at chest-level, palm next to the heart and facing downwards) and its customary Sanskrit prayer to the Motherland.[2] A few of these visiting dignitaries addressed the gathered thousands in the mid-day heat, talking about the vital role that the RSS had played in their lives. Advani told the audience that the 'RSS exercises a moral influence on the government and both Prime Minister Atal Bihari Vajpayee and I share a historical bonding with it'.[3] On the other hand, some senior RSS leaders, in speeches from the same platform, publicly expressed their dissatisfaction with the political class and listed their key concerns. Although the RSS chief later denied that this meant that there were differences between the Vajpayee government and the Sangh,[4] the open criticism was a reflection of the growing tension between the two at the time. As I followed BJP leaders around the camp, I was struck by the genuine deference they showed to senior RSS leaders like Rajendra Singh (Rajju Bhaiyya), who had stepped down as RSS chief earlier that year due to poor health. After hanging out with RSS volunteers in their khakhi-white-black uniforms for three days, I headlined my TV report from Mahabalipuram, 'Show of Strength by RSS'.[5]

In retrospect, I was only half-right. The political message to the government was indeed one of strength, showcased in the leaders' speeches and through synchronised martial displays by hundreds of lathi-carrying RSS volunteers in full view of the invited cameras. Despite having a BJP-led government in power, the RSS was grappling with a serious crisis of growth that year. Its leaders at the camp were deeply worried about the decline in new membership numbers and the reluctance of young Indians to join up.

Mohan Bhagwat, then RSS sarkaryavah (general secretary) and later appointed sarsanghchalak (chief) in 2009[6], blamed the rising popularity of satellite TV for falling recruitment. As he lamented to a visiting reporter in Agra, 'Children don't know their mother tongue. They don't call their father Pitaji but Daddy and Papa. They watch too much TV.' He was right. A young RSS volunteer, fourteen-year-old Navin Sagar from the RSS-affiliated Saraswati Shishu Mandir in Agra, aptly summed up the organisation's crisis to the same reporter: 'I watch TV. Cartoon Network and "Aahat" are my favourites. I learn computers and want to go to the US. What they teach in the RSS is good but irrelevant.'[7]

The growth of television and its impact on membership had long been a worry for RSS leaders, who had started devising countermeasures. Seshadri Chari, then editor of the RSS magazine *Organiser*, pointed out that, in 2000, when TV penetration first deepened, the Sangh began introducing 'more games to attract the youth'. It even started inter-shakha (branch) cricket matches to woo younger recruits.[8] RSS leaders at the time were worried that annual growth rates of shakhas were stagnating at about 15 per cent, and so the Sangh announced a major expansion programme. Then RSS leader Ram Madhav announced in 2001 that the organisation had reached '30-40 per cent of the revenue blocks in the country'. Its aim was to 'reach 100 per cent by the year 2006, the birth centenary year of Guruji Golwalkar'.[9]

By 2003, the organisation had about 4,000 full-time pracharaks, but the 'base from which to draw them' was still decreasing. A senior RSS paracharak told the journalist Manini Chatterjee that the Sangh was suffering from 'the three Ts: television, tuitions and technology'. This crisis was existential because its primary recruiting ground had always been students: it had shishu shakhas (six–ten years), bala shakhas (ten–thirteen years), kishore shakha (fourteen–twenty-one years), tarun shakhas (twenty-one–forty-five years) and praudh shakhas (those above forty-five years).[10] Its most prominent leaders, like Vajpayee and Advani, had all been drawn to the Sangh before they were teenagers.[11]

Yet, despite the dip in recruitment, by 2003, the RSS was already what Chatterjee called the 'biggest NGO in India', with 45,960 daily shakha meetings. Assuming a base number of fifteen members on average in each shakha, this was close to seven lakh men and boys. At the time, the RSS was also conducting an additional 7,923 Saptahik Milans (weekly meetings) and 7,200 monthly Mandalis (gatherings).[12]

By 2019, the number of daily shakhas had gone up by 28 per cent to 59,266 per year, Saptahik Milans by 117 per cent to 17,229 and monthly Mandalis by 13 per cent to 8,302.

While the RSS does not officially publish data on its primary membership, it does document the daily, weekly and monthly meetings and training camp numbers in its annual reports. I have made an informed estimate of active RSS members from these reports. In 2019, the lower range of its membership was 8,88,990 members and the higher range was 59,26,600.[13]

After a decade of decline and stagnation, the inflection point for RSS growth came in 2012, as the anti-corruption movement against the Congress-led UPA government grew in strength. While the RSS

Figure 12.1: RSS Daily Shakhas: Annual Growth (1977–2018)

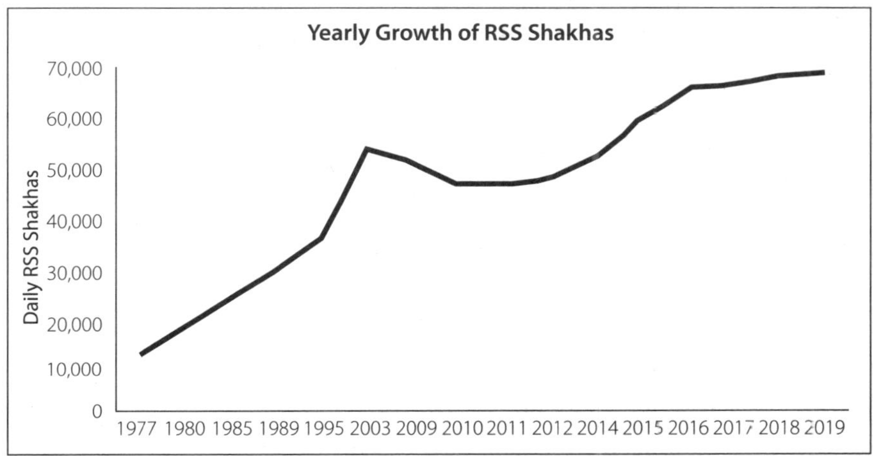

Source: 2009–2019 data from RSS Annual Reports. 1977–2009 data from Manini Chatterjee, 'Repackaging the RSS', The Indian Express, *16 March 2003*

supported the India Against Corruption movement, and its cadres formed a large proportion of the mobilisation that drove it,[14] it is unclear whether the Sangh's growth spurt around that time was caused by this involvement or whether it was just a coincidence. Between 2010 and 2014, the daily shakhas went up by 12.9 per cent, weekly Milans by 69.7 per cent and monthly Mandalis by 29.6 per cent. Thereafter, the rate of growth accelerated even further. Between 2014 to 2019, daily shakhas increased by 31.7 per cent and the weekly Milans by 37.9 per cent. However, monthly Mandalis declined by -6.9 per cent (see Figure 12.2).[15] By mid-2019, the RSS's Sahakaryavaha Manmohan Vaidya could claim that the organisation was active in 90 per cent of the blocks in India.[16]

RSS data shows that the number of daily shakhas saw a spurt after the first Modi government came to power in 2014. As one RSS leader in UP told me, 'We are growing fast but we are also very conscious that some of the new people who come to us may be coming only because they may have an impression that they could somehow get closer to power through the Sangh. Our biggest challenge is to keep estimating who is joining us because of such perceptions and who is genuine. We are only interested in people who genuinely believe in our thinking.'[17]

Figure 12.2: Annual Growth of RSS Daily Shakhas, Saptahik Milans, Monthly Mandalis and Places Where Shakhas are Held (2009–2018)

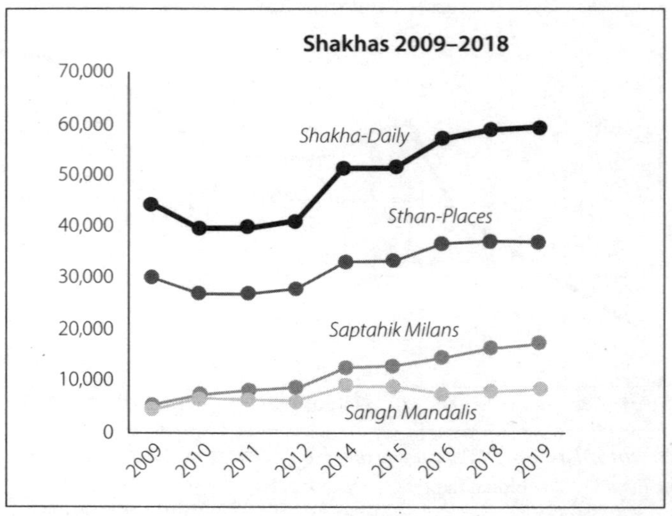

Source: RSS Annual Reports
Note: Membership information for 2013 not available.

Anyone who knows the Sangh knows that 'shakhas' (literally, branches), or daily gatherings—at the bottom of the RSS organisational pyramid—are its lifeblood.[18] They were set up by RSS founder Keshav Baliram Hedgewar as the central organism at the heart of the Sangh when he founded it on Vijayadashami (Dussehra), 27 September 1925.[19] Hedgewar envisaged a strong network of shakhas where 'Hindus would gather and refurbish the values of life'. According to K.S. Sudarshan, who headed the RSS between 2000 and 2009, Hedgewar forged the 'shakha with its auto-financing system and deep-rooted traditions as moorings to mould the Hindus so that we can stand before the world as a mighty confident nation'.[20]

Daily shakhas are thus the fundamental building blocks of the Sangh. They consist, according to one description, of physical warm-up and jogging (five minutes), yoga and surya namaskar (forty minutes), Sanskrit shlokas called Subhashit or Amrit Vachan or patriotic songs (ten minutes) followed by prayers for five minutes.[21] Hedgewar saw the shakhas as 'incubators for vyakti-nirman [personality development]'. As senior Sangh leader Sunil Ambekar puts it, for Hedgewar, 'Sangh means Shakha and Shakha means programmes for personality development'.[22]

The expansion of shakhas was accompanied by a major increase in RSS training camps for existing members between 2014 and 2019 (see Figure 12.3). Annual RSS Officer Training Camps (Level 1) increased by 49.8 per cent in this period (from 10,435 to 15,639), Level 2 Training Camps by 49.4 per cent (from 2,231 to 3,335) and Level 3 Training Camps by 15.8 per cent (from 607 to 703).

Figure 12.3: Annual Growth of RSS Officer Training Camps—Levels 1, 2 and 3 (1994–2019)

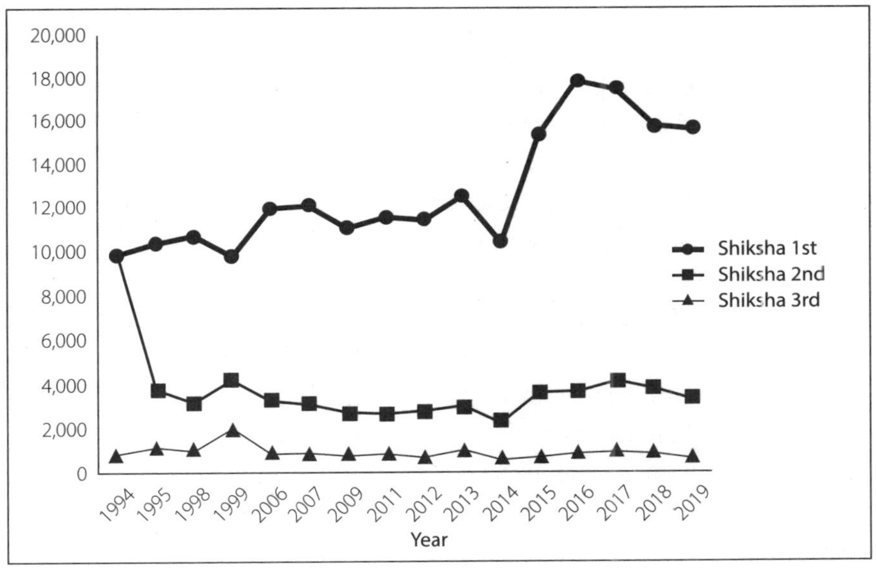

Source: RSS Annual Reports

How the RSS Grew: A Case Study of Karnataka

It is equally important to understand what has driven the expansion of the RSS in recent years. Sangh leaders say that online outreach has been the biggest source of expansion since the early 2010s. In 2018, it launched a 'Join RSS' initiative on its website, which a senior Sangh functionary claimed was yielding about 10,000 new recruits per month on average.[23]

The RSS's growth strategy in Karnataka is an instructive case study. In February 2020, I travelled to Bengaluru to meet with a group of state Sangh leaders and understand how they viewed these changes. At the state headquarters in Chamarajpet in Old Bengaluru, Radhakrishna Holla, RSS communications head for Karnataka, told me that that over the last 'six–seven years' they had focused on their website. 'Anybody can register with an email and a number,' he said. 'The result is that in Bengaluru City we get about 200-400 memberships each month as registrations from website alone. It is a new way of growing. From the rest of the state overall, we get about 400 a month. This totals up to about 8,000–10,000 a month on average new registrations in Karnataka. They are mostly young students and young people.'[24]

By early 2020, the RSS had about 4,000 shakhas in Karnataka: 62.5 per cent of these were in north Karnataka (2,500); 37.5 per cent in south Karnataka (1,500). Holla, who is an IT engineer working for the RSS in his spare time, explained that traditionally Bengaluru had been the biggest growth area for RSS shakhas, along with the districts of Shivamogga and Mangalore (in Dakshin Kannada). In recent years though, there had been a major expansion in the south Karnataka districts of Tumkur, Kolar, Mysore and Mandya—'very good growth', as he put it.[25]

Coastal Karnataka and the areas around Mangalore were where the RSS set up its first shakhas in Karnataka in the 1940s and 1950s. It was an early start, but a major factor that held back further expansion until the 1990s was the language barrier (see Chapter 15 for more on this).[26] The early RSS pracharaks were all from Maharashtra and spoke Marathi, not Kannada. Their message was received and found an audience in Karnataka's coastal areas, where most people speak Konkani, or in Bangalore, where a large mass of north Indian migrants spoke Hindi. Vadhiraj, an RSS worker who has worked for over two decades with SC/ST groups and headed communications for the Karnataka South zone for ten years, explained that 'language was not an issue in the [Bengaluru] city here' and in the 'coastal areas, the language was Konkani, so they could talk.'[27]

Local RSS leaders in Karnataka attributed the Sangh's recent growth to the use of social media and its recourse to communication in the local languages. 'Now in Karnataka,' said Vadhiraj, 'all pracharaks are from Karnataka, so they can expand and reach out. All our activities happen now in Kannada.'[28] Holla said, 'I should credit this growth to social media also. So, areas where we had less presence earlier, like Tumkur, are now growing.' Sangh leaders say that, typically, it is easier to organise weekly gatherings in new areas. In Karnataka, they said, 'daily gatherings and weekly gatherings called Milans are both growing in new places'.[29]

By the early 2010s, the RSS started expanding its social reach in the state through daily and weekly videos on dedicated Facebook and YouTube channels. Its Facebook page in the state is 'largely in Kannada'.[30] By September 2021, the Kannada RSS Facebook page had 8,56,279 followers; its Kannada YouTube channel 2,70,000.[31] The state media in-charge explained to me that they approach Twitter and Facebook with different content strategies. Twitter, he said, 'is not that important for people in vernacular audiences … it's more to reach opinion-makers but Facebook is for mass-connect and we do it in Kannada.' Each administrative region in the RSS has a media centre called Vishwa Swamvad Kendra (World Dialogue Centre). In Karnataka, this team comprised a central team of five people and a social media team of about four or five people, with one person each handling every zone in the state (the RSS divides Karnataka into six zones).[32]

Figure 12.4: RSS Online Membership—Interactive Live Tracker

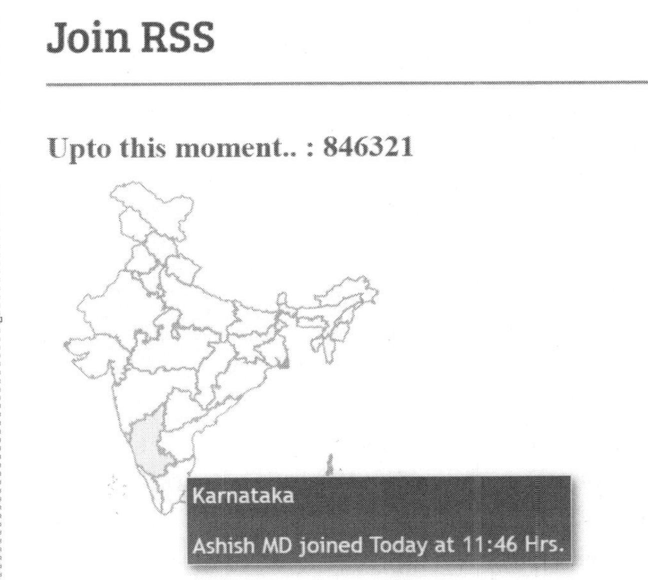

Source: By September 2020, RSS had a live interactive new membership tracker on its website. Hovering the cursor over a state throws up the name of the latest person to have joined the RSS from that state that day, and the time of joining. The screengrab above is from 24 September 2020. It displays the name of the latest person who had joined RSS that day from Karnataka. https://www.rss.org/

The roots of these social-media strategies can be traced back to 1999 when the RSS started its first 'cybershakha' on the occasion of its Hindi magazine *Panchjanya* going online. This was the pre-smartphone era, when the internet was mostly accessed through dial-up modems. The then RSS chief Rajju Bhaiyya delivered a brief 'Baudhik' (intellectual discourse) on the internet from Delhi, and then replied to emails from all over the world. In 1999, the Sangh announced three new departures for these cyber shakhas: attendees did not have to wear RSS uniforms, they could approach the RSS supremo directly and women could 'send messages to the RSS chief'. Never before had 'women been permitted access to the RSS leadership, leave aside the chief himself'.[33] That first cybershakha on 25 September 1999 was aimed at NRIs.[34]

By 2003, the RSS had started organising software shakhas or 'IT Milans', which were first reported from Pune (Maharashtra), Bengaluru (Karnataka), Hyderabad (Andhra Pradesh), Chennai (Tamil Nadu) and Noida (UP). They included everything from 'Powerpoint presentations on the RSS's community work to Yoga' and 'video conferences'. BJP leader Ram Madhav, then still with the RSS, said that 'the first software shakha was held in 2003-04. It's a new experiment to connect with emerging sections of professionals.'[35] Initiatives like these were later localised and scaled up in local languages in states like Karnataka.

The Sangh also aggressively uses publications in local languages, neatly differentiated and targeted. In Karnataka, for example, it publishes two Kannada magazines. According to Holla, '*Vikrama*[36] [for mass connect] has a weekly circulation of about 20,000 in Kannada, and *Aseema*[37] is for intellectuals, with a monthly circulation of 5,000 plus.'[38]

Importantly, the BJP being in power in Karnataka was of great help to the RSS. As Vadhiraj said, 'BJP has increased in Karnataka because of RSS, but RSS has also increased because of BJP.'[39] He pointed to the controversy over Tipu Sultan, the eighteenth-century Muslim ruler of Mysore who died fighting the British in 1799, but whose legacy is bitterly divided between those who revere him as a freedom fighter and Hindu nationalists who see him as an oppressor of Hindus. Since the early 2000s, controversies around the legacy of Tipu have regularly erupted into political slugfests between the Congress and the BJP. When the Congress-led Siddaramaiah government decided to celebrate Tipu Jayanti from 10 November 2015 onwards as an annual event to commemorate India's 'first freedom fighter', the BJP protested vociferously. The Yediyurappa-led BJP government, which won power in Karnataka in 2019, scrapped these plans within three days of taking office, a move that Siddaramaiah characterised as being 'against minorities'.[40] In Vadhiraj's view, this controversy played a role in the growth of the RSS. 'Even Siddaramaiah helped us by introducing Tipu Jayanti,' he said. 'Valmikis in the state had suffered under Tipu in the eighteenth century and they came to us. Many people got into discovering us because of the BJP and realised that most issues are not political but social. So, they went to RSS thereafter.'[41]

Power acts as a powerful recruitment tool. Karnataka's example is not unique. In Haryana, when M.L. Khattar of the RSS was made chief minister in 2014, the Sangh grew stronger in the state. Journalist Manvir Saini observed that as 'stories of Khattar spending time with another Swayamsevak, PM Narendra Modi, in their earlier years started circulating, many were attracted'. As a result, the number of RSS shakhas in Haryana rose by over 400 per cent—from nearly 400 in 2014 to about 1,700 (covering 6,909 villages) by 2017.[42] In just over three years, a state that had been a lukewarm area for the RSS had shakha penetration almost as dense as Gujarat's. By 2017, Gujarat, with a population of about 6 crore, had 3,500 shakhas, while Haryana, with a population of 2.5 crore, had grown to 1,700 shakhas.[43]

The numbers clearly show that Modi's national victories in 2014 and 2019 also served to strengthen the RSS. According to RSS Saha Sarkaryavaha (Joint General Secretary) Manmohan Vaidya, between 2014 and 2016, an average of 90,000–95,000 Indians put in requests to join the RSS every year.[44] This, he claimed, went up to 1,25,000 in 2017; 1,50,000 in 2018, and stood at 1,30,000 as of September 2019. Crucially, even as the RSS expanded its footprint, it was also claiming a younger demographic. As Vaidya said in Bhubaneshwar in October 2019, students and youth were running 60 per cent of all shakhas. The number of shakhas run by individuals above the age of forty, he said, stood at just 11 per cent. This 'partially explains the rise of vote share for BJP among the first-time voters,' he said emphatically.[45]

How Much RSS in the BJP: 50:50

The RSS has a complicated relationship with power. It does not formally take part in politics—indeed, that has been a cardinal principle for the Sangh since its inception. As Chapter 9 shows, the RSS's second sarsanghchalak (chief), M.S. Golwalkar, counselled and advised Syama Prasad Mookerjee when he set up the Jan Sangh but also warned him that, as a matter of policy, the 'RSS could not be drawn into politics, that it could not play second fiddle to any political or other party, since no organisation, devoted to the wholesale regeneration of the real, that is cultural, life of the Nation, could ever function if it was to be used as a handmaid of political parties'.[46] Yet, RSS cadres formed the sinews of the Jan Sangh and were at the core of its political base, just as they provided a powerful core base for its successor.

At the same time, RSS leaders have consistently refuted talk of political ambitions. Most recently, in 2018, RSS Sarsanghchalak Mohan Bhagwat reiterated: 'There are questions regarding the political ambitions of the Sangh. Right from its inception, the Sangh had taken a conscious decision to stay away from electoral politics. No officer-bearer of the Sangh is allowed to be a member of any political party and will stay away from politics.'[47] He added, 'It is not our concern as to why other political parties do not have a large number of swayamsevaks. Why don't they (swayamsevaks) feel like going to other parties, is the question they (other political parties) need to think on. We don't ask the swayamsevaks to work for any specific party.'[48]

Yet, few would doubt that the BJP considers itself a part of the wider Sangh Parivar. It cannot be otherwise in a government led by a former RSS pracharak, Narendra Modi, and a party that has never been led by a politician who did not spend his early years with the RSS or its affiliates. Amit Shah, the co-architect of the BJP's expansion since 2014, started his career with the ABVP, as did his successor as party president, J.P. Nadda.[49]

How exactly does the RSS interface with the BJP, though? Meeting over lunch in his office in Bengaluru, I put this question to Karnataka's then deputy chief minister, Ashwathnarayan. 'The Sangh plays an important role, but we can't say we win because of it,' he responded. 'It is a separate but centralised cord between the Sangh and the BJP. The Sangh sends us people in various roles, such as organising secretary etc., in the party itself. It is an independent entity, but is also well integrated. It is time-tested …'[50]

While few doubt the influence of the RSS on the BJP and the multiplier effect its cadres bring to the party, it is necessary to more precisely quantify their relationship. To map this with exactitude, I carried out a special sorting exercise of the backgrounds of three categories of national BJP leaders: the first Modi cabinet of ministers in Delhi (2014–2019), the second Modi cabinet (2019) and the BJP's top office-bearers.

The journalist Rajiv Pundir and I studied publicly available information about each Union cabinet minister in both Modi regimes and the central office-bearers of the BJP at the national level to ascertain how many of these leaders had an RSS background. We aimed to identify the penetration of the RSS into the BJP, at least to the extent that could be numerically measured. To round off this analysis, we also studied one BJP state government, the cabinet of BJP's Shivraj Singh Chauhan in Madhya Pradesh, to understand just how many of its ministers had been with the RSS. It is important to clarify here that having an RSS background does not mean that a BJP functionary is currently a member of the Sangh. In fact, under RSS rules, any pracharak working for the BJP would have to resign his role in the Sangh.

The purpose of our exercise was to quantify the influence of RSS ideas on the BJP's top leadership. We found that exactly half of Modi's first cabinet—every second minister, that is—in 2014 (seventeen of thirty-four ministers) had an RSS or RSS-affiliate background (see Figure 12.5).

The second Modi cabinet appointed in 2019 also had a similar (but slightly lower) representation of leaders with an RSS background: 48 per cent (twelve of twenty-five cabinet ministers). A major cabinet addition in 2019 was that of ex-foreign secretary, S. Jaishankar, who had no political background, as external affairs minister. The larger council of ministers also had ministers of state with independent charge, like R.K. Singh (Power) and Hardeep Singh Puri (Urban Development), who had bureaucratic experience and no RSS background. A senior BJP leader, when questioned by the news portal *The Print* on the party's links with the

Figure 12.5 Ministers with RSS Background Accounted for 50 per cent of Modi's First Cabinet (2014–2019)

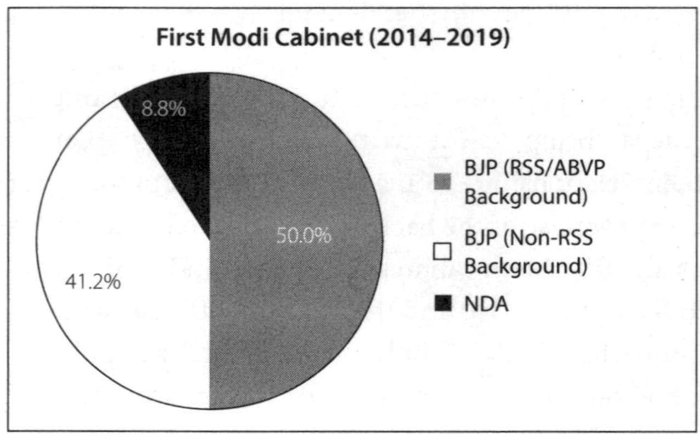

Source: Author's fieldwork, with research support from Rajiv Pundir. Note: Breakdown based on Union cabinet list as of 13 November 2018. It does not include erstwhile ministers with an RSS background, like Venkaiah Naidu, who in 2017 was appointed vice president, or Ananth Kumar, who passed away on 12 November 2018.[51]

RSS, made it clear that 'having an affiliation with the RSS is not a criterion to become a minister ... to say someone is being promoted merely because they have links with the RSS is not a fair comment'.[52] An RSS functionary also stressed that the organisation has 'no role in deciding tickets for the party or deciding the portfolio. Yet, at the same time, RSS only believes in two things—there are those who are already with us and those who are yet to come under the fold.'[53]

The RSS's influence on the BJP and its ideas becomes even clearer when we examine the backgrounds of the party's office-bearers at the national level. Specifically, we looked at sixty-one leaders (fifty-seven national office-bearers and four members of the Margdarshak Mandal). Here, the number of those with an RSS background came to 45.9 per cent (see Figure 12.7). Among them were J.P. Nadda, who like Amit Shah had started his political career with the RSS, and B.L. Santhosh, party general secretary, who was on loan to the BJP from the RSS. The actual influence of those with an RSS background may be higher than the numbers indicate. The vital post of the BJP's national general secretary (organisation) and all three joint general secretaries in charge of party organisational work were held by leaders on loan from the RSS to the BJP. Furthermore, *The Print*,

Figure 12.6: Ministers with RSS Background Accounted for 48 per cent of Modi's Second Cabinet (2019–)

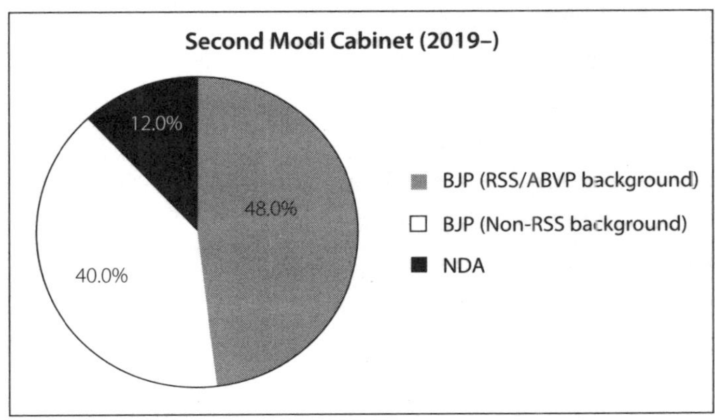

Source: Author's fieldwork, with research support from Rajiv Pundir. Note: Breakdown is based on Union cabinet list, accurate as of 12 December 2019.

in January 2020, counted as many as 48 per cent of the BJP's Lok Sabha MPs (146 of 303) and 41.4 per cent of its then Rajya Sabha MPs (thirty-four of eight-two) as having an RSS link.[54]

Figure 12.7: Leaders with RSS Background Accounted for 47 per cent of BJP National Office-bearers (2020)

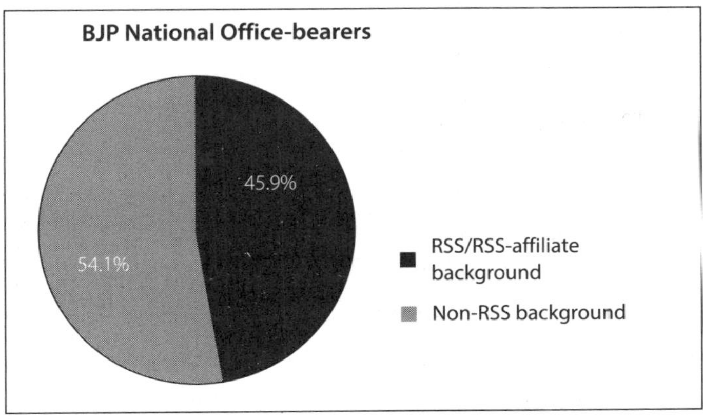

Source: Author's fieldwork, with research support from Rajiv Pundir. Data is accurate as of 24 September 2020. Note: We did not count the Parliamentary Board or Central Election Committee since many office-bearers overlapped with these bodies.

Make no mistake, the Modi government and the BJP are not controlled by the RSS, but the RSS has a higher imprint on both than it did when Vajpayee was prime minister. Under Modi, the BJP is happy to proclaim its RSS links. Many of its ministers are deeply driven by RSS thinking and its cultural agenda. A separate Ministry of Animal Husbandry, Dairy and Fisheries was created in 2019, following a suggestion that is said to have chiefly emerged from the VHP. The National Education Policy (NEP) also listed several suggestions in the draft policy from Sangh-affiliated organisations.[55]

A step below the Centre, a similar pattern of representation is replicated in BJP-ruled states. We examined the Shivraj Singh Chouhan-led BJP government of Madhya Pradesh between 2013 and 2020. We came across an interesting contrast between the Chouhan government that was in power in 2013–2018 and the government he formed on 24 March 2020, after twenty-three Congress MLAs defected to the BJP, along with senior leader Jyotiraditya Scindia, to bring down the Kamal Nath-led government that had come to power in December 2018. The earlier Chouhan cabinet had only twenty cabinet ministers and 40 per cent of them had an RSS background. When the BJP came back to power in 2020, Chouhan expanded his cabinet to thirty-five ministers to accommodate the Congress defectors who had made his new government possible. The new entrants constituted over one-third of the new cabinet and the proportion of ministers with an RSS background fell by almost half to 23 per cent. These numbers indicate the BJP's ability to be flexible in order to gain or retain power (see Figure 12.8).

A cadre of ex-RSS leaders is not the only form of soft power the Sangh has within the party. The real power it has is of a moral nature. The late BJP leader Pramod Mahajan, often derided by some RSS leaders as a 'lapsed' swayamsevak, used to call the RSS a 'third umpire'. The Sangh's authority, he said, also 'came from its neutrality', its strength from its 'sacrifice, from a simple lifestyle, from objectivity, from ideology'. In his view, as long as the Sangh was seen by BJP leaders to have these qualities, it would always have a moral authority.[56] As Pyarelal Khandelwal, then vice president of the BJP, told the journalist Manini Chatterjee, 'those who want to do election politics do not remain pracharaks. If he joins politics, he will have to resign, and therefore the respect for the pracharak remains intact within the parivar'.[57]

Figure 12.8: Cabinet Ministers with RSS Backgrounds Fell in Madhya Pradesh After Congress Defectors Were Given Ministerial Portfolios in 2020

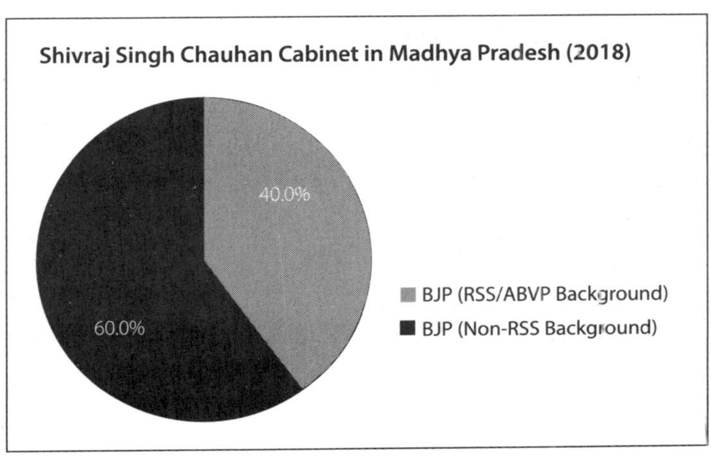

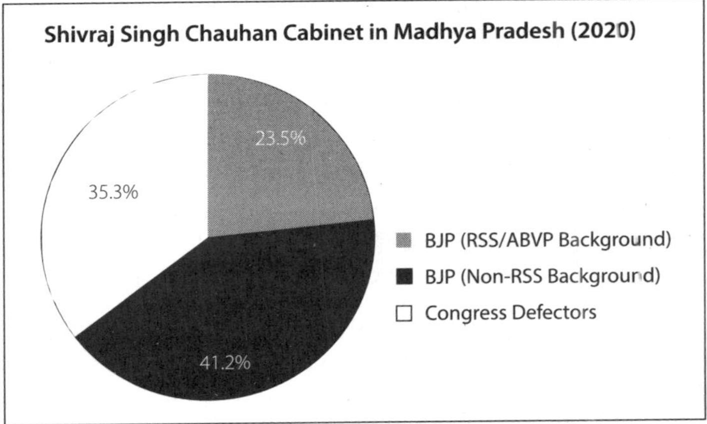

Source: Author's fieldwork, with research support from Rajiv Pundir. The upper chart is accurate as of 1 November 2018. The lower chart is accurate as of 24 September 2020.

It is also important to recognise the understanding with which RSS pracharaks are formally sent by the Sangh to work within the BJP, as Narendra Modi was at the beginning of his career. In 2009, when thirty-five pracharaks were said to be working in the BJP, RSS Chief Mohan Bhagwat was questioned about their influence. He responded by saying that it 'is not compulsory that they report to us. We only want them to stick to their principles. We don't interfere in their work.'[58]

The crucial question is: who is the boss in this relationship? Bhagwat has insisted in the past that the 'RSS never intervenes, only gives advice when asked'. Yet, it is also true that, in 2013, when the ascendance of Narendra Modi as the BJP's prime ministerial candidate was not yet clear and there was a power tussle within the party—with several Delhi leaders' names doing the rounds—it was Bhagwat who publicly said that 'the new leadership will be someone from outside Delhi other than these four [Sushma Swaraj, Arun Jaitley, Ananth Kumar and Venkaiah Naidu]. This is what I have been told. That is what has been agreed on and I believe the process has begun.'[59]

The BJP–RSS relationship is essentially a symbiotic one. On 15–16 November 1987, then RSS chief Balasaheb Deoras reportedly said that the RSS planned to enter politics. It was the only time that the Sangh came close to formally entering the domain of electoral politics. Three years later, on 17 March 1990, Advani announced in a famous speech at an RSS meeting in Coimbatore: 'We have to intensify our efforts to project the viewpoint of the RSS ... There has been a conscious effort on the part of Swayamsevaks who are working in the BJP to make each one understand the ideological base to which we belong and our connections with sister organisations like the VHP, the ABVP, the BMS, the Sena Bharati and the Kalyan Ashram which are all based on the inspiration from the RSS.'[60]

Fundamentally, the BJP and the RSS are conjoined. The fact that so much of the party's top leadership is populated by the RSS means that the two organisations may be separate but come from a common fountainhead of ideas. In 2000, when the journalist Rajesh Joshi asked RSS Joint General Secretary Madan Das Devi if 95 per cent of the BJP was RSS, he famously retorted, 'If you say 95% I don't agree. It's a different thing to say that the BJP draws most of its strength from the RSS ... Nobody gets along 100% with his wife. The BJP is closest to us with respect to other parties. Which other party is there for us to support in the country? Sonia Gandhi?'[61]

This is not to say that the BJP and RSS imports do not have discords. Power brings its own challenges. In Karnataka, before the assembly elections of 2018, B.L. Santhosh, a former RSS pracharak who had been appointed general secretary (organisation), and the party's chief ministerial candidate and former pracharak B.S. Yediyurappa were known to have political differences. They 'couldn't get along'. As a senior

Karnataka BJP leader told me, 'Something happened and Yediyurappa said to the media, if Santhosh wants to control the party, he should run it. I will not do it. That shook up the party high command. Santhosh never speaks in public, but the enmity is not gone. It got resolved then because the High Command called and said "what is happening, it is an election year, sort it out". The local party was with Yediyurappa.'[62] Senior BJP MLC in the state, Lehar Singh, when asked about the RSS–BJP relationship, summed it up diplomatically: 'They have almost a good equation. It is not much of a problem and the political class is clever enough to have its way.'[63]

The current BJP–RSS relationship is very unlike what it used to be during the Vajpayee years, which were characterised by a permanent state of tension between the two. The RSS top brass would often go public with their critiques. In March 2000, for instance, RSS Chief K.S. Sudarshan called the PMO incompetent and lamented that the BJP had become 'Congressised'. A month later, senior RSS leader and SJM founder Dattopant Thengdi attacked Finance Minister Yashwant Sinha. The then SJM convener Murlidhar Rao went to the extent of saying that 'the government is not being led by political leadership but by people who are insensitive to national interests'. RSS Joint General Secretary H.V. Seshadri castigated the government for a kind of 'tandav [dance of death] of corruption'.[64] In the Vajpayee years, the RSS and the BJP were enmeshed in multiple crises: on the finance ministership of Jaswant Singh, on SJM opposition to economic reforms, and BMS criticism of the Insurance Regulation Authority Bill.[65]

Things became so bad that RSS Spokesperson M.G. Vaidya wrote a signed piece in *Organiser* in 2001 arguing that the 'RSS believes in the eminence of the party, whether in power or not, must be maintained. No question should be raised about its supremacy … the workers of the party should not play second fiddle to the legislative wing, wagging their tails at the Government's bidding.' Such a party, he said, would be 'useless'.[66] These familial discords became so common that *India Today* would write tongue-in-cheek, 'Every family has an uncle it is embarrassed about. For the NDA government led by Atal Behari Vajpayee, it is the Sangh Parivar patriarchs in Nagpur.'[67] That is certainly not the case with the Modi government, where the two move much more in tandem with one another.

It would be simplistic to see the penetration of the BJP by RSS leaders as a permanent Sangh conspiracy to micro-manage. The pulls and pressures of politics are far more nuanced. BJP's Rajya Sabha MP Swapan Dasgupta analysed this perceptively in 2009 when he argued that the 'overwhelming majority' of RSS workers in 'all probability, vote for BJP candidates', nurture a 'distaste for the Nehruvian legacy', and that the more ambitious of them may also see linking with the BJP as a 'worthwhile career graph'. 'Indeed, within the BJP, there is a discernible divide between those who came to the party from the RSS and those who entered through other routes.' Yet, the RSS constitutes 'only a small fraction of those who drive the BJP at the grassroots'.[68]

As Chapter 8 of this book shows, the BJP's own expansion since 2014 means that its membership base had significantly dwarfed that of the RSS by 2019. Further, as Dasgupta pointed out, the demands of politics often ensure that even imports from the RSS or its affiliates 'end up disavowing the austere exclusivism of the RSS and accepting the more worldly logic of political mobilisation. Kalyan Singh moulded himself as a caste leader of western Uttar Pradesh; Narendra Modi became a passionate advocate of modernity and efficient governance; and Atal Bihari Vajpayee took to consensual coalition-building. All of them came into conflict with the RSS at one point or another.'[69]

In that sense, those who think the BJP is simply the political arm of the Sangh are wrong. It is a far more complicated relationship than that. In 2003, RSS Chief K.S. Sudarshan was asked precisely this question. His response was clear: 'There is no political wing as such. The Sangh prepares individuals who are sent to different fields according to their abilities but their main task is to spread the Hindutva ideology. The only relationship we have is that we are swayamsevaks. At times we get together to discuss how to reach our goals. But we don't accept that BJP is a wing of the RSS or that RSS is a volunteer core of the BJP.'[70]

Where the Sangh does have a major influence is in the realm of ideas, and through that on policy. The RSS saw Modi's twin electoral victories in 2014 and 2019 as the triumph of Hindu nationalist ideas. After the 2014 win, in a signed editorial, *Organiser*'s editor argued that the 'most fundamental shift' it heralded was a 'departure from pseudo-secular divisive politics'.[71] In 2019, he argued even more forcefully that the result showed the 'so-called "Khan-Market consensus" based on the elitist approach is irrelevant for the masses'. For the RSS, the 'most important faultline' in the 2019 election was whether what it saw as an 'elitist "Idea of India", that would decide what is good or bad for Bharat is acceptable or not.' The RSS seems to have interpreted Modi's second national election victory as the triumph of a 'new narrative for new Bharat'[72] that, in its view, was clearly based on a return to Hindu-ness and a Hindu-focused moral order.

13

WHAT THE RSS SAYS

Issues That Matter the Most to the Sangh

There is a big difference in the public approaches taken by the BJP and the RSS. While individuals in both entities arguably subscribe to a common world view, the weightage that they give to various issues in their outward-facing discourse varies greatly. The RSS speaks much more about Hinduism than anything else, for instance. It also speaks about 'Hindu' issues far more than the BJP does.

We put all articles published by the RSS fortnightly magazine *Organiser* (230 issues in the May 2015–December 2019 period); all Facebook posts by the RSS, the BJP, Narendra Modi, Amit Shah, the Congress and Rahul Gandhi (January 2016–December 2019: 4,76,827 posts); and all the annual Vijayadashami speeches by the RSS sarsanghchalak over a three-year period (2016–2019) through our Narad Index[1] to get a broader sense of how the RSS communicates, and how this compares with the BJP, Narendra Modi and the Congress. The Narad Index shows that on all platforms, online and offline, RSS-speak on issues around Hindus or Hindu-related topics (like the Ram Temple in Ayodhya) outscored every other topic by a wide margin. This is followed by education, an issue that the Sangh focuses its energies on in its outreach. The only exception to this pattern is *Organiser*, where education came in second to Pakistan and Kashmir in 2019 (see Figure 13.1).

Figure 13.1: The RSS Communicates Differently from the BJP: Speaks More about Hinduism than Anything Else, Education Is a Close Second (Facebook, Vijayadashami Speeches, *Organiser*)

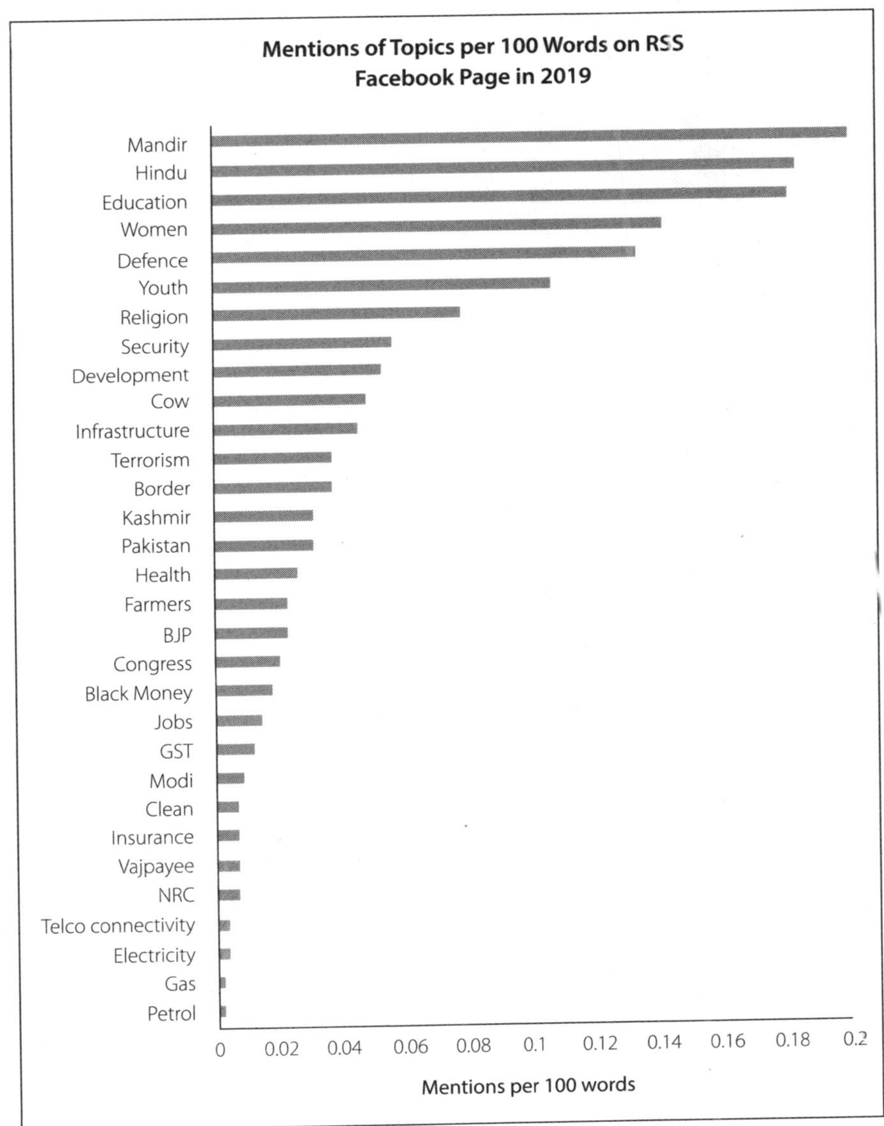

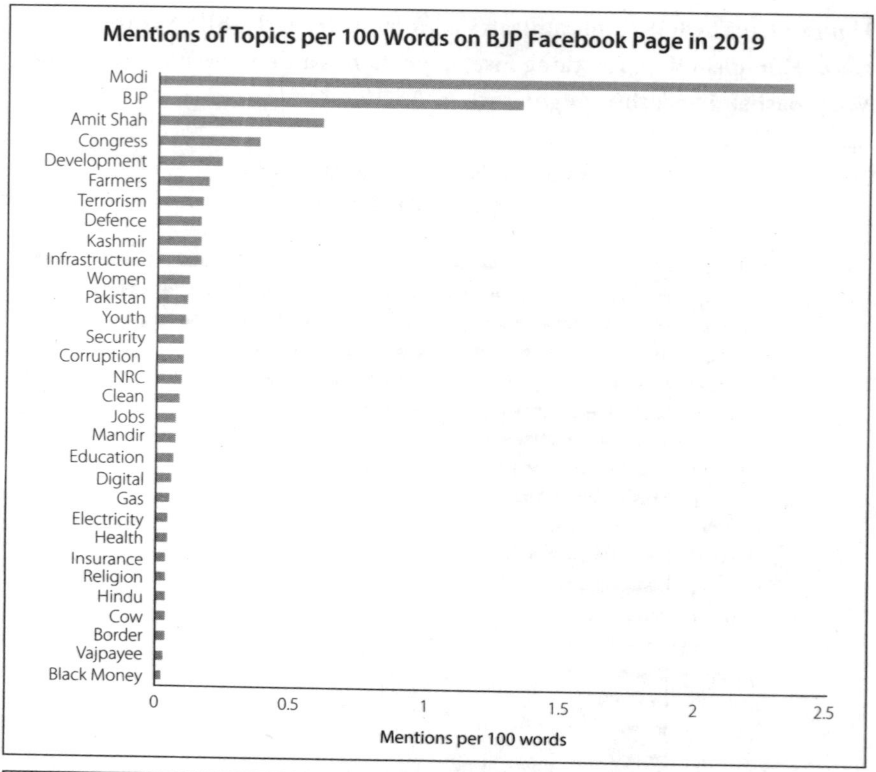

Mentions of Topics per 100 Words on BJP Facebook Page in 2019
Modi
BJP
Amit Shah
Congress
Development
Farmers
Terrorism
Defence
Kashmir
Infrastructure
Women
Pakistan
Youth
Security
Corruption
NRC
Clean
Jobs
Mandir
Education
Digital
Gas
Electricity
Health
Insurance
Religion
Hindu
Cow
Border
Vajpayee
Black Money
0
0.5
1
1.5
2
2.5
Mentions per 100 words

Mentions of Topics per 100 Words in RSS Vijayadashami Speech in 2019
Hindu
Education
Health
Corruption
Security
Jobs
Development
Women
Border
Kashmir
Terrorism
Infrastructure
Clean
Religion
Youth
0
0.1
0.2
0.3
0.4
0.5
Mentions per 100 words

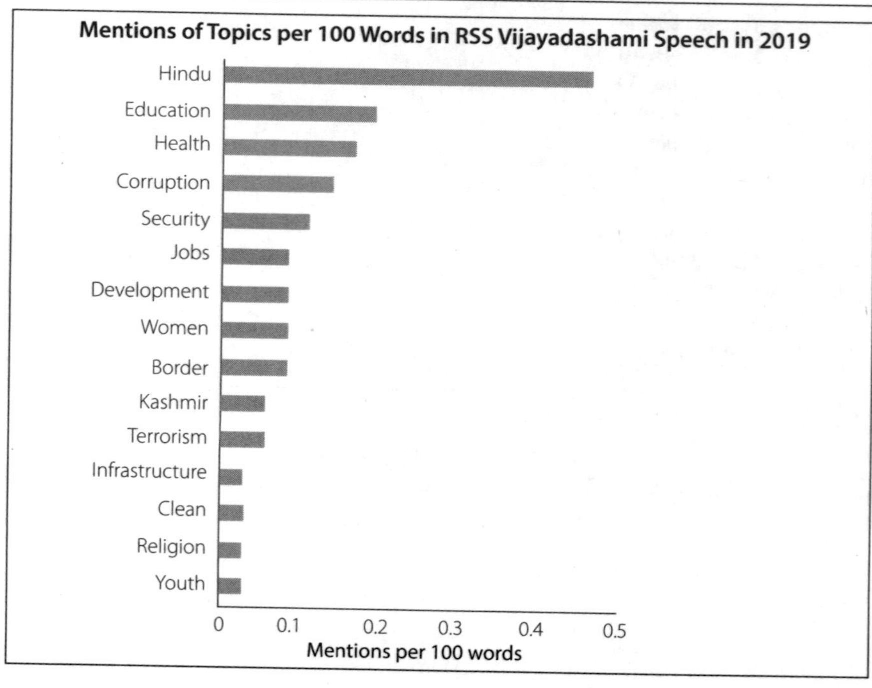

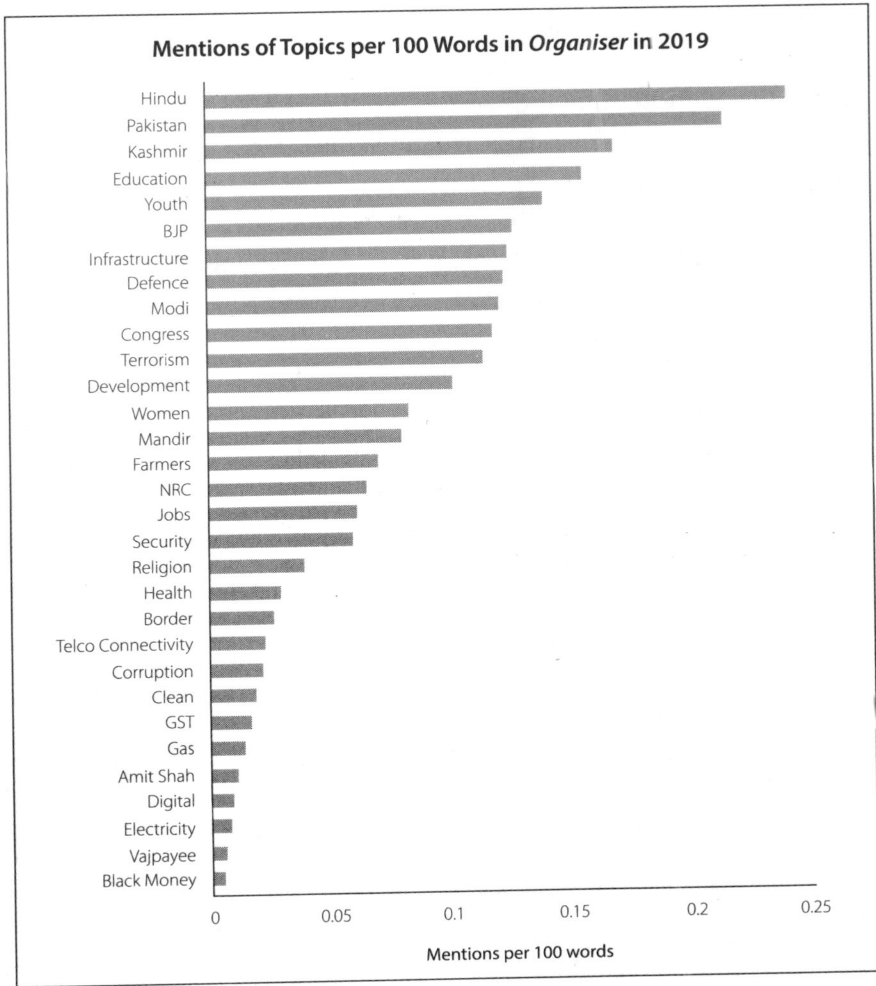

Source: Narad Index, Nalin Mehta and Rishabh Srivastava; for details see Appendix 4/online on nalinmehta.in

The pattern holds over time as well. Hindu issues and education are the two topics that have most animated the RSS's discourse over the years on all three platforms. On Facebook, for example, in 2016–2019, the Ram Mandir and Hindu-related issues were closely followed by education as the third most important topic. This is different from the BJP's usage of Facebook: the top topics were Narendra Modi, the BJP, Amit Shah, the Congress (in that order); the Ram Mandir came in nineteenth and 'Hindu' issues at twenty-seventh. This does not at all mean that these issues are less important to the BJP: they remain at the heart of its political differentiation. The patterns only reflect the party's wider communications strategy, which is much more spread out across political issues as a whole.

The interesting thing is that the RSS focuses much less on Narendra Modi than the BJP and Modi himself do. The Narad Index shows that, in the 2016–2019 period, the Sangh spoke the least about Modi. Even less than the Congress did (see Figure 13.2). This may be rooted in a long-held Sangh belief, inculcated by its founder Hedgewar (often referred to as Doctorji), that individuals must not be venerated. Hedgewar himself is said to have only reluctantly accepted the title of sarsanghchalak[2] on 9–10 November in 1929, four years after he founded the RSS.[3] He also ensured that the RSS considers the saffron flag its real 'Guru', rather than any individual.[4] Hedgewar also started the RSS tradition of commencing 'daily activities with [a] salutation to the Bhagwa Dhwaj' in 1926.[5]

Figure 13.2: RSS Speaks Much Less about Modi than the BJP or the Congress (2016–2019)

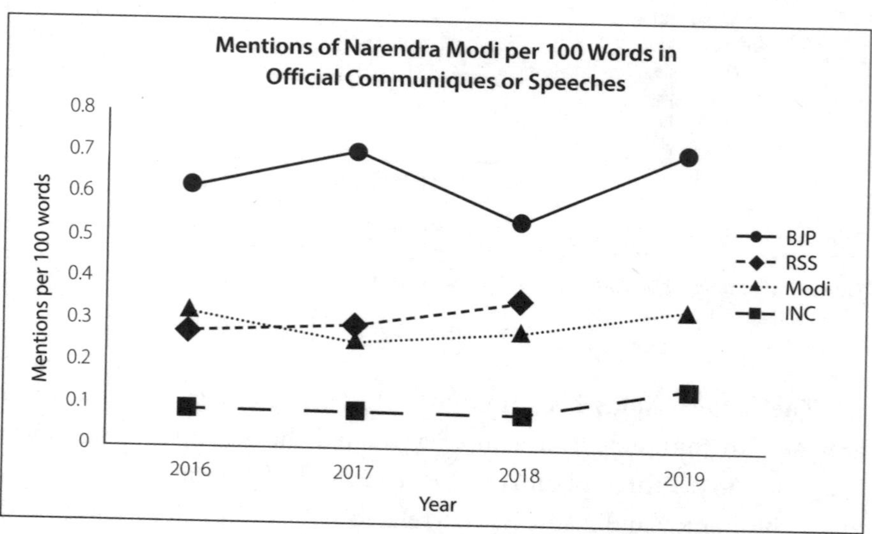

Source: Narad Index, Nalin Mehta and Rishabh Srivastava; for details see Appendix 4/online on nalinmehta.in.

The BJP is a political party that needs to win votes. The Sangh is linked to it in ideational terms but it is not in the business of electoral politics. This distinction impacts how the two organisations portray individual leaders. For the BJP, these leaders are vote catchers: Modi from 2014 onwards, Vajpayee in the 1990s and early 2000s.

Between 2016 and 2019, the RSS consistently spoke far more about the Ram Temple than either the BJP or Modi did. While the party's discourse was more about development, anti-Congressism and Pakistan (as detailed in Chapter 6), the Sangh did much of the heavy-lifting on hardcore 'Hindu' political issues (see Figures 13.3 and 13.4). In fact, the volume gap between their discourses on 'Hindu'-related issues and the Ram Temple is surprisingly large.

This suggests a useful political division, given the shared thinking of the RSS and BJP on wider cultural issues.

That the RSS speaks most about Hinduism is not surprising. This is, after all, an organisation where, in the words of a senior functionary, 'every swayamsevak takes the oath to work for "*Hindu Rashtra ki sarvangin unnati* [Hindu nation's all-encompassing progress]"'. Underlying the

Figure 13.3: The RSS Talks More Often of Ayodhya's Ram Temple: Much More than Modi/BJP (2016–2019)

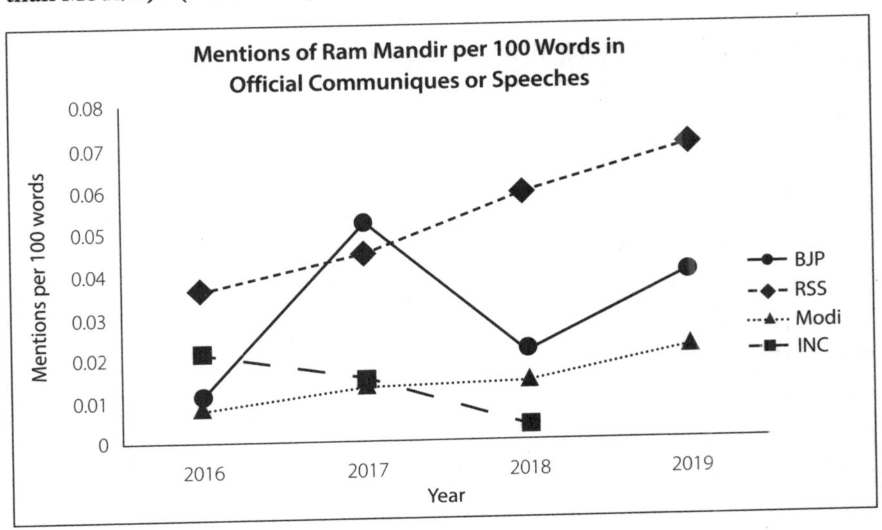

Source: Narad Index, Nalin Mehta and Rishabh Srivastava; for details see Appendix 4.

Figure 13.4: The RSS Speaks Far More than the BJP on Hindu Issues (2016–2019)

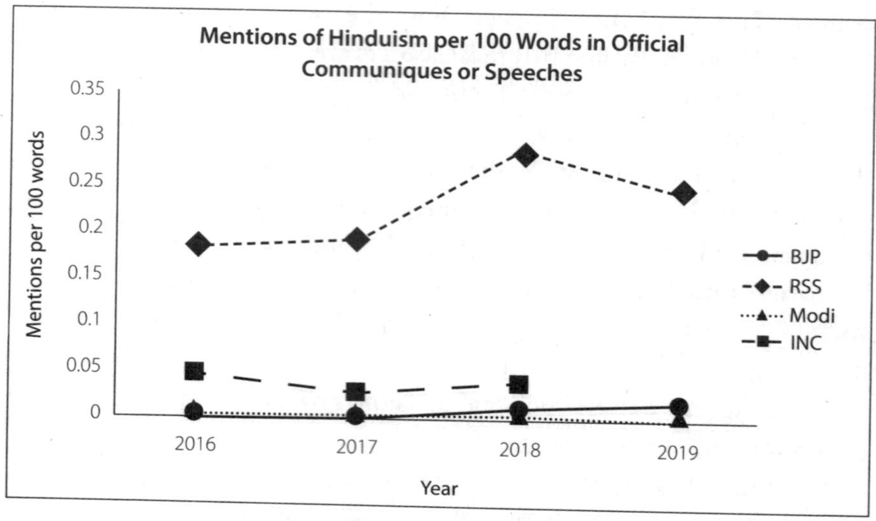

Source: Narad Index, Nalin Mehta and Rishabh Srivastava; for details see Appendix 4.

Sangh programme is its 'vow for the comprehensive development of Hindu Rashtra, the protection of Hindu dharma, Hindu culture and Hindu society'.[6]

The RSS, Hindutva and the Hindu Rashtra

Why the RSS Thinks Hindutva Is the Same as Hinduism and Bharatiyata

While the RSS's quantitative focus on what it sees as 'Hindu' issues is clear, it is important to understand what it means by these terms in qualitative terms. As a number of scholars who have studied the RSS and its thinking over the decades have shown, these positions are not static and keep evolving. When the Sangh uses terms like 'Hindutva' and 'Hindu Rashtra', the question is, how does it understand them in the 2020s, beyond what its leaders thought in the 1920s or 1930s. Hedgewar had started his political activism as a Congressman who organised young volunteers at the party's 1920 Nagpur session where Gandhi emerged as the 'undisputed leader'. Until then, there had been differences among Congress leaders over Gandhi's linking of the anti-British Non-Cooperation Movement with the Khilafat Movement in support of the Caliph of Istanbul. As Walter Andersen, a historian of the RSS, has noted, the original uniform Hedgewar designed for the RSS—khaki shirt and shorts, a black khaki cap, long socks and boots—was 'much like' what was worn by Congress volunteers at 'the 1920 Congress session at Nagpur'.[7] Equally, there is a view that the dress code seemed to replicate the British police uniform of the time,[8] just as there is a view that the black caps may have been influenced by the Italian Fascist Benito Mussolini's black caps.[9]

The RSS was banned by the Government of India on 4 February 1948, four days after the assassination of Gandhi, and 17,000 of its members were arrested. The ban was lifted on 12 July 1949.[10] Yet, Gandhi is now so central to the RSS's iconography that Sarsanghchalak Mohan Bhagwat chose to begin his annual Vijayadashami speech with an incantation to Gandhi on his 150th birth anniversary for two years running: in 2018 and 2019.[11]

On the other hand, few leaders have been as influential in defining the RSS as Madhav Sadashiv Golwalkar (often referred to as Guruji), who succeeded Hedgewar as the RSS's second sarsanghchalak on 3 July 1940[12] and oversaw the organisation for three decades. His 1939 book, *We, Our Nationhood Defined*, which came out of his abridged translation of G.D. Savarkar's Marathi work *Rashtra Mimansa* (Nation Worship), was for a long time regarded as a systematic exposition of RSS thinking.[13] Yet, the RSS publicly disowned *We, Or Our Nationhood Defined* in 2006 as 'neither representing the views of Guruji nor of the RSS'.[14]

The 1939 book was, for decades, considered a foundational RSS document, separating Hindus from others. In its pages, Golwalkar argued that India was the holy land for Hindus, that the country needed a 'national regeneration' and this could only come from a revival of the 'great Hindu race' professing its 'illustrious Hindu religion'. Hinduism, for Golwalkar, had been grievously hurt by 'degenerating contact with the debased civilisations of Mussalmans and the Europeans', and the revival of India was inseparable from the revival of Hinduness. As he put it, 'All those not belonging to the national, i.e. Hindu Race, Religion, Culture and Languages, naturally fall out of the pale of real "National" Life.'[15]

In 2006, the RSS's Suruchi Prakshan published a booklet by Rakesh Sinha (later appointed a BJP Rajya Sabha MP), *Shri Guruji and Indian Muslims*. It was formally released by the Sangh in Nagpur and stated that Golwalkar's book 'neither represents the views of the grown Guruji nor of the RSS. He himself acceded this when he revealed that the book carried not his own views but was "an abridged version of G. D. Savarkar's work *Rashtra Mimnsa*"...Yet secularist social scientists find great solace to quote "We" extensively. In fact the journey of his thought begins with his succession as the Sarsanghchalak of the RSS in 1940 and it continued till 1973 when he died.' [16]

Former RSS spokesperson M.G. Vaidya too claimed that the book was not representative of the Sangh's views because it was from a time before Golwalkar became sarsanghchalak. Golwalkar had met Hegdewar in Banaras in 1931 while working as a zoology teacher. He joined the RSS in 1934 when he was made karyavah of its Nagpur branch. However, he left the Sangh in 1936 to join the Sargachi Ramakrishna Mission Ashram in West Bengal to renounce the world as a sanyasi and became a disciple of Swami Akhandananda, who was himself a colleague of Swami Vivekananda and a disciple of Ramakrishna Paramahamsa. He finally returned to the RSS in 1937 after the Swami's death and was initially made in-charge of its All-India Officers Training Camp.[17] Vaidya, who had been the RSS's first spokesperson and also served as its Akhil Bharatiya Baudhik Pramukh (all India head for intellectual activities), declared that he approved of the removal of *We, Or Our Nationhood Defined* from the RSS pantheon. He stressed that the book which was central to understanding Golwalkar was his *Bunch of Thoughts* (published in 1966) because it contained his views after he became sarsanghchalak in 1940. '*We or Our Nationhood Defined* is not the Bible as everyone would like to believe,' said Vaidya. 'If it were the Bible, then every Sangh worker would have read it and it could have been found in every house. But it's not the case.' He claimed that the seven volumes of Golwakar's collected works that were issued after his death did not include it, neither did the twelve-volume collection published on his birth centenary.[18]

In 2018, RSS Sarsanghchalak Mohan Bhagwat publicly announced that even parts of *Bunch of Thoughts* were not representative of the Sangh's current views. Talking specifically to the parts where Golwalkar referred to Muslims as enemies, Bhagwat responded that '*Bunch of Thoughts* is a collection of speeches made in a particular context and cannot be eternally valid. Sangh is not dogmatic. Times change, and accordingly our thoughts transform. Dr Hedgewar, RSS founder, said we are free to adapt to times as they change. Sangh acknowledges as valid only those parts of *Bunch of Thoughts* which remain relevant in the current circumstance and have been put together in an in-house publication on Golwalkar, *Guruji: Vision and Mission*.'[19]

So, where does the RSS stand today on key cultural flashpoints? It is essential to understand that it sees Hindutva, Hinduism and Bharatiyata (Indianness) as essentially the same thing. For its opponents, Hinduism is politically perverted in the RSS's version of Hindutva, which has been reinventing a variegated collection of multiple beliefs as a unitary identity from the nineteenth century onwards.[20] In other words, it was a political project that sought to reconstruct Hinduism. For the RSS, on the other hand, Hindutva is the core tradition that has bound India for centuries and the thread that bound religious figures as diverse as Ram, Parashuram, Krishna and Buddha to later historical figures as diverse as Shivaji, Vivekananda, Ambedkar, Tagore and Gandhi. All of these icons, in the RSS's view, were proponents of Hindutva.

Mohan Bhagwat illustrated this viewpoint in 2018, in a rare interview to *Organiser*, with the cover-page title 'Hindutva Is One'. To a question on the difference between the original Hindutva versus more aggressive versions of it, the sarsanghchalak answered that the term 'Hindutva' encapsulated several eternal values that the Sangh believed in: 'Satya (Truthfulness), Ahimsa (Non-violence), Asteya (not stealing), Aparigrah (non-possessiveness), Brahmacharya (consciousness of a higher ideal), Tap (Austerity), Shouch (Purity), Santosh (contentment) and Ishwara-Pranidhana (Surrender to Almighty).' Crucially, Bhagwat invoked the Mahatma. 'Gandhi Ji also talked about a consistent search for Truth, that Truth is Hindutva,' he said. Then he mentioned a range of nationalist leaders—few of whom are generally identified with Hindu nationalism—as early pathfinders of Hindutva. 'It is the same Hindutva, not necessarily Hindu society, about which Vivekananda, Subhas Chandra Bose, Gurudev Rabindranath Thakur, Dr Babasaheb Ambedkar, etc. have spoken about,' he said. 'The expression of those values depends on the person and the situation.'[21]

Hindutva, for the RSS, extends to the pre-historic past, when even the word 'Hindu' had not been invented. It encompasses the ancient epics and their gods, including Ram and Krishna. From the heroes in those epics to medieval rulers like Maharana Pratap and Shivaji, who fought the Mughals, the RSS sees an unbroken chain of Hindutva. 'There was no word called "Hindu" at the time of Maryada Purushottam Shri Ram, but He is still an icon of Hindutva,' Bhagwat asserted. 'The principles that He practised were considered to be ideal and they are later called Hindutva. On the other hand, Sri Krishna, who in a way broke all the norms of propriety of conduct but still He was following Hindutva. The same is true about Parshuram, who used violence and Karunavatar Buddha who practised and preached non-violence. All of them, gave expression to Hindutva as per the need of the then society. Shivaji Maharaj extended respect to Mirza Raja. He was also following the Hindutva.'[22]

Bhagwat disagreed that there were multiple ways of being Hindu that differed from Hindutva. For example, he explained, there was no difference between his understanding of Hindutva vis-à-vis the polytheism of Gandhi or the brilliant exposition of a thinker like Swami Vivekanand, who wowed the 1893 Parliament of the World's Religions in Chicago with his characterisation of Hinduism as a tolerant faith of 'universal acceptance' which accepted 'all religions as true'.[23] As Bhagwat put it:[24]

> ... Hindutva is one. It cannot be different even if one looks at it with different prisms. I believe in Truth and non-violence, but if somebody is attacking me, indirectly to kill the Truth and non-violence I believe in, then to protect those values I will have to fight. Whether to fight or not is not Hindutva, to live or to die for Truth is and non-violence is Hindutva. To fight for a practice of Truth and non-violence is Hindutva. When to suffer and when one should not, can be an individual decision. That decision can be right or wrong. If one takes wrong decision and fights, that fight is not Hindutva. In a wrong decision, someone decides to keep quiet, then keeping quiet is not Hindutva. The fundamental values for which that decision is being taken is Hindutva. The talk of Swami Vivekananda's Hindutva and the Hindutva of the Sangh, assertive Hindutva and the moderate one, all this is irrelevant. The nature is of an individual being and not that of Hindutva. Human nature can be assertive or moderate, not Hindutva.

> As there is growing attraction towards Hindutva these confusions and distortions are deliberately created ... As a Hindu, we do not consider anyone as our enemy, nor do we consider anyone as alien. But for the sake of Hinduness we have to protect Hindu Dharma, Hindu Sanskriti and Hindu Society. In the process, we may have to explain, we may have to fight, if necessary. That explaining or fighting is not Hindutva, but the fundamental values that we carry forward, on the basis of which we take a call for action, that is Hindutva. In every sense it is one. That is why in Meerut I had said, 'If Hindus become more kattar (fundamentalist), it actually means they will be more liberal'. In this sense, Mahtama Gandhi was a 'Kattar' Hindu. In one his writings in *Harijan*; he declared that he was a 'Kattar Sanatani Hindu' in the same sense. Now how to practice and perfect that Hindutva is an individual decision. There is no differentiation in Hindutva. You can say someone's understanding of Hindutva is wrong. You can say my interpretation and practise is right and other's is wrong. There is no meaning in saying our Hindutva or their Hindutva.

In other words, Hindutva, for the RSS, is the same as Hinduism. A February 2018 issue of *Organiser* quoted senior RSS leader J. Nandakumar as saying, '"Hindutva" (or Hindu-ness) is the correct word to indicate Sanatan Dharma and not Hinduism, as "ism" means a closed book of thought or a set of dogmas or a blind belief system.' In this view, 'Shivaji's guru Samarth Ramdas, Swami Vivekananda, Bal Gangadhar Tilak, Gandhiji and Guru Golwalkar had taken upon themselves the task of protecting Hindu Dharma in their own ways. They were not like Nehru or EMS Namboothiripad who were ashamed of being called a Hindu.'[25]

This conflation of Hindutva with Hinduism, of course, is a claim that remains deeply contested, and has been challenged by many. In early 2020, I debated ideas of Hinduism with the Congress politician and former diplomat Shashi Tharoor as we discussed his book, *Why I Am a Hindu*. Tharoor argued strongly that his Hinduism harked back to the multi-formed polytheistic traditions of Hinduism, which were the very opposite of the uniform notion of Hinduism that the RSS upholds.[26]

In fact, when Tharoor's book on Hinduism was first published in 2018, *Organiser* published an angry response titled 'Exasperating Farrago'. Its reviewer argued that Tharoor's thesis was symptomatic of a 'race for proving Hindu credentials among secular politicians'. The magazine rejected his argument as an attempt to 'impose a Western framework of Hinduism on Hindus' and a 'dangerous ploy to snatch away Hindutva from the common Bharatiyas'. It attacked him for 'forgetting the fact that what he calls "Hinduism" includes many religions and what he differentiates as "Hindutva" are the common characteristics of these religions'. The reviewer was further incensed by Tharoor's defence of individual Hinduisms and his usage of the expression 'My Hinduism' because '"My Hinduism" is the most un-Hindu expression one can have staying and living within the fold of Hindutva'. *Organiser* went on to argue that 'Hindutva has no "ism", like the way one would have Islamism, Christianism or Judaism', and that it could never be 'mine or your Hinduism or Hindutva'. It asked, 'Do you say "my Sikhism" or "Islamism"?' before concluding that Tharoor was 'trivialising the entire narrative on a matter which has thousands of years of penance and thought behind it'. For the RSS, Tharoor's construction of 'Hindutva versus Hinduism, secularism versus nationalism' was an example of 'RSS bashing'.[27]

Tharoor, on the other hand, contended that the 'Islamicised Hinduism' of the Sangh Parivar and the 'sectarian notion of Hindutva', as he put it, was a 'travesty of what Hinduism really is'. The Sangh's idea of Hinduism, he argued, 'does not speak' for Hindus like him.[28] For secular liberals, the basic divide has always been that Hindutva is political while Hinduism is not; Hinduism is secular while Hindutva is not; Hinduism is a positive while Hindutva is negative. The RSS, of course, rejects such a distinction between the two concepts and these positions.

What the RSS Understands by the Term 'Hindu Rashtra'

What does this mean for those who believe that the RSS will impose upon India a Hindu Rashtra? The RSS says it does not need to, because India is already a Hindu Rashtra.[29] This needs some explanation. Hindutva, for the RSS, is not only Hinduism, but the very essence of Indianness. As Mohan Bhagwat made clear in a series of public lectures in Delhi in 2018: 'We refer to Hindutva as a value system. There are those who prefer to call it "Indic", others call it "Bharatiya"—we accept all these terminologies as the same ... What is called as Hinduism today is not the same as the religion of the Hindus. There exists no specific Hindu "*shastra*" because they were composed before the word Hindu became prevalent. Our ancient scriptures are meant for everyone, not limited to a few … Bharat is not merely a geographic term … Bharat is explained by the word Hindu. Hence Sangh is insistent on the word Hindu.'[30] In this view, India has long been a Hindu Rashtra. As Bhagwat put it, 'Hindutva is essentially all-inclusive. It will be the basis of a strong and prosperous Bharat … Living life with this discipline is Hindutva. It is the collective wisdom of all the sects originating out of India. That is why we say that ours is a Hindu Rashtra.'[31]

This opinion is a core belief in an organisation where every member swears allegiance to the Bhagwa Dhwaj and considers it his 'Guru'. It also explains why *Organiser* often publishes articles on the theme of Hindu Rashtra. A typical piece, in 2018, for example, on Hindutva and the concept of Hindu Rashtra, argued that to 'all the people, who regularly say, that a Hindu Rashtra will be declared soon—sorry. Bharat is a Hindu Rashtra and all its citizens are Hindus, irrespective of their mode of worship. It will remain so until there is a single Hindu by birth or belief in this geography. All that is necessary is the awareness within everyone that this is a Hindu Rashtra, which is the means and the goal of the Hindu movement in itself.'[32]

The idea that Hindutva is synonymous with the Indian nation and nationalism is not a new one. Vajpayee made exactly the same point in 1992, several months before the demolition of the Babri Masjid in 1992, when he told *Panchjanya* that Hindutva is the basis of Indian nationalism and he saw no difference between the two.[33] Similarly, when L.K. Advani was asked as deputy prime minister in 2003 if a Hindu Rashtra as understood by the RSS would turn India into a theocratic state, he argued, 'Hindu rashtra and theocratic state are contradictory.' Advani pointed to a conversation he had with Guru Golwalkar on the two disputes the Indian state had with the RSS at the time of Independence: on it being a secret organisation and on secularism. The first one was settled easily after the RSS adopted a written constitution. On the second, as he recalled, the 'Government was then involved in the process of drafting the Constitution of India, and the RSS was believed to have been holding contradictory views on both. Shri Guruji cited the example of Great Britain, which has no written Constitution. If a country can be run without a Constitution, why can't an organisation? Even so, RSS had no basic objection drawing up a formal Constitution. Guruji emphasised that Hindi Rashtra has nothing to do with the nature of the state. Just as the Christian-majority European countries have a secular government, we in India have always had a secular state in a Hindu-majority country. So, there is no contradiction between the views of the RSS and the view that there can be no theocratic state here ...'[34]

When speaking of a Hindu Rashtra, Sangh leaders often make a subtle distinction between 'rajya' (state) and 'rashtra' (nation). K.S. Sudarshan, joint general secretary of the RSS in 1998, made this point emphatically. 'We must remind ourselves of our "rajyadharma" and "rashtradharma",' he said, 'and understand the subtle difference between rajya and rashtra. The concept of Hindu rashtra should not be confused with a theocratic Hindu rajya which is something absolutely non-existent, like the proverbial flower-in-the-sky.'[35]

The question, of course, is that if India is Hindu, where does it leave the country's religious minorities? And who defines what is Hindu, to begin with? Bhagwat specifically addressed these questions in his annual Vijayadashami address of 2018: 'Those sections of the society who consider themselves "separate" because of their religion, tradition and lifestyle or [are] apprehensive of the word "Hindu" need to understand that Hindutva is the eternal ethos of this country. Hindutva has intrinsic identification with the undivided land of Bharat from the Himalayas up to the seas. All the Bharatiyas should immerse themselves in the hue of Bharat's culture ingrained in its ethos is a sincere wish of the Sangh. The practices of all the sects and traditions of Bharat derive themselves from this cultural ethos ... Hindutva is behind Bharat's capacity to embrace the entire universe with acceptance and appreciation of all its distinct diversities.' That is why, he concluded, 'Bharat is the Hindu Rashtra.'[36]

The Place of Muslims and Christians in the Hindu Rashtra

The big question is whether Muslims and Christians—the two religions with their 'birthplaces' outside India—have any place in this cultural Hindu Rashtra? The RSS is at pains to insist that they do. Mohan Bhagwat declared in Delhi in 2018 that 'Hindu Rashtra does not mean that it has no place for Muslims. The day it is said that Muslims are unwanted here, the concept of Hindutva will cease to be.'[37] But the real question is this: will Muslims have a place of equality with Hindus in the Hindu Rashtra? What sort of Muslims are acceptable in this world view? To understand this, one must go back to the argument that the BJP often made during the height of the Ram Janmabhoomi movement, for Muslims to accept Ram as a 'Imam-e-Hind' and to give Hindus cultural primacy.

The BJP's late K.R. Malkani said in 1992: 'The Hindu has no intention of going theocratic and setting up a Hindu State … The Hindu is secular by conviction. He believes in pluralism … The Indian Union is one only because it is Hindu from the Himalayas to the Seas, and from Gujarat to Bengal. And it will remain one only if its Hindu character is recognised, not eroded. This does not mean that the non-Hindu will have fewer rights; but it does mean that the basic character of India shall not be challenged in the name of "secularism". Even Iqbal, the philosopher of Partition, had hailed Ram as "Imam-e-Hind". Let Muslims Indians accept Rama as "Imam-e-Hind"—even as Indonesian Muslims accept him as their hero par excellence—and all Hindu-Muslim problems will melt away.'[38] In other words, accept the cultural primacy of Hindus and all are then equal. It follows then that, if every Indian is culturally a Hindu, as the RSS thinks they are, what need is there to declare a Hindu state?

As Sudarshan explained in a May 1998 article, the 'issue of Hindus vis-a-vis non-Hindus has been dealt with by the late MC Chagla more emphatically than probably any other RSS sympathiser. "In the true sense, we are all Hindus although we may practice different religions. If the distinction (between Hindus and non-Hindus) were to go then there will be no conflict between Hindus and non-Hindus." (Bhawan's Journal, August 27-September 9, 1978) … But assimilation presupposes an accommodating philosophy and the realisation of its inherent strength by society which is predominantly Hindu. The expression Hindu has a totally national aspect that takes in its stride the whole gamut of the tradition, culture and other civilisational aspects of social behaviour as evolved on this soil through millennia. Hindu should not be seen in any context other than dharma, which not in the least means religion in the sense of an ecclesiastical order. Dharma is the Hindus' eternal point of reference.' This is what, the RSS says, Hedgewar tried to inculcate. The

Sangh's founder, according to Sudarshan, was 'not in favour of adopting any ready-made ism as the Sangh's philosophy, no Hedgewarism, and certainly not Hinduism.'[39]

At the heart of these arguments is the belief that India is essentially a secular state because Hindus, in the RSS view, are more secular and pluralist as a society. Equally, it believes that everyone who lives in India is anyway Hindu by culture.

One of Mohan Bhagwat's predecessors, Rajju Bhaiyya, summed this up when he argued in 1994 that 'it is erroneous to speak of "India that is Bharat". Instead, it should be "Bharat that is Hindustan"'. He said, 'Hindu *rashtra* is not just the Hindu state. The land and the people constitute the country. After hundreds of years of living together, they developed a culture, then became a nation. Thus, three things are essential for a nation—the land, people and culture. The basic concept of Hindu *rashtra* is that the culture is nurtured here. Those who think that this culture is right—they are *Bharatiya*. When anyone feels that his or her culture is Arabic or Roman, then differences crop up. The predecessors of 98 per cent of Christians and Muslims are actually Hindu by race.'[40]

This is why, at the seventy-fifth Vijayadashami speech of the RSS, Bhagwat's predecessor K.S. Sudarshan made an impassioned plea to Muslims, saying that they have the 'blood of Rama and Krishna in their veins'. He said, 'Indian Muslims should realise that their ancestors did not come from a foreign land. So why don't they work for the Indianisation of Islam and give a new shape to their religion?'[41] This theme of indigenising Islam and Christianity is a familiar trope in RSS messaging. Sudarshan's 2000 speech was typical: calling for both a 'swadeshikaran' (indigenisation) of Christianity (through the setting up of a nationalised church) and an 'Indianisation' of Islam (asking Muslims to adopt Ram and Krishna as national icons that were part of their ancestral heritage).[42]

In the same vein, in 2020, the RSS listed a question on the FAQs page of its website on whether a Muslim or a Christian can join up as a member. Its answer deserves to be quoted in full:[43]

> Christians and Muslims who live in Bharat have not come from an alien land, rather they are all children of this nation. All our forefathers and ancestors are from this country. If for any reason, a person changes his

> religion then that does not mean that they should change their values and vision towards life. So Christians, Muslims or people following any other religion who live in Bharat & who subscribe to the world view of Bharat are all 'Hindus'. They are welcome to be in the RSS. In fact, several such 'Hindus' do come into RSS, take active part in Sangh's activities towards nation building and work with full responsibility. They are neither discriminated against nor do they receive any special treatment.

The RSS often says that it draws its intellectual lineage from late-nineteenth and turn-of-the-century spiritual figures like Swami Vivekanand, Swami Dayanand, Lokmanya Tilak and Sri Aurobindo as well as mid-twentieth-century leaders like Guru Golwalkar. Yet, its construction of 'Hindu' and 'Hindutva' is predicated on the concept of defence against an 'other'. This 'other' may not necessarily be Muslim or Christian. It could be rival concepts of India, rival notions of Hinduism or even the distinction that the RSS draws between Bharat (the indigenous nation) and India (the Western construct). The 'chief theoretician of modern Hindu nationalism', V.D. Savarkar, was never part of the RSS, but his celebration of the word 'Hindutva' in the celebrated 1923 pamphlet, *Hindutva: Who Is a Hindu?*, remains a critical theoretical underpinning for much of Hindutva thinking, as Swapan Dasgupta has pointed out.[44] For Savarkar, Hindutva was not a 'word, but a history'; 'Hinduism' was only a 'derivative, a fraction, a part of Hindutva'.[45]

Yet, there is a crucial difference between Savarkar's idea of Hindutva and that of the RSS. Syama Prasad Mookerjee left the Hindu Mahasabha in 1949 because Savarkar did not give in to his insistence on membership for non-Hindus. Savarkar's definition of being Hindu meant a person who regarded 'the land of Bharatvarsha from the Indus to the seas as his fatherland (pitribhumi) as well as his holy land (punyabhumi), that is the cradle land of his religion'. This narrow definition, predicated on religion, automatically put Muslims and Christians (whose holy lands are outside India) outside the ambit of nationalism.[46]

The Sangh's notion of cultural Hindu nationalism—where it accepts those from other religions and promises equality of religion, language and food habits, with the caveat that they accept the cultural primacy of Hinduness—as Indianness itself, is different from the Nehruvian idea of India, but it is also distinct from Savarkar's conception. Mohan Bhagwat pointed out in his 2019 Vijayadashami address that, although the RSS was focused on 'organising the Hindu society', this did not mean that it harboured 'hatred against those sections, especially Muslims and Christians, who do not call themselves Hindu'. He said, 'Those who belong to Bharat, those of who are descendants of Bharatiya ancestors, those who are working for the ultimate glory of the nation and joining hands in enhancing peace by mingling with each other and accepting, respecting and welcoming all diversities; all those Bharatiyas are Hindus.' Whether they denoted themselves as 'Bharatiya', or 'Indic', or negated the word 'Hindu', and 'whatever may be their mode of worship, language, food habits, lifestyle, and native place', it would not 'make any difference' and they 'are also acceptable to the Sangh', he concluded.[47]

There is a difference between this cultural conception and the Savarkarite tradition, which feeds vicious and hateful anti-minority feelings, as Dasgupta wrote soon after the demolition of the Babri Masjid.[48] It is precisely these tensions and fissures at the ground-level—as well as the fears of minority groups who do not accept the Hindutva claim of cultural primacy—that the RSS and the BJP will have to resolve.

14

THE SANGH PARIVAR AND EDUCATION

Tribal Communities, Vanvasi Kalyan Ashram and Christian Missionaries

The holy fire in the Vedic altar rose up in flames, the smell of incense was everywhere and Sanskrit shlokas rent the air as the former prince sat on his haunches and washed the feet of a poor Adivasi in a large copper plate. There were over a hundred of them sitting in long queues, and one by one the prince cleaned their feet, welcoming them 'back' into the Hindu fold as the priests chanted in the background.

It was October 2003. The new tribal-majority state of Chhattisgarh was about to conduct its first-ever state assembly election[1] and I was following the campaign of the BJP's chief ministerial face, Dilip Singh Judeo. The moustachioed, swashbuckling scion of the royal family of Jashpur, who was fond of driving around in all-terrain jeeps, Judeo was a minister in Vajpayee's BJP-led government and a Rajya Sabha MP.[2] Presiding over such 'reconversion' ceremonies of tribals who had converted to Christianity had become a hallmark of his regional political imagery.

When journalist Sanjeev Singh and I met him on the election trail, he insisted that we come along to witness a ceremony deep in a tribal area of the state. He called it 'shuddhi' (purification),[3] and stressed that it was a crucial part of the regeneration of Hindutva. The ceremony was conducted by the Akhil Bharatiya Vanvasi Kalyan Ashram (ABVKA), a

Sangh Parivar outfit. Its activists had been working in the tribal districts of central India for over five decades. So crucial was Judeo's support to this work, which was clearly intended to counter Christian missionaries working in the same areas, that a month later, when he was ensnared in a sting operation that showed him accepting money over drinks and bad-mouthing Prime Minister Vajpayee, the RSS publicly defended him. Sangh leaders called the sting operation a 'Christian conspiracy'[4] during a campaign that the BJP and ABVKA framed as an electoral battle (against Congress's Ajit Jogi) between 'real' tribals and 'false' ones[5]. The BJP eventually won that election.[6]

I had met ABVKA workers a couple of years earlier in the remote villages of Gujarat's southern tribal district of Dang, where I was covering the aftermath of violence against Christian missionaries. There, I also spent time with the Christian missionaries from Kerala who were managing their parish from a colonial-era village church and running a Christian school in a village where many tribal houses now sported fluttering saffron flags. When Prime Minister Vajpayee visited Dang after the violence, he called for a 'national debate' on conversion.[7] In Gujarat, ABVKA was a relatively recent entrant at the time, but it had already altered social dynamics in the tribal villages. In Jashpur, on the other hand, it had been working continuously at least since 1952. In fact, it was here that ABVKA was born.

Surprisingly, the genesis of ABVKA was an initiative by the then Congress chief minister of Madhya Pradesh, Pandit Ravishankar Shukla, a Hindu traditionalist, to counter Christian missionaries. Founded by Ramakant Keshav Deshpande, its work was initially funded by the Jashpur royal court and Dilip Singh Judeo's grandfather, Vijay Bhushan Singh Deo. At the time, I did not know that the BJP candidate I was travelling with was continuing a royal family legacy that dated back to independent India's founding moment. Dilip Singh Judeo, who first became a BJP MP in 1989 and passed away in 2013, claimed to have 'brought back' over 1,50,000 tribals into the Hindu fold.[8]

Fresh evidence unearthed from the archives in the course of my research shows that the ABVKA was birthed amidst a major national debate—on the role of foreign Christian missionaries and conversions—within Nehru's government as well as the larger Congress Party between

1953 and 1955. This debate raged over three years in Parliament, once again pitting Nehru against the Congress's Hindu traditionalists whom he had vanquished in 1951 to take back control of the party machinery (see Chapter 9). This was the second major debate on 'communal' issues, after the 1950-51 dispute on Hindus left behind in Pakistan, which set Congressman against Congressman.

The debate on conversions became such a flashpoint that, three years after his decision to attend the opening of the newly reconstructed Somnath Temple in Gujarat, President Rajendra Prasad clashed yet again with the prime minister. Twice in the year 1954, the president of India publicly warned missionaries to stop conversions. Nehru reacted with reassurances to minorities in Parliament, detailed missives to Congressmen and a nuanced pushback. Importantly, several Congress-run state governments (UP, Madras, Assam, Madhya Pradesh) sent in detailed reports to Home Minister K.N. Katju, asking for measures to end conversion. Katju himself made strong statements in Parliament. This relatively less-known debate ended with the Government of India and Prime Minister Nehru issuing a new policy in 1955, imposing restrictions on foreign missionaries. The debate on religious conversion was unfolding at a time when Nehru faced serious internal opposition from the Congress's Hindu traditionalists as he piloted the Hindu Code Bills for religious reform. All of this formed the backdrop to the creation of the RSS-run ABVKA.

Most opponents of the Sangh think of it as a hydra-headed monolithic entity, all the components of which work in unison as part of a masterplan to re-engineer society. The origins of the ABVKA, dedicated to inculcating a Hindu identity among tribal communities and one of forty-plus organisations that make up the wider Sangh Parivar, show how simplistic such a notion is.

The Congress's Missionary Impulse and the Origins of the ABVKA

The most surprising thing about the creation of the ABVKA was the catalytic role played by a Congress chief minister. In 1946, when Ravishankar Shukla took over as premier of the Central Provinces and

Berar (which later became Madhya Pradesh through reorganisation in 1952 and 1956), he was welcomed 'everywhere with enthusiasm and slogans of Bharat Mata ki jai were raised'. However, when he went to the tribal areas of Jashpur, 'black flags were shown and protest gatherings held' in several places.[9] According to an official history of ABVKA, published by it on its sixtieth foundation day, when Shukla questioned why he was facing such protests, he was told that the 'instigating elements (Christian missionaries and foreign elements who controlled them) were behind the scenes and it was like they were making the puppets dance'. Shukla turned for advice to veteran Congressman Thakkar Bappa (Amritlal Vithaldas Thakkar), a conservative Gandhian who had been working in tribal areas for years.[10] Bappa had founded the Bhil Seva Mandal in 1922 and been general secretary of the Harijan Seva Mandal founded by Gandhi in 1932. Because the Jashpur area had 'no nationalist organisation', he suggested to Shukla that the state open a 'Backward Community Society Welfare Department'. Bappa's confidante Pandurang Govind Vanikarji was sent as the director of this work. The department was established in 1947.

Working in Jashpur was difficult in every way, as Vanikarji knew it would be. However, he found an able candidate in Ramakant Keshav Deshpande, who practised law in Ramtek.[11] Deshpande, the RSS's city in-charge in Ramtek, had been arrested and sentenced to death in the 1942 Quit India movement, but was later released by the British.[12] This RSS pracharak, whom the ABVKA's history praises as being 'suffused in RSS ideals', was now handpicked by an appointee of a Congress chief minister. Deshpande and his wife first went to Jashpur in 1948.[13] He was hired by the state government to work on tribal welfare programmes there as area organiser. Atul Jog, ABVKA's national organising secretary, told me in a phone interview that Chief Minister Shukla himself 'created' Deshpande's Jashpur job, which he started in 1951.[14] The administration gave him a budget for eight village schools, but after 'intense requests', he managed to get the resources for 108 and began to set them up.

In 1952, after the death of Thakkar Bappa, Deshpande decided that he wanted to work full-time on tribal welfare and that he could not do this while still in government service. So he approached RSS Sarsanghchalak Guru Golwalkar for help with setting up a social organisation. Golwalkar sent in the Sangh's Madhya Bharat prant head, Haribhau Ketkar, to help.

Meanwhile, Deshpande approached the ruler of Jashpur, Vijay Bhushan Singh Deo, for assistance. Judeo provided rooms free of cost for a school, held a Vedic sacrifice with his nobles in his old palace on 26 December 1952, and announced a plan to build the new organisation's first tribal hostel, which would house thirteen children. Singh Deo's royal patronage was so intrinsic that the organisation remained unnamed for a year until he invited Deshpande and Ketkar for a conference at his palace along with several city notables in 1953. There, the royal priest of Jashpur suggested a new name: Kalyan Ashram. To meet the tribal students' expenses, Judeo decided to donate one-tenth of his personal yearly income to the project.[15] Shortly after Guru Golwalkar inaugurated ABVKA's first permanent premises in 1963, Judeo joined the Jan Sangh.[16] When princely privy purses were abolished by Indira Gandhi in 1971, he donated about 150 acres of land in the villages of Bageecha and Kardana to the ABVKA.[17]

From its inception, the Ashram defined itself as a Hindu counter to Christian missionary work in Jashpur. Its official history listed the large Christian presence in Jashpur in the 1950s as among the organisation's biggest challenges. The ABVKA claimed that, at the time, Jashpur had '10-12 big centres of the Christian Mission', 'about 200 nuns and priests' and '40-50 foreigners'. It said the missionaries had access to 'tonnes of porridge, oil, milk' to distribute, '8-10 big hostels' and 'one big hospital'. Presenting itself as a 'Hindu' social service challenger in Jashpur, the Kalyan Ashram school, in contrast, had '12 [students] and the hostel had 13 boys'. It was administered at the time by 'two people' and part-funded by a 'portion of what Deshpande earned from his law practice'.[18] At the heart of this enterprise was a belief that Christian missionaries were instrumental in creating a divide between tribal communities and urban Hindus. The Ashram's official history claims, 'The cultural predecessor [agraj] forest dweller [vanvasi] was called adivasi and given a separate identity—the vanvasis were given weapons against their own rule—calling Adivasi this land's original resident and Hindu society as attacking [aakramak] they created the base for creating several nations within the Indian nation—then they gave this fertiliser and water and created a poison fruit tree. In a planned manner they created a conspiracy so that town-dwelling Hindus and forest-dwelling Hindus started seeing each other as enemies instead of as brothers.'[19]

Nehru, Prasad and the Congress Traditionalists: Foreign Missionaries and Independent India's First Conversions Debate (1953–1955)

While ABVKA itself was too small to make it to the national headlines in the 1950s, the manner in which it framed itself locally as a 'Hindu' counter-reaction to foreign missionaries mirrored a much larger debate on the evangelical activities of Christian churches that unfolded in Delhi between Nehru, Rajendra Prasad, the Home Ministry and several Congress chief ministers. Coming soon after the controversy over Rajendra Prasad's decision to attend the installation of idols at the reconstructed Somnath Temple in Gujarat,[20] this controversy reflected yet another episode in the tensions over religion, freedom of expression, the role of the state and a Hindu backlash that animated the ruling Congress.

The debate started with Home Minister K.N. Katju telling Parliament on 15 April 1953 that, while Indians were free to propagate their religion, the new government 'did not want people from outside [missionaries] to come and do that'. Katju flatly declared that 'if they come here for evangelical work, then the sooner they stop it the better'.[21] Five months later, in September 1953, he announced that Nehru's government had already expelled three foreign missionaries for 'undesirable activities'. When he was questioned, Katju declared that the expelled missionaries had 'moved about among the primitive tribes and indulged in various activities which from the national point of view were not considered satisfactory'.[22]

Congress ministers from five states added to this narrative. The Madras state government, headed by former governor general of India, C. Rajagopalachari, sent the Home Ministry a report on 'anti-Indian' activities by two Italian missionaries in Fort Cochin.[23] Assam Chief Minister Bishnuram Medhi accused the American Baptist Mission of 'abetting a foreign conspiracy to separate the Naga Hills from India and to retain it as an imperialist foothold'.[24] UP Home Minister Sampurnanand too announced that he was consulting with the Central government about 'concerns' on American missionaries who, he said, had become particularly active in rural areas and on the state's borders with Tibet and Nepal. The UP assembly's deputy speaker, Hargovind Patel, alleged that some of these missionaries carried 'wireless transmitters'.[25] The UP assembly separately discussed a dispute on 250 conversions in Mathura by Catholic and Methodist missionaries, which led to the arrest of Arya Samaj activists who alleged 'monetary inducements'.[26] A minister from Bihar told the States Council that if Christian missionaries continued their 'wrongful activities', his state government would force them to leave.[27] With a number of MPs now asking questions linking espionage with foreign missionaries, Home Minister Katju informed the Rajya Sabha that he had begun collecting data on the number of missionaries in Kashmir (his office had counted nine thus far).[28]

Ravishankar Shukla's Madhya Pradesh government too sent a critical report on 'objectionable activities' to Delhi. It alleged, Katju told Parliament, that some missionaries were engaged in 'anti-Indian movements', such as the 'formation of a separate "Jharkhand State" to be affiliated with Pakistan'.[29] Jharkhand, of course, was founded five decades later in 2000 by the BJP-led Vajpayee government (and had nothing to do with Pakistan). Such was the paranoia at the time that Katju formally warned foreign missionaries that India was not open for conversions by people who decried Hinduism as 'hopeless[ly] idolatrous'.[30]

ABVKA's work in Jashpur came to be indirectly linked to this debate when President Prasad visited Surguja (another former princely state near Jashpur) to see two new colonies for forest-dwellers built as a pilot scheme. There he met locals, some of whom seemed to have complained about conversions. A newspaper account of this meeting reported that 'nearly 300,000 people are stated to have been converted during the last few years' in Raigarh, Surguja and neighbouring districts. Many missionaries countered that they were being unfairly maligned. Their work, they said, was being tarnished by communal propagandists.[31] Prasad leaned into the raging debate, issuing two public statements on conversions in 1954. Speaking in open forums, the president said that India guaranteed full freedom to preach Christianity, but warned churches that 'none' of their activities should be inspired by a desire for conversion.[32] In Mysore, he told church groups in a public meeting to 'avoid activities which cause suspicion'.[33] This hysteria over foreign missionaries arose at a time when their numbers had almost doubled after independence, to 4,683 (1947–1952) compared with 2,271 (1942–1947).[34]

India's encounter with Christianity can be traced back to the arrival of Saint Thomas the Apostle, who is said to have reached Kerala's Malabar coast in 52 CE.[35] There was a second phase when the first Protestant missionaries (from Germany) arrived in the Danish colony of Tranquebar on the Coromandel coast in 1706,[36] and a third phase under the British, who introduced 'prohibitory measures against Christian missionaries' and drastically reduced state subsidies to them after the 1857 Uprising because 'aggressive' proselytising by Evangelicals was seen as one of the causes of the upsurge.[37] Now, independent India was all astir on the issue of proselytisation. This was also the time when Nehru was formulating what came to be known as his Tribal Panchsheel Policy, influenced by the anthropologist Verrier Elwin, which broadly aimed to protect the cultures of various Indian tribes and ring-fence them from too many outside interventions.

The churches, including the Catholic Bishops' Conference of India, fought back, saying they had co-existed peacefully in the country for centuries and that a 'deliberate attempt' was being made to 'ignore the Constitution', with 'extremist elements' attacking 'Christians with impunity even with the help of the authorities'.[38] Church groups argued that they were being unfairly maligned for political reasons.[39]

Nehru initially reacted to the attacks on Christian missionaries by clarifying governmental policy, saying that, while there would be no religious interference by the Indian state, it had a pressing political and security imperative for imposing controls in border areas. There were nine foreign missions in border areas at the time, said the government. Nehru announced that no new ones would be allowed, though there would be no restrictions on indigenous Christian missions.[40]

Yet, he was entirely sensitive to the impact this controversy could have on Indian Christians, their right to equality and perceptions of bias. Much like he had done in his 1951 speech in Nasik when faced with a similar debate, Nehru now despatched a powerful letter as Congress president in his monthly circular to state Congress Committees. The prime minister argued that, while he personally disapproved of conversion, he was equally opposed to the counter Hindu 'Shuddhi' movement. He said that while he had imposed controls on foreigners only in border areas, the debate on conversion could not but have an impact on Indian

Christians. In his clearest enunciation yet of what he meant by a 'secular' state, Nehru told Congressmen that it signified an 'equal' space where 'minority communities' were free to practise their religion. Furthermore, he wrote, the 'majority community' should 'fully realise it' and not use its 'dominant position in any way which might prejudice our secular ideal'. If organisations talking of a 'Hindu Rashtra' triumphed, he said, it would be 'neither nationalism nor democracy'. It would be a 'throwback to some ideas of a medieval period', thundered Nehru. A majority's dominance as a 'religious community' would be 'totally undemocratic', he argued, because there was 'no chance of a minority gaining this position in a democratic set-up'.[41] It was yet another episode in the long-standing face-off between Nehru and his party's Hindu traditionalists on the question of Hinduism and its role in the new India.

The debate eventually ended with the Union government instituting new curbs on foreign missionaries in 1955. They would henceforth be required to take prior government approval to enter India, and would not be welcome if they devoted themselves only to proselytisation. They would also need to have suitable qualifications in fields like education, medicine and social work.[42] It was only after this new regulation that Rajendra Prasad issued a new and reassuring statement to foreign missionaries. Speaking at a function to celebrate the 1,903rd anniversary of the arrival of St Thomas in India, the president of India said that the country had 'no intention of curtailing their freedom or come in the way of their missions'.[43] It was in this political atmosphere that the ABVKA was born.

Hanuman Statues and Jagrans vs Missionaries: ABVKA's Early Strategies

While the president and the prime minister jousted, in Madhya Pradesh, Chief Minister Shukla appointed two enquiry commissions on religious conversions. The first one, headed by former Madhya Bharat High Court judge M.B. Rege, announced that 1,200 conversions had taken place in the state since Independence.[44] The second and better known Justice M. Bhavani Shankar Niyogi-led 'Christian Missionary Activities Enquiry Committee' (1954–1956) was even more scathing. It recommended a forced withdrawal of missionary activity and the takeover of foreign mission properties by what it called 'national churches' or to an 'international holding body', arguing that:[45]

> Evangelism in India appears to be part of the uniform world policy to revive Christendom for re-establishing western supremacy and it is not prompted by spiritual motives. The objective is apparently to create Christian minority pockets with a view to disrupting the solidity of non-Christian societies, and the mass conversions of a considerable section of Adivasis with the ulterior motive is fraught with danger to the security of the State.

Crucially, ABVKA, along with Sangh pracharak Krishnarao Sapre and Bhimsen Chopra, and Hindu Mahasabha leaders,[46] assisted the Niyogi Commission in its meetings. The commission, which is often cited on Hindu nationalist websites,[47] claimed to have a record of nearly 4,000 conversions by Lutheran missionaries in Sarguja alone.[48] Its conclusions had a strong political impact in what is present-day Chhattisgarh, where the princely states of Sarguja and Raigarh had already enacted anti-conversion laws in the 1930s. The UN described the Niyogi Commission's charges as 'exaggerated',[49] but it became the ideational genesis of new anti-conversion laws that were enacted a decade later, in Odisha (1967), Madhya Pradesh (1968) and six other Indian states.[50]

The Ashram also began inviting religious leaders to Jashpur. The first among these were Rambhikshuji Maharaj, Swarupanandji Maharaj and Prabhuduttji Brahmachari.[51] The ABVKA's own account celebrates this intervention as a moment when 'after centuries, their religious brothers had knocked on the doors of vanvasis'. The arrival of Hindu religious leaders from other areas added a new layer to ABVKA's work on education. Long-time Sangh supporter and Lok Sabha TV CEO Ashish Joshi, who hails from Madhya Pradesh, pointed out that Deshpande began to counter Christian missionary work by placing statues of Hanuman, the monkey god, in tribal villages across Jashpur.[52] This strategy was seen as an important visual marker of what the Ashram saw as Hindu nationalist resistance. It was a key driving impulse for both Deshpande and his first patron, the ruler of Jashpur. By 1975, the Ashram had taken on two more core activities: medical care and financial aid to tribal communities.[53]

ABVKA's National Expansion (1978–2020): An NGO Model and a Church Emulation Strategy on Social Welfare

The Ashram began to expand to other Indian states from 1978 onwards. Speaking on the phone from Ranchi in September 2020, Atul Jog told me that the decision to expand beyond Madhya Pradesh was taken during a discussion between Deshpande and RSS Sarsanghchalak Balasaheb Deoras.[54] The foundations of its growth, interestingly, were laid in a seminar at the Tata Institute of Social Sciences, Mumbai, where the Ashram's state and national officer-bearers were trained in 1975. ABVKA leaders found the seven-day training of such 'special use' that, in 1976, they set up their own national training centre in Dadar and Nagar Haveli's Motra Randha village. It operated for many years, with several officials moving there to develop the training centre.[55] ABVKA's objective in expanding nationwide was to directly reach the 8.2 per cent of Indians who identify as tribals.[56]

To do this, it adopted the methods of modern NGO management and emulated the social-welfare work done by church bodies on education, medicine and financial support. In the 1980–2000 period, new ABVKA branches were registered as separate entities in each state. 'The country is so big,' says Jog. 'Languages are so different in each state. You can't run it centrally.'[57] By 1992, it had 563 full-time employees working in 119 districts with large tribal populations. ABVKA further estimated that its workers were in touch with over one-sixth of the country's villages (11,000 of 60,893 villages) at the time. K. Bhaskaran, ABVKA's then all-India organising secretary, explained that, in order to reach all 450 tribal groups in the country, his organisation focused on building primary and secondary schools, libraries, primary health centres and hospitals. 'The workers had also built temples for tribals in its efforts to spread the message of Hindutva in the country.' Outside of tribal communities in Hindi-speaking states, the Northeast emerged as a new focus area. By 1992, ABVKA had set up operations in eighteen of the sixty-four districts at the time in the eight north-eastern states.[58] In the south—specifically, Andhra Pradesh, Karnataka, Tamil Nadu and Kerala—its reach had expanded to sixteen of the twenty-eight districts where tribals formed a majority.[59]

Ironically, ABVKA's growth strategy replicated the social-welfare work done by the Christian missionaries it had been formed to oppose and whom it saw as a civilisational threat. It emulated and adapted many of the outreach tactics of these missions as it expanded across India. Just as Church missionaries created hospitals, schools and orphanages,[60] by 2019, ABVKA was directly benefitting 5,87,768 tribals in one way or another. Its biggest emphasis was on healthcare (67.8 per cent), followed by education (23.9 per cent) and direct financial aid (8.3 per cent), as Figure 14.2 shows.

By 2019, in fact, the ABVKA had significantly scaled up its growth. It claimed to have initiated contact in 345 of India's 727 districts in its online interactive management dashboard. It estimated that as many as 447 of India's districts had tribal populations.[61] The data illustrates a determined push into this demography. ABVKA claimed to have established committees in 323 districts; its committees were actively working in 52,323 villages (see Figure 14.1).[62] This increased penetration was, of course, focused largely on tribal districts. Therefore, in Karnataka, for example, according to the RSS workers I met in Bengaluru, the ABVKA was growing in Coorg, Goondlepet, Ambikanagar, Dandeli and Sulya in Dakshin Kannada.[63]

Figure 14.1: ABVKA's Penetration by District, Block and Village in Tribal Populations

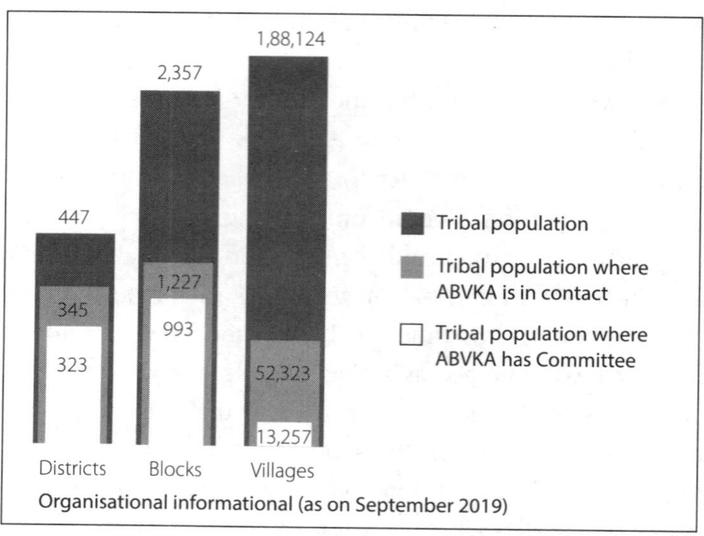

Source: Akhil Bharatiya Vanvasi Kalyan Ashram Organisational Information, http://kalyanashram.org/organisational-information-as-on-oct-2018/

Figure 14.2: ABVKA's Missionary Model: Medical Centres, Education and Economic Aid

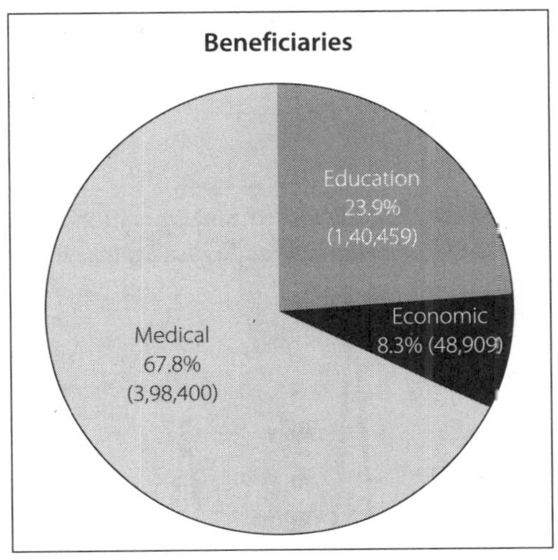

Source: Akhil Bharatiya Vanvasi Kalyan Ashram Service Projects Information, http://kalyanashram.org/service-project-at-a-glance/

Figure 14.3: ABVKA's National Spread: Social Welfare Projects

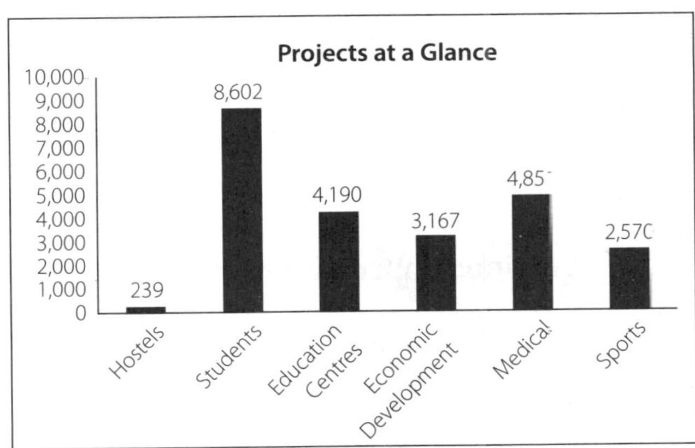

Source: Akhil Bharatiya Vanvasi Kalyan Ashram Service Projects Information, http://kalyanashram.org/service-project-at-a-glance/

In states that do not have significant tribal populations, the ABVKA targeted tribal-majority districts. By 2020, its website had detailed, geo-tagged, state-specific pages, where visitors could see micro-details of each welfare project in every state.[64] In education, its largest beneficiaries were concentrated in West Bengal, Rajasthan, Maharashtra, Bihar and Andaman. In economic aid, Jharkhand, Odisha and western Maharashtra accounted for the largest chunk (see Figures 14.3 and 14.4).

Figure 14.4: ABVKA's Tribal Outreach: Education and Economic Aid Beneficiaries (State-wise)

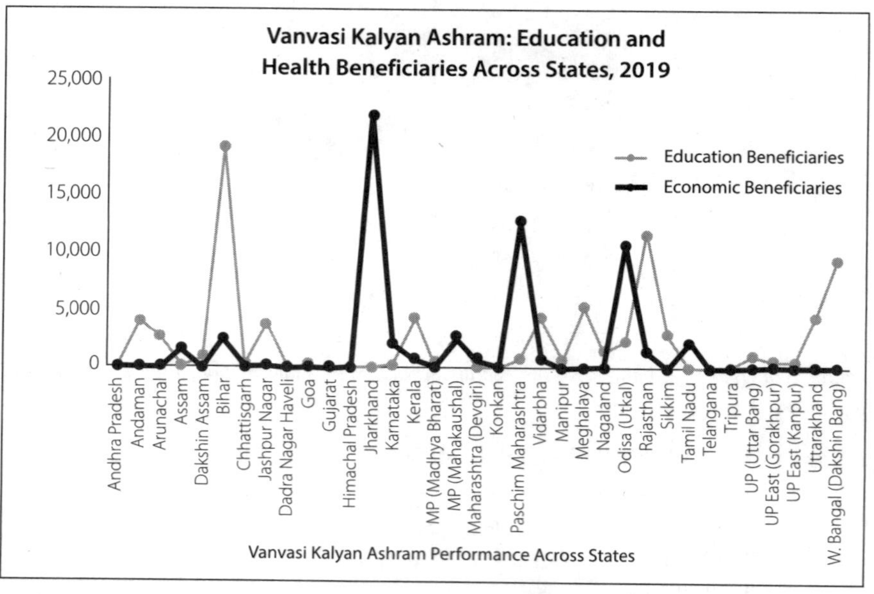

Source: Akhil Bharatiya Vanvasi Kalyan Ashram Service Projects Information, http://kalyanashram.org/service-project-at-a-glance/

The RSS and Education: Impressions from Deendayal Dham

In July 2020, I visited the Deendayal Upadhyaya Research Library, managed by the Sangh-affiliated Deendayal Dham in the late Jan Sangh's leader's hometown of Mathura. The Coronavirus lockdown had not yet been lifted and the sprawling Deendayal Dham complex—which includes a large school (Saraswati Shishu Mandir), a student hostel (Bhaurau Deoras Hostel), a large rural employment self-help centre and an Ayurvedic pharmacy selling cow-based products (Kamdhenu Gaushala Pharmacy)—was largely deserted. As I perused the archival shelves for the rare Sangh literature I had gone to find, I got into a conversation with two teenaged schoolboys. They were the only other people in the library, and had been engrossed in deep study when we reached. Surrounded by writing papers, both boys were feverishly scribbling notes from the competition books they were studying. Both also had installed in front of them their mobile phones, set on small portable stands and connected to earphones. They seemed to be simultaneously listening to a video and writing notes, while constantly also consulting the books in front of them. Impressed by their discipline, I asked what examination they were studying for. National Defence Academy, they both responded enthusiastically. They were students from the Saraswati Shishu Mandir and did not want to lose time preparing for their entrance examination, I discovered. As I got back to my own reading, I realised that the archival library shelves, near which we were all sitting, occupied only half the floor. The other half served as a traditional RSS altar of veneration, carefully adorned with images of the Sangh's pantheon of reverence: the customary photo of Bharat Mata, which has pride of place in every RSS and BJP office; the Om symbol; portraits of the Sangh's first two sarsanghchalaks, Dr Hedgewar and Guru Golwalkar; a large saffron banner depicting the Ram Temple in Ayodhya and the original version of Sangh Pratigya (pledge) that every swayamsevak takes. The pledge on the wall read:

> I hereby, remembering the Almighty and my ancestor, take the pledge that I have become a member of the Rashtriya Swayamsevak Sangh to protect the sacred Hindu Dharma, Hindu Sanskriti and Hindu society and to make this Hindu Rashtra independent. I will carry on the Sangh work honestly, selflessly and with all my physical, mental and monetary strength and will stick to this resolve throughout my life.

This original pledge was instituted as a Sangh tradition by Dr Hedgewar as part of the first RSS initiation ceremony with a select group of ninety-nine Sangh members in 1928.[65] The line in the pledge on making the Hindu Rashtra 'independent' was changed after Independence to '*Hindu Rashtra ki sarvangin unnati*' (all-round development of the Hindu Rashtra).[66] I do not know what the boys in the library thought about the Sangh or the pledge. They were studying so hard, I did not have the heart to disturb them any further. But they would have seen the images on the wall just a few feet away and would likely have been aware of the discourse.

Figure 14.5: Education Is a Key Part of Sangh Parivar Work: Snapshots from Deendayal Upadhyaya Shodh Pustakalaya

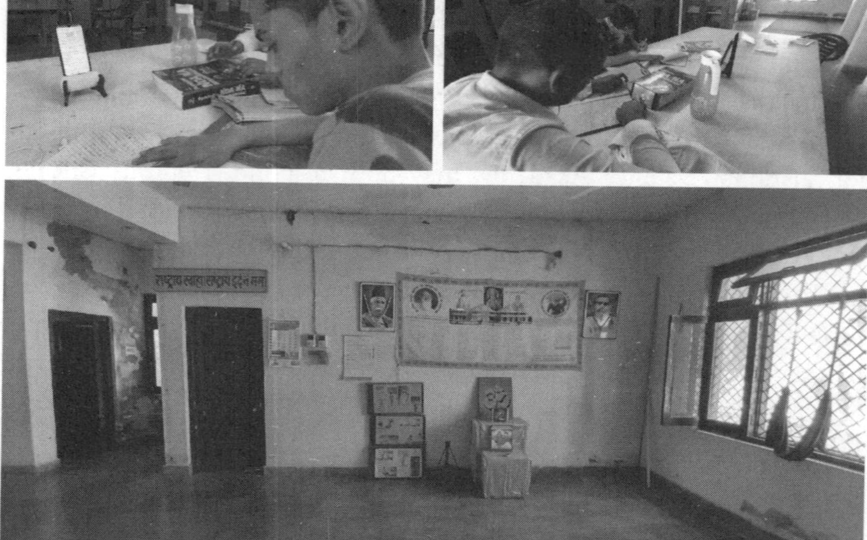

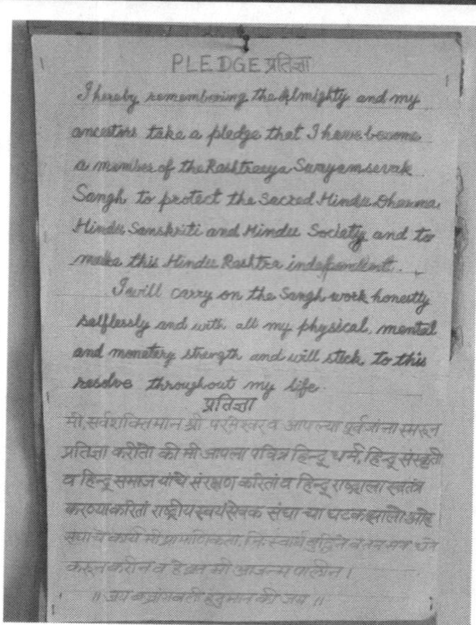

Note: L to R: Students preparing for a competitive national defence examination. In the far corner is a Sangh altar adorned with its images of veneration. Photos by Rajiv Pundir and Nalin Mehta, Deendayal Dham, Mathura, 26 July 2020.

Our tour of the Deendayal Dham, conducted by a senior RSS leader, reminded me once again that ABVKA is only one among multiple Sangh initiatives focused on education. Even as Golwalkar mentored the creation of the Ashram in 1952, he laid the foundation of Gita Mandir in Kurukshetra. Parallel to this, the first Saraswati Shishu Mandir was set up in Gorakhpur in 1952. The Shishu Mandirs initially grew as a network of schools in UP. In 1958, a state-level committee was set up to supervise them.[67] As this education network expanded nationwide, in 1977, the Sangh set up the Vidya Bharati Akhil Bharatiya Shiksha Sansathan, a pan-India coordinating body, to supervise it. By 2020, Vidya Bharati's scholastic system included 12,363 educational institutions, including forty-nine colleges, 935 senior secondary schools, 2,232 middle schools, 4,369 primary schools, 2,951 pre-primary centres and 1,557 informal single-teacher schools.[68] The scholars Walter K. Andersen and Shridhar D. Damle have claimed that this constitutes 'by far the largest private school system in India'. In a sense, this education system had 'turned the tables on the concerns the Sangh once had regarding Christian missionary schools educating Hindus, as it now enrols a considerable number of Muslims and Christians'.[69] This is not surprising. The spick-and-span Saraswati Shishu Mandir we toured in Mathura had a large scholarship programme, a subsidised hostel and a significant student population from lower-income households.[70]

'In the decade after the [1948] ban, these schools provided an alternative way to spread the RSS's message of national unity and pan-Hinduism,' Andersen and Damle point out. 'Teachers at these schools often insert nationalist narratives into the social science and history books prescribed by national authorities, as these texts are held by some RSS circles to be devoid of respect for the country's distinct civilization. These schools also celebrate Hindu festivals and their facilities are typically adorned by Hindu religious symbols ... these schools, like the shakhas, play a major role in engendering a sense of common solidarity among their participants, and we were told this is an important objective.'[71]

While it is important to understand that these education-focused institutions fulfil a major welfare need and bridge wide gaps in the state's education system, they also help in moulding new generations into Hindutva thinking. In that sense, the ABVKA's cultural influence

Figure 14.6: Saraswati Shishu Mandir and Balasaheb Deoras Student Hostel, Deendayal Dham, Mathura

Above: An image of Lord Krishna atop Kalia, the snake (representing a popular Krishna legend) in the courtyard of the Saraswati Shishu Mandir high school in Mathura. Below: A student hostel named after the RSS's third Sarsanghchalak Balasaheb Deoras. Source: Photos by Rajiv Pundir and Nalin Mehta, 26 July 2020.

had a fundamental role in helping the BJP make political inroads into tribal areas.

ABVKA's Academic Focus: Higher Pass Percentages, Cultural Layering and Competitive Exams

The ABVKA is organically linked to the Sangh scholastic network. It runs two types of schools: formal institutions and informal ones called Ekal

Vidyalayas, which consist of a single mobile teacher holding open classes in remote and tribal villages without formal schools. It was managing 4,190 schools in India's tribal areas by 2019 (see Table 14.1). When I asked ABVKA's Atul Jog about the primary difference between schools run by his organisation and those run by the government or other private entities, he explained that the 'academic curriculum is the same' in ABVKA schools. So, they follow curricula set by central education boards like CBSE or the state education boards. But the schools add two additional layers of cultural education. 'We always ensure that tribal community's custom is celebrated and we celebrate its festivals,' he said. Along with this, the schools focus on teaching students the stories of 'mahapurush [great men] who have done something for society, so that a feeling of deshbhakti [patriotism] grows in them'. In the border areas of Assam and Nagaland, for example, he said that ABVKA schools organise trips to the army's border outposts on the festival of Rakhi. Students ritualistically tie rakhis (symbolising sibling-bonding) on soldiers' wrists. 'This is to increase emotional bonding both ways to increase patriotism,' Jog added. Naturally, all ABVKA schools teach the Saraswati Vandana (an ode to the Hindu goddess of learning) and impart Hindu cultural messaging.

Table 14.1: Vanvasi Kalyan Ashram Network of Schools Nationwide

Year	*Schools*	*Students*	*Workers, full-time*	*Workers, part-time*	*Villages*	*Districts*
1992	-	-	563	-	11,000	119
2015	4,460	1,25,415	820	650	-	-
2019	4,190	1,40,459	926	853	1,88,124	674

Source: Akhil Bharatiya Vanvasi Kalyan Ashram Service Projects Information, http://kalyanashram.org/service-project-at-a-glance/

When I asked Jog what had changed in ABVKA schools over the last few years, he said that their main challenge earlier had been to get students to graduate. The baseline for academic performance had shifted upwards significantly in recent years. Speaking on the phone from the capital of Jharkhand, he excitedly pointed out that, of the 1,249 Class XII students in twenty-five ABVKA schools in the state, 68.5 per cent had scored a first division, 22.4 per cent a second division and 1.2 per cent a third division in 2020. One of the girl students, Abha Kumari from Betalsood village, ranked eighth in Jharkhand. 'Earlier, for our children, passing Class X was big, graduating college was even bigger,' he said. 'Now they are getting selected in medical schools, engineering and IITs.'

In fact, the ABVKA's focus now is on training schoolchildren for competitive examinations in different sectors including government, banking and engineering. In early 2020, three of its students—Prashant Hendrm, Manisha Tirkey and Pankaj Bhagat—cleared the Jharkhand Public Service Commission examination and qualified to join the state civil service. In Chhattisgarh's Bilaspur district in 2013 alone, fifty-five ABVKA students qualified for different levels of government. 'Each of them was the first in their families to ever get a government job,' said Jog. Ensuring post-education recruitment for its students has emerged as the organisation's new priority area. By 2020, it had set up free coaching centres for government recruitment examinations in Ranchi, Bhilai and Bhopal.[72]

ABVKA's Cultural Messaging: What It Talks About and Why That Matters

It is important to acknowledge that the ABVKA schools fulfil a critical education gap for hundreds of thousands of children who have few other options in India's tribal areas. Equally, given the exponential growth of these schools, it is necessary to understand the cultural value system they are embedded in: the ABVKA's understanding of the world, its views on key issues and how it communicates them.

As in the 1950s, the organisation's major focus, even in 2020, was on opposing conversions. The ABVKA sees missionary proselytisation as secessionist anti-India work. In 2016, for instance, its Kendriya Karyakari Mandal met in Pindwara, Rajasthan, and passed a resolution demanding a law against conversions, arguing:[73] 'Population of the Christian converts in Janjati communities was limited in some parts of North East and central India at the time of independence, has now spread rapidly across the [sic] in spite of all resistance of Janjatis. It shows that successive Governments have failed in protecting freedom of religion as far as the native Indian religions are concerned. Some communities are totally converted into

Christianity while many other communities are having more than 50% converts ... If this is left unchecked, the cultural identity of Janjati communities will be perished and the Constitutional guarantee to protect their identity and existence will remain mere ornamental letters. In this contemporary age the world has witnessed that the East Timor has been bifurcated from Indonesia and became a new country and Sudan has been divided into two nations as North and South Sudan.'

The ABVKA bunched missionary activity by organisations like World Vision with the actions of extreme Islamists, opposing what it saw as the Christian equivalent of 'Love Jihad'. It demanded that existing state laws against conversion be implemented, and that the Centre bring in new legislation and a national White Paper on the issue. As its 2016 Pindwara Resolution said:[74]

> The activities of World Vision, CASA [Church's Auxiliary for Social Action] and CCF [Church's Commission Fellowship] are not unknown. Religious conversions as well as cross border Muslim infiltration are causing a new threat. They are now getting engaged in marital relationship with local Janjati girls and get access to their land, forests and other natural resources. They are trying to gain power in the local self government institutions through such marital relations [....]
>
> 1. Since the religious conversion is a national problem, the Union Government should take immediate measures and enact a Central Act for freedom of religions.
> 2. Immediate steps should be taken to implement and enforce the Freedom of Religion Act in Arunachal Pradesh, MP; CG; Odisha and HP where such Acts have been passed by their respective State Assemblies and these States should publish a White Paper on status and implementation of this Act.
> 3. A National Commission should be appointed to enquire and recommend the adverse impact of religious conversions on the social harmony, tensions and conflicts prevailing in the Janjatis and their areas.

This is a concern long shared by many BJP leaders in tribal areas and underpins the older arguments that the party makes for 'reconversion' of tribals from Christianity. In some ways, the ABVKA's anti-conversation rhetoric brought full circle the political journey of a project that had begun as an educational enterprise for young tribal children in the 1950s. Animosity to Christian missionaries was central to BJP leader Dilip Singh Judeo's local messaging in Chhattisgarh. He told me, when we met in 2003, that keeping tribal groups within the Hindu fold was his primary motive for entering politics. After Australian missionary Graham Staines was burnt to death in Odisha with his two minor children in 1999, Judeo openly declared that he would help fight the case of the main accused, Dara Singh, who was arrested in 2000. However, the then BJP president Kushabhau Thakre, facing large-scale public condemnation of the killings, issued a statement washing his hands of the controversy. Judeo was then forced to retract his statement.[75]

BJP state governments have long shared a close relationship with the ABVKA. Gujarat's minister for tribal development, for instance, attended the 8 May 2016 release of the organisation's 'Vision Statement', which called for increased government assistance to tribals to stop conversions. The minister, Mangubhai Patel, asserted, 'We led a revolution and today we can say for sure that conversion has stopped because of government's intervention.'[76]

Conversions are a fundamental concern for the wider Sangh Parivar as well. As senior pracharak Sunil Ambekar argued in his book, *The RSS: Roadmaps for the 21st Century*, 'What successive governments have acknowledged, the Sangh announced loudly. Conversion is a threat, particularly in tribal and underprivileged areas. The Sangh has expanded its footprint in these spheres. It is a high-priority focus. The Sangh runs a wide range of diverse programmes through its Vanvasi Kalyan Ashram.'[77]

This distrust of missionaries and framing them as anti-Indian is a trope that goes back to Golwalkar, who had argued in *A Bunch of Thoughts*, 'Their [Christians'] activities are not merely irreligious, they are also anti-national … So long as the Christians here indulge in such activities and consider themselves as agents of international movement for the spread of Christianity, and refuse to offer their first loyalty to the land of their birth … they will remain here as hostiles [sic] and will have to be treated as such.'[78] Yet, paradoxically, as we have seen, the Sangh emulated the growth strategies of the missionaries on education. Interestingly, Vidya Bharti stalwart and its then head, Lajjaram Tomar, told his national executive at Smriti Mandir in Nagpur in 2000 that they should appreciate the sacrifices made by the missionaries, not criticise them unnecessarily, and learn from their spirit and faith so 'that the enemies in the clashes of civilisation can be defeated'.[79]

What the RSS Wants in Education

On the Narad Index, the Sangh's emphasis on education is way higher than mentions of education by the BJP or in Prime Minister Modi's communications outreach (see Figure 14.7). The RSS primarily has four broad concerns on education: reviving indigenous education practices, wresting control of the historical narrative on the Indian past from what it sees as a dominant Leftist perspective, reviving Indian language education and reversing what it thinks of as a colonial-minded education inherited from the British (driven by those it derisively refers to as 'Macaulay-putras', or the sons of Macaulay). Lord Macaulay's 1835 'Minute on Education' had set the template for British policies to impart English education to the 'natives' in British India. In the view of Hindu nationalists, independent India had continued to let its education policies be defined by the metaphorical 'sons of Macaulay' who, they believe,

Figure 14.7: RSS Focuses More on Education than BJP: Second Highest Priority after Hindutva

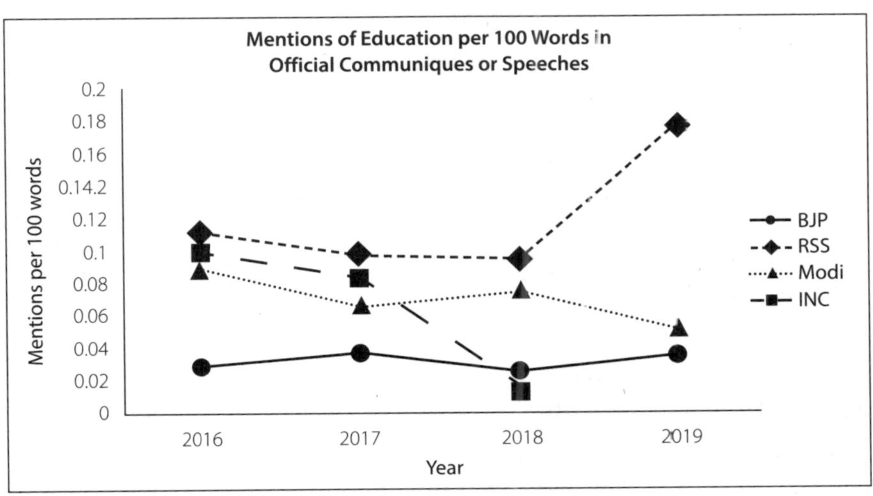

Source: Narad Index, Nalin Mehta and Rishabh Srivastava; for more details, see Appendix 4

scorned local languages, indigenous forms of knowledge and Hindu-nationalist narratives. These beliefs, and the need to reverse the situation as the RSS sees it, form the basis of all Sangh Parivar education initiatives.

Thus, when the Modi government adopted the NEP in July 2020 (the first such policy after 1986),[80] *Organiser* welcomed it with a gushing cover story headlined 'Foundation for Freedom'. In a signed editorial, its editor, Prafulla Ketkar, hailed the structural changes that the NEP proposed as a 'major breakthrough'. Tellingly, he framed the new language policies as a tool of decolonisation, linking them to the legacy of the freedom movement leader (and Hindu traditionalist) Lokmanya Tilak, who had declared that the 'classification of letter and sounds on which we have bestowed so much labour in India and which we find perfected in the works of Panini is not to be found in any other language in the world'. For the RSS, criticism of the NEP was akin to the opposition Tilak faced in colonial India. Just as he was 'mocked' for trying to bring a 'national character to education', argued *Organiser*, 'people with the same colonised mindset' were now criticising NEP 2020.[81] Similarly, Sangh-affiliated outfits like the Shiksha Sanskriti Utthan Nyas (SSUN) saw the NEP as a 'resurgence of Bharatiyata'.[82] They also interpreted it as a negation of the 'deep shadow of Marxist policy makers' who had been influenced by what one writer called the 'socialist and secular framework' of politics.[83] The Bharatiya Shikshan Mandal, among the most prominent Sangh affiliates involved in deliberations on the NEP, hailed it as a 'new revolution'. It announced that 'almost 60%' of its suggestions had found a place in the NEP, including the renaming of the Ministry of Human Resource Development as Ministry of Education.[84]

The Sangh's exultation over NEP 2020 comes from a long history of battles over the design of Indian education. In the RSS's view, the Radhakrishnan Commission of 1948 and the Kothari Committee of 1964 had spoken of decolonising education, but no tangible measures had followed thereafter. From the 1960s onwards, the RSS saw the 'outsourcing of the education baton to the Communists in 1967, denigrating whatever is Bharatiya' as the 'crux of education'. It argued that this was essentially an 'imitation' strategy that led to a big gap between national needs and education outputs in the post-liberalisation period.[85] This is why the RSS focuses so much on education, its main goal

Figure 14.8: RSS-affiliated Outfits Pushed for and Welcomed NEP 2020

Organiser *cover story: 9 August 2020, Vol. 72, No. 7*

being the introduction of what it sees as 'Indian knowledge treasures' in primary school.[86]

It believes that this fundamental Sangh impulse for the 'Indianisation of education' is often 'negated with allegations of saffronisation, even without understanding the content and structure of such education'. Reviving what it sees as indigenous models of education is a vital tool for the RSS's strategy to develop India.[87] As Mukul Kanitkar argued in 2015, many in the Sangh saw the coming of the Modi government and its move to create the NEP as a call to action: they would now create 'an indigenous mode of education', and 'genuine patriots of Bharat' could work to 'de-Macaulay-ise the education system'.[88] This is why the RSS prioritised the building of educational institutions. 'This was an especially urgent priority in the first years after Independence,' argue Andersen and Damle. It was 'prompted both by the growing demand for education on the part of the

RSS's largely urban, middle-class base and by the sangh's conviction that national values were inadequately represented in the curriculum, both in public schools and in private Christian schools'.[89]

The RSS's emphasis on education in local languages is the other side of the same coin: a battle against what it sees as a colonial legacy. For the RSS, if Japan and Germany could become economic powers without English, why not India? As a leading piece in *Organiser* argued in 2015, 'It has been categorically proved through scientific research that education is best imparted through the mother tongue. Twenty nations with the highest GDP across the world use their own language as medium of education as well as governance. Only four nations—England, America, Australia and Canada—have English as their medium, for the simple reason that English is their mother tongue. On the other hand, the 20 most backward countries are the ones that have a foreign language or a mix of foreign and regional (like in India) as medium of education.'[90]

The RSS's Akhil Bharatiya Pratinidhi Sabha (ABPS), its highest decision-making body, met in March 2018 and came out with a clear resolution on the preservation of Indian languages and dialects. As many as 1,496 pratinidhis (representatives) from various prants and Sangh associations signed on to the 'need to protect and promote Bharatiya languages'. The ABPS lamented that 'the declining trend in practice and usage of Bharatiya languages, elimination of their words and replacement by words of foreign languages are emerging as a serious challenge'. It demanded that 'Primary education across the country should only be in mother tongue or any Bharatiya language. For this, parents should make up their mind and governments should formulate suitable policies.' Furthermore, it called for teaching and study materials as well as examinations for higher education in technical and medical colleges to be in 'Bharatiya languages too'. Finally, the RSS also wanted preference for Bharatiya languages in 'all governmental and judicial works' and asked that the 'entire society including the Swayamsevaks should give preference to the mother tongue in conversations and day-to-day interactions in the family'.[91] This was the second major resolution passed by the ABPS on education in the mother tongue.

Sarsanghchalak Mohan Bhagwat underscored this priority when he told swayamsevaks that while 'we should respect all the languages and consider them at par with our mother-tongue,' they should 'interact in our [own] languages'. He was appealing, he said, not only to the government but also to the media that 'language should be used in its pristine form'.[92]

Textbooks, Changes and the SBAS

The Sangh Parivar's concerns on education narratives are exemplified by the single-minded focus of the controversial Shikhsha Bachao Andolan Samiti (SBAS), spearheaded by the RSS's Dinanath Batra and set up in 2004. With the BJP having recently lost power and with a new HRD minister and many leftist historians and educationists calling for 'detoxification' of education, several Sangh Parivar individuals came together on 2 July 2004 in Delhi to form the SBAS.[93] Among the first causes it took up, in 2007, was the reversal of what it saw as the introduction of 'graphic sex education' in secondary school textbooks from Class Six onwards by the UPA. The introduction of sex education in school was seen as a triumph of scientific knowledge by many educationists. In the RSS's view, it was a perversion: 'Whether by design or sheer negligence, textbook content started yielding negativity, untruths, distortion of facts and at times even perversity.' In the eyes of the SBAS, sex education was a move 'by certain forces in the education sector to sabotage young minds'.[94]

In 2008, after forcing NCERT to initially withdraw what is perceived as objectionable passages, pressure from SBAS caused the UPA government to backtrack and significantly modify sex education modules taught in schools.[95]

The list of causes that the Samiti took up says all there is to say about its outlook on education. It filed eleven cases in court and won all of them: the removal of A.K. Ramanujan's celebrated essay, 'Three Hundred Ramayanas: Five Examples and Three Thoughts on Translation',[96] from the Delhi University syllabus; the removal of seventy-five passages from NCERT Class VI–XII books; and the withdrawal of University of Chicago historian Wendy Doniger's book, *The Hindus: An Alternative History*.[97] After a two-year legal battle, Penguin, the publisher of Doniger's book, signed an 'amicable settlement' with SBAS, agreeing to pulp all the copies it had.[98] The book was eventually republished in India by Speaking Tiger, another publisher, but the point had been made.[99] One of the

SBAS's moving forces, its secretary Atul Kothari, saw each of the cases his organisation took up as proof of a 'global conspiracy to disconnect the Indians from their roots'. As he told *Organiser*, 'We fought against it [Ramanujan's essay, 'Three Hundred Ramayanas', in the Delhi University curriculum] for about five years. We had to approach Delhi High Court and then the Supreme Court against it and finally it was withdrawn.'

'Till the year 2004,' Kothari said, 'whenever the matter of education came up, only the left intellectuals dominated the discourse. Now they have been thrown out along with their devious plans. Objectionable chapters and words from the textbooks were removed. There were many other victories too.'[100]

The SBAS was conceptualised as a protest movement. After the early successes, its founders met in Bhopal in 2007 to create the Shikshaa Sanskriti Uttan Nyas (SSUN), which intended to build on its work to create alternatives to education practices rooted in 'Bharatiya moral and national values'.[101] The big question after blocking sex education in schools was what it would be replaced with. The SSUN's members met in Pune in February 2009 and prepared a new curriculum focused on 'Character Building', a move reminiscent of evangelical sects in the United States. Soon after, the Rajya Sabha's Petition Committee, headed by the then BJP Rajya Sabha MP Venkaiah Naidu, proposed introducing 'Character Building' courses in education instead of sex education. The new syllabus was readied by 2010 and first implemented in schools in the tribal district of Jhabua in Madhya Pradesh in 2012. By 2019, the curriculum was being taught in 300 schools nationwide, and the SSUN had held 400 workshops for teachers on the subject.[102] By 2020, the SSUN had also created syllabi on indigenous knowledge systems like Vedic mathematics for Grades 1–12, had plans for introducing six-month certificate courses and also a one-year diploma.[103]

Since 2014, there have been protracted battles between the Sangh and historians over the portrayal of key historical figures in school textbooks, such as the one over the importance of the sixteenth-century Rajput ruler of Chittor, Maharana Pratap, and his battles with the Mughal emperor Akbar. In 2017, the then Union home minister Rajnath Singh questioned why Maharana Pratap was not referred to as 'Great' while Akbar was.[104] Such critiques often led to changes in school textbooks. When revised

NCERT history books for Grade 6–10 hit the bookshelves in 2018, an analysis by *The Indian Express* found that several new historical figures—spiritual leaders Sri Aurobindo and Swami Vivekananda, freedom fighters Lala Lajpat Rai and Vallabhbhai Patel, Peshwa and Maratha General Bajirao, Jat king Suraj Mal, Maharana Pratap and Chhatrapati Shivaji, founder of the Maratha empire—had 'either been introduced' or had 'more space dedicated to them'.[105]

The Sangh as a 'Network of Networks'

The ABVKA, Vidya Bharati and SBAS, all working on education in their different ways, are only three among more than forty entities that the RSS says are part of the wider Sangh Parivar.[106] In 1997, when Suruchi Prakashan, an RSS publishing house, published *Param Vaibhav ke Path Par*, detailing various organisations supported by the RSS for different tasks, the BJP was third on the list. As RSS pracharak Sunil Ambekar has pointed out, 'Various Sangh bodies, such as ABVP, BMS, Bharatiya Kisan Sangh [BKS], Vanvasi Kalyan Ashram [VKA], VJP, Swadeshi Jagran Manch [SJM] and Vidya Bharati, are among the best known. But there is an entire gamut of Parivar organisations. There is no sphere that is left untouched. For the armed forces, for instance, there is an organisation for ex-servicemen named Purva Sainik Parishad; for the welfare of those living near border areas, there is Seema Jagran Manch; the lawyers' body is known as Adhivakta Parishad; for sports there is Kreeda Bharati; in medicine there is National Medicos Organisation; and the Aarogya Bharati that promotes Indian systems of healing. Saksham works for the rights of the differently abled and is a respected name in the field of disability services.'[107]

For RSS ideologues, the Sangh is 'a network of networks'. As Ambekar put it, 'There is no limit on the number of organisations that can be seeded to support the multiple issues that necessitate intervention. Thus, a large number of front organisations can be created with Sangh inspiration ... Parivar organisations are referred to as Sangh Srishti, or creation, but the fact is that these are India's creations born out of Indian visions. The Sangh's mantra is the synergy of constructive energies in national interest.'[108]

Exactly how many organisations are affiliated to the Sangh remains unclear, but these groups span a 'broad spectrum of interests, including politics, agriculture, public health, education, veterans' affairs, religion, entrepreneurship and tribal welfare. Moreover, new groups continue to form to address fresh challenges, including a new affiliate that focuses on strengthening family bonds (the Kutumb Prabodhan) and another for female empowerment (the Stree Shakti).'[109] There are many that are not counted as full affiliates till they show they can be autonomous. The Kutumb Prabodhan, for example, started outreach work in 2010 and Stree Shakti in the 1990s, but they only became full affiliates in 2017.[110]

RSS leaders insist that these affiliate organisations are not remote-controlled, that they work as autonomous 'domain experts'. The ground for creating what the RSS calls the 'Sangh Vividh Kshetra Sanghathan' [the Sangh's structure of organisations working in various fields] was prepared during the first sarsanghchalak Dr Hegdewar's lifetime. However, most Sangh-linked bodies are independent and autonomous.'[111] They 'are called Parivar because they share the same genealogy of ideas. But they are all autonomous and independent in structures and functions. A large number of activists, or karyakartas, in these organisations are not swayamsevaks. However, there are swayamsevaks among them, who move from the RSS to work in Parivar organisations, while some new karyakartas over time become swayamsevaks. If any coordination is required, Sangh communicates through swayamsevaks working in these organisations, by giving advice whenever demanded.'[112]

For the Sangh, these structural linkages mean that activists are exposed to, and come to be converted to, the Sangh's world view during the course of their work. It sees the Parivar organisations, therefore, as a 'conveyor belt of Sangh ideas in society'.[113]

Parallelly, Sangh ideologues see organisations like the ABVKA as a way of re-engineering society into their own ideal. According to Ambekar, 'different sectors—farmers, workers, students—may be discrete units, but they are not separate silos. There are inherent linkages and mutual coordination which results in a nation-building vision. This is known as "Sangh-samanvay", or coordination, essential in society. As Swami Vivekanand said in his speech at Madurai, "There are three stages necessary for the future of India. The whole secret lies in organisation, accumulation of power and coordination of wills." In the Sangh's life, the first two stages are already true. We are in the third stage and the Sangh is working on the coordination of wills.'[114]

There is no question that the RSS, and its multiple affiliated organisations, are a major political force multiplier for the BJP. Under Vajpayee's prime ministership, the party was sensitive to public criticism of its RSS link. The Gujarat government of Keshubhai Patel lifted the ban on RSS members joining the bureaucracy in January 2000, but was forced to withdraw after Prime Minister Vajpayee faced immense criticism in Parliament. There was strong opposition in Gujarat, with Amarsinh Chaudhary, leader of the Congress, terming it a blatant attempt to 'saffronise the bureaucracy which has so far remained largely free from communal bias'.[115] The issue then grew into a wider crisis for Vajpayee's coalition government as the Opposition brought in a censure motion. Keshubhai initially refused to back down, but his hand was forced by the BJP top brass after Vajpayee, it is said, threatened to resign if the censure passed in Parliament.[116] In sharp contrast to this, there have been no controversies about the RSS link under the Modi regime, which wears its Sangh lineage proudly.

PART V

BEYOND THE DOMINANT NARRATIVE

THE SOUTH, THE NORTHEAST AND WOMEN

15

THE BJP'S SOUTH MODEL

The Karnataka Formula

Ever since Australian John MacArthur published his upside-down 'universal corrective' map of the world in 1979, depicting the southern countries of the world on top, it has served as a useful reminder of how geographic representations subliminally shape our perception of the world. The northern Hindi heartland dominates the national political narrative. The road to Delhi passes through Lucknow, as the old adage goes. But turn the map of India upside down and the political battlefield looks very different from the rhetoric that animates conversations above the Vindhyas: 'Ali vs Bajrang Bali',[1] 'Hindu terror' or 'national/anti-national'.

From the beginning of the coalition era in 1989, the southern states have often tilted the balance of power in Delhi. The BJP, for example, lost power in 2004 largely because its then allies, the AIADMK in Tamil Nadu and the Telugu Desam Party (TDP) in Andhra Pradesh, were routed. Conversely, Vajpayee's two national electoral triumphs in 1998 and 1999 were linked to having the right winning ally in Tamil Nadu (the DMK) and a winning political arrangement in Andhra Pradesh. The 2014 and 2019 elections bucked the historical pattern because the Narendra Modi wave overrode the traditional caste-based political arithmetic in the Hindi heartland and in western India. These landslide victories masked the fact that that they were largely predicated on electoral advances in just twelve (ten in the Hindi heartland and two in the west) of India's twenty-eight states, which accounted for 85 per cent of all BJP seats in 2014 and 58.4 per cent in 2019.

Invert the map and the political landscape looks very different for the BJP. Karnataka, Tamil Nadu, Andhra Pradesh, Telangana, Kerala and the Union Territory of Puducherry account for 130 seats in southern India: over one-fifth of the Lok Sabha's 543 seats. In 2014, in sharp contrast to the north, the BJP won only 16.1 per cent (twenty-one) of these seats; they accounted for only 7.4 per cent of its total tally. In 2019, it won only 22.3 per cent (twenty-nine), accounting for just 9.57 per cent of its final tally.

Karnataka is the region's outlier—the big question is why.

The party's model of political mobilisation, based on north India-focused identity politics, remained largely ineffective in the rest of south India. So, what was the BJP's secret sauce in Karnataka? How has it consistently won a majority of parliamentary seats in four successive general elections between 2004 and 2019 in this state? Of Karnataka's twenty-eight Lok Sabha seats, the BJP won eighteen in 2004, nineteen in 2009, seventeen in 2014 and twenty-five in 2019. It remains the only southern state where a saffron government has ever come to power.[2] As with people or companies, the failures of political parties tell us as much about them as their successes—and the south was definitely a bridge too far for the BJP until 2021. Except for Karnataka, where it managed to become the pre-eminent party despite being likened to 'north Indian imperial invaders' from the ancient past by local regional parties. Is there a Karnataka model of BJP politics? How does it work and why does it not work in the other southern states? Are the BJP's Karnataka gains replicable? Will this one state become the base from which the party will grow out into the rest of south India?

The Tumkur Factor: The View from Siddaganga Math

The shaded grand courtyard of the Sree Siddaganga Math (monastery), one of the oldest and most influential shrines of the Shiva-focused Lingayat sect, is an unlikely place for a political conversation. It is nestled amid rocky hillocks—the Ramalinga, Siddaganga and Shivagange Hills—that house several sacred caves. The monastery was founded in the fifteenth century as a Sharana (Shiva devotee) abode for spreading the teachings of the twelfth-century Lingayat statesman-saint-social reformer Basavanna. As a centre for Sharana Sahitya (literature) and 'Shunya Sampadane' (an anthology of Kannada poems by several medieval Lingayat saints), it developed as a critical node for the Bhakti movement during the time of the Vijayanagar empire. Located in Karnataka's Tumkur district, it is also home to a gurukul (traditional school) that provides education, free food and shelter to over 10,000 poor children.[3]

The Siddaganga Math became the epicentre of a heated political exchange in the summer of 2018 when the then Congress Chief Minister Siddaramaiah tried to reduce the BJP's recent dominance among Lingayat voters by recommending minority status for the sect.[4] This meant that the Lingayats would be recognised as a distinct religious community, outside of Hinduism, and be eligible for reservation benefits as a minority community under state laws. While many Lingayats also call themselves Veerashaivas,[5] the cabinet order simultaneously recognised Veerashaiva-Lingayats as a separate Lingayat subsect, opening up another contentious religious argument.[6] 'The government is dividing us. Mark my words, this move has changed the election. Lingayats will not forgive Congress for this,' T.B. Shekhar, the agitated head of the Tumkur Veerashaiva Samaj, told me during a live video discussion in the Math's courtyard on 6 May 2018, as we tried to make sense of Karnataka's caste matrix. State assembly elections were due a week later, and we had travelled to Tumkur for a broadcast on how Lingayat voters viewed the poll campaign.

As we talked in the afternoon sun, the then presiding seer of the Math, the legendary 112-year-old Shivakumar Swamiji, stepped out. Locally known as 'Nadedaaduva Devaru' (Walking God), he had come out to the courtyard, dressed in his customary saffron robes, to give 'darshan' despite his ill-health. He sat on his sanctified 'aasan' with its finely carved Shivling on a polished wooden panel. Swamiji's appearance electrified the hundreds of devotees standing around us, all of whom instantly queued up for their turn to touch his feet.[7]

Just over a month earlier, in April 2018, the then BJP president Amit Shah had also visited Swamiji, along with the party's chief minister candidate, B.S. Yediyurappa, to start the poll campaign. In full view of the TV cameras, Shah reverentially prostrated on the ground and touched the octogenarian seer's feet with his forehead. Later, he announced that the aashirwaad (blessing) he had received from Swamiji would 'increase' the BJP's 'strength', giving it greater 'energy' and 'confidence' in the elections.[8] A week later, the then Congress president Rahul Gandhi followed suit. Visiting the Math, also in full view of the cameras, Gandhi presented Swamiji with a large bouquet of red-and-white roses before seeming to engage him in an animated conversation.[9] The televised visits of the two politicians underscored the seriousness with which both sides viewed the Lingayat vote, as also the role of caste and religion in the election campaign.

'Without Caste and Without Religion, There Is No Politics in India'

How do religious leaders at the Math view the politics of Lingayat reservations? What is their own positioning and how do they evaluate their influence? Curious about these questions, we paid a visit to the monastery. We were granted an audience with the institution's operative head, Sri Sri Siddalinga Mahaswamy, junior swamy and president of the Siddaganga Math. He was saffron-clad and turbaned, with white ash on his forehead, and sat in his office under a colourful portrait of a bejewelled Basavanna on a throne. He chose not to get drawn into political matters. Yet, his cryptic answer to my question on how he viewed the elections was revealing. 'Elections are for voting by each and everyone, but wherever you go, religion and caste are ridden with politics,' the fifty-five-year-old monk said. 'Without caste and without religion, there is no politics in India. That is bad, but we will hope that one day all will come out without religion and caste. But today we are seeing everyone running behind caste and religion.'

He denied that his Math had supported the reservation move for Lingayats and emphasised 'unity' as its core goal. 'The country, society and community need unity,' he said. 'That is the only purpose.'[10] The monk diplomatically avoided the question of whether Lingayat voters should support the BJP or the Congress.

T.B. Shekhar of the Veerashaiva Samaj was proven right when the results were declared. The BJP emerged as the single largest party in the polls. Its lead was powered by wins in a majority of the seventy assembly seats where Lingayat voters were dominant (over 15 per cent of voters).[11]

The 2018 Karnataka election initiated a year of messy coalition-building and changing governments, but the Tumkur factor also underscored the vast tonal contrast between politics in the Hindi heartland and south of the Vindhya ranges—the traditional boundary between north and south India.

Presaging the BJP: Lingayats, Vokkaligas and Karnataka's Changing 'Dominant' Caste Patterns

The political attendance at the Siddaganga Math underscores the changing 'dominant caste'—to use a term coined by the sociologist M.N. Srinivas in 1959[12]—politics in Karnataka. The Ekikaran (Unification) movement had led to Kannada-speaking regions from the adjoining states of Madras, Hyderabad and Bombay being incorporated into the old princely state of Mysore. Before this reorganisation in 1956, Vokkaligas, a land-owning farming community, were the biggest caste in Mysore. The Congress's Lingayat leaders had led the demand for Karnataka's unification and came to constitute the largest caste community in the enlarged state. Lingayats also formed a major support base for the party in the non-Mysore regions of the new state.[13]

By way of background, while the Lingayat lineage goes back to the twelfth century, they were first listed as a caste within Hinduism in the Mysore state's 1881 Census[14] and first referred to as a 'sect' in 1928 by the scholar R.G. Bhandarkar. The community's unique religious attributes—the wearing of an Ishtalinga (a symbol of Shiva) on the body, strict vegetarianism, rejection of temple worship, the substitution of Brahmins with their own priests in life-death ceremonies, their rejection of the caste system and their practice of burying the dead instead of cremation—meant that, by the time of Independence, some caste scholars had begun referring to them as a 'caste-sect'. Others, like M.N. Srinivas, regarded the Lingayats as a 'status-honour' group linked with the process of 'Sanskritisation'.[15] It was this long-standing debate that Congress Chief Minister Siddaramaiah had waded into with his minority-status proposal in 2018.

These two traditionally powerful caste groups, Lingayats and Vokkaligas, virtually controlled state politics between 1956 and 1972[16]—

the L–V caste equation that powered the Congress's political hold over Karnataka until the mid-1970s. As political scientist James Manor summed up, 'This system worked well so that the period between 1956 and the early 1970s can be seen as an era of Lingayat raj (with Vokkaliga support) in which the dominant groups had rather smooth sailing.'[17]

The political dominance of these castes was so pronounced that, in the 1952–1972 period, Lingayats accounted for an average of 31 per cent of the Karnataka assembly's legislators (despite being only 15.5 per cent of the population at the time). Vokkaligas made up an average of 27.9 per cent of legislators (despite being 12.98 per cent of the population then).[18] In other words, for several decades, every second Karnataka legislator belonged to one of these two castes. This is also reflected in the choice of chief ministers. Before the 1956 reorganisation, two of Mysore state's first three chief ministers were Vokkaligas (1947–1956). After the reorganisation, the first four chief ministers were all Lingayats (1956–1971). Thereafter, leaders from other caste groups started occupying the seat of power in Bengaluru as new caste coalitions began to challenge the traditional structures of power. But Lingayat leaders still made up 45 per cent (nine of twenty) of all state chief ministers between 1956 and 2021 (see Table 15.1).

After Lingayat regional satrap S. Nijalingappa (chief minister in 1956–1958 and then 1962–1968) broke away from the Congress in the great split of 1969—between Indira Gandhi and the Old Guard (called the 'Syndicate')—state Congress leaders wove together a new rainbow caste coalition. Chief Minister Devaraj Urs in 1972 sought to break the stranglehold of the Lingayats and the Vokkaligas by giving political representation to other caste groups that had so far been relatively marginalised.[19] He coined a new acronym for this fresh social coalition: AHINDA. This was a Kannada acronym for 'Alpasankhyataru' (minorities), Hindulidavaru (backward classes) and Dalitaru (Dalits). This is also the caste formulation that Congress Chief Minister Siddaramaiah tried to harness in the 2018 Karnataka assembly poll. Presaging V.P. Singh's 1989 move to change the politics of the Hindi heartland with his adoption of the Mandal Commission report, Urs sought to stir up Karnataka politics with the appointment of the state's first Backward Classes Commission. It was headed by L.G. Havanur, who himself hailed from the backward

Beda (hunter) community. This commission identified fifteen backward communities, 128 backward castes and sixty-two backward tribes, and created a new basis for affirmative reservation in the state. The Havanur Commission's findings, as the political scientist Valerian Rodrigues has shown, led to strong protests by upper castes and a challenge in the Karnataka High Court, which upheld its findings. Subsequent Backward Classes Commissions in Karnataka—Venkataswamy Commission (1983–1986) and Justice Chinnappa Reddy Commission (1988–1990)[20]—led to Vokkaligas also being classified as OBCs.[21]

Table 15.1: The Lingayat–Vokkaliga Factor in Karnataka Politics: Chief Ministers and Their Castes (1947–2021)[22]

S. No.	*Name*	*Tenure*	*Caste*	*Party*
Mysore State: Before Reorganisation (1947–1956)				
1.	K. Chengalaraya Reddy	1947–1952	Reddy	Congress
2.	K. Hanumanthaiah	1952–1956	Vokkaliga	Congress
3.	Kadidal Manjappa	1956–56	Vokkaliga	Congress
Mysore State: After Reorganisation (with Kannada-speaking areas previously administered by Bombay, Hyderabad, Madras as well as Coorg): 1956–1973				
4.	S. Nijalingappa*	1956–1958; 1962–1968	Lingayat	Congress
5.	B.D. Jatti	1958–1962	Lingayat	Congress
6.	S.R. Kanthi	1962–62	Lingayat	Congress
7.	Veerendra Patil*	1968–1971; 1989–1990	Lingayat	Congress/ Congress (O); Congress
Karnataka (after renaming of Mysore State): 1973–2020				
8.	D. Devaraj Urs*	1972–1977; 1978–1980	Urs** (OBC)	Congress
9.	R. Gundu Rao	1980–1983	Brahmin	Congress
10.	Ramakrishna Hegde*	1983–1984; 1985–1986; 1986–1988	Brahmin, with Lingayat support	Janata Party
11.	S.R. Bommai	1988–1989	Lingayat	Janata Party
12.	S. Bangarappa	1990–1992	Ediga*** (SC)	Congress

S. No.	*Name*	*Tenure*	*Caste*	*Party*
13.	M. Veerappa Moily	1992–1994	Tuluva (OBC)	Congress
14.	H.D. Deve Gowda	1994–1996	Vokkaliga (OBC)	Janata Dal
15.	J.H. Patel	1996–1999	Lingayat	Janata Dal
16.	S.M. Krishna	1999–2004	Vokkaliga (OBC)	Congress
17.	Dharam Singh	2004–2006	Rajput	Congress
18.	H.D. Kumaraswamy*	2006–2007; 2018–2019	Vokkaliga (OBC)	Janata Dal (Secular)
19.	B.S. Yediyurappa*	2007–07; 2008–2011; 2018–18; 2019–2021	Lingayat	BJP
20.	D.V. Sadananda Gowda	2011–2012	Vokkaliga (OBC)	BJP
21.	Jagdish Shettar	2012–2012	Lingayat	BJP
22.	Siddaramaiah	2013–2018	Kuruba (OBC)	Congress
23	Basavaraj Bommai	2021–	Lingayat	BJP

Source: Author's fieldwork, with T.M. Veeraraghav. Note: Veerendra Patil first became Congress chief minister in 1968, but switched to Congress (O) when the party split and continued as chief minister till 1971. The renaming of Karnataka in 1973 happened during the tenure of Devaraj Urs.

*Note: * Indicates those who were elected more than once as chief minister. ** Also referred to as Arasu. ***Also referred to as Idiga.*

Politically, this meant that many Lingayat leaders drifted away from the Congress in the 1970s. They realigned, instead, with the anti-Congress JP movement. This political shift by a dominant caste in Karnataka mirrored what happened further north in Gujarat. Just as the origins of the BJP's dominance in Gujarat can be traced to the dominant caste group of Patels moving away from the Congress in the early 1980s, the party's rise in Karnataka owes a great deal to the Lingayat vote shifting away from the Congress and towards the BJP from the 1990s.

Gujarat's political switch—of the Patels aligning with the JP movement—was also accelerated by the then Congress state chief Jinabhai Darjee carving out a new KHAM (Kshatriya Harijan Adivasi Muslim) social coalition for the party in the late 1970s.[23] Later, Chief Minister Madhavsinh Solanki built on the KHAM formula to drive Congress dominance in the early 1980s, further alienating the Patels, who felt they were being cut out of the power structure. Eventually, this caste group became the bedrock of the BJP's political rise in Gujarat. A similar shift happened with the Lingayats in Karnataka.

When Rajiv Gandhi Sacked a Chief Minister at an Airport: Veerendra Patil and the Origins of the BJP's Lingayat Breach

The career of Lingayat leader Veerendra Patil is instructive for understanding this change. He was the Congress chief minister at the time of the great split of 1969, and chose to leave the party with another two-time former chief minister, S. Nijalingappa. Patil continued as Karnataka chief minister in the Congress (O) that was formed in opposition to Indira Gandhi's Congress (I), before losing the elections in 1972. Through the 1970s, ex-Congress Lingayat leaders cast their lot with the anti-Congress Janata Party. However, after the Emergency, when Indira Gandhi contested a by-election from Karnataka's Chikmagalur in 1978, Patil, who now headed the Janata Party's Karnataka unit, was chosen to stand against her.[24] Indira won easily, giving birth to the famous poll slogan 'Ek Sherni Sau Langur, Chikmagalur Bhai Chikmagalur' (One tigress, 100 langurs, Chikmagalur brother Chikmagalur).

In 1980, when the BJP was formed, some Lingayat leaders remained with the Janata Party, others had returned to the Congress. Patil was among the latter. Despite their Chikmagalur battle, Indira Gandhi appointed him a cabinet minister in 1980.[25] In the decade that followed, the Congress tried to woo Lingayat voters. As part of this outreach, when it came back to power in Karnataka in 1989, Patil was appointed chief minister again—the first time such apex leadership was given to a Congress Lingayat leader in two decades, thus signalling a shift in Congress strategy. His subsequent unceremonious removal from power in 1990 by Rajiv Gandhi, similarly, came to signify an important turning point in Karnataka politics. It was seen by many in the community as an insult to Lingayat pride and heralded the first breach by the BJP into the community's vote. A year later, in the parliamentary elections, it won the party its very first victories in Karnataka.[26]

This is how Patil's public sacking came to be. In October 1990, communal riots broke out in some parts of Karnataka. Patil, who had just suffered a minor stroke, was convalescing at home. Congress leader Rajiv Gandhi, having recently lost the 1989 elections, decided to cut short the Sadbhavana Yatra he had embarked upon in north India and make a sudden, 'unexpected' visit to Bangalore to take stock. After a helicopter ride to the riot-hit Channapatna town on 7 October, he met Patil at his home and drove back to Bangalore airport to board a chartered aircraft. Several ministers and hundreds of party workers had gathered to see him off. As they waited outside the VIP lounge, Gandhi met with waiting reporters. One of them asked him when the state government would start functioning properly again. Gandhi replied, 'In four days.' Before the startling announcement could be fully digested, he added that the Congress Legislature Party would meet in a couple of days to 'elect a new leader' and that Patil 'was not really well' and had 'agreed to step down'. As he took their leave, Rajiv Gandhi added 'with a twinkle in his eye': 'You have got good copy.'[27]

To the large number of Congressmen gathered on the tarmac, the impact of this off-the-cuff announcement was 'to put it mildly, as shocking as it was dramatic'. Gandhi had no doubt expected that the change of guard would be smooth. But Patil fought back, and publicly. He invited journalists and a Doordarshan TV crew to his house. He told them that, while he had been temporarily unwell, his faculties were intact and he would keep working as chief minister. Speaking to Doordarshan, Patil was 'more or less declaring war against his own party'. 'I was not asked to step down and I am not stepping down,' he said in his televised speech,[28] adding that the leadership issue 'did not arise when Gandhi had met him'.[29] This was now a full-blown constitutional crisis. With the chief minister remaining adamant, the Congress calling a legislators' meeting to elect a new leader and both sides claiming to have the required numbers, President R. Venkataraman declared President's Rule in the state on 10 October, after duly seeking advice from Governor Bhanu Pratap Singh.[30]

V.P. Singh was then serving as prime minister of a Janata Dal-led coalition government in Delhi. His party offered Patil unconditional support towards winning the floor test. Its state leader Jeevaraj Alva accused Rajiv Gandhi of a 'dictatorial attitude' that must be 'condemned by all those who still have some dignity irrespective of political affiliations'.[31] The airport sacking had become such a public spectacle that the prime minister now personally entered the debate, directly targeting Rajiv Gandhi. He released a statement saying, 'Despite its huge majority in the house, the Congress government had been destabilised by the party president, Mr Rajiv Gandhi.'[32] As *The Times of India* noted, 'under normal circumstances, Congress leaders should have been angry with the National Front and the governor. But it appears they were angrier with Mr Patil for bringing the situation to such a pass.' The 'coup' at the airport, the newspaper concluded, had 'boomeranged'.[33] In the event, Patil lost the battle. S. Bangarappa was elected as his replacement and President's Rule was finally revoked on 17 October.[34]

The drama around Patil's public humiliation handed the BJP a vital opening: it created a new narrative of injured Lingayat pride. Around this time, the BJP's B.S. Yediyurappa, who had started as an RSS pracharak and entered politics with the Jan Sangh, was just beginning to establish his credentials as a Lingayat leader. Yediyurappa, then president of the party's state unit, declared that Patil's removal by Rajiv Gandhi was the 'most uncultured way to treat a chief minister'. He alleged that the communal riots that claimed forty lives and led to Patil's sacking had, in fact, been 'instigated' by a group of Congress leaders, led by C.K. Jaffer Sharief. According to Yediyurappa, Sharief had the Congress High Command's tacit approval for the 'coup' against Patil.[35]

A decade earlier, in neighbouring Andhra Pradesh, Telugu film actor N.T. Rama Rao had formed the TDP on a platform of regional sub-nationalism after Rajiv Gandhi, as Congress general secretary, publicly admonished the then Andhra chief minister Tanguturi Anjaiah in 1982 on the tarmac of Hyderabad's Begumpet airport. Gandhi had been annoyed by a crowd of partymen welcoming him with a band playing drums and other instruments. He was there on a private visit, and is said to have admonished Anjaiah, calling him a 'buffoon', when he learnt that the crowd was brought by the chief minister.[36] Patil himself indirectly compared his fall from grace at the airport with the Anjaiah incident. 'In this very state, and in next-door Andhra Pradesh, powerful chief ministers were humiliated at the polls because people thought they were corrupt,' he said in an interview. 'Unless Rajiv Gandhi gets rid of the power peddlers around him, his own political career will be finished.'[37]

A year after the Patil incident, in the 1991 parliamentary elections, the BJP opened its account in Karnataka, winning four seats. Patil, who remained opposed to the saffron party until he died, immediately saw the link. This was more about anti-Congress-ism and regional pride than religious identity. In an interview shortly after the 1991 election, he explained how the BJP's fortunes had suddenly changed. People were 'turning to the BJP', he said. 'During the last assembly poll [1989], the BJP was hard-pressed even to find candidates who were willing to contest on their symbol. Then they got only four seats. But in the 1991 Lok Sabha polls, the BJP candidates came first or a close second in over a hundred assembly constituencies and raised their percentage of the vote from 2.5 percent to 30 percent. Now there is a queue for BJP tickets, and if they are not careful, the Congress will once again sit in the opposition in Karnataka.'[38]

For many Lingayat voters, Patil's removal was a sign of the 'eclipse of Lingayat power in Karnataka. Within the Congress Party, there was no other Lingayat leader who could be projected as a substitute.'[39] It was a critical moment because, although Yediyurappa was Lingayat too, 'this community was never with BJP till the late-1980s', says V. Anand, who managed Yediyurappa's social media and communications campaign in 2018. We were meeting over lunch in Bengaluru in February 2020. Anand emphasised the critical role of the Lingayat vote in the BJP's growth. By now, it was estimated to be between 17 and 19 per cent of the state's population.[40] 'That incident with Patil changed things forever and helped BJP in 1990,' he said. 'It was seen as the humiliation of the Lingayat community, and Congress never recovered from that. This 17–19 per cent of the population, which was committed to the Congress, was now alienated and more. Thanks to Yediyurappa, BJP could catch this group. Since then, they have never left the BJP or Yediyurappa, and that was the price Congress paid.'[41]

It is important to stress that the Lingayat vote did not shift immediately, nor can it be regarded as a monolith. However, the Patil incident began a process whereby, through the 1990s, a major chunk of Lingayat voters, who had initially shifted to the Janata Party in the 1980s, gradually began moving to the BJP. Initially, this vote bank was split between the Janata Party, the Janata Dal, the Janata Dal (S) and the BJP. Over time, it came to form a solid caste-based block that served as the fulcrum of the BJP's growth in north and central Karnataka. The Lingayat vote was particularly potent for the party because it was concentrated in about seventy seats, with influence in another thirty. In comparison, by 2018, former prime minister H.D. Deve Gowda's JD(S)'s primary vote base had narrowed down geographically to the Vokkaliga-dominant areas of Old Mysore in southern Karnataka.[42] The BJP capitalised on the erosion of the caste alliance Urs had stitched together for the Congress, as well as the decline of the Congress (O), Ramakrishna Hegde's Janata Dal and JD(S) to emerge as the primary anti-Congress force in Karnataka.

By contrast, the Congress's support base remained more evenly spread out across Karnataka, among other OBC castes, like Siddaramaiah's Kuruba community, as well as among Dalits and Muslims. However, because these communities are generally more dispersed across constituencies, in several state elections after 2004, the Congress has ended up in the peculiar position of winning more overall vote share than the BJP but considerably fewer seats. This happened in 2004, 2008 and 2018.[43] The only exception was 2013, when Yediyurappa had briefly separated from the BJP to form his own regional outfit and split the BJP vote. Simply put, winning the Lingayat vote has been the making of the BJP in Karnataka.

Karnataka's Mini-Ayodhya: Hubli's Idgah Maidan, Hindutva and the Making of the BJP

If the Ayodhya movement was the turning point for the BJP in north India, in Karnataka it would be the five-year-long dispute over Hubli's Idgah Maidan or the Kittur Rani Chennamma Maidan, which flared up between 1992 and 1995. Chatting over lunch in his office, C.N. Ashwathnarayan, then deputy chief minister of Karnataka, attributed the rise of the BJP in big part to the party having a 'no appeasement policy of minorities'.[44] This is a common response from state party leaders when asked why Karnataka is different from the other south Indian states and what explains the BJP's rise here. 'By and large, Karnataka has a mindset of the rightist ideology from the beginning,' said Lehar Singh Siroya, senior BJP MLC and former state unit treasurer, who was said to be close to both B.S. Yediyurappa, former chief minister, and the central party leadership.

'It's not like West Bengal or others. *Yahan rightist vichardhara hai* [we have right-wing thinking here]. The reason for our growth is a rightist approach. Leftist thinking is not acceptable to the public in this state. They are averse to it.'[45]

The only difference between Hindutva sentiments in the Hindi heartland and Karnataka, many leaders believe, is in the public emphasis, packaging and volume of it in party communications. 'BJP is a relatively moderate party here,' observed V. Anand. 'What you see in UP is not here. Lord Ram is important here, but you don't have to live for it like in UP. Even in coastal areas, they are very vocal. They won't let you take them for a ride, but they will not be of a violent kind. That streak is there in Karnataka. We have a silent, strong community but accountable cadre.'[46]

This was not always so. The Jan Sangh won only four of 216 seats in the 1967 state assembly polls. When Ram Sewak, a Jan Sangh candidate, managed to save his deposit in the polls in 1967, such was his joy that he remembers having taken out a victory procession despite having lost the election. As he told the journalist Veeraraghav, 'Those were the pitiable days. Nobody was willing to touch us. We were almost untouchables.'[47] Even a decade later, in 1977, only nine of the sixty Janata Party MLAs were from the Sangh. The BJP then won eighteen of 224 seats in 1983 before being virtually wiped out in the late 1980s.

It was at this point that, in tandem with the Ayodhya movement in the north, a local religious dispute over a playing ground in the eastern town of Hubli proved to be a game changer. From just four seats in the state assembly in 1989, the BJP jumped fourfold to forty seats in 1994. All its leaders agree that the Idgah Maidan was pivotal here. In the north, the Ayodhya dispute had festered for over a hundred years as a localised property dispute before becoming the political flashpoint that transformed the BJP's political fortunes in the 1990s. The roots of the Hubli dispute lay in a 999-year lease agreement that the Anjuman-e-Islam (AeI), a local Muslim body, had signed with the local municipality in 1921. The lease conferred on it the right to use the 1.5-acre maidan, also called the Kittur Rani Chennamma Maidan, twice a year for prayers. The rest of the year, it was a playground for cricket and other sports, for holding fairs during jatras and public meetings by political parties. The problem began when the AeI decided to 'construct a building there' in 1990.[48] 'It was opposed by everybody,' recalls Lehar Singh. 'Otherwise that ground was for playing. It was used for namaaz only on Ramadan and Id, rest of the time for cricket.'[49] The dispute assumed political overtones when the Congress state government gave the AeI permission to construct this building. Many local residents argued that they would no longer be able to play cricket there and a group opposed to the construction (B.S. Shettar and 105 others) went to court.

The government's order was overturned by a local munsif court, which held it 'illegal and ineffectual' and upheld the 'right of people to use the Idgah maidan for jatras and other activities'.[50] The court also ordered the removal of the structure built by the AeI. Both the additional sessions judge and the Karnataka High Court in July 1992 agreed with the munsif order and directed the Hubli-Dharwad Municipal Corporation (HDMC) to demolish the building. The AeI then appealed to the Supreme Court, which stayed the demolition of the building at the time, while keeping the main appeal pending.[51] The BJP's local leadership organised around this complex local dispute and that 'small piece of land became synonymous with Hindu mobilisation in the state'.[52]

In the north, the then BJP president Murali Manohar Joshi had gone on an Ekta Yatra to Kashmir to hoist the national flag in Srinagar. Coinciding with this, in the south, the local BJP leadership decided to launch a movement to hoist the national flag at Hubli's Idgah Maidan. On Republic Day 1992, a group of BJP, RSS and VHP leaders planned to hoist the tricolour at the Idgah Maidan in sync with Joshi's flag-hoisting at Srinagar's Lal Chowk. When the AeI refused to allow the flag-hoisting, arguing that this was private property, Hubli erupted. The Congress state government under S. Bangarappa backed the AeI. It denied the protesters permission for flag-hoisting, but despite prohibitory orders, a group of young men managed to enter the ground and hoist the tricolour. As *The Times of India* reported later, 'the matter would have ended there, but for the panicky reaction of the police, who removed the flag. This made the issue contentious.'[53]

Sure enough, a case was filed in a local court against the police for insulting the national flag. The BJP, the RSS and the VHP set up a Rashtra Dhwaj Gaurav Sanrakshan Committee (Committee for Protecting the Honour of the National Flag).[54] What had begun as a local property dispute now became a larger controversy that involved the national flag. The Sanrakshan Committee declared that it did not care who hoisted the flag as long as it was hoisted—implying that refusal to allow flying the tricolour on the disputed spot by anyone was problematic—and the matter turned into a political flashpoint.[55] The state government took a limited, legalistic view, thus playing into the BJP's hands. As an official told reporters at the time, 'The collection of a crowd was what aggravated the Ayodhya problem. We are not apprehending an Ayodhya-type situation but we are convinced that once people are allowed to collect at a place, it could lead to trouble.' The legal view was that, since the Idgah Maidan was disputed property, nobody could hoist a flag in it. 'Even the Anjuman-e-Islam has no right to hoist a flag there,' local officials argued. 'If anyone wants to hoist a flag, they can do so in places specified by the flag code, but not on a disputed land.'[56]

Records from that time show that the state government's decisions on the Idgah Maidan issue were directly monitored not just by the Congress chief minister but also by Prime Minister Narasimha Rao, with Union minister Sikandar Bakht acting as his eyes and ears on the controversy. Between 1992 and 1995, the BJP made five abortive bids to hoist a flag at the Idgah Maidan. It became a rallying point for party leaders across the state and a powerful magnet for the leading lights of the Ayodhya movement. Uma Bharti, for example, was barred from entering the state in 1994. She somehow managed to reach Hubli before she was arrested by the local police. 'I was arrested before I entered the Idgah maidan,' she later recalled. 'I didn't hoist the national flag and had not made any provocative speech … In the entire country this was the only place where hoisting the national flag was banned.'[57] Soon after her arrest, four people were killed and over a hundred injured when the police opened fire to disperse a 5,000-strong crowd that had gathered at the Sawai Gandharva Hall in Hubli's Deshpande Nagar after being turned away from flag-hoisting. The BJP called for a 'black day' across Karnataka, while Chief Minister Veerappa Moily accused the BJP of being responsible for the deaths.[58]

Why did the flag-hoisting become such a contentious issue? For the Congress government, as officials briefed reporters at the time, the BJP's call for a huge crowd to gather 'clearly indicates that the intention is to provoke people and create a violent atmosphere not just in Hubli but in the entire state'. To the AeI, the flag-hoisting seemed like a threatened land grab and they feared that a crowd could bring down the disputed structure.[59] Former Hubli mayor Firdous Kunoon told the journalist Veeraraghav, 'Muslims were scared that if you want to put a pole and hoist a flag, you will prove it's your property or public property.' The BJP projected it as the litmus test of patriotism. As Firdous put it, 'In my schooldays, in the same ground, there were firecracker shows at night on the last day of Ganesh pooja, but that has now stopped.'[60]

As the dispute festered and communal tensions mounted, the BJP's critics accused it of playing 'divisive politics'. A newspaper editorial at the time argued, 'The BJP's objective in flaunting its patriotic credentials and taking upon itself the onerous task of checking the nationalist credentials of all citizens, especially the Muslims, is in keeping with its divisive politics, intended to strengthen its electoral base. It has not been averse in this context to adopt provocative postures and play politics with the national flag … Admittedly, if the BJP's motivated campaign to depict the Muslims as unpatriotic has influenced the gullible, it is because of the reluctance of Muslims to hoist the flag themselves at the maidan. One reason for this was that until the BJP chose the site in 1992, it had occurred to no one, including the BJP, that a flag needed to be hoisted there to prove one's devotion to the motherland.'[61]

BJP's Lehar Singh points out, 'We got a big boost with the Ayodhya movement plus what happened in the Idgah Maidan in Hubli. The Yediyurappa and Ananth Kumar combination did really well for us … Ananth Kumar and Yediyurappa successfully exploited the issue and in the process brought our MLAs from four to forty in 1994. Because of this combination and jodi [couple], we could win thirteen seats in 1999 Lok Sabha poll.'[62] BJP's Jagdish Shettar, who won an MLA election from Hubli Rural in 1994 and has been the BJP's candidate from that seat ever since, summed up this political bump for Network18: '10,000 votes was our vote bank in Hubli before 1994 in 1989 and 1985. I got 46,000 votes in 1994.'[63]

The Idgah controversy was finally put to rest politically by H.D. Deve Gowda when he was chief minister in 1995. After an all-party meeting, he persuaded the AeI itself to hoist the national flag at the maidan. Yediyurappa had threatened a dharna with all forty BJP MLAs and a state-wide Hubli-chalo agitation if the issue was not resolved,[64] so Gowda's was a prudent solution. The Ram Temple issue did not cut it for the BJP in Karnataka, but the Idgah movement's appeal, melding a dispute over a religious space with the national tricolour and patriotic sentiments, successfully turned it into the 'Ayodhya of the south',[65] albeit at a much lower temperature. Legally, the case reached its denouement in 2010, when a two-member bench of the Supreme Court upheld the orders of the lower courts and ordered the demolition of the AeI structure. The apex court also ruled that the ground was the exclusive property of the HDMC, with the AeI having the right to conduct prayers twice a year.[66]

The Idgah Maidan movement was not an aberration. In the coastal town of Chikkamagaluru, the BJP has been involved in a similar political mobilisation around a disputed religious site—the Sree Guru Dattatreya Bababudan Swamy Dargah on the Bababudangiri Hill. For decades, the site has been a syncretic shrine. Hindus consider it the final resting place of Dattatreya, considered an incarnation of Vishnu, Shiva and Brahma, while Muslims believe that the dargah is one of the earliest centres of Sufism in India, with Sufi saint Dada Hayat Mir Qalandar having lived there for years. In the late 1980s, the BJP, VHP and RSS cadres started demanding that the shrine be declared a Hindu temple. 'Prior to 1964, the shrine Shree Guru Dattatreya Bababudan Swamy Dargah was a symbol of religious harmony, where both Hindus and Muslims offered prayers at the same shrine.'[67] The area became disputed in 1964 when it was allotted to the Waqf Board by the Karnataka government. When local Hindus went to court, a district court pronounced in 1978 that the shrine was venerated by both Hindus and Muslims and ordered that status quo be maintained, a decision that was also endorsed by the Karnataka High Court in 1991.[68] The matter took a political turn when the BJP sought to turn Bababudangiri into yet another Ayodhya. While efforts to galvanise more Hindu pilgrims to the shrine began in the early 1990s, the Bajrang Dal and the VHP together organised a pilgrim procession on a noticeably large scale in 1997. The number of pilgrims undertaking the annual journey by foot to the shrine began to swell in size thereafter. In 2002 and 2003, over 20,000 devotees were estimated to have visited the shrine annually in December to observe Datta Jayanti.[69] 'Both issues of the Idgah Maidan and Baba Budangari were not of the same emotive appeal as the Ram Temple. They did not turn into such a test of identity as the Ayodhya dispute did,' says Veeraraghav. But 'they certainly helped the BJP to consolidate its constituency in Karnataka as it made its first political inroads'.[70]

How fundamental is the usage of political Hindutva for the BJP in general? 'It is a by-product [of] whatever we do,' said a senior BJP minister in Karnataka, speaking off-the-record. Hard-line Hindutva leaders, he said, 'don't regret whatever they do. They feel that we do it for our culture, our sentiment and our feelings. The sense of Hindutva is our very strength.' Politics, in his view, was about identity and 'identity is what we will ask about most. If you ask the question, who are we, the answer to that question is most important. Preservation and propagation of our culture is our first and foremost priority. Then comes everything else. As an organisation we can talk about it. People appreciate it. As a government we can't do it.'[71]

A Question of Language: Konkani, Hindi and Why the BJP Made Early Coastal and Urban Inroads

Political movements can provide a push for a political party, but they may not be quite enough. To grow, parties need a critical mass of voters, key social groups on their side and a strong machinery. Since 1991, when it first won four of the state's twenty-eight Lok Sabha seats, the Karnataka BJP has always maintained a vote share in the high-twenties in every national poll. The party had its first wins in the parliamentary constituencies in Bidar on the state's northernmost tip, Mangalore on its southern coastline, Tumkur in the south and Bangalore South in the state capital. It won each of these seats by large margins (with over 40 per cent of the votes in each constituency) and steadily used these areas as a base to expand its footprint outwards. Each of these seats was also representative of the early social coalition that the party was creating in Karnataka.

In Bidar, the party won because of Ram Chandra Veerappa, a Dalit farmer leader who was known as a 'progressive nationalist' in the constituency. 'We won on his shoulders,' says Lehar Singh.[72] He represented the party's social push with farmers. Yediyurappa himself was a farmer leader who had won his first assembly election from Shikaripura after going on Cycle Yatras.[73] Tumkur, the seat of the Siddaganga shrine, came to the party because of S. Mallikarjunaiah, a Lingayat leader.[74] He represented the Lingayat base that the party would subsequently build under Yediyurappa. The party has never lost Bangalore South, a seat first won by the late Ananth Kumar, since 1991. It represents the urban constituency that the party was beginning to appeal to. Yediyurappa and Ananth Kumar were later to become the twin engines of the BJP's growth.

Mangalore, on the coast, is symbolic of Hindutva's increasing acceptability in the state. In the 1940s and '50s, the Sangh set up its first Karnataka shakhas along the coast. The coastal areas also had a large Muslim population, were prosperous, and were home to Saraswat Brahmins from Maharashtra and Goa. Mangalore has often seen communal flare-ups and these tensions mean that even inadvertent accidents could take on a communal colour there. The suspicion of cow slaughter was among the most common flashpoints for such flare-ups. As a former senior police office recounted, 'There was a typical example of a van which people suspected of carrying cows. It wasn't, but the driver panicked and sped up to escape those chasing him. While speeding like this, he ended up hitting a person from that community purely by accident and this became a big communal riot.'[75] By 1996, the party expanded further along the coastline, adding the seats of Dharwad North and Kanara. It expanded next in the areas of Kolar, Gulbarga and Bellary.[76] By 1998, virtually all of the Karnataka coast, from Belgaum in the north to Mysore in the south, was saffron. Despite a major dip in 1999 (when the party was reduced to just seven seats), the BJP has remained a dominant state party in all the national elections since (see Table 15.2). However, in contrast to its dominance in parliamentary elections in four successive elections in Karnataka (2004–2019), it had never managed to win a full majority in provincial elections until 2018, although it did emerge as the single largest party in 2004, 2008 and 2018 and formed the state government then (see Table 15.3).

Table 15.2: The BJP in Karnataka: Lok Sabha Elections (1980–2019)

Year	*Lok Sabha Elections: Party-wise Details (Total Seats: 28)*	*BJP's Inflection Points*
1980	Congress: 27; Janata Party: 1	No BJP wins, Congress dominant

Year	*Lok Sabha Elections: Party-wise Details (Total Seats: 28)*	*BJP's Inflection Points*
1984	Congress: 24; Janata Party: 4	No BJP wins, Congress dominant
1989	Congress: 26; Janata Dal: 2	No BJP wins, Congress dominant
1991	Congress: 23, BJP: 4, Janata: 1	First BJP breakthrough, a year after the Veerendra Patil sacking
1996	Janata Dal: 16; BJP: 6; Congress: 5; KCP: 1	Slight expansion by BJP, Janata Dal replaces Congress as the leading party
1998	NDA: 16 (BJP: 13 and Lok Shakti: 3); Congress: 9; Janata Dal: 3	The first time that the BJP wins a majority of Karnataka parliamentary seats, as part of the NDA alliance with Ramakrishna Hegde's Lok Shakti formed in 1997 (after Hegde, a former Janata chief minister, is expelled from JD-S)
1999	Congress: 18; BJP: 7; JD(U): 3	BJP declines
2004	BJP: 18; Congress: 8; JD(S): 2	BJP resurgence
2009	BJP: 19; Congress: 6; JD(S): 3	BJP dominance consolidated
2014	BJP: 17; Congress: 9; JD(S): 2	BJP dominance continues
2019	BJP: 26 (25 + support for 1 independent); Congress: 1; JD(S): 1	BJP sweeps state

Source: ECI, research and analysis by Nalin Mehta, Rajiv Pundir

Table 15.3: The BJP in Karnataka: Vidhana Soudha Elections (1983–2019)

Year	*Vidhana Soudha Elections: Party-wise Details (Total seats: 224)*	*BJP Inflection Points*
1983	Janata: 95; Congress (I): 82; BJP: 18; Independents: 22	BJP's first inroads
1985	Janata: 139; Congress: 65; BJP: 2; Independents: 13	BJP declines
1989	Congress: 178; JD: 24; BJP: 4; Independents: 12	BJP support remains negligible
1994	JD: 115; BJP: 40; Congress: 34; KCP: 10; Independents: 18	First BJP expansion, after Idgah Maidan agitation and Veerendra Patil sacking

Year	*Vidhana Soudha Elections: Party-wise Details (Total seats: 224)*	*BJP Inflection Points*
1999	Congress: 132; BJP: 44; JD(U): 18, JD(S): 10; Independents: 19	BJP consolidates
2004	BJP: 79; Congress: 65; JD(S): 58	The first time that the BJP becomes the single largest party in a hung house, aligns with the JD-S. Both parties agree to have a chief minister each for twenty months. Yediyurappa becomes first BJP deputy chief minister—under JD-S Chief Minister H.D. Kumaraswamy—and the first BJP chief minister in south India in 2007, but his government lasted only five days as JD (S) withdrew support
2008	BJP: 110; Congress: 80; JD(S): 28	BJP wins much bigger tally, forms its first full-term government in south India (though it did not win a simple majority, falling short of the half-way mark)
2013	Congress: 122; BJP: 40; JD(S): 40; KJP: 6; BSR Congress: 4	BJP tally declines substantially after Yediyurappa leaves the party and forms a new regional party that splits the BJP vote
2018	BJP: 104; Congress: 80; JD(S): 38; KPJP: 1; BSP: 1; Independent: 1	BJP again voted in as single largest party, though short of simple majority. Forms government that fell in 2.5 days; JD (S)–Congress post-poll alliance takes power, but falls in 2019 after sixteen MLAs resign. Yediyurappa-led BJP formed government again in 2019. BJP appoints new chief minister, Basavaraj Bommai in July 2021

Source: ECI, research and analysis by Nalin Mehta, Rajiv Pundir

Figure 15.1: The BJP's Spatial Expansion in Karnataka Explained in Five Charts (Lok Sabha Elections)

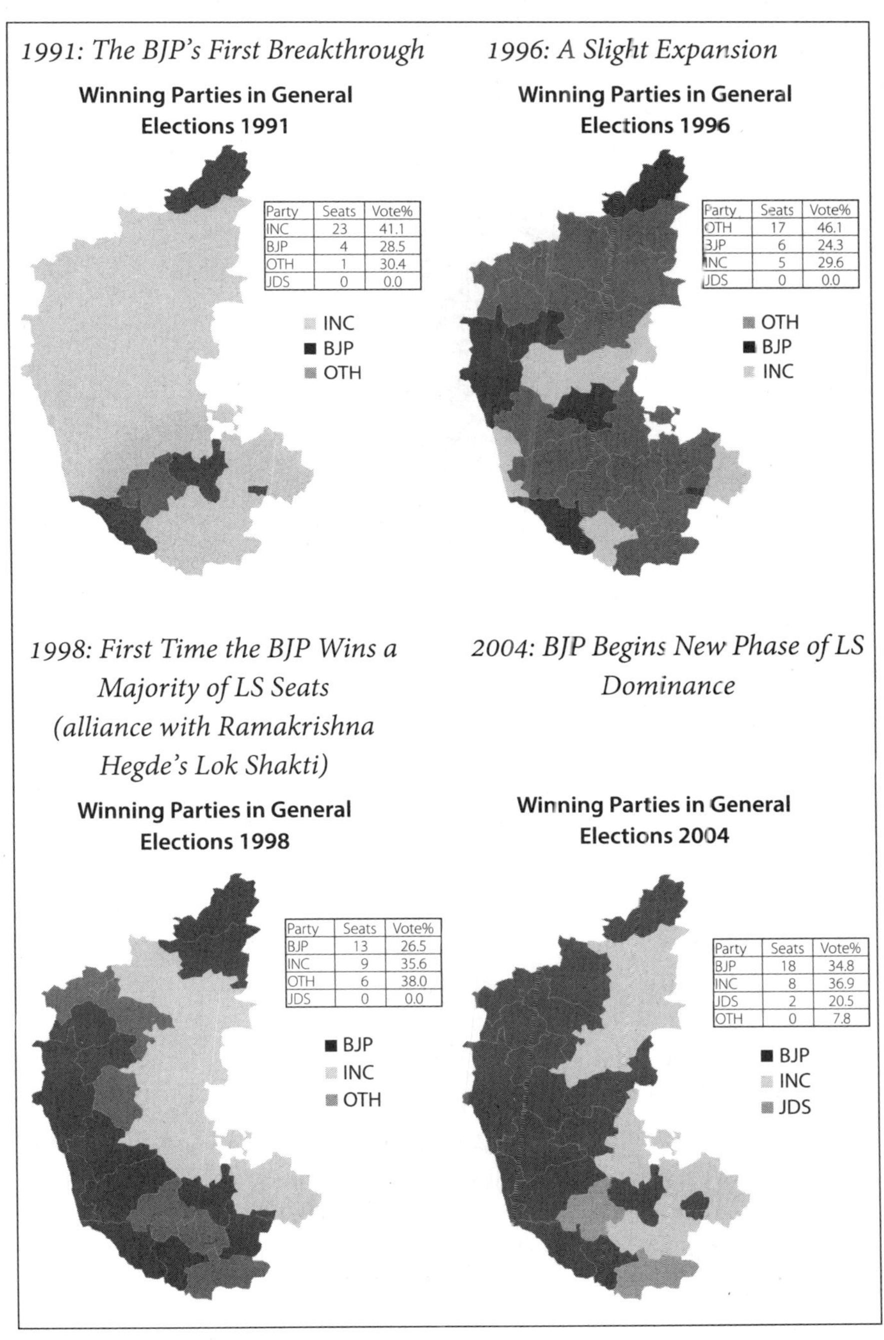

2009: The BJP Consolidates Dominance, a pattern that repeats in the 2014 and 2019 Lok Sabha Polls

Source: ECI data, spatially analysed and visualised by Nalin Mehta, Rishabh Srivastava on https://pollniti.com/#!

B.Y. Vijayendra, the BJP's state vice-president and son of former chief minister Yediyurappa, recalled how his father had laid the foundations of the party. BSY (as Yediyurappa senior is known) went on 'padyatras in the early 1990s which really helped', he says. 'The party grew first in coastal areas, then later in the north ... So, our first stage of growth was in urban areas like Bengaluru, the second stage was in coastal areas because of RSS and the third stage was in north Karnataka because of BSY and his padyatras and our outreach to farmers.'[77]

Coastal Karnataka was, so to say, the 'cradle of the Sangh' in Karnataka. As V. Anand puts it, 'There are huge shakhas there and people are deeply committed to RSS there. Tomorrow, say if they give a ticket to me and those guys hate my face, they will say, it's okay—they would say that he is appointed by BJP, so they will still vote for me. That is the commitment of our cadre on the entire coastal Karnataka.' Before the BJP, the Jan Sangh too had won its first-ever election victory of any kind in south India in coastal Karnataka when Dr V.S. Acharya was elected president of the Udupi City Municipality in 1968.[78] He later became home minister in the second Yediyurappa government in 2008.[79]

Until the late 1980s, the party was largely sustained by RSS pracharaks. Among them was Bhaurao Deshpande, originally from the RSS and later organising secretary of the Jan Sangh,[80] who is regarded as the party's chief builder in its early days in Karnataka.[81] Deshpande, after whom the BJP office in Bengaluru is named, is said to have also groomed Yediyurappa. Also from the RSS were pracharaks like Yadav Rao Joshi (1914–1992), a Nagpur Brahmin who initiated the Sangh's work in Karnataka in 1941.[82] He is regarded as a father figure by many RSS workers, who say he was also a 'good musician like Bhimsen Joshi'.[83]

The interesting question here is, why did the BJP not expand outwards from the coastal areas until the 1990s? The answer lies in the language barrier. The early pracharaks were all from Maharashtra and spoke Marathi, not Kannada. Radhakrishnan Holla, RSS communications head for Karnataka, told me that 'in the early days, in the 1960s and '70s, we were big in Bangalore and Mangalore and areas like Shivamogga. In those days, the pracharaks came from Maharashtra, so language was a huge problem.'[84] RSS worker Vadhiraj added that linguistic barriers did not matter in the coastal areas where 'the language was Konkani, so they could talk there in the old days'.[85] BJP MLC Lehar Singh explained that 'initially the party grew with north Indians from Bangalore, who were attracted to Jan Sangh'. He too had moved to the city in 1969 from Udaipur.[86] In the early 2000s, however, the RSS began training local pracharaks who spoke Kannada. This is borne out by the Karnataka Sangh's social-media pages, which by 2020 were predominantly in Kannada (see Chapter 12).[87]

Two Leaders, Hindutva and a New BJP Caste Coalition: The Ananth Kumar–Yediyurappa Era

Until the late 1980s, the BJP, and the Jan Sangh before it, had no stable social base in Karnataka. 'Big people come to a party when there is a base,' said Lehar Singh. 'Dedicated karyakartas were always there, but what can they do beyond a point without social leaders?' This changed in the 1990s, under the twin leadership of former RSS pracharaks Yediyurappa and Ananth Kumar, who forged a new social combination, expanding into new geographies. Yediyurappa is a Lingayat[88] from KR Pet in Mandya. He had, in fact, been named after the presiding deity of a twelfth-century Shaivite temple in Tumkur. The late Ananth Kumar, a Brahmin from Hubli, was a lawyer who practised in the Karnataka High Court.[89]

Yediyurappa initially made inroads as a farmer leader in this region, earning the sobriquet 'Raitha Nayaka' (Farmer Leader).[90] He first came into the 'limelight after he undertook a padayatra of bonded labourers from Shikaripur to Shimoga in 1981'. Two years later, in 1983, he was one of the BJP's first eighteen MLAs in Karnataka.[91] After Veerendra Patil's sacking in 1990, Yediyurappa became the fulcrum of Lingayat mobilisation. 'Lingayats are in large numbers in at least ten–twelve districts and in eighty to ninety assembly seats and ten–twelve Lok Sabha seats,' Anand explained, adding:[92]

> When they shifted towards BJP, the whole game changed. After Veerendra Patil was sacked, within two–three years, the whole scenario changed. They [Congress] still haven't recovered from that ... It is because of this leadership that the growth of the BJP in Karnataka was bigger than in any other than any state in South India. Yediyurappa expanded the party, brought in a committed group of Lingayats and we grew because of his leadership in north and central Karnataka. We moved from being four to forty to seventy-ninety to 110 in the state assembly because we expanded into new areas. Similarly, credit has to be given to Ananth Kumar. We have won Bangalore South so many times that it seems so easy, and today some people feel that any donkey can contest and win from that seat, that was not the case at that time. Because Bangalore South has a huge population of Vokkaligas who were not exactly BJP's pals at the time. Despite all this, Ananth Kumar won that seat six times, even though the caste balance of that constituency was not in favour of Brahmins. That is a good credit to him and the party.

'We were a Brahmin-based party,' says B.Y. Vijayendraa. 'But BSY identified other people in the coalition like C.J. Halnol, a Dalit leader, H.N. Nanjegowda for Vokkaligas. They were successfully roped into the BJP. We couldn't have got people of such stature earlier. A lot of Dalits moved into BJP due to this move. This was a big turning point for BJP in 1994–95. In earlier days, we were a Brahmin-dominated party and an urban party. We then expanded our base. Pre-2000, we were seen as a Lingayat and Brahmin party. Now, after the 2019 Lok Sabha elections, we are a Brahmin plus Lingayat plus Backward plus Vokkaliga party.'[93]

Growth did not come without battles over control, both within the state unit and between the state unit and the central leadership. During his first term as chief minister, there were allegations of corruption in mining contracts in Bellary against Yediyurappa,[94] which undermined the BJP's national campaign against corruption and caused deep intra-party tensions.[95] It led to Yediyurappa leaving the BJP in 2012 and fighting the 2013 elections as the head of a new regional party, the Karnataka Janata Paksh (KJP). Though his outfit won only six seats, it bagged a crucial 9.79 per cent of the vote share,[96] badly damaging the BJP, which plunged to its lowest tally in the state in two decades. This demonstrated Yediyurappa's personal influence in rural areas, leading to his return to the party in 2013.

While both Ananth Kumar and Yediyurappa expanded the party, their deep rivalry also set back some of the advances. 'Yediyurappa became leader of opposition in 1994. In 1996, Ananth became MP. From there, their differences started,' recalls Lehar Singh. 'Both started having a rivalry. This came to a peak in 2004 when Yediyurappa was not allowed to become Opposition leader for two months … All the deterioration later for BJP was because of their rivalry. This rivalry was also caused by the party's central high command which was a divided house with two factions—for and against Yediyurappa.'[97]

While the Lingayats moved to the BJP, the other big social group in Karnataka, the Vokkaligas, who make up about 15 per cent of the population, moved to Deve Gowda's JD(S), the social base for which continues to be the Old Mysore region. Interestingly, while the BJP did appropriate some Vokkaliga leaders, it has never really targeted the community's vote aggressively, like it has with other social groups. Partly, this was because the BJP's own Vokkaliga leaders felt it was a pointless exercise. 'They have a huge inferiority complex in our party and are always in awe of the Deve Gowda family. Nobody ever wanted to personally antagonise the Deve Gowda family,' said a senior party leader. 'Even some of our senior Vokkaliga leaders played convenient politics not to antagonise Deve Gowda. They would go to take his aashirwad to win and do morning hazri at his house [rather than] try and beat him. They never thought of challenging the Gowda family directly. They used to say "aashirwad dein" [please give blessings].'[98] This began to change after 2019, with the BJP making a determined push into Vokkaliga areas. 'In Bengaluru City, we got 28 per cent of Vokkaliga vote, Congress got 17–19 per cent, JD(S) got 10–11 per cent. So Vokkaligas are turning more in favour of us now,' said B.Y. Vijayendra. 'We are now trying to have a positive presence in Old Mysore. We never attempted anything here but now we do.'

Traditionally, the BJP has had very little presence in Hyderabad–Karnataka (dominated by the Congress) and Mysore–Karnataka (dominated by the JD(S)). 'Now we have chance there [Hyderabad–Karnataka] because Mallikarjun Kharge is getting old. We are aggressively looking to target Old Mysore and Hyderabad-Karnataka,' he said.[99]

BJP leaders regard their victory in the Krishnarajpet by-election in Mandya district in December 2019 as a turning point for them in the Old Mysore region. It was a seat that the BJP had never won before and was followed by the defeat of Deve Gowda's grandson, Nikhil Kumaraswamy, in Mandya in the 2019 Lok Sabha election. Says B.Y. Vijayendra, 'If JD(S) continues like this, it will disintegrate. Nikhil Kumaraswamy was defeated in Lok Sabha election in Mandya. KR Pet by-election has changed the dynamic of the old Mysore region. This is a golden opportunity for us. We have to prove ourselves in three years.'[100] The BJP's new positioning on caste balancing in Karnataka was also reflected in the choice of its ministers in 2019. Of its three deputy chief ministers in the state, one was a Vokkaliga (C.N. Ashwathnarayan), one a Dalit (Govind Karjol) and the third a Lingayat (Laxman Savadi). By 2020, as a senior state BJP leader told me, the changed political scenario meant that the party's 'attitude to Vokkaligas is changing'. 'We are getting aggressive. We always wanted to challenge them earlier, but our own Vokkaliga leadership never allowed it. They are now ready to do so because Deve Gowda is weaker. Yediyurappa was ready earlier also, but the leadership of the party didn't have the courage to take them on earlier. Now they do.'[101]

Absorbing the Janata Dal and Fusing It with the Sangh

Although its core Sangh cadre has been the bedrock of the BJP's expansion, the party was significantly helped by the break-up of the Janata Dal in the

1980s. While one Janata faction turned into the JD(S) under Deve Gowda, many JD leaders joined the BJP and gave it muscle in areas where it had no prior presence. They created the second and third tier of its leadership in many districts. As Lehar Singh said, 'In districts where we didn't have any registration, we got in place a new structure with many of these leaders from the Janata Dal. In many districts, we had no leaders, but with JD split we got a new rung of leaders from JDS at the zila level.'[102]

Apart from Yediyurappa and Ananth Kumar, in the 1990s, the BJP had already built a second rung of core leaders from the Sangh: leaders like C.T. Ravi from Chikamagalur, Vishweshwar Hegde Kageri, who became Karnataka assembly speaker in 2019, R. Ashoka in Bengaluru, K.S. Eshwarappa from Shimoga and Jagadish Shettar from Hubli. Now it got an infusion of new leaders from the Janata Dal: Ramesh Vishwanath Katti in Belgaum, Basavaraj Bommai in Hubli, J.C. Madhu Swamy from Tumkur, Govind Karjol from Mudhol, who later became deputy chief minister, and Srinivas Prasad, who switched in 2016. Even Ashwathnarayan moved into the party from the JD(S) in the early 2000s. When I asked him how difficult it was to adjust to a cadre-based and ideological party, he said, 'It's about integration and function. We have objectives and programmes. It's a clear mandate, and if you change you can join us. Each organisation has its own mechanism. You have to fit into it. Other parties are used to big boss deciding everything. Here you don't see big bosses.'[103] Another BJP leader said, 'A lot of people came in because they have a shot at power. They came in because they can be ministers[,] which they can't be with JD(S). They think, why waste time. It's a big motivation for them to come to power.'[104]

Did the entry of defectors from other parties dilute the BJP? 'Ideology kept getting diluted,' lamented a senior leader. 'Power has become the ideology now. Power is necessary, and ideology *ka sawal kahan raha ab* [where's the question of ideology then].' He pointed to the first BJP alliance with JD(S) in 2004, which broke up in 2007, leading to the collapse of the BJP-led government. At the same time, he explained, 'JD(S) was a stepping stone to power for us. We had eighteen ministers. By taking power, the party became resourceful.'[105] In that sense, it was only following the advice that B.L. Mehta gave to the Jan Sangh in the 1960s (see Chapter 8): use power as a means of expansion.

Similarly, the national ascent of Vajpayee in the late 1990s and of Modi after 2014 helped the BJP in Karnataka. 'People get attracted to power,' said a senior BJP legislator. 'People want power. People start gravitating towards a party that has power as they can see the benefit of that. Once you are in power, people start getting attracted to you. So, we won 110 seats in 2008 ... Coming to power at the Centre under Vajpayee in the late 1990s hugely helped us because it attracted people from other parties and it strengthened our party.' Few remember that, in 2004, when Vajpayee's BJP lost the general election nationally, it still won a majority in Karnataka, taking seventeen of the twenty-eight state seats in Parliament. In the 2018 state assembly poll, the 'Narendra Modi factor worked in at least fifteen seats in assembly election', says a Bengaluru-based journalist who covered the 2018 poll campaign. 'It provided a critical push for BJP to jump to 105 seats.'

Multilingual Identity: Why Karnataka Is Different from the Rest of South India

In the 2018 Karnataka state election, Congress Chief Minister Siddaramaiah likened himself to the legendary seventh-century Chalukya ruler Pulakesin II, who defeated the north Indian emperor Harsha. His attempt to create a Kannada First vs Outsider narrative clearly could not stave off a saffron surge. One of the reasons this narrative did not work was because—unlike say Tamil Nadu's Dravidian parties or Telangana's regional identity-based politics or Andhra Pradesh's politics forged in the idea of Telugu pride—Karnataka has never had language-focused politics. In other south Indian states, especially Tamil Nadu, the BJP could be more easily portrayed as a Hindi-speaking party of the north, espousing a Sanskritised 'Aryavrat' at odds with non-Brahmanical and non-Sanskritic regional identities as symbolised by the Dravidian movement. Unlike Andhra Pradesh, Telangana, Kerala or Tamil Nadu, Karnataka is 'multilingual state, with people speaking Telugu, Marathi, Kannada, Tamil'. While Kannada is by far the most widely spoken language in the state, Urdu is the second-largest mother-tongue group. There are Telugu speakers in the Hyderabad–Karnataka region, Tamil speakers in Bengaluru, Tulu speakers in the Dakshin Karnataka region, and Konkani is spoken on the coastline.[106] Karnataka is the most multilingual state in south India, the third-most in India—in terms of people who speak more than one language—according to Census data.[107] BJP MLC Lehar Singh argues that 'the majority of people here are bilingual. They speak Marathi/Tamil, Telugu/Marathi or some such combination. This is why there is no linguistic identity fanaticism here like in Tamil Nadu. We don't have linguistic nationalism because Karnataka is a multilingual state and most people speak at least two languages. Language-based politics doesn't work here and people don't like it.'[108]

Siddaramiah's gambit to take on the BJP by creating a 'Tamil type of north-south divide' didn't succeed for this reason. While other states have a history of political mobilisation around language or regional identity, Karnataka has been a conglomeration of four or five language groups, each concentrated in specific regions. The state's diversity and multilingualism mean that, relatively speaking, the fear of a north Indian hegemon does not evoke the same reaction as it does in other southern states. 'There is no regional force in Karnataka. When Indira Gandhi constituted a task force for Chikmagalur, the actor Dr Raj Kumar was asked to contest, but he refused. So, no regional force was created in Karnataka,' the journalist and academic Veeraraghav explained to me in early 2020. 'Karnataka is a combination of four–five regions with contradictions between them. JD(S) is largely a regional force of Vokkaligas but has a base only in Old Mysore, where BJP finds it difficult to win.'

While the BJP never had a presence in Tamil Nadu, it used to win about five or six assembly seats in Hyderabad and outer Hyderabad in the 1980s, at a time when it was winning only about a dozen seats in Karnataka. So why did it not grow in Andhra like it did in Karnataka? Some Karnataka BJP leaders say the difference lies in the leadership and its ability to create a rural base. 'It is because we got everything wrong there [in Andhra]. We didn't have a top leader and they didn't have the vision to grow outside the city, like we did in Karnataka. We were seen in Andhra as an urban party focused on Hyderabad and not concerned with the agrarian issues. The agrarian issues are never touched by them, but in Karnataka that was the basis of Yediyurappa's initial growth as Rayatu Bandhu,' a BJP leader explained. 'Yediyurappa appealed to farmers, SC/STs. Even today, if you ask Muslims or Christians, they find BSY the most secular leader you will find among all parties. What Amit Shah is today, what Modi is today, he was that all those years ago in Karnataka but he can't speak in Hindi. He had the moderate face of Vajpayee and this killer instinct of Shah and Modi. It was a deadly combination for us.'[109]

The BJP had similar origins in Andhra and Karnataka, but its paths in the two states diverged in the 1990s. Party leaders say they made no progress in Andhra because 'there was no primary leader' and TRS and TDP 'gave us no space to expand'. The TDP emerged first as the political articulation of Telugu pride, and TRS later, to create a separate Telangana. In Karnataka, on the other hand, no local sons-of-the-soil party emerged to take on the Congress. When Janata Dal/JD(S) were the primary anti-Congress force in the state in the 1990s, neither focused its politics on becoming a vehicle of Kannadiga pride. This was a crucial difference.

Besides, Vajpayee also needed the TDP's support for his national coalition in Delhi, so the BJP could not afford to be aggressive in Andhra. Like Karnataka (with Lingayats, Vokkaligas and Kurubas), Andhra Pradesh has two major caste groups: Reddys and Kammas. Most chief ministers there have been Reddys or Kammas. Reddys have tended to be supportive of the Congress, while the Kammas moved to the TDP with the coming of N.T. Rama Rao in 1983. As a senior Karnataka BJP political strategist explained to me, 'Till NTR, Kammas had largely voted for Congress. That changed in 1986 when N.T. Rama Rao, who was a Kamma, came in. So, they also have two dominant castes, like in Karnataka, and one which is a balancing caste: Kapus which was around 8–10 per cent. So, it was like balancing a scale … You had a similar situation here in Karnataka with Vokkaligas and Lingayats. There is a community called Kuruba, which are like Kapus, basically they are OBCs. They play the balancing act. In Karnataka, it was to Yediyurappa's credit that BJP could exploit the Lingayat resentment after the Veerendra Patil incident. He understood the importance of it and grew our base among the Lingayat and SCs. We didn't have equivalent leadership in Andhra Pradesh.'[110]

There were opportunities in both states, but what the BJP lacked in Andhra was 'a leader who was ambitious like Amit Shah', said Anand. 'People forget that Yediyurappa formed the first BJP government in south India in 2008 when Narendra Modi had just started his second term as chief minister in Gujarat. If we had a leader like that in Andhra Pradesh or

Tamil Nadu or Kerala, we would be in a different place today. Yediyurappa had the face of Vajpayee and was a street fighter like Amit Shah. This combination helped the party to grow in a big way. This is something that made a big difference.' In other words, the difference lay in the creation of 24x7 political leaders who had their ears to the ground and took the long view.

To illustrate this point, he narrated the story of two by-poll elections that the BJP lost in January 2017. 'Yediyurappa took those two by-polls damn seriously. He stayed there for twenty days, planned every aspect of the campaign and it looked like his life is depending on these by-poll results.' Eventually, the BJP lost both contests, though it increased its vote share. This strategist said that he asked Yediyurappa why he had staked so much on these elections, knowing it was a losing battle anyway and that it would adversely affect his standing. He says Yediyurappa's response was to point out that these two elections were in two different districts where the BJP cadre had not been galvanised and were not active. Yediyurappa told him that 'in those twenty days, half a dozen district guys became active and they all started to do some work. Now they are taking the party work seriously which will help me in 2018 elections. Our focus made Siddaramaiah think that Congress might ending up losing there, so three-fourth of his cabinet and twenty ministers were given the responsibility to win these two seats: ten ministers each. BJP lost these by-polls but it was a moral victory and it helped us in the assembly polls that followed in 2018 in these two districts. That's how you build a cadre.'[111]

Karnataka as the BJP's Springboard for the South

In January 2020, the Karnataka government sought to reopen an alleged rape case of a girl who lived in Kasaragod in neighbouring Kerala. The allegation was that she had been raped by three boys but the Kerala police had not registered a case. Unusually for an incident that had occurred in another state, the BJP's Udupi-Chikkamagaluru MP Shobha Karandlaje took up the case and accompanied the victim for a meeting with Chief Minister Yediyurappa, who in turn asked the Bengaluru police chief to look into the matter. The BJP MP then raised the 'love jihad' angle, alleging that the victim was under pressure from the alleged perpetrators to convert to Islam.[112]

The Kasaragod district police chief, meanwhile, said that his force had indeed received a missing person's complaint, traced the girl to Bengaluru, and that her statement had been recorded both by the police and a magistrate. District Police Chief James Joseph said 'no love jihad angle' was alleged by the girl or had come up in the investigation.[113] Karandlaje, on the other hand, alleged that three boys had been blackmailing the girl's family to convert to Islam, saying they would release the alleged rape video if the family refused to do so. She declared that such cases were happening regularly in the 'border areas with Kerala', and demanded a thorough investigation. After the Karnataka BJP took up the case, the Bangalore police registered a case and it was subsequently transferred to the Karnataka CID.[114] The political blame-game over the incident reflected how Karnataka politics was now leaching into Kerala, where the BJP believed it was growing. Karandlaje was also said to have later taken up the pro-CAA cause in the border areas in Kerala.

At the Bengaluru RSS headquarters, local workers told me that, by 2020, the Kerala RSS had more 'organisational growth than in the Gujarat chapter in terms of full-time workers'. As one worker put it, 'Our political growth is not there in Kerala so far in terms of victories but we have a political dividend there because we have shakha density.' Then why did the BJP not grow there as much as it did in Karnataka, I asked. 'Because in Kerala, Hindus are 53 per cent,' he responded. 'Muslims are 27 per cent, Christians are 18 per cent. That's why we have not grown and BJP has not grown as much.' Meanwhile, Karnataka has emerged as the springboard for RSS activities in Kerala. 'Most RSS pracharaks in Kerala are from Karnataka. We also send pracharaks for Northeast.'[115]

In Tamil Nadu, which remains divided between the DMK and the AIADMK, the BJP was relying on the support base of actor Rajinikanth and the often discussed possibility that he would launch a new party to create an opening through an anti-Periyar faultline. (Periyar, or Erode Venkatappa Ramasamy [1879–1973], is regarded as the father of the Dravidian Movement and started the Self-respect Movement and the Dravidar Kazhagam.) 'This has parallels with how Nehru was treated like a demigod by Congress,' said the journalist Veeraraghav. 'In Tamil Nadu politics, Periyar has been a demigod for Dravidian politics. When you question Periyar's legacy, you can open new political space.' The basis of such a political challenge is the belief that a cultural transformation had taken place in Tamil Nadu over the years through soft saffron leaders who, while espousing the ideas of the Dravidian movement, had simultaneously financed temple repair funds and schools for temple priests. As the scholar Mahesh Rangarajan once pointed out, the late AIADMK leader Jayalalithaa supported the BJP's right to kar seva in Ayodhya as far back as 1991.[116]

Appeals to a shared religiosity could, theoretically, break the ideological divide. 'It needn't be a Hindutva/Dravida faultline in Tamil Nadu. It can also be Rajni vs Dravida faultline,' Veeraraghav pointed out. 'Who said Periyar is not challengeable? BJP is keen to challenge Periyar. In a personality-focused state, they have found an ideological opposition and have started it. When was the last time Periyar was questioned in Tamil Nadu? Rajnikanth is opening the door for them.'[117] In the same vein, BJP Rajya Sabha MP and former Vice Chairman of Kerala NDA Rajeev Chandrashekhar told me in late 2019: 'If I was a predicting man, Tamil Nadu in my opinion presents any political party an opportunity because the two Dravidian parties there have been governing with almost identical styling between the two of them. They both give lots of giveaways and have lived off the Karunanidhi and Jayalalitha mystique charisma for so many decades. So, their successes are dependent on all the same kind of leaders. There is, in my opinion, a vacuum there and an opportunity for BJP.'[118] The BJP has also been trying to take advantage of the vacuum created in the AIADMK by Jayalalithaa's death in 2016. In September 2020, AIADMK leaders told reporters that BJP leaders had been mediating as their party and the rebel Sasikala faction held talks for a merger.[119] Even so, Tamil Nadu remains an uphill task for the BJP.

Many BJP leaders believe the party can make faster inroads in Telangana. The fact that it won four Lok Sabha seats[120] in the state in the 2019 national elections is seen by party strategists as a 'golden opportunity'. 'This is the first time. This is huge,' one of them told me. One of those seats was won by defeating Telangana Chief Minister K.C. Rao's daughter K. Kavitha in Nizamabad. Another key seat was wrested by the BJP's new Hindutva icon in Telangana, Bandi Sanjay Kumar, who defeated TRS stalwart B. Vinod Kumar in Karimnagar—a constituency KCR himself had won from in 2004. Following this victory, the BJP appointed Sanjay Kumar as its Telangana president in March 2020. The former RSS and ABVP leader has a hard-line Hindutva reputation and his appointment indicated the party's new strategy. 'If they play their cards right, they have a fantastic chance to do something in Telangana,' said a BJP strategist in Bengaluru. 'The win in Karimnagar was important because it was so close to KCR. It was the place of the launch of fight for Telangana. He hit them inside their house. BJP was never taken seriously there but he did this. He is aggressive and sharp.'

In the months leading up to his appointment as Telangana BJP chief, Sanjay Kumar announced that the BJP would 'fly the saffron flag on Golconda Fort sooner than later'. After stones were thrown at a BJP rally in Hanamkonda, he also sent Asaduddin Owaisi's AIMIM and Telangana's ruling TRS a sharp message: 'If they use sticks to attack us, we will retaliate with knives, and if knives are used, we will respond with guns. The war has already begun.'[121]

In the same vein, when the Telangana government adopted a resolution in the state assembly against CAA, NPR and NRC, the BJP state unit president announced that, if Chief Minister K. Chandrashekhar Rao and Asaduddin Owaisi did not want to register for NPR due to political reasons, they could 'seek refuge in Pakistan'.[122] Just as Karnataka was built as a BJP bastion because of its local leadership and 'local spine', the party was now looking to grow in Telangana through aggressive Hindutva positioning.

It is a sign of how serious the BJP is about Telangana that a number of Karnataka BJP leaders were sent to the state in 2019 to oversee the poll campaign. The first-time BJP MP from Secunderabad, G. Kishan Reddy, was appointed minister of state for home affairs in the second Modi government. Another sign of this new focus on the state was the sheer central leadership firepower deployed in a Hyderabad municipal poll in December 2020. The result was that, in a city where almost every second voter is Muslim, the BJP finished as the second largest party with forty-eight seats in the Greater Hyderabad municipal polls. Furthermore, it finished within striking distance of the ruling TRS, which went down drastically to fifty-five seats.[123] The BJP's stunning rise in Hyderabad's

2020 municipal poll demonstrated yet again the fresh inroads the party was now making in the state.

Rajeev Chandrashekhar told me, 'In the South, there is a simple issue you cannot hide. South is an issue of political leaders. If we had an Amit Shah in the South; or we had an Arun Jaitley in the South who speaks Tamil, who speaks Malayalam, we would do better. The other problem in the South is that, unlike in the North—where there's one Hindi link language—the South has multiple languages. So, if I'm a leader from UP, I can work across North India. Here you have Telugu, Tamil, Kannada and Malayalam, Konkani and many other languages. It is not so easy for one leader.' So, what did the party need, I asked him. 'We need five leaders, five solid local leaders,' he responded. 'Those local leaders have not developed yet. In Karnataka, we have a good bench-strength. But in Telangana, Tamil Nadu or Kerala, the focus now of our PM is that he will build these good, solid local leaders who will be able to communicate, take the message.' The BJP's aim, he pointed out, was to replace the Congress in the southern states. He too saw Telangana as a 'big opportunity'. 'KCR is vulnerable and Telangana is good hunting ground for BJP because Congress is diminished here. Chandrababu Naidu is non-existent, so BJP naturally can be a counter to KCR. Similarly, in Andhra, there's only YSR-Congress. Now that Congress is disappearing in Andhra and N. Chandrababu Naidu, in my opinion, is at the end of his political career, we have a huge opportunity to expand here.'[124]

By 2021, the political chessboard of Kerala too looked like Karnataka's from the early 1990s. Kerala had at least five Lok Sabha constituencies (of a total of twenty) where the BJP had been consistently winning over 20 per cent of the vote share. In the south: Thiruvananthapuram (31.3 per cent), Attingal (24.7 per cent) and Pathanamthitta (29.7 per cent), the centre of the Sabarimala agitation; in central Kerala: Thrissur (28.7 per cent) and Palakkad (21.3 per cent); and in the north, Kasargod (16 per cent).[125] In these areas, it had a large RSS shakha presence, a cadre and some centres of influence. Somewhat like the Idgah Maidan movement in Karnataka, the BJP spearheaded the Sabarimala movement in Kerala against the Supreme Court's judgement allowing women pilgrims to the holy site, although it did not yield political dividends. However, the agitation did help create a ground-base for the party, so that it emerged from the whole controversy as a player. In the future, given the right conditions, this could be the basis for political advances—that is, if the Congress declines, as has happened in other states like West Bengal and Assam.

Rajeev Chandrashekhar summed it up thus: 'If you look at the history of BJP, its leaders have been traditionally north Indian leaders. They started in pockets in the North and expanded into the Hindi belt. Meanwhile, we have built a significant Sangh Parivar presence in the South. Political activity and the political momentum in the South was very belated and it began only in the late 1990s. There were a lot of reasons for this, including linguistic problems for BJP. South and north India are very different places. While there was considerable bench strength for the BJP in the North, the development of BJP's political leaders in the South was really a 1990s phenomena when you had a Yediyurappa and an Ananth Kumar that built the party in Karnataka and made it electorally successful here. Now, if we can find such leaders in other states, we have the basis for expansion, the opportunity and the timing.'[126]

16

MERGERS, ACQUISITIONS AND THE 'EIGHT GODDESSES'

The BJP's Northeast Push

What does the ancient Hindu legend of Lord Krishna and how he eloped with Rukmini, when she was being married against her will to the Chedi King Shishupal, have to do with India's Northeast and BJP's expansion? Actually, quite a lot. At the 2018 Madhavpur Magh Mela near Gujarat's Porbandar port, Gujarat Chief Minister Vijay Rupani claimed that Rukmini was a princess from Arunachal Pradesh, and that the region had been a part of India since the Dwapar Yug of the Hindu epics. The BJP's Manipur chief minister, N. Biren Singh, also at the event, agreed: 'By marrying Rukmini, Krishna had bound the Northeast to Krishna ... Lord Krishna made them [Northeastern states] part of India during his time.' Arunachal Chief Minister Pema Khandu, also of the BJP, who had specially flown in for the event, concurred: 'We watch in news channels today that some other country is claiming some part of Northeast. But nobody can change the history and the ancient history says that Arunachal was not a separate state but entire Northeast was one. For centuries, we have been with India, mainland India.'[1] In one quick leap, BJP chief ministers had connected the tribal cultures of the Northeast with the cosmology and lore of the Hindu epics.

Rupani also tweeted a video titled 'Madhav se Madhavpur' (From Madhav to Madhavpur), in which breathtaking visuals of Hindu temples in Gujarat, like the legendary Somnath Temple, are intercut with old

Hindu temples and places of worship in the Northeast. A voice-over says, 'Gujarat and the Northeast region are separated by thousands of kilometres but have been relatives [sambandhis] for centuries ... We will tell you a love story that centuries ago tied the two regions in a love bond [prem-bandhan]. This is a story of the Dwapar Yug, when a king of Gujarat did a love marriage with a princess of Arunachal ... this is the story of the Lord of Dwarka Shri Krishna and Queen Rukmini.' The video then cuts to a clip of Prime Minister Modi, wearing traditional Arunachal tribal headgear with hornbill feathers, speaking at a rally from a podium designed like a lotus: 'Gujarat and Arunachal have a relationship that is thousands of years old,' he says. 'From Dwarka, Bhagwan Shri Krishna and our Arunachal Pradesh's Rukmini, this is a relationship joining the East and the West, a relationship joining me and you.'[2] Having seamlessly connected the cultural past to the political present, the video transitions from religious imagery to Modi's Look-East Policy (to cultivate links with Southeast Asia) and how the Northeast would be its central lever. It speaks of increased developmental funding through the DONER (Development of Northeast Region) ministry and moves on to images of smiling women from Arunachal who had received LPG cylinders under the Ujjwala scheme. It drew a straight line from what it called a relationship begun by 'Gujarat's bahurani [daughter-in-law]' and the damaad (son-in-law) of the Northeast to the dream of #EkBharatShresthaBharat, a hashtag which trended that day on Twitter, with BJP ministers tweeting the messages and the prime minister retweeting them.[3]

This narrative of a primordial connection between the Northeast and the world of Hindu epics and legends is central to the message of cultural unity promoted by the BJP and the wider Sangh Parivar in India's north-eastern states. Religious and mythological pasts speak of unity in diversity and a deeper cultural oneness as a central pillar of the BJP's regional strategy. The Ram Janmabhoomi movement of the 1990s sought to break down divisions of caste and language to reimagine a new Hindu identity; the Krishna messaging in the Northeast is a subtle cultural variation.

Some observers dismissed the harnessing of the Krishna–Rukmini legend as make-believe.[4] This critique, however, misses the point of this process of acculturation. From the 1950s, several academic experts on Arunachal's tribal cultures have documented the belief of the Idus—a sub-group of the Mishmi tribe—that Rukmini was one of them, and that they developed an ethnic identity around this.[5] One account of the tribe noted in 1958 that there are 'archaeological relics in Bishmaknagar in Lohit Frontier, which are said to mark the capital of King Bishmak, whose daughter Rukmini was carried away by Lord Krishna himself'.[6] The Idu Mishmis have spring love songs around the Krishna–Rukmini tale, as well as Rukmini Haran (kidnapping) dances and plays.[7] As P.N. Luthra explained in the *Economic and Political Weekly* in 1971, the Idus also call themselves 'Chulikata' (hair-cut) because of this legend: 'Rukmini, according to Idus, was carried away by Lord Krishna, which infuriated them and led to conflict between the two. The Idus admit that they came off worse and, to symbolise the humiliation of their defeat, they decided to partly cut off their hair. This earned them the name "Chulikata", a descriptive term whose origin was only recently unveiled when Bhishmaknagar fort was unearthed 18 miles from Roing in Lohit District. As to the authenticity of the legend, mythologists and historians will, no doubt, have a good deal to say.'[8]

In 1968, when figurines of Hindu yakshas, yakshinis and gods from the pantheon were unearthed in Bishmaknagar, the North East Frontier Agency (NEFA) authorised an officer with the designation of Director of Research (History) to undertake further excavations in the area. These archaeological remains, on the river Kundil near Sadiya, are part of a wider network of ancient Hindu ruins and associated legends in the area including a Parshuram Kund in Lohit district and Malinithan, a grove said to have been tended by Shiva's consort, Parvati, where Krishna and Rukmini rested on their way back to Dwarka.

The archaeological evidence shows without doubt that classical Hindu legends, influence and culture penetrated the region in ancient times. When this happened and whether these were later reconstructions—continuous and methodical records of the region's tribes are only available from the thirteenth century[9]—is, of course, conjecture and beside the point for our purposes. As one scholar noted, one way to understand the vexed 'identity of the people of this civilisation' is to see it from the lens of the 'Sanskritisation' theory[10] propounded by the sociologist M.N. Srinivas in the 1950s, which suggested that castes or tribes lower down in the hierarchy sought to gain upward mobility by emulating rituals and practices of dominant or upper castes. Seen from that angle, 'the claim of the Mishmis that they descended from Bhishmaka, the legendary king of Kundil ... can be resolved'.[11] The political use of the Krishna-Rukmini legend encapsulated the idea of 'Ek Bharat', or One India, that is at the centre of the BJP's core messaging in the state. There is a direct link between such political imagery and the RSS's groundwork in the Northeast over the past few decades to inculcate a wider Hindu identity in the region.

The BJP's national election victory in 2014 presaged the most dramatic realignment of political power equations in the north-eastern states since Independence. Until 2016, the party had never been elected to power in any of these eight states. It had briefly formed a government once in Arunachal Pradesh (2003) when Gegong Apang, the Congress's longest-serving chief minister in the state, defected and merged his new regional outfit with the party and ran a BJP-led government for a year, before he returned to the Congress.[12] However, in that one-year rule, coinciding with Vajpayee's premiership, the party had not been elected to power. Moreover, until 2016, the BJP had never even finished as the second-best party in an electoral contest in any of the north-eastern states, whether in the national or state assembly polls. Yet, it held office in six of the eight states in the region by 2021. In four of these—Assam (on 24 May 2016 and again on 10 May 2021), Tripura (on 9 March 2018), Arunachal Pradesh (on 31 December 2016, then 29 May 2019) and Manipur (on 15 March 2017)—BJP chief ministers assumed power at the head of multi-party coalitions.[13] The party's first-ever victories in Assam (where it trounced the Congress twice in succession) and Tripura (where it ousted the CPI(M), which had held power for twenty-five years) were historically significant milestones. In two other states, Nagaland (8 March 2018) and Meghalaya (6 March 2018), the BJP assumed power as a junior coalition partner in alliance governments led by larger regional parties. In Nagaland, the party even had a deputy chief minister.[14] By mid-2021, the only north-eastern states that the BJP did not control were Mizoram and Sikkim. Even here, however, ruling parties in both states were formally still members of the North East Democratic Alliance (NEDA; a BJP-led coalition of non-Congress political parties from the region formed on 24 May 2016).[15] The region's political shift away from the Congress also reflected in parliamentary elections. In 2014, the BJP had won just 32 per cent (eight of twenty-five) Lok Sabha seats in the Northeast. By 2019, its tally went up to 56 per cent (fourteen of twenty-five).

Figure 16.1: The BJP Emerged as the Single-largest Party in the Northeast in the 2019 Parliamentary Poll

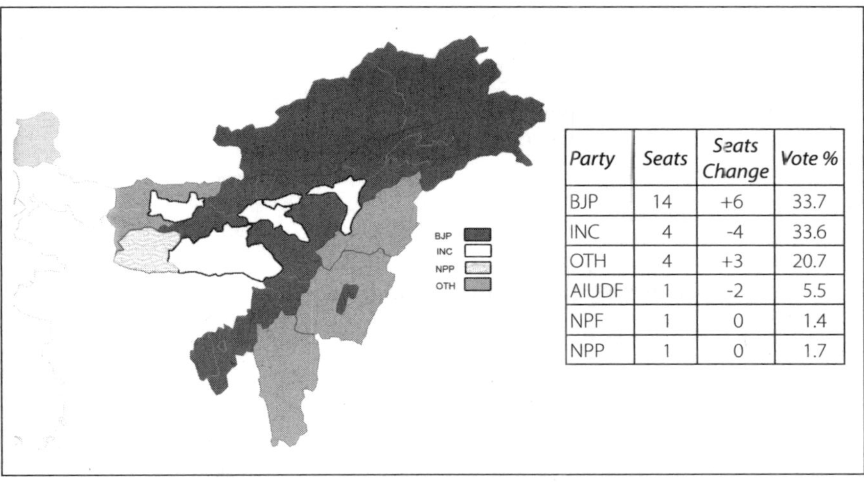

Party	Seats	Seats Change	Vote %
BJP	14	+6	33.7
INC	4	-4	33.6
OTH	4	+3	20.7
AIUDF	1	-2	5.5
NPF	1	0	1.4
NPP	1	0	1.7

Note: There are twenty-five Lok Sabha seats in the Northeast. Source: Election Commission of India data, graphic mapping by Nalin Mehta, Rishabh Srivastava, PollNiti, https://pollniti.com/live.html#!

To put the BJP's rise in the Northeast in perspective, it is important to underscore the low base it started from. In Tripura, until a few weeks before the March 2018 assembly election, the party did not have even a councillor-level elected representative. It won zero seats (1.5 per cent votes) in the 2013 assembly polls. To go from that to bagging thirty-five of sixty assembly seats and 43 per cent of vote share in 2018 was an astonishing feat, especially in a largely tribal state. Only AAP in Delhi in 2013 and NTR's TDP in Andhra in the early 1980s offer comparable political start-up stories. But they were new formations, unknown quantities. The BJP, on the other hand, has been a known ideological entity in the Northeast for decades, working closely with the RSS's grassroots outreach in the region. In Tripura, the BJP won not only Congress bastions—the urban areas around Agartala—but also Left strongholds: huge swathes of forested tribal areas across south, central and eastern Tripura (see Figure 16.2).[16] It had a similar growth spurt pattern in Assam. The best that the party had

Figure 16.2: The BJP's Stunning Rise in Tripura

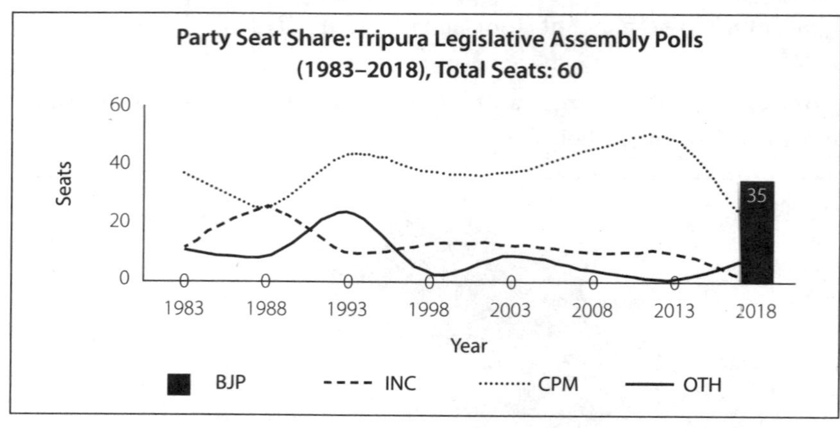

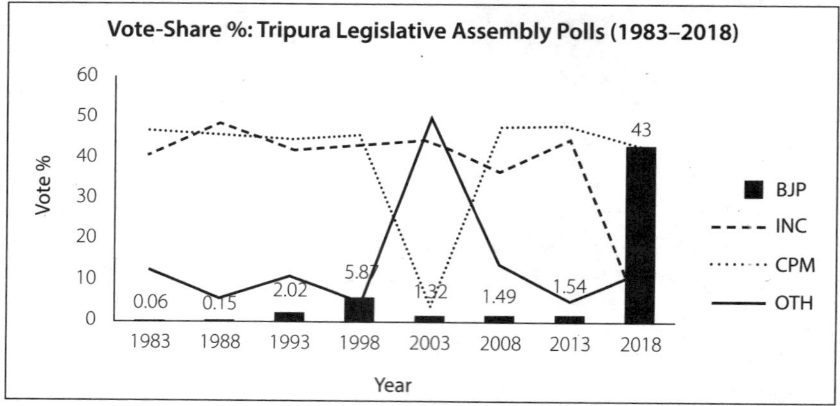

Source: ECI data, analysis and graphic visualisation by Nalin Mehta, Rajiv Pundir

ever performed before the 2016 showing was in 2006: ten seats (12 per cent vote share) in Assam's 126-member assembly. From there, it grew by 500 per cent, catapulting to sixty seats (29.8 per cent vote share) in 2016. It repeated this feat after five years in power, winning 60 seats again (33.21 per cent vote share) in 2021 (see Figure 16.3). Similarly, in Arunachal Pradesh, the BJP accelerated from eleven seats (30.97 per cent vote share) in 2014 to forty-one (50.86 per cent votes) in the 2019 provincial polls. In Manipur, it went from a previous best of four seats in 2002 to twenty-one in 2017 (36.29 per cent votes); and in Nagaland, from a previous best of seven seats (10.8 per cent vote share) in 2002 to twelve (15.3 per cent votes) in 2018 (see Appendices 11–14).

Figure 16.3: The BJP's Assam Model: Sudden Growth Spurt

Party Seat Share: Assam Legislative Assembly Elections (1983–2021)

Seats
110
90
70
50
30
10
2 0
2 0
2 10
2 4
0 8
2 10
0 5
0 60
1 60
1983 1985 1991 1996 2001 2006 2011 2016 2021
Year
BJP INC AUDF AGP OTH

Note: Total Seats – 126 (112 in 1996, 109 in 1983)

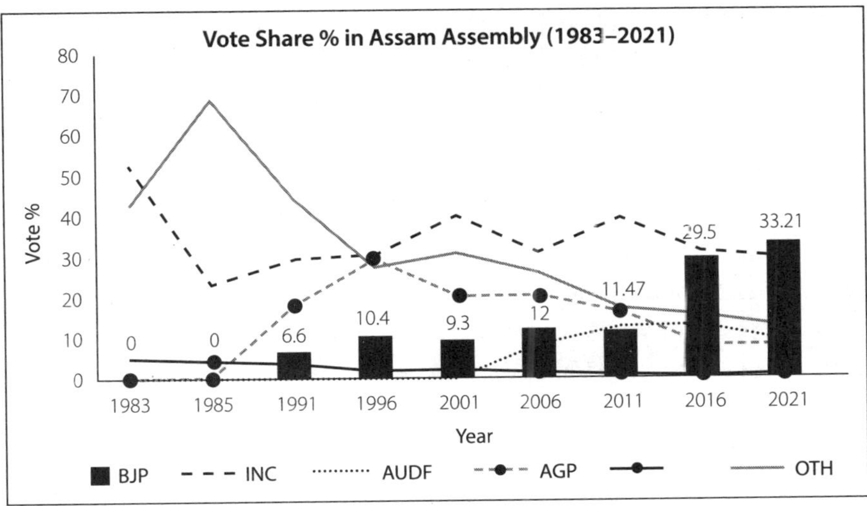

Source: ECI data, analysis and graphic visualisation by Nalin Mehta, Rajiv Pundir

Agartala, Itanagar, Imphal and Kohima are so far away from the heat and dust of Delhi that elections in the Northeast have too often been seen by the capital's political and intellectual elites as footnotes to the larger story, at best—or ignored, at worst. The big tectonic shift between 2016 and 2019 saw the lifting of these self-limiting blinkers. In that sense, the planting of the saffron flag in Guwahati, Agartala, Imphal, Itanagar, Kohima and Shillong is not only a historic advance for the BJP, but also a significant shift of registers for India's polity.

These victories also signify three big political messages. For one, they legitimately allowed the BJP to claim that it was more than a Hindi–Hindu party and was thus the national inheritor of the Congress's traditional mantle as the only pan-Indian party. The party can assert this claim because many north-eastern states have a very high proportion of religious minorities. BJP-ruled Assam has the highest proportion of Muslims in any large Indian state after Kashmir: 34.2 per cent of its people profess Islam (only Lakshadweep has more—96.5 per cent Muslims—but in a population of only 64,473).[17] Several north-eastern states where the BJP won power have a very high density of Christian populations. As much as 87.9 per cent of Nagaland, 74.5 per cent of Meghalaya, 41.2 per cent of Manipur and 30.2 per cent of Arunachal Pradesh is Christian.[18] For a party accused of being majoritarian and Hindu-centric, the symbolism of victories in these states was huge. This is why, on the day the party won victories in Tripura, Nagaland and Meghalaya in March 2018, Amit Shah declared: 'Our victory in the Northeast shows that the taunt about us, especially among you in the media, that the BJP is not an all-India [Akhil Bharatiya] party, has been proved wrong. We now have an MP in Ladakh. We rule in Kohima and we rule also in Kutch. The Northeast victories have brought the real all-India character of the BJP in front of the whole world.'[19] The political message was not lost on the Opposition either. As the Congress's former Assam chief minister Tarun Gogoi said, 'They want it all. They want to show that they are an all-India party.'[20]

Significantly, the BJP's advances in the Northeast also signalled a retreat of the Congress in states it had dominated for decades. The Congress was literally reduced to zero seats in Tripura and Nagaland in 2018. If the BJP had not been able to achieve a 'Congress-mukt' Bharat, it seemed to be moving towards a 'Congress-mukt' Northeast, even if it was not winning outright. Furthermore, its wipe-out of the CPI(M) government in Agartala was its first-ever victory in a direct election face-off with the Left. The Marxist party had held power for over two decades continuously in the state.

To the party, the Tripura victory in particular meant that the geographical Kurukshetra of the great ideological battles that have defined the Republic since its inception—between the red Left and the saffron Right—had been remapped. Sunil Deodhar, the BJP's Tripura in-charge, exulted: 'We have cultivated "kesar" [saffron] in the red desert' and 'broken the Communist spine'.[21] The BJP saw here portents for possible realignments in Kerala, the one other state where the Left still rules. 'The biggest happiness today is with our Kerala and West Bengal colleagues,' Amit Shah declared on the day of the Northeast victories. 'It is now proven that Left is not right for any part of India. This has been decided first in West Bengal, now in Tripura.'[22] Modi was even more ecstatic, emphasising the point with triumphant imagery: '*Jab sooraj dhalta hai to laal rang dikhta hai, aur jb ugta hai to kesariya rang hota hai* [When the sun sets, it is red in colour, and when it rises, it is saffron]'.[23] This was received with thunderous applause at the BJP office.

So, how did the party turn its fortunes around in the Northeast? Locally led by erstwhile foes, like ex-Congress leader Himanta Biswa Sarma, who drove an aggressive policy of mergers, acquisitions and alliances with regional power groups; pushed by its central leadership's aggressive expansion strategy; supported by a growing network of RSS shakhas in the region; and riding a cycle of anti-incumbency with the Congress in these states, the BJP upended conventional Northeast politics between 2016 and 2019. This chapter examines whether the shift is a passing one, dependent on the BJP's control of Delhi, or whether it reflects a subterranean churning in the Northeast.

The BJP and Its Reimagining of the Northeast as the 'Eight Lakshmis'

The Northeast has been a prize that the BJP has long been focused on. Speaking at a gathering in Guwahati in February 2014, during his first prime-ministerial campaign, Narendra Modi used vivid Hindu religious imagery to showcase this ambition: 'Earlier they used to call it Seven Sisters. In my view, this is "Asht-Lakshmi", these eight states are "Asht-Lakshmi",' he said. 'And where does Lakshmi-ji reside? On the lotus [Kamal]. Lakshmi-ji's seat is the lotus. If you shower your blessings on the lotus once, and after Asht-Lakshmi takes its seat on it, we will achieve new heights in the development in all the eight states. We want to move forward with this aim.'[24] The term 'Asht-Lakshmi' refers to the eight-goddess manifestation of the Hindu goddess of wealth, who is traditionally depicted as sitting on a lotus,[25] which also serves as the BJP's election symbol. Once elected prime minister, Modi stressed again on this reimagining of the Northeast, also alluding this time to Vastu-shastra, the traditional Hindu art of architecture, and the importance it places on the East in construction design. As he put it, while flagging off the first train from Meghalaya to Guwahati in 2014:[26]

> There are those of us who believe in Vaastu though I must confess that I do not know much about it. But if I were to believe what the experts say then the North East corner of the house should be well kept. It should be clean and its sanctity should be maintained at all times. If this is done the house will forever prosper. Well, I cannot verify these claims but what I do know is that if we are able to take care of North East India, the 'Ishan' corner of our homeland, then the entire India will prosper.... It is my firm belief that these 8 North Eastern states, our Ashta Lakshmi (eight goddesses of wealth), have the potential of bringing in prosperity for the entire nation ... By connecting the North East, this Asht Lakshmi of India, by rail, we intend to make this region the most prosperous in India.

It was a novel characterisation of a region[27] that had thus far been marginal in the 'Hindu' imagination. Modi was recasting the Northeast as a region with pre-modern cultural linkages to India's old Sanskritic cultures. The influence of these ancient cultures once ranged from 'as far west as Puruṣāpura in Gandhāra (Peshawar, in today's northwest Pakistan) to Pāndurānga in Champa (central Vietnam) and Pramambanan on the plains of Java,' wrote the Sanskrit scholar Sheldon Pollock.[28] He famously characterised this vast sphere of Indian cultural influence in the early part of the Common Era as a 'Sanskrit Cosmopolis'.[29] It is telling that Modi's speeches in the Northeast stress on epic connections while simultaneously emphasising the centrality of the region to India's Look-East Policy and the material benefits this would bring. In that sense, if 'the Northeast is seen as the connecting tissue that links parts of the

Indian subcontinent with their south-eastern counterparts,' writes the Northeast scholar Arkotong Longkumer, 'then the Northeast has to be "reconstructed" to establish the region as the centre of the "Sanskrit Cosmopolis".'[30] Such ideas lie at the heart of the BJP's new framing of the Northeast as 'Asht-Lakshmi'.

Equally, the BJP's expansion into the Northeast was only possible because the party operates very differently in the region than it does in the Hindi heartland. Within the region, the party followed differentiated and localised growth strategies in each state, based on its specific demographic make-up and historical lineage. It is an adaptability and flexibility that is in contrast to most mainstream depictions of the BJP as a unitary organisation with a highly centralised command and control system. 'The BJP is very flexible as far as Northeast is concerned,' a senior journalist in Guwahati, speaking on condition of anonymity, told me. 'Wherever it has to talk about Vedic religions, it will talk about it, like in Tripura. But elsewhere this doesn't work, in Meghalaya, Nagaland or where there are Christian majorities. There they have a different face. They project themselves there as the champions of the tribal cause and tribal identity. Tribal groups perceive some kind of danger to themselves, especially from the presence of Bengali-speaking Muslims. So, in Nagaland, BJP follows a policy where they look more pro-tribal than anything else, but in Assam their politics is about Assamese identity and Hindu identity. In Tripura, it is about Hindu identity.'[31] The party has built a multi-layered identity in the Northeast, emphasising different things in different states.

To make sense of this, it is vital to understand the make-up of the region. Colonial Assam—loosely analogous to what was known in ancient India as Pragjyotisha-Kamarupa—encompassed India's Northeast, barring the princely states of Manipur and Tripura and the kingdom of Sikkim.[32] The primary fault-line in old Assam, which came under British control in 1826 after the Treaty of Yandaboo,[33] was between people in the 'plains' and the tribes in the 'hills'. This was formalised by the Bengal Eastern Frontier Regulation of 1873, which instated an 'inner line' along the foothills as a way of demarcating these areas. The British saw the hill people as different as from those in the plains, and governed them—much as they governed the North West Frontier Province (now in Pakistan)—by essentially leaving them alone.[34] The difference was that, in the Northeast, the British allowed a host of foreign Christian missionaries: the Baptists and the Welsh Presbyterians in Meghalaya's Cherrapunji in the 1830s,[35] followed by the American Baptist Mission in Sibsagar from 1836.[36] Their presence had a profound impact on tribal communities even as, after Indian independence, the Sixth Schedule of the Constitution guaranteed autonomy to tribal communities in several north-eastern states through Autonomous District Councils.[37]

Simultaneously, India's independence opened up years of political ferment in the Northeast, leading to the country's longest-running separatist insurgencies—starting with Naga leaders who proclaimed a 'Naga National Council' in 1946 and a Naga Federal Government in 1955; the Mizo National Front uprising in 1966 that led to the Indian Air Force aerially strafing insurgent targets in Aizawl the same year (the only time IAF has been used in offensive operations on Indian soil);[38] as well as insurgencies in Manipur, Tripura and Assam.[39] It was this instability that led to the enactment of the Armed Forces (Special Powers) Act, 1958[40] that remained in force in some parts of the region in 2021. The Northeast has been India's 'Troubled Periphery' for decades—to quote the title of a fine book by Subir Bhaumik—and 'South Asia's most enduring theatre of separatist guerrilla warfare'.[41] The exigencies of managing this instability led to the creation of several new states in the Indian Union. Nagaland was created in 1963, Meghalaya and Manipur in 1972, Mizoram and Arunachal Pradesh in 1987.[42] Sikkim (previously an autonomous monarchy) merged with India in 1975.

The region has the highest number of tribes anywhere in India and among the most diverse group of languages and sub-languages. It is home to as many as 121 Scheduled Tribes, with multiple sub-tribes.[43] An early Indian Census counted as many as 192 languages and dialects.[44] Added to this was the tyranny of distance: Partition cut off old rail links between the Northeast and the rest of India, which were only revived with the construction of the Takilagram–Siliguri rail link in 1950.[45] It is this diversity and complexity of the Northeast, so far removed from the politics of the Hindi heartland, that makes the BJP's rise all the more remarkable.

The BJP in the Northeast Is Very Different from the BJP in Hindi-speaking States: Cow Politics, Food Habits and Strategic Adaptability

Nothing illustrates the BJP's strategic adaptability in the Northeast more than its approach to the cow question. On the Narad Index, we compared all Facebook posts by BJP chief ministers, as well as BJP handles, in the eight north-eastern states versus all Facebook posts by their counterparts in UP, Rajasthan, Madhya Pradesh and Bihar over a two-year period: 2017–2019. We found that, while BJP leaders in the Hindi heartland focus a great deal on cows, cow-welfare and related issues, there are virtually no mentions of it on BJP handles in the Northeast, where large sections of the population eat beef (see Figure 16.4). When issues related to cows did feature (like they did on occasion in Arunachal or Tripura), they were in response to controversies over beef-eating or cow-protection in the Hindi-speaking states. In these states, BJP chief ministers like Vasundhara Raje (Rajasthan chief minister: 2013–2018, 2003–2008) and Yogi Adityanath of UP (in his 2019-20 budget) earmarked increased budgets for cow

Figure 16.4: A Comparison of 'Cow' Mentions by BJP Chief Ministers/State Handles in Hindi-speaking States vs BJP Chief Ministers/Handles in the Northeast on Facebook

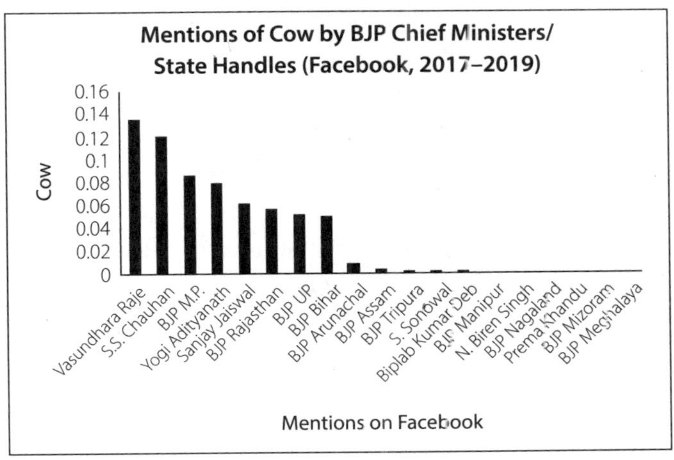

Source: Narad Index, Nalin Mehta and Rishabh Srivastava; for more details, see Appendix 4/online at nalinmehta.in

shelters.[46] Vasundhara Raje declared that in Rajasthan, during her tenure, cow-protection measures had increased the number of these animals in cowsheds by three times.[47] In Madhya Pradesh, Shivraj Singh Chouhan, while in Opposition, questioned the Congress state government in 2019 about its election promise to build more cowsheds. The Congress's failure to build them after promising to do so, he said, amounted to a 'sin like cow killing'.[48]

The BJP's Facebook handles in Hindi-speaking states promoted this aggressively, while its Facebook handles in the Northeast stayed away from the issue entirely (see Figure 16.5). Occasionally, when such controversies challenged BJP narratives, party chief ministers like Pema Khandu of Arunachal Pradesh pushed back, saying that 'beef cannot be the only point of reference when it comes to the North East'. He said that it was taking attention away from 'real issues', and that there was no cultural issue or gap 'between us and BJP', and gave assurances that 'even on the issue of beef', the Centre had already said that 'there would be consultations'.[49]

This strategic adaptability is most evident in the fact that some long-time RSS workers actually changed their dietary habits while working with tribes in the Northeast. Sunil Deodhar, a key BJP strategist who is regarded as the architect of the party's election triumph in Tripura, told the journalist Sanjib Baruah that he found 'gahori [pork in Assamese and Nagamese] very delicious' and that it was one of his 'favourite foods'. A Chitpavan Brahmin from Maharashtra, Deodhar said he had 'reservations on beef' but had eaten 'wild rats in Meghalaya', quoting a Sanskrit shloka, '*Yasmin deshe hi yo jate: tazz tasvoyaya hitam* [The medicines of a country are the best cure for ailments in that country]'. Another former RSS man, Atul Jog, a top ABVKA functionary, said he ate 'pork and rice beer, whatever we are offered'. He offered a telling comment to explain the diet change: '*Jaisa desh vaisa bhesh* [Take the form of the country you are in].' Like Deodhar, Jog too drew the line at beef, saying, 'We don't consume beef and the tribes know it. We refuse with respect and they acknowledge it ... But now even they are realising the importance of, utility and significance of raising cows—something that they have also started. Take, for example, in the Tangsa community in Arunachal Pradesh, there is a group called Raangfra, which is trying to encourage vegetarianism.'[50] Deodhar, who started wearing the ethnic scarf worn by some tribes in Tripura after he

Figure 16.5: BJPs Chief Ministers in Hindi-speaking States Take a Different Approach from the Party's Northeast Chief Ministers on Cows

Shivraj Singh Chouhan
17 October 2019

Congress had promised to build a cowshed in its promise. If the administration had taken the cow to the cowshed, it would not have been locked in any room and would not have been a victim of death. Refusing after giving promise, then dying of cow, is a sin like cow killing. Government should take initiative, so that such cows do not die.

See original · Rate this translation

1.7K 168 comments 58 shares

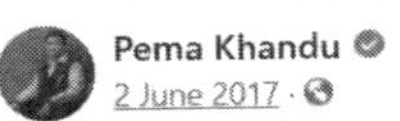

In the northeast, majority are non-vegetarian but it doesn't mean that everyone eats beef. In fact, pork is much more popular than beef. Beef cannot be the only point of reference when it comes to North East.

The beef controversy is taking away attention from the real issues of northeast, which is development, governance and jobs.

Spoke with DNA India in an interview today. You can read the full transcript here:
http://www.dnaindia.com/.../interview-exclusive-beef-ban...

Source: Facebook Posts by BJP UP, Vasundhara Raje, Shivraj Singh Chouhan and BJP Arunachal Pradesh (2017–2019), curated through the Narad Index arrived there, told another reporter that he started eating pork only after moving to the state. He said it was not easy to make dietary changes, but that he did so to start building a base for the party in the state. He also learnt Bengali, a major language there, and engaged a tutor to learn tribal languages.[51] According to one account, between them, Deodhar and Jog, both of whom have worked in the Northeast for at least a decade each, 'speak a variety of languages and dialects like Assamese, Khasi, Jaintia, Angami, Naga, Manipuri etc.'[52]

This strategic adaptability was not without its challenges. When Amit Shah visited Mizoram in 2014, one of the questions the BJP's state unit leaders put to him was about a possible nationwide beef ban. At a time when beef politics and the BJP's support for an end to 'illegal' cow slaughter was becoming a major issue in the northern states, Mizoram BJP President J.V. Hluna told reporters that he had asked the party's national president how a beef ban was possible in the state. According to him, Shah responded by asking, 'if the Bible allows you to eat [beef]'.[53] Hluna said that Shah assured him that 'there is nothing to worry and asked us to follow our tradition. And, as per Bible and our tradition, consumption [of] beef is allowed.'[54] However, when the Central government approved a new rule banning the sale of cattle for slaughter nationwide—the Regulation of Livestock Markets Rules, 2017, under the Prevention of Cruelties to Animal Act, 1960—beef and cow politics emerged as a major issue in the Northeast. This caused BJP leaders in virtually every north-eastern state to declare that there would be no end to beef-eating and that the BJP did not intend to dictate food habits in the region. As Manipur Chief Minister Biren Singh told a newspaper: 'Beef is very important here. All Christians eat it, most tribal communities, valley people eat beef. It is part of traditional diet now. Even the younger generation has taken to it now. The BJP is only trying to regulate the beef industry to avoid illegal slaughter for hygiene purposes.' He categorically assured voters that the party 'will not violate people's right to eat what they have been traditionally eating for many years'.[55]

Within a week, the issue flared up again in Meghalaya, where there was a controversy around BJP district-level office-bearers announcing a proposed beef-bitchi (a local drink) party to celebrate three years of the Modi government. The party's North Garo Hills District President Bachu

C. Marak posted an invitation to the proposed beef party on Facebook, earning a rebuke from the BJP's Meghalaya in-charge Nalin Kohli. The West Garo Hills President, Bernard Marak, quit over the issue, although a central BJP leader claimed they had found a convenient excuse to 'play the martyr card'.[56] The Meghalaya fracas demonstrated how easily differences over food habits could derail the BJP's political project in the region. Like Biren Singh did in Manipur, clarifications were also issued by the party in Nagaland, Meghalaya, Arunachal Pradesh and Mizoram. In each state, local party leaders insisted that the BJP's central leadership was well aware of the need for flexibility. 'Ban on cow slaughter like the one in UP won't take effect in Nagaland if our party comes to power,' explained Nagaland BJP Chief Visasolie Lhoungu to a newspaper. 'The reality here is very different and our central leaders are aware of that.'[57] Similarly, in Aizawl, the Mizoram BJP chief announced that 'with the consent of Amit Shahji, national president of BJP, we are not supporting the ban'. In Itanagar, Tapir Gao, the state BJP chief, added, 'In the northeastern state, we are taking all kinds of meat except human ... The individual food habits are not the BJP's concern. It is the Opposition that is politicising the issue.'[58]

The discomfiture over beef is indicative of the cultural tensions inherent in the BJP's Northeast expansion. Cow slaughter is not banned in Arunachal Pradesh, Mizoram, Meghalaya, Nagaland, Tripura and Sikkim. In Manipur, it was decreed as an offence by the maharaja in 1939 but is still heavily consumed. In Assam, only 'cattle fit for slaughter' may be killed.[59] Government data shows that beef is the highest consumed meat in Meghalaya. In Nagaland, it is a close second to pork. In Manipur, it is the second most consumed meat after fish and prawns. In the Northeast overall, it is the fifth most consumed meat after fish/prawns, chicken, pork and mutton.[60] At a Manipur election rally in 2017, for example, one of the BJP's allies, the Naga People's Front, followed up political speeches with a feast for the assembled crowd, serving up pork stew and chunky beef curry.

As the journalist Smita Gupta has pointed out, the BJP has put 'the issue of beef, which is part of the diet for a large section of the people here, on the back-burner, even as it runs a virulent and vigorous campaign against its consumption elsewhere in the country'.[61] Rajat Sethi and Shubrastha, both of whom have worked for the party in the region, went so far as to write that the party's 'North-East foot-soldiers like to call it the Bharatiya Jesus Party!' However, they noted that the BJP will have to 'go through ideological churning afresh. Its hitherto majoritarian outlook would need to give some political space to a "minority darshan" or philosophy.'[62] It was the kind of flexibility that led the BJP's opponents, like Hyderabad MP Asaduddin Owaisi, to quip tongue-in-cheek: 'BJP's hypocrisy is that in Uttar Pradesh cow is mummy but in the Northeast it's yummy.'[63]

The constant tension caused by this balancing act is best illustrated by the flip-flops of two BJP central ministers on the beef issue in 2015. It began with Mukhtar Abbas Naqvi, then minister of state for parliamentary affairs and Rajya Sabha MP from UP, who declared at a media conclave, 'Those who are dying without eating beef can go to Pakistan or Arab countries or any other part of world where it is available.' He added, 'Even Muslims are against it.'[64] A week later, Kiren Rijiju, then minister of state for home and BJP MP from Arunachal Pradesh, retorted at a press conference in Aizawl: 'I'm from Arunachal Pradesh, can somebody stop me? So let us not be touchy about somebody's practices ... This is a democratic country. Sometimes, some statements are made which are not palatable.'[65] Rijiju later claimed that he had been misquoted, strongly denied that he personally ate beef and insisted that he was speaking hypothetically about how no one could stop individual food choices. 'To calm down the situation, I had the responsibility as a Union minister whereby I gave a hypothetical example of myself that I am from Arunachal Pradesh and if I have a particular food habit, no one can stop.'[66]

Rijiju's argument, essentially, was this: different states, different rules. As he put it, 'If a Mizo Christian says that this is the land of Jesus, why should someone have a problem in Punjab or Haryana? We have to honour the sentiments of each place and each location ... If Maharashtra is Hindu majority, or if Gujarat is Hindu majority, Madhya Pradesh is Hindu majority, if they are to make laws which are conducive to the Hindu faith, let them be. But in our place, in our state where we are majority, where we feel whatever steps we take, you know, laws which are conducive to our beliefs, it should be. So they also should not have a problem with the way we live, and we also should not have a problem with the way they live.'[67]

This is the tightrope the BJP must walk on the issue of beef and cow slaughter in the Northeast. As Sethi and Shubrastha write, 'Issues like the beef ban will continuously implore the BJP leadership to dovetail two very contrasting viewpoints—respecting the customary food habits of the North-east on the one hand and balancing the pressures emanating from the Hindi heartland to ban cow slaughter. How effectively the party leaders can take these challenging issues head-on will determine the future prospects of the party in the region.'[68]

The BJP's Five Strategies Within the Northeast

The party adopted five broad strategies within the Northeast to drive its expansion in these new catchment areas. The cornerstone of its approach was mergers and acquisitions, that is, to bring into its tent a range of defectors from rival parties as well as local notables with diverse followings. It also focused on building coalitions and new anti-Congress alliances to broaden its political support base. This meant strategic realignments to co-opt core electoral groups and adroit management of the electoral arithmetic of communities in each state to build winning alliances. The BJP also leveraged its position as the party in office in Delhi. This is especially crucial for states in the Northeast and gave an additional incentive to parties in the region to align with it. It combined these strategies with a sharp focus on the delivery of development projects. Significantly, its grassroots membership drive in the region unfolded in tandem with longer-term ideological penetration by the wider RSS network. Finally, its success in Assam was built on a model of ethno-religious mobilisation predicated on a narrative of Hindus in peril and the social fissures opened up by 'illegal immigration'.

Strategy 1: Mergers and Acquisitions

AT LEAST 50 PER CENT OF ALL BJP MINISTERS IN FIVE NORTH-EASTERN STATES DEFECTED FROM OTHER PARTIES

The BJP grew exponentially because many senior leaders from other parties joined it. They brought with them their own support bases and influence networks. Very much like a corporation looking to expand into new areas, the party focused on winning the market by looking at the competition and acquiring as much of the rival talent as possible. Of course, it had to be attractive enough to pull in those it wooed. Himanta Biswa Sarma—who became the key strategist and the national face of the BJP's Northeast drive as convener of the NEDA as well as Assam chief minister—is only the most famous example of this strategy. Sarma was considered the Congress's second most powerful leader in Assam before he fell out with then chief minister Tarun Gogoi over the party's succession plans. Gogoi had recently introduced his son Gaurav into politics. He switched to the BJP, joining the party in August 2015.[69] Sarma had started his political career decades earlier with the Asom Gana Parishad (AGP), which emerged out of the Assam movement of the 1980s. In the 2019 general election, he was the only BJP leader, apart from Narendra Modi and Amit Shah, who campaigned in every north-eastern state.

Sarma is certainly the best known among those who defected to the BJP before it came to power, but he was not the only one. In Assam, the top rungs of the BJP government formed in 2016 were full of former AGP and Congress stalwarts. Former chief minister Sarbananda Sonowal—a tribal leader from the Sonowal Kachari community, who was appointed minister of ports, shipping and waterways in the Central government in 2021—won his first election as an AGP MLA from Moran in 2011 before joining the BJP. Assam Assembly Speaker Hitendra Nath Goswami served three terms as an AGP legislator before joining the BJP in 2014. The state's parliamentary affairs minister, Chandra Mohan Patowary, served as president of the AGP in the 2008–2011 period and was leader of the Opposition in the state assembly between 2006 and 2011 before he joined the BJP.[70] Similarly, the party's ministerial list in Assam included a former State Congress Youth president (Pijush Hazarika)[71] and a former Congress district president from the tribal area of Karbi Anglong (Sum Ronghang).[72]

As many as 50 per cent of ministers in the BJP's first Assam government were important leaders in other parties before they hitched their fortunes to the BJP (see Table 16.1). All of them had left their original parties before assembly polls in these states—they defected and contested elections on BJP tickets. The party opened its doors to top leaders from both the AGP and the Congress before the 2014 Lok Sabha elections, and leaders from these parties joined it in droves.[73] Twelve of the BJP's sixty Assam MLAs (20 per cent) elected in 2016 had served as MLAs of other parties in the previous assembly.[74] That so many of them were rewarded with ministerial berths established their importance and sent out a message to other regional leaders about the BJP's flexibility and willingness to co-opt.

When I analysed the backgrounds of all BJP ministers in five north-eastern states between 2016 and 2020, I found that Assam was not an aberration. In fact, it turned out that 50 per cent of the ministerial berths for defectors from other parties was the lowest benchmark in the five states I analysed (see Table 16.1). In Manipur, this ratio was as high as 80 per cent in favour of defector-ministers. In Meghalaya and Arunachal, it was 100 per cent.

In Tripura, the chief minister at the time was a BJP true-blood with an RSS background. Even so, 50 per cent of its first ministers (three of six) had previously been legislators with the Congress or the Trinamool Congress.[75] As in Assam, a host of senior leaders from across Tripura's political spectrum joined the party in the months leading up to the election.[76] And, like in Assam, as many as ten (28 per cent) of the BJP's thirty-five winning MLAs in 2018 had previously been legislators or ministers with other parties.[77]

Thanks to this conscious policy of rewarding defectors, the BJP became the party of upward mobility for many leading politicians in the Northeast. This also meant that it could co-opt big leaders with minimal disruption to existing power structures. When they switched sides, it was a simple exchange of the patronage of older parties with that of the BJP, without radical social shifts below that level. Besides, this policy meant that future defectors continued to have an incentive to shift their allegiance.[78]

Table 16.1: Defectors from Other Parties are Crucial to the BJP's Expansion, Became Key Ministers

State	*Ministers*	*BJP Ministers*	*BJP Ministers Who were Earlier in Other Parties*	*Percentage of BJP Ministers Who were Earlier in Other Parties*
Assam	18	12	6	50%
Tripura	8	6	3	50%
Nagaland	11	6	3	50%
Manipur	12	5	4	80%

State	*Ministers*	*BJP Ministers*	*BJP Ministers Who were Earlier in Other Parties*	*Percentage of BJP Ministers Who were Earlier in Other Parties*
Meghalaya	12	1	1	100%
Arunachal Pradesh	11	11	11	100%

Source: Author's analysis of ministerial lists as displayed on respective state government home pages on 10 May 2020[79]

Nagaland Deputy Chief Minister Yanthungo Patton had been home minister in the previous Naga People's Front (NPF) government before he resigned and joined the BJP just before the March 2018 assembly election.[80] Three of the BJP's six ministers in the state (50 per cent) had also defected from other parties, as did the former chief minister, Jacob Zhimomi.[81] Similarly, as many as seven of the BJP's twelve legislators in the state had previously been MLAs or ministers in other parties.[82] In Manipur too, the BJP's first chief minister, Nongthombam Birendra Singh, had defected from the Congress in 2016 and had once been a Congress minister. More than a dozen other senior leaders from both the Congress and the Trinamool Congress defected in the lead-up to Manipur's 2017 election. Most of them were given BJP tickets to contest and many were rewarded with ministerial berths.[83] As many as 80 per cent of BJP ministers in the state (four of five) came from either the Congress, the Trinamool Congress or the National People's Party (NPP).[84] In fact, the entire Manipur unit of P.A. Sangma's NPP defected to the BJP. [85] Similarly, the party's lone minister in Meghalaya, Alexander Laloo Hek, who became the leader of its legislator party and a cabinet minister holding several portfolios, was a former Congress minister.[86] He too defected to the party just a month before the state elections, along with other legislators.

Arunachal Pradesh was a separate category of defections altogether. Here, the BJP won the entire state through defections in 2016. It started when Chief Minister Pema Khandu, then with the Congress, defected with forty-three party MLAs to join the People's Party of Arunachal and formed a new government in September 2016.[87] Three months later, in December 2016, he defected to the BJP with thirty-two MLAs to form a new government in Itanagar.[88] It was another three years before he formed the BJP's first 'elected' government in Arunachal, in 2019—'elected' in the sense that he fought the 2019 state assembly elections for the first time as a BJP man, campaigned on the party banner, asked for votes in its name and won a full majority.

Strategy 2: Strategic Alliances, Co-option and Partnerships

NEDA AS AN ANTI-CONGRESS ALLIANCE UMBRELLA

The BJP's second big pillar of growth in the Northeast was the creation of a network of alliances with regional parties, aimed at replacing the Congress in the region. The first step towards this was the formation of the NEDA coalition in 2016. Launched a day after the BJP's first Assam government was sworn in to office, with a meeting of regional chief ministers and the enunciation of what was called the Guwahati Declaration, NEDA was kicked off with the slogan of a 'Congress-mukt North-East'. As NEDA Convenor Himanta Biswa Sarma explained, the coalition's aim was the 'expansion of the base of BJP and its NE allies to make a Congress-free region at the local or regional level'.[89] It was also meant to 'institutionalise broader political cooperation' as 'not just a political alliance, but also a regional, alliance, geo-cultural alliance'.[90] Ten regional parties joined at the time. Since then, some have left and others have joined, while some remained members of the regional alliance even as they also fought electoral battles with the BJP at the state level. As the scholar Tarun Gogoi (no connection to the Congress MP by the same name) has pointed out, NEDA can be seen as a 'strategic move for BJP to exploit the anti-Congress sentiment among regional parties and garner it for their electoral benefit as well as expand their support base as insider party in a localised form'.[91] In other words, regional parties became conduits for the BJP's expansion. In the 2014 Lok Sabha poll, the party had only won eight of twenty-five seats. By 2019, the BJP had won fourteen seats on its own, while NEDA won eighteen seats. In effect, the coalition helped shrink the electoral space for the Congress in the region (see Table 16.2).

Table 16.2: The Role of NEDA in Expanding the BJP's Footprint in the Northeast: 2019 General Election Results

State	*Congress*		*BJP*		*NEDA*	
	Seats	*Vote %*	*Seats*	*Vote %*	*Seats*	*Vote*
Arunachal Pradesh (2)	0	20.69	2	58.22	2	58.22
Assam (14)	3	35.44	9	36.05	9	46.76
Manipur (2)	0	24.63	1	34.22	2	56.7
Meghalaya (2)	1	48.28	0	7.93	1	30.2
Mizoram (1)	-	-	0	5.75	1	50.64
Nagaland (1)	0	48.11	-	-	1	49.73
Sikkim (1)	0	1.13	0	4.71	0	48.64
Tripura (2)	0	25.34	2	49.03	2	53.19
North-East India (25)	4	33.6	14	33.7	18	-

Source: ECI data, Tarun Gogoi, 'North East Democratic Alliance (NEDA) and Political Change in Northeast India', Dialogue, *Vol. 20, No. 4, 2019, p. 116. Cumulative Northeast vote percentage data for BJP and Congress from Nalin Mehta, Rishabh Srivastava, PollNiti, https://pollniti.com/live.html#!*

LOCAL ALLIANCES, STRATEGIC FLEXIBILITY AND CO-OPTING KEY GROUPS

While co-opting influential defectors from other parties, the BJP focused equally on building networks of power with multiple regional parties in each state. Given that it was starting from a low base, the gambit of building a patchwork of alliances was smart strategy. This becomes clearer when you examine state-specific alliances by the BJP in each of the north-eastern states: in Assam with AGP and Bodoland People's Front (BPF) in its first government, and then AGP and United People's Party Liberal (UPPL) for its second term; in Manipur with NPP, NPF and Lok Janshakti Party (LJP); in Meghalaya with United Democratic Party (UDP), People's Democratic Front (PDF) and Hill State People's Democratic Party (HSPDP); and in Nagaland with NPP (see Table 16.3).

The model was to forge partnerships with regional parties that brought with them specific vote bases in order to build a wider social coalition. While the alliances in each state were different, so was the party's political messaging. The BJP's biggest disadvantage in the Northeast was the perception of being a Hindu/Hindi-focused outsider. It sought to offset this, state by state, by aligning with indigenous parties that represented large local interest groups. Tripura and Nagaland are two examples of this differentiated approach.

Table 16.3: The BJP's Coalitions in the Northeastern States (2016–2021)

State	*Govt Since*	*Chief Minister*	*Chief Minister's Party*	*BJP's Alliance Partners*	*BJP+ Seats in Assembly*
Assam	24 May 2016	Sarbananda Sonowal	BJP	AGP, BPF	86/126
*Assam (second term)	10 May 2021	Himanta Biswa Sarma	BJP	AGP, UPPL	75/126
Arunachal Pradesh	16 September 2016	Pema Khandu	BJP	JD(U), NPP	55/60
Manipur	15 March 2017	N. Biren Singh	BJP	NPP	37/60
Nagaland	7 March 2008	Neiphiu Rio	NDPP	NDPP	34/60
Meghalaya	8 March 2018	Conrad Sangma	NPP	UDP, PDF, HSPDP	39/60
Tripura	8 March 2018	Biplab Kumar Deb	BJP	IPFT	44/60

Source: Analysis by the author

THE TRIPURA MODEL: ALLIANCE WITH INDIGENOUS TRIBAL PARTY

In Tripura, where Bengali-speaking Hindus constitute a majority (about 65 per cent of the population), the BJP had natural advantages. Yet, along with appealing to Bengali Hindus, it also sought to assuage fears of cultural engulfment of the state's indigenous tribal groups by aligning with the Indigenous People's Front of Tripura (IPFT). This BJP–IPFT alliance, with its slogan of 'Chalo Paltai' (Let's Overturn) ended up winning a majority of the state's tribal seats. As Ram Madhav—the senior leader who oversaw that campaign and who was entrusted by the BJP with its Northeast expansion till 2020—explained, 'Tripura has two distinct groups: Bengali-speaking people and the tribals who are about 35 per cent … Tribals felt they were being discriminated against, that their language, culture and way of life was endangered. So we promised them "unity" and entered into an alliance with IPFT.'[92] This alliance was significant because the IPFT was one of the key groups demanding a separate state for the tribal regions of

Tripura. It had shot into the national limelight in 2017 when hundreds of its supporters blocked railway tracks as well as a national highway on the outskirts of the capital Agartala, demanding the creation of 'Twipraland'. Though the ruling Left Front government rejected the demand, the BJP took a more measured line, saying that it 'recognised the deprivation of the tribals of the state'.[93] Even as this demand turned into a major electoral issue, IPFT forged a pre-poll alliance with the BJP. It was a temporary win-win for both sides.

The alliance allowed the BJP to present itself as a pro-tribal party. According to Ram Madhav, the party first got 'IPFT to issue a statement that they are committed to unity and integrity of Tripura'. In turn, the BJP 'promised the tribals that we would take care of their economic, cultural and social concerns'. The alliance gave this promise local credibility. 'It is because of this partnership,' he told *Organiser*, 'that we won 17 out of 19 tribal seats we contested.'[94] For the IPFT too, an alliance with Delhi's ruling party offered several benefits. N.C. Debbarma, the party chief, said that he felt his party's best chances lay with the BJP. 'They control the Centre, and are most likely to continue,' he argued. 'This is a Constitutional demand and has to be supported by the Centre.'[95] The alliance suited and complimented the strengths of both parties. It was potent enough for the Left's chief minister at the time, Manik Sarkar, to accuse the BJP of trying to divide the state by tying up with tribal groups. This message had no impact and the alliance's arithmetic succeeded in outflanking the powerful Left Front (see Table 16.4).

Table 16.4: The BJP's Rise in Tripura: 2018 Assembly

Party	*Seats*	*Vote-Share*
BJP	35	43%
IPFT	8	7.5%
CPI-M	16	42.7%
TOTAL	60	

Note: Election to one seat, Charilam, was countermanded. Source: ECI

It helped the BJP that, compared to the IPFT, another state tribal outfit, the Indigenous Nationalist Party of Twipra (INPT) led by former militant-turned-leader Bijoy Kumar Hrangkhaw, could not strike a chord with the Janjati population. This is why Amit Shah made it a point to stress in his victory speech that the party's pro-tribal outreach had worked. The BJP–IPFT won all twenty ST-reserved seats in Tripura, with the IPFT winning eight of the nine seats it contested.[96] The challenges of this alliance became clearer in 2019, when the IPFT's insistence on Twipraland meant that the IPFT and the BJP, while remaining allies in the state government, fought against each other in Tripura's two seats in the national election. 'Ideological differences with the BJP are there,' IPFT's general secretary and the tribal welfare minister in the alliance government, Mevar Kumar Jamatia, was quoted as saying. 'Being a regional party, our focus is on regional issues such as the demand for a separate Twipraland in the scheduled areas.'[97] Even so, the fact that the unlikely alliance persisted on the state level showed that the BJP was prepared to be pragmatic and make compromises for political gains in the region.

NAGALAND'S SPLIT-AND-MERGE MODEL

The BJP's challenge in Nagaland, a Christian-majority state, was of a very different order from what it faced in Tripura. The apex body of Baptist churches, the Nagaland Baptist Churches Council, had directly attacked the party, accused it of being anti-minorities and asked believers not to support those who sought to 'pierce the heart of Jesus Christ'.[98] In such a situation, the BJP needed local faces and much more flexibility. Though it had a fifteen-year-old alliance with the NPF, some senior leaders from its long-time ally too accused the party of being anti-Christian in the months leading up to the 2018 assembly election. NPF leader and former Nagaland chief minister, Shurhozelie Liezietsu, for example, reportedly told voters that the BJP had a larger agenda of declaring India a 'Hindu Rashtra'. 'If the BJP comes to power in this Christian state,' he said at a public meeting in Kohima, 'they [the BJP] will tell the rest of the world that, since Christian Nagaland has voted for BJP, Christians want to convert to Hinduism and then they will force us into paganism. Our faith is destined to die and very soon, Nagaland will stop being the abode of Christ and will become the den of anti-Christ where idols will be worshipped and the heathen will rule.'[99] The Christian–Hindu binary became a key fault line of Naga identity. Liezietsu characterised it as a choice between 'outsiders' and 'Naga identity' and asked voters not to gamble with their 'faith, identity and culture'.[100]

The BJP responded to this challenge with two countermoves. It downplayed the Hindutva narrative in Nagaland, especially on the issue of beef. Further, it countered the outsider/anti-Christian charge by stitching together a new alliance with another regional party, the Nationalist Democratic Progressive Party (NDPP), which had emerged after a split within the then ruling NPF, a few months before the state went to the polls in 2018. The NPF split was caused by differences among its senior leaders and the BJP played what one observer called a 'masterly and shrewd tactical game' in managing the political fallout. It chose not to disown the parent NPF, which was also a BJP ally at the Centre. But it struck a parallel deal with the new NDPP just before the election. The BJP 'had calculated that the two were evenly matched and did not want to put all its eggs in one basket', *Imphal Press Journal* editor Pradip Phanjoubam observed. 'Given the power balance, the NPF could not muster the courage to protest the BJP move, nor did NDPP insist on the BJP severing ties with the NPF ... Till the last moment before the BJP took the decision, both the NPF and NDPP were profusely pledging allegiance to the BJP.'[101]

The NPF had split into two halves with equal influence in the state, and one half, led by Neiphiu Rio, renamed itself as NDPP. The new party's breakaway leaders needed the BJP as a national ally in their fight with the NPF. So the new faction gave the BJP, a party that had won only one seat in Nagaland's previous state elections of 2013, the space to contest in as many as twenty seats in Nagaland's sixty-member assembly. With backing from NDPP cadres, the BJP won twelve of these seats, its highest ever performance so far in the state. Its best until then had been seven seats in 2003. The NDPP itself won eighteen seats, giving its alliance with the BJP a majority in the Nagaland assembly (see Table 16.5).

One interpretation of the BJP's rise is that it was actually the 'outcome of the party riding on the support base of Rio's party, which in turn is roughly half of the original NPF's support base.' If there had not been a split in the NPF, and if the BJP had gone to the polls on its own, the journalist Pradip Phanjoubam felt that 'in all likelihood, its performance would not have been any better than in the 2013 assembly election.'[102]

What is certain is that the BJP got the better end of the bargain in the alliance. 'We contested 40 seats but won 18. The BJP did much better, winning 12 out of 20 seats,' said Neiphiu Rio, the chief-ministerial face of the BJP–NDPP alliance. As Ram Madhav later explained, the alliance was very 'significant' because its 'adversaries like the NPF, who were fellow travelers until a few months ago, projected the BJP as a Hindutva party and unleashed the most communal campaign in the state. Yet, people supported the BJP.'[103]

Table 16.5: The BJP's Rise in Nagaland: 2018 Assembly Poll

Party	*Seats*	*Vote Share*
BJP	12	15.3%
NPF	27	38.8
JDU	1	4.5%
NDPP	18	25.2%
Independent	1	4.3%
Total	60	

Note: Elections were held in in fifty-nine seats; ECI data

The BJP's high strike rate in Nagaland illustrates the wider trend of its emergence as the predominant national party in the region. The Sangh saw the victory of the alliance as a vindication of the BJP's allegation that it had been vilified as a communal party. With the victories in Christian-dominated Nagaland and Meghalaya, *Organiser* declared that the 'tag of "Hindu Chauvinism" would now be countered forcefully'. Law and IT Minister Ravi Shankar Prasad delineated this further when he said, 'In spite of very vicious campaign against the BJP among the Christian minorities, the BJP has won 12 out of the 20 seats we fought polling 15% of votes in Nagaland'[104]

Rapidly shifting local alliances, irrespective of ideological affinity, are not unusual in the Northeast. Even the Congress and the BJP entered into a historic local alliance in the Chakma Autonomous Development Council (CADC), one of the forums under the Sixth Schedule of the Constitution that grants special safeguards to tribal areas. It lasted for a year before unravelling.[105] The BJP had always had alliances in the Northeast. The point is that, once it was firmly in power in Delhi and looked like it was making a serious bid in the Northeast, its value for prospective allies and defectors began rising. All of this took a lot of deft manoeuvring by the BJP's coalition architects like Himanta Biswa Sarma and Ram Madhav—a reflection also of how deeply invested the BJP was in the region from 2014.

Strategy 3: Narratives of Development and the Importance of the Centre in the Northeast

The promise of development and greater efficiency has been a key BJP plank in the Northeast. As one way of testing this, we decided to look at independent satellite data to see how the region had changed under the UPA and NDA governments. For several years now, NASA satellites have been taking publicly available pictures across India every month. Since these images are available over several years, they allow us to observe change visually. My research colleague Rishabh Srivastava extracted NASA VIIRS images for India stretching over a fourteen-year period (2004–2018) to measure nightlights in the Northeast. Nightlights are a good proxy measure to check the progress of electricity connectivity as well increasing economic activity. Srivastava collected over 150 GB of data, wrote a software programme to empirically measure the change in nightlights visible in monthly satellite photos, and then we overlaid them on a parliamentary constituency map of India. In the north-eastern states, the changes were remarkable.

The satellite images showed that nightlights increased across the region:

- in Arunachal Pradesh by 80 per cent in the 2014–2018 period (compared with 30 per cent in 2009–2013, 20 per cent in 2004–2009);
- in Manipur by 114 per cent (28 per cent in 2009–2013, 23 per cent in 2004–2009);
- in Assam by 50 per cent (33 per cent in 2009–2013, 19 per cent in 2004–2009);
- in Mizoram by 63 per cent (29 per cent in 2009–2013, 38 per cent in 2004–2009);

- in Nagaland by 59 per cent (15 per cent in 2009–2013, 41 per cent 2004–2009);
- in Sikkim by 41 per cent (28 per cent in 2009–2013, 23 per cent in 2004–2009);
- in Tripura by 42 per cent (55 per cent in 2009–2013, 3 per cent in 2004–2009).

To be sure, the increase in electrification and nightlights was built on work done by the previous Congress-led UPA governments. Indeed, the early progress on this by UPA-1 (2004–2009) was impressive, but the independent NASA satellite data showed that the pace of growth slowed down in UPA-2 (2009–2013). It accelerated significantly after 2014, when the Modi government built on the successes of the previous governments, but increased the pace. So much so that in Arunachal, Manipur, Mizoram

Figure 16.6: Nightlights Changed Drastically in the Northeast After 2014

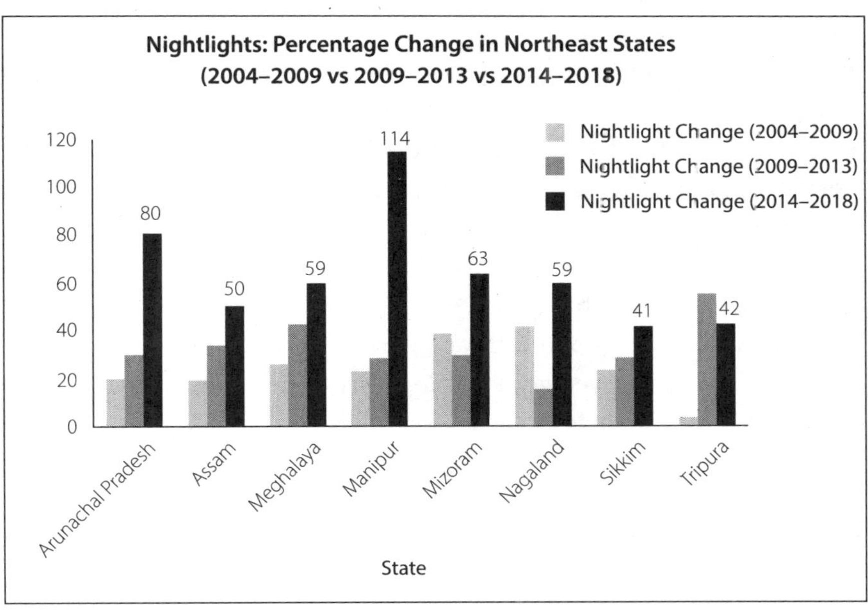

Source: Satellite data extracted from NASA VIIRS Night-time Monthly Lights Composites. (Radiance measured in nanowatts/cm²/sr.) Data analysis by Rishabh Srivastava, who aggregated data by year, using Python programming, and then mapped it on to all parliamentary constituencies to calculate state-by-state growth.[106]

and Nagaland, the nightlight growth rate doubled. These figures testify to changes taking place in the Northeast and also explain why, when the Modi government talks of development in the Northeast, its slogans are not easily dismissed as the usual propaganda by local constituencies.

The role of money and the clout that any Central government wields with its developmental funding is crucial. Narendra Modi indicated as much when he asked Arunachal Pradesh voters to choose 'double-engine growth' (with BJP governments at the Centre and in the state) while addressing a public rally in Aalo in April 2019.[107] This has been a standard BJP slogan in every election since the party came to power in Delhi. Yet, in the Northeast, it has a special resonance because these states are far more dependent on the Central government for funding than most others.

The north-eastern states, like many others, were created on linguistic principles or based on political exigencies. Their tax revenue base, which was not a criterion for their creation, is much lower than the national average. States such as Haryana, Maharashtra, Gujarat, Tamil Nadu, Telangana or Delhi raise about 70 per cent of their own budgets. The north-eastern states, on the other hand, depend on Central transfers for most of their revenue (as much as 70 per cent of their spending on average).[108] As the North Eastern Council Regional Plan put it, they were 'not economically viable and had to depend heavily on the Central Government for financial assistance, especially Plan assistance, which continues to be given on a 90:10 basis, i.e. 90% is central assistance while the States themselves raise only 10% of the budget'.[109] All the north-eastern states were, therefore, characterised as 'special category states'.[110]

This means that the political party controlling the Central government has always had more leverage in the Northeast than other parties have. The BJP has had this advantage in recent years because 'money plays a big role in our politics', as a veteran political observer in Guwahati put it, speaking on condition of anonymity. 'Our states need monetary help for everything and depend a great deal on Delhi. Sikkim, for instance, has the highest per capita income in the country, but hardly generates any revenue of its own. Without Central government assistance, you will find its people very destitute. The district of Darjeeling alone, with its tea gardens, probably generates more revenue than all the Northeast combined. We have hardly any manufacturing, relatively less farming, few jobs and few revenue-growth programmes in most states, and hence the dependence.'[111] The Central government spends up to ten times more per person each year in the north-eastern states than it spends in other less developed states like Madhya Pradesh or UP. The spending is, on average, ₹55,253 per person per year in Arunachal Pradesh, ₹51,127 in Sikkim, ₹42,276 in Mizoram, ₹34,023 in Nagaland, ₹23,637 in Manipur, ₹20,521 in Tripura and ₹16,070 in Meghalaya. These are huge spends when compared with the average per capita spending in general category states: ₹5,030 (see Table 16.6).

Table 16.6: Delhi Spends Far More on North-eastern States Per Capita Than on Other States[112]

Differences in Per Capita Income and Fiscal Variables Among States (2014-15), in ₹

State	*Per Capita GSDP*	*Per Capita Revenue*	*Total Transfers from Centre*
General Category States			
Andhra Pradesh	1,06,263	10,687	7,393
Bihar	33,954	2,026	5,095
Chhattisgarh	87,354	7,629	6,414
Gujarat	1,41,405	11,187	3,329
Haryana	1,65,728	12,095	3,207
Jharkhand	62,091	4,199	4,827
Karnataka	1,44,869	11,788	4,609
Kerala	1,55,005	12,512	4,542
Madhya Pradesh	63,323	6,135	5,450
Maharashtra	1,52,853	10,887	3,221
Odisha	71,184	6,411	6,686
Punjab	1,26,606	9,787	3,637
Rajasthan	84,837	7,193	5,463
Tamil Nadu	1,46,503	11,668	4,749

State	*Per Capita GSDP*	*Per Capita Revenue*	*Total Transfers from Centre*
Telangana	1,41,979	9,719	4,163
Uttar Pradesh	49,450	4,460	4,707
West Bengal	94,711	4,853	5,378
All General Category States	**95,802**	**7,895**	**5,030**
Special Category States			
Arunachal Pradesh	1,10,217	6,185.6	55,253.8
Assam	60,621	3,630.2	8,054
Himachal Pradesh	1,47,330	3,630.2	8,054
Jammu and Kashmir	77,559	11,323.6	13,864.8
Manipur	58,442	2,269.2	23,637.8
Meghalaya	75,156	4,005.2	16,070.5
Mizoram	93,136	4,297.2	42,276.9
Nagaland	89,607	3,207.8	34,023
Sikkim	2,40,274	19,361.1	51,127.9
Tripura	77,358	3,572.1	20,521.1
Uttarakhand	1,53,076	8,929.2	10,203.8
All Special Category States	**85,572**	**5,604.4**	**14,080.1**
All States	**95,802**	**7,419**	**5,399.15**

Source: Finance Accounts of State Governments, Comptroller and Auditor General, Government of India. Reproduced from M. Govinda Rao, 'Central Transfers to States in India Rewarding Performance While Ensuring Equity (Final Report of a Study Submitted to NITI Aayog)', p. 11. The report was sponsored by NITI Aayog and conducted by the National Institute of Public Finance and Policy, 25 September 2017, New Delhi.

While governments at the Centre have always allocated generous funds for the Northeast, the BJP argues that, since 2014, the money its government has sanctioned is being spent more effectively. Amit Shah claims this to be one of the major reasons for the party's victories. 'The biggest reason for our win is that money was always allocated for North-

East but development did not happen. Under Modiji, this money started getting converted into development ... The way development began to happen, people started thinking we should also join this development journey and this is the reason why people voted for us and change.'[113] This narrative of development is at the centre of the BJP's political messaging in the region. 'Our vision is Act-East and Act-Fast on East,' declared Modi at a public rally in Silchar in early 2019.[114] His decision to hold a meeting of the North Eastern Council in Shillong, as opposed to Delhi, soon after he was elected, symbolised precisely this. 'He was the first prime minister after Morarji Desai to hold a North Eastern Council meeting in Shillong,' claimed Amit Shah. 'Every fifteen days, a Central government minister goes on some work or the other to visit the Northeast region.'[115] Ram Madhav said, 'Today, if you find any good roads in these states it is simply central funded i.e. national highways. Today, except in Arunachal, in other states we have achieved near 100% electrification. Now we are taking it to the next level by ensuring 100% electrification of every household.'[116]

The BJP also makes much of the fact that the Ministry of Development of North Eastern Region was established by the first Vajpayee government in 2001. The funding for this ministry increased by 14 per cent in 2020-21 (from ₹2,670 crore in 2019-20 to ₹3,049 crore), which shows how important the Modi government considers it. In fact, government data shows that actual expenditure on gross budgetary support to the north-eastern states in fifty-four ministries rose by 142 per cent (from ₹23,819 crore to ₹60,112 crore) between 2014-15 and 2020-21. Simultaneously, the budget for the North Eastern Council doubled between 2015 and 2020, from ₹700 crore to ₹1,747 crore.[117]

Government data shows that Central government funding for most states in the region increased significantly between 2014-15 and 2018-19. In Assam, where the BJP formed its first government in 2016, central funding increased by over fifty per cent in this period, in Manipur by over sixty-six per cent, and it more than doubled in Mizoram (see Table 16.7).

Being in power at the Centre clearly increased the BJP's bargaining power in the Northeast. Regional parties and influential local politicians began to see the benefit of aligning with the BJP, just as they had seen the benefits of doing so with the Congress in the days of its hegemony. The

BJP combined this advantage with its aggressive ground campaigning, tactical alliances and messaging on the narrative of development fronted by Prime Minister Modi.

Table 16.7: Increases in Central Funding for North-eastern States (2014–2019)*

State	*State*	*Funds Released During Last Five Years (₹ Crore)*			
	2014-15	*2015-16*	*2016-17*	*2017-18*	*2018-19*
Arunachal Pradesh	251.52	197.76	195.68	248.72	210.78
Assam	293.59	323.34	359.12	313.24	453.20
Manipur	219.59	259.51	324.00	363.35	366.11
Meghalaya	157.15	193.69	194.54	298.00	118.92
Mizoram	95.22	166.06	133.03	242.03	192.00
Nagaland	157.41	160.28	177.68	195.11	108.92
Sikkim	126.16	77.61	111.18	110.40	160.68
Tripura	103.02	104.82	139.51	107.77	57.34
Total to States	1403.66	1483.07	1634.74	1914.52	1667.95
Central Agencies	51.7	80.62	180.31	104.89	166.25
Grand Total	**1455.36**	**1563.69**	**1815.05**	**2019.41**	**1834.2**

Source: FIB Delhi, Ministry of Development of North Eastern Region, 'Funds for North-East States', 4 December 2019, https://pib.gov.in/PressReleasePage.aspx?PRID=1594968

**Funds released under schemes of Ministry of Development of North Eastern Region and North Eastern Council.*[118]

Strategy 4: Hindu Acculturation, the RSS and Grassroots Expansion

The RSS has made deep inroads in two states in particular: Assam and Tripura. On 21 January 2018, the Sangh organised its biggest ever rally in Assam: the Luitporia (Sons of Brahmaputra) Hindu Samavesh, a giant gathering in Guwahati of swayamsevaks from upper Assam. With sixty-five Hindu saints and religious leaders attending, along with heads of village bodies and twenty tribal kings—from the Karbi, Naga, Khasi, Hajong, Tiwa, Garo, Jaintia, Mising and Hajong communities as well as over ten chiefs of different Satras in Assam[119]—the RSS leadership congratulated itself on 'the growing acceptability of the Sangh in an unprecedented manner'.[120] It claimed that over 75,000 people attended the gathering in total, including over 30,000 swayamsevaks representing 96 per cent blocks (239), 70 per cent circles (1,511) and 90 per cent urban localities in upper Assam. As many as 14,000 families in Guwahati, it said, had contributed to organising the programme. In Tripura, a year earlier, the RSS's sarsanghchalak, Mohan Bhagwat, had attended a similarly large Hindu Sammelan in Agartala. The Sangh claimed that it reached 1 lakh households, each of which hoisted saffron flags on its directive. 'The invitations were delivered personally and not through the usual technological tools.' As many as 26,000 people attended the public meeting, and there were representatives from half the region's villages (505 of 1,043). As the Sangh's annual report reported, 'A plan to contact each and every tribal group was prepared and Gurupujan, Raksha Bandhan, Vijaydashami programmes took the process forward ... This programme organized in the Northeastern state of Tripura was effective in every sense.'[121] Bhagwat underlined the fact that the gathering took place while Tripura was still under Communist rule and thus showed 'the growing acceptability of RSS in the cross-sections of the society'.[122]

The cultural integration of the Northeast has always been one of the core priorities of the Sangh. Former pracharak and then BJP general secretary Ram Madhav pointed out in 2018 that, for years, not a single annual gathering of the Sangh's highest decision-making bodies—the Karyakarini or the Pratinidhi Sabha—had concluded without passing a Northeast-linked resolution. 'These were treated as challenges for our ideological cause.'[123] Such is the Northeast's importance that Tripura was created as a separate 'prant' in the RSS's organisational hierarchy in 2018.[124] As Mohan Bhagwat declared, 'For us, in Tripura, the Sangh work has increased, we have developed a team there to take care of the work and, therefore, now it is considered as a separate Prant.'[125]

Ram Madhav attributed regional growth to this kind of penetration by the RSS and its network of institutions like the ABVKA, Ekal Vidyalayas and other affiliates. 'Today, the BJP has grown into a big entity in a number of Northeastern states, but the core remains those who have been brought forward by the Sangh years ago. In Tripura, four of the Sangh Pracharaks were kidnapped and we never found even their dead bodies. But today we see a flood of people into the BJP in Tripura. We have secured 43 seats there but the core remains those who had joined the party when there was nothing. Originally inspired by the Sangh they came into the politics and gradually built the party in their respective states. The Sangh workers worked there at the time when a severe sense of alienation was there. They created a constituency for India. That constituency has become our core. Even in different political parties there, people still mention that they participated in the SEIL (Students' Experience in Interstate Living) programme. Even in states like Nagaland and Meghalaya, where the Sangh had little scope to grow, our karyakartas worked through Vanvasi Kalyan Ashram and other frontal organisations. Now we see lot of people there with India at the heart.'[126]

The RSS worked in the Northeast for decades before it could make headway. In October 1946, a few months before Independence, three pracharaks—Dadarao Parmarth, Vasantrao Oak and Krishna Paranjpe—set up the first shakhas in Guwahati, Shillong and Dibrugarh. They were followed by Eknath Ranade, who set up the first Vivekananda Kendra in the region as well as several residential schools in Arunachal Pradesh.[127] By 1975, the RSS had shakhas in every district of Assam. As national organisational growth became a priority, from 2003, it started to focus on 'Bengal and North-East'.[128] By 2019, it had 813 shakhas in Upper Assam—which in the Sangh's administrative division constitutes the Brahmaputra Valley, Nagaland and Meghalaya—275 in Tripura and several dozen each in Manipur and Arunachal Pradesh.[129]

The groundwork for the BJP's 2018 Tripura victory was, in fact, driven by former RSS pracharaks. Sunil Deodhar, who joined the RSS in 1985, was made BJP in-charge of Tripura in 2014, after having managed its work in Meghalaya. Ram Madhav and Ram Lal, who was then general secretary in charge of organisation, were also former RSS pracharaks.[130] Deodhar camped in the state for 500 days. He later explained to *Organiser* the challenges of the job: 'There was nothing to start with in Tripura. Everything had to be built from the grassroots. I was expected to strengthen the organization there. Specifically, a place where you are new and there is no base of your organisation, then you have to socialise with people, you have to hit the ground zero time and again, spend hours and hours with the local people, eat what they eat, learn and speak their language, take part in their festivals, be part of their life, only then you will be able to make space in their hearts. We tried to understand their problems and then share them with our people and later found right solution. The training I got from RSS helped me a lot to build organisation there. I worked in Tripura along the same lines as I worked in Meghalaya. I was able to convince 60 new karyakartas to work as Vistaraks.'[131]

In tandem with this local mobilisation, the RSS sent 250 workers in 2016 to Tripura. The number of shakhas in the state doubled from eighty in 2015 to 250 by the time of the election in 2018. It was the 'RSS's boots on the ground that eventually helped breach the Left citadel of Tripura'.[132]

RANI GAIDINLIU AND RESISTANCE TO CHRISTIAN MISSIONARIES: CORE RSS BELIEFS IN THE NORTHEAST

RSS expansion in the Northeast has been driven by three core beliefs: that the region has been part of Greater Bharat since ancient times, that the British wrongly drove a wedge in this ancient cosmology of networks by characterising the region's tribal groups, with their animist beliefs, as separate from Hindus and the idea of Hinduism, and that the growth of Christian missionary work and the rise in conversions in the Northeast are a threat to Indian security stability. Prafulla Ketkar, the editor of *Organiser*, summed up the cultural core of these beliefs in a signed editorial in early 2018. 'Right from Mahabharata period we find references to the sacred places and personalities from the region in our discourse. These brave people did not allow Moghuls to cross Brahmaputra and therefore, remained protected from the Muslim invasions. Taking benefit of this the British, again finding the region difficult to govern, kept it underdeveloped and allowed missionaries to carry on their activities openly. Unfortunately, in the post-independence period instead of rekindling the ancient linkages, we also bought the British narrative and were caught in the tyranny of distance. It was physical as well as cultural. Only nationalist organisations like the RSS brought Lachit Borphukan [commander of an indigenous Ahom army that defeated an invading Mughal army in the Battle of Saraighat in 1671] and Rani Ma Gaidinliu in the limelight by giving them the due recognition in the national discourse.

Taking this process forward rest of Bharat should completely break the colonial shackles about our geography and nationhood.'[133]

The RSS demand to award India's highest honour, the Bharat Ratna, to the late Rani Gaidinliu of Nagaland is meant to embody both its belief in preserving the animist cultures of the tribes from Christian conversion and its nationalist messaging. The demand was first made by ABVKA in 2014. Rani Gaidinliu had spent fourteen years in British jails, opposed Naga secessionist movements after Independence and fought for the preservation of traditional Naga animist beliefs.[134] As a seventeen-year-old, she had raised a three-tribe Zeliangrong army against the British to establish Naga Raj and resist Naga conversions to Christianity. She lost the Battle of Hangrum (Assam) in 1932. As Rahul Karmakar has pointed out, 'Naga converts were primarily held responsible for her capture and imprisonment until 1947.' Interestingly, Jawaharlal Nehru met her while she was incarcerated in Shillong jail and gave her the sobriquet of Rani (queen), and she became Nehru's 'poster girl' of the Northeast after Independence.[135] The Heraka movement she headed was a minority among the Nagas, but it was strongly opposed to Christian conversion, just as the Sangh was. Masoyo Hunphun Awungashi has shown that, since the 1970s, the 'RSS has backed the Zeliangrong Heraka Association, which sought to reconvert Christian members of the Zeme, Liangmai and Rongmei tribes.'[136]

To understand why a primary driver of the RSS's expansion in the Northeast is its resistance to Christian missionary expansion, we must look at the patterns of religious change in the region. While Christians make up 16.94 per cent of the population, they are primarily concentrated in the hill states. If you take out Assam and Tripura, Census data shows that Christians make up as much as 68.42 per cent of the population in the Northeast. The Christianisation of the hill states—Meghalaya, Mizoram, Nagaland and Arunachal Pradesh—is largely a product of conversions in the twentieth century. In Meghalaya, Christians made up just 6.16 per cent of the population in 1901. This went up to 24.67 per cent in 1951 and 74.59 per cent in 2011. Similarly, Mizoram had only 0.05 per cent Christians in 1901. By 1951, the state was almost entirely converted, with Christians making up 90.05 per cent of the population (down to 87.16 per cent in 2011). Nagaland was half-Christianised by 1951 at 46.05 per cent and almost entirely converted by 2011 (87.9 per cent). Arunachal Pradesh saw a different pattern, with conversions primarily occurring after 1971, when the area was brought under civilian control. The state had only 0.79 per cent Christians in 1971. By 2011, this proportion had gone up to 30.26 per cent.[137]

Opposition to the expansion of Christianity is a fundamental article of faith with the Sangh. Then RSS chief K.S. Sudarshan, speaking in Agra in 2000, accused Christian missionaries of using the Northeast to establish 'military bases' in 'strategic areas' to work against India. He argued that Christianity as it was practised in the region had 'more to do with politics and less with religion' and that 'Church politics is detrimental to the country'. As he put it, 'The Church has a special interest in the Northeast because it is a sensitive, border area and they wanted a base in strategic areas to establish military bases. All this is politics in the name of religion.' Sudarshan also floated the idea of a new 'Indian' church, asking Christians to set up an indigenous church, delinked from foreign churches, if they did not believe in 'anti-national' activities. This call for an indigenous Indian church is not very different from the RSS's call for Indianising Islam.[138]

Linking the church with foreign influences, especially in the context of the Northeast, is a recurring theme in Sangh literature. On the RSS's seventy-fifth anniversary Dashami speech in Nagpur, Sudarashan once again called on Christians to free themselves of 'divisive' foreign missionaries 'in particular in north east' who, he said, were encouraging 'extremism and separatism'. The church, in this view, was part of a 'foreign conspiracy' to destabilise India[139]—a view that goes back to Golwalkar. He had argued in *A Bunch of Thoughts*: 'Their [Christian] activities are not merely irreligious, they are also anti-national ... So long as the Christians indulge in such activities and consider themselves as agents of international movement for the spread of Christianity, and refuse to offer their first loyalty to the land of their birth ... they will remain here as hostile [sic] have to be treated as such.'[140] Much like it did in the tribal areas of Madhya Pradesh and Chhattisgarh (see Chapter 14), the RSS chose to focus on education and the setting up of a wide network of schools in the Northeast as a tool to counter what it saw as the threat of Christian expansion. It is to this story that we now turn.

SANKAR DEVA NIKETANS, ABVKA AND EKAL VIDYALAYAS: EDUCATION AS A CULTURAL TOOL

Education is a key focus of the RSS's deep expansion into the Northeast. In 2016, Himanta Biswa Sarma tweeted a picture of himself with Sarfaraz Hussain, a tea-shop employee's son who had topped the state's CBSE board examination. A Muslim student, he had graduated from the Sankardev Shishu Niketan, scoring 590 out of 600 marks. This network of schools, named after the fifteenth-century Assamese poet-saint Sri Sankar Deva, is known as Saraswati Shishu Mandir in other states[141] and is run by the Sangh Parivar's Vidya Bharati network, which was set up in 1977. Sarma, then education minister of Assam, announced that schools with RSS ideals would soon be set up in each of the 2,202 panchayats in Assam.[142] Whether that happens or not, the Sangh Parivar was already running hundreds of schools across the Northeast. By 2020, Vidya Bharati was running 578 schools in Assam, with 16,347 students. Across seven north-eastern states, it ran a total of 670 schools—all geo-located on its website—with 28,488 students and 9,510 teachers,. A vast majority of these were in Assam (578), followed by Arunachal Pradesh (thirty), Sikkim (twenty-four), Meghalaya (eighteen), Manipur (twelve), Tripura (five) and Nagaland (three).

Table 16.8: Vidya Bharati Schools in the Northeast

State	*Schools*	*Students*	*Teachers*
Assam	578	16,347	8,775
Arunachal Pradesh	30	3,123	293
Sikkim	24	1,683	176
Meghalaya	18	4,081	335
Manipur	12	2,050	128
Tripura	5	916	65
Nagaland	3	248	31
Total	670	28,448	9,510

Source: Vidya Bharati data collated by the author from its state-wise online database: http://vidyabharti.net/

Sangh Parivar-affiliated Ekal Vidyalayas in the Northeast numbered 6,070 by 2020. This model of a single teacher running a school under a tree or in an open area allows for rapid expansion in backward areas because infrastructure costs are minimal.[143] The Parivar's ABVKA also runs 600 schools in the Northeast and twenty-seven hostels for tribal children. Again, a majority of these are in Assam (127 schools and eleven hostels), Meghalaya (124 schools), Manipur (forty-four schools and three hostels) and Tripura (forty-six schools and eight hostels). These educational institutions form the bedrock of the Sangh's growing cultural influence in the region.

Table 16.9: ABVKA Educational Institutions in the Northeast

State	*Educational Institutions*	*Hostels*
Assam	100	11
Arunachal Pradesh	51	-
Manipur	44	3
Tripura	46	8
Sikkim	201	1
Nagaland	34	4
Mizoram	-	-
Meghalaya	124	0
Total	600	27

Source: ABVKA data collated by the author from its state-wise online database https://kalyanashram.org/about-us/where-we-work/

Strategy 5: Hindu–Muslim Fault Lines and the Assam Model

The BJP's Assam model of ethno-religious mobilisation forms the fifth pillar of its growth. It is predicated on a sense of Hindus being in danger, a narrative of demographic change driven by the immigrant as 'Muslim' and the BJP's projection of itself as the protector of Hindu identity. An emergent communal divide powered the BJP's rise to ruling-party status in the state. This template also drove its growth in neighbouring West Bengal. We could call it the Assam/Bengal model. A large influx of migrants after the 1971 war with Pakistan and the Assam movement of the 1970s led to the state's politics being split along the 'insider–outsider' narrative. The BJP's demand for the deportation of all 'illegal migrants to Bangladesh'—which preceded the Supreme Court-mandated NRC in 2019—is at least as old as 2006.[144] That is why Himanta Biswa Sarma termed the 2019 general election in Assam as the 'final battle of Saraighat'.[145] It was a reference to the famous 1671 victory of the Ahom king, Raja Chakradhwaj Singha, and his general Lachit Borphukan, over the invading Mughal forces in a battle on the banks of the river Brahmaputra. That battle ended Mughal attempts to conquer Assam. This Saraighat narrative of beleaguered Hindus fighting a back-against-the-wall war against invading Mughal armies also formed the subtext of its 2016 assembly election victory, which resulted in Assam's first BJP government.

Rajat Sethi and Shubrashtha have argued in their history of that campaign that 'calling the elections "The Last Battle of Saraighat" against the demographic, cultural and political aggression of the illegal Bangladeshis threatening the essence of the state made this a people's movement'.[146] As mentioned before, Assam has the highest proportion of Muslims of any large state in India, after Jammu and Kashmir: 34 per cent. West Bengal has more Muslims—24.6 million—but they make up a slightly lower proportion of the population at 27.01 per cent.[147] It is no accident that the two states became home to an ethno-religious mobilisation based on notions of Hindu identity, starting with areas where Muslims were demographically dominant or large enough to be the primary factor in elections.

Tellingly, from the early 1990s, the first BJP political breakthroughs came in areas with significant Muslim populations. The creation of a Hindu political identity worked best in areas where the 'Other' was seen as a threat. This led to a Hindu consolidation of voters, just as there was Muslim consolidation against the BJP. While the Muslim vote could be split between the Congress and other regional forces, the Hindu votes counter-mobilised and coalesced around the BJP. There is a strong pattern of its dominance in these Muslim-dominated areas in national elections between 1991 and 2019. The BJP won its first Assam Lok Sabha seats in 1991 in the southernmost tip of the state: Karimganj and Silchar. Of these, Karimganj is a Muslim-dominant (56.36 per cent) constituency.[148] Even Silchar had a 12 per cent Muslim population. In 1996, the BJP won Karimganj again, its lone victory in that election. In 1999, it won two Lok Sabha seats: Nowgong (Nagaon) and Guwahati in Upper Assam. Of these, Nagaon district had a Muslim population of 55.36 per cent,[149] while Guwahati had 12.45 per cent Muslims. In 2004, the BJP won again in Nagaon and Mangaldoi (27.59 per cent Muslim population).[150] The pattern repeated in 2009, when the BJP won four Lok Sabha seats: Mangaldoi, Guwahati, Nagaon and Silchar. It was only in 2014, when it won seven parliamentary seats (three of these with a significant Muslim presence) and 2019, when it had a majority of nine seats, that the percentage of Muslim-dominant seats in its portfolio declined. Even then, over 40 per cent of its wins were in seats with a significant Muslim presence.

Table 16.10: The BJP Grew through Hindu Consolidation in Muslim-significant Seats in Assam

Year	*Lok Sabha Seats Won by BJP in Assam*	*Muslim-significant Lok Sabha Seats Won by BJP in Assam*	*Muslim-significant Seats BJP Won of Its Assam Tally %*
1980	0	0	–
1984	0	0	–
1989	0	0	–
1991	2	1	50
1996	1	1	100
1998	1	1	100
1999	2	1	50
2004	2	2	100
2009	4	4	100
2014	7	3	42.8
2019	9	4	44.4%

Source: Analysis by Nalin Mehta with Rishabh Srivastava of Lok Sabha data and Muslim-dominant seats, https://pollniti.com/live.html

This is not to say that the BJP grew on Hindu issues alone. An election is seldom won on a single issue. Yet, the electoral results showed a correlation between Muslim-significant seats and wins for the party, repeating over two decades. Eleven of Assam's thirty-three districts are Muslim-majority districts.[151] The BJP's initial bridgeheads mostly came in these districts as it became the political vehicle for articulating Hindu unease over Muslim migration. Unlike the Hindi heartland, Assam never had a Hindu–Muslim political fault line until recently. In fact, until the early 1990s, the primary praxis of identity politics in the state was on the question of language: Bengali speakers vs non-Bengali speakers.

Although the BJP had a presence in Assam from the 1950s onwards and focused on issues of illegal Muslim migration from Bangladesh from the very beginning, its message found little traction. Within a week of its formation, in the early 1950s, the Jan Sangh had set up an ad hoc committee to organise an Assam branch under the presidentship of I.P. Barooah, but it made little headway.[152] The growth of the BJP in the early 1980s was 'halted', as H. Srikanth has argued, 'to a considerable extent by the Assamese caste Hindus, who used to see BJP only as a Marwari party'. The Assam movement to protect indigenous populations from illegal migrants from Bangladesh defined the state's politics from the late 1970s to the 1980s. But it was focused on *all* outsiders—whether Hindu or Muslim—not on religious identity. As one observer put it,[153]

> BJP's policy of being soft to the Hindu immigrants and hard on the Muslim immigrants did not find many takers among influential section of Assamese society, who were more obsessed with the fear of domination by the Bengalis—both Hindus and Muslims—in all public spheres. Fear that their language and culture would be wiped out and the Assamese people would become minorities in their own land drove them to the so-called 'anti-foreigners' movement in the late seventies.

In the 1980s, the RSS started supporting the Assam movement, and this is what created an initial platform for the BJP. Its backing, the journalist Shekhar Gupta has argued, helped change the 'national imagery of the Assam movement, which was seen as anti-national because it blockaded crude supplies to the mainland'.[154] This meant that many of the movement's leaders, who later created the AGP, the state's pre-eminent regional party, started seeing the Sangh as an ally. In turn, the RSS, which had always opposed Muslim migration but not Hindu refugees from Bangladesh, gradually succeeded in shifting the popular focus from 'anti-immigrant to anti-Muslim immigrant'.[155] In this formulation, Hindu immigrants became 'sharnarthee', or asylum-seekers, while Muslim migrants became classified as 'anupraveshkaari', or infiltrators who had to be sent back.[156]

RSS leaders like the late Bansilal Soni and Padmanabha Acharya (later appointed governor, first of Nagaland, then additionally of Tripura and Assam, and also given charge briefly of Arunachal Pradesh and Manipur) were among those who worked to lay this foundation. By the time L.K. Advani began his Ayodhya Rath Yatra, the 'BJP in Assam had a strong platform'.[157] It won its first Lok Sabha seat in 1991. A number of cadres from the AGP, the political successor to the Assam movement, started moving to the BJP around this time. It gave the party new local leadership and credibility over and above its old Sangh base. 'Wherever Assamese Hindus were unhappy, BJP started growing. Now they portray themselves as saviours of Assamese Hindus,' explained a local editor.[158]

Once the political canvas was thus reframed, the BJP's turning point came with the 2008 Hindu–Muslim riots.[159] As one senior editor told me, 'Everything changed in 2008 when anti-Muslim riots happened in Udalguri and Nalbari [districts]. This was the first time that Hindu Bengalis and Nepalis fully aligned with Bodos against Muslims. In Assam, communal violence in the past had mostly been about Bengalis versus non-Bengalis. It was not because of religion earlier.'[160]

While it is true that Assam had seen the Nellie massacre in 1983, where over 2,000 Muslim migrants had been killed in horrific election-linked violence over illegal migration in Nagaon, communal tensions were never the default template for the state's politics. 'In 2008, Bengali Muslims were isolated,' the editor told me. 'Bengali Hindus started getting together and sided against them. This is why Congress leaders in Barak Valley are so quiet about these issues even now. Many Bengali Hindus now see themselves as threatened by Bengali-speaking Muslims [not Assamese Muslims who are seen as sons of the soil] and have bought into the idea of resistance to Muslim outsiders. This helps explain why the BJP was voted in.'[161]

The BJP initially supported the Assam movement and then aligned with the political heir to the movement, the AGP, in 2006. Eventually, as the regional party started declining, the BJP captured its political mantle and drew in large numbers of its leadership as well. 'The detection, deletion and deportation of illegal foreigners were the main electoral plank of the AGP which has been, in the last two decades, gradually hijacked by the electoral agenda of the BJP.'[162] While some critics have questioned the veracity of the infiltration narrative and whether Muslim migration was as widespread as those who opposed it argued,[163] it became the leitmotif of the BJP's politics in Assam. This is why, long before the Supreme Court's 2015 directive on implementing the NRC in Assam, Narendra Modi's primary political message while campaigning there in 2014 was on illegal migration. 'It is the need of the hour to stop the influx and we take this as our responsibility,' he said at an election rally in Gogamukh. 'After May 16 [when the election result comes out], *hum chun chun ke hisaab lenge* [we will settle each and every account].'[164]

The second historical turning point was the rise of a Muslim party in Assam in 2005—All India United Democratic Front (AIUDF). It was founded by Badruddin Ajmal, the patriarch of a trading family that sold attar oil, perfumes and textiles, as a party of Muslim migrants who carried the 'Bangladeshi stigma'. Ajmal, who is also the president of the Assam branch of the Jamiat Ulema-e-Hind and is rated as among the 500 most influential Muslims in the world,[165] created the party within months of the Supreme Court scrapping the Illegal Migrants (Determination by Tribunal) Act of 1983.[166] Several observers in Assam trace the decline of the Congress in the state to the rise of Ajmal's party. As Assamese politics got divided along a Hindu–Muslim axis, AIUDF became the counterpoint to the BJP. The Congress was left in a virtual no-man's land in this politics of religious identities. On one end was the BJP, which warned of Assam going the 'Jinnah' way if Ajmal was voted in,[167] and on the other was Ajmal, who compared Assamese Muslims with Rohingya Muslims in Myanmar, arguing for 'all Muslims to come together'[168] because they were being 'treated like insects'.[169] From 2005 onwards, AIUDF began to split the Muslim vote, which earlier went only to the Congress in the one-third of Assam's districts that were Muslim-dominant. Tactical alliances between the Congress and AIUDF also drove away the sections of Assamese Hindus who were now opposed to Muslim migration. AIDUF won ten assembly seats (9.05 per cent votes) in Assam's 2006 assembly elections, eighteen (12.5 per cent votes) in 2011, thirteen (13.05 per cent votes) in 2016, and 16 (9.29 per cent votes) in 2021, making it a significant Opposition party. Muslim electoral assertion was a consequence of Hindu identity politics, but it also served as a fuel for further Hindu consolidation.

The Challenges of Expansion

While the BJP has metamorphosed into the largest national party in the Northeast, it also faces significant challenges. The anti-NRC protests[170] in Assam and those against the CAA in early 2020 reflect some of these. The original intent of the NRC was to identify and deport illegal migrants. For the BJP, this denoted Muslim migrants. Yet, lakhs of Hindus were excluded in the final NRC lists. As many as 19.07 lakh Assamese residents (almost 6 per cent of the 3.29 crore who applied) were left out of these. The rate of exclusions in the border districts with Bangladesh, such as South Salmara (7.22 per cent), Dhubri (8.26 per cent) and Karimganj (7.57 per cent) was much lower than in districts like Karbi Anglong (14.31 per cent) and Tinsukia (13.25 per cent), where Assam's bhumiputras[171] have lived for centuries.

In Assam, public unhappiness was rooted in the fact that, while CAA would allow Indian citizenship to non-Muslim immigrants, the Assam movement had been against all migrants, irrespective of religion. The Assam Accord of 1985 had also put down a migration cut-off date of 24 March 1971, the year of the India–Pakistan war. The CAA extended that cut-off by over four decades, to 31 December 2014. Faced with prolonged protests in the first half of 2020, the BJP now sought to get out of this political bind by promising to activate Clause VI of the Assam Accord, which promised guarantees to ethnic Assamese in government positions.[172] Essentially, Clause VI promised 'Constitutional, legislative and administrative safeguards, as may be appropriate' to 'protect, preserve and promote the cultural, social, linguistic identity and heritage of the Assamese people'.[173] This is more or less what the Government of India had done in Sikkim in the 1970s when it became a part of India. To protect indigenous Bhutias and Lepchas in the state, sixteen seats in the thirty-two-member Sikkim assembly were reserved for them, even though their share in the population was only about 20–25 per cent. In Assam, such a safeguard would mean that, even if Bengali migrants were to form a majority in a particular area, they would be unable to contest elections. In February 2020, a committee appointed by the Central government to implement Clause VI gave its recommendations on how this might work at the administrative level.[174] How the BJP plays this card will be pivotal for its future in the region.

The NRC also opened up old discords in other north-eastern states. In November 2019, Meghalaya brought in an ordinance that virtually closed its borders with Assam, requiring all 'outsiders' staying more than twenty-four hours to register with the government.[175] In Tripura, indigenous tribes began demanding their own NRC in 2019 to expel Hindu Bengalis.[176] Many indigenous groups in these states were worried that the safeguards may not be enough. Their primary concern was a fear of engulfment by outsiders. Unlike in Assam, 'outsiders' in other states is not a dog-whistle for Muslim immigrants. In Tripura, by 2020, the immigrant Bengali population accounted for over 65 per cent of the state's population. Even though there are laws to protect the interests of the local tribes, the state has only had Bengali chief ministers since 1977. In Meghalaya, Manipur and Arunachal Pradesh, 'outsiders' denoted any settlers.

The BJP's big challenge as it seeks to consolidate its gains in the Northeast is one of trust. In 2018, for example, its expansion effort in Mizoram also opened up old Bru–Mizo tribal rivalries. When the Election Commission sought to allow displaced Bru refugees located in relief camps in Tripura to vote in state assembly elections, Mizo groups protested. They feared that Bru groups backing the BJP were being illegally included in the electoral rolls. Such was the intensity of the opposition that the Election Commission had to remove Mizoram's chief electoral officer, S.B. Shashank.[177]

By early 2021, the BJP, through a combination of strategies, organisational commitment, smart alliances and tactical flexibility had replaced the Congress as the primary national party in the Northeast. But this success also brought with it new kinds of challenges, reopened old legacy issues and brought into sharp focus the dissonance between the party's driving impulses in the Hindi-speaking states and the demographic diversity in the eastern states. How the BJP negotiates these new tensions will be crucial for its own political future as well as for Indian democracy.

17

THE MAKING OF A NEW WOMEN'S VOTE

Gender, Politics and Hindutva

In October 2007, I landed in Ahmedabad to cover Narendra Modi's second chief-ministerial election campaign for a television channel. The ECI had just announced the election dates for Gujarat, the official campaign was yet to start, and we were catching up on local gossip. The journalist Brajesh Kumar Singh, then Ahmedabad bureau chief at Star News, turned to me and said, 'What campaign have you Delhi journalists come to cover? Modiji has already finished his campaign.' He must have noticed the incredulous smile that these big-sounding political claims tend to bring to my face. So he added quietly, 'You may not believe it, but did you know Modi in the past year has held women-only public meetings in almost every district in Gujarat? The official campaign is the official campaign and it will start now, but do you understand the importance of what he has done with these women's meetings? His real campaign and support base at this level was long done before Congress woke up to the official campaign.'[1]

Government records showed that the Gujarat chief minister had personally presided over twenty-seven mahila sammelans (women's meetings) in various districts between 10 March and 20 September 2007 in the months leading up to the election announcement.[2] These women's empowerment meetings were organised through various government departments and the chief minister made it a point to attend each one of them. Modi had one message at these sammelans: 'If you have any problem, then you write a letter to me. Your brother, your son is sitting in Gandhinagar. Just send a postcard.'[3] The 2007 Gujarat campaign is now primarily remembered for Modi's return to Hindutva as the primary poll plank. It was an election in which he accused the Manmohan Singh-led UPA government in Delhi of replacing the map of India on rupee coins with a cross (the BJP called it a plan by the 'government machinery to push Christian beliefs') and alleged that Sohrabuddin was a 'hero for the Congress'. Hardline Hindutva combined with a focus on what was later to be marketed nationally as the Gujarat model of development became the BJP's primary differentiator in that campaign.[4] Yet, beneath the sharp edges of the communal–secular divide, it was the strategic wooing of the women's vote that would be the bedrock of the party's political mobilisation.

This was so crucial to the Gujarat BJP's political outreach in 2007 that a drop in male voting in the state's first polling phase in Saurashtra and South Gujarat—vis-à-vis women voting which remained as high as in 2002—caused a 'lot of excitement in the Narendra Modi camp'.[5] A Modi confidante, speaking before votes were counted, told *The Times of India* that the chief minister's strategy of reaching out to women through the district-wise mahila sammelans had 'probably helped in offsetting the Sonia factor' as well as the internal discontent and rumblings of 'Patel power'. Gujarat BJP Spokesperson Yamal Vyas summed up this view, saying, 'There is no doubt Modi is popular among women and they came out to vote because of him.'[6] The issue of Modi's mahila sammelans became so potent locally that the leader of the Opposition in the state, the Congress's Arjun Modhwadia, raised the matter in the state assembly, asking who had paid for these women-only meetings that Modi attended. The Gujarat government answered with administrative details on the floor of the assembly. It explained that a total of thirty-one such meetings were held. A sum of ₹10.8 crore had been spent on them by various boards and state corporations, including ₹9.9 lakh (0.1 per cent) by the Central government and ₹21.88 lakh by various government departments situated in these areas.[7]

When Modi briefed a journalist in May 2007 about his pre-election campaign approach, he too highlighted the mahila sammelans. Through these—and other such targeted events, like vanbandhu sammelans (forest friend, or Adivasi, meetings) and sagarkhedu (seafarer) sammelans—Modi estimated that he had addressed over 28 lakh women in a two-month period before the ECI's announcement of poll dates.[8]

Modi as a 'Sex Symbol': Masculinity, the 'Chhappanee Chhatee' Discourse and Outreach on Women's Issues

The genesis of Modi's 2007 political outreach to Gujarati women lay in how the crowds had responded to him in 2002 during his first election campaign. That was when he first evolved a language of political machismo. Modi's public references to his 'chhappanee chhatee' (fifty-six-inch chest) became the signature of a new political persona, along with a new discourse of 'asmita' (Gujarati pride). In an election in which the chief minister accused those who raised questions about the post-Godhra riots of maligning '5 crore Gujaratis', he simultaneously presented himself as the manly defender of Gujarati pride.[9] Looking back, as a TV journalist following Modi's Gaurav Yatra (Pride Journey) between September and December 2002, the one thing that stood out was how often he used the phrase 'chhappanee chhatee' in his speeches as he traversed the state in a modified bus, starting from the Bhatiji temple in Mehsana's Phagvel to Godhra and back to Ahmedabad.[10] In a speech he delivered in Godhra in October 2002, a colleague did the count: the chief minister had mentioned his 'chhappanee chhatee' over a dozen times. He was clearly positioning himself as the masculine defender of Gujarati and Hindu pride. This is why the most common slogan one heard every time Modi entered an election rally in 2002 was: '*Dekho dekho kaun aaya, Gujarat ka sher aaya* [Look, look, who has come, the lion of Gujarat has come]'. We had first heard this slogan earlier that year when he arrived at the Ahmedabad Collectorate to file his nomination papers for the Maninagar constituency. It remained a constant refrain at Modi rallies thereafter.

Back then, Modi also seemed to attract more women attendees than men in rally after rally. Many of us reporting on him noticed that they seemed to react more visibly to his speeches than the men did, especially when he used his catchphrases like 'chhappanee chhatee'. In my memory, the many Gaurav Yatra rallies I attended were less like political roadshows and more like an Indian version of what a Beatles rock concert might be like, where people came for darshan. At one particular rally in a village in Mehsana district, as Modi was speaking, the village temple's bells began to ring to signify the evening aarti, or prayer. Mid-speech, he stopped and said, '*Meri mataon aur behenon, mandir mein aartee shuru ho gayee hai, iska intezaar karte hain* [My mothers and sisters, the temple prayer has begun, let's wait for it].' There was pin-drop silence in the crowd, as he waited for the aarti to finish before resuming his speech. We did not realise it then, but Modi seemed to have become a Gujarati sanskari sex symbol. This phenomenon was noted by several commentators, including the Gujarati newspaper editor Aakar Patel, who later headed Amnesty International in India. 'Gujarati women absolutely adore him,' Patel wrote. 'Modi, though he may not acknowledge this, is a sex symbol in his home state. The ratio of women to men for his meetings and gatherings is higher than it is for other politicians in the state. He has the aura of a king or emperor, someone who exudes absolute power and authority, and therefore someone irresistible to women.'[11]

By 2007, this tactic had been turned into women-focused outreach and development strategies. When Modi addressed election rallies that year, they all featured special messages for the attending women. Often, he exhorted women to remember him before they cooked food in their homes on voting day. He would turn to the women and say in Gujarati, '*Behenon, pehle NaMo, fir jamo* [Sisters, first NaMo, then cooking].' This one-liner on voting and cooking 'always won laughs from the women in the audience and applause', remembers the journalist Sanjeev Singh, who covered several Modi rallies.[12] By 2012, his third election as a sitting chief minister, this outreach had been further fine-tuned.

The journalist Nistula Hebbar too described Modi as 'India's unlikeliest sex symbol'. His political projection was, in her view, that of an 'alpha male who set things right', who was not 'afraid to speak out his mind' and combined this personality projection with a focus on developmental issues around women.[13] 'Modi, according to those in the know, has always been more than conscious of the female vote,' she wrote. 'Apart from a helping hand to women to run small-scale businesses and expressing concern about their general safety in public spaces, he made a conscious effort to reach out to women voters. During the 2012 Assembly polls in Gujarat, he deployed Nirmala Sitharaman, Meenakshi Lekhi and

Smriti Irani to especially target women voters in rural areas. His rallies have consistently attracted a more female audience than male in Gujarat. The general atmosphere of a rise of crime against women, especially following the December 16 gang rape in Delhi [the Nirbhaya case] and the Central government's complete misreading of the popular mood, has allowed Modi's muscular image to gain traction among women.'[14]

This gender-focused image was an important but underrated building block of Modi's prime-ministerial bid in 2014. If women felt unsafe, then 'we have no right to call ourselves "mard" [man]', he declared at a 2013 rally in Chhotaudepur. Talking of attacks on women in the land of 'Sita and Savitris', the prime ministerial-candidate declared that 'some men with pervert brains blame women for such acts', further asserting that such assaults were 'no fault of the woman' and that the 'fault lies in the pervert minds of men'.[15] Similarly, Modi denounced female infanticide at a FICCI meeting that year, saying that India had 'regressed back to the 18th century' with such practices. Arguing that 'we, particularly men, underestimate the power of women', he said 'women are two steps ahead of men' and a 'modern India' could only be built by 'taking pride in our women and their powers'.[16]

This image of being a 'mard' is what Modi subliminally tapped into in 2014. As the sociologist Sanjay Srivastava argued, his first national campaign and the appeal of his pre-prime ministerial persona 'significantly focused upon his "manly" leadership style: efficient, dynamic, potent, and capable of removing all policy-roadblocks through sheer force of personality. In this narrative, he was implicitly contrasted with his predecessor Manmohan Singh and more generally against an "effeminate" Indian type who is unable to strike hard at both external enemies (Pakistan and China, say) and internal threats ("Muslim terrorists", most obviously). His "56-inch chest"—able and willing to bear the harshest burdens in the service of "Mother India"—was a frequently invoked metaphor in the election.'[17]

The BJP banked on Modi's muscularity to show up what it saw as the weak administrative response of the UPA government to matters of law and order, concerns that are paramount for women. The titles bestowed on Modi, like 'Bharat Maa ka Sher' (Mother India's Lion) and 'Hindu Hriday Samrat' (King of Hindu Hearts), blended narratives of masculinity and security with wider Hindutva messaging.[18] So, one actress, Mallika Sherawat, could call him India's most eligible bachelor in 2014, while another, Sherlyn Chopra, said she would like to be his personal assistant. These could have been publicity stunts, of course. Another actress, Meghna Patel—somewhat like the 'Obama Girl' of 2007, whose sexually suggestive serenade to Barack Obama went viral on the internet—shot a series of nude photographs of herself, her intimate parts covered only by lotuses in bloom or images of Modi. These served as online posters, put out with the message 'Vote for Narendra Modi'. As the Baroda-born actress told a news magazine, 'Women from the rest of India have only now discovered Modiji's appeal … In Gujarat, we have known it for over 13 years.'[19]

In Bengaluru, during the 2014 poll campaign, Modi's appeal among women led to the formation of a female volunteer group, NaMo Bharathi, created solely to ensure that all four constituencies in the city voted BJP.[20] Rasita Anand, one of the founders of this group, told *Open*, 'All of us have just two similarities—we are all women and we all support Modiji.' Members of the group set up a temporary office, helped register new voters, went on door-to-door campaigns, and even organised talks and meets with various BJP leaders. Another member of the group, Poonam Vinod Lal, a software engineer, explained, 'Just look at how respectfully [Modi] speaks to and about women. None of those pretentious, politically-correct, cutesy speeches, where they say something and do something else. Modiji says he cares about us and wants to protect us.'[21]

Women Protesters, Women Voters and Some Key Questions

This background raises critical questions about how the BJP as a party views women voters, its attitudes on gender-parity and the political impact of its women-focused strategies. These questions are critical, especially in light of the fact that it was women—from Delhi's Shaheen Bagh to Kolkata's Circus Maidan—who largely led and powered the anti-CAA protests that engulfed India between December 2019 and February 2020. By one count, women led at least 426 such protests nationwide (229 protest sit-ins, 119 rallies and eighty-seven protest marches).[22] The active involvement of so many women in protests against the government, such as the activists from the Pinjra Tod (Break the Cage) collective, which initially began in Delhi as a movement against restrictive hostel rules for women students,[23] further strengthened the general assumption that the BJP is a male-dominated and male-centric party, that it does not have the support of women and that support for the cultural right-wing is split along gender lines. This is a common enough assumption in the liberal discourse in India. It could not be more wrong.

The fact is that women accounted for 48.08 per cent of Indian voters in the 2019 Lok Sabha polls. Almost every second voter was a woman.[24] The BJP could simply not be winning massive mandates without large numbers of women supporting it—that would be electorally impossible. Furthermore, as many as 67.17 per cent of women voters actually cast their vote in 2019—on par with the overall voting percentage of 67.4 per cent—and higher than the male turnout rate of 67 per cent.[25] In other words, women voters voted as much as men voters did in 2019. There was no gender divide in voter turnout patterns among registered voters. The BJP may ignore Muslim voters electorally—like it did in the UP elections of 2017—but women are a key constituency that the party has systematically targeted between 2004 and 2020. They are at the vanguard of the party's rise as India's pre-eminent political formation. While the BJP had always had women leaders—starting with the Gwalior royal Vijaya Raje Scindia from the Jan Sangh days; Sushma Swaraj, who moved from the Janata Party after 1980; and Uma Bharati, who became a star campaigner during the Ram Temple movement—it had suffered from a gender gap in its support base. Until 2014, more men used to vote for it than women.

There was a dramatic gender shift in 2019, when more women voted for the party than men for the first time. The making of a new women's vote was the foundation for Modi's re-election in 2019. It was driven by three factors: Modi's personal political outreach to women through a discourse focused on the glorification of women's achievements, a major shift in the representation of women in elections and internal party organisation, and specific policy initiatives by the government aimed at women.

New research in this chapter shows that, by 2020, the party organisation had more women's representation in its central decision-making levels than any other national political party in India. This was accompanied by a new strategy for reserving a significant share of party positions for women at all levels of party organisation—down to the voting-booth level. Similarly, both Modi governments, NDA-1 and NDA-2, had a slightly higher proportional representation of women ministers (12.7 per cent on average) when compared to Manmohan Singh's two UPA governments (11.2 per cent on average), and significantly higher than Vajpayee's BJP-led NDA government (9 per cent).

In policy outcomes too, women beneficiaries had a large share in general non-women-specific Modi-government schemes: 81 per cent of the total financial beneficiaries in Stand Up India, 68 per cent of loans under the Pradhan Mantri Mudra Yojana and 53 per cent of banking accounts under the Pradhan Mantri Jan-Dhan Yojana (PMJDY). A whopping 11.4 million (66.9 per cent) of 17.1 million rural houses sanctioned under PMAY-G were registered in the names of women individually or as joint holders with their husband. This government decision to privilege poor women in the registration of welfare housing on an unprecedented scale—in a country where legal inheritance rights on parental property were only extended fully to all women in August 2020 by a Supreme Court judgement[26]—embodied revolutionary new possibilities and a major shift for rural women.

This chapter shows how these policies collectively led to the remaking of the women's vote in India and powered the BJP's political ascendance. The initiatives to create a new national constituency for the party on gender lines changed the conventional rules of Indian politics. They also raise vexing questions around women's empowerment, patriarchy, modernity and Hindu nationalism that deserve deeper examination.

Women Voted More for the BJP than Men Did in 2019, Especially in Hindi-speaking States

The 2019 Lok Sabha poll marked a watershed. Women voters in India had always lagged behind men since 1962, which is when the ECI started making available separate figures for men and women voters. That year, 62.1 per cent of men voters turned out to vote, compared to 46.7 per cent women. The gender gap in turnout was a huge 15.4 per cent, wrote Prannoy Roy and Dorab Sopariwala. By 2014, the year Modi won his first national election for the BJP, this gap had narrowed down to just 1.5 per cent (67 per cent men vs 65.5 per cent women).[27] In 2019, however, when Modi won his second mandate, the gender gap in turnout had not only disappeared, it was now slightly in favour of women. The women's turnout during Modi's second, and bigger, national triumph was 67.17 per cent (29,41,01,483 women voted out of 43,78,06,707 registered women voters) compared to 67 per cent for men (31,67,19,158 men voted out of 47,26,66,414 registered men voters).[28] For the first time, women overtook men in turnout.[29] This was also the first general election in which women voted more than men in favour of the BJP-led NDA.

The significance of the women's vote for the BJP must not be underestimated. Earlier, the party's support base amongst women had 'tended to be lower than among men'. In 2014, the BJP-led NDA outscored the UPA by 19 per cent votes among men, but only by 9 per cent among women. In other words, in 2014, according to Roy and Sopariwala's calculations, 'If no women, only men had voted … NDA would have won by an enormous landslide with 376 seats [compared to its actual number of 336]. However, if no men, only women had voted, the NDA would have won 265 seats—which would have been seven seats short of the majority mark.'[30] Within five years, by 2019, this gender divide in voting underwent a seismic shift.

In the 2019 Lok Sabha election, according to the India Today–Axis My India post-poll survey, 46 per cent of women voted for the BJP, as opposed to 44 per cent of men. Women overwhelmingly supported Narendra Modi, according to this post-poll survey, the only one to accurately predict the election results. It was based on a sample size of 7,42,187 respondents and conducted in each of the 543 Lok Sabha seats (an average of around 1,366 respondents per seat). In contrast to the 46 per cent of women voters who said they voted for the BJP and its allies, 27 per cent said they had voted for the Congress and its allies and 27 per cent for other parties.[31]

Interestingly, it was in the less economically developed Hindi heartland states that the BJP-led NDA alliance had a net gender advantage, with more women voting for it than men: in UP, Bihar, Madhya Pradesh, Rajasthan, Haryana and Uttarakhand. In more economically developed states, in sharp contrast, the BJP still had a gender disadvantage (see Table 17.1). The more developed a state, the less women are likely to vote for the BJP when compared to men (with the exception of Gujarat). Consider the states of Delhi, Karnataka and Maharashtra—all of which voted overwhelmingly for the BJP in 2019. In these three states, unlike the rest of the Hindi heartland, the BJP depended more on men than women voters: Delhi with 54 per cent women voters compared to 60 per cent men, Karnataka with 48 per cent women voters compared to 54 per cent men and Maharashtra with 50 per cent women voters compared to 52 per cent men voters. Moreover, at the national level, as many as 50 per cent women who mentioned their occupation as housewives voted for BJP+. This was double the 23 per cent of housewives who voted for Congress+—despite an aggressive campaign by the Congress in favour of NYAY, which promised ₹6,000 every month to 25 per cent of the poor, and indicated that the money would go to the bank account of the housewife or the woman head in the household.[32]

Figure 17.1: Women Outvoted Men in Favour of the BJP+ Alliance in 2019 for the First Time: Women in Less Developed States Voted More for the BJP

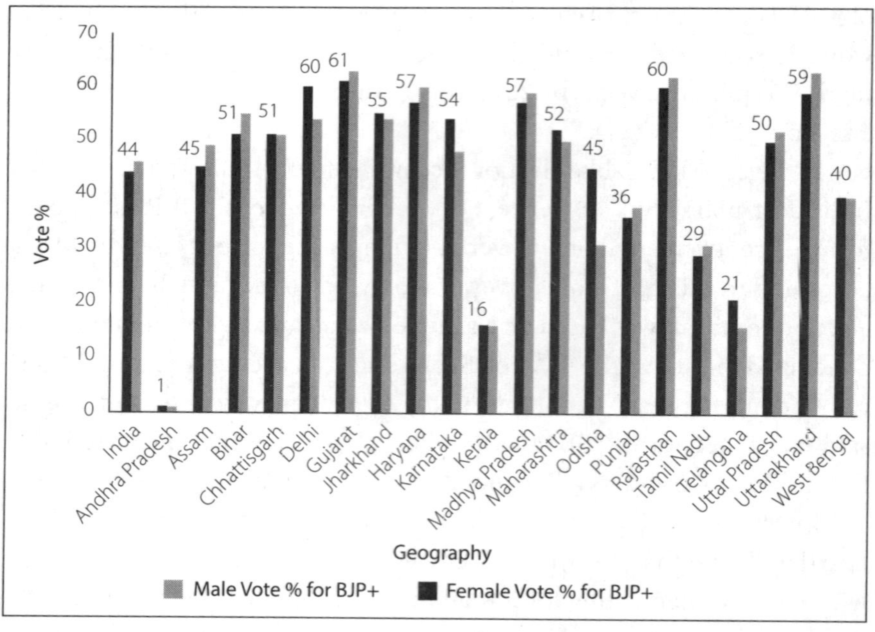

Source: India Today Axis–My India Post-Poll Survey 2019. Sample size: 7,42,187 respondents. Data analysis by Nalin Mehta, Rishabh Srivastava of full data-set available on Samarth Bansal, India Today, 31 May 2019, https://www.indiatoday.in/diu/story/how-india-voted-2019-lok-sabha-election-india-today-axis-my-india-poll-1539617-2019-05-31

This shift in women voters in key states towards the BJP is a recent political development. The data scientist Rukmini S. found that, between 1996 and 2014, successive rounds of CSDS-Lokniti National Election Studies showed that the BJP generally had a '2 to 3 point disadvantage among women voters as compared to the Congress Party'. This state of affairs was 'broadly similar to the situation in the United States, where women have historically leaned more toward the Democratic Party than the Republican Party.'[33]

Yet, by 2018, the BJP had 'largely shed its gender disadvantage'. As Rukmini S. pointed out, the CSDS-Lokniti's May 2018 survey found that virtually all of the modest increase in the BJP's vote share between 2014 and 2018 came from women voters. In May 2014, 33 per cent of men and 29 per cent of women preferred the BJP (see Figure 17.2). Four years later, male support remained at the same level, but women's support had risen to 31 per cent. Many BJP leaders attributed this rise to the government's numerous welfare schemes.[34] This process reached its culmination in 2019 with more women voting for the BJP than men.

Figure 17.2: BJP's Gender Disadvantage (1996–2014), Which Was Overturned in 2019

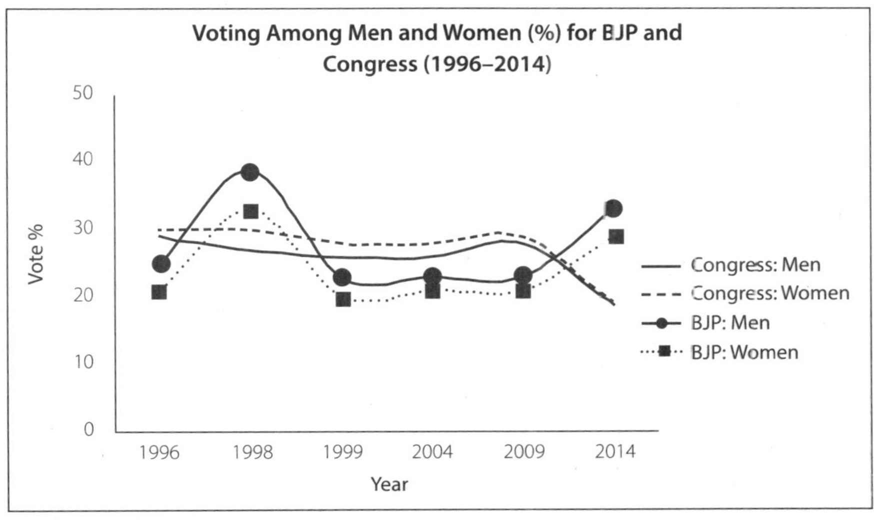

Source: Lokniti-CSDS NES data. Quoted in Rukmini S., 'Women Voters Make Political Parties Take Notice', Seminar, *No. 720, August 2019, http://www.india-seminar.com/2019/720/720_rukmini_s.htm*

When Women Did Not Vote BJP: Mahila Morcha and a Prehistory to the BJP's Gender Shift

The BJP's first organised attempt at targeting women's votes can be traced to the launch of the party's Mahila Morcha (Women's Front) at its first plenary meeting in Mumbai on 28–30 December 1980. Convened by Jayawantiben Mehta, a BJP MLA from Maharashtra (later MP and minister in the Vajpayee government)[35] and inaugurated by the party's first female vice-president, Vijaya Raje Scindia, the inaugural meeting of the Mahila Morcha drew about 15,000 women in a convention that was attended by about 44,000 people in all.[36] Earlier that year, the BJP's poll manifesto for elections in Maharashtra had, for the first time, made significant promises on women-specific issues, something that had never explicitly been part of the Jan Sangh's agenda. The party promised that, if elected to power in Maharashtra, it would create a separate government department for the welfare of women and children.[37]

While its various state-level manifestos in 1980 drew heavily from the undivided Janata Party in 1977,[38] the introduction of women's issues followed in the wake of new social debates engendered by the report of the seminal Committee on the Status of Women in India. Titled *Towards Equality*, this 1974 document commissioned by the Ministry of Education and Social Welfare highlighted alarming figures on how women fared in terms of employment, political participation and health. It showed that the status of Indian women had 'not improved much since independence' despite many 'progressive social legislations and constitutional guarantees'.[39] It led to 'A Blue Print of Action Points and National Plan of Action for Women 1976', which for the first time laid the basis for gender-based programming in government ministries. The result was that India's Five Year Plan (Sixth Plan, 1980–1985) devoted a separate chapter to Women and Development—resulting in 'women being perceived as productive contributors to the national economy' in governmental planning.[40] This was also the year that the BJP launched its Mahila Morcha. The *Towards Equality* report, a 'founding text for the women's movement in India', marked the beginning of 'women's studies in India' and a 'radically altered perspective on the women's questions for activists, the State and researchers alike'.[41]

The creation of the Mahila Morcha in 1980 was thus the BJP's response to a major debate in India at the time on the status of women. Morcha workers welcomed Vajpayee to their enclosure with the slogan '*Ham Bharat ki naari hain, phool nahin chingari hain* [We are the women of India. We are not flowers, we are embers].' The feminist historian Tanika Sarkar heard this 'beautifully feminist slogan' being chanted by women karsevikas in Ayodhya a decade later.[42] The foundation for that mobilisation too was laid with the creation of the Mahila Morcha.

The Morcha's first resolution, titled 'Equal Rights & Equal Dignity for Women' and adopted in that 1980 Bombay meeting, had six demands: 'free education for women of families with incomes within Income Tax limits', more stringent anti-dowry laws, trial of rape cases before 'lady judges in camera', 'Equal Pay for Equal Work', 'Justice and social security for divorcee women' and education to diminish the impact of caste and untouchability on women.[43] These were progressive, forward-looking demands which echoed—at least in theory—the broader thrust of India's rising feminist movement. Yet, the low representation of women at senior levels, an inability to go beyond the party's core constituencies and the failure to give prominence to women's issues in its wider politics meant that the initiative did not immediately gain traction.

The BJP's first National Executive in 1980 had only five (4.7 per cent) women members, out of a total 106 members who were listed in the party's apex body.[44] The social profiles of these five original women members of the National Executive, who made up a tiny minority in the party's initial leadership, showcased the origins of BJP's initial women cohort. Rajmata Scindia, the dowager queen of the princely state of Gwalior, was a major party patron from Madhya Pradesh. Initially a Congress MP from Guna,[45] she switched to the Swatantra Party and finally to the Jan Sangh in 1967.[46] She played a big part in the downfall of the Madhya Pradesh Congress government in 1967 and became the leader of the Samyukta Vidhayak Dal (SVD) that took power as the first non-Congress regime in the state under Govind Narayan Singh.[47] A founding vice-president of the BJP in 1980, she was the only woman office-bearer in the party's central leadership at the time. Later, she played a big part in the Ram Janmabhoomi movement.

Jayawantiben Mehta, appointed as National Executive member, was a Gujarati from Bombay who first became a Jan Sangh corporator, then an

MLA and finally a three-time MP from Mumbai South, where she felled Congress heavyweight Murli Deora in parliamentary elections in 1996 as well as 1999. Mohinder Kaur, the third female appointee on the party's apex body, was a Sikh woman leader from Delhi. Sumatibai Suklikar from Nagpur had fought and lost several municipal elections in the 1960s. Finally, Dr Kamla Verma, president of the BJP's Haryana wing, had been with the party since its Jan Sangh days and had served as a minister in the Lok Dal–BJP coalition government headed by Chaudhary Devi Lal and the Haryana Vikas Party–BJP government of Bhajan Lal. While Suklikar was appointed 'special invitee' to the National Executive, Verma was both a 'permanent invitee' and president of the party's Haryana unit.

This founding women cohort was thereafter joined by Sushma Swaraj, a lawyer who started her political career in the 1970s Navnirman movement and became a cabinet minister in the Janata Party government in Haryana in 1977;[48] Sumitra Mahajan, from a Vaishya family in Indore, who started as a corporator; Uma Bharti, who started as a young prodigy singing religious texts in Tikamgarh (Madhya Pradesh) before becoming a major figure in the Ram Temple movement and an OBC leader; and Vasundhara Raje (Vijaya Raje Scindia's daughter and titular queen of Dholpur). Swaraj became the BJP's first female chief minister (Delhi) in 1998 and Leader of the Opposition (2009–2014). Mahajan went on to become the party's longest-serving female Lok Sabha MP (1989–2019) and India's second woman speaker in the Lok Sabha (2014–2019). Vasundhara Raje eventually became the party's first female chief minister in Rajasthan (2003–2008 and 2013–2018).

Despite such beginnings, the BJP failed to attract women voters through the early 1980s. The Mahila Morcha's political outreach to women at the time was focused almost entirely on social issues: such as its nationwide campaign against dowry as a 'social evil' in 1982[49] or its move to set up a legal cell for rape cases in 1984.[50] Women's issues were not at the forefront of its politics. For example, when Vijaya Raje Scindia circulated a signed ten-page vision paper for discussion at the BJP's National Executive in 1981, the word 'woman' did not feature in it even once.[51] The failure to attract women voters was a major reason why the party fell to an abysmal two seats in the 1984 general election. When Vajpayee commissioned a twelve-member inquiry into the reasons behind this

Figure 17.3: BJP Mahila Morcha's Inaugural Meeting at the BJP's First Plenary, 1980

Source: This meeting in Bombay was attended by 15,000 delegates. Sudhakar Raje (ed.), Onward March: BJP First National Convention Speeches and Resolutions 28–30 December 1980 Bombay, Published by Madhu Deolekar, Publicity Chief BJP (Bombay: Mouj Printing Bureau), p. 50.

wipe-out, the Working Group listed several—key among which was the 'poor response from women and Party units' failure to pay special attention and care towards this section'.[52] Arguing that the BJP 'cannot grow merely on traditional cadres' who may be a strong core group, but were 'too small in numbers looking to the needs of an all Indian wide political party', the Working Group made eight specific recommendations to attract new voters. The need to attract women voters featured high on this blueprint at Number 3. As the report put it, 'Bring in women leadership at all levels of organisation and encourage youth in our party.'[53]

Women, the Ram Janmabhoomi Movement and Hindu Nationalism: The Second Phase of the BJP's Growth

If L.K. Advani and his 'rath' had been the 'visual emblems' of the Ram Janmabhoomi movement, 'then the voice and words that fixed its message belonged to a woman'.[54] So wrote Tanika Sarkar while studying the role of women in the Ayodhya agitation. This was the second phase of the

BJP's growth among women voters. Audio cassettes of fiery speeches by Uma Bharti and Sadhvi Ritambhara and poetry collections like *Shraddha Suman Mala* (Flower Garland of Devotion) by women poets played an important role in the Hindu nationalist upsurge that drove the movement. VHP leaders estimated that about 50,000 female karsevikas were involved in the December 1990–January 1991 Satyagraha in Ayodhya, and about 20,000 of them courted arrest on 4 January 1991.[55] Women were at the vanguard of the temple movement, which thrust a number of Sangh-related women's groups into the limelight: the BJP Mahila Morcha, the VHP's Matri Shakti and Durga Vahini, and the RSS-affiliated Rashtrasevika Samiti.[56] Women were 'active and prominent in the bloody riots that swept across India' in the wake of the movement in Ahmedabad, Bhagalpur and Mumbai. As Sarkar explained, the 'role of Rithambhara's audio-cassetted speech and Uma Bharati's propaganda tours in stoking ferocious anger and aggression against Muslims was memorable'.[57] After the Babri Masjid was demolished, Vijaya Raje Scindia reportedly said that she could now die in peace for she had seen her dream come true.[58]

Importantly, many of the women in the Ayodhya mobilisation, at various levels, were not simply mouthing or repeating narratives created by men. They had agency. Unlike 'most South Asian women, who achieve political prominence because of their relationships with influential men, women like Scindia, Rithambara and Uma Bharti were relatively independent of men in both their personal and political lives', the political scientist Amrita Basu noted. In fact, she went so far as to argue that they had found 'within Hindu nationalism a vehicle for redressing their experiences of gender inequality and for transgressing sex-typed roles'.[59] Tanika Sarkar, who wrote a series of papers and a fine book on Hindu nationalism and women in the 1990s, described her fieldwork with the RSS's women's wing workers as profoundly 'confounding and disconcerting'. This, she explained, was because Leftist feminist thinkers had 'always celebrated the release of women from pure domesticity' and their politicisation 'had always been assumed to be an emancipatory possibility'. In other words, feminist movement leaders had always thought of the 'relationship between communal violence and women' as one of 'male-inflicted violence and female victimhood'. But the reality 'confounded certainties and forced new trajectories'.[60]

The Hindu nationalist women challenged the certitudes and ideas of the Left-led feminist movement. An earlier generation of RSS leaders had extolled traditional roles for women. Yet, Sarkar's study found that the women she dealt with were independent-minded and aware of their rights. Importantly, they were 'little concerned about westernised modernity'. 'In fact, the new Hindu woman citizen,' she wrote, 'is cast in a mould which is very close to that of bourgeois feminism ... The new Hindu woman is therefore, a person with professional and economic opportunities, secure property ownership, legal rights to ensure them and some amount of political power to enforce these rights.' Even on specific questions of gender, when Sarkar studied issues of *Jagruti* (the magazine of the RSS's women's wing) and spoke to office-bearers, she found that the verdict was 'unequivocally modernist'. As she summed it up, this manifestation and celebration of woman power by the Hindu Right paradoxically empowered many women, giving them a public role, 'even leadership', a 'recognition as full-fledged citizens' and 'access to serious intellectual cognition'.[61] In other words, many Hindu nationalist women were independent actors. They did not believe in Western or Leftist notions of feminism and, paradoxically, were not that different from Leftist feminists themselves. Except for one big difference: their political beliefs came from the opposite end of the spectrum.

While the Ayodhya movement drew in committed Hindu nationalist women to the BJP, its overall support base was still largely male-based. By the mid-1990s, it started fronting elected women representatives in legislatures and executive bodies. Its record on this was already 'far better than that of the Left', as Sarkar noted. Yet, the BJP's growth was also simultaneously limited by the patriarchal gender blinkers of many of its own leaders. Despite the Ayodhya spurt, even as late as 1999, Leftist women's outfits like the All India Democratic Women's Association (AIDWA) had much deeper organisational roots nationally.[62] While the BJP had built a core ideological group of female supporters after the temple movement, the vast majority of Indian women had not begun voting for the party. After the highs of the Ayodhya movement and the Vajpayee era of coalition governments in the 1990s, female support for the BJP remained static through the early 2000s. It started rising sharply in 2009, but election data shows that the real upward shift came with Modi in 2014, and finally in 2019 (see Table 17.2).

Why More Women Moved to the BJP after 2014: Three Strategies for Walking the Talk

That the BJP became a more attractive party to Indian women after 2014 is clear. The interesting question is whether this reflected a deeper social and political churn in India or was the outcome of a change in the BJP and the result of new policies targeted at women. In other words, did the party start doing something dramatically different to usher in this gender shift? Or was it only the beneficiary of wider social changes? The evidence is overwhelming that the women's vote shifted after the party made major changes in its approach to women.

The BJP had taken a mahila turn in 1980 and started talking the talk. But women voters did not shift in large enough numbers until it made significant changes in its outreach and started being perceived by many women as walking the talk too. These changes are encapsulated in four specific targeted interventions that were personally led by Modi, who has had a marked focus on women in his public messaging. At the organisational level, after 2014, the BJP made major changes in its party organisation, giving more proportional representation to women nationally (in government, party structure and as election candidates) than any other national political party in India. At the policy level, it was driven by a targeted deepening of women-focused initiatives in governmental development programmes and a focus on publicising these. Of course, some of these programmes were built on ideas developed and piloted by Manmohan Singh's UPA, but the Modi government doubled down on them, scaled up the initiatives and built a new political narrative around them. At the discourse level, the cultural superstructure was driven by the RSS, whose thinking on women has also evolved over time.

Strategy 1: 'When a Woman Gets Convinced in a Family, the Whole Family Gets Convinced': Modi's Women Outreach and Discourse

An examination of Narendra Modi's speeches as prime minister reveals that he speaks more about women than he does about core BJP issues like defence, security, terrorism, Hindutva or Pakistan. This is a striking revelation of how crucial women are to his political positioning. On the Narad Index, our analysis of all Modi speeches as prime minister showed that women were the fifth-biggest focus area for him in 2019 when measured in terms of how often he mentioned them (see Figure 17.4). Moreover, Modi's focus on women has increased over time. Examining all of his speeches between 2014 and 2019, we found that the focus on women went up substantially each year. Between 2014 and 2019, mentions of women increased by 114 per cent in Modi's speeches.

Figure 17.4: Women High Priority in Modi's Speeches, Above Core BJP Issues

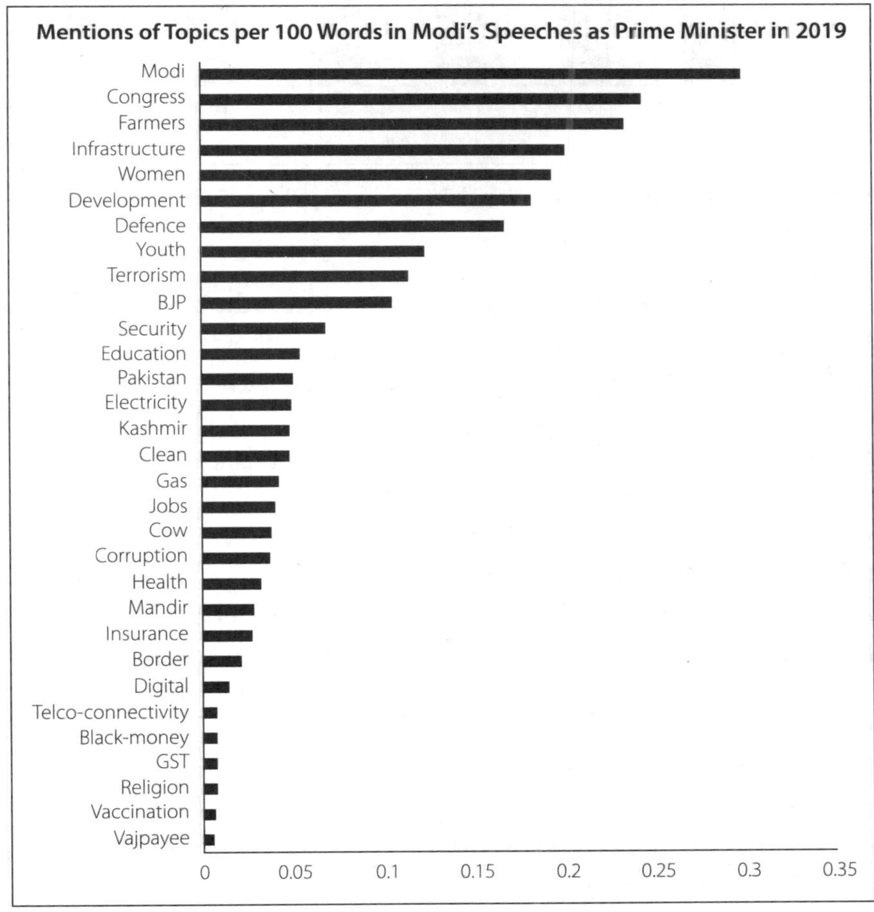

Source: Narad Index, Nalin Mehta and Rishabh Srivastava, for more details, see Appendix 4/online on nalinmehta.in

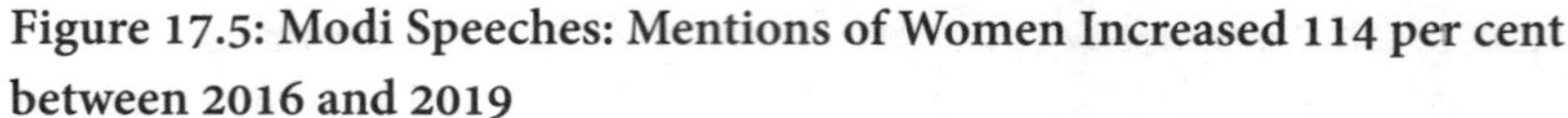

Figure 17.5: Modi Speeches: Mentions of Women Increased 114 per cent between 2016 and 2019

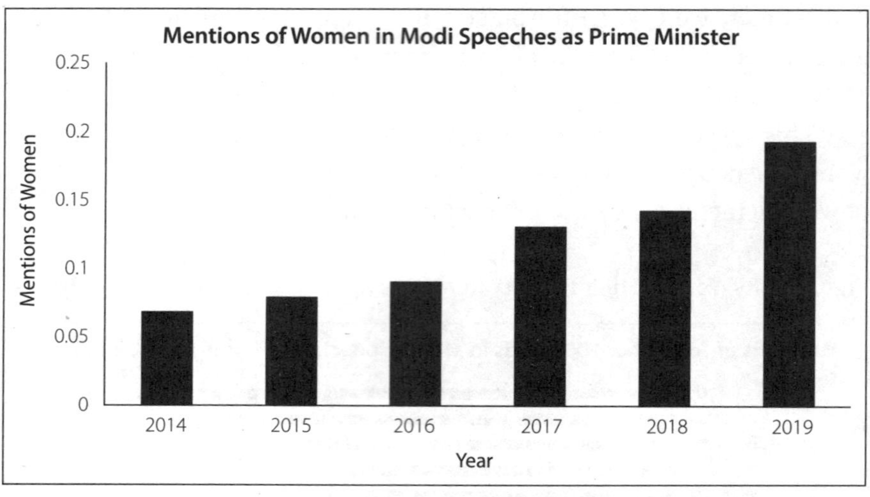

Source: Narad Index, Nalin Mehta and Rishabh Srivastava, for more details see Appendix 4/online on nalinmehta.in

Women cadre became a key BJP priority because the party saw female supporters as political galvanisers within households. Addressing a gathering of BJP Mahila Morcha workers in Karnataka in 2018, Modi spelt this out clearly. 'We will have to go house to house to expose Congress propaganda… I can say with experience that our Mahila Morcha workers are the most effective in this task,' he said. 'When women do this work, when they go house-house, sit down and talk, it has a double effect. First, when a woman convinces someone, she uses everyday domestic arguments, explains it in normal language. She does not do big lofty talk, she explains in simple terms and wins confidence like that. Being credible has a lot of power. You would have seen that when a woman gets convinced in a family, then the whole family gets convinced. We have always tried from the beginning that women have an equal share in every aspect of the social and economic spheres.'[63]

Modi has also been keenly aware of the symbolism of women leaders in power and often refers to this in his speeches. He told that same gathering that the country was now moving towards 'women-led development and not just development for women'. Arguing that his party, his government and its programmes were all following a mantra of 'Women First', he pointed to his cabinet: 'You will see that women have been given important portfolios.' He went on to point out two photographs from the China-hosted Shanghai Cooperation Organisation which had gone viral on social media at the time. 'In both photos,' Modi said, 'among all the men you can see only two women. Everybody else was a man. This photo was of defence and foreign ministers of many countries. Among them was a photo of Sushma Swaraj, who was the only [female] foreign minister, and the second was of Nirmala Sitharaman.'[64]

The Modi government also focused on the message of women entering hitherto male-dominated fields, especially in the military domain. From the Republic Day parade in 2020 being commanded for the first time by a woman officer to the Air Force commissioning its first women combat fighter pilots in 2019 and announcing in 2020 that women pilots were being trained to fly its new Rafales to announcing an all-women crew on board Air India—each of these has been promoted by the BJP as a political triumph.

For instance, Modi, speaking on his *Mann ki Baat* radio programme in October 2021, pointed out that the number of women in police and central armed forces had more than doubled in six years. He declared that the Army and the police were no longer all-male bastions and that this trend would lead to 'new age policing' with women in uniform becoming role models for 'lakhs of daughters'. He was referring to Bureau of Police Research and Development data which showed that the number of women in police forces had risen to 2.15 lakh in 2020, up from 1.05 lakh in 2014, the year he took over as prime minister.[65] Similarly, when his government decided to open up admissions in Sainik Schools—managed by Sainik School Societies and overseen by the Ministry of Defence to prepare students for entry into the defence services—Modi announced the decision from the ramparts of the Red Fort during his Independence Day speech. 'I used to receive messages from lakhs of daughters of our country that they, too, want to study in Sainik Schools,' he said. 'Two-and-a-half years ago, in the Sainik School in Mizoram, we started the experiment of admitting girl students. The government has now decided that all Sainik Schools in the country will be open for daughters of the country.'[66] Admissions to the tri-services National Defence Academy in Khadakwasla, a hitherto male preserve, were also opened up to girls in October 2021, after a landmark Supreme Court order on 18 August 2021. Almost one-third of the 5,70,000 students who applied thereafter for the maiden co-educational entrance examination for National Defence Academy in November 2021, were girls (1,78,000).[67]

Earlier, in 2018, Modi had devoted the year's first episode of his *Mann Ki Baat* programme entirely to the theme of women's achievements. Reading from a letter sent to him by a certain Prakash Tripathi on the Narendra Modi app, the prime minister told viewers that 'the flight of our courageous Defence Minister Nirmala Seetharaman [then defence minister] in a Sukhoi 30 fighter plane is inspirational for him [Tripathi]. He also refers to INSV Tarini, with an all-women crew on board under the command of Vartika Joshi, which is currently circumnavigating the globe. Three braveheart women, Bhavna Kanth, Mohana Singh and Avani Chaturvedi, have become fighter pilots and are undergoing training on the Sukhoi-30. An Air India Boeing jet with an all-women crew led by Kshamata Vajpayee flew from Delhi to San Francisco, USA and back. These are all women achievers. You are absolutely right. Today women are not just advancing in myriad fields; they are leaders.' Calling them 'First Ladies', Modi went on to list a host of women breaking glass ceilings: 'the first female Merchant Navy Captain, the first female passenger train driver, the first female fire fighter, the first female Bus Driver, the first woman to set foot on Antarctica, the first woman to reach Mount Everest … Our woman power … breaking the age old shackles of social mores, creating new records.' The prime minister concluded by telling his viewers that all these details had been compiled into a book on 'first ladies' so that the 'entire country comes to know about the power of these women', and that this was now available as an eBook on the Narendra Modi website.[68] Subsuming both nation and gender, the political packaging was complete.

There is enough evidence to show that the BJP's political outreach to women is personally led by Modi. He speaks far more on the issue than his own party, the Congress or the RSS. This was starkly evident when we compared women-mentions in all Modi speeches with all BJP press releases and speeches and all articles in *Organiser* and *Congress Sandesh* in the 2016–2019 period. In 2016, the BJP, RSS and Modi all spoke about women in roughly similar volumes. Thereafter, the prime minister's focus on women skyrocketed (see Figure 17.6).

Figure 17.6: Modi Speaks about Women Much More than the BJP or the RSS

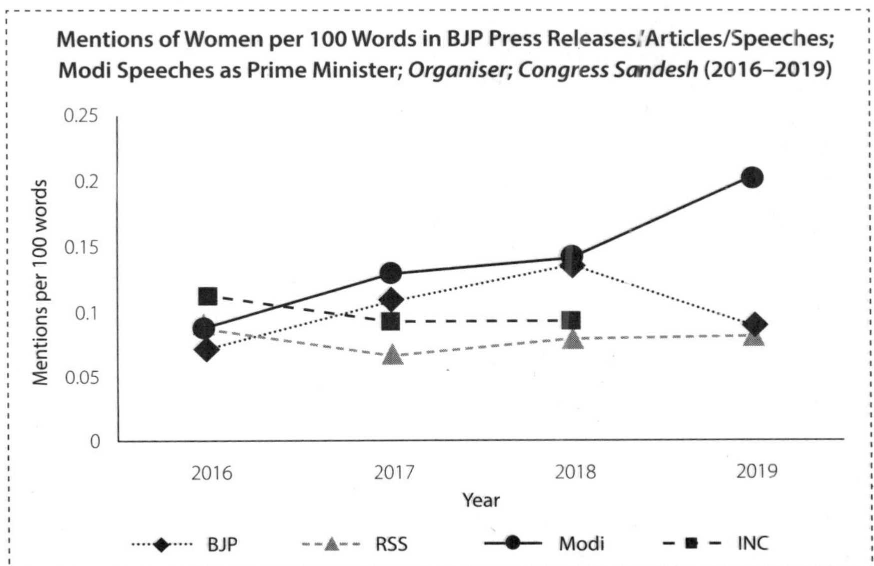

Source: Narad Index, Nalin Mehta and Rishabh Srivastava; for more details see Appendix 4/online on nalinmehta.in

A determined focus on women is clear in these charts. In his gender-focusing, Modi often harks back to women scholars in ancient India, linking them to various government developmental initiatives focused on women. As he said in *Mann ki Baat*,[69]

> In our country, respect for women, their status in society and their contribution has proved to be awe inspiring to the entire world, since ancient times. There has been a long tradition of Vidushis ... women exponents or women champions. Many Vidushis of India have contributed in composing the verses of the Vedas. Lopamudra, Gargi, Maitreyee ... it's a long list of names. Today, we talk about 'Beti Bachao, Beti Padhao', 'save the girl child, educate her'. But centuries ago, it has been mentioned in our ancient texts, in the Skand Puran:
>
> *Dashputra-samakanya, dashputran pravdharyan*
> *Yat falam labhte marya, tata, labhyam kanyakaikeya*
>
> This means, a daughter is the equivalent of ten sons. The 'Punya' that you earn through ten sons amounts to the same earned through just one

> daughter. This underscores the importance that has been given to women in our society. And that is why, in our society, women have been accorded the status of 'Shakti'. This woman power binds closely together society as a whole, the family as a whole, on the axis of unity & oneness. Be it the erudition of the Vidushis of the Vedic Period … Lopamudra, Gargi, Maitreyee; be it the learning & devotion of Akka Mahadevi or Meerabai, be it the governance of Ahilyabai Holkar or the valour of Rani Lakshmibai, woman power has always inspired us. They have always brought glory to the Nation.

Equally, Modi has been criticised for largely speaking of women in relational terms (sisters, mothers, daughters).[70] Be that as it may, the gender focus in his messaging is clear.

Step 2: The BJP Fielded More Women Candidates, Gave Women Higher Share in Party Leadership and Central Government than Other Parties Did

Between 2004 and 2019, the BJP became far more accommodative of women candidates than it had ever been before. Until the early 2000s, it had a low representation rate for women it fielded for the Lok Sabha: only 8.2 per cent in 2004. The thirty women candidates fielded by the party that year were substantially lower than the Congress's forty-five (10.8 per cent of all its candidates). By 2019, the BJP had radically improved its representation of women. In the 2019 Lok Sabha poll, it fielded more women than any other political party in India: fifty-five. It narrowly pipped the Congress, which fielded fifty-four women. In proportional representation terms, the BJP's share of women candidates (12.6 per cent) was only marginally behind the Congress's (12.8 per cent). And the party did not just field more women candidates, it fielded strong women candidates who had a substantially higher success rate than female candidates from all the other parties.[71] Two out of every three women who fought on the BJP banner got elected.[72] The result was that the party had the largest number of women MPs in Parliament in 2019: forty-one. A measure of its success was that the BJP's women contingent in the Seventeenth Lok Sabha was over four times larger than the next biggest female cohort, from the Trinamool Congress (nine), and over six times bigger than that of the Congress (six) .[73]

Table 17.1: How the BJP Started Giving More Lok Sabha Tickets to Women Candidates than Other Political Parties in the Lok Sabha Polls (2004–2019)

Party	*2004*	*2009*	*2014*	*2019*
BJP	30	44	48	55
INC	45	43	60	54
BSP	20	28	27	24
SP	11	8	11	2
CPI	2	4	6	4
CPM	8	6	11	10
JD (U)	1	3	5	2
Shiv Sena	2	1	1	12
NCP	6	7	4	1
Trinamool Congress	6	5	13	23
BJD	1	0	2	7
AIADMK	2	2	4	1
DMK	2	2	2	2
TDP	4	1	1	3
YSR-CP	-	-	5	4
TRS	-	1	1	2
AAP	-	-	58	3

Women Candidates % Fielded by Political Parties in Lok Sabha Polls (2004–2019)

Party	*2004*	*2009*	*2014*	*2019*
BJP	8.2	10.2	8.9	12.6
INC	10.8	9.8	12.9	12.8
BSP	4.6	5.6	5.4	6.3
SP	4.6	8.4	14.1	16.2
CPI	5.9	7.1	9.0	8.2
CPI (M)	11.6	7.3	11.8	14.5

Party	*2004*	*2009*	*2014*	*2019*
JD (U)	2.1	5.8	5.4	8.3
Shiv Sena	3.6	4.5	5.0	52.2
NCP	18.2	10.3	11.1	2.9
Trinamool Congress	18.18	18.5	28.8	37.09
BJD	8.3	0	9.52	33.3
AIADMK	6.06	8.6	10.0	6.6
DMK	12.5	9.09	5.7	8.6
TDP	12.1	3.2	3.3	12.0
YSR-CP	-	-	13.1	11.7
TRS	-	11.1	5.8	11.7
AAP	-	-	13.4	15

Source: ECI data on women participation in Lok Sabha polls analysed by Nalin Mehta, Rishabh Srivastava. This has been cross-referenced with year-wise datasets on women's representation made available by the Association of Democratic Reforms (ADR). Where there were discrepancies between ECI's original source data/its subsequent analytical tables and the ADR's data analysis, we have gone by ECI numbers.[74]

Of course, merely giving tickets to women is not necessarily a marker of greater women's participation. The Samajwadi Party in 2019 gave more tickets to women as a proportion of its total candidates (16.2 per cent) than either the BJP or the Congress. Many of these women were wives or relatives of political leaders and nobody thinks of the SP as a paragon of women's empowerment. Yet, representation does matter, especially in political formations that are not family-controlled. The BJP, which was way behind other major political parties in giving tickets to women in the early 2000s, drastically changed its strategies and overtook them all by 2019 (see Table 17.1). The party's increase of women candidates served as an important signal. As the BJP became more established as the party of upward social mobility, it was also signalling to ambitious women looking for political careers that its doors were open.

Five smaller parties fielded a higher proportion of women than the BJP in 2019. These included Maharashtra's Shiv Sena, more than 50 per cent of the candidates of which were female. West Bengal's Trinamool Congress (37 per cent), Odisha's Biju Janata Dal (33.3 per cent) and Delhi's AAP

(15 per cent) also embraced a more gender-equal candidature. However, these parties were all regional forces, each with a narrow geographic base. At the national level, the BJP's real comparison was with the Congress, and under Modi and Shah, the BJP drew level with its rival on this register. Interestingly, the BJP was also more accommodative of women candidates than the CPI (8.2 per cent women candidates) and only marginally lesser than the CPI(M) (14.5 per cent).

The female turn of the Shiva Sena, which competed for the same Hindu nationalist vote as the BJP in Maharashtra, has a long history. The gender studies scholar Sikata Banerjee,[75] the activist Teesta Setalvad[76] and the women's rights lawyer Flavia Agnes[77] have shown how, from the 1990s onwards, the Shiv Sena started focusing on women's issues and mobilising large numbers of women more successfully than liberal women's groups, raising vexing questions about gender and the Hindu cultural Right.[78] The Trinamool Congress, led by the woman satrap Mamata Banerjee, and BJD, led by India's longest-serving chief minister, Naveen Patnaik, both embraced far greater gender representation. Yet, these parties remained the exceptions. Across India, other regional political outfits, including the Dravidian parties (DMK and AIADMK), the Telugu parties (TDP and YSR-Congress) and the Dalit party, BSP, all gave less representation to women than the BJP did (see Table 17.1).

The BJP's woman-candidate share fell well short of the 33 per cent target of the long-debated Women's Reservation Bill, which is yet to pass in Parliament. Yet, it was much higher than the historical pattern of women members who were elected to Parliament between 1957 and 2014 (see Figure 17.7). In a country where women MPs never made up even one-tenth of Parliament until even as late as 2009, the BJP's gambit of giving more tickets to women took it well above the national average on this gender yardstick.

A second marker of inclusiveness is the number of women included in leadership positions as ministers in the Union government. While Lok Sabha seats are about political winnability, ministerial positions represent the importance given to individuals and their social groups within a party. On this yardstick, Modi's two governments on average had a larger share of women ministers than Manmohan Singh's two governments that preceded it as well as Vajpayee's NDA regimes. The first full-term BJP-

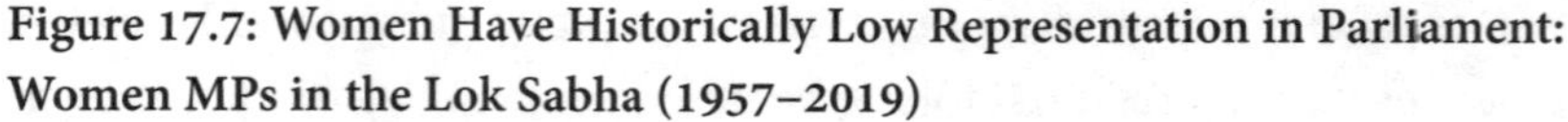

Figure 17.7: Women Have Historically Low Representation in Parliament: Women MPs in the Lok Sabha (1957–2019)

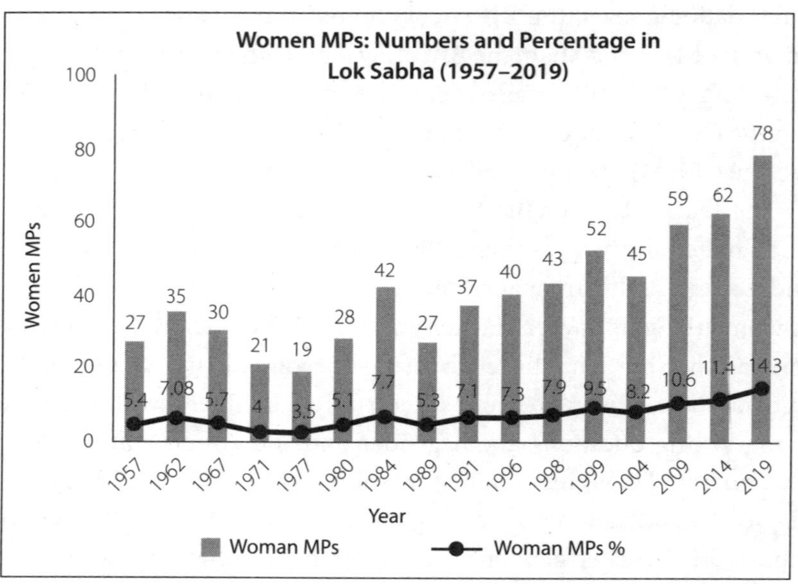

Source: Social Statistics Division, National Statistical Office, Women and Men in India: A Statistical Compilation of Gender Related Indicators in India, 21st Issue (New Delhi: Ministry of Statistics and Programme Implementation, Government of India, 2019), p. 102. Research inputs by Rajesh Sharma.

led government under Vajpayee (1999–2004) had a yearly average of 9 per cent women ministers. Manmohan Singh's UPA-1 and UPA-2 upped women's representation in the Union government's council of ministers to 11.2 per cent on average. Modi's NDA-1 and NDA-2 further increased women's share of ministerial portfolios to an average of 12.7 per cent. While the number of ministers kept changing with periodic reshuffles, the average yearly count tells the story of a growing gender balancing at the political level that started towards the end of Manmohan Singh's prime ministership and increased under Modi.

In fact, Modi's second year in power, 2015, saw the ratio of women ministers rising to 17.8 per cent. Government data shows that this was the highest ever share of women ministers since gender statistics started being counted in 1985. Since then, the share of women ministers under Modi has fallen somewhat. Yet, women's share on average still remains higher than in the Congress governments (see Figures 17.8 and 17.9). Furthermore, from the late Sushma Swaraj as foreign affairs minister (2014–2019) to Smriti Irani as human resources minister in NDA-1 and Nirmala Sitharaman as defence minister and then finance minister (from 2017 onwards), women have held major portfolios in the two Modi governments.

Figure 17.8: Modi's NDA-1 and NDA-2 Have Higher Averages of Women Ministerial Representation than Manmohan Singh's UPA-1, UPA-2 and Vajpayee's NDA

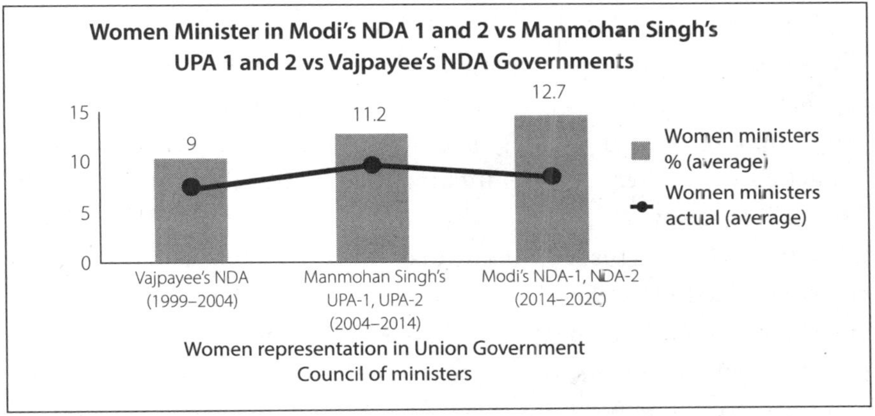

Figure 17.9: Women Ministers Have Historically Had Low Representation in Central Governments

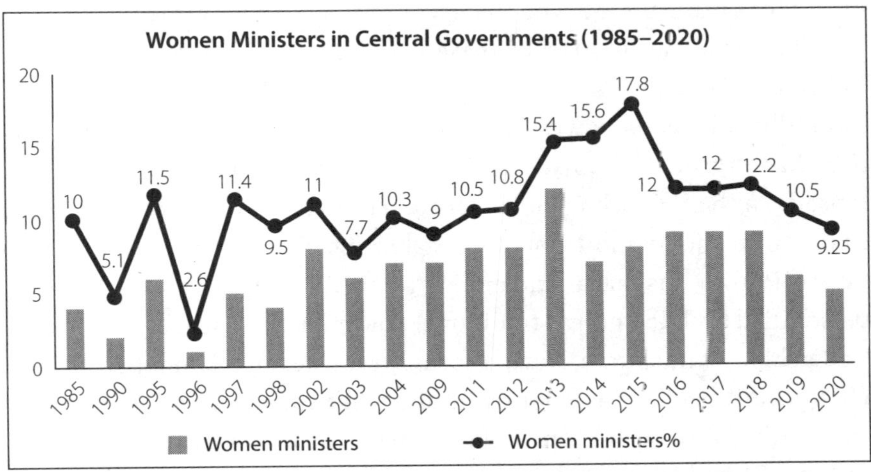

Source: Social Statistics Division, National Statistical Office, Women and Men in India: A Statistical Compilation of Gender Related Indicators in India, 21st Issue (New Delhi: Ministry of Statistics and Programme Implementation, Government of India, 2019), p. 100. Research inputs by Rajesh Sharma.

To put this in context, the presence of important women leaders in Delhi is not new in itself. India has had influential women ministers since Nehru's first cabinet included Rajkumari Amrit Kaur. There have been powerful women leaders like Indira Gandhi at the national level and several regional female leaders like AIADMK's late Jayalalithaa, Trinamool's Mamata Banerjee and BJP's Vasundhara Raje. However, the ratio of women ministers overall in successive Union governments was always low (see Figure 17.9).

Thirdly, under Modi and Shah, the BJP instituted important course-corrections on the representation of women in the party's central organisation. These leadership changes ensured for the BJP the highest proportion of women among national office-bearers in India when compared with other major outfits that had 'national party' status. The BJP had as many as 16.9 per cent women as central officer-bearers in October 2020. This was more than women's representation in the central leadership of the CPI(M) (14.7 per cent), Trinamool Congress (13 per cent), CPI (11.1 per cent), NCP (10.8 per cent) and Congress (8.5 per cent). Numbers, of course, tell only half the story. The nature and seniority of the positions these women held was equally important. It is instructive that, when BJP President J.P. Nadda announced his new central leadership team in September 2020, as many as five of his twelve party vice presidents—a whopping 41 per cent—were women.

The social background of these new women vice-presidents is also indicative of the party's changing growth strategy. Apart from the veteran Vasundhara Raje, there was Rita Verma, a Kurmi (OBC) leader and two-time MP from UP who had defeated the former Congress minister Jitin Prasada in the Lok Sabha polls. Verma represented the party's new caste coalition in India's most populous state.[79] Dr Bharti-ben Shiyal, a two-time MP from Bhavnagar and among six women BJP MPs from Gujarat, personified both the party's traditional power base and its bet on younger leadership.[80] Annapurna Devi, a former minister in Manmohan Singh's UPA government and previously head of Lalu Yadav's RJD in Jharkhand, was credited with the RJD's revival in the tribal state after 2014. She defected to the BJP in March 2019 and was rewarded with a senior position.[81] D.K. Aruna from Telengana, a Reddy leader from an old Congress family who had previously held ministerial positions in Congress governments

Table 17.10: The BJP Has the Highest Ratio of Women as National Office-bearers Among National Political Parties, the Congress Has the Lowest

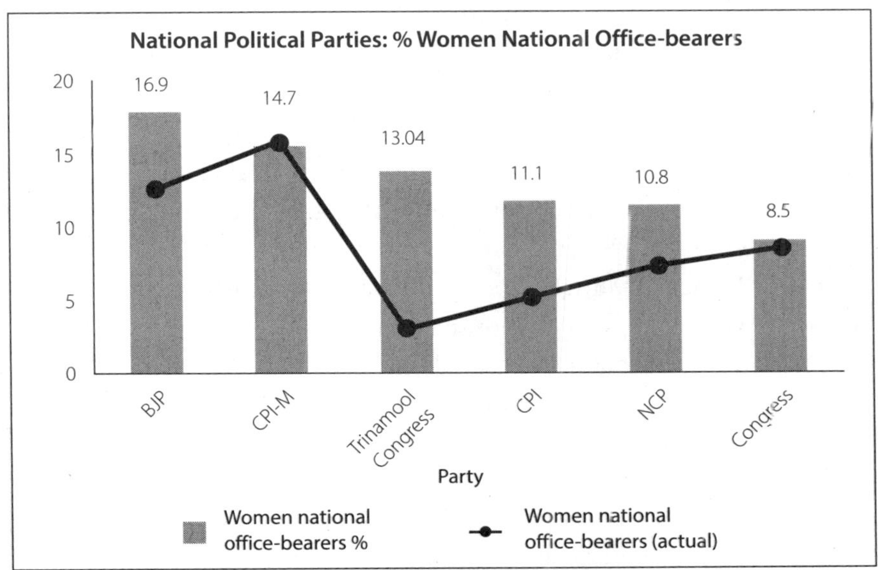

Source: The author's analysis of central leadership of six national parties recognised by the ECI. In October 2020, the BJP had twelve women out of seventy-one national office-bearers, CPI(M) had fifteen women out of 102, the CPI had seven of sixty-three, the NCP five of forty-six and the Congress eight out of ninety-four. Note: For a meaningful comparison, we chose national parties with a minimum threshold of at least ten central officer bearers. The BSP, also a national party, had only four national officer bearers, including its president Mayawati (25 per cent representation) but its proportional representation of women is not comparable with others because of the small size of its central leadership. Data from: https://www.bjp.org/en/nationalofficebearers; https://cpim.org/leadership; https://www.communistparty.in/blank-1; https://www.ncp.org.in/about/; https://www.inc.in/aicc-office-bearers; https://www.bspindia.org/our-leadership/. Accurate as of 21 October 2020.

in undivided Andhra Pradesh, was also a defector. She joined the BJP in 2018. Her elevation, and that of another former Congress leader, D. Purandeswari (from Andhra Pradesh), to the important post of general secretary represented the party's southern ambitions.[82]

This is in sharp contrast to the Congress. It is led by a woman president, Sonia Gandhi. However, including her and her daughter Priyanka Gandhi—both dynastic leaders—the proportion of women in the Congress's central leadership is half that of the BJP. The primary difference between the two parties on this issue is that the BJP embraced a wider social coalition of women as part of a methodical growth plan. The Congress did not. Similarly, in the Left, in 2020, the CPI(M)'s all-powerful Politburo had only two women members: Brinda Karat and Subhashini Ali, both from an older generation of leadership. In Maharashtra's NCP too, while Supriya Sule, Sharad Pawar's daughter, is the anointed heir, the overall representation of women in leadership positions is way lower than in the BJP. The Trinamool Congress, led by Mamata Banerjee, is a different case. Banerjee is all-powerful in her party, and while she brought in more women leaders at the state-party level in 2020, its impact was only relevant in Bengal. Tellingly, even her council of ministers, in which she holds the lion's share of portfolios, had only 6 per cent women leaders in October 2020, if you count individuals. Mayawati's iron hold over the BSP similarly failed to build a recognisable second-line of women leadership.

These comparisons show that the BJP systematically broad-based its leadership in terms of gender representation after 2014 in a way that other parties did not. On every measurable quantitative yardstick of gender representation—the number of women who voted for it, the number of women who were given Lok Sabha tickets, the number of women who were made ministers and the number of women appointed as national office-bearers—the new BJP did better than its national political rivals.

The BJP's UP Model of Reservation for Women at the Booth and District Levels: Veerangana Sammelans and Gender-based Mobilisation

Just as the BJP reached out to Dalits and OBCs in UP by reserving positions for them at the booth and district levels, after 2014, it instituted a gender-based reservation system in the state as part of an organisational overhaul. Twenty-five per cent of posts were reserved for women in BJP executive councils (karyakarani) set up in each booth and district. In these twenty-one-member councils, five seats were reserved for women and two each for SCs and OBCs, at every level of the party. When I met up with a group of BJP district-level leaders in Mathura in July 2020, they told me this was a big turning point for the party.[83] Initially, the party found it very difficult to fill these women's quotas, so it relied on relatives of local leaders. As a BJP district general secretary explained to me. 'If you want to fill five women, then you make someone's wife, someone's sister and so on. If we had to choose five women, then four we did only to fill the quota, but one woman that was genuinely new. That one woman turned into ten, but those ten new ones came from that first one. They came slowly. They did not come together.' Just as with Dalits and OBCs, however, this reservation forced local party leaders to reach out to families that had never before voted BJP. 'If we talked to fifty people, then maybe five came in, but these five became the starting point for reaching out to others,' summed up Pradeep Goswami, BJP general secretary in Mathura.[84]

This move had a deep impact at the constituency voting-booth level. 'Elections are a kind of war and the mantra to win an election depends on 50 per cent planning and 50 per cent implementation on the pratyaksh [clearly visible] battlefield,' explains the BJP's *Mahila Morcha: Training Manual*, outlining its 'Mahila Booth Rachna' (Women's Booth Formation). 'Victory and defeat are dependent on booth planning.' This is why the quotas for women in voting booths were so crucial. Because 'in the end the final fight in an election is fought only at the booth'.[85] This is why, by the time of the Karnataka election of May 2018, Modi was directly telling party workers that the poll would be won on 'naari shakti'—woman power. As he told a gathering of the BJP's Karnataka Mahila Morcha:[86]

> You will have to go out, reach house-to-house and you will have to acquaint people with the lotus sign. You will have to teach them how to press the button next to the lotus sign. You will have to fit into people's minds that voting [matdaan] comes before jalpaan [drinking water]. Let mothers in families decide that until you go and vote, you will not get morning tea, won't get morning breakfast. See what a big revolution this will be. And can you decide that in the polling booths you work in, you can get more women to vote than men? If men give 350 votes, women must give 400 votes. If men give 500 votes, women must put 600 votes. You make your minds determined on this. Be competitive. Let women decide. Encourage women to come forward to protect women.

While the deep focus on women was part of the 'Modi model',[87] as one BJP office-bearer told me, some of the early groundwork for reaching out to women voters and incorporating the lessons of the Gujarat model started under the presidency of Rajnath Singh (2005–2009) and Nitin

Gadkari (2009–2013). This period, when the BJP was still recovering from its shock election loss in 2004, was also when it started new organisational initiatives, of which outreach to women was an important part, following on from the party's formal commitment in 2003 to support legislation for 33 per cent reservation for women in Parliament and state legislatures.[88] While that promise has since languished, its adoption within the party structure signalled the beginning of a shift. 'Many more women started coming into the party,' recalls Vani Tripathi Tikoo, who served as BJP national secretary at the time. 'Rajnath Singh started being in favour of 33 per cent reservation for women at the party.' Smriti Irani, already a national face as the ideal bahu in Ekta Kapur's television blockbuster, *Kyunki Saas Bhi Kabhi Bahu Thi*, was among the new recruits to the party at the time. She was appointed women's wing president and party spokesperson.

This was around the time of the Nirbhaya incident in Delhi and the BJP made women's safety a core concern in the MCD elections in Delhi, with a focus on sexual harassment as a primary political issue. 'This campaign was national in character,' says Tikoo, who played a central role in creating the campaign. 'It was about women's security and deeper issues like sexual harassment against women.' The BJP in Delhi created slogans like '*Har ladki har beti kare pukar, kyon hota uski izzat par hamla baar baar. Jaagrok bano, bhajpa ko chuno* [Every girl, every daughter cries out, why is her honour attacked each time. Wake up, choose BJP]'. 'This almost sounded like a national-level campaign,' said Tikoo. 'This is no way about municipality or garbage or the sewers and the gutters. This was about the condition of women.'[89] It culminated in the BJP emerging as the single largest party in Delhi's 2012 municipal elections. In all the three councils it won, the party nominated women mayors.[90]

This early local experiment was accompanied by a national recruitment drive for the BJP's youth wing, called the Veerangana Sammelans (Women Warriors' Meetings), to specifically target younger women. Vani Tripathi Tikoo, who crafted this campaign, said, 'I targeted young women who were between eighteen to thirty-five years of age ... About 70 per cent of India was under thirty years of age but there had been no targeted attempt in the party till then to change our orientation to this generational shift. The Veerangana Sammelan was born out of this realisation.'[91]

In 2009, the BJP held women-only meetings in eighteen Indian states over a six-month period. These state-level meetings focused on the eighteen to thirty-two age group and culminated in a large Veerangana Mahila Sammelan in Delhi's Mavalankar Hall. Handpicked women activists were brought to Delhi for a national leadership conclave with the party's top leadership. 'Thousands of girls travelled to Delhi for the first time for the two-day conclave which was about young women cadres alone,' explained Tikoo. Its primary aim was to provide a ready reckoner to the women on how to fight and manage election campaigns. 'We were trying to demolish that "Panch Pati" syndrome out of the Indian electoral system. Many young women leaders in that auditorium met with national leaders like Sushma Swaraj who spoke about how election management should be done … Many of them had not faced more than five men out of their ghungat before… We thought it was important to focus on the women themselves and work with them on how to learn to communicate their ideas, how to look at elections from a managerial point of view and finding money and finance to raise to fight an election.'

The Women's Reservation Act was still being debated in Parliament at the time that this BJP initiative focused on the 'basics in election management' with women leaders.[92] The Veerangana recruitment drive was run by the BJP's state youth units. Among those selected for the Delhi conclave, '90 per cent were rank newcomers who eventually became members of the party. Many of them became state-level leaders within the next decade.'[93] As a key organiser recalled, 'The outcome of doing such activity was so ecstatic that the party for the first time started taking notice of the under-thirty-five segment of women.'

The choice of name—Veerangana—drew on older Sangh traditions that valorise female nationalist warriors. 'It was chosen in a conversation with Sushma Swaraj because it had a "veer ras" [bravery element],' said Tikoo. 'The RSS already had [a] wing and there was a Durga Vahini. Veerangana is softer and we also attached it with Rani of Jhansi. It was a name of joy, not just a victory, but also of joy, of putting up a brave face. We often used to refer to Rani of Jhansi in our meetings and recited Subhadra Kumari Chauhan's famous poem, "*khoob larhee mardani voh toh Jhansi vaali rani thee* [how splendidly she fought, in a manly way, she was the queen of Jhansi]".'[94]

This tradition of focusing on veeranganas has since become a part of BJP Mahila Morcha events. In May 2018, for example, Prime Minister Modi, while addressing the Karnataka BJP Mahila Morcha workers on a live video chat, began his interaction by first paying homage to a range of female veeranaganas from the state: Kittur Rani Chennamma, Keladi Chenamma, Belawadi Mallamma, Rani Abbakka Chowta and the Chitradurga warrior Onake Obavya.[95] The BJP's 2018 training manual for women workers, in fact, has a whole section listing women heroes. Starting with Vedic sages like Gargi, Kapila, Arundhati, Maitreyi, and even Ayodhya's warrior queen Kaikeyi from the Ramayana, the list is long and religion-agnostic. It includes Rani Padmavati, who committed jauhar while resisting Sultan Alauddin Khilji's assault on Chittor; Razia Sultan, the first female sultan of Delhi; the Maratha hero Shivaji's mother, Jijabai; the eighteenth-century Indore queen Ahilyabai Holkar; Lucknow's Begum Hazrat Mahal, who fought the British in 1857; and Captain Lakshmi Sehgal, who led the Rani Jhansi women's regiment in Subhash Chandra Bose's Indian National Army during the Second World War.[96]

The Veerangana meetings also worked to convince women workers that campaigning would not be unsafe for them. 'Women cannot be taken seriously unless they themselves take themselves seriously. We are so very dependent on the patriarchy around us,' said Tikoo. 'Sushma Swaraj focused on this a lot in her speeches. We said it doesn't take too much for a booth-level karykarta to go out at night and leave her home to campaign, but then her parents and relatives immediately complain saying that it is unsafe and that politics is dirty. So how do I know that she's going to be safe for the campaign? This thought was vitally debated in the party.' The new focus on women also created 'deep division between a lot of party leaders'. This was important because a woman getting a ticket or a party position was not in itself sufficient. 'Preparing, managing and using the campaign to empower yourself is also a big deal,' Tikoo explained. The question of giving more tickets to women, especially in important seats held by the BJP, was widely debated in the party. Then Rajnath Singh and Nitin Gadkari came out and said that 'when there was a discrepancy on seats, why not err on the side of giving it to a woman'.[97] Interestingly, the 2009 Lok Sabha election, under Rajnath Singh's stewardship, was the first in which the BJP fielded more women candidates than any other party in any Lok Sabha election (see Table 17.1).

Strategy 3: Women Beneficiaries High in Modi's Developmental Policies: How Much of the Woman Talk Did His Government Walk?

We have seen how much Prime Minister Modi and the BJP focus on women in their discourse and party mobilisation as well as the resultant impact on voting patterns. Obviously, mere political rhetoric—without action to match—would not be enough to draw women voters. The BJP started winning because it was acting differently from the other parties. Its policy actions contributed to more women voting for the BJP than men did in 2019. They did so partly because the Modi government fulfilled many of its promises in terms of governmental benefits, especially for rural women. If it had only been about creating women-focused schemes, then all governments in the past have done so. What then differentiated the BJP politically on the women question? In mid-2018, Modi provided some clarity on this issue. His strategy had two pillars: one, collating diverse women-focused schemes in a single basket so there was one direction and it became possible to have cohesive political communications around it, and, two, pushing gender-focused welfare measures for women at every stage in their lifecycle, from the cradle to the grave. Addressing a group of BJP workers, Modi acknowledged that 'for women's empowerment, earlier too many schemes were made', but 'there was no one direction' and they were 'not connected to the small-small needs of women'. Stressing on the point that 'collecting all schemes in one direction' creates 'a new kind of power', the prime minister pushed a narrative of gender-based welfare interventions. 'This is why Bharatiya Janata Party started working with one approach,' he said. 'From the time a woman gets pregnant, gives birth to children, education of children, career of the children—in one way, from the time of a woman's birth to death, at every milestone, our approach has been, how can government be helpful and provide governmental support. How can we increase the speed of this work and we have focused all our schemes in this manner.'[98]

The biggest marker of Modi's approach was the large share of women beneficiaries in general government schemes that were not women-specific (see Figure 17.11). Women accounted for 68 per cent of loans under the PMMY, which provides credit to micro enterprises to bring them into the formal economy. Loans were given to 16.64 crore women from a cumulative credit of ₹5,43,943 crore over a five-year period (2016–2020).[99] One of the three categories of loans given under the Mudra scheme was, of course, targeted at women's groups alone. However, women also accounted for a significant percentage of the overall scheme benefits. Each of these 16.64 crore women who got Mudra loans represented a family or a self-help group.[100] Similarly, women accounted for 53 per cent of banking accounts (20.33 crore of 38.13 crore) opened under the PMJDY.[101] This large representation of women in Jan Dhan accounts (launched in 2014) is particularly important. Having these accounts (they require no minimum balance) is a prerequisite for eligibility to the government's social security schemes on life insurance of ₹30,000, accident insurance of ₹2 lakh, overdraft of up to ₹10,000 and Mudra loans.[102] Moreover, Jan Dhan accounts are the conduit for direct-benefit cash transfers under a host of government schemes.

Of the 17.1 million rural houses sanctioned under the PMAY-G, those registered in women's names or in joint ownership with their husbands accounted for as much as 66.9 per cent by October 2020.[103] This was the result of a 2016 decision by the Modi government to prioritise the commissioning of houses built in the name of a woman or jointly with her husband. In urban areas, registration of houses in women's names was made mandatory in 2016. This was done, Modi explained, so that women 'get security'.[104] The impact of this is revolutionary in a country where daughters have long been denied legal inheritance. Hindu women only got the legal right to inherit parental property in the same way as male heirs and their families in 2005 through an amendment of the Hindu Succession Act of 1956. This legal right was further expanded to women whose fathers had died before 2005 by a landmark Supreme Court judgement on 11 August 2020.[105] In a milieu in which women had faced so many barriers to equality in property rights, the fact that as many as 4.54 million rural houses built under PM Awaas Yojana-Gramin were registered in the names of women and another 6.9 million were registered jointly in the names of wives and husbands is truly significant. Put another way, of the 17.1 million houses sanctioned under this scheme, only 5.6 million were registered in the names of men alone, and 11.4 million women had new residential property registered in their names (as single or joint owners).[106] Interestingly, a very large proportion of these women-registered houses—as many as 5.02 million—were built in Hindi heartland states, where patriarchal norms have traditionally been strong and where the women's vote eventually shifted to the BJP: UP, Rajasthan, Madhya Pradesh and Bihar.[107] In other words, almost one-third of all houses sanctioned nationwide under this scheme went to women in the politically important Hindi heartland states.

Figure 17.11: Women Accounted for a Large Share of General (Not Specific to Women) Developmental Schemes of the Modi Government

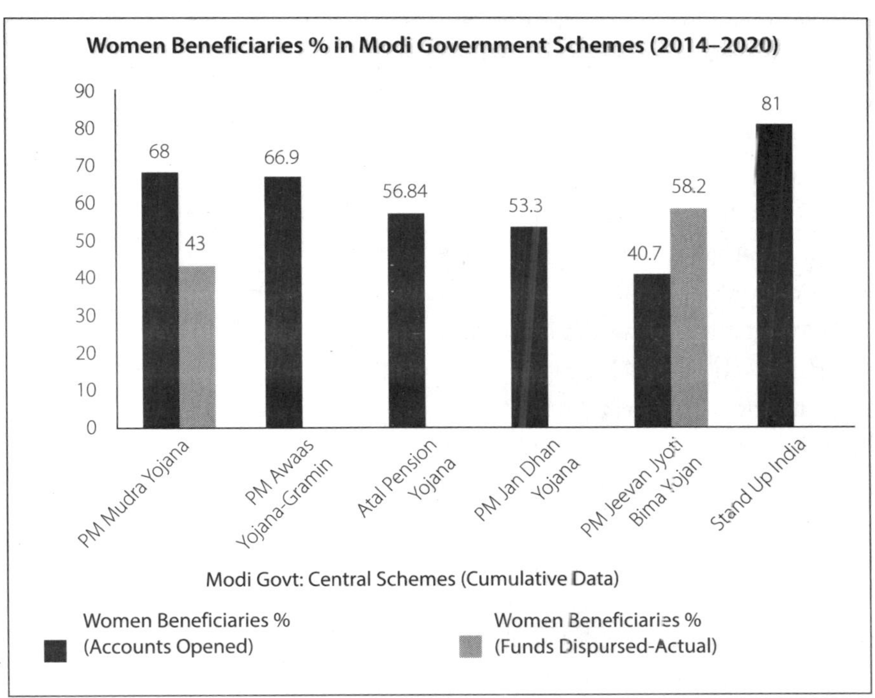

Source: Mudra Yojana Annual Report 2019-20, p. 16; PMAY-G Social Reports, 24 October 2020: https://rhreporting.nic.in/netiay/SocialProgressReport/Ownershipdetailsofhousessanctionedreport.aspx; Atal Pension Yojana Gender-Wise Enrolments, 31 March 2020: https://www.npscra.nsdl.co.in/enrollment-details-of-apy.php; PMJDY Progress Report, 24 October 2020: https://pmjdy.gov.in/account; Stand Up India and PMJJBY data from PIB Delhi, 3 March 2020: https://pib.gov.in/PressReleseDetailm.aspx?PRID=1604929

Conventional analyses of the BJP's gender politics often misses the acute focus it places on women and how it managed to turn its traditional gender disadvantage around, especially in the Hindi heartland. India has long been among the eighty-odd countries counted by the International Monetary Fund (IMF) that practise gender budgeting. It started under Prime Minister Manmohan Singh in 2005-06 when the Union government began to apply a gender lens to government expenditures in order to prioritise gender-specific outcomes and tackle stark gender inequalities. According to a data analysis of the gendered sections of successive Union government budgets—which include schemes specifically targeted at women (such as Beti Bachao Beti Padhao) and those where women are also beneficiaries (like Mid-Day Meal initiatives)—this averaged to 5.04 per cent of the total government expenditure per year between 2005-06 and 2013-14.

Under Modi, this average came down to 5 per cent between 2014-15 and 2020-21.[108] While financial expenditures for gender-based outcomes generally fell or stagnated after hitting a high point of 5.9 per cent in the middle of UPA-2, the BJP focused on two things: a much greater political focus on how many women became beneficiaries of its general developmental schemes and more targeted cohesion and messaging around women-only schemes. A case in point is how, on Women's Day in 2020, the finance ministry pushed out a press release listing six general financial schemes where women had turned out to be the primary beneficiaries.[109] A great deal has been said of the Modi government's focus on the women-centric Ujjwala scheme—which provides LPG cylinders and a direct-cash transfer to women below the poverty line—but the political focus has been just as much on giving women a bigger share of the wider financial schemes.

On more conventional women-centric programmes, it is important to break down what Modi means when he talks of supporting women from the cradle to their death. In his personal public outreach, he divides this into four milestones. The first milestone is birth. For this, pregnant women not employed by the Union or any state government became entitled to direct-cash benefits from the state for the first time under PM Matru Vandana Yojana (PMMVY), started in January 2017. As many as 15.4 million pregnant women enrolled for maternity cash transfers as part of this scheme between 2017 and 2020. Of these, 13.8 million women received cash benefits. They each received payments of ₹4,138, on average, in their bank accounts.[110] Additionally, the government amended the Maternity Act in 2017 to increase maternity leave for women working in establishments with over ten employees from the earlier requirement of twelve weeks to twenty-six weeks.[111] As Modi reminds his listeners often in public meetings, this means 'half a year, six months. When the world's developed countries hear what a developing country like ours has done and taken such a big decision for women, even they must be feeling what a wonder this is. They must be surprised. More so that we have mandated creches in offices with more than fifty employees.'[112]

The second milestone is education. For this, Modi often counts three schemes, the first of these being Beti Bachao, Beti Padhao, for educating girl children and to improve India's sex ratio. Initially tested in 140 districts, the scheme was extended to 640 districts in 2017.[113] Ministry of Health data shows that one of its targets—India's Sex Ratio at Birth—improved from 918 in 2014-15 to 931 in 2018-19.[114] Under Swachh Bharat, over 107 million household toilets were built nationwide between 2014 and 2020.[115] Revealingly, from a gender point of view, Modi in 2017 lauded Swachh Bharat toilets as 'Izzat Ghar' or House of Respect after seeing this title-plate being used on toilets in Varanasi by the UP government. In October 2017, the Union government issued a circular to all states, asking Hindi-speaking states to start formally referring to Swachh Bharat toilets as 'Izzat Ghar' and non-Hindi speaking states to come up with similar nomenclature in regional languages.[116] Finally, the Sukanya Samriddhi scheme was launched in December 2014. It allows parents to save money for girl children under the age of ten by depositing a minimum of ₹250, which matures after twenty-one years at an 8.1 per cent interest rate. Over 1.7 crore Sukanya Samriddhi accounts were opened between 2014 and 2019, with 25,979.6 crore being deposited in them till 2018.[117]

The third milestone is careers. Modi speaks of Mudra loans to over 16 crore women as the centrepiece of his idea of self-empowerment. As he told the BJP's Mahila Morcha workers in 2018, 'Our country's daughters can now make their own careers, fulfil their dreams themselves ... Without bank guarantees, people have been given loans over ₹5 lakh crores. It is a very important thing that 70 per cent of those who have got financial help from Mudra scheme are women and our daughters. I feel proud hearing this. The success of this scheme proves how our country's women are breaking old chains and coming forward for self-employment.'[118] Women also accounted for as much as 81 per cent of all financial beneficiaries (who received over 20,000 crore cumulatively in sanctioned loans) under the Stand Up India scheme between April 2016 and March 2020.[119]

The fourth peg is old-age support. Women across India accounted for 43 per cent of new pensioners (93 lakh of 2.15 crore subscribers) under the Atal Pension Yojana. Launched in May 2015, this guaranteed minimum monthly pensions of up to ₹5,000 for those above sixty years of age.[120] Women also accounted for over 40 per cent of beneficiaries under both the Pradhan Mantri Jeevan Jyoti Bima Yojana (PMJJBY) and the Pradhan Mantri Suraksha Bima Yojana (PMSBY).[121] Both schemes were launched in 2015. PMJJBY offers life insurance of ₹2 lakh for a premium of ₹330 per annum, while PMSBY provides accident/disability insurance of up ₹2 lakh for a premium of ₹12 per annum. Modi's speeches often highlight the fact that both these schemes provided security cover for women for just 90 paise per day (life insurance) and Re 1 per month (accident insurance). As he put it, 'If you see all these decision and schemes from a broader perspective and from a big canvas, you will find how our government understands the little-little needs of our women, daughters and sisters, understands their worries and is standing with them at every milestone and turning point in the lives of our daughters.'[122] By mid-2019, as many as 25 million women account-holders had signed up for the life insurance scheme (62.8 million Indians enrolled in all). Furthermore, a whopping 66.2 million women signed up for the accident insurance policy (a staggering 165.5 million Indians enrolled overall) by 2019.[123] This widening of the social welfare net is crucially important in a country where most people below the poverty line have hitherto not had access to insurance or social welfare of this kind.

Modi's focus on women reflects a Lohiaite vision. He often quotes a parliamentary speech by the socialist leader Ram Manohar Lohia in the 1960s. 'He said that India's women have two primary problems: one is toilets, the other is water. This means there are no toilets for women and women don't have water to run their households … Lohia ji is gone, many governments have come and gone, leaders have come and gone, but only we have determined that each house will have a toilet as well as water.'[124]

A key part of Modi's gender narrative focuses on changing traditional gender hierarchies in official documentation. The move to give priority to women in house registrations under PM Awaas Yojana is a case in point. Modi argues in his speeches that 'we know that if you ask any woman, even today in our society, the situation is that if you ask in whose name is the house, it will be in the name of the husband or son; whose name is the car, it will be in the name of the husband or son. If you buy even a scooter, it will be in the name of the husband or the son.' To ensure that property can be in the name of women, several rules were changed between 2014 and 2019. For instance, it was no longer necessary for women to provide either their marriage or divorce documents to apply for passports. 'It would be enough for them to provide names of their father or mother … This is our complete commitment towards naari shakti,' said Modi in 2018. 'If women's contributions increase in the country, the country will develop. This is what the dream of New India is about: where women are strong, confident and equal stakeholders in development.'[125]

It is nobody's case that these schemes have no flaws. The Ujjwala scheme, which provided over 80 million free LPG connections between April 2016 and September 2019, could only be availed by women below the poverty line, and these beneficiaries also received direct cash transfers of up to ₹1,600 each.[126] In the initial phases, over 40 per cent of Ujjwala connections were released on single Aadhar cards alone (without the mandatory bank account details, as the guidelines mandated), which created problems while resolving concerns on ending duplication.[127] Other critics have described the problems that women face when it comes to refilling the LPG cylinders. While these are valid concerns, the fact is that, on women, Modi and the BJP have a story to tell. Whatever the flaws in their story, its broad contours have been convincing enough for large numbers of women to switch to the party as never before, especially in the Hindi heartland states. Consider how Modi sells the Ujjwala story in his public outreach. In a speech to the Indian Merchants' Chamber Ladies' Wing in April 2017, he said:[128]

> Mothers and sisters can imagine that when a wood stove is burnt, when a mother makes food by burning a wood stove, her body ingests smoke equal to that from 400 cigarettes a day. When children play in

> the house, imagine what would be happening to them with the smoke? What would be happening to their bodies? Understanding this pain and problem, I initiated a campaign to save these mothers and sisters from wooden stoves ... we took up the big challenge to save these families from smoke ... The law, rules and schemes are one thing, but in day-to-day life, change happens when they are implemented, [when] facilities reach the person sitting at the last end [of the process]. This government's identity is that when schemes are made, roadmaps are made, and to fulfil them, continuous monitoring is done.

Politically, it may not matter to voters if such schemes have some leakages, as long as they are seen to be working by and large. Like Swachh Bharat, their importance lies as much in the symbolism as in the final delivery. They were central to the Modi government's primary political messaging: that its achievements on women-focused welfare were better than those of governments that came before.

The BJP, the RSS and Questions of Gender

Vijaya Raje Scindia, the original BJP woman torchbearer, created a furore in 1990 when she defended 'voluntary sati' in Parliament. She argued that, while the ancient Hindu practice of 'pushing women into their husbands' funeral pyre was condemnable, there was nothing wrong if a woman wanted to commit sati voluntarily'.[129] For Scindia, who led a pro-sati march in 1987 after the infamous burning of Roop Kanwar, a widow in Rajasthan's Deorala, sati was 'very much part of our tradition'.[130] She argued in the Lok Sabha that voluntary widow self-immolation was no different from self-immolation by some DMK workers in Tamil Nadu after the death of their leader M.G. Ramachandran.

The BJP, which had condemned 'sati', quickly distanced itself from Scindia's position. Yet, in many ways, this debate reflected the chasm between the party's long-held notions of patriarchy and tradition and its aim of attracting women voters.[131] The internal contradictions were highlighted again in 1994 when Sushma Swaraj officially condemned the Shankaracharya of Puri for his public opposition to women chanting Vedic verses. At a time when there was a deep disquiet over the Hindu Right's positioning on women, Swaraj declared that, for the BJP, 'anything attributed to scriptures or any practice followed which denigrates the position of Indian women deserves outright rejection'.[132] This tension between the party's ambitions for the women vote and the patriarchal notions of some of its members was a constant through the 1990s. On the one hand, the Mahila Morcha would hold a rally comparing its women workers to the angry Hindu goddess Chandika.[133] On the other, there would be headlines such as the one made by Mridula Sinha, then president of the BJP's Mahila Agadi, when she blamed women for domestic violence. 'Yes, it's often the woman's fault,' she declared. 'She can provoke the man to such an extent that he beats her. And sometimes the woman can be so *ziddi*. We tell the woman to try and adjust. After all, it is her family.'[134] At one point in the late 1990s, Sangh leaders in Delhi were even saying that girls should not wear skirts, ostensibly because mosquitoes would bite their legs.[135] Until the early 2000s, instances like these confirmed for many liberals that the BJP and the wider Sangh Parivar subscribed to regressive patriarchal notions that were at odds with modern values like individual agency.

Those days are long gone. At a policy level at least, the BJP has fundamentally changed its attitudes to women. From the early 2000s, the BJP and the RSS worked hard to course-correct. They actively reached out to Indian women with a new gender-focused discourse, higher representation and refocused governmental schemes. They did so by focusing on a highly public strategy that was centred on fields that involve physical activity and were hitherto seen as male domains. It is telling that so many leading women athletes—from Paralympics silver medallist Deepa Mehta to Olympics bronze medallist Saina Nehwal to wrestler Babita Phogat—joined the BJP after Modi came to power.

This shift was exemplified by Modi's 2017 speech to women business leaders. 'Today, this country's women are flying combat jets, are going to space, winning medals at the Olympics for the country,' said Modi. 'From panchayats to Parliament, from villages to Silicon Valley, Indian women are shining. And so this imagination that women are only home-bound is a myth.'[136] When speaking to women party leaders in 2018, he focused on the need to change the social norms that differentiate between men and women, specifically in the context of sexual harassment:[137]

> We ask fifty questions to daughters. Who is the daughter speaking to, why did she come late, what is she doing, who came? But do we, who ask questions to our daughters, ever question our sons? Where do you go, who are your friends, who do you meet, who do you speak to, why did you come late at night, where did you spend the night, if you are going out, then with whom? We don't even ask our sons. Only when sons keep in mind their values and boundaries, will they keep in mind society's rules.

Not surprisingly, there continue to be contradictions in the party's positions on gender questions. In 2017, for instance, the Congress demanded an apology from the BJP, quoting from a 2014 blog by newly appointed UP Chief Minister Adityanath, in which he had ostensibly written that 'women power ... does not require freedom, but protection'.[138] From Unnao MP Sakshi Maharaj asking all Hindu women in 2015 to 'produce four children'[139] to the then BJP UP vice president Dayashankar Singh comparing BSP chief Mayawati to a 'prostitute' in 2016,[140] there are enough examples of regional party leaders expressing objectionable views. Yet, the BJP has done dramatically well with women voters under Modi because of wider changes it made on women's representation and its overall discourse, as this chapter has outlined.

In tandem with the official shift in the BJP's positioning, the RSS's views on women also changed over time. In the 1960s, Golwalkar had extolled the ideal of a woman as a mother and wife, upholding traditional cultural norms. In recent years, by contrast, the Sangh has taken progressive and assertive positions on women's roles outside the family. In March 2016, it passed a resolution calling for eliminating restrictions on women in Hindu temples, saying that in religious matters 'both men and women are considered to be equal partners'. The RSS also supported women priests.[141] When Walter Andersen and Sridhar Damle updated their study of the RSS in 2018, they found that married members of the Sangh's women-affiliate body, the Rashtra Sevika Samiti, 'tended to describe themselves and their husbands (almost always RSS members) as equal partners, both in terms of managing family matters and in their respective civic lives'.[142] Like the BJP, the Rashtriya Sevika Samiti talks up the idea of women taking on combat roles and encourages such activities. An account of this by BJP Mahila Morcha leader Priti Gandhi in *Organiser* is instructive: 'With a strong belief that women are by no standards the weaker gender, the Rashtriya

Sevika Samiti trains their Sevikas not only in outdoor sports but also teaches them skills like horse riding and sword fighting which help them develop their physical capacity and are confidence-building exercises. The Samiti recognises and celebrates the inherent qualities of a women—"Matrutva", i.e. Universal motherhood, "Kartrutva", or Efficiency and Social Activism and "Netrutva", i.e. Leadership. An exemplary mother like Jijabai, a capable administrator like Ahilyabai Holkar and a brave, fearless leader like Rani Lakshmibai of Jhansi are the role models of Sevikas.'[143]

By 2018, the Sevika Samiti, formed by Laxmibai Kelkar in 1936, had 5,215 active shakhas, 875 centres, 475 fully operational projects across India—on health, education, value education and self-reliance—and almost 4,00,000 members.[144] The Samiti has its own uniform, and much like its male counterpart, holds three levels of training camps, training about 10,000 women each year.

The Sangh then formed a central body, Mahila Samanvay, to coordinate the work among women in its various bodies. Geetatai Gunde was relieved from the ABVP in 2009 to take charge and to 'ensure procedural competence in Parivar organizations to encourage women's participation'. Women activists working with her included ABVP's Mamata Yadav, BMS's Gita Gokhale, VHP's Srimati Meenakshi and ABVKA's Ranjana Khare. This coordination meant that a number of related RSS bodies began focusing in parallel on women's issues. According to senior ABVP leader Sunil Ambekar, the Adhivakta Parishad began organising meetings on women's legal rights, while Krida Bharti did the same on the subject of women athletes, Itihas Sankalan Samiti organised conferences of women historians and on the history of women. When the BMS, for example, organised a march in Delhi in 2017, one lakh of the two lakh attendees were women. Such activities led to the creation of new Sangh-supported women-focused organisations: Bharatiya Stree Shakti Jagran in Pune, Maitreyi in Pune and the All-India Women's Organisation (also called Stree Shakti).[145]

Different Feminisms: The BJP and Sangh Feminism vs the Older Feminist Movement

The BJP draws a distinction between 'Western' notions of feminism and its own. The older women's movement drew on early global feminist movements to stress on the individual agency of women—outside of familial relationships (as mother, wife or daughter) and outside of religion and culture. The BJP, on the other hand, emphasised their agency as career women but equally their role in families and as upholders of culture. The *Mahila Morcha: Training Manual* valorises independent career women like tennis player Sania Mirza, badminton Olympic medallist P.V. Sindhu, boxer Mary Kom, astronaut Kalpana Chawla, singer Lata Mangeshkar and corporate chieftains like former Pepsi Chairman and CEO Indira Nooyi and Biocon's Kiran Mazumdar-Shaw. It also has sections on the contributions of women as mothers, wives, housewives, protectors of culture and tradition that sit side-by-side with their contributions as scientists, politicians and administrators. While the BJP stresses on the equality of women, it regards the traditional feminist movement as an imported 'Western' concept.[146] This is an important distinction.

Citing ancient Vedic sages like Gargi, Kapila, Arundhati and Maitreyi as examples of women's agency in ancient India, the BJP argues that the historical contexts of women's movements in the West and India are different. 'In the Western view, woman was regarded as lower,' says the training manual. Speaking of Christian traditions, it argues that 'her Creation was from Adam's ribs and so she is a sub-part and her work is to keep man happy and serve him'. Many Western women's rights movements initially had to fight for their rights 'first from religion and the Church and then from the sovereign and the State'. This is why, in the BJP's view, their 'practices cannot be replicated to solve the problems of Indian women because India's intellectual, historical context and way of thinking towards women is different'. Acknowledging that, over several centuries, 'some bad customs were born', the BJP sees the degradation of the status of women in India as the result of centuries of political instability. Working women in India, it argues, are only regaining 'their ancient respected status', and bringing 'bad customs' to an end. 'They [women] don't need to fight with Dharmashastra [religious text] or to be freed from anyone,' says the BJP. In this view, women need equality and 'shakti' (power), not 'mukti' (emancipation).[147]

The RSS agrees with this critique of Western as well as traditional Indian feminism that defines women's empowerment in terms of sexual politics and the philosophy of power. The Sangh's critique of feminism is best encapsulated by ABVP's Sunil Ambedar:[148]

> For them [Western feminists], the nature-defined role of women as mothers and carers was a model of femininity based on a patriarchal past, like cages associated with a gendered identity. Feminism is the language of male oppression and class struggle and it shows no flexibility to account for diverse experiences. Improvements in economic condition and education are not considered transformative enough. All contestations are about the woman's body. The hippie culture of the West in the 60s and 70s became the coda of this stream of thought. It is, therefore, natural for most women to be uneasy with Western feminist thinkers and their tropes, which have come to inhabit the social science space in India. In any case, whatever pretensions it had as an academic discipline soon degenerated into a fad and reckless lifestyle choices ... It can be safely stated that the march of women's empowerment in India has no traces of Western feminist thinking. It follows the Indian trajectory of integration, where women and men work together to remove social ills that are incapacitating for women.

In other words, the BJP and the RSS talk of a new Indian model of feminism, focused as much on the family as it is on women's empowerment. The Sangh says 'it is reaching out to families with the message of women's empowerment, education, democratic participation and fighting evil practices like dowry. If a woman wants to go out for studies or work, she ought to be encouraged. If a woman decides to enter public life, she should be supported. We are seeing this change quietly sweep across the country in a uniquely Indian manner.'[149]

This notion of feminism is more sophisticated than what most liberals believe it to be. The default view has been that it aimed at 'maintain[ing] the highly subordinate position of women in India'.[150] The reality is different and much more complex. Swati Dyahadroy's work on Dnyana Prabodhini (DP), founded in 1962, has shown, for instance, that its women's wing had women doing things that men normally did, like beating drums in religious processions and learning martial skills. This countered the patriarchal idea of women's bodies and 'physical separation in public'. As Dyahadroy wrote, 'Women, thus, enter the public space claiming hitherto male domains by performing feats considered masculine in nature like beating drums, doing the lezim (local dance form similar to the drill) but encircled by male colleagues from the DP.' They claim the public space and get agency, and also work outside the home.[151] In many ways, the BJP's focus on the mobilisation of women is informed by this broad worldview.

The Sabarimala Conundrum: Tradition Vis-à-vis Women's Equality

The BJP's decision, in 2018, to oppose the Supreme Court's decision on opening up the Sabarimala Ayyappa shrine in Kerala to women of menstruating age illustrated the tensions between its new outreach to women and the older cultural notions it was moved by. BJP President Amit Shah declared that the apex court should desist from passing judgements that could not be enforced. The party, he said, stood on the side of Ayyappa devotees, framing the conflict as a battle for 'dharma, belief and bhakti'.[152] When Prime Minister Modi was asked why the BJP supported the criminalisation of triple talaq among Muslims but was opposing the entry of Hindu women into Sabarimala, he answered that triple talaq was a matter of gender equality, while Sabarimala was one of tradition. He told ANI that many 'Islamic countries', including Pakistan, had banned triple talaq and, therefore, it was 'not an issue of religion or belief'. On Sabarimala, conversely, he insisted that 'India is of the view that everyone should get equal rights' and pointed to diverse traditions: 'In India, there are also some small temples where men cannot go and men do not go.' Pointing to the one dissenting note, by Justice Indu Malhotra, in the 5–1 Supreme Court Sabarimala ruling, the prime minister said, 'a woman judge in the Supreme Court has made certain observations. It needs to be read minutely. She has seen the issue as a woman also and given her views. There should be a debate on that as well sometimes.'[153] Shah too insisted that the limitation on entry was 'not discrimination', it was 'part of worship' and about the 'protection of the uniqueness' of the Sabarimala shrine, the only Ayyappa temple that had restrictions on women because of the celibate form of the deity there.[154]

While the BJP was roundly criticised for its stance, it is important to note that the Congress took precisely the same position on this issue. The BJP's agitation against women activists trying to enter Sabarimala in November 2018 was matched by Congress–UDF leaders staging protests on precisely the same grounds at various places in Kerala, including a march led by former Kerala chief minister Oomen Chandy and Opposition leader Ramesh Chennithala from Nilakkal to Pamba.[155] The Congress's turn away from the liberal position was best articulated by Thiruvananthapuram MP Shashi Tharoor. Having initially welcomed the Supreme Court verdict, he later changed his mind, arguing that a 'significant majority of women' had demonstrated that their 'faith is offended by the Supreme Court verdict', and that it would be 'preposterous to tell women that their faith is really a form of Stockholm syndrome. When you disturb the belief of worshippers, you violate a space beyond reasoning.' He admitted that this left liberals like him 'torn', but insisted that in 'religious matters, beliefs must prevail'.[156] As Tharoor told me later in a public discussion, he changed his mind after he 'saw the reactions from my own people' whom he represented in Parliament and on 'seeing the depth of feeling, particularly among women'. As he put it, 'when you see it from the outside, you see it as an issue of equality and you frame it that way but from the point of believers ... they frame it as an issue of sanctity', which would damage the centuries-old beliefs around the temple.[157] Rahul Gandhi too changed his position on Sabarimala after initially supporting the Supreme Court verdict. Shorn of all the spin, the Congress and the BJP were essentially saying the same thing.

The Sabarimala debate demonstrates how all Indian political parties are conflicted on questions of gender. In a political landscape characterised by double-speak on gender, the gaps in the BJP's discourse may not necessarily be a disadvantage—in comparison to the Congress—especially if it is doing more on the ground for the representation of women than the other parties are.

The BJP's Mobilisation of Women and Questions for the Women's Movement

The large-scale mobilisation of women by the BJP after 2014 raises serious questions for the wider women's and Left movements in India. The fact that many women, especially in rural India, chose to vote for the BJP, and that non-BJP women's movements were unable to seriously expand their presence outside of their existing pockets, raises several questions that these groups must confront. The feminist movement first dealt with these fundamental challenges in the early 1990s, when large numbers of women joined the BJP's mobilisation on the Ram Temple. Writing on that first upsurge, Tanika Sarkar and Urvashi Butalia recognised that 'We do have before us a large-scale movement among women of the right who bring with them an informed consent and agency, a militant activism.'[158] While left-wing women writers conceded that the ground was shifting, they largely felt at the time that these women had shifted because of religious causes like the Ayodhya Temple, and that they would shift back when these emotions receded into the background. Their understanding of the Hindu right-wing cultural vision as only privileging familial roles for women, as mothers or housewives, led them to assume that, at some point, many of these women would realise its limitations. This view was best summed up by Sarkar and Butalia, who argued that 'Feminist convictions are not given or inherent in women, after all.'[159]

The evidence in this chapter shows that these assumptions need serious revisiting. If religion was the only opium that moved women to the BJP through the Ayodhya movement, that is certainly not the case any longer. At the party, government and development beneficiary levels, the BJP is more gender-representative that any other party in India. If patriarchal ideas had imposed limits on its expansion among women, we have also seen how the views of the BJP and the RSS have evolved over time. The BJP's growth among women also raises deeper questions about what it means to be a feminist in India. It valorises women achievers and career women as well as housewives and mothers. Celebrating familial roles is anathema to a certain kind of feminism. While seeing women as only upholders of cultural values or as child-producing vessels is, of course, deeply problematic, what happens if a party upholds both emancipatory ideas and some traditional norms? Is that kind of feminism not feminism at all?

In some ways, the BJP's ideas on woman power draws from what is globally referred to as the 'third wave' of feminism. The 'first wave' in the mid-nineteenth and early twentieth century focused on getting equal rights for women. In India, the Constitution wrote equal rights for women into law in 1947, long before many developed countries did, though the social position of Indian women did not change for decades.[160] 'Second-wave' feminism from the 1960s and 1970s saw discrimination against women as the outcome of cultural, political and religious inequality and focused on issues of identity. It argued that women had to get out of these bonds to be truly free. A product of the American Cultural Revolution of the 1960s, it was epitomised by the slogan 'The Personal is Political' that became synonymous with the women's liberation movement. The 'third wave' from the 1990s challenged the 'second wave' and emerged as a backlash against it. Broadly stacked under the rubric of 'post feminism', its adherents largely 'agreed with the goals of feminism, but did not identify themselves as feminists'. Unlike 'second-wave' activists, the 'third wave' rejected the idea that women are independent islands and argued that they could be both independent and have familial or cultural roles.[161]

The BJP's women's outreach arguably drew from this way of thinking but added a Hindu twist to it. Modi often uses religious imagery to portray women, for example. During Durga Puja celebrations in October 2020, he announced that women of India should be respected like the goddess herself.[162] He also published a collection of poems titled *Letters to Mother*, which conflated the nation with the universal idea of motherhood.[163] Despite the BJP's success in mobilising women, most gender-based critiques of Hindu right-wing movements have failed to grapple with its nuances, much like the widespread mainstream academic reluctance to engage with gender and spirituality as a subject meriting serious study. The Pakistani scholar Ayesha Jalal has argued that women and spirituality did not receive enough attention because academic theology had relegated it to the margins of intellectual discourse. 'The feminist movement for the most part too has skirted around it because of the distaste with which its luminaries look upon matters to do with religion.'[164] The same can be said about the wider left-wing Indian women's movement and how it approached the BJP and the RSS.

Even as the feminist movement remained deeply engaged in vociferous debates on identity and patriarchy, the evidence in this chapter shows that the BJP significantly widened its ambit and drastically increased its gender mobilisation. I am not a specialist on women's issues. However, as someone examining the BJP's growth and looking into this arena from that vantage point, I was surprised that I found virtually no serious research from gender scholars on the BJP and its mobilisation of women in the post-2000 period. While a number of scholars did fine studies of the Hindi nationalist movement and the woman question in the 1990s, there has been no substantial work since. This is a surprising gap because women have been at the centre of the BJP's rise as India's predominant political party after 2014. Their modes of mobilisation and the impact of governmental polices obviously needs new research that gender theorists and activists must engage with and examine more deeply. In some ways, the BJP's rise under Modi embodies a clash of different versions of feminism. Simply rejecting its ideas on women as regressive is not enough. Even those who oppose it must try and understand why more Indian women agree with the BJP's notion of women's equality than theirs. It necessitates a fresh interrogation of old assumptions and a new debate on women and Indian politics. If this chapter can provoke such debates and more research into how operates, I would consider its work done.

At the time of writing, the BJP was initiating another gender-initiative to bring the minimum legally acceptable marriage age of Indian women on par with men to twenty-one, from eighteen years of age. Announcing that he had been getting 'a lot of letters from aware daughters from across the country for an early decision on the matter', Prime Minister Modi declared in October 2020 that his government would decide soon after a high-powered committee headed by Jaya Jaitly, former president of the Samata Party, gave its report. Like the triple talaq case before it, the proposal was opposed by several women's rights groups on various technical grounds because they saw it as a way of reducing women's agency in cases of elopement and love marriages.[165] The BJP, on the other hand, portrayed it as one of gender-equality. Either all Indian men and women should be allowed to marry at eighteen or all at twenty-one. Politically, this can be framed as a simple yes and no question to voters. Common sense dictates that the disparity in age limits clearly makes no sense.[166] Yet, the move seemed to tie up several rights groups in knots. Whichever way this plays out in the future, it showed once again how the BJP was deploying women's issues to plot its future political growth.

CONCLUSION

18

'PARTY OF RAM'

A Hindu Suratrana, the Idea of 'New India' and Its Global Message

It is the death of the Republic, lamented one of the few liberals on my school alumni WhatsApp group. As the image of Prime Minister Narendra Modi presiding over the bhoomi-pujan of the new Ram Temple in Ayodhya streamed on television screens and other devices across India on 5 August 2020, the WhatsApp group erupted. The morning started with 'Ram-Ram' messages and people posting celebratory Ram imagery on the group. Then one of the Modi-bhakts on the group posted a 'Nation with Namo' political pamphlet, listing 'decades-long pending issues' the Modi government had 'resolved' in 'just six years'. Prominently listed was the Ram Temple dispute. To this, my liberal friend answered, 'You must add on the list highest unemployment in 45 years, highest territory ceded to China in 60 years, highest diesel prices'. It was the kind of argument that had become almost a daily ritual on this group between the same set of Left- and Right-leaning individuals. But that day, as the puja began in Ayodhya, some of the political neutrals jumped in. 'Bhai, let it be today,' one counselled the liberal. 'Today is a historic day. Please keep agendas aside.' On screen, Modi had just been anointed with a saffron turban and a silver mukut (crown) by the priests of the Hanumangarhi temple. He was now doing a dandvat pranam,[1] lying prostrate on the floor with his hands folded before the idol of Ram Lalla. Another school friend weighed in. He felt bad, he said, about 'Libtard Sikular Hindus who grew up hating their culture, history, roots and their identity. They have no ethics, grace, moral values to hold onto as they navigate life.'

Now, this WhatsApp group, with its 100-odd members, is not a scientific sample. But it is a microcosm of the wider social debate in middle India that Modi's fronting of the Ram Temple construction unleashed, and a demonstration of the renewed potential of the Ayodhya movement as a political lightning rod.[2] Modi was hailed as the Hindu Hriday Samrat when he began his electoral career in Gujarat. Now, the carefully choreographed symbolism of the Vedic yajna in Ayodhya, with him as its karta (doer), subliminally posited Modi as a new Hindu suratrana (protector of the gods).[3]

Celebratory 'Jai Sri Ram' messages started pouring in on WhatsApp. The lonely liberal valiantly pushed back, saying that he actually taught yoga for a living and spent most of his time reading the Hindu scriptures. But the group admin moved in swiftly, unceremoniously removing him as well as the vociferous bhakts from the group. 'Enough is enough,' said the admin. 'It's a good day today.' It was a revealing epitaph for a day that ended with most of my neighbours in the Noida high-rise apartment complex we live in lighting lamps outside their flats, like it was Diwali. On Zee News, meanwhile, the anchors, broadcasting from a faux Ram Temple set, had begun dancing to a Ram-dhun. Some of the studio guests were touching the feet of actors dressed up as Ram, Sita and Hanuman—specially brought on to the set—as is customary in many Ram Lilas, where the actors are said to embody the gods for the duration of the performance. It was that kind of day.

Modi's yajna at Ayodhya can be directly contrasted with Nehru's firm opposition to the state playing any role in reconstructing the Somnath temple in 1951. His intense debates with K.M. Munshi, the minister in his cabinet who spearheaded that initiative, and his insistence that Rajendra Prasad, India's first president, attend the Somnath ceremony in his personal capacity, not as the Republic's first citizen, set a template for a newly independent country that had just been partitioned on religious lines. Importantly, Nehru's opposition to the government rebuilding temples was framed in a state that, at least constitutionally, was not yet 'secular'. The words 'secular' and 'socialist' were added to the Preamble by

Indira Gandhi in 1976 during the Emergency through the Forty-second Constitutional Amendment.[4]

Many liberals wrongly decried Modi's decision to lead the Ram Temple ceremony as an abandonment of the Constitution. A political move, it certainly was. Yet, as Yogi Adityanath pointed out in his speech at the consecration ceremony, the construction was 'within the legal framework, within the democratic and constitutional system and done peacefully'.[5] As the leader of a political party that explicitly listed the construction of the Ram Temple in its election manifesto, Modi was well within his rights to front such a construction once the Supreme Court ruled in favour of it (however flawed many thought the court's unanimous 5–0 judgement was).[6]

The fact is that, by 2020, the BJP had won the culture war on Ram. Congress leader Priyanka Gandhi's message welcoming Ram Lalla and genuflecting before his image, Manish Tiwari's social media recitation of a Ram bhajan, Kamal Nath changing his Twitter profile picture to that of a Hindu pilgrim reciting the Hanuman Chalisa—all of this reflected the tricky position that the Congress found itself in. It chose to side with the Ram Temple, but stood to gain nothing politically from being the BJP's B-team on Hinduness.

Modi, meanwhile, sought to appropriate Ram within the reframing of a new 'Ram Rajya'. Speaking in Ayodhya, he attempted to link the Ram story to his own political project. He spoke of the subterranean shift he had spearheaded within the new BJP: on women and gender relations, on caste and the poor, neatly linking what he posited as the ideals of Ram to his own political messaging. Ram's appeal was built on the support of those on the margins, Modi argued: 'vanars and vanvasis', the poor and women. The promise of this new Ram Rajya was, he said, similarly focused on the lower castes, backward classes and the poor. In a subtle nod to the BJP's wooing of smaller OBC castes like Rajbhars, Modi explicitly referenced the eleventh-century king Suheldev, revered by both OBC Rajbhars and Dalit Pasis.

One major critique of the Ram Temple movement was that it reduced a multifaceted god to only his angry image. Modi addressed this head-on, speaking at length on the many sides of Ram and the multiplicity of the Ramayana in its hundreds of regional versions: both Indian and non-

Indian. His speech at Ayodhya was different from the Sangh boilerplate messaging on the temple and Ram on several levels. He mentioned the Tamil Ramayana at least five times, even quoting from it a couple of times. (Tamil Nadu has been a key focus area for the BJP, which is eying the political vacuum left by the demise of AIADMK supremo J. Jayalalithaa. It is hoping for new expansion in a major southern state.) Sikhs, Buddhists and Jains featured again and again as part of the new Ram Rajya's respect for minorities. There was no explicit mention of Muslims, except in a passing reference to foreign invaders who attacked the temple of Ram—though he did say repeatedly that 'Ram is for all and Ram is in all'. It was typical Modi-speak, but the references to the many Ramayanas was certainly atypical of the movement's usual rhetoric. He repeatedly exhorted the audience to chant the name of Ram, but used the local religious slogan 'Jai Siya Ram' (which places Sita before Ram), not 'Jai Sri Ram', which was the aggressive slogan of the Ram Janmabhoomi movement.

Hindutva has always had global ambitions. That day, three of its top leaders—Modi, Adityanath and Bhagwat—chose to dwell on why the message of the Ayodhya movement had ramifications far beyond India's borders, saying it was the duty of the young to spread this message worldwide. Speaking of the 'New India' under Modi, Bhagwat argued that 'in the time of Corona', the world was looking for answers. 'Does anyone have answers?' he asked. 'The world has tried two methods [presumably capitalism and communism]. Is there a third way? Yes—we have a third way. *This temple is just the beginning of the preparation of spreading that message of an alternative way*.' (Emphasis added.)

None of the three spelt out the contours of this third Indian way, beyond the usual homilies about Hindu tolerance and ancient wisdom-liners like 'Vasudhaiva Kutumbakam' (The World is One Family)—themes that Modi and the RSS often refer to. Yet, they were hinting at deeper, more tantalising possibilities.

The BJP and Sangh leaders were clearly positioning India as the fount of a Hindu civilisation as compared to, say, a Sinic/Chinese or Western civilisation. This concept may be a bit nebulous, as was the 'Gandhian socialism' of Deen Dayal Upadhyaya that the BJP had briefly adopted in the 1980s. It is, however, rooted in the civilisational notion of India as a Hindu power that is steeped in 'parampara', or tradition. This is an India wielding the soft power of ancient Hindu practices, acting as a swing state—probably in the sense that Samuel Huntington meant it when he wrote *The Clash of Civilizations*. Huntington's thesis, first fleshed out as an article in 1993, basically argued that the praxis of local politics would shift to the 'politics of ethnicity', while that of global politics would shift to the 'politics of civilizations'. In other words, 'cultural entities' would become the central dividing axes of power, locally and internationally: Sinic (Chinese), Islamic, Japanese, Orthodox (Russia), Western (Europe, North America, Australia, New Zealand), Latin American, African and Hindu (India).[7] While this idea was severely critiqued for simplifying the complexity of international relations—such as the huge differences among Islamic states— its central thesis of essentialist 'cultural' norms acting as a powerful guiding force for states willing to use them is undeniable.

Yogi Adityanath's assertion on Diwali 2020 that the government-organised ritual lighting of over 606,569 lamps by the banks of the Sarayu river in Ayodhya was meant to connect 'Bharatvanshis' (descendants of Bharat), whatever their 'mat-mazhab' (views-religion), to the 'ideals of Sri Ram' should be seen in this context.[8] At one level, it was simply a spectacle for the faithful—going up to 941,551 lamps on Diwali in 2021. For five years in a row, the Uttar Pradesh government's department of tourism even received a certificate from representatives of the Guinness Book of World Records for the lamp-lighting, which was monitored through drone-mounted cameras.[9] Yogi Adityanath framed Ayodhya's Deep Mahotsav (Great Festival of Lamps) as a 'symbol of public faith in our culture getting stronger' and dedicated the Guinness record to 'all Ram-Bhakts'.[10] Tellingly, the UP chief minister said that it was his job to take such a celebration to the world, so it would not only help 'brand' Ayodhya but also take 'Sri Ram's blessings' to the people of the world.[11] Statements like these merged seamlessly with his declaration that Ayodhya would become a 'vaishwik nagri' (global city), and with the plans for an airport that would have air-routes to South Korea, Fiji, Japan, Nepal and Thailand.[12] You do not have to agree with his formulation to see its ambition.

The political strategy of using religious spectacles is also underpinned by the economic logic of religious tourism. Agra's Taj Mahal has long been the global face of Indian tourism. Yet, UP government officials have asserted that, while Agra consistently gets the highest number of foreign tourist arrivals in the state each year (over 2 million foreigners and 83.5 million Indians in 2019), the religious sites of Prayagraj[13] (289.1 million because of the Kumbh that year), Ayodhya (over 30 million), Govardhan (16.9 million) and Vrindavan (16 million) consistently receive a substantially higher number of travellers, mostly domestic pilgrims. In fact, Prayagraj, with its confluence of rivers considered holy by Hindus, continues to be the most popular city in UP for domestic tourists. Even in non-Kumbh Mela years, it draws a substantial number of tourists: 49.4 million in 2018, for instance. This is true of Ayodhya as well.[14]

This is why Yogi Adityanath, in his maiden state budget as chief minister, pushed to allocate ₹1,240 crore towards developing the Ram, Krishna and Buddha tourism circuits in the state. In 2019-20, his government allocated significant funds to this project—over ₹300 crore to Ayodhya, over ₹125 crore to UP Brij Tirtha (tourism for the Mathura–Vrindavan circuit) and over ₹200 crore for roads leading up to the Kashi Vishwanath temple in Varanasi.[15] Tourism numbers also underlay the Central government's 2021 plans to connect Delhi and Ayodhya via a high-speed bullet train (to run on high-speed rail corridors, which are, of course, Modi's signature project, started with the Japanese government's technical and financial support). Also on the anvil is connectivity for the religious sites of Mathura and Prayagraj, as well as Agra, on the proposed Delhi–Varanasi bullet train route.[16]

Where China uses Mandarin and a host of cultural tools for its soft power projection,[17] the BJP seeks to deploy the cultural power of Hinduism for India's global branding. A good example of this is the Modi regime's celebration of yoga, which is personally fronted by the prime minister, both nationally and internationally. It is not an accident that the BJP made much of the establishment of the International Yoga Day by the UN on 14 December 2014. The UN Resolution was proposed by Prime Minister Modi himself in an address during the opening of the 69th session of the General Assembly. 'Yoga is an invaluable gift from our ancient tradition,' he told the UN. 'Yoga embodies unity of mind and body, thought and action … a holistic approach … Yoga is not just about exercise; it is a way to discover the sense of oneness with yourself, the world and the nature.'[18] The idea of Hindu cultural power is an incipient concept still, but what these statements indicate is a visualisation of

India as a Hindu power (probably like Israel is a Jewish power) without territorial aspirations.

Such a projection, using civilisational markers, also seems explicitly linked now to India's long-held aspiration as a rising power for a bigger seat in global forums, such as its bid for a permanent seat on the UN Security Council.[19] For the purveyors of 'New India'—a slogan formally adopted by the BJP in a political resolution on 9 September 2018[20]—the signs from Ayodhya indicated that such a country would overwhelmingly look to its Hindu traditions as markers of identity. It may not become a Hindu democracy constitutionally (unlike, say, Israel's Jewish democracy), it may not initiate military conscription for all, it may not look to grab land from its neighbours and Muslims may not become de jure second-class citizens (unlike Arabs in Israel), but the ambition to visibly demonstrate Hindu power is clear. The desire to be acknowledged globally is precisely why a billboard displaying the Ram Temple on bhoomi-pujan day at New York's Times Square was important for the BJP and its supporters.[21] It is another matter that its advertising coincided with pro-Kashmir and anti-Indian state advertising on the same billboards.

The BJP is deeply invested in the notion of correcting what it sees as past wrongs, an impulse that is intrinsically linked to the desire to rewrite history from 'India's point of view', as Amit Shah advised historians at Banaras Hindu University to do in late 2019. 'Putting together our history, improving our history and rewriting our history again is the responsibility of the country, the people and the country's historians. How long will we go on cursing the British saying that an injustice was done to us. Who is stopping us from writing (history)? … We do not have to get in conflict with anyone … We will write history as we see it, and because it will contain the truth, it will be popular … Can our historians not make 200 personalities who helped Indians reach here, and 25 dynasties which gave a lot to the world, a part of our history? This is the time when our historians need to rewrite our history as per a new vision,' he said.[22]

Speaking at a seminar on the fifth-century Gupta king Skandagupta, he said, 'India never invaded any foreign territory, but we have our own heroes like Skandagupta who defeated the Hunas when they had conquered a large part of Asia and Europe and had seemed invincible. It is unfortunate that our children don't know about the great ruler who extended our boundaries from Afghanistan to Junagadh. It is also unfortunate that his merits and contributions are ignored and there are not enough historical references about him.'[23] Modi's New India is thus as much about redefining the Indian past as it is about reshaping the future; as domestic in its ambition as it is global.

On the first Diwali after the Ram Temple decision in 2020, for example, the only news a prominent Hindi newspaper had on the front page of its UP district editions was a picture of hundreds of thousands of lamps lighting up the city and Yogi Adityanath's assertion that this was the 'dream of five centuries coming true'. This banner headline was accompanied by others like '*Gaurav-bodh se alokit Ram-Nagri*' (A feeling of pride lights up Ram's town), which used a poetic and religious turn of phrase to convey a political message. Another front-page headline declared: '*Ayodhya Banegi Vaishwik Nagri*' (Ayodhya will become a global city).[24] Not only did Yogi Adityanath emphatically declare that 'after 492 years' Sri Ram Janmabhoomi was glittering with celebration,[25] the UP government also distributed formal 'certificates' of participation to those who joined the ritual by lighting a virtual lamp through a special government website.[26] Such a website would, of course, serve a religious purpose as well as yield a database of prospective BJP voters at scale. It was an initiative that blended the BJP's use of technology and religious idiom with the end goal of political mobilisation.

Figure 18.1: Online Virtual Utsav by UP Government to Supplement Its Diwali Deep-Utsav in Ayodhya

Source: UP government-run website, 13 November 2020: https://virtualdeepotsav.com/

Figure 18.2: Ayodhya Lit Up With 606,569 Lamps on Diwali Deep-Utsav

Source: Picture tweeted by UP Chief Minister Yogi Adityanath on 13 November 2020, with a message saying 'the world record is dedicated to all Ram-Bhakts', https://twitter.com/myogiadityanath/status/1327288747558199296?s=20

Doordarshan's UP channel broadcast the lamp-lighting in Ayodhya live for almost seven hours on 13 November 2020. With drone-mounted cameras relaying aerial pictures of 'darshan' from the city, this programming on the state-owned network was unambiguous about what it thought the first Diwali in Ayodhya after the SC judgement signified. It was presented by commentators on the network as the 'ending of 500 years of darkness', as a 'gaurav-poorn pal' (pride-filled moment) coming after a 'centuries-long struggle' by 'itni peedhiyan' (so many generations) and the 'aahuti' (religious sacrifice) of 'lakhs of followers' for 'asmita'. Doordarshan also glorified the role of two leaders of the Ram Temple movement: Mahant Digvijay Nath (Hindu Mahasabha leader and Gorakhpur MP in 1967), who played a leading role in the emergence of the Ram Lalla idols in the Babri Masjid in 1949, and Mahant Avaidyanath (MLA from Maniram in 1967, 1969, 1974 and 1977; Gorakhpur MP in 1970, 1989, 1991 and 1996)—both Yogi Adityanath's predecessors as head of the Gorakhnath Math. The narrative virtually legitimised the demolition of the Babri Masjid, without actually saying so. It simultaneously positioned Yogi Adityanath as the inheritor of a religio-political tradition going back several decades, and as the one who heralded the transformation of the holy city from a 'sooni-see [sad] Ayodhya' to 'sundar [beautiful] Ayodhya'. The state TV anchor then went on to say that this was not just 'Ram's Ayodhya' on Diwali, but a metaphor for '*satta mei Ram: chaahe Dilli mein ya Lucknow mein*' (Ram in power, whether in Delhi or in Lucknow). 'Nature chooses its best sons,' said the DD anchor. He concluded that it was up to today's 'adhunik Ram' (modern Rams) to decide the future direction of India, and praised Narendra Modi and Yogi Adityanath for 'redefining India'.[27]

In fact, the Modi government's ₹971-crore[28] Central Vista redevelopment plan, an overhaul of New Delhi's imperial heart, is a physical manifestation of this redefinition as well as of Modi's 'New India'. The plan envisages a new Parliament building, the redevelopment of the 3-kilometre-long ceremonial avenue linking the Rashtrapati Bhawan and the iconic India Gate, new residences for the prime minister and vice president, and new office blocks for fifty-one Union government ministries. A number of conservationists, architects and urban planners have opposed it and called it 'vulgar'.[29] When activists went to court against construction work at the Central Vista during the pandemic, the Delhi High Court, on 31 May 2021, dismissed their petition as 'motivated', declared the plan an 'essential project of national importance' and imposed a ₹1 lakh fine on the petitioners. A three-judge bench of the Supreme Court upheld this verdict on 29 June 2021. The apex court said 'no interference is required' because the Central Vista project had 'complied of all protocols'. It also observed that the petitioners were selective in choosing the Central Vista project alone and did not research about such similar public projects where construction was ongoing.[30]

The Central Vista's principal architect, Bimal Patel, initially countered heritage concerns with a utilitarian argument about the administrative and practical needs of a changing and dynamic capital city,[31] while the government argued for the project in epochal terms. He emphasised that while the colonial British built Delhi's most important imperial buildings on top of Raisina Hill that 'exemplified the Raj ruling over the people of India' and created a 'big processional route [to them] that you have to go up as supplicants,' the Modi government's approach was the opposite. 'What we are doing here, and this present Prime Minister has sort of mandated, is that all the government facilities are going to come in the area on the plains, so to say, including the Prime Minister's office. And these magnificent buildings, which were the symbol of the government on top of the hill, are going to become museums ... Now you're going to be able to walk up with your kids, go into these buildings, to the museums, where you will be able to enjoy our culture. Now, this is a complete reversal. You're putting the people on top, and you're putting the government below, in a sense.'[32]

The current governmental heart of Delhi, with its imposing central structures and colonial bungalows, was originally built by the British architects Sir Edward Lutyens and Sir Herbert Baker in the 1920s. Nehru's India added a new layer of ministerial offices—like Krishi Bhawan and Udyog Bhawan—to it after Independence. 'These buildings built in the 1960s are hideous,' Hardeep Singh Puri, Union minister for housing and urban affairs, has said. 'You have to build to new, higher environmental standards.'[33] Durga Shanker Mishra, secretary for housing and urban affairs, wrote that the 'roots of the country's democracy date back to ancient times. However, the six centuries of the Sultanate and Mughal era were a period of regression.' The new Parliament, designed to be a 'People's Parliament' was being built, he said, 'for the first time in the history of the country' as an 'intrinsic part of the vision for New India@75'.[34] In their view, then, central Delhi was built by colonial overlords, with Nehruvian India appropriating it. Shahjahanabad, the Delhi that preceded it, was built by the Mughals in the seventeenth century, following a long pedigree of rulers who built similar citadels. The Central Vista project would be very much a part of this history of a permanent architectural legacy.

Modi's 'New India' was essentially recasting the nation's capital for itself—a monument to the electoral triumphs that endorsed its thinking. 'Our vision is of a new India that will be in tune with its glorious past,' the prime minister announced in an election rally in Meerut in March 2019.[35] This is partly why Modi refused to suspend the project in spite of the pandemic-induced economic crisis—a demand made by Congress President Sonia Gandhi, among others, as a cost-saving measure.[36] Modi tellingly chose the inauguration ceremony of new office complexes for 7,000 defence officers on Delhi's Kasturba Gandhi Marg and Africa Avenue to personally respond in public for the first time to criticism of the Central Vista project. The officers deputed to these new complexes on Kasturba Gandhi Marg and Africa Avenue had earlier been working out of colonial-era hutments. They were now relocating to spanking new buildings. Addressing them and an audience consisting of the top brass from the Army, Navy and Air Force, Modi said, 'Those people who are after the Central Vista project with a stick, with great cleverness they kept totally quiet on the fact that this is also a part of the Central Vista, that a facility where more than 7,000 armed forces officers work is being developed. Because they knew that their intent of spreading doubts and lies, their loose talk won't work as soon as this fact came out. Today the country is watching what we are doing behind the Central Vista. Now see, these modern offices built on K.G. Marg and Africa Avenue will greatly help in effectively managing all work linked to national security. This is a big and important step towards the construction of a modern defence enclave in the capital.'[37]

The BJP: Challenges and Prospects from 2021 Onwards

'The revolution is coming,' a prominent businessman said to me. 'The BJP will soon fall.' This is a deeply held view among many of my friends who dislike the BJP's cultural politics. They hold that it somehow became the dominant Indian party through a sleight of hand by appealing to Hindutva sentiments. Ergo, when emotions calm, the party will collapse. Are they right? Or is this the vain hope of out-of-touch liberals who feel marginalised in a country that has changed enormously since the BJP came to power?

Admittedly, the BJP was at the peak of its political fortunes in 2020 and is therefore facing the challenge of staying there. It comes up against five big challenges today, but the party has two major advantages as it navigates these problems.

Challenge 1: The Coronavirus Fallout and the Economy

The BJP's first big political challenge, going forward, is the long-term fallout of the second wave of the coronavirus which engulfed India in early-2021. Painful memories of loss or illness in virtually every family, oxygen shortages in many parts of the country, images of dead bodies floating in the Ganga and concerns over adequate vaccination availability at the time raised serious questions for the party, the Union government and state governments across India. Although Narendra Modi remained India's most popular political leader by far even in August 2021, the devastation caused by the pandemic was a major reason why *India Today's* bi-annual 'Mood of the Nation' survey showed a big dip in his ratings, compared to the same period the previous year. When asked how they rated Modi's performance as prime minister, 54 per cent Indians rated it as 'good' or 'outstanding' in August 2021—down from 74 per cent in January 2021 and 78 per cent in August 2020. When asked who they thought was best suited to be India's next prime minister, 24 per cent still said Modi. In comparison, the highest rated opposition leader on this question was Rahul Gandhi, at 10 per cent. However, Modi's rating on this very question had fallen from 38 per cent in January 2021 and 66 per cent in August 2020.[38] As the magazine's editorial director, Raj Chengappa, summed up, 'For Prime Minister Narendra Modi', the message coming out from this survey was clear: Indians were 'unhappy with the Centre's performance over the past six months' though they still 'saw the Modi government as the best bet' at the time.[39]

Conscious of the discontent caused by the pandemic, Modi undertook three major moves. First, he hit the 'reset' button in his government with major changes to his ministerial team on 8 July 2021. He brought into his government a new set of leaders in key roles, with thirty-six fresh faces. These included a new health minister, Mansukh Mandaviya from Gujarat's Bhavnagar, who was also given dual charge of chemicals and fertilizers (which includes the department of pharmaceuticals). A Rajya Sabha MP, Mandaviya had been on the core COVID-19 response team for over a year, and replaced Dr Harshavardhan.[40]

Second, Modi purged the entire government in his home state of Gujarat in September 2021. The Vijay Rupani-led state government had been particularly criticised for its response to the pandemic and, after he quit as state chief minister, the BJP replaced his entire erstwhile council of twenty-two ministers. In came twenty-four fresh ministers, who took office under the new chief minister, Bhupendra Patel, himself a first-time MLA.[41] Replacing the old with the new is an old but under-appreciated

Modi strategy that had helped him retain power in Gujarat earlier too. The BJP had replaced a significant number of its sitting legislators in the Gujarat assembly elections in 2002, 2007, 2012 and 2017 as a tactic to beat anti-incumbency sentiments. The gambit worked each time—with the party attaining high strike rates in such constituencies.[42] Whether it will work this time too depends a great deal on the performance of the incoming leaders who have a little over a year to perform, with polls due in the state in December 2022.

Similarly, in Uttar Pradesh too, where there had been public rumblings within the state BJP itself on the handling of the pandemic,[43] Yogi Adityanath revamped his government by inducting seven new ministers to consolidate the BJP's rainbow caste coalition of Savarn, non-Yadav OBC and non-Jatav Dalits ahead of the assembly polls in 2022. The social profile of the new ministers he inducted into the state government in September 2021 (three OBCs, two SCs, one ST and one Brahmin) was tellingly 'the same as the seven inducted in the Modi ministry from the state just two months ago.'[44]

Finally, at the national level, the Modi government recalibrated and focused intensely on vaccinations after the second wave.[45] By early-November 2021, over 53 per cent of Indians had received at least one dose of vaccinations, and over 23 per cent had been fully vaccinated.[46] This meant a cumulative vaccine coverage of 107.6 crore doses.[47] Globally, this meant that only China had vaccinated more people (228.5 crore doses) in comparison. India's vaccine count was followed by the US (42.3 crore), Brazil (27.5 crore), Indonesia (19.5 crore), Japan (19 crore), and Mexico (12.6 crore). Of course, these countries had vaccinated a much higher proportion of their populations, but the absolute vaccine numbers in India reflect the nature of the governmental drive.[48] Whether such numbers will be enough and how people, on balance, perceive the government's handling of the pandemic were still open questions at the time of writing. How governmental actions to combat the coronavirus play out on the ground over the next two years will be crucial to the BJP's political fortunes, at least till 2024.

Linked to this is the big challenge of the economy, a crisis that has been greatly aggravated by the pandemic. When *India Today's* 'Mood of the Nation' survey asked Indians what they thought was the single-biggest failure of the Modi government in August 2021, the most common response was price rise/inflation (29 per cent), followed by unemployment (23 per cent), and then the handling of the pandemic (11 per cent).[49] As a die-hard BJP supporter, businessman and regular party fund contributor in Mathura told me, 'The only challenge for BJP is the economy. They don't know what to do. They fail here. Rest all is fine.' The Indian economy was in a crisis even before the national lockdown in March 2020. The BJP may have won the cultural war on Ram but if the economy does not recover, if more jobs are not created, the negative political implications are obvious—'the economy cannot run "Ram Bharose" (up to Ram).'

A recovery is not about higher growth rates alone.[50] This book has shown how the BJP skilfully scaled up social welfare schemes through DBTs and a whole host of schemes after Modi came to power in 2014. He has been a statist; more Left than the Left, as a BJP MP put it.[51] His government wholly embraced the DBT welfare system that was initially tried and piloted under Manmohan Singh. Total DBT payments, in fact, rose twenty-nine-fold (from ₹7,367 crore to ₹2.14 lakh crore) and DBT beneficiaries rose seven-fold (from 10.8 crore to 76.7 crore) between 2013-14 and 2018-19. This has been a central pillar of the Modi era's political economy.[52] Around this welfare system—powered by linked Aadhar cards, mobile phones and cheap data—the BJP targeted its outreach through a new booth-level cadre structure that was deployed to mobilise labharthees of schemes like PM Awas, PM Kisan, Swachh Bharat and Ujjwala. The government also consciously privileged poor women in welfare housing registrations on an unprecedented scale. Importantly, whether it was houses or personal toilets, the government did not build these for the beneficiaries. The labharthees managed the construction themselves. This expansion of the social welfare net has been at the heart of the party's new model. This is why, after the BJP won the Bihar assembly election in November 2020, party president J.P. Nadda announced that it had won partly because of 'DBT-raj'.[53]

And therein lies the rub: for a regime so focused on building a DBT-enabled welfare state, the availability of strong public finances is a must. A tanking economy would simply dry up the funds for such welfare measures. As the economist Rathin Roy has pointed out, the government's total expenditure fell to 12.2 per cent of the GDP in 2019-20, compared to 13.9 per cent in 2013-14.[54] If the economy is not fixed, then the Modi government's ambition to significantly expand the footprint of its welfare programmes would become untenable. The fragility of Union government expenditures is more apparent when you factor in the rising budget deficit—and the situation may be worse than official figures suggest, because of borrowings through public sector enterprises that do not fully reflect in budget documents, as former RBI deputy governor Viral Acharya has pointed out.[55] While the India story is far from over, and it is certainly an overreaction to be 'losing hope in India',[56] sustaining heavy welfare spending without sustainably high growth rates is a challenge. Without serious disinvestment as well as further reforms and changes in the fiscal management system, the BJP's political project could run into a major economic roadblock. In other words, the money would simply run out. Unless this is managed well, economic strife could lead to multiple adverse political consequences.

Challenge 2: The China Border Stand-off

The emerging border crisis with China is another political risk for a government so invested in a muscular national-security narrative. The Chinese incursions across the Line of Actual Control (LAC) in Depsang, Pangong Tso, Galwan and Hot Springs emerged as a sort of 'Kargil redux'—as one former military officer put it—by May 2020.[57] Just as Pakistani soldiers surprised India in 1998 by taking over some heights on the Indian side of the Line of Control during a winter break in patrolling, the Chinese took advantage of a pause in regular military exercise due to Covid-19 in early 2020 to take over previously unheld barren areas that had so far only been periodically patrolled by both sides. Unless status quo ante is restored, this could mean a resetting of the LAC by several hundred square kilometres from earlier settled patterns of patrolling. After several soldiers on both sides died in border-fighting for the first time since 1975, Modi denied any loss of territory in a nationally televised address on 19 June 2020. India also made strong military counter-moves of its own after the initial Chinese troop movements, occupying some previously unoccupied areas in that sector, until mutual withdrawals were organised in some areas. While troops disengaged in the Galwan

Valley, the north and south sides of the Pangong Lake and Gogra, several other 'friction points' remained until late-2021. So much so that India's ambassador to Beijing publicly listed three 'clear obstacles' blocking progress in talks: the 'need to avoid shifting goalposts', taking a 'one-sided view of concerns and sensitivities, where one's own preoccupations trump any of those flagged by the other side' and 'viewing bilateral relations through the prism of relations with other countries'.[58] By late 2021, both militaries remained deployed in an unprecedented stand-off on border mountain peaks in areas that had never been occupied by either side during winters. New friction points also began to emerge along other parts of the LAC—in Arunachal Pradesh and Uttarakhand.[59] Meanwhile, Modi's government embraced the new Quad grouping of United States, Japan, Australia and India—whose subtext remained China's assertiveness—with its leaders participating in two summits in six months. While the border crisis receded from the headlines, the longer it lingers, the more the chance of escalation and the more difficult the domestic political fallout.

On the other hand, a national crisis can also unite the nation. Vajpayee won a national election in 1999 after the Kargil War. The BJP's security narrative was always predicated on staring down Pakistan. With the surgical military strikes of September 2016 and the Balakot airstrikes of February 2019, it had the security narrative firmly under control. China's concerted border intrusions upset that balance. By June 2020, Modi had met Xi Jinping eighteen times since coming to power in 2014. He had visited China five times, the most by any Indian prime minister.[60] External Affairs Minister S. Jaishankar has argued that the higher engagement was because India 'counts for more and is more active' and that Modi's foreign engagements with Japan, Europe and the US would also yield higher results than before.[61] Even so, for a leader who had invested so much in the China relationship, the charge of being misled by China, just as Nehru was in 1962, is a risk. However, by aggressively publicising the deployment of previously covert battalions like the Special Frontier Force, consisting of Tibetan refugees, on the LAC,[62] and through strategic border appearances with the troops by Prime Minister Modi, who delivered messages of strength dressed in camouflage gear, the political narrative largely remained under control for the BJP until the close of 2021. It seemed that India was settling down for the long haul. A previous stand-off at Sumdorong Chu with China in 1986 had only ended nine years later, as Jaishankar pointed out to *The Hindu* journalist Suhasini Haider.[63]

And yet, the longer the military stand-off, the more it will bleed India economically. Even more so, if the friction expands beyond the Ladakh–Leh sector to other sectors along the LAC, which is 4,065 kilometres long, extending right up to Arunachal Pradesh. The Ladakh deployment entailed a great deal of emergency-buying of equipment for the Army's frontline troops. Any extension of such deployments would entail much higher defence spends. In short, an expansionist China looking to tie up India could do so by forcing expenditures that Beijing (with an annual GDP that is almost five times larger than India's and 2.2 per cent of annual GDP spending on defence) has deeper pockets for than New Delhi (2.35 per cent of GDP spending on defence).[64]

Challenge 3: New Caste Coalitions and the Problems of Expansion

This book has shown how the BJP's political growth was driven by a major expansion of its social base in the northern Hindi heartland, especially with OBCs. The Mehta–Singh Social Index demonstrated how the BJP shifted from being an upper caste-dominated party to becoming the most socially representative party by caste in UP.[65] These findings showed how our understanding of the BJP's caste representation has so far not kept pace with ground realities. OBCs (mostly non-Yadav) made up exactly half of the party's MPs elected from general category seats nationwide in 2019. Similarly, the BJP also significantly upped SC (mostly non-Jatav) representation among its MPs, MLAs, state-level office-bearers and ministers. So much so that OBCs and SCs, taken together, came to occupy half or more than half the leadership positions at virtually every level of the party in UP—barring district presidents. This Mandalisation of the BJP was built on the forging of new caste coalitions that significantly increased the party's influence.

However, its current growth pattern also runs the risk of turning the BJP into a new Congress. In its heyday, the Congress was an umbrella group of multiple factions, interests and sections, many of them inimical to each other. Now that the BJP has supplanted the Congress as the country's dominant party with its new caste coalitions, it runs the same risk of internal tussles that the older party struggled with. Caste equations are not static, nor are castes monolithic. Smaller castes like Nishads or Rajbhars moved to the BJP because they were given greater representation, but sustaining this equation requires nimble political skills on both sides. Furthermore, for a party that has invested so much in accommodating defectors and giving them key positions in almost every state—from Himanta Biswa Sarma in Assam to Jyotiraditya Scindia in Madhya Pradesh—how the newcomers mesh with, and engage with, the core party faithful in the long term will be a crucial factor to watch.

Managing this mélange of interest groups will be a major challenge for a party that, until 2014, was comparatively unidimensional. It will require sagacious leadership. As Amit Shah put it to a 2017 meeting of intellectuals in Palampur, 'The Congress had many people of many ideologies. They didn't have any principles, only the aim of somehow capturing power. That is why later, many parties at different times kept leaving it.'[66] This is precisely the problem the BJP is likely to face as it expands. As this book has documented, it is now as large a social hold-all tent as the Congress was at its peak. Managing the contradictions of this expansion and aligning them with its own ideological principles will hold the key to its future.

Challenge 4: The Question of Leadership after Modi

Prime Minister Modi has undoubtedly been the catalyst and harbinger of the new BJP. Election after election has revealed that his personal popularity with voters remains undiminished. Survey after survey has shown that he continues to bring a huge premium to the party. Modi (born in 1950) remains the driving engine of his party's political juggernaut. Therefore, given that the party has radically shape-shifted on Modi's watch, the ability of his eventual successor to manage the system that Modi–Shah built will be critical. Modi has several years of active politics ahead of him. The big question for the BJP is: who can lead it next?

Amit Shah (born 1964) is fourteen years younger than Modi, and only six years older than the Congress's Rahul Gandhi. Not only did Shah co-create the BJP's new organisational structures under Modi, putting his stamp on its revamp, he has been the face of some of the party's biggest ideological projects in governance: revoking Article 370 on Kashmir and ushering in the CAA. He has also been the BJP's most prominent orator, after Modi, since 2016. What could a possible Shah prime ministership look like? Would it be ideologically harder on Hindutva? And would it garner the same national voter enthusiasm that Modi evokes? Shah declared in a piece he wrote on the Modi government completing its sixth year in power that the 'BJP-led central government has implemented every promise in its manifesto'. He went on to list these promises: the repeal of Article 370, CAA, the Triple Talaq law and 'paving the way for the construction of the Shri Ram Temple'. The Modi government, he stressed, 'has rectified the historical mistakes after Independence'.[67] Similarly, Shah argued in his first speech as party president to the BJP's National Council that 'for almost six decades, society was influenced essentially on the basis of the Congress ideology. In fact, politics was over-shadowed by a Congress culture. Now, it is our duty that our ideology should positively influence the thinking and work culture of our society.'[68] For a leader who sees the BJP's ideological differentiation as its life-force, and who has played a fundamental role in reorganising and expanding the party's organisational machinery, one thing is certain: there can be no softening on the BJP's core issues.

In the party's second tier, Yogi Adityanath (born 1972) has long been the leader most in demand for election rallies, after Modi and Shah. Modi became the BJP's prime ministerial candidate in 2013 on the back of his 'Gujarat model'. He came to Delhi after a decade as chief minister in one of India's most prosperous states, one that was also the original 'laboratory' of Hindutva. Gujarat remains Modi's citadel, but his ascent to power was made possible by the party's breakthrough in UP, which delivered seventy-one (25.1 per cent) BJP MPs in 2014 and sixty-two (20.4 per cent) in 2019. Modi himself fronted the UP breakthrough, contesting from the ancient city of Varanasi in both parliamentary elections. He also fronted the 2017 UP assembly election campaign, which resulted in a BJP sweep and Adityanath's ascent to power in Lucknow.

Undoubtedly, the political road to Delhi runs through Lucknow. Yogi Adityanath is already the BJP's most nationally visible chief minister. If he retains UP in the 2022 assembly elections, he will emerge as the most influential party chief minister. [Yogi Adityanath eventually returned to power in the state with a historic sweep in the 2022 poll.] He has age on his side, and many years of politics ahead of him. He, like Modi in his chief-ministerial avatar, is a political lightning rod whose very presence sharply polarises opinion. His ideological facade is even harder than that of the Modi–Shah combine. Crucially, no individual UP chief minister has ever been returned to power for back-to-back terms since Independence. If Yogi does it in 2022, he will have a power base like none other in the BJP, with at least two decades of politics still ahead of him. [Yogi's 2022 triumph with an absolute majority (255 of 403 seats for the BJP) and an increased vote-share (41.3 per cent) was also the first time in 37 years that an incumbent party returned to power in UP.]

Challenge 5: A Hindu Party? The Hindu–Muslim Question and the Future of Secularism

The fifth political risk for the BJP is the possibility of increased social strife if it goes further down the route of Hindu identity-based ethnic politics. During his address in Ayodhya in 2020, Modi signalled a dialling down of temperature on the Hindu card after the BJP won the political battle on Ram, but the party has enough absolutist hardliners on religious issues. The social forces unleashed by Hindu triumphalism may also prove to be beyond the party's control. For example, by early 2020, the Karnataka BJP's Twitter handle had started pushing out such divisive messaging on CAA that some of the old guard in the party were uncomfortable. As one told me, 'This is immature. This kind of messaging affects only a few thousand people. People are mature now. They don't associate with this.' Flexing saffron muscles often works to the BJP's advantage in polarised areas, but some party leaders also saw the need to keep this tendency in check.

Even at a time when the new love jihad laws in BJP-ruled states have added a fresh twist to the debates on personal freedoms and religion, the central question for the party is an old one, and Vajpayee had raised it in 1991. Does the BJP see itself as a religious party or as a political party with a Hindu cultural tint? 'There are elements who would like to see the BJP become a religious party,' said Vajpayee. He was responding to the debate generated by the slogan '*Jo Hindu Hit Mein Baat Karega, Vahi Desh Pe Raj Karega*' (Only he who speaks in the Hindu interest will rule the country). Both Advani and Vajpayee objected to the slogan at a BJP plenary session that year. The next day, another slogan was raised, '*Jo Rashtra Hit Mein Baat Karega, Vahi Desh Pe Raj Karega*', in which 'Hindu interest' was replaced by 'national interest'.[69]

The big question is whether the BJP can reconstitute itself as a right-wing party that respects tradition and order without necessarily positioning itself as a 'Hindu' party.[70] This is a question that has been at the heart of inner-party debate since the late 1980s. It is now clear that the new BJP has reinvented itself as a part steeped in Hinduness. And this identity politics is too deeply embedded in its DNA for the party to turn away from it. Its position today is not too far away from the idea expressed by Advani in 1991 that India is 'essentially a Hindu country'.[71] Yogi Adityanath and Amit Shah's politics especially exemplify this. When questioned about whether he would attend a similar ceremony for a mosque in Ayodhya as he did for the Ram Temple, the UP chief minister was unequivocal: 'If you ask me as a chief minister, then I don't abstain from any religion or community. But if you ask me as a yogi, then I will definitely not go. I will not go because I am a Hindu. As a Hindu, I have a right to worship and lead life as per the laid religious rules. But I don't have the right to intervene in others' works or meddle into others' affairs.'[72] The statement also reflected the BJP's current understanding that Hindutva had been a necessary condition for the party to grow. At another level, the Taliban's conquest of Kabul in 2021, and its establishment of a hardline sharia-based state in Afghanistan, strengthens the seeding power of Hindu nationalist messaging. It is too early to say how this will pan out, but the Taliban's ascent has already become a cipher for global jihad in many debates at the local political level.

Each time the BJP has focused on sharpening its position on Hindutva, the party's ranks have swelled. Every time it has waffled on this issue, after the 1990s phase of consolidation under Vajpayee, for instance, it has entered into periods of decline. Yet, Hindutva positioning has never been sufficient on its own to win elections, as this book has documented. Hindutva was the engine that gave it electoral momentum, but election victories were fashioned by creating a unique cocktail of Hinduness, caste reengineering and a deep focus on welfarism. In short, as a UP government official working closely with Yogi Adityanath told me, Hindutva gave the BJP's wheel speed, but the wheel that drove its expansion was welfare.[73] 'Welfare' or 'development' here refers specifically to the government's focus on cash transfers through a dozen-plus schemes, not 'hard infrastructure'. The embracing of this system is what created the new BJP system of politics.

Yet, it is undeniable that Hindutva provided the glue that held together the party's core supporters and informed its recasting of secularism after 2014. As then Home Minister Rajnath Singh told the Lok Sabha in an important debate in 2015, the Constitution-makers did not insert the words 'secular' and 'socialist' in the Preamble. These words were inserted only by the 42nd Amendment in 1976. 'If the words "secularism" and "socialism" had been essential,' he said, 'then definitely Babasaheb Bhimrao Ambedkar would have used them in the Preamble to the Constitution.' He did not use them, said Singh, because he believed that it was already included in India's 'core nature', its 'core character'. 'There is no need to add it separately in the Preamble', which was the spirit, or 'aatma', of the Constitution. Where does this leave secularism as we have understood it? As Singh put it, 'Translating the Indian Constitution, the formal translation of secular is *panth-nirpeksh* [community-neutral], not *dharm-nirpeksh* [religion-neutral]. India's religion by itself is *panth-nirpeksh* [community-neutral].'

This redefinition of 'secularism'—the most 'misused' word in India politics, according to the BJP—is precisely what Yogi Adityanath often refers to (see Chapter 1). It is also what RSS chief Mohan Bhagwat alluded to in Ayodhya when he spoke of the 'Vasudhaiva Kutumbakam' philosophy of ancient India. Based on what the BJP sees as an essential tolerance in Hinduism itself, which saw ancient migrants like Parsis finding a home in India, it seeks to do away with all 'tokenism' to minorities. How the party plays this card and manages social balance will be crucial to its future.

As Rajnath Singh said in the Lok Sabha, 'The Muslim community has 72 sects ... India is the only country in the world which has all 72 sects ... yet Babasaheb Ambedkar did not use the word secular.' For those who think of secularism as 'dharm-nirpeksh', Singh pointed to the ancient Mauryan seal above the Lok Sabha Speaker's chair in Parliament, with the Mauryan lion and its pre-Common Era slogan 'Dharm-chakra Pravartanay' (protector of the dharm chakra). 'Should we remove that too?' he asked.[74]

BJP's Advantage 1: A Robust Booth-level Cadre and Organisational Structure

In the distant future, a post-Modi BJP may see a short-term decline, since many new voters came to the party due to the prime minister's personal popularity. Yet, this is likely to be only temporary. This book has shown how the new BJP has built a deep and fundamentally new organisational structure in the districts, down to the voting-booth level. It fused a major offline restructuring of its party organisation and oversight mechanisms with the clever adoption of new technologies and digital tools. Leveraging digital 3G/4G technologies enabled a vast yet tight party structure that could be monitored on a daily basis. It also enabled its leaders to organise large-scale campaigns and verify this expansion in a way that was not feasible earlier for any political party.

The old BJP was much more dependent on the RSS's cadre network for mobilisation. While the party continues to have a symbiotic relationship with the Sangh, as this book shows, its massive cadre expansion after 2014 at the district and voting-booth levels was not only a structural transformation in its DNA but also a fundamental enabler of its political power. The BJP's expansion also changed the balance of power between it and the RSS. Between 2014 and 2020, it became the world's largest political party, overtaking the Chinese Communist Party. Unlike the Chinese one-party system, the BJP's massive expansion unfolded within a multi-party democratic system. By 2019, its cadre network was large enough to dwarf the RSS's—it had 174 million signed-up members, about twenty-nine times the estimated size of the RSS (see Chapter 8). It remains tied to the RSS for ideological reasons, but does not need the Sangh to mobilise votes anymore. If anything, the Sangh is now more dependent on the party.

When the Congress system started to decline in the 1970s, it took the party another two decades to wither away. Similarly, the party structure that the CPI(M) built in West Bengal after 1977 carried it through for another decade in power after Jyoti Basu's exit as its face in 2000. The BJP may lose power, but 'even if this new BJP system stops doing anything today', says the psephologist Jai Mrug, 'it will take fifteen years to dismantle this system.'[75] The BJP's consolidation phase as the hegemonic Indian political party is now over. It has a significant local footprint in at least 500 of India's 543 parliamentary constituencies. By the end of 2020, it had emerged as the second pole of politics in its new catchment areas of West Bengal and Odisha in the east, turned into the dominant national party in most of the north-eastern states and was growing fast in Telangana as well as Andhra Pradesh. It was also looking to expand in Kerala and using alliances to gain a foothold in Tamil Nadu.

Many opponents of the party have convinced themselves that Modi's special appeal is a black-swan event. When it goes away, the BJP will collapse. This is wishful thinking. Scholarship around the BJP has so far failed to account for its structural growth at the micro-level. Even the most thoughtful scholars studying it continue to squabble over whether the BJP has only 'built an election machine' or a real 'system' like the Congress before it.[76] Academics can continue to squabble over definitions of what constitutes a political system. The fact is that you cannot switch a party machinery off and on with the press of a button. People and voters are not galvanised like that. The new BJP's 'election machine' is built on a system that works all year round at the district level. This is precisely why it works at election time.

To be clear: the BJP's 303 seats (with 37.36 per cent votes) in the 2019 Lok Sabha constituted the largest majority in Parliament in over three-and-a-half decades. It ranked next to Rajiv Gandhi's 404 (49.1 per cent votes) seats in 1984, Indira Gandhi's 352 seats (43.6 per cent votes) in 1971 and Nehru's 361 tally (44.7 per cent votes) in 1962. To be sure, the Congress won greater vote shares in all those elections than Modi's BJP. But it is not with the 1970s or 1980s Congress that the new BJP must be compared. The 1980s Congress was already in deep decline as a system of power. Also, the earlier Congress victories occurred in a different era and in a vastly different political domain from post-1980s India, which saw the rise of caste-based and regional parties in most states. They also occurred in a world before the internet, digital connectivity and new information systems, and in a polity that was powered by older patterns of local patronage. The BJP's election triumphs under Modi have come in a vastly reordered and digitally connected society. And yet, the BJP's political dominance today is actually more akin to the Congress of the 1950s. It will lose and win elections, but the systemic dominance of the BJP in India's polity is of that order.

When the political scientist W.H. Morris-Jones visited the Congress's party office in Bhopal in 1967 to research what held the party together, he was waved off by a committed party worker 'hard at work over a desk' who told him he was 'busy'. When Morris-Jones persisted, the worker responded, 'Look, you must understand. I am working for the party and nobody can interfere with this work.'[77] The political scientist finally got what he was looking for from other party officials, but he later recalled that this encounter 'opened' his eyes. There were, he wrote, 'several of his kind to be found in dusty Congress offices up and down the country, slaves dedicated to the cause'. These party workers were legatees of Gandhi's exhortation to the service ethic, which had harnessed the 'traditional call of *seva* to the modern party machine'. By 2020, it was possible to find such dedicated men and women—karyakartas—in brand-new BJP offices across India. I met and had conversations with many of them—from UP, Rajasthan, Chhattisgarh and Madhya Pradesh in the Hindi heartland to Karnataka and Telangana in the South and Gujarat in the West—while researching this book. It was almost impossible to find a comparable cohort of dedicated ideological workers (as opposed to leaders) in the Congress offices.

What is the big differentiator between the old BJP and the new BJP? When I put this question to a district leader in Mathura, he told me: 'Earlier, as a party worker, we used to work only during election times. In the new BJP, we work daily. We are given daily tasks and we send in a daily report to the level above us. They don't let us sit for a moment. That is the difference. Earlier, we used to have our district-level party meetings only in the evenings, after we finished work and closed our shops. Now we have it daily at 11 a.m. and everyone turns up. Attendance is marked.' Many scholars of the BJP, not abreast of the shift at the ground level, continue to believe that the BJP is somehow winning elections only because of the power of money or by subverting institutions. The party does have money-power. For decades, so did the Congress. But to think that the BJP is growing only because of this is wishful thinking based on an older style of studying politics that is well past its use-by date.

The BJP is growing because the acquisition of power has made it the party of upward mobility and aspiration in middle India. When Brajesh Pathak, once the BSP's deputy leader in the Lok Sabha, switched to the BJP, he explained his motives to the journalist Pranshu Mishra thus: 'A political leader has an average career of 20 years unless you are from a political family. Then it can go up to 30 years. Of 20 I had done 10 in BSP, I will do my remaining 10 in BJP. Congress is good but what's the point in joining it.' He is currently a minister in Yogi Adityanath's government.[78] The RSS too is seeing a similar spurt in growth. As a regional head of the Sangh in UP told me, 'We are growing fast but we are very aware that many people are coming to us because they want the spoils of power. Our job is to figure out which of these are genuine and which ones are here only till we have power.'

The bottom line is that the BJP's vote share in India has never gone below 18 per cent in parliamentary elections since 1991. Between 1999 and 2009, it hovered around the 20 per cent mark. Even when it lost two successive elections in 2004 and 2009, it's 22.2 per cent vote share only fell to 18.8 per cent. 'It didn't become 12–13 per cent,' says Jai Mrug. In 2014, the BJP upped this to 31.3 per cent, and in 2019 to 37.7 per cent. These numbers mean that, in a worst-case scenario, even if one in three voters leave the BJP by 2024, it will still retain over 25 per cent of the vote share. By way of comparison, that is roughly what brought the Congress and Manmohan Singh to power in 2004 (26.5 per cent vote share) and again in 2009 (28.5 per cent vote share). Unless there is a landslide, this is the scale of the challenge for the Opposition.

BJP's Advantage 2: The Congress's Weakness Is an Asset

The BJP's biggest asset is the continuing decline of the Congress as a national party under Sonia and Rahul Gandhi. Engulfed in its leadership crisis, the Congress remains strong in the two-party polity states of the Hindi belt—MP, Chhattisgarh, Uttarakhand, Himachal, Rajasthan—but is a declining force in the South (Telangana, Andhra), where the

BJP is replacing it as the main opponent of the regional parties. Outside the Hindi heartland, the real challenge to the BJP comes from regional parties like the Trinamool Congress in West Bengal or the DMK in Tamil Nadu. Even in these areas, it is looking to follow an acquisition model, like usurping the BJD's space in Odisha in a post-Naveen Patnaik era or aligning with the AIADMK in Tamil Nadu. The fact is that regional parties can push the BJP back in state elections. Nationally, however, the absence of a strong opposing national party with ground strength gives it an inordinate advantage in parliamentary polls.

A telling illustration of the rising gap between the BJP and the Congress is the number of Lok Sabha seats in which candidates from the two parties forfeited their security deposits. Candidates forfeit their deposits with the Election Commission when they fail to win more than one-sixth of the votes polled in their constituency.[79] It is, therefore, a good measure for gauging the rising irrelevance of a party in a particular area. In 2009, BJP candidates forfeited their deposits in as many as 170 seats, the Congress only in seventy-one. By 2019, that equation had almost reversed. The BJP forfeited deposits in only fifty-one seats nationally in 2019. The Congress did so in almost three times as many seats (148). In other words, in almost one-third of India's parliamentary seats, the Congress had become electorally irrelevant within the course of a decade. What this shift means for both parties is evident (see Figure 18.3).

By the beginning of 2021, as the Congress continued to grapple with the question of Rahul Gandhi and the dynasty's leadership, one fact was inescapable. Not only had Sonia Gandhi been president of the party for over two decades (with a short interval for her son in between), most of its top faces had also virtually been the same in this period. Most of the party's top leaders, including the so-called 'Gang of 23', which asked for leadership changes, came from the same cohort that I had encountered as a young beat reporter covering the party two decades earlier. They were essentially the same generation that had battled Vajpayee and Advani's BJP in the late 1990s. By contrast, the BJP's top office-bearers under Modi in 2020 were virtually unrecognisable from the team he and Shah inherited in 2014.

The average age of the BJP's national office-bearers appointed under J.P. Nadda's presidency in 2019 was about fifty. In that same year, the party

Figure 18.3: A Tale of Forfeited Deposits: The BJP Reduced Such Seats Significantly, While the Congress Forfeitures Zoomed to Almost One-Third of All Lok Sabha Seats (2009–2019)

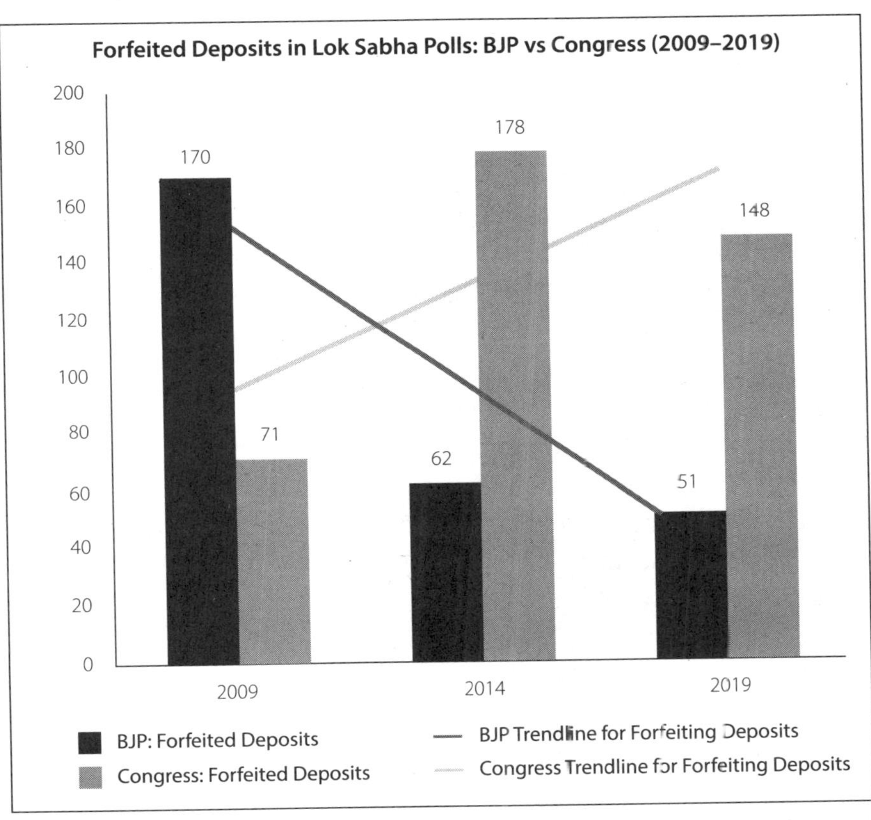

Source: Author's analysis of ECI Statistical Reports: 2009–2019. Note: The BJP contested 433 seats in 2009, 428 in 2014 and 436 in 2019. The Congress contested 440 in 2009, 464 in 2014 and 421 in 2019.

instituted new age-limit rules for its local office-bearers in the states.[80] In UP, for example, the BJP stipulated that no mandal president would be over fifty years of age, no district president above sixty. In a country with one of the youngest populations in the world, this was a political investment in a new generation of leaders. As the BJP's district vice president in Mathura told me, 'The party felt that we need such leaders that can work for us for the next fifteen years. We have now got totally new people. We are developing these people so that this generation can lead us after ten years and so that our generation can do the mentoring after that.'[81] This illustrates a fundamental difference between the two parties: a focus on cadre-building and workers. Much of the public debate on the Congress, meanwhile, remains focused on Rahul Gandhi and his leadership style.

Another instance of the growing power gap between the two parties emerged while I was travelling to Raebareli, Sonia Gandhi's parliamentary constituency, in June 2020. The road to Raebareli ran through a gate of saffron: the imposing Deen Dayal Upadhyaya Dwar. Named after one of the BJP's early founding figures, and sporting the smiling visages of UP Chief Minister Yogi Adityanath and Prime Minister Narendra Modi, it towered over all visitors driving south into Raebareli on National Highway No. 30 from Lucknow, the state capital. Saffron paint and BJP leaders replaced the more neutral colouring and older images of former prime minister Manmohan Singh and Sonia Gandhi in 2017 after Yogi Adityanath came to power as the head of the first BJP-majority government in UP in almost two decades. The Election Commission had ordered that the political imagery on the gateway be whitewashed during the 2019 polls. But, once the polls were over, the smiling saffron icons were back—typical of the aggressive political intent of the ruling party and the scale of the new BJP's ambition.

Few places in India, after all, are as emblematic of the Gandhi family and the Congress as Raebareli, a small town 63 kilometres south-east of Lucknow. It is the parliamentary constituency of the Congress matriarch Sonia Gandhi. The seat was first won for the party in India's inaugural democratic national election of 1952 by her father-in-law Feroze Gandhi. It later became the electoral home of her mother-in-law, former prime minister Indira Gandhi. The Congress might have virtually disappeared from the electoral map of Uttar Pradesh from the 1990s onwards, with the rise of regional caste-based parties like the Samajwadi Party and Bahujan Samaj Party, but it has never lost its parliamentary bastion of Raebareli after Sonia became party leader in 1998.

The Gandhi family's other UP bastion of Amethi, parliamentary home to Sonia Gandhi's son, Rahul, was famously lost in 2019. Amethi, which was initially wrested from the BJP's Sanjay Sinh by Sonia Gandhi in 1999, has been won by non-Congress candidates only thrice since 1967. It will be a symbolic prize-catch again in 2024. This is why the emergence of the Deen Dayal Upadhyaya Dwar at the gates of Raebareli itself is so deeply significant. For the Congress, it is an attack right on its homestead. For the BJP, it signifies an assertive new brand of total politics, an in-your-face aggression that takes no prisoners.

Opposition leaders have so far put their hopes in an 'anti-BJPism' counter-force. Like anti-Congressism earlier, this is predicated on the idea that, even at its height, the ruling party does not win more than 40 per cent of the vote share, and therefore, the coming together of anti-BJP forces (what psephologists measure as the index of Opposition unity) can beat it. This was the basis of the unlikely SP–BSP alliance in UP in 2019, which failed. Perhaps because anti-BJPism, like anti-Congressism before it, sounds good in theory but is likely to work only if the party in question blunders big time—like Rajiv Gandhi did with Bofors—or if the government is overwhelmed by a massive economic crisis. As the psephologist Jai Mrug put it, 'Past experiences in India with the Janata Party and Janata Dal have shown that an alternative built on a purely negative approach is never enduring. The BJP managed to upset the electoral calculus in 1991 not because it was anti-Congress, but it because it offered an alternative vision for India. Ayodhya was the party's cutting edge, its distinctive identity.'[82] The same applies now to the Congress. It cannot just be the not-BJP party. It must offer an alternative vision to differentiate itself.

The BJP's rise as the dominant pillar of Indian polity has given rise to vociferous debates on a whole range of contentious issues: freedom of speech, the future of dissent, the changing nature of federalism, democracy, Centre–state relations, and indeed, on the changing idea of India. These are crucial questions. How they play out will be pivotal for the country's future. Whether you support the BJP or oppose it, it is vital to understand how it grew, its differentiated modes of mobilisation across states and the interface between technology and ideas in today's transformed political and social landscape. This book will be a catalyst, I hope, for new and more informed debates on politics, democracy, technology and the future—in India and elsewhere.

POSTSCRIPT

The edifice of this book was built on new digital research tools that were specifically built for this research project on the BJP with the data scientist Rishabh Srivastava: the Narad Index (comprising 11,588 BJP-linked documents between 2006 and 2019); the Mehta–Singh Social Index (with caste backgrounds of 4,415 political leaders in UP spread across three decades and four parties); Twitter Listening Post (which monitors seventy-five political accounts) and Pollniti (a centralised digital repository of 218 interactive data dashboards). In order to spark further conversation, debate and informed discussion, most of these datasets are available online on www.nalinmehta.in and www.pollniti.com.

NOTES

All weblinks in notes accessed last on 29 November 2021.
All listed designations of interviewees are accurate as of date of interview, unless otherwise stated.

Introduction

1. PTI, '1,000 BJP men held in Gujarat', *The Times of India*, 31 December 1988. Modi was then general secretary of the BJP's Gujarat unit. His name appeared twice earlier in the newspaper in the 1970s: in 1978 as a participant in a television programme, *Yuvadarshan*, on 'The youth struggle during the Emergency', and in 1979, where, as an RSS pracharak, he receives a cheque of Rs 5 lakh for work in relief camps after the Morvi dam disaster. 'Television', *The Times of India*, 23 May 1978; Staff Reporter, 'RSS Wing donates Rs 5 lakh', *The Times of India*, 2 October 1979.
2. Law Kumar Mishra, TOINS, 'Keep out, BJP tells police', *The Times of India*, 25 September 1990.
3. In June 2016, then Union minister of state for personnel and PMO, Jitendra Singh responded to a controversy on denial of government jobs to RSS members saying, 'the central government has not issued any such order [prohibiting government staff from joining RSS activities] recently', and 'if any old order exists, we will review it'. The RSS's publicity head, Manmohan Vaidya said, 'Banning RSS members from joining government service is unjust and undemocratic. Such bans hardly affect RSS work and morale of swayamsevaks.' By way of background: in 1964, the Union government brought in a rule under Central Civil Service (Conduct) Rules (Rule 5 (1)) stating that 'No Government servant shall be a member of, or be otherwise associated with, any political party or any organisation which takes part in politics[,] nor shall he take part in, subscribe in aid of, or assist in any other manner, any political movement or activity.' After questions on whether this applied to RSS, the Ministry of Home Affairs issued a circular on 30 November 1966 saying, 'Certain doubts have been raised about Government's policy with respect to the membership or any participation in the activities of the Rashtriya Swayamsevak Sangh and the Jamaat-e-Islami by Government servants, it is clarified that Government have always held the activities of these two organisations to be

of such nature that participation in them by Government servants would attract the provisions of sub-rule (1) of Rule 5 of the CCS (Conduct) Rules, 1964. Any government servant, who is a member of or otherwise associated with the aforesaid organisations or with their activities, is liable to disciplinary action.' The Union government on 28 October 1980 issued another circular which reiterated the 1966 circular. On 27 November 2014, the Narendra Modi government amended the Conduct Rules to add a few clauses to Rule 3(1). One of these said, 'Every government employee shall at all times maintain political neutrality.' On 5 January 2016, the Department of Personnel and Training (DoPT) informed *The Indian Express* after an RTI query that 'No such orders withdrawing the OMs [office memorandums] dated 1966 and 1980 has been issued.' *The Indian Express* also found that the Himachal Pradesh government on 24 January 2008, the Madhya Pradesh government on 21 August 2006 and Chhattisgarh government in February 2015 had issued instructions saying there were no restrictions on government employees joining RSS activities. The UP government on 20 February 2013 also said that there were no restrictions on RSS membership for government employees. All details quoted from Shyamlal Yadav, 'Express RTI: The revolving door between BJP, Govt and RSS', *The Indian Express*, 16 June 2016, https://indianexpress.com/article/explained/narendra-modi-government-rss-manmohan-vaidya-mohan-bhagwat-bjp-and-rss-links-2855319/. Government of India Central Civil Services (Conduct) Rules, 1964, are available on https://dopt.gov.in/forewordnotification.

4. Swapan Dasgupta, 'Waning interest worries me: Advani', *The Times of India*, 13 June 1991.
5. The Times of India News Service (TOINS), 'BJP demands access to Ram idols', *The Times of India*, 24 December 1992.
6. While Joshi led the Yatra as the then BJP president, newspaper reports of the time refer to Modi variously as convener, coordinator and chief coordinator. Narendra Modi quotes are from TOINS, 'BJP invites RV to unfurl flag in J&K', *The Times of India*, 22 November 1991. A picture of the Yatra's flag-hoisting in Srinagar shows Joshi unfurling the flag, standing next to Modi and K.L. Sharma, surrounded by security men. TOINS, 'Give forces a free hand: BJP', *The Times of India*, 27 January 1992. Also see picture of Modi with Murali Manohar Joshi, L.K. Advani, Atal Bihari Vajpayee and Vijaya Raje Scindia during Ekta Yatra at Jammu Parade Ground, which was published as a standalone Page 1 picture, without title, in *The Times of India*, 25 January 1992. Details on Kesari Vahini from several Modi interviews quoted in TOINS, 'Tie up only for polls: BJP', *The Times of India*, 7 January 1992; TOINS, 'Rumblings in BJP, allies over yatra climax', *The Times of India*, 31 January 1992. For more on Ekta Yatra, see TOINS, 'No enthusiasm for yatra in MP', 1 January 1992; TOINS, 'Ensure DD coverage: BJP', *The Times of India*, 21 January 1992.
7. This conversation took place while on a TV reporting assignment and in the presence of Sanjeev Singh, then NDTV's Ahmedabad correspondent, and Vinay Menon, then covering the campaign for *Hindustan Times*. Quoted in Nalin Mehta,

'Gujarat beyond Gandhi: Notes on identity, conflict and society', in Nalin Mehta, Mona G. Mehta (eds), *Gujarat beyond Gandhi: Identity, Society and Conflict* (London, New York: Routledge, 2011), p. 1.

8. Kanak Bhawan is one of the more famous temples in Ayodhya, situated north-east of Ram Janmaboomi, Ramkot. It was built in 1891 by Vrishbhanu Kumari, Queen of Tikamgarh, Madhya Pradesh. (Details from UP Tourism and official Ayodhya District online portals, available on: http://uptourism.gov.in/post/kanak-bhawan; https://ayodhya.nic.in/tourist-place/kanak-bhawan/.)
9. Literally 'elder' in Persian, this term is used to denote a Sufi master or guide.
10. We have used the spelling 'Jan Sangh' for the BJP's predecessor, as opposed to the more commonly used 'Jana Sangh', unless quoted otherwise. This is because the original spelling of the organisation—Jan Sangh—changed over time in contemporary records through the 1960s. The Election Commission of India General Election Archive (1951–2004) variously recorded the official party name as 'All India Bhartiya Jan Sangh' in its 1951 and 1957 general election reports, as 'Jan Sangh' in 1962, 'Bharatiya Jana Sang' in 1967 and as 'Bharatiya Jana Sangh' in 1971.
11. BJP, 'Salient points of speech of BJP national president, Shri Amit Shah addressing intellectuals meet at Budha Mal Castle, Palampur, Kangra, Himachal Pradesh', 4 May 2017, https://www.bjp.org/en/pressreleasesdetail/299215/Salient-points-of-speech-of-BJP-National-President-Shri-Amit-Shah-addressing-Intellectuals-meet-at-Budha-Mal-Castle-Palampur-Kangra-Himachal-Pradesh-
12. Ibid.
13. This was the phrase used by Trinamool Congress MP Derek O'Brien in his response to the CAA Bill when he compared it to the 'Nazi Playbook' of pre-WW-II Germany in Rajya Sabha. Video clip of his Parliament speech is available on: https://www.youtube.com/watch?v=YroWXUBQ8rM.
14. 'vegetarian but tasty party', *The Times of India*, 29 December 1980.
15. P. Chidambaram speaking at his book launch, *Undaunted: Saving the Idea of India*, 7 February 2019, Teen Murti Bhawan, New Delhi.
16. Roy and Sopariwala note three phases in Indian politics. Phase 1: 1952–1977, when there was 84 per cent pro-incumbency record favouring parties ruling state governments to win a clear majority of MPs from that state; Phase 2: 1977–2002, when pro-incumbency rate dropped to 48 per cent; and Phase 3: 2002–2019, when it went up to 54 per cent. Prannoy Roy, Dorab R. Sopariwala, *The Verdict: Decoding India's Elections* (New Delhi: Penguin Random House, 2019), pp. 24–26.
17. See, for instance, Sunil Khilnani, *The Idea of India* (New Delhi: Penguin, 1998).
18. 'Mr Nehru's call for war against communalism', *The Times of India*, 1 October 1951, p .1.
19. 'Dr Mookerjee explains reasons for resignation: Doubts about efficacy of India-Pakistan pact', *The Times of India*, 20 April 1950.
20. A good summation of this is in Rafiq Zakaria, 'The Tandon-Nehru conflict', *The Times of India*, 21 December 1969.

21. Special Correspondent, 'Mr P. Tandon elected Congress president, reorientation of policy likely in future', *The Times of India*, 3 September 1950.
22. 'Congress session's overwhelming support for resolution on communalism', *The Times of India*, 22 September 1950.
23. 'Fate of Congress: Issue before Nasik Ssession', *The Times of India*, 17 September 1950.
24. This internal Congress debate is best summed up in B.D. Graham, 'Syama Prasad Mookerjee and the communalist alternative', in D.A. Low (ed.), *Sounding in Modern South Asian History* (Berkeley, LA: University of California Press, 1968), pp. 330–366.
25. Special Representive, 'Congress faces sudden crisis: Mr Nehru resigns from executive, deep anxiety among leaders', *The Times of India*, 11 August 1951.
26. Modi's victory speech is available at: 'Victory celebrations at BJP HQ. #VijayiBharat', 23 May 2019, https://youtu.be/VruL38kjEBY.
27. Ibid.
28. Ibid.
29. The Bombay Plan, published in 1944-45, by eight leading Indian industrialists, proposed state intervention in the economic development of the nation after Independence. Though it was never officially accepted by Nehru, its basic ideas are said to have influenced the first three Five-Year Plans of India. For the full text of the Bombay Plan, see Purushottamdas Thakurdas (ed.), *A Brief Memorandum Outlining a Plan of Economic Development for India* (2 vols.) (London: Penguin, 1945), http://www.isec.ac.in/Plan_%20of_%20economic_%20development_%20for_%20India.pdf Also see Amal Sanyal, 'The curious case of the Bombay Plan', *Contemporary Issues and Ideas in Social Sciences*, 2010, http://citeseerx.ist.psu.edu/viewdoc/download?doi=10.1.1.680.334&rep=rep1&type=pdf.
30. Details from Bluekraft Digital Foundation, *Mann ki Baat: A Social Revolution in Radio* (New Delhi: Rupa, 2019).
31. HT Correspondent, 'HT-Nielsen top 10: PM Narendra Modi's Exam Warriors continues to lead non-fiction list', *Hindustan Times*, 3 May 2018, https://www.hindustantimes.com/books/ht-nielsen-top-10-pm-narendra-modi-s-exam-warriors-continues-to-lead-non-fiction-list/story-4jy8KryNz8fjf1ldO2tgCO.html.
32. Narendra Modi, *Exam Warriors* (New Delhi: Penguin, 2018), p. 46.
33. Ibid., p. 94.
34. BlueKraft Digital Foundation, *Mann ki Baat: A Social Revolution on Radio* (New Delhi: Rupa, 2019), p. 27.
35. Ibid., p. 198.
36. See, for example, IANS, 'KVC turnover touches nearly 90k crore on PM Modi's appeal', *Outlook*, 8 May 2020, https://www.outlookindia.com/newsscroll/kvic-turnover-touches-nearly-rs-90k-crore-on-pm-modis-appeal/1827885; Sarika Malhotra, 'Khadi sales went up by 34% in FY16 due to PM Modi's efforts', *Business Today*, 18 January 2017, https://www.businesstoday.in/opinion/interviews/leaderspeak-striving-to-build-brand-khadi/story/244339.html; TNN, 'With PM as

face of khadi, sales up 89% in first half of this fiscal', *The Times of India*, 30 October 2017, http://timesofindia.indiatimes.com/articleshow/61329183.cms. Data is from *Khadi India: 2 Years Progress Report, November 2015 to February 2018: A Journey of Transformation* (Khadi and Village Industries Commission: MSME, New Delhi), http://www.kvic.gov.in/kvicres/update/e_Book/mobile/index.html#p=1. For a critical analysis, see Noor Mohammad, 'Spinning tales: Modi claims on khadi don't add up', *TheWire.in*, 31 October 2017, https://thewire.in/economy/spinning-tales-modis-claims-on-khadi-sales-dont-add-up.

37. See, for instance, Brijesh Pandey, 'Modi deletes Gandhi from Khadi Gram Udyog calendars: No KVIC rules on photos, says government', *India Today*, 13 January 2017, https://www.indiatoday.in/india/story/narendra-modi-mahatma-gandhi-khadi-gram-udyog-charkha-954810-2017-01-13.
38. Barack Obama, *A Promised Land* (New York: Penguin, 2020), pp. 337, 600.
39. The Modi government, between 2020 and 2021, subsequently added further measures to the initial announcement as the Coronavirus pandemic changed shape, especially after the second wave. Critics have, however, argued that the Indian financial relief measures were more tilted towards a monetary stimulus, compared to the US and several European countries where the COVID-19 relief packages were more about direct transfers related to income. For a detailed breakdown of the Indian package: between money spent by the government and measures by the RBI, see the presentation made by Finance Minister Nirmala Sitharaman at a press conference on 17 May 2020. It is available at: Government of India, *Atmanirbhar Bharat, Part 5: Government Reforms and Enablers*, p. 23, https://static.pib.gov.in/WriteReadData/userfiles/Aatma%20Nirbhar%20Bharat%20%20Presentation%20Part%205%2017-5-2020.pdf.
40. Rajni Kothari, 'The Congress "system" in India', *Asian Survey*, Vol. 4, No. 12, Dec. 1964, pp. 1161–1173.

CHAPTER 1 The BJP as the Party of the Village

1. The meeting in Pratapgarh was held on 23 April 2018. It was followed the same week with a similar chaupal in Amroha. All quotes for this public meeting are from video recordings of the event and interviews given by Yogi Adityanath after it to local reporters. Some of these are available on Pratapgarh Hub, 'Chief Minister Yogi in Pratapgarh Uttar Pradesh', 23 April 2018, https://www.youtube.com/watch?v=88B75-gDTAA; Aaj Tak, 'Nayak ke avatar mei CM Yogi, Pratapgarh Chaupal mei afsaro kee sare-aam class', 23 April 2018, https://www.youtube.com/watch?v=Gg8lvdTwGKE; India TV, 'UP: Yogi Adityanath holds first chaupal in Pratapgarh, dines at houses of dalits', 23 April 2018, https://www.youtube.com/watch?v=PiS0TaOvuw8.
2. Delhi Aaj Tak, 'UP ke gao mei Yogi kee chaupal, exclusive interview of CM Yogi Adityanath', 23 April 2018, https://youtu.be/6JZx3wSZgpw.

3. We took district-level Census demographic data and overlaid onto Lok Sabha constituencies, geotagging them. We used the psephologist Jai Mrug's classification for this book to divide Lok Sabha seats into three categories: Urban (with urban populations above 80 per cent); Rurban (having urban population between 33 per cent and 60 per cent) and Rural (with less than 33 per cent urban population).
4. The late Kalyan Singh was a Lodh Rajput, an OBC community. He was chief minister of UP when his government submitted a four-page affidavit to Supreme Court on 27 November 1992 on the disputed Ram Janmabhoomi case, providing an assurance of its record in 'maintaining law and order, particularly in maintaining communal harmony'. The Supreme Court, on this basis, allowed 'symbolic kar seva' on 6 December 1992, which led to the demolition of the Babri Masjid on that day. Kalyan Singh resigned as UP chief minister on the evening of the demolition and the Union government subsequently put the state under President's Rule. Details of affidavit from: *State (Through Central Burau of Investigation) v. Shri Kalyan Singh (Former CM Of UP) and Others*, Criminal Appeal Number 751 of 2017, 19 April 2017. Full text available at: https://indiankanoon.org/doc/76812356/. Also see Manoj Mitta, 'When even Supreme Court let down nation', *TheWire.in*, 6 December 2017, https://thewire.in/politics/babri-masjid-demolition-supreme-court; Manoj Mitta, 'Supreme Court judges face awkward questions over Babri Masjid demolition', *India Today*, 15 November 1993.
5. Quoted in Mahesh Rangarajan, 'Hindutva's "accursed problem"', *Seminar*, No. 485, January 2000, https://www.india-seminar.com/2000/485/485%20rangarajan.htm.
6. Booth numbers from ECI, 'Electors data summary', in *Uttar Pradesh General Legislative Election 2017*, 16 August 2018, https://eci.gov.in/files/file/3471-uttar-pradesh-general-legislative-election-2017/.
7. Interview with Dinesh Sharma, deputy chief minister, UP; former vice president, BJP; former BJP in-charge, Gujarat; and ex-mayor of Lucknow, 8 June 2020, Lucknow.
8. The Census of India 2011 counted 17,22,45,148 Muslims out of a total Indian population of 121,08,54,977. In UP, it counted 3,84,83,967 Muslims out of a total population of 19,98,12,341. Data from Office of the Registrar General and Census Commissioner of India, 'C1- Population by religious community', https://censusindia.gov.in/2011census/C-01.html.
9. Interview with Pranshu Mishra, UP bureau chief, Network18, 9–10 June 2020. BJP did win the Ayodhya seat (Faizabad) in the 1991 Lok Sabha elections.
10. In 1991, the BJP won 221 seats with 31.45 per cent of the votes. However, the INC had 17.32 per cent, the JD had 18.84 per cent, JP 12.52 per cent and BSP 9.44 per cent. The combined vote share of the last three pro-Mandal parties amounted to 40.8 per cent. Data from ECI, *Statistical Report on General Election, 1991, to the Legislative Assembly of Uttar Pradesh*, 14 August 2018, https://eci.gov.in/files/file/3257-uttar-pradesh-1991/.

11. Interview with a senior official in the UP chief minister's office, 9 June 2020, Lucknow.
12. Rajni Kothari, 'The Congress "system" in India', *Asian Survey*, Vol. 4, No. 12, Dec. 1964, pp. 1161–1173. On the Congress's one-party dominance, see W.H. Morris-Jones, 'Dominance and dissent: Their inter-relations in the Indian party system', *Government and Opposition*, Vol. 1, No. 4, August 1966 and W.H. Morris-Jones, 'The Indian Congress Party: A dilemma of dominance', *Modern Asian Studies*, Vol. 1, No. 2, 1967. Both essays are reproduced in W.H. Morris-Jones, *Politics Mainly Indian* (New Delhi: Orient Longman, 1978), pp. 213–265.

CHAPTER 2 Becoming the Hindi Heartland's Predominant Rural Party

1. In multipolar election contests in the first-past-the-post system, the effective number of political parties/players increases. Bipolarity represents a two-way concentration of votes. The minimal level of a multipolar configuration would be a three-way contest. In states like UP, it could be even higher. While there are often a large number of parties contesting a particular seat, there are various ways to statistically compute the 'effective' number of political parties (i.e., the number of key contenders) in the contest. One of the most common techniques is to use the inverse of the square root of the sum of the squares of their vote share. The formula is as below: Effective Number of Political Parties = 1/SQRT((A)^2+(B)^2+(C)^2). As per this, if we are to assume that UP has at a minimum number of three parties in contest, the formula is written as 3 = 1/SQRT((A)^2+(B)^2+(C)^2).

   Repeated iterations of this formula show that the value of the LHS remains around three (the conservative case we are trying to establish in the case of UP, if at least one of the variables of A, B and C remain above 0.4, which is 40 per cent. At its point of inflexion, it assumes that even if two of the three parties obtain 30 per cent each, one of them still needs to touch the 40 per cent mark to obtain an effective number of political parties as three. With the vote share of one party at larger than 40 per cent, the number starts dropping below three and the contest starts getting closer to a bipolar scenario marking a definitive departure from a purely triangular contest and signifying the dominance of one party among the three. We, therefore, set 40 per cent as a premium performance benchmark for saying that a party has indeed made a decisive presence in three-way (or more) contests. I am grateful to Jai Mrug for this calculation and explanation.
2. Interview with Keshav Prasad Maurya, deputy chief minister, UP; former president, UP BJP; former BJP MP from Phulpur, 8 June 2020, Lucknow.
3. Interview with Dinesh Sharma, deputy chief minister, UP; former vice president, BJP; former BJP in-charge, Gujarat; and ex-mayor, Lucknow, 8 June 2020, Lucknow.
4. Diego Maiorana, 'The 2019 Indian elections and the ruralization of the BJP', *Studies in Indian Politics*, Vol. 7, No. 2, 2019, pp. 177, 183.

5. Similarly, in the 2021 West Bengal assembly elections where the BJP, with 77 of 294 seats, came a distant second to Trinamool Congress, the majority of its wins were in the state's rural and rurban constituencies. Of the BJP's 77 seats, as many as 58 (75.3 per cent) were rural or rurban, 38 (49.3 per cent) rural and 20 (25.9 per cent) rurban. TOI Data Hub: https://timesofindia.indiatimes.com/elections/assembly-elections/west-bengal/constituency-map. Note: Results were declared on 2 May 2021 for 292 seats (as polls in two seats were postponed due to the death of candidates).
6. Interview with Jai Mrug, CEO, M76 Analytics and Director, VotersMood Research, 21 and 28 May 2020.
7. Ibid.
8. Ibid.

CHAPTER 3 The Caste Game

1. Akhilesh Singh, 'Modi hails BJP workers for "Seva Yagna" in Covid times', *The Times of India*, 5 July 2019.
2. If you leave out BJP MPs elected from seats reserved by law only for SC or ST, the party still had 113 OBC and a further nineteen MPs who were either SC or ST who got elected from 226 general constituencies. Among reserved constituencies, BJP won thirty-one of the forty-seven ST-reserved seats nationwide with 41.7 per cent vote share, and forty-six of the eighty-four SC-reserved seats with 35.3 per cent vote share across India. Analysis by author from ECI data and SC/ST seat analysis is available at: https://pollniti.com/live.html#.
3. Christophe Jaffrelot, *Modi's India: Hindu Nationalism and the Rise of Ethnic Democracy* (New Delhi: Context, 2021), first published Princeton University Press, 2021, pp. 344-346. Jaffrelot is regarded as the preeminent global scholar of the Hindu nationalist movement and lower caste mobilisation in India. In this regard, see, for example, his body of work: *The Hindu Nationalist Movement and Indian Politics: 1925 to the 1990s* (New Delhi: Penguin, 1999, first published 1996); his *India's Silent Revolution: The Rise of Low Castes in North Indian Politics* (New Delhi: Permanent Black, 2003); and a collection of his essays published in *Religion, Caste & Politics in India* (New Delhi: Primus, 2010).
4. Jaffrelot and Vernier produced their analysis working with researchers at the Trivedi Centre for Political Data (Ashoka University) and CERI (Sciences Po, Paris) using data from SPINPER (The Social Profile of the Indian National and Provincial Elected Representatives) project. Christophe Jaffrelot, Gilles Verniers, 'Explained: In Hindi heartland, upper castes dominate new Lok Sabha', *The Indian Express*, 27 May 2019, https://indianexpress.com/article/explained/in-hindi-heartland-upper-castes-dominate-new-house-5747511/.
5. Christophe Jaffrelot, Gilles Verniers, 'Explained: In Hindi heartland, upper castes dominate new Lok Sabha', *The Indian Express*, 27 May 2019, https://indianexpress.

com/article/explained/in-hindi-heartland-upper-castes-dominate-new-house-5747511/.

6. Christophe Jaffrelot, Gilles Verniers, 'The reconfiguration of India's political elite: Profiling the 17th Lok Sabha', *Contemporary South Asia*, Vol. 28, No. 2, 18 May 2020, pp. 242–254, https://www.tandfonline.com/doi/full/10.1080/09584935.2020.1765984.
7. They used data from SPINPER project co-funded by Trivedi Centre for Political Data (Ashoka University); CNRS, France; CERI and University of Bordeaux.
8. Upper-caste Rajputs are commonly referred to as Thakurs in the Hindi heartland.
9. Interview with Tarit Prakash, VMR, 1 June 2020.
10. SC data is from Census of India 2011. OBC data is from NSSO Report No. 563: *Employment and Unemployment Situation among Social Groups*, 2011-12. Quoted in Ministry of Social Justice and Empowerment, Government of India, *Handbook on Social Welfare Statistics 2018* (New Delhi: Department of Social Justice and Empowerment, Plan Division, 2018), pp. 29, 238, http://socialjustice.nic.in/writereaddata/UploadFile/HANDBOOKSocialWelfareStatistice2018.pdf. For the SC caste breakdown of UP, see, for instance, Census of India 2001, *Uttar Pradesh—Data Highlights: The Scheduled Castes*, https://censusindia.gov.in/tables_published/scst/dh_sc_up.pdf.
11. And STs are 0.57 per cent of the population in UP. Calculated by the author from UP caste data in Ministry of Social Justice and Empowerment, Government of India, *Handbook on Social Welfare Statistics 2018* (New Delhi: Department of Social Justice and Empowerment, Plan Division, 2018), http://socialjustice.nic.in/writereaddata/UploadFile/HANDBOOKSocialWelfareStatistice2018.pdf.
12. For more on the earlier Congress model of caste-based mobilisation in UP and its decline after the rise of caste-based parties, see Zoya Hasan, 'Transfer of power? Politics of mass mobilisation in UP', *Economic & Political Weekly*, Vol. 36, No. 46/47, 24–30 November 2001, pp. 4401–4409; Christophe Jaffrelot, *India's Silent Revolution: The Rise of Low Castes in North Indian Politics* (New Delhi: Permanent Black, 2003), pp. 48–143, 426–452; Christophe Jaffrelot, 'The rise of the Other Backward Classes in the Hindi belt', *The Journal of Asian Studies*, Vol. 59, No. 1, February 2000, pp. 86–108.
13. Interview with Brijesh Shukla, columnist, *Navbharat Times*, 11 June 2020, Lucknow. Also see his piece, 'BJP ke paas hai ati-pichhdon kee sanjeevani', *Navbharat Times*. The piece was written in May 2019, before the general election results were declared, after he had travelled 7,000 km to cover the poll campaign across UP.
14. Interview with one of the longest-serving MLAs in UP, who spoke off-the-record for this book, 9 June 2020.
15. This was the house of UP party leader and local magnate Sudhir Halwasiya. Rajiv Srivastava, 'Finally, a house for Amit Shah in Lucknow', *The Times of India*, 9 February 2014, https://timesofindia.indiatimes.com/india/Finally-a-house-for-Amit-Shah-in-Lucknow/articleshow/30075957.cms. For more on his 2013-14 UP

campaign, see Lalmani Verma, 'The build-UP: Amit Shah's gameplan to conquer UP for Narendra Modi', *The Indian Express*, 6 April 2014, https://indianexpress.com/article/india/politics/the-build-up/.

16. Conversation with the Resident Editor of a major newspaper in Lucknow who did not wish to be named, 12 June 2020.
17. Amit Shah interview with TNN, 'My mission was to deliver in UP, Amit Shah says', *The Times of India*, 17 May 2014, https://timesofindia.indiatimes.com/news/Election-results-2014-My-mission-was-to-deliver-in-UP-Amit-Shah-says/articleshow/35233049.cms.
18. Overall, India has a total of 2,479 castes notified as OBCs across all states. Ministry of Social Justice and Empowerment, Government of India, *Handbook on Social Welfare Statistics 2018* (New Delhi: Department of Social Justice and Empowerment, Plan Division, 2018), p. 237, http://socialjustice.nic.in/writereaddata/UploadFile/HANDBOOKSocialWelfareStatistice2018.pdf. For a detailed breakdown of UP's seventy-six OBC castes, see: 'Central list of OBCs for the state of Uttar Pradesh', http://www.bcmbcmw.tn.gov.in/obc/faq/uttarpradesh.pdf.
19. According to the 1931 Census. Christophe Jaffrelot, 'The rise of the Other Backward Classes in the Hindi belt', *The Journal of Asian Studies*, Vol. 59, No. 1, February 2000, p. 102.
20. A total of 1,284 castes are notified as SC across all Indian states. Ministry of Social Justice and Empowerment, Government of India, *Handbook on Social Welfare Statistics 2018* (New Delhi: Department of Social Justice and Empowerment, Plan Division, 2018), p. 37. The full Ministry of Social Justice and Empowerment list of sixty-six castes notified as SC in UP is available at: http://socialjustice.nic.in/writereaddata/UploadFile/Scan-0019.jpg.
21. Census 2011 data. See analysis by Swati Mathur, 'Jatavs on top of SC population in UP', *The Times of India*, 4 July 2015, https://timesofindia.indiatimes.com/city/lucknow/Jatavs-on-top-of-SC-population-in-UP/articleshow/47931787.cms; Census of India 2001, *Uttar Pradesh—Data Highlights: The Scheduled Castes*, https://censusindia.gov.in/tables_published/scst/dh_sc_up.pdf. For further sub-caste SC details, see Ministry of Social Justice and Empowerment, Government of India, *Handbook on Social Welfare Statistics 2018* (New Delhi: Department of Social Justice and Empowerment, Plan Division, 2018), pp. 52–105, http://socialjustice.nic.in/writereaddata/UploadFile/HANDBOOKSocialWelfareStatistice2018.pdf.
22. Bhavna Vij-Arora, 'The caste of poll saffron', *Outlook*, 21 May 2018, https://www.outlookindia.com/magazine/story/the-caste-of-poll-saffron/300140; Faisal Fareed, 'Tug of war in UP over legacy of Rajbhar king', *The Indian Express*, 29 February 2016, https://indianexpress.com/article/cities/lucknow/tug-of-war-in-up-over-legacy-of-rajbhar-king/.
23. PMO India YouTube video, 'PM Modi releases commemorative stamp on Maharaja Suheldev and address public rally in Ghazipur', 28 December 2018, https://www.youtube.com/watch?v=ood3ZDg6Koc. For an account on the historical traditions

for Raja Suheldev among Pasis, see Badri Narayan, 'Memories, saffronising statues and constructing communal politics', *Economic & Political Weekly*, Vol. 41, No. 45, 11–17 November 2006, pp. 4697–4698. For a critical account of Suheldev, see, for example, Ajaz Ashraf, 'How Amit Shah and BJP have twisted the story of Salar Masud and Raja Suheldev', 17 July 2017, https://scroll.in/article/841590/how-amit-shah-and-the-bjp-have-twisted-the-story-of-salar-masud-and-raja-suheldev. Suheldev's battle with Mahmud of Ghazni is also the subject of a recent novel by the best-selling writer Amish, *Legend of Suheldev: The King Who Saved India* (New Delhi: Westland, 2020).

24. The Lok Sabha constituencies where Nishads are said to have influence include: Firozabad, Badaun, Shahjahanpur, Kairana, Machhlishahr, Jaunpur. They also have a sizeable presence in Ghazipur, Phulpur, Sitapur, Jalaun, Fatehpur, Unnao, Gorakhpur, Ballia and Deoria, according to UP Backward Class Finance and Development Corporation Chairperson Baburam Nishad. PTI, 'Amit Shah woos Nishads, promises to build 8-feet tall statue of Nishadraj', News18.com, 10 May 2019, https://www.news18.com/news/politics/in-up-amit-shah-woos-nishads-promises-to-build-80-feet-tall-statue-of-nishadraj-2135337.html. For an analysis on the political importance of Nishads in eastern UP, see Sanjay Pandey, 'Why Nishads are so important in eastern UP', *Deccan Herald*, 4 April 2019, https://www.deccanherald.com/national/why-nishads-are-so-important-in-eastern-up-727018.html.
25. Interview with Brijesh Shukla, columnist, *Navbharat Times*, 11 June 2020, Lucknow.
26. BJP also lost Kairana and Phulpur in that round of by-elections in 2018.
27. See, for example, IANS, 'Nishads emerge as major votebank in UP elections', *Business Standard*, 18 May 2019, https://www.business-standard.com/article/news-ians/nishads-emerge-as-major-vote-bank-in-up-elections-119051800408_1.html.
28. This switch by Praveen Nishad showed that Nishad groups were not passive recipients of a BJP indoctrination drive. Far from it. Nishad leaders responded to the BJP's overtures by playing the game instrumentally. For a detailed background on Nishad identity and politics, see Assa Doron, 'Caste away? Subaltern engagement with the modern Indian state', *Modern Asian Studies*, Vol. 44, No. 4, 2010, pp. 753–783.
29. Aman Sharma, 'High Court stays UP's move to shift 17 OBCs to SC list', *The Economic Times*, 17 September 2019, https://economictimes.indiatimes.com/news/politics-and-nation/high-court-stays-ups-move-to-shift-17-obcs-to-sc-list/articleshow/71160095.cms?from=mdr.
30. IANS, 'Uttar Pradesh adds 17 OBC groups to SC list', *The Hindu*, 30 June 2017, https://www.thehindu.com/news/national/other-states/up-adds-17-obc-groups-to-sc-list/article28231615.ece.
31. Pankaj Shah, 'UP panel suggests 7% quota for Yadavs & Kurmis, says they are politically influential', *The Times of India*, 18 December 2018, https://timesofindia.indiatimes.com/city/lucknow/up-panel-suggests-7-quota-for-yadavs-kurmis-says-they-are-politically-influential/articleshow/67137290.cms.

32. Interview with Dinesh Sharma, deputy chief minister, UP, 8 June 2020, Lucknow.
33. Details from https://www.keshavprasadmaurya.com/ and PTI, 'Keshav Prasad Maurya, the deputy CM rewarded for BJP win in UP', *The Times of India*, 18 March 2017, https://timesofindia.indiatimes.com/elections/assembly-elections/uttar-pradesh/news/keshav-prasad-maurya-the-deputy-cm-rewarded-for-bjp-win-in-up/articleshow/57710427.cms.
34. Muslim Telis were classified as OBC vide Resolution 12011/68/93-BCC(C) dt 10/09/1993; Modh Ghanchis were added vide Resolution 12011/36/99-BCC dt 04/04/2000. Full list of OBCs in Gujarat is available at: National Commission for Backward Classes, 'Central list of OBCs for the state of Gujarat', http://ncbc.nic.in/Writereaddata/cl/gujarat.pdf. For a short background, see TNN, 'Modi didn't add his caste to OBC list', *The Times of India*, 11 May 2014, https://timesofindia.indiatimes.com/news/Modi-didnt-add-his-caste-to-OBC-list/articleshow/34941744.cms.
35. Quoted in Rohit Bhan, 'Congress, BJP spar on Narendra Modi's backward caste status', NDTV.com, 9 May 2014, 'https://www.ndtv.com/elections-news/congress-bjp-spar-on-narendra-modis-backward-caste-status-560811.
36. This argument on birth is also one made by some Dalit intellectuals. See, for example, Kancha Illaiah Shepherd, 'If caste is about experience, PM Modi has never spoken about discrimination he faced on account of his birth', *The Indian Express*, 8 May 2019, https://indianexpress.com/article/opinion/columns/narendra-modi-obc-backward-caste-dynast-lok-sabha-elections-5715807/.
37. 'Sharing stage with Mulayam, Mayawati says Modi a fake OBC leader, slams Rahul Gandhi's NYAY—key takeaways from Mainpuri Rally', *FE Online*, 19 April 2019, https://www.financialexpress.com/elections/mayawati-mulayam-singh-yadav-akhilesh-mainpuri-rally-lok-sabha-election-uttar-pradesh-modi/1553238/.
38. Narendra Modi speech in Kannauj, 26 April 2019, available on Narendra Modi YouTube channel, https://www.youtube.com/watch?v=JCSMN_ju7YE&feature=emb_logo.
39. Interview with Dinesh Sharma, deputy chief minister, UP, 8 June 2020, Lucknow.
40. Full text of Narendra Modi's speech in Alwar on 25 November 2018, available in Hindi at: https://www.narendramodi.in/text-of-pm-s-address-at-public-meeting-at-alwar-rajasthan-542495.
41. Sunetra Choudhury, 'Panel may recommend splitting 27% OBC quota into three bands', *Hindustan Times*, 31 December 2019, https://www.hindustantimes.com/india-news/panel-may-recommend-splitting-27-obc-quota-into-three-bands/story-9XUA9UWxL9qE6vVABUeINN.html. For a critical analysis, see Yogendra Yadav, 'From Mandal to Modi, OBC categorisation caught up in bad politics', 15 July 2020, https://theprint.in/opinion/mandal-modi-obc-sub-categorisation-caught-up-in-bad-politics/461498/.
42. PIB Delhi, 'Cabinet approves extension of term of the Commission constituted under Article 340 of the Constitution to examine the issue of sub-categorization within Other Backward Classes in the Central list', 14 July 2021, https://pib.gov.in/

PressReleaseIframePage.aspx?PRID=1735389; Damini Nath, 'OBC Commission's tenure extended by 6 months', *The Hindu*, 24 June 2020, https://www.thehindu.com/news/national/obc-commissions-tenure-extended-by-6-months/article31904996.ece.

43. The National Commission for Backward Classes was reconstituted as a constitutional body w.e.f. 15.08.2018 by insertion of a new Article 338B in the Constitution through the Constitution (One Hundred and Second Amendment) Act, 2018. This made the powers available to the NCBC as per Article 338B the same as those available to the National Commission for Scheduled Castes as per Article 338. Krishan Pal Gurjar, Minister of State for Social Justice and Empowerment, Lok Sabha Unstarred Question No. 1761, 2 July 2019, http://loksabhaph.nic.in/Questions/QResult15.aspx?qref=1957&lsno=17. Further, the Constitution (One Hundred and Twenty Seventh Amendment) Act, 2021, was passed by Parliament on 11 August 2021. It amended the 2018 legislation to allow states and union territories to make their own lists of socially and economically backward classes. It was necessitated after a Supreme Court judgment on 5 May 2021 which ruled that the legislation had taken away the power hitherto held by states to identify and list such classes for education and job quotas. Subsequently, the 2021 Constitutional Amendment clarified that the 2018 Act listed similar powers of notifying class lists only for the purposes of the union government. Ritika Chopra, Krishn Kaushik, '187-0: Bill to restore states' power on OBC list passed', *The Indian Express*, 15 August 2021, https://indianexpress.com/article/india/187-0-bill-to-restore-states-power-on-obc-list-passed-7449656/; PRS Legislative Research, 'The Constitution (One Hundred and Twenty Seventh Amendment) Act, 2021', https://prsindia.org/billtrack/the-constitution-one-hundred-and-twenty-seventh-amendment-bill-2021.

44. National Commission for Backward Classes, *Report Relating to the Proposal for Sub-Categorisation Within the Other Backward Classes*, 27 February 2015, http://ncbc.nic.in/Writereaddata/Report%20on%20Sub-Categorization%20within%20OBCs%20-2015-%20Pandey635681469081640773.pdf.

45. Narendra Modi speech in Dhanbad on 12 December 2019. Full text in Hindi available at: https://www.narendramodi.in/text-of-pm-modi-s-speech-at-public-meeting-in-dhanbad-jharkhand-547632.

46. The Constitution (One Hundred and Twenty Fourth) Amendment Bill. For a background on this, see PRS Legislative Research, 'Bill summary', https://www.prsindia.org/node/838346/chapters-at-a-glance. For a critique of how hurriedly this constitutional amendment was passed, see M.R. Madhavan, 'Hurrying though legislation: On reservation quota', *The Hindu*, 12 January 2019, https://www.prsindia.org/content/hurrying-through-legislation-reservation-quota.

47. Narendra Modi's speech in Dhanbad on 12 December 2019. Full text in Hindi available at: https://www.narendramodi.in/text-of-pm-modi-s-speech-at-public-meeting-in-dhanbad-jharkhand-547632.

48. 'Empowering the marginalised though the legislative route', 19 March 2019, https://www.narendramodi.in/empowering-the-marginalised-through-the-legislative-route-19-march-2019-544128.
49. Interview with Brijesh Shukla, columnist, *Navbharat Times*, 11 June 2020, Lucknow.
50. Interview with Keshav Prasad Maurya, deputy chief minister, UP, 8 June 2020, Lucknow.
51. Conversation with the resident editor of a major newspaper in Lucknow, 12 June 2020.
52. Interview with Pranshu Mishra, UP bureau chief, Network18, 9 and 10 June 2020.
53. Interview with Keshav Prasad Maurya, deputy chief minister, UP, 8 June 2020, Lucknow.
54. Ibid.
55. Interview with Dinesh Sharma, deputy chief minister, Uttar Pradesh, 8 June 2020, Lucknow.
56. Ibid.
57. Interview with Keshav Prasad Maurya, deputy chief minister, UP, 8 June 2020, Lucknow.
58. Interview with Brijesh Shukla, columnist, *Navbharat Times*, 11 June 2020, Lucknow.
59. Chandra Bhan Prasad's interview to Avijit Ghosh, 'India cheers Dalits riding donkeys but fears Dalits riding horses ... caste society and government have dissolved into one', *The Times of India*, 5 October 2020.
60. Isabel Wilkerson, *Caste: The Origins of Our Discontent* (New York: Random House, 2020).
61. Journalists covering UP have been writing accurately about the BJP's OBC and SC mobilisation in its ticket-distribution during each of the relevant post-2014 poll campaigns mentioned in this chapter. This was rightly pointed out to me by Kunal Pradhan, executive editor, *Hindustan Times*, June 2020. Also see, for example, Brijesh Shukla's pieces published on this theme in May 2019: 'BJP ke paas hai ati-pichhdon kee sanjeevani', 'Dimple ke liye aasaan nahi hai Kannauj ki larhayee', published in *Navbharat Times* in May 2019 before the general election results were announced.
62. I am deeply grateful to Mahesh Rangarajan for this particular formulation in response to these findings.

CHAPTER 4 The BJP's Political Mobilisation of Welfare

1. The Swachh Bharat Mission was launched on 2 October 2014, Gandhi's birthday, by modifying the UPA government's erstwhile Nirmal Bharat Abhiyan, and putting in place a five-year target. The scheme increased allocation for individual household toilets to Rs 12,000 from Rs 10,000. Of this, the Union government's share of funding was 60 per cent (Rs 7,200 per toilet), while the state governments' share was 40 per cent (Rs 4,800 per toilet). For states in the Northeast, Jammu

and Kashmir and Special Category States, the Centre–State ratio of funding was 90 per cent (Rs 10,800 per toilet): 10 per cent (Rs 1,200 per toilet). Details from Swachh Bharat Mission, 'FAQs—SBM Phase I', https://swachhbharatmission.gov.in/SBMCMS/faq.htm, and Swachh Bharat Mission, Guidelines for Swachh Bharat Mission (Gramin), revised October 2017, p. 17, https://swachhbharatmission.gov.in/SBMCMS/writereaddata/portal/images/pdf/sbm-ph-II-Guidelines.pdf.

2. Indira Awas Yojana was restructured into PMAY-G with effect from 1 April 2016—and the revised scheme formally launched on 20 November 2016—with an initial target of building 1 crore pucca house by 2018-19, with a final end-target of 2022. Aimed at providing pucca housing to all, the scheme increased unit assistance from Rs 70,000 to Rs 1.2 lakh per beneficiary in the plains and from Rs 75,000 to Rs 1.3 lakh in hilly states, difficult areas and IAP districts. The beneficiary is entitled to ninety to ninety-five person days of unskilled labour from MGNREGS. The scheme is administered by the Ministry of Rural Development. Separately, the PMAY-U is administered by the Ministry of Housing and Urban Affairs. PMAY-U was launched on 25 June 2015 and focuses on 'urban housing shortage among the EWS/LIG and MIG categories including the slum dwellers by ensuring a pucca house to all eligible urban households by the year 2022.' Essentially, in operational terms, they are separate schemes—one rural, one urban—run by two different ministries with different reporting lines and administrative hierarchies but both fall within the broad rubric of the Modi's government's 'Housing for All' Mission. For PMAY-G, see https://pmayg.nic.in/netiay/about.aspx; PIB, Ministry of Rural Development, 'PM launches "housing for all" in rural areas', 20 November 2016, https://pib.gov.in/newsite/printrelease.aspx?relid=153931. For PMAY-U, see details on https://pmaymis.gov.in/, Pradhan Mantri Awas Yojana, *Housing for All (Urban)—Scheme Guidelines 2015* (New Delhi: Ministry of Housing and Urban Poverty Alleviation, 2015) and Kaushal Kishore, minister of state for housing and urban affairs, in response to Lok Sabha Unstarred Question No. 1827, answered on 29 July 2021.

3. Interview with Hemant Chouhan, gram _andhi_, Shahpur Bans Must village, Saharanpur district, UP, 17 June 2020.

4. This point was made to me by the journalist Brijesh Shukla. Interview with Brijesh Shukla, columnist, *Navbharat Times*, 11 June 2020, Lucknow.

5. Ibid.

6. Ashwani Kumar, 'Is cash transfer a "Congress calling card"?', *Business Standard*, 29 January 2013, https://www.business-standard.com/article/ opinion/ashwani-kumar-is-cash-transfer-a-congress-calling-card-113010200040_1.html.

7. See, for example, Saba Naqvi, 'Freshly minted cheer', *Outlook*, 10 December 2012, https://www.outlookindia.com/magazine/story/freshly-minted-cheer/283179.

8. The UPA government initiated DBT with effect from 1 January 2013 in forty-three identified districts for twenty-four selected schemes. The NDA government

(vide O.M. No. I-11011/58/2013-DBT dated 13.2.2015 and 19.2.2015) expanded the scope of DBT to cover all central sector schemes/centrally sponsored schemes in which cash benefits are transferred to individual beneficiaries. Source: Jayant Singh, minister of state for finance, answer to Lok Sabha Unstarred Question No. 2077, 6 May 2016.

9. RBI gave approval to banks for e-KYC verification through Aadhaar only on 2 September 2013 vide RBI/2013-14/209. DBOD.AML.BC.No.44/14.01.001/2013-14, https://www.rbi.org.in/scripts/Notification User.aspx?Id=8357&Mode=0.

10. According to the Ministry of Finance data tabled in Parliament, as of 26 December 2018, 434 schemes of fifty-six ministries/departments had been onboarded on to the DBT portal. One example is the Ministry of Petroleum and Natural Gas's modified DBT for LPG (DBTL/PAHAL) Scheme launched in fifty-four districts on 15.11.2014 and across the country on 01.01.2015. LPG consumers who join the PAHAL scheme get the LPG cylinders at non-subsidised price and receive LPG subsidy (as per their entitlement) directly into their registered bank accounts. As on 27.03.2017, out of 19.81 crore active LPG consumers, 16.95 crore had joined the PAHAL Scheme. Subsidy amount of more than Rs 46,000 crore had been transferred to the beneficiaries' bank accounts since its launch. A second example is that of MNREGA. As per NREGASoft, around 99 per cent of MNREGA wages were being paid electronically (FY 2018-19 as on 24.07.2018) into the Bank/Post Office accounts of MGNREGA workers through Electronic Fund Management System (eFMS). In FY 2013-14, only 37 per cent of the wages were paid electronically. Overall, DBT schemes include subsidies and benefits, such as scholarships, pension, wages and other social benefits under various centrally sponsored schemes and central sector schemes. Till 31 March 2017, Union government ministries reported savings of Rs 57,029 crore due to DBT. DBT data from P. Radhakrishnan, minister of state for finance, answer to Unstarred Question 2827, Lok Sabha, 28 December 2018, http://164.100.24.220/loksabhaquestions/annex/16/AU2827.pdf.

MNREGA details from Ram Kripal Yadav, minister of state for rural development, answer to Lok Sabha Unstarred Question No. 1507, 26 July 2018, http://164.100.24.220/loksabhaquestions/annex/15/AU1507.pdf. DBT savings estimate from P. Radhakrishnan, minister of state for finance, answer to Unstarred Question 18, Lok Sabha, 2 February 2018, http://164.100.24.220/loksabhaquestions/annex/14/AU18.pdf. LPG PAHAL; data from Arjun Ram Meghwal, minister of state for finance, Lok Sabha Unstarred Question 4922, 31 March 2017, http://164.100.24.220/loksabhaquestions/annex/11/AU4922.pdf.

11. This data tabled in Lok Sabha is available at: http://164.100.24.220/loksabhaquestions/annex/174/AU1183.pdf and http://164.100.24.220/loksabhaquestions/annex/16/AU2827.pdf.

12. The ECI allowed the Union agriculture ministry to transfer the first and second tranche of the payment to all those beneficiaries registered under the scheme before 10 March 2019. Ahead of the Lok Sabha polls, the Centre announced the

Rs 75,000-crore Pradhan Mantri Kisan Samman Nidhi (PM-Kisan) scheme under which Rs 6,000 per year would be disbursed in three instalments to around 12 crore farmers who hold cultivable land up to 2 hectares. PTI, 'PM Kisan Scheme: 4.74 crore farmers to get second instalment from next month', *Economic Times*, 23 March 2019, https://bit.ly/2JnB3id.

13. Narendra Modi's speech in Kannauj, 26 April 2019, available on Narendra Modi YouTube channel, https://www.youtube.com/watch?v=JC3MN_ju7YE&feature=emb_logo.
14. The Rythu Bandhu programme reaches 57,15,870 farmers across thirty-two Telangana districts. For details, see http://rythubandhu.telangana.gov.in/Default_RB1.aspx. Implementation details from Government of Telangana, Agriculture and Cooperation Department, *Guidelines for Implementation of Agriculture Investment Support Scheme ('Rythu Bandhu') in Telangana State: Orders Issued*, G.O. Rt. No 231, 4 April 2018. For a critical analysis, see Sai Manish, 'Winning elections Telangana style: Pay farm land owners, ignore the tillers', *Business Standard*, 20 December 2018, https://bit.ly/3qahbjw.
15. Congress, 'Congress schemes repackaged/renamed by NDA', https://www.inc.in/en/congress-schemes-renamed-by-bjp.
16. Neelanjan Sircar, 'The politics of vishwas: Political mobilization in the 2019 national election', *Contemporary South Asia*, Vol. 28, No. 2, 26 May 2020, pp. 178–194, https://doi.org/10.1080/09584935.2020.1765988. Also see Christophe Jaffrelot, Gilles Verniers, 'The BJP's 2019 election campaign: Not business as usual', *Contemporary South Asia*, Vol. 28, No. 2, 18 May 2020, pp. 155–177, https://doi.org/10.1080/09584935.2020.1765985; Christophe Jaffrelot, 'Class and caste in the 2019 Indian election–Why have so many poor started voting for Modi?', *Studies in Indians Politics*, Vol. 7, Issue 2, pp. 149–160, first published online on 12 November 2019, Issue published on 1 December 2019, https://doi.org/10.1177/2321023019874890; Rajeshwari Deshpande, Louise Tillin, K.K. Kailash, 'The BJP's welfare schemes: Did they make a difference in the 2019 elections?', *Studies in Indian Politics*, Vol. 7, Issue 2, November 2019, pp. 219–233, https://doi.org/10.1177/2321023019874911.
17. Yamini Aiyar, 'Modi consolidates power: Leveraging welfare politics', *Journal of Democracy*, Vol. 30, No. 4, p. 84.
18. Anant Zanane, 'Akhilesh Yadav's free laptops for students boot up with Mulayam photo', 11 March 2013, https://www.ndtv.com/india-news/_andhi_a-yadavs-free-laptops-for-students-boot-up-with-mulayam-photo-515845; Agencies, 'UP CM Akhilesh Yadav launches free laptop scheme for students', *Economic Times*, 11 March 2013, https://economictimes.indiatimes.com/nation-world/up-cm-akhilesh-yadav-launches-free-laptop-scheme-for-students/laptop-bags-have-images-of-yadav-his-father/slideshow/18923275.cms.
19. Priyangi Aggarwal, 'UP begins distributing school bags with pictures of former CM Akhilesh Yadav', *Economic Times*, 21 April 2017, https://economictimes.indiatimes.com/news/politics-and-nation/up-begins-distributing-school-bags-with-

pictures-of-former-cm-akhilesh-yadav/articleshow/58294440.cms?from=mdr; HT Correspondent, 'Schoolkids to get bags with Akhilesh Photo', *Hindustan Times*, 3 March 2017, https://www.hindustantimes.com/lucknow/schoolkids-to-get-bags-with-akhilesh-photo/story-QygzNo03aO91FU3dG72IUJ.html.

20. Interview with a senior official in the UP CMO, 9 June 2020, Lucknow.
21. Ibid.
22. Aman Sharma, 'In stance shift, Congress adopts Aadhaar in Madhya Pradesh', *Economic Times*, 11 January 2019, https://economictimes.indiatimes.com/news/politics-and-nation/in-stance-shift-congress-adopts-aadhaar-in-madhya-pradesh/articleshow/67480516.cms?from= mdr.
23. Interview with a senior official in the UP CMO, 9 June 2020, Lucknow.
24. Interview with Dinesh Sharma, deputy chief minister, UP, 8 June 2020, Lucknow.
25. Interview with Keshav Prasad Maurya, deputy chief minister, UP, 8 June 2020, Lucknow.
26. Interview with a senior official in UP CMO, 9 June 2020, Lucknow.
27. Interview with Keshav Prasad Maurya, deputy chief minister, UP, 8 June 2020, Lucknow.
28. Conversation with Pravin Kumar, author of *Yogi Adityanath: The Rise of a Saffron Socialist* (New Delhi: Times Books, 2017), 12 June 2020, Lucknow.
29. Interview with Keshav Prasad Maurya, deputy chief minister, UP, 8 June 2020, Lucknow.
30. Interview with a senior official in UP CMO, 9 June 2020, Lucknow.
31. Ibid.
32. UP Government, *100 Din Vishwas Ke* (Lucknow: UP Government, 2017).
33. UP Government, *Vikas Evam Sushasan Ke 30 Mah* (Lucknow: UP Government, 2019).
34. Interview with Dinesh Sharma, deputy chief minister, UP, 8 June 2020, Lucknow.
35. Data from Swachh Bharat Mission Gramin Dashboard, 27 November 2020, https://sbm.gov.in/sbmdashboard/IHHL.aspx.
36. Narendra Modi's speech in Kannauj, 26 April 2019, available on Narendra Modi YouTube channel, https://www.youtube.com/watch?v=JCSMN_ju7YE&feature=emb_logo.
37. Aman Sharma, 'Call Swachh Bharat toilets "izzat ghar": Centre to states', *Economic Times*, 17 October 2017, https://economictimes.indiatimes.com/news/politics-and-nation/call-swachh-bharat-toilets-izzat-ghar-centre-to-states/articleshow/61123473.cms?from=mdr.
38. Narendra Modi's speech in Kannauj, 26 April 2019, available on Narendra Modi YouTube channel, https://www.youtube.com/watch?v=JCSMN_ju7YE&feature=emb_logo.
39. Data from PMAY-G, Awassoft Dashboard, 'C2- Category-wise houses sanctioned and completed', 27 November 2020, https://rhreporting.nic.in/netiay/SocialProgressReport/Categorywisehouses completedreport.aspx.

40. The Centre–state funding ratio is 90:10 in the Northeast and Himalayan states, https://pmayg.nic.in/netiay/about.aspx. Also see PMAY-G, Ministry of Rural Development, *Framework for Implementation—Pradhan Mantri Awas Yojana Gramin*, https://pmayg.nic.in/netiay/Uploaded/English_Book_Final.pdf.
41. Additional data from Ram Kripal Yadav, minister of state for rural development, answer to Lok Sabha Unstarred Question No. 1061, 8 February 2018, http://164.100.24.220/loksabhaquestions/annex/14/AU1061.pdf & Answer to Lok Sabha Unstarred Question No. 1337, 9 February 2017, http://164.100.24.220/loksabhaquestions/annex/11/AU1337.pdf; Narendra Singh Tomar, minister for rural development, answer to Lok Sabha Unstarred Question No. 414, 19 November 2019, 2018, http://164.100.24.220/loksabhaquestions/annex/172/AU414.pdf.
42. Interview with a senior functionary in UP government, who spoke on the condition of anonymity, 9 June 2020.
43. The absolute number of poor declined from 407 million in 2004-05 to 355 million in 2009-10 to 269 million in 2011-12. The percentage of poor fell from 29.8 per cent in 2009-10 to 21.9 per cent in 2011-12. Montek Singh Ahluwalia, *Backstage: The Story Behind India's High Growth Years* (New Delhi: Rupa, 2020), p. 295. Also see Ahluwalia's interview with Nalin Mehta, Sanjiv Shankaran, 'If a bank chief isn't beholden to a FinMin joint secretary, he will behave differently', *The Times of India*, 16 February 2020, https://timesofindia.indiatimes.com/home/Sunday-times/all-that-matters/if-a-bank-chief-isnt-beholden-to-a-finmin-join-secretary-he-will-behave-differently-says-montek-singh-ahluwalia/articleshow/74152939.cms.
44. Interview with Hemant Agarwal, BJP district vice president, Mathura Mahanagar, 26 July 2020.
45. Interview with a long-standing UP MLA who spoke on the condition of anonymity, 9 and 10 June 2020.

CHAPTER 5 The BJP's Muslim Model

1. Census 2011 counted 17,22,45,158 Muslims in India. In UP, it counted 3,84,83,967 Muslims. Data from the Office of the Registrar General and Census Commissioner, India, 'C1—Population by religious community', https://censusindia.gov.in/2011census/C-01.html.
2. Interview with Dinesh Sharma, deputy chief minister, UP, 8 June 2020, Lucknow.
3. Ibid.
4. Christophe Jaffrelot, 'The fate of secularism in India', in Milan Vaishnav (ed.), *The BJP in Power: Indian Democracy and Religious Nationalism*, 4 April 2019, https://carnegieendowment.org/2019/04/04/fate-of-secularism-in-india-pub-78689
5. Harsh Mandar, 'Sonia, sadly', *The Indian Express*, 24 March 2018, https://indianexpress.com/article/opinion/columns/_andh-sadly-congress-muslims-party-sonia-gandhi-5100506/. For a more nuanced perspective, see Suhas Palshikar,

'The BJP and Hindu nationalism: Centrist politics and majoritarian impulses', *South Asia: Journal of South Asian Studies*, Vol. 38, No. 4, 2015, pp. 719–735.

6. Narendra Modi's victory speech on 23 May 2019 is available on the BJP YouTube Channel, 'Victory Celebrations at BJP Headquaters #VijayiBharat', https://www.youtube.com/watch?v=VruL38kjEBY.
7. This was a point often made by Advani in the late 1980s and early 1990s. See, for example, his interview to Manini Chatterjee, 'We should not shy away from the fact that this is essentially a Hindu country', *The Telegraph*, 14 February 1991; and his interview to A. Surya Prakash, 'Advani trains guns on "pseudo-secularists"', *The Indian Express*, 4 February 1991. Advani's successor as BJP president, Murali Manohar Joshi, made the same argument in an interview to Rajiv Saxena, 'The Hindu majority makes india secular', *Observer*, 13 January 1991. Atal Bihari Vajpayee in 1991 also argued that the Ayodhya issue 'is not a religious issue. It's a national issue in the sense that Ram is a national hero.' See his interview to Vinod Sharma, 'There are elements who want the BJP to become a religious party', *Hindustan Times*, 10 February 1991.
8. Yogi Adityanath's interview to *Network 18* at India Summit, 17 March 2018. Full video available at: https://www.news18.com/news/politics/nobody-is-more-secular-than-hindus-says-yogi-adityanath-at-news-18-rising-india-summit-1692553.html. Yogi's usage of the word 'panth' echoed a sentiment first articulated by the then BJP Union home minister, Rajnath Singh, in a 2015 speech in Parliament during a ceremony to commemorate the Constitution and its framer Dr B.R. Ambedkar. Singh argued that 'The official translation of the word "secularism" is *panth-nirpeksh* [sect neutral], not *dharm-nirpeksh* [religion-neutral]. Bharat's dharam in itself is *panth-nirpkesh*.' He was referring to the fact that the official translation of India's Constitution in Hindi translates the word 'secularism' as 'panth-nirpeksh'. This ignited a wider debate on secularism and its meaning and the BJP's political intentions at the time, with Congress leaders accusing the BJP of 'playing games' with the meaning of the term. Clips of Rajnath Singh's speech on 26 November 2015 available at https://www.youtube.com/watch?v=CPNiLB9jXr8&t=2s. Full text of the official Hindi translation of India's Constitution is available at https:/legislative.gov.in/hi/constitution-of-india.
9. In multipolar election contests in the first-past-the-post system, the effective number of political parties/players increases. Bipolarity represents a two-way concentration of votes. The minimal level of a multipolar configuration would be a three-way contest. In states like UP, it could be even higher. While there are often a large number of parties contesting a particular seat, there are various ways to statistically compute the 'effective' number of political parties (i.e., the number of key contenders) in the contest. One of the most common techniques is to use the inverse of the square root of the sum of the squares of their vote share. The formula is as below: Effective Number of Political Parties = 1/SQRT((A)^2+(B)^2+(C)^2).

As per this, if we are to assume that UP has at a minimum number of three parties in contest, the formula is written as 3 = 1/SQRT((A)^2+(B)^2+(C)^2).

Repeated iterations of this formula show that the value of the LHS remains around three (the conservative case we are trying to establish in the case of UP, if at least one of the variables of A, B and C remain above 0.4, which is 40 per cent. At its point of inflexion, it assumes that even if two of the three parties obtain 30 per cent each, one of them still needs to touch the 40 per cent mark to obtain an effective number of political parties as three. With the vote share of one party at larger than 40 per cent, the number starts dropping below three and the contest starts getting closer to a bipolar scenario marking a definitive departure from a purely triangular contest and signifying the dominance of one party among the three. We, therefore, set 40 per cent as a premium performance benchmark for saying that a party has indeed made a decisive presence in three-way (or more) contests. I am grateful to Jai Mrug for this calculation and explanation.

10. Shreyas Sardesai, 'The religious divide in voting preferences and attitudes in the 2019 election', *Studies in Indian Politics*, Vol. 7, Issue 2, pp. 161–175. First published online on 6 November 2019; issue published on 1 December 2019.
11. PTI, 'BJP fares well in "minority-concentration" districts, wins over 50% seats', *The Times of India*, 29 May 2019, https://timesofindia.indiatimes.com/india/bjp-fares-well-in-minority-concentration-districts-wins-over-50-seats/articleshow/69556665.cms; Samyak Pandey, Ruhi Tiwari, 'BJP's _andhi_ation strategy pays off as party wins 37% seats with high Muslim population', *ThePrint.in*, 24 May 2019, https://theprint.in/india/bjps-polarisation-strategy-pays-off-as-party-wins-37-seats-with-high-muslim-population/240228/. Also see Kaushik Deka, 'Consolidation of the Muslim vote bank?' *India Today*, 27 May 2019, https://www.indiatoday.in/india-today-insight/story/lok-sabha-election-muslim-votebank-bjp-congress-1535453-2019-05-27.
12. Interview with a senior official in the UP CMO, speaking on the condition of anonymity, 9 June 2020, Lucknow.
13. Ibid.
14. PNS, 'Yogi most sought after campaigner in Bihar', *Pioneer*, 13 October 2020, https://www.dailypioneer.com/2020/state-editions/yogi-most-sought-after----campaigner-in-bihar.html.
15. Pankaj Shah, 'Yogi Adityanath swings votes for NDA in Bihar with 67% strike rate', *The Times of India*, 10 November 2020, https://timesofindia.indiatimes.com/elections/assembly-elections/bihar/yogi-adityanath-swings-votes-for-nda-in-bihar-with-67-strike-rate/articleshow/79155612.cms.
16. Amit Shah speaking in a joint press conference with Narendra Modi, 17 May 2019. Full video available at: https://www.youtube.com/watch?v=_h3eIji3P6k.
17. Details from http://upcmo.up.nic.in/, 26 November 2020. See Raza's profile in Jagat Narayan Singh, 'Meet Yogi Adityanath's lone Muslim minister Mohsin Raza in UP cabinet', *India Today*, 19 March 2017, https://www.indiatoday.in/assembly-

elections-2017/uttar-pradesh-assembly-election-2017/story/yogi-adityanath-muslim-minister-mohsin-raza-966411-2017-03-19.

18. See, for example, PTI, 'Mukhtar Abbas Naqvi: Lone Muslim face in Modi govt. 2.0', *India Today*, 31 May 2019, https://www.indiatoday.in/fyi/story/mukhtar-abbas-naqvi-lone-muslim-face-modi-govt-2-1538945-2019-05-31.
19. Pradeep Chhibber, Rahul Varma, 'The rise of the second dominant party system in India: BJP's new social coalition in 2019', *Studies in Indian Politics*, Vol. 7, No. 2, 1 December 2019, pp. 131–148.
20. He also praised Mayawati for what he saw as soft Hindutva and 'Hindu social engineering' like Indira Gandhi did in the 1980s. Quoted in Suddheendra Kulkarni, 'Reality shirking Sangh', *The Indian Express*, 18 May 2007.
21. Ibid.
22. Balraj Madhok, 'Back to the roots', *Hindustan Times*, 8 November 2001.
23. Interview with a long-standing UP MLA who spoke on the condition of anonymity, 9 and 10 June 2020.
24. TNN, 'I'm a Hindu; No need to celebrate Eid: Yogi Adityanath', *The Times of India*, 7 March 2018, http://timesofindia.indiatimes.com/articleshow/63195659.cms.
25. Pankaj Shah, 'Yogi Adityanath doubles financial grant for pilgrims of Kailash Mansarovar', *The Times of India*, 25 March 2017, http://timesofindia.indiatimes.com/articleshow/57829099.cms. For details, see state government orders listed on Department of Religious Affairs, Government of Uttar Pradesh website: http://updharmarthkarya.in/booking/Home. Parallel to this, the UP government's Minority Welfare and Waqf Department's budgets were significantly increased: going up from Rs 1,365.31 crore in 2015-16 (under the previous Akhilesh Yadav-led SP government) to Rs 3,159.26 crore in 2020-21. Data from Minority Welfare and Waqf Department, Government of Uttar Pradesh, 'Vittiya Avashyaktao ka Uddeshyavaar Vargikaran', http://minoritywelfare.up.gov.in/en/page/progress-reports.
26. The Union government used to provide subsidies on airfare for Haj pilgrims since the 1950s. The Supreme Court, in a two-bench judgment by Justice Aftab Alam and Justice Ranjana Prakash Desai in 2012, ruled that the Haj subsidy should be 'done away with' by 2022. The apex court found the subsidy both unsustainable in law and inconsistent with the Quran, which enjoins it for those believers who can 'afford the expenses (for one's conveyance, provision and residence)'. The ruling, based on its reading of the Quran, hence specifically distinguished between subsidies for the Haj and those for other religious activities by other religions. Following this judgment and the recommendations of a Haj Policy Review committee set up by Ministry of Minority Affairs, this subsidy was gradually reduced from 2013 and withdrawn by the Modi government in 2018. The Union government's subsidy for Haj pilgrims provided to the airlines amounted to Rs 577.07 crore in 2014-15, Rs 529.51 crore in 2015-16 and Rs 405.39 crore in 2016-17. Expenditure details from Mukhtar Abbas Naqvi, Minister of Minority Affairs, Lok Sabha Unstarred

Question No. 915 answered on 07.02.2018 and General V.K. Singh (retd.), Minister of State for External Affairs, Lok Sabha Unstarred Question No. 4282 answered on 21.03.2018. For the Supreme Court's full Haj verdict see, *Union of India & Ors vs Rafique Shaikh Bhikan & Anr* on 30 April 2012, Special Leave Petition (Civil) No. 28609 of 2011 with Special Leave Petition (Civil) Nos 33190-33217 of 2011 and Transfer Petition (Civil) No. 191 of 2012. Full judgment available on: https://indiankanoon.org/doc/124837377/.

27. Interview with a long-standing UP MLA who spoke on the condition of anonymity, 9 and 10 June 2020.
28. Interview with Hemant Chouhan, gram _andhi_, Shahpur Bans Must village, Saharanpur district, UP, 17 June 2020.
29. Ibid.
30. Data from PMAY-G, Awassoft Dashboard, 'C2- Category-wise houses sanctioned and completed', 17 December 2020, https://rhreporting.nic.in/netiay/SocialProgressReport/Categorywisehouses completedreport.aspx.
31. PMMY was launched on 8 April 2015, for providing loans up to Rs 10 lakh to non-corporate, non-farm small/micro enterprises. These Mudra loans are given by commercial banks, RRBs, small finance banks, MFIs and NBFCs. *Mudra Yojana Annual Report 2019-2020*, p. 16.
32. Quoted in PTI, 'Mukhtar Abbas Naqvi: Lone Muslim face in Modi govt. 2.0', *India Today*, 31 May 2019, https://www.indiatoday.in/fyi/story/mukhtar-abbas-naqvi-lone-muslim-face-modi-govt-2-1538945-2019-05-31.
33. Narendra Modi's speech in Dhanbad, 12 December 2019. Full text in Hindi available at: https://www.narendramodi.in/text-of-pm-modi-s-speech-at-public-meeting-in-dhanbad-jharkhand-547632.
34. PTI, 'India's Muslim neighbours among 23 countries that have banned triple talaq', *Hindustan Times*, 19 September 2018, https://www.hindustantimes.com/india-news/india-s-muslim-neighbours-among-23-countries-that-have-banned-triple-talaq/story-J8b9HkOCwdMAIWyscwxZMK.html.
35. Asaduddin Owaisi, 'Present generation is lucky to see this Indian team with three good pacers', *The Indian Express*, 21 May 2019, https://indianexpress.com/article/opinion/present-generation-is-lucky-to-see-this-indian-team-with-three-good-pacers-5739334/.
36. On 10 December 2018; video at: https://twitter.com/ANI/status/1072044067423440896?s=20.
37. Gulam Jeelani, 'How Asaduddin is emerging as the rising star of Muslim politics in India', 19 November 2020, https://www.moneycontrol.com/news/politics/how-asaduddin-owaisis-aimim-champions-the-rise-of-muslim-politics-in-india-6135651.html. For further background on AIMIM, also see Rochana Bajpai, Adnan Farooqui, 'Non-extremist out-bidding: Muslim leadership in majoritarian India', *Nationalism and Ethic Politics*, Vol. 24, No. 3, 2018, pp. 276–298; Mahtab Alam, 'Love and hate in Hyderabad: The incendiary political life of Akbaruddin

Owaisi', 11 December 2018, https://thewire.in/politics/love-and-hate-in-hyderabad-the-fiery-political-life-of-akbaruddin-owaisi.

38. This was the charge by Pawan Khera, Congress spokesperson, in a TV debate hosted by Rajdeep Sardesai on India Today TV, 10 November 2020, https://www.youtube.com/watch?v=U1Xz5K29Igk.
39. Nalin Mehta and Sanjeev Singh's interview with Asaduddin Owaisi, broadcast on 'Elections with Times—Owaisi: Telangana's Kingmaker', *The Times of India*, 30 November 2018, https://timesofindia.indiatimes.com/videos/news/_andhi-telanganas-kingmaker/videoshow/66874909.cms.
40. Ibid.
41. It won 1,07, 779 votes (13.46 per cent) in Sant Kabir Nagar, 73,235 (12.1 per cent) in Gonda, 79,801 (10.85 per cent) in Domariyaganj, 67,897 (8.79 per cent) in Basti and 44,691 votes (7.38 per cent) in Shrawasti.
42. Owaisi's 22 July 2008 speech in Lok Sabha on the nuclear deal, where he specifically took umbrage at the _andhi_ation_ion of Indian Muslims as being against the deal as a 'canard', is available on: https://www.youtube.com/watch?v=gjxxYoHnIJI.
43. Mohamad Siddique, 'AIMIM's MP Owaisi to Support UPA', 20 July 2008, https://www.rediff.com/news/2008/jul/20upavote3.htm.
44. Special Correspondent, 'MIM withdraws support to UPA, Kiran government', *The Hindu*, 12 November 2012, https://www.thehindu.com/news/national/_andhi-pradesh/mim-withdraws-support-to-upa-kiran-government/article4090292.ece.
45. For exact seat break-up of Muslim-significant seats in Bihar in 2020, see *TOI* Data Hub: https://timesofindia.indiatimes.com/elections/assembly-elections/bihar/constituency-map.
46. XVII Lok Sabha records. Research by author.
47. Yogi Adityanath's speech on 28 November 2020. Video clip available at: https://twitter.com/ANI/status/1332675702580101122?s=20. For a background on the idea of Bhagyanagar and the Bhagyalakshmi temple, adjacent to Charminar, see Sreenivas Janyala, 'A Hyderabad temple, And the city's name', *The Indian Express*, 1 December 2020; Rohini Swamy, 'Yogi is wrong: There is not a shred of evidence to prove Hyderabad was called Bhagyanagar', 2 December 2020, https://theprint.in/statedraft/yogi-is-wrong-theres-not-a-shred-of-evidence-to-prove-hyderabad-was-called-bhagyanagar/160024/.
48. Sreenivas Janyala, 'Massive BJP surge in Hyderabad GHMC election results, says Telangana next', *The Indian Express*, 6 December 2020.
49. Shruti Tomar, 'MP plans law against "love jihad" with 5-year jail term', *Hindustan Times*, 18 November 2020.
50. Vatsala Gaur, Aman Sharma, 'UP clears ordinance "to stop love-jihad" provision for 1-5 year jail', *Economic Times*, 24 November 2020.
51. 'Love jihad: Reality or rhetoric?', *Organiser*, 7 September 2014.
52. ET Bureau, 'Kerala HC asks govt to frame laws to stop "love jihad"', *Economic Times*, 10 December 2009, https://economictimes.indiatimes.com/news/

politics-and-nation/kerala-hc-asks-govt-to-frame-laws-to-stop-love-jihad/articleshow/5320856.cms.

53. Christophe Jaffrelot, 'Law of unfreedom', *The Indian Express*, 26 November 2020.
54. For an overview of anti-conversion laws in Indian states, see James Andrew Huff, 'Religious freedom in India and analysis of the constitutionality of anti-conversion laws', *Rutgers Journal of Law and & Religion*, 10(2), 1(4), 2009, archived at https://perma.cc/7Z7Y-9U8Q; Laura Dudley Jenkins, 'Legal limits on religious conversion in India', *Law and Contemporary Problems*, 109, 113 (2008), http://scholarship.law.duke.edu/cgi/viewcontent.cgi?article=1469&context=lcp.
55. Sonam Joshi, 'Tied up in a knotty law, some interfaith couples opt to convert', *The Times of India*, 30 November 2020, https://timesofindia.indiatimes.com/india/tied-up-in-a-knotty-law-some-interfaith-couples-opt-to-convert/articleshow/79483259.cms. The Special Marriage Act, 1954 enshrines the provision of civil marriage for all Indians, irrespective of religion or faith followed by either party. One does not have to be interfaith to marry under this Act. The legislation is for everyone. However, it is primarily used by interfaith couples (and a small number of atheists) or those marrying across caste divides and impacts them the most.
56. Christophe Jaffrelot, 'Law of unfreedom', *The Indian Express*, 26 November 2020.
57. For an analysis of the legal issues raised by the Uttar Pradesh Prohibition of Unlawful Conversion of Religion Ordinance No. 21 of 2020, see, for instance, the questions raised by former IPS officer (former DGP Kerala) N.C. Asthana, 'Legal howlers in UP's "anti-conversion" law expose its real intent', *The Wire*, 3 December 2020, https://thewire.in/communalism/legal-howlers-in-ups-anti-conversion-law-expose-its-real-intent.
58. Rajesh Kumar Pandey, 'Allahabad HC upholds the right to choose partner irrespective of religion', *The Times of India*, 25 November 2020.

CHAPTER 6 What the BJP Says

1. A further 46 million listed English as their third language. Census 2011 data, from Office of the Registrar General and Census Commissioner of India, https://censusindia.gov.in/2011Census/Language_MTs.html.
2. Ibid.
3. *Kamal Sandesh* is a fortnightly magazine published by the BJP in both English and Hindi. It is published by the Dr Mookerjee Smruti Nyas from New Delhi, along with twenty-one other magazines, for the BJP. In 2017, the BJP claimed the magazine had a circulation of 8,00,000. See http://www.kamalsandesh.org/about-kamal-sandesh/. Circulation figures from Simontini Bhattacharjee's interview with Amit Shah: 'We are a party of ideology', *Millennium Post*, 10 July 2017, http://www.millenniumpost.in/opinion/we-are-a-party-of-ideology-251695.
4. *Organiser*, an English weekly, was launched as an RSS mouthpiece in July 1947, followed by the Hindi-language *Panchjanya*, in January 1948. Published by Bharat

Prakashan (Delhi) Ltd, it claims a readership of 5 lakh for its print edition and has a large digital presence. For a short background on various RSS publications, see Walter K. Andersen, Shridhar D. Damle, *The RSS: A View to the Inside* (New Delhi: Penguin/Viking, 2018), p. 25. Also see https://www.organiser.org/encyc/2019/8/23/About-Us.html.

5. *Congress Sandesh* was launched by the Congress as an official magazine in 1999. It started as a monthly in both English and Hindi, but since 2018 has been published sporadically. See https://www.inc.in/en/congress-sandesh/pdf/archives. In 2019, a party leader estimated its circulation to be 20,000: Sanjay K. Jha, 'Congress mouthpiece falls silent', *The Telegraph*, 1 January 2019, https://www.telegraphindia.com/india/congress-mouthpiece-falls-silent/cid/1680618.
6. The BJP won three of seventy seats in the Delhi state assembly election in February 2015, with 32.19 per cent vote share. It won eight of seventy seats, with 38.51 per cent vote share in the Delhi assembly election of February 2015. ECI data, Statistical Reports on General Election 2015 to the Legislative Assembly of NCT of Delhi, https://eci.gov.in/files/file/3878-delhi-2015/ and https://eci.gov.in/files/file/12027-general-legislative-election-2020/.
7. Arun Jaitley, 'Is Congress becoming ideologyless? Is anti-Modism its only ideology?', https://www.bjp.org/en/pressreleasesdetail/304037/Article-Is-Congress-Becoming-Ideologyless-Is-Anti-Modism-its-only-ideology-by-Union-Minister-Shri-Arun-Jaitley, 13 June 2018.
8. There is a paradox here: families, kin, clans remain at the heart of party politics for most Indian political parties. At the apex levels of party _andhi_ation, the exceptions to this generally have been the BJP, the CPI-M and the early BSP under Kanshi Ram. See, for instance, the essays in Kanchan Chandra (ed.), *Democratic Dynasties: State, Party, and Family in Contemporary Indian Politics* (New York: Cambridge University Press, 2016). In the context of Rahul Gandhi and dynastic politics, see in particular the arguments by the sociologist Dipankar Gupta, 'How Modi won the status war: The sociology of a landslide', *Open*, 7 June 2019, https://openthemagazine.com/cover-stories/how-modi-won-the-status-war/. A similar argument has been made by the historian Ramachandra Guha, '5 reasons why _andh _andhi cannot take on Modi for PM', 18 August 2020, https://www.ndtv.com/opinion/why-my-assessment-of-rahul-gandhi-remains-unchanged-2281181.
9. Emphasis is mine. BJP Press Release, 'Salient points of speech of BJP national president, Shri Amit Shah addressing intellectuals meet at Budha Mal Castle, Palampur', Kangra, Himachal Pradesh, 4 May 2017, https://www.bjp.org/en/pressreleasesdetail/299215/Salient-points-of-speech-of-BJP-National-President-Shri-Amit-Shah-addressing-Intellectuals-meet-at-Budha-Mal-Castle-Palampur-Kangra-Himachal-Pradesh-.
10. BJP, '*Congressi netaon dvara Pradhan Mantri Modi ko kahe gaye apshabd*', 15 May 2018, https://www.bjp.org/en/pressreleasesdetail/303981/-.

11. See, for example, Saba Naqvi, 'It's jingles all the way', *Outlook*, 1 March 2004, https://www.outlookindia.com/magazine/story/its-jingles-all-the-way/223068.
12. For a background note on the three laws, see, for instance, the legislative briefs by PRS Legislative Research, available at: https://www.prsindia.org/ministry/agriculture-and-farmers-welfare.
13. Modi's address in a video call with farmer groups from Madhya Pradesh on 18 December 2020, https://twitter.com/narendramodi/status/1339913010031169536?s=20.
14. Modi announced the decision on Guru Nanak Jayanti, 19 November 2021, saying he was 'sorry' and that 'there must have been some deficiency in our efforts, due to which we could not explain the truth like the light of the lamp to some farmers'. The laws were repealed on 30 November in Parliament. Full video of Modi's speech announcing the law repeal is available at: https://youtu.be/q0grrP8ufuo.
15. Bharatiya Janata Party, National Council Meeting, 'Resolution on agriculture', 11–12 January 2019, https://www.bjp.org/en/speechdetail/239883/RESOLUTION-ON-AGRICULTURE-.
16. The eight-member National Farmers Commission, chaired by Prof. M.S. Swaminathan, was set up on 18 November 2004 by UPA-2 to assess the extent of India's agrarian crisis. It submitted five reports between 2004 and 2006, all of which are available at: https://ruralindiaonline.org/en/articles/all-reports-by-the-swaminathan-commission/. For a perspective on and succinct explanation of how the MSP formula at 1.5 times the input cost was calculated and the debates around it, see Explained Desk, 'How the 1.5-times formula for crops MSP is calculated', *The Indian Express*, 2 December 2020, https://indianexpress.com/article/explained/explained-how-the-1-5-times-formula-for-crops-msp-is-calculated-7075865/.
17. By 31 August 2020, a total of 1.67 crore farmers, 1.44 lakh traders and 83,958 commission agents and 1722 farmer producer organisations (FPOs) have been registered on eNAM platform. A total trade value of Rs. 1,04,313 crore had been recorded on eNAM platform. PIB Delhi, Ministry of Agriculture, 'Success rate of E-NAM', 18 September 2020. https://pib.gov.in/PressReleaseIframePage.aspx?PRID=1656145.
18. Bharatiya Janata Party, National Council Meeting, 'Resolution on agriculture', 11–12 January 2019, https://www.bjp.org/en/speechdetail/239883/RESOLUTION-ON-AGRICULTURE-. For more details, also see PIB, Ministry of Agriculture and Farmers Welfare, 'Pulses and oilseeds amounting to Rs 44,142 crore procured from farmers during 2014-15 to 2018-19', 4 December 2018, https://pib.gov.in/newsite/PrintRelease.aspx?relid=186101.
19. Bharatiya Janata Party Press Release, 'Salient points of press conference of BJP national president Shri Amit Shah at Sindhu Bhawan, Gandhidham, Kutch (Gujarat)', 4 November 2017, https://www.bjp.org/en/pressreleasesdetail/300029/Salient-points-of-Press-Conference-of-BJP-National-President-Shri-Amit-Shah-at-Sindhu-Bhawan-Gandhidham-Kutch-Gujarat-.

20. BJP Press Release, 'Dear Congressmen and your other pseudo-secular friends, please note what Gandhiji has said on proselytization, cow slaughter', 6 October 2008, https://www.bjp.org/en/pressreleasesdetail/281620/Dear-Congressmen-and-your-other-pseudo-secular-friends-please-note-whatGandhiji-has-said-on-proselytization-cow-slaughter.
21. BJP Press Release, 'Salient points of BJP national president, Shri Amit Shah addressing "Haridwar-Tehri" Lok Sabha Trishakti Sammelan in Dehradun (Uttarakhand) and Booth Presidents Sammelan of Western India', 2 February 2019, https://www.bjp.org/en/pressreleasesdetail/992901/Salient-points-of-BJP-National-President-Shri-Amit-Shah-addressing-Haridwar-Tehri-Lok-Sabha-Trishakti-Sammelan-in-Dehradun-Uttarakhand-and-Booth-Presidents-Sammelan-of-Western-.
22. Ibid.
23. See full text of the Supreme Court of India's Ayodhya judgement on 9 November 2019. Reproduced here: https://www.scribd.com/document/434115991/Supreme-Court-judgment-in-Ayodhya-title-dispute-case#from_embed.
24. I have analysed the implications of this elsewhere; see Nalin Mehta, 'Party of Ram', *The Times of India*, 8 August 2020, https://timesofindia.indiatimes.com/blogs/academic-interest/party-of-ram-bjp-has-won-the-culture-war-on-ram-time-now-to-focus-on-the-economy/. Also see Conclusion.

CHAPTER 7 Modi@Digital

1. An earlier version of this chapter was published in Nalin Mehta, 'Digital politics in India's 2019 general elections', *Economic & Political Weekly*, Vol. 54, Issue 28, December 2019. It was also presented at the National University of Singapore, ISAS-Konrad-Adenauer-Stiftung panel on 'Role of digital media in the 2019 general elections' and a closed-door seminar on 27–28 June 2019; SOBA FG Pierce Memorial Symposium in Delhi, India Islamic Centre, July 2019; and 'Review of general election 2019' at Indian Institute of Democratic Leadership, Rambhau Mhalgi Prabodhini, Thane, 24 September 2019.
2. 'Narenda Modi G+ Hangout', 31 August 2012, https://www.youtube.com/watch?time_continue=12&v=OzUTCXKnmZg&feature=emb_logo.
3. Ibid.
4. TNN, 'Narendra Modi on Google Hangout, Ajay Devgn to host event', 31 August 2012, https://www.gadgetsnow.com/social/Narendra-Modi-on-Google-Hangout-Ajay-Devgn-to-host-event/articleshow/16068578.cms?utm_source=contentofinterest&utm_medium=text&utm_campaign=cppst.
5. '3 days to go to "Hangout" with Narendra Modi', *NarendraModi.in*, 27 August 2012, https://www.narendramodi.in/amp/6-days-to-go-to-hangout-with-narendra-modi.
6. Modi crossed Shashi Tharoor's following on Twitter in July 2013. As the BJP's recently appointed poll campaign chief, he reached 18,26,469 followers on Twitter,

while Tharoor moved to second position with 18,21,868 followers. India Today Online Desk, 'Narendra Modi topples Tharoor to become most popular on Twitter', *India Today*, 4 July 2013, https://www.indiatoday.in/india/gujarat/story/narendra-modi-topples-tharoor-to-become-most-popular-on-twitter-169087-2013-07-04.

7. Rahul Gandhi joined Twitter on 7 May 2015 as @officeofrg, https://www.livemint.com/Politics/NXjnawAnPuxmqiMcXapqxH/Rahul-Gandhi-joins-Twitter.html. He later moved to tweeting in his own name on 16 May 2018. *TOI* Online, 'Rahul Gandhi changes his Twitter handle', 16 May 2018, https://timesofindia.indiatimes.com/india/rahul-gandhi-changes-his-twitter-handle/articleshow/63340587.cms.
8. 'Address by Shri Narendra Modi at the Google Big Tent Active Summit on Technology in Politics', *NarendraModi.in*, 21 March 2013, https://www.narendramodi.in/address-by-shri-narendra-modi-at-the-google-big-tent-active-summit-on-technology-in-politics-2767.
9. See, for example, Peter Manuel, *Cassette Culture: Popular Culture and Technology in North India* (Chicago: Chicago University Press, 1993); Nalin Mehta, *India on Television: How Satellite News Channels Changed the Ways We Think and Act* (New Delhi: HarperCollins, 2008).
10. For background on the use of audio cassettes by the BJP in the 1980s, see 'BJP MP Uma Bharati and Sadhvi Ritambhara become a stumbling block to L.K. Advani's plans', *India Today*, 15 January 1991, https://www.indiatoday.in/magazine/indiascope/story/19910115-bjp-mp-uma-bharati-and-sadhvi-ritambhara-become-a-stumbling-block-to-l.k.-advanis-plans-813895-1991-01-15; Kaveree Bamzai, 'The Soldier Sadhvi', 25 April 2019, *Open*, https://openthemagazine.com/shorts/the-soldier-sadhvi/; Tanika Sarkar, 'The women of the Hindutva brigade', *Bulletin of Concerned Asian Scholars*, Vol. 25, Issue 4, pp. 16–24, DOI: 10.1080/14672715.1993.10416135. For an in-depth analysis on how the BJP used television and technology to change the discourse of the Ram Temple, Arvind Rajagopal, *Politics after Television: Hindu Nationalism and the Reshaping of the Public in India* (New York: Cambridge University Press, 2001). Also see Nalin Mehta, *India on Television: How Satellite News Channels Have Changed the Way We Think and Act* (New Delhi: HarperCollins, 2008), chapter on pre-satellite TV in India, pp. 22–55 and chapter on how Modi appropriated satellite TV news as Gujarat chief minister in 2002, pp. 274–298.
11. I am grateful to Mahesh Rangarajan for this reference. Also see Kavita Karan, 'Political communication in the 1991 general election in India with special reference to Andhra Pradesh', PhD dissertation submitted to the London School of Economics, 1997, pp. 100, 168, http://etheses.lse.ac.uk/2230/1/U615177.pdf.
12. For an academic overview of ideas on two-step communication, first introduced by the sociologists Paul Lazarsfeld, Bernard Berelson and Hazel Gaudet in 1944, elaborated on by Elihu Katz and Lazarsfeld in 1955, see Elihu Katz, 'The two-step flow of communication: An up-to-date report on a hypothesis', *Political Opinion Quarterly*, Vol. 21, Issue 1, 1957, pp. 61–78, https://doi.org/10.1086/266687. Reproduced on

University of Pennsylvania Scholarly Commons, Departmental Papers, https://repository.upenn.edu/cgi/viewcontent.cgi?article=1279&context=asc_papers. In recent years, digital media has led to many media scholars taking up the one-stop flow model of communication, where information is directly sent to recipients without an intermediary, somewhat like the 'Hypodermic Needle'/'Magic Bullet' idea of communication that became fashionable in the 1930s with the rise of mass radio. For an analysis of this school of thought, see W. Lance Bennett, Jarol B. Manheim, 'The one-step flow of communication', *The Annals of the American Academy of Political and Social Science*, Vol. 608, No. 1, pp. 213–232, https://doi.org/10.1177/0002716206292266.

13. See NaMo app e-greeting posted online by Radhakrishnan K. Koppillil, chairman, board of governors, IIT Kanpur, and former chairman, Indian Space Research Organisation, on 29 August 2020, https://twitter.com/radhakr272/status/1299608051175927810?s=20.
14. Pt Deendayal Upadhyaya Prashikshan Mahabhiyan 2018, *Media Approach and Strategy: Quick Guidebook for Handling Media and Social Media* (New Delhi: BJP, 2018).
15. Canalys, 'Indian smartphone shipments up 10% to 137 million in 2018, unfazed by global decline', 7 February 2019, https://www.canalys.com/newsroom/indian-smartphone-shipments-up-10-to-137-million-in-2018-unfazed-by-global-decline. Also see PTI, 'India beats US to become 2nd-largest smartphone market in Q3: Canalys', *Business Standard*, 9 November 2018, https://www.business-standard.com/article/current-affairs/india-pips-us-to-become-2nd-largest-smartphone-market-in-q3-canalys-118110801258_1.html.
16. 'Data usage per smartphone is the highest in India—Ericsson', *Ericsson.com*, 19 June 2019, https://www.ericsson.com/en/press-releases/2/2019/6/data-usage-per-smartphone-is-the-highest-in-india--ericsson. By 2019, India accounted for 12 per cent of the world's internet users, China 21 per cent and USA 8 per cent. See Mary Meeker's Internet Trends 2019 Report, 11 June 2019, https://www.bondcap.com/report/itr19/#view/1.
17. See, for example, Robin Jeffrey, Assa Doron, 'Mobile-izing: Democracy, organization and India's first "mass mobile phone" elections', *The Journal of Asian Studies*, Vol. 71, No. 1, February 2012, pp. 63–80.
18. Telecom Regulatory Authority of India (TRAI) in mid-2019 reported 581.51 million internet users in India. Information Note to the Press (Press Release No. 49/2019), TRAI, New Delhi, 19 July 2019, https://www.trai.gov.in/sites/default/files/PR_No.49of2019.pdf; Information Note to the Press (Press Release No. 37/2014), TRAI, 7 July 2014, https://trai.gov.in/sites/default/files/PR-TSD-May%2C%2014.pdf.

    By 21 August 2019, TRAI was reporting that wireless data subscribers had increased to 578.21 million, https://trai.gov.in/sites/default/files/PR_No.61of2019.pdf.

19. India had 91,05,12,091 voters in the 2019 general election. Source: ECI, https://eci.gov.in/files/file/10991-2-highlights/.
20. Google estimated average mobile data consumption per user to be about 8 GB/month in early 2019. Google, *Unlocking Digital for Bharat* (Delhi: Google, 2019). Data from Bain & Company, quoted in the report, p. 2.
21. CSDS, *Social Media and Political Behavior* (New Delhi: Lokniti-CSDS, 2019), pp. 11–22.
22. Saba Naqvi, 'Mobile politics: Why I think Lok Sabha 2019 was not a post-Mandal but a post-Jio election', *DailyO*, 19 June 2019, https://www.dailyo.in/politics/bjp-wins-lok-sabha-2019-mobile-revolution-in-india-narendra-modi-rahul-gandhi/story/1/31162.html.
23. Author's interview with Caesar Sengupta, Google vice president, Next Billion Users and Digital Payments, at Google HQ in May 2019, published as '95% of video consumption in India is in regional languages; Hindi internet users will outnumber English by 2021', *The Times of India*, 17 May 2019, https://timesofindia.indiatimes.com/blogs/academic-interest/95-of-video-consumption-in-india-is-in-regional-languages-hindi-internet-users-will-outnumber-english-users-by-2021/.
24. Author's interview with Ajit Mohan, vice president and managing director, Facebook India, published as 'There is clearly a shift from offline to online … people are looking for richer experiences on virtual presence', *The Times of India*, 22 July 2020, https://timesofindia.indiatimes.com/blogs/academic-interest/there-is-clearly-a-shift-from-offline-to-online-people-are-looking-for-richer-experiences-on-virtual-presence/.
25. Data from Google, Political Advertising for India, https://transparencyreport.google.com/political-ads/region/IN?creative_by_advertiser=region:IN;q:;start:1550534400000;end:1558569599999; spend:;impressions:;type:;sort:3&lu=creative_by_advertiser; Facebook Ad Library Report, https://www.facebook.com/ads/library/report.
26. *The Times of India*, 'BJP earned five times more than Congress in 2017', 29 March 2019, https://timesofindia.indiatimes.com/india/bjp-earned-five-times-more-than-congress-in-2017-18/articleshow/68624311.cms.
27. Bharti Jain, TNN, 'BJP spent over Rs 1,200 crore in polls to Lok Sabha, four state assemblies last year', *The Times of India*, 16 January 2020, https://timesofindia.indiatimes.com/india/bjp-spent-over-rs-1200-cr-on-polls-to-lok-sabha-four-assemblies-last-year/articleshow/73284418.cms; TNN, 'Cash-strapped Congress spent Rs 820 crore on 2019 Lok Sabha polls', *The Times of India*, 8 November 2019, https://timesofindia.indiatimes.com/india/cash-strapped-congress-spent-rs-820-crore-on-2019-lok-sabha-polls/articleshow/71963145.cms. Also see PTI, 'BJP declares Rs 1027 crore in FY-18: Report', *The Economic Times*, 17 December 2018, https://m.economictimes.com/news/politics-and-nation/bjp-declares-rs-1027-crore-income-in-fy18-report/articleshow/67133806.cms.

28. Newly Purnell, Jeff Horwitz, 'Facebook's hate speech rules collide with Indian politics', *Wall Street Journal*, 14 August 2020, https://www.wsj.com/articles/facebook-hate-speech-india-politics-muslim-hindu-modi-zuckerberg-11597423346. Also see Jeff Horowitz, Newly Purnell, 'Facebook executive supported India's Modi, disparaged opposition in internal messages', *Wall Street Journal*, 30 August 2020, https://www.wsj.com/articles/facebook-executive-supported-indias-modi-disparaged-opposition-in-internal-messages-11598809348. Ankhi Das, the Facebook executive at the centre of the controversy, stepped down from her role in October 2020, saying she wanted to pursue her 'personal interest in public service', PTI, 'Facebook's Head of Public Policy Ankhi Das quits company', 27 October 2020, https://timesofindia.indiatimes.com/business/india-business/facebooks-india-head-of-public-policy-ankhi-das-quits-company/articleshow/78894033.cms.
29. Full letter posted online by *Bar and Bench*, https://twitter.com/barandbench/status/1300797901988274178?s=20. There was a similar spat between Twitter and the Government of India in the backdrop of India ushering in a new regulatory framework for digital media in early 2021. The Ministry of Electronics and IT notified the new Information Technology (Intermediary Guidelines and Digital Media Ethics Code) Rules 2021 on 25 February 2021, and they came into effect from 26 May 2021. Ahead of this, Twitter on 21 May tagged a tweet by BJP spokesperson Sambit Patra as 'manipulated media'. The tweet referred to an alleged Congress social media 'toolkit' against the Modi government's handling of the COVID-19 pandemic—which the Congress denied as 'fake'. The IT Ministry condemned Twitter's action as 'prejudged', 'biased' and 'arbitrary' while the Congress said it was 'vindicated'. After Delhi Police asked Twitter to explain the grounds for its tag, and officers from its Special Cell visited two Twitter offices to serve a notice, Twitter publicly argued that there was 'a potential threat to freedom of expression' while the IT ministry accused it of trying to 'undermine the legal system' and attempting to 'dictate its terms to the world's largest democracy'. Twitter went to the Delhi High Court to challenge the new digital media rules. Separately, the rules have also been challenged in the same court by WhatsApp, which termed them 'unconstitutional', Press Trust of India, The Wire, Quint, The News Minute, Digital News Publishers Association (in Madras High Court) and News Broadcasters Association (in Kerala High Court). The Union government informed the Delhi High Court that Twitter was in 'abject non-compliance' with the IT Rules regarding mandated requisite appointments of grievance officers. The court on 28 July 2021 ruled that this was 'not acceptable' and asked Twitter to comply in full. The matter was sub-judice at the time of writing. Ravi Shankar Prasad was replaced as IT Minister by Ashwini Vaishnav in a cabinet reshuffle on 7 July 2021.

    For details on new IT and digital media rules, see PIB, Ministry of Electronics and IT, 'Government notifies Information Technology (Intermediary Guidelines and Digital Media Ethics Code) Rules 2021', 25 February 2021, https://pib.gov.in/PressReleseDetailm.aspx? PRID=1700749. Twitter's public statement on the issue is available at: https://twitter.com/Policy/status/1397818577432891394?s=20; the IT ministry's response is available at: https://twitter.com/GoI_MeitY/status/139789548 6904836096?s=20; also see Liz Mathew, Aashish Aryan, Manoj C.G., 'Twitter marks BJP leader's post on Cong "toolkit" manipulated; IT ministry steps in, calls it biased', *The Indian Express*, 22 May 2021, https://indianexpress.com/article/india/sambit-patra-tweet-manipulated-media-toolkit-twitter-7324737/;

PTI, 'Delhi High Court expresses displeasure over non-compliance of IT Rules by Twitter', *The Times of India*, 28 July 2021, https://timesofindia.indiatimes.com/business/india-business/delhi-high-court-expresses-displeasure-over-non-compliance-of-it-rules-by-twitter/articleshow/84823291.cms. For WhatsApp's legal positioning, see Pankaj Doval, Abhinav Garg, 'WhatsApp moves High Court against new IT Rules, terms them unconstitutional', *The Times of India*, 27 May 2021, https://bit.ly/3s9B4c3. For more on the legal challenges to the IT Rules, see Express News Service, 'NBA challenges new IT Rules in Kerala HC', *The Indian Express*, 10 July 2021, https://indianexpress.com/article/india/nba-challenges-new-it-rules-in-kerala-hc-7397487/; Akshaya Nath, Nalini Sharma, 'Madras High Court issues notice to Centre on Digital News Publishers Association's plea against new IT Rules', *India Today*, 23 June 2021, https://www.indiatoday.in/law/story/madras-hc-issues-notice-to-centre-on-digital-news-publishers-association-s-plea-against-new-it-rules-1818600-2021-06-23.

30. For a perspective on this larger debate, see, for instance, *The Economist*, 'Big tech and free speech: Silicon Valley should not be given control over free speech', 16 January 2021, https://www.economist.com/leaders/2021/01/16/big-tech-and-censorship; and Emily Bell, 'Off-label: How tech platforms decide what counts as journalism', in the 'Existential Issue', *Columbia Journalism Review*, 3 May 2021, https://existential.cjr.org/who/tech-platforms-labels/.

31. See, for example, the argument by BJP MP and former Union minister for information and broadcasting, Rajyavardhan Singh Rathore that the attacks on hate speech are wrongly framed by the Left to malign the Right. 'Facebook is in the dock; we need to resist Left-Congress assault on free speech', *The Indian Express*, 17 August 2020. Or the debate in the Parliamentary Committee on IT, where its chairman, Congress MP Shashi Tharoor, summoned Facebook for an explanation, but was opposed by BJP MPs on grounds of procedure and bias. See Liz Mathew, 'Explained: Why Shashi Tharoor could summon Facebook before parliamentary panel', *The Indian Express*, 19 August 2020, https://indianexpress.com/article/explained/simply-put-house-panel-summons-power-6560374/. Similarly, when the Pegasus Project, a collaborative investigation by seventeen news organisations in ten countries, alleged in July 2021 that mobiles phones of scores of people in India could have been compromised by military-grade spyware software produced by an Israeli company and only made available to governments or government agencies, and the government refused to accept the opposition's demand for debate in Parliament's monsoon session, government officials skipped a scheduled meeting

of the Parliamentary Standing Committee on IT and BJP MPs refused to sign the committee's attendance register forcing the meeting to be called off due to a lack of quorum. The Supreme Court appointed a three member committee to examine the Pegasus allegations on 27 October 2021. Special Correspondent, 'Government officials skip house panel meeting on Pegasus', *The Hindu*, 28 July 2021, https://www.thehindu.com/news/national/parliamentary-panel-not-allowed-to-discuss-pegasus/article35588921.ece. Also see Manoj C.G., 'Last week of house session, no sign of thaw, opposition wants to be heard on Pegasus,' *The Indian Express*, 9 August 2021, https://indianexpress.com/article/india/last-week-of-house-session-no-sign-of-thaw-opposition-wants-to-be-heard-on-pegasus-7444821/.

32. https://twitter.com/sagarikaghose/status/8141129179?lang=en.
33. For more details on these Times of India Online surveys, see https://timesofindia.indiatimes.com/india/mega-times-group-poll-71-9-of-indians-say-they-will-vote-for-narendra-modi-as-pm-again-in-2019/articleshow/64324490.cms; https://timesofindia.indiatimes.com/india/times-group-survey-79-of-people-say-they-will-vote-for-modi-in-2019/articleshow/62090389.cms; https://timesofindia.indiatimes.com/india/timesmegapoll-83-say-modi-led-government-is-most-likely-outcome-after-2019-general-election/articleshow/68086731.cms.
34. Kunal Pradhan, Jayant Sriram, 'Rise of the cyber Hindu', 1 November 2013, *India Today*, https://internetdemocracy.in/media/rise-of-the-cyber-hindu/.
35. Sanjeev Ratna Singh, 'Narendra Modi vs Rahul Gandhi on Twitter: A comparison of social media strategies for political mobilisation (2017–19)', *International Research Journal of Management Sociology and Humanity*, Vol. 10, Issue 5, 2019, pp. 371–384, http://www.irjmsh.com/Artical_details?id=8381; Sanjeev Ratna Singh, 'BJP vs Congress on Twitter: A comparison of social media strategies for political mobilisation during late 2018 assembly elections', *International Journal of Research and Analytical Reviews*, Vol. 6, Issue 2, June 2019, pp. 383–397, http://www.ijrar.org/IJRAR19K5665.pdf; Sanjeev Ratna Singh, 'BJP vs opposition parties on Twitter: A comparison of social media strategies for political mobilisation during 2017 Uttar Pradesh and Gujarat assembly elections', *International Journal of Advanced Science and Technology*, Vol. 28, No. 9, November 2019, http://sersc.org/journals/index.php/IJAST/article/view/677.
36. Joyojeet Pal, 'Booths, brickbats, brands, and Bollywood: Social media in the 2019 Indian general election', Presentation at the Institute of South Asian Studies, National University of Singapore, 28 June 2019. Also see Joyojeet Pal, 'How #BJP fused with #StrongIndia in #2019', *Mint*, 9 May 2019, https://www.livemint.com/elections/lok-sabha-elections/how-bjp-fused-with-strongindia-in-2019-1557414405626.html.
37. By 19 December 2019, Narendra Modi had 3,26,00,000 Instagram followers, while Rahul Gandhi had 9,32,000 followers. On Facebook, in December 2019, Modi had 4,40,44,370 followers while Rahul had 32,05,849 followers. Rahul Gandhi's Instagram account: https://www.instagram.com/rahulgandhi/?hl=en; Modi's Instagram account: https://www.instagram.com/narendramodi/?hl=en; Modi's

Facebook account: https://www.facebook.com/narendramodi/; Rahul Gandhi's Facebook account: https://www.facebook.com/rahulgandhi/.

38. By August 2020, Modi's YouTube followers had jumped to 7.32 million, while Rahul Gandhi's had jumped to 3,30,000. Rahul Gandhi's YouTube channel: https://www.youtube.com/channel/UC1DtEMePmr4O6F2do6BVI7A/playlists; Modi's YouTube channel: https://www.youtube.com/user/narendramodi/playlists; Modi's Pinterest account: https://in.pinterest.com/NarendraModi/.

39. Narendra Modi's LinkedIn account: https://www.linkedin.com/in/narendramodi/detail/recent-activity/posts/. Also see, Vardaan, 'PM Narendra Modi joins LinkedIn', 30 December 2014, https://www.indianweb2.com/2014/12/pm-narendra-modi-joins-linkedin.html; 'PM Modi joins LinkedIn? On lookout for a job?', 9 October 2014, https://www.thenewsminute.com/lives/347.

40. Narendra's Modi's LinkedIn post on 20 March 2014, https://www.linkedin.com/pulse/20140320073143-274826784-ict-for-one-nation-one-mission/.

41. Pt. Deendayal Upadhyaya Prashikshan Mahabhiyan 2018, BJP, *Media Approach and Strategy: Quick Guidebook for Handling Media and Social Media* (New Delhi: BJP, 2018).

42. Personal interview with Jairam Ramesh, Congress leader, MP and chief whip in the Rajya Sabha, 17 November 2019. Ramesh served as rural development minister in UPA-II and also, at various points, was minister of state for power, environment and forests, daily water and sanitation.

43. Personal interview with Amit Malviya, National Head, Information and Technology, BJP, 18 November 2019.

44. Personal interview with Joyojeet Pal, senior researcher, Microsoft, 15 November 2019.

45. Ibid.

46. Personal interview with Jairam Ramesh, Congress MP and chief whip in the Rajya Sabha, 17 November 2019.

47. BJP's Batman tweets are available at: https://twitter.com/BJP4India/status/1090826822697259008. Also see Neeta Sharma, '"PM Modi like Batman": BJP brags about Augusta Westland extraditions', 31 January 2019, https://www.ndtv.com/india-news/pm-narendra-modi-like-batman-bjp-brags-about-agustawestland-extraditions-1986011; Newsroom, 'Modi is Batman, at least according to BJP's Twitter handle', *HuffingtonPost*, 31 January 2019, https://www.huffingtonpost.in/entry/modi-is-batman-at-least-according-to-bjps-twitter-handle_in_5c52b30ae4b0ca92c6dd5165.

48. Personal interview with Jairam Ramesh, Congress MP and chief whip in the Rajya Sabha, 17 November 2019.

49. Kumar Uttam, 'BJP plans a WhatsApp campaign for 2019 Lok Sabha election', 29 September 2018, https://www.hindustantimes.com/india-news/bjp-plans-a-whatsapp-campaign-for-2019-lok-sabha-election/story-lHQBYbxwXHaChc7Akk6hcI.html.

50. PTI, '2019 polls: BJP to form chain of WhatsApp groups to strengthen communication between party workers', *The Economic Times*, https://economictimes.indiatimes.com/news/politics-and-nation/2019-polls-bjp-to-form-chain-of-whatsapp-groups-to-strengthen-communication-between-party-workers/articleshow/67219816.cms?from=mdr.
51. Ishita Ayan Dutt, Avishek Rakshit, 'BJP created 55,000 WhatsApp groups to take on Mamata', 4 June 2019, https://www.rediff.com/news/special/bjp-created-55000-whatsapp-groups-to-take-on-mamata/20190604.htm.
52. Chandrashekhar G., 'BJP's war room equipped with 20000 WhatsApp groups', *Deccan Chronicle*, 27 April 2018, https://www.deccanchronicle.com/nation/current-affairs/270418/bjps-war-room-equipped-with-20000-whatsapp-groups.html.
53. Author interview with Caesar Sengupta, Google vice president, Next Billion Users and Payments, 16 May 2019, Google Campus, Mountain View, California, published as '95% of video consumption in India is in regional languages, Hindi internet users will outnumber English users by 2021', *The Times of India*, 16 May 2019.
54. Joyojeet Pal, 'Elections 2019: What tweet for tat tells you about Rahul Gandhi', *Mint*, 224 April 2019, https://www.livemint.com/elections/lok-sabha-elections/elections-2019-what-tweet-for-tat-tells-you-about-rahul-gandhi-1556058743723.html.
55. A'ndre Gonawela, Joyojeet Pal, Udit Thawani, Elmer van der Vlugt, Wim Out, Priyank Chandra, 'Speaking their mind: Populist style and antagonistic messaging in the tweets of Donald Trump, Narendra Modi, Nigel Farage, and Geert Wilders', *Comput Supported Coop Work*, 27, 2018, pp. 293–326, http://joyojeet.people.si.umich.edu/wp-content/uploads/2018/05/Gonawela.pdf.
56. Ibid.
57. Ibid.
58. See Joyojeet Pal, Priyank Chandra, V.G. Vinod Vydiswaran, 'Twitter and the rebranding of Narendra Modi, *Economic & Political Weekly*, Vol. 51, Issue No. 8, 20 February 2016, https://www.epw.in/journal/2016/8/twitter-and-rebranding-narendra-modi.html Also see Joyojeet Pal, Anmol Panda, 'Narendra Modi matinee show: Inside India's celeb Twitter', *Mint*, 28 January 2019, https://www.livemint.com/politics/news/narendra-modi-matinee-show-inside-india-s-celeb-twitter-1548616373119.html.
59. Google, Political Advertising for India, https://transparencyreport.google.com/political-ads/region/IN?hl=en.
60. See TOI campaign tracker at: https://timesofindia.indiatimes.com/elections/campaigntracker.
61. Aman Sharma, 'New engagement platform: NaMo app a big campaign and feedback tool', *The Economic Times*, 20 March 2019, https://economictimes.indiatimes.com/news/elections/lok-sabha/india/new-engagement-platform-namo-app-a-big-campaign-and-feedback-tool/articleshow/68474625.cms.

62. See, for example, Venkat Ananth, 'When a project to empower left Congress stranded', *The Economic Times*, 17 June 2019, https://economictimes.indiatimes.com/news/politics-and-nation/when-a-project-to-empower-left-congress-stranded/articleshow/69818494.cms; Pankaj Vohra, 'Rahul's own team fed his PM hopes right up to poll defeat', *Sunday Guardian*, 15 June 2019, https://www.sundayguardianlive.com/news/rahuls-team-fed-pm-hopes-right-poll-defeat.
63. Betwa Sharma, 'How project "Shakti" misled Rahul and deepened Congress's Lok Sabha rout', *HuffingtonPost*, 30 May 2019, https://www.huffingtonpost.in/entry/bogus-app-rahul-gandhi-congresss-lok-sabha-rout_in_5cee2e83e4b0793c23476816.
64. Venkat Ananth, 'When a project to empower left Congress stranded', *The Economic Times*, 17 June 2019, https://economictimes.indiatimes.com/news/politics-and-nation/when-a-project-to-empower-left-congress-stranded/articleshow/69818494.cms?from=mdr.
65. Ibid.
66. Ibid.
67. Personal interview with Amit Malviya, National Head, Information and Technology, BJP, 18 November 2019.
68. Samarth Bansal, 'Narendra Modi app has a fake news problem', 27 January 2019, https://medium.com/disfact/narendra-modi-app-has-a-fake-news-problem-d60b514bb8f1, originally posted in DisFact.
69. See, for example, Swati Chaturvedi, *I am a Troll: Inside the Secret World of the BJP's Digital Army* (New Delhi: Juggernaut, 2016); Shivam Shankar Singh, *How to Win an Indian Election: What Political Parties Don't Want You to Know* (New Delhi: Ebury, 2019).
70. Personal interview with Amit Malviya, National Head, Information and Technology, BJP, 18 November 2019.
71. Amit Shah's speech, available on BJP YouTube, 'Shri Amit Shah addresses social media volunteers' meet in Kota, Rajasthan: 22.09.2018', https://www.youtube.com/watch?v=1OW7AQxpf2g.
72. Ibid.
73. 'Sonia Gandhi names interim Congress president after day long CWC meet', 10 August 2019, https://timesofindia.indiatimes.com/india/sonia-gandhi-named-interim-congress-president-after-day-long-cwc-meet/articleshow/70623738.cms.

CHAPTER 8 How the BJP Became the World's Largest Political Party

1. Vinay Sahasrabuddhe served as BJP vice president from August 2014 to September 2020. He also headed the BJP's organisational effort in Madhya Pradesh since 2014. He became a Rajya Sabha MP in 2016, was appointed president of the Indian

Council for Cultural Relations in 2018 and chairman of the Parliamentary Standing Committee on Human Resource Development in 2020. He headed the BJP's Training Cell during 1999–2009.

2. https://twitter.com/vinay1011/status/1247033508112949249?s=20. The research for this chapter was concluded in December 2020, and it covers the period until the end of the first phase of COVID-19 pandemic.
3. https://twitter.com/vinay1011/status/1246991332519772160?s=20.
4. https://twitter.com/vinay1011/status/1247070541296500736?s=20.
5. See, for example, Anirban Ganguly, Shiwanand Dwivedi, *Amit Shah and the March of the BJP* (New Delhi: Bloomsbury, 2019).
6. Madan Das Devi, then RSS joint general secretary, in interview to Rajesh Joshi, 'RSS dumping the BJP: "It's for the Future to Tell"', *Outlook*, 30 October 2000.
7. Swapan Dasgupta, 'Meshed in adolescence', *Telegraph*, 3 April 2009.
8. For background on the BJP/Jan Sangh–RSS relationship, see Craig Baxter, *The Jana Sangh: A Biography of an Indian Political Party* (Philadelphia: University of Pennsylvania Press, 1969); Walter K. Andersen, Shridhar D. Damle, *The RSS: A View from the Inside* (New Delhi: Penguin/Viking, 2018); Christophe Jaffrelot, *The Hindu Nationalist Movement and Indian Politics: 1925 to the 1990s* (New Delhi: Penguin, 1996) and Pralay Kanungo, 'Sangh and sarkar: The RSS power centre shifts from Nagpur to New Delhi', in Angana P. Chatterjee, Thomas Blom Hansen, Christophe Jaffrelot (eds), *Majoritarian State: How Hindu Nationalism Is Changing India* (New Delhi: HarperCollins, 2019), pp. 133–150.
9. This is how the BJP describes itself on its Twitter account: https://twitter.com/bjp4india. The party's National Executive officially celebrated this milestone in Bengaluru on 3 April 2015. Party spokesperson Prakash Javadekar claimed that the BJP now had the 'largest databank'. See https://youtu.be/eTgckcn5PNk.
10. 'Mahamantri Report' (2013–2016) submitted by Ram Lal, national general secretary of the BJP. Quoted in Anirban Ganguly, Shiwanand Dwivedi, *Amit Shah and the March of the BJP* (New Delhi: Bloomsbury, 2019), p. 116.
11. Chinese Communist Party data is based on numbers released by CCP Organisation Department and reported by Statista, https://www.statista.com/statistics/281378/number-of-chinese-communist-party-ccp-members-in-china/; Hudson Lockett, 'Chinese Communist Party's membership growth slows down', *Financial Times*, 30 June 2016, https://www.ft.com/content/3b92a4c4-876d-3d44-b547-a4b4fedd8524.
12. If we assume about fifteen workers per shakha, the RSS's 2014 membership would have been 6,74,730. At an average of fifty per shakha, this would have been 2.24 million. We have used the upper range of 100 per shakha on average for this analysis: 4.49 million. Shakha data from RSS annual reports.
13. On 31 March 2015, the BJP claimed a membership number of 8,67,00,000, whereas the CCP had 6,88,00,000 members. Data quoted in Anirban Ganguly, Shiwanand Dwivedi, *Amit Shah and the March of the BJP* (New Delhi: Bloomsbury, 2019), p. 116.

14. RSS data based on estimates by author calculated from RSS Annual Reports 2009–2019. RSS 1977–2003 data from Manini Chatterjee, 'Repackaging the RSS', *The Indian Express*, 16 March 2003. CCP data until 1988 from Stanley Rosen, 'The Chinese Communist Party and Chinese society: Popular attitudes toward party membership and the party's image', *The Australian Journal of Chinese Affairs*, July 1990, No. 24, July 1990, pp. 51–92; subsequent CCP data from Statista, https://www.statista.com/statistics/281378/number-of-chinese-communist-party-ccp-members-in-china/. BJP data as reported by the party in several public sources. 2019 numbers from PTI, 'BJP's strength to rise by 70 million, totalling 180 million: J.P. Nadda', 14 January 2020, *Business Standard*, https://www.business-standard.com/article/pti-stories/bjp-to-add-7-cr-new-members-totalling-18-cr-nadda-119082900946_1.html; 2015 numbers from PTI, 'BJP membership near 18 crore, only seven countries have more population: JP Nadda', *The Times of India*, 29 August 2015, https://timesofindia.indiatimes.com/india/bjp-membership-near-18-crore-only-seven-countries-have-more-population-jp-nadda/articleshow/70897742.cms, BJP press conference, 31 March 2015: https://www.youtube.com/watch?v=qfXkU_HZOp8; 2014 numbers from 'Saath aaye desh banaaye: Narendra Modi', *Kamal Sandesh*, 16–30 November 2014, http://ofbjpuk.org/wp-content/uploads/2014/12/ks_nov_02_204_e.pdf; 1980–1985 comparison is over a year-range: RSS estimates from 1985, BJP from 1980 and CCP from 1982.
15. BJP YouTube channel, 'Press conference by Shri Amit Shah at BJP head office', New Delhi, 17 May 2019, https://www.youtube.com/watch?v=_h3eIji3P6k. Shah spoke in Hindi; translation mine.
16. 'Narendra Modi launches BJP's membership drive', 1 November 2014, https://www.narendramodi.in/pm-narendra-modi-launches-bjps-membership-drive-5826; 'BJP launches membership drive, PM first member', *Outlook*, 1 November 2014, https://www.outlookindia.com/newswire/story/bjp-launches-membership-drive-pm-first-member/866247; PTI, 'PM Modi launches BJP membership drive from Varanasi', *The Times of India*, 6 July 2019, https://timesofindia.indiatimes.com/india/pm-modi-launches-bjps-membership-drive-from-his-ls-constituency/articleshow/70104952.cms.
17. See, for instance, Gargi Parsai, 'BJP eyes 10 crore new members', *The Hindu*, 1 November 2014, https://www.thehindu.com/news/national/modi-launches-bjp-membership-drive/article6555553.ece.
18. 'PM launches BJP sadasyata abhiyan', *Kamal Sandesh*, 16–30 November 2014, p. 6, http://ofbjpuk.org/wp-content/uploads/2014/12/ks_nov_02_204_e.pdf.
19. Anirban Ganguly, Shiwanand Dwivedi, *Amit Shah and the March of the BJP* (New Delhi: Bloomsbury, 2019), pp. 121–122.
20. Quoted in Manu Balachandaran, Saptarishi Dutta, 'Here's how the BJP surpassed China's communists to become the largest political party in the world', *Quartz*, 31 March 2015, https://qz.com/india/372466/heres-how-the-bjp-surpassed-chinas-communists-to-become-the-largest-political-party-in-the-world/.

21. Interview with Hemant Agarwal, BJP district vice president, Mathura Mahanagar, 26 July 2020.
22. Interview with Rajesh Singh Pintu, Mathura Nagar Nigam Parshad, 26 July 2020.
23. Ibid.
24. Interview with Hemant Agarwal, BJP district vice president, Mathura Mahanagar, 26 July 2020.
25. Ibid.
26. Interview with a BJP district leader in UP, July 2020. His identity has not been disclosed on his request.
27. Original Modi quote is in Hindi; translation mine. 'Country is moving towards women-led development', 4 May 2018, https://www.narendramodi.in/country-is-moving-towards-women-led-development- 539996.
28. Personal interview with N. Ravi Kumar, BJP general secretary and MLC, Karnataka, 10 February 2020, Bengaluru.
29. Interview with Pradeep Goswami, general secretary, Mathura Mahanagar, 26 July 2020.
30. Interview with Rajesh Singh Pintu, Mathura Nagar Nigam Parshad, 26 July 2020.
31. Interview with Pradeep Goswami, general secretary, Mathura Mahanagar, 26 July 2020.
32. Interview with Rajesh Singh Pintu, Mathura Nagar Nigam Parshad, 26 July 2020.
33. Interview with N. Ravi Kumar, BJP general secretary and MLC, Karnataka, 10 February 2020, Bengaluru.
34. Press Conference by Amit Shah at the BJP Head Office, New Delhi, 17 May 2019, https://www.youtube.com/watch?v=_h3eIji3P6k. Amit Shah spoke in Hindi. The translation is by me.
35. Anirban Ganguly, Shiwanand Dwivedi, *Amit Shah and the March of the BJP* (New Delhi: Bloomsbury, 2019), pp. 131–132.
36. Numbers quoted from Amit Shah's press conference at the BJP Head Office, New Delhi, 17 May 2019, https://www.youtube.com/watch?v=_h3eIji3P6k. Amit Shah spoke in Hindi; translation mine.
37. Ibid.
38. PTI, 'BJP to reach out to government beneficiaries on February 26', *Business Standard*, 21 February 2019, https://www.business-standard.com/article/pti-stories/bjp-to-reach-out-to-govt-scheme-beneficiaries-on-feb-26-119022101160_1.html.
39. Interview with Hemant Agarwal, BJP district vice president, Mathura Mahanagar, 26 July 2020.
40. Interview with Pradeep Goswami, general secretary, Mathura Mahanagar, 26 July 2020.
41. Ibid.
42. Ibid.
43. Ibid.

44. Interview with Rajesh Singh Pintu, Mathura Nagar Nigam Parshad, 26 July 2020.
45. Ibid.
46. Interview with Hemant Agarwal, BJP district vice president, Mathura Mahanagar, 26 July 2020.
47. Ibid.
48. Ibid.
49. Ibid.
50. Ibid.
51. Interview with Pradeep Goswami, general secretary, Mathura Mahanagar, 26 July 2020.
52. Amit Shah's speech, available on the BJP's YouTube page: 'Shri Amit Shah addresses social media volunteers' meet in Kota, Rajasthan: 22.09.2018', https://www.youtube.com/watch?v=1OW7AQxpf2g.
53. Interview with N. Ravi Kumar, BJP general secretary and MLC, Karnataka, 10 February 2020, Bengaluru.
54. Ibid.
55. Ibid. Details also from Sundeep Moudgal, Bengaluru-based *The Times of India* journalist, who covered the meeting.
56. Interview with N. Ravi Kumar, BJP general secretary and MLC, Karnataka, 10 February 2020, Bengaluru.
57. Interview with Vinay Sahasrabuddhe, BJP vice president and MP, 5 August 2019, New Delhi. Part of this quote was in Hindi; translation is mine.
58. Interview with Pradeep Goswami, general secretary, Mathura Mahanagar, 26 July 2020.
59. Conversation with Sundeep Moudgal, Bengaluru-based *The Times of India* journalist, 9–10 February 2020.
60. Ibid.
61. Quoted in Anirban Ganguly, Shiwanand Dwivedi, *Amit Shah and the March of the BJP* (New Delhi: Bloomsbury, 2019), pp. 104–105.
62. PTI, 'New BJP office bigger than any party office in the world', *The Economic Times*, 18 February 2018, https://economictimes.indiatimes.com/news/politics-and-nation/new-bjp-hq-bigger-than-any-other-party-office-in-world-shah/articleshow/62970724.cms.
63. Quoted in Anirban Ganguly, Shiwanand Dwivedi, *Amit Shah and the March of the BJP* (New Delhi: Bloomsbury, 2019), p. 168.
64. Interview with N. Ravi Kumar, BJP general secretary and MLC, Karnataka, 10 February 2020, Bengaluru.
65. Conversation with Sundeep Moudgal, Bengaluru-based *The Times of India* journalist, 9–10 February 2020.
66. Interview with N. Ravi Kumar, BJP general secretary and MLC, Karnataka, 10 February 2020, Bengaluru.
67. Interview with Rajesh Singh Pintu, Mathura Nagar Nigam Parshad, 26 July 2020.

68. Interview with Pradeep Goswami, general secretary, Mathura Mahanagar, 26 July 2020.
69. Information from BJP district office construction project, in Anirban Ganguly, Shiwanand Dwivedi, *Amit Shah and the March of the BJP* (New Delhi: Bloomsbury, 2019), p. 168.
70. Details on Amit Shah's website, 6 February 2019, http://amitshah.co.in/2019-02-06-inaugurated-51-district-bjp-offices-from-bulandshahr-uttar-pradesh/.
71. The ceremony was held at Tiruvallur. ANI, 'Nadda lays foundation stone for BJP offices in 16 TN districts', 30 November 2019, https://www.aninews.in/news/national/politics/nadda-lays-foundation-stone-for-bjp-offices-in-16-tn-districts20191130151428/.
72. PTI, 'Bihar has PM Modi's blessings: JP Nadda's message to BJP workers', *Financial Express*, 22 February 2020, https://www.financialexpress.com/india-news/bihar-has-pm-modis-blessings-jp-naddas-reach-out-message-for-bjp-workers/1875929/.
73. PTI, 'BJP inaugurates its head office in Union Territory of Ladakh', *The Times of India*, 7 November 2019, https://timesofindia.indiatimes.com/india/bjp-inaugurates-its-head-office-in-union-territory-of-ladakh/articleshow/71955288.cms.
74. PTI, 'New BJP office bigger than any party office in the world', *The Economic Times*, 18 February 2018, https://economictimes.indiatimes.com/news/politics-and-nation/new-bjp-hq-bigger-than-any-other-party-office-in-world-shah/articleshow/62970724.cms.
75. Tabeenah Anjum, 'Rajasthan becomes the first state to give land to bjp offices in 28 districts', *Deccan Herald*, 8 August 2017, https://www.deccanherald.com/content/627096/rajasthan-becomes-first-state-give.html.
76. https://twitter.com/AmitShah/status/808323575958540289?s=20.
77. Ibid.
78. https://twitter.com/AmitShah/status/808323644761874432?s=20.
79. See the documents available online on BJP's e-library, http://library.bjp.org/jspui/.
80. Ibid. The documents referred to are available online: *Personal Secretary/Personal Assistant Training Guidebook: Pt. Deendayal Upadhyaya Prashikshan Mahabhiyan 2019* (New Delhi: BJP, 2019); *Kisan Morcha Training Guidebook: Pt. Deendayal Upadhyaya Prashikshan Mahabhiyan 2018* (New Delhi: BJP, 2018); *Working Papers Mandal Varg: Pt. Deendayal Upadhyaya Prashikshan Mahabhiyan 2015* (New Delhi: BJP, 2015); *Mahila Morcha: Prashikshan Praroop* [Women's Front: Training Manual] *Pt. Deendayal Upadhyaya Prashikshan Mahabhiyan 2018* (New Delhi: BJP, 2018).
81. See the documents available online on BJP's e-library, http://library.bjp.org/jspui/.
82. Amit Shah, quoted in Anirban Ganguly, Shiwanand Dwivedi, *Amit Shah and the March of the BJP* (New Delhi: Bloomsbury, 2019), p. 166.
83. Ibid.

84. Press conference by Shri Amit Shah at the BJP head office, New Delhi, 17 May 2019, https://www.youtube.com/watch?v=_h3eIji3P6k. Modi spoke in Hindi; translation mine.
85. BJP e-library, 12 December 2016, http://library.bjp.org/jspui/handle/123456789/453; http://amitshah.co.in/2016-12-12-inaugurating-the-nanaji-deshmukh-memorial-library-in-state-bjp-office-raipur-chhattisgarh/.
86. BJP e-library, 20 August 2017, http://library.bjp.org/jspui/handle/ 123456789/ 719.
87. BJP e-library, 21 July 2017, http://library.bjp.org/jspui/handle/ 123456789/ 487.
88. BJP e-library, 12 August 2017, http://library.bjp.org/jspui/handle/ 123456789/ 518.
89. BJP e-library, 25 September 2017, http://library.bjp.org/jspui/handle/123456789/1845.
90. TNN, 'Shah launches Nanaji Deshmukh Library at BJP office in Jammu', *The Times of India*, 1 May 2017, https://timesofindia.indiatimes.com/city/jammu/shah-launches-nanaji-deshmukh-library-at-bjp-office-in-jammu/articleshow/58457092.cms.
91. Written response to emailed query by author from Aseervatham Achary, member, Documentation and Library Cell, BJP, 19 August 2020.
92. Interview with Vinay Sahasrabuddhe, BJP vice president and MP, 5 August 2019.
93. Ibid. The quote was in Hindi; translation mine.
94. Amit Shah, quoted in Anirban Ganguly, Shiwanand Dwivedi, *Amit Shah and the March of the BJP* (New Delhi: Bloomsbury, 2019), p. 181.
95. Personal interview with Vinay Sahasrabuddhe, BJP vice president and MP; vice chairman, Rambhau Mhalgi Prabodhini, Thane, 24 September 2019.
96. Conversation with Prabodhini executive who wanted to remain unnamed.
97. Ibid.
98. Rhambhau Mhalgi Prabodhini website, https://rmponweb.org/about-rmp/.
99. Interview with Vinay Sahasrabuddhe, BJP vice president and MP, 5 August 2019.
100. Ibid.
101. Interview with Vani Tripathi Tikoo, former secretary, BJP, 27 August 2019, New Delhi.
102. Interview with senior BJP leader who spoke on condition of anonymity.
103. Ibid.
104. Interview with Vani Tripathi Tikoo, former secretary, BJP, 27 August 2019, New Delhi.
105. Vajpayee, quoted in *Working Group Report, Presented to National Executive Bhopal* (New Delhi: BJP, 20 July 1985), p. 5.
106. Ibid.
107. *General Secretary's Report (1981–82)* by LK Advani, 4th National Council Session (New Delhi: BJP, 15, 16, 17 April 1983), p. 1.
108. Ibid., p. 2.
109. The Working Group's convener was Krishanlal Sharma. Its members included: Bhairon Singh Shekhawat (later Rajasthan chief minister and India's vice

president), Shanta Kumar (later Union minister under Vajpayee), Makrand Desai, Pramod Mahajan (later Union minister under Vajpayee), Vijay Kumar Malhotra (later BJP's chief whip in Lok Sabha), Sunder Lal Patwa, Jana Krishnamurthi (later BJP president), Murli Manohar Joshi (later BJP president), Surah Bhan, Arif Baig and Mridula Sinha. *Working Group Report, Presented to National Executive Bhopal* (New Delhi: BJP, 20 July 1985), p. 41.

110. The Working Group was set up during the BJP National Executive, held on 15–17 March 1985, with twin objectives: review the party's functioning, achievement and shortcomings in the past five years and to draw up an 'Action Plan for the future on all fronts—ideological, organisational, agitational, constructive and electoral'. The Working Group met first on 2–3 April in Delhi and sent 4,000 questionnaires to prominent party functionaries. Five hundred and forty-nine responses were received, along with twenty detailed notes. Sub-groups toured the country and met about 1,000 friends of the BJP. The Working Group met five times in Delhi before finalising its report. Source: Krishnalal Sharma, convenor of the Working Group, in 'Introduction', *Working Group Report, Presented to National Executive Bhopal* (New Delhi: BJP, 20 July 1985), p. 1
111. *Working Group Report, Presented to National Executive, Bhopal* (New Delhi: BJP, 20 July 1985), pp. 6–7.
112. Ibid.
113. Ibid., p. 23.
114. Ibid., p. 27.
115. Ibid., pp. 23, 27.
116. Ibid., p. 31.
117. Ibid., p. 35.
118. Anirban Ganguly, Shiwanand Dwivedi, *Amit Shah and the March of the BJP* (New Delhi: Bloomsbury, 2019), pp. 96–97.
119. Ibid., p. 100.
120. *Working Group Report, Presented to National Executive Bhopal* (New Delhi: BJP, 20 July 1985), p. 40.

CHAPTER 9 Roots of the BJP

1. Mookerjee was first elected to Bengal's Legislative Council as a Congress representative in 1929 but quit a year later. I am grateful to Prof. Mahesh Rangarajan for pointing out that, of Nehru's first cabinet of fourteen (including himself), six were not from the Congress. These members included: C.H. Bhabha (Commerce), Shanmukam Chetty (Finance), S.P. Mookerjee (Industries and Supplies), K.C. Neogy (Relief and Rehabilitation) and B.R. Ambedkar (Law). The first cabinet list is from 'The first cabinet', *Hindustan Times*, 15 August 1947, https://www.hindustantimes.com/india-news/ht-archives-the-first-cabinet-of-independent-india-comes-into-existence/story-GZmqCqmX5ilSjEUX1gB97J.html.

2. Mookerjee served as acting president due to Savarkar's prolonged illness in these years. Walter Andersen, 'The Rashtriya Swayamsevak Sangh-III: Participation in politics', *Economic and Political Weekly*, Vol. 7, No. 13, 25 March 1972, pp. 679, 680.
3. Mookerjee resigned as Hindu Mahasabha vice president in a working committee meeting in May 1949. Mahasabha 'Record Book', quoted in Walter Andersen, 'The Rashtriya Swayamsevak Sangh-III: Participation in politics', *Economic & Political Weekly*, 25 March 1972, Vol. 7, No. 13, p. 681.
4. Quoted by the then BJP President Amit Shah, 15 July 2017, http://amitshah.co.in/salient-points-of-speech-by-bjp-national-president-shri-amit-shah-released-a-book-syama-prasad-mookerjee-his-vision-of-education/.
5. *Organiser*, '#SyamaPrasadMookerjee: Live up to the legacy', Vol. 71, No. 2, 7 July 2019, https://epaper.organiser.org/index.php?edition=Mpage&date=2019-06-29&page=1.
6. Quoted in Pulse of the Press, 'Jan Sangh upsurge', *The Times of India*, 12 February 1967, p. 8.
7. Ibid.
8. Staff Correspondent, 'Akhil Bhartiya Jan Sangh formed', *The Times of India*, 22 October 1951, p. 7.
9. Stage description from the account quoted in Ramachandra Guha, 'Democracy's biggest gamble: India's first free elections in 1952', *World Policy Journal*, Vol. 19, No. 1 (Spring, 2002), p. 97.
10. A Bengal Jan Sangh was formed on 28 April 1951, a Punjab–PEPSU–Himachal Pradesh–Delhi branch in Jullunder on 23 May and a UP party on 2 September. Details from B.D. Graham, 'Syama Prasad Mookerjee and the communalist alternative', in D.A. Low (ed.), *Sounding in Modern South Asian History* (Berkeley, LA: University of California Press, 1968), p. 352.
11. Voting in India's first general election after Independence was spread across sixty-eight phases between 25 October 1951 and 21 February 1952. *Report on the First General Elections in India 1951-52, Vol. 1* (New Delhi: ECI, 1955), https://eci.gov.in/files/file/7448-first-general-elections-in-india-vol-i-1951-1952/.
12. 'Mr Nehru's call for war against communalism', *The Times of India*, 1 October 1951, p. 1.
13. Staff Correspondent, 'Akhil Bhartiya Jan Sangh formed', *The Times of India*, 22 October 1951, p. 7.
14. Staff Correspondent, 'Bharatiya Jan Sangh election campaign', 4 November 1951, *The Times of India*, p. 10.
15. For Nathuram Godse's full argument, see the account of his appeals trial at Simla's Peterhoff by the Punjab High Court in Justice G.D. Khosla, *Murder of the Mahatma, and Other Cases from a Judge's Notebook* (London: Chatto & Windus, 1963). Eight people were charged: Nathuram Godse, editor, *Hindu Rashtra*, Poona; his brother, Gopal Godse, storekeeper, Army Depot, Poona; Narayan Apte, managing director, *Hindu Rashtra*, Poona; Vishnu Karkare, restaurant proprietor, Ahmed

Nagar; Madanlal Pahwa, Refugee Camp, Ahmednagar; Shankar Kistayya, domestic servant, Poona; Dattatraya Parchure, medical practitioner, Gwalior and Vinayak Savarkar, president of the Hindu Mahasabha from 1937–1942. Of these eight, Savarkar was acquitted, Godse and Apte sentenced to death and the remaining five sentenced to life imprisonment by the initial trial court. The High Court upheld the findings and sentences of the lower court, except in the case of Parchure and Kistayya, who were also acquitted.

16. 'Mr Nehru's call for war against communalism', *The Times of India*, 1 October 1951, p. 1.
17. B.D. Graham, 'Syama Prasad Mookerjee and the communalist alternative', in D.A. Low (ed.), *Sounding in Modern South Asian History* (Berkeley, LA: University of California Press, 1968), p. 333.
18. Details from Walter Andersen, 'The Rashtriya Swayamsevak Sangh-III: Participation in politics', *Economic & Political Weekly*, Vol. 7, No 13, 25 March 1972, pp. 678–681; and B.D. Graham, 'Syama Prasad Mookerjee and the communalist alternative', in D.A. Low (ed.), *Soundings in Modern South Asian History* (Berkeley, LA: University of California Press, 1968), pp. 331–333. Andersen and Graham differ on the date of Mookerjee's exit from the Mahasabha. I have chosen to go with Andersen's date of 1949.
19. The Citizenship (Amendment) Bill, 2019 was introduced in Lok Sabha by Home Minister Amit Shah on 9 December 2019 and passed by the house on 10 December with a vote count of 311–80. The Rajya Sabha passed it on 11 December with a vote count of 125–99. The Bill became law on 13 December, with the President of India giving his assent. For a background on the Act, see PRS Legislative Research, 'Bill Summary: The Citizenship (Amendment) Bill', 9 December 2019, https://prsindia.org/files/bills_acts/bills_parliament/2019/Bill%20Summary%20-%20The%20Citizenship%20(Amendment)%20Bill,%202019.pdf.
20. See full text of Agreement Between Governments of India and Pakistan Regarding Security and Rights of Minorities (Nehru–Liaquat Agreement) New Delhi, 8 April 1950, https://mea.gov.in/Portal/LegalTreatiesDoc/PA50B1228.pdf.
21. 'Sunday News' Special Representative, 'Two ministers resign: Central cabinet differences', *The Times of India*, 9 April 1950. Also see 'Sunday News' Special Representative, 'Resignations of both ministers accepted: Speculation on cabinet changes', *The Times of India*, 16 April 1950.
22. B.D. Graham, 'Syama Prasad Mookerjee and the communalist alternative', in D.A. Low (ed.), *Soundings in Modern South Asian History* (Berkeley, LA: University of California Press, 1968), p. 341.
23. 'Sunday News' Special Representative, 'Two ministers resign: Central cabinet differences', *The Times of India*, 8 April 1950.
24. B.D. Graham, 'Syama Prasad Mookerjee and the communalist alternative', in D.A. Low (ed.), *Soundings in Modern South Asian History* (Berkeley, LA: University of California Press, 1968), pp. 341, 345. Nehru's quotes are from Graham's account.

25. Ibid., p. 345.
26. Emphasis is mine. 'Dr Mookerjee explains reasons for resignation: Doubts about efficacy of Indo–Pakistan pact', *The Times of India*, 20 April 1950.
27. B.D. Graham, 'Syama Prasad Mookerjee and the communalist alternative', in D.A. Low (ed.), *Soundings in Modern South Asian History* (Berkeley, LA: University of California Press, 1968), p. 348.
28. Walter Andersen, 'The Rashtriya Swayamsevak Sangh-III: Participation in politics', *Economic & Political Weekly*, Vol. 7, No. 13, 25 March 1972, p. 680.
29. Walter Andersen, 'The Rashtriya Swayamsevak Sangh-IV: Jan Sangh and other organisations', *Economic & Political Weekly*, Vol. 7, No 14, 1 April 1972, p. 724. This is also what Oak told the scholar Myron Weiner. Quoted in B.D. Graham, 'Syama Prasad Mookerjee and the communalist alternative', in D.A. Low (ed.), *Soundings in Modern South Asian History* (Berkeley, LA: University of California Press, 1968), p. 349. Also see Balraj Madhok, *Dr Syama Prasad Mookerjee: A Biography* (Delhi: Deepak Prakashan, 1954).
30. Walter Andersen, 'The Rashtriya Swayamsevak Sangh-III: Participation in politics', *Economic & Political Weekly*, Vol. 7, No 13, 25 March 1972, p. 678.
31. Ibid., p. 680.
32. Ibid. J.A. Curran also noted that the RSS may have been comfortable with such a Congress: J.A. Curran, *Militant Hinduism in Indian Politics: A Study of the RSS* (New York: Institute of Pacific Relations, 1951).
33. Details from B.D. Graham, 'Syama Prasad Mookerjee and the communalist alternative', in D.A. Low (ed.), *Soundings in Modern South Asian History* (Berkeley, LA: University of California Press, 1968), p. 342.
34. 'Refugee influx not being stopped by Delhi pact: Dr Gidwani', *The Times of India*, 18 June 1950.
35. Staff Correspondent, 'Capital levy to meet refugee relief: Mr Tandon's suggestion at Delhi Conference', *The Times of India*, 30 July 1950.
36. Special Representative, 'Mr P. Tandon elected Congress president: Reorientation of policy likely in future', 3 September 1950, *The Times of India*, p. 1.
37. Kripalani's interview to Graham in Lucknow, 1964. B.D. Graham, 'Syama Prasad Mookerjee and the communalist alternative', in D.A. Low (ed.), *Soundings in Modern South Asian History* (Berkeley, LA: University of California Press, 1968), p. 371.
38. Special Representative, 'Future of Congress: Nasik may prove turning point', *The Times of India*, 12 September 1950.
39. 'Pandit Nehru asks for clear mandate from Congress: Statement on significance of presidential election result', *The Times of India*, 13 September 1950.
40. Quoted in 'Fate of Congress issue before Nasik session', *The Times of India*, 16 September 1950.
41. Gobind Sahay, former parliamentary secretary, UP, quoted in 'Conflict will be aggravated: UP leader's view', *The Times of India*, 3 September 1950.

42. PTI, 'Indian delegates from overseas', *The Times of India*, 26 August 1950.
43. Special Representative, 'Future of Congress: Nasik may prove turning point', *The Times of India*, 12 September 1950.
44. Ibid.
45. 'Congress session's overwhelming vote for resolution on communalism: Pandit Nehru's firm stand on democratic Principles', *The Times of India*, 22 September 1950.
46. Ibid.
47. Special Representative, 'Faith in secular democracy: Nasik Congress defines India's policy, session ends in Pandit Nehru's triumph', *The Times of India*, 21 September 1950.
48. Quoted in Rafiq Zakaria, 'The Tandon–Nehru conflict', *The Times of India*, 21 December 1969.
49. The dispute dated back to a 'unity' resolution against internal dissension passed by the AICC in its February 1951 Ahmedabad session soon after Sardar Patel's death. It was followed by Kidwai and Acharya Kripalani dissolving, on Tandon's insistence, a 'Democratic Front' they had formed within the Congress for internal reform. In return they were promised adequate representation on the party's Central Election Committee. When this did not materialise despite a series of unity talks, Acharya Kripalani quit the Congress. Tandon was also critical of Congress dissidents forming an independent party, the Kisan Mazdoor Praja Party, after the dissolution of the Democratic Front, and Kidwai's close association with it. Kidwai asked for a special session of the AICC to resolve internal conflicts which was held in Bangalore and passed a resolution asking for 'ways and means should be devised to avert the impending rift in the Congress so that it may function as a consolidated and integrated body to tide over the national crisis'. Kidwai, who was disappointed by the Bangalore outcome, returned to Delhi and resigned immediately from the cabinet and the party. Kidwai's resignation was also accompanied by that of union food minister Ajit Prasad Jain on the same grounds. Nehru accepted the former, and he was replaced by Rajkumari Amrit Kaur, who was given additional charge of Kidwai's ministry along with her existing portfolio of health. The prime minister, however, persuaded Jain to stay on, citing the dire situation on the ground with refugees and rehabilitation. All details from Rafiq Zakaria, 'The Tandon Nehru conflict', *The Times of India*, 21 December 1969. Special Correspondent, 'Mr Kidwai decides to quit office', *The Times of India*, 3 August 1951. For more on the AICC's unity resolution, see 'United about what?', *The Economic & Political Weekly*, 3 February 1951.
50. Special Representative, 'Congress faces sudden crisis: Mr Nehru resigns from Executive, deep anxiety among leaders', *The Times of India*, 11 August 1951, p. 1.
51. Special Representative, 'Rapprochement at Indore merely ephemeral: Mr Nehru alone capable of maintaining unity', *The Times of India*, 19 September 1952.
52. B.D. Graham, 'Syama Prasad Mookerjee and the communalist alternative', in D.A. Low (ed.), *Soundings in Modern South Asian History* (Berkeley, LA: University of California Press, 1968), p. 348.

53. 'Activities of Hindu Sabha condemned: Charges by Mr Nehru', *The Times of India*, 4 December 1951, p. 7.
54. Ibid.
55. Ibid.
56. Staff Correspondent, 'Threat to crush Jan Sangh: Charge against Mr Nehru', *The Times of India*, 30 November 1951, p. 8.
57. Ibid.
58. Own Correspondent, 'Congress government has abused people's trust', *The Times of India*, 17 December 1951, p. 5.
59. Ibid.
60. 'Grave threat to unity', *The Times of India*, 26 May 1962, p. 8.
61. Atal Bihari Vajpayee, 'Foreword', in *Bharatiya Jana Sangh Party Documents, Vol. 4: Resolutions on Internal Affairs* (New Delhi: Bharatiya Jan Sangh, 1973), p. 1.
62. Staff Correspondent, 'Akhil Bhartiya Jan Sangh formed', 22 October 1951, *The Times of India*, p. 7.
63. Own Correspondent, '"Congress government has abused people's trust": Dr Mookerjee's charge', *The Times of India*, 17 December 1951.
64. India Today Web Desk, 'Indian Muslims have nothing to fear, says Amit Shah as Lok Sabha passes Citizenship Amendment Bill', *India Today*, 10 December 2019, https://www.indiatoday.in/india/story/delhi-air-quality-very-poor-1643381-2020-02-05.
65. 'Refugees' Rehabilitation in W. Bengal urged', *The Times of India*, 6 April 1958, p. 10.
66. Staff Correspondent, 'Refugee rehabilitation being speeded up', *The Times of India*, 10 November 1952, p. 6.
67. PTI, 'Reversal of policy in D.P. exodus: Criticism by Jan Sangh', *The Times of India*, 23 April 1956, p. 5.
68. Amit Shah statements on 23 April, 1 May, 20 November in the Rajya Sabha and 18 December. Video links available at: https://twitter.com/AmitShah/status/1123581776415399937?s=20, https://youtu.be/Z__6E5hPbHg, https://twitter.com/BJP4India/status/1197163315148910593?s=20, https://twitter.com/DilliDurAst/status/1207263602148724736?s=20.
69. Video of Modi's full speech available at: https://youtu.be/AgElqM9Op_Y.
70. Jatin Anand, 'Pan-India NRC was never on the table', *The Hindu*, 22 December 2019, https://www.thehindu.com/news/cities/Delhi/pan-india-nrc-was-never-on-the-table-says-narendra-modi-at-delhi-rally/article30372096.ece.
71. India Today Web Desk 'No talk on nationwide NRC right now, PM Modi was right, says Amit Shah', *India Today*, 24 December 2019, https://www.indiatoday.in/india/story/no-talks-on-nationwide-nrc-now-amit-shah-interview-1631224-2019-12-24; Neeta Sharma, 'No plans for pan-India NRC for now, government tells parliament', 4 February 2020, https://www.ndtv.com/india-news/no-decision-to-prepare-nrc-on-national-level-government-to-parliament-2172891.
72. 'Failure of Congress policy on refugees: Dr Mookerjee's criticism', *The Times of India*, 24 September 1952.

73. On the question of why Muslims were left out, Shah argued that 'where there is in an Islamic state, Muslims cannot be termed religious minorities'. He questioned if Muslims in Pakistan, Afghanistan and Bangladesh could be termed minorities and argued that the possibility of their religious prosecution in these countries was very low. If it did still happen, then provisions to grant citizenship to such Muslims from these countries existed in the law. Shah emphasised that in the five years of the Modi government, over 566 Muslims from these countries had been given citizenship. He quoted several court judgements to argue that CAA did not hurt Article 14 of the Constitution that guarantees the Right to Equality. He further argued that, in the past, the Congress chief minister of Rajasthan had written to the Congress's then Union home minister, P. Chidambaram, to provide refugee status to Hindu and Sikh communities from Pakistan—and it was then given to 13,000 of them. Shah's full speech in Rajya Sabha on 11 December 2019 available at: https://www.youtube.com/watch?v=kKyx89AUaQM.
74. The full text of this judgment is available on *Supreme Court of India, Romesh Thappar vs The State of Madras, 26 May 1950, Equivalent Citations: 1950 AIR 124, 1950 SCR 594*, https://indiankanoon.org/doc/456839/.
75. In a fascinating debate in Parliament on the First Amendment, when an exasperated Nehru reacted to opposition complaints by announcing that he had 'put up so much from a few members who had dared to oppose us', Mookerjee responding by accusing the prime minister of using the 'language of a dictator'. The prime minister shot back saying that 'hard dealing' would lead to 'hard blows' all around. He laid down the gauntlet saying 'we challenge them [the opposition] to a combat here, in the marketplaces, in the country, everywhere and on every level'. Mookerjee interjected saying, 'Except in physical combat, to much comic relief in the house'. Staff Correspondent, 'First amendment to 17-month-old Constitution passed', *The Times of India*, 3 June 1951. It was given presidential assent on 18 June 1951.
76. All details on first amendment and Nehru–Patel quotes on this from Abhinav Chandrachud, *Republic of Rhetoric: Free Speech and the Constitution of India* (New Delhi: Penguin, 2017), extract in *Scroll*, https://scroll.in/article/849499/freedom-of-expression-was-once-absolute-in-india-then-jawaharlal-nehru-asked-for-changes, and Abhinav Chandrachud, 'Of curbs to free speech', *The Hindu*, 27 July 2016, https://www.thehindu.com/opinion/op-ed/Of-curbs-to-free-speech/article14509786.ece.
77. Staff Correspondent, 'Akhil Bhartiya Jan Sangh formed', 22 October 1951, *The Times of India*, p. 7.
78. 10 February 1952, Delhi, CWC, in *Bharatiya Jana Sangh Party Documents, Vol. 4: Resolutions on Internal Affairs* (New Delhi: Bharatiya Jan Sangh, 1973), p. 19.
79. 31 December 1952, Kanpur, CWC, *in Bharatiya Jana Sangh Party Documents, Vol. 4: Resolutions on Internal Affairs* (New Delhi: Bharatiya Jan Sangh, 1973), p. 21–24.

80. ANI, 'Sardar Patel was right and Nehru was wrong: RS Prasad', 11 September 2019, https://timesofindia.indiatimes.com/videos/news/sardar-patel-was-right-nehru-was-wrong-on-kashmir-issue-rs-prasad/videoshow/71090339.cms.
81. Srinath Raghavan, 'BJP wants to revoke Article 370, ironically Sardar Patel was its architect', 26 June 2018, https://theprint.in/opinion/ironical-that-bjp-wants-article-370-revoked-sardar-patel-was-its-architect/74804/ and his 'Kashmir: The state and status' at https://www.youtube.com/watch?v=OgXVMC5rdHg&feature=youtu.be. For a counterview, see Arghya Sengupta, 'The complex history of Article 370', *The Telegraph*, 17 October 2019, https://www.telegraphindia.com/opinion/the-complex-history-of-article-370-sardar-vallabhbhai-patel-and-kashmir/cid/1712373.
82. Own Correspondent, 'Full accession of Kashmir: Jan Sangh demand', *The Times of India*, 1 January 1953.
83. Background from B.D. Graham, 'Syama Prasad Mookerjee and the communalist alternative', in D.A. Low (ed.), *Soundings in Modern South Asian History* (Berkeley, LA: University of California Press, 1968), pp. 358–366.
84. 54.13, 'Integrate Kashmir', 25 January ,1954, Bombay II AIS, 'Integrate Kashmir', in *Bharatiya Jana Sangh Party Documents 1951–72, Vol. 4: Resolutions on Internal Affairs* (New Delhi: Bharatiya Jan Sangh, 1973), p. 34.
85. 55.06, 'Integrate Kashmir', 1 January 1955, Jodhpur III AIS, in *Bharatiya Jana Sangh Party Documents 1951–72, Vol. 4: Resolutions on Internal Affairs* (New Delhi: Bharatiya Jan Sangh, 1973), pp. 36–38.
86. 58.21, 'Integrate Kashmir', 15 October 1958, Delhi CWC, *Bharatiya Jana Sangh Party Documents 1951–72, Vol. 4: Resolutions on Internal Affairs* (New Delhi: Bharatiya Jan Sangh, 1973), pp. 48–49.
87. Ibid.
88. 66.03, 'Abrogate Article 370', 15 January 1966, Kanpur, CWC, in *Bharatiya Jana Sangh Party Documents 1951–72, Vol. 4: Resolutions on Internal Affairs* (New Delhi: Bharatiya Jan Sangh, 1973), pp. 79–80.
89. Staff Correspondent, 'Akhil Bhartiya Jan Sangh formed', 22 October 1951, *The Times of India*, p. 7.
90. Prof. Balraj Madhok, *What Bharatiya Jana-Sangh Stands For (Full Text Including Questions and Answers of the Speech of Prof. Balraj Madhok, President Bharatiya Jana Sangh, Delivered at Ahmedabad on August 7, 1966 as Part of the Project 'Towards Better Political Understanding')* (Ahmedabad: Ahmedabad Junior Chamber), Rhambhau Mhalgi Prabodhini archives, file No. PB-0097, Mumbai.
91. Ibid. Emphasis mine.
92. For a background, see Nandini Gondhalekar and Sanjoy Bhattacharya, 'The All India Hindu Mahasabha and the end of British rule in India, 1939–1947', *Social Scientist*, Vol. 27, No. 7/8, July–August 1999, pp. 48–74.
93. See the essays in Myron Weiner (ed.), *State Politics in India* (Princeton: Princeton University Press, 1968).

94. 'Jan Sangh convention in Delhi: "No communal outlook"', *The Times of India*, 23 October 1951, p. 3.
95. Golwalkar's article in *Organiser*, 25 June 1956. Quoted in K.S. Sudarshan (as told to Seshadri Chari), 'No ism but dharma', *Outlook*, 27 April 1998.
96. B.D. Graham, 'Syama Prasad Mookerjee and the communalist alternative', in D.A. Low (ed.), *Soundings in Modern South Asian History* (Berkeley, LA: University of California Press, 1968), p. 354.
97. B.D. Graham, 'The leadership and organisation of the Jana Sangh, 1951 to 1967', excerpts from *Hindu Nationalism and Indian Politics: The Origins and Development of Bharatiya Jana Sangh* (Cambridge: Cambridge University Press, 1990), reproduced in Zoya Hasan (ed.), *Parties and Party Politics in India* (New Delhi: Oxford University Press, 2014, first published 2002), p. 163.
98. Statement by Sharma, *The Statesman*, 4 November 1954, pp. 1, 2.
99. Letter from Madhok to L.K. Advani, 7 March 1973, quoted in Manga Ram Varshney, *Jana Sangh–RSS and Balraj Madhok*, quoted in B.D. Graham, 'The leadership and organisation of the Jana Sangh, 1951 to 1967', an excerpt from B.D. Graham, *Hindu Nationalism and Indian Politics: The Origins and Development of the Bharatiya Jana Sangh* (Cambridge: Cambridge University Press), reproduced in Zoya Hasan (ed.), *Parties and Party Politics in India* (New Delhi: Oxford University Press, 2014, first published 2002), p. 172.
100. Figures from B.D. Graham, 'Syama Prasad Mookerjee and the communalist alternative', in D.A. Low (ed.), *Sounding in Modern South Asian History* (Berkeley, LA: University of California Press, 1968), pp. 352–353.
101. Pralay Kanungo, 'The myth of the monolith: The RSS wrestles to discipline its political progeny', *Social Scientist*, November–December 2006, pp. 51–69.
102. 'Morarji Desai government collapsed due to internal contradictions', *India Today*, 2 July 2007, https://www.indiatoday.in/magazine/cover-story/story/20070702-1979-non-congress-government-collapsed-748333-2007- 07-02.
103. Narandas I. Mehta, *Bharatiya Jana Sangh and the Rule of 75%* (Bombay: Bharatiya Jan Sangh Bombay Vibhag, 1969) (324.23 Meh PA0067, Rhambhau Mhalgi Prabodhini), p. 13.
104. Bruce Graham, *Hindu Nationalism and Indian Politics: The Origins and Development of the Bharatiya Jana Sangh* (Cambridge: Cambridge University Press, 1990).
105. Kiran Bala, *Electoral Performance of the Bharatiya Janata Party in Indian Parliamentary Elections 1984 to 2004: A Geographical Analysis*, Ph.D Thesis submitted at Maharashi Dayanand University, 2016, p. 67.
106. Pralay Kanungo, 'The Myth of the Monolith: The RSS Wrestles to Discipline its Political Progeny', *Social Scientist*, November–December 2006, pp. 51–69.
107. Jan Sangh Upsurge, *The Times of India*, 12 February 1967, p. 8.
108. Ibid.
109. Initially it had four seats in 1962, but Balraj Madhok later won a by-election from New Delhi, taking the tally up to five.

110. Narandas I. Mehta, *Bharatiya Jana Sangh and the Rule of 75%* (Bombay: Bharatiya Jan Sangh Bombay Vibhag, 1969) (324.23 Meh PA0067, Rhambhau Mhalgi Prabodhini), pp. 8–9.
111. Ibid., p. 13.
112. Ibid., pp. 16–19.
113. Ibid., p. 19.
114. Ibid., p. 21.
115. Ibid., p. 24.
116. Ibid., p. 25.
117. Ibid.
118. Prof. Balraj Madhok, *What Bharatiya Jana-Sangh Stands For (Full Text Including Questions and Answers of the Speech of Prof. Balraj Madhok, President Bharatiya Jana Sangh, Delivered at Ahmedabad on August 7, 1966 as Part of the Project 'Towards Better Political Understanding')* (Ahmedabad: Ahmedabad Junior Chamber), Rhambhau Mhalgi Prabodhini archives, file No. PB-0097, Mumbai, p. 3.
119. Resolutions 61.11, 52.25 and 56.27 in *Bharatiya Jana Sangh Party Documents, Vol. 4: Resolutions on Internal Affairs* (New Delhi: Bharatiya Jan Sangh, 1973), quoted on p. 14.
120. Resolutions 52.25, 53.06, 53.23 quoted in *Bharatiya Jana Sangh Party Documents, Vol. 4: Resolutions on Internal Affairs* (New Delhi: Bharatiya Jan Sangh, 1973), p. 17.
121. Prof. Balraj Madhok, *What Bharatiya Jana-Sangh Stands For (Full Text Including Questions and Answers of the Speech of Prof. Balraj Madhok, President Bharatiya Jana Sangh, Delivered at Ahmedabad on August 7, 1966 as Part of the Project 'Towards Better Political Understanding')* (Ahmedabad: Ahmedabad Junior Chamber), Rhambhau Mhalgi Prabodhini archives, file No. PB-0097, Mumbai, p. 4.
122. Ibid.
123. Ibid. p. 6.
124. 'Citizenship law & NRC have nothing to do with Indian Muslims: PM Narendra Modi', *The Times of India*, 22 December 2019, https://timesofindia.indiatimes.com/india/citizenship-law-nrc-have-nothing-to-do-with-indian-muslims-pm-narendra-modi/articleshow/72924298.cms.
125. Prof. Balraj Madhok, *What Bharatiya Jana-Sangh Stands For (Full Text Including Questions and Answers of the Speech of Prof. Balraj Madhok, President Bharatiya Jana Sangh, Delivered at Ahmedabad on August 7, 1966 as Part of the Project 'Towards Better Political Understanding')* (Ahmedabad: Ahmedabad Junior Chamber), Rhambhau Mhalgi Prabodhini archives, file No. PB-0097, Mumbai, p. 41.
126. Ibid., p. 41–42.
127. Atal Bihari Vajapyee in Foreword, *Bharatiya Jana Sangh Party Documents, Vol. 4: Resolutions on Internal Affairs* (New Delhi: Bharatiya Jan Sangh, 1973), p. 7.
128. Prof. Balraj Madhok, *What Bharatiya Jana-Sangh Stands For (Full Text Including Questions and Answers of the Speech of Prof. Balraj Madhok, President Bharatiya Jana Sangh, Delivered at Ahmedabad on August 7, 1966 as Part of the Project 'Towards*

Better Political Understanding') (Ahmedabad: Ahmedabad Junior Chamber), Rhambhau Mhalgi Prabodhini archives, file No. PB-0097, Mumbai, p. 45.

129. Ibid.
130. PMO Press Release, 30 July 2019, https://pib.gov.in/newsite/PrintRelease.aspx?relid=192390.
131. Prof. Balraj Madhok, *What Bharatiya Jana-Sangh Stands For (Full Text Including Questions and Answers of the Speech of Prof. Balraj Madhok, President Bharatiya Jana Sangh, Delivered at Ahmedabad on August 7, 1966 as Part of the Project 'Towards Better Political Understanding')* (Ahmedabad: Ahmedabad Junior Chamber), Rhambhau Mhalgi Prabodhini archives, file No. PB-0097, Mumbai, p. 4.
132. Ibid.
133. Ibid., pp. 5–6.
134. Bharatiya Jan Sangh, *Principles and Policy, Adopted by the Bharatiya Pratinidhi Sabha at Vijaywada (Andhra) on 25 and 26 January 1965*, Rhambhau Mhalgi Prabodhini archives, File No. B-46 Mumbai, p. 3.
135. Ibid., pp. 12–13.
136. Prof. Balraj Madhok, *What Bharatiya Jana-Sangh Stands For (Full Text Including Questions and Answers of the Speech of Prof. Balraj Madhok, President Bharatiya Jana Sangh, Delivered at Ahmedabad on August 7, 1966 as Part of the Project 'Towards Better Political Understanding')* (Ahmedabad: Ahmedabad Junior Chamber), Rhambhau Mhalgi Prabodhini archives, file No. PB-0097, Mumbai, p. 7.
137. *Bharatiya Jana Sangh Election Manifesto 1962*, p. 17
138. Prof. Balraj Madhok, *What Bharatiya Jana-Sangh Stands For (Full Text Including Questions and Answers of the Speech of Prof. Balraj Madhok, President Bharatiya Jana Sangh, Delivered at Ahmedabad on August 7, 1966 as Part of the Project 'Towards Better Political Understanding')* (Ahmedabad: Ahmedabad Junior Chamber), Rhambhau Mhalgi Prabodhini archives, file No. PB-0097, Mumbai, p. 52.
139. Ibid.
140. Ibid., pp. 51–52.
141. UNI, 'Jan Sangh support', *The Times of India*, 3 November 1966, p. 9.
142. Nalin Mehta, interview with Jairam Ramesh, 'Indira Gandhi put RSS Guru Golwalkar on Cow Slaughter Committee … wound up after 12 years without a report', *The Times of India*, 16 June 2017, https://timesofindia.indiatimes.com/blogs/academic-interest/indira-gandhi-put-rsss-guru-golwalkar-on-cow-slaughter-committee-wound-up-after-12-years-without-a-report/. Also see Jairam Ramesh, *Indira Gandhi: A Life in Nature* (New Delhi: Simon and Schuster, 2017).
143. Ibid.
144. TOI Q&A, 'Meat exporters feel they're not doing business but committing a crime … officials closing slaughterhouses on flimsy reasons', *The Times of India*, 29 March 2017, https://timesofindia.indiatimes.com/blogs/the-interviews-blog/meat-

exporters-feel-theyre-not-doing-business-but-committing-a-crime-officials-closing-slaughterhouses-on-flimsy-reasons/. Also see ANI, 'Issue new licenses, renew old licenses for slaughterhouses: HC to UP govt', *Business Standard*, 12 May 2017, https://www.business-standard.com/article/current-affairs/issue-new-licenses-renew-old-licenses-for-slaughterhouses-hc-to-up-govt-117051200903_1.html; Manu Moudgil, 'Slaughterhouse crackdown in UP: Butchers and farmers hit, big businesses gain', *Hindustan Times*, 15 July 2017, https://www.hindustantimes.com/india-news/slaughterhouse-crackdown-in-up-butchers-and-farmers-hit-big-businesses-gain/story-SE3ha4M3FArgc3n28wtqqM.html; PTI, 'Issue licenses as per rules: HC on UP meat ban', *The Times of India*, 12 May 2017, https://timesofindia.indiatimes.com/city/lucknow/issue-new-licences-as-per-rules-hc-on-up-meat-ban/articleshow/58649222.cms.

145. TOI Q&A, 'Meat exporters feel they're not doing business but committing a crime ... officials closing slaughterhouses on flimsy reasons', *The Times of India*, 29 March 2017, https://timesofindia.indiatimes.com/blogs/the-interviews-blog/meat-exporters-feel-theyre-not-doing-business-but-committing-a-crime-officials-closing-slaughterhouses-on-flimsy-reasons/.
146. Ibid.
147. TNN, 'Govt finally dilutes rule on cattle', *The Times of India*. https://timesofindia.indiatimes.com/india/govt-finally-dilutes-rules-on-cattle-sale/articleshow/63705093.cms.
148. TOINS, 'Swatantra-Jan Sangh merger: Proposal under study', *The Times of India*, 23 January 1964, p. 5.

CHAPTER 10 When Right Is Left

1. Rohit David, interview with Anil Bokil in 'Demonetisation being addressed partially ... replace flawed taxation system with banking transaction tax', *The Times of India*, 16 December 2016, https://timesofindia.indiatimes.com/blogs/the-interviews-blog/demonetisation-being-addressed-partially-replace-flawed-taxation-system-with-banking-transaction-tax/.
2. This is the phrase used by Arvind Subramanian, who was chief economic advisor, Government of India, when demonetisation was announced. He also used it in his book on his tenure: Arvind Subramanian, *Of Counsel: The Challenges of the Modi–Jaitley Economy* (New Delhi: Penguin, 2018), p. 101.
3. *Jana Sangh's Economic Policy* (Bombay: RM Sheth), containing full text of Vajpayee interview with J.N. Parimoo, 'No Instability—Vajpayee', *The Economic Times*, 12 February 1971, pp. 1, 4. In PB-051, Rhambhau Mhalgi Prabodhini archive.
4. Ibid.
5. 'Demonetisation demanded by Jan Sangh', *The Times of India*, 19 November 1972, p. 7; TOINS, 'Jan Sangh council pleads for demonetisation', *The Times of India*, 17 July 1973, p. 1.

6. 'Demonetisation of hundred-rupee notes suggested', *The Times of India*, 2 August 1973, p. 9; 'Demonetisation ruled out by T.T.K.: Campaign against unaccounted funds', *The Times of India*, 19 November 1964, p. 1.
7. See, for example, TOINS, 'Demonetisation no solution: Chavan', *The Times of India*, 20 March 1974, p. 5; TOINS, 'Demonetisation is "no answer to black money"', *The Times of India*, 18 March 1972, p. 11; TOINS, 'TKK will not resort to demonetisation', *The Times of India*, 29 August 1964, p. 1.
8. TOINS, 'Demonetisation wanted by U.P. govt.', *The Times of India*, 4 July 196, p. 6.
9. Prem Shankar Jha, 'The demonetisation debate: Wanchoo Committee's interim report', *The Times of India*, 28 August 1972, p. 6. The final report of the committee, headed by a distinguished civil servant, was called *Final Report of the Direct Taxes Enquiry Committee*, 1971, Government of India. For more on this, see M.J. Thavaraj, 'Wooing black money: The Wanchoo committee way', *Social Scientist*, Vol. 1, No. 5, December 1972, pp. 30–39.
10. 'Non-official motion on demonetisation', *The Times of India*, 10 October 1971, p. 7.
11. 'Bengal PCC for demonetisation', *The Times of India*, 22 April 1971, p. 5.
12. See, for instance, the demand by Congress Forum for Socialist Action in Staff Reporter, 'Plea for demonetisation of 100-rupee notes', *The Times of India*, 4 May 1971, p. 4; 'Black money: MPs for demonetisation', *The Times of India*, 3 May 1973, p. 13.
13. 'Frantic rush to change Rs 100 notes in Delhi', *The Times of India*, 7 August 1973, p. 4; 'A Times of India notebook', *The Times of India*, 13 August 1973, p. 6.
14. Finance Minister H.M. Patel reported to Parliament that the exercise had yielded Rs 128 crore (worth of Rs 1,000 notes), Rs 18.15 crore (worth of Rs 5,000 notes) and Rs 34.6 lakh (worth of Rs 10,000 notes). 'Demonetisation details', *The Times of India*, 22 February 1978, p. 5.
15. This was the claim made by former finance minister and Reddi Congress leader C. Subramaniam. 'Political motive behind demonetisation: CS', *The Times of India*, 18 January 1978, p. 16.
16. 'Demonetisation news leaked out: Indira', *The Times of India*, 10 February 1978, p. 1. This issue was also raised by CPI. 'Demonetisation leak raised in Lok Sabha', *The Times of India*, 21 February 1978, p. 14.
17. Even in 1983, Finance Minister Pranab Mukherjee had to deny speculation on demonetisation. See PTI, 'No demonetisation', *The Times of India*, 2 March 1983, p. 9.
18. This was in a report by the Institute of Parliamentary Affairs. PTI, 'Demonetisation suggested', *The Times of India*, 24 July 1991, p. 7.
19. Rahul Gandhi tweets on 3 September 2020. https://twitter.com/RahulGandhi/status/1301376885369180160?s=20; https://twitter.com/RahulGandhi/status/1300703359905783813?s=20.
20. Arvind Subramanian, *Of Counsel: The Challenges of the Modi–Jaitley Economy* (New Delhi: Penguin, 2018), pp. 99–100.

21. The growth in the first quarter (April–June) of 2021-22 reflected a resumption of economic activity to near-similar levels as persisted before the first national pandemic lockdown in 2020 when all economic activity ground to a halt. India's GDP in Q1 of 2021-22 was Rs 32,38,020 crore, compared to Rs 26,95,421 crore in Q1 of 2020-21. Even so, the GDP size in the first quarter of 2021 was a little lower than what it was in the first quarter of 2019-20, Rs 35, 66, 708 crore. Economic growth soared to a new high of 20.1% in the April–June quarter in 2021-22 because it grew from a low base, compared to the record 24.4% contraction in the year-ago period. By the second quarter of 2021-22, GDP size was Rs 35,73,451 crore, 0.33 per cent higher than the per-pandemic level of Rs 35,61,530 crore in Q2, 2019-20, indicating that the economy had recovered lost ground. Data from PIB Delhi, Ministry of Statistics and Programme Implementation, 'Estimates of Gross Domestic Product for the second quarter (July-September) of 2021-22, 30 November 2021, https://pib.gov.in/PressReleasePage.aspx?PRID=1776500 and 'Estimates of Gross Domestic Product for the first quarter (April-June) of 2021-22, 31 August 2021, https://pib.gov.in/PressReleasePage.aspx?PRID=1750782. For a short analysis of the change in GDP growth numbers in 2021-22, see 'Covid didn't crush it', *The Times of India*, 1 September 2021, https://timesofindia.indiatimes.com/blogs/toi-editorials/covid-didnt-crush-it-gdp-wasnt-bruised-badly-by-second-wave-but-q1-data-shows-economy-below-2019-level-boost-demand/; TNN, 'GDP growth in Q1 records 20.1% recovery on low base', *The Times of India*, 1 September 2021, https://timesofindia.indiatimes.com/business/india-business/gdp-growth-in-q1-records-20-1-recovery-on-low-base/articleshow/85818730.cms. Also see former finance minister P. Chidambaram's critique on https://twitter.com/PChidambaram_IN/status/1432701058137182218?s=20. I am grateful to Sanjiv Shankaran for providing a detailed perspective on the GDP numbers.
22. On unemployment, in September 2020, the Central government's own data estimates are based on the annual Periodic Labour Force Survey (PLFS) conducted by the National Statistical Office (NSO), Ministry of Statistics and Programme Implementation and the Employment & Unemployment Survey conducted by the Labour Bureau. These surveys showed unemployment rate as follows: 2018-19: 5.8 per cent, 2017-18: 6 per cent, 2015-16: 3.7 per cent, 2013-14: 3.4 per cent, 2012-13: 4 per cent. Details from Minister of State (Independent Charge) for Labour and Employment Santosh Gangwar's reply to Lok Sabha on 14 September 2020 to Unstarred Question No. 214.
23. CMIE data, reproduced here: https://pollniti.com/data/unemployment.html.
24. For more on the social and economic shifts that changed American politics and led to Donald Trump's presidency, see, for example, J.D. Vance, *Hillbilly Elegy: A Memoir of a Family and a Culture in Crisis* (New York: HarperCollins, 2016) and Arlie Russell Hochschild, *Strangers in Their Own Land: Anger and Mourning on the American Right* (New York: The New Press, 2016). Also see the arguments explored by American historian Thomas Frank in his *What's The Matter with*

Kansas? How Conservatives Won the Heart of America (New York: Metropolitan Books, 2004).

25. Congress, 'Bhakt ka chashma', 9 May 2019. Full video is available at: https://twitter.com/INCIndia/status/1126313591030706176?s=20.
26. See Nalin Mehta, interview with Bruce Stokes, director of Global Attitudes, Pew Research Centre, '8 in 10 Indians have a favourable view of Modi ... 50% were critical of his Pakistan policy before Kashmir unrest', *The Times of India*, 30 September 2016, https://timesofindia.indiatimes.com/blogs/academic-interest/8-in-10-indians-have-a-favourable-view-of-modi-50-were-critical-of-his-pakistan-policy-before-kashmir-unrest/.
27. After the second wave of the pandemic in early 2021, these consumer perception numbers in the RBI survey dropped significantly. However, by July 2021, at the time of writing, they had begun to change again. Crucially, the wider trend persisted: of a huge gap between people's negative perception of their own employment prospects and the economy as a whole in the present vis-à-vis their expectations over the next twelve months on both counts. The RBI reported that its respondents in May 2021 rated their net perception of the economic situation in percentage response terms at -75 and their own employment prospects at -74.9. By July 2021, these net perception numbers had improved only marginally to -69 and -68.2 respectively. However, when asked about future expectations about the economy over the next twelve months, compared to the present, the net perception changed significantly from -18.3 in May 2021 to -4.8 in July 2021. When people were asked about their own future employment prospects, the net sentiment changed from -13 in May 2021 to +0.9 in July 2021. RBI, *Consumer Confidence Survey*, 6 August 2021, conducted in 5,384 households in thirteen cities and available on https://m.rbi.org.in/scriptS/BimonthlyPublications.aspx?head=Consumer%20Confidence%20Survey%20-%20Bi-monthly.
28. Arvind Subramanian, *Of Counsel: The Challenges of the Modi–Jaitley Economy* (New Delhi: Penguin, 2018), pp. 94–101.
29. Details from Minister of State (Independent Charge) for Labour and Employment Santosh Gangwar's various replies to Lok Sabha on 14 September 2020 to Unstarred Questions Nos, 174, 197, 188; and on 15 September 2020 to Unstarred Question No. 294. Rations constitute 5 kg of wheat or rice and 1 kg of preferred pulses per person per month.
30. Initial data from author's interview with Dinesh Sharma, deputy chief minister, UP. A briefer version of this was published as 'We want companies leaving China to come to India instead of going to Vietnam or elsewhere', *The Times of India*, 14 June 2020. Updated later from UP government's internal note on 16 September 2020. I am grateful to Pravin Kumar for providing updated government numbers.
31. See the critique on 'administrative approach' to economy by Rathin Roy, managing director (research and policy), Overseas Development Institute, who tweeted the UP government's RFP advertisement on 10 September 2020, calling it 'ridiculous'.

Similarly, Jairam Ramesh called it 'absolutely bogus' while former finance secretary Arvind Mayaram termed it 'simply delusional', https://twitter.com/EmergingRoy/status/1303897139173490688.

Roy had served as a member of the prime minister's Economic Advisory Council until September 2019. For a critique on the need for a strategic economic vision, as opposed to an administrative approach, see Rathin Roy's series in *Business Standard*, 'It's not too late, but soon it will be', *Business Standard*, 7 August 2020; 'Articulate an economic strategy', *Business Standard*, 8 May 2020. The UP government had called for bids for a global consultant on 19 June 2020, opened the financial bids on 27 November 2020 but cancelled the bid process on 22 March 2021, with a government statement saying that a 'fresh tender notice is likely in this regard'. Umesh Raghuvanshi, 'trillion dollar economy goal: 13 months on, Uttar Pradesh still weighing its options', *The Hindustan Times*, 26 July 2021, https://www.hindustantimes.com/cities/lucknow-news/trilliondollar-economy-goal-13-months-on-uttar-pradesh-still-weighing-its-options-101627322440496.html.

32. Initial details from UP government data note, 'Skill wise registrations and interests in employment', 6 May 2020. Updated UP government details on 15 September 2020 provided by Pravin Kumar.
33. P. Chidambaram, 'The worst effected economy', *The Indian Express*, 6 September 2020, https://indianexpress.com/article/opinion/columns/india-economy-slowdown-act-of-god-p-chidambaram-6584615/.
34. TNN, 'BJP wins 41 of 59 bypoll seats, 31 of them at expense of Congress', *The Times of India*, 11 November 2020, https://timesofindia.indiatimes.com/india/bjp-wins-41-out-of-59-bypoll-seats-31-at-congs-expense/articleshow/79158640.cms.
35. Narendra Modi's address at BJP office 11 November 2020. Full video available at: https://www.youtube.com/watch?v=nhtA2WyAQ9k.
36. The BJP did lose a big prestige battle in West Bengal to the Trinamool Congress in May 2021. However, the Bengal result must be seen in context. The BJP won seventy-seven seats (of the 292 that went to elections in the 294-member state assembly) and 38.3 per cent vote share in the May 2021 West Bengal state assembly election. This was down from the 121 state assembly segments it led in, with 40.3 per cent vote share, in the 2019 Lok Sabha polls. In comparison, the BJP had won only three seats (10 per cent vote share) in the 2016 assembly polls, two seats (18 per cent vote share) in the 2014 Lok Sabha polls and zero seats (4 per cent vote share) in the 2011 state election. In 2021, its vote share fell marginally from 2019, but seat share fell drastically because the election became a two-horse race—with the Congress (zero seats) and the CPI-M (zero seats) getting wiped out. For data comparisons, see TOI West Bengal datahub, available at: https://timesofindia.indiatimes.com/elections/assembly-elections/west-bengal/constituency-map; also see Ashish Ranjan, 'Mamata vs BJP: who had the edge in Bengal's close contest seats?', *India Today*, 5 May 2021, https://www.indiatoday.in/elections/story/west-bengal-2021-assembly-election-result-analysis-tmc-bjp-1799196-2021-05-05.

37. Swapan Dasgupta, 'The right course', *Open*, 17 February 2020, p. 33.
38. Raj Chengappa, 'Modinomics 2.0', *India Today*, 7 February 2020, https://www.indiatoday.in/magazine/cover-story/story/20200217-modinomics-2-0-1643717-2020-02-07.
39. Nalin Mehta, Interview with Montek Singh Ahluwalia, 'If a bank chief isn't beholden to a FinMin joint secretary, he will behave differently', *The Times of India*, 16 February 2020, https://timesofindia.indiatimes.com/blogs/academic-interest/if-a-bank-chief-isnt-beholden-to-a-finmin-joint-secretary-he-will-behave-differently-montek-singh-ahluwalia/.
40. The full paper is available at: https://www.hks.harvard.edu/sites/default/files/centers/cid/files/publications/faculty-working-papers/2019-12-cid-wp-369-indian-growth-diagnosis-remedies-final.pdf.
41. In April 2021, Wholesale Price Index (WPI) based inflation rose to 10.49 per cent (the highest in eleven years), because of higher oil and commodity prices and a low base effect, while food inflation accelerated by 4.92 per cent. Asit Ranjan Mishra, 'WPI Inflation Rises to 11-Year-High in April', *Mint*, p. 1. The Office of the Economic Advisor, Ministry of Commerce and Industry reported that the annual rate of inflation in July 2021 was at 11.16 per cent (provisional) for the month of July 2021 as compared to (-0.25 per cent) in July 2020. See figures in Ministry of Commerce and Industry, Department for Promotion of Industry and Internal Trade, Office of the Economic Advisor, 'Press release: Index numbers of wholesale price in India for the month of july, 2021 (base year: 2011-12)', 16 August 2021. For a discussion on whether this streak of inflation in 2021 was just a passing or 'transitory' phenomenon, see Udit Misra, 'Growth, inflation: Decoding RBI monetary policy stance', *The Indian Express*, 10 August 2021, p. 13.
42. Narendra Modi's victory speech on 23 May 2019 is available on the BJP YouTube channel, 'Victory Celebrations at BJP HQ. #VijayiBharat', https://www.youtube.com/watch?v=VruL38kjEBY.
43. Gurcharan Das, 'Modi needs to give India its Thatcher moment', *The Financial Times*, 18 May 2014, https://www.ft.com/content/06c3d5f0-dcf8-11e3-b73c-00144feabdc0.
44. See, for instance, Soutik Biswas, 'Will India's Narendra Modi be a reformer?', 26 May 2014, https://www.bbc.com/news/world-asia-india-27534163; Sreeram Chaulia, 'Comparisons of Narendra Modi to world leaders inevitable, but he is here to stamp his own personality', *The Economic Times*, 25 May 2014, https://economictimes.indiatimes.com/news/politics-and-nation/comparisons-of-narendra-modi-to-world-leaders-inevitable-but-he-is-here-to-stamp-his-own-personality/articleshow/35568592.cms?from=mdr.
45. This was a comparison made by *The Wire*'s Founding Editor, Siddharth Varadarajan.
46. Personal interview with Vinay Sahasrabuddhe, vice president, BJP, 5 August 2019.
47. R. Vijayraghavan, 'BJP search for an economic policy', *The Hindu*, 16 June 1992.

48. Gyan Varma, 'Buy Indian, helps Indians, urges Modi', *Mint*, 1 October 2018, https://www.google.com/amp/s/www.livemint.com/Politics/mNN9kUVMRf50aDHoPqjSbK/Buy-Indian-help-Indians-urges-Modi.html%3ffacet=amp.
49. *Jana Sangh's Economic Policy* (Bombay: RM Sheth), containing full text of Vajpayee interview with J.N. Parimoo, 'No instability—Vajpayee', *The Economic Times*, 12 February 1971, pp. 2, 7. In PB-051, Rhambhau Mhalgi Prabodhini archive.
50. Moushumi Das Gupta, 'To cut cost, PM Modi cuts size of his personal staff by almost 50%, PMO by at least 15%', *The Print*, 1 January 2020, https://www.google.com/amp/s/theprint.in/india/governance/to-cut-cost-pm-modi-cuts-size-of-his-personal-staff-by-almost-50-pmo-by-at-least-15/342987/%3famp.
51. *Jana Sangh's Economic Policy* (Bombay: RM Sheth), containing full text of Vajpayee interview with J.N. Parimoo, 'No instability—Vajpayee', *The Economic Times*, 12 February 1971, pp. 1, 4. In PB-051, Rhambhau Mhalgi Prabodhini archive.
52. Ibid., p. 3.
53. Bharatiya Jan Sangh, *Principles and Policy, Adopted by the Bharatiya Pratinidhi Sabha at Vijaywada (Andhra) on Jan. 25 and 26, 1965*, p. 10. File No. B-46, Rhambhau Mhalgi Prabodhini archive.
54. Bharatiya Jan Sangh, *Nationalisation of Banks*, p. 5. Undated policy document in File No. B-72, Rhambhau Mhalgi Prabodhini archive.
55. The banks were nationalised on 19 July 1969. See chronology on RBI website, https://www.rbi.org.in/Scripts/chro_1968.aspx.
56. Press clipping kindly shared by Jairam Ramesh on 19 November 2019.
57. Emphasis in italics is mine. TOINS, 'Similarity of different programmes', *The Times of India*, 8 February 1957, p. 12.
58. Ibid.
59. Ibid.
60. Prof. Balraj Madhok, *What Bharatiya Jana-Sangh Stands For (Full Text Including Questions and Answers of the Speech of Prof. Balraj Madhok, President Bharatiya Jana Sangh, Delivered at Ahmedabad on August 7, 1966 as Part of the Project 'Towards Better Political Understanding')* (Ahmedabad: Ahmedabad Junior Chamber), p. 32. File No. PB-0097, Rhambhau Mhalgi Prabodhini Archive.
61. Atal Bihari Vajpayee in 'Foreword', *Bharatiya Jana Sangh Party Documents, Vol. 4: Resolutions on Internal Affairs* (New Delhi: Bharatiya Jan Sangh, 1973), p. 4.
62. *Jana Sangh's Economic Policy* (Bombay: RM Sheth), containing full text of Vajpayee interview with J.N. Parimoo, 'No instability—Vajpayee', *The Economic Times*, 12 February 1971, pp. 1, 4. In PB-051, Rhambhau Mhalgi Prabodhini archive.
63. Ibid.
64. This was formally adopted in the party's General Council at its Indore session in 1954 and incorporated in its manifesto. In 1956, at its Delhi session, the Jan Sangh clarified that income in this context meant 'expendable income'. It further stated that if 'any individual by dint of honest labour or his ability earns more than the

permitted maximum, the excess income would be procured for "development needs through contribution, taxation, compulsory loans and investment". All manifestos issued for various elections held since, have reiterated the Party's stand on limiting the disparity between the maximum and the minimum expendable incomes.' All details from Atal Bihari Vajpayee in 'Foreword', *Bharatiya Jana Sangh Party Documents, Vol. 4: Resolutions on Internal Affairs* (New Delhi: 1973), p. 6.

65. Ibid, p. 4.
66. R. Vijayaraghavan, 'BJP search for an economic policy', *The Hindu*, 13 June 1992.
67. Ibid.
68. Nilanjan Mukhopadhyay, 'BJP puts economics before mythology', *The Economic Times*, 14 March 1992.
69. Manini Chatterjee, 'BJP to launch countrywide agitation on budget', *The Telegraph*, 16 March 1992.
70. 'BJP's new image', *The Indian Express*, 17 March 1992.
71. R. Vijayaraghavan, 'BJP search for an economic policy', *The Hindu*, 13 June 1992.
72. Ibid.
73. Emphasis in original. 'Swadeshi is a fundamental value for the nation, says BJP', *Organiser*, 19 April 1992.
74. R. Vijayaraghavan, 'BJP search for an economic policy', *The Hindu*, 13 June 1992.
75. Rakesh Sinha, 'Saffron contemplation on economic issues', *Pioneer*, 6 June 2001.
76. The first major Indian industrialist to express public scepticism of the reforms was Rahul Bajaj, the owner of the scooter manufacturing giant Bajaj Auto. For more on Bombay Club, see Baldev Raj Nayyar, 'Business and India's economic reforms', *Economic & Political Weekly*, Vol. 33, No. 38, 19–25 September 1998.
77. Quoted in Jay Dubashi, 'India first', *Seminar*, Vol. 417, May 1994, p. 19.
78. 'An affair of the purse: The BJP is the new darling of industrialists', *India Today*, 21 February 1993.
79. Rohit Saran, 'The return of the bombay club', *Business Today*, 7–21 April 1996.
80. Jay Dubashi, 'India first', *Seminar*, Vol. 417, May 1994, pp. 19–20.
81. Ibid., pp. 20–21.
82. Ibid, p. 21
83. Farzand Ahmed, 'Swadeshi time bomb', *India Today*, 25 September 2000, pp. 20–22.
84. Ibid.
85. Ibid.
86. Ibid.
87. Geeta Puri, 'BJP's salvation lies in Swadeshi not Hindutva', *The Indian Express*, 10 January 1992.
88. Ibid.
89. Smita Gupta, 'BJP shifting from Swadeshi stance', *The Times of India*, 15 March 1994.

90. Ibid.
91. Mani Shankar Aiyar, 'An economic agenda for the BJP', *India Today*, 4 April 1992.
92. Quoted in TOI, 18 March 1992, as attributed in Mani Shankar Aiyar, 'An economic agenda for the BJP', *India Today*, 4 April 1992.
93. Aiyar's satirical document, which started with the incantation 'Har Har Mahadev', and ended with 'Om Namo Narayana!', was called 'A third model of development: The BJP alternative'. Published in Mani Shankar Aiyar, 'An economic agenda for the BJP', *India Today*, 4 April 1992.
94. Quoted in Ashutosh Kumar Sinha, 'The Sangh Parivar speaks in different tongues on economic policies, but the BJP treads the middle path on poll-eve', *Outlook*, 26 January 1998, p. 65.
95. A.S. Panneerselvan interview with S. Gurumurthy, 'There's a limit to marketisation', *Outlook*, 26 January 1998, p. 66.
96. Swapan Dasgupta, 'The right course', *Open*, 17 February 2020, p. 31.
97. Ibid.
98. *The Times of India* budget front pages (2014–2020). I am grateful to Sanjay Kalia for compiling these.
99. Saurabh Sinha, TNN, 'Return of the prodigal son: Air India back in founder Tata fold after 68 years', *The Times of India*, 8 October 2021, https://timesofindia.indiatimes.com/business/india-business/return-of-the-prodigal-son-air-india-back-in-founder-tata-fold-after-68-years/articleshow/86865871.cms. The highest price bid was awarded to M/s Talace Pvt. Ltd., a wholly owned subsidiary of M/s Tata Sons Pvt. Ltd. for sale of 100 per cent equity shareholding of Government of India in Air India along with equity shareholding of Air India in AIXL and AISATS. The winning bid was for Rs 18,000 crore as Enterprise Value (EV) consideration for AI (100 per cent shares of AI along with AI's shareholding in AIXL and AISATS). The transaction did not include non-core assets including land and building, valued at Rs 14,718 crore, which were to be transferred to GoI's Air India Asset Holding Limited (AIAHL). The government announced that the next steps in the transaction for the Letter of Intent and signing of the Share Purchase Agreement were expected to be completed by December 2021. PIB, Ministry of Finance, 'Government approves Air India disinvestment: Tatasons' SPV – Talace Pvt. Ltd – wins bid for Air India, 8 October 2021, https://pib.gov.in/PressReleaseIframePage.aspx?PRID=1762146.
100. The first attempt for a strategic sale of Air India was in 2001 by the Vajpayee government when 40 per cent of its equity was put on the block. Thereafter in 2018, the Government of India bid to sell Air India again, this time putting 76 per cent equity on the block but it did not receive a single bid. In January 2020, the government reinitiated the strategic sale of Air India, but with 100 per cent equity up for prospective buyers. Timeline details from Pranav Mukul, 'Air India disinvestment: History suggests still some way to go', *The Indian Express*, 20 December 2020, https://indianexpress.com/article/business/aviation/air-india-

divestment-history-suggests-still-some-way-to-go-7111741/. For an analysis of the 2021 deal, see Arvind Panagariya, 'Why nothing less than 100% sale worked for Air India', *The Times of India*, 13 October 2021, https://timesofindia.indiatimes.com/india/why-nothing-less-than-100-sale-worked-for-air-india/articleshow/86996597.cms.

101. Swaminathan Aiyar, 'A burst of privatisation in India looks imminent', *The Financial Times*, 8 October 2019, https://www.ft.com/content/5d491d12-e90f-11e9-aefb-a946d2463e4b.
102. Anilesh S. Mahajan, 'Highways of growth', *India Today*, 7 February 2020, https://www.indiatoday.in/magazine/cover-story/story/20200217-highways-of-growth-1643716-2020-02-07.
103. '5 years of Modi government: How you fared ...', TOI Budget Special, *The Times of India*, 2 February 2019.
104. Anilesh S. Mahajan, 'Highways of growth', *India Today*, 7 February 2020, https://www.indiatoday.in/magazine/cover-story/story/20200217-highways-of-growth-1643716-2020-02-07.
105. Swaminathan Aiyar, 'A burst of privatisation in India looks imminent', *The Financial Times*, 8 October 2019, https://www.ft.com/content/5d491d12-e90f-11e9-aefb-a946d2463e4b.
106. Anilesh S. Mahajan, 'Highways of growth', *India Today*, 7 February 2020, https://www.indiatoday.in/magazine/cover-story/story/20200217-highways-of-growth-1643716-2020-02-07.
107. RBI, 'Assessment of the progress of digitisation from cash to electronic' (Mumbai: RBI, Department of Payment and Settlement Systems, 24 February 2020), https://rbidocs.rbi.org.in/rdocs/Publications/PDFs/CASHB74203395BD64E2ABC1BD5F68D8AEF13.PDF.
108. This data is available online at: https://www.rbi.org.in/scripts/AnnualReportPublications.aspx?Id=1293, https://m.rbi.org.in/Scripts/BS_ViewBulletin.aspx?Id=18290.
109. Author's interview with Caesar Sengupta Google vice president, Next Billion Users and Payments, published as '95% of Video Consumption in India is in regional languages, Hindi will outnumber English users by 2021', *The Times of India*, 17 May 2019, https://timesofindia.indiatimes.com/blogs/academic-interest/95-of-video-consumption-in-india-is-in-regional-languages-hindi-internet-users-will-outnumber-english-users-by-2021/.
110. Data in Digbijay Mishra and Rachel Chitra, 'E-payments industry counts the costs after zero mdr jolt', *The Times of India*, 24 February 2020.
111. Ibid.
112. Nandan Nilekani, Keynote address, 'India@70: Rebooting the republic', and Q&A with Nalin Mehta, Times Lit Fest—Delhi, 26 November 2016. Full video at: https://timesofindia.indiatimes.com/videos/news/Times-Litfest-Delhi-Nandan-Nilekani-talks-about-rebooting-the-Republic/videoshow/55635017.cms.

113. Nishant Chadha, presentation on 'Social sector and budget' at '5-Institute Budget Seminar 2020-21: Reforms and Development Perspectives', New Delhi, 8 February 2020.
114. Rema Nagarajan, 'Centre's health outlay woefully off-course for 2.5% of GDP target', *The Times of India*, 9 February 2020.
115. Rathin Roy, 'Union budget 2020: The fiscal crisis worsens' at '5-Institute Budget Seminar 2020-21: Reforms and Development Perspectives', New Delhi, 8 February 2020.
116. Ibid.
117. ET Bureau, 'FY 20 deficit likely to be 4.5-5% of GDP: Ex-Fin Secy', *The Economic Times*, 16 January 2020, https://economictimes.indiatimes.com/news/economy/indicators/fy20-deficit-likely-to-be-4-5-5-of-gdp-ex-fin-secy/articleshow/73287128.cms. Also see Subhash Chandra Garg, 'How much and on what government of India spends over Rs 31 lakh crore', 24 January 2020, https://subhashchandragarg.blogspot.com/search?updated-max=2020-01-31T04:30:00-08:00&max-results=7&start=1&by-date=false.
118. *CAG Presentation to XV Finance Commission*, made available to author on condition of anonymity.
119. TNN, 'Budget 2020: The deceptive rise in India's income tax base', *The Economic Times*, 2 February 2020, https://economictimes.indiatimes.com/wealth/tax/budget-2020-the-deceptive-rise-in-indias-income-tax-base/articleshow/73868046.cms.
120. India Today Web Desk, 'Tax terrorism widespread, pressurizes People: TV Mohandas Pai', *India Today*, 4 August 2019, https://www.indiatoday.in/business/story/tax-terrorism-widespread-pressurizes-people-tv-mohandas-pai-1577045-2019-08-04.
121. Interview with Brajesh Kumar Singh, group consulting editor, Network18, 9 December 2019.
122. Modi statement in Hindi in Lok Sabha, 27 February 2015. Video available at: https://youtu.be/5nBRKUf6AAo.
123. Rahul Gandhi statement in Lok Sabha, 20 April 2015. Video available at: https://youtu.be/Z0uioKWABqo.
124. Interview with Rajeev Chandrasekhar, BJP Rajya Sabha MP, 26 August 2019, New Delhi. Chandrasekhar was subsequently appointed, in July 2021, as Union minister of state for skills development and entrepreneurship as well as for electronics and information technology.
125. Nalin Mehta, interview with Dinesh Sharma, 'We want companies leaving China to come to India instead of going to Vietnam or elsewhere', *The Times of India*, 14 June 2020.
126. Interview with Rajeev Chandrasekhar, BJP Rajya Sabha MP, 26 August 2019, New Delhi.
127. Nalin Mehta, interview with Montek Singh Ahluwalia, 'If a bank chief isn't beholden to a FinMin joint secretary, he will behave differently', *The Times of India*, 16 February 2020, https://timesofindia.indiatimes.com/blogs/academic-interest/if-a-

bank-chief-isnt-beholden-to-a-finmin-joint-secretary-he-will-behave-differently-montek-singh-ahluwalia/.

128. Private conversation with a former bureaucrat who preferred to remain unnamed.
129. PTI, 'In a first, nine private sector specialists selected as joint secretaries in govt departments', *The Economic Times*, 12 April 2019, https://economictimes.indiatimes.com/news/economy/policy/in-a-first-nine-private-sector-specialists-selected-as-joint-secretaries-in-govt-departments/articleshow/68854312.cms.
130. Arup Roychoudhury, 'Govt expands PM's Economic Advisory Council', *Business Standard*, 17 October 2019, https://www.business-standard.com/article/economy-policy/govt-appoints-3-part-time-members-to-eac-pm-119101700406_1.html.
131. The decision to create the post of CDS was announced by PM Modi on 15 August 2020. General Bipin Rawat was appointed as India's first CDS on 30 December 2020. For more, see Anit Mukherjee, 'Three pitfalls of CDS, Dept of Military Affairs and why it should make US sceptical', 6 March 2020, https://theprint.in/opinion/three-pitfalls-of-cds-dept-of-military-affairs-and-why-it-should-make-us-sceptical/376468/.
132. PIB Delhi, 'Cabinet approves amendment in the Terms of Reference for the Fifteenth Finance Commission: Provision to address concerns regarding funds for defence and internal security', 17 July 2019, https://pib.gov.in/PressReleasePage.aspx?PRID=1579116, Dinesh Narayanan, 'Central funds to states may be cut to create internal security fund', *Economic Times*, 23 September 2019, https://economictimes.indiatimes.com/news/defence/nk-singh-headed-finance-commission-working-on-proposal-cabinet-cleared-enabling-approvals-on-july-17/articleshow/70384389.cms, Nikunj Ohri, '15th Finance Commission forms panel for separate defence and internal security fund', Bloomberg, 13 February 2020, https://www.bloombergquint.com/law-and-policy/15th-finance-commission-forms-panel-for-separate-defence-and-internal-security-fund.
133. Quoted in Asit Ranjan Mishra, Anil Padmanabhan, 'Fifteenth Finance Commission prepares defence funding framework', 6 February 2020, https://www.livemint.com/news/india/fifteenth-finance-commission-prepares-defence-funding-framework-11580927443150.html.
134. Nirmala Sitharaman, minister of finance, 'Explanatory memorandum as to the action taken on the recommendations made by the Fifteenth Finance Commission in its final report submitted to the president on November 9, 2020', 1 February 2021, Ministry of Finance, Government of India. The Fifteenth Finance Commission's reports are available at: https://fincomindia.nic.in/ShowContent.aspx?uid1=3&uid2=0&uid3=0&uid4=0.
135. For challenges in military reform, see, for instance, Nalin Mehta, 'The challenge begins now', *The Times of India*, 22 February 2020, https://timesofindia.indiatimes.com/blogs/academic-interest/the-challenge-begins-now-cds-is-off-to-a-blistering-start-but-serious-reform-to-integrate-armed-forces-requires-painful-decisions/; Anit Mukherkjee, 'India's civilian leadership must step up', *The*

Hindustan Times, 5 July 2021, https://www.hindustantimes.com/opinion/indias-civilian-leadership-must-step-up-101625491333170.html.

136. Quoted in Asit Ranjan Mishra, Anil Padmanabhan, 'Fifteenth Finance Commission prepares defence funding framework', 6 February 2020, https://www.livemint.com/news/india/fifteenth-finance-commission-prepares-defence-funding-framework-11580927443150.html.

CHAPTER 11 The BJP's RSS Link

1. PTI, 'BJP will never sever RSS link', *The Times of India*, 21 April 1980, p. 7.
2. Express News Service, 'Janata Party bans dual membership', *The Indian Express*, 30 July 1979, p. 1.
3. The RSS 'dual membership' of erstwhile Jan Sangh members in Janata Party became a lightning rod for infighting and factionism at least from 1978 onwards. The Charan Singh/Raj Narain faction, supported by ex-socialist leader Madhu Limaye, sought to attack Prime Minister Morarji Desai by attacking his ex-Jan Sangh allies, Atal Bihari Vajpayee and L.K. Advani. The resulting crisis led to the expulsion of Raj Narain from Janata Party on 12 June 1979. He formed the Janata Party (Secular) with a group of forty-seven breakaway MPs, which led to the collapse of the Morarji Desai government. Charan Singh became prime minister on 28 July 1979, leading a minority government, supported by Janata (S), Yashwantrao Chavan of Congress (Socialist) and outside support of Indira Gandhi's Congress (I). Singh had to resign on 20 August 1979 when Congress (I) withdrew support. Details here from Christophe Jaffrelot, *The Hindu Nationalist Movement and Indian Politics: 1925 to the 1990s* (New Delhi: Penguin, 1999), pp. 307–312.
4. PTI, 'RSS issue—it's a fight to finish: Ram', *The Times of India*, 29 February 1980, p. 1.
5. Special Correspondent, 'Jan Sangh group to form new party', *The Times of India*, 5 April 1980, p. 1.
6. The ECI on 24 April 1980 initially gave the BJP recognition as a national party on the basis of its claim that it represented the majority of the undivided Janata Party. The BJP said it would not claim the flag or the symbol of the Janata Party. The ECI also accepted the BJP's pitch for the 'lotus' as a party symbol after an earlier proposal for allotment of a 'wheel (with five spokes) and the elephant' was not accepted by the ECI. However, the ECI's initial decision left the residuary Janata Party with the problem of recognition as a national party, after its symbol, the 'haldhar within wheel', was frozen by the Commission. Once an election symbol is frozen, it amounted to automatic withdrawal of recognition to a political party. This meant that the Chandra Shekhar-led Janata Party would have had to fight the upcoming election that year under a new name, unless its symbol was unfrozen. Chandra Shekhar protested and asked for a review. On review, the ECI eventually changed its mind, gave recognition to the party led by Chandra Shekhar as 'Janata

Party' and unfroze its 'haldhar within wheel' symbol six months later on 9 October 1980. See Special Correspondent, with PTI, 'National party status: BJP', *The Times of India*, 25 April 1980, p. 1. Special Correspondent, 'Janata plea to review decision', *The Times of India*, 25 April 1980, p. 1. PTI, 'Haldhar symbol allotted to JP', *The Times of India*, 10 October 1980, p. 2.

7. PTI, 'BJP will never sever RSS Link, *The Times of India*, 21 April 1980, p. 7.
8. 'New party, old problem', *The Times of India*, 8 April 1980, p. 6.
9. Special Correspondent, 'Jan Sangh group to form new party', *The Times of India*, 5 April 1980, p. 1.
10. The inaugural convention was attended by 3,643 delegates. Vajpayee was authorised by the delegates to lead the party and appoint the party's working committee and office-bearers whose names were announced: Vice-presidents: Vijaya Raje Scindia, Ram Jethmalani; General Secretaries: L.K. Advani, Sikander Bakht, Murali Manohar Joshi; Secretaries: Suraj Bhan, K. Krishnamurthy; Treasurer: S.S. Bhandari. Vajpayee's presidency was subsequently formally ratified unopposed by all state units of the party on 12 December 1980. Special Correspondent, 'Jan Sangh group to form new party', *The Times of India*, 5 April 1980, p. 1; Special Correspondent, 'Vajpayee elected BJP president', *The Times of India*, 13 December 1980, p. 1.
11. Special Correspondent, 'Vajpayee chief of Bharatiya Janata Party', *The Times of India*, 7 April 1980, p. 1.
12. Special Correspondent, 'Jan Sangh group to form new party', *The Times of India*, 6 April 1980, p. 1.
13. Ibid.
14. The third member of the drafting committee was S.S. Bhandari. Special Correspondent, 'Vajpayee chief of Bharatiya Janata Party', *The Times of India*, 7 April 1980, p. 1.
15. 'Schizophrenic party', *The Times of India*, 9 May 1980, p. 6.
16. Ibid.
17. Ibid.
18. Ibid.
19. Ibid.
20. Special Correspondent, 'BJP policy stress on Gandhism', *The Times of India*, 7 May 1980, p. 1.
21. 'Schizophrenic party', *The Times of India*, 9 May 1980, p. 6.
22. The plenary with over 44,000 delegates took place in a specially constructed tent city called 'Samata Nagar' (Equality City) on reclaimed land in Bombay's Bandra West. It was specially designed by the architect Ramesh Sheth and BJP leaders said it cost Rs 16 lakh. Staff Reporter, 'Big township for BJP session', *The Times of India*, 20 December 1980, p. 15; Staff Reporter, 'Impressive show', *The Times of India*, 29 December 1980, p. 1. Also see Staff Reporter, 'BJP firm on party goal', *The Times of India*, 29 December 1980, p. 1. Full details from BJP, *Onward March: First National*

Convention: Speeches and Resolutions, December 28-30, 1980, Bombay, Rhambhau Mhalgi Prabodhini archives, File No. PC-44, Thane.

23. After the initial plenary at 'Samata Nagar', Vajpayee and the delegates moved in a large procession to Shivaji Park, where Vajpayee gave another public speech. Vajpayee's Shivaji reference is from B. Dixit, letter to the editor, 'Bharatiya Janata Party', *The Times of India*, 19 May 1980, p. 6. For more on the Shivaji Park rally, see Staff Reporter, 'Biggest ever rally', *The Times of India*, 29 December 1980. On Shivaji and Yakutbaba, the official Ratnagiri Tourism website says that 'a meeting between Yakutbaba and Shivaji Maharaj also took place when Maharaj was leaving for Dabhol. It was Shivaji Maharaj who expressed the desire to build a Dargah at Kelshi that time. And so, the Dargah was built with beautiful carvings on stone on a total area of 534 acres, that was awarded for this purpose.' See https://ratnagiritourism.in/en/temples/yakutbaba-darga-kelshi/.
24. 'New party, old problem', *The Times of India*, 8 April 1980, p. 6.
25. The BJP's new policy statement containing its five core commitments—nationalism and national integration, democracy, 'positive secularism', Gandhian socialism, value-based politics—was first made public on 6 May 1980. This eventually took the shape of a thirty-three-page policy document, 'Our five commitments', that was readied by 14 December 1980 for formal ratification by the party's first plenary on 28 December 1980. See Special Correspondent, 'BJP policy stress on Gandhism', *The Times of India*, 7 May 1980, p. 1; UNI, 'Gandhian philosophy acceptable to BJP', *The Times of India*, 15 December 1980, p. 1.
26. PTI, 'Vijaya Raje Scindia questions party line', *The Times of India*, 27 December 1980, p. 1.
27. Special Correspondent, 'BJP's Gandhian tag resented', *The Times of India*, 25 December 1980, p. 1.
28. Christopher Jaffrelot, *The Hindu Nationalist Movement and Indian Politics: 1925 to the 1990s* (New Delhi: Penguin, 1999), p. 319.
29. UNI, 'Vijaya Raje Scindia has no objection to "socialism"', *The Times of India*, 28 December 1980, p. 1.
30. Delegates proposed 257 amendments to the economic resolution over a seven-hour debate. Only seven were accepted. See Staff Reporter, 'BJP session votes for Gandhian line', *The Times of India*, 31 December 1980, p. 1.
31. PIB, Ministry of Housing and Urban Affairs, 'Swachh Bharat mission logo and tagline contest winners to be facilitated by prime minister', 30 September 2014. https://pib.gov.in/newsite/PrintRelease.aspx?relid=110172. For more on Modi's emphasis on Gandhi's legacy as a driving force for Swachh Bharat, see 'Swachh Bharat on the airwaves', in *Mann ki Baat: A Social Revolution on Radio* (New Delhi: BlueKraft Digital Foundation/Rupa, 2019) pp. 26–46.
32. The Mahatma Mandir Convention Centre was built by Larsen & Toubro and Shapoorji Pallonji and Company Limited in two phases. See promotional video on Narendra Modi YouTube channel, https://youtu.be/xX1Ray-kiK4.

33. Staff Reporter, 'BJP talks start sans Nanaji', *The Times of India*, 27 December 1980, p. 1.
34. Staff Reporter, 'BJP firm on party goal', *The Times of India*, 29 December 1980, p. 1.
35. *Organiser*, 17 February 1985. Quoted in Christophe Jaffrelot, *The Hindu Nationalist Movement and Indian Politics: 1925 to the 1990s* (New Delhi: Penguin, 1999), p. 329.
36. Quoted in Christophe Jaffrelot, *The Hindu Nationalist Movement and Indian Politics: 1925 to the 1990s* (New Delhi: Penguin, 1999), p. 329.
37. On this, see former Madhya Pradesh chief minister and senior Congress leader Kamal Nath's statement giving credit to Rajiv Gandhi for 'opening the locks' of the Babri Masjid, for saying in 1989 that 'Ram Rajya' (rule of Ram) will be created and that Ram Mandir should be built. Video interview available at: https://youtu.be/4ARhuayfOr4.
38. BJP, *Opening Remarks by Shri LK. Advani: Resolutions Adopted by National Executive: National Executive Meeting*, 9, 10 and 11 June 1989, Palampur.
39. Atal Bihari Vajpayee, L.K. Advani, Murali Manohar Joshi, Kushabhau Thakre, Bangaru Laxman, Jana Krishnamurthi, Rajnath Singh all started their careers with the RSS. Venkaiah Naidu also joined the RSS and started his political career with the ABVP, the RSS-affiliated student wing. Nitin Gadkari, considered close to the RSS, also started his career with the ABVP. Amit Shah joined the RSS as a student and then the ABVP. J.P. Nadda also started with the ABVP.
40. 'I am a state-level worker, he [Togadia] works at the international level now, his canvas is wider', Narendra Modi interview with N.K. Singh, *The Indian Express*, 1 November 2007.
41. A.B. Bardhan, 'Swayamsevak Vajpayee', *Observer*, 19 September 2000.
42. Rajesh Ramachandran, 'Here's why', *Hindustan Times*, 12 March 2000.

CHAPTER 12 The Growth of the RSS

1. The RSS was founded by Dr Keshav Baliram Hedgewar on Vijayadashami day, 27 September 1925, at his house in 'Sukravari' in Nagpur. The name 'Rashtriya Swayamsevak Sangh' was selected on 17 April 1926 during a meeting at Hedgewar's house, from a list of four names: Jaripatka Mandal, Bharat Uddharak Mandal, Hindu Swayamsevak Sangh and Rashtriya Swayamsevak Sangh. The tradition of commencing daily activities with a salutation to the saffron flag (bhagwa dhwaj) and concluding with the RSS prayer—prarthana—in Hindi and Marathi was instituted in 1926. See https://www.rss.org/Timeline.html.
2. Advani and Gupta's photo performing the RSS salute was published on page 1 of *The Times of India*, 16 October 2000. The RSS Prarthana, 'Namastee sada vatsale', is an ode to the Motherland in Sanskrit, with its last line in Hindi. It is compulsory to sing this prayer in all Sangh functions. It was first sung publicly by RSS pracharak Yadav Rao Joshi on 18 May 1940. Written by Narhar Narayan Bhide, the first line

is, 'Namaste sada vatsale matribhume' ('Namaste, oh ever-loving Motherland'). The last line 'Bharat Mata ki jai' is in Hindi. Details from the RSS website, which also carries translations of the song in Kannada, Tamil, Malayalam and Bangla. See https://samvada.org/2015/news/75-years-for-rss-prarthana/. Full video of the RSS prayer, with Hindi translation, is available at: https://youtu.be/4Si8U02s8cQ.

3. Quoted in S. Prasannarajan, 'Vision Hindutva', *India Today*, 30 October 2000.
4. See, for instance, Rajesh Ramachandran, 'RSS leader lashes out at political class in his annual address', 14 October 2000; Dilip Chaware, 'No differences with NDA, says RSS chief', *The Times of India*, 20 November 2000.
5. Nalin Mehta, 'RSS show of strength in Agra', NDTV broadcast, 15 October 2000, recording in author's collection.
6. The RSS defines this term, based on Sanskrit words, as 'the topmost leader of the RSS revered and venerated as "Friend, Philosopher and Guide" by all'. See https://www.rss.org//Encyc/2017/6/3/basic-faq-on-rss-eng.html.
7. Quoted in S. Prasannarajan, 'Vision Hindutva', *India Today*, 30 October 2000.
8. Quoted in Bishakha De Sarkar, 'With friends like these', *The Telegraph*, 13 March 2000.
9. Vivek Deshpande interview of Ram Madhav, 'Second-class Citizenship (for Muslims) against Hindu ethos', *The Indian Express*, 16 March 2003.
10. Manini Chatterjee, 'Repackaging the RSS', *The Indian Express*, 16 March 2003.
11. Ibid.
12. Ibid.
13. First, I discounted the monthly and weekly shakhas—assuming that some people who go to daily shakhas may also be going to weekly and monthly ones. Then, I used the RSS's officially reported number of daily shakhas in a year to make three projections: based on whether the average number of attendees at each shakha was fifteen, fifty or a hundred. The calculation gave us a range of rough minimum (calculated at an average of fifteen members per shakha) and maximum (calculated at an average of 100 members per RSS shakha) range for RSS membership numbers. If we use the middle estimate of an average of fifty attendees per shakha per year, then membership would amount to 29,63,300 members in 2019. Estimate by Nalin Mehta and Rajiv Pundir.
14. RSS chief Mohan Bhagwat said on 10 November 2011 that the RSS supported the Anna-led anti-corruption movement. This is a point made in September 2020 by Prashant Bhushan, one of the key leaders of the movement as well. Also see Ashutosh, 'Movement and the mask', *The Indian Express*, 13 September 2020.
15. Data from RSS annual reports, analysed by the author. In this regard, also see Anahita Mukherjee, 'RSS is on a roll: Number of shakhas up 61% in 5 years', *The Times of India*, 16 August 2015. The data in this report does not match entirely with the data in RSS annual reports. We have gone with the original RSS data. However, data points used in this TOI report indicate the same direction of change, http://timesofindia.indiatimes.com/articleshow/48498034.cms.

16. IANS, 'RSS active in 90% of blocks in India: Manmohan Vaidya', *Outlook*, 16 October 2019, https://www.outlookindia.com/newsscroll/rss-active-in-90-of-blocks-in-india-manmohan-vaidya/1641746.
17. Personal conversation with senior city-level RSS leader in UP, July 2020.
18. A number of shakhas (three to ten) form a Mandal (group of colonies) and a number of Mandals (five to ten) club together to form a Nagar (town/tehsil/block). A number of Nagars form a Zila (district). A number of Zilas form a Vibhag. Five to fifteen Vibhags form a Sambhag (division), and several of these form a Prant (province). A number of Prants make a Kshetra (region). By 2019, the RSS had eleven Kshetras: 1. South: Kerala, South Tamil Nadu, North Tamil Nadu; 2. South-Central: South Karnataka, West Andhra Pradesh, East Andhra Pradesh 3. West: Konkan, West Maharashtra, Devagiri, Gujarat, Vidarbha; 4. Central: Malwa, Madhya Bharat, Mahakaushal, Chhattisgarh; 5. North-West: Chittor, Jaipur, Jodhpur; 6. North: Delhi, Haryana, Punjab, Jammu and Kashmir, Himachal Pradesh; 7. West UP: Uttarakhand, Meerut and Braj; 8. East UP: Kanpur, Awadh, Kashi, Gorakhpur; 9. Northeast: North Bihar, South Bihar and Jharkhand; 10. East: North Bengal, Utkal, South Bengal; and 11. Assam: North Assam, Arunachal Pradesh, South Assam, Manipur. Details from Arun Anand, *Know about the RSS* (New Delhi: Prabhat, 2019), pp. 25–26.
19. Arun Anand, *Know about the RSS* (New Delhi: Prabhat, 2019), p. 53.
20. K.S. Sudarshan, then joint general secretary, RSS (as told to Seshadri Chari), 'No ism but dharma', *Outlook*, 27 May 1998.
21. Arun Anand, *Know about the RSS* (New Delhi: Prabhat, 2019), pp. 35–36.
22. Sunil Ambekar, *The RSS: Roadmaps for the 21st Century* (New Delhi: Rupa, 2019), p. 128.
23. PTI, 'Sangh starts "join RSS" initiative on website to boost base among youth', *Business Standard*, 29 April 2018, https://www.business-standard.com/article/pti-stories/sangh-starts-join-rss-initiative-on-website-to-boost-base-among-youth-118042900477_1.html.
24. Personal interview with Radha Krishna Holla, communications head, RSS Karnataka, RSS office, Bengaluru, 10 February 2020. The RSS Karnataka weblink is: https://samvada.org/.
25. Ibid.
26. Ibid.
27. Personal interview with Vadhiraj, RSS worker in Bengaluru and former head of communications, RSS Karnataka South Zone, 10 February 2020.
28. Ibid.
29. Personal interview with Radha Krishna Holla, communications head, RSS Karnataka, RSS office, Bengaluru, 10 February 2020.
30. Ibid.
31. RSS's Vishwa Samvad Kendra Karnataka Facebook page is at: https://www.facebook.com/Samvada. Its YouTube page is at: https://www.youtube.com/channel/UCeHTzY_gxSLC4M9i80s1D9Q.

32. Personal interview with Radha Krishna Holla, communications head, RSS Karnataka, RSS office, Bengaluru, 10 February 2020.
33. Dilip Chaware, 'RSS zooms into the virtual world with a "cyber shakha"', *The Times of India*, 23 September 1999.
34. From our Correspondent, 'The first CyberShakha of RSS', *Organiser*, 10 October 1999.
35. Gautam Siddharth, 'Software shakhas draw techies to RSS', *The Times of India*, 28 January 2008.
36. Available online at: https://vikramaweekly.in/.
37. Available online at: https://aseemamag.com/e-magazine/.
38. Personal interview with Radha Krishna Holla, communications head, RSS Karnataka, RSS office, Bengaluru, 10 February 2020.
39. Personal interview with Vadhiraj, RSS worker in Bengaluru and former head of communications, RSS Karnataka South Zone, 10 February 2020.
40. Yediyurappa stepped down as chief minister on 26 July 2021. He was replaced by Basavaraj Bommai. Details on the Congress response to the BJP government's move on the Tipu Sultan controversy from India Today Web Desk, 'BJP scrapped Tipu Jayanti because they hate minorities: Karnataka Congress leader Siddaramaiah', *India Today*, 30 July 2019, https://www.indiatoday.in/india/story/bjp-scrapped-tipu-jayanti-because-they-hate-minorities-karnataka-congress-leader-siddaramaiah-1575275-2019-07-30.
41. Personal interview with Vadhiraj, RSS worker in Bengaluru and former head of communications, RSS Karnataka South Zone, 10 February 2020. Tipu Sultan, reviled in British accounts of the period because of his alignment with the French, engaged in a long correspondence with Napoleon Bonaparte for a French invasion of India against the British. He was undoubtedly a nationalist hero to many: in 1990-91, the state broadcaster Doordarshan broadcast a historic drama on his life, *The Sword of Tipu Sultan*. Several Kannada plays were written about him in the nineteenth century, and the great playwright Girish Karnad wrote his iconic Kannada–English play, 'Dreams of Tipu Sultan', in 1997 to commemorate fifty years of India's independence. The record shows that Tipu built a strong economy, worked with Hindu advisors and donated to temples. Equally, he was responsible for the killing of thousands of Kodavas in Coorg and the forcible conversion of the Catholic Christians of Mangalore into Islam. For more on this, Chandan Gowda, 'All about Tipu Sultan', *The Hindu*, 2 December 2016, https://www.thehindu.com/opinion/op-ed/All-about-Tipu-Sultan/article16440247.ece. For Girish Karnad's play on Tipu, see Julia Neslie, 'Nailed to the past: Girish Karnad's plays', *Journal of South Asian Literature*, 1996/1997, Vol. 31/32, No. 1/2, pp. 50–84. For a historical account in defence of Tipu, see Bhupendra Yadav, 'Tipu Sultan: Giving "the devil" his due', *Economic & Political Weekly*, Vol. 25, No. 52, 29 December 1990, pp. 2835–2837; Mohammad Moienuddin, 'Distortions of Indian history with reference to Tipu Sultan', *Proceedings of the Indian History Congress*, Part One: Millennium,

Vol. 61, 2000–01, pp. 660–666. For more details on Tipu, see William Dalrymple, *The Anarchy: The East India Company, Corporate Violence and the Pillage of an Empire* (London: Bloomsbury, 2019). For the RSS counterview, see, for instance, Prashant Vaidyaraj, '"Historical tyrant" Tipu continues to be eulogised for votes', *Organiser*, 10 November 2018.

42. Manvir Saini, 'BJP win helped RSS grow deep roots in Haryana', *The Times of India*, 5 May 2019, http://timesofindia.indiatimes.com/articleshow/69181307.cms.
43. Ibid.
44. IANS, 'RSS active in 90% of blocks in India: Manmohan Vaidya', *Outlook*, 16 October 2019, https://www.outlookindia.com/newsscroll/rss-active-in-90-of-blocks-in-india-manmohan-vaidya/1641746.
45. Ibid.
46. In an article for *Organiser* (25 June 1956), Golwalkar wrote that after SP Mookerjee resigned from the government, he did not find any of the existing parties suitable. He says they met often on his decision to form a new party. Recounted by K.S. Sudarshan, then joint general secretary, RSS (as told to Seshadri Chari), 'No ism but dharma', *Outlook*, 27 May 1998.
47. Mohan Bhagwat quoted in 'The Sangh as it is', *Organiser*, Vol. 70, N. 14, 30 September 2018, p 15.
48. Ibid.
49. Atal Bihari Vajpayee, L.K. Advani, Murali Manohar Joshi, Kushabhau Thakre, Bangaru Laxman, Jana Krishnamurthi, Rajnath Singh all started their careers initially with the RSS. Venkaiah Naidu also joined the RSS and started with ABVP, the RSS-affiliated student wing. Nitin Gadkari, considered close to RSS, and started his career with ABVP. Amit Shah joined the RSS as a student and then the ABVP. J.P. Nadda also started with the ABVP.
50. Interview with Ashwathnarayan C.N., deputy chief minister, Karnataka, Bengaluru, 10 February 2020. Also minister for higher education; IT & BT, science and technology; skill development, entrepreneurship and livelihood. Dr Ashwathnarayan lost his portfolio of deputy chief minister on 4 August 2021 when the BJP decided to do away with its three-deputy chief ministers formula in Karnataka after Basavaraj Bommai took as state chief minister, succeeding B.S. Yediyurappa.
51. Note on methodology: We looked for written evidence for the RSS/RSS-affiliate membership of BJP leaders on the lists we examined. Only if we could find such a reference, did we classify a minister as having an RSS/RSS-affiliate background. If we could not find a written reference, even in cases where we heard verbal references of a leader being 'close to the RSS' or other such allusions, as a thumb rule we chose to be cautious and did not classify the leader as being from RSS. So, the actual number of RSS/RSS-affiliate members may be higher. We followed this methodology for all the BJP lists we examined for RSS backgrounds.
52. Neelam Pandey, Shankar Animesh, 'RSS in Modi government in numbers: 3 of 4 ministers are rooted in Sangh', *The Print*, 27 January 2020, https://theprint.

in/politics/rss-in-modi-govt-in-numbers-3-of-4-ministers-are-rooted-in-the-sangh/353942/.

53. Ibid.
54. Ibid.
55. RSS-affiliated bodies, the Bharatiya Shikshan Mandal (BSM), the Shiksha Sanskriti Utthan Nyas and the Bharatiya Bhasha Manch, were deeply involved in generating inputs through seminars across the country. The name of the Ministry of Human Resources and Development, which deals with education, was changed on 20 August 2020 to Ministry of Education. Renaming the ministry had figured prominently at a BSM conference in 2018. The Sangh affiliates submitted their suggestions to two key NEP drafting committees—Subramanium committee and another headed by K. Kasturirangan. Rahul Shrivastava, 'The RSS impact on New Education Policy', *India Today*, 3 August 2020, https://www.indiatoday.in/india/story/new-education-policy-rss-sangh-parivar-impact-sanskrit-1706340-2020-07-31. Also see Shyam Lal Yadav, Ritika Chopra, 'RSS wanted more, government walked the tightrope', *The Indian Express*, 30 July 2020, https://indianexpress.com/article/education/new-education-policy-rss-wanted-more-government-walked-the-tightrope-6530113/; Asmita Nandy, '"60-70% demands met', decoding RSS impact on NEP 2020', *The Quint*, 1 August 2020, https://www.thequint.com/news/education/rss-impact-on-new-education-policy-2020-decoding-demands.
56. Manini Chatterjee, 'Repackaging the RSS', *The Indian Express*, 16 March 2003.
57. Ibid.
58. Prabhu Chawla interview with Mohan Bhagwat on *Seedhi Baat*. Interview of the Week, *India Today*, 16 November 2009.
59. Ibid.
60. A.G. Noorani, 'RSS and Services-II', *The Statesman*, 15 January 2000.
61. Rajesh Joshi interview with Madan Das Devi, 'RSS dumping the BJP: "It's for the future to tell"', *Outlook*, 30 October 2000.
62. Interview with a BJP leader in Karnataka who spoke on condition of anonymity, 9 February 2020.
63. Interview with Lehar Singh Siroya, BJP MLC in Karnataka, Bengaluru, 9 February 2020.
64. Shamsul Islam, 'The failed Swayamsevaks', *The Hindu*, 7 July 2001.
65. Radhika Ramaseshan, 'Power levels shishya and guru in Sangh', *The Telegraph*, 30 March 2000
66. Pradeep Kaushal, 'Govt can't make the party brass wag its tail, says RSS', *The Indian Express*, 30 July 2001.
67. Ashok K. Damodaran, 'Furore over khaki', *India Today*, 13 March 2000
68. Swapan Dasgupta, 'Meshed in adolescence', *The Telegraph*, 3 April 2009.
69. Ibid.
70. 'We don't consider anyone Atalji's successor', *India Today*, 30 June 2003.

71. Prafulla Ketkar, 'Vote for a tectonic shift', *Organiser*, 25 May 2014, Vol. LXV, No. 48, p. 5.
72. Prafulla Ketkar, 'New narrative for new Bharat', *Organiser*, 2 June 2019, 2014, Vol. 70, No. 49, p. 5.

CHAPTER 13 What the RSS Says

1. Essentially, the Narad Index we developed for this project (as outlined in the Introduction and Chapter 6) measures the number of times a topic (or related keywords in English and Hindi) is mentioned per 100 words. The more times a particular topic, say Hindutva, is mentioned, the higher it ranks on the Narad Index. This allowed us to see patterns of political communication holistically. We took care to define both Hindi and English keywords for each topic and then ran the algorithm over the thousands of documents we had gathered to see how patterns of discourse between the RSS and its linked outfits change and how. See detailed methodology note in Appendix 4.
2. Christophe Jaffrelot, *The Hindu Nationalist Movement and Indian Politics: 1925 to the 1990s* (New Delhi: Penguin, 1996), p. 41.
3. This was at a meeting at Dole Math, Nagpur. See https://www.rss.org/Timeline.html.
4. See the RSS website, https://www.rss.org//Encyc/2017/6/3/basic-faq-on-rss-eng.html.
5. See the RSS website, https://www.rss.org/Timeline.html.
6. Sunil Ambekar, *The RSS: Roadmaps for the 21st Century* (New Delhi: Rupa, 2019), p. 128.
7. Walter Andersen, 'The Rashtriya Swayamsevak Sangh-I: Early concerns', *Economic & Political Weekly*, 11 March 1972, Vol. 7, No. 11, p. 589.
8. D. Gold quoted in Christophe Jaffrelot, *The Hindu Nationalist Movement and Indian Politics: 1925 to the 1990s* (New Delhi: Penguin, 1996), p. 34.
9. For this view, see for instance, Suprakash Majumdar, 'Dress how you want to be addressed: RSS and fascism', *National Herald*, 13 August 2019, https://www.nationalheraldindia.com/eye-on-rss/dress-how-you-want-to-be-addressed-rss-and-fascism.
10. The RSS was banned by the Government of India twice thereafter: 22 March 1977–4 July 1977 during the Emergency; and 10 December 1992–4 June 1993 after the demolition of the Babri Masjid. See https://www.rss.org/Timeline.html.
11. He also mentioned the first Sikh Guru, Nanak Dev. Speeches on 8 October 2019 and 18 October 2019.
12. RSS website, https://www.rss.org/Timeline.html.
13. G.D. Savarkar, better known as Babarao Savarkar, was the brother of Hindutva ideologue V.D. Savarkar and a co-founder, with him, of the revolutionary group Abhinav Bharat. Walter K. Andersen, Shridhar D. Damle, *Brotherhood in Saffron:*

The Rashtriya Swayamsevak Sangh and Hindu Revivalism (New Delhi: Penguin, 2019, first published 1987), p. 48.

14. Akshaya Mukul, 'RSS disowns Golwalkar's book', *The Times of India*, 9 March 2006, https://timesofindia.indiatimes.com/india/rss-officially-disowns-golwalkars-book/articleshow/1443606.cms.
15. M.S. Golwalkar, *We, Or Our Nationhood Defined* (Nagpur: Bharat Publications, second edition, 1947), p. 52.
16. Rakesh Sinha, *Shri Guruji and Indian Muslims*, pp. 2–3; eBook available at chrome-extension://efaidnbmnnnibpcajpcglclefindmkaj/viewer.html?pdfurl=http%3A%2F%2Fwww.archivesofrss.org%2FEncyc%2F2014%2F1%2F21%2F23_07_02_19_muslim.pdf&clen=238506& chunk=true. The booklet was released by the Sangh on 24 February 2006, Akshaya Mukul, 'RSS disowns Golwalkar's book', *The Times of India*, 6 March 2006.
17. Details from Walter K. Andersen and Shridhar D. Damle, *Brotherhood in Saffron: The Rashtriya Swayamsevak Sangh and Hindu Revivalism*, pp. 47–48; Des Raj Goyal, *Rashtriya Swayamsevak Sangh* (Delhi: Radhakrishnan Prakashan, 1987), p. 78
18. Akshaya Mukul, 'RSS disowns Golwalkar's book', *The Times of India*, 9 March 2006, https://timesofindia.indiatimes.com/india/rss-officially-disowns-golwalkars-book/articleshow/1443606.cms.
19. Mohan Bhagwat quoted in 'Myths busted: Sarsanghchalak ji answers', *Organiser*, Vol. 70, No. 14, 30 September 2018. RSS Sahsarkaryavah Manmohan Vaidya further clarified that while the Sangh had not distanced itself from Golwalkar as a whole, *Bunch of Thoughts* 'must be seen in the context of its times'—'from 1940–1965 (not his [Golwalkar's] entire tenure as Sarsanghchalak), a specific time' which had 'unique circumstances'. Manmohan Vaidya 'Sangh and Shri Guruji', *Organiser*, 28 October 2018, Vol. 70, No. 18.
20. For a historical background, see, for example, Christophe Jaffrelot, *The Hindu Nationalist Movement and Indian Politics: 1925 to the 1990s* (New Delhi: Penguin, 1996), pp. 11–75.
21. Mohan Bhagat's interview with Prafulla Ketkar and Hitesh Shankar, 'don't forget fundamentals in favourable atmosphere', *Organiser*, 25 March 2018, Vol. 69, No. 39.
22. Ibid.
23. Full text of Swami Vivekanand's 1893 speech is available at: https://belurmath.org/swami-vivekananda-speeches-at-the-parliament-of-religions-chicago-1893/.
24. Mohan Bhagat interview with Prafulla Ketkar and Hitesh Shankar, 'Don't forget fundamentals in favourable atmosphere', *Organiser*, Vol. 69, No. 39, 25 March 2018.
25. G. Sreedathan, 'Dharmo rakashati rakshitaha', *Organiser*, Vol. 64, No. 34, 18 February 2018.
26. Shashi Tharoor in conversation with Nalin Mehta on *Why I Am a Hindu*, Scindia Old Boys' Association's FG Pearce Symposium, India International Centre, Delhi, 3 February 2020.

27. Ajay Bharadwaj, 'Exasperating Farrago', *Organiser*, Vol. 69, No. 34, 18 February 2018.
28. Shashi Tharoor, *Why I Am a Hindu* (New Delhi: Aleph, 2018), pp. 195–197.
29. See, for example, Seshadri Chari, 'Decoding "Hindu Rashtra"', *India Today*, 8 November 2019, https://www.indiatoday.in/magazine/cover-story/story/20191118-decoding-hindu-rashtra-1616717-2019-11-08.
30. Mohan Bhagwat quoted in 'The Sangh as it is', *Organiser*, Vol. 70, No. 14, New Delhi, 30 September 2018.
31. Ibid.
32. Nachiketa Iyengar, 'Hindutva sans "ism"', *Organiser*, Vol. 69, No. 34, 18 February 2018.
33. TOINS, 'Hindutva is nationalism: Vajpayee', *The Times of India*, 24 March 1992.
34. Seshadri Chari interview of L.K. Advani in 'Liberal Hindutva', *Pioneer*, 15 February 2003.
35. K.S. Sudarshan, then joint general secretary, RSS (as told to Seshadri Chari), 'No ism but dharma', *Outlook*, 27 May 1998.
36. Speech at Nagpur, 18 October 2018. Text available at: https://www.firstpost.com/politics/mohan-bhagwat-vijayadashami-2018-speech-full-text-rss-chief-discusses-2019-elections-ramjanmabhoomi-and-urban-naxals-5401441.html.
37. Mohan Bhagwat quoted in 'The Sangh as it is', *Organiser*, Vol. 70, No. 14, New Delhi, 30 September 2018.
38. K.R. Malkani (then BJP vice president), 'Significance of Ayodhya', *The Indian Express*, 3 August 1992.
39. K.S. Sudarshan, then joint general secretary, RSS (as told to Seshadri Chari), 'no ism but dharma', *Outlook*, 27 May 1998.
40. Quoted in Rakesh Sinha, 'Rajjubhayya: Wax and steel', *The Economic Times*, 19 March 1994.
41. Radhika Ramaseshan, 'RSS accuses church of military designs', *Telegraph*, 16 October 2000.
42. Farzand Ahmad, 'Missionary imposition', *India Today*, 23 October 2000. Also see Rajesh Ramachandran, 'Christianity is more about politic than religion, says RSS chief', *The Times of India*, 16 October 2000. Several churches condemned this call. See Staff Reporters, 'Catholics' body condemns RSS chief's call for national church', *The Times of India*, 9 October 2000.
43. RSS website, https://www.rss.org//Encyc/2017/6/3/basic-faq-on-rss-eng.html. This view is also explained in 'RSS - Ek parichay', a video with Sangh Sahsarkaryavah Manmohan Vaidya, https://www.rss.org//Encyc/2017/5/20/RSS-Ek-Parichay-Dr-Manmohan-Vaidya-.html.
44. Swapan Dasgupta, 'Nationhood specified: Hindutva as a double-edged sword', *The Times of India*, 9 June 1993. Savarkar's book was first published as *Essentials of Hinduism* (Bombay: Veer Savarkar Prakashan, 1923); republished with a new title in 1928.
45. Ibid.

46. Swapan Dasgupta, 'Nationhood specified: Hindutva as a double-edged sword', *The Times of India*, 9 June 1993.
47. Rashtriya Swayamsevak Sangh, 'Summary of the address by param poojniya sarsanghchalak Dr Mohan Bhagwat Ji on the occasion of Sri Vijayadasami Utsav 2019 (Tuesday, 8 October 2019', available on chrome-extension://efaidnbmnnnibpcajpcglclefindmkaj/viewer.html? pdfurl=https%3A%2F%2Fwww.rss.org%2Fvijayadashmi-2019-english-speech.pdf&clen=703645&chunk=true.
48. Swapan Dasgupta, 'Nationhood specified: Hindutva as a double-edged sword', *The Times of India*, 9 June 1993.

CHAPTER 14 The Sangh Parivar and Education

1. Voting in Chhattisgarh's first state assembly election took place on 1 December 2003.
2. Judeo was first elected to Parliament in 1989 and was Union minister of state for environment and forests from 29 January–17 November 2003, http://loksabhaph.nic.in/Members/MemberBioprofile.aspx?mpsno= 3297&lastls=15. He passed away in 2013.
3. The 'shuddhi' movement was first started by the Arya Samaj, led by Swami Dayanand Saraswati, who is said to have performed the first such ceremony on a Muslim from Dehradun in 1877. It reflected a modern development in Hinduism, in response to Islam and Christianity. The first attempt at mass conversion was in 1908 in Deegh in Bharatpur State and was aimed at a group of Muslims. The 'shuddhi' movement gained steam from 1923 in the United Provinces with the formation of the Bharatiya Hindu Shuddhi Mahasabha and the launch of large-scale reconversion efforts by the Hindu Mahasabha and the Arya Samaj. Details from 'Yogendra Sikand on Muslim response to the Shuddhi Movement of the '20s', *Muslim India*, Vol. 770, April 2011, pp. 171–172. Also see Charu Gupta, 'Articulating Hindu masculinity and feminity: "Shuddhi" and "Sangathan" movements in United Provinces in the 1920s', *Economic & Political Weekly*, Vol. 33, No. 13, 26 March–3 April 1998, pp. 727–735.
4. Rajesh Ramachandran, 'Christian hand in Judeo Case: RSS', *The Times of India*, 19 November 2003. https://timesofindia.indiatimes.com/india/christian-hand-in-judeo-case-rss/articleshow/290484.cms.
5. ABVKA organising secretary in charge of Mahakaushal, Nishikant Joshi, quoted in Rajesh Ramachandran, 'Hindutva made the difference: RSS', *The Times of India*, 5 December 2003, https://timesofindia.indiatimes.com/india/Hindutva-made-the-difference-RSS/articleshow/340296.cms.
6. BJP chose Raman Singh as its chief minister after the election and he won two more terms (in 2008 and 2013) before losing power to Congress in 2018.
7. Uday Mahurkar, Sheel Raval, 'Champions of reconversion dominate amid debate over Gujarat violence against Christians', *India Today*, 25 January 1999.
8. Ibid.

9. Snehlata Vaid, *Vanvasi Kalyan Ashram: Karya Parichay* (Jashpur: Kalyan Ashram, 2011), p. 14. The text is in Hindi; translation is mine.
10. Telephone interview with Atul Jog (who was in Ranchi), national organising secretary, ABVKA, 13 September 2020.
11. Snehlata Vaid, *Vanvasi Kalyan Ashram: Karya Parichay* (Jashpur: Kalyan Ashram, 2011), p. 14. The text is in Hindi; translation is mine.
12. RSS website, https://www.rss.org/Timeline.html.
13. Telephone interview with Atul Jog (who was in Ranchi), national organising secretary, ABVKA, 13 September 2020.
14. Ibid.
15. Snehlata Vaid, *Vanvasi Kalyan Ashram: Karya Parichay* (Jashpur: Kalyan Ashram, 2011), pp. 15–16. The text is in Hindi; translation is mine. Details on the role of the Jashpur court also confirmed by Atul Jog of ABVKA.
16. Christophe Jaffrelot, *The Hindu Nationalist Movement and Indian Politics: 1925 to the 1990s* (New Delhi: Penguin, 1996), p. 322.
17. Snehlata Vaid, *Vanvasi Kalyan Ashram: Karya Parichay* (Jashpur: Kalyan Ashram, 2011), pp. 15–16. The text is in Hindi; translation is mine.
18. Ibid, p. 18.
19. Ibid, p. 13.
20. Special Correspondent, 'Idol installed in Somnath Temple: Dr. Prasad stresses need for religious tolerance', *The Times of India*, 12 May 1951.
21. 'Activities of missionaries: Govt. attitude clarified', *The Times of India*, 16 April 1953.
22. 'Three foreign missionaries so far externed: Undesirable activities', *The Times of India*, 16 September 1953.
23. '"Anti-Indian" activities by missionaries: Madras govt.'s report under consideration', *The Times of India*, 2 September 1953.
24. TOINS, 'Missionaries in Naga Hills: Chief minister's charge', *The Times of India*, 10 March 1954. This caused another debate in Parliament. 'Charge against U.S. Baptist Mission: State will take necessary action', *The Times of India*, 25 March 1954.
25. TOINS, 'Steps against foreign missionaries in UP: Government consulting centre', *The Times of India*, 24 April 1954.
26. TOINS, 'Conversions by Christian missionaries in Mathura—Monetary inducements: UP assembly debate', *The Times of India*, 10 May 1954.
27. TOINS, 'Propaganda by missionaries: Bihar minister's view', *The Times of India*, 4 March 1954.
28. TOINS, 'Activities of missionaries in Kashmir: Data being collected', *The Times of India*, 5 May 1954.
29. TOINS, '"March of civilisation" among tribes: Controversy over work of missionaries', *The Times of India*, 4 May 1954.
30. TOINS, '"Do not attempt to convert": Missionaries warned', *The Times of India*, 7 April 1954.

31. TOINS, '"March of civilisation" among tribes: Controversy over work of missionaries', *The Times of India*, 4 May 1954.
32. 'Full freedom to preach Christianity assured: But Dr Prasad cautions against conversions', *The Times of India*, 19 February 1954.
33. '"Avoid activities which cause suspicion": Dr Prasad's advice to missionaries', *The Times of India*, 12 August 1954.
34. Figures tabled in Parliament by Home Minister Katju. TOINS, '"Do not attempt to convert": Missionaries warned', *The Times of India*, 7 April 1954.
35. Mario Bussali, 'The Apostle St. Thomas and India', *East and West*, Vol. 3, No. 2, July 1952, pp. 88–94.
36. D. Dennis Hudson, 'The first Protestant mission to India: Its social and religious development', *Sociological Bulletin*, Vol. 42, No. 1/2, March–September 1993, pp. 37–63; 'Missionaries', Letter to the Editor by Hari Prasad Gupta, *The Times of India*, 11 June 1955.
37. Belkacem Belmekki, 'A wind of change: The New British colonial policy in post-revolt India', *Atlantis*, Vol. 30, No. 2, December 2008, p. 117.
38. 'Anti-Christian incidents in some parts: Call to centre for firm steps', *The Times of India*, 3 November 1955.
39. See, for example, 'Christians are concerned', *The Times of India*, 16 November 1955; 'Full religious tolerance, assures Mr. Nehru', *The Times of India*, 21 May 1954; TOINS, 'Vilification of missionaries: Plea to premier to intervene', *The Times of India*, 19 April 1955
40. TOINS, 'Work of foreign missionaries: Centre's policy clarified', *The Times of India*, 19 May 1954.
41. TOINS, 'Congressmen must work for social equality: Mr Nehru's call: "Shuddhi" movement condemned', *The Times of India*, 10 August 1954.
42. TOINS, 'New Govt. Policy Towards Foreign Missionaries: "Must also devote time to social work"', *The Times of India*, 27 August 1955.
43. TOINS, 'Alien missionaries given assurance: No intention to curtail freedom, says Dr. Prasad', *The Times of India*, 19 December 1955.
44. The eight-member M.B. Rege Committee was appointed on 10 May 1954. '1,200 conversions in six years: Activities of Christian missionaries in M.B', *The Times of India*, 15 December 1954; 'Alleged unfair conversions: M.B. inquiry ordered', *The Times of India*, 11 May 1954.
45. The six-member committee was appointed on 14 April 1954. Justice Niyogi, who headed it, had been a former chief justice of the Nagpur High Court. The committee, which included S.K. George, a professor at Commerce College, Wardha, visited seventy-seven centres, contacted 11,360 persons, received written statements from 375 people and interviewed residents of 700 villages. 'Withdraw Christian missionaries: MP inquiry committee's recommendations', *The Times of India*, 18 July 1956.
46. Hindu Mahasabha's V.D. Deshpande visited Jashpur and gave a memorandum to the committee. TOINS, 'Adivasis' allegations', *The Times of India*, 16 June 1954.

47. Full text of the report available at: http://www.voiceofdharma.org/books/ncr/.
48. The UN report was drafted by Dr A. Krishnaswami, MP, as part of a world-wide study on discrimination on religious rights and practices for the UN Sub-Commission on the Prevention of Discrimination and Protection of Minorities. Dr Krishnaswami, an Indian member of parliament, was entrusted this task as Special Rapporteur by the ninth session of the Sub-Commission and his report included information from thirty countries and a large number of NGOs. 'Withdraw Christian Missionaries: MP inquiry committee's recommendations', *The Times of India*, 18 July 1956.
49. 'Niyogi Committee charges termed "exaggerated": UN Report on Christian Missionaries', *The Times of India*, 16 November 1957.
50. For an overview of anti-conversion laws in Indian states, see James Andrew Huff, 'Religious freedom in India and analysis of the constitutionality of anti-conversion laws', 10(2) *Rutgers Journal of Law and & Religion*, 1(4), 2009, archived at https://perma.cc/7Z7Y-9U8Q; Laura Dudley Jenkins, 'Legal Limits on Religious Conversion in India', *Law and Contemporary Problems*, 109, 113 (2008), http://scholarship.law.duke.edu/cgi/viewcontent.cgi?article=1469&context=lcp.
51. Snehlata Vaid, *Vanvasi Kalyan Ashram: Karya Parichay* (Jashpur: Kalyan Ashram, 2011), p. 18. The text is in Hindi; translation is mine.
52. Interview with Ashish Joshi, CEO, Lok Sabha TV, New Delhi, 15 September 2019, in his office in the Parliament building.
53. Snehlata Vaid, *Vanvasi Kalyan Ashram: Karya Parichay* (Jashpur: Kalyan Ashram, 2011), p. 18. The text is in Hindi; translation is mine.
54. Balasaheb Deoras's full name was Madhukar Dattatraya Deora. Details from http://kalyanashram.org/about-us/background/; telephone interview with Atul Jog (who was in Ranchi), national organising secretary, ABVKA, 13 September 2020.
55. Snehlata Vaid, *Vanvasi Kalyan Ashram: Karya Parichay* (Jashpur: Kalyan Ashram, 2011), pp. 19–20. The text is in Hindi; translation is mine.
56. ABVKA website, http://kalyanashram.org/about-us/background/.
57. Telephone interview with Atul Jog (who was in Ranchi), national organising secretary, ABVKA, 13 September 2020.
58. The 1991 Census enumerated sixty-four districts in the eight north-eastern states. The number of districts increased to eighty-six by 2015. 1991 data is from M. Vijayanunni, *1991 Census Handbook* (New Delhi: Registrar General and Census Commissioner of India, 1996), available at: https://censusindia.gov.in/DigitalLibrary/data/Census_1991/Publication/India/45969_1991_CHN.pdf; 2015 data is from North Eastern Council Secretariat (Evaluation and Monitoring Sector), Government of India, *Basic Statistics of North Eastern Region 2015* (Shillong: 2015), p. xxvii, available on: http://necouncil.gov.in/sites/default/files/uploadfiles/BasicStatistic2015-min.pdf.
59. 1992 details and quotes from Staff Reporter, 'RSS organ aims to reach tribal pockets', *The Independent*, 20 March 1992.

60. A good example is Chhattisgarh's Raigarh district. In 1992, there were twenty-five Roman Catholic churches in the district. The churches also ran fifteen higher-secondary schools and 250 balwadis in remote pockets, two hospitals, three leprosy treatment centres, one TB control unit, an orphanage, an old-age home and seed banks for tribal cultivators. Azizur Rahaman, 'Convertible issue', *Sunday*, 12 April 1992.
61. Overall, Census of India in 2001 estimated 593 districts with ST populations of varying degrees. District-wise ST data from Census 2011 is available at: https://censusindia.gov.in/2011census/pca_st/pca-st.html, 2001 ST data is on https://censusindia.gov.in/census_and_you/scheduled_castes_and_sceduled_tribes.aspx. India had a total of 727 districts in September 2021. District count is from http://districts.nic.in/.
62. Details from ABVKA reports and organisational information at: https://kalyanashram.org/about-us/where-we-work/.
63. Personal interview with Radha Krishna Holla, communications head, RSS Karnataka, RSS office, Bengaluru, 10 February 2020.
64. ABVKA organisational information at: https://kalyanashram.org/about-us/where-we-work/.
65. RSS website, https://www.rss.org/Timeline.html.
66. RSS website, https://www.rss.org/Encyc/2012/10/22/rss-vision-and-mission.html.
67. Vidya Bharti website, http://vidyabharti.net/about-vidya-bharati.
68. Vidya Bharti Akhil Bhartiya Shiksha Sansthan Brochure, http://vidyabharti.net/sites/default/files/vb-brochure-english.pdf.
69. Walter K. Andersen, Shridhar D. Damle, *The RSS: A View to the Inside* (New Delhi: Penguin/Viking, 2018), p. 34–35.
70. Information from a senior RSS leader and board member of Deendayal Dham, Mathura, 26 July 2020.
71. Walter K. Andersen, Shridhar D. Damle, *The RSS: A View to the Inside* (New Delhi: Penguin/Viking, 2018), p. 34.
72. Telephone interview with Atul Jog (speaking from Ranchi), national organising secretary, ABVKA, 13 September 2020.
73. ABVKA Resolution Passed in KKM Meeting, 22 September 2016, Pindwara, Rajasthan: Resolution No. 6. 'Ban illicit religious conversions and appoint A-8 central commission of inquiry to study & report impact thereof', http://kalyanashram.org/wp-content/uploads/2018/02/Ban-on-Conversions-1.pdf.
74. Ibid.
75. Shailendra, 'Hindutva's effort to claim tribals', *People's Democracy*, 2 July 2000. Also see Dara Singh interview in *Bharatiya Pragna*, Vol. 2, No. 6, June 2000, http://www.geocities.ws/free_dara_singh/interview.htm.
76. Quoted in Walter K. Andersen, Shridhar D. Damle, *The RSS: A View to the Inside* (New Delhi: Penguin/Viking, 2018), p. 35.

77. Sunil Ambekar, *The RSS: Roadmaps for the 21st Century* (New Delhi: Rupa, 2019), p. 26.
78. Quoted in Rajesh Joshi, 'Season of bad blood', *Outlook*, 30 October 2000.
79. HT Correspondent, 'RSS body "lauds" missionaries', *Hindustan Times*, 24 September 2000.
80. DD News, 'Cabinet approves New Education Policy', 29 July 2020, https://ddnews.gov.in/national/cabinet-approves-national-education-policy-2020#:~:text=The%20Union%20Cabinet%20chaired%20by,school%20and%20higher%20education%20sectors.
81. Prafulla Ketkar, 'Returning to Tilak's concept of Swaraj', *Organiser*, 9 August 2020, Vol. 72, No. 7.
82. Atul Kothari, National Secretary, SSUN, 'Resurgence of Bharatiyata in education', *Organiser*, 9 August 2020, Vol. 72, No. 7.
83. Swadesh Singh, 'Revolution through knowledge: Harbinger of massive reforms', *Organiser*, 9 August 2020, Vol. 72, No. 7.
84. Vasudha Venugopal, 'RSS Affiliates Welcome the NEP, say over 60% of their suggestions met', *The Economic Times*, 30 July 2020, https://economictimes.indiatimes.com/news/politics-and-nation/rss-affiliates-welcome-the-nep-say-over-60-of-their-suggestions-met/articleshow/77249418.cms.
85. Prafulla Ketkar, 'Making education national', *Organiser*, Vol. 70, No. 51, 16 June 2019.
86. Interview with M.K. Sridhar, member of the NEP drafting committee, in 'Integrated and holistic approach to a child's education', *Organiser*, Vol. 70, No. 51, 16 June 2019.
87. Anirban Ganguly, 'Indianising education for harnessing humanism', *Organiser*, Vol. 66, No. 49, 7 June 2015.
88. Mukul Kanitkar, 'Bharatiya education: A holistic and integrated approach', *Organiser*, Vol. 66, No. 49, 7 June 2015.
89. Walter K. Andersen, Shridhar D. Damle, *The RSS: A View to the Inside* (New Delhi: Penguin/Viking, 2018), p. 33.
90. Parwati Prema Jagati Saraswati Vihar, 'Where Traditions Meet Modernity', *Organiser*, Vol. 66, No. 49, 7 June 2015.
91. RSS ABPS Resolution: 'Need to protect and promote Bharatiya languages', Nagpur, 10 March 2018, https://www.rss.org/Encyc/2018/3/10/abps-rsolution-2018.html.
92. See Akhil Bharatiya Pratinidhi Sabha, 'Full text of the resolution adopted at RSS Akhil Bharatiya Pratinidhi Sabha, 2018 in Nagpur' and Mohan Bhagat interview with Prafulla Ketkar and Hitesh Shankar, 'Don't forget fundamentals in favourable atmosphere', in *Organiser*, Vol. 69, No. 39, 25 March 2018.
93. Interview with Atul Kothari by Pramod Kumar, 'We are reconnecting education to Indian roots', *Organiser*, 30 June 2019.
94. Abha Khanna Gupta, 'A crusade for healthy education', *Organiser*, Vol. 66, No. 49, 7 June 2015.

95. See, for instance, Kaveree Bamzai, 'Indian schools still not ready for sex education', *India Today*, 18 June 2007, https://www.indiatoday.in/magazine/education/story/20070618-no-sex-education-in-indian-schools-743388-2007-06-18; PTI, 'NCEART to remove objectionable portions on sex-education', *Outlook*, 29 July 2008, https://www.outlookindia.com/newswire/story/ncert-to-remove-objectionable-portions-on-sex-education/593552.
96. Available to read here: https://publishing.cdlib.org/ucpressebooks/view?chunk.id=d0e1254&docId=ft3j49n8h7.
97. Abha Khanna Gupta, 'A Crusade for Healthy Education', Organiser, Vol. 66, No. 49, 7 June 2015.
98. Smriti Singh, TNN, 'Penguin pulls out Wendy Doniger's book "The Hindus" from India', *The Times of India*, 12 February 2014, https://timesofindia.indiatimes.com/india/penguin-pulls-out-wendy-donigers-book-the-hindus-from-india/articleshow/30240558.cms.
99. Rashmi Menon, ET Bureau, 'Indian publishers nervous about taking books that might offend Hindutva: Wendy Doniger', *The Economic Times*, 11 February 2016, https://economictimes.indiatimes.com/magazines/panache/indian-publishers-nervous-about-taking-books-that-might-offend-hindutva-wendy-doniger/articleshow/50940104.cms?from=mdr.
100. Interview with Atul Kothari by Pramod Kumar, 'We are reconnecting education to Indian roots', *Organiser*, 30 June 2019.
101. Ibid.
102. Ibid.
103. Parwati Prema Jagati Saraswati Vihar, 'Where traditions meet modernity', *Organiser*, Vol. 66, No. 49, 7 June 2015.
104. Indroneil Biswas, 'Maharana Pratap did not get due place in history, says Home Minister Rajnath Singh', *NDTV.com*, 9 May 2017, https://www.ndtv.com/india-news/maharana-pratap-did-not-get-due-place-in-history-says-home-minister-rajnath-singh-1691526.
105. Ritika Chopra, 'New icons in NCERT books: Bajirao to Maharana Pratap', *The Indian Express*, 30 May 2018, https://indianexpress.com/article/education/new-icons-in-ncert-books-bajirao-to-maharana-pratap-5196491/.
106. RSS website, https://www.rss.org//Encyc/2017/6/3/basic-faq-on-rss-eng.html.
107. Sunil Ambekar, *The RSS: Roadmaps for the 21st Century* (New Delhi: Rupa, 2019), pp. 128–129.
108. Ibid.
109. Walter K. Andersen, Shridhar D. Damle, *The RSS: A View to the Inside* (New Delhi: Penguin/Viking, 2018), p. 23.
110. Ibid.
111. Sunil Ambekar, *The RSS: Roadmaps for the 21st Century* (New Delhi: Rupa, 2019), pp. 128–129.
112. Ibid, p. 129.

113. Ibid., pp.130–131. Also see Mohan Bhagat interview with Prafulla Ketkar and Hitesh Shankar, 'Don't forget fundamentals in favourable atmosphere', *Organiser*, 25 March 2018, Vol. 69, No. 39.
114. Sunil Ambekar, *The RSS: Roadmaps for the 21st Century* (New Delhi: Rupa, 2019), p.130.
115. Uday Mahurkar, 'Sangh takes charge', *India Today*, 17 January 2000. The Gujarat government sent a query to the Home Ministry and it sent a positive reply. Gujarat Home Minister Haren Pandya revealed the contents of the Centre's letter on 13 July 1999. It cited the report of the Unlawful Activities Tribunal of 1993 to that say that they had not found anything 'unlawful' about the RSS activities. This Tribunal was led by Justice P.K. Bahri of the Delhi High Court, which on 4 June 1993 under Unlawful Activities (Prevention) Act, 1967, stuck down GOI order of 10 December 1992, banning the RSS. See A.G. Noorani, 'RSS and Services-I', *Statesman*, 14 January 2000.
116. V. Venkatesan. 'A Saffron Move Stopped', *Frontline*, 31 March 2000.

CHAPTER 15 The BJP's South Model

1. When BSP leader Mayawati asked Muslim voters not to waste their votes in the 2019 poll campaign, the UP chief minister responded by saying, 'SP-BSP have faith in Ali. We also have faith in Bajrang Bali.' Video available at: https://www.youtube.com/watch?v=MRkZYYbmQLQ.
2. See interactive election data sets (1980–2019), state-wise and region-wise, that we have made available for this analysis at: https://pollniti.com/.
3. Sree Siddaganga Math website, https://www.siddagangamath.org/siddaganga/home.html. For more details on Basavanna (also known as Basaveshwara, Basava) and the Lingayat/Veerashaiva tradition, see Julia Leslie, 'Understanding Basava: History, hagiography and a modern Kannada drama', *Bulletin of the School of Oriental and African Studies*, University of London, Vol. 61, No. 2, 1998, pp. 228–261.
4. The announcement was made on 19 March 2018, following the recommendations of a seven-member committee headed by former High Court judge Nagamohan Das. The Congress government moved to recognise Lingayats and Veerashaiva-Lingayats who believe in Basava Tattva (philosophy) as a religious minority community under Section (D) of the Karnataka Minorities Act. This opened up a political controversy on three counts.

a. A section of the community saw the reservation move as a political ploy to attract Lingayat voters who are traditionally regarded as pro-BJP;

b. A section of Lingayats complained that they were not distinct from Hinduism;

c. Some Lingayat groups argued that Veerashaivas and Lingayats were the same and alleged that treating them as separate communities (with the government regarding the Veerashaivas as a subsect of the Lingayats) was a cynical ploy aimed at political division.

Manu Aiyappa, 'Karnataka cabinet grants minority status to dominant Lingayats community', *The Times of India*, 18 March 2018, https://timesofindia.indiatimes.com/city/bengaluru/karnataka-govt-grants-separate-religion-status-to-lingayat-community/articleshow/63366151.cms; TNN, 'Karnataka govt clears minority status for Lingayats', *The Times of India*, 20 March 2018, https://timesofindia.indiatimes.com/india/karnataka-govt-clears-minority-status-for-lingayats/articleshow/63373048.cms.

5. On this, see S.H. Patil, 'Impact of modernisation and democratisation on a dominant community: A case study of the Lingayat community in Karnataka', *The Indian Journal of Political Science*, Vol. 68, No. 4, October–December 2007, p. 665; R. Blake Michael, 'Foundation myths of the two denominations of Vīraśaivism: Viraktas and Gurusthalins', *The Journal of Asian Studies*, Vol. 42, No. 2, February 1983, pp. 309–322.
6. Vikram Gopal, 'Lingayats and Veerashaiva-Lingayats notified as a religious minority, subject to central approval', *Hindustan Times*, 23 March 2018, https://www.hindustantimes.com/karnataka/lingayats-and-veerashaiva-lingayats-notified-as-religious-minority-subject-to-central-approval/story-cswoP1Dlbcz3T2qnfNP8YM.html.
7. This was broadcast as part of the *Times of India*'s 'Election with Times Series', which I anchored and reported for. 'Why Lingayat vote is decisive in Karnataka elections', 8 May 2018, https://timesofindia.indiatimes.com/why-lingayat-vote-is-decisive-in-karnataka-elections/videoshow/64073381.cms.
8. ABP, 'BJP's Lingayat mission: Party chief Amit Shah bows head to Shivakumara Swami of Siddaganga', 26 March 2018, https://www.youtube.com/watch?v=fffAxv8y79E.
9. TOI, 'Rahul Gandhi visits Siddaganga Mutt, seeks Shivakumara Swami's blessings', 4 April 2018, https://www.youtube.com/watch?v=2tMs3yWGcek.
10. Nalin Mehta, interview with Swamy Sri Sri Siddalinga Mahaswamy, broadcast as part of the *Times of India*'s 'Election with Times Series', 'Why Lingayat vote is decisive in Karnataka Elections', 8 May 2018, https://timesofindia.indiatimes.com/why-lingayat-vote-is-decisive-in-karnataka-elections/videoshow/64073381.cms. For a full profile of the Swamy, who succeeded Shivakumar Swamyji after his death in January 2019, see https://www.siddagangamath.org/siddaganga/junior.html.
11. The BJP won thirty-eight of seventy seats where Lingayat voters were dominant in the Karnataka assembly election of 12 May 2018. Overall, in the 224-member state assembly, it won 104 seats (36.35 per cent vote share), Congress eighty (38.14 per cent vote share), JD-S thirty-eight (18.3 per cent vote share). See TOI Karnataka Data Hub, https://timesofindia.indiatimes.com/elections/assembly-elections/karnataka/constituency-map.
12. M.N. Srinivas, 'The dominant caste in Rampura', *American Anthropologist*, New Series, Vol. 61, No. 1, February 1959, pp. 1–16. For more on how caste remains fundamental to Indian politics, see Ronojoy Sen, 'The persistence of caste in Indian politics', *Pacific Affairs*, Vol. 85, No. 2, June 2012, pp. 363–369.

13. Vokkaligas had constituted 20.4 per cent of the old Mysore State's population, while Lingayats were 12 per cent in the 1930 Caste Census. Valerian Rodrigues, 'Political power and democratic enablement: Devaraj Urs and lower caste mobilisation in Karnataka', *Economic & Political Weekly*, Vol. 49, No. 25, 21 June 2014, p. 64.
14. Chandan Gowda, 'Terms of separation', *The Hindu*, 23 March 2018.
15. All details from a summary of the studies on Lingayats by William McCormack, 'Lingayats as a sect', *The Journal of the Royal Anthropological Institute of Great Britain and Ireland*, Vol. 93, No. 1, January–June 1963, pp. 59–60.
16. Valerian Rodrigues, 'Political power and democratic enablement: Devaraj Urs and lower caste mobilisation in Karnataka', *Economic & Political Weekly*, Vol. 49, No. 25, 21 June 2014, pp. 62–70.
17. James Manor, 'Structural changes in Karnataka politics', *Economic & Political Weekly*, Vol. 12, No. 44, 29 October 1977, p. 1867.
18. Based on an average of year-wise figures in Valerian Rodrigues, 'Political power and democratic enablement: Devaraj Urs and lower caste mobilisation in Karnataka', *Economic & Political Weekly*, Vol. 49, No. 25, 21 June 2014, p. 64.
19. James Manor, 'Changes in Karnataka over the last generation: Villages and the wider context', *Economic & Political Weekly*, Vol. 42, No. 8, 24 February–2 March 2007, p. 653.
20. Valerian Rodrigues, 'Political power and democratic enablement: Devaraj Urs and lower caste mobilisation in Karnataka', *Economic & Political Weekly*, Vol. 49, No. 25, 21 June 2014, pp. 65–66.
21. NCBC, 'Central list of OBCs for the state of Karnataka', http://www.ncbc.nic.in/Writereaddata/cl/karnataka.pdf.
22. Mysore State was first reorganised on 1 November 1956, with the addition of new areas vide the States Reorganisation Act. It was renamed Karnataka on 1 November 1973 vide the Mysore State (Alteration of Name) Act, 1973.
23. See, for instance, TNN, 'Darji, a poor man's Congressman', *The Times of India*, 31 August 2004, https://timesofindia.indiatimes.com/city/ahmedabad/Darji-A-poor-mans-Congressman/articleshow/834014.cms.
24. PTI, 'Veerendra known as good administrator', *The Times of India*, 1 December 1989.
25. Chidanand Rajghatta, 'The gentle mutineer', *The Times of India*, 14 October 1990.
26. Interview with T.M. Veeraraghav, former resident editor, *The Hindu*, Bengaluru, and former South India editor, Network 18, 9 February 2020.
27. E. Raghavan and Imran Qureshi, 'A coup that boomeranged', *The Times of India*, 14 October 1990.
28. Ibid.
29. For full details of Patil's televised statement of defiance and good-health, see PTI, 'Veerendra Patil defies Rajiv', *The Times of India*, 8 October 1990.
30. Patil claimed 103 MLAs vs a claim of 145 by the party top brass. TOINS, 'President's Rule in Karnataka', *The Times of India*, 11 October 1990.

31. TOINS, 'JD offers support to Veerendra', *The Times of India*, 16 October 1990.
32. TOINS, 'President's Rule to be revoked in Karnataka', *The Times of India*, 15 October 1990.
33. E. Raghavan and Imran Qureshi, 'A coup that boomeranged', *The Times of India*, 14 October 1990.
34. PTI, 'End of political turmoil', *The Times of India*, 18 October 1990.
35. UNI, 'CLP ousts Veerendra', *The Times of India*, 12 October 1990.
36. Modi referred to this story in a public meeting in 2018. See India TV News Desk, 'PM Modi recalls how Rajiv Gandhi publicly insulted T Anjaiah, 'Dalit' CM of Andhra Pradesh: Here's what actually happened', 7 February 2018, https://www.indiatvnews.com/news/india-pm-modi-recalls-how-rajiv-gandhi-publicly-insulted-t-anjaiah-dalit-cm-of-andhra-pradesh-here-s-what-actually-happened-426523. For details of that incident, also see: Radhika Ramaseshan, 'Rajiv shadow in Rahul snub', *The Telegraph*, 29 March 2008.
37. Veerendra Patil interview with M.D. Nalapat, '"Liquor kings found me unreasonable": Patil', *The Times of India*, 2 December 1990.
38. Veerendra Patil interview with M.D. Nalapat, '"Elect leader democratically": Veerendra', *The Times of India*, 3 September 1991.
39. S.S. 'Caste and power game in Karnataka', *Economic & Political Weekly*, Vol. 25, No. 42/42, 20–27 October 1990.
40. James Manor in 2013 estimated Lingayats to be about 17 per cent of the population. James Manor, 'Lucky in its adversaries, a slipshod Congress gains a majority in the Karnataka election', *Economic & Political Weekly*, Vol. 48, No. 47, 23 November 2013, p. 54.
41. Personal interview with V. Anand, director, Octobuzz Analytics Pvt. Ltd., and in-charge of Yediyurappa's communications and social media campaign in the 2018 election, 9 February 2020, Bengaluru.
42. On this, see, for instance, Sandeep Shastri, B.S. Padmavathi, 'Karnataka: The lotus blooms … nearly', *Economic & Political Weekly*, Vol. 44, No. 6, 7–13 February 2009, p. 45.
43. In 2004, the Congress (35.28 per cent votes) significantly outpolled the BJP (28.49 per cent) but won only sixty-five seats compared to the BJP's seventy-nine. In 2008, again, the Congress won more votes (34.59 per cent) than the BJP (35.86 per cent), but won only eighty seats, compared to the BJP's 110. In 2013, the Congress won more votes (38.04 per cent) than the BJP (36.22 per cent), but underperformed on seats with seventy-eight, compared to the BJP's 104. 2004 and 2008 data quoted in James Manor, 'Letting a winnable election slip away: Congress in Karnataka', *Economic & Political Weekly*, Vol. 43, No. 41, 11–17 October 2008, p. 23. 2018 data from https://eci.gov.in/files/file/6933-karnataka-2018/.
44. Personal interview with Ashwathnarayan C.N., deputy chief minister, Karnataka, Bengaluru, 10 February 2020. Also minister for higher education; it & bt, science & technology; skill development, entrepreneurship & livelihood. Dr

Ashwathnarayan lost his portfolio of deputy chief minister on 4 August 2021 when the BJP decided to do away with its three-deputy chief ministers formula in Karnataka after Basavaraj Bommai took over as state chief minister, succeeding B.S. Yediyurappa.

45. Personal interview with Lehar Singh Siroya, Karnataka BJP MLC and former state party treasurer, 9 February 2020.
46. Personal interview with V. Anand, director, Octobuzz Analytics Pvt. Ltd, and in-charge of Yediyurappa's communications and social media campaign in the 2018 election, 9 February 2020, Bengaluru.
47. T.M. Veeraraghav, *Battleground South India*, Documentary on CNN-IBN, telecast in 2008.
48. Personal interview with Lehar Singh Siroya, Karnataka BJP MLC and former state party treasurer, 9 February 2020.
49. Ibid.
50. TOINS, 'Karnataka to foil Idgah flag hoisting', *The Times of India*, 10 August 1994, p. 1.
51. For a full legal timeline of this case, see Rishikesh Bahadur Desai, 'Idgah Maidan belongs to HDMC, rules SC', *The Times of India*, https://timesofindia.indiatimes.com/city/hubballi/Idgah-Maidan-belongs-to-HDMC-rules-SC/articleshow/5441838.cms. Further details from TOINS, 'Karnataka to foil Idgah flag hoisting', *The Times of India*, 9 August 1994, p. 1. This case was linked to an older property dispute at the Idgah Maidan from 1971 when AeI initially got permission from HDMC to build a commercial complex. A group of Hubli residents immediately went to court against the HDMC, AeI and the state government in the munsif court (through OS 359/72) which ruled in their favour. The additional sessions judge (vide RA No/1974) and Karnataka High Court (vide RSA no. 754/82) upheld this judgment and when the litigation reached the Supreme Court, it put an interim stay on demolitions in 1992. Details on original legal case from People's Democratic Forum, *The Flag Without Tears: A Report on the Hubli Idgah Maidan Issue*, December 1994 (Bangalore, People's Democratic Forum), pp. 10–12, 31–35.
52. Interview with T.M. Veeraraghav, former resident editor, *The Hindu*, Bengaluru, and former south India editor, Network 18, 9 February 2020.
53. M. Ahiraj, 'Tension in Hubli over I-Day flag hoisting', *The Times of India*, 15 August 1993, p. 9.
54. Ibid.
55. Ibid.
56. TOINS, 'Karnataka to foil Idgah flag hoisting', *The Times of India*, 9 August 1994, p. 1.
57. TNN, 'Her story: What happened in Hubli', *The Times of India*, 22 August 2004, p. 5.
58. TOINS, 'Four killed in Hubli firing', *The Times of India*, 16 August 1994, p. 1.

59. M. Ahiraj, 'Tension in Hubli over I-Day flag hoisting', *The Times of India*, 15 August 1993, p. 9.
60. T.M. Veeraraghav, *Battleground South India*, Documentary on CNN-IBN, telecast in 2008.
61. 'Back to Hubli', *The Times of India*, 25 January 1995.
62. Personal interview with Lehar Singh Siroya, Karnataka BJP MLC and former state party treasurer, 9 February 2020.
63. T.M. Veeraraghav, *Battleground South India*, Documentary on CNN-IBN, telecast in 2008.
64. 'Flag hoisting issue hots up again', *The Times of India*, 21 January 1995.
65. Amulya Ganguly, 'Ayodhya to Idgah', *The Times of India*, 22 August 1994.
66. Rishikesh Bahadur Desai, 'Idgah Maidan belongs to HDMC, rules SC', *The Times of India*, 13 January 2010, https://timesofindia.indiatimes.com/city/hubballi/Idgah-Maidan-belongs-to-HDMC-rules-SC/articleshow/ 5441838.cms.
67. Theja Ram, 'BJP's Ayodhya in Karnataka: Troubles at Bababudangiri on Datta Jayanti', 4 December 2017, https://www.thenewsminute.com/article/bjp-s-ayodhya-karnataka-trouble-bababudangiri-datta-jayanti-72635.
68. For legal details, see Karnataka High Court, *Sri Syed Ghouse Mohiuddin Shah ... vs State of Karnataka - By its chief ... on 14 February, 2007*, order by H. Ramesh, available on https://indiankanoon.org/doc/796868/. Also see Veekhar Ahmad Sayeed, 'A battlefront in the south', *Frontline*, 14 February 2018, https://frontline.thehindu.com/the-nation/a-battlefront-in-the-south/article10074157.ece/amp/.
69. T.M. Veeraraghav, *Battleground South India*, Documentary on CNN-IBN, telecast in 2008.
70. Interview with T.M. Veeraraghav, former resident editor, *The Hindu*, Bengaluru, and former south India editor, Network18, 9 February 2020.
71. Personal interview with a senior BJP minister in the Karnataka government, who did not wish to be identified. February 2020, Bengaluru.
72. Personal interview with Lehar Singh Siroya, Karnataka BJP MLC and former state party treasurer, 9 February 2020.
73. T.M. Veeraraghav, *Battleground South India*, Documentary on CNN-IBN, telecast in 2008.
74. Personal interview with Lehar Singh Siroya, Karnataka BJP MLC and former state party treasurer, 9 February 2020.
75. Suresh Babu, former ADG police, Karnataka, in T.M. Veeraraghav, *Battleground South India*, Documentary on CNN-IBN, telecast in 2008.
76. Personal interview with Lehar Singh Siroya, Karnataka BJP MLC and former state party treasurer, 9 February 2020.
77. Personal interview with B.Y. Vijayendra, Karnataka BJP vice president, 10 February 2020, Bengaluru. He was general secretary of the BJP's State Yuva Morcha (youth wing) when we met.
78. Details available at: http://kla.kar.nic.in/mlc'list/Sri%20V%20s%20Acharya.htm.

79. Personal interview with V. Anand, director, Octobuzz Analytics Pvt. Ltd, and in-charge of Yediyurappa's communications and social media campaign in the 2018 election, 9 February 2020, Bengaluru.
80. See L.K. Advani, *A Prisoner's Scrapbook* (New Delhi: Ocean Books, 2003 edition).
81. Sudheendra Kulkarni, 'Karnataka lessons for Congress and BJP', *The Indian Express*, 1 June 2008.
82. RSS Samvada, 'Images that inspire: A life sketch of Yadav Rao Joshi', 7 July 2014, https://samvada.org/?p=21684.
83. Personal interview with Radha Krishna Holla, communications head, RSS Karnataka, RSS office, Bengaluru, 10 February 2020.
84. Ibid.
85. Personal interview with Vadhiraj, RSS worker in Bengaluru and former head of communications, RSS Karnataka South Zone, 10 February 2020.
86. Personal interview with Lehar Singh Siroya, Karnataka BJP MLC and former state party treasurer, 9 February 2020.
87. See RSS Samvad website, https://samvada.org/; RSS Karnataka Facebook page: https://www.facebook.com/Samvada/.
88. Pradeep Kaushal, 'Many yatras later, finally there', *The Indian Express*, 11 November 2007.
89. Yediyurappa quoted in Bharath Joshi, 'Ananth Kumar was a lawyer but I made him a politician', *Deccan Herald*, 12 November 2018, https://www.deccanherald.com/state/i-was-lawyer-ananth-kumar-made-702651.html.
90. Personal interview with V. Anand, director, Octobuzz Analytics Pvt. Ltd, and in-charge of Yediyurappa's communications and social media campaign in the 2018 election, 9 February 2020, Bengaluru.
91. Pradeep Kaushal, 'Many yatras later, finally there', *The Indian Express*, 11 November 2007.
92. Personal interview with V. Anand, director, Octobuzz Analytics Pvt. Ltd, and in-charge of Yediyurappa's communications and social media campaign in 2018 election, 9 February 2020, Bengaluru.
93. Personal interview with B.Y. Vijayendra, Karnataka BJP vice president, 10 February 2020, Bengaluru.
94. PTI, 'Yeddyurappa, 3 family members acquitted in Bellary mines graft case', *The Hindu*, 26 October 2016, https://www.thehindubusinessline.com/news/national/yeddyurappa-3-family-members-acquitted-in-bellary-mines-graft-case/article21743484.ece1.
95. For a critique of Yediyurappa's leadership style, see James Manor, 'The trouble with Yeddyurappa', *Economic & Political Weekly*, Vo. 46, No. 13, 26 March–1 April 2011, pp. 16–17.
96. ECI data, https://eci.gov.in/files/file/3784-karnataka-2013/.
97. Personal interview with Lehar Singh Siroya, Karnataka BJP MLC and former state party treasurer, 9 February 2020.

98. Interview with a senior BJP leader who spoke on condition of anonymity.
99. Personal interview with B.Y. Vijayendra, Karnataka BJP vice president, 10 February 2020, Bengaluru.
100. Ibid.
101. Interview with a senior BJP leader who spoke on condition of anonymity.
102. Personal interview with Lehar Singh Siroya, Karnataka BJP MLC and former state party treasurer, 9 February 2020.
103. Personal interview with Ashwathnarayan C.N., deputy chief minister, Karnataka, Bengaluru, 10 February 2020. Also minister for higher education; it & bt, science & technology; skill development, entrepreneurship & livelihood. Dr Ashwathnarayan lost his portfolio of deputy chief minister on 4 August 2021 when the BJP decided to do away with its three-deputy chief ministers formula in Karnataka after Basavaraj Bommai took over as state chief minister, succeeding B.S. Yediyurappa.
104. Interview with a senior BJP leader who spoke on condition of anonymity.
105. Personal interview with Lehar Singh Siroya, Karnataka BJP MLC and former state party treasurer, 9 February 2020.
106. In Karnataka, for languages spoken as mother-tongue, Census 2011 recorded: Kannada speakers: 4,06,51,090; Urdu: 66,18,324; Hindi: 20,13,364; Konkani: 7,88,294; Marathi: 20,64,906; Tamil: 21,10,128, Telugu: 35,69,400. Census 2011 data from Office of the Registrar General and Census Commissioner of India, Ministry of Home Affairs, Government of India, 'C-16 population by mother tongue', available at: https://censusindia.gov.in/2011census/C-16.html.
107. Chethan Kumar, 'Karnataka No. 1 multilingual state in south, third in country', *The Times of India*, 24 November 2018, https://timesofindia.indiatimes.com/city/bengaluru/karnataka-no-1-multilingual-state-in-south-third-in-the-country/articleshow/66779735.cms.
108. Personal interview with Lehar Singh Siroya, Karnataka BJP MLC and former state party treasurer, 9 February 2020.
109. Interview with a senior BJP leader who spoke on condition of anonymity.
110. Ibid.
111. Personal interview with V. Anand, director, Octobuzz Analytics Pvt. Ltd, and in-charge of Yediyurappa's communications and social media campaign in 2018 election, 9 February 2020, Bengaluru.
112. TNN, 'Kerala rape survivor goes to CM BS Yediyurappa for justice, told to meet Bengaluru top cop', *The Times of India*, 6 January 2020, https://timesofindia.indiatimes.com/city/bengaluru/kerala-rape-survivor-goes-to-bsy-for-justice-told-to-meet-bluru-top-cop/articleshow/73113259.cms.
113. Arjun Raghunath, 'Love jihad twist to rape case raises eyebrows', *Deccan Herald*, 6 January 2020, https://www.deccanherald.com/national/south/love-jihad-twist-to-rape-case-raises-eyebrows-791897.html.
114. TNN, 'Kerala rape survivor goes to CM BS Yediyurappa for justice, told to meet Bengaluru top cop', *The Times of India*, 6 January 2020, https://timesofindia.

indiatimes.com/city/bengaluru/kerala-rape-survivor-goes-to-bsy-for-justice-told-to-meet-bluru-top-cop/articleshow/73113259.cms.

115. Personal interview with Vadhiraj, RSS worker in Bengaluru and former head of communications, RSS Karnataka South Zone, 10 February 2020.
116. Quoted in Sagarika Ghose, 'How the south was wooed', *Outlook*, 16 March 1998.
117. Interview with T.M. Veeraraghav, former resident editor, *The Hindu*, Bengaluru, and former south India editor, Network 18, 9 February 2020.
118. Interview with Rajeev Chandrasekhar, BJP Rajya Sabha MP, 26 August 2019, New Delhi. Chandrasekhar was subsequently appointed, in July 2021, as union minister of state for skills development and entrepreneurship as well as for electronics and information technology.
119. Arun Janardhanan, 'BJP as mediator, AIADMK and Sasikala hold talks for merger', *The Indian Express*, 23 September 2020.
120. BJP won Secunderabad, Nizamabad, Adilabad and Karimnagar in 2019.
121. Express News Service, 'If you use stones, we will reply with bombs: Telangana BJP MP Bandi Sanjay Kumar to AIMIM, TRS', *The New Indian Express*, 9 January 2020, https://www.newindianexpress.com/states/telangana/2020/jan/09/if-you-use-stones-we-will-reply-with-bombs-telangana-bjp-mp-bandi-sanjay-kumar-to-aimim-trs-2087029.html.
122. PTI, 'KCR, Owaisi can "seek refuge in Pakistan": BJP', *The Week*, 17 March 2020, https://www.theweek.in/news/india/2020/03/17/kcr-owaisi-can-seek-refuge-in-pakistan-bjp.html.
123. Sreenivas Janyala, 'Massive BJP surge in Hyderabad GHMC election results, says Telangana next', *The Indian Express*, 6 December 2020.
124. Interview with Rajeev Chandrasekhar, BJP Rajya Sabha MP, 26 August 2019, New Delhi.
125. ECI data for 2019 Lok Sabha, https://pollniti.com/live.html#!.
126. Interview with Rajeev Chandrasekhar, BJP Rajya Sabha MP, 26 August 2019, New Delhi.

CHAPTER 16 Mergers, Acquisitions and the 'Eight Goddesses'

1. Quoted in Jyoti Malhotra, 'Krishna-Rukmini bind Gujarat with North East', *The Indian Express*, 28 March 2018, https://indianexpress.com/article/opinion/krishna-rukmini-bind-gujarat-with-north-east-madhavpur-mela-porbandar-mahesh-sharma-rupani-5114997/. Also see TNN, 'Vijay Rupani, Northeast states' governors visit Madhavpur fair', *The Times of India*, 28 March 2018, https://timesofindia.indiatimes.com/city/rajkot/cm-ne-states-guvs-visit-madhavpur-fair/articleshow/63494128.cms.

   Vijay Rupani's tweet with a picture of north-eastern chief ministers together with Central and Gujarat government ministers at the mela is available at: https://twitter.com/vijayrupanibjp/status/978601006874447873.

2. Narendra Modi sound-byte in 'Madhav se Madhavpur' video. He spoke in Hindi; translation is mine. The video was tweeted by Gujarat Chief Minister Vijay Rupani on 27 March 2018, https://twitter.com/vijayrupanibjp/status/978684544068046849. See also Manipur Post Staff, 'Manipur part of India since time of Krishna', *The Manipur Post*, 28 March 2018, http://www.manipurpost.com/2018/03/manipur-part-of-india-since-time-of-krishna-n-biren/.
3. 'Madhav se Madhavpur' video, tweeted by Vijay Rupani on 27 March 2018, https://twitter.com/vijayrupanibjp/status/978684544068046849.
4. Jyoti Malhotra, 'Krishna-Rukmini bind Gujarat with North East', *The Indian Express*, 28 March 2018, https://indianexpress.com/article/opinion/krishna-rukmini-bind-gujarat-with-north-east-madhavpur-mela-porbandar-mahesh-sharma-rupani-5114997/.
5. See, for instance, M.C. Behera, 'Change and continuity in the tribal society of Arunachal Pradesh: A study of cultural syncretism', *International Journal of Cross-Cultural Studies*, Vol. 2, No. 2, December 2016, p. 115. Also see Tamo Mibang, M.C. Behera (eds), *Marriage and Culture: Reflections for Tribal Societies of Arunachal Pradesh* (New Delhi: Mittal, 2006).
6. P. Chaliha, *The Outlook on NEFA* (Jorhat, Assam: Assam Sahitya Sabha, 1958), p. 97. Quoted in Savitri Burman, 'NEFA—The land and its people', *India Quarterly*, Vol. 19, No. 4, October–December 1963, p. 345.
7. See, for example, Jumyir Basir, professor of tribal studies, Rajiv Gandhi University, Itanagar, quoted in Adrija Roychowdhury, 'Fact check: Did Rukmini come from Arunachal Pradesh? Here is what we know', *The Indian Express*, 29 March 2018, https://indianexpress.com/article/research/fact-check-did-rukmini-come-from-arunachal-pradesh-madhavpur-mela-guajat-vijay-rupani-mahesh-sharma-5116300/.
8. P.N. Luthra, 'North-East Frontier Agency tribes: Impact of Ahom and British policy', *Economic & Political Weekly*, Vol. 6, No. 23, 5 June 1971, p. 1144.
9. Ibid.
10. For more on the Sanskritisation theory, see M.N. Srinivas, *Religion and Society among the Coorgs of South India* (Oxford, UK: Oxford University Press, 1952).
11. The NEFA officer tasked with excavations was L.N. Chakravarty. M.L. Bose, *A History of Arunachal Pradesh* (New Delhi: Concept, 1997), pp. 41–43. In some versions of the Krishna–Rukmini story, she is depicted as a princess of Vidarbha in Maharashtra. The story is mentioned in the Udyog Parv of the Mahabharat, and the Bhagvat and Vishnu Puranas. Her father Bhishnak's capital in these versions is a village in Maharashtra. As Byomkesh Tripathy has pointed out, the Arunachal version of this tale transplanted the entire setting of Vidarbha to local habitations in the state. See Byomkesh Tripathy, S. Dutta (eds), *Religious History of Arunachal Pradesh* (New Delhi: Gyan, 2008).
12. See Special Correspondent, 'Arunachal Pradesh former chief minister Gegong Apang quits BJP', *The Hindu*, 16 January 2019, https://www.thehindu.com/

news/national/other-states/arunachal-pradesh-former-chief-minister-gegong-apang-quits-bjp/article26004433.ece and https://www.rediff.com/news/2004/aug/28apang.htm.

13. In Assam, BJP's Sarbanand Sonowal headed the eighty-six-member coalition that took office in 2016: sixty BJP, fourteen Asom Gana Parishad (AGP,) twelve Bodoland People's Front (BPF) after winning a majority in the 126-member Assam assembly. Himanta Biswa Sarma, took office as the state's second BJP chief minister in 2021 as the head of a seventy-five member coalition majority: sixty BJP, nine AGP, six United People's Party Liberal (UPPL). In Manipur, the Congress was the single largest party with twenty-eight seats, but Nongthombam Biren Singh assumed power as part of a coalition of twenty-one BJP, four NPF, four NPP and one LJP MLAs, supported by some other legislators. In Tripura, the BJP won a full majority on its own, with Biplab Kumar Deb taking office as chief minister. In Arunachal, the BJP's first government was formed through defections when thirty-three MLAs of the People's Party of Arunachal joined the BJP in 2016. In 2019, the party won power after winning an election. See PTI, 'BJP forms government in Arunachal Pradesh with PPA MLAs joining it', *The Economic Times*, 31 December 2016, https://economictimes.indiatimes.com/news/politics-and-nation/bjp-forms-government-in-arunachal-pradesh-with-33-ppa-mlas-joining-it/articleshow/56271718.cms; Sumir Karmakar, 'First BJP govt in Arunachal, CM wins first election', *Deccan Herald*, 23 May 2018, https://www.deccanherald.com/assembly-election-2019/first-bjp-govt-in-arunachal-cm-wins-first-election-735676.html.

14. In Nagaland, Neiphiu Rio of NDPP became chief minister with his eighteen NDPP MLAs, supported by twelve from BJP, one JDU and one NDP MLA. In Meghalaya, Conrad Kongkal Sangma of National People's Party became chief minister in a coalition where the BJP had two seats. The BJP's Yanthungo Patton became deputy chief minister of Nagaland. All political parties in Nagaland, including the BJP, subsequently agreed to form an 'opposition-less' unity government and to re-term the combined alliance as United Democratic Alliance on 18 September 2021. See tweet by Nagaland CM Neiphiu Rio, https://twitter.com/Neiphiu_Rio/status/1439159434748387331?s=20.

15. IANS, 'MNF will never support BJP, says Mizoram minister', *Business Standard*, 6 June 2019, https://www.business-standard.com/article/news-ians/mnf-will-never-support-bjp-says-mizoram-chief-minister-119060600012_1.html; Archis Mohan, 'BJP main opposition party in Sikkim as 10 SDF MLAs join party', *Business Standard*, 14 August 2019, https://www.business-standard.com/article/politics/bjp-now-main-opposition-in-sikkim-as-10-sdf-mla-s-join-party-119081400088_1.html.

16. This was apart from eight seats won by BJP's ally Indigenous People's Front of Tripura (IPFT).

17. Of Assam's total population of 3,12,05,576 in 2011, 1,06,79,345 were Muslim. Census 2011 data, https://censusindia.gov.in/2011census/Religion_PCA.html.

18. Census 2011, data tables, https://censusindia.gov.in/2011census/Religion_PCA.html.
19. Amit Shah press conference on 3 March 2018, https://youtu.be/v6Kd5CJKhvM.
20. At Ideas Exchange hosted by *The Indian Express*, quoted in Rajat Sethi and Shubhrastha, *The Last Battle of Saraighat: The Story of the BJP's Rise in the North-East* (New Delhi: Penguin, 2017).
21. Nishant Kumar Azad interview with Sunil Deodhar, 'We have cultivated "kesar" (saffron) in the red desert', *Organiser*, Vol. 69, No. 38, 18 March 2018.
22. Amit Shah press conference on 3 March 2018: https://youtu.be/v6Kd5CJKhvM.
23. BJP YouTube: 'सूरज जब ढलता है तो लाल रंग का होता है और जब उगता है तो केसरिया रंग का होता है: पीएम मोदी', 4 May 2018, https://www.youtube.com/watch?v=Cz7rtInD45s.
24. Narendra Modi YouTube Channel video in Guwahati, 'North East is the Ashta Lakshmi of India; Lotus and Lakshmi are closely linked: Shri Modi', 10 February 2014, https://youtu.be/R65kan8fM3k. Modi spoke in Hindi; translation is mine.
25. For more on Lakshmi manifestations, see Vasudha Narayanan, 'ŚRĪ: Giver of fortune, bestower of grace' in John Stratton Hawley, Donna Marie Wulff (eds), *Devī: Goddesses of India* (Berkeley: University of California Press, 1996), p. 104.
26. Narendra Modi speech on 29 November 2014. Full text available at: https://www.narendramodi.in/text-of-prime-ministers-address-at-the-flagging-off-of-the-first-train-from-mendipathar-meghalaya-to-guwahati-2908. See the video of the speech at: https://www.youtube.com/watch?v=y0SQ5mPzcDc.
27. BJP President Amit Shah further emphasised this point on June 2018. Abhishek Saha, 'Amit Shah: Prime Minister Narendra Modi regards North East as Ashta Lakshmi', *The Indian Express*, 19 June 2018, https://indianexpress.com/article/india/amit-shah-pm-narendra-modi-regards-northeast-as-ashta-lakshmi/.
28. Sheldon Pollock, *The Language of Gods in the World of Men: Sanskrit, Culture, and Power in Premodern India* (New Delhi: Permanent Black, 2007 edition, originally published by University of California Press, Berkeley), p. 14.
29. Ibid.
30. Arkotong Longkumer, 'Playing the waiting game: The BJP, Hindutva, and the Northeast', in Angana P. Chatterjee, Thomas Blom Hansen, Christophe Jaffrelot (eds), *Majoritarian State: How Hindu Nationalism Is Changing India* (New Delhi: HarperCollins, 2019), p. 284. Also see Arkotong Longkumer, 'The power of persuasion: Hindutva, Christianity, and the Discourse of Religion and Culture in Northeast India', *Religions*, Vol. 47, No. 2, 2017, pp. 203–227.
31. Phone interview with a senior newspaper editor in Guwahati, speaking on condition of anonymity.
32. Historians debate the exact geographic contours and dates of these kingdoms but there is general agreement that ancient Pragjyotish at various points extended over an area bigger than modern Assam, extending to the eastern boundary of Assam. It is 'generally believed' that Pragiyotisha-Kamarupa 'included a vast tract of land: viz., the North Bengal, north and east Bangladesh, modern Assam and its

neighbouring hilly regions with the boundary in the north reaching the foot hills of the border of Tibet …' Nirode Boruah, 'The Kingdom of the Doiyangdhansiri Valley of Assam', *Proceedings of the Indian History Congress*, 2000–2001, Vol. 61, Part One: Millennium (2000–2001), p. 174; K.N. Dutt, 'Problems in the history of Assam', *Proceedings of the Indian History Congress*, 1960, Vol. 23, Part - II (1960), pp. 164–169. Also see Nirode Boruah, 'The Kingdom of the Kapili Valley of Assam', *Proceedings of the Indian History Congress*, 2001, Vol. 62 (2001), pp. 135–143; Suchandra Ghosh, 'Kamarupa and Early Bengal: Understanding their political relationship', *Proceedings of the Indian History Congress*, 2010–2011, Vol. 71 (2010–2011), pp. 110–118; Nirode Boruah, 'Sanskritization and detribalization in early Assam: Some geographical aspects', *Proceedings of the Indian History Congress*, 2008, Vol. 69, 2008, pp. 167–179.

33. The Yandabo Treaty signed on 24 February 1826 between the British and an invading Burmese force ceded to the British control of the old Ahom kingdom, which had controlled the whole Brahmaputra Valley from 1750, along with other areas in Assam. The British annexed the Cachar kingdom in 1853 and added it to Assam in 1874. The Garo Hills were annexed in 1822 and added to Assam in 1874. V. Venkata Rao, 'Government and politics in North East India', *The Indian Journal of Political Science*, Vol. 48, No. 4, October–December 1987, pp. 459–460.
34. Navine Murshid, 'Assam and the foreigner within', *Asian Survey*, Vol. 56, No. 3. May/June 2016, pp. 584–585. Also see Sanjib Baruah, 'Territoriality, indigeneity and rights in North-east India', *Economic & Political Weekly*, Vol. 43, No. 12/13, 22 March–4 April 2008, p. 15.
35. Hoineilhing Sitlhou, 'Straying beyond conquest and emancipation: Exploring the fault lines of missionary education in North East India', *Indian Anthropologist*, Vol. 39, No. 1/2, January–December 2009, pp. 65–84. Also see Magdalyne Syiemlieh, 'Early Khasi response to Christian missions: Challenges, acceptance and assertion', *IOSR Journal of Humanities and Social Science*, Vol. 14, Issue 2, July–August 2013, pp. 36–43.
36. Munin Saikia, 'Historical writings on North-East India and the American Baptist Missionaries', *Proceedings of the Indian History Congress*, Vol. 72, Part I, 2011, pp. 906–912.
37. Navine Murshid, 'Assam and the foreigner within', *Asian Survey*, Vol. 56, No. 3, May/June 2016, pp. 584–586.
38. TNN, 'Mizoram remembers day of IAF bombing', *The Times of India*, 7 March 2015, https://timesofindia.indiatimes.com/city/guwahati/Mizoram-remembers-day-of-IAF-bombing/articleshow/46479179.cms.
39. For more on the early insurgencies and north-eastern politics in the early years after Independence, see V. Venkata Rao, 'Government and politics in North East India', *The Indian Journal of Political Science*, Vol. 48, No. 4, October–December 1987, pp. 458–486; C. Nunthara, 'Peace and conflict in the "frontier" areas of North-east India', *Sociological Bulletin*, Special Issue on South Asia: The State of Sociology:

Issues of Relevance and Rigour, Vol. 54, No. 3, September–December 2005, pp. 585–602; Prabhat Datta, 'Secessionist movements in North East India', *The Indian Journal of Political Science*, Vol. 53, No. 4, October–December 1992, pp. 536–558.

40. Full text of the Act is available at: http://legislative.gov.in/sites/default/files/A1958-28.pdf.
41. Subir Bhaumik, *Troubled Periphery: Crisis of India's North East* (New Delhi: Sage, 2009), p. xiv.
42. Rupam Saikia and Anjan Saikia, 'Assam–Nagaland border dispute vis-à-vis stability in regional politics (A micro-analysis from historical perspective)', *Proceedings of the Indian History Congress*, Vol. 75, 2014, Platinum Jubilee, p. 1,301.
43. Tripura has eighteen tribes (inclusive of thirty-seven Kuki sub-tribes); Meghalaya seventeen (inclusive of thirty-seven Kuki sub-tribes); Assam has fourteen in autonomous districts (inclusive of thirty-seven Kuki sub-tribes) and nine in the rest of the state; Sikkim has two; Arunachal Pradesh has twelve; Nagaland has five; Manipur has twenty-nine; Mizoram has twelve (inclusive of thirty-seven Kuki sub-tribes). Data from 'List of Notified Tribes', Census of India 2011, https://censusindia.gov.in/tables_published/SCST/ST%20Lists.pdf.
44. For more on tribes in the region and linguistic diversity, see V. Venkata Rao, 'North East India: Problems and prospects', *The Indian Journal of Political Science*, Vol. 36, No. 1, January–March 1975, pp. 1–12.
45. V. Venkata Rao, 'Reorganisation of North East India', *The Indian Journal of Political Science*, Vol. 33, No. 2, April–June 1972, pp. 123–124.
46. Relevant Facebook posts by Vasundhara Raje: https://www.facebook.com/VasundharaRajeOfficial/posts/1389117867896802; https://www.facebook.com/VasundharaRajeOfficial/posts/1025353140939945; https://www.face book.com/VasundharaRajeOfficial/posts/1145320118943246.

    Yogi Adityanath's Facebook post: https://www.facebook.com/BJP4UP/posts/2263671590511592.
47. Vasundhara Raje on Facebook: https://www.facebook.com/VasundharaRajeOfficial/posts/1205202912954966.
48. Shivraj Singh Chouhan on Facebook: https://www.facebook.com/BJP4UP/posts/2263671590511592.
49. Kartikeya Sharma's interview with Pema Khandu, 'Beef ban being blown out of proportion, pork more popular in Northeast, says Pema Khandu', *DNA*, 2 June 2017, https://www.dnaindia.com/india/interview-exclusive-beef-ban-being-blown-out-of-proportion-pork-more-popular-in-north-east-says-pema-khandu-2459467.
50. Quoted in Sanjib Kr. Baruah, 'Where RSS men love their pork', 9 February 2019, https://www.firstpost.com/india/where-rss-men-love-their-pork-6053551.html.
51. Quoted in Dailybite, 'Do you know secret recipe of the man who helped BJP win hearts over in Tripura was Pork?', *DailyO*, 7 March 2018, https://www.dailyo.in/variety/tripura-elections-sunil-deodhar-bjp-congress-pork-beef-ban/story/1/22712.html.

52. Sanjib Kr. Baruah, 'Where RSS men love their pork', 9 February 2019, https://www.firstpost.com/india/where-rss-men-love-their-pork-6053551.html.
53. Quoted in Ipsita Chakravarty, '"It is impossible here": Centre's cattle slaughter rules have BJP leaders in the Northeast worried', 3 June 2017, https://scroll.in/article/839509/it-is-impossible-here-centres-cattle-slaughter-rules-have-bjp-leaders-in-the-north-east-worried.
54. Quoted in Aakarshuk Sarna, '"Bible allows us to eat beef": Mizoram BJP chief on new cattle rules', 7 June 2017, https://www.news18.com/news/politics/bible-allows-us-to-eat-beef-says-mizoram-bjp-chief-on-new-cattle-rules-1425653.html.
55. Quoted in Vasudha Venugopal, 'BJP has no issues with Northeast's beef-eating: Manipur CM Biren Singh', *The Economic Times*, 4 June 2017, https://economictimes.indiatimes.com/news/politics-and-nation/bjp-has-no-issues-with-northeasts-beef-eating-manipur-cm-biren-singh/articleshow/58990216.cms.
56. Utpal Prashar, 'Meghalaya BJP leader quits over beef party, another may be asked to resign', *Hindustan Times*, 14 June 2017, https://www.hindustantimes.com/india-news/meghalaya-bjp-leader-quits-over-beef-party-another-may-be-asked-to-resign/story-b0Q5zfRQECSlH88AhNIVbK.html.
57. Utpal Prashar, 'No beef ban if we come to power in poll-bound NE states: BJP', *Hindustan Times*, 28 March 2017, https://www.hindustantimes.com/india-news/no-beef-ban-if-we-come-to-power-in-poll-bound-ne-states-bjp/story-s73qgNWp0gWNf3B6NAJIbM.html.
58. Quoted in Ipsita Chakravarty, '"It is impossible here": Centre's cattle slaughter rules have BJP leaders in the Northeast worried', 3 June 2017, https://scroll.in/article/839509/it-is-impossible-here-centres-cattle-slaughter-rules-have-bjp-leaders-in-the-north-east-worried.
59. Express News Service, 'The states where cow slaughter is legal in India', *The Indian Express*, https://indianexpress.com/article/explained/explained-no-beef-nation/; Ipsita Chakravarty, 'Beef and the BJP: What happens to Hindutva in the states of the North East?', 30 March 2017, https://scroll.in/article/833168/beef-and-the-bjp-what-happens-to-hindutva-in-the-states-of-the-north-east, https://indianexpress.com/article/explained/explained-no-beef-nation/.
60. State-wise estimates of meat-consumption by type from NSSO (National Sample Survey Organisation) unit-level data on household consumption, 66th round (2009–10)—with a sample size of 9,153 households in eight Northeast states by Sumit Mahajan, J.S. Papang, K.K. Datta, 'Meat consumption in North-east India: Pattern, opportunities and implications', *Journal of Animal Research*, Vol. 5, No. 1, April. 2015, p. 38, https://ndpublisher.in/admin/issues/JARV5N1g.pdf.
61. Smita Gupta, 'How the RSS grew roots in the North East', *The Hindu BusinessLine*, 9 March 2018, https://www.thehindubusinessline.com/blink/know/how-the-rss-grew-roots-in-the-north-east/article22991950.ece.
62. Rajat Sethi and Shubhrastha, *The Last Battle of Saraighat: The Story of the BJP's Rise in the North-East* (New Delhi: Penguin, 2017), Kindle edition, p. 22.

63. 'Cow "mummy" in UP, "yummy" in Northeast', *The Times of India*, 1 April 2017, https://timesofindia.indiatimes.com/videos/news/cow-mummy-in-up-yummy-in-northeast-owaisi/videoshow/57960946.cms; also see ANI tweet quoting Owaisi, 1 April 2017, https://twitter.com/ANI/status/848067900573335552?s=20.
64. HT Correspondent and Agencies, 'Those who want to eat beef should go to Pakistan: Mukhtar Abbas Naqvi', *Hindustan Times*, 22 May 2015, https://www.hindustantimes.com/india/those-who-want-to-eat-beef-should-go-to-pak-mukhtar-abbas-naqvi/story-kTyciMp58MrUhrWJfp5kFK.html.
65. See video of Rijiju's statement in Adam Halliday, 'Video: Kiren Rijiju gives it back to Naqvi: "I eat beef, can somebody stop me?"', *The Indian Express*, 28 May 2015, https://indianexpress.com/article/india/politics/kiren-rijiju-gives-it-back-to-naqvi-i-eat-beef-can-somebody-stop-me/.
66. Outlook Web Bureau, 'Beef is not an issue for BJP, focus is on development, Says Kiren Rijiju in an Interview', *Outlook*, 4 March 2018, https://www.outlookindia.com/website/story/beef-not-an-issue-for-bjp-focus-is-on-development-says-kiren-rijiju-in-an-interv/309064.
67. See video of Rijiju statement in Adam Halliday, 'Video: Kiren Rijiju gives it back to Naqvi: "I eat beef, can somebody stop me?"', *The Indian Express*, 28 May 2015, https://indianexpress.com/article/india/politics/kiren-rijiju-gives-it-back-to-naqvi-i-eat-beef-can-somebody-stop-me/.
68. Rajat Sethi and Shubhrastha, *The Last Battle of Saraighat: The Story of the BJP's Rise in the North-East* (New Delhi: Penguin, 2017), Kindle edition, p. 22.
69. Samudra Gupta Kashyap, 'Tarun Gogoi's ex-confidante Himanta Biswa Sarma joins BJP in style', *The Indian Express*, 29 August 2015, https://indianexpress.com/article/india/india-others/tarun-gogois-ex-confidante-himanta-biswa-sarma-joins-bjp-in-style/. Also see, Himanta Biswa Sarma interview on *Walk the Talk* with Shekhar Gupta, NDTV, 15 April 2016, https://www.ndtv.com/video/shows/walk-the-talk/rahul-gandhi-acts-like-god-assam-bjp-s-himanta-biswa-sarma-412046.
70. See, for instance, Saibal Sen, 'Two AGP leaders Join BJP, Gorkha Janmukti Morcha pledges support in West Bengal', *The Times of India*, 10 March 2014, https://timesofindia.indiatimes.com/india/Two-AGP-leaders-join-BJP-Gorkha-Janmukti-Morcha-pledges-support-in-West-Bengal/articleshow/31777522.cms.
71. Hazarika's profile available at: http://assamassembly.gov.in/pijush-hazarika.html.
72. Assam government ministerial list, http://assamassembly.gov.in/minister-list-2016.html.
73. From the AGP these included: Hitenda Nath Goswami, Chandra Mohan Patowary, Naba Doley, Padma Hazarika and Jagdish Bhuyan. From the Congress, these included: Bolin Chetia Saikia, Pradhan Baruah, Pallab Lochan Das, Piyush Hazarika, Rajen Borthakur, Abu Taher Bepari, Kripa Nath Mallah, Binanda Kumar, Jayanta Mallah Baurah. Details from Shubhrajeet Konwer, 'BJP and coalition politics: Strategic alliances in the states of Northeast', *Social Change and Development*, Vol. XVI, No 1, 2019, p. 41. Also see: 'Senior AGP leader joins BJP with supporters at

Jorhat', *The Sentinel*, 20 April 2015, https://www.sentinelassam.com/news/senior-agp-leader-joins-bjp-with-supporters-at-jorhat/.

74. This count is by Sangeeta Barooah Pisharoty, 'How Modi government brought the Northeast into its fold', *The Wire*, 18 March 2018, https://thewire.in/politics/how-modi-government-brought-the-northeast-into-its-fold.
75. Based on full list of Tripura Council of Ministers available at: https://tripura.gov.in/councilminister. The three former Congressmen who became BJP ministers were Ratan Lal Nath, Pranajit Singha Roy and Manoj Kanti Deb. See Bikash Singh, 'Congress MLA Ratan Lal Nath to join BJP in Tripura', *The Economic Times*, 21 December 2017, https://economictimes.indiatimes.com/news/politics-and-nation/congress-mla-ratan-lal-nath-to-join-bjp-in-tripura/articleshow/62196958.cms; PTI, 'Former Congress MLA Manoj Kanti Deb joins BJP', *The Financial Express*, 7 September 2017, https://www.financialexpress.com/india-news/former-congress-mla-manoj-kanti-deb-joins-bjp/845346/lite/; 'Recognise ex-TMC MLAs as BJP members in Tripura: BJP', *North East Today*, 20 September 2017, https://web.archive.org/web/20170924001722/https://www.northeasttoday.in/recognise-ex-tmc-mlas-as-bjp-members-in-tripura-bjp/.
76. These included a host of leaders from the Trinamool Congress; Congress leaders like Sudip Roy Burman (MLA from Agartala), Ashish Kumar Saha (MLA from Town Borwoali), Diba Chandra Hrangkhwal (Karamchchara), Biswa Bandhu Sen (Dharmanagar), Pranajit Singh Roy (Radhakishorepur) and Dilip Sarkar (Badarghat). Details are from Shubhrajeet Konwer, 'BJP and coalition politics: Strategic alliances in the states of Northeast', *Social Change and Development*, Vol. XVI, No 1, 2019, p. 41.
77. This count is by Sangeeta Barooah Pisharoty, 'How Modi government brought the Northeast into its fold', *The Wire*, 18 March 2018, https://thewire.in/politics/how-modi-government-brought-the-northeast-into-its-fold.
78. For more on the mass of defections to BJP that followed its election victories, see, for instance, Bikash Singh, 'It's destination BJP for Assam Congress netas', *The Economic Times*, 13 August 2019, https://economictimes.indiatimes.com/news/politics-and-nation/its-destination-bjp-for-assam-congress-netas/articleshow/70649271.cms; HT Correspondent, '15 AGP leaders join BJP in Dima Hasao', *The Hills Times*, 7 March 2019, https://www.thehillstimes.in/regional/15-agp-leaders-join-bjp-in-dima-hasao/; NE Now News, 'Assam: Former senior Congress stalwarts join BJP', *North East Now*, 11 August 2019, https://nenow.in/north-east-news/assam-former-senior-congress-stalwarts-formally-join-bjp.html; Anup Biswas, 'Many AGP leaders join BJP in Dima Hasao', 8 March 2019, https://www.apnnews.com/many-agp-leaders-join-bjp-in-dima-hasao/.
79. Data from Manipur cabinet list: http://www.cmmanipur.gov.in/cabinet/; Tripura Council of Ministers list: https://tripura.gov.in/councilminister; Assam council of ministers list: http://assamassembly.gov.in/minister-list-2016.html (this list was updated as of 26 May 2016); Nagaland cabinet list: https://www.nagaland.gov.in/

portal/portal/StatePortal/Government/CabinetMinisters; Meghalaya Council of Ministers list: http://meghalaya.gov.in/megportal/ministerslist; Manipur cabinet list: http://www.cmmanipur.gov.in/cabinet/.

80. 'Former Home Minister Patton joins BJP', *Morung Express*, 16 January 2018, https://morungexpress.com/former-home-minister-patton-joins-bjp.
81. Details of defectors from: IANS, 'Former Nagaland CM Chishi, independent legislator Jacob Zhimomi to join BJP', *The New Indian Express*, 22 January 2018, https://www.newindianexpress.com/nation/2018/jan/22/former-nagaland-cm-chishi-independent-legislator-jacob-zhimomi-to-join-bjp-1760757.html; PTI, 'Three NCP MLAs join BJP in Nagaland', *The Times of India*, 17 June 2014, https://timesofindia.indiatimes.com/india/Three-NCP-MLAs-join-BJP-in-Nagaland/articleshow/36709646.cms; Sanchari Chatterjee, 'JDU and an independent prove kingmakers in Nagaland, but will BJP form government?', News18.com, 4 March 2018, https://www.news18.com/news/politics/jdu-and-an-independent-prove-kingmakers-as-bjp-npf-weigh-options-in-nagaland-1677719.html; Amitabh Sinha, 'Membership drive a success, BJP makes inroads in far east Nagaland', News18.com, 2 November 2019, https://www.news18.com/news/politics/membership-drive-a-success-bjp-makes-deep-inroads-in-far-east-nagaland-2371197.html.
82. This count is by Sangeeta Barooah Pisharoty, 'How Modi government brought the Northeast into its fold', *The Wire*, 18 March 2018, https://thewire.in/politics/how-modi-government-brought-the-northeast-into-its-fold.
83. These included Congress leaders like Francis Ngajokpa, Y. Erabot Singh, Vungzagin Valte, S. Achouba, T. Shyam Kumar, Y. Suryachandra, Ngamthang Haokip, S. Bira, Ginsuanhau, Paonam Brojen, T. Lokweshwar Singh. From Trinamool Congress, the leaders who joined the BJP included N. Biswajit Singh, Joykishan Singh, Oinam Luknoi, T. Robindra Singh. This tally is by Shubhrajeet Konwer, 'BJP and coalition politics: Strategic alliances in the states of Northeast', *Social Change and Development*, Vol. XVI, No. 1, 2019, p. 42.
84. Details of defectors from: TNN, '3 disqualified Manipur TMC MLAs join BJP', *The Times of India*, 1 June 2015, https://timesofindia.indiatimes.com/city/guwahati/3-disqualified-Manipur-TMC-MLAs-join-BJP/articleshow/47492922.cms; *The Sangai Express*, 'Two former Congress MLAs Valte, Nemcha join BJP, Kim Gangte follows suit from AITC', 25 March 2017, http://e-pao.net/GP.asp?src=1..260117.jan17.
85. Khelen Thokchom, 'Manipur NPP unit joins BJP', *The Telegraph*, 16 March 2015, https://www.telegraphindia.com/states/north-east/manipur-npp-unit-joins-bjp/cid/1529120.
86. 'Congress leaders who joined BJP bag cabinet berths', *The Economic Times*, 17 March 2018, https://economictimes.indiatimes.com/news/politics-and-nation/congress-leaders-who-joined-bjp-bag-cabinet-berths/articleshow/63339166.cms.
87. Anuja, 'Congress lose Arunachal as chief minister, 43 MLAs defect to BJP ally', *Mint*, 17 September 2016, https://www.livemint.com/Politics/

hX40OqyuxZKwiudAS8FOvO/Arunachal-Pradesh-Congress-in-turmoil-again-as-CM-Khandu-4.html.

88. Supratim Dey, 'Arunachal CM Pema Khandu suspended from PPA, joins BJP', *Business Standard*, 31 December 2016, https://www.business-standard.com/article/politics/arunachal-cm-prema-khandu-suspended-from-ppa-joins-bjp-116123100430_1.html.
89. Quoted in India TV Politics Desk, 'As Amit Shah launches Northeast alliance, big blow to BJP's grip in Arunachal', 13 July 2016, https://www.indiatvnews.com/politics/national-as-amit-shah-launches-northeast-alliance-big-blow-to-bjp-s-grip-in-arunachal-339206.
90. Himanta Biswa Sarma quoted in Tarun Gogoi, 'North East Democratic Alliance (NEDA) and political change in Northeast India', *Dialogue*, Vol. 20, No. 4, 2019, p. 118.
91. Ibid.
92. Ram Madhav interview with Prafulla Ketkar, Promod Kumar, 'Need to view North East with different prism', *Organiser*, Vol. 69, No. 38, 18 March 2018.
93. Scroll Staff, 'Tripura elections: Tribal outfit IPFT emerges as a major player', 3 March 2018, https://scroll.in/latest/870677/tripura-assembly-elections-tribal-outfit-ipft-emerges-as-a-major-player.
94. Ram Madhav interview with Prafulla Ketkar, Promod Kumar, 'Need to view North East with different prism', *Organiser*, Vol. 69, No. 38, 18 March 2018.
95. Quoted in Scroll Staff, 'Tripura elections: Tribal outfit IPFT emerges as a major player', 3 March 2018, https://scroll.in/latest/870677/tripura-assembly-elections-tribal-outfit-ipft-emerges-as-a-major-player.
96. Swati Deb, 'Saffron surge in Red Fort: Assembly polls results report', *Organiser*, Vol. 69, No. 38, 18 March 2018.
97. Quoted in Armstrong Chanambam, 'As BJP faces ally IPFT in Tripura, Congress calls it ploy to divide tribal votes', 4 April 2019, https://www.firstpost.com/politics/lok-sabha-election-2019-as-bjp-faces-ally-ipft-in-tripura-congress-calls-it-ploy-to-divide-tribal-votes-6383401.html.
98. Kallol Dey, 'Nagaland Elections: Baptist Church Body appeals political parties not to support BJP', *The Indian Express*, 11 February 2018, https://indianexpress.com/article/north-east-india/nagaland/nagaland-assembly-election-baptist-churches-body-appeals-political-parties-not-to-support-bjp-5059696/.
99. Quoted in Jaideep Mazumdar, 'BJP battling vicious communal campaign by the Church and Congress in Nagaland', *Swarajya*, 25 February 2018, https://swarajyamag.com/politics/bjp-battling-vicious-communal-campaign-launched-by-the-church-and-congress-in-nagaland.
100. 'Voters endorse Moditva', *Organiser*, Vol. 69, No. 38, 18 March 2018.
101. Pradip Phanjoubam, 'How BJP won without winning in Nagaland', *Economic & Political Weekly*, Vol. 53, No. 10, March 2018.
102. Ibid.

103. Ram Madhav interview with Prafulla Ketkar, Promod Kumar, 'Need to view North East with different prism', *Organiser*, Vol. 69, No. 38, 18 March 2018.
104. 'Voters endorse Moditva', *Organiser*, Vol. 69, No. 38, 18 March 2018.
105. Adam Saprisanga, 'How Congress unraveled in Mizoram, its last bastion of power in Northeast', 21 September 2019, https://theprint.in/politics/how-congress-unraveled-in-mizoram-its-last-bastion-of-power-in-northeast/294335/.
106. Methodology: 150+ GB of TIFF files were acquired from the NASA website, and then processed using a Python programme that Srivastava wrote. The data was mapped on to all 543 Lok Sabha constituencies by time period.
107. Utpal Prashar, 'PM Narendra Modi urges Arunachal voters to vote for "double-engine" growth', *Hindustan Times*, 30 March 2019, https://www.hindustantimes.com/lok-sabha-elections/lok-sabha-elections-2019-pm-narendra-modi-urges-arunachal-voters-to-vote-for-double-engine-growth/story-7KglM3GRY29YIoNV4sR04H.html.
108. Reserve Bank of India, *State Finances: A Study of Budgets of 2019–20* (Mumbai: RBI, 2019), p. 11.
109. *North Eastern Council Regional Plan (2017–18 to 2019–20)*, p. 4, http://megplanning.gov.in/circular/NEC%20Regional%20Plan%202017-18%20to%20 2019-20.pdf.
110. After the erstwhile Planning Commission was replaced by the NITI Aayog in January 2015, the nomenclature of 'special category states'—which had first started in 1969 with Jammu and Kashmir, Assam and Nagaland—was no longer used. But financial benefits for such states from the Union government continued. To the original list, eight more states were added over the years (Arunachal Pradesh, Himachal Pradesh, Manipur, Meghalaya, Mizoram, Sikkim, Tripura and, in 2010, Uttarakhand). I am grateful to Sanjiv Shankaran for this insight. Details on 'special category states' and the importance of this categorisation, from P. Vaidyanathan Iyer, 'Nothing special about special category states any longer', *The Indian Express*, 28 July 2015, https://indianexpress.com/article/explained/nothing-special-about-special-category-states-any-longer/.
111. Personal interview with a newspaper editor in Guwahati, speaking on condition of anonymity.
112. Data from M. Govinda Rao, *Central Transfers to States in India Rewarding Performance While Ensuring Equity (Final Report of a Study Submitted to NITI Aayog)*, p. 11. The report was sponsored by NITI Aayog and conducted by National the Institute of Public Finance and Policy, New Delhi.
113. BJP, 'Press conference by Shri Amit Shah on BJP's success in Tripura, Nagaland and Meghalaya Elections', 3 March 2018. He spoke in Hindi; translation is mine. Full video available at: https://youtu.be/v6Kd5CJKhvM.
114. 'Our vision is act-east and act-fast on east, says PM Modi in Silchar', 4 January 2019. He spoke in Hindi; translations are mine. Full speech text available at: https://www.narendramodi.in/text-of-pm-s-speech-at-public-rally-in-silchar-assam-543133.

115. BJP, 'Press conference by Shri Amit Shah on BJP's success in Tripura, Nagaland and Meghalaya Elections', 3 March 2018. Full video available at: https://youtu.be/v6Kd5CJKhvM.
116. Ram Madhav interview with Promod Kumar, 'Need to view North East with different prism', *Organiser*, 18 March 2018.
117. Data from PIB Delhi, Ministry of Development of North Eastern Region, Press Release, 3 February 2020, https://pib.gov.in/PressReleasePage.aspx?PRID=1601757.
118. Release of funds under these schemes is based on the progress of implementation of projects. In addition, each Union ministry/department is expected to spend 10 per cent of its Gross Budgetary Support (GBS) as per prescribed norms in North Eastern Region. However, no state-wise allocations for this category of spending and funds are released to the states based on requirements against sanctioned projects/schemes. Ibid.
119. Details of attendees from 'Hindu revivalism, BJP-RSS and the future of the Indian state system', *Nagaland Post*, 3 January 2020, https://www.nagalandpost.com/hindu-revivalism-bjp-rss-and-the-future-of-the-indian-state-system/212300.html.
120. RSS Sarkaryavah Bhaiyyaji Joshi noted triumphantly in his 2018 annual report that the 'admiration expressed by eminent personalities from social, religious, industrial fields' at such functions 'indicates the growing acceptability of our work'. RSS, 'Prativedan—2018 Presented by Ma. Sarkaryavah in the Akhil Bharatiya Pratinidhi Sabha', 9 March 2018, http://rss.org//Encyc/2018/3/9/Prativedan-2018.html.
121. RSS, 'Prativedan—2018 Presented by Ma. Sarkaryavah in the Akhil Bharatiya Pratinidhi Sabha', 9 March 2018, http://rss.org//Encyc/2018/3/9/Prativedan-2018.html.
122. Mohan Bhagwat in interview with Prafulla Ketkar, Hitesh Shankar, 'Don't forget fundamentals in favourable atmosphere', *Organiser*, Vol. 69, No. 39, 25 March 2018.
123. Ram Madhav interview with Promod Kumar, 'Need to view North East with different prism', *Organiser*, Vol. 69, No. 38, 18 March 2018. Also see Ram Madhav's comments on this in his foreword to Rajat Sethi and Shubhrastha, *The Last Battle of Saraighat: The Story of the BJP's Rise in the North-East*, (New Delhi: Penguin, 2017).
124. The Northeast prants in the RSS hierarchy are: North Assam, Arunachal Pradesh, South Assam, Manipur. Arun Anand, *Know About the RSS* (New Delhi: Prabhat, 2019), pp. 25–26.
125. Mohan Bhagwat in interview with Prafulla Ketkar, Hitesh Shankar, 'Don't forget fundamentals in favourable atmosphere', *Organiser*, Vol 69, No. 39, 25 March 2018.
126. Ram Madhav interview with Promod Kumar, 'Need to view North East with different prism', *Organiser*, Vol. 69, No. 38, 18 March 2018.
127. Smita Gupta, 'How RSS grew its roots in the North-East', *The Hindu BusinessLine*, 9 March 2018, https://www.thehindubusinessline.com/blink/know/how-the-rss-grew-roots-in-the-north-east/article22991950.ece.

128. Ram Madhav interview with Vivek Deshpande, 'Second-class citizenship (for Muslims) against Hindu ethos', *The Indian Express*, 16 March 2003.
129. Figures from Shankar Das, RSS head of publicity in Assam. Quoted in Masoyo Hunphun Awungashi, 'Land of the rising Sangh', *Caravan*, 1 April 2019, https://caravanmagazine.in/reportage/the-rsss-expansion-into-northeast.
130. Smita Gupta, 'How RSS grew its roots in the North-East', *The Hindu BusinessLine*, 9 March 2018, https://www.thehindubusinessline.com/blink/know/how-the-rss-grew-roots-in-the-north-east/article22991950.ece.
131. Nishant Kumar Azad interview with Sunil Deodhar, 'We have cultivated "kesar" (saffron) in the red desert', *Organiser*, Vol. 69, No. 38, 18 March 2018, pp. 16–17.
132. Smita Gupta, 'How RSS grew its roots in the North-East', *The Hindu BusinessLine*, 9 March 2018, https://www.thehindubusinessline.com/blink/know/how-the-rss-grew-roots-in-the-north-east/article22991950.ece.
133. Prafulla Ketkar, 'New narrative for the North East', *Organiser*, Vol 69, No. 38, 18 March 2018, p. 4.
134. See Jagdamba Mall, *Swatantrata Senani Rani Gaidinliu*, at ABVK website, https://kalyanashram.org/publications/.
135. Rahul Karmakar, 'Rani Gaidinliu: A Naga queen and BJP's spin machine', *Hindustan Times*, 14 June 2015, https://www.hindustantimes.com/india/rani-gaidinliu-a-naga-queen-and-bjp-s-spin-machine/story-kfQG1IggxU6j4Frs7haBFK.html.
136. Masoyo Hunphun Awungashi, 'Land of the rising Sangh', *Caravan*, 1 April 2019, https://caravanmagazine.in/reportage/the-rsss-expansion-into-northeast.
137. Census of India data. Analysis is available at: https://blog.cpsindia.org/2016/08/religion-data-of-census-2011-xxviii.html.
138. Radhika Ramaseshan, 'RSS accuses church of military designs', *The Telegraph*, 16 October 2000.
139. Farzand Ahmad, 'Missionary imposition', *India Today*, 23 October 2000.
140. Quoted in Rajesh Joshi, 'Season of bad blood', *Outlook*, 30 October 2000.
141. Hirain Gohain, 'BJP plans for Assam: An RSS-run school in every panchayat', *The Wire*, 15 June 2016, https://thewire.in/communalism/the-bjps-plans-for-assam-an-rss-run-school-in-every-panchayat.
142. Ibid.
143. *Ekal Bharathi, Annual Report 2018–19*, https://www.ekal.org/pdf/ekal-abhiyan-annual-report-2018-19-v1.pdf.
144. Rajeev Ranjan Roy, 'Deport all illegal migrants from Bangladesh: BJP', *The Pioneer*, 6 December 2006.
145. Sarma speech broadcast on News Live. 'Final battle of Saraighat has begun: Himanta Biswa Sarma', https://www.youtube.com/watch?v=IQIAgYKjSI0.
146. Rajat Sethi and Shubhrastha, *The Last Battle of Saraighat: The Story of the BJP's Rise in the North-East* (New Delhi: Penguin, 2017), Kindle edition, p. 16.
147. Census 2011 data, https://censusindia.gov.in/2011census/Religion_PCA.html.

148. Data on Muslim population is from the Assam government, quoted in Staff Reporter, 'Nine Districts in Assam Muslim-majority: Sarma', *The Sentinel Assam*, 1 March 2017, https://www.sentinelassam.com/top-headlines/nine-districts-in-assam-muslim-majority-himanta/?infinitescroll=1.
149. Data on Muslim population is from https://www.census2011.co.in/census/city/188-nagaon.html.
150. Data on Muslim population is from https://www.censusindia.co.in/towns/mangaldoi-population-darrang-assam-801630.
151. As per 2011 Census, Dhubri district has 79.67 per cent, Barpeta 70.74 per cent, Darrang 64.34 per cent, Hailakandi 60.31 per cent, Goalpara 57.52 per cent, Karimganj 56.36 per cent, Gaon 55.36 per cent, Morigaon 52.56 per cent and Bongaigaon 50.22 per cent people of Islamic faith. In a written reply to a question raised by BJP MLA Mril Saikia in the House, data given by State Planning and Development Minister Himanta Biswa Sarma. Staff Reporter, 'Nine districts in Assam Muslim-majority: Sarma', *The Sentinel Assam*, 1 March 2017, https://www.sentinelassam.com/top-headlines/nine-districts-in-assam-muslim-majority-himanta/?infinitescroll=1.

    Assam has nine Muslim-majority districts. See Bharti Jain, 'Muslims majority districts in Assam up', *The Times of India*, 26 August 2015, https://timesofindia.indiatimes.com/india/Muslim-majority-districts-in-Assam-up/articleshow/48682463.cms.
152. PTI, 'Jan Sangh in Assam', *The Times of India*, 30 October 1951, p. 5.
153. H. Srikanth, 'Communalising Assam: AGP's loss is BJP's gain', *Economic & Political Weekly*, Vol. 34, No. 49, 4–10 December 1999, p. 3,412.
154. Sarbanand Sonowal quoted in Shekhar Gupta, 'How the RSS plans to win Assam for the BJP', Rediff, 11 April 2016, https://www.rediff.com/news/column/how-the-rss-plans-to-win-assam-for-the-bjp/20160411.htm.
155. Ibid.
156. Masoyo Hunphun Awungashi, 'Land of the rising Sangh', *Caravan*, 1 April 2019, https://caravanmagazine.in/reportage/the-rsss-expansion-into-northeast.
157. Personal interview with a senior Guwahati newspaper editor speaking on condition of anonymity.
158. Ibid.
159. A judicial enquiry later blamed the 2008 violence on the All Assam Minority Students Union and intelligence failures by the Assam police. Sushanta Talukdar, '2008 riots probe: Panel blames MUSA, Assam Police intelligence wing', *The Hindu*, 21 July 2010, https://www.thehindu.com/news/national/other-states/2008-riots-probe-panel-blames-MUSA-Assam-police-intelligence-wing/article16204027.ece.
160. Personal interview with Guwahati newspaper editor speaking on condition of anonymity.
161. Ibid.

162. Nani Gopal Mahanta, 'Lok Sabha elections in Assam: Shifting of traditional vote bases to BJP', *Economic & Political Weekly*, Vol. 49, No. 35, 30 August 2014, p. 20. For a background on this, also see, Udayon Misra, 'Immigration and identity transformation in Assam', *Economic & Political Weekly*, Vol. 34, No. 21, 22–28 May 1999, pp. 1,264–1,271.
163. See, for instance, Navine Murshid, 'Assam and the foreigner within', *Asian Survey*, Vol. 56, No. 3, May–June 2016, pp. 581–604.
164. PTI, 'Narendra Modi slams Congress for encouraging vote bank politics leading to influx that is destroying Assam', *The Economic Times*, 31 March 2014, https://economictimes.indiatimes.com/news/politics-and-nation/narendra-modi-slams-congress-for-encouraging-vote-bank-politics-leading-to-influx-that-is-destroying-assam/articleshow/33023692.cms.
165. 'Maulana Badruddin Ajmal Qasmi', *The Muslim 500*, https://www.themuslim500.com/profiles/badruddin-ajmal-qasmi/.
166. Rahul Karmakar, 'Badruddin Ajmal: The scent of a Kingmaker?', *Hindustan Times*, 5 April 2016, https://www.hindustantimes.com/assembly-elections/follow-the-leader-badruddin-ajmal-scent-of-kingmaker/story-CZCxqG80ZXmFRlPBKe2BfO.html.
167. Abhishek Saha, 'Tempo over Citizenship Amendment Bill lost, don't think it will hurt BJP: Badruddin Ajmal, AIUDF President', *The Indian Express*, 13 March 2019, https://indianexpress.com/elections/assam-citizenship-bill-bjp-badruddin-ajmal-aiudf-president-5623371/.
168. Krishna N. Das, 'Modi's BJP vows to strip Muslim immigrants of vote in Assam', Reuters, 11 March 2016, https://www.reuters.com/article/india-politics/modis-bjp-vows-to-strip-muslim-immigrants-of-vote-in-assam-idUSKCN0WC2WR.
169. Hemanta Kumar Nath, 'Muslims not considered as human beings, treated like insects in the BJP regime: Badruddin Ajmal', 12 January 2020, https://www.indiatoday.in/india/story/muslims-not-considered-as-human-beings-treated-like-insects-in-the-bjp-regime-badruddin-ajmal-1636089-2020-01-12.
170. The NRC is a legacy of the Assam Accord of 1985 and the Assam movement that preceded it. A key demand of that movement against 'foreigners' was for 'detection, deletion and deportation' of illegal Bangladeshi migrants. It was a demand that was specifically coded into the Assam Accord signed by the Rajiv Gandhi-led Central government. The Assam government under Tarun Gogoi tried to start a project to update the 1951 NRC list with a pilot project in 2010 in Barpeta and Kamrup. It was put on the backburner after serious pushback. Things changed only after the Supreme Court mandated an updation exercise in 2013 after a writ petition filed by the Assam Public Works. The exercise began in early 2015, and the court has been constantly monitoring the exercise since then. It has reportedly cost over Rs 1,220 crore, engaged 40,000 government employees, 8,200 contractual employees and took over five years. Nalin Mehta, 'NRC's political googly', *The Times of India*, 10 September 2019.

171. Literally 'sons of the soil', a term used by several tribal indigenous communities to denote themselves in the state
172. 'Bodo accord will bring progress and prosperity for the community and Assam: PM'. Full text of his speech in Kokrajhar on 7 February 2020 available at: https://www.narendramodi.in/text-of-prime-minister-narendra-modi-s-address-at-kokrajhar-in-assam-548326.
173. Full text of Assam Accord available at: https://assam.gov.in/en/main/ASSAM%20 ACCORD.
174. Special Correspondent, 'Assam Accord Clause 6: Panel submits report to chief minister', *The Hindu*, 25 February 2020, https://www.thehindu.com/news/national/other-states/assam-accord-clause-6-panel-submits-report-to-chief-minister/article30912307.ece.
175. Moonmoon Ghosh, 'Planning to Visit Meghalaya? Outsiders will now have to register with govt', News18.com, 2 November 2019, https://www.news18.com/news/india/planning-to-visit-meghalaya-outsiders-will-now-have-to-register-with-govt-as-cabinet-approves-new-rule-2370913.html.
176. Rahul Karmakar, 'Tripura, where demand for Assam-like NRC widens gap between indigenous people and non-tribal settlers', *The Hindu*, 27 October 2018, https://www.thehindu.com/news/national/other-states/tripura-where-demand-for-assam-like-nrc-widens-gap-between-indigenous-people-and-non-tribal-settlers/article25348269.ece.
177. PTI, 'After protests, poll body removes Mizoram chief electoral officer', *NDTV.com*, 15 November 2018, https://www.ndtv.com/india-news/after-protests-poll-body-removes-mizoram-chief-electoral-officer-1948005.

CHAPTER 17 The Making of a New Women's Vote

1. Conversation with Brajesh Kumar Singh, then Ahmedabad bureau chief, Zee News, Ahmedabad, 10 October 2007, reproduced with permission. Later, he was editor of ABP Asmita; group consulting editor, Zee Network; and group consulting editor, Network 18.
2. '31 Mahila Sammelans organised and attended by CM Narendra Modi', *The Times of India*, Ahmedabad edition, 30 September 2008. Also see data on these meetings released by general administrative department, Gujarat, in November 2007, in response to an RTI. 'Narendra Modi caught in RTI web on travel expenses', *Rediff.com*, 3 October 2012, https://www.rediff.com/news/slide-show/slide-show-1-modi-s-travel-cost-during-2007-mahila-sammelans-was-zero/20121003.htm; TNN, 'Narendra Modi didn't divulge his own traveling expenses', *The Times of India*, 3 October 2012, https://timesofindia.indiatimes.com/city/vadodara/Narendra-Modi-didnt-divulge-his-own-2007-travelling-expenses/articleshow/16649344.cms.
3. Interview with Brajesh Kumar Singh, group consulting editor, Network 18, New Delhi, 14 October 2020.

4. Narendra Modi interview in Uday Mahurkar, 'Gujarat: Modi back to Hindutva', *India Today*, 23 November 2007, https://www.indiatoday.in/magazine/states/story/20071203-gujarat-modi-back-to-hindutva-734610-2007-11-23. Also see: TNN, 'Its Maha Modi Vs Aam Aadmi', *The Times of India*, 15 October 2007.
5. The drop was more pronounced in first-phase voting in Saurashtra and South Gujarat, where male voting fell by almost 3 per cent from 64.65 per cent in 2002 to 61.87 per cent in 2007, while women voting remained at 57.19 per cent in 2007 compared to 57.91 per cent in 2002. Rajiv Shah, Paul John, 'Modi magic on fair sex?' *The Times of India*, 13 December 2007. Male voting percentage in Gujarat fell from 64.91 per cent in 2002 to 62.31 per cent in 2007. Women voting in 2007 was 57.02 per cent in 2007, compared to 57.99 per cent in 2002. Data for 2002 from the ECI: https://eci.gov.in/files/file/3838-gujarat-2002/. Data for 2007 from the ECI: https://eci.gov.in/files/file/3839-gujarat-2007/.
6. Rajiv Shah, Paul John, 'Modi magic on fair sex?', *The Times of India*, 13 December 2007.
7. '31 Mahila Sammelans organised and attended by CM Narendra Modi', *The Times of India*, Ahmedabad edition, 30 September 2008.
8. Sushil Pandit, '"Focus on big picture was Modi's brief": A member of CM's campaign reveals how Gujarat was won', *The Times of India*, 26 December 2007.
9. See Nalin Mehta, *India on Television: How Satellite News Channels Have Changed the Way We Think and Act* (New Delhi: HarperCollins, 2008), Chapter 7, pp. 274–298.
10. TNN, 'Modi kicks off Gujarat Gaurav Yatra', *The Time of India*, 8 September 2002, https://timesofindia.indiatimes.com/city/ahmedabad/Modi-kicks-off-Gujarat-Gaurav-Yatra/articleshow/21590967.cms.
11. Aakar Patel, 'The Narendra Modi you didn't know', *Hindustan Times*, 9 June 2013 (first published 16 October 2012), https://www.hindustantimes.com/india/the-narendra-modi-you-didn-t-know/story-Qd4aGsqf4b4YRKzLHHeScI.html.
12. Interview with Sanjeev Singh, editor, digital broadcast, Times Internet, who covered these 2007 rallies for Times Now, New Delhi, 12 October 2020.
13. Nistula Hebbar, 'Sex symbol status: Narendra Modi attracts female audience but needs to show more tenderness', *The Economic Times*, 29 September 2013, https://economictimes.indiatimes.com/news/politics-and-nation/sex-symbol-status-narendra-modi-attracts-female-audience-but-needs-to-show-more-tenderness/articleshow/23216479.cms.
14. Ibid.
15. PTI, 'If women feel unsafe, we shouldn't call ourselves "mard"', *The Indian Express*, 30 August 2013, http://archive.indianexpress.com/news/if-women-feel-unsafe-we-shouldnt-call-ourselves-mard-narendra-modi/1162401/.
16. Express News Service, 'Empower women for a prosperous India, says Narendra Modi', *The Indian Express*, 8 April 2013, http://archive.indianexpress.com/news/empower-women-for-a-prosperous-india-says-narendra-modi/1099254/.

17. Sanjay Srivastava, 'Modi-masculinity: Media, manhood, and "traditions" in a time of consumerism', *Television and New Media*, Vol. 16, No. 4, 2015, p. 331.
18. Nistula Hebbar, 'Sex symbol status: Narendra Modi attracts female audience but needs to show more tenderness', *The Economic Times*, 29 September 2013, https://economictimes.indiatimes.com/news/politics-and-nation/sex-symbol-status-narendra-modi-attracts-female-audience-but-needs-to-show-more-tenderness/articleshow/23216479.cms.
19. Lhendup G. Bhutia, 'The Modi hotness quotient', *Open*, 15 May 2014, https://openthemagazine.com/features/india/the-modi-hotness-quotient/.
20. See, for instance, https://www.facebook.com/namobharathi.in/.
21. Lhendup G. Bhutia, 'The Modi hotness quotient', *Open*, 15 May 2014, https://openthemagazine.com/features/india/the-modi-hotness-quotient/.
22. Bhanu K. Pragnya Reddy, Bhanupriya Rao, 'Women lead 426 protests anti-CAA-NRC protests in India', BehanBox.com, 23 January 2020, https://www.behanbox.com/women-led-protest-map-against-citizenship-laws-in-india/; Namita Bhandare, 'Anti-CAA protests have shown women can lead', *Hindustan Times*, 27 December 2019, https://www.hindustantimes.com/columns/anti-caa-protests-have-shown-women-can-lead/story-xpZ6lruoWhk4oo8pzhQaGM.html.
23. Pinjra Tod Facebook page, https://www.facebook.com/pinjratod/; Aishwarya S. Aiyar, 'Delhi riots: Who are Pinjra Tod and why did they join anti-CAA stir?', *The Quint*, 29 May 2020, https://www.thequint.com/news/india/pinjra-tod-anti-caa-protests-delhi-police-probe-north-east-delhi-riots.
24. Women accounted for 43,78,06,707 of 91,05,12,091 voters in the 2019 Lok Sabha poll. Among those who actually voted, women accounted for 47.93 per cent. ECI data, https://eci.gov.in/files/file/10949-23-participation-of-women-electors-in-poll/.
25. Overall numbers include votes cast by men, women, third gender, NRIs, postal ballots and services. ECI data, https://eci.gov.in/files/file/10975-10-voters-information/.
26. The full judgement, *Vineeta Sharma vs Rakesh Sharma and Others, 2020*, is available at: https://main.sci.gov.in/supremecourt/2018/32601/32601_2018_33_1501_23387_Judgement_11-Aug-2020.pdf.
27. Prannoy Roy, Dorab R. Sopariwala, *The Verdict: Decoding India's Elections* (New Delhi: Vintage, Penguin Random House, 2019), pp. 38–39.
28. Author calculations from ECI data in EDM Division, 'Participation of women electors in poll', 11 October 2019, https://eci.gov.in/files/file/10949-23-participation-of-women-electors-in-poll/ and EDM Division, 'Voters information', 11 October 2019, https://eci.gov.in/files/file/10975-10-voters-information/.
29. Overall turnout was 67.4 per cent in 2019. EDM Division, 'Voters information', 11 October 2019, https://eci.gov.in/files/file/10975-10-voters-information/.
30. Prannoy Roy, Dorab R. Sopariwala, *The Verdict: Decoding India's Elections* (New Delhi: Vintage, Penguin Random House, 2019), pp. 43–45.

31. The poll predicted 339–365 seats for the NDA. The actual result was 353 seats. Data from analysis by Samarth Bansal, ‘How India voted in 2019 election? Here is what India Today-Axis My India poll tells us’, *India Today*, 31 May 2019, https://www.indiatoday.in/diu/story/how-india-voted-2019-lok-sabha-election-india-today-axis-my-india-poll-1539617-2019-05-31; Samarth Bansal, ‘Behind the numbers: How India Today-My Axis forecast seats’, *India Today*, 21 May 2019, https://www.indiatoday.in/elections/lok-sabha-2019/story/behind-the-numbers-how-india-today-axis-my-india-forecasts-seats-1531359-2019-05-21.
32. UP (52 per cent women vs 50 per cent of men), Bihar (55 per cent women vs 51 per cent men), Madhya Pradesh (59 per cent women vs 57 per cent men), Rajasthan (62 per cent women vs 60 per cent men), Uttarakhand (63 per cent women vs 59 per cent men). Analysis by Rishabh Srivastava of Axis My India Poll’s state-wise data. Full data set available on Samarth Bansal, ‘How India voted in 2019 election? Here is what India Today-Axis My India poll tells us’, *India Today*, 31 May 2019, https://www.indiatoday.in/diu/story/how-india-voted-2019-lok-sabha-election-india-today-axis-my-india-poll-1539617-2019-05-31.
33. Rukmini S., ‘The BJP’s electoral arithmetic’, in Milan Vaishnav (ed.), *The BJP in Power: Indian Democracy and Religious Nationalism*, Carnegie Endowment for International Peace, 4 April 2019, https://carnegieendowment.org/2019/ 04/04/bjp-s-electoral-arithmetic-pub-78678.
34. Ibid.
35. Mehta was elected thrice as MP, variously from Mumbai North East and Mumbai South (1989, 1993, 1996). Express News Service, ‘Former Union minister Jayawantiben Mehta passes away’, *The Indian Express*, 7 November 2016, https://www.newindianexpress.com/nation/2016/nov/07/former-union-minister-jayawantiben-mehta-passes-away-1535866.html.
36. Staff Reporter, ‘BJP plans women’s conference’, *The Times of India*, 21 December 1980; ‘Staff Reporter, ‘Impressive show’, *The Times of India*, 29 December 1980.
37. Staff Reporter, ‘Antyodaya in each village, says BJP plank’, *The Times of India*, 5 May 1980.
38. Ibid.
39. Rekha Pande, ‘The history of feminism and doing gender in India’, *Estudos Feministas*, Vol. 26, No. 3, 2018, pp. 8–9.
40. Ibid., p. 8.
41. Mala Khullar, ‘Introduction: Writing the women’s movement’ in Maya Khullar (ed.), *Writing the Women’s Movement: A Reader* (New Delhi: Zubaan, an Imprint of Kali for Women, 2005), p. 11.
42. Tanika Sarkar, ‘The woman as communal subject: Rashtrasevika Samiti and Ram Janmabhoomi Movement’, *Economic & Political Weekly*, 31 August 1991, Vol. 26, No. 35, p. 2,062.
43. Sudhakar Raje (ed.), *Onward March: BJP First National Convention Speeches and Resolutions 28–30 December 1980 Bombay*, published by Madhu Deolekar, publicity chief, BJP (Bombay: Mouj Printing Bureau), pp. 50–51.

44. The five women were Vijaya Raje Scindia from Gwalior, Mohinder Kaur from Delhi, Jayawantiben Mehta from Bombay, Sumatibai Suklikar from Nagpur and Dr Kamla Verma from Haryana. Of the 106 members of the National Executive, fifteen were central office-bearers (including one woman), thirty-six were members (including two women), fourteen were special invitees (including one woman), twenty-three were permanent invitees as state presidents (including one woman), fourteen were BJP party leaders in legislative assemblies and four were leaders of the party in legislative councils. The author's calculation from National Executive members list published in Sudhakar Raje (ed.), *Onward March: BJP First National Convention Speeches and Resolutions 28–30 December 1980 Bombay*, published by Madhu Deolekar, publicity chief, BJP (Bombay: Mouj Printing Bureau), pp. 67–72.
45. Harihar Swarup, 'Maharani all the way', *The Tribune*, 13 June 1999, https://www.tribuneindia.com/1999/99jun13/edit.htm#1.
46. TOINS, 'Rajmata will resist bid by Congress to woo her back', *The Times of India*, 10 August 1967.
47. TOINS, 'MP assembly is prorogued after vote on account: Regular budget only after four months', *The Times of India*, 1 August 1967; TOINS, 'SVD Rift Widens Over Issue of MP Cabinet Changes', *The Times of India*, 5 November 1968; 'Rajmata denies "bias" towards Jana Sangh', *The Times of India*, 17 June 1968.
48. Ira Pande interview of Sushma Swaraj, 'The sky is the limit', *Seminar*, April 1996, No. 440, pp. 43–45. Swaraj served as cabinet minister for labour. Special Correspondent, 'Minister's resignation a setback to Haryana govt', *The Times of India*, 16 November 1977; Special Correspondent, 'Party sore: Sushma episode', *The Times of India*, 18 November 1977; Special Correspondent, 'Haryana crisis blows over', *The Times of India*, 23 November 1977.
49. PTI, 'BJP to start crusade against dowry', *The Times of India*, 13 July 1982.
50. TOINS, 'Vajpayee's call to educated women', *The Times of India*, 3 August 1984.
51. Vijaya Raje Scindia, 'Need for a modern outlook' (A paper presented to the National Executive of the BJP on 24 April 1981) (New Delhi: Bharatiya Janata Party, 1981).
52. The Working Group's convener was Krishanlal Sharma. Its members included: Bhairon Singh Shekhawat (later Rajasthan chief minister and India's vice-president), Shanta Kumar (later Union minister under Vajpayee), Makrand Desai, Pramod Mahajan (later Union minister under Vajpayee), Vijay Kumar Malhotra (later BJP's chief whip in the Lok Sabha), Sunder Lal Patwa, Jana Krishnamurthi (later BJP president), Murli Manohar Joshi (later BJP president), Surah Bhan, Arif Baig and Mridula Sinha. *Working Group Report, Presented to National Executive Bhopal* (New Delhi: BJP, 20 July 1985), p. 11.
53. Ibid.
54. Tanika Sarkar, 'The woman as communal subject: Rashtrasevika Samiti and Ram Janmabhoomi Movement', *Economic & Political Weekly*, Vol. 26, No. 35, 31 August 1991, p. 2,057.
55. Ibid.

56. See for instance, Kalyani Devaki Menon, '"We will become Jijabai": Nationalist women in India', *The Journal of Asian Studies*, Vol. 64, No. 1, February 2005, pp. 103–126.
57. Tanika Sarkar, 'Pragmatics of the Hindu Right: Politics of women's organisations', *Economic & Political Weekly*, Vol. 34, No. 31, 31 July 1991, p. 2,161.
58. Quoted in Naunidhi Kaur, 'Sifting the truth', *Frontline*, 27 April 2002, https://frontline.thehindu.com/other/article30244706.ece.
59. Amrita Basu, 'The gendered imagery and women's leadership of Hindu Nationalism', *Reproductive Health Matters*, Vol. 4, No. 8, November 1996, pp. 71, 74.
60. Tanika Sarkar, 'Pragmatics of the Hindu Right: Politics of women's organisations', *Economic & Political Weekly*, Vol. 34, No. 31, 31 July 1991, p. 2,162.
61. Tanika Sarkar, 'The woman as communal subject: Rashtrasevika Samiti and Ram Janmabhoomi Movement', *Economic & Political Weekly*, Vol. 26, No. 35, 31 August 1991, p. 2062.
62. Ibid., p. 2166.
63. Full text of Narendra Modi's live address and interaction with Karnataka BJP Mahila Morcha, 4 May 2018, https://www.narendramodi.in/country-is-moving-towards-women-led-development-539996. Text is in Hindi; translations are mine.
64. Ibid.
65. TNN, 'Army, police no longer all-male bastions', *The Times of India*, 25 October 2021, https://timesofindia.indiatimes.com/india/army-police-no-longer-all-male-bastions-modi/articleshow/87245162.cms. The total number of women in India's police forces rose by 16 per cent in 2020, compared to the previous year. Overall, women amounted to 10.3 per cent of the total strength of police forces in 2020. PIB Delhi, Ministry of Home Affairs, Bureau of Police Research & Development (BPR&D) releases data on police organizations as on 01.01.2020', 29 December 2020, https://pib.gov.in/PressReleasePage.aspx?PRID=1684384
66. TOI.in, 'Sainik Schools now open for girls also: PM Modi in his I-Day speech', *The Times of India*, 15 August 2021, https://timesofindia.indiatimes.com/videos/news/sainik-schools-now-open-for-girls-also-pm-modi-in-his-i-day-speech/videoshow/85343000.cms. There were thirty-three Sainik Schools in India in 2020. The Modi government gave cabinet approval to a proposal to set up 100 additional 100 Sainik schools from academic year 2022-23 in partnership with states, NGOs and private entities. Express News Service, 'Union cabinet nod to 100 affiliate Sainik Schools across India', *The New Indian Express*, 13 October 2021, https://www.newindianexpress.com/nation/2021/oct/13/union-cabinet-nod-to-100-affiliate-sainik-schools-across-india-2371064.html.
67. The Supreme Court of India order followed an earlier judgment by the apex court order on 17 February 2020 that allowed permanent commission to women in the defence forces (beyond just short-service commission). Deeksha Bharadwaj, '178,000 women apply for NDA as forces lift gender barrier', *The Hindustan Times*, 30 October 2021, https://www.hindustantimes.com/india-news/178k-women-

apply-for-nda-as-forces-lift-gender-barrier-101635531114904-amp.html?utm_source=whatsapp&utm_medium= social&utm_campaign=ht_AMP.

68. Full transcript in Bluekraft Digital Foundation, *Mann ki Baat: A Social Revolution on Radio* (New Delhi: Rupa, 2019), pp. 632–633.
69. Ibid., p. 632.
70. See, for example, the critique in one analysis of sixty-eight Modi speeches in Rukmini Bhaya Nair, 'Man-watching Mr Modi', *Outlook*, 24 June 2013, https://www.outlookindia.com/magazine/story/manwatching-mister-modi/286143.
71. The success rate of the BJP's women candidates, 74.5 per cent, was also slightly higher than the success rate of its male candidates: 68.7 per cent. Author calculations from ECI data in EDM Division, 'Participation of women electors in poll', 11 October 2019, https://eci.gov.in/files/file/10949-23-participation-of-women-electors-in-poll/; EDM Division, 'Performance of national parties', 11 October 2019, https://eci.gov.in/files/file/10955-20-performance-of-national-parties/.
72. Success rate of the BJP's women candidates was 74.5 per cent. Next highest was Trinamool Congress at 39.1 per cent and then the Congress at 11.1 per cent. ECI data in EDM Division, 'Participation of women candidates in national parties', 11 October 2019, https://eci.gov.in/files/file/10943-26-participation-of-women-candidates-in-national-parties/.
73. Data from Lok Sabha, 'Seventeenth Lok Sabha: Women members', http://164.100.47.194/loksabha/Members/women.aspx.
74. 2004 ECI data: https://eci.gov.in/files/file/4126-general-election-2004-vol-i-ii-iii/; 2009 ECI data: https://eci.gov.in/files/file/2869-participation-of-women-in-national-parties/, https://eci.gov.in/files/file/2868-participation-of-women-in-state-parties/, https://eci.gov.in/files/file/2881-performance-of-national-parties/, https://eci.gov.in/files/file/2880-performance-of-state-party/; 2014 ECI data published on 10 August 2018: https://eci.gov.in/files/file/2809-participation-of-women-in-national-parties/; https://eci.gov.in/files/file/2807-participation-of-women-in-state-parties/, https://eci.gov.in/files/file/2820-performance-of-national-parties/, https://eci.gov.in/files/file/2818-performance-of-state-parties/, https://eci.gov.in/files/file/2815-performance-of-registered-unrecognised-parties/, https://eci.gov.in/files/file/2805-participation-of-women-in-registered-unrecognised-parties/, https://eci.gov.in/files/file/2815-performance-of-registered-unrecognised-parties/; 2019 ECI data published on 11 October 2019: https://eci.gov.in/files/file/10955-20-performance-of-national-parties/, https://eci.gov.in/files/file/10953-21performance-of-state-parties/, https://eci.gov.in/files/file/10943-26-participation-of-women-candidates-in-national-parties/, https://eci.gov.in/files/file/10941-27participation-of-women-in-state-parties/. Cross-referenced ADR data from its public data platform MyNeta: https://myneta.info/loksabha2004/index.php?action=summary&subAction=women_candidate&sort=candidate#summary.

75. Sikata Banerjee, 'Hindu nationalism and the construction of woman: The Shiv Sena organises women in Bombay', in Tanika Sarkar, Urvashia Butalia (eds.), *Women and the Hindu Right: A Collection of Essays* (New Delhi: Kali for Women/Zubaan, 2020 eBook edition, first published 1995). Also see Sikata Banerjee, 'The feminization of violence in Bombay: Women in the politics of the Shiv Sena', *Asian Survey*, Vol. 36, No. 12, December 1996, pp. 1213–1225.
76. Teesta Setalvad, 'The woman Shiv Sainik and her sister Swayamsevika', in Tanika Sarkar, Urvashia Butalia (eds.), *Women and the Hindu Right: A Collection of Essays* (New Delhi: Kali for Women/Zubaan, 2020 ebook edition, first published 1995).
77. Flavia Agnes, 'Redefining the agenda of the women's movement within a secular framework', in Tanika Sarkar, Urvashia Butalia (eds), *Women and the Hindu Right: A Collection of Essays* (New Delhi: Kali for Women/Zubaan, 2020 eBook edition, first published 1995).
78. See Sikata Banerjee, 'Hindu nationalism and the construction of woman: The Shiv Sena organises women in Bombay', in Tanika Sarkar, Urvashia Butalia (eds.), *Women and the Hindu Right: A Collection of Essays* (New Delhi: Kali for Women/Zubaan, 2020 ebook edition, first published 1995).
79. Manish Chandra Pandey, 'Nadda's team has 11 leaders from UP as party eyes 2022 state polls', *Hindustan Times*, 27 September 2020, https://www.hindustantimes.com/india-news/nadda-s-team-has-11-leaders-from-up-as-party-eyes-2022-state-polls/story-pe73KMEcSkvuKaxnx9tvkJ.html.
80. Megha Bhatt, 'It's a huge win for women candidates', Ahmedabad *Mirror*, 24 May 2019, https://ahmedabadmirror.indiatimes.com/loksabha-elections/its-a-huge-win-for-women-candidates/articleshow/69471839.cms.
81. Bedanti Saran, 'Jharkhand RJD chief Annapurna Devi joins BJP', *Hindustan Times*, 26 March 2019, https://www.hindustantimes.com/lok-sabha-elections/lok-sabha-elections-2019-jharkhand-rjd-chief-annapurna-devi-joins-bjp/story-OwbGGMdjnHhntTVhIalDAM.html.
82. Balakrishna Ganeshan, 'DK Aruna made BJP VP: What this means for the party in Telangana', 29 September 2020, https://www.thenewsminute.com/article/dk-aruna-made-bjp-vice-president-what-means-party-telangana-134140.
83. Interview with Hemant Agarwal, BJP district vice-president, Mathura Mahanagar, 26 July 2020.
84. Interview with Pradeep Goswami, general secretary, Mathura Mahanagar, BJP, 26 July 2020.
85. BJP, *Mahila Morcha: Prashikshan Praaroop* (New Delhi: Pandit Deen Dayal Upadhyaya Prashikshan Mahaabhiyan, 2018), pp. 64–68.
86. Full text of Narendra Modi's live address and interaction with Karnataka BJP Mahila Morcha, 4 May 2018. https://www.narendramodi.in/country-is-moving-towards-women-led-development-539996. The text is in Hindi; translations are mine.
87. Interview with a former BJP national office-bearer, speaking on condition of anonymity, 29 June 2020.

88. BJP, *Resolution on Reservation for Women in Parliament and State Legislatures at National Executive Meeting, Raipur, July 18–20, 2003*, https://www.bjp.org/en/articledetail/226483/Resolution-on-Reservation-for-Women-in-Parliament-and-State-Legislatures-at-National-Executive-Meeting-Raipur---July-18-20-2003.
89. Interview with Vani Tripathi Tikoo, former national secretary, BJP, 27 August 2019.
90. Pragya Kaushika, 'BJP women to become mayors in north and east Delhi', *The Indian Express*, 27 April 2012, http://archive.indianexpress.com/news/bjp-women-to-become-mayors-in-north-and--east-delhi/942199/; Gaurav Vivek Bhatnagar, 'All you need to know about Delhi's MCD elections', 22 April 2017, https://thewire.in/politics/explainer-mcd-elections-delhi.
91. Interview with Vani Tripathi Tikoo, former national secretary, BJP, 27 August 2019.
92. Ibid.
93. Ibid.
94. Ibid.
95. https://www.narendramodi.in/country-is-moving-towards-women-led-development-539996.
96. BJP, *Mahila Morcha: Prashikshan Praaroop* (New Delhi: Pandit Deen Dayal Upadhyaya Prashikshan Mahaabhiyan 2018), pp. 90–91.
97. Interview with Vani Tripathi Tikoo, former national secretary, BJP, 27 August 2019.
98. Full text of Narendra Modi's live address and interaction with the Karnataka BJP Mahila Morcha, 4 May 2018, https://www.narendramodi.in/country-is-moving-towards-women-led-development-539996. Text is in Hindi; translations are mine.
99. PMMY was launched on 8 April 2015 for providing loans up to Rs 10 lakh to non-corporate, non-farm small/micro enterprises. These Mudra loans are given by commercial banks, RRBs, small finance banks, MFIs and NBFCs. *Mudra Yojana Annual Report 2019-20*, p. 16.
100. 'Naari shakti is breaking the barriers of society: PM during Mann ki Baat', 28 January 2018. Full transcript of this *Mann ki Baat* episode available at: https://www.narendramodi.in/pm-modi-s-mann-ki-baat-january-2018-538680.
101. The scheme was launched on 28 August 2014. The scheme envisages universal access to banking facilities with at least one basic banking account for every adult. Data from PIB Delhi, Ministry of Finance Release, 3 March 2020, https://pib.gov.in/PressReleseDetailm.aspx?PRID=1604929.
102. From 28 August 2018, Jan Dhan account-holders were eligible for: Over Draft (OD) limit of Rs 10,000 (revised from Rs 5,000), accident insurance cover for new RuPay card holders of Rs 2 lakh (raised from Rs 1 lakh). Jan Dhan accounts also provided a platform for three social security schemes, viz., Pradhan Mantri Jeevan Jyoti Bima Yojana (PMJJBY), Pradhan Mantri Suraksha Bima Yojana (PMSBY), Atal Pension Yojana (APY) and Pradhan Mantri Mudra Yojana (PMMY). See https://pmjdy.gov.in/scheme.
103. PM Awaas Yojana-Gramin MIS, 'C.1 Gender-wise houses sanctioned and completed', 24 October 2020, https://rhreporting.nic.in/netiay/SocialProgressReport/

Ownershipdetailsofhousessanctionedreport.aspx 24/10/2020. Also see NIPFP Research Team, *Evaluation of Governance Parameters of Pradhan Mantri Awaas Yojana- Gramin (PMAY-G) Third Report Submitted to Ministry of Rural Development Government of India* (New Delhi: National Institute of Public Finance and Policy, December 2019), p. 87.

104. Full text of Narendra Modi's live address and interaction with the Karnataka BJP Mahila Morcha, 4 May 2018, https://www.narendramodi.in/country-is-moving-towards-women-led-development-539996. Text is in Hindi; translations are mine. Also see PTI, 'PMAY-Urban: Registration to Include Woman's Name Mandatorily', *Financial Express*, 30 May 2016, https://www.financialexpress.com/economy/pmay-urban-registeration-to-include-womans-name-mandatorily/269459/.

105. Apurva Viswanath, 'Explained: Reading SC verdict on Hindu women's inheritance rights', *The Indian Express*, 17 August 2020.

106. PM Awaas Yojana-Gramin MIS, 'C.1 Gender-wise houses sanctioned and completed', 24 October 2020, https://rhreporting.nic.in/netiay/SocialProgressReport/Ownershipdetailsofhousessanctionedreport.aspx 24/10/2020. Also see NIPFP Research Team, *Evaluation of Governance Parameters of Pradhan Mantri Awaas Yojana- Gramin (PMAY-G) Third Report Submitted to Ministry of Rural Development Government of India* (New Delhi: National Institute of Public Finance and Policy, December 2019), p. 87.

107. In Bihar, women-only or joint-women-ownership houses built under the scheme amounted to 20,68,280; in MP: 10,74,198; Rajasthan: 9,44,018; in UP: 9,37,433 houses. PM Awaas Yojana-Gramin MIS, 'C.1 Gender-wise houses sanctioned and completed', 24 October 2020, https://rhreporting.nic.in/netiay/SocialProgressReport/Ownershipdetailsofhousessanctionedreport.aspx 24/10/2020.

108. Sneha Alexander, Vishnu Padmanabhan, 'How much does the Indian government spend on women?', *Mint*, 8 March 2020, https://www.livemint.com/news/india/how-much-does-the-indian-government-spend-on-women-11583662675936.html.

109. PIB Delhi, Ministry of Finance Release, 3 March 2020, https://pib.gov.in/PressReleseDetailm.aspx?PRID=1604929.

110. Beneficiaries, through Aadhar-linked mobile phones, received maternity benefits in more than one instalment through total direct-benefit cash transfers of Rs 5,710.98 crore in this period. Average calculated by author from data submitted by Smriti Irani, minister for women and child development, reply to Lok Sabha Unstarred Question No. 4507 on 20 March 2020. Average days taken for cash payments after registration went from 20.4 in 2017-18 to 32.3 in 2018-19 to 36.3 in 2019-20. Smriti Irani, minister for women and child development, reply to Rajya Sabha Unstarred Question No. 205 on 12 March 2020.

111. This move was aimed at specifically helping women working in the formal sector, approximately 1.8 million. Full text of the Maternity Benefit (Amendment) Act,

2017 available at: https://labour.gov.in/sites/default/files/Maternity%20Benefit%20Amendment%20Act%2C2017%20.pdf. Also see Jean D'Cunha, Special Advisor to UN Women (India, Bhutan, Maldives, Sri Lanka), 'India's bold Maternity Benefits Act can become a game changer if it addresses current limitations', *Economic & Political Weekly*, Vo. 53, Issue 31, 8 August 2018, https://www.epw.in/node/152339/pdf.

112. Full text of Narendra Modi's live address and interaction with the Karnataka BJP Mahila Morcha, 4 May 2018. https://www.narendramodi.in/country-is-moving-towards-women-led-development-539996. The text is in Hindi; translations are mine.
113. PIB, Ministry of Women and Child Development Release, 8 February 2018.
114. Funding for 'Beti Bachao, Beti Padhao' increased from Rs 9,194.42 lakh in 2017-18 to Rs 10,479.84 lakh in 2018-19 to Rs 11,012.37 lakh in 2020-21. Data from Smriti Irani, minister for women and child development, reply to Lok Sabha Unstarred Question No. 4592 on 20 March 2020.
115. Swachh Bharat Dashboard, 'Households toilets coverage across India', 28 October 2020, https://sbm.gov.in/sbmdashboard/IHHL.aspx.
116. Aman Sharma, 'Call Swachh Bharat toilets "Izzat Ghar": Centre to states', *The Economic Times*, 17 October 2017, https://economictimes.indiatimes.com/news/politics-and-nation/call-swachh-bharat-toilets-izzat-ghar-centre-to-states/articleshow/61123473.cms?from=mdr.
117. Anurag Thakur, minister of state for finance, answer to Lok Sabha Unstarred Question No. 4669, 22 July 2019, http://164.100.24.220/loksabhaquestions/annex/171/AU4669.pdf; Piyush Goyal, finance minister, answer to Lok Sabha Starred Question No. 346, 10 August 2018, http://164.100.24.220/loksabhaquestions/annex/15/AU1655.pdf.
118. Full text of Narendra Modi's live address and interaction with the Karnataka BJP Mahila Morcha, 4 May 2018. https://www.narendramodi.in/country-is-moving-towards-women-led-development-539996. The text is in Hindi; translations are mine.
119. Anurag Thakur, minister of state for finance, answer to Lok Sabha Unstarred Question No. 4750, 23 March 2020, http://164.100.24.220/loksabhaquestions/annex/173/AU4750.pdf. The Stand Up India scheme was launched on 5 April 2016, to facilitate bank loans between Rs 10 lakh and Rs 1 crore to at least one SC or ST borrower and at least one woman borrower per bank branch of Scheduled Commercial Banks for setting up a greenfield enterprise. PIB Delhi, Ministry of Finance Press Release, 3 March 2020, https://pib.gov.in/PressReleseDetailm.aspx?PRID=1604929.
120. APY was launched on 9 May 2015. It offers guaranteed minimum monthly pension of Rs 1,000–5,000 at the age of sixty years. As on 22 February 2020, more than 93 lakh subscribers (43 per cent) out of a total of around 2.15 crore subscribers under APY were women. PIB Delhi, Ministry of Finance Release, 3 March 2020, https://

pib.gov.in/PressReleseDetailm.aspx?PRID=1604929. Further background from Anurag Singh Thakur, minister of state for finance, answer to Lok Sabha Question No. 4744, 22 July 2019, http://164.100.24.220/loksabhaquestions/annex/171/AU4744.pdf.

121. PMJJBY was launched on 9 May 2015. Under PMJJBY, 40.70 per cent enrolments were of women members and 58.21 per cent of claim beneficiaries are women (as on 31 January 2020). 1,91,96,805 females had enrolled out of a total of 4,71,71,568 enrolments. 95,508 claims had been paid to female beneficiaries out of a total of 1,69,216 claims paid (as on 31 January 2020). PIB Delhi, Ministry of Finance Release, 3 March 2020, https://pib.gov.in/PressReleseDetailm.aspx?PRID=1604929.
122. Full text of Narendra Modi's live address and interaction with the Karnataka BJP Mahila Morcha, 4 May 2018, https://www.narendramodi.in/country-is-moving-towards-women-led-development-539996. The text is in Hindi; translations are mine.
123. Anurag Singh Thakur, minister of state in the ministry of finance, answer to Lok Sabha Unstarred Question No. 3277, 9 December 2019, http://164.100.24.220/loksabhaquestions/annex/172/AU3277.pdf.
124. 'Naari Shakti is breaking the barriers of society: PM during Mann ki Baat', 28 January 2018. Full transcript of this *Mann ki Baat* episode available at: https://www.narendramodi.in/pm-modi-s-mann-ki-baat-january-2018-538680.
125. 'From panchayats to parliament, women are leading from the front: PM Modi', 13 April 2017. Full text of his speech to Indian Merchant Chambers Ladies Wing, Mumbai, available at: https://www.narendramodi.in/text-of-pm-modi-s-speech-on-the-50th-year-celebrations-of-indian-merchants-chamber-ladies-wing-via-video-conferencing-535046. Speech was in Hindi; translations are mine.
126. Total direct cash transferred to women beneficiaries amounted to Rs 1.21 lakh crore in this period. Of the 80 million beneficiaries, nearly 86 per cent returned for a second refill. Average per capita income consumption of Ujjwala beneficiaries is around 4.87 cylinders. Overall Ujjwala beneficiaries accounted for almost one-third of total LPG consumers in India. Data from Dharmendra Pradhan, minister for petroleum and natural gas, answer to Rajya Sabha Unstarred Question No. 1896, 4 December 2019; Dharmendra Pradhan, minister for petroleum and natural gas, answer to Rajya Sabha Unstarred Question No. 2690, 11 December 2019; Dharmendra Pradhan, minister for petroleum and natural gas, answer to Lok Sabha Unstarred Question No. 1537, 1 July 2019. Ujjwala Scheme guidelines are available at: http://petroleum.nic.in/sites/default/files/ujscheme.pdf.
127. See, for instance, Report of the Comptroller and Auditor General of India on Pradhan Mantri Ujjwala Yojana: Union Government (Commercial), Ministry of Petroleum and Natural Gas, No. 14 of 2019, https://cag.gov.in/en/audit-report/details/55961.
128. 'From panchayats to parliament, women are leading from the front: PM Modi', 13 April 2017.Full text of his speech to Indian Merchant Chambers Ladies Wing,

Mumbai, available at: https://www.narendramodi.in/text-of-pm-modi-s-speech-on-the-50th-year-celebrations-of-indian-merchants-chamber-ladies-wing-via-video-conferencing-535046. Speech was in Hindi; translations are mine.

129. TOINS, 'Rajmata earns wrath on "sati"', *The Times of India*, 27 August 1990.
130. Ravi Shankar, 'Women 2nd class citizens in Hindutva parivar', *Asian Age*, 30 August 1999.
131. TOINS, 'Rajmata earns wrath on "sati"', *The Times of India*, 27 August 1990.
132. 'Puri priest's remarks on women derogatory: BJP', *The Statesman*, 21 January 1994.
133. TOINS, 'Women power at BJP rally', *The Times of India*, 28 September 1991.
134. Ravi Shankar, 'Women 2nd class citizens in Hindutva parivar', *Asian Age*, 30 August 1999.
135. Ibid.
136. 'From panchayats to parliament, women are leading from the front: PM Modi', 13 April 2017 Full text of his speech to Indian Merchant Chambers Ladies Wing, Mumbai, available at: https://www.narendramodi.in/text-of-pm-modi-s-speech-on-the-50th-year-celebrations-of-indian-merchants-chamber-ladies-wing-via-video-conferencing-535046. Speech was in Hindi; translations are mine.
137. Full text of Narendra Modi's live address and interaction with Karnataka BJP Mahila Morcha, 4 May 2018, https://www.narendramodi.in/country-is-moving-towards-women-led-development-539996. Text is in Hindi; translations are mine.
138. Express News Service, 'On Yogi's website: "Women's power does not require freedom, but protection"', *The Indian Express*, 18 April 2017, https://indianexpress.com/article/india/on-yogis-website-women-power-does-not-require-freedom-but-protection-4617177/.
139. Relevant portion from Sakshi Maharaj's speech is available at: https://www.youtube.com/watch?v=OQ7mKZPpLeg.
140. PTI, 'BJP revokes suspension of Dayashankar Singh', *The Hindu*, 12 March 2017, https://www.thehindu.com/elections/uttar-pradesh-2017/bjp-revokes-suspension-of-dayashankar-singh/article17451450.ece.
141. Walter K. Andersen, Shridhar D. Damle, *The RSS: A View from the Inside* (New Delhi: Penguin/Viking, 2018), p. 24.
142. Ibid., p. 25.
143. Priti Gandhi, 'Matrushakti & Sangh', *Organiser*, Vol. 70, No. 18, 28 October 2018, p. 25.
144. Ibid.
145. Sunil Ambekar, *The RSS: Roadmaps for the 21st Century* (New Delhi: Rupa, 2019), pp. 177, 193–196.
146. BJP, *Mahila Morcha: Prashikshan Praaroop* (New Delhi: Pandit Deen Dayal Upadhyaya Prashikshan Mahaabhiyan, 2018), pp. 100–102.
147. Ibid., pp. 100–101
148. Sunil Ambekar, *The RSS: Roadmaps for the 21st Century* (New Delhi: Rupa, 2019), pp. 198–199.

149. Ibid., p. 199.
150. Gail Omvedt, 'Hindu nationalism and women-I', *The Hindu*, 27 April 2000. Also see, Sarvar V. Sherry Chand, Vijay Shery Chand, 'The gender divide', *The Times of India*, 10 February 1991; Kamla Bhasin, Ritu Menon, Abha Bhaiya, 'Why women fear the fundamentalists', *Sunday Review*, 20 January 1991; Lalita Panicker, 'Women's worth: Parivar's brand of liberation', *The Times of India*, 5 June 1997.
151. Swati Dyahadroy, 'Exploring gender, Hindutva and seva', *Economic & Political Weekly*, Vol XLIV, No. 17, 25 April 2009, pp. 65–73.
152. Shaju Philip, 'Amit Shah asks on Sabarimala: Why issue orders that can't be enforced?', *The Indian Express*, 28 October 2018, https://indianexpress.com/article/india/amit-shah-asks-on-sabarimala-why-issue-orders-that-cant-be-enforced-5421715/; Amit Shah tweet on 27 October 2018, https://twitter.com/AmitShah/status/1056133606186409990?s=20.
153. PM Modi's interview with Smita Prakash, ANI, 1 January 2019. Relevant video clip available at: https://www.youtube.com/watch?v=sjTxneIIiak&t=1s.
154. Scroll Staff, 'Sabarimala: BJP workers will uproot Kerala government if it arrests more devotees, says Amit Shah', *Scroll.in*, 27 October 2018, https://scroll.in/latest/899877/sabarimala-row-centre-will-dissolve-kerala-government-if-it-arrests-more-devotees-says-amit-shah.
155. P.S. Gopalakrishnan Unnithan, 'Sabarimala protests bring BJP, Congress on same side in Kerala', *India Today*, 20 November 2018, https://www.indiatoday.in/india/story/sabarimala-protests-bring-bjp-congress-on-same-side-in-kerala-1392598-2018-11-20.
156. Shashi Tharoor, 'Why Sabarimala issue leaves instinctive liberals like me torn: Shashi Tharoor', *The Print*, 10 November 2018, https://theprint.in/opinion/why-sabarimala-issue-leaves-instinctive-liberals-like-me-torn-shashi-tharoor/147759/.
157. Shashi Tharoor in conversation with the author at the Times Lit Fest Delhi, November 2018. Full video available at: https://www.youtube.com/watch?v=6FNnEWit_rE.
158. Tanika Sarkar, Urvashi Butalia, 'Introductory remarks', in Tanika Sarkar, Urvashia Butalia (eds.), *Women and the Hindu Right: A Collection of Essays* (New Delhi: Kali for Women/Zubaan, 2020 ebook edition, first published 1995).
159. Ibid.
160. In this context, see, for instance, Sanjay Seth, 'Nationalism, modernity, and the "woman question" in India and China', *The Journal of Asian Studies*, Vol. 72, No. 2, May 2013, pp. 273–297.
161. Rekha Pande, 'The history of feminism and doing gender in India', *Estudos Feministas*, Vol. 26, No. 3, 2018, pp. 2–3.
162. Santanu Chowdhury, 'PM addresses Bengal on Puja: Respect women of India like you respect Durga', *The Indian Express*, 23 October 2020.
163. Narendra Modi (tr. Bhawana Somaaya), *Letters to Mother* (New Delhi: HarperCollins, 2020). First published in Gujarati as *Sakshi Bhaav* in 2014.

164. Ayesha Jalal, 'Women and Religion', *Economic & Political Weekly*, 8 February 2003, p. 529. See also Duree S. Ahmed (ed.), *Gendering the Spirit: Women, Religions and the Post-Colonials Response* (New York: Zed, 2002).
165. Jagriti Chandra, 'Should the age of marriage for women be raised to 21?', *The Hindu*, 4 September 2020, https://www.thehindu.com/opinion/op-ed/should-the-age-of-marriage-for-women-be-raised-to-21/article32517084.ece.
166. The Law Commission in 2008 recommended a common minimum marriage age of eighteen for both men and women. Full report available at: https://lawcommissionofindia.nic.in/reports/report205.pdf.

CHAPTER 18 'Party of Ram'

1. 'Danda-vat', a Sanskrit word, literally means lying on the floor like a stick. Devotees perform dandvat pranam by lying fully prostrate on the floor with their arms stretched out. It is a symbol of complete submission. The full video of Modi's dandvat pranam before the Ram Lalla idol in Ayodhya on 5 August 2020 is available at: https://navbharattimes.indiatimes.com/state/uttar-pradesh/ayodhya/faizabad/narendra-modi-offers-prayers-to-ram-lalla-in-ayodhya-before-ram-mandir-bhumi-pujan/videoshow/77366857.cms.
2. For critiques of the Ayodhya bhoomi-pujan, see, for instance, Yogendra Yadav, 'Secularism gave up language of religion. Ayodhya Boomi Pujan is a result of that', *The Print*, 5 August 2020, https://theprint.in/opinion/secularism-language-religion-ayodhya-bhoomi-pujan-ram-mandir-kashmir/475307/; Pratap Bhanu Mehta, 'Ram, I will not find you there', *The Indian Express*, 5 August 2020. For a counter-view, see Ram Madhav, 'Great unifier, universal hero', *The Indian Express*, 5 August 2020, and Vinay Sahasrabuddhe, 'Temple as turning point', *The Indian Express*, 5 August 2020.
3. 'Suratrana' is a Sanskrit term which literally is interpreted to mean protector/saviour of the gods or as a transliteration of the word 'Sultan' into Sanskrit. It featured, among other places, in an inscription on the Qutab Minar in Delhi, coins of the early Delhi Sultanate sultans and inscriptions of the Vijayanagar empire in Hampi and several other places. The copper plates of Devaraya II of the Vijayanagara kingdom use the term 'Hinduraya Suratrana'. For details on the Qutab Minar inscription, see Sheldon Pollock, 'Ramayana and political imagination in India', *The Journal of Asian Studies*, Vol. 52, No. 2, May 1993, p. 285; for the origins of the term, see A.R. Kulkarni, 'Social relations in the Maratha period in the medieval period', *Proceedings of the Indian History Congress*, Vol. 32, Volume I, 1970, p. 235.
4. See, for instance, Adrija Roychowdhury, 'Secularism: Why Nehru dropped and Indira inserted the S-word in the Constitution', *The Indian Express*, 27 December 2017, https://indianexpress.com/article/research/anant-kumar-hegde-secularism-constitution-india-bjp-jawaharlal-nehru-indira-gandhi-5001085/.

5. UP Yogi Adityanath's speech at Ayodhya bhoomi-pujan, 5 August 2020. https://bit.ly/39RXgjI.
6. Full text of the SC's Ayodhya judgement is available at: https://www.sci.gov.in/pdf/JUD_2.pdf.
7. Samuel P. Huntington, *The Clash of Civilizations and the Remaking of the World Order* (London: Simon & Schuster, 1996), pp. 28, 45–46. Huntington's thesis was first published as 'The clash of civilizations?', *Foreign Affairs*, Vol. 7, No. 3, Summer 1993, https://www.foreignaffairs.com/articles/united-states/1993-06-01/clash-civilizations.
8. Special Correspondent, 'Panch sadi ka swapn poora hoga: Yogi', *Dainik Jagran* (Fatehpur edition), 14 November 2020, p. 1.
9. Yusra Husain, 'Ayodhya Deepotsav sets fifth Guinness Record in a row', *The Times of India*, 4 November 2021, https://timesofindia.indiatimes.com/city/lucknow/ayodhya-deepotsav-sets-5th-guinness-record-in-a-row/articleshow/87517743.cms; AP, 'Ayodhya lights record number of diyas, retains Guinness World Record for second year', *The Hindu*, 14 November 2020, https://www.thehindu.com/news/national/other-states/ayodhya-lights-record-number-of-diyas-retains-guinness-world-record-for-second-year/article33099954.ece.
10. Yogi Adityanath's tweet, 13 November 2020, https://twitter.com/myogiadityanath/status/1327288747558199296?s=20. See also his tweet on 3 November 2021, https://twitter.com/myogiadityanath/status/ 1455910462344728584?s=20.
11. Special Correspondent, 'Panch sadi ka swapn poora hoga: Yogi', *Dainik Jagran* (Fatehpur edition), 14 November 2020, p. 1.
12. 'Ayodhya banegi vaishwik nagari', *Dainik Jagran* (Fatehpur edition), 14 November 2020, p.1; 'Gaurav-bodh se alokit huee Ram nagari', *Dainik Jagran* (Fatehpur edition), 14 November 2020, p. 3.
13. The UP government, under Chief Minister Yogi Adityanath, renamed Allahabad as Prayagraj on 16 October 2018. The change was ratified by the Union government on 1 January 2019, a day before the Kumbh Mela. The chief minister justified the name-change saying, 'Five hundred years ago the name of the place was Prayagraj as it is at the "Triveni Sangam" (a confluence of three rivers) ... There are many Prayags on the bank of the sacred rivers coming from the Himalayas but this place is Prayagraj [King of Prayags].' PTI, 'UP cabinet approves renaming of Allahabad to Prayagraj', *The Economic Times*, 17 October 2018, https://economictimes.indiatimes.com/news/politics-and-nation/uttar-pradesh-cabinet-renames-allahbad-to-prayagraj/articleshow/66234532.cms; Rahul Tripathi, 'Days before Kumbh Mela, Centre approves renaming of Allahabad as Prayagraj', *The Indian Express*, 2 January 2019, https://indianexpress.com/article/india/home-ministry-allahabad-prayagraj-kumbh-mela-5518766/.
14. Regional Tourism Offices data from the UP government, 'The Indian and foreign tourist visits in important tourist places of Uttar Pradesh in year 2015 to 2019', 12 February 2020, internal note by UP government. Similar data, along the same

trendline, was also presented by the state government at the UP Investors Summit, 2018. UP Government PPT presentation at UP Investors Summit, 21–22 February 2018, *UP Nahi Dekha to India Nahi Dekha*. I am grateful to Pravin Kumar for providing a copy of this 2018 government presentation and the 2020 data note.

15. UP state budgets, year-wise, available at: http://budget.up.nic.in/. Figures on Yogi Adityanath's first state budget from Anuja Jaiswal, 'Prayagraj, Ayodhya & Vrindavan see rush of domestic tourists', *The Times of India*, 25 April 2019.
16. The National High Speed Rail Corporation Limited (NHRSCL) was working on detailed project reports (DPR) for seven new high-speed rail corridors: 1. Delhi–Varanasi (865 km) 2. Delhi–Ahmedabad (886 km) 3. Mumbai–Nagpur (753 km) 4. Mumbai–Hyderabad (711 km) 5. Chennai–Mysore (435 km) 6. Delhi–Amritsar (459 km) 7. Varanasi–Howrah (760 km). Of these, by August 2021, the DPR for the Delhi–Varanasi route was the most advanced and in its final stages. It envisaged a Delhi–Varanasi journey by bullet train in four hours. Ayodhya is one of the twelve stations on the route (Sarai Kale Khan, Noida, Jewar, Mathura, Agra, Etawah, Kannauj, Lucknow, Ayodhya, Raebareli, Prayagraj, Bhadohi, Varanasi) with the Delhi–Ayodhya leg planned in two hours. Details on planned high speed corridors from Vinod Kumar Yadav, Chairman NHRSCL in 'Chairman's Address', 28 September 2020, *National High Speed Rail Corporation Limited Annual Report 2019-20*, p. 4, https://nhsrcl.in/index.php/en/about-us/annual-report. Details on Delhi–Ayodhya leg as part of the proposed Delhi–Varanasi corridor from Aaj Tak, 'Bullet train se jaa sakenge Ayodhya, Delhi–Varanasi ke beech honge yeh 12 station', 12 August 2021, https://www.aajtak.in/india/news/video/delhi-varanasi-corridor-dpr-for-ayoodhya-and-kashi-by-bullet-train-1308464-2021-08-12?jwsource=cl; Also see Dipak Dash, 'Bullet train to link Delhi and Agra', *The Times of India*, 8 December 2020, https://timesofindia.indiatimes.com/india/bullet-train-to-link-delhi-and-ayodhya/articleshow/79611962.cms.
17. For an analysis of Chinese soft power projection, see, for example, Joshua Kurlantzick, *Charm Offensive: How China's Soft Power Is Transforming the World* (New York: Yale University Press, 2007); Hongyi Lai, Yiyi Lu (eds), *China's Soft Power and International Relations* (London, New York: Routledge, 2012); Parama Sinha Palit, *Analysing China's Soft Power Strategies and Comparative Indian Initiatives* (New Delhi: Sage, 2017).
18. UN, 'International Day of Yoga', 21 June 2020, https://www.un.org/en/observances/yoga-day.
19. See, for instance, the book by Modi's foreign minister, S. Jaishankar: *The Indian Way: Strategies for an Uncertain World* (New Delhi: HarperCollins, 2020).
20. BJP, *Political Resolution Passed in BJP National Executive Meeting at Dr Ambedkar International Centre, 15 Janpath, New Delhi*, 9 September 2018, https://www.bjp.org/en/articledetail/240014/POLITICAL-RESOLUTION-PASSED-IN-BJP-NATIONAL-EXECUTIVE-MEETING-AT-DR-AMBEDKAR-INTERNATIONAL-CENTRE-15-JANPATH-NEW-DELHI.

21. PTI, 'Lord Rama's image displayed at iconic Times Square to celebrate bhoomi-pujan in Ayodhya', Network18, 5 August 2020, https://www.news18.com/news/india/lord-ramas-image-displayed-at-iconic-times-square-to-celebrate-ram-temple-bhoomi-poojan-in-ayodhya-2762405.html.
22. Express News Service, 'Amit Shah has a history lesson: Don't blame others, rewriting it our responsibility', *The Indian Express*, 18 October 2019, https://indianexpress.com/article/india/amit-shah-has-a-history-lesson-dont-blame-others-rewriting-it-our-responsibility-6075169/.
23. Binay Singh, 'Need to rewrite history from India's point of view: Amit Shah', *The Times of India*, 18 October 2019, https://timesofindia.indiatimes.com/india/need-to-rewrite-history-from-indias-point-of-view-amit-shah/articleshow/71640037.cms; https://economictimes.indiatimes.com/news/politics-and-nation/need-to-rewrite-history-from-indias-point-of-view-amit-shah/articleshow/71631391.cms.
24. 'Ayodhya banegi vaishwik nagari', *Dainik Jagran* (Fatehpur edition), 14 November 2020, p.1; 'Gaurav-bodh se alokit huee Ram nagari', *Dainik Jagran* (Fatehpur edition), 14 November 2020, p. 3.
25. Yogi Adityanath's tweet on 13 November 2020, https://twitter.com/myogiadityanath/status/1327211493251633153?s=20.
26. UP government website to light virtual lamp in Ayodhya, www.virtualdeepotsav.com.
27. Full Doordarshan UP broadcast from Ayodhya on 13 November 2020 is available at: https://youtu.be/Q-scNwXc7r0.
28. This is the estimated cost of the new Parliament building. Tata Projects Ltd emerged as the lowest bidder for construction with a bid for Rs 861.91 crore. Union minister of state (independent charge) for housing and urban affairs, Hardeep Singh Puri, answer to Lok Sabha Unstarred Question No. 1896, 22 September 2020, http://164.100.24.220/loksabhaquestions/annex/174/AU1896.pdf.
29. See, for instance, Amy Kazmin, 'Modi ignores criticism and lays foundation stone for "vulgar" new capital', *The Financial Times*, 10 December 2020. For a critique of the Central Vista Plan, also see, Narayani Gupta, 'The staging ground of our democracy is being bulldozed without debate', *The Times of India*, 23 May 2021, p. 14.
30. The petitioners in the Delhi High Court were translator Anya Malhotra and documentary film-maker Sohail Hashmi. Express Web Desk, 'Supreme Court dismisses appeal against Delhi HC's order that allowed Central Vista construction', *The Indian Express*, 29 June 2021, https://indianexpress.com/article/india/supreme-court-central-vista-delhi-high-court-7380891/; A. Vaidyanathan, '"No interference" required: Supreme Court rejects plea on Central Vista, Delhi High Court order', NDTV, 29 June 2021, https://www.ndtv.com/india-news/supreme-court-rejects-plea-on-central-vista-delhi-high-court-order-no-interference-required-2475087; Abraham Thomas, 'SC refuses to stay HC order which allowed central vista work to go on', *Hindustan Times*, 29 June 2021, https://www.

hindustantimes.com/india-news/supreme-court-refuses-to-stay-hc-order-which-allowed-central-vista-work-to-go-on-101624949113756.html.

31. Bimal Patel, Director HCP, 'Central Vista Project: Reimagining and renewing a national icon', Public Presentation at CEPT University, 1 February 2020, Full video of presentation available at: https://www.youtube.com/watch?v=BXbvc3oLIBk.
32. Bimal Patel interview to Meenal Baghel, 'Change is essential, so heritage of place shouldn't paralyse architecture', *The Times of India*, 24 September 2021, p. 6.
33. Quoted in Amy Kazmin, 'Modi ignores criticism and lays foundation stone for "vulgar" new capital', *The Financial Times*, 10 December 2020. For more on this view, also see Ram Madhav, 'Vista project is both a matter of pride and necessity. It won't hit Covid work', *The Times of India*, 28 May 2021, p. 14.
34. Durga Shanker Mishra, 'A people's parliament', *The Indian Express*, 10 December 2020.
35. Subrat Patnaik, 'Modi promises "New India" as he launches election campaign', Reuters, 28 March 2019, https://www.reuters.com/article/us-india-election-campaign-idUSKCN1R90W3.
36. The demand was made in a letter from Sonia Gandhi to the prime minister as one of five measures she suggested to save money for the fight against COVID-19 in April 2020. PTI, 'Suspend Central Vista Project, stop media ads to save funds for COVID-19: Sonia Gandhi to Prime Minister Modi', *BloombergQuint*, 7 April 2020, https://www.bloombergquint.com/politics/suspend-central-vista-project-stop-media-advts-to-save-money-to-fight-covid-19-sonia-to-pm; PTI, '12 opposition leaders write to PM Modi, demand free vaccination, suspension of Central Vista Project', *The Economic Times*, 12 May 2021, https://economictimes.indiatimes.com/news/politics-and-nation/12-opposition-leaders-write-to-pm-modi-demand-free-mass-vaccination-suspension-of-central-vista-project/articleshow/82576121.cms.
37. Narendra Modi's speech on 16 September 2021 at the inauguration of new defence office complexes in Delhi. He spoke in Hindi; translation is mine. Video clip from his speech is available at: https://twitter.com/ANI/status/1438390948233302018?s=20. For a comparison of the old armed forces complexes and new ones, see the reportage by Padmaja Joshi, 'Vista for veers', Newshour@10, Times Now, broadcast on 23 September 2021, available at: https://twitter.com/PadmajaJoshi/status/1440979609202282502?s=20
38. The bi-annual survey was conducted for *India Today* by Karvy Insights between 10 July and 20 July 2021, across 115 parliamentary and 230 assembly constituencies in nineteen states. A total of 14,559 interviews were conducted—71 per cent in rural and 29 per cent in urban areas—with a mixed methodology (50 per cent face-to-face and 50 per cent telephonic interviews) adopted due to COVID-19-related restrictions. *India Today*, 'India Today Mood of the Nation Survey', August 2021, https://www.indiatoday.in/mood-of-the-nation-survey-august-2021.

39. Raj Chengappa, 'Motion poll: Economy the big worry', *India Today*, 16 August 2021, https://www.indiatoday.in/magazine/cover-story/story/20210823-mood-of-the-nation-poll-economy-the-big-worry-1841399-2021-08-16.
40. TNN, 'PM Modi hits reset with big cabinet changes', *The Times of India*, 8 July 2021, https://timesofindia.indiatimes.com/india/pm-modi-hits-reset-with-big-cabinet-changes/articleshow/84218785.cms; TNN, 'Cabinet rejig bid to ensure faster delivery', *The Times of India*, 8 July 2021, https://timesofindia.indiatimes.com/india/cabinet-rejig-bid-to-ensure-faster-delivery-synergy/articleshow/84219962.cms.
41. TNN, 'Clarion Cull: 24 new faces replace entire Gujarat cabinet', *The Times of India*, 17 September 2021, https://timesofindia.indiatimes.com/india/clarion-cull-24-new-faces-replace-entire-gujarat-cabinet/articleshow/86280206.cms.
42. https://timesofindia.indiatimes.com/blogs/academic-interest/why-gujarat-verdict-heralds-a-new-bjp-3-0/; https://www.hindustantimes.com/india/bjp-plays-it-safe-repeats-sitting-mlas-to-avoid-defection/story-YzTPq9zgZVF4Epc1Xq4lFP.html.
43. Liz Mathew, Harikishan Sharma, A. Maulshree Seth, 'Covid rumblings within: BJP leaders in UP complain as govt puts up brave face', *The Indian Express*, 11 May 2021, p. 1.
44. The new ministers brought in by Yogi Adityanath were Jitin Prasada (Brahmin and former Congress Union minister), Paltu Ram (Dalit), Dinesh Khatik (Dalit), Dharmveer Prajapati (Kumhar, OBC), Chhatrapal Gangawar (Kurmi, OBC), Sangeeta Balwant Bind (Nishad, OBC) and Sanjeev Kumar Gond (ST). Their caste profiles mirrored the social backgrounds of seven new UP leaders who Modi too inducted into his Union government in July 2021: Ajay Mishra (Brahmin), Anupriya Patel (Kurmi, OBC), Pankaj Choudhary (Kurmi, OBC), BL Verma (Lodh, OBC), Bhanu Pratap Singh (Kori, SC), SP Baghel (Baghel, SC) and Kaushal Kishor (Pasi, SC). Rajiv Srivastava, Akhilesh Singh, 'Ahead of polls, Yogi revamps team to give caste balance', *The Times of India*, 27 September 2021, pp. 1, 12. Also see Rajiv Srivastava, 'Eye on polls, Yogi castes the net wide with UP MLC picks', *The Times of India*, 27 September 2021, p. 12.
45. For a critique of the government's vaccine policy see, for instance, K. Sujatha Rao, 'Injecting confusion', *The Indian Express*, 4 June 2021, https://indianexpress.com/article/opinion/columns/we-need-a-vaccine-policy-based-on-fairness-and-justice-not-the-current-centre-vs-state-vs-private-sector-mess-7343074/.
46. Data from Coronavirus tracker, 4 November 2021, *The Times of India*, https://timesofindia.indiatimes.com/coronavirus.
47. Government of India data, valid as on 4 November 2021, https://www.mygov.in/covid-19/.
48. International data from *The New York Times* Covid Vaccinations Tracker, 28 September 2021, available at: https://www.nytimes.com/interactive/2021/world/covid-vaccinations-tracker.html. India's big vaccine push followed after its second

wave with the announcement of a major vaccine drive in mid-May 2021, when officials declared they would make 217 crore vaccine shots available between August and December 2021, to cater to the 95 crore Indians who are above the age of eighteen. At the time, responding to concerns on vaccine-availability, the government announced the following emerging schedule for vaccine availability as likely between August and December 2021: Covishield – 75 crore, Covaxin – 55 crore, Bio E Sub Unit – 30 crore, Zydus Cadila DNA – 5 crore, SII-Novavax – 20 crore, BB Nasal Vaccine – 10 crore, Gennova mRNA – 6 crore, Sputnik – 15.6 crore. Sushmi Dey, 'Govt vows vax push, says will get 217 Cr shots from Aug to Dec', *The Times of India*, 14 May 2021, p. 1. Subsequently, Bharati Pravin Pawar, minister of state for health and family welfare, told Parliament in July 2021 that a total 135 crore COVID-19 vaccine doses were expected to be available between August and December 2021. Dr Bharati Pravin Pawar, minister of state in the ministry of health and family welfare, Lok Sabha Unstarred Question No. 716 answered on 23 July 2021.

49. *India Today*, 'India Today Mood of the Nation Survey', August 2021, https://www.indiatoday.in/mood-of-the-nation-survey-august-2021.
50. The Indian economy in September 2020 was 'not yet past the 2019-20 figures in terms of actual, absolute levels of real GDP'. Union finance secretary T.V. Somanathan interview in 'We are pulling out of the worst … problem with stimulus is its easier to start a spending programme than to stop it', *The Indian Express,* Idea Exchange, 20 September 2021, p. 12.
51. Interview with Rajeev Chandrasekhar, BJP Rajya Sabha MP, 26 August 2019, New Delhi. Chandrasekhar was subsequently appointed, in July 2021, as Union minister of state for skills development and entrepreneurship as well as for electronics and information technology.
52. Collated from Anurag Singh Thakur, minister of state for finance, answer to Lok Sabha Unstarred Question No. 1183, 19 September 2020; P. Radhakrishnan, minister of state for finance, answer to Lok Sabha Unstarred Question No. 2827, 28 December 2018; cash and kind break-up of all 2017-18 and 2018-19 transfers from DBT Mission, Government of India, https://dbtbharat.gov.in/.
53. Quoted in PTI, 'Development only basis for politics now, women BJP's silent voters: PM', *Hindustan Times*, 12 November 2020, https://www.hindustantimes.com/india-news/development-only-basis-for-politics-now-women-bjp-s-silent-voters-pm-modi/story-SdrkdYS7gwhGEVBV9BI4FP.html.
54. Rathin Roy, 'It's not too late, but it could soon be', *Business Standard,* 7 August 2020, https://www.business-standard.com/article/opinion/it-is-not-too-late-but-it-soon-will-be-120080700063_1.html.
55. Idea Exchange with Viral Acharya, 'Can't make transfers to household in Covid because we haven't had an open debate on Fisc', *The Indian Express*, 10 August 2020. In September 2020, the government was 'at a budgeted deficit of 6.8%'. Idea Exchange with Union finance secretary T.V. Somanathan, 'We are pulling out of the

worst … problem with stimulus is its easier to start a spending programme than to stop it', *The Indian Express*, 20 September 2021, p. 12.

56. Andy Mukherjee, 'Why I am losing hope in India', *Bloomberg*, 28 November 2020, https://www.bloomberg.com/graphics/2020-opinion-india-and-modi-are-losing-china-battle/.
57. Quoted in Ajai Shukla, 'Playing into China's hands on Ladakh', *Business Standard*, 7 August 2020, https://www.business-standard.com/article/opinion/playing-into-china-s-hands-in-ladakh-120080700061_1.html.
58. Vikram Misri, India's ambassador to China, 'Ambassador's remarks at MP-IDSA—Sichuan University Virtual Dialogue, Sept 23, 2021', https://www.eoibeijing.gov.in/eoibejing_pages/MTA1NQ. Also see the statement on 'provocative behavior and unilateral attempts by the Chinese side to alter status quo …' by Ministry of External Affairs, 'Official spokesperson's response to media queries regarding Chinese MFA spokesperson's comments on the Galwan Valley incident', 24 September 2021, https://mea.gov.in/response-to-queries.htm?dtl/34314/Official_Spokespersons_response_to_media_queries_regarding_Chinese_MFA_Spokespersons_comments_on_the_Galwan_valley_incident. For background, see Lt Gen H.S. Panag, 'India sits on black top with helmet under its boots. A 1962 tactic by China is now likely', *The Print*, 9 September 2020, https://theprint.in/opinion/india-sits-on-black-top-with-helmet-under-its-boots-a-1962-tactics-by-china-is-now-likely/498462/; also see Suhasini Haider's interview with External Affairs Minister S. Jaishankar, 'India approaches China bilaterally, with the challenge of global rebalancing, says external affairs minister', *The Hindu*, 2 December 2020, https://www.thehindu.com/news/national/lac-standoff-india-will-not-accept-less-than-bottom-line-in-talks-with-china-says-jaishankar/article33234296.ece.
59. Abhishek Bhalla, '200 Chinese troops stopped at Arunachal border in latest face-off with Indian Army', *India Today*, 8 October 2021, https://www.indiatoday.in/india/story/chinese-troops-stopped-at-arunachal-border-faceoff-with-india-1862214-2021-10-08; PTI, 'Chinese PLA yransgressed LAC into Uttarakhand's Barahoti Sector last month: Sources', *The Times of India*, 30 September 2021, https://timesofindia.indiatimes.com/india/chinese-pla-transgressed-lac-in-uttarakhands-barahoti-sector-last-month-sources/articleshow/86648365.cms.
60. Shubhajit Roy, '18 Xi meetings, several pacts: Killings breach consensus, dent diplomacy', *The Indian Express*, 17 June 2020, https://indianexpress.com/article/india/india-china-standoff-diplomacy-lac-incident-mea-6462195/.
61. Suhasini Haider's interview with External Affairs Minister S. Jaishankar, 'India approaches China bilaterally, with the challenge of global rebalancing, says external affairs minister', *The Hindu*, 2 December 2020, https://www.thehindu.com/news/national/lac-standoff-india-will-not-accept-less-than-bottom-line-in-talks-with-china-says-jaishankar/article33234296.ece.
62. Man Aman Singh Chinna, Krishn Kaushik, 'Special frontier force: Why is a covert force now under the spotlight?' *The Indian Express*, 13 September 2020,

https://indianexpress.com/article/explained/what-is-special-frontier-force-vikas-battalion-6578568/.

63. Suhasini Haider's interview with External Affairs Minister S. Jaishankar, 'India approaches China bilaterally, with the challenge of global rebalancing, says external affairs minister', *The Hindu*, 2 December 2020, https://www.thehindu.com/news/national/lac-standoff-india-will-not-accept-less-than-bottom-line-in-talks-with-china-says-jaishankar/article33234296.ece.
64. The World Bank listed India's 2019 GDP as US$ 2.875 trillion in 2019. China's GDP in the same year was US$ 14.343 trillion. See: https://data.worldbank.org/?locations=CN-IN.
65. See Chapter 3 for details. Fieldwork and analysis by Mehta–Singh Social Index. Lok Sabha and Vidhan Sabha candidates analysed from ECI data. UP BJP office-bearers analysed from party list issued on 23 August 2020. UP BJP government ministers list is accurate as of 30 October 2020. UP BJP district presidents' list is based on party listing as of 25 July 2020.
66. BJP, 'Salient points of speech of BJP National President Shri Amit Shah addressing intellectual meeting at Budha Mal Castle Palampur, Kangra, Himachal Pradesh', 4 May 2017, https://www.bjp.org/en/pressreleasesdetail/299215/Salient-points-of-speech-of-BJP-National-President-Shri-Amit-Shah-addressing-Intellectuals-meet-at-Budha-Mal-Castle-Palampur-Kangra-Himachal-Pradesh-.
67. Amit Shah, 'Undoing 6 decades in 6 years', *The Times of India*, 30 May 2020, https://timesofindia.indiatimes.com/blogs/toi-edit-page/undoing-6-decades-in-6-years-modi-has-turned-india-into-a-self-reliant-country-brimming-with-self-confidence/.
68. 'Presidential address of Shri Amit Shah', BJP National Council Meeting, 9 August 2014, Delhi, http://amitshah.co.in/presidential-speech-by-shri-amit-shah-at-bjp-national-council-meeting-at-new-delhi/.
69. Atal Bihari Vajpayee interview with Vinod Sharma, 'There are elements who want the BJP to become a religious party', *Hindustan Times*, 10 February 1991.
70. This was the question asked by Ramachandra Guha in 2009. 'Beyond redemption', *The Telegraph*, 9 July 2009.
71. L.K. Advani in conversation with Manini Chatterjee, 'We should not shy away from the fact that this is essentially a Hindu country', *The Telegraph*, 14 February 2019.
72. Express News Service, 'Won't Attend Mosque Inauguration Even If Invited', *The Indian Express*, 7 August 2020, https://indianexpress.com/article/india/wont-attend-mosque-inauguration-even-if-invited-yogi-adityanath-6543406/. He spoke in Hindi; translation is mine.
73. Interview with a senior official in the UP CMO, 9 June 2020, Lucknow.
74. Rajnath Singh speaking in 'Discussion on the Commitment to India's Constitution as Part of 125th Birth Anniversary Celebration of Dr BR Ambedkar', Lok Sabha, 26 November 2015, http://loksabhaph.nic.in/Debates/textofdebate.

aspx?tab=1&lsno=16. Full video of the speech is available at: https://www.youtube.com/watch?v=39asmXghBVM.s.

75. Interview with Jai Mrug, CEO, VMR, 21 and 28 May 2020.
76. This was the question asked by the scholar Suhas Palshikar at an online seminar on 'The BJP System' organised by the Institute of South Asian Studies, National University of Singapore, 27 May 2020.
77. W.H. Morris-Jones, 'India 40 years on', *South Asia: Journal of South Asian Studies*, Vol. 10, No. 2, 1987, p. 79.
78. Interview with Pranshu Mishra, UP bureau chief, Network18, 9 and 10 June 2020.
79. ECI, 'Contesting for elections', 3 April 2018, https://eci.gov.in/faqs/elections/contesting-for-elections/faqs-contesting-for-elections-r4/.
80. J.P. Nadda, BJP president, interview with Ashutosh Jha, 'Rashtrahit se bhatakne vaale dal sudhrenge ya bahar honge', *Dainik Jagran* (Fatehpur edition), 14 November 2020.
81. Interview with Hemant Agarwal, BJP district vice-president, Mathura Mahanagar, 26 July 2020. The age caps vary across regions. Also see Rohan Dua, 'BJP eyes gennext, cuts age cap by 20 years of Uttar Pradesh district chiefs', *The Times of India*, 15 November 2019, https://timesofindia.indiatimes.com/city/lucknow/bjp-eyes-gennext-cuts-age-cap-by-20-years-of-uttar-pradesh-district-chiefs/articleshow/72064015.cms. Nadda claimed that the age cap for district presidents nationwide was forty-five years: J.P. Nadda, BJP president, interview with Ashutosh Jha, 'Rashtrahit se bhatakne vaale dal sudhrenge ya bahar honge', *Dainik Jagran* (Fatehpur edition), 14 November 2020.
82. Interview with Jai Mrug, CEO, VMR, 21 and 28 May 2020.

APPENDIX 1

Breakdown of OBC Candidates Fielded by the BJP in the 2017 Assembly Poll in Uttar Pradesh

Caste Category	*Sub-caste*	*2017, BJP Candidates*	*2017, BJP Candidates % OBC*
OBCs	Kurmi	28	22.5
	Lodh	20	16.12
	Jat	14	11.29
	Yadav	9	7.25
	Maurya	8	6.45
	Gujjar	7	5.64
	Saini	6	4.83
	Kushwaha	5	4.03
	Nishad	5	4.03
	Shakya	5	4.03
	Rajbhar	4	3.22
	Pal	2	1.61
	Chauhan	2	1.61
	Patel	2	1.61
	Bind	2	1.61
	Banjara	1	0.8
	Khadakvanshi	1	0.8
	Prajapati	1	0.8
	Badhai	1	0.8
	Saithwar	1	0.8
Total		124	100

Note: This includes six OBC candidates (all non-Yadav) fielded by BJP allies.
Source: Mehta-Singh Index

APPENDIX 2

Breakdown of SC Candidates fielded by the BJP in the 2017 Assembly Poll in UP

Caste Category	*Sub-caste*	*2017, BJP Candidates*	*2017, BJP Candidates % SC*
SC	Jatav	22	26.1
	Pasi	22	26.1
	Dhobi	12	14.2
	Khatik	5	5.9
	Kori	5	5.9
	Valmiki	3	3.5
	Sonkar	2	2.3
	Gaud	2	2.3
	Kabir	1	1.1
	Paswan	1	1.1
	Baghel	1	1.1
	Kaul	1	1.1
	Charo	1	1.1
	Anuragi	1	1.1
	Ahirwar	1	1.1
	Kathariya	1	1.1
	Beldar	2	2.3
	Banjara	1	1.1
Total		84	100

Note: This includes seven SC candidates (five non-Jatav) fielded by BJP allies.

Source: Mehta-Singh Index

APPENDIX 3

Table 4.15: Percentage of Lok Sabha Candidates Aged Under Fifty-five in UP: 2004–2019

Party	*2004*	*2009*	*2014*	*2019*
BJP	57.33	72.06	58.9	45.45
BSP	81.8	69.74	63.7	62.16
INC	53.62	48.48	59.7	43.08
SP	75.76	63.01	53.95	32.43

APPENDIX 4

Narad Index: A Core Methodology Note

The text analysis in this project is split into two parts:

1. Analysis of party press releases, periodicals and speeches
2. Analysis of posts by parties on Facebook pages
3. Analysis of posts by parties on Twitter

Part 1. Press releases and periodicals

Unstructured data in the form of HTML files and PDFs was obtained from the websites of the organisations listed below. A custom software was then created to clean and convert these into text files.

A total of 11,558 documents—totalling more than 17.9 million words—were analysed.

- 8,579 BJP speeches, press releases, and articles from 2006 onwards (4.98M words)
- 168 issues of *Kamal Sandesh* from 2009 onwards (2.69M words)
- 230 issues of the RSS's *Organiser* from May 2015 onwards (6.12M words)
- 1,060 articles published in *Congress Sandesh* from 2015 (0.63M words)
- 1,305 speeches of PM Modi from June 2014 onwards (3.44M words)

- 216 documents of the Vanvasi Kalyan Ashram from June 2018 (43,000 words)

Once the data was cleaned, mentions of individual topics per 100 words were calculated. This was done by defining keywords for each topic, and taking note of each instance that such keywords were found in the document.

Keywords for individual topics are listed in the table below:

Topic	*Topic Keywords*
jobs	job, employ, रोजगार, रोज़गार, नौकरी
kashmir	kashmir, कश्मीर
infrastructure	road, electric, सड़क, पानी, highway, water, रेल, infrastructure
farmers	farm, खेत, कृषि, किसान, फ़सल, crop, खाद, fertilize, fertilise, agri
gas	एलपीजी, गैस, lpg, gas
petrol	petrol, diesel, पेट्रोल, डीज़ल
development	develop, vikas, विकास
telco_connectivity	इंटरनेट, internet, फ़ोन, phone
electricity	बिजली, electric
vaccination	टीकाकरण, vaccine
corruption	corrupt, भ्रष्ट
health	health, स्वस्थ
clean	clean, स्वच्छ, toilet, शौचालय
black_money	demonetisation, नोट, black money, black-money, blackmoney, काला धन
education	study, degree, education, educate, शिक्षा, पढ़
insurance	insurance, insure, बीमा
defence	defence, army, navy, रक्षा, जवान
gst	gst
digital	digital, डिजिटल, computer, कंप्यूटर, laptop, लैपटॉप
women	women, महिला, माता, बेटि
congress	congress, कांग्रेस

Topic	*Topic Keywords*
pakistan	pakistan, पाकिस्तान, neighbour, neighbor, पड़ोसी
mandir	ram, mandir, मंदिर, राम, अयोध्या, ayodhya, babri, बाबरी, जन्मभूमि
cow	गाय, गौ, गऊ, cow
terrorism	terror, आतंक
security	security, सुरक्षा
border	border, सीमा
modi	मोदी, modi
amit shah	amit shah, अमित शाह
hindu	hindu, हिंदू, हिंदुत्व
religion	religion, धर्म
bjp	bjp, janata party, भाजपा, जनता पार्टी
youth	youth, children, student, युवा, नौजवान, छात्र, kids, बच्चे
vajpayee	vajpayee, vajpai, वाजपेयी
advani	advani, आडवाणी
NRC	NRC, register of citizenship, NPR, population registry, CAA, citizenship amendment act, citizenship amendment bill, refugee, immigration, immigrants

Part 2. Facebook posts

A similar approach was used to analyse the Facebook posts of political groups and leaders from January 2016 to December 2019. All posts by the official pages of the BJP, RSS, Congress, Narendra Modi, Amit Shah and Rahul Gandhi were downloaded and analysed.

Cumulatively, this amounted to 40,251 posts and 1.2 million words.

Part 3. Twitter posts

476,827 posts from January 2016 to May 2019 by seventy-five political accounts.

APPENDIX 5

Narendra Modi and BJP vs Rahul Gandhi and Congress on Facebook: Followers (2018–2019)

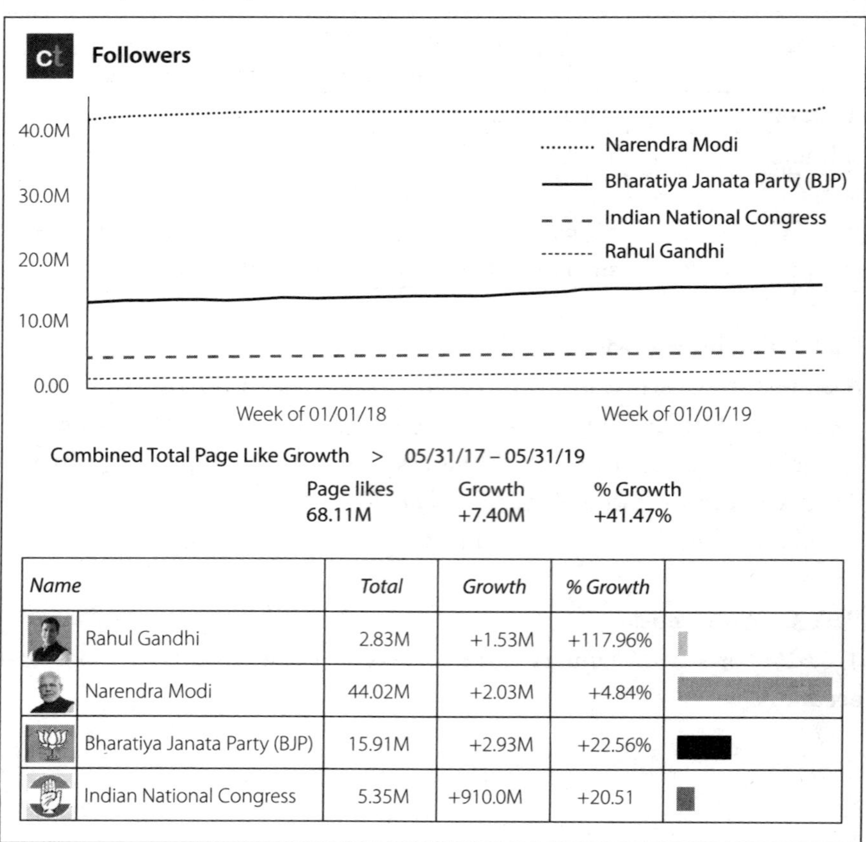

Name	Total	Growth	% Growth	
Rahul Gandhi	2.83M	+1.53M	+117.96%	
Narendra Modi	44.02M	+2.03M	+4.84%	
Bharatiya Janata Party (BJP)	15.91M	+2.93M	+22.56%	
Indian National Congress	5.35M	+910.0M	+20.51	

Source: Crowd Tangle, 2019

APPENDIX 6

Narendra Modi and BJP vs Rahul Gandhi and Congress on Facebook: Interaction Rate (2018–2019)

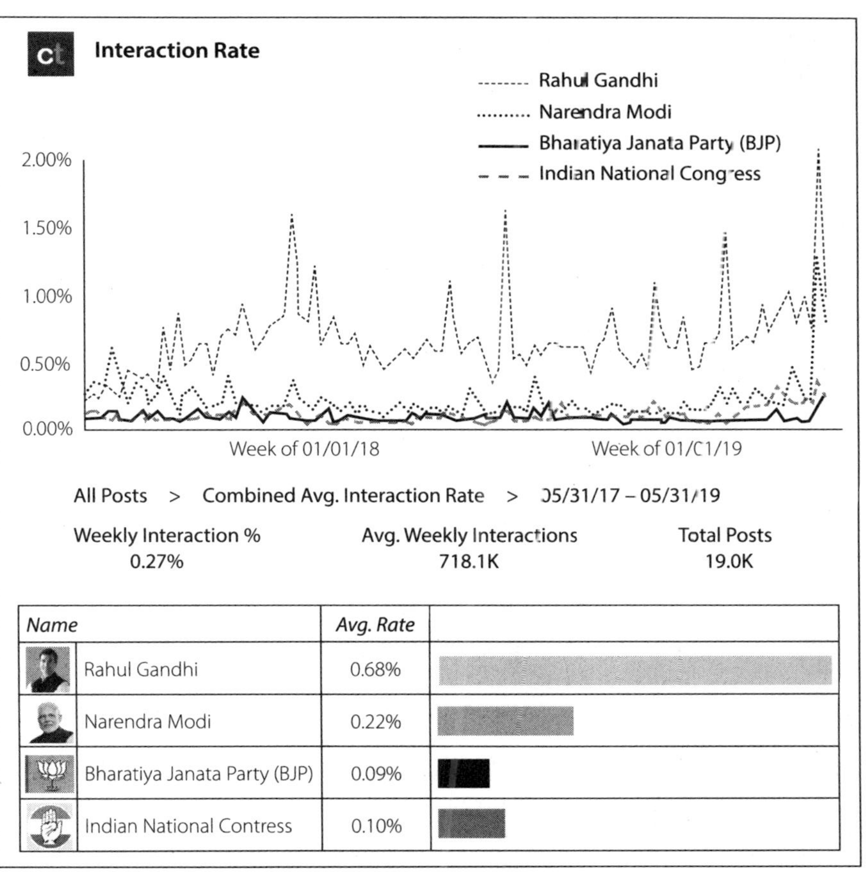

Source: Crowd Tangle, 2019

APPENDIX 7

Narendra Modi and BJP vs Rahul Gandhi and Congress on Facebook: Interactions (2018–2019)

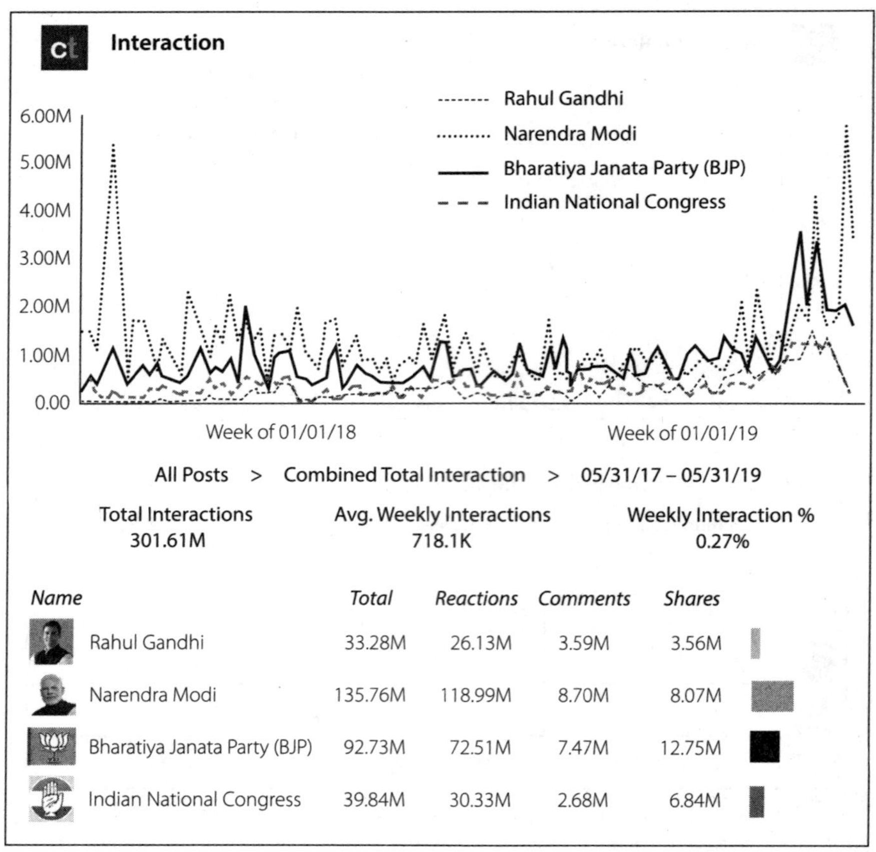

Name	Total	Reactions	Comments	Shares
Rahul Gandhi	33.28M	26.13M	3.59M	3.56M
Narendra Modi	135.76M	118.99M	8.70M	8.07M
Bharatiya Janata Party (BJP)	92.73M	72.51M	7.47M	12.75M
Indian National Congress	39.84M	30.33M	2.68M	6.84M

Source: Crowd Tangle, 2019

APPENDIX 8

Narendra Modi and BJP vs Rahul Gandhi and Congress on Instagram: Interactions (2018–2019)

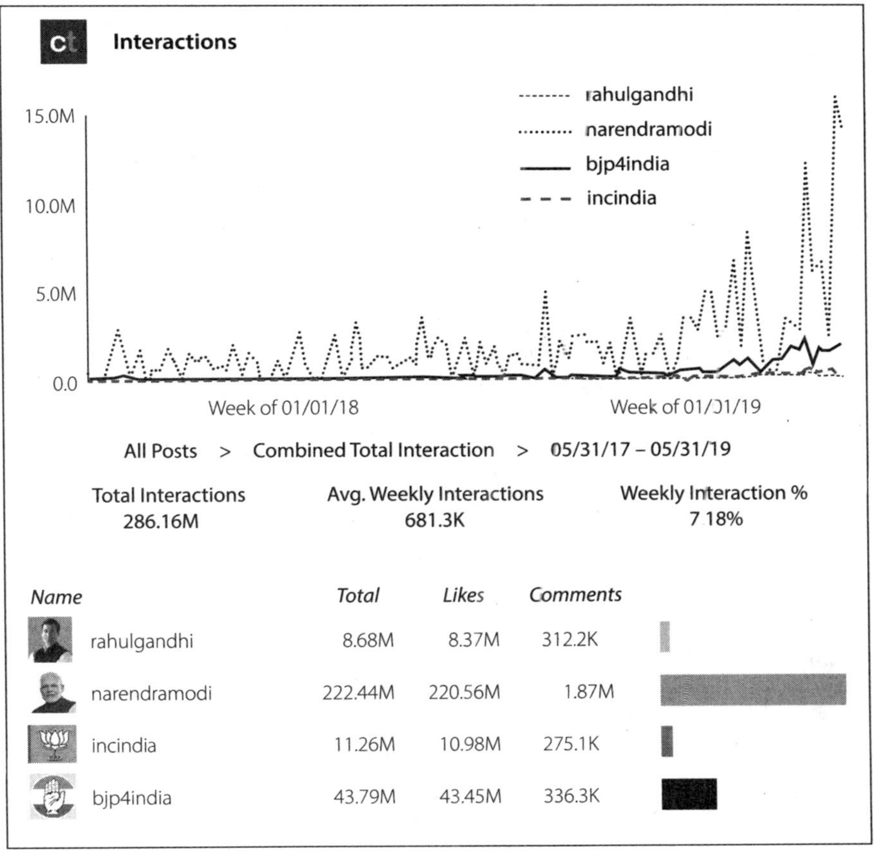

Name	Total	Likes	Comments
rahulgandhi	8.68M	8.37M	312.2K
narendramodi	222.44M	220.56M	1.87M
incindia	11.26M	10.98M	275.1K
bjp4india	43.79M	43.45M	336.3K

Source: Crowd Tangle, 2019

APPENDIX 9

Narendra Modi and BJP vs Rahul Gandhi and Congress on Instagram: Interaction Rate (2018–2019)

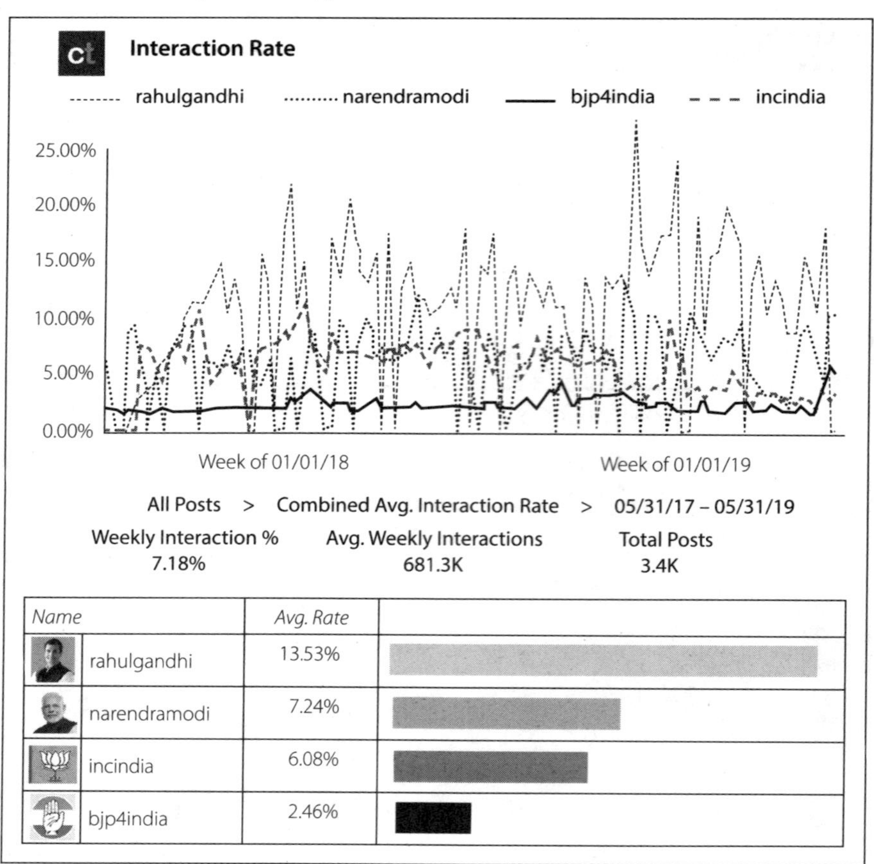

Name	Avg. Rate	
rahulgandhi	13.53%	
narendramodi	7.24%	
incindia	6.08%	
bjp4india	2.46%	

Source: Crowd Tangle, 2019.

APPENDIX 10

Narendra Modi and BJP vs Rahul Gandhi and Congress on Instagram: Followers (2018–2019)

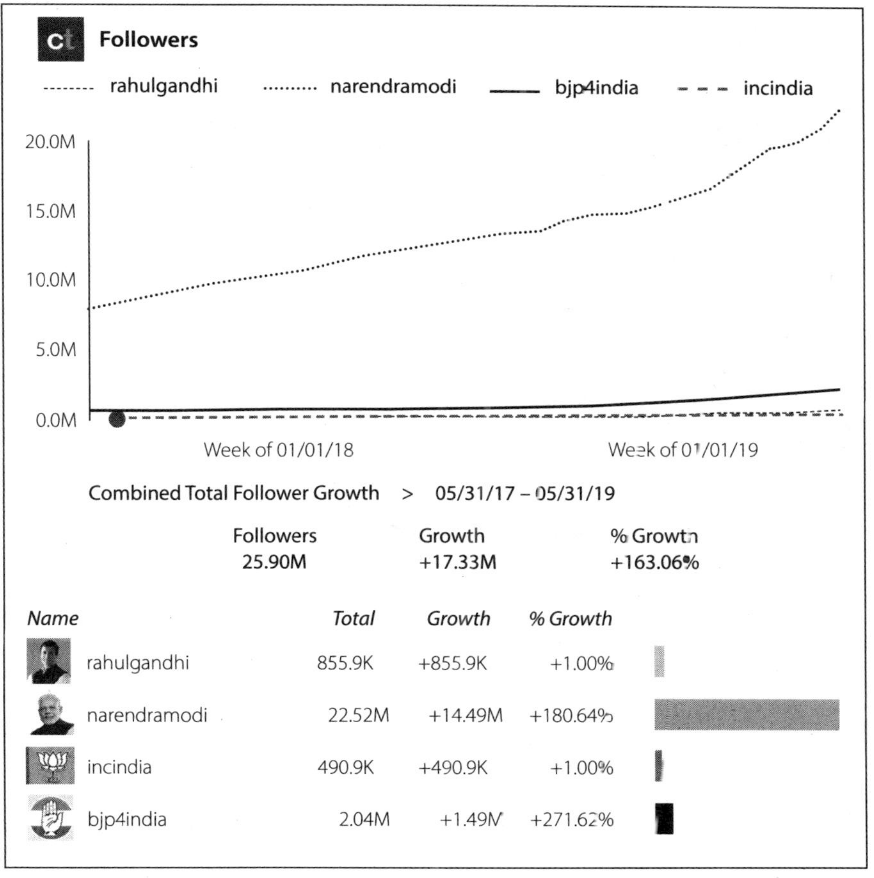

Name	Total	Growth	% Growth
rahulgandhi	855.9K	+855.9K	+1.00%
narendramodi	22.52M	+14.49M	+180.64%
incindia	490.9K	+490.9K	+1.00%
bjp4india	2.04M	+1.49M	+271.62%

Source: Crowd Tangle, 2019.

APPENDIX 11

The BJP's Nagaland Foray—Nagaland Legislative Assembly: 1982–2018

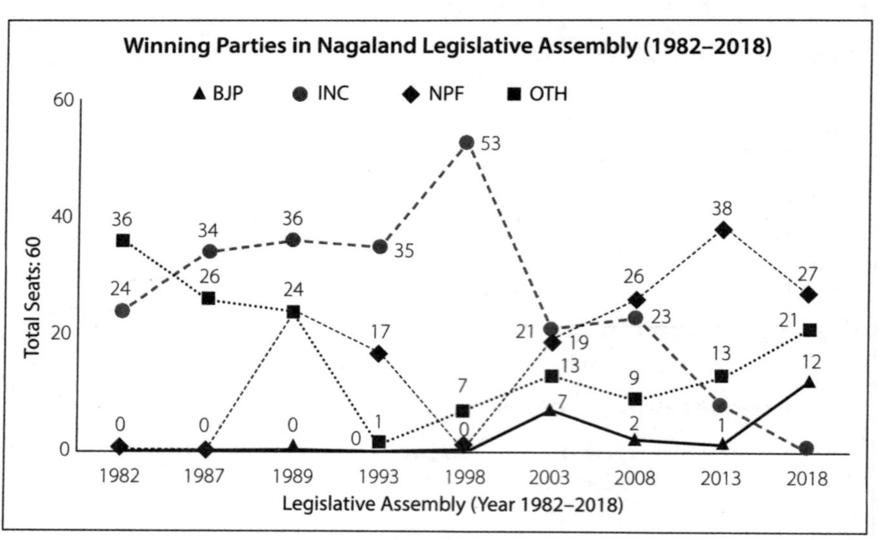

APPENDIX 12

Nagaland Legislative Assembly Vote Shares of Winning Parties: 1982–2018

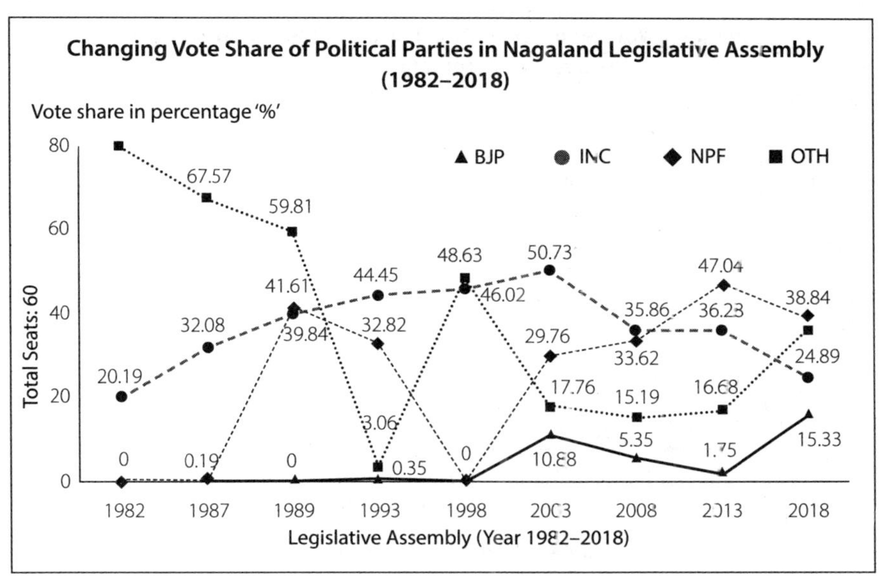

APPENDIX 13

The BJP in Arunachal—Vote Share of Parties in Assembly Polls (1985–2019)

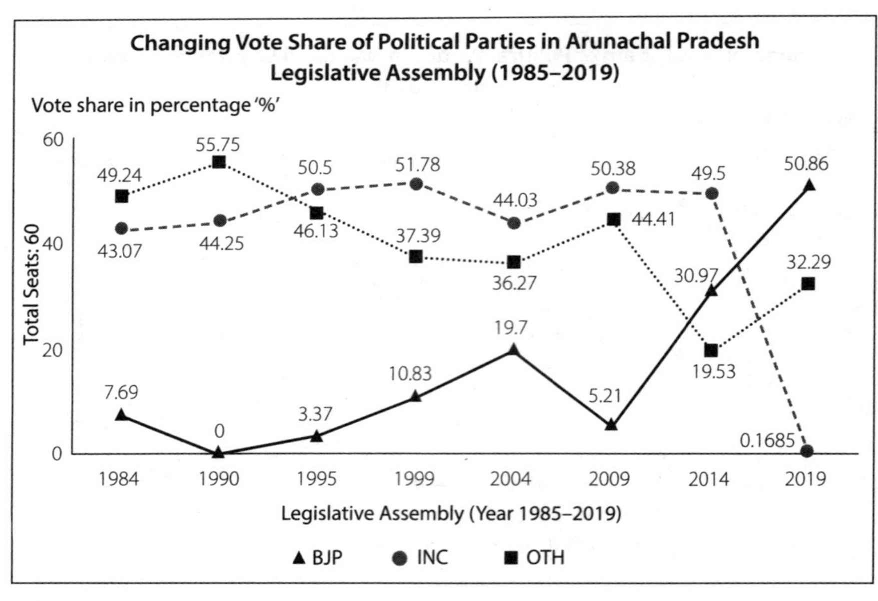

APPENDIX 14

The BJP's Manipur Advances

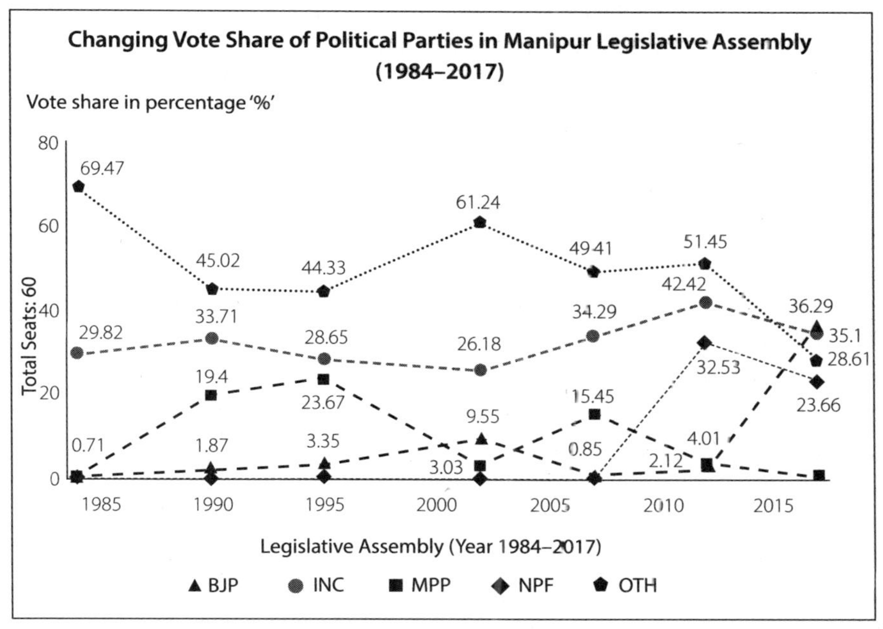

APPENDIX 15

The State/UT and Year-wise Details of the Number of Beneficiaries of the Pradhan Mantri Ujjwala Yojana (PMUY)

Beneficiaries and targets of PMUY					
S. No.	*State*	*LPG connections released under PMUY*			
		2016-17	*2017-18*	*2018-19*	*2019-20*
1	Andaman and Nicobar Islands	1,189	522	6,178	5,154
2	Andhra Pradesh	63,428	16,616	2,62,554	50,528
3	Arunachal Pradesh	-	6,362	32,953	5,385
4	Assam	2	11,28,137	17,07,801	6,56,107
5	Bihar	24,76,953	24,36,197	29,81,636	6,55,896
6	Chandigarh	-	-	88	-
7	Chhattisgarh	11,05,441	8,46,679	7,40,584	2,99,588
8	Dadra and Nagar Haveli	3,211	8,226	2,671	640
9	Daman and Diu	73	130	219	5
10	Delhi	516	161	73,120	3,099
11	Goa	954	30	88	10
12	Gujarat	7,52,354	5,16,660	12,52,052	3,83,415
13	Haryana	2,78,751	78,361	3,23,344	50,504
14	Himachal Pradesh	1,601	28,140	83,177	23,133
15	Jammu and Kashmir	2,65,787	1,07,133	6,80,098	1,88,842
16	Jharkhand	5,36,912	6,66,631	17,01,032	3,59,008
17	Karnataka	15,840	8,93,174	19,13,808	3,24,866

Beneficiaries and targets of PMUY					
S. No.	State	LPG connections released under PMUY			
		2016-17	2017-18	2018-19	2019-20
18	Kerala	11,241	27,152	1,71,530	46,441
19	Lakshadweep	-	134	156	2
20	Madhya Pradesh	22,39,821	10,75,351	31,30,613	7,29,564
21	Maharashtra	8,58,808	10,18,570	21,86,426	3,68,164
22	Manipur	25	32,592	97,760	26,221
23	Meghalaya	-	36,844	1,03,467	10,433
24	Mizoram	-	902	24,879	2,341
25	Nagaland	-	9,225	40,177	5,745
26	Odisha	10,11,955	12,88,380	19,25,954	5,20,263
27	Puducherry	760	1,861	10,753	204
28	Punjab	2,45,008	1,37,343	8,26,611	15,568
29	Rajasthan	17,22,694	9,02,940	30,69,891	6,86,317
30	Sikkim	-	687	7,111	953
31	Tamil Nadu	2,72,749	7,45,302	21,23,792	1,00,589
32	Telangana	41	-	9,23,800	1,48,708
33	Tripura	-	46,379	1,92,014	33,523
34	Uttar Pradesh	55,31,159	9,54,957	64,76,981	18,00,869
35	Uttarakhand	1,13,866	23,574	2,15,481	51,787
36	West Bengal	25,20,479	25,36,306	30,05,534	8,02,399

Source: Minister of Petroleum and Natural Gas reply to Rajya Sabha Unstarred Question No. 1560 for 4 March 2020 regarding 'Beneficiaries and targets of PMUY'

THE BJP

A Timeline

I. Nehru's Power Struggle with Congress Traditionalists, Jan Sangh and the Hindu Right

> **Pre-1950s:**

27 September 1925: The RSS was founded by Dr Keshav Baliram Hedgewar on Vijayadashami day in Nagpur. The name 'Rashtriya Swayamsevak Sangh' was selected on 17 April 1926. The tradition of commencing daily activities with a salutation to the saffron flag (Bhagwa Dhwaj) and concluding with the RSS prayer, Prarthana, in Hindi and Marathi was instituted in 1926.

1928: Vinayak Damodar Savarkar publishes *Hindutva: Who is a Hindu?*, which remains a critical theoretical underpinning for much of Hindutva thinking. It was first published in 1923 as *Essentials of Hinduism* and republished with a new title in 1928.

1929: Syama Prasad Mookerjee elected as Congress member of the Bengal Legislative Council.

1930: Mookerjee resigns and leaves the Congress.

1931: Mookerjee re-elected independent legislator from same constituency.

1940–1944: Mookerjee is acting president of the Hindu Mahasabha.

15 August 1947: Mookerjee joins Nehru's cabinet as minister for industries and supplies as a member of the Hindu Mahasabha, along with N.C. Chatterjee.

4 February 1948: RSS banned after the assassination of M.K. Gandhi. Ban lifted on 12 July 1949.

1949: Mookerjee resigns from the Hindu Mahasabha because it refuses to allow non-Hindu members.

> 1950

26 January: The Constitution of India is adopted.

8 April: Mookerjee resigns from Nehru cabinet, with M.C. Neogi, to protest against the Nehru–Liaquat Pact, signed the same day in Delhi between the prime ministers of India and Pakistan.

19 April: Mookerjee gives speech in Parliament explaining reasons for his resignation, cheered by the whole House.

26 May: Supreme Court rules that the ban on Bombay's *Cross Roads* newspaper and pre-censorship on the RSS's *Organiser* is unconstitutional.

June: Nehru writes to Sardar Patel with concerns on the Hindu Mahasabha and Mookerjee's critique of the Nehru–Liaquat Pact; says it is inimical to smooth functioning of the pact.

3 July: Patel replies saying that he had found 'no legal powers to deal with either Press or people like Syama Prasad Mookerjee' after the Supreme Court judgement in the *Cross Roads* and *Organiser* case; says 'very soon we shall have to sit down and consider constitutional amendments.'

29 July: Mookerjee attends refugee meeting in Delhi, in the presence of UP Congress chief and assembly speaker Purshottam Das Tandon, where anti-Nehru slogans are raised. Tandon presides over the conference, give speech saying Pakistan has not fulfilled its part of the agreement to protect Hindus.

27 August: Tandon says the PM must take his party's views seriously on policy after his name is proposed as a candidate for the Congress president election.

1 September: Nehru writes letter disapproving of Tandon's candidature for Congress president.

2 September: Tandon, supported by deputy PM Sardar Patel, defeats Acharya Kripalani, supported by Nehru, in the Congress election, and is appointed AICC president.

12 September: Nehru issues public statement saying 'communal' elements are celebrating Tandon's election, asks his party for a mandate on his policies on refugees, Pakistan and communalism at the Congress's upcoming Nasik session.

15 September: In presence of UP Chief Minister Govind Ballabh Pant, Tandon publicly says that the Nasik session will decide if Congress will 'live or die'.

21 September: Nehru delivers a rousing speech at the Nasik session; says if his party does not back his policies he will resign and fight it from outside; argues 'majority rule' cannot be 'mob rule'. Presents Resolution on Communalism, which is passed; wins party mandate for his policies. Patel attends all sessions but does not speak at the session.

19 October: Nehru writes to Ambedkar, suggesting a constitutional amendment to add more restrictions to free speech.

15 December: Sardar Patel dies.

> 1951

12 May: President Rajendra Prasad attends ceremony to consecrate installation of idols at the reconstructed Somnath temple in Gujarat despite Nehru's opposition. Attends as private citizen, not in his official capacity.

2 June: Parliament passes the First Amendment to the Constitution adding further restrictions on free speech, including criticism of friendly countries.

2 August: Nehru confidante and communications minister, Rafi Ahmad Kidwai, resigns as Union government minister under pressure from Tandon, holds press conference criticising Tandon.

9 August: Nehru resigns from Congress Working Committee, Central Election Board.

21 August: Nehru wins support of Congress Parliamentary Board.

8 September: Nehru elected Congress president.

1 October: Nehru launches poll campaign in Punjab, says main issue in election is fight against communalism. Master Tara Singh, president of the Shiromani Akali Dal, at the time was campaigning for a new Punjabi Suba (province).

21 October: Jan Sangh is formed.

25 October: Voting begins in sixty-eight-phase first general election of independent India, to be concluded on 21 February 1952.

1 November: Nehru writes to Congress chief ministers: says he can understand 'communal' sentiments in non-Congress leaders but is 'amazed' that 'any Congressmen should so mislead himself' and others to 'ignore' them; says such 'dangerous tendencies' grew because the party 'partly ignored them' and this created an 'inner weakness' in the Congress itself, leading to a change by the party to a 'straightforward and frontal approach to the problem'.

II. Nehru, the Christian Missionary Debate of the 1950s and the Vanvasi Kalyan Ashram

1948: Central Provinces and Berar CM Pandit Ravishankar Shukla, on the advice of veteran Congressman and Gandhian Thakkar Bappa, invites RSS pracharak and lawyer Ramakant Keshav Deshpande to work on a state government tribal welfare programme in Jashpur as area organiser.

1951: Deshpande formally begins working as a state government official in Jashpur, tasked with creating schools for tribals.

1952: RSS Sarsanghchalak Guru Golwalkar sends the Madhya Bharat prant head, Haribhau Ketkar, to help Deshpande when he decides to set up a separate tribal education initiative.

26 December 1952: Ruler of Jashpur, Vijay Bhushan Singh Deo, provides rooms free of cost for a school, holds a Vedic sacrifice with his nobles in his old palace, and the plan for the new organisation's first tribal hostel for thirteen tribal children is announced.

1953: Deshpande's tribal education organisation is named 'Kalyan Ashram' by the royal priest of Jashpur; Judeo donates one-tenth of his personal yearly income to the project. It is later renamed All India Vanvasi Kalyan Ashram (ABVKA).

15 April 1953: Union Home Minister K.N. Katju tells Parliament that, though Indians were free to propagate their religion, the Nehru government wanted missionaries to stop evangelical work.

September 1953: Home Minister K.N. Katju announces expulsion of three foreign missionaries for 'undesirable activities' from a 'national point of view'.

- Madras state government, headed by former governor general of India C. Rajagopalachari, sends the home ministry a report on 'anti-Indian' activities by two Italian missionaries in Fort Cochin.

19 February 1954: President Rajendra Prasad publicly says that India guarantees full freedom to preach Christianity, but warns churches that 'none' of their activities should be inspired by a desire for conversions.

25 March 1954: Assam Chief Minister Bishnuram Medhi accuses the American Baptist Mission of 'abetting a foreign conspiracy to separate the Naga Hills from India and to retain it as an imperialist foothold'.

24 April 1954: UP Home Minister Sampurnanand announces consultations with the Central government about his 'concerns' on American missionaries who, he said, had become particularly active in rural areas and on the state's borders with Tibet and Nepal.

4 May 1954: Ravishankar Shukla's Madhya Pradesh government sends a critical report on 'objectionable activities' of missionaries to Delhi, says some of their activities were 'anti-Indian'.

5 May 1954: A Congress Bihar government minister says that if Christian missionaries continued their 'wrongful activities', his state government would force them to leave.

10 May 1954: UP assembly discusses a dispute on 250 conversions in Mathura by Catholic and Methodist missionaries, which led to the arrests of Arya Samaj activists who alleged 'monetary inducements'.

10 August 1954: Nehru writes to Congress CMs saying he personally disapproved of conversions, but was equally opposed to the counter Hindu 'Shuddhi' movement. He insists that, while he had imposed controls on foreigners in border areas, the debate on conversions could not but have an impact on Indian Christians.

12 August 1954: President Rajendra Prasad tells church groups in Mysore at a public meeting to 'avoid activities which cause suspicion'.

27 August 1955: Nehru's government institutes new curbs on foreign missionaries. They would henceforth be required to take prior government approval to enter India and would not be welcome if they devoted themselves only to proselytisation. They would also be required to have suitable qualifications in fields like education, medicine and social work.

19 December 1955: President Prasad tells church groups that India had 'no intention of curtailing their freedom or come in the way of their missions'.

18 July 1956: The MP government's Justice Bhavani Shankar Niyogi Commission recommends a forced withdrawal of missionary activity and the takeover of foreign mission properties by indigenous churches or international holding bodies.

1963: The RSS's Guru Golwalkar inaugurates ABVKA's first permanent premises in 1963.

1967: Odisha enacts first anti-conversion law in India.

1968: Madhya Pradesh becomes second state to pass an anti-conversion law.

1978: ABVKA begins expanding nationally.

22 September 2016: ABVKA demands national law against conversions.

29 September 2018: ABVKA passes resolution opposing demand by some tribal groups to list them with a separate religious code in the next Census of India. Says it is a conspiracy to divide Hindus and weaken tribals.

III. The 1950s to 1977: Jan Sangh—Its Politics and Economics

21 October 1951: The Jan Sangh is formed. Party President Syama Prasad Mookerjee announces in its inaugural function that India should withdraw the Kashmir issue from the UN as 'the state was an integral part of India'.

10 February 1952: Jan Sangh passes its first political resolution on internal affairs, emphasising that India's constitutional provisions on Kashmir were 'of a temporary character'.

1 January 1953: Jan Sangh demands 'full accession' of Kashmir state to India, failing which it asks for integration of Jammu and Ladakh with Indian territory.

24 June 1953: Syama Prasad Mookerjee dies in police custody in Kashmir. He had gone there in support of the Praja Parishad's agitation organised around the slogan '*Ek Vidhan, Ek Nishaan, Ek Pradhan*' (One Constitution, one symbol, one premier).

25 January 1954: Jan Sangh directly asks for the integration of Kashmir into the Indian Union, passes resolution titled 'Integrate Kashmir', saying that Article 370 is 'undesirable'.

4 November 1954: Mauli Chandra Sharma, Jan Sangh's second president, issues a public statement alleging interference by the RSS, resigns and is later expelled from the party.

1955: Jan Sangh demands that Kashmir 'should be completely merged with India and fully brought on the level of other States' and that the 'National Flag of India should be honoured in the State as the highest flag and not on the same level with the State flag of Kashmir'.

1956: Jan Sangh passes resolution against Government of India decision to restrict migration certificates to Hindu migrants from East Pakistan, accuses government of 'weak-kneed policy'.

1956: Jan Sangh calls for a basic minimum income for citizens as well as a cap on their private incomes and the size of their houses. It wanted incomes to be capped to 'a maximum of Rs 2000 p.m. and a minimum of Rs 100 p.m. with efforts to raise the minimum so that in the foreseeable future the highest and the lowest incomes may bear a ratio of 10:1'.

8 February 1957: Jan Sangh manifesto demands nationalisation of basic and defence industries, says private sector's role is to aid the development of India.

1962: Jan Sangh crosses double figures in Parliament for the first time, winning fourteen Lok Sabha seats.

- The cow first appears on the Jan Sangh's manifesto in 1962 when it declared that it would 'amend the Constitution to prohibit the slaughter of the bovine species and enact necessary legislation'. The party also promised to establish dairies, goshalas and gosadans.

3 November 1966: Jan Sangh adopts a resolution extending all-out support to the all-party Cow Protection Movement for a total ban on cow slaughter. The resolution said the Constitution must be amended to enact a law to ban cow slaughter and said the blame should not be shifted to state governments.

1967: Deen Dayal Upadhyaya becomes Jan Sangh president, reorganises party into regional zones, each headed by a former pracharak.

1967: Jan Sangh enters into alliances with ideologically different parties for the first time, under a policy spearheaded by Nanaji Deshmukh and Atal Bihari Vajpayee, with Deen Dayal Upadhyaya's approval.

- Jan Sangh joins Samyukta Vidhayak Dal (SVD), a grand alliance of Opposition parties, against the Congress in national and state elections in 1967.
- New SVD government comes to power in several states with Jan Sangh as a key partner. In UP, Jan Sangh wins ninety-eight (the highest after Congress's 199) of 425 assembly seats as part of the alliance. Jan Sangh leaders join the new UP government in an alliance that includes two Communist Parties and several others.

1967: Jan Sangh wins thirty-five Lok Sabha seats, crossing an important threshold.

1968: Deen Dayal Upadhyaya killed in a train under mysterious circumstances.

- Atal Bihari Vajpayee becomes Jan Sangh president.

IV. A Pre-history of Demonetisation

19 July 1969: Indira Gandhi nationalises the fourteen largest commercial banks in India; Jan Sangh responds with an economic policy document that does not oppose it in principle, only the form of implementation. Passes economic resolution urging takeover of all big foreign firms.

12 February 1971: Future BJP prime minister Atal Bihari Vajpayee, as Jan Sangh president, says he will implement demonetisation to eliminate black money if voted to power.

- Vajpayee also pushes for swadeshi products, like in the days before Independence; says imperative to revive local products and 'people are getting crazy over imported things and even pay fabulous prices for them'.

- Vajpayee further demands exemption from all income tax for those earning up to ₹7,500, following the recommendations of the Boothalingam Committee; argues for 'heavy consumer tax' on 'luxuries' like refrigerators, transistors, fans and the like.
- Future prime minister I.K. Gujral, then a Congress Rajya Sabha MP, had earlier demanded demonetisation on 18 November 1964.
- On 3 July 1967, the Uttar Pradesh cabinet, including Jan Sangh ministers in an alliance government led by Charan Singh, had also passed a cabinet resolution demanding that the Central government demonetise all notes above ₹10.

1971: Wanchoo Committee, set up by the Indira Gandhi government, unanimously recommends demonetisation as a measure to end black money.

22 April 1971: West Bengal Pradesh Congress Committee passes resolution demanding demonetisation.

9 October 1971: Group of 100 AICC members demand demonetisation.

18 November 1972: Jan Sangh passes economic resolution demanding demonetisation.

16 July 1973: Jan Sangh Council again passes resolution demanding demonetisation.

1 August 1973: Future prime minister Chandra Shekhar, then a Congress MP, demands demonetisation.

12 August 1973: Rumours of demonetisation cause panic selling of notes in Delhi and a spike in gold prices. Finance Minister Y.B. Chavan publicly denies plans for demonetisation.

V. The Emergency, Janata Party Merger and Break-up

1977: Jan Sangh merges into the Janata Party, with four other Opposition parties, in response to Indira Gandhi's declaration of Emergency in 1975.

22 March–4 July 1977: RSS banned during Emergency.

16 January 1978: The Janata Party government, which includes erstwhile Jan Sangh members as ministers, demonetises ₹1,000, ₹5,000 and ₹10,000 notes.

23 July 1978: Indira Gandhi, now in opposition, alleges selective leaks of demonetisation news to 'certain private banks' prior to announcement for commercial benefits.

30 July 1979: Janata Party bans its members from having membership of 'any organisation having faith in a theocratic state'.

28 February 1980: Janata Party's Jagjivan Ram announces he would 'not leave' the RSS 'dual membership issue' undecided and would 'pursue it to the end'.

VI. BJP's Vajpayee–Advani Era: 1980 to the Early 2000s

5 April 1980: Ex-Jan Sangh faction and several other leaders walk out of Janata Party and create the BJP. They have with them fifteen of the Janata Party's twenty-eight Lok Sabha MPs, all fourteen of its Rajya Sabha MPs, five former cabinet ministers, eight former ministers of state and six former chief ministers. The newly formed BJP claims it is the 'real' Janata Party, not a breakaway faction.

- Atal Bihari Vajpayee, BJP's inaugural president, says new party would fight upcoming elections on the basis of the 1977 election manifesto of the Janata Party because there was nothing wrong with the Janata Party's policies and programmes.
- L.K. Advani says there would be 'no compromise' in accepting 'Gandhism as the ideology of the new party'.
- Three member-committee tasked with drafting the BJP's new constitution: S.S. Bhandari, Ram Jethmalani and Sikandar Bakht.

21 April 1980: BJP General Secretary L.K. Advani says party 'would never sever its link with the Rashtriya Swayamsevak Sangh'.

24 April 1980: Election Commission initially sides with the BJP, gives it 'national party status' and freezes the Janata Party's election symbol for a few months until it took a final call. EC later recognised Chandra Shekhar's rump as the Janata Party in October 1980.

28–30 December 1980: Vajpayee says the BJP has embraced 'samata' (equality) as the Constitution-maker and Dalit leader Dr Ambedkar had argued for. Also invokes a new notion of 'positive secularism'.

27 December 1980: BJP Vice President Vijaya Raje Scindia publicly objects to adoption of 'socialism' as a BJP policy, says it a Western concept and that it would turn party into a 'photocopy' of the Congress.

28 December 1980: Scindia withdraws objection saying party's senior leaders had clarified that the BJP's socialism actually had 'Indian content', unlike that of Karl Marx. Says the 'socialism' the party was adopting was actually the 'jan-kalyanwad' of Indian tradition and the 'integral humanism' advocated by Deen Dayal Upadhyaya.

- BJP formally adopts 'Gandhian socialism' as a founding ideology for the new party in its inaugural policy statement.

28–30 December 1980: The BJP's first organised attempt at mobilising the women's vote with the launch of the BJP Mahila Morcha (women's front) convened by Jayawantiben Mehta and inaugurated by the party's first female vice president, Vijaya Raje Scindia.

December 1980: Nanaji Deshmukh withdraws from the party's organisational affairs, moves to Gonda (Madhya Pradesh), and later to Chitrakoot, to work on rural education and farming cooperatives.

1984: After Indira Gandhi's assassination, Nanaji Deshmukh says the Congress's Rajiv Gandhi deserved 'cooperation and sympathy' for larger causes.

1984: The BJP wins only two Lok Sabha seats: its lowest ever in national elections.

1985: Vajpayee commissions a twelve-member working group to review the party and asks if Jan Sangh made a mistake merging with the Janata Party in 1977. Asks if BJP should go back and revive Jan Sangh. Working Group says no and creates a blueprint for revival.

1985: Assam Accord by the Rajiv Gandhi government specifically lists a key demand of the Assam movement for 'detection, deletion and deportation' of illegal Bangladeshi migrants. Puts a migration cut-off date of 24 March 1971, the year of the India–Pakistan war.

1 February 1986: Rajiv Gandhi-led Union government enables the opening of the locks on the disputed Babri Masjid for 'Hindu worshippers'.

1986: The BJP issues its first Economic Policy.

25 September 1988: Narendra Modi's name first appears as a politician in the pages of *The Times of India* as the organiser of an anti-Congress rasta-roko agitation on farmers' demands in Gujarat. His name appeared twice earlier in the newspaper in the late 1970s as an RSS pracharak.

9–11 June 1989: BJP formally embraces the political aim of building a Ram temple, initially started by VHP, through its Palampur Resolution. That resolution categorically framed the Ram temple as an article of faith and committed the party to building it at the site of the Babri Masjid.

1989: The BJP wins eighty-five of 543 seats in Parliament.

August 1990: PM V.P. Singh announces the implementation of the Mandal Commission Report for 27 per cent reservations in education and government jobs for OBCs.

September 1990: L.K. Advani embarks on a 10,000-kilometre Rath Yatra (chariot journey) from the Somnath temple to the disputed Babri Masjid site in Ayodhya. Narendra Modi is a key organiser of the Gujarat leg.

7 October 1990: Rajiv Gandhi announces the sacking of the Congress's Lingayat CM in Karnataka, Veerendra Patil, at Bengaluru airport; President's Rule is declared.

12 October 1990: The BJP's B.S. Yediyurappa says Patil's removal by Rajiv Gandhi was the 'most uncultured way to treat a chief minister'.

24 June 1991: Kalyan Singh sworn in as first BJP CM of UP.

1991: The BJP wins four Lok Sabha seats in Karnataka, its first-ever wins in the state; opens its electoral account in the South.

1991: The BJP crosses the 100-seat mark in Parliament for the first time, winning 120 seats.

November 1991–January 1992: As chief organiser of the BJP's Kanyakumari-to-Kashmir Ekta Yatra, Modi accompanies then BJP president Murali Manohar Joshi to unfurl the Indian tricolour in Srinagar's Lal Chowk in a symbolic ceremony.

1992: BJP launches movement to plant the national flag over Idgah Maidan in Hubli, Karnataka, when Anjuman-e-Islam (AeI), a local Muslim body, conferred with the right to use the 1.5-acre maidan for prayers, decides to construct a building there. Court overturns decision, orders demolition of the building. The BJP launches political movement after SC stay on demolition without a decision on the final matter.

14 March 1992: L.K. Advani expresses broad support for Manmohan Singh's economic reforms and the government's liberalisation policies.

15 March 1992: The BJP reverses its position on reforms, announces a nationwide agitation against the Union budget, which Murli Manohar Joshi calls 'highly inflationary' and 'anti-poor'. The BJP announces 26 March as 'Anti-Budget Day', with protest rallies around the country. Party rejects Dunkel proposals and calls Rao's budget a 'great fraud' on Parliament.

May 1992: The BJP issues its second Economic Policy statement in Gandhinagar titled 'Humanistic Approach to Economic Development—A Swadeshi Alternative'. Says it is:

- against 'unbridled capitalism', supports 'spirit of Swadeshi' and that 'self-reliance cannot be lost',
- India 'must liberalise, industrialise and modernise—but it must do so the Indian Way',
- 'consumer goods will not be kept open for foreign investment while existing multinationals in the consumer goods sector will have to dilute their control within five years, existing employees being given preference in the equity dilution',
- simultaneous focus on domestic Swadeshi industry and caution on the impact of foreign investments even as it supported the opening up of the economy.

6 December 1992: Babri Masjid is demolished. The BJP's Kalyan Singh resigns as UP CM and his government is dismissed by the Union government, which imposes President's Rule.

10 December 1992–4 June 1993: The RSS is banned after the demolition of the Babri Masjid.

1993: The BJP opposes Coca-Cola's takeover of Parle, which it thought was 'injurious to our economy and therefore anti-national'.

1994: The BJP wins forty seats in the Karnataka state assembly, a jump from just four in 1989.

15 March 1994: L.K. Advani declares that the BJP is opposed to the jingoism on MNCs. Says 'if the BJP is to take its place in the Indian polity as a "modern party", it will have to articulate an economic policy that is taken seriously not merely in India but in the world'.

1994: The Gujarat government adds Hindu Modh Ghanchis to the OBC list, the Union government does so in 1999. These circulars mean Modi is legally classified as an OBC leader at forty-nine, halfway into his political career.

1996: The BJP emerges as the single-largest party in the Lok Sabha, with 160 seats. Atal Bihari Vajpayee sworn in as the party's first prime minister but his government falls in thirteen days.

1998: Vajpayee becomes prime minister again after winning a mandate as head of the BJP-led National Democratic Alliance.

- India conducts its second nuclear tests in Pokharan.

1998: The BJP wins a simple majority of Lok Sabha seats in Karnataka for the first time as part of an alliance with Ramakrishna Hegde's Lok Shakti.

1999: India fights the Kargil War with Pakistan; Vajpayee government falls after AIADMK withdraws support. Vajpayee returns to power for third time as PM, heading the NDA as the BJP wins its highest-ever Lok Sabha tally (till then) of 183.

25 September 1999: RSS starts its first 'cybershakha'. Cybershakha attendees:

- do not have to wear RSS uniforms,
- can approach the RSS supremo directly,
- women can 'send messages to the RSS chief'.

March 2000: RSS chief K.S. Sudarshan calls the PMO incompetent and laments that the BJP had become 'Congressised'.

April 2000: Senior RSS leader and SJM founder Dattopant Thengdi attacks Finance Minister Yashwant Sinha. RSS Joint General Secretary

H.V. Seshadri castigates the Vajpayee government for its 'tandav [dance of death] of corruption'.

September 2000: The RSS's Swadeshi Jagran Manch (SJM) opposes the Vajpayee government's ban on the sale of non-iodised salt; says it would play into the hands of MNCs. On 12 September, the Vajpayee government withdrew its ban.

15 October 2000: L.K. Advani says that the 'RSS exercises a moral influence on the government and both Prime Minister Atal Bihari Vajpayee and I share a historical bonding with it'.

October 2000: RSS chief K.S. Sudarshan accuses Christian missionaries of using the north-eastern states to establish 'military bases' in 'strategic areas' to work against India. Calls for a new 'Indian' church, asking Christians to set up an indigenous church, delinked from foreign churches.

16 March 2001: RSS announces major membership-expansion programme.

7 October 2001: Narendra Modi becomes Gujarat chief minister.

27 February 2002: Fifty-seven kar-sevaks returning from Ayodhya are burnt to death in the Sabarmati Express at the Godhra railway station after an altercation.

28 February–June 2002: Communal riots in Gujarat.

22 December 2002: Modi wins his first Gujarat election as a sitting CM.

2003: RSS starts organising software shakhas or 'IT Milans'.

2004: Vajpayee calls polls six months ahead of schedule, loses elections. The Congress-led UPA comes to power. Manmohan Singh becomes prime minister.

2004: The BJP wins an absolute majority of Lok Sabha seats in Karnataka, the start of a pattern that continues till 2019.

2004: The BJP becomes the single largest party in the Karnataka assembly for the first time, Yediyurappa becomes the first BJP deputy CM in the South in an alliance government with JD(S).

2 July 2004: Shiksha Bachao Andolan Samiti (SBAS) set up by the RSS's Dinanath Batra. Files eleven cases in court, wins all of them: the removal of A.K. Ramanujan's celebrated essay on 'Three Hundred Ramayanas: Five

Examples and Three Thoughts on Translation' from the Delhi University syllabus, the removal of seventy-five passages from NCERT books for Classes VI to XII and the withdrawal of University of Chicago historian Wendy Doniger's book, *The Hindus: An Alternative History*.

2007: Yediyurappa becomes first BJP CM in the South, but the government lasts only five days after the JD(S) withdraws support.

23 December 2007: Modi re-elected Gujarat CM for his second term.

2008: The BJP forms its full-term state government in the South with Yediyurappa as CM after winning elections with a much bigger tally.

2010: Modi, as Gujarat CM, leads a move to build a large Mahatma Mandir (temple) Convention Centre in Gandhinagar. Sand is brought in urns from all 18,066 villages in Gujarat to be emptied into the foundation of the Mahatma Mandir. The convention centre includes a memorial to Gandhi's Dandi March and a large charkha (spinning wheel) installation.

2010: The Assam government under Tarun Gogoi tries to start a project to update the 1951 NRC list with a pilot project in 2010 in Barpeta and Kamrup.

31 August 2012: Modi does live Google+ Hangout with Bollywood star Ajay Devgn on 'Strong and Glorious India long cherished by Vivekanand'.

VII. Modi's BJP and His National Ascent

20 December 2012: Modi re-elected Gujarat CM for his third term.

1 January 2013: UPA government initiates Direct Benefit Transfer (DBT) in forty-three identified districts for twenty-four selected schemes.

March 2013: Modi tells Google Big Tent summit 'technology in politics' plays a crucial role in the age of internet democracy.

2013: Amit Shah, as BJP's UP in-charge, pushes district-level elections in the party's state unit.

2013: The Supreme Court mandates an NRC updation exercise in Assam after a writ petition filed by the Assam Public Works. NRC exercise begins in Assam in 2015.

2014: Modi opens a LinkedIn account at the height of the Lok Sabha election campaign in 2014. His first post titled: 'ICT for One Nation-One Mission'.

10 February 2014: Modi calls Northeast states 'Asht-Lakshmi', says Lakshmi's seat is on the 'lotus' (BJP symbol).

May 2014: Modi becomes PM after BJP wins full majority in the Lok Sabha, winning 282 seats.

August 2014: Amit Shah appointed BJP president. The BJP claims to have 35 million members, about half of the Chinese Communist Party of China (CCP).

2 October 2014: Modi launches Swachh Bharat mission with an aim to make India open-defecation-free by Gandhi's 150th birth anniversary in 2019.

- The scheme modified the UPA government's erstwhile Nirmal Bharat Abhiyan, and put in place a five-year target. It increases allocation for individual household toilets to ₹12,000 from ₹10,000.

3 October 2014: Modi launches his *Mann Ki Baat* radio show, with messaging on Gandhi, cleanliness and khadi.

2014: The BJP begins setting up parallel IT teams in each district and voting booth that mirror its organisational structure at each administrative level.

2014: The BJP expands its panna-pramukh model, which was first tried successfully in Gujarat, to UP in the 2014 and 2019 general elections, the 2017 assembly elections and to Karnataka in the 2018 assembly elections.

1 November 2014: The BJP launches Sadasyata Maha-Abhiyan (great membership campaign) after winning elections.

- Does away with previous methods of filling paper forms to enrol members, switching entirely to digital form-filling and phone-based SMS and digital verification methods.
- Launched with the specific aim of increasing the party's strength five-fold and to overtake the CCP in cadre numbers.

29 November 2014: In a speech in the Northeast while flagging off the first Meghalaya–Guwahati train, Modi invokes Vaastu Shastra, the traditional Hindu art of architecture, and the importance it places on the East in construction design.

14 December 2014: The UN establishes International Yoga Day after a proposal by PM Modi himself in his address during the opening of the sixty-ninth session of the General Assembly.

27 February 2015: Modi says in Parliament that the MNREGA programme is the biggest failure of the decades of Congress rule.

April 2015: The BJP decides to own an office in 635 of the country's 694 districts. Till 2017, it owned land for its offices in only 190 districts.

20 April 2015: Rahul Gandhi accuses the Modi government of being 'suit-boot ki sarkar'.

2015: The BJP institutes caste- and gender-based quotas at the organisational level in UP: in local twenty-one-member committees at every level, the party begins to reserve 2 seats each for OBCs and SCs and five seats (23.8 per cent) for women.

May 2015: Mukhtar Abbas Naqvi, then minister of state for parliamentary affairs, says those 'who are dying without eating beef, can go to Pakistan or Arab countries or any other part of world where it is available'.

- Kiren Rijiju, then minister of state for home and BJP MP from Arunachal Pradesh, says 'I'm from Arunachal Pradesh, can somebody stop me?' Later claimed he had been misquoted, strongly denied that he personally ate beef and insisted that he was speaking in hypotheticals that no one could interfere with individual food choices.

August 2015: Himanta Biswa Sarma joins the BJP after quitting Congress, becomes fulcrum of its new Northeast outreach.

1 April 2016: Indira Awas Yojana restructured into PM Awas Yojana with an initial target of building 1 crore pucca houses by 2018-19, with a final end-target of 2022.

- Scheme provides ₹1.2 lakh per beneficiary in the plains and ₹1.3 lakh in hilly states, difficult areas and IAP districts. The beneficiary is entitled to ninety to ninety-five person days of unskilled labour from MGNREGS.

April 2016: K.P. Maurya, an OBC leader, becomes head of UP BJP.

24 May 2016: The BJP forms its first-ever state government in Assam with its alliance winning a majority in state polls.

- The BJP launches the NEDA coalition with ten regional parties, raising the slogan of a 'Congress-mukt North-East'.

July 2016: The BJP starts booth-level sammelans in UP.

September 2016: Jio phone network launched, revolutionises cheap data on mobile phones.

8 November 2016: Prime Minister Narendra Modi announces demonetisation.

December 2016: Amit Shah inaugurates Nanaji Deshmukh Memorial Library at the Chhattisgarh state BJP office in Raipur. BJP puts online a massive e-library of thousands of digitised documents.

- Between 2016 and 2019, the BJP creates new Nanaji Deshmukh libraries and e-libraries in six states: Raipur (Chhattisgarh), Bhopal (Madhya Pradesh), Jaipur (Rajasthan), Bengaluru (Karnataka), Ranchi (Jharkhand) and Jammu.

31 December 2016 and **29 May 2019:** The BJP forms government in Arunachal Pradesh.

March 2017: The BJP fields more OBC candidates than any other party in UP (127, 31.5 per cent) in the state assembly polls.

- Yogi Adityanath appointed UP chief minister after the BJP sweeps the state in the assembly polls.

April 2017: The BJP launches the Vistarak (expander) Yojana from Naxalbari in West Bengal, where the Naxalite movement had begun in the 1960s. It encompassed thousands of party workers, who the BJP characterised as vistarakas, agreeing to spend between fifteen days, six months and a year in specific booths. The party claims that 277,922 vistaraks committed to fifteen-day booth visits.

2017: The BJP launches Shakti Kendra Yojana, which involves the setting up of cluster heads to supervise four or five voting booths each.

June 2017: Manipur's BJP chief minister, Biren Singh, says beef is 'very important' in his state. Says BJP 'will not violate people's right to eat what they have been traditionally eating for many years'.

October 2017: Modi government sets up the Rohini Commission to decide how to further sub-divide the 27 per cent quota for OBCs among the 2,400-plus OBC castes (which range across five broad categories) nationally.

November 2017: Yogi Adityanath launches the 'chaupal' (village gathering) programme for targeted political outreach on the government's social welfare schemes.

2017: The UP BJP deploys 'vistaraks' (expanders). In each of the 403 UP vidhan sabha constituencies in 2017 and eighty Lok Sabha seats for 2019, the party posted a vistarak. These were deeply ideological party workers who volunteered to spend between six and twelve months working for the party in constituencies away from their homes.

21 January 2018: The RSS organises its biggest ever rally in Assam: the Liuparia (sons of Brahmaputra) Hindu Samavesh, a giant gathering of swayamsevaks from upper Assam held in Guwahati. Sixty-five Hindu saints and religious leaders attend, along with the heads of village bodies and twenty tribal kings and over ten chiefs of different satras in Assam.

February 2018: The BJP national headquarters in Delhi moves to a new complex on Delhi's Deen Dayal Upadhyaya Marg.

March 2018: The BJP loses the Gorakhpur parliamentary by-election to a Nishad candidate. Defeat signals the first coming together of the SP–BSP Mahagathbandan (grand alliance).

6 March 2018: The BJP assumes power as a junior coalition partner in an alliance government in Meghalaya.

8 March 2018: The BJP assumes power in Nagaland as a junior alliance partner, in a state that has an 87.9 per cent Christian population.

9 March 2018: The BJP forms its first ever state government in Tripura, after ousting the CPI(M) which had been in power for twenty-five years.

2018: Tripura created as separate prant (province) in the RSS's organisational hierarchy.

17 March 2018: Yogi Adityanath says that the government should be 'panth-nirpeksh' (community-neutral) not 'dharm-nirpeksh' (religion-neutral). Says 'secularism as a word means panth-nirpkeshta not dharm nirpekshta'.

27 March 2018: Gujarat Chief Minister Vijay Rupani claims that Lord Krishna's consort Rukmini in the Hindu epics was a princess from Arunachal Pradesh and that the region had been a part of India since the

Dwapar Yug of Hindu cosmology. BJP's Manipur Chief Minister N. Biren Singh and Arunachal Chief Minister Pema Khandu concur.

April 2018: The BJP completes the task of purchasing land for district offices in 522 districts and construction starts on most of these.

29 April 2018: The Sangh launches a 'Join RSS' initiative on its website, which a senior Sangh functionary claims yields about 10,000 new recruits per month on average.

August 2018: National Backwards Castes Commission given constitutional status by an Act of Parliament.

9 September 2018: The BJP passes a political resolution on the slogan 'New India'.

22 September 2018: Amit Shah says the BJP won the 2014 polls because of the support of rural Indians, Adivasis, Dalits and OBCs as well as its work on cyber communications. Says the 'cyber-yoddhas' (warriors) and 'young workers' were the 'most important' factors behind the victory.

2018: The BJP launches 'Mera Booth Sab Se Mazboot' (My booth is the strongest) programme using NaMo app.

1 October 2018: On his *Mann Ki Baat* show, PM Narendra Modi urges Indians to buy Indian, says it helps Indians.

December 2018: Commission set up by Yogi Adityanath's government suggests a further carving out and streamlining of OBC reservation quotas into three broad categories.

- PM Modi launches commemorative stamp on Raja Suheldev, an eleventh-century king of Shravasti, said to be both a Rajbhar and a Pasi icon, who many believe led local resistance against the forces of the Afghan invader Mahmud of Ghazni centuries ago.

January 2019: The Modi government, through a constitutional amendment bill, legislatively enables 10 per cent reservation for economically weaker sections (EWS, i.e. the poor among non-reserved general category castes).

14 February 2019: Suicide bombing in Pulwama kills over forty Indian CRPF jawans.

26 February 2019: IAF surgical strikes on Balakot, in retaliation for the Pulwama bombings.

March 2019: NaMo app had been downloaded 10 million times across Android and iOS and sold merchandise worth over ₹5 crore.

19 April 2019: BSP chief Mayawati accuses Modi of being a 'zabardasti ka pichhda' (forced backward).

26 April 2019: Modi says he is born not just in a pichhda, but in an ati-pichda (most-backward) caste.

May 2019: Amit Shah addresses rallies in constituencies where Nishads form a sizeable chunk of voters. He promises an 80-foot statue of Nishadraj, the Nishad king in the ancient epic, Ramayana.

17 May 2019: Amit Shah says BJP had 2.5 crore workers in 2014, was fighting 2019 polls with 11 crore workers. Claims to have set up booth-level committees in 83 per cent of India's voting booths between 2014 and 2019.

23 May 2019: Modi elected for second term as PM, with the BJP winning 303 seats, its highest ever tally.

- Modi says in victory speech that there are only two castes in India: those who are 'poor' and 'those who are trying to help make the country free of poverty'.
- The BJP wins a majority of the Lok Sabha seats in the Northeast (fourteen of twenty-five).

6 July 2019: The BJP launches its second big membership drive after winning second national election. Claims over 174 million members by year-end, higher than the Chinese Communist Party's 88.76 million that year.

2019: NRC exercise completed in Assam; 19.07 lakh Assamese residents (almost 6 per cent of the 3.29 crore who applied) excluded from the final NRC list, including lakhs of Hindus.

18 October 2019: Amit Shah advises historians at Banaras Hindu University to write history from 'India's point of view', saying it is 'our responsibility to write our history'.

9 November 2019: Supreme Court rules for a Ram temple in a 5–0 judgement. Says Babri Masjid demolition illegal, but orders construction of Ram temple at the disputed site by a government-appointed trust.

December 2019: The Modi government passes CAA in Parliament to allow Indian citizenship to non-Muslim immigrants from select neighbouring countries. Act also extends the cut-off by over four decades to 31 December 2014.

2019: Yogi Adityanath-led state government accepts the demands of seventeen non-Yadav OBC castes to reclassify them instead as Scheduled Castes (traditionally considered lower down the caste hierarchy).

- Reclassification issued in June 2019, but stayed three months later by the Supreme Court.

7 February 2020: After anti-CAA protests in Assam, the BJP promises to activate Clause VI of the Assam Accord, which promised constitutional, legislative and administrative safeguards to local Assamese.

May 2020: Chinese incursions in Ladakh, which lead to deaths of several Indian soldiers and an unknown number of Chinese soldiers.

June 2020: Modi says the BJP was represented by over 113 OBC, forty-three ST and fifty-three SC members of Parliament in Lok Sabha, i.e. 68.9 per cent (209) of its 303 Lok Sabha MPs elected in 2019 were non-upper castes.

July 2020: The Modi government adopts India's New Education Policy (NEP; the first such policy after 1986). RSS magazine *Organiser* welcomes it with a cover story headlined 'Foundation for Freedom'. The Bharatiya Shikshan Mandal, among the most prominent Sangh affiliates involved in deliberations on the NEP, hailed it as a 'new revolution'. It announces that 'almost 60%' of its suggestions had found place in the NEP, which included renaming the ministry of human resource development as the ministry of education.

5 August 2020: PM Modi presides over the Ram temple consecration ceremony at Ayodhya.

14 August 2020: Facebook becomes embroiled in a controversy documented by the *Wall Street Journal*, where its then public policy head for India, South Asia and Central Asia was accused of ensuring that posts by some BJP leaders flagged as hate speech by Facebook's community guidelines team were not removed.

31 August 2020: The impact of COVID-19 leads to India GDP growth numbers in Quarter 1 of 2020-21 contracting by -23.9 per cent, the sharpest decline since quarterly numbers started being collected in 1996.

1 September 2020: Union IT Minister Ravi Shankar Prasad writes to Facebook CEO Mark Zuckerberg that the 'Facebook India team, right from the India Managing Director to other senior officials, is dominated by people who belong to a particular political belief'.

28 September 2020: Parliament passes three Farm Bills for agricultural reforms.

13 November 2020: Yogi Adityanath's UP government organises ritual lighting of over 606,569 lamps by the banks of the Sarayu river in Ayodhya, dedicates Guinness World Records for the lamp-lighting to 'all Ram-Bhakts'.

November 2020: Two BJP state governments announce plans for a 'love-jihad' law: UP and MP.

10 December 2020: PM Modi lays the foundation stone of a ₹971 crore plan for a new Parliament building, which is part of an overhaul of New Delhi's imperial heart, with the redevelopment of the 3 kilometre-long ceremonial avenue linking the Rashtrapati Bhawan and the iconic India Gate, representing a physical manifestation of Modi's idea of a 'New India'.

10 May 2021: Himanta Biswa Sarma sworn in as BJP's second chief minister of Assam, when the party wins the state's assembly election again after five years in power.

21 October 2021: India crosses milestone of one billion COVID-19 vaccine doses

29 November 2021: The Farm Laws Repeal Bill passed in Parliament

VIII. DBT: Key Dates and Figures: 2013-14 to 2018-19:

- Modi government doubled down on DBTs, significantly expanded it fifteen-fold to 434 schemes by 2018-19.
- The initial number of 10.8 crore beneficiaries reported in 2013-14 (many of which were added under UPA) went up by seven times to 76.3 crore beneficiary accounts by 2018-19.
- Actual direct cash payments into people's bank accounts went up by over twenty-nine times from ₹7,367 crore in 2013-14 to ₹2.14 lakh crore in 2018-19. If you add transfers in kind, then total transfers went up by forty-four times in the same period.

- Women beneficiaries had a large share in general non-women-specific Modi government schemes:
  - » 81 per cent of total financial beneficiaries in Stand Up India, 68 per cent of loans under the Pradhan Mantri Mudra Yojana (PMMY),
  - » 53 per cent of banking accounts under Pradhan Mantri Jan-Dhan Yojana (PMJDY),
  - » 11.4 million (66.9 per cent) of 17.1 million rural houses sanctioned under PM Awas Yojana-Gramin (registered in the names of women individually or as joint holders with their husbands),
  - » 43 per cent of new pensioners (93 lakh of 2.15 crore subscribers) under the Atal Pension Yojana (launched in May 2015, this scheme guaranteed minimum monthly pensions of up to ₹5,000 for those above sixty years of age),
  - » Over 40 per cent of beneficiaries under both the Pradhan Mantri Jeevan Jyoti Bima Yojana (PMJJBY) and the Pradhan Mantri Suraksha Bima Yojana (PMSBY); by mid-2019, as many as 25 million women account holders had signed up for the life insurance scheme (of the 62.8 million Indians who enrolled); 66.2 million signed up by 2019 for the accident insurance policy (of 165.5 million Indians who enrolled overall).

IX. Modi's Women Outreach: Key Dates and Figures

10 March–20 September 2007: As Gujarat chief minister, Modi personally presides over twenty-seven mahila sammelans (women meetings) in various Gujarat districts as part of his outreach to women voters.

After 2014: Almost 25 per cent of posts were reserved for women in BJP executive councils (karyakarani) set up in each booth and district. In these twenty-one-member councils, five seats each were reserved for women, two each for SCs and for OBCs at 'every level' of the party.

January 2017: Modi government launches PM Matru Vandana Yojana (PMMVY) for pregnant women not employed by any Central or state government for direct-cash benefits from the state for the first time.

- 15.4 million pregnant women enrolled for maternity cash transfers as part of this scheme between 2017 and 2020.

- Of these, 13.8 million women received cash benefits. They each received payments of ₹4,138 on average in their bank accounts.
- Government amends the Maternity Act in 2017 to increase maternity leave for women working in establishments with over ten employees from the earlier requirement of twelve weeks to twenty-six weeks.

April 2016–September 2019: The Ujjwala scheme, which provided over 80 million free LPG connections between April 2016–September 2019, could only be availed by women under the poverty line who also received direct cash transfers of up to ₹1,600 each.

2019: Women accounted for 48.08 per cent of Indian voters in the 2019 Lok Sabha polls; 67.18 per cent of women voters cast their vote in 2019—on par with the overall voting percentage of 67.4 per cent—and higher than the male turnout rate of 67 per cent. In other words, women voters voted as much as men voters did in 2019.

2014–2020: Modi's two governments (NDA-1 and NDA-2) gave slightly higher proportional representation to women ministers (12.7 per cent average) compared to Manmohan Singh's two previous ones (11.2 per cent average in UPA-1 and UPA-2), and significantly higher than Vajpayee's previous BJP-led NDA government.

2019: BJP fields more women than any other political party in India, with fifty-five female candidates. It narrowly pipped the Congress, which fielded fifty-four women. In proportional representation terms, the BJP's share of women candidates (12.6 per cent) is marginally behind the Congress (12.8 per cent).

- Two out of every three women who fought on the BJP banner got elected.
- BJP in 2019 had the largest number of women MPs in Parliament: forty-one. The next largest women MP contingent in the Seventeenth Lok Sabha—from the Trinamool Congress (nine) and Congress (six)—were over four times lower.

2020: The BJP makes leadership changes to ensure the highest proportion of women among national office bearers in India when compared with other major outfits with 'national party' status.

- BJP had 16.9 per cent women as central officer bearers in October 2020. This was more than women's share in the central leadership of the CPI(M) (14.7 per cent), Trinamool Congress (13 per cent), CPI (11.1 per cent), NCP (10.8 per cent) and Congress (8.5 per cent).
- When BJP President J.P. Nadda announced his new central leadership team in September 2020, as many as five of his twelve party vice presidents (41 per cent) were women.

INDEX

ACKNOWLEDGEMENTS

This book couldn't have been written without the 'four musketeers', says my literary agent Jaya Bhattacharji Rose. She is right. Rishabh Srivastava is the first of them and he built the amazing data tools that informed much of it. An exhilarating conversation on caste over coffee led to him putting together our first election data hub for the 2017 UP assembly elections. He didn't sleep for three days till he had built the initial protype. That first experiment reframed my understanding of much that was happening. It also taught us what not to do and began a journey that culminated in this book.

Sanjeev Singh was a perfect sounding board, always finding answers to questions each time we got stuck, but also constantly raising more questions to answer. His unmatched feel of ground-level micro politics, deep understanding of caste, and his ability to leaven even the most serious political argument with a wry sense of humour were invaluable. Rajiv Pundir heroically kept track of all the data, meticulously managed thousands of documents, catalogued our archives, marshalled the research backend and made many of the charts and graphics. He, along with Pradeep Nagarkoti, also took pictures on our book-related travels. Sanjiv Shankaran, the wise one, fact-checked the manuscript. He always knew something I did not and always had a lead on where to look for evidence when all else seemed lost.

Jai Mrug generously provided deep psephological perspective and detailed demographic filters, state by state and constituency by constituency. He and Tarit Prakash at VMR also mobilised their network of surveyors across every district in UP to independently peer-review our data. In Lucknow, Pranshu Mishra at Network18 and Brijesh Shukla at *Navbharat Times* corrected many of our data lists. So did scores of other district-level journalists, academics and social notables. Rajesh Sharma helped immensely with the research.

I only really had the courage to begin this book after Robin Jeffrey endorsed the idea of it over a long dinner in Jaipur. It grew at every stage, and after countless conversations with him. Robin read and corrected every draft of the manuscript 'as if he had been paid' to do it. Mahesh Rangarajan, whose nuanced understanding of politics I have always admired, examined the manuscript with a historian's critical lens and a political analyst's sharp eye for detail in record time. He never took more than twenty-four hours to read any chapter and his long and meticulously handwritten annotations and comments on each page filled the gaps, driving me in new directions. The thoughtful Assa Doron improved the draft with an anthropologist's scepticism and kept providing reality checks, including on my health and heart rate. Shubhashis Gangopadhyay put the manuscript through an economist's microscope and told me to 'stop beating around the bush and say it as it is'. T.M. Veeraraghav read every word, was a constant tutor in the intricacies of politics in South India and never complained, though I drove him up the wall till the end, urging him to make phone calls to sources for checking obscure details from ages ago. Soma Wadhwa's angry, shouting pushback on the first draft of the chapter on women and a passionate three-hour-long phone argument with her made me rewrite it in significant measure.

Support and advice from Rohit Saran, peerless editor and storyteller of numbers, was particularly precious. It was Rohit who first introduced me to the world of data journalism and visualisation. This book, in many ways, is an unintended by-product of the baby lessons I initially learnt from him in two different newsrooms. So, getting a thumbs up from him on the draft felt truly special, though, as always, he told me to improve the graphics and wanted to know every little detail of how they would finally appear ('delete that map there and move this one here, it breaks the flow,' he said as he handed back the manuscript).

Vikas Singh, brilliant wordsmith and editor, who never misses a thing, read each chapter at super-speed, as he always does. So did the formidable Sharvani Pandit, who never minces her words. Only when they both gave a head-up did I know this book was finally ready to travel.

At TOI, I benefitted hugely from the support of Jojo, Neelam Raj, Asha Rai, Robin David, Shankar Raghuraman, Praveen Kumar, Keshav Pradhan, Raja Bose and many other wonderful colleagues who are too numerous to be named here. At my new academic home at UPES, Sharad Mehra, Sunil Rai, Jaya Suri and Ram Sharma smoothened many paths to provide a lovely, enabling environment which allowed me to finish the book. At the Institute of South Asian Studies, National University Singapore, C. Raja Mohan provided stimulating discussion platforms where I could try out early versions of some of my ideas on the BJP. He kept asking when the book would be out and his support was hugely encouraging. Ronojoy Sen and Amitendu Palit were equally supportive. Rohit Pal Sharma pulled out all the stops in facilitating an unbelievable array of interactions and also provided delicious rasmalai. I also greatly benefitted from S.G. Gupta's deep understanding of the rural welfare economy and Gaurav Gupta, always a darling, solved many a problem.

A sincere, heartfelt thank you to everyone who agreed to be interviewed for this book, to others who gave me deep background or facilitated access to many previously closed doors. Several of you are named in the preceding pages. Apologies for not naming others here for paucity of space and other obvious reasons, but you know who you are.

The indomitable and erudite Jaya Bhattacharji Rose is formally my literary agent but, in practice, she was also this book's initial editor who reshaped it in fundamental ways. Endless daily conversations, round-the-clock WhatsApp messages and her constant questions became such a way of life that halfway through it, she became the voice in my head, the person I was writing the whole thing for. Though she was deeply confronted by what this book was finding, she believed in the project and its method wholeheartedly. Jaya threw herself totally into this as an intellectual sparring partner and entire sections were born in our daily conversations as I sought to make sense of it all. It was V.K. Karthika who had first suggested writing a chapter on how the BJP sees women but when I dithered while writing, Jaya insisted, 'you cannot write a book on the BJP without writing about women'. She became my tutor on the world of gender studies and her refusal to take no for an answer forced me out of my usual comfort zone and turned what was originally a 500-word section into a 20,000-word chapter. Similarly, though I was reluctant to insert myself into the narrative and write about personal histories in the Introduction, she persisted for a week, simply refusing to relent until I finally agreed and wrote them in. Despite the lockdown, she also conducted the riveting auction with India's top six publishers that led to this book being published. I have been lucky to have her as a partner in this project.

I am also deeply grateful to Rajneesh Chopra, of C&C Associates Advocates and Solicitors, who represents the book as a lawyer, and provided an all-encompassing legal covering brief after reading two drafts. Rajneesh's friendship and immense belief and confidence in the project was hugely encouraging. His valuable advice helped keep out unnecessary howlers.

Finally, the magical and brilliant Karthika, my editor. She has literally chiselled every sentence, debated every word and argued over the nuance of meaning in every translation I put in. Karthika has always had my heart as an editor ever since she commissioned and published my first book over a decade ago. So, naturally, I was ecstatic when she pulled out all the stops to bag the auction for this one. I naively thought I had it all done already but putting the manuscript through the very special Karthika microscope and wringer streamlined and made it significantly better. I am never quite sure how she does it, while managing her entire stable and all the complex things she has to do as a publisher, but her deeply thoughtful and razor-sharp editing—across three line-edit versions—showed how much she truly believed in this book. An editor who respects the author's voice (even when it strongly confronts her own), gets the larger point of it all and is willing to do whatever it takes to make a better product (while balancing editorial sanctity with commercials) is a dream to work with. Karthika is that rare publisher who does all this effortlessly: without showing her stress, without putting any pressure, and she is always open to a debate on even the smallest word and throwaway line in a footnote. Sonia Madan meticulously copy-edited the text and with Jojy Philip valiantly recreated each of the graphics multiple times—no small feat for a book with over a hundred of these—without ever complaining. For that, and such detailing, a big thank you to the whole team at Westland.

At home, this book would simply not have happened if Nitika Mansingh, who always holds the universe together, had not bravely put up with my long absences (physical and mental), crazy hours and long stretches of not sleeping; if my Dad and Mum hadn't kept asking daily if I had finished; and if the boys—Arjun and Raghav—hadn't been so patient with what they saw as my nerdiness. Raghav kept asking in exasperation why I was still working on the book, as more versions kept coming in ('Didn't you finish this six months ago?') while Arjun kept trying to close the multitudes of open tabs on my computer ('Why do you have so many of them open?'). Nitin Mehta brought me down to earth when he clinically analysed my chapter-production rate two years ago and bluntly said, 'Dude, at this pace, you book will not finish before 2024'. Miranda Jenkins has always been wonderfully supportive. A big thank you also to Tej and Reeta Mansingh—as well as to Yash, Gaurav, Shefali and Jaya—for agreeing to put the very personal histories of the Mansingh clan of Fatehpur out there.

I have been truly fortunate to have had such a large support team for this project. Any errors, of course, are mine alone.

NALIN MEHTA
UPES, Dehradun, December 2021

Note: Subsequent to the publication of the first edition of this book, the BJP retained power in four of the five state assembly elections held in March 2022: Uttar Pradesh (255 of 403 seats, 41.3 per cent vote-share), Uttarakhand (47 of 70 seats, 44.3 per cent vote-share), Manipur (32 of 60 seats, 37.8 per cent vote-share, Goa (20 of 40 seats, 33.3 per cent vote-share). It only did poorly in Punjab (2 of 117 seats, 6.6 per cent vote-share) with the Aam Aadmi Party sweeping the state and replacing the Congress as the party in power.

These results—with Yogi Adityanath becoming the first UP chief minister since Independence to return to power for back-to-back terms—demonstrated that the political processes which drove the party's growth and electoral victories between 2014 and 2019, strengthened between 2019 and 2022. Far from reversing, these processes took deeper roots.

NALIN MEHTA
UPES, Dehradun, June 2022